I TRIED TO WARN YOU

I TRIED TO WARN YOU

The Collected Works
of
James George Jatras

PONTIC PRESS

ALEXANDRIA, VIRGINIA

I TRIED TO WARN YOU
The Collected Works of James George Jatras

Pontic Press
P.O. Box 1
Alexandria, VA 22313

HARDBACK ISBN: 978-0-9910169-2-1
PAPERBACK ISBN: 978-0-9910169-3-8
EBOOK ISBN: 978-0-9910169-4-5

All previously published works contained herein are reprinted with the permission of the original publisher. See the title index on page 651 for complete list.

Cover art: Photography by Madison (Melania) Marino, enhanced by Patrick Mason of the zydeco band Bayou Boogie. (Cigarette provided in 2023 by Emilia Braun—my first since 1962, so I won't smoke another one until at least 2084, though there will certainly be the occasional cigar—J.G.J.)

10 9 8 7 6 5 4 3 2 1

To Kathy

TABLE OF CONTENTS

PREFACE

As for man, his days are as grass:
  as a flower of the field, so he flourisheth.
For the wind passeth over it, and it is gone;
  and the place thereof shall know it no more.

Psalms 102 (LXX): 15–16

My father, George, was fond of pointing out the folly of thinking ourselves indispensable. He'd put his finger into a glass of water, withdraw it, then quip: "See the hole it left?"

Notwithstanding, perhaps it doesn't require the megalomania of Shelley's Ozymandias to hope that some trace of one's earthly endeavors might merit passing interest before fading into oblivion along with their author.

Hence this present volume.

It is published, I believe, as the decline of European, Christian civilization, and perhaps that of humanity as a whole, accelerates with breathtaking intensity. How different our world is from the one imagined just over a century ago! Whether Christendom's two-phase autogenocide of 1914–1945 and its ongoing unhealed wounds (the culmination of rot setting in at least from the time of the so-called Enlightenment, and even from seeds planted at the Great Schism) might yet prove fatal remains to be seen.

Thus, while the title speaks of "warning," perhaps it is one that was in vain from the start. I do not pretend that these writings evidence any special wisdom or exceptional insight, only that they are those of a man born in the mid-20th century who, to the best of his ability, tried to discern the larger meaning of what was happening around him. Time will prove whether he succeeded, if there's anyone left with the inclination to make the assessment—or anyone left at all.

The contents represent the greater portion of my observations over five decades. Much material has been lost, particularly my analyses from the U.S. Senate Republican Policy Committee (1985–2002). (Those who say the internet is forever evidently are mistaken.) At the time of this writing, some works, notably those published on *Strategic Culture Foundation*, are only occasionally accessible due to U.S. government censorship necessary to protect our democracy™ and the freedoms we all enjoy as Americans©. Video material

ix

has not been included due to format. Accordingly, a major purpose of this book is to record what can be saved before it disappears.

The reader may be able to discern an evolution from my youthful idealism, especially with regard to the American republic and—as I had hoped—its bright future to what some might regard as pessimism, even cynicism. That, I hope, will not be misconstrued. To be sure, there's an aspect by which one projects one's own sense of mortality onto external phenomena: just as with each of us, states, *ethnē*, civilizations have their own life cycles of birth, flourishing (some of them, anyway), decay, and death. (Where today are the Hittites?) Historians routinely speak of ethnogenesis. Few address the question of ethnothanatos.

Does America—or more properly, do Americans as such—have a future? I am convinced that the United States, as a unified polity, does not. Or rather, if it does, it would be as a monstrous parody of the country I grew up in and loved. As tweeted by someone: "America is a corpse being consumed by maggots. Liberals are rooting for the maggots. Conservatives are rooting for the corpse." My sympathies are of course with Team Corpse, but whether an American *ethnos* can survive the effective end of the constitutional order that has been its political expression *ab initio* is at best an open question. In any case, as countries go, 250 years or so is a pretty good run.[1]

During the past few years, I have been privileged to address the Student Seminar at the annual Ron Paul Institute conference, the contents of which are found herein. From the perspective of the ebullient, youthful hearts constituting my audience, one might think the black-pilled, cranky Boomer projection of what they could expect for the rest of their lives would be received as quite the downer. But that hasn't been the case. I suspect the absence of old landmarks in the era in which they've grown up has prepared them in some way to take events as they come without any false expectations of stability, proportion, or reason. In any case, my closing exhortation to them seems to have been received as I intended.

In the end (as I told my young friends), the impact any one of us can expect to have in the face of world-historic trends before which the fates of nations and empires fly like leaves in the autumn winds is vanishingly small. Already baked into the cake will be, I believe, hardships that we've become accustomed to think only happen to "other people" in "other countries" far away, not seen here since the Revolution and the Civil War, or maybe in isolated instances during the Great Depression: financial and economic disruption and, in some places, especially in urban areas, collapse; supply chains, utilities, and other aspects of basic infrastructure ceasing to function (what happens in major cities when food deliveries stop for a week?), even widespread hunger; rising levels of violence, both criminality and civil strife, coupled with repression of "racists," "homophobes," "deniers," and other retrogrades. Our ability to impact the "big picture" regarding any of this is slim to none.

---

[1] Editor's Note: This line was written months before the *Babylon Bee* quoted George Washington saying much the same thing.

Nevertheless, for what it is worth, I put before my bright young listeners three practical tasks for their consideration.

Firstly, I urged them to be vigilant against deception, in a day when assuredly evil men and impostors will grow worse and worse, deceiving, and being deceived.

Admittedly, this is a tough one, given the ever-present lying that surrounds us and the suppression of dissent. We must try to sift truth from falsehood but we can't become obsessed because, in many cases, we won't be able to be sure anyway. We must focus most on what's proximate to us and on the people most important to us. Everyone who's denoted as an "expert" or an "authority" isn't necessarily unreliable, but that's a good starting assumption. We must be skeptical—about everyone. In communist countries, this was the norm: listen to what the establishment media say, to foreign sources if we can access them, and to anti-establishment dissidents (then it was *samizdat*, now it's internet "conspiracy theorists"—but beware of Trojan Horses like the infamous QAnon): then triangulate and take our best guess. There may be a cost. As Solzhenitsyn said, "He who chooses the lie as his principle inevitably chooses violence as his method."

Secondly, as stewards of every worldly charge placed on us by God and by other people—as fathers and mothers, as husbands and wives, as sons and daughters, as neighbors, as students, as workers, as citizens, as patriots—we must prudently care for those to whom we have a duty within the limited power and wisdom allotted to us. We must start with ourselves. Be as self-sufficient as possible. Get involved in our community; that leftist slogan is actually a good one: think globally, act locally. Befriend our neighbors. Learn a real skill: electricity, plumbing, carpentry. Farm! *Don't* go to law school, for goodness' sake. Get in shape. Eat and sleep right. Have plenty of the essentials: food, fuel, gold, ammunition. Learn to shoot. Limit computer and phone time. Cultivate healthy personal relationships—real ones, not virtual ones. Marry young, have lots of kids—especially women, don't get seduced by all that "career" nonsense. Read old books. Cultivate virtue. Go to church.

Third, for those of us who are believers, particularly Christians, we must pray without ceasing, firm in faith that, through whatever hardships may lie ahead, even the very hairs of our head are all numbered, and the final triumph of Truth is never in doubt.

If these admonitions are all that anyone draws from this book, I feel I have done my job. May they serve as my epitaph.

Spotsylvania, Virginia
July 2024

Acknowledgements

With gratitude to my cherished wife Kathy, my other half, with whom I patiently await reunion; to my parents George and Stella (Stavroula) and my brother Jeffrey (Leonidas), who imbued in me my love for truth and a burden of obligation to it; to my grandparents August (Agesilaos Iatrides), Coula, Leonidas, and Marini, whose Laconian bones rest in Pennsylvanian soil in anticipation of the General Resurrection, and whom I thank for making me a child of what once was the most wonderful country in the world; to my daughters Alexandra and Christina, to my son-in-law Brian (the son Kathy and I never had), and to my grandchildren (who are not named here, both because they are minors and because the roster may still grow), whose future I hope will not be as grim as I suppose; and to my editor and publisher, Protodeacon (Brian) Patrick Mitchell, Ph.D., without whose able assistance you would not be reading this now.

NOTE ON TEXT

In most of my writing I was meticulous, perhaps obsessive, in documenting my assertions in the form of hyperlinks to sources. Again, due to format, these do not appear in the present work, resulting in the occasional incongruous "here" or in other seeming anomalies in the text. Links may be available on some of the entries that still can be located online.

J.G.J

Solzhenitsyn and the Liberals

Solzhenitsyn and the Liberals

James George Jatras | *Modern Age* | Spring 1985

SINCE HE WAS EXILED from his homeland over a decade ago, it has become increasingly clear that liberals, whatever they may regard as his merits as a writer, do not like Aleksandr Solzhenitsyn or what they represent to be his social and political views. What is not immediately clear is why they dislike him so intensely.

Liberalism, according to Webster's dictionary, is a philosophy which includes, among other principles, a belief in "the autonomy of the individual" and in "the protection of political and civil liberties." Now, certainly Solzhenitsyn is a conservative, and conservatives and liberals do have significant differences which should not be underestimated. But I would like to think these differences would not, generally, include any basic disagreements about the rapacious nature of communist totalitarianism, unarguably the greatest single threat in today's world to the continued existence of "the autonomy of the individual" and "political and civil liberties." Liberals today, to the extent that they remain genuine liberals (and have not degenerated, as some conservatives claim they inevitably must, into collectivists), have every obligation to be actively anti-communist—as much, say, as genuine conservatives in the 1930s were obligated to be actively anti-Nazi and anti-fascist, as too many sadly were not. Solzhenitsyn is considered by many the world's foremost living anticommunist: others, Sakharov for example, have struggled valiantly against Soviet injustices, but it was Solzhenitsyn who for the first time forced us to admit to ourselves the reality of all the horrible things about the USSR that we had always known but preferred to overlook.

I have in mind here the desire to engage in *mythmaking* about the Soviet Union. For example, in the *New Republic* of February 26, 1936, Robert M. MacGregor praised "the speed, effectiveness, and accuracy" of work performed under the fraudulent Stakhanovite system, heralding the movement as pointing "to the possibility of wiping out the difference between manual and mental labor, one of the principal attributes, as Stalin interprets it, of actual communism." That Stakhanovism was in fact a cynical and brutal scheme to extort vastly increased work norms out of the shackled and impoverished Soviet worker seems to have been beyond MacGregor's knowledge or interest. Not only liberals believed in such myths. In his 1946 book *I Chose Freedom* the soon-to-defect Victor Kravchenko relates his excruciating inability to disabuse "some thoroughly anti-labor capitalists" of the notion that there prevailed in the USSR a hateful system in which "the workers ruled" and "everybody was equal."

Herein lies the value of Solzhenitsyn's art. The major difficulty with foreign perceptions of the Soviet Union is not that the facts have not been available but that our imagination was not up to admitting them to our consciousness. "The chief problem confronting the expert in Soviet affairs is not to keep his information up to date, as it is in other fields," wrote the French Sovietologist Alain Besançon in his 1978 book *The Soviet Syndrome,* a scant hundred pages well worth the reading. "His main difficulty lies in accepting as true what most people deem improbable, in believing the unbelievable." The facts, I emphasize, were there: nobody who has read S.P. Melgounov's 1926 book *The Red Terror in Russia* will find much shock value in Stalin's misdeeds. But it was Solzhenitsyn, through some artistic alchemy or fortuitous timing that cannot be entirely explained, who made the world admit as true what could not be true. Today it is commonly accepted that Soviet rule has cost Russia several tens of millions of lives, that the USSR is one vast prison peppered with concentration camps, that "real socialism" is a great engine of murder, torture, slavery. "The main result," wrote Robert Conquest in the *New Republic* in 1978, "has been that it is now no longer possible in any country with reasonably free publication for the Soviet system to find serious defenders. . . . The word *Gulag* entered the language—every language." This was Solzhenitsyn's doing. It must be among the regime's greatest errors—perhaps a fatal one—that they did not kill him when they had the chance.

As we move through this perilous decade which, I suggest, could very well see the final resolution, one way or the other, of what Communists call "the international class struggle," I think we would do well to listen to what Solzhenitsyn has to say—not agree necessarily, but at least listen—for the sake of his tortured country and for the preservation of liberal values in what remains of the free world. It is not all just Gulag and the camps. Recently he has spoken, with insight and originality, on religion in the USSR and in today's world as a whole (the Templeton address, "Men Have Forgotten Cod"), on China (during a visit to Taiwan), and to the Japanese people (calling for a "genuine Japanese-Russo-Chinese friendship" in the Far East). But since his initial fanfare greeting in the West—and especially since his 1978 Harvard commencement address—Solzhenitsyn has all but disappeared from the major media, mostly, that is, from the liberal media. Today about the only place one can find his recent statements (such as the three noted above) is in *National Review*. To my knowledge, no other major periodicals—mostly liberal periodicals, or at least more liberal than *National Review*—have seen fit to give him more than passing coverage, usually not even that. There seems to be a common desire that he go away or at least just shut up. And the reason for this is not difficult to discern.

Mention Solzhenitsyn to just about any liberal. He is, you will hear (many times over), an "anti-democrat," an "authoritarian," a "theocrat," an unreconstructed "Russian imperialist," an extremist who borders on being a "fascist," as well as a "monarchist," and, of course, an "anti-Semite." Is it not enough—or, as some suggested after his 1978 Harvard commencement address, maybe too much—that we let him stay here? Why dignify the ravings of this scoundrel and ingrate by quoting him? (Ronald Reagan does in fact quote Solzhenitsyn in his speeches on occasion; so did Ambassador Kirkpatrick. Come to think of it, that's one more count against the three of them.)

There is, however, one public service that Solzhenitsyn performs that even his severest critics will probably concede, the utility of which must be appreciated: he is "Solzhenitsyn, Bogeyman of the Right." By associating people or institutions, however tangentially, with Solzhenitsyn, their credibility is instantly and effortlessly compromised. There are those for whom such a device is indispensable. For example, in a recent article in the *Washington Post*, Josef Joffe and Dimitri Simes sought to illustrate that "extremist" views run rampant at Radio Free Europe (RFE) and Radio Liberty (RL) by quoting an unnamed RL editorialist who, in introducing the speech given by Solzhenitsyn in Taiwan, called the author an "unofficial envoy of the Russian people to the Chinese island of freedom." Joffe and Simes note this characterization without comment, as if it were so patently absurd as to need no explanation.

From here others pick up the theme. Three liberal human rights organizations—Americas Watch, Helsinki Watch, and the Lawyers Committee for

International Human Rights—in their subtly titled report *Failure: The Reagan Administration's Human Rights Policy for 1983* cite the *Post* article in support of their claims that RL lauds "Alexander Solzhenitsyn's diatribes against Western ideas of free expression" and that "broadcasters with anti-Western, monarchist, even fascist tendencies often monopolize the programming." See how easy it is. Just string the words together—Solzhenitsyn, anti-Western, monarchist, fascist.

And on it goes. In a report for the Senate Foreign Relations Committee by Minority Staff Director Geryld B. Christianson (submitted by Senators Percy and Pell), both the *Post* article and the concerns of Helsinki Watch are used to justify proposals to muzzle the radios, RL in particular. Christianson tosses around names from Russian history like Stolypin, Wrangel, and Vlasov in a manner designed to take advantage of the ignorance of readers unacquainted with the historical facts. (For example, he notes "favorable broadcasts" on Generals Alexeyev and Wrangel, who—and this apparently discredits them in Christianson's mind—"fought on the White Russian side in the Russian civil war." But the White armies represented every non-communist shade of political view in Russia, from monarchists on the Right to Social Revolutionaries on the Left, and included the democratic Center. In fact these political divisions—the only thing the Whites really agreed on was their opposition to the Communists—contributed to their eventual defeat. But what, in Christianson's mind, is objectionable *per se* about service with the Whites? Does he prefer the Reds?) Solzhenitsyn makes his obligatory appearance in the report. Airing of his Taiwan speech is characterized by Christianson as "the most egregious case" of RL's political bias. He calls Solzhenitsyn's views "clearly outrageous"—this, commenting on a speech where Solzhenitsyn's main point was that the Chinese and Russian peoples should free themselves from communism and should not allow the vicious regimes in Moscow and Peking to stir up hostility between them.

In short, the use of Solzhenitsyn's name and "well-known" political views is a handy cudgel for those desiring to smear Russian anticommunism and, it seems, anti-communism generally. Interestingly, however, his reputed views are usually simply characterized, often in the most extreme terms. Seldom are his opinions on anything exactly described and documented or his works quoted in detail.

There is a certain circularity here. Solzhenitsyn is damned for his supposedly reactionary views, but those who so portray him are loath to waste paper or ink letting him demonstrate just how reactionary he really is—or is not. One would think that giving him the opportunity to parade his "extremism" would be letting him have just so much rope with which to hang himself. In any case, it is an opportunity which his liberal critics have missed time and again. Consequently, I thought it might be useful to pick out those passages which give the sense of Solzhenitsyn's actual political orientation so that we can all see just what sort of reactionary he really is. For those who have taken the time to read him (and even among his fellow conservatives one rarely finds anybody who has managed to plow past the first half of *The Gulag Archipelago*, volume 1) this may seem somewhat pedantic, but there may be some value in having the evidence in concentrated form.

To begin with, those who do have some familiarity with his writings are aware that Solzhenitsyn does not, strictly speaking, view his message as "political" but rather as moral. He believes that the essential matters for human beings and nations are not those relating to governmental structures but rather to choices between right and wrong, good and evil, truth and falsehood. As one of his characters in *August 1914* puts it, the differences that matter are not those between parties and nations but rather "the difference between decency and swinishness." For instance, in his *Letter to the Soviet Leaders* (sent late in 1973) he states:

> This universal, obligatory force-feeding with lies is now the most agonizing aspect of existence in our country—worse than all our material miseries, worse than any lack of civil liberties.

Similarly, he believes that the way for his country to free itself from communism is for each person to refuse to participate in the lie (from the essay "The Smatterers," which appears in the anthology *From Under the Rubble*, 1974):

> . . . in our country the daily lie is not the whim of corrupt natures but a mode of existence, a condition of the daily welfare of every man. In our country the lie has been incorporated into the state system as the vital link holding everything together, with billions of tiny fasteners, several dozen to each man.
>
> This is precisely why we find life so oppressive. But it is also precisely why we should find it natural to straighten up. When oppression is not accompanied by the lie, liberation demands political measures. But when the lie has fastened its claws on us, it is no longer a matter of politics! It is an invasion of man's moral world, and our straightening up and *refusing to lie* is also not political, but simply a retrieval of our human dignity. [Emphasis in original.]

To Solzhenitsyn the sphere of government is purely secondary (from the essay "As Breathing and Consciousness Return," in *Rubble*):

> It would be more correct to say that in relation to the true ends of human beings here on earth . . . the state structure is of secondary significance. That this is so, Christ himself teaches us. "Render unto Caesar what is Caesar's"—not because every Caesar deserves it, but because Caesar's concern is not the most important thing in our lives.

Solzhenitsyn is often accused of advocating authoritarianism over democracy. However, since he does not see the state structure as a question of overriding importance, he has never, in any passage of which I am aware, stated a preference for any form of government (from "The Mortal Danger," *Foreign Affairs*, Spring 1980):

> As concerns the theoretical question whether Russia should choose or reject authoritarianism in the future, I have no final opinion, and have not offered any.

Regarding practical considerations, he suggests that authoritarianism would be a realistic first step away from the current state of affairs ("Breathing," in *Rubble*):

> If Russia for centuries was used to living under autocratic systems and suffered a total collapse under the democratic system which lasted eight months in 1917, perhaps—I am only asking, not making an assertion—perhaps we should recognize that the evolution of our country from one form of authoritarianism to another would be the most natural, the smoothest, the least painful path of development for it to follow? It may be objected that neither the path ahead, nor less still the new system at the end of it, can be seen. But for that

matter we have never been shown any realistic path of transition from our present system to a democratic republic of the Western type. And the first-mentioned transition seems more feasible in that it requires a smaller expenditure of energy by the people.

He is concerned that Russia is not immediately prepared for democracy (from *Letter*):

> Here, in Russia, for sheer lack of practice, democracy survived for only eight months. . . . The *emigré* groups of Constitutional Democrats and Social Democrats still pride themselves on it to this very day and say that outside forces brought about its collapse. But in reality that democracy was *their* disgrace; they invoked it and promised it so arrogantly, and then created merely a chaotic caricature of democracy, because first of all they turned out to be ill-prepared for it themselves, and then Russia was worse prepared still. Over the last half-century Russia's preparedness for democracy, for a multi-party parliamentary system, could only have diminished. I am inclined to think that its sudden reintroduction now would merely be a melancholy repetition of 1917.

Aside from his discerning no realistic immediate path to a democracy of the Western type, Solzhenitsyn, who describes himself as an "opponent of all revolutions and all armed convulsions, including future ones" *(Letter)*, assesses the "realistic" possibilities for change starting from the present rulers' obvious determination to retain at least their own personal power. This entire outlook was summed up in "The Mortal Danger":

> But this letter was a genuine address to very real rulers possessed of immeasurable power, and it was plain that the very most one could hope for would be concessions on their side, certainly not capitulation: neither free general elections nor a complete (or even partial) change of leadership could be expected. The most I called for was a renunciation of communist ideology and of its most cruel consequences, so as to allow at least a little more breathing space for the national spirit, for throughout history only nationally-minded individuals have been able to make constructive contributions to society. And the only path down from the icy cliff of totalitarianism that I could propose was the slow and smooth descent via an authoritarian system. (If an unprepared people were to jump off that cliff directly into democracy, it would be crushed to an anarchical pulp.) This "authoritarianism" of mine also drew immediate fire in the Western press.

Solzhenitsyn's idea of a tolerable authoritarian structure includes a number of qualities which are usually considered prerequisites if not integral parts of a viable constitutional democracy. Again, his point of departure is "the lie" (from *Letter*):

> It is not authoritarianism itself that is intolerable, but the ideological lies that are daily foisted upon us. Not so much authoritarianism as arbitrariness and illegality, the sheer illegality of having a single overlord in each district, each province and each sphere, often ignorant and brutal, whose will alone decides all things. An authoritarian order does not necessarily mean that laws are unnecessary or that they exist only on paper, or that they should not reflect the

notions and will of the population. Nor does it mean that the legislative, executive and judicial authorities are not independent, any of them, that they are in fact not authorities at all but utterly at the mercy of a telephone call from the only true, self-appointed authority. May I remind you that the *soviets,* which gave their name to our system and existed until July 6, 1918, were in no way dependent upon ideology: ideology or no ideology, they always envisaged the widest possible *consultation* with all working people. [Emphasis in original.]

Indeed, notwithstanding his views on the primacy of morality, the necessity of legality in place of arbitrariness is a recurring theme in Solzhenitsyn's writings. He suggests (in *Letter*) that the Soviet Constitution (superseded in 1977), which, in his view, "from 1936 . . .has not been observed for a single day," may not be entirely beyond hope but may present a basis for future improvements.

He also notes that authoritarian systems, though having certain virtues ("stability, continuity, and immunity from political ague"), have "great dangers and defects":

> . . . the danger of dishonest authorities, upheld by violence, the danger of arbitrary decisions and the difficulty of correcting them, the danger of sliding into tyranny. (from "Breathing," in *Rubble*)

He concludes that a sense of responsibility, "before God and their own conscience," is a necessary restraint on rulers:

> The autocrats of our own time are dangerous precisely because it is difficult to find higher values which would bind them.

In cleansing Russian society of the moral legacy of the Soviet period he says (in *The Gulag Archipelago,* volume I):

> We have to condemn publicly the very *idea* that some people have a right to repress others. [Emphasis in original.]

But as Solzhenitsyn states in "The Mortal Danger": "My criticism of certain aspects of democracy is well known." However, his criticisms do not relate to the principle of democratic government but rather to what he sees as some difficulties of application:

> 1. *That the will of the people is not always served* when, for instance, governments rule in the minority or with only a slim majority and when great parts of the electorate are disillusioned to the point of not voting ("Mortal Danger"); "when a tiny party holds the balance between two big ones," "when superpowers are rocked by party struggles with no ethical basis." ("Breathing," in *Rubble*)
> 2. *That democracies are often weak* against terrorists ("Breathing," in *Rubble; Letter;* and "Mortal Danger"), "when unlimited freedom of discussion can wreck a country's resistance to some looming danger and lead to capitulation in wars not yet lost" ("Breathing," in *Rubble);* and that democracies have an apparent "inability to prevent the growth of organized crime, or to check unrestrained profiteering at the expense of public morality." ("Mortal Danger")
> 3. *That "the terrifying phenomenon of totalitarianism,* which has been born into our world perhaps four times, did not issue from authoritarian systems, but in each case from a weak democracy: the

one created by the February Revolution in Russia, the Weimar and Italian republics, and Chiang Kai-shek's China. The majority of governments in human history have been authoritarian, but they have yet to give birth to a totalitarian regime." ("Mortal Danger")

On top of his "authoritarianism," Solzhenitsyn has been accused of advocating a theocratic form of government. He denies the charge (from "Mortal Danger"):

This is a flagrant misrepresentation; I have never said or written anything of the sort. The day-to-day activity of governing in no sense belongs to the sphere of religion. What I do believe is that the state should not persecute religion, and that, furthermore, religion should make an appropriate contribution to the spiritual life of the nation. Such a situation obtains in Poland and Israel and no one condemns it; I cannot understand why the same thing should be forbidden to Russia a land that has carried its faith through ten centuries and earned the right to it by sixty years of suffering and the blood of millions of laymen and tens of thousands of clergy.

In his *Letter* he states:

I myself see Christianity today as the only living spiritual force capable of undertaking the spiritual healing of Russia. But I request and propose no special privileges for it, simply that it should be treated fairly and not suppressed.

Nevertheless, Solzhenitsyn's strong commitment to religious and patriotic principles has prompted some critics to accuse him of seeking to revive the pre-1917 Russian imperial tradition. Indeed, it is safe to say that the supposed similarity between Solzhenitsyn's reputed Russian "imperialism" and Soviet expansionism has become bound up with the perennial question of whether Soviet policy is specifically Russian rather than communist. While an adequate examination of this subject is beyond the scope of this paper, it is reasonable to speculate whether Solzhenitsyn has simply been dragged into an effort to attribute the Soviet regime's demonstrable aggressiveness to some incorrigible Russian urge for conquest rather than to one of the idols of our age, socialism. In any event, in "The Mortal Danger" Solzhenitsyn summarizes the position he took in his *Letter* on Russia's role in the world:

In the sphere of foreign policy, my proposal foresaw the following consequences: We were not to "concern ourselves with the fortunes of other hemispheres," we were to "renounce unattainable and irrelevant missions of world domination," to "give up our Mediterranean aspirations," and to "abandon the financing of South American revolutionaries." Africa should be left in peace; Soviet troops should be withdrawn from Eastern Europe (so that these puppet regimes would be left to face their own people without the support of Soviet divisions); no peripheral nation should be forcibly kept within the bounds of our country; the youth of Russia should be liberated from universal, compulsory military service. As I wrote: "The demands of internal growth are incomparably more important to us, as a people, than the need for any external expansion of our power."

In his *Letter* he notes:

For the next half-century our only genuine military need will be to defend ourselves against China, and it would be better not to go to war with her at all. A well-established Northeast is also our best defense against China [Note: after jettisoning Marxist-Leninist ideology, Solzhenitsyn proposes that Russia shift her energies from promoting world revolution to internal development, primarily in Siberia and northeast Russia.] *No one else on earth* threatens us, and no one is going to attack us. [Emphasis in original.]

Among the epithets too commonly tossed around today is the word "fascist," and Solzhenitsyn, as have other conservatives, has on occasion been labeled as such. As to its applicability to him and his views, Solzhenitsyn seems to mention "fascism" (actually, Naziism) only once in *The Gulag Archipelago*, volume 111, where he calls it a "quadruped" comparable to communism. It is noteworthy that in his observation that totalitarianism has come into being "four times" he apparently considers Italian Fascism and German National Socialism in a category with Marxism-Leninism and Maoism. It is worth mentioning that other notable Russians who share Solzhenitsyn's general perspective, including academician I.R. Shafarevich, the author of *The Socialist Phenomenon,* do not consider Fascism and National Socialism as "right-wing" or "conservative" movements (as they are generally regarded in the West) but rather as varieties of left-wing collectivist movements, types of socialism closely akin to communism.

Similarly, I could not find any direct reference to Solzhenitsyn's reputed preference for monarchy as opposed to republicanism. However, in his essay "Repentance and Self-Limitation in the Life of Nations," in *From Under the Rubble,* he characterizes 'the whole Petersburg period" in Russia as one of "external greatness, of imperial conceit." He considers that the Imperial Russian government managed "to preserve serfdom for a century or more after it had become unthinkable, keeping the greater part of our own people in a slavery which robbed them of all human dignity." He notes that in "what we may call the neo-Muscovite," *i.e.,* Soviet period, "the conceit of the preceding Petersburg period has become grosser and blinder."

In general, whatever idealization of a previous period of Russian monarchy which may exist seems to be directed toward pre-Petrine Muscovy, which, in his essay "The Courage to See" *(Foreign Affairs,* Fall 1980), he terms "the virtual antithesis" of St. Petersburg Russia.

As an illustration, in his view of pre-Petrine Russia Solzhenitsyn speaks favorably of the then-existing proto-parliamentary institution of the Zemskiy Sobor (Assembly of the Land), whose decisions, he says, "while not legally binding on the tsar" were "morally incontestable." The Zemskiy Sobor of 1612, which elected the first Romanov tsar and ended the "Time of Troubles," arranged, according to the historian S.V. Utechin, to meet regularly; at first its members were appointed by various nobility, clergy, and local assemblies, but later they were elected (by whom Utechin does not say). The Zemskiy Sobor as an institution was abolished by Peter the Great. Peter, the founder of Imperial Russia, is viewed negatively by Solzhenitsyn: in "The Mortal Danger" he says that "nationally minded Russians" regard Peter as an "object of censure" and notes that in the popular folklore he was considered "an anti-Christ"; one of Solzhenitsyn's co-contributors to *From Under the Rubble,* the dissident historian Vadim Borisov, calls Peter "the first Russian Nihilist."

In addition to his putative sympathy for "fascism" and "monarchism," there is a common perception that there is something at least vaguely anti-Semitic about Solzhenitsyn. This is somewhat puzzling in that neither Jews nor issues specifically relating to Jews figure prominently in his works, which are mostly, as one might expect, on Russian themes. Such Jewish characters as do exist—for instance Rubin in *The First Circle* (the honest, idealistic Jewish Communist, patterned after Lev Kopelev); the fellow exile identified only as M_____z in *The Gulag Archipelago*, volume III; and the "highly intelligent and respected" engineer Ilya Isakovich Arkhangorodsky from *August 1914*—are usually portrayed in a positive light.

It has been suggested that Solzhenitsyn, along with other (usually unidentified) members of what can be loosely described as the Russian patriotic or nationalist movement, "blames" the Revolution and its catastrophic consequences on the Jews, considering it something perpetrated on Russia by non-Russians in general, Jews in particular. However, to the extent that Solzhenitsyn concerns himself with ethnically non-Russian, including Jewish, contributors to the Revolution, his goal seems to be to demonstrate that communism is not an inherently Russian phenomenon—as it is often taken to be—but one which representatives of other peoples had a big part in shaping as well. Nonetheless, in "Repentance and Self Limitation" he accepts Russia's collective responsibility for the multimillion death toll of Soviet repression in that country:

> . . . *we, all of us,* Russia herself, were the necessary accomplices.
> [Emphasis in original.]

Later in the same essay he states:

> This article has not been written to minimize the guilt of the Russian people. Nor, however, to scrape all the guilt from mother earth and load it onto ourselves. True, we were not vaccinated against the plague. True, we lost our heads. True, we gave way, and then caved in altogether. All true. But we have not been the first and only begetters in all this time since the fifteenth century! [The reference to the fifteenth century represents Solzhenitsyn's view that modern totalitarianism is the logical culmination of philosophical trends beginning at that time.]

As Shafarevich, who also contributed to *Rubble,* puts it in his essay "Separation or Reconciliation? The Nationalities Question in the USSR":

> We have all had a hand in creating the problem that now confronts us: the Russian Nihilists, the Ukrainian "Borotbists," the Latvian riflemen and many others have each done their bit. How can we hope, separately, to disentangle the knot we all helped to tighten?

A theme related to the Jews/Revolution question is the extent to which Russian patriotism is inherently anti-Semitic. Michael Agursky, another of the contributors to *Rubble* and a self-described Jewish nationalist now resident in Israel, addressed this issue both generally and with regard to Solzhenitsyn personally in the article "Russian Isolationism and Communist Expansion" in the journal *Russia:*

> But no matter what the Russian roots of the revolution were like, not only anti-Semites and monarchists have pointed to the mass Jewish participation in the revolution. . . .
>   But many Russian nationalists, including Solzhenitsyn himself, occupy a position in the question of the participation of Jewish revolutionaries in the Russian revolution which scarcely differs from that of Zionism, calling for Jews to refuse to participate in social

movements in other countries and to devote themselves to the building of their own national home. Many Jews had a heavy presentiment of what the Trotskys, Zinovyevs and Sverdlovs would lead the Jews to in Russia.

Not without reason does Solzhenitsyn, who has been falsely accused of anti-Semitism, relate sympathetically to Zionism and to the State of Israel, and he has spoken out on this problem many times. And for me this is much more important than his attitude towards the Jewish and non-Jewish revolutionaries and leaders of the Soviet state in its first period.

Notwithstanding his favorable attitude toward Israel and Zionism, Solzhenitsyn has been criticized for not being more concerned with the question of Jewish emigration:

> How can the problems of any major country be reduced to the issue of who is allowed to depart from it? (from "Mortal Danger")

Solzhenitsyn's determination to view events from a specifically Russian perspective no doubt has an influence here; his concern, like charity, begins at home: *his* religion persecuted, *his* nation stagnating demographically. That is, he seems to have no objection to Jews' reasserting their Jewish identity, and he would certainly encourage them to do so. But his duty, as a Russian, is to be primarily concerned with Russia and Russians. He rejects the notion that Russian patriotism may be manipulated by the Soviet regime for evil purposes:

> But then the Soviet authorities also try to exploit the Jewish emigration from the U.S.S.R. in order to fan the flames of anti-Semitism, and not without success. ("See that? They're the only ones allowed to escape from this hell, and the West sends goods to pay for it!") Does it follow that we are entitled to advise Jews to forgo the quest for their spiritual and national origins? Of course not. Are we not all entitled to live our natural life on the earth and to strive toward our individual goals, without heed for what others may think or what the papers may write, and without worrying about the dark forces that may attempt to exploit those goals for their own ends? (from "Mortal Danger")

Finally, it should not be ignored that the Soviet regime, trying to discredit Russian patriotism, has since the mid-1970s itself attempted to foster the notion that Solzhenitsyn is an anti-Semite. However, prior to this (in 1971–1973), they had attempted to give the impression that Solzhenitsyn was himself Jewish:

> There was a time when they happily made play with my patronymic, Isayevich. They would say, trying to seem casual: "Incidentally, his real name is Solzhenit*ser* or Solzhenit*sker*; not, of course, that this is of any importance in our country." (from the memoir *The Oak and The Calf*)

Later,

> . . . the *racial* line was again revived. Or more precisely, the Jewish line. A special major of state security named Blagovidov rushed off to check the personal files of all the "Isaakii's" in the archives of

Moscow University for 1914 in the hope of proving that I was Jewish.
. . . Alas, the racist researchers were thwarted. I turned out to be a
Russian. (from *The Oak and The Calf*)

But by the time the Russian writer Vladimir Voinovich was called in for a
"chat" with the KGB in mid-1975, the line had changed:

From Marchenko we switch to Solzhenitsyn. In my letter to the
Writers' Union I had called him a very great citizen. But they find he
is not a very great citizen. He is a bad man and an anti-Semite (VV's
note: "Previously he was counted a Jew.") to boot. And in general his
ideas—orthodoxy, autocracy, national character—well, all doors are
shut to these nowadays. (from "Incident at the Metropole (Facts
Resembling a Detective Story)," in *Kontinent 2*)

In addition to the allegation of anti-Semitism—as if the KGB were in a position
to call anyone anti-Semitic—it is interesting to note the references to "autocracy" and "national character," which are likewise absent from Solzhenitsyn's
writings. One is tempted to wonder to what extent the attribution of certain
views to Solzhenitsyn derives ultimately from KGB sources.

In conclusion, it does not appear that there is anything in Solzhenitsyn's
views which is specifically incompatible with democratic principles or with
"the autonomy of the individual" and the protection of "civil and political
liberties." In addition, many of the negative characterizations commonly attributed to him appear to be groundless.

It is still to be explained, then, why his detractors, particularly liberal
detractors, view him so negatively. No doubt Solzhenitsyn's indictment of the
West's weakness is a discomfort to those who have devoted their professional
lives to making it weak, an endeavor in which liberals have been at least as
active as conservatives during these past thirty years of declining American
power. Similarly, far too many liberals regard the idea of active resistance to
communism as some sort of dangerous provocation, a threat to "peace."

However, there seems to be more to it. No one who has made an honest
examination of Solzhenitsyn's works could find in them any indication of
"fascism," "anti-Semitism," or the like. Rather, these characterizations have
all the appearance of having been thrown up as diversions from what one
suspects is the true reason liberals dislike Solzhenitsyn: the fact that the power
of his vision and the values that embody it expose the hollowness of contemporary liberalism. Indeed, even Solzhenitsyn's attacks on communism are
a source of discomfort, for most liberals know, or at least understand
instinctively, that they and the Communists ultimately worship at the altar of
the same secular pantheon: Man, Progress, Reason, among other gods. They
both seek to build the same earthly paradise; they differ only in their
methodology. Solzhenitsyn's reminder that man and society cannot survive
without God, that the twentieth century has become a slaughterhouse
precisely because "men have forgotten God," is anathema to them. And
because they are unable to refute him, they slander him.

And perhaps this should not come as a surprise. As the Romans said:
Veritus odium parit. Truth purchaseth hatred.

Pravoslavophobia

"Religious Victims"

James George Jatras | *Policy Review* | Spring 1986

Dear Sir:

Professor Ewa Thompson's attack on Reverend Michael Bourdeaux for his excellent survey of religious persecution in the Soviet Union ("Secular Inhumanism: The Soviet Union's War against Christians, Muslims, and Jews," Fall 1985) should not go unanswered. In her distortion of the religious picture in the U.S.S.R., she not only unjustly defames Reverend Bourdeaux, a man of the highest scholarly standards and sterling personal qualities, for being concerned for all persecuted believers regardless of denomination, she also grossly and unfairly insults all Russians and all Orthodox Christians.

Professor Thompson largely bases her argument as to the "favored" position of Russian Orthodoxy in the U.S.S.R. on a mechanical comparison of numbers and population percentages of believers, underground publications, clergy, prisoners of conscience, and so on, with particular attention to the relative indices between Lithuanian Catholics and Russian Orthodox.

This is extremely misleading. The particular intensity of Catholicism in Lithuania is well known. That intensity is a tribute not only to the faith of the Lithuanians but reflects the organizational strength of Roman Catholicism and the fact that, unlike the Orthodox or the Protestants, the leaders of the Catholic Church are abroad and not subject to Soviet repression.

The comparative weakness of the institutional Protestant churches in Latvia and Estonia, for instance, serves to highlight the exceptional case of Lithuania. This is not to say that ordinary Protestant believers in Latvia or Estonia—or ordinary Orthodox in Russian or Georgia—do not believe as strongly as Lithuanian Catholics, only that they can generally expect less support from their own leaders and from co-religionists abroad.

More importantly, the differing levels of open religious participation among denominations and ethnic groups also reflects tactical changes in Soviet anti-religious policy. In the first years of the post-revolutionary period, when Soviet policy was one of open persecution of believers and extermination of clergy, the main target was the Orthodox Church. By the time of the Baltic annexations the Soviets had discovered the relative merits of the more protracted and insidious policy they pursue now.

The effects of this change are apparent even in Russia itself, where to this day a disproportionate number of functioning Orthodox churches are located in areas occupied by the Germans during World War II. Churches closed by the Communists were allowed to reopen—the Nazis had little interest in the religious peculiarities of people they regarded as subhuman. Today there are only 16 Orthodox monasteries in the whole (out of well over 1,000 before the revolution), and only two of these are in Russia proper.

In its early period, the Soviet regime virtually wiped out or forced into exile the entire Orthodox episcopate, a loss of leadership from which no religious community easily recovers under conditions of continued harassment and discrimination. The question here is: does the apparently lower level of Russian Orthodox religious activity and resistance denote favoritism, or is it evidence of even fiercer persecution in the not too distant past?

Soviet religious persecution is constant and directed at religion per se, not just at certain churches. Russian Orthodox, like other believers, are severely restricted in instructing their children in their faith, in opening or keeping open places of worship, and getting access to religious literature. Like other believers, their faith all but guarantees a life of religious apartheid with respect to employment, housing, education, and virtually all other social activity.

Also, contrary to the impression given by Professor Thompson, Orthodox believers are prominent for their resistance to the Soviets, both as believers and as patriots. Besides the obvious name of Aleksandr Solzhenitsyn, the Soviets are well aware of such Russian believers as Father Gleb Yakunin, Sergei Khodorvich, Dmitry Dudko, Leonid Borodin, Vladimir Osipov, Igor Ogurtsov, Igor Shafarevich, Father Aleksandr Pivovarov, Anatoly Levitin-Krasnov, Ima Ratushinskaya, and many, many others who carry on the struggle for God and their country against, literally, Godless Communism.

In their efforts to defend their faith and human dignity, religious believers have made great progress in learning to put aside historic animosities and to work together. Understandably, the Soviets do everything they can to exacerbate lingering religious and national suspicions, keeping their unfortunate subjects weak and divided. Professor Thompson's efforts serve only to obscure the true nature of the pitiless Soviet anti-religious policy and are a cruel betrayal of all those who suffer for their faith.

James George Jatras
Executive Board Member
Committee for the Defense of Persecuted Orthodox Christians
Alexandria, VA

"Pravoslavophobia"

James George Jatras | *Chronicles* | February 1997

Item: An American of Greek origin calls a congressional office to protest United States policies in Bosnia that would place Christian Serbs at the mercy of a hostile Muslim regime. "So-called Christians," corrects a member of the congressman's staff, ignorant of the caller's religion.

Item: A national opinion magazine carries on its cover a harsh caricature of Russian "nationalism" personified by three vicious bears, costumed as a peasant, a "czarist" officer, and an Orthodox bishop in liturgical vestments!

Item: In another issue of that magazine, one writer, for whom Orthodox-baiting has been a preoccupation, conjures up an "Orthodox revanche" involving Greece, Serbia, Bulgaria, and Russia that has "drenched" Eastern Europe in "Muslim blood." And in yet another issue of the magazine the "near genocide" of Muslims in Bosnia is cited as "virtually consecrated by the Orthodox church."

Item: A distinguished retired American general, commenting on possible NATO expansion, states his view that (traditionally Roman Catholic) Poland, Hungary, the Czech Republic, and, maybe, Slovakia should be rapidly admitted to the Western alliance, but (Orthodox) Romania and Bulgaria should never be allowed in—and Greece should be ejected!

Item: The Sunday magazine of a leading national newspaper depicts, in appropriate iconographic style, with the Kremlin looming in the background, a mounted Saint George as a black-shirted member of the extremist Pamyat ("Memory") organization.

Reviewing American media coverage of a series of ethnic conflicts in Eastern Europe—Ukrainian Uniates vs. Ukrainian Orthodox, Hungarians vs. Romanians in Transylvania, Croats and Albanians vs. Serbs in the former Yugoslavia, Bulgarian Turks vs. Bulgarian Bulgarians—*St. Sophia Quarterly* editor Fr. Alexander Webster, author of *The Price of Prophecy: Orthodox Churches on Peace, Freedom, and Security*, observed in a 1990 *Washington Post* op-ed that historical complexities are invariably reduced to identification of "oppressor and victims," with the Orthodox contenders predictably wearing the black hats. The message is clear: the Orthodox East is the home of troublemakers. "They" (Americans are told) are evidently not like "us"—and the difference is not for the better.

There is an odd consistency to slanted, snidely anti-Orthodox, Western observations of Eastern European phenomena. First, one seldom if ever sees overt, explicit condemnation of Orthodoxy as a religion or of Orthodox national cultures as such. (But there are those who come awfully close. Christopher Hitchens in the *Nation* has made it his specialty to pepper his commentaries with gratuitous slaps at the "Serbian fundamentalist Orthodox"—whatever that means—and the presumed victimization of Muslim Chechens and Bosnians by "a sort of neo-czarist and Christian Orthodox imperium.") Generally, though, there is the use of images (the vicious bears, the Pamyat Saint George, the ubiquitous editorial cartoon villain labeled "the Serbs") that drive home the notion that "the Orthodox are bad." Or a mood is woven with seductively vague language: Romanian culture, wrote Robert D. Kaplan, author of *Balkan Ghosts*, in 1993, is "a blend of Latin sexuality and flair, Eastern Orthodox mysticism and superstition, and Byzantine intrigue." Now, he doesn't actually claim that "mysticism" and "superstition" are more or less the same thing, both equally "Orthodox." Nor does he come out and say Romanians are lecherous, irrational, and deceptive, but his reader will hardly miss the point. Or the broadcast media routinely and pointedly (one has to assume this is deliberate) match footage of Bosnian Serb officials attending church, crossing themselves, exchanging a threefold kiss, in the company of what to Western eyes must look like outlandish, if not threatening, hirsute figures wearing garish clerical robes—while the voice-over recounts the atrocities the officials are accused of having committed.

Second, it doesn't seem to matter whether the Western observer is Protestant, Roman Catholic, or Jewish (or most likely, not religious at all, though some might identify with one creed or another). The sense of the Western "us" versus the Eastern "them" is identical. Likewise, the specific religious identity of the presumptive victimized population juxtaposed to that of the supposed Orthodox oppressor likewise seems to make little difference. Whether the conflict is with Roman Catholics or with Muslims, the Orthodox are in the wrong.

Third, to the extent that the historical dimensions of current conflicts are noted at all, any past sins committed against the Orthodox are well past the moral statute of limitations. The annexation of the Ukrainian Uniates by the Russian Orthodox Church "counts," but the "Union" of Brest doesn't. The last two centuries of Polish subjugation by Russia is a moral reflection on the latter, but the two centuries before that, when the shoe was on the other foot, are irrelevant. Romanian discrimination against Transylvanian Magyars (between the world wars and since 1945) is a disgrace, but Hungarian treatment of Romanians under the Habsburgs and the Arrow Cross is forgotten. Serbia's repression of the Albanian Muslim majority in Kosovo since 1989 is roundly condemned, but the violent means employed by the Albanians under Turks, Nazis, and communists alike to *become* the majority are overlooked. The "international community" fairly cheered when the renascent fascist regime of Franjo Tudjman in Croatia, with American and German assistance, blasted their way past U.N. peacekeepers and depopulated the Serb Krajinas in the summer of 1995. But of course the Serbs "had it coming" for having had the temerity to take control of the Krajinas in the summer of 1991, on the flimsy grounds of being the majority population in the disputed areas. Conveniently omitted from news coverage was any mention of the horrendous slaughters perpetrated against the same Krajina (and Bosnian) Serbs during World War II, or even the reminiscent expulsions often of thousands of Serbs from Croatia in the spring of 1991 even *before* Croatia declared its independence.

Fourth and finally, the Orthodox can be defamed with impunity. Call us names, mock our icons, ridicule our clergy, demand we be bombed, applaud our *eradication—it's all in good fun.* No journalist or camera-jockey fears a lawsuit from an Orthodox Christian version of the Anti-Defamation League, much less a *fatwa* of the type placed on Salman Rushdie. Even a letter of protest to the editor of the offending publication is unlikely to be published. We are a soft target.

To what do we attribute this phenomenon? For that matter, is it a single phenomenon—more than just a combined Serbophobia, Russophobia, Hellenophobia, etc.? We might simply call it Pravoslavophobia, thus pinpointing the Orthodox religion, with its distinctive cultural stamp.

In his aforementioned *Washington Post* essay, Fr. Alexander suggested the seeming anti-Orthodox slant in media coverage "is due largely to an affinity of reporters and pundits for 'Western' culture, meaning Western [i.e., Protestant and Roman Catholic—or even post-Christian] Europe and often only Northwestern Europe. These cultural blinders preclude recognition of the full range of Western civilization, which includes Byzantine political and religious culture too."

Undoubtedly, that factor—an affinity for one's own Western experience coupled with ignorance of the separate cultural development of Orthodox Eastern Europe—is important. But there seems to be more to it than that. To start with, many of the Westerners who denigrate the Orthodox have not even the slightest idea who we are or what makes us different from the West. Even a semi-educated Westerner (and probably most Orthodox Easterners) could take a stab at explaining, say, Roman Catholicism as having something to do with the Pope of Rome and Protestantism as a Bible-based protest against papalism. But when they come to Orthodoxy, they draw a blank. They can't really hate us, because they don't even have any clear idea who we are. In fact, most Western Christians have a fairly positive attitude toward Orthodoxy. (Protestants generally regard Orthodoxy as superior to Roman Catholicism and vice versa. We're everybody's second-favorite religion.)

A few years ago, I had the opportunity to discuss this matter, in the context of the current Balkan war, with His Grace, Bishop Atanasije (Jevtic) of Herzegovina, one of the infamous, supposedly "nationalist" bishops close to the Bosnian Serb leadership. He had come to Washington to plead his people's case to Western politicians and media, to point out that while Serbs were sinners, not angels, they were certainly not the demons our media made them out to be. In particular, he hoped to present documentary evidence of recent Croatian atrocities against the Orthodox in his diocese, mainly near the town of Medjugorje, the site both of World War II massacres and of an ongoing "Marian apparition" particularly popular among "charismatic" Roman Catholics. Naturally, no one was interested. Only atrocities committed—or said to have been committed—by Serbs have news value. (His Grace told me about little children running from him in terror in a Swiss airport when they heard he was a Serb.)

As we discussed the West's hostility to his plight, I advanced the following theory, which His Grace believed to have some merit: Yes, Pravoslavophobia does exist, but it is a prejudice in the purest sense of the word—a prejudgment based on ignorance, a bias resting on regional parochialism. This prejudice reflects the fact that we are different from Westerners, but they themselves are only vaguely aware of the nature of the difference. It is something they feel rather than think.

This requires some explanation. One of the shibboleths of contemporary Western thought is multiculturalism: an exaggerated, if condescending, affirmation of the worth of other races and nations, religions and cultures. In addressing a non-Christian, non-European civilization, a high-minded Westerner feels obligated to emphasize that their folkways are not only just as good as his but maybe even better ("They have so much to teach us!"). Indeed, in "celebrating their diversity," he may feel the need to denigrate his own social traditions, which, after all, are largely the handiwork of white, Christian, heterosexual males. However, the same enlightened Westerner does not experience the same pressures when confronting the Orthodox East as he would when speaking to or about, say, Mohawks, Zulus, Chinese, or Afghans. We Orthodox are different enough for him to feel that we are alien but not different enough for him to feel obligated to respect us.

In sum, he perceives us as warped, distorted versions of himself. When he looks at us, he sees a mangled version of his own face, which produces a vague, inarticulate sense of unease, if not revulsion. And since he can't be in the wrong—the problem must be us.

Here is perhaps the greatest irony of the East/West divide within Christendom. After all, the West was once Orthodox—while we were never Roman Catholic or Protestant. The ancient Christian kingdoms of England, France, Spain, etc., began their emergence from barbarism as *sub-Byzantine states and cultures*, displaying, of course, their own distinctive features, much as Greece, Bulgaria, Romania, etc., differ from each other. In time, history was kinder to the West, which achieved its own distinctive cultural synthesis in the High Middle Ages, while the Orthodox East was crippled first by Ottoman/Mongol conquests (often aided by the depredations of our Western brethren) and then by a host of imported Western psychoses, like socialism. Even so, it is still clear, as a historical matter, that in the area of culture no less than religion, the West is derivative of the East, not the other way around.

In the closing decade of this millennium, sensitizing the West to its anti-Orthodox prejudice should not be seen as just one more example of whining and special pleading by yet one more "aggrieved" group. In the wake of two devastating intra-Christian civil wars (World War I and II), the once globally dominant European civilization—what some still quaintly refer to as Christendom—finds itself culturally, morally, religiously, and, perhaps worst of all, demographically moribund. At the same time, the non-European world, spearheaded by a reinvigorated and militant Islam no longer cowed by Western technical and military superiority, is on the offensive. As it happens, along virtually the entire front between Christendom and Islam (from the Balkans through the Caucasus and all through central Asia to the Chinese frontier) the frontline Christian states, *all of them Orthodox*, are not only actively engaged against the Muslim advance but, in most cases, must contend with the West's tacit or explicit support for their foes. If for no other reason than self-interest, the West should seriously think out long-term consequences of a possible collapse of the Orthodox East. The throat you help slit today may turn out to be your own.

A version of this article ran previously in the St. Sophia Quarterly.

"If God Ran the State Department"

James George Jatras | *Chronicles* | December 1997

"In the Name of the most Holy & undivided Trinity." Thus begins the Treaty of Paris (1783), by which Great Britain formally conceded the existence of the independent United States of America. This matter-of-fact invocation of the Triune God of Christianity stands in sharp contrast to the stirring tributes to human authority in the opening words of the documents usually cited as the foundations of the American republic: the Declaration of Independence ("When in the Course of human events . . .") and our second, and theoretically our current, constitution ("We the People of the United States . . ."). In fact, as the deed to our national existence, the Treaty of Paris is arguably *the* American founding document. The fact that the Christian invocation was *pro forma* for the times says as much about the times as the principle: the United States took its place among the nations of the world as an explicitly Christian polity.

With the possible exceptions of Puritan New England and the incipient state of Deseret, the United States has never been a *theocracy* in the sense that the ecclesiastical establishment ruled the civil. But until recently, it was unarguably a *thearchy* since public authorities, at all levels, from the schoolmarm leading her students in the Lord's Prayer to the President and the Supreme Court, openly affirmed Christianity (in its Protestant iteration) as the uncontested ruling ethos. The herald of liberty, Patrick Henry, proclaimed: "It cannot be emphasized too strongly or too often that this great nation was founded, not by religionists, but by Christians, not on religions but on the Gospel of Jesus Christ."

In sharp contrast to our current legal fictions, Justice Joseph Story, a preeminent expositor of our constitutional order (when we still had one), elucidated: "The real objective of the First Amendment was not to countenance, much less to advance, Mohammedanism, or Judaism, or infidelity, by prostrating Christianity, but to exclude rivalry among Christian sects, and to prevent any national ecclesiastical establishment patronage of the national government," and, in particular, to protect the then-established churches of several states. That a Christian America had an international mission was attested to by John Adams: "The destiny of America is to carry the Gospel of Jesus Christ to all men everywhere." Even as late as 1905, U.S. Supreme Court Justice David Josiah Brewer could state at Harvard University: "This Republic is classified among the Christian nations of the world. . . . We constantly speak of this Republic as a Christian nation—in fact, as the leading Christian nation of the world. The popular use of the term certainly has significance. It is not a mere creation of the imagination."

Today, in what Don Feder has rightly called Pagan America, such sentiments have only a quaint antiquarian significance; if uttered today, they would be offensive and subversive. The constitutionalism of Story and Brewer has long since given way to the lawlessness of Stevens and Breyer and their ilk. As if their conscious intent were to vex the shade of Justice Story, our judicial authorities act precisely to prostrate Christianity while giving official protection to pernicious cults that would have scandalized the Founding Fathers. The exemplar, of course, is the Supreme Court's extension of First Amendment protections to Afro-Caribbean animal sacrifices in *Church of The Lukumi Babalu Aye, Inc. v. City of Hialeah* (1993).

The United States no longer prides itself on exporting ministers of the Gospel of Jesus Christ; instead, as Irving Kristol has put it, "our missionaries live in Hollywood"—missionaries not of Christ, as John Adams had hoped, but of "a dominant secular hedonistic ethos. It is an imperium with a minimum of moral substance." As is true of our domestic policy, our globalist foreign policy reflects the values of a ruling pseudo-elite that is estranged not only from our country's Christian heritage but from the inarticulate and half-forgotten residue of that heritage among ordinary Americans. That is, the moral plunge of our international agenda from exporting the Gospel to exporting cash and condoms for the cooperative, sanctions and bombs for the recalcitrant, is inseparable from the progressive de-Christianization of American society and of the larger European civilization which gave it birth.

Recently, someone asked the not entirely rhetorical question in reference to what has long been called the "American experiment" in republican, "pluralistic" self-government: When can we say an experiment has failed? To answer that question, it is necessary to recall that in the long history of Christendom, republicanism has been the rare exception—and "pluralism," a modern marketing term for de-Christianization, was unknown. That a public religious establishment can exist while allowing a reasonable degree of toleration of private dissent was obvious to the premodern mind; Swift, speaking through the giant king of Brobdingnag, gave the classic justification for limited forbearance: "A man may be allowed to keep poisons in his closet, but not to vend them about for cordials."

It should be remembered that in the Roman Empire, the legalization of Christianity under Constantine after three centuries of persecution and the establishment of Christianity as the official religion under Theodosius the Great coincided with the culmination of the progressive evolution of the office of the emperor—originally, in theory, just the "first citizen" (*princeps*) of the Republic—into a true monarch. By the beginning of the fifth century, in both Rome and Constantinople the emperor was a visible icon of Christian thearchy, the divinely anointed successor of David and Solomon, ruler of the New Israel: in a word, king (*basileus*). The indissoluble symphony between crown and cross, state and church, *imperium* and *sacerdotium* was in turn adopted by the sub-Roman successor states established by the barbarians, as new peoples—Celt, German, Slav—adopted the Faith, along with many aspects of classical Greco-Roman culture, under the command of a Clovis or an Ethelbert, an Olaf or a Vladimir. (In keeping with Ephesians 3:14–15 and 5:20–33, the same derivative understanding sanctified authority on the family level in the form of patriarchy; as late as the 18th century, wives in England who killed their husbands suffered not hanging but burning, the penalty for traitors, since their crime was not just murder but "petty treason.")

In sum, the growth and consolidation of European Christian civilization took place in a context in which Christianity—in the form of an established church—was the exclusive public creed of states ruled by autocratic monarchs (invariably styled "defender of the faith") in consultation with—but not under the command of—such councils, senates, and so forth as tradition provided. It is during this millennium and a half before the ironically misnamed "Enlightenment" that the true Light, the Word Incarnate, became implanted in the European heart: the vestigial Christian consciousness in modern America and

Europe is nothing less (and alas, nothing more) than the small change in copper left over from the moral gold bullion amassed during that time.

In contrast, modernity might best be defined as a rejection of divinely anointed, legitimate authorities in the world in favor of the moral nihilism that became intellectually respectable during the 18th century, received its fullest elaboration in the 19th, and achieved political dominance in the 20th. Today, not a single historically Christian country can truthfully claim to be a functional Christian society. On the state level, no government, whether nominally a republic or a monarchy (the latter being, in practice, a republic in ermine drag, where not even the monarch would claim that "the people" are not sovereign), would stake its legitimacy on the cross on its flag or would claim Christ as its ruler. The ideological assault on monarchy—first by democracy (*vox populi, vox dei*), then by socialism—is inextricably linked to the notion that God no longer rules the world, if He exists at all. (It is significant that the great revolutions of modern European history—English, French, Russian— each culminated in regicide, the national analog of deicide and patricide, an anti-sacrament, a blood sacrifice upon the altar of human self-will.) In due course, having killed, deposed, or emasculated our kings, and having intellectually expelled the Creator from His creation under the tutelage of Darwin, Marx, and Freud, it is hardly surprising that in recent decades our rebellion has now worked its way down to the family in the destruction of fatherhood: feminism as moral patricide.

America, despite the best intentions and emphatic Christian aspirations of the Founders, has not been immune from this progression and in some respects has been its showcase. Perhaps the most *experimental* thing about the American experiment was the apparently unexamined assumption that a stable, Christian social order that reflected 14 centuries of Christian monarchy and church/state cooperation could be preserved and even strengthened under a political order explicitly based on then-current fantasies about the idealized civic virtues of pagan Greece and Rome. We thought we could declare every man to be his own king as well as his own pope, while under the guidance of a "natural aristocracy," the inherited moral and social order would not suffer. We were wrong. The progressive degeneration over the years from a confederal republic, to a federal democracy, to our current demagogic unitary state can be traced in the decline from Jefferson's apologetics for sans-culottic obscenities in France, to the rule of King Mob under Jackson, to Lincoln's anti-constitutionalism, to Wilson's sanctimonious one-worldism, to the bush-league Bolshevism of Roosevelt and Johnson, and finally to the Gramscian prevarications of Bush, Clinton, and Gingrich.

It is specious to believe, as do many American Christians (particularly evangelicals), that the prevailing corruption has not seduced and degraded "the people" as badly as our rulers, and that the Humpty-Dumpty of Christian society can (and will) be reassembled by a political movement like the Moral Majority or the Christian Coalition. Sadly, there are more Americans who are depraved enough to vote for the kind of government we now have than there are who will vote against it. Just as unlikely is national salvation in the form of "revival," a new Great Awakening. Americans' Christianity has almost entirely lost its savor. Social regeneration cannot be expected from a few more group hugs for "reconciliation" by Promise Keepers, much less from "designer" megachurches specializing in "Christian aerobics" for yuppies or from the babbling, barking, and backflopping of the Toronto Airport Blessing, the Pensacola Outpouring, and the rest of the demonic "signs and wonders" deception.

But . . . *if* God has not irrevocably withdrawn His grace from our corrupted world, and if He were, by some miracle unforeseen and undeserved by us, to restore an American Christian society and the constitutional republic that the Founding Fathers envisioned and which, for however short a time, existed—what should be its place in the world? What should be its policy toward other nations?

One good place to start would be with the old John Birch Society slogan, an oldie but goodie: "U.S. out of the U.N., and the U.N. out of the U.S." Most American Christians, to the degree that they have any kind of spiritual compass, as well as many people who are anything but Christian, have an instinctive and valid mistrust of the growing threat that world government presents to American national sovereignty. A Christian America would cease its participation in the United Nations and throw that organization's headquarters out of New York; the U.N. Participation Act of 1947 should be repealed. As Saint Paul told the Athenians, God "hath made of one blood all nations of men for to dwell on all the face of the earth, and hath determined the times before appointed, and the bounds of their habitation" (Acts 17:26). That is, even though all men are of the same flesh. Holy Scripture suggests that each kindred, tongue, people, and nation has its foreordained place and time. That the United States has become Frank Nitti to the U.N.'s Al Capone, breaking the knees of any nation (or at least the relatively weak ones, like Iraq, Somalia, Haiti, or Serbia) so crass as to want to preserve its independence and pursue its sovereign interests should be particularly repugnant to us. A Christian America would zealously preserve its own sovereignty—trade, immigration, and citizenship policy would be restructured to protect, not break down, the American nation—and respect the sovereignty of other nations. We would seek, with nations as with individuals, to "do good unto all men, especially unto them who are of the household of faith," as the Apostle writes.

A Christian foreign policy would mean the end of foreign aid and, in general, the end of most officially approved meddling in other nations' business. Congress should repeal the 1961 Foreign Assistance Act and abolish the Kennedy-era Agency for International Development and the Peace Corps. If we object—as we should—to the efforts by the Chinese government to buy the Clinton administration, why do we expect other countries to thank us when we use the National Endowment for Democracy, funded with tax dollars, to influence foreign elections and pick winners and losers, or when an armed U.S. force embarks upon nonsensical "nation-building"? Why does our Gauleiter in Bosnia, Robert Gelbard, think he has the right to threaten Bosnian Serbs with the "most serious imaginable" consequences (more "serious" than the bombs and sanctions we have already inflicted on them?) unless they vote to ratify the leaders we have preselected for them? Why does the International Republican Institute conduct programs in Russia and Eastern Europe to encourage greater female participation in the political process, as if there is something inherently wrong with the traditional attitude (still stronger in the post-communist world than in the West) that politics mostly concerns men and that women's major responsibility is the home? Most of what our money goes for is neither good nor Christian, and even if it were, there is no compelling reason why Americans should be taxed to pay for work that would be better done on a voluntary basis.

In general, an American Christian foreign policy that championed national sovereignty over internationalism would heed the long-neglected warning of George Washington against "permanent, inveterate antipathies against particular nations and passionate attachments for others." At the same time, a sovereign, Christian America would take a realistic and principled attitude toward two issues that should provoke the conscience of any Christian people: persecution of Christians and the march of militant Islam.

"Precious in the sight of the Lord," sang the psalmist, "is the death of his saints." An amazed and stupefied Washington establishment has lately discovered the obvious fact that more Christians have suffered a martyr's fate in the 20th century than in the previous 19 combined. (As a side observation on the abysmal level of Christian knowledge and solidarity, how many American Christians now fond of citing this know that today most Christian victims of Islam are Roman Catholics, or that the vast majority of this century's horrendous communist death toll were Orthodox?) Typically, the bipartisan establishment has managed to trivialize even this belated awareness of Christian persecution and has relegated it to the generic status of "human rights," unwilling to show any particular concern for Christians without throwing in Tibetan Buddhists, Iranian Baha'is, Chinese Muslims, and anybody and everybody else to avoid even the suspicion that American Christians might be especially concerned about fellow Christians. An American Christian policy would bar or severely limit goods from persecuting states and keep our political contacts with persecuting regimes at appropriately minimal levels.

Similarly, the United States should reverse its pro-Muslim bias in the conflicts that currently rage between Muslims and Christians in the Balkans, the Caucasus, Central Asia, and along the southern Sahara and extend toward the Christians what traditional diplomacy called "benevolent neutrality"; we should encourage the moral unity of traditionally Christian peoples and should abandon misguided policies, like NATO expansion and our Bosnia deployment, that promote disunity. It is not the job of even a Christian America to go to war to protect Christians abroad, but we should be in solidarity with, not hostile to, Christian communities that are increasingly subject to physical eradication by the devotees of a crazed false prophet.

Of all the items on the Christian Coalition's voters' guide, in all likelihood the only one never to be faulted by the ACLU or People for the American Way on the ground of church/state separation is the notion that American Christians have a *religious* obligation to insist on unqualified American support for the state of Israel. This is not to suggest that the United States could not justify a cooperative relationship with Israel purely on prudent foreign policy grounds, given the latter's antipathy toward Islamic radicalism. However, we should terminate Israel's peremptory claim to over four billion dollars in various forms of American assistance every year, the benefit of which even many Israelis are now questioning; the Cranston Amendment, for example, which requires that American annual aid to Israel be no less than Israel's annual interest payment on past loans, should be repealed. Likewise, it is natural and—if it were kept within certain limits—tolerable that American Jews would have an inclination to interpret Israel's interests as harmonious with America's, even as Americans of other ethno-religious stock maintain their emotional bond with their countries of origin.

But there is no justification for the conviction of so many American Christians, mostly evangelicals but including members of other denominations, that American support for a non-Christian foreign state is an *absolute* divine mandate. This superstition derives almost entirely from a novel— indeed, heretical—method of biblical exegesis called Dispensationalism, which holds, among other things, that the covenant given to Israel in the Old Testament continues to run concurrently with the New Covenant; in its extreme form, its adherents go so far as to suggest that there are in effect two paths of salvation, one for Jews and the other for Gentiles, a clear perversion of Scripture (especially Saint Paul's Epistle to the Romans, chapters 9 through 11) and of any Christian teaching to be found from the first century to the 19th. Some Dispensationalists even expect in the not-too-distant future to hail the returned Christ in the guise of an earthly king and messiah ruling from a rebuilt Temple of Solomon in Jerusalem—and have provided moral and material support to a radical Israeli group called the Temple Mount Faithful, which has repeatedly provoked violent tensions in its campaign to rebuild the Temple destroyed by Titus in A.D. 70. For any serious Christian, especially one familiar with the writings of the Church Fathers, less important than the political consequences of a rebuilt temple (the site is now occupied by the Dome of the Rock and the al-Aqsa mosque) or the Jewish religious significance of rebuilding the Temple (the last serious attempt to do so was under Julian the Apostate in the fourth century) is that there could be absolutely no doubt as to *who* will be the "Christ" ruling the earth from that Temple: "that man of sin . . . , the son of perdition, who opposeth and exalteth himself above all that is called God, or that is worshipped; so that he as God sitteth in the temple of God, shewing himself that he is God," as Saint Paul warned.

Of course, speculation as to how specific political events relate to the unfolding of the "mystery of iniquity" have no more proper place in setting policy than do those of Dispensationalism and should not bias American policy for or against either Israel or any other country. But as a purely religious question, the effect of Dispensationalism on American perceptions of world events deserves urgent and immediate examination by all American Christians.

Unfortunately, that examination is about as likely as the United States having a Christian foreign, or domestic, policy any time soon—or ever again. God gave the Christian world 15, maybe 16, good centuries after Constantine. We cannot expect Him to be so generous again.

The foregoing was originally published under the nom de plume *D. George Leech.*

"Oriental Fumin'"

J.G. Jatras | *Chronicles* | October 2001

It was not what we have come to expect when John Paul II arrives in a Christian country—or in any country, for that matter. In place of adoring crowds lining the streets along which the popemobile made its stately progress, there were scattered groups of demonstrators hurling imprecations both angry and somewhat bizarre: "arch-heretic, two-horned, grotesque monster of Rome." Was something lost in the translation?

These words, often quoted in the Western media, were those of a parish priest, presumably more moderate than the monastic zealots who constituted the core of the antipapal reaction to John Paul's historic pilgrimage to Greece. Some Roman Catholics—particularly conservatives who, like John Paul himself, are generally favorable toward the Orthodox East—were at least as puzzled as they were offended. All right, they figured, we could understand protests from the usual bunch of communists, feminists, and sodomites. But monks? And he even apologized! What more do you people want?

To begin with, let's get the part about the apology out of the way. Frankly, I wish he hadn't extended it, and not only because apologies to every group with an ax to grind have become the order of the day, with Bill Clinton the universally recognized master emeritus. (By contrast, John Paul, we can be sure, was sincere.) Saying "I'm sorry" for something he did not personally do not only is beneath his pontifical dignify, but serves to evoke a sappy emotional response on the part of some Orthodox that obscures the real points of division. (While we're on the apology issue, let me add a footnote: If Rome really is sorry for 1204 and all that, how about giving us back some of the loot—notably, the relics those sticky-fingered *Frangoi* grabbed and which now hallow virtually every major cathedral in Western Europe. If you break into my house, trash the place, steal all my stuff, and then apologize, isn't it reasonable for me to reply: "OK, but how about giving me back my VCR and my toaster"? Dibs on the Shroud of Turin!)

The more profound significance of the Greek reaction is that it is finally beginning to dawn on those decent Roman Catholics who see the Orthodox as natural allies in an immoral, neopagan world that sacramental union between Eastern and Western Christianity is not in the cards anytime soon—even if they do not fully understand why. As one commentator describing himself as "a Roman Catholic admirer of Orthodoxy" lamented:

> Isn't working closely to combat the functional nihilism that accompanies the spread of consumerist values a more pressing concern than fussing over the fate of the *Filioque* clause? The pope knows that the key question in the era of postmodernism and globalization is not what brand of Christianity the world will follow; it is whether the world will follow Christianity at all.

Well, setting aside Orthodox suspicions that papal supremacy is likely to remain less negotiable than other differences, and that any prospective union would mean, as it always has in the past, Orthodox subordination to Rome, and therefore precisely a question of what brand of Christianity the union produces, this seeming indifference to dogmatic questions is indicative of how little the West understands the East. Some of the over-the-top Greek rhetoric obscured the fact that, for many Orthodox, *"Filioque"* (not to mention "Vicar of Christ") is still fightin' words. Catholic ecumenists may prefer to think the vehement anti-Romanism of doctrinally and morally conservative Orthodox is simply the mark of retrogrades and obscurantists (oh, flatterers!), and they are entitled to their opinion. They may console themselves with the notion that the Orthodox simply have not come to terms with modernism or, as has been suggested by some (both Catholic and Orthodox), have not even noticed it. To which I reply: Oh, we've noticed modernism all right; it's just that we don't like it very much. In fact, Orthodoxy in the last century alone has suffered at its hands to an extent the Western confessions can scarcely imagine. But it is hard for conservative Roman Catholics to understand that, from our perspective, Rome (and not just post-Vatican II) is not an antidote to modernism but part of it, John Paul's own moral witness on some important issues notwithstanding. (One very important distinction should be noted here: Some Roman Catholics who pass for moral "conservatives" nowadays, mostly because they are pro-life, have long since made their peace with modernism up to Vatican II and beyond. Some of the "conservatives" who make a point of hailing John Paul II, perhaps mistakenly, as one of their own barely conceal their underlying disdain for what they see as Orthodox backwardness. Their interest in the East does not, I believe, extend much beyond an urge to devour us. More tragic, at least from the Orthodox perspective, are those truly conservative exemplars of the best of the Roman Catholic tradition who, like some of their Protestant counterparts, desire reconciliation with East precisely because they see our backwardness for what it is: loyalty to the ancient traditions. But they are caught in a circle that cannot be squared: If they think

Dostoevsky's parable of the Grand Inquisitor in *The Brothers Karamazov* is just about socialism, they had better read it again.)

Part of the reason for Catholic ecumenists' incomprehension is that their understanding of Orthodoxy is derived almost exclusively from contacts with Orthodox ecumenists, too many of whom are exactly the type of Eastern-rite Episcopalians (in the Bishop Spong sense) that Rome would end up with if there were a union. Any foreseeable union would cause a schism in our Church, and Rome would mostly find itself in communion with people who, as much or more than Catholic modernists, want nothing so much as the approval of a godless world. There are exceptions, of course, but Catholics should ask themselves: If these Orthodox are willing to unite with Catholics professing views on authority in the Church, the *Filioque*, etc., that run counter to their own tradition, how pro-life would they turn out to be? Those Catholics who see union as a means to reinforce the best elements in their own confession might find that it leads to the exact opposite.

In sum, the Greek trip was a big setback for John Paul II's well-known desire to go to Russia, and prospects for union during his pontificate are virtually dead. Even as far as his own agenda is concerned, it was almost entirely counterproductive. Try to see it from the perspective of real Orthodox Greeks: the Church of Greece, which knew he wanted to advance his ecumenical agenda, did not want him to come. So the socialist government (pro-abortion, pro-homosexual, pro-"Europe") preempts the Greek Church by inviting John Paul as a head of state. And then he doesn't expect to be received as a political figure? When you sincerely court someone and the answer is "no," why force your attentions? Isn't this just asking for things to get ugly, notwithstanding efforts by the Greek hierarchy to strike a note of civility during the visit itself? On this Rome—probably not the Pope himself but his diplomats—has made an unfortunate blunder.

From the Orthodox perspective, we can unite with Roman Catholicism when, and only when, what we sincerely regard as the latter's errors of the past millennium are rejected, and the former patriarchate of the old imperial capital returns to Orthodoxy. No one expects that to happen anytime soon. Trying to force the issue by dismissing the disagreements as so much fussing, and by placing unity above truth, is an insult to faithful Catholics and Orthodox alike. Better that we accept that we fundamentally disagree on important matters of faith but can still—and must—cooperate on moral and cultural issues. The primate of the Greek Church, Archbishop Christodoulos of Athens, made that appeal in his meeting with John Paul II, stating that—

> the time has come for us to co-ordinate our efforts to assure that Europe remains a Christian land, away from the apparent tendency to transform her nations into atheist states, denying their Christian identity.

Likewise, there is little for any Roman Catholic or Protestant worthy of his own tradition to disagree within the social concept published by the Moscow patriarchate in August 2000. Serious Christians of various confessions have plenty of reasons to view one another as friends and comrades in the twilight struggle against the modern social pathologies and their effects, exemplified by the demographic crisis that threatens all of Christian Europe. If moral alliance, not Eucharistic unity, were the focus of the Pope's eastern policy, even many Orthodox zealots would be receptive. But his Greek pilgrimage, however well-intentioned, was not the way to go about it.

J.G. Jatras, an occasional contributor, writes from Virginia. His disturbing resemblance to certain monks seen in news photos of the Pope's visit to Greece is purely coincidental.

"The Patriarch of Russia's Restoration"

James George Jatras | American Orthodox Institute | 2009

Russian Orthodoxy Resurgent: Faith and Power in the New Russia
By John Garrard and Carol Garrard
Princeton University Press, 326 pp., $29.95

The recognized godfather of modern Orthodox-inspired Russian patriotism, Aleksandr Solzhenitsyn, once characterized Bolshevism as a promethean effort to rub off the age-old face of Russia and to replace it with a new, ersatz Soviet face. Historians will argue for years if that monstrous experiment was doomed to failure, when and how that failure might have occurred at critical historical junctures, and especially who the indispensable figures in communism's eventual demise were. But there is little question that in the chronicles of Russia's restoration as a recognizably Orthodox Christian country the late Patriarch ALEKSY II of Moscow and All Russia will figure high on that list.

While few could realistically expect the end of communism to entail the reinstatement of dispossessed noble families' lands and estates or formal reestablishment of the Church and monarchy (not yet, anyway), "restoration" is indeed the right term. After the long, sub-rosa civil war that constituted the communists' decades-long efforts to overcome Russians' obstinate unwillingness or inability to conform their lives and consciences to the insane scribblings of Marx, Engels, and Lenin, Americans and other westerners familiar with Russia today can only be astounded at the miraculous—there is no other word for it—degree to which the Orthodox Church has become the national moral conscience, including in state and, especially, military affairs. While Americans, with our history of government neutrality among churches, might be a bit taken aback at state officials' participating in Orthodox services to bless the launch of a new nuclear submarine or to celebrate the patron Saint's Day of a military unit, given the degree to which Christianity is being ruthlessly purged from our own public life we might feel just a twinge of envy.

That this state of affairs came into being relatively peacefully during the dangerous days of the Soviet regime's final death agony is largely Aleksy's doing. Indeed, though his name does not appear in the title or subtitle, Aleksy is really the subject of the Garrards' book, far more than Russia or Orthodoxy per se. The book is especially enlightening in detailing Aleksy's actions during the failed August 1991 putsch, when Soviet diehards sought to overthrow the government of the Russian Republic (the largest of the USSR's 15 Union Republics) headed by President Boris Yeltsin. The Garrards credit (correctly in this reviewer's opinion) Aleksy's stern anathema against the shedding of civil blood for the fact that the military refused to take action in support of the coup and that the death toll was kept to just three persons:

> Every person who raises arms against his neighbor, against unarmed civilians, will be taking upon his soul a very profound sin which will

separate him from the Church and from God. It is appropriate to shed more tears and say more prayers for such people than for their victims. May God protect you from the terrible sin of fratricide. I solemnly warn all my fellow-citizens: The Church does not condone and cannot condone unlawful and violent acts and the shedding of blood. I ask all of you, my dear ones, to do everything possible to prevent the flame of civil war from bursting forth. Cease at once!

The success of Aleksy's warning, issued in response to an appeal by Yeltsin, is all the more remarkable in that it would be heeded by officers and men of a Red Army originally created to crush Russian resistance to an earlier Bolshevik *coup d'etat*, in October 1917. The army's response did not materialize out of thin air. The Garrards record Aleksy's amazingly deft cultivation of the armed forces, and even elements of the KGB, well before his rise to the patriarchate. During the 1980s, first as Metropolitan of his native Tallinn (Estonia) and of Leningrad (now once again Saint Petersburg), Aleksy was remarkably successful in securing the Soviet authorities' acquiescence to the restoration to the Church of the celebrated Danilov Monastery—now once again official headquarters of the patriarchate—and the KGB's return of the relics of the famous military saint and champion of Orthodoxy against the Roman Catholic Swedes and Teutonic Knights, Prince Aleksandr Nevsky. His masterful use of the 1988 celebration of the millennium of the Baptism of Rus' under Saint Prince Vladimir of Kiev was a major milestone in the Church's assumption of its current commanding role. At the same time, the authors, despite their clearly positive attitude toward Aleksy and his accomplishments, do not hide the fact that little of this would have been possible if Aleksy had not himself been a longtime operative of the KGB.

Taken as a whole, *Russian Orthodoxy Resurgent* is a valuable book and the Garrards should be commended for ably bringing to light facets of one of recent history's little known but most significant chapters. At the same time, the work includes two minor oddities and one major, indeed deplorable, defect.

In a prolonged digression, the Garrards explore the bases of the thousand-year-old dispute between Orthodoxy and Roman Catholicism as an intended insight on Aleksy's distrust of the Vatican, his refusal to allow Pope John-Paul II visit Russia as he dearly wanted, and his insistence that Orthodoxy, not Catholicism or Protestantism, be acknowledged as *the* Christian confession in Russia in relation to other historic faiths: Islam, Judaism, and Buddhism. In doing so, however, they embark on a long, and essentially irrelevant, explanation that the claims of Rome and Moscow depend on how one reads the Gospel accounts of Christ's first calling to His apostolate, respectively, Saint Peter or his brother Saint Andrew. Aside from the fact that the see of Constantinople also takes its founding honorific from Andrew and Antioch and (through Saint Mark) Alexandria from Peter, no such who-was-summoned-before-whom controversy has much bearing on the real points of division: Rome's own formulation of its Petrine claims of supremacy (and infallibility), the *filioque*, the forced unions of Lyons, Ferrara-Florence, and Brest, and repeated armed incursions by western armies into Orthodox countries to subdue people regarded by Rome as schismatics if not heretics. Writing as no stranger to Orthodox-Latin polemics, this reviewer is puzzled as to why the authors would include such a strange and, frankly, inaccurate explanation.

Perhaps even more peculiar is the Garrards' repeated insistence that the Russian Orthodox Church Outside of Russia (ROCOR) and the Russian Orthodox Church Abroad (ROCA) are two different bodies when in fact they are the same thing. I have consulted numerous sources, including many in ROCOR/ ROCA—both of which names are in fact found on their own website—and they are as baffled as I am as to what the source of misunderstanding might be. (In common parlance, even more common than "ROCOR" and "ROCA" are "the Synod" or "the Synodal Church," which is not used in the book.) While the confusion can be regarded as a minor quirk the topic to which it is relevant— the 2007 reunion of the branches of the Russian Church abroad and at home, of which then-President Vladimir Putin was hardly less a champion than Aleksy—is not. In any case, the reunion was a bilateral, not trilateral, event.

These blemishes are insignificant compared to the Garrards' absolutely inexcusable vilification of the Serbian Orthodox Church and the Serbian people. It is understandable that the authors wished to juxtapose Aleksy's successful navigation of the Russian Church through the treacherous shoals of Russian politics, both civil and ecclesiastical, and it was no doubt tempting to hold up a negative point of comparison. Given the magnitude of the disinformation about and demonization of Serbia and the Serbian Church, and the close national and spiritual ties between Russians and Serbs, the Serbian example might seem a suitable illustration of the "road not taken" (as the Garrards indeed refer to it). They compare what they see as Aleksy's positive handling of sensitive issues like the glorification of the Royal Martyrs Nicholas II and his family, the return to Sarov of the relics of Saint Seraphim, and the veneration of warrior saints such as Nevsky and Prince Dmitry Donsky to "Serbian bloodlust" and supposedly Church-blessed massacres of Croats and Muslims stirred up by Serbian churchmen eager for Serbs to see them- selves as victims of their neighbors through manipulation of such events as the translation of the relics of Saint Prince (not "King") Lazar on the 600th anniversary of the epic battle of Kosovo in which he championed the Christian forces fighting Ottoman invaders. The authors seemingly are unaware of the fact that Serbs *are* indeed victims of their neighbors, having been subjected not only to the physical depredations of mass murder and eradication from their homes during World War II under Croatian *Ustaše* and their Muslim allies but in the 1990s by Croats and Bosnian and Kosovo Albanian Muslims—the last continuing today in slow-motion under Wash- ington's sponsorship. Likewise missing is any awareness that Aleksy, as well as Putin, and everyone else featured positively in the book, and in fact almost everyone in Russia, has remained fully in support of the Serbian cause and would see no difference at all between the Russian and Serbian national, religious, and martial traditions. It certainly does not help that the Garrards took as their authorities on Balkan events two unreliable authors noted for their vicious Serbophobia and Pravoslavophobia.

In short, the Garrards should have observed Rule One for the writing of nonfiction: stick to what you know, stay away from subjects about which you are ignorant. While at their worst on Serbia, with regard to Russia, a subject they clearly know very well, they are perceptive and effective. As an elucidation of pivotal events of recent history, *Russian Orthodoxy Resurgent* is, despite its flaws, a valuable public service, for Orthodox Christians especially. Espe- cially with the repose of Patriarch Aleksy, John Garrard and Carol Garrard have written a book well worth reading and a fitting memorial to a hierarch whose reputation will only grow with the passage of time.

Statement of James George Jatras Regarding Allegations of Misuse of Funds to Support Lobbying in the United States on Behalf of Serbs in Kosovo and Metohija

James George Jatras | February 19, 2010

In connection with the suspension of His Grace, Bishop ARTEMIJE, from supervision of his Eparchy, allegations have been made to the effect that funds allocated for other purposes (variously reported as earmarked for humanitarian relief or for repair of churches) instead were used to pay for lobbying service by two firms with which I have been associated, Venable and Squire Sanders. To the best of my knowledge, this was first raised in Blic <http://www.blic.rs/Vesti/Drustvo/176948/Vladika-Atanasije-Iguman-Simeon-cemorati-na-sud> yesterday. Later that same day, an item appeared in a website purporting to be that of the Diocese of Ras and Prizren and Kosovo and Meto-hija, denouncing me <http://raskoprizrenska.blogspot.com/2010/02/blog-post_1108.html> for beginning circulation of an open appeal in defense of Vladika Artemije <http://www.thepetitionsite.com/2/open-appeal-for-the-reinstatement-of-his-grace-bishop-artemije-of-ras-and-prizren-and-kosovo>, which started yesterday.

I will address the accusation of the alleged misuse of funds in due course, below. But first it needs to be made clear what is going on here: that a concerted effort is being made to destroy the man who, more than anyone else, has become the symbol of Serbia's resistance to amputation and annihilation of Serbia's most important spiritual and national patrimony. Can anyone doubt that should it succeed what would be the consequence for the Serbs of Kosovo and Metohija and for the whole Serbian nation? Even if there are legitimate questions to be asked about administrative matters in the Diocese, everyone can see the methods being used to obliterate Vladika Artemije's public witness and to terrorize and intimidate his supporters. Who benefits from that?

With regard to my contract for lobbying services on behalf of Vladika Artemije and of the Serbian people of Kosovo and Metohija, I have and always will regard the fact that His Grace asked me, and not someone else, to perform this task in Washington as the great honor of my life. It should be kept in mind that beginning with my work at the U.S. Senate, and subsequently during my testimony as the trial of Slobodan Milosevic at The Hague, I have tried to be conscientious regarding both the damage my own country was doing to itself through its misguided Balkan policy (and particularly support of radical Islamic elements in Bosnia and Kosovo) and the obscene unfairness of the demonization the Western powers, especially the United States, attached to the Serbs during the Balkan wars of the 1990s. For that, well before being engaged by the Serbs of Kosovo, I was attacked from many quarters, notably by Islamic organizations and the Albanian lobby. Perhaps for that reason, when Vladika Artemije decided that something on a professional basis needed to be done on behalf of his people, he selected me knowing that it would not be just a "job" performed by a "hired gun" who could just as happily represent Serbia's enemies but someone committed to his cause.

In March 2006, I signed on behalf of Venable an agreement with the Serbian National Council of Kosovo and Metohija <http://www.fara.gov/docs/54

35-Exhibit-AB-20060404-5.pdf> (SNC), under the signature of its president, Mr. Dragan Velic. It should be kept in mind there was then no official Serbian government lobbying effort in the United States, at a time when the U.S. government clearly was moving towards a "final solution" of the province's status. (Several months later the government did sign an agreement with another firm <http://www.fara.gov/docs/5430-Exhibit-AB-20060829-12.pdf> but not, as far as I know, with specific reference to Kosovo.) Vladika Artemije concluded that if no action was going to be taken by official Belgrade, he had no choice but to try to do something himself as the centerpiece of a professional effort to put the truth about Kosovo in front of the face of the American people and decision-makers. This is the same decisiveness and courage he displayed when I first met him, when I was working at the Senate, during the period 1997-1998, when he was, as far as I know, the only Bishop willing to speak against Milosevic and to come to Washington on a mission of peace.

Upon signing of the March 2006 agreement with the SNC, Venable immediately launched the American Council for Kosovo <http://www.save kosovo.org/>. Our goal was to provide a real American voice against the wrong-headedness of our country's policy of supporting a group of Islamic terrorists and organized crime organizations (the KLA) under the command of the criminals Thaci, Ceku, and Haradinaj; and to show t,hat far from perpetrators of genocide in Kosovo, Serbs are the victims. We knew we were starting a fight with an entrenched policy position in Washington, which held that all the merits were on the Albanian side and none on the Serbian side. We also were fighting against an Albanian lobby that had been active, literally, for decades, and which had vast sources of funds (of course, including criminal proceeds), the amounts of which can only be speculated, and which lavishly gave to American politicians' campaigns.

The reaction to our beginning operations was hysterical. One of the Albanian-American groups accused us of trying to "hijack American policy toward Kosova http://blog.aacl.com/?s=hijack," to which, of course, the Albanians were accustomed to full and uncontested enjoyment. (It is quite meaningful that the information in the Blic article is taken almost word-for-word from this Albanian-American site.) They hacked our website. They launched a phony mirror site <http://www.savekosova.org/> (which even fooled some people into thinking we were working for the Albanians too!). They denounced us as racists, extremists, etc., for pointing out the truth of Kosovo and the "friends" America had adopted there. We believed we could win only by changing the terms of debate. When we began, "Kosovo" meant only "the place where America stopped genocide of peaceful Albanians by evil Serbs." Due to our efforts, for many, many Americans "Kosovo" now means "the place where our government insanely helps jihadists and gangsters terrorize Christian Serbs."

Were we successful? Let us remember that when we began our efforts Washington fully expected smoothly to arrange the "final status" of Kosovo well before the end of 2006. The architects of American policy expected minimal resistance from Belgrade and were sure the Russians were not serious in their opposition to independence. And of course there were virtually no dissenting voices in the United States. While our efforts may not have been early enough to have accomplished a reversal of American policy, I am confident that if not for this campaign under Vladika Artemije's guidance and direction Washington would have moved much faster than it did to "resolve" the issue. Instead, we threw enough sand in the gears that contributed to a delay of almost two years, by which time the Russian position had become rock-solid and it had become impossible for anyone (openly, anyway) in

Serbian politics to consent to losing Kosovo. Even when Washington did make its move in early 2008, in concert with the KLA kingpins and with unprecedented bullying of our European allies, they did so with the increasingly desperate knowledge they were losing ground and that it was "now or never." The result—the ongoing, unresolved crisis—is not one anyone wants to see but is far better than what likely would have been the case if we had not moved when we did at Vladika Artemije's initiative. I sincerely believe we helped give Serbia a fighting chance, which it is still her option to take advantage of or not.

With respect to the money, there is a curious assumption behind the accusation that moneys were "diverted" to lobbying: that while Serbia's enemies should take full advantage of all the influence money can buy, Serbs should rely solely on goodhearted, voluntary, nonprofessional efforts. That assumption is a large part of why Serbia and Serbs ended up where they did in the propaganda wars of the 1990s. It is an assumption Vladika Artemije wisely understood he had to reject if he was to have any hope of saving his flock. In any case, the cost for services in the agreement signed between SNC and Venable in March 2006 was for an initial six-month period for $600,000, and continuing thereafter unless cancelled at the same rate of $100,000 per month. Any search of lobbying records for international clients <http://www.fara.gov> shows that is this is well within the range of such services, with two provisos:

- First, that the payments under the SNC/Venable agreement were inclusive of out-of-pocket costs (like media buys, travel, conferences, etc.), and was not just for professional fees to the firm for its work. This is not usual. In most agreements the contract amount is what goes for the work, with costs added on top. This means that out of the SNC/Venable contract from one-third to up to forty percent of the funds paid went not for professional fees but for things like ads in papers read by officials, like Roll Call and The Hill; in well-read political sites like DrudgeReport and Daily Kos; conferences at locations like the Capitol Hill Club (Washington's most well-regarded Republican gathering place); for travel around the U.S., Britain, Germany, Russia, India, Israel, Belgium (EU), Rome, and other locations; and similar expenses. This also means that the actual amount paid for the work of Venable's professionals was far exceeded (by a factor of two or three times) by the amount of time devoted to the mission.

- Second, that funding ($600,000) for the initial six months, which was paid out over the period March-December 2006, virtually exhausted the sources available for support of the representation. In February 2007, because I had changed firms, the agreement with Venable was reassigned to Squire Sanders Public Advocacy <http://www.fara.gov/ docs/5791-Ex hibit-AB-20070208-3.pdf>, under the signature of Fr. Simeon (Vilovski), continuing at $100,000 per month, though by then no further funds were available. Notwithstanding, the work continued at the same intensity throughout 2007 and 2008, and into 2009. Since then, it has been necessary to scale back the work but it has never fully ended despite having, in effect, ceased to be professional effort and transformed into essentially a volunteer activity.

So, that means that since the signing of the March 2006 contract, that initial $600,000 for six months has bought almost four years worth of work of varying levels of intensity. That's an average of about $12,500 per month, of which, as noted above, a sizeable portion went to costs.

None of what is related above is a state secret, however. As noted, all of this has been public record since March 2006, and in a sense it is absurd and insulting to have to explain it. How, then, to understand the sense of breathless discovery by those trying to discredit Vladika Artemije? When all is said and done, there is only one legitimate question than can be asked that relates to the lobbying issue: did the funds for it come from some specific source for which it was absolutely impermissible to be used for any other purpose, such as lobbying? Not being party to the Eparchy's ledgers, I would strongly doubt it. First, money is fungible. If money is given to the Eparchy for various purposes and then is spent for a number of legitimate activities, how is it determined which money went for what purpose? Second, I categorically reject any suggestion that Vladika Artemije, Fr. Simeon, or any of the monastics and laity associated with him would perform any clearly improper action, financial or otherwise. If, on the other hand, we are talking about questions of judgment, that should be left to the Bishop's discretion. For example, if Vladika Artemije decides that instead of spending a dollar to help restore a damaged church (so the Albanians can attack it again) it would be better to spend it to help ensure churches won't be destroyed, who better than he to be the judge of it?

In any case, such questions can be asked in a reasonable and humane way. That is not, however, what we see before us today, which can only feed the sense that something else is at work. It is hard to escape the conclusion that what really is unfolding is a political agenda reminiscent of the Milosevic era, to silence Vladika Artemije's courageous and irreplaceable voice that is so offensive to some in Washington, Brussels, and Belgrade.

In closing, I note that the item posted on the "new" Eparchy site accuses me not only of hypocrisy but of attacking the Holy Synod. To appeal respectfully but firmly is not to attack. So, once again, I appeal to His Holiness, Patriarch IRINEJ, to the Holy Synod, and to the whole Serbian people, that this unjust and unjustified persecution of Vladika Artemije stop at once and that he be restored to authority over his Diocese.

Letter to Todorović & Šebek

Re: Bishop Artemije of Ras and Prizren

James George Jatras | January 27, 2014

Aleksandar Todorović, attorney
Dušan Radosvljević, attorney
Advokatska kancelarija
"Todorović & Šebek"
Svetogorska br. 22
B e o g r a d

VIA EMAIL to toseb@open.telekom.rs

Dear Mr. Todorović and Mr. Radosavljević:

This is in response to your letter to me of December 27, 2013, inquiring about specifics of lobbying activities under the direction of His Grace, Vladika Artemije of Ras and Prizren. I will address your specific questions below to the best of my ability, following three initial observations.

First, since you are attorneys with a private law firm and not public officials, it seems to me that professional ethics and courtesy should have led you to include in your letter a disclosure of the entity on whose behalf you are acting and the scope of your responsibilities. In any case, since you clearly directed this inquiry to me in furtherance of the unjust and unwarranted accusations made against Vladika Artemije, my response is being made public contemporaneously with its delivery to you.

Second, there is nothing in your inquiry that has not been already publicized in detail, either as posted on the website of the Foreign Agents Registration Act (FARA) unit of the U.S. Department of Justice (DOJ; at www.fara.gov), or included in my "Statement by James George Jatras Regarding Allegations of Misuse of Funds to Support Lobbying in the United States on Behalf of Serbs in Kosovo and Metohija" of February 18, 2010 (in English at http://www.mail-archive.com/news@antic.org/msg12924.html) or my response to the scurrilous attack by the Greek publication *Romfea* (in English at http://dijaspora.wordpress.com/2010/03/15/attacks-on-vladika-artemije-and-jim-jatras-are-not-subsiding/). Nonetheless, I will answer your questions with as little redundancy as possible. Where appropriate, these earlier responses are cited.

Third, on the face of it the purpose of your request is unclear. You state: "Since the objective of Serbian Orthodox Church is not to pursue [His Grace] without merit, and since the reasons of payments to 'Venable LLP' are not completely clear, . . . it would help to put the case ad acta and thereby avoid the conduct of proceedings for offenses against" him if the amounts paid for lobbying could be "covered," presumably to dispel "doubt" as to "the real motive" of the payments. Regarding this aspect:

- It is unclear whether you are inquiring on behalf of the Public Prosecutor (which the subject heading on your letter would suggest) or on behalf of the Serbian Orthodox Church (per the above quotation from your letter). Your clarification is requested.
- If there is no desire to pursue His Grace and Fr. Simeon (Vilovski) "without merit," and if you (or the entity on whose behalf you are working) wish "to solve this unpleasant case, that burdens both Orthodox Christians and the public in the Republic of Serbia," then by all means advise your client to desist from this pointless, unfounded, and destructive vendetta.
- Perhaps most puzzling is the novel suggestion that there is any doubt that the "real motive" for the payments at issue was anything other than lobbying and related services. Indeed, until receiving your letter, my entire understanding of the unjustified accusations against Vladika Artemije and Fr. Simeon (and by association, against me) was that funds intended for another purpose (church repairs to be made by substandard Albanian firms, so that the churches would be in a presentable state for renewed desecration and demolition) were used for supposedly illicit purposes, i.e., lobbying. With respect to such use, as I asked in my February 18, 2010, statement, referenced above, for which no answer has yet been provided by any of Vladika Artemije's accusers:

> When all is said and done, there is only one legitimate question than can be asked that relates to the lobbying issue: did the funds for it come from some specific source for which it was **absolutely impermissible** to be used for any other purpose, such as lobbying? Not being party to the Eparchy's ledgers, I would strongly doubt it. First, money is fungible. If money is given to the Eparchy for various purposes and then is spent for a number of legitimate activities, how is it determined which money went for what purpose? Second, I categorically reject any suggestion that Vladika Artemije, Fr. Simeon, or any of the monastics and laity associated with him would perform any clearly improper action, financial or otherwise. If, on the other hand, we are talking about questions of judgment, that should be left to the Bishop's discretion." [Emphasis added]

Vladika Artemije having decided that due to the emergency situation and extraordinary pressures on his flock it was imperative to devise a sustainable security and protection program, including a deterrent against any further destruction and desecration of Orthodox holy places, and that such a program took precedence over non-sustainable repairs, such use of funds would better serve the same objective in a much more efficient manner. Indeed, this would be an appropriate decision corresponding to accepted "best business practices" of budget administration. Instead of "throwing good money after bad" he wisely sought to eliminate the *political* root cause of the danger to his people: the wrong-headed policy of the western powers, particularly of the United States. To that end, His Grace chose lobbying among the very few peaceful and effective options open to him, to engage professional services with the required qualifications and capabilities to present the case of those under the care of his Eparchy in order to put a halt at the source of the problem to the suffering of his people and to set conditions for securing their lives and property. *Keep in mind that there was nothing secret* about any of this at the initiation of this program, or at any time since.

- But the current suggestion—which I emphasize, is totally new to me—that the funds in question were *not* used for lobbying is an even more outrageous and baseless speculation. If you have any shred of evidence that payments made for lobbying were for some other, surreptitious purpose ("the real motive"), simple decency would suggest that you provide it. If you are unable to do so, I expect your prompt and public apology for this groundless, unsubstantiated, and defamatory conjecture.

Let me now address your specific questions.

1.   "Were there any reports on performed legal and lobbying activities?"

The activities described were not in the nature of legal services but were confined to lobbying and related media services. As required by FARA, these were duly reported to the FARA unit at DOJ, which later posted some of them—but for some reason not all of—at www.fara.gov. Since my departure from Venable in January 2007, I no longer have access to those reports; whether Venable still does, I am unable to say. Why the FARA unit would not have posted all of the reports submitted to them, and whether the additional reports not posted online are available for public inspection in hard copy at the FARA office, are questions you are welcome to submit to them.

However, let me draw your attention to two reports that are publicly posted at the FARA unit, at:

http://www.fara.gov/docs/5435-Supplemental-Statement-20060630-4.pdf
http://www.fara.gov/docs/5435-Supplemental-Statement-20061229-5.pdf

These are for two six-month periods of 2006, during which time the "Registrant" (Venable LLP) performed the described services for the Republic of the Philippines, the Embassy of India, the Rodina Political Party (of Russia), and the Serbian National Council of Kosovo and Metohija (the account in question). The various contacts, meetings, media placements relevant to the Kosovo work are listed in a manner comparable to those pertaining to the other matters, which you may take as a representative—but not exhaustive—description of the lobbying work performed under Vladika Artemije's direction. (Please note that it was probably unnecessary to register this project under FARA at all, since His Grace is not a foreign official under the meaning of FARA. However, since the Serbian National Council could conceivably be construed as a "political party," and since we anticipated close scrutiny for our opposition to U.S. policy on Kosovo, we decided to register under FARA in an excess of caution.)

2. "If not, what actions were taken in order to justify the amount of 700.000,00 USD, which was paid by invoices (that we have) for a period of 6 months, as of 22 March, 2006?"

Per the response to the first question above, I presume the phrase "if not" in this question is inoperable, since there is indeed a publicly available, repressentative listing of such actions, per the links provided above.

Concerning the amount of payments, please note the following, from my February 18, 2010, statement:

With respect to the money, there is a curious assumption behind the accusation that moneys were "diverted" to lobbying: that while Serbia's enemies should take full advantage of all the influence money can buy, Serbs should rely solely on good-hearted, voluntary, nonprofessional efforts. That assumption is a large part of why Serbia and Serbs ended up where they did in the propaganda wars of the 1990s. It is an assumption Vladika Artemije wisely understood he had to reject if he was to have any hope of saving his flock. In any case, the cost for services in the agreement signed between SNC and Venable in March 2006 was for an initial six-month period for $600,000, and continuing thereafter unless cancelled at the same rate of $100,000 per month. Any search of lobbying records for international clients http://www.fara. gov shows that is this is well within the range of such services, with two provisos:

• First, that the payments under the SNC/Venable agreement were inclusive of out-of-pocket costs (like media buys, travel, conferences, etc.), and was not just for professional fees to the firm for its work. This is not usual. In most agreements the contract amount is what goes for the work, with costs added on top. This means that out of the SNC/Venable contract from one-third to up to forty percent of the funds paid went not for professional fees but for things like ads in papers read by officials, like *Roll Call* and *The Hill*; in well-read political sites like DrudgeReport and Daily Kos; conferences at locations like the Capitol Hill Club (Washington's most well-regarded Republican gathering place); for travel around the U.S., Britain, Germany, Russia, India, Israel, Belgium (EU), Rome, and other locations; and similar expenses. This also means that the actual amount paid for the work of Venable's professionals was far exceeded (by a factor of two or three times) by the amount of time devoted to the mission.

- Second, that funding ($600,000) for the initial six months, which was paid out over the period March-December 2006, virtually exhausted the sources available for support of the representation. In February 2007, because I had changed firms, the agreement with Venable was reassigned to Squire Sanders Public Advocacy <http://www.fara.gov/docs/5791-Exhibit-AB-20070208-3.pdf>, under the signature of Fr. Simeon (Vilovski), continuing at $100,000 per month, though by then no further funds were available. Notwithstanding, the work continued at the same intensity throughout 2007 and 2008, and into 2009. Since then, it has been necessary to scale back the work but it has never fully ended despite having, in effect, ceased to be professional effort and transformed into essentially a volunteer activity.

So, that means that since the signing of the March 2006 contract, that initial $600,000 for six months has bought almost four years worth of work of varying levels of intensity. That's an average of about $12,500 per month, of which, as noted above, a sizeable portion went to costs.

3. "Was there a specification of costs?"

No. As noted above, the payments in support of this project were inclusive of out-of-pocket costs, not according to the standard arrangement whereby the agreed payments are allocated entirely to professional fees, with costs incurred added on top. A partial, though hardly exhaustive, list of outside disbursements appears in the two FARA postings provided at the links in my response to your first question.

+++++

In closing, allow me to again address the absurdity and injustice of the persecution to which Vladika Artemije (with Fr. Simeon, and others loyal to him) have been and continue to be subjected. The underlying premise of these false accusations is either that His Grace "wasted" funds on lobbying or (as your letter now suggests) that the lobbying payments were a cover for some mysteriously unidentified "real motive." It should be patently obvious that the *opposite* is the case: that Vladika Artemije is being maltreated precisely because the lobbying and media services he procured for even a limited time were far too effective and had become a threat to the policy of those governments (sadly, that of my own country in the forefront) wishing to wrest Kosovo and Metohija from Serbia, and a discomfort to their Serbian collaborators. As observed in my February 18, 2010, statement:

We believed we could win only by changing the terms of debate. When we began, "Kosovo" meant only "the place where America stopped genocide of peaceful Albanians by evil Serbs." Due to our efforts, for many, many Americans "Kosovo" now means "the place where our government insanely helps jihadists and gangsters terrorize Christian Serbs." [. . .]

Let us remember that when we began our efforts Washington fully expected smoothly to arrange the "final status" of Kosovo well before the end of 2006. The architects of American policy expected minimal resistance from Belgrade and were sure the Russians were not serious in their opposition to independence. And of course there were virtually no dissenting voices in the United States. While our efforts may not have been early enough to have accomplished a reversal of American policy, I am confident that if not for this campaign under Vladika Artemije's guidance and direction Washington would have moved much faster than it did to "resolve" the issue. Instead, we threw enough sand in the gears that contributed to a delay of almost two years, by which time the Russian position had become rock-solid and it had become impossible for anyone (openly, anyway) in Serbian politics to consent to losing Kosovo. Even when Washington did make its move in early 2008, in concert with the KLA kingpins and with unprecedented bullying of our European allies, they did so with the increasingly desperate knowledge they were losing ground and that it was "now or never." The result—the ongoing, unresolved crisis—is not one anyone wants to see but is far better than what likely would have been the case if we had not moved when we did at Vladika Artemije's initiative. I sincerely believe we helped give Serbia a fighting chance, which it is still her option to take advantage of or not.

The proof of our effectiveness is in the fact that there is reason to suspect that the campaign (of which you evidently are a part) to eliminate His Grace as an obstacle to the policy of the Western powers was undertaken in direct response to a NATO, and perhaps specifically U.S., initiative. As reported by NATO, U.S. Admiral Mark P. Fitzgerald, then Commander, U.S. Naval Forces Europe and Africa, and Commander, Allied Joint Force Command (JFC) Naples, "with operational responsibility for NATO missions in the Balkans, Iraq and the Mediterranean," took part in meetings in Kosovo in January 2010 ("JFC Com Visits Kosovo" at http://www.jfcnaples.nato.int/page8840506. aspx; note, this occurred on January 8, the second day of Orthodox Christmas according to the Old Calendar) and February 2010 ("JFC Commander visits [sic] Viskoki [sic] Decane [sic] Monastery" at http://www.jfcnaples.nato.int/page8840281.aspx). During his January visit the Admiral publicly stated that he considered Serbian so-called "parallel institutions"—that is, the legitimate structures of the sovereign Serbian state, as opposed to the Albanians' illegal separatist administration installed under NATO patronage—to be a "security threat." Further, an unconfirmed report indicates that a high NATO officer—whether Admiral Fitzgerald or someone else is not specified—stated in the course of one of the January meetings (this is verbatim or a close paraphrase) "What we need here is a more cooperative bishop."

Again, I cannot confirm this report or firmly identify the speaker of the comment. But the timing is indicative. Just over a month after Admiral

Fitzgerald's earlier visit, and just before his later one, Vladika Artemije's authority over his Eparchy was "temporarily" suspended. This was followed in due course by his physical removal from the province of Kosovo and Metohija and by an unlawful and legally void declaration of the Holy Hierarchical Assembly of the Serbian Orthodox Church that he had been stripped of the Episcopal dignity and reduced to the level of a monk. (For a further account of these developments, see "ANY PRETEXT WILL DO: Totalitarianism in Service to the West: Serbia Betrays God, Helps Evict Last of Kosovo Christianity," by Julia Gorin, at http://www.juliagorin.com/ word press/?p=2324; the speaker in question is identified, perhaps imprecisely based on available information as "a KFOR officer"; and "Eleven Years Later: NATO Powers Prepare Final Solution In Kosovo," by Rick Rozoff, http://rickrozoff.wordpress.com/2010/03/19/11-years-later-nato-powers-prepare-final-solution-in-kosovo/.)

There is little question that the removal of Bishop Artemije was undertaken in the service of a broader policy initiative to "resolve" Kosovo's status. I will leave it to those in the upper echelons of the Serbian State and Church who behind the scenes unworthily acted to comply with NATO's evident wishes, to explain their motives and answer to their consciences.

I trust this answers your questions, if not quite to your satisfaction.

James George Jatras, Esq.*

*Admitted in the District of Columbia, the Commonwealth of Pennsylvania, and the Supreme Court of the United States

---

"No Partition of Kosovoand Metohija"

Jim Jatras | *Strategic Culture* | January 16, 2017

If all of America's foreign policy observers were ranked for their realism, honesty, integrity, and sound thinking, few could come close to Dr. Steven Meyer, a longtime CIA analyst and Professor of Political Science at Washington's prestigious National Defense University. If his recommendations had held sway over the last quarter century, the world and especially Europe would be a much, much better place than what has resulted from listening to the inferior minds and deficient personalities that actually guided U.S. policy.

Dr. Meyer recently authored a critique of the Serbian government's approach to negotiations with the "Kosovars" (sic) regarding the fate of Serbs in the occupied province of Kosovo and Metohija. His observations as why the current approach is unproductive and contrary to Serbia's interest and those of the Serbs in Kosovo are entirely correct. But his recommended alternative—

that Belgrade initiate an entirely new round of talks with an eye to partition on ethnic grounds (basically, along the Ibar River)—is ill-advised, in my opinion.

Dr. Meyer's critique of Belgrade's policy is spot-on:

> So far, the Brussels process has been a failure, just like every other effort since 1999, to find a just and equitable solution. As with past efforts, the Brussels process has failed because the questions of political legitimacy, and authority and mostly sovereignty are ignored. Until these questions are addressed honestly there will be very little—if any—progress on Kosovo.
>
> The Kosovars are working from the perspective that the Serbs will do anything to please the EU and that Pristina can continue to be difficult because time is on their side. Leaders in Pristina believe that they have the West, especially the U.S., on their side and that Serbia has never had the initiative and never will have it. To a large extent, Pristina is right. The Vucic government has been so determined to sacrifice Kosovo on the EU altar that Belgrade has put Serbia on the defensive. Belgrade says Serbs will never surrender sovereignty over Kosovo. But bit by bit that is exactly what Belgrade is doing. [. . .]
>
> Most recently, the Serbian government's agreement to 'bottom-up technical negotiations' required by the Brussels process also has failed. In fact, it is a tacit surrender of sovereignty by Belgrade with nothing in exchange. To be clear, whenever Belgrade surrenders authority over even minor 'technical' areas, it is surrendering sovereignty—and this is a violation of the Serbian Constitution as well as being a detriment to Serbia's national interests.

Truer words were never written. Dr. Meyer suggests that instead of continuing down this disastrous path, which only can result in losing Kosovo with nothing to show for it, Belgrade should quit the stacked game. Instead, he calls for Belgrade "to take a leadership role in the process, not assume the position of a weak supplicant", to set the stage for a "new approach [that] needs to establish a framework that actually engages the question of sovereignty."

The centerpiece would be partition, with Serbia exercising "full sovereignty north of the Ibar River, where Serbs constitute more than 90 percent of the population", while "the region south of the Ibar River should be under Kosovar sovereignty." Members of either ethnic group who didn't want to live under the authority of the other could move to the other zone with humanitarian funding. International guarantees would protect those minorities that remain.

The sentiment Dr. Meyer's proposal is admirable, certainly as compared with the policy Belgrade is now following. Unfortunately, there are two serious problems with Dr. Meyer's recommended solution:

1. It is politically and morally wrong; and
2. It wouldn't work.

The fundamental wrongness of Dr. Meyer's proposal relates to the cornerstone issue on which his proposal rests: "questions of political legitimacy, and authority and mostly sovereignty." For Serbia, that question is definitively answered in the Constitution. If, as Dr. Meyer correctly observes, surrender of authority over even seemingly minor "technical" areas is "surrendering sovereignty", "a violation of the Serbian Constitution", and "a detriment to Serbia's national interests", what can we say about the de jure renunciation of the large majority of the province? What kind of new negotiations can proceed on the rightful owners' a priori concession to give up most of what is legally theirs as the basis of the negotiation? If you steal my car, do I "negotiate" by agreeing to let you keep most of it in the hopes of your giving me back one of the tires? By conceding the sovereignty question at the beginning, Serbia would lose her entire stakes before any talks could begin.

The practical defects are as fatal as that of principle. Belgrade has walked down the misguided path of "technical" negotiations while claiming not to have sacrificed principle based on two factors Dr. Meyer describes: that the current Belgrade leadership "will do anything to please the EU" and that the Albanians' leaders believe, rightly, that "they have the West, especially the U.S., on their side." As long as all of Belgrade's policies are governed by the mirage of EU membership, nothing in Dr. Meyer's proposal will disabuse Pristina of their conviction that they need not concede anything, that time is on their side, and that their outside sponsors will back them up. That would not change just because the topic of discussion has shifted to one of territorial division, which the Albanians would almost certainly reject anyway while reaping the proceeds of Belgrade's fatal concession of principle.

Perhaps the biggest defect in Dr. Meyer's proposal is insufficient regard for the fact that the world, and Europe, are changing. He alludes to that indirectly by noting—

> Recently, according to the media, Foreign Minister Ivica Dacic said that he did not think that President-elect Trump would return Koso- vo to Serbia. This is certainly correct. In the first place, Trump does not have the power, authority or right to return Kosovo to Serbia.

I agree, Trump will not return Kosovo to Serbia, though I expect he would have the "power" to do so if he wanted. As for whether he has the "authority and right", I suppose he has no less than Bill Clinton and George W. Bush had to take it away in the first place.

But that's not really the point. Much more relevant is that the Washington foreign policy establishment is in full-scale panic over someone taking up residence in the White House who doesn't burn incense before the same idols as the neoconservative and liberal-interventionist crowd for whom the 1999 Kosovo aggression was their first big "success," a template for later misad- ventures in the broader Middle East. Trump is someone who wants to get along with Russia, who says that NATO is "obsolete", who wants an end to idiotic nation-building, and who thinks fighting Islamic terror is actually a priority, not a cover for supporting jihadists as a policy tool. (It is for that very reason that there is right now a full-blown conspiracy in the U.S. to de- legitimate Trump, with the bipartisan foreign policy establishment, politicizes leadership of the intelligence community, and the major media all in confederation against him.)

At the same time, the European Union, the false god before which Serbia's leaders grovel, is falling apart under the pressure of rising nationalism. How much will Belgrade surrender on the slim hope that by the time their country is invited there will still be an EU to join? Maybe time is not on Pristina's side after all. . .

So, if Belgrade's current approach is wrong, and Dr. Meyer's recom- mendation is wrong, what do I suggest? In a word, patience. For the time being, a "frozen conflict" is not the worse state of affairs. Maintain the princi- ple of sovereignty. Negotiate, to the extent possible, on small things, not for the purpose of "making progress" but with only one goal: how to keep as many Serbs in Kosovo, as safe as possible, for as long as possible. (With regard to

Dr. Meyer's suggestion that minority Serbs south of the Ibar in partitioned Kosovo could be protected by outside guarantees, as someone of Greek origin I have to ask how much that was worth for the Greeks of Constantinople and the islands of Imbros and Tenedos under the Treaty of Lausanne.)

Serbia needs to start thinking of the EU as already in the past tense, as a thing that has no future. Make friends with the patriotically oriented movements in Britain, France, Germany, Austria, Hungary, of course in the United States. Above all, stay close to Russia.

Dr. Meyer's clinching argument is the "hard fact that Serbia will not get most of Kosovo back. Any attempt to do so would reignite war—a war Serbia could not win." Nobody is talking about a war but about a rapidly changing international context that may provide opportunities that are not apparent now.

The last time Serbia lost Kosovo seemingly forever it took half a millennium to get it back. This time it will not take as long.

"Will Trump Succeed in Restoring America, or Will His Enemies Drag Him—and Our Country—Down?"

Jim Jatras | *Strategic Culture* | February 13, 2017

After barely two weeks in office, Donald Trump has stunned the world with his "shock and awe" campaign to keep promises made when he was a candidate. The mere fact of a politician doing what he said he would do seems to have unsettled the nerves of his opponents. What is called "Trump Derangement Syndrome" is already reaching critical proportions.

Withdrawing from the Trans-Pacific Partnership, ordering a start on his Mexican border wall, ordering an investigation into voter fraud (if conducted properly, almost certain to uncover widespread unlawful voting by non-citizens both legally and illegally present in the U.S., since no proof of citizenship is required to register), insisting he wants to get along with "killer" Vladimir Putin, and cutting short a call with Australia's prime minister over Barack Obama's idiotic promise to take in Muslim refugees that our mates Down Under don't want themselves—all of these have infuriated the usual suspects.

But the declaration of war was his order to impose restrictions on entry from seven majority-Muslim countries designated as trouble spots by Obama with nary a peep from the progressive watchdogs of "tolerance" and anti-"Islamophobia." As Srdja Trifkovic has noted, Trump's order is the first step in instating an ideological test to bar jihad ideologues from the United States. (See "The Real 'Muslim Ban'" and my "If He Doesn't Like Trump's Exclusion of All Muslims, Obama Must Exclude Advocates of Sharia and Caliphate").

If Trump prevails on his exclusion order, he has the high ground to crush his opponents in both political parties—and they know it. That's why the reaction has been both hysterical and cynical. Mainstream media, inveterate enemies of Trump and the American people, rarely mention the list of countries was Obama's. (Frankly, it's a bad list. Iran is on it—how many terrorist attacks by an Iranian, or by any Shiite, have we seen in the U.S. or

Europe? But look who's not on it: Saudis (9/11), Pakistanis (San Bernardino), Palestinians (Fort Hood), Afghans (Orlando). For that matter, where's the Federation of Bosnia and Herzegovina and the criminal pseudo-state of "Kosova"?) Still, you have to start someplace, and the order can be refined as it moves forward.

If it gets a chance. In a barefaced political move, a federal district judge in Washington State enjoined the order, and his injunction was upheld by three judges of the Ninth Circuit, the worst in the country. (As they say at the Supreme Court: "This case comes on appeal from the Ninth Circuit. Other reasons for reversal include. . .") Trump can ask for review by the full Circuit en banc (a futile undertaking) or more likely turn to the Supreme Court. If the Supreme Court agrees to hear the case, which is far from certain, a probable split of 4 to 4 (at best) would affirm the injunction. Or, as some consider likely, pseudo-conservative Justice Anthony Kennedy, of same-sex marriage infamy, could side with the terrorists-welcome crowd, handing Trump a 5 to 3 defeat. Either result would kill Trump's order. He could always withdraw it and reissue it in modified form crafted to survive judicial scrutiny, but the lesson would be clear: questions of who can safely be let into the U.S. will no longer be governed by the duly elected president, whom the Constitution and federal statute empower to make such assessments, but by unelected judges' according to their personal preferences. This is the antithesis of the rule of law.

Clipping Trump's wings early to prevent his protecting our country from dangerous intruders is only one element of the threat he faces. Of even greater menace is the effort to create what amounts to a "color revolution" on the streets, in a replay of the tried-and-true method used in other countries: Philippines, Serbia, Georgia, Ukraine (twice), Egypt, Lebanon, just to name some that succeeded. Now the same Deep State and George Soros team are setting their sights on overturning the will of the American people to restore and preserve our country.

Violence against political speech of the wrong kind is being legitimated and mainstreamed by the media. Black-clad "anti-fascist action" reincarnations of Mao's Red Guards and Röhm's brownshirts beat up and mace peaceful citizens. So-called journalists openly mull whether the president should be assassinated. A celebrity fantasizes about blowing up the White House.

Americans are more divided than any time since 1861. The term "civil war" is heard more and more, both in the "cold" variety and the prospect it could turn hot. Half of America hates the other half. We have become virtual aliens to one another who don't agree on even the most basic principles of God, man, and the purpose of life. Secessionist movements are gathering unprecedented levels of support (notably in California—please, please, please let them go and take their 55 Democratic Electoral Votes with them!).

Taken together, there's reason to be cautiously pessimistic. Trump beat his GOP rivals, he beat Hillary, and maybe he can beat the confederacy of scoundrels mobilizing against him. But it's far from a sure thing. It's a fight in which he's virtually alone, with few trustworthy allies within his own party and even in his own nascent administration. (This is a particular concern in the national security area, which I will touch upon at another time.)

If Trump is to win, he needs to stick to his own instincts and vision. Compromising in the hopes of wooing those opposed to him would be fatal. Those who can be reconciled will be won only by delivering on his primary pledge to restore the economy and jobs for working people.

Actually, Trump is not totally alone. There are still the tens of millions of people who voted for him and who disdain his enemies as much as Trump's enemies hate him.

For the media, the "antifa" thugs, the fantasists of assassination, it may now seem all in good fun to trash every rule of civil and moral restraint in their quest to bring Trump down. But they should think twice, and then think again. The side that starts a civil war isn't necessarily the side that wins it.

"Flynn's Resignation is Blood in the Water for Attack on Trump and His Russia Policy"

Jim Jatras | *Strategic Culture* | February 16, 2017

The resignation of Donald Trump's National Security Adviser Lt. Gen. Mike Flynn is a major coup for Establishment forces trying to hobble the new administration before it can get to its feet. With a single-minded mania that would do Captain Ahab credit, the anti-Trumpers will now redouble their efforts to harpoon their great white whale in the White House.

It all pretty much comes down to Russia. Congressional critics of both parties are demanding that Flynn's talking with the Russian ambassador in Washington be subsumed into inquiries about unproven allegations of Russian hacking of the U.S. election and the president's dogged unwillingness to denounce Vladimir Putin as a murderer, thug, war criminal, and so forth. Obviously, no one but a cabal of Kremlin agents could consider a worthy goal of American policy a respectful, give-and-take policy toward so deplorable an adversary. The fact that discussion of sanctions against Russia imposed by the Obama Administration came up in Flynn's talk with the ambassador will spur efforts on Capitol Hill to codify them in law to prevent Trump from lifting them.

Trump is guilty of many unpardonable crimes and heresies against the Establishment. His insistence on controlling our borders, his America-first trade policy, and his rejection of nation-building and "regime change" as standard U.S. policy are bad enough. But anything less than a full-throated detestation of Russia is totally intolerable and must be stopped by any means necessary. It remains to be seen whether the full story of Deep State management of leaks to produce Flynn's political assassination will be revealed.

Throughout the campaign, despite the neoconservative Russophobia of his GOP rivals and Hillary Clinton's effort to run against a Trump-Putin ticket, Trump refused to take the easy way out and back off his stated purpose to "get along with Russia." While few accuse him of having a wonkish, detailed knowledge of strategic issues—for example, mocking accusations that he doesn't know what the nuclear triad is—he seems to have an instinctive understanding that nothing good can happen under his tenure if our current collision course with Russia isn't abated.

To be sure, it was unclear where Flynn fit into that understanding. Already widely accused of being a Putin toady, largely based on sitting next to the Russian president at a 2015 dinner for the RT television network, Flynn doesn't come across in his writing as particularly pro-Russian. In a book co-authored with über-neoconservative Michael Ledeen, Flynn depicted Russia as part of an enemy combination consisting of North Korea, China, Iran, Syria, Cuba, Bolivia, Venezuela, Nicaragua, al-Qaida, Hezbollah, and ISIS.

Flynn also advocated the creation of an Arab "NATO-like structure" of our Sunni so-called allies, starting with Saudi Arabia, who have exercised such a baneful influence on U.S. policy in pushing regime changes in Iraq, Libya, and Syria. With Flynn's recently putting Iran "on notice" concerning a recent missile test, even some Trump supporters are concerned that this administration could repeat George Bush's disaster in Iraq but on a far larger scale.

Still, this needs to be clear: while restoring normal ties with Russia is a prerequisite for Trump's having a successful foreign and security policy, it's not a guarantee. If the administration thinks it can cuddle up with the Kremlin so the U.S. and Russia can team up against China, or if they expect Russia to throw Iran under the bus, they don't know the first thing about Russians or strategy. This is not a time for gimmicks or facile rhetoric; it's time to find some real understanding on mutual interests and cooperation against real dangers.

Sometimes it seems Trump is the only one in his administration who understands that, though I have high hopes for Steve Bannon and Stephen Miller. (Maybe Trump should only listen to people named Στέφανος!) In her maiden speech at the United Nations, his ambassador, Nikki Haley, condemned Russia in language that could have been drafted by Samantha Power (and in fact, was perhaps drafted by her residual staff in New York). White House spokesman Sean Spicer recently insisted that Russia must return Crimea to Ukraine, or else. Vice President Mike Pence has openly differed from Trump on Russia.

It will be important to see who replaces Flynn. Of the names being mentioned, the absolute worst choice would be General David Petraeus. This is someone who in Senate testimony, just before the 14th anniversary of the 9/11 attacks advocated arming al-Qaeda—al-Qaeda!—in Syria. (But only the moderate terrorists, of course.) Amazingly, there was no burst of outrage from even one of the assembled solons.

Finally, a note about the Balkans. Just as America's post-Cold War venture into global hegemony featured Balkan interventions calculated in large part to box in the Russians and curry favor with the Islamic world, a reversal of those policies—rapprochement with Moscow, treating Islamic terror as an enemy, not an item in our toolkit—eventually would help rebalance the Balkans in a positive way for Serbia and Republika Srpska. The key word is "eventually", where a more rational global policy from Washington would in time be felt locally as well. Conversely, if the Establishment succeeds in confining Trump, that larger change in context might not occur, perpetuating the current anti-Serbian policies for some time longer.

"Establishment Struggles to Maintain Anti-Russian Narrative as the Ice Starts to Crack Under Them"

Jim Jatras | *Strategic Culture* | April 7, 2017

As I have noted before in *Strategic Culture Foundation*, the infant Trump Administration is engaged in a life and death struggle with the Deep State, the mainstream media (MSM), all of the Democrats in Congress, and a lot of the Republicans too. One issue lies at the heart of the struggle: the determination of Trump's enemies not to allow any sort of warming of ties between Washington and Moscow.

Day after day the MSM run story after story alleging, with no evidence whatsoever, that Trump is a puppet of Vladimir Putin, who stole our election to put Trump in the White House. Congressional hearings on "Russian interference" in elections in America—and France, Germany, and wherever else—have turned into a veritable Witches' Sabbath of Russophobic hysteria and of the dangers of "populism" of the sort represented by Trump and Marine Le Pen.

Meanwhile, the other side of the crisis is starting to slip out of the anti-Trumpers' control. In recent days it has become clear that Barack Obama's former Assistant Secretary of Defense Evelyn Farkas admitted on TV to what amounts to knowledge of criminal leaking of classified information. Potentially even more damaging to the "soft coup" is the revelation that Obama's former National Security Adviser Susan Rice—notorious for her lies about the 2012 Benghazi terror attack—was involved in the "unmasking" of Trump transition team names captured in intelligence surveillance. The MSM is panicking, insisting Rice did nothing wrong: don't look behind that curtain, nothing to see here, just move along, folks. . .

That isn't going to work. In coming weeks, we will start to get some answers. Who—which agencies, American or foreign like GCHQ—spied on Trump and his people? Whom were they surveilling, the Trump people directly or "only" the people the team were talking with, Russian or otherwise? Under what legal authority, if any, did the surveillance operate? What was done with the data, and to whom was it passed on—violating what laws?

Meanwhile, the more dignified elements of the Deep State pretend has nothing has changed. The ship of state sails majestically forward, no storm is on the horizon. The usual well-funded "experts" explain the world to us, and even honest and intelligent people are expected to nod deferentially and drink in great draughts of Establishment wisdom.

A case in point is the recent report of the über-Establishment Brookings Institution: "Putin's no populist, but he can gain from populist movements worldwide." It can be summed up in two sentences: Putin is a scared little man fishing in troubled waters. Trump doesn't know what he's doing and needs to be careful not to give Putin an opening for mischief.

Frankly, it's not the worst think tank analysis about Russia and America—almost anything from American Enterprise Institute or Heritage would be ten times worse. The Brookings report rests on a straw man, namely the issue of what constitutes "populism/populist" (used 38 times in the piece). The closest the authors come to giving us a definition is "uncontrollable political and economic forces for which no one was prepared." Whatever that means.

By that definition, "populism" never has existed and never can, except for very brief, unviable episodes. Its repeated use in the piece is a symptom of the progressive authors' faith in the Bolshevik myth of spontaneous movements of "the people" (you know, like .05 percent of the population on the streets of Kiev, twice, counts as "the Ukrainian people have chosen to be part of Europe!"). That myth, closely linked to the myth of democracy (as wielded as a weapon by Western ideologues), is contrasted to the reality: the inevitability of oligarchy, in modern times usually plutocratic in nature. (Though not always. The USSR was an oligarchy but not based on wealth. Rather, membership in the ruling oligarchy temporarily gave one a semblance of wealth, unless and until your number finally came up.)

Brookings writes: "Last but not least, populists target the power of elite establishments. In Russia, Putin is the establishment." To be in power effectively is, ipso facto, to be the establishment. There are few ways an outsider can do that:

One, shoot the old establishment and create a new one (the Bolsheviks, again).

Two, give in and sell out to the establishment (what some on the left accuse Bill Clinton and Obama of doing, and what some hope, or fear, Trump may do).

Or, three, a hostile takeover: instill enough fear in the members of the establishment so they serve your purposes not theirs. That pretty much is what Putin did, in a pattern somewhat reminiscent of the centralizing monarchs of European absolutism of the 17th and 18th centuries, with the Russian oligarchs serving as poor stand-ins for the traditional nobility in the earlier era. The last seems the most prudent course, and probably what Trump is trying to do under somewhat different conditions.

Brookings disputes that Putin really wants to see populists elected in other countries:

> Contrary to popular belief, the Russian president is no fan of populism. His support for populist parties in Europe and the United States is simply opportunistic: he will seek to bolster their chances, if they can fracture support for mainstream parties that tend to view Russia as a threat and the transatlantic bond as vital for countering it. His support is a pure calculation in order to survive.

Well, that's one way to put it. A less snarky way to say it would be that Putin prefers political forces in Europe and the US that are less hostile to Russia than those that are more hostile. How horrible!

He rightly identifies the latter with globalist, anti-traditionalist, anti-national, anti-Christian, pro-jihad, pro-migration multicultural elites who are destroying their own countries, while the former are not just "populists" but patriots, whether they be American, French, English, Serbian, etc. Isn't that what different countries are for?

Irony of ironies: when the Soviets used their proxy General Jaruzelski to crush Solidarnoszcz in December 1981, the Reagan administration aptly demanded the Soviets "Let Poland be Poland." Great idea! And let France be France, Germany Germany, America America, Serbia Serbia—and let Russia be Russia.

But somehow that's bad. Russia must be America, or at least be Holland.

This week we'll see if Washington will give permission for China to be China.

"While the Deep State 'Death Star' Seeks to Finish Off Trump, 'Mr. Massacre' Returns Pushing for Greater Albania"

Jim Jatras | *Strategic Culture* | May 19, 2017

The fake news is flying thick and fast in Washington this week. On the heels of Donald Trump's Oval Office visit with Russian Foreign Minister Sergey Lavrov and other American and Russian officials, it finally seemed the fledgling US administration was turning the corner and beginning to focus on moving forward on cooperation with Moscow against radical Islamic terrorism, particularly in Syria.

Then the Deep State and mainstream media (MSM) counterattacked. First, they questioned why a TASS photographer was allowed access to the meeting while the American fake news purveyors were not. Then they speculated that maybe Lavrov or Ambassador Sergey Kislyak had planted a bug in the president's office. Then they charged that Trump had compromised sensitive intelligence (received from Israel) by revealing it to the Russians. Finally they accused Trump of obstruction of justice—an impeachable offense—by his reportedly suggesting to now-fired FBI Director James Comey that he should go easy on short-lived National Security Adviser Michael Flynn, whose scalp was the first the Deep State/MSM gang had nailed to the wall.

The whole anti-Trump campaign has been based on criminal leaks of classified or privileged material from within the government. Still, there is no sign of a counterattack. Perhaps Attorney General Jeff Sessions has secretly empaneled a grand jury and indictments of leakers are forthcoming. More likely he has not and is more concerned with whether prosecutors are using too much discretion in the severity of offenses they choose to charge criminal suspects with, or whether states are playing fast and loose with federal marijuana laws.

The only brief respite Trump has received against this onslaught has been when he launched cruise missiles against Syria over a false flag chemical attack by jihadists in Idlib, for which the MSM and Deep Staters applauded him. There is reason to fear that Trump, guided by advisers whose policy proclivities mirror those of his critics, may seek the path of least resistance by further bellicose measures. These could take place in Korea, against Russia (for example in Ukraine), or in the broader Middle East. For example, while in Saudi Arabia—surreally touted by National Security Adviser H.R. McMaster as a paragon of a moderate, tolerant, peaceful Islamic ally—Trump is set to announce a coalition against Iran characterized as an "Arab NATO." As though one NATO weren't bad enough.

The icing on the cake is the baseless allegation this week that the Syrian government is running a crematorium adjoining Saydnaya prison north of Damascus, where, the State Department's Stuart Jones claims, up to 50 inmates' bodies are burned daily. But even Jones admits he doesn't know the facility is a crematorium at all. The offered "proof"? On satellite images the snow melts faster on that roof than on others nearby. . .

Nonetheless Holocaust rhetoric, the 800-pound gorilla of atrocity porn, was unleashed. A Google News search of "Syria, crematorium, Holocaust" yields over 6,000 hits. US Ambassador to the UN Nikki Haley called the unproven accusation "reminiscent of the 20th century's worst offenses against humanity." An Israel cabinet minister has called for Syrian President Bashar al-Assad's assassination.

Which brings us to the Balkans and William Walker.

For those old enough to remember, nothing we are now hearing about Syria is new. (Not even anything in Syria is new—remember "Aleppo Boy"?) The art and science of manipulating events and images to "justify" attacks on other countries may have cut its teeth in the first Gulf War ("incubator babies" in Kuwait) but reached a perfect level of sophistication in the dissolution of Yugoslavia: the Omarska "death camp" that wasn't, the Srebrenica "genocide", "boxcars" transporting Albanian civilians (not to death camps but away from the fighting), the tens of thousands of Albanian men falsely reported held at a stadium in Pristina.

One of the most vivid cases was of course the "Racak massacre" of Albanian civilians by Yugoslav police in January 1999. As I wrote five months before the events at Racak in an analysis for the US Senate Republican leadership, the administration of Bill Clinton had already decided on an attack and was only waiting for a suitable "trigger":

> As of this writing, planning for a U.S.-led NATO intervention in Kosovo is now largely in place, while the Clinton Administration's apparent willingness to intervene has ebbed and flowed on an almost weekly basis. The only missing element appears to be an event—with suitably vivid media coverage—that would make intervention politically salable, even imperative, in the same way that a dithering Administration finally decided on intervention in Bosnia in 1995 after a series of 'Serb mortar attacks' took the lives of dozens of civilians—attacks, which, upon closer examination, may in fact have been the work of the Muslim regime in Sarajevo, the main beneficiary of the intervention. . . . That the Administration is waiting for a similar 'trigger' in Kosovo is increasingly obvious: 'A senior U.S. Defense Department official who briefed reporters on July 15 noted that "we're not anywhere near making a decision for any kind of armed intervention in Kosovo right now." He listed only one thing that might trigger a policy change: "I think if some levels of atrocities were reached that would be intolerable, that would probably be a trigger."' [Washington Post, August 4, 1998]. The recent conflicting reports regarding a purported mass grave containing (depending on the report) hundreds of murdered Albanian civilians or dozens of KLA fighters killed in battle should be seen in this light. ["Bosnia II: The Clinton Administration Sets Course for NATO Intervention in Kosovo", United States Senate Republican Policy Committee, August 1998]

The key figure in selling the Racak trigger was of course William Walker, a top contender for the "Worst Job of Not Looking Like a Spook Award." As described by Mark Ames and Matt Taibbi in "Meet Mr. Massacre," published in the now-defunct The Exile of February 10, 2000:

> Years from now, when the war in Serbia is over and the dust has settled, historians will point to January 15, 1999 as the day the American Death Star became fully operational.
> That was the date on which an American diplomat named William Walker brought his OSCE war crimes verification team to a tiny Kosovar village called Racak to investigate an alleged Serb massacre of ethnic Albanian peasants. After a brief review of the town's 40-odd bullet-ridden corpses, Walker searched out the nearest television camera and essentially fired the starting gun for the war.
> 'From what I saw, I do not hesitate to describe the crime as a massacre, a crime against humanity,' he said. 'Nor do I hesitate to accuse the government security forces of responsibility.'
> We all know how Washington responded to Walker's verdict; it quickly set its military machine in motion, and started sending out menacing invitations to its NATO friends to join the upcoming war party." [NOTE: For anyone who assumes the Internet is forever, it

appears there has been a concerted effort to throw the Mr. Massacre article into the Memory Hole. It is still available here.]

Walker recently returned to the scene of his 1999 handiwork to promote what any reasonable person took as a call for forming a Greater Albania:

> This project that I'm working on is meant for all Albanians in Kosovo, in diaspora, in Albania. I'm working on a joint project, on their unification. Albanians worldwide were united in the 1990s with the sole purpose of the liberation of Kosovo. I was with them when they declared independence. Albanians have won and they came to celebrate together, now is the time after the independence, for the final step, for us all to be together, to accomplish this achievement."

Walker's words prompted a vocal response even from the usually passive authorities in Belgrade, with Serbian Prime Minister and President-elect Aleksandar Vucic denouncing Walker's words and false depiction of Racak:

> . . . it was a pretext for war. It all started with William Walker's lies. This is a man who now openly shows that he is in fact a Greater Albania lobbyist. This is the same man because of whom (NATO) carried out an aggression against the Republic of Serbia. This is the same man. This is a man who now stands for the 'Greater Albania' and says so openly. He is no longer even hiding it."

Walker, whose statue today presides over Racak, claims that he was in no way advocating for Greater Albania, in a response that sounded as much a confirmation of the accusation as a refutation: "I meant that Albanians in Kosovo, Albania and Macedonia, would be in far better position if they work together." He has also established a Kosovo-based "Walker Foundation", to "to help Kosovo citizens for a better future." If the numbers of migrants from Kosovo (and Albania) flooding into the European Union along with people from places like war-torn Syria, Iraq, and Afghanistan are any indication, he has his work cut out for him.

Meanwhile, the "Death Star", whose activation Ames and Taibbi warned of in 1999 Kosovo, remains fully operational. Its media and Deep State custodians perceive Trump as a threat and hope first to break him to their yoke, then remove him. At this point, they seem to have the upper hand.

"When Washington Think Tanks Call for 'Action' in the Balkans, Expect Trouble"

Jim Jatras | *Strategic Culture* | May 9, 2018

Any time two prestige think tanks in Washington issue a report calling for US "action" in any region of the world, hold onto your hat—you can be sure that trouble is a-brewing. That's doubly true if the call relates to the Balkans, the place where in the 1990s the post-Cold War pattern was set for American wars of choice and then taken on the road to Iraq, Libya, and Syria.

On May 1, the *über*-establishment National Committee on American Foreign Policy and the East-West Institute jointly issued a report, "Time for Action in the Western Balkans." As stated in the summary:

> 'Since the end of the Cold War, the United States has been engaged in the Western Balkans to ensure a Europe that is "whole, free and at peace" and a reliable partner for dealing with global challenges. Our goal has been to stabilize the Balkans, and to enhance security throughout Europe, through the integration of the Western Balkans into trans-Atlantic structures. We have succeeded only in part. Although the Western Balkans are better off now than they were in the 1990s, they are stagnating and risk instability as a result of three factors: deficient internal governance and weak economies, continuing tense relations between ethnic groups and neighboring states, and the malign influence of outside forces.'

One is reminded of the famous quip by Mary McCarthy about Lillian Hellman: "every word she writes is a lie, including 'and' and 'the.'

Perhaps that's too harsh. Not every word in the summary paragraph is false. There is indeed a region in Europe known as the Balkans, and as the report notes, some countries lie in the western part of it: "Albania, Bosnia-Herzegovina, Kosovo, Macedonia, Montenegro, and Serbia." (Wait, there's some fibbing here too. Kosovo is not a country, it's an occupied province of Serbia. Nobody is quite sure what exactly Bosnia-Herzegovina is supposed to be. Why no Croatia, is it located in another part of Europe now?)

Each sentence in the summary encapsulates a deception further elaborated in the main report. The following is a handy sentence-by-sentence explanation in normal, straightforward English:

> 'Since the end of the Cold War, the United States has been engaged in the Western Balkans to ensure a Europe that is "whole, free and at peace" and a reliable partner for dealing with global challenges.'

The phrase "whole, free and at peace" is ideological claptrap. It is reminiscent of the Soviet Union's claims of advancing "peace, progress, and socialism." No one can say precisely what the words really mean but they're meant to evoke a favorable psychological and emotional response, especially—and ironically—the "peace" reference common to both formulations.

The current phrase seemingly originated in 1989, even before the reunification of Germany or the breakups of Yugoslavia and the USSR, in remarks by George Bush the Elder, but only as "Europe whole and free." The Orwellian addition of the words "and at peace" evidently occurred in 2001 under the peace-loving, NATO-expanding, and Iraq-invading Bush the Younger.

Still, how does the expression relate to the United States' being a "reliable partner for dealing with global challenges"? As summarized in 2014 by the Atlantic Council, another top-flight Washington think tank:

> In 1989, with Central and Eastern Europe still dominated by the Soviet Union and its Warsaw Pact alliance, President George H. W. Bush, addressed the citizens of then-divided Germany with his vision for Europe's future. He foresaw a united continent, built on a foundation of lasting security and shared values of democracy, freedom, and prosperity. That vision of a "Europe Whole and Free" became a cornerstone of President Bill Clinton's foreign policy and of NATO's "open door" policy for membership. At its 1999 Washington summit, NATO swept aside much of Europe's Cold War division by welcoming

three former foes—Poland, the Czech Republic, and Hungary—to the Alliance. Five years later [under George H.W. Bush], Bulgaria, Estonia, Latvia, Lithuania, Romania, Slovakia, and Slovenia joined NATO in the broadest enlargement of its history. In 2009 [under Barack Obama], the Alliance welcomed Albania and Croatia as members. [JGJ: *Now, under Donald Trump add Montenegro in 2017.*]

In 1993, the European Union established its "Copenhagen criteria," the principles under which it would welcome new members, unifying most of the continent. This paved the way for the transformation of Central and Eastern Europe toward democracy, the rule of law, respect for fundamental human rights, and market economies. Austria, Finland, and Sweden joined the EU in 1995, followed on May 1, 2004 by eight Central and Eastern European countries (the Czech Republic, Estonia, Hungary, Latvia, Lithuania, Poland, Slovakia, and Slovenia), and two Mediterranean countries (Malta and Cyprus). Bulgaria and Romania became EU member states in 2007, and Croatia in 2013.

In other words, the phrase that never leaves the lips of establishment figures of both parties, from Bush 41 down to the present day, almost exclusively means one thing: expansion of NATO and the European Union. The corollary is isolation, exclusion, vilification, and encirclement of Russia:

'Our goal has been to stabilize the Balkans, and to enhance security throughout Europe, through the integration of the Western Balkans into trans-Atlantic structures.'

If tearing apart Yugoslavia by unilateral recognitions (Slovenia and Croatia, 1991; Bosnia-Herzegovina, 1992) and illegally bombing Serbia (1999) are examples of efforts to "stabilize" the Balkans, one shudders to think what a goal to destabilize would look like.

The report also warns that "Kosovo and Bosnia have been recruiting grounds for radical groups in Syria and Iraq, and a potential staging area for radical incursions in Western Europe." There's no hint that the presence of these "radical groups" (What kind? Buddhist? Rastafarian?) has anything to do with earlier US/NATO/EU efforts to "stabilize" the areas in question by arming and funding jihadist fighters, including those affiliated with al-Qaeda.

As for "trans-Atlantic structures" (a rough equivalent of another ideological buzzword, "Euro-Atlantic integration"), we're back again to the inexorable expansion of NATO and the EU. It seems the goal of stabilization boils down to little more than making sure every country in the region eventually is under secure lock and key as a member of at least one and preferably both of the Brussels-based bureaucracies.

Throughout the report, puzzlingly little attention is given to another certified Goodthink word, *democracy*. Perhaps that's because no regard is given to what people in the region really think or whether or not they want to join NATO or the EU under the conditions demanded. For example, despite polls showing pro-NATO sentiment in Montenegro was at best a bare majority, and more probably the minority position, the corrupt administration of Milo Đukanović in Podgorica and the NATO countries insisted on ramming membership through without risking a popular referendum. The same contempt for democracy is shown in the report's recommendation that the unelected so-called "High Representative" of Somebody or Other should autocratically "use his powers to intervene, to include drafting and promulgating" a new election law for Bosnia-Herzegovina whether the benighted locals like it or not.

Regarding Serbia, the report states: "NATO membership should remain an option for Serbia, but any U.S. expectations must be tempered by the historical legacy of NATO's military operations in the region, as well as the likelihood of vociferous Russian opposition." As euphemisms go, "the historical legacy of NATO's military operations in the region" as a stand-in for "people resenting the aggressive alliance that bombed them" is hard to beat. Still, Serbs no doubt would be banging on NATO's door if not for the machinations of those nasty Russians.

As for the EU, the report urges the US to support Belgrade's accession "while supporting the E.U.'s position that new members comply with its Russia policy and that Serbia will not join unless it recognizes Kosovo." Translation: Just roll over and die, and you're in . . . maybe. The report continues:

> We have succeeded only in part. [JGJ: Such humility!] Although the Western Balkans are better off now than they were in the 1990s, they are stagnating and risk instability as a result of three factors: deficient internal governance and weak economies, continuing tense relations between ethnic groups and neighboring states, and the malign influence of outside forces.

Here it's time to cut to the chase: "malign influence of outside forces" means Russia, Russia, Russia. The entire region, Serbia included, would long since have happily been absorbed by the NATO-EU Borg if not for Moscow's malign meddling:

> The U.S. and the E.U. should counter Russian interference by (i) reaffirming the continued opportunity for Western Balkan countries to join the E.U., NATO, or both, (ii) countering Russian media manipulation with objective alternative sources of information, and support for independent media [JGJ: *Like those "independent" media controlled by western governments and George Soros fronts, one presumes*], (iii) advancing the region's cooperation with NATO and E.U. efforts to promote cyber-security [JGJ: *You can never have too much NATO and EU!*], and (iv) analyzing the extent to which other energy sources, including U.S. liquefied gas (LNG), can serve as exceptional alternatives to Russian energy [JGJ: *According to the report, cheap Russian energy is a "potential threat to some countries in the region" providing "an opportunity for significant economic leverage" that could be "abused to achieve Russian geopolitical desires," while by contrast expensive US energy is strictly nonpolitical*].

To sum up, "action" means intensification of the same policies that not only have made a wreck of the Balkans for a quarter of a century but now have brought us a new Cold War and the renewed threat of another world war. But the only warning for American and western policy identified in the report is the "dangers of continued inaction"—we just haven't been *aggressive enough!*

Get ready for that to change.

Alright, though—so what? This is just a report from a couple of non-governmental, independent think tanks. Why does it matter?

In Washington think tanks are far more dangerous than the kind of tanks that have gun turrets and caterpillar tracks. No less than the other organs of power, such as government agencies and the obedient corporate media, think tanks are an integral part of the governing establishment. Like government contractors (who provide a significant portion of think tank funding), think tanks almost exclusively represent the views of a few hundred certified "experts" sharing a remarkable uniformity of opinion regardless of party affiliation. These experts, who inhabit a closed loop of Executive Branch departments and agencies, Congress, media, contactors, think tanks, and NGOs, are responsible for the generation of policy initiatives and their implementation. It should also be noted that many of the most prominent NGOs themselves receive significant funding from government agencies and could more properly be termed "quasi-nongovernmental," or QuaNGOs.

The people who play key roles in the government and purportedly nongovernmental sectors like think tanks not only think alike, in many cases they are in fact *the very same people* who have simply switched positions within what could best be understood as a single, hybrid public-private entity that in recent years has come to be known as the Deep State. These sources of expert views also overwhelmingly dominate the content of news and information (for example, serving as media "talking heads" or publishing commentaries), ensuring that what the public sees, hears, and reads is in accord with the analytical papers issued by think tanks, Congressional reports, and official press releases. The result is a closed loop that is almost completely impervious to views regarded as "outside the mainstream" because they do not originate in or accord with the incestuous "consensus" that exists inside the loop.

In short, think tanks like those cited above are an integral part of the ruling apparatus. Their policy recommendations in reports like "Time for Action in the Western Balkans" will be seriously heeded and put into action by the official organs of government. In fact, those recommendations very likely were solicited by the latter precisely for the purpose of providing rationales for a course of action already decided upon.

"Poland Unwisely Plays the 'American Card' Against the EU and Russia"

Jim Jatras | *Strategic Culture* | June 2, 2018

To start with, let's point out that there is much to admire about the current Polish government under the Law and Justice (*Prawo i Sprawiedliwość*, PiS) party. It is socially and culturally conservative (prolife, pro-family); opposed to the non-European, largely Islamic, migratory invasion threatening the demographic replacement of native, Christian Europeans (and which may already be irreversible in some countries, like Sweden); and takes a strong patriotic stand for Polish sovereignty against the Moloch in Brussels. The European Union (EU) even threatens sanctions over absurd claims that the PiS's strictly domestic judiciary and media practices violate "democratic freedoms."

In contrast, "democratic freedoms" evidently weren't much of a concern in the corrupt EU establishment's (now hopefully failed) attempt to block the validly elected populist coalition in Italy. Nor are Europe's "democracy" champions troubled by the arrest, muzzling, and peremptory sentencing—and possible death sentence—of activist-journalist Tommy Robinson in the United

Kingdom. What the EU calls "democracy" of the elites and actual citizens' democracy clearly are two very different things. The voters' choice is only valid when it delivers items on the EU's anti-traditional, anti-Christian, anti-national, anti-human values, like the tragic abortion referendum outcome in Ireland.

In such a context, any European government that so upsets the mandarins in Brussels as much as the PiS in Warsaw does must have something good going for it. Together with the other three members of the Visegrád Group—and especially of Viktor Orbán's Hungary, which if anything is even more of a *bête noir* of the neo-liberal, Sorosite Eurocrats than Poland is—Poland is at the cutting edge of the nationally, religiously, and culturally based Euroskeptic movement, one which now includes the populist coalition in Austria.

Bravo! Let's give credit where credit is due.

But seemingly alone of the countries of the Visegrád plus one (V+1), Poland appears unduly attached to an outsized, anachronistic sense of its weight in continental affairs. This is combined with a visceral, unselfconscious antipathy towards Russia and, perhaps to a slightly lesser degree, towards Germany (which in practice means towards the EU itself, a "Fourth Reich" that has succeeded economically where Berlin had twice in the past failed militarily). However painful the nostalgic phantom limb pain of a once-great power whose borders formerly reached to Smolensk, encompassed all of Belarus and much of Ukraine, and which even briefly occupied Moscow during the Time of Troubles, such antipathies are not useful today for anyone—certainly not for Poland, nor for the rest of Europe.

An early inkling that Poland would seek to punch above its weight in prosecuting its anti-Russia vendetta was in February 2014 (prior to PiS's accession to power) when then-Foreign minister Radosław Sikorski stood shoulder-to-shoulder with his German and French counterparts in brokering a political compromise between Ukrainian president Viktor Yanukovych and the Maidan opposition. Of course, neither Poland, nor Germany, nor France (nor their American backers) murmured a peep of protest when the opposition proceeded over the space of a few hours to trash the arrangement, which was little more than a sly ruse for the seizure of total power that sent Yanukovych fleeing for his life. While for many Poles the anti-constitutional regime change in Kiev may have been a gratifying jab at Russia it also empowered Ukrainian nationalists who honor as heroes criminal perpetrators of the butchery of many tens of thousands of Polish victims of the massacres in Volhynia, the Lublin region, and Eastern Galicia from 1943 to 1945 by the Organization of Ukrainian Nationalists-Bandera faction (OUN-B) and its armed wing, the Ukrainian Insurgent Army (UPA).

But with the PiS in power, Poland's bid to again play with the big boys shifted into high gear. Key to this is a special relationship with Washington, which Warsaw sees as a powerful counterweight to its immediate neighbors. While other manifestations will surely follow, at the moment "playing the American card" involves two key initiatives:

1. *Against the EU*: Warsaw is positioning itself as the critical mediator between the United States (Poland's friend) and the EU (Poland's antagonist) with respect to US threats to hit European companies with secondary sanctions on trade with Iran following American withdrawal from the JCPOA (Joint Comprehensive Plan of Action); and

2. *Against Russia*: Warsaw has offered the US up to two billion dollars in support for a permanent American base in Poland.

Regarding the Iran sanctions, because of the need for unanimity in any EU-wide countermeasures, Poland has a lot of leverage. While EU midgets like Donald Tusk, Jean-Claude Juncker, and Federica Mogherini talk a brave fight against US sanctions, the outcome at the EU and in European capitals is very much in doubt. The US will try to pick off one or another of the top three European governments (United Kingdom, France, or Germany) to cave to the US position, then expect the others to follow. The almost certain pullout of the French company Total from Iran is a good indicator of how things may go.

Moreover, since standing firm against Washington's threats requires solidarity with Russia (as well as with China) the US will rely on the most anti-Russian members—not only Poland but the Baltic states and maybe Romania—to block any concerted resistance. The US will count on the leading role to be played by Poland, which, as noted above, already has its other problems with Brussels. Washington will expect Warsaw to jump at the chance to not only poke the EU (and Germany) in the eye but Russia too.

It cannot be emphasized too strongly that European resistance to reimposition of Iran sanctions is not just a test for the EU institutionally (in which case, who cares) but is a critical measure of whether European countries individually as well as collectively can reassert their sovereignty against the hegemon across the Atlantic. At this juncture, Poland appears ready to help Washington maintain dominance over our European satellites.

How that helps Poland is less than clear. Certainly it is understandable, perhaps even praiseworthy, for the PiS government to want to deliver a sharp riposte to Brussels for its threats against Poland over migration policy and meddling in Poland's internal constitutional affairs. But a binary identification of "Brussels bad, Washington good" doesn't logically follow. This relates not just to interests but values. US elites overwhelmingly share the postmodern, post-Christian values of Western Europe. As Patrick Buchanan observes: "A scholarly study sums it up: 'The statistical trends in religion show two separate Europes: the West is undergoing a process of secularization while the post-socialist East, de-secularization.' One Europe is turning back to God; the other is turning its back on God." (Ironically, along with Poland and Hungary, one of the primary examples of post-communist Christian revival is Russia—something many Poles might not choose to acknowledge.)

Thus, despite the Trump administration's blowing up the US relationship with the EU over the Iran nuclear deal, there is still more that unites than divides the unelected bureaucracy in Brussels with its American counterpart—no, not Trump himself, who was legitimately elected, but the Deep State oligarchy that has been attempting to overthrow him. Consider the contrast: Poland now has indicated its willingness to torpedo concerted EU resistance to Washington's demand for new sanctions on Iran (plus secondary sanctions on Europe) just as Brussels (with likely American involvement, according to Tom Luongo) tried to torpedo formation of a new, right-left populist Italian government that would have been a powerful partner for V+1. Why? Because a Five-Star/Lega government might pull the plug on sanctions against Russia.

Even more momentous than what Warsaw chooses to do about Iran-related sanctions is the offer of an American base in Poland, which creates a positive and direct danger to the Polish people. Poland needs neither an American base (nor the American "defensive" missiles set to be deployed there) for the simple reason that there is no military danger to Poland, neither from "Russian aggression" nor from a non-existent Iranian missile threat.

Rather, these measures themselves run the risk of creating a menace where there wasn't one before. As Washington and our NATO satellites continue to step up pressure on Russia—through "forward basing" in the East, arming Kiev with Javelin missiles, naval and aerial probing in the Black and Baltic seas—the possibility of a mishap that leads unintentionally (one hopes it would be unintentional) to hostilities goes up accordingly. (We should also add US provocations against Russia in Syria.) In that case, any US presence would be of zero value as military protection to Poland, but it would ensure that Poland would be a primary target if war were to break out.

Moscow warns that a permanent US base in Poland would be a violation of the 1997 NATO-Russia Founding Act, which states that "in the current and foreseeable security environment, the Alliance will carry out its collective defence and other missions by ensuring the necessary interoperability, integration, and capability for reinforcement rather than by additional permanent stationing of substantial combat forces." NATO has already moved to skirt this provision by claiming that "force rotation" in Poland and the Baltics and the Nordic region is neither "permanent" nor "substantial." Moreover, as the neoconservative-dominated think tank Heritage Foundation asserts, due solely to Russian actions in its Near Abroad "the 'current and foreseeable security environment' in Europe has changed dramatically since 1997. This alone justifies permanently basing NATO troops in Central and Eastern Europe."

In other words, the Founding Act is a dead letter. That would have to include its key assertion: "NATO and Russia do not consider each other as adversaries." An adversarial stance towards Russia is the heart of the so-called "Three Seas Initiative"—lauded by US President Donald Trump during his 2017 visit to Warsaw—which seems nothing more than a warmed-over version of earlier Polish effort to isolate Russia from Europe, Józef Piłsudski's "Prometheism" and "Intermarium" initiatives.

Unless Poland intends to levitate itself to some other place in Europe, even with America's favor Poles will have to contend with the fact that they have Germany on one side and (in effect, not really counting Belarus) Russia on the other. These are the neighbors God gave the Poles, with which they can be friends or enemies.

With a looming confrontation between the US and the EU over trade and Iran sanctions, and with ties to Russia locked in a deep freeze, there are those in Washington happy to use Poland as a cat's paw against both. How that is in Poland's interest is another matter.

"A Two-Pronged Attack on Orthodoxy and Russia"

Jim Jatras | *Strategic Culture* | July 7, 2018

As US President Donald Trump and Russian President Vladimir Putin prepare to meet in Helsinki, all eyes are on what generally are regarded as the "usual" political issues that divide the world's two foremost military powers: Ukraine, Syria, sanctions, claims of election interference, and so forth. This reflects the near-universal but erroneous view that this current, second Cold War is not ideological, as opposed to the first Cold War that pitted atheistic Soviet communism against America's "in God we trust" capitalism. (Leave aside whether "capitalism," an anarcho-socialist term popularized by Marxists, is the proper description of contemporary neoliberal corporatism.)

No, we are told, the current Washington-Moscow standoff is a turf war, nothing more. Unlike the 1945–1991 rivalry it "lacks an ideological dimension" beyond the authoritarian determination to elevate "the Russian state, ruled by him and his clan."

Such a view totally dismisses the fact that following the demise of communism as a global power bloc there has been an eerie spiritual role reversal between East and West. While it's true that during original Cold War the nonreligious ruling cliques in Washington and Moscow held basically compatible progressive values, ordinary Christian Americans (mainly Protestants, with a large number of Roman Catholics) perceived communism as a murderous, godless machine of oppression (think of the Knights of Columbus' campaign to insert "under God" into the Pledge of Allegiance). Conversely, today it is western elites who rely upon an ideological imperative of "democracy" and "human rights" promotion to justify a materialist global empire and endless wars, much like the old Soviet nomenklatura depended on Marxism-Leninism both as a working methodology and as a justification for their prerogatives and privileges. In that regard, promotion of nihilist, post-Christian morality—especially in sexual matters—has become a major item in the West's toolkit.

This has a special importance with regard to Russia, where under Putin the Orthodox Church has largely resumed its pre-1917 role as the moral anchor of society. This elicits not only political opposition but a genuine and heartfelt hatred from the postmodern elites of an increasingly post-Christian West, not only for Putin personally and Russia generally but against the Russian Orthodox Church—and by extension against Orthodox Christianity itself.

This antipathy has many facets, too many to be detailed at one time in this short space. But for now it is sufficient to note two current attacks, both of them arising from within Orthodoxy itself, though no doubt with outside encouragement. One such attack relates to ecclesiastical structures and is overtly political. The other is in the moral sphere and seeks to inject into Orthodoxy the moral decay that has undermined so much of western Christianity.

The first, overtly political attack aims to split Ukraine from the main body of the Russian Orthodox Church under the authority of Patriarch Kirill of Moscow. The post-Maidan authorities in Kiev, namely Ukrainian President Petro Poroshenko and the Verkhovna Rada (parliament), have asked Ecumenical Patriarch Bartholomew of Constantinople (Istanbul) to issue a Tomos of autocephaly to the self-styled "Ukrainian Orthodox Church of the Kyiv Patriarchate" led by former Metropolitan Filaret (Denysenko). In such case, the Ukrainian authorities declare that the canonical Ukrainian Orthodox Church, which is an autonomous part of the Russian Orthodox Church under the authority of Metropolitan Onufry, would be forbidden to call itself "Ukrainian" would regarded as a representative of an "aggressor" power. Issuance of a Tomos would also set the stage for the government's forcible seizure of churches and monasteries from Metropolitan Onufry's canonical Church and handing them over to the state-approved schismatic body, with the world-renowned Kiev Pechersk (Caves) Lavra and the Holy Dormition Pochayiv Lavra in west Ukraine the most prominent likely targets.

For their part, Ukrainian officials state their chances of getting the Tomos are virtually certain, but so far public signals from Ecumenical Patriarch Bartholomew have been mixed. Recently, it was announced by pro-Moscow observers that the Ecumenical Patriarch had turned down Poroshenko's request after a visit of bishops from the Moscow-affiliated Ukrainian Church. Other reports, however, indicate that Constantinople considers it an open question whether the areas now constituting Ukraine were ever permanently transferred to Moscow's jurisdiction in the first place—which one voice, "Orthodoxy in Dialogue" (to which we shall return below), cheered as "taking Moscow down a peg."

Viewed from western countries, where ecclesiastical matters have long ceased to have life-and-death political consequences, the Ukrainian church situation may seem archaic, even bizarre, especially taking place in a part of the world that not too long ago was under the domination of militant secularists. Be that as it may, the current Ukraine crisis fits into a dismal pattern of powers hostile to Orthodoxy attempting to create new church bodies to serve their political purposes. The most notorious of these were the purported creation of a "Croatian Orthodox Church" in 1942 under the genocidal regime of Ustaša dictator Ante Pavelić as a cover for the genocide of Orthodox Serbs in the so-called "Independent State of Croatia," and the so-called "Renovationist Church" formed in early Soviet Russia during the most murderous period of communist anti-religious persecution.

At stake today is not only the peace of Ukraine—where violence over state-imposed church transfers is a real concern—but peace within the Orthodox world as a whole. While the honor accorded the Ecumenical Patriarch in Orthodoxy doesn't remotely approximate that of the Pope of Rome within his confession, as the bishop of the former imperial capital and once-foremost city in Christendom he speaks with great honor and authority. On the other hand, the flock of the Church of Russia under the Patriarchate of Moscow as currently structured (including Ukraine) constitutes an absolute majority of the world's Orthodox Christians. An incautious move could trigger a major rupture, not just in Ukraine but worldwide, with the constituent national churches forced to take sides. For his part, Patriarch Irinej of the Serbian Orthodox Church has spoken strongly against the Kiev authorities and their aspiring autonomous church: "Anyone who helps the Ukrainian schismatics is an enemy not only of the Russian Church and the Russian world, but also of all Orthodox Slavic nations and the entire Orthodox world."

Shifting now from the structural to the moral sphere, recently there appeared on the excellent websites *Fort-Russ* and *Pravmir* a commentary, "ORTHODOXY, CAPITALISM, AND 'THE WEST': IS ORTHODOX CHRIST-IANITY STUCK IN THE PAST?" by Nathaniel Wood, identified as a scholar of Orthodox theology and political theology and associate director of the Orthodox Christian Studies Center of Fordham University. The piece opens with an unobjectionable observation mainly relating to economic issues:

> Orthodox political theology has often been strongly communitarian, skeptical of rationalist legal order, and reliant on the benevolence of autocratic rule. In . . . Russia, for instance, the influential Slavophile movement of the 19th century praised the Russian peasant commune as the highest expression of Orthodox social principles and even made it a basis for their model of the Church (the notion of sobornost'). The Slavophiles' ideal Orthodox society was not only explicitly anti-capitalist, going as far as to ground all property ownership in social obligation, but was critical of the "rationalist" culture of legal relations standing behind the Western capitalist order, even to the point of investing all political authority in the autocrat out of fear that a society based on legal rights was antithetical to Orthodoxy.

In addressing Mr. Wood's comment on economics, Professor Jonathan Chaves of George Washington University, observes as an Orthodox Christian:

It is perfectly possible and respectable to be a Christian conservative and unhappy with "Plutocracy." Plutocracy is the conglomeration or aggregation of small businesses into vast multinational corporations. In the 1920's G.K. Chesterton and Hilaire Belloc, both devout Roman Catholics, founded a tint party, the Distributist Party. Distributism said, "No" to Socialism, recognizing that private property is a foundation-stone of Liberty; and "No" to Plutocracy, realizing that it led to vast entities aggregating power to themselves. They said "Yes" to private, small business. And so must we all. If this discussion takes place only within the Orthodox Church, it will remain a tempest in a teapot. Let us link arms with those in agreement on the specific issues we can agree on.

So far so good. It's one thing to question whether Orthodox Christians should uncritically accept the neoliberal global order and its corporatist economic and financial system ("capitalism"). Neither Scripture, nor the Canons of the Ecumenical and Regional Synods, nor the Church Fathers had much specific to say about this system simply because it didn't exist in their day. Neither did socialism, for that matter.

But it's quite another thing to redefine, under the guise of scholarship, moral principles that far precede the modern era and are central to Christian anthropology. Today, as noted above, those principles are under threat in increasingly godless Western Europe and North America. Moreover, in a manner reminiscent of the 20th century Bolshevik assault on Christianity (including the so-called "Renovationist" church), the West has made moral aggression against the socially conservative countries of formerly communist Europe a key element of its foreign policy. (See my "The West's Quest to 'Save the World Through Degeneracy.'")

It is clear that such a redefinition of Christian morality, not economics, is the real deliverable in Mr. Wood's essay and of the Fordham program he represents. Moreover, Russia is the particular target. The following is from website of the Orthodox Christian Studies Center of Fordham University:

Fellow co-director Aristotle Papanikolaou, Ph.D., professor of theology and the Archbishop Demetrios Chair in Orthodox Theology and Culture, said the Russian Orthodox Church has been trying to redefine human rights language in such a way that allows them to uphold "traditional values" for the last decade. This understanding of human rights doesn't protect a band like Pussy Riot from protesting in a Church, or art that's deemed blasphemous, and it's consistent with laws that ban gay marriage and homosexual "propaganda."

"Normally people would say, that's a violation of human rights, and some Orthodox Christians want to say 'No it's not. We have our own particular interpretation of human rights, and we are justified in doing that because the West's concept of human rights is biased and anti-Christian,'" he said. "Our project hopes to offer a more nuanced understanding of Orthodox Christianity's relation to human rights language than the diametrical opposition proposed by certain Orthodox Christians, especially in the post-communist context."

Papanikolaou further noted that the Russian government also uses the language of human rights and the defense of religious freedom to justify its ongoing military intervention in Syria.

So, "a more nuanced understanding of Orthodox Christianity's relation to human rights language" doesn't have a problem with blasphemous antics in Moscow's Christ the Savior Cathedral (lovingly rebuilt after being blown up by the Bolsheviks)? With sacrilegious "art" (which in the west is often subsidized with believers' tax money)? With indoctrinating innocent young children in alternative sexual morality (for example, in several US cities "Drag Queen Story Hour")? With marriage not restricted to one man and one woman? With western-supported head-choppers seeking to kill, enslave, or uproot the Christians of Syria, and have been prevented from doing so mainly through Russia's heroic intervention in that country?

Also, as an Orthodox Christian of Greek origin myself, I can't help but notice more than a whiff of Hellenic intellectual and academic arrogance in the way mainly Greek principals of the Fordham project formulate their criticisms of the Russian Church's positions. (Similarly, it is important to bear in mind that if the Ukrainian schism spreads further, the fault lines will partly though far from entirely split between Russians and Greeks, with disastrous results.) Rather than a case of the Russian Church's seeking to 'redefine human rights language in such a way that allows them to uphold "traditional values"' it is quite clear that it is the Fordham academics who are themselves seeking to redefine authentic Orthodox Christian traditional values (without the quotation marks) as stated forthrightly, clearly, and faithfully in the Social Concept of the Russian Orthodox Church (which link, to give Mr. Wood credit, he did include in his posting).

Sadly, the Fordham program is not alone in cutting-edge Orthodox academia. Another effort, "Orthodoxy in Dialogue," cited above with respect to the Ukrainian crisis, displays the same agenda, including demanding that Orthodox clergy advocate open borders in the US on a par with opposing abortion, being Orthodox and "genderqueer," explaining the finer points of "intersex" vs. "transgender" (and faulting the esteemed Metropolitan Hierotheos of Nafpaktos and Agiou Vlasiou for ignoring the priceless "contributions that empirical sciences have made to our understanding of sexual and gender variance in human nature"), trashing respected American Orthodox Christian voices like Fr. John Whiteford and Rod Dreher, and—well you get the idea.

What is perhaps most tragic is that while ever-growing numbers of western Christians, lapsed Christians, and non-Christians are attracted to the Holy Orthodox Church precisely because they perceive Her, correctly, to be the Ark of Salvation that—with the powerful global support of the Russian state—does not change course with the gales and storms of a tempestuous and darkening world, revisionist Orthodox scholars would have us trim our sails to match the course of some western confessions that are increasingly rendered Christian in name only, if that. It is counsel we dare not heed.

"US State Department on Ukraine: 'Any Decision on Autocephaly Is an Internal Church Matter'"

Jim Jatras | *Strategic Culture* | September 21, 2018

Last week the website of Ukrainian President Petro Poroshenko posted an account of his meeting in Kiev with Ambassador Sam Brownback, former US Senator and Governor of Kansas, currently Ambassador at Large for International Religious Freedom. According to the posting, "President Poroshenko outlined the measures taken to establish the Ukrainian Autocephalous Orthodox Church. The Head of State thanked the American party [i.e., Brownback] for an active support in this process." Moreover, according to Kiev, Brownback assured Poroshenko that the United States would further support Ukraine in its struggle for "the right to have the Ukrainian Autocephalous Orthodox Church."

Poroshenko's administration thus claimed explicit and public American official endorsement for his quest for the Ecumenical Patriarchate in Constantinople to grant autocephaly (complete self-rule among the various member Churches of the Orthodox Christian communion) to a schismatic body headed by self-styled "Patriarch Filaret" Denysenko—an entity recognized as canonical by no local Orthodox church in the world, including (as of this writing) by the Ecumenical Patriarchate itself. As noted in this space two months ago when hardly anyone was paying attention, this effort by Poroshenko, Denysenko, and their supporters is part of a two-pronged attack against Russia and against the Holy Orthodox Church itself, in part to further the agenda of academic purveyors of moral/sexual LGBT and "genderqueer" theology like "Orthodoxy in Dialogue" and the hardly less revolutionary "Orthodox Christian Studies Center" at Fordham University—both, unsurprisingly, staunch supporters of Constantinople's neo-papal pretensions.

Kiev's account of the Brownback-Poroshenko meeting immediately seemed suspicious when it was first noticed by this analyst. Brownback is a careful and principled advocate for religious freedom. While as a State Department official he is bound by administration policy—which is overtly anti-Russian, whatever President Donald Trump's preferences may be—Brownback would know better than to wade into the internal canonical affairs of Orthodoxy, in which he has no particular authority. Upon investigation it seems he said nothing of the sort attributed to him concerning Poroshenko's claimed "right to have the Ukrainian Autocephalous Orthodox Church."

Support for that suspicion is found in the words of a high State Department official, Ambassador Michael Kozak, speaking at the 2018 Human Dimension Implementation Meeting of the Organization of Security and Cooperation in Europe, who stated on September 13: " . . . the United States is a staunch supporter of religious freedom, including the freedom of members of religious groups to govern their religion according to their tenets. We therefore believe any decision on autocephaly is an internal church matter." Granted, Kozak introduced and concluded his short remarks with the standard anti-Russian rhetoric, but the point is clear: contra Poroshenko, the US government has not taken an overt official stand in support of Ukrainian autocephaly.

One would hardly know that from the behavior of Poroshenko and Denysenko, who seem to think that the status of the Orthodox Church in Ukraine is not only a matter to be decided from on high by the Ecumenical Patriarchate (about which more below) but by western geopolitical "experts" who wouldn't know Orthodoxy from orthodontia. Like mushrooms in Ukraine's forests, analyses of the Ukrainian church situation have popped up in learned Orthodox theological journals like *The Economist* and *Newsweek*. Taras Kuzio, writing for the Atlantic Council, a top establishment think tank funded heavily by US and foreign government agencies and their corporate contractors (at page 64) but not particularly renowned for its spiritual perspicacity, weighed in with what clearly are the real goals of the push for autocephaly, which are entirely political and directed at Russia:

> It's no exaggeration to write that the granting of autocephaly from the Russian Orthodox Church to Ukraine's millions of Orthodox believers is as significant as the disintegration of the USSR for Ukraine. Granting Ukraine's Orthodox Church a Tomos [from Orthowiki: a small book that contains a major announcement or similar text promulgated by a holy synod, such as a recognition of autocephaly] is the last step Ukraine needs to take in order to become truly independent. [. . .]
>
> With the Russian Orthodox Church as the last source of Putin's soft power now gone, Ukraine's movement out of Russia's orbit is irreversible. The creation of an autocephalous Ukrainian Orthodox Church is Ukraine's ultimate answer to Putin's aggression.

Not surprisingly Denysenko was reverently received in Washington by the Atlantic Council on September 19, which also by pure coincidence was International Talk Like a Pirate Day. In an address heavy on politics and hostility to Russia and meager on anything relevant to tradition or spirituality, Denysenko confirmed that his own "church" is currently illicit in the eyes of the whole Orthodox world and would (he contended with no supporting authority) be legitimated by a Tomos, absent which many people would remain hesitant to join it. He also confirmed it would be up to the Ukrainian government to decide upon the seizure from their rightful owners, the canonical Ukrainian Orthodox Church of the Moscow Patriarchate, of major centers like the Kiev Pechersk (Caves) Lavra and the Holy Dormition Pochaev Lavra—all "peacefully," of course, and in accordance with law.

The abbot of Pechersk reports that violent threats have already begun. If and when fighting breaks out, we can be sure that western governments, think tanks, and media will with one voice rush to blame it all solely on Russian meddling, not on militant nationalist supporters of autocephaly, many of whom are not even believers, so *Radio Free Europe* tells us:

> "Soon there will be one unified national church," says Crimean Tatar journalist Aider Mudzhabayev in his videoblog, "I see this as a big step forward. God willing . . . hmmm, I'm an atheist, but God willing it'll go that way."
>
> For many "church passers-by" [i.e., occasional or nominal] and atheists like Mudzhabayev, "our" "Ukrainian" church should be recognised and receive a Tomos on autocephaly. [. . .]
>
> The main thing, after all, is to create a symbol: an Independent United National Ukrainian Church—patriotic and recognised by Orthodoxy around the world.
>
> In the circumstances, however, this united church is very unlikely to be genuinely united. Practicing believers, who mostly belong to the Moscow Patriarchate, will not join it. This will be for various reasons: their conservatism, their conception of the unity of the Russian Church and their reputation in the eyes of the public. In this sense, the united national church—if it receives its Tomos—will be merely a symbolic victory for Ukraine's patriotic "church passers-by."

Poroshenko, who hopes achievement of a united national church will be his ticket to reelection next year, is also making his pitch to the DC Swamp's powerbrokers. Via a *Washington Post* interview with Lally Weymouth, whose lack of interest in the issue is palpable even through the medium of print, once the important stuff like Ukraine's becoming a "full member of the European Union and of NATO" has been dealt with, it's evident that Poroshenko's case is entirely a political one against Russia:

> We have another topic—the independence of the Ukrainian Orthodox Church from Russia.
>
> Q: I hear that you're the architect of an imminent deal regarding the orthodox church.
>
> A: I am proud of that. I hate the idea that the Ukrainian church is manipulated from Moscow.
>
> Q: Has it been manipulated by Moscow?
>
> A: Yes, because the formal patriarch of part of our church is Russian, Patriarch Kirill of Moscow. We hate to accept that. We asked the ecumenical patriarch of Constantinople, Bartholomew I, to give us independence. Shortly, we will have an independent Ukrainian church as part of an independent Ukraine. This will create a spiritual independence from Russia.

Now the next step is up to Ecumenical Patriarch Bartholomew and his purported "exarchs" sent from North America to Kiev without agreement from Metropolitan Onufry of Kiev, who heads the only canonical Orthodox Church in Ukraine. Metropolitan Hilarion (Alfeyev) of the Moscow Patriarchate suggests they may be planning to reconsecrate Denysenko's schismatic "hierarchs" to "at least give them the appearance of legitimacy," as "at least two bishops are needed to celebrate an episcopal consecration." Such an action, which would be the equivalent of a declaration of war against Moscow, is itself a tacit admission that the priestly orders of Denysenko's "church" are invalid, and that in Ukraine the only canonical hierarchy recognized by the entire world—including Constantinople!—is the one led by Metropolitan Onufry, who has not asked for autocephaly.

Almost ignored in western accounts of the dispute is the fact that Constantinople has no lawful power to reach into the territory of another autocephalous church to consecrate bishops and confer canonical status on schismatics. The contrast is painfully apparent between Patriarch Bartholomew's increasingly extravagant claims of papal or even imperial authority (for example, in his failed bid, after decades of preparation, to convene an "Eighth" Ecumenical Council, a modernizing Orthodox "Vatican II" in 2016) and the virtual absence of an organic flock within his own home area. If it were not for administration of the Greek Diaspora (including this analyst) in places like the Americas, Australia, and parts of Western Europe—which Constantinople has only by virtue of its status of the once-great capital of the Christian East Roman Empire, Constantine's "New Rome," Цариград (Tsargrad) to the Slavs, Miklagard (Great City) to the Vikings—the Constantinopolitan synod is revealed as a group of bishops almost without any people, a rotten borough able to count perhaps only a few hundred mostly elderly Greeks left huddled in Istanbul's Fener district. As Saint John (Maximovich) of Shanghai and San Francisco observed decades ago, Constantinople had even then become in truth only a "pitiful spectacle," a sorry shadow of its former glory, even while "in theory embracing almost the whole universe." If the Ecumenical Patriarch imprudently unleashes the worldwide schism now looming, forcing other autocephalous Churches to choose sides, it cannot be excluded that one casualty may be his own See's fictional and anachronistic standing.

Returning to the official position of the US government, Kozak at least is correct in stating that the status of Ukraine's church is an internal Orthodox affair. Whether that can be relied on is another matter, in light of Denysenko's open appeal for American support during his Atlantic Council talk. It should also be noted that the Greek government, which has been moving towards closer cooperation with NATO in light of growing discord between Washington and Ankara, has undertaken a campaign of harassment against Russian clergy seeking visas to Greece and specifically to enter as pilgrims en route to Mount Athos. A few months ago, as the church controversy was building, Ernst Reichel, the German Ambassador in Kiev, openly endorsed autocephaly for Ukraine.

In short, given the level of political interest in sowing havoc in the Orthodox Church and taking a jab at Russia, a hands-off approach from Washington, Brussels, Berlin, etc. cannot be taken for granted—whatever the pro forma stated position of the State Department. All Orthodox believers, as well as anyone genuinely dedicated to freedom of conscience, should join in inviting the US and NATO governments to just butt out of where they don't belong.

"For US, Meddling in Orthodox Church Affairs Is Just Another Tool Against Russia"

Jim Jatras | *Strategic Culture* | September 29, 2018

Probably not many people who follow international affairs think the intricacies of Orthodox Church governance are particularly important.

Well, the US Department of State does.

Barely a week ago, the State Department, via the statement of a senior official, Ambassador Michael Kozak, publicly pledged that Washington would stay out of the contentious question of the status of the Orthodox Church in Ukraine: "any decision on autocephaly is an internal church matter." (Without repeating all of the details of my previous commentaries on what some may regard as an arcane and peripheral issue, there is reason to expect that Patriarch Bartholomew of Constantinople may soon issue a "tomos" [decree] of autocephaly [self-rule] for the Orthodox Church in Ukraine, thereby purporting to rip it out from the Russian Orthodox Church, of which the canonical Ukrainian Orthodox Church, which has not asked for autocephaly, is an autonomous part.)

Especially for a government like that of the United States, which claims to have no particular religious agenda, respecting the internal canonical integrity of the Orthodox Church as a spiritual community was the only correct position.

But it didn't last long.

Kozak's declaration must now be considered inoperative. On September 25, the noted theologian Heather Nauert, the State Department's spokesperson, issued the following statement:

Press Statement

Heather Nauert
Department Spokesperson
Washington, DC

September 25, 2018

> The United States strongly supports religious freedom, including the freedom of members of groups to govern their religion according to their beliefs and practice their faiths freely without government interference. The United States respects the ability of Ukraine's Orthodox religious leaders and followers to pursue autocephaly according to their beliefs. We respect the Ecumenical Patriarch as a voice of religious tolerance and interfaith dialogue.
>
> The United States maintains unwavering support for Ukraine and its territorial integrity in the face of Russian aggression in eastern Ukraine and the Russian occupation of Crimea. We also support Ukraine as it charts its own path and makes its own decisions and associations, free of external interference.

No doubt drafted not by Nauert herself but by someone in the Bureau of European and Eurasian Affairs (EUR) the press statement avoids directly calling for autocephaly while unmistakably giving the impression of such endorsement, which is exactly how it was reported in the media, for example, "US backs Ukrainian Church bid for autocephaly." The State Department's praise for the Ecumenical Patriarchate reinforces that clearly intended impression.

Thus, the State Department must now be considered a party to triggering violent religious strife that will soon grip Ukraine and cause a split in the Orthodox world rivaling even the Great Schism between Orthodoxy and Roman Catholicism that took place in 1054. (Unlike the US, the Vatican commendably has maintained a principled position of non-interference. The Papal Nuncio in Kiev even issued a statement answering Ukrainian government spin that falsely claimed the support for autocephaly: "In order to partially correct the news given by official Government sources with regard to the meeting that took place yesterday. . . the Apostolic Nunciature in Ukraine wishes to once again state the position of the Holy See in the question of the creation of one Local Ukrainian Orthodox Church, namely that this is an internal question of the Orthodox Church, on which the Holy See never did and has no intention whatsoever of expressing any evaluation, in any venue.")

No doubt the official US imprimatur will be taken both by Kiev and the Phanar (the district in Istanbul, formerly Constantinople, where the Ecumenical Patriarchate is located) as a green light to press forward with the impending schism. That in turn will inevitability lead to violence—which of course will be blamed exclusively on Ukrainians loyal to the canonical Church and on Russia.

The game plan for such seizures was laid out by false "Patriarch Filaret" Denysenko last week in Washington, in his remarks to the Atlantic Council. He specified that following expected recognition of autocephaly by Constantinople (which uncanonically claims such authority) members of Ukrainian parishes can choose which jurisdiction to adhere to by a two-thirds vote. This opens the door to packing the putative membership in a parish by people who have no connection to it and who might not even be Orthodox believers, who will then "democratically" outvote the genuine parishioners. As for monastic establishments, that's simple according to Denysenko: the Ukrainian government will grab them. The Ukrainian Ministry of Culture has already begun compiling an inventory of properties belonging to the canonical Ukrainian Orthodox Church in preparation for their forcible seizure by state authorities, to be turned over the Denysenkoite schismatics.

One should not suppose that the Nauert statement means the US government or the State Department has taken a sudden interest in theology and ecclesiology. Rather, it is a new twist in what always must be kept in mind (and certainly officials in Kiev never forget): that nobody in Washington really cares much about Ukraine or Ukrainians per se. They matter only to the extent to which US officials believe that keeping Ukraine out of Russia's orbit means preventing Moscow from regaining superpower status.

To that end, pulling Ukraine firmly in to the western camp of NATO (the 2008 Bucharest declaration that Ukraine, along with Georgia, will become a member has never been rescinded) and the European Union presents Russia with an insoluble security vulnerability. Ukraine's President Petro Poroshenko repeated insists Ukraine will become a "full member of NATO and of the European Union."

Hence, Poroshenko's drive for autocephaly has exactly zero to do with spiritual values and everything to do with slamming Russia: "We will have an independent Ukrainian church as part of an independent Ukraine. This will create a spiritual independence from Russia." His rival for the presidency, front-runner and former prime minister, Yulia Tymochenko supports it for the same reason. If that results in bloodshed, well, too bad . . .

The State Department's decision to become involved in a religious matter that does not concern the US is likewise narrowly political and reflects the schizophrenia in the Trump administration concerning Russia. Trump's 2016 declarations that he wanted to improve ties with Moscow terrified the post-Maidan leadership in Kiev, who were overtly in Hillary's camp. When Trump unexpectedly won, they were afraid he would make a deal with Moscow over their heads.

However, with the moving into political positions of influence strongly anti-Russian figures, many of them Bush retreads and even some with "Never Trump" credentials, Ukrainian officials have good reason to feel that that danger has largely been averted. With hostility toward Russia seemingly permanent and deepening, they believe they have Washington back where they want them.

Viewed through that lens, egging on religious dissension is just another item in the toolkit.

"Whose Money Stoked Religious Strife in Ukraine—and Who Tried to Steal It?"

Jim Jatras | *Strategic Culture* | November 17, 2018

Was $25 million in American tax dollars allocated for a payoff to stir up religious turmoil and violence in Ukraine? Did Ukrainian President Petro Poroshenko (unsuccessfully) attempt to divert most of it into his own pocket?

Last month the worldwide Orthodox Christian communion was plunged into crisis by the decision of Ecumenical Patriarch Bartholomew I in Constantinople to recognize as legitimate schismatic pseudo-bishops anathematized by the canonical Ukrainian Orthodox Church, which is an autonomous part of the Russian Orthodox Church. In so doing not only has Patriarch Bartholomew besmirched the global witness of Orthodoxy's two-millennia old

Apostolic faith, he has set the stage for religious strife in Ukraine and fratricidal violence—which has already begun.

Starting in July, when few were paying attention, this analyst warned
about the impending dispute and how it facilitated the anti-Christian moral
agenda of certain marginal "Orthodox" voices like "Orthodoxy in Dialogue,"
Fordham University's "Orthodox Christian Studies Center," and *The Wheel*.
These "self-professed teachers presume to challenge the moral teachings of
the faith" (in the words of Fr. John Parker) and "prowl around, wolves in
sheep's clothing, forming and shaping false ideas about the reality of our life
in Christ." Unsurprisingly such groups have embraced Constantinople's neo-
papal self-aggrandizement and support for the Ukrainian schismatics.

No one—and certainly not this analyst—would accuse Patriarch Bartholomew, most Ukrainian politicians, or even the Ukrainian schismatics of
sympathizing with advocacy of such anti-Orthodox values. And yet these
advocates know they cannot advance their goals if the conciliar and traditional
structure of Orthodoxy remains intact. Thus they welcome efforts by
Constantinople to centralize power while throwing the Church into discord,
especially the Russian Church, which is vilified in some Western circles
precisely because it is a global beacon of traditional Christian moral witness.

This aspect points to another reason for Western governments to support
Ukrainian autocephaly as a spiritual offensive against Russia and Orthodoxy.
The post-Maidan leadership harp on the "European choice" the people of
Ukraine supposedly made in 2014, but they soft-pedal the accompanying
moral baggage the West demands, symbolized by "gay" marches organized
over Christian objections in Orthodox cities like Athens, Belgrade, Bucharest,
Kiev, Odessa, Podgorica, Sofia, and Tbilisi. Even under the Trump admin-
istration, the US is in lockstep with our European Union friends in pressuring
countries liberated from communism to adopt such nihilistic "democratic,
European values."

Perhaps even more important to its initiators, the row over Ukraine aims
to break what they see as the "soft power" of the Russian Federation, of which
the Orthodox Church is the spiritual heart and soul. As explained by Valeria
Z. Nollan, professor emerita of Russian Studies at Rhodes College:

> 'The real goal of the quest for autocephaly [i.e., complete self-
> governing status independent of the Moscow Patriarchate] of the
> Ukrainian Orthodox Church is a de facto coup: a political coup al-
> ready took place in 2014, poisoning the relations between western
> Ukraine and Russia, and thus another type of coup—a religious one—
> similarly seeks to undermine the canonical relationship between the
> Ukrainian Orthodox Church and Moscow.'

In furthering these twin objectives (morally, the degrading of Orthodox Christianity; politically, undermining the Russian state as Orthodoxy's powerful
traditional protector) it is increasingly clear that the United States government—and specifically the Department of State—has become a hands-on
fomenter of conflict. After a short period of appropriately declaring that "any
decision on autocephaly is an internal [Orthodox] church matter," the
Department within days reversed its position and issued a formal statement
(in the name of Department spokesperson Heather Nauert, but clearly drafted
by the European bureau) that skirted a direct call for autocephaly but gave the
unmistakable impression of such backing. This is exactly how it was reported
in the media, for example, "US backs Ukrainian Church bid for autocephaly."
Finally, Secretary of State Mike Pompeo weighed in personally with his own
endorsement as did the US *Reichskommissar* for Ukraine, Kurt Volker.

The Threat . . .

There soon became reason to believe that the State Department's involvement was not limited to exhortations. As reported by this analyst in October, according to an unconfirmed report originating with the members of the Russian Orthodox Church Outside of Russia (an autonomous New York-based jurisdiction of the Moscow Patriarchate), in July of this year State Department officials (possibly including Secretary Pompeo personally) warned the Greek Orthodox Archdiocese of America (also based in New York but part of the Ecumenical Patriarchate) that the US government was aware of the misappropriation of a large amount of money, about $10 million, from estimated $37 million raised from believers for the construction of the St. Nicholas Greek Orthodox Church and National Shrine in New York. The State Department warning also reportedly noted that federal prosecutors have documentary evidence confirming the withdrawal of these funds abroad on the orders of Ecumenical Patriarch Bartholomew. It was suggested that Secretary Pompeo would "close his eyes" to this theft in exchange for movement by the Patriarchate of Constantinople in favor of Ukrainian autocephaly, which helped set Patriarch Bartholomew on his current course.

[Further details on the St. Nicholas scandal are available here, but in summary: Only one place of worship of any faith was destroyed in the September 11, 2001, attack in New York and only one building not part of the World Trade Center complex was completely destroyed. That was St. Nicholas Greek Orthodox Church, a small urban parish church established at the end of World War I and dedicated to St. Nicholas the Wonderworker, who is very popular with Greeks as the patron of sailors. In the aftermath of the 9/11 attack, and following a lengthy legal battle with the Port Authority, which opposed rebuilding the church, in 2011 the Greek Archdiocese launched an extensive campaign to raise funds for a brilliant innovative design by the renowned Spanish architect Santiago Calatrava based on traditional Byzantine forms. Wealthy donors and those of modest means alike enthusiastically contributed millions to the effort. Then—poof! In December 2017, suddenly all construction was halted for lack of funds and remains stalled to this day. Resumption would require having an estimated $2 million on hand. Despite the Archdiocese's calling in a major accounting firm to conduct an audit, there's been no clear answer to what happened to the money. Both the US Attorney and New York state authorities are investigating.]

This is where things get back to Ukraine. If the State Department wanted to find the right button to push to spur Patriarch Bartholomew to move on the question of autocephaly, the Greek Archdiocese in the US is it. Let's keep in mind that in his home country, Turkey, Patriarch Bartholomew has virtually no local flock—only a few hundred mostly elderly Greeks left huddled in Istanbul's Phanar district. (Sometimes the Patriarchate is referred to simply as "the Phanar," much as "the Vatican" is shorthand for the Roman Catholic papacy.) Whatever funds the Patriarchate derives from other sources (the Greek government, the Roman Catholic Church, the World Council of Churches), the Phanar's financial lifeline is the ethnic Greek community (including this analyst) in what is still quaintly called the "Diaspora" in places like America, Australia, and New Zealand. And of these, the biggest cash cow is the Greek-Americans.

That's why, when Patriarch Bartholomew issued a call in 2016 for what was billed as an Orthodox "Eighth Ecumenical Council" (the first one since the year 787!), the funds largely came from America, to the tune of up to $8 million according to the same confidential source as will be noted below. Intended by some as a modernizing Orthodox "Vatican II," the event was doomed to failure by a boycott organized by Moscow over what the latter saw as Patriarch Bartholomew's adopting papal or even imperial prerogatives—now sadly coming to bear in Ukraine.

... and the Payoff

On top of the foregoing, it now appears that the State Department's direct hand in this sordid business may not have consisted solely of wielding the "stick" of legal threat: there's reason to believe there was a "carrot" too. It very recently came to the attention of this analyst, via an unsolicited, confidential source in the Greek Archdiocese in New York, that a payment of $25 million in US government money was made to Constantinople to encourage Patriarch Bartholomew to move forward on Ukraine.

The source for this confidential report was unaware of earlier media reports that the same figure—$25 million—was paid by Ukrainian President Petro Poroshenko to the Phanar as an incentive for Patriarch Bartholomew to move forward on creating an independent Ukrainian church. Moreover, Poroshenko evidently tried to shortchange the payment:

'Peter [Petro] Poroshenko—the president of Ukraine—was obligated to return $15 million US dollars to the Patriarch of Constantinople, which he had appropriated for himself.

'As reported by Izvestia, this occurred after the story about Bartholomew's bribe and a "vanishing" large sum designated for the creation of a Unified Local Orthodox Church in Ukraine surfaced in the mass media.

'As reported, on the eve of Poroshenko's visit in Istanbul, a few wealthy people of Ukraine "chipped in" in order to hasten the process of creating a Unified Local Orthodox Church. About $25 million was collected. They were supposed to go to the award ceremony for Patriarch Bartholomew of Constantinople for the issuing of a tomos of autocephaly. [A tomos is a small book containing a formal announcement.] However, in the words of people close to the backer, during the visit on April 9, Poroshenko handed over only $10 million.

'As a result, having learned of the deal, Bartholomew cancelled the participation of the delegation of the Phanar—the residence of the Patriarch of Constantinople, in the celebration of the 1030th anniversary of the Baptism of Russia on July 27 in Kiev.

"'Such a decision from Bartholomew's side was nothing other than a strong ultimatum to Poroshenko to return the stolen money. Of course, in order to not lose his face in light of the stark revelations of the creation of the tomos of autocephaly for the Ukrainian Orthodox Church, Peter Alexeevich [Poroshenko] had to just return those $15 million for the needs of Constantinople," a trusted source explained to reporters.

'For preliminary information, only after receiving the remaining sum, did Bartholomew finally give his consent to sending a delegation of the Phanar to Kiev ...'

Now, it's possible that the two identical figures of $25 million refer to two different pots of money (a cool $50 million!) but that seems unlikely. It's more probable the reports refer to the same sum as viewed from the sending side (the State Department, the Greek Archdiocese) and the delivery side (Poroshenko, Constantinople).

Lending credibility to the confidential information from New York and pointing to the probability that it refers to the same payment that Poroshenko reportedly sought to raid for himself are the following observations:

When Poroshenko generously offered Patriarch Bartholomew $10 million, the latter was aware that the full amount was $25 million and demanded the $15 million Poroshenko had held back. How did the Patriarch know that, unless he was informed via New York of the full sum?

If the earlier-reported $25 million was really collected from "a few wealthy people of Ukraine" who "chipped in," given the cutthroat nature of disputes among Ukrainian oligarchs would Poroshenko (an oligarch in his own right) have risked trying to shortchange the payment? Why has not even one such Ukrainian donor been identified?

Without going into all the details, the Phanar and the Greek Archdiocese have a long relationship with US administrations of both parties going back at least to the Truman administration, encompassing some decidedly unattractive episodes. In such a history, a mere bribe for a geopolitical shot against Moscow would hardly be a first instance or the worst.

As one of this analyst's Greek-American connections puts it: "It's easy to comprehend the Patriarchate bowing to the pressure of State Dept. blackmail . . . not overly savory, but understandable. However, it's another thing altogether if Kiev truly "purchased" their autocephalous status from an all too willing Patriarchate... which would relegate the Patriarch to 'salesman' status and leave the faithful wondering what else might be offered to the highest bidder the next time it became convenient to hold a Patriarchal 'fire sale' at the Phanar?!"

To add insult to injury, you'd think Constantinople at least could pay back some of the $7–8 million wasted on the Crete 2016 debacle to restart the St. Nicholas project in New York. Evidently the Phanar has better things to spend it on, like the demonstrative environmentalism of "the Green Patriarch" and, together with Pope Francis, welcoming Muslim migrants to Europe through Greece. Of course maybe there's no need to worry, as the Ukraine "sale" was consistent with Constantinople's papal ambitions, an uncanonical claim to "universal" status, and misuse of incarnational language and adoption of a breathtakingly arrogant tone that would cause even the most ultramontane proponent of the Rome's supremacy to blush.

Finally, it seems that, for the time being at least, Constantinople doesn't intend to create an independent Ukrainian church but rather an autonomous church under its own authority. It's unclear whether or not Poroshenko or the State Department, in such event, would believe they had gotten their money's worth. Perhaps they would. After all, the issue here is less what is appropriate for Ukraine than what strikes at Russia and injures the worldwide Christian witness of the Orthodox Church. To that end, it doesn't matter whether the new illegal body is Constantinopolitan or Kievan, just so long as it isn't a "Moskal church" linked to Russia.

"What's Really Behind the State Department's Meddling in Ukraine?"

Jim Jatras | *Chronicles* | April 11, 2019

On March 31 the first round of Ukraine's presidential election was held. In line with all polls, the top spot (with about 30 percent of the vote) was taken by Volodymyr Zelensky, a comic actor who played President of Ukraine in a popular TV series, making him the leading candidate for the position he once spoofed. He was followed (with about 16 percent) by incumbent President

President Poroshenko, known as the oligarchic "Chocolate King" because of his confectionary company, *Roshen*. Poroshenko has also sought to emulate another king, England's Henry VIII, through creation of his own Ukrainian church, which late last year Poroshenko declared independent of the Russian Orthodox Church with assistance from an unlikely duo, the Greek Orthodox Patriarch in Istanbul and the US State Department.

(Trailing behind Poroshenko with about 13 percent was perennial candidate and former prime minister Yulia Tymoshenko, also known as the "Gas Princess" (for her prominent role in the shady natural gas industry), "goddess of the Revolution" (for her firebrand image in Ukraine's turbulent post-Soviet history), and the "Princess Leia of Ukrainian politics" (for her trademark folk-motif braids). Tymoshenko claims, quite plausibly, that Poroshenko stole the second spot from her but that Ukraine's judicial system has been "privatized" by Poroshenko and it's pointless to challenge the results in court.)

Zelensky and Poroshenko will now square off in an April 21 second round. The smart money favors Zelensky, given how badly he trounced Poroshenko in the first round. The smart money is probably wrong. Poroshenko—for whom the stakes are likely either self-imposed exile to avoid prosecution or continued slopping at a lucrative trough—has a lot of cards he can play, both what they call locally "administrative measures" to pad his vote and goodies to get former rivals to support him.

Most of all, he can count on western governments, notably that of the United States, and their hangers-on to not only turn a blind eye but to positively enthuse over Ukraine's democratic vitality.

In world in which Washington routinely thunders from on high about other countries' democratic legitimacy, the see-no-evil attitude toward Ukraine speaks volumes. (Imagine if, say, Venezuela's Nicolas Maduro, Russia's Vladimir Putin, or Syria's Bashar al-Assad had while in office racked up a 10,000 percent income increase, mainly from a shady Zurich-based fund.)

At this point it's appropriate to stop and ask: why should anyone in the US care about Ukraine and its elections? Perhaps the more important question is, why does the State Department care so much? The answer has many facets: historical, geopolitical, ideological, ethnic, moral, and—perhaps surprisingly for some who may not think of "mere religion" as being particularly important in a postmodern Europe—spiritual.

In fact, upon examination Ukraine is a revealing showcase of all that's wrong with American global policy, including a fanatical determination to impose a post-Christian moral order on what are still unexpectedly vibrant Christian societies rebounding from decades of communist repression. Sadly, this determination has not slackened under the Trump administration but has continued as though the previous administration had never left. In this regard, whatever his very public professions of his Christian faith, whited sepulchre Secretary Mike Pompeo and his State Department area at the forefront.

One of the major claimed accomplishments of incumbent Ukrainian President Petro Poroshenko's reelection campaign of "army, language, faith" is creation of an autocephalous Ukrainian Orthodox Church (*i.e.*, completely self-governing, with no tie at all to the Russian Orthodox Church). Western governments and media have uniformly—and inaccurately—hailed this as a reality already fulfilled with the awarding of a tomos (literally, a small book containing an authoritative pronouncement or declaration) from Ecumenical Patriarch Bartholomew I of Constantinople to Poroshenko and religious figures in Ukraine who had up until then been universally shunned as schismatics by all Orthodox jurisdictions. As of this writing, no other autocephalous Church has endorsed Constantinople's actions, and several, notably the

Patriarchates of Belgrade and Antioch—and notably, the Church of Albania, which is largely Greek by ethnicity—have taken sharp exception to it.

The Ukrainian Church situation is complex and contentious. It will be months if not years before it works itself out. Indeed, it may lead to a permanent split within Orthodoxy, not only in Ukraine but worldwide. Also, despite Patriarch Bartholomew's stated intention to foster accord and reconciliation in Ukraine, his actions clearly have aggravated already raw feelings among believers there. Far from creating a united Ukrainian autocephalous Church, he has only managed to cobble together a new body under the authority of Constantinople in opposition to the canonical Moscow-linked Church, which continues to exist under its primate Metropolitan Onufriy. Violence in various forms is inevitable as Ukrainian authorities harass the canonical Church and prepare to seize its parishes and monasteries, notably the historic Kiev Perchersk Lavra and the Pochaev Lavra in western Ukraine.

Conspicuously, Poroshenko's blatant politicking in Church affairs—which has been criticized even from quarters favoring autocephaly—has been applauded by western governments, notably by American officials. Just a few days after a high State Department career officer commendably declared in September 2018 that "any decision on autocephaly is an internal [Orthodox] church matter" he was reversed by endorsements of autocephaly by Secretary Pompeo, US Special Representative for Ukraine Kurt Volker, and US Ambassador in Kiev Marie Yovanovitch (an Obama appointee but still in place). Following the Robber Council of Kiev on December 15, the US Embassy tweeted out its congratulations in English and in Ukrainian (not in Russian of course). Secretary of State Mike Pompeo placed a personal call to the "newly elected head of the Orthodox Church of Ukraine Metropolitan Epifaniy" (Dumenko). US Ambassador Marie Yovanovitch extended her congratulations to Dumenko in person. It should also be noted that The Atlantic Council, an *über*-Establishment Washington-based think tank operating in close coordination with the US government (and heavily funded by US and allied governent agencies and contractors), has been an active advocate for autocephaly in the policy community and media.

Moreover, there is reason to believe the US State Department's involvement was not just hortatory. As reported by this analyst in October 2018, according to an unconfirmed report originating with the members of the Russian Orthodox Church Outside of Russia (an autonomous New York-based part of the Moscow Patriarchate), in July 2018 State Department officials, possibly including Secretary Pompeo personally, warned the scandal-ridden and broke Greek Orthodox Archdiocese of America (also based in New York but under authority of the Ecumenical Patriarchate) that the US government was aware of the misappropriation of a large amount of money, about $10 million, from an estimated $37 million raised from believers for the (now stalled) construction of the St. Nicholas Greek Orthodox Church and National Shrine in New York (to replace the original St. Nicholas church destroyed in the 9/11 attack on the World Trade Center). The State Department warning also reportedly noted that federal prosecutors have documentary evidence confirming the withdrawal of these funds abroad on the orders of Ecumenical Patriarch Bartholomew. It was suggested that Secretary Pompeo would "close his eyes" to this theft in exchange for movement by the Patriarchate of Constantinople in favor of Ukrainian autocephaly, which helped set Patriarch Bartholomew on his current course. Moreover, the State Department's direct hand in this sordid business may not have consisted solely of wielding the "stick" of legal threat: there's reason to believe there was a "carrot" too. There are numerous unproven reports of a $25 million payoff to Constantinople from Poroshenko (although allegedly Poroshenko initially attempted to hold back $15 million for himself). Attributions of the original source of that money differ. Some claim it came from organized crime bosses in Dnipro. This analyst was told by an unsolicited, confidential informant in the Greek Archdiocese in New York that the funds came from the State Department.

We may never know the truth about any such payment. But whatever the details, one still has to ask why the US is so keenly committed to creating an autocephalous Church in Ukraine. Aside from the obvious impropriety of the United States' taking sides in a question of the Orthodox Church's internal governance, *why* is the State Department so committed to promoting a transparently political power grab by Poroshenko, the Ukrainian schismatics, and Patriarch Bartholomew of Constantinople?

Given the various lobbies with a lot of influence in Washington, including those of foreign states and ethnic communities, it is natural to look in that direction to identify relevant actors and driving forces on the American side with respect to formulation of policy toward Ukraine. Among those that might come to mind are the Ukrainian diaspora in the United States (just under a million people), the Greek-American community (variously estimated at between one and three million, depending on self-identification), and so forth. There is precedent for such influences on US policy in Eastern Europe. One is reminded of the role the Croatian and Albanian diaspora communities played in the breakup of Yugoslavia. It should be noted that the Yugoslav conflicts took place as the post-Cold War drive for US global hegemony was only beginning to take form, and Bosnia and Kosovo were catalytic in its development.

It is true that some Ukrainian-Americans (heavily weighted by those with western Ukraine origins) have long taken part in activities of various "Captive Nations" and "ethnic heritage" groups operating after World War II, notably the CIA front "American Committee for Liberation from Bolshevism" and the "Anti-Bolshevik Bloc of Nations" (originally spun off by the United Kingdom's MI6 from the earlier "British League for European Freedom"). Mainly though not exclusively oriented toward the Republican Party they operated under the banner of anti-communism but really (to an extent many non-"ethnic" Americans may not fully have understood) were vehicles for their various ethnic agendas. These agendas related less to communism than dissatisfaction with the territorial arrangements that existed after 1945, giving these groups the character of World War II losers' associations. Russophobia (and with respect to the Balkans, Serbophobia) was a common point of agreement.

It should also be noted that while American Greeks were not notable in these activities the US government has valued the utility of the Constantinopolitan Patriarchate since at least the 1940s. Today, while his flock within Turkey dwindles to almost nil (in effect, it is what in English parliamentary context was known as a "rotten borough"), Patriarch Bartholomew has sought to expand his profile as a "player" on the world stage, exemplified by his demonstrative environmentalism as "the Green Patriarch" and, together with Pope Francis, welcoming Muslim migrants to Europe through Greece. Moreover, his actions in Ukraine are an expansion of Constantinople's longstanding quasi-papal ambitions built on uncanonical claims to "universal" status as a kind of "Eastern Pope," misuse of doctrinally troubling incarnational language, and adoption of a breathtakingly arrogant tone that would cause even the most ultramontane proponent of the Rome's supremacy to blush. Given strong support for Ukrainian Orthodox autocephaly from the Ukrainian Greek Catholic Church, which now sees a new opportunity for it to be elevated to a patriarchate within Roman Catholicism, Ukraine also advances Constantinople's warm ecumenical embrace aimed at reunion with the Roman Papacy, with a Ukrainian church in communion with both Rome and Constantinople as a possible catalyst. In short, whatever the carrots and sticks involved, the State Department was pushing on an open door at the Phanar.

However, as described below, by 2005 the ideological and methodological aspects of the US policymaking establishment's aspirations for global hegemony were already fully formed. A key part of this was turning Ukraine into a forward salient against Russia, as attested to in the "Orange Revolution" of 2004–5 and the 2008 NATO Bucharest declaration regarding Ukraine's (and Georgia's) destiny as part of NATO. Today, attacking the Orthodox Church in Ukraine is another logical—and well-targeted—element of that aggressive aim. While some elements in the Greek and (especially) Ukrainian communities no doubt had a hand in it, they don't have the influence to set the agenda and should be regarded more as implementing a program thought up by others. I would compare the US *apparat* in this regard to that of the Soviet Union: the imperatives are ideological and bureaucratic; while ethnic lobbies (comparable in their day to pro-Soviet Third World "national liberation movements") are useful, they are the tools of policy, not its masters.

The origin of the US focus on Ukraine and its religious issues must instead be sought within the larger perspective of American policy since the end of the first Cold War in 1991 and the development of the current one in the course of the 1990s: the American "unipolar moment," as the bipartisan US policy establishment sought to consolidate and perpetuate its hegemonic control over the entire planet, taking advantage of the vacuum left by the demise of the USSR. Perhaps the fullest expression of this was a 1996 article by neoconservative ideologists William Kristol and Robert Kagan, misleadingly titled "Toward a Neo-Reaganite Foreign Policy," in which they called for the US to establish and maintain indefinitely "benevolent global hegemony"—American world domination. As scrutinized by this analyst in *Chronicles* magazine the following year, Kristol and Kagan laid down virtually all of the elements that have guided US foreign policy during the ensuing years. It is no accident that GOP neoconservatives were enthusiastic supporters of Bill Clinton's Balkan interventions of 1990s, under the guidance of people like then-Secretary of State Madeleine Albright, who once opined regarding the sanctions-related deaths of a half million Iraqi children that "the price is worth it." In the US establishment, there is little dissent on either side of the partisan aisle with Albright's sincere conviction that a militant United States has a special wisdom: "If we have to use force, it is because we are America; we are the indispensable nation. We stand tall and we see further than other countries into the future . . . "

The result is a kind of neo-Bolshevism, where, as the vanguard of all progressive humanity, the United States sees itself as the midwife of history to advance the principles not of the USSR's "peace, progress, and socialism" but of a similarly ideologized triad of "democracy, human rights, and free markets."

Viewed this way, a revived, non-ideological, nationally minded Russia is an obstacle that must be overcome—one way or the other. (A similar attitude exists toward China and Iran.) Recently the administration of US President Donald Trump, who as a candidate repeatedly stated his desire to improve ties with Russia but has been prevented from doing so, has taken to describing the neoconservative program of previous administrations as (in Secretary Pompeo's words) as reassertion of sovereignty (but *only* for the US and our allies!) and "reform" of "the liberal international order." The rhetoric is new but the policies are the same as under Trump's predecessors.

Sometimes we are told that the current Washington-Moscow standoff is just a turf war, that unlike the 1945–1991 rivalry it "lacks an ideological dimension" beyond the authoritarian determination to elevate "the Russian state, ruled by [Vladimir Putin] and his clan." Such a view totally dismisses the fact that following the demise of communism as a global power bloc there has been an eerie spiritual role reversal between East and West. While it's true that during original Cold War the nonreligious ruling cliques in Washington and Moscow held basically compatible progressive values, ordinary Christian Americans (mainly Protestants, with a large number of Roman Catholics) perceived communism as a murderous, godless machine of oppression (think of the Roman Catholic men's organization Knights of Columbus' campaign to insert "under God" into the Pledge of Allegiance). Conversely, today it is western elites who rely upon an ideological imperative to justify a materialist global empire and endless wars, much like the old Soviet *nomenklatura* depended on Marxism-Leninism both as a working methodology and as a justification for their prerogatives and privileges. In that regard, promotion of nihilist, post-Christian morality—especially in sexual matters—under the guise of "democracy and human rights" has become a major item in the West's toolkit.

This has a special importance with regard to Russia, where under Putin the Orthodox Church has largely resumed its pre-1917 role as the moral anchor of society. This elicits not only political opposition but a genuine and heartfelt hatred from the postmodern elites of an increasingly post-Christian West, not only for Putin personally and Russia generally but against the Russian Orthodox Church—and by extension against Orthodox Christianity itself.

This points to why, from the point of view of the State Department, the Russian Orthodox Church—and hence the canonical autonomous Ukrainian Orthodox Church—is nothing more than an instrument of the Kremlin's soft power. According to one person rather new to the relevant issues but nonetheless considered authoritative by the State Department:

> The Church, for its part, acts as the Russian state's soft power arm, exerting its authority in ways that assist the Kremlin in spreading Russian influence both in Russia's immediate neighborhood as well as around the globe. The Kremlin assists the Church, as well, working to increase its reach. Vladimir Yakunin, one of Putin's inner circle and a devout member of the ROC, facilitated in 2007 the reconciliation of the ROC with the Russian Orthodox Church in Exile (which had separated itself from the Moscow Patriarchate early in the Soviet era so as not to be co-opted by the new Bolshevik state), which reconciliation greatly increased [Patriarch of Moscow] Kirill's influence and authority outside of Russia. Putin, praising this event, noted the interrelation of the growth of ROC authority abroad with his own international goals: "The revival of the church unity is a crucial condition for revival of lost unity of the whole 'Russian world', which has always had the Orthodox faith as one of its foundations."

Hence, weaken "Russian state's soft power arm," weaken the Russian state.

But there is even more to it than that. The authors of the current US anti-Russia, anti-Orthodox Church policy know, or at least instinctively sense, that the revival of Russia's Church-State *symphonia* after a hiatus of eight decades is not just a political alliance of convenience but is the source of deep spiritual, moral, and social strength. This is reflected, for example, in Putin's warm remarks on the dedication of a Moscow monument to Aleksandr Solzhenitsyn, the acknowledged godfather of Russia's restoration as a Christian country, on the centenary of the writer's birth.

In Russia's reborn *symphonia*, President and Patriarch speak as one:

At the height of the Cold War, it was common for American conservatives to label the officially atheist Soviet Union a "godless nation."

More than two decades on, history has come full circle, as the
Kremlin and its allies in the Russian Orthodox Church hurl the same
allegation at the West.

"Many Euro-Atlantic countries have moved away from their roots,
including Christian values," Russian President Vladimir Putin said in
a recent keynote speech. *"Policies are being pursued that place on
the same level a multi-child family and a same-sex partnership, a
faith in God and a belief in Satan. This is the path to degradation."*
[. . .]

Mr. Putin's views of the West were echoed this month by Patriarch
Kirill I of Moscow, the leader of the Orthodox Church, who accused
Western countries of engaging in the "spiritual disarmament" of
their people.

In particular, Patriarch Kirill criticized laws in several European
countries that prevent believers from displaying religious symbols,
including crosses on necklaces, at work.

"The general political direction of the [Western political] elite
bears, without doubt, an anti-Christian and anti-religious character,"
the patriarch said in comments aired on state-controlled television.

"We have been through an epoch of atheism, and we know what it
is to live without God," Patriarch Kirill said. "We want to shout to the
whole world, 'Stop!'" ["Who's 'godless' now? Russia says it's U.S.:
Putin seizes on issue of traditional values," by Marc Bennetts, *The
Washington Times*, January 28, 2014]

Such sentiments can hardly sit well with Western elites for whom celebration
of the same-sex partnerships decried by Putin is a mark of social enlightenment. That's why an inseparable part of the "European choice" the people of
Ukraine supposedly made during the 2014 "Revolution of Dignity" is wholesale acceptance of "European values," including the kind of "Pride" symbolized by LGBT marches organized over Christian objections in Orthodox cities
like Athens, Belgrade, Bucharest, Kiev, Odessa, Podgorica, Sofia, and Tbilisi.
(Note that after the march in Odessa in August of this year a priest of the
canonical Church targeted by Poroshenko cleansed the street with Holy
Water.)

There is no doubt that the moral/sexual component of undermining
Orthodox Christianity in Ukraine is a key factor in US policy. There is a curious
consistency between advocacy for non-traditional, post-Christian sexual morality and support for the schismatics sponsored by Poroshenko and Patriarch
Bartholomew. This is well understood by Constantinople's pseudo-Church in
Ukraine. In December, shortly after his "enthronement," "Metropolitan Epifaniy" Dumenko responded to a phone caller claiming to be a western parliamentarian (but in fact was a Russian prankster), suggesting that "if the new
church will soften its position regarding the LGBT community, the gays of
Ukraine, and it will take liberal values, it will be a great stimulus to develop
European values. We spoke with Secretary Pompeo and he agrees that you
should the increase your LGBT and gay values in the future." Taking the bait,
Dumenko said that "because we are moving towards Europe . . . we should
depart from the Russian conservative tradition" and adopt a progressively
more "open" position on such matters.

Indeed, the relevant US government officials cheering on Poroshenko and
the Ukrainian church schismatics are remarkably up-front and visible in their

advocacy of the LGBT agenda in Ukraine. The US Embassy Kiev website displays Pompeo's declaration on behalf of all Americans that "The United States joins people around the world in celebrating Lesbian, Gay, Bisexual, Transgender, and Intersex (LGBTI) Pride Month, and reaffirms its commitment to protecting and defending the human rights of all, including LGBTI persons."

Ambassador Yovanovitch has really gone the extra mile—literally. Not only did she tweet out her own Pride message, she also participated in the parade (and took 60 Embassy personnel and family members with her!) proudly marching behind the American flag (as shown in this MUST WATCH video tweeted by the embassy—your American tax dollars at work!). Additional video posted by *HromadskeUA*, an "independent" Ukrainian media outlet reportedly funded by, among others, the US Embassy, the Canadian Embassy, and George Soros's International Renaissance Foundation (though the cited *HromadskeUA* financial reports no longer seem to be available). Both Yovanovitch's remarks in the video and the posted text draw an explicit connection between the "freedom" of the 2014 regime change and the new sexual morality (Google auto-translation from Ukrainian):

> The atmosphere is wonderful. It is important for us because we maintain equal rights. *In 2014, people in Ukraine were in favor of freedom, and this is an organic continuation*—US Ambassador Marie Yovanovich goes to the March of Equality Column. With her together with about 60 representatives of the American embassy. [emphasis added]

The locals were quick to make the same connection. "KyivPride," a local LGBT advocacy group unsurprisingly supported by the US Embassy (again, our tax dollars at work), the Canadian government, the German embassy, the US Agency for International Development (USAID), and Freedom House were quick to hail creation of the new pseudo-church, no doubt reflecting the deep Orthodox piety of the group's members. As posted by *OrthoChristian.com*, The organization posted a message on several platforms, including Facebook and Instagram, reading:

> KyivPride congratulates all LGBTI Orthodox believers on the formation of a united and independent Ukrainian Orthodox Church and reminds everyone that love does no harm to others! Also remember that article 35 of the constitution of Ukraine states: "Everyone has the right to freedom of personal philosophy and religion. This right includes the freedom to profess or not to profess any religion." Human rights above all!

Last but certainly not least should be noted the involvement of certain fringe elements in the Orthodox Church itself, who perhaps can be compared to the Roman Catholic Church's far more powerful "Lavender Mafia." As this analyst warned months ago the Ukrainian church crisis seemingly facilitates the anti-Christian moral agenda of certain marginal "Orthodox" voices like "Orthodoxy in Dialogue," Fordham University's "Orthodox Christian Studies Center," and *The Wheel*. As Anatoly Karlin points out, "many of the biggest supporters of Ukrainian autocephaly in the West are for all intents and purposes SJWs [social justice warriors]. The website Orthodoxy in Dialogue, for instance, wants Orthodoxy to get with the times and start sanctifying gay marriage:"

> We pray for the day when we can meet our future partner in church, or bring our partner to church.

We pray for the day when our lifelong, monogamous commitment to our partner can be blessed and sanctified in and by the Church.

We pray for the day when we can explore as Church, without condemnation, how we Orthodox Christians can best live our life in Christ in the pursuit of holiness, chastity, and perfect love of God and neighbour.

We pray for the day when our priests no longer travel around the world to condemn us and mock us and use us as a punching bag.

We pray for the day when the one, holy, catholic, and apostolic Church of Christ ceases to be our loneliest closet.

In sum, US official involvement in Ukrainian Church affairs is not really about Ukraine or Ukrainians at all. It is about hostility to Russia, which in turn reflects Washington's own drive for unlimited worldwide political and moral supremacy. Breaking Ukraine's spiritual ties with Russia is at least as important to breaking of political ties and enlisting Ukraine as part of NATO's anti-Russian deployment. Even something as simple as Poroshenko's making (western) December 25 Christmas a public holiday along with (Orthodox) January 7 is hailed by *The Daily Signal*, a publication of the Heritage Foundation, as "a leap of faith" towards "ditching Russian influence."

But underlying this geopolitical aspect is another, darker motive: to inflict on Ukraine and indeed all Orthodoxy the social, especially sexual, pathologies that have wrought havoc in western societies. As an ideological imperative built on Cultural Marxist dichotomies of oppressor and victim classes according to sex, race, language, religion, etc. (as described by this analyst in *Chronicles*) this effort to transform all human society supplies a missionary zeal no less relevant to American officials' and their fellow travelers' efforts than their aspirations of global political dominion.

"Serbian Church Defeats US Agenda in Ukraine but Not in Serbia—Yet"

Jim Jatras | *Strategic Culture* | May 4, 2019

The importance of comedian Volodymyr Zelensky's victory in the second round of Ukraine's presidential election is not that he won but that incumbent Petro Poroshenko lost—badly. The nervousness of Poroshenko's western patrons (and his client, in the case of US Special Representative Kurt Volker) at losing their faithful factotum is evident. For example, the Atlantic Council immediately called for "technical assistance to help [Zelensky] shape the transition, connect him with Western experts, and begin a dialogue." Translation: Let's make sure this new chief keeps the Indians on the reservation.

In the same vein, Poroshenko and his parliamentary cronies moved fast to try to ensure that Zelensky's freedom to govern would be restricted. Immediately following the vote, legislation was advanced in the Verkhovna Rada to transfer powers from the president to the Rada (and hence to the prime minister), to limit the president's power to appoint cabinet ministers, to lock in exclusive official use of the Ukrainian language, and to impair Zelensky's ability to call early elections (his new Servant of the People party currently holds no seats). Predictably no western government or "democracy" watchdog group has cried foul over these blatant attempts to clip the wings of the voters' overwhelming favorite. *Nothing to see here folks*—now let's get back to regime change to install "democracy" in Venezuela . . .

Even without obstructionism from the old guard it's doubtful Zelensky can achieve much. During the campaign, parallels were drawn to fellow "outsider" Donald Trump and his improbable 2016 win. Whatever Trump's intentions to #DrainTheSwamp and institute an #AmericaFirst policy, they have come to naught in the face of a united, bipartisan establishment. If anything, the Kiev "Swamp" facing Zelensky is worse than the one that bested Trump in Washington—in fact, it's fair to say that the former is to a great extent just a function of the latter. Whatever his intentions and personal qualities, which remain in doubt, Zelensky is being set up to be the latest failed president of a failing state.

However, one area in which we can expect some improvement is the crisis in the Orthodox Church, which last year was plunged into an ugly schism over Ukraine. As noted earlier, while many people, especially some of a secular mind who scorn mere *"religion,"* tend to underestimate the importance of spiritual matters in relation to politics and society, there are some parts of the world where they are taken very seriously. Paradoxically, this is especially true in parts of eastern and central Europe that until recently were under the sway of militant atheists. Indeed, that legacy—and the eventual failure of communism—seems to be a factor in Christianity's revival as a potent societal force in much of that region, in most cases allied with national identity, in sad contrast to progressively secularizing (and morally self-destructing) western Europe and North America.

Without repeating all the details here, Poroshenko had sought to create his very own "Orthodox Church of Ukraine" as a prop for his reelection bid with the enthusiastic (and reportedly monetary) involvement of the US State Department and Ecumenical Patriarch Bartholomew in Constantinople, along with cheerleading from the global LGBT lobby (itself weaponized against Christianity by western governments and the Soros network). Under Poroshenko's and Patriarch Bartholomew's patronage, the "Robber Council" of Kiev on December 15, 2018, purported to transform a hodgepodge of schismatics into a new "autocephalous" Ukrainian church, though in fact the new illegitimate body would be totally subject to Constantinople, with even less independence than that enjoyed by the existing, canonical Ukrainian Orthodox Church (UOC). Patriarch Kirill of Moscow, who heads the Russian Orthodox Church, of which the UOC is an autonomous part, responded by breaking communion with Constantinople.

While Zelensky has met *pro forma* with the supposed primate of the phony church—as well as with the first hierarch of the canonical Church, Metropolitan Onufry—for obvious reasons he's unlikely to involve himself too deeply in sustaining his predecessor's pet project. That project now seems to be failing quicker than anyone had dared hope. Not a single autocephalous Orthodox Church has responded positively to Constantinople's call to recognize the new entity.

Perhaps most significantly, recently the Patriarchs of Alexandria, Antioch, and Jerusalem gathered on Cyprus with the Archbishop of that country's Church, ostensibly to discuss problems of Christians in the Middle East. Thankfully, they seem to have resolved a schism between Antioch and Jerusalem unrelated to the Ukraine imbroglio, but by all indications Ukraine was the real purpose of the meeting—with Constantinople pointedly absent. To the extent that the rift between Moscow and Constantinople threatened to break down globally along ethnic lines with "Greeks" on the one hand and Russians or "Slavs" generally on the other, the conclave of the culturally Greek Churches seems to have averted that danger. The Church of Albania, also largely Greek, has also strongly criticized Constantinople.

Hopefully, we will soon see floated an initiative to give Patriarch Bartholomew a face-saving way to back down from his misstep in Ukraine. Sadly, he as yet shows no sign of doing so, despite the Ukrainian schismatics' he has taken under his wing having given him more than ample grounds to disavow them.

Among the strongest bulwarks against the schismatic schemes of Kiev, Constantinople, Washington, and the Soros/LGBT network has been the Serbian Orthodox Church, based on a principled rejection of Constantinople's anti-traditional, neo-papal claims. The vehemence of the Serbian Church's stand on Ukraine also reflects particular internal threats Serbia faces from politically motivated schismatic groups that could provide tempting targets for meddling by Patriarch Bartholomew and his western backers. These include the "Macedonian Orthodox Church," which claims to be independent of the Serbian Church but is recognized by no other Church (and where state authorities in the NATO puppet and newly renamed "Republic of North Macedonia" harass the canonical Autonomous Archbishopric of Ohrid), as well as attempts to create a separate "Montenegrin Orthodox Church." In this context, never far from anyone's consciousness is the formation of an ersatz "Croatian Orthodox Church" in 1942 under the World War II-era regime of Ustaša dictator Ante Pavelić, as a cover for the genocide of Orthodox Serbs in the so-called "Independent State of Croatia."

Thus, the approaching failure of Poroshenko's, the State Department's, and Patriarch Bartholomew's project in Ukraine is a victory not only for the Orthodox Church as a whole but for the Serbian Church in particular. The Archpastors and faithful of that Church deserve praise for their bold witness. That said, it is unfortunate to note that at the same time the same hierarchs (Orthodoxy does not regard any bishop or synod of bishops as infallible) have failed to correct a grave injustice *within their own Church*—one evidently prompted from Washington, the very same point of origin as the Ukrainian crisis.

I refer to the 2010 removal without an ecclesiastical trial of His Grace, Bishop Artemije from his Eparchy of Raška and Prizren, which includes the province of Kosovo and Metohija, and his later (purported) reduction to the status of a simple monastic. The ostensible reasons for the action taken against Vladika Artemije are allegations against him and Fr. Simeon (Vilovski) concerning improper use of funds earmarked for repairs to places of worship (to put Serbian churches and monasteries in good order for further vandalism and destruction from NATO-empowered Albanian Muslim militants) for lobbying in Washington, starting in 2006, on behalf of his flock and against western plans to separate Kosovo from Serbia. As the lead lobbyist for that effort, I can personally attest to the emptiness of these accusations, on which I have written in detail [see pp. 33–42]. The charges against him are unfounded, which is why, in addition to suffering at the hands of the Holy Synod in Belgrade, Vladika Artemije has never been brought to trial by state authorities despite an ongoing campaign of defamation and legal harassment that continues to this day.

Why has he been treated this way? First, because he has been openly defiant of the bogus charges labeled against him. Unwilling to "repent" for allegations of wrongdoing he has not committed, he insists that he is the true Bishop of the Raško-Prizrenska Eparchy in Exile—leading to his being falsely being accused of schism. Second, he is an outspoken opponent of ecumenism, which offends many in all Orthodox jurisdictions, which sadly are infected with this spiritual malady to a greater or lesser degree.

But the chief reason is flatly political. Vladika Artemije was punished for his forthright opposition to US and NATO policy in Kosovo and his spearheading the lobbying effort to oppose creation of that terrorist-mafia pseudostate (and hotbed of Islamic jihad) under NATO protection. In addition, he sued the NATO powers in the European Court of Human Rights in Strasbourg, and in 2009 sought to bar a visit by then-US Vice President and current 2020 presidential candidate Joe Biden (a belligerent proponent of war against Serbs in Bosnia and Kosovo and of detaching Kosovo from Serbia, not to mention a Ukraine profiteer via his son Hunter Biden) from visiting Visoki Dečani monastery—a decision overturned by the Serbian Church at the behest of the Serbian government, then headed by western quisling Boris Tadić.

But the final push evidently came from the US military. The proof of Vladika's effectiveness is in the fact that there is reason to suspect that the campaign to eliminate him as an obstacle to Western policy was undertaken in direct response to a NATO, and specifically US, initiative. As reported by NATO, US Admiral Mark P. Fitzgerald, then Commander, US Naval Forces Europe and Africa, and Commander, Allied Joint Force Command (JFC) Naples, "with operational responsibility for NATO missions in the Balkans, Iraq and the Mediterranean," took part in meetings in Kosovo in January 2010 ("JFC Com Visits Kosovo," with this link now evidently pulled down from the Naples Command website; note, this occurred on January 8, the second day of Orthodox Christmas according to the Julian Calendar) and on February 2010 ("JFC Commander visists [sic] Viskoki [sic] Decane [sic] Monastery," also now pulled down). During his January 2010 visit Admiral Fitzgerald (who retired later that year, becoming, unsurprisingly, a consultant "with numerous defense and commercial maritime and aviation contractors") publicly stated that he considered Serbian so-called "parallel institutions"—that is, the legitimate structures of the sovereign Serbian state, as opposed to the Albanians' illegal separatist administration installed under NATO patron-age—to be a "security threat" to the NATO occupying forces. Further, an unconfirmed report indicates that a high NATO officer (whether Admiral Fitzgerald or someone else is not specified) stated in the course of one of the January meetings (this is verbatim or a close paraphrase) "*What we need here is a more cooperative bishop.*"

While it is impossible to authenticate this report definitively or firmly identify the speaker of the comment the timing is highly indicative. Just over a month after Admiral Fitzgerald's earlier visit, and just before his later one, Vladika Artemije's authority over his Eparchy was "temporarily" suspended. This was followed by his physical removal from the province of Kosovo and Metohija and by a declaration of the Holy Hierarchical Assembly of the Serbian Orthodox Church that he had been stripped of the episcopal dignity and reduced to the status of a monk. (For further accounts of relevant western pressure on Serbian Church and state authorities, see "ANY PRETEXT WILL DO: Totalitarianism in Service to the West: Serbia Betrays God, Helps Evict Last of Kosovo Christianity," by Julia Gorin; the speaker in question is identified, perhaps imprecisely based on available information as "a KFOR officer"; and "Eleven Years Later: NATO Powers Prepare Final Solution In Kosovo," by Rick Rozoff.)

In sum, Vladika Artemije was victimized by the same aggressive, anti-Christian western powers who now seek to use the Ukrainian schism as a political and moral weapon against Orthodoxy, with compliant Serbian government and Church authorities acting on their behalf. With the effort in Ukraine visibly withering, and with it Washington's ability to meddle in Orthodox Church affairs, it is long past time for the Holy Hierarchical Assembly of the Serbian Orthodox Church to rectify the injustice done to Vladika Artemije.

May they now display the same courage and commitment to principle in this matter that they have shown with respect to Ukraine.

"My Role in Weaponizing 'Moral Equivalence' and 'Religious Freedom'"

Jim Jatras | *Strategic Culture* | May 11, 2019

It's confession time . . .

Without getting overly autobiographical, it is worth noting that my perspectives (whatever their value) on American public policy and global affairs reflect decades of first-hand, professional experience in both the Executive and Legislative branches of the US government. The former was at the Department of State as a commissioned US Foreign Service Officer, the latter at the US Senate as a policy adviser to the Republican leadership.

I'd like to believe that at all times my intentions were to serve the best interests of my country as viewed in light of the most venerable principles of the American nation, as well as the Christian, European, and human values that once undergirded that nation.

However, the consequences of my efforts, together with those of others, sometimes went horribly wrong. On at least two occasions, there was, to say the least, a disconnect between good intention and sound judgment, between what I had hoped and expected could be achieved—and what turned out to be the results.

For example, as the (first) Cold War was entering its terminal phase, I was one of the primary planners and organizers of the May 1985 international conference in Washington, DC, "Moral Equivalence: False Images of U.S. and Soviet Values," sponsored by the State Department and the Shavano Institute for National Leadership. As described by *Imprimis*, a publication of Hillsdale College, which later incorporated Shavano and published the remarks of some of the speakers, the conference brought together "forty-five participants from the United States, Russia, Great Britain, France, Italy, Latin America, and Central Europe accepted the invitation to examine the issue of an alleged 'moral equivalence' between the two 'superpowers.' The attention this conference has received has been substantial. Articles have appeared in dozens of national publications such as *Time, the Wall Street Journal, National Review, Policy Review, the Washington Post, the Washington Times, the New York Post,* and *the New York Times*, as well as in over 500 other newspapers throughout the nation."

Among the headline participants were UN Ambassador Jeane Kirkpatrick, Tom Wolfe, the late, great Joseph Sobran, Richard Pipes, Sidney Hook, and many others spanning the spectrum from paleoconservatism, to libertarianism, to social democracy. As conceived by myself and other planners, the conference had a single message: that the godless ideology of Marxism-Leninism with its record of mass murder, destruction, and degradation (exemplified then by the USSR and its satellites) was not morally comparable to normal, non-ideological societies and states (then represented—so I believed at the time—by the United States and our allies.)

The conference was a smashing success (definitely worth the $45,000 allocated by the Department, though in the end Shavano commendably declined to accept the public funds, as reported by *Imprimis*). The phrase "moral equivalence"—which had been launched by Kirkpatrick a year earlier—became a widespread meme, with the communist Evil Empire weighed in the balances and found wanting.

Unfortunately "moral equivalence" is a meme that now just won't die, even though the context for it receded into history a few years following our conference. What has since become evident (and maybe already was to eyes more discerning than mine at the time) was that the US and our (let's be honest) satellites are every bit as ideological as the old Soviet Union. In fact, in some ways ours is the *same ruling ideology* as communism but shifted from economic class conflict of Bourgeoisie/Proletariat to new Oppressor/Victim paradigms defined by sex, race, religion, ethnicity, language, sexual orientation, migration status, and so forth.

The result is an eerie and deepening moral role reversal between East and West, under which western elites rely upon bogus ideological imperatives like "democracy," "human rights," and "free markets" to justify a global empire and endless wars, much like the old Soviet *nomenklatura* depended on Marxist-Leninist "world revolution" both as a working methodology and as a justification for their prerogatives and privileges. In that regard, promotion of nihilist, post-Christian morality—especially in sexual matters—has become a major item in the West's toolkit, promoted with a messianic fanaticism that would do Leon Trotsky proud.

To be fair, in retrospect it's doubtful that many of the conference participants could have foreseen such a future or would have welcomed it. As Joseph Duggan, former adviser and speechwriter to Ambassador Kirkpatrick, notes:

> Reagan and Kirkpatrick never advocated pre-emptive war. Nor did they believe it was America's national vocation to pursue, as George W. Bush proclaimed in his second inaugural address, "the ultimate goal of ending tyranny in our world." They pursued a realistic strategy to win the Cold War and roll back Soviet Communism without having to unleash nuclear missiles in a Pyrrhic World War III.
>
> Following the West's victory in the Cold War, Kirkpatrick told a forum hosted by Midge Decter that it was time for the United States to become "a normal country, in a normal time."
>
> At the same time, Kirkpatrick wrote, "There is no mystical American 'mission,' or purpose to be 'found' independently of the U.S. Constitution. . . . There is no inherent or historical 'imperative' for the U.S. government to seek to achieve any other goal—however great—except as it is mandated by the Constitution or adopted by the people through elected officials."

Unfortunately, though, far from becoming "a normal country, in a normal time," America took the path of (as characterized by Russian Foreign Minister Sergey Lavrov) the "replication of the experience of Bolshevism and Trotskyism"—morphing ourselves into a new Evil Empire in place of the old one. In a devolution from anything resembling the best of American values, rejection of "moral equivalence" between post-communist Russia and the US has become a mindless rhetorical prop amounting to ritualistic hate speech against Russia in particular and generally against anyone or anything targeted by the Washington *nomenklatura* and its fellow travelers and hangers-on. For example, our self-imposed mission of "democracy promotion" means that "Russia and America aren't 'morally equivalent,'" because "there is no comparison between Russian efforts to undermine elections and American efforts to strengthen them." Or this gem from some snotty kid who wasn't even alive when the 1985 conference took place, blazing away with all the unthinking fervor of a Maoist Red Guard or a member of the *Hitlerjugend*:

> Drawing moral equivalences where they do not exist is a dangerous game that enables the world's tyrants. . . . If we are not vigilant, we'll wake up one day, having forgotten the vocabulary of American moral leadership, and worse, we'll have ceded a unique global role that makes the promotion of human freedom the ultimate goal of foreign policy. Dismissing Russian interference because we do it too is bad, but blaming America for a downturn in relations provoked by a journalist-assassinating, dissident-assassinating, civilian-airline-downing, chemical-weapons-dictatorship-supporting regime, is downright unconscionable.

Now for a second confession . . .

Your Working Boy also was one of the primary Senate staffers responsible for the drafting and enactment of the International Religious Freedom Act (IRFA) of 1999 (P.L. 105–292). For these efforts I was mentioned by the bill's chief sponsor on the Senate floor as "one of the most distinguished analysts of foreign policy on Capitol Hill" and someone who "contributed vitally, both to the substance of the bill and to the process of negotiation which led to its passage"—as I now regret.

To borrow a phrase from Peter Van Buren, we meant well. IRFA was a response to a growing awareness in the 1990s even in some quarters of polite, secular company that persecution of Christians was rampant in some countries, and that indeed more Christians died for their faith in the 20th century alone than in all the 19 centuries preceding it—chiefly at the hands of communist regimes (mainly earlier in the century) and Muslim militants (now). Especially for some on the Republican side of the aisle, taking up the cause of Christian persecution also made political sense. For example, liberal-Democrat-turned-liberal-Republican Pennsylvania Senator Arlen Specter (who eventually returned to the Democratic Party), facing a possible conservative primary challenger in 1998, seized upon the issue.

In my defense, I naively tried to craft legislation that would specifically address the plight of Christians. Why not? Awareness of Christian persecution was the reason the whole issue had come up in the first place. The US had earlier enshrined in statutory language religion-specific concern for evangelical Christians and Pentecostals. Helping Muslims *as Muslims* was explicit in US policies in Bosnia and Kosovo. But instead of a focus on Christians, what emerged in the form of IRFA was a promotion of generic "religious freedom," including an annual report from the State Department on the practices of every country in the world and establishment of an Ambassador at Large for International Religious Freedom, currently former Kansas Senator and Governor Sam Brownback. IRFA also established an advisory bipartisan Commission on International Religious Freedom (USCIRF), which among other things recommends which bad actors should be designated "Countries of Particular Concern" (CPCs) by the president and subject to possible sanctions.

Predictably, "religious freedom" became little more than another subjective standard under which countries the Washington apparat wants to hammer can be cited (accurately or not), along with "sponsorship of terrorism" (Syria and Iran yes, Saudi Arabia no) and the former "Narcotics Certification Process" that penalized countries not fully cooperating with US counternarcotics efforts (but ended in 2002, having become too divorced from reality even for the Washington Swamp). Thus, pluralistic countries like Syria and Russia with a high degree of religious freedom are, for obvious geo-political reasons, designated CPCs along with the likes of Saudi Arabia (which for some time after IRFA's enactment the State Department managed to protect from the CPC label) and North Korea—which allow the practice of, respectively, only one religion and none. (To be fair, in the Syria section of its April 2019 report. USCIRF does express concern about the fate of Christians and others in areas controlled by "Other Islamist and Non-Islamist Opposition Groups," without however mentioning that such groups are armed by the US and our allies.)

USCIRF and the State Department are concerned about religious freedom in Western Europe—no, not so much about Christians prosecuted for offending certified Victims—but for disfavor shown to cults like Scientology and violating Muslim women's "freedom" to wear headscarves (leaving aside whether or not these women and girls are being forced to wear the hijab in the first place). It is significant that the 2019 report devotes its entire cover to the plight of Muslim Uighurs in China's Xinjiang province, where there is reason to believe the usual US agencies are already stirring up jihadists against Beijing to undermine the Belt and Road Initiative.

Finally, on another geopolitical front, Ambassador Brownback has now seen fit to weigh in personally on behalf of the schismatic pseudo-Church in Ukraine fostered by recently defeated Ukrainian Petro Poroshenko, Ecumenical Patriarch Bartholomew, and the State Department. Upon receiving notification of Brownback's involvement from the redoubtable George Michalopulos of Monomakhos, I immediately emailed several State Department officials and representatives of religious freedom NGOS—some of whom I have known for many years—as follows:

Dear Friends,

Up to now, based on my personal respect for him, I had been content to give Ambassador Sam Brownback the benefit of the doubt when it came to the unconscionable meddling of the Department of State in the internal canonical order of the Orthodox Church, preferring to assign blame on the US side to Secretary Pompeo, Special Rep for Ukraine Volker, Ambassador Yovanovitch, and Ambassador Pyatt, as well as to EUR generally.

However, Ambassador Brownback's current mission to the Balkans, and specifically to Greece and Mt. Athos, with the clear aim of jawboning the Church of Greece into recognizing the false autocephaly of the so-called "Orthodox Church of Ukraine" is intolerable! His job is promoting religious freedom, not interfering in internal Orthodox Church governance, fomenting civil strife, and promoting the neopapal pretentions of the Patriarch of Constantinople to further a geopolitical agenda. Doing so under the guise of "religious freedom" makes a mockery of his portfolio.

I have no illusions that others in our government who have seen fit to intrude into matters about which they know little or nothing will back off. Truly, they know not what they do. But I expected better from Ambassador Brownback.

Respectfully: Mr. Ambassador, please get back into your lane!

Jim Jatras

Don't expect the foregoing to have much impact. Some mistakes, once made, are not easily remedied.

"Western Campaign Against Orthodox Church Turns to Montenegro"

Jim Jatras | *Strategic Culture* | December 28, 2019

"Religion is the sigh of the oppressed creature, the heart of a heartless world, and the soul of soulless conditions. *It is the opium of the people.*" So Karl Marx wrote in 1843. For three generations over the course of the 20th century his atheist disciples violently sought to break their subjects of this "opium" addiction.

They failed. In many though not all parts of the former communist bloc Christianity not only survived but provided the impetus for national and social revival. In some countries, like Poland, Hungary, and Lithuania, this meant Roman Catholicism. In others, like Russia, Ukraine, Serbia, and Georgia, this means Orthodoxy.

For the no-less-godless successors of the commissars now ruling most of Europe through the twin bureaucracies of NATO and the European Union, religion—or at least Christianity—remains a retrograde force that needs to be overcome. They are helped by the fact that in western Europe (and increasingly in the United States) consumerism, feminism, LGBT, multi-culturalism, and other materialistic post-modern alternatives have proved to be far more corrosive of Christianity than dynamite, bullets, concentration camps, and punitive psychiatric hospitals.

There is also a geopolitical element. Because NATO/EU's biggest target is Russia, and because revival of the Orthodox Church is central to Russia's revival—including its military determination to resist western aggression as it has so many times in the past from Germany, Sweden, Poland, France, etc.—*the Orthodox Church is itself in the crosshairs.* From the soulless perspective of western bureaucrats Orthodox Christianity is nothing more than an instrument of the Kremlin's soft power. According to one person rather new to the relevant issues but nonetheless considered authoritative by the State Department:

> The Church, for its part, acts as the Russian state's soft power arm, exerting its authority in ways that assist the Kremlin in spreading Russian influence both in Russia's immediate neighborhood as well as around the globe. The Kremlin assists the Church, as well, working to increase its reach. Vladimir Yakunin, one of Putin's inner circle and a devout member of the ROC, facilitated in 2007 the reconciliation of the ROC with the Russian Orthodox Church in Exile (which had separated itself from the Moscow Patriarchate early in the Soviet era so as not to be co-opted by the new Bolshevik state), which reconciliation greatly increased [Patriarch of Moscow] Kirill's influence and authority outside of Russia. Putin, praising this event, noted the interrelation of the growth of ROC authority abroad with his own international goals: "The revival of the church unity is a crucial condition for revival of lost unity of the whole 'Russian world', which has always had the Orthodox faith as one of its foundations."

Thus the 250-million-plus-member Orthodox Church needs to be brought to heel, or better yet, broken. Over the past few years we have seen several episodes pointing to that end:

- Removal of Bishop Artemije of Raška and Prizren. The Serbian Orthodox eparchy that includes the NATO-occupied province of Kosovo and Metohija. In 2010 Vladika Artemije, an outspoken opponent of ecumenism, was accused on spurious corruption charges for which he's never been brought to trial, expelled from his eparchy without an ecclesiastical trial, and later reduced to the status of a simple monk. (He insists that he is the true Bishop of the Raško-Prizrenska Eparchy in Exile, leading to his being falsely being accused of schism.)

The real reasons for this were transparently political. Vladika Artemije was punished for his forthright opposition to US, NATO, and EU policy in Kosovo and his spearheading a Washington lobbying effort to oppose creation of that terrorist-mafia pseudo-state (and hotbed of Islamic jihad) under NATO protection. In addition, he sued the NATO powers in the European Court of Human Rights in Strasbourg, and in 2009 sought to bar a visit by then-US Vice President and current 2020 presidential candidate Joe Biden (a belligerent proponent of war against Serbs in Bosnia and Kosovo and of detaching Kosovo from Serbia, not to mention a Ukraine profiteer via his son Hunter Biden) from visiting Visoki Dečani monastery—a decision overturned by the Serbian Church at the behest of the Serbian government, then headed by western quisling Boris Tadic. The Biden snub reportedly prompted a high NATO official (probably US Admiral Mark P. Fitzgerald, then Commander, US Naval Forces Europe and Africa, and Commander, Allied Joint Force Command (JFC) Naples) to demand: "What we need here is a more co-operative bishop." They soon got it, with the shameful submission of the Serbian Church under pressure from Washington, Brussels, and Belgrade officialdom. (As noted below, the Serbian Church leadership's betrayal of Vladika Artemije has now come back to haunt them in Montenegro.)

- The Ukrainian Orthodox Church schism. A year ago, His All-Holiness, Bartholomew I, the Patriarch of Constantinople, recognized as a new "autocephalous" (entirely self-ruling) "Orthodox Church of Ukraine" ("OCU") persons who had up until then been universally shunned as schismatics and frauds by all Orthodox jurisdictions. Since then Constantinople, with the overt help of the US State Department and the Greek government, has been able to round up a few additional endorsements, notably from the Patriarch of Alexandria and All Africa and the Archbishop of Athens (both dependent on Greek state subsidies) but pointedly rejected by many of the bishops, clergy, and faithful in the African and Greek jurisdictions. A number of Churches, notably Antioch and Serbia, have been outspokenly supportive of the canonical Ukrainian Orthodox Church, which remains an autonomous part of the Russia Orthodox Church.

US officials who wouldn't know Orthodoxy from orthodontia have taken a keen interest in the Church's internal canonical arrangements, insisting that creation of the bogus "OCU" is an exercise in human rights and "religious freedom," despite violence against clergy and believers of the canonical Church and plans to seize churches and monasteries. Among the outspoken supporters of the OCU are celebrated theologians like US Secretary of State Mike Pompeo (who placed a personal call to the "newly elected head of the

"OCU" "Metropolitan Epifaniy" (Dumenko), Geoffrey Pyatt (current US Ambassador to Greece, who was also Ambassador to Ukraine during the 2014 regime change operation), Sam Brownback (US Ambassador at Large for International Religious Freedom), and—recognizable to many Americans from their impeachment testimony—US Special Representative for Ukraine Kurt Volker and US Ambassador in Kiev Marie Yovanovitch (noted for her over-the-top LGBT promotion in Ukraine). Pyatt and Brownback are notable for their round-robin visits to Orthodox Church leaders, notably in the Balkans, to "encourage" their recognition of the Ukrainian schismatics.

- <u>Violence over LGBT in Georgia</u>. Governments of formerly Christian countries in North America and Europe have made LGBT ideology an integral element of their promotion of "human rights" and "democracy" in formerly communist countries where the locals generally have a far less "progressive" view than is common in western Europe or "blue" America. This includes pressuring compliant governments of European countries recently emerged from communism to hold "Pride parades" that offend local sensibilities. The message to traditional societies still grounded in Christian morality but with elites committed to "a European course," meaning membership in NATO and (perhaps *someday* . . .) the European Union is that it's a package deal. You don't get to pick which part of western "democracy, human rights and free markets" you want and which you don't. You can't have transatlanticism without transgenderism. So shut up, grit your teeth, and *take it* . . .

The sexual social subversion campaign arrived in Georgia this summer, when the usual suspects—foreign embassies and their controlled NGOs, working in concert with George Soros's Open Society groups—were determined to hold Tbilisi's first Pride parade. With strong opposition from Orthodox faithful led by activist businessman and father of eight children Levan Vasadze, the parade was cancelled. Forced to back down, the pro-western, pro-LGBT forces responded with violence, using as their pretext a visit by international (including—Russian!) lawmakers to the Georgian parliament under the auspices of the Athens-based Interparliamentary Assembly on Orthodoxy (IAO). Endorsed by Tbilisi Pride organizers, the parliamentary attack was spearheaded by the United National Movement, the party of disgraced former president and Western favorite Mikheil Saakashvili (who is in self-imposed exile, fleeing from his conviction on corruption charges). The Georgian parliamentary Speaker was compelled to resign and questions were raised as to whether the ruling Georgian Dream reformist party could retain power—which surely was the point in the first place. The country's politics continue to be unstable, with forces defending Georgia's Orthodox Christian integrity denounced as "far right" by hatemongers in the west.

- <u>Montenegro's new anti-Serbian Orthodox Church law</u>. Now in the crosshairs is the Serbian Orthodox Church in spanking-new NATO member and EU aspirant Montenegro, with passage of a new law (with the approval of the Council of Europe's Orwellian-named "EUROPEAN COMMISSION FOR DEMOCRACY THROUGH LAW." a/k/a the Venice Commission) that requires religious bodies to prove their ownership of properties before 1918. As reported by *RT*'s Nebojsa Malic:

    Montenegro's ruling regime rammed the controversial law through the parliament in the dead of night between Thursday and Friday. Every single amendment of the opposition Dem-

ocratic Front (DF)—proposed to alleviate concerns that the bill
was deliberately targeting the Serbian Orthodox Church (SOC)—
was rejected. When some DF members disrupted the session in
protest, all of them were arrested and jailed. [. . .] [JGJ: Some of
the detained legislators have declared a hunger strike.]

The government in Podgorica has waved off criticism, saying
that the law is in line with the highest EU and international
human rights standards. [JGJ: A *de facto* endorsement from the
Vienna Commission says it all.] Most journalists have been
happy to take that at face value. Not being most journalists, I
actually read its text.

Article 11 mandates that any religious community in Montenegro must be headquartered there and cannot extend outside
its borders. That's absurd for a country that's about the size of
Connecticut, with a population estimated at around 620,000.

Article 16 says that no religious community may have in its
name *"an official name of another country or its emblems."*
Article 7 bans *"abuse of religious feelings for political ends,"*
whatever that may mean. And Article 24 says that the state can
seize the property of any religious community that is determined
by police to have violated the terms of its registration and been
stricken from the rolls, without appeal. Need one go on?

Now consider that President Milo Djukanovic has recently
accused the SOC of *"promoting pro-Serb policies that are aimed
at undermining Montenegrin statehood,"* as Reuters phrased it,
and it becomes blindingly obvious for whom the bell tolls.

In a close replay of the Ukraine situation, the new Montenegrin law sets the
stage for state seizures of Church properties and turning them over to an un-
recognized schismatic group, the so-called "Montenegrin Orthodox Church,"
sponsored by the corrupt regime of President Milo Djukanovic. Protests have
broken out in both Montenegro and Serbia, with Montenegrin police very
democratically beating some protesters, including a Bishop of the canonical
Church. In Belgrade, the ruling Holy Synod of the Serbian Orthodox Church
denounced the new law and stated its support for the canonical Church.
(Belgrade has been stalwart in its support for the legitimate Church in Ukraine. But perhaps, now that they're being targeted themselves, some of the
Serbian hierarchs may remember how shabbily they treated Vladika Artemije
in their vain attempt to appease western demands—*and will take steps to
remedy that shameful mistake?*)

It remains to be seen what western governments will do, but based on the
Ukraine precedent it isn't hard to guess. Comments Malic: "Adopting a 'religious freedom' law that opens the door to persecuting a particular faith would
normally be seen as a horrifying breach of human rights, but when done to
Orthodox Serbs in Montenegro, the West doesn't seem to mind." As of this
moment, except for a non-specific demonstration alert, there is no posted
statement from the US Embassy in Podgorica, either in English or in some
language written exclusively in the Latin (not Cyrillic) alphabet called
"Crnogorski," evidently a reference to Serbian. (Foreign embassies in Washington take note! Start posting your websites in "American," not English!)

Now all that's needed to ice the cake is for the State Department's human
rights, religious freedom and democracy mavens and the US Commission on
International Religious Freedom—which, with Your Working Boy's culpability, has long since become little more than another subjective standard
under which countries the Washington *apparat* wants to hammer can be cited

(accurately or not)—to hail Montenegro's latest step into the radiant, post-Christian, post-national future of Euro-Atlantic integration.

But who knows. Maybe we'll be pleasantly surprised and Washington and Brussels will demand that their Montenegrin flunkies back off. Don't bet on it though. There's still a lot more of the Orthodox Church left to disrupt.

"Why Did Washington Insist on the Kosovo War?"

James George Jatras | Ron Paul Institute | April 9, 2024

The following remarks were delivered at a conference marking the 25th anniversary of the NATO bombing of Serbia: "The 1999 Red-Green Bombing Terror against Serbia," held on March 20, 2024, at the Bundestag in Berlin hosted by MdB Dr. Rainer Rothfuß and his Alternative for Germany parliamentary group.

In 2004, I appeared as the second defense witness called by Slobodan Milošević at his so-called "trial" before the so-called "International Criminal Tribunal for the former Yugoslavia" at The Hague. My testimony was not as an expert witness but as a witness of fact concerning the formulation and implementation of US and western policy. I addressed one specific charge: that—*beginning no later than October 1998*—Mr. Milošević was the initiator of a criminal conspiracy to drive the Albanians out of Kosovo and Metohija on the basis of their ethnicity.

There was one little problem with this accusation: There was absolutely zero direct evidence for it. No written order to this effect was ever produced. No person testified as to having received, transmitted, or even heard of such an instruction. Rather, the claim was based solely on circumstantial inferences of events starting from October 1998.

Thus, the heart of my testimony related to a paper I issued on August 12, 1998, as an analyst at the US Senate Republican Policy Committee, titled "Bosnia II: The Clinton Administration Sets Course for NATO Intervention in Kosovo." In that paper, working solely from open sources, I detailed how, at that time—fully *two months before* the Milošević-led supposed "criminal conspiracy" came into effect—

> . . . planning for a U.S.-led NATO intervention in Kosovo is now largely in place, . . . The only missing element appears to be an event—with suitably vivid media coverage—that would make intervention politically salable, even imperative, in the same way that [the] Administration finally decided on intervention in Bosnia in 1995 after a series of "Serb mortar attacks" took the lives of dozens of civilians—attacks, which, upon closer examination, may in fact have been the work of the Muslim regime in Sarajevo, the main beneficiary of the intervention. . . . That the Administration is waiting for a similar "trigger" in Kosovo is increasingly obvious: [As reported in the *Washington Post*, August 4, 1998], "A senior U.S. Defense Department official who briefed reporters on July 15 noted that 'we're not anywhere near making a decision for any kind of armed

intervention in Kosovo right now, . . . [but] I think if some levels of atrocities were reached that would be intolerable, that would probably be a trigger.'"

Now, if I was aware of this as early as August 1998, so were a lot of other people in Washington. I submitted to the "Tribunal" that in light of my paper, all interpretations of events would have to be drastically reevaluated. The issue wasn't any longer whether Belgrade was planning an expulsion but that Washington was looking for a pretext for aggression.

(My cross-examination by prosecutor Geoffrey Nice (later *Sir*, based on his work at The Hague), asked me barely a word about my testimony. Rather, he interrogated me about my ethnic origins (Greek, from four Spartan grandparents), my religion (Orthodox Christian), and my opinions about the Islamic challenge to European, Christian civilization (negative).)

As we know, in due course the suitable "trigger" was found, with the so-called "Račak massacre" of January 1999. The key figure in "selling" Račak was William Walker. As described by Mark Ames and Matt Taibbi (now of *Rolling Stone*) in their article "Meet Mr. Massacre," published in the now-defunct *The Exile* of February 10, 2000:

> Years from now, when the war in Serbia is over and the dust has settled, historians will point to January 15, 1999 as the day the American Death Star became fully operational.
>
> That was the date on which an American diplomat named William Walker brought his OSCE war crimes verification team to a tiny Kosovar village called Račak to investigate an alleged Serb massacre of ethnic Albanian peasants. After a brief review of the town's 40-odd bullet-ridden corpses, Walker searched out the nearest television camera and essentially fired the starting gun for the war.
>
> "From what I saw, I do not hesitate to describe the crime as a massacre, a crime against humanity," he said. "Nor do I hesitate to accuse the government security forces of responsibility."
>
> We all know how Washington responded to Walker's verdict; it quickly set its military machine in motion, and started sending out menacing invitations to its NATO friends to join the upcoming war party.

Focus on that phrase: "the American Death Star became fully operational." Kosovo became the template that we then took on the road in one form or another in Afghanistan, Iraq, Libya, Syria, Yemen. Ukraine.

But the question still lingers: *Why?* Why was Washington so insistent that we and our NATO satelli–oops—"allies" needed to launch that war? Why did then-Secretary of State Madeleine Albright reveal in confidence, according to a reliable source, that at Rambouillet "We intentionally set the bar too high for the Serbs to comply. They need some bombing, and that's what they are going to get"?

Some people will tell you it was about putting a NATO base, Camp Bondsteel, in a strategic location. Or that we wanted to clear the way for an East-West energy pipeline across the Balkans. Or that we coveted the mineral wealth of the Trepča mines. Or to secure the transit route for Afghan opium processed into heroin bound for Europe.

Certainly, all of our various interventions line a lot of a pockets, but in more than three decades of work in and around the Washington *apparat,* I never heard anyone point to such concrete and, frankly, normal if immoral imperial considerations.

Rather, answers must instead be sought within the larger perspective of American policy since the end of the first Cold War in 1991 and the development of the current one in the course of the 1990s: the American "unipolar moment," as the bipartisan US policy *nomenklatura* sought to consolidate and perpetuate its hegemonic control over the entire planet, taking advantage of the vacuum left by the demise of the USSR. Perhaps the fullest expression of this was a 1996 *Foreign Affairs* article by neoconservative ideologists William Kristol and Robert Kagan (NOTE: Victoria Nuland's husband), misleadingly titled "Toward a Neo-Reaganite Foreign Policy," in which they called for the US to establish and maintain indefinitely "benevolent global hegemony"—in other words, perpetual American world domination.

Kristol and Kagan laid out virtually all of the elements that have guided US global policy during the ensuing years. It is no accident that Republican neoconservatives were enthusiastic supporters of Bill Clinton's Balkan interventions of the 1990s, under the guidance of people like then-Secretary of State Madeleine Albright, who once opined regarding the sanctions-related deaths of a half-million Iraqi children that "the price is worth it." In the US establishment, there is little dissent on either side of the partisan aisle with Albright's view that a militant United States has a special wisdom: "If we have to use force, it is because we are America; we are the indispensable nation. We stand tall and we see further than other countries into the future . . ."

The result is a kind of neo-Bolshevik ideology, where, as the vanguard of all progressive humanity, the US leadership class sees itself as the midwife of history. America took the path (as characterized by Russian Foreign Minister Sergey Lavrov) of the "replication of the experience of Bolshevism and Trotskyism"—morphing ourselves into a new Evil Empire in place of the old one. (Anyone familiar with the origins of America's neoconservatives understands that the Trotskyite reference is not just rhetorical.)

Which brings us back to the "Why?" regarding Kosovo. When the dissolution of Yugoslavia kicked off in June 1991, largely at the initiative of Austria and Germany, official Washington was terrified that with the end of the Soviet bloc Europe might become "whole and free"—but without us. What then could be the future of Lord Hastings Lionel Ismay's mission for NATO of keeping the Americans *in* Europe, the Russians *out*, and the Germans *down*? Europe, the crown jewel of the Global American Empire (the GAE) was slipping away.

Hence, as former Chairman of the Senate Foreign Relations Committee Richard Lugar (R-Indiana) indicated, NATO needed to go "out of area or out of business." Starting in spring 1992, Washington moved swiftly to expand the conflict from Slovenia and Croatia (where it had been relatively contained) to Bosnia and Herzegovina. There the US became the vociferous champion of the Muslim faction, illegally shipping in al-Qaeda fighters and Iranian weapons via covert C–130 flights into Tuzla. We then engaged in a little demonstrative bombing of the Bosnian Serbs to set the stage for the Dayton Agreement. The arsonist sets the fire, so then he can be the hero rushing to the rescue: "See, you silly 'dispensable' European children? You just can't get along without us . . ."

Following Dayton, Kosovo was the other shoe that needed to drop—with appropriate violence—to ensure that Europe was totally, abjectly, humiliatingly subservient to the United States through NATO, with the passive complicity of NATO's concubine, the European Union. The corollary was that, just as the Serbs had no legitimate voice in determining post-Yugoslav structures, the Russians understood they had no legitimate voice in European security arrangements. These would be decided without them.

Now, of course, with defeat looming in Ukraine and with the broader Middle East on the edge of a regional conflagration, with many in Washington beating the drums for war with Iran or even China, the GAE's "unipolar" moment is coming to an end, one way or the other, either with a bang or with a whimper. Unfortunately, neither in Washington, nor in Berlin or other European capitals, with the exception of Budapest, are decisions made by people who can be regarded as mentally and morally healthy human beings, much less patriots.

The next few months and years promise to be a period of disorder and acute danger. The question is, can we—Americans and Europeans alike—find a path to governance that can secure a future for our peoples?

Russophobia

"Post–Soviet World"

James George Jatras | *Policy Review* | Summer 1988

Dear Sir:

David Moro's "The National Re-birth of Russia" is a bold departure from the usual, tired analysis of the Soviet problem.

Mr. Moro proceeds from what one would assume would be an elementary premise of any discussion of the Russian problem: that the Soviet regime is an aberration in the progress of both Russian and world history. A narrowly based, ideological "vanguard party," drawing its claimed legitimacy from an economic model considered laughable even before the end of the 19th century, now manages to hang on to power principally through the cynical exploitation of its subjects' security concerns and national loyalties. The continued retention of power by that party ensures the perpetuation of the atmosphere of insecurity and disorder that has plagued the world community since the last stable international system collapsed in 1914. Thus, for both Russia and the world, a return to some sort of normalcy requires the replacement of the totalitarian Soviet regime with a normal government.

So accustomed are we to the abnormality of the last seven decades that too many of us are incapable of understanding how much more relaxed and nonthreatening would be international life in a post-Soviet age. Clearly, as critics of Mr. Moro will suggest, the emergence of a non-communist, nationally oriented Russian government will not be without its difficulties—especially with respect to the many non-Russian nationalities of the Soviet Union. But it must be emphasized that these difficulties (which are only suppressed and festering for the moment, not absent) are of a secondary order of magnitude; they are on a par with the Falklands/Malvinas and Cyprus disputes (today) or the Alsace-Lorraine and Schleswig-Holstein questions (yesterday). These issues pale in comparison with the Soviet regime's unwavering pursuit of world domination and "the triumph of socialism on a world scale." The Soviet Union of necessity must seek power in Central America, in Africa, throughout Asia; a nationally minded Russian government, even more than the former Russian empire, would care less about these places. Even on a regional basis, in the unlikely event that the Russian successor government had the slightest imperial aspirations, it would be forced to come to terms with its neighbors, as have the other former imperialists of Britain, France, and Germany.

The uncertainties of a post-Soviet world appear so daunting because they are unknown, precisely because our leading analysts have been far more interested in the impossible task of trying to find a way to a modus vivendi with militant Communism than a way to supersede it. We imagine that fascism, national socialism, apartheid, and a host of petty tyrannies are all mortal—but Communism is forever.

James George Jatras
Alexandria, VA

"Feeling Like Russians Again"

James George Jatras | *Chronicles* | April 1999

The Russian Question: Nationalism, Modernization, and Post-Communist Russia
By Wayne Allensworth
Lanham, MD; Rowman & Littlefield, 368 pp. $69.00

"The status of the American Negro is that of an oppressed national minority, and only a Soviet system can solve the question of such minorities," William Z. Foster, long-time chairman of the Communist Party, U.S.A., wrote in his 1932 book, *Toward Soviet America*:

> Accordingly, the right of self-determination will apply to Negroes in the American Soviet system. In the so-called Black Belt of the South, where the Negroes are in the majority, they will have the fullest right to govern themselves and also such white minorities as may live in this section.

Thus, by sheer sleight of hand, an ethnic majority would be transformed into a minority on its own home territory. Thankfully, Foster and company never got the opportunity' to enact their program for rectifying what they believed to be America's irredeemably racist past.

But suppose they had? Following the model actually put into effect by the Soviet Union on the territory of the former Russian empire, it is not hard to see how this principle would have worked out in practice: an African-American republic in the Deep South, a Spanish-speaking republic in most of the Mexican Cession, large territories in the West assigned to various Indian nations ("Navajo Autonomous Republic"), small francophone enclaves in Louisiana and northern Vermont and Maine, and so forth—all under the tight control of an avowedly non-national, even anti-national, regime determined to efface any memory of the former American nation. A truncated "American" (i.e., white, English-speaking) republic would occupy most of the Midwest, Upper South, and Northeast, itself riddled with autonomous regions for Indians and real or imagined ethnic minorities, like Pennsylvania Germans, Chicago Poles, and Cape Cod Portuguese. Even within the borders of this rump America, the residual non-minority American identity, still suspect as the former oppressing power, would be subject to unblinking scrutiny for any signs of reawakening chauvinism.

And now, suppose that—after the better part of a century—the whole system were to collapse, and all the arbitrarily drawn lines to become the borders of internationally recognized states. The resulting "America"—that is, the territory that had not been assigned to one or another of the formerly oppressed minorities—finds itself the mutilated remnant of its former, pre-Foster domain, while millions of non-minority Americans, literally overnight, find themselves "foreigners" under the not-too-tender rule of African-American, Hispanic, etc., governments, which consider their very presence an offense to their "national" dignity. Is there any doubt that, among non-minority Americans, there would be a nationalist reaction, not only over the treatment of dispossessed "Americans" in the minority-ruled statelets but against the dismemberment itself?

This, roughly, is the position that Russia and the Russians now find themselves in, with the dismantling of the Soviet Union. To be sure, as Wayne Allensworth insightfully describes the spectrum of Russian national opinion, there has been a reaction against the vivisection of Russia's national territory' that occurred in 1991, by which the Soviet regime was finally laid to rest. Yet what is surprising is not that this reaction has occurred but that, given the increasing misery into which most Russians have been plunged in the post-Soviet era, it has not been a more forceful one. A stock theme of some of the more extreme (and numerically insignificant) nationalist elements, such as Aleksandr Barkashov's proto-Nazi movement, Russian National Unity, is the international anti-Russian conspiracy, in which

> the United States works in concert with the International Monetary Fund (IMF), the U.N., NATO, and an internationalist-oriented elite in the mass media to undermine Russian sovereignty, military security, and cultural identity.

Given, however, the role of U.S. "experts" in turning Russia's post-Soviet privatization into the biggest looting of a nation's resources in world history (estimated by some authorities at upward of $400 billion), coupled with a U.S. policy (begun under Bush but compounded under Clinton) that is cynically contemptuous of Russia's legitimate interests in the Caucasus, the Balkans, and the "near abroad" (that is, the newly independent states, first delineated as administrative subdivisions within the U.S.S.R. by Lenin and Stalin, the borders of which the United States now considers sacred), and the threat posed by an unnecessary and gratuitous expansion of NATO, the mystery is not why some Russians go in for conspiracy theories but why most have not— yet. (Back in the days of communism, the United States meekly acquiesced in the "Brezhnev Doctrine," under which the Soviet Union had the right to ensure that socialist states would remain eternally socialist. But today, not only is post-communist Russia not entitled to a Monroe Doctrine in its own neighborhood, it is regarded as aggression *per se* if Moscow objects to the establishment of an American sphere of influence in areas vital to Russia, but of negligible importance to America.)

Allensworth, a Russia analyst at the U.S. government's Foreign Broadcast Information Service, is superbly equipped to explain the complexities and nuances of the kaleidoscopic variations of Russian nationalist opinion. Allowing, perhaps, the wish to become father to the thought, Allensworth confronts the dominant anti-nationalism of American policy—anti-nationalist in its hostility not only to Russian nationalism but to American nationalism and to every other manifestation, in any country, of a patriotic consciousness not completely subordinate to globalist ideology—with the fact (or at least the hope) that Russia is down but not yet out.

"Russia is at a crossroads. A choice must be made, not between nationalism and internationalism but between Russian nationalisms." From among the contenders to succeed the terminally decrepit Boris Yeltsin and his hopelessly corrupt U.S.-supported regime, he clearly prefers retired general Aleksandr Lebed, now governor of Siberia's Krasnoyarsk region and a leading advocate of what Allensworth calls "reform nationalism." As the most constructive variant of nationalist opinion, reform nationalism, Allensworth suggests, not only can restore Russia to the status of a respectable great power in a very dangerous neighborhood; it has the moral authority to pull the country out of the domestic morass into which it has sunk. Echoing Aleksandr Solzhenitsyn, the acknowledged godfather of Orthodox Christian patriotism in Russia, Lebed believes that a healthy Russia must be reestablished on authentic national traditions—notably, the mutual reinforcement of the army and the Church. (While Solzhenitsyn is, of course, a professed Orthodox Christian, Lebed, so far as this reviewer knows, has never declared his religious faith. He has criticized former Soviet *apparatchiki* who have opportunistically rushed to declare themselves believers in the post-communist era; on the other hand, Lebed was the only presidential contender to attend the recent interment of the royal martyrs, Nicholas II and his family, at the Peter and Paul Fortress in St. Petersburg.) As Lebed puts it in his autobiography:

> So let us remember what Russia stands on, and return the Church, which was separated from the state, to its bosom and create a powerful spiritual state institution. And seriously, thoughtfully, as we can be when we want to be, let us reform the army and bring it back to its former might and grandeur. The Church strengthens the army; the army defends the Church. And on this restored spiritual axis—the two forces of our great power—we can begin to feel like Russians again.

To feel like Russians again. It is hard to read Allensworth's book without mentally comparing, more than once, the parallels between nationalism in Russia and the quandary of American national identity. When will we be permitted to feel like Americans again? While Foster's Soviet-style plan for American denationalization never made it past the drawing board, other programs, structurally different but kindred in spirit—multiculturalism in education, multilingualism, affirmative action, dual citizenship, uncontrolled immigration—have confused and demoralized Americans' national consciousness. In the final analysis, despite the genocidal ministrations of the Soviet regime and the dashed hopes of de-communization, Russians still know they are Russians. Yet how many Americans, by comparison, can describe with any degree of coherence who we are as a people? Indeed, apart from the universalist cant about "one nation, many peoples" that has become *de rigueur* in public discourse today, is it even permissible to speak of an American "nationality" at all?

The question is hardly an idle one. Allensworth aptly closes his book with a chapter on "The Global Regime and the Nationalist Reaction":

> The conclusive stage of the economic, political, and social rationalization that began in early modern Europe is its globalization. The fear that all nationalists express of the developing hegemonic global monoculture is inextricably tied to their intuitive grasp of the fundamental meaning of modernism's final drive toward dominance: The real question facing both the Russians and other nations is the question of survival.

The fact that Russians are addressing that question—sometimes, admittedly, in reprehensible (the Nazism of Barkashov), unattractive (the "national bolshevism" of communist leader Gennadi Zyuganov), and bizarre (the ranting of "liberal democrat" Vladimir Zhirinovsky) ways—is itself unacceptable to the global managerial elite that dominates their country and ours: hence Russian nationalism's bogeyman status among the "democratic" intelligentsia of America and Russia alike. If Allensworth is right in believing that a nationalist of some sort will come to power after Yeltsin, we can expect a full-blown "Who Lost Russia?" hysteria from the globalist apparatus in Washington, and maybe even a new Cold War. But a survey of the current American political scene, alas, offers little hope that the globalists may soon be crying in their Perrier, "Who Lost America?"

"Trump's Opponents Are Trying to Cripple Him by Playing 'Russian Card'"

Edward Lozansky and Jim Jatras | *Chronicles* | January 9, 2017

Departing presidents tend to fade from public consciousness surprisingly quickly once they leave office. Most at least have the good grace to assume a low profile on their way out to give their successors room to launch.

Not Barack Obama though. The closing weeks of his tenure have seen a contrived imbroglio over a non-veto of a U.N. resolution condemning Israeli settlements, grudging unwillingness to accept that his "regime change" policy in Syria is a wretched failure, and slapping sanctions on Moscow for supposed Russian hacking to skew the U.S. election in favor of Donald Trump. Obama plans to stay in Washington and remain engaged in policy—which means sniping at his successor.

Whether or not one thinks that material released by Wikileaks was the fruit of Russian cyber activity—we think it highly implausible—there is no doubt of the *intent* lurking behind the claims. First, to cast a cloud over Trump's election and the legitimacy of his presidency. Second, to throw as much sand in the gears of Trump's oft-stated desire to improve ties with Russia, most importantly on the critical question of presenting a common front against (WARNING: the following phrase may offend acolytes of Hillary Clinton and Obama) radical Islamic terrorism.

Regarding the legitimacy of the election, the hypocrisy of some Democrats and their pet mainstream media is breathtaking. Trump's opponents shrieked that he was "undermining our democracy" when during a debate he refused to state absolutely in advance he wouldn't challenge the outcome. No sooner had the same opponents picked their shocked selves off the floor the morning of November 9 than we witnessed the launch of #NotMyPresident mobs and a vain attempt to suborn the votes of Electors pledged to Trump, efforts denounced by neither Obama nor Clinton.

Obama's attempt to undermine Trump was stepped up a notch in late December. Imposition of new sanctions on Moscow, including expulsion of 35 Russian diplomats and closure of two diplomatic compounds, was clearly designed to trigger tit-for-tat retaliation. Instead, Russian President Vladimir Putin refused to take the bait, preferring to wait for grown-ups to take over in Washington on January 20 and inviting American diplomats' kids over to the Kremlin to see the Christmas tree. Trump then rubbed salt in the Russophobes' wounds by praising Putin as "very smart" for his restraint.

The next escalation was a Senate hearing that featured Democrats and Republicans alike treating the hacking allegations as proven fact and calling for tougher measures. Then, on the very day Trump was officially elected president in the Congressional tally of Electoral College votes—and was briefed by intelligence community honchos—the Empire Struck Back with release of an unclassified report from the Director of National Intelligence (DNI), already conveniently leaked to *NBC*. The key assertion:

> We assess Russian President Vladimir Putin ordered an influence campaign in 2016 aimed at the US presidential election. Russia's

goals were to undermine public faith in the US democratic process, denigrate Secretary Clinton, and harm her electability and potential presidency. We further assess Putin and the Russian Government developed a clear preference for President-elect Trump. We have high confidence in these judgments.

This claim, and others in the same vein, is presented with no actual evidence. (For those unfamiliar with spook-speak, "high confidence" means "we think so but don't know for sure.") Instead, Americans are expected to accept such allegations on faith from the same people who brought us Benghazi and WMDs in Iraq. Anyone failing to do so is presumptively a witting or unwitting tool of the Kremlin.

Aside from the unproven hacking claims themselves (at the Senate hearing, Lt. Gen. James Clapper conceded that the U.S. hacks other countries and vice versa) nothing in the DNI report indicates that any Russian efforts of political influence involved falsification of information. ("Disclosures through WikiLeaks did not contain any evident forgeries.") Or put differently, whatever their provenance, the disclosures released by Wikileaks regarding, for example, John Podesta's emails and efforts to tilt the Democratic primary race against Bernie Sanders, were *true*. So even if we accept for the sake of argument it was the Russians, how dare they tell us what those corrupt Democrats were up to!

The real tipoff is found in the DNI report's political assertions regarding a narrative that reinforces what we agree is most Russians' preference for Trump over Clinton, as reflected in opinion polls, as well as in Russian media and officials' public comments:

> *Hillary Clinton*: " . . . focused on her leaked e-mails and accused her of corruption, poor physical and mental health, and ties to Islamic extremism," whose "election could lead to a war between the United States and Russia."

> *Donald Trump*: " . . . the target of unfair coverage from traditional US media outlets that [the Russians] claimed were subservient to a corrupt political establishment," and "an outsider victimized by a corrupt political establishment and faulty democratic election process that aimed to prevent his election because of his desire to work with Moscow" in "an international counterterrorism coalition against the Islamic State in Iraq and the Levant (ISIL)."

Which of the above characterizations attributed to Russian messaging are Americans supposed to disagree with?

Following his briefing on the *classified* version of the DNI report—which presumably detailed all the real evidence redacted from the public version to protect "sources and methods"—Trump appeared underwhelmed, producing a string of three tweets:

> "Having a good relationship with Russia is a good thing, not a bad thing. Only 'stupid' people, or fools, would think that it is bad! We have enough problems around the world without yet another one. When I am President, Russia will respect us far more than they do now and both countries will, perhaps, work together to solve some of the many great and pressing problems and issues of the WORLD!"

Trump's short message, when compared to the thrust of the DNI report, is what it all boils down to: the defeated Obama apparatus, a politicized intelligence community leadership, a bipartisan foreign policy establishment, and a mainstream media treated with increasing skepticism and derision by the American people are doing their level best to knock the legs out from under Trump largely because he wants to shift U.S. policy from a sterile and counter-productive antagonism toward Russia to cooperation on common concerns. At the top of those concerns—as identified in the DNI report itself!—is joint U.S.-Russian action against the Islamic State.

As Trump tweeted, "Only 'stupid' people, or fools, would think that it is bad!" Or maybe he needs to add smart people in an American version of the defunct Soviet *nomenklatura* that has built generations of lucrative careers on East-West confrontation, not to mention arming and training Islamic radicals in successive "regime change" wars like Libya and Syria.

Do the DNI report and Congressional calls for new sanctions to poison the well against Trump's agenda constitute a desperate last stand? Or will they manage to pull it off, crippling Trump before he can even get started?

We shall soon see. The confirmation fight over Secretary of State-designate Rex Tillerson will be an early indicator.

Edward Lozansky is president of the American University in Moscow. He is the author of the book Operation Elbe, *which describes joint US-Russia anti-terrorist efforts.*

Jim Jatras is a former U.S. diplomat and foreign policy adviser to the Senate GOP leadership. He is the author of a major study, "How American Media Serves as a Transmission Belt for Wars of Choice."

"Appointment of Special Counsel for 'Russiagate' Could Derail Trump's MAGA Agenda, Lead to War"

Jim Jatras | *Chronicles* | May 19, 2017

Letter from Pergamum-on-the-Potomac

On the heels of Donald Trump's Oval Office visit with Russian Foreign Minister Sergey Lavrov and other American and Russian officials, it finally seemed the fledgling US administration was turning the corner and making progress toward cooperation with Moscow against radical Islamic terrorism, particularly in Syria.

Then the fake news came flying thick and fast as the Deep State and MSM counterattacked. First, they questioned why a Russian photographer was allowed access to the meeting while the American fake news purveyors were not. Then they speculated that maybe Lavrov or Ambassador Sergey Kislyak had planted a bug in the president's office. Then they charged that Trump had compromised sensitive intelligence (received from Israel) by revealing it to the Russians. Finally they accused Trump of obstruction of justice—an impeachable offense—by his reportedly suggesting to former FBI Director James Comey (fired the day before the Russian meeting) that he should go easy on short-lived National Security Adviser Michael Flynn, whose scalp was the first the Deep State/MSM gang had nailed to the wall.

The whole anti-Trump campaign has been based on criminal leaks of classified or privileged material from within the government. Still, there is no sign of a counterattack. Perhaps Attorney General Jeff Sessions has secretly empaneled a grand jury and indictments of leakers are forthcoming. More likely he has not and is more concerned with whether prosecutors are using too much discretion in the severity of offenses they choose to charge criminal suspects with, or whether states are playing fast and loose with federal marijuana laws.

The steady drumbeat of negative stories designed to keep Trump and his team (or whatever minority of his personnel might actually support him and his agenda) has had the desired effect of keeping the Administration on the defensive. It led to the decision by Deputy Attorney General Rod Rosenstein to appoint former FBI Director Robert Mueller to take over the Bureau's investigation into claims of Russian interference into the 2016 and collusion with members of Trump's campaign. Reportedly, the decision was solely Rosenstein's and the White House was only informed of the fact about a half hour before the public announcement.

If anyone is hoping Mueller's appointment will yield a respite from the barrage of attacks, they are likely to be disappointed. Ideally, Mueller would simply look at the work the FBI has done so far, take note of the fact that there's no evidence of any crime was committed—without which there shouldn't even be an investigation in the first place—and wrap it up. That's unlikely. It is in the nature of Special Counsels to justify their existence by finding something, anything, even if it's only catching people in inconsistent statements that can be packaged as perjury—crimes that would not have existed if not for the investigation itself. This can drag out for many months, if not years. At the same time, we can expect the media lynch mob to keep the pot boiling by one unsubstantiated, unsourced leak after another, as the Administration struggles to implement its agenda under an ever-present cloud: "the Trump Administration, under criminal investigation of collusion with Russia."

The impact on the weak sisters among Congressional Republicans is obvious. Leaving aside Never-Trumpers who are only too happy to conspire with Democrats to reverse the 2016 vote in a "soft coup" by the Deep State and MSM, many GOP legislators will be loath to go to the mat for an Administration tainted by a criminal probe, whose very longevity is at issue. It may be too soon to stick a fork in Trump's agenda, but as one commentator has put it, it may be time to get the fork out of the drawer. All now in jeopardy: Obamacare repeal and replace, tax reform, the Wall, renegotiating NAFTA and other bad trade deals, infrastructure revitalization, defunding Planned Parenthood. (That's in addition to Trump's border security initiatives already blocked by the courts.)

Most of all, the issue that triggered this latest onslaught—rapprochement with Russia and teaming up against the jihadists—is very much in doubt. Even the appearance of being less than 100 percent hostile to Russia is evidence of treason, as shown by a senior Republican's recent statement caught on audio that Trump and California Congressman Dana Rohrabacher must be on the Kremlin's payroll.

Perhaps most dangerously, keep in mind that the only brief respite Trump has received against the onslaught has been when he launched cruise missiles against Syria over what was almost certainly a false flag chemical attack by jihadists in Idlib, for which the MSM and Deep Staters applauded him. Now we have a baseless allegation that the Syrian government is running a crematorium adjoining Saydnaya prison north of Damascus, where, the State Department's Stuart Jones claims, up to 50 inmates' bodies are burned daily. But even Jones admitted he doesn't know the facility is a crematorium at all. The offered "proof"? On satellite images the snow melts faster on that roof than on others nearby. Nonetheless, Holocaust rhetoric, the 800-pound gorilla of atro-city porn, was unleashed. A Google News search of "Syria, crematorium, Holocaust" yields over 5,000 hits. US Ambassador to the UN Nikki Haley called the unproven accusation "reminiscent of the 20th century's worst offenses against humanity." An Israel cabinet minister has called for Syrian President Bashar al-Assad's assassination.

There is reason to fear that Trump, guided by advisers whose policy pro-clivities mirror those of his critics, may seek the path of least resistance by further bellicose measures. These could take place in Korea, against Russia (for example in Ukraine), or in the broader Middle East (especially Syria, where the GOP-led Congress is reinvigorating the call for regime change). For example, while in Saudi Arabia—surreally touted by National Security Adviser H.R. McMaster as a paragon of a moderate, tolerant, peaceful Islamic ally—Trump is set to announce a coalition against Iran characterized as an "Arab NATO." As though the one NATO we already have weren't dangerous enough.

"Can Angela Merkel Avoid Trapping Germany in Another Two-FrontWar?"

Jim Jatras | *Strategic Culture* | June 2, 2017

To anyone with even a trace of patriotic feeling for his own country, perhaps the most stinging rebuke Donald Trump aimed at Hillary Clinton last year was when he compared her to German Chancellor Angela Merkel, a "catastrophic leader" who has "ruined Germany":

> Hillary Clinton wants to be America's Angela Merkel. And you know what a disaster this massive immigration has been to Germany and the people of Germany—crime has risen to levels that no one thought they would ever see. We have enough problems in our country, we don't need another one.

The soft-hearted Trump was being far too charitable to both Clinton and Mer-kel. Had Hillary been given control of a country far more powerful than Ger-many, there's no limit to the harm she might have inflicted on and the world. And of course Merkel's open door migrant policy is a mortal danger to all of Europe, not just to Germany.

When Trump showed up in Brussels and Sicily to meet with NATO, EU, and G7 leaders, there was already no love lost between him and Merkel, as evidenced by his apparently deliberate snub of her proffered handshake when they met in Washington in March. Rather than use the May meetings as an opportunity to smooth ruffled feathers, Trump doubled down by lecturing our European satellites on their failure to meet NATO military spending targets and by his unwillingness to declare America's absolute commitment to defend the very same deadbeats. He also complained about the EU's trade practices, meaning really Germany's trade practices.

To top things off, he declined to burn incense before one of the globalists' most sacred idols, the Paris Climate Change Agreement. Merkel wasted no time in denouncing the blaspheming infidel who had befouled the holy precincts. Front and center in her admonishment was Trump's questioning (not rejecting yet, just questioning) the Paris Agreement, which Merkel called "very dissatisfying." She then unleashed what in her mind and those of globalists elsewhere what she regarded the worst of all possible insults—that Trump was going "out on a limb" by putting his own country's interests first:

> "Recent days have shown me that the times when we could rely completely on others are over to a certain extent," Merkel said.
> "We also know that we Europeans must really take our fate into our own hands, of course in friendship with the United States of America, in friendship with Great Britain and as good neighbors wherever that is possible also with other countries, even with Russia."
> "Anyone who today puts on national blinkers and no longer has eyes for the world around him is, I am convinced, ultimately out on a limb."

No doubt Merkel's comments were largely geared to a domestic German audience in advance of elections in September. Leaders of her main opposition (and current "grand coalition" partners) in the SPD, who are even more anti-Trump and anti-nationalist than Merkel, if that's possible, were quick to second her remarks.

The anti-Trump establishment in the United States also piled on to take Merkel's side against Trump in what many outlets described as an impending U.S.-Europe "divorce":

- "If the President of the United States calls that a huge success, I'd hate to see failure," said Adam Schiff, Democratic lawmaker and high-ranking member of the House Intelligence Committee.

- Richard Haas, President of the Council on Foreign Relations, the leading voice of the bipartisan U.S. foreign policy establishment, called Merkel's comments a "watershed" in relations between the two allies. "(It's) what the US has sought to avoid since World War II," said Haas.

- "I realize that some of President Trump's actions and statements have unsettled America's friends. They have unsettled many Americans as well," commented Republican Senator John McCain, a leading Trump critic.

But the trophy goes to former Hillary Clinton *consigliere* Jamie Rubin (and husband of *CNN*'s top propagandist for aggression Christiane Amanpour), notorious for his blatant lying as State Department spokesman in support for Bill Clinton's and NATO's illegal attack on Serbia in 1999. Praising Merkel as the new "leader of the free world," Rubin lauded the German chancellor for her migration open door and deep-seated hostility to Russia, neither of which is particularly in Germany's interest.

This is of course the root problem of any go-it-alone "leadership" from Merkel. In the end, she is standing up not for Germany but for the basket of politically correct issues Chinese social media users mock as *baizuo* (literally, "white left"), a term that perfectly describes Merkel and her admirers on both sides of the Atlantic:

... *baizuo* is used generally to describe those who "only care about topics such as immigration, minorities, LGBT and the environment" and "have no sense of real problems in the real world"; they are hypocritical humanitarians who advocate for peace and equality only to "satisfy their own feeling of moral superiority"; they are "obsessed with political correctness" to the extent that they "tolerate backwards Islamic values for the sake of multiculturalism"; they believe in the welfare state that "benefits only the idle and the free riders"; they are the "ignorant and arrogant westerners" who "pity the rest of the world and think they are saviors."

Oddly, one of the first speculations raised by commentators on Merkel's "take our fate into our own hands" remark is whether it would lead to the formation of an "EU army" to replace the departing Americans. (To be fair, perhaps the ideological changeover from American-led trans-Atlanticism to German-led transgenderism wouldn't be all that great, given trends in recent years.) Still, one wonders which European countries would sign up for a military structure dominated by Berlin on a continent already subject to German economic hegemony. Starting with Germany itself, would countries that bristle at Trump's demand for spending two percent of GDP on the military be more forthcoming with Merkel in charge? To defend themselves from whom, exactly—the mobs of migrants, liberally interspersed with jihadists and rapists, that Merkel is determined to let in? Would the Poles, who already spend more than two percent and who hate and fear Germans and Russians in roughly equal measure, participate?

Of course there are some nostalgic attractions. For example, there are many in Latvia and Estonia who no doubt would be thrilled to get their old SS uniforms out of mothballs. Merkel can surely count on the HDZ-led government in Croatia, which is openly rehabilitating that country's Ustaša past. (Hint to Merkel: Maybe Culture Minister Zlatko Hasanbegović would allow the new EU army to borrow under license their copyrighted slogan, "*Za dom spremni!*" ©). No doubt the effort would be cheered along by some Americans, like former U.S. Director of Central Intelligence James Clapper, who recently declared that "historical practices of the Russians" are "almost genetically driven"...

Which brings us back to the thorny question of Russia. The anti-Russian hysteria in the U.S. (which recently has taken a curious anti-Jewish turn) has so far blocked any serious attempt by the Trump administration to achieve normalization of U.S.-Russia ties. But if the decoupling of the U.S. from Europe dreaded by the globalists in fact comes to pass, we may see both Washington and Berlin seeking to mend some fences with Moscow. In her anti-Trump tirade, Merkel magnanimously made a point of suggesting she would get along "even" with dastardly Russia. Would her Paris satrap Emmanuel Macron have proceeded with Vladimir Putin's recent visit commemorating 300 years of French-Russian relations if Merkel had been opposed?

Whatever her preferences, maybe Merkel has no choice to seek her own "Rappallo" if she is to avoid the bind Germany has found itself in twice in the last century—a two-front war. (Presumably this time it would be only ideological and moral, not a shooting war.) Simply put, she may have to decide which of the two, Trump or Putin, she hates more.

Actually, from an America First point of view, confronting Germany and the failing EU/NATO complex from both east and west isn't a bad idea. As pro-Trump commentator Ann Coulter suggested in a tweet, "We should form a military alliance with Russia to protect it from Western Europe" and its migrant hordes. Maybe that's what Trump had in mind in the first place.

"It's the Russia, Stupid"

Jim Jatras |*Strategic Culture* | June 16, 2017

It's another week in Washington and another horror show. This time it was Attorney General Jeff Sessions being grilled by Senators on whether, when, and how he might have met with certain Russians, or any Russian, or someone who might actually know a Russian. In addition to fishing for any inconsistency that could be used to support an accusation of obstruction of justice or perjury—the usual sleazy methodology of politically motivated investigations here—the transparent aim was to further poison the well on any possible initiative to improve ties with Moscow.

The strategy appears to be working. The Russian Embassy in Washington confirms that for the first time since the Russian Federation's founding the State Department did not send pro forma national day greetings. Perhaps the bureaucrats were afraid they would be tainted and themselves become targets of multiple investigations into "collusion" with the Kremlin. (Luckily, this intrepid Washington analyst has no qualms about such associations.)

Or more likely, they themselves are part of the Russophobic mob undermining the White House. It has been reported that soon after the inauguration Trump sought to open dialogue with the Kremlin and set an early summit with President Vladimir Putin. This produced a hysterical counter-action from the Deep State. As reported by conservative columnist and former presidential candidate Patrick Buchanan:

> The State Department was tasked with working out the details.
>
> Instead, says Daniel Fried, the coordinator for sanctions policy, he received "panicky" calls of 'Please, my God, can you stop this?"
>
> Operatives at State, disloyal to the president and hostile to the Russia policy on which he had been elected, collaborated with elements in Congress to sabotage any detente. They succeeded.
>
> "It would have been a win-win for Moscow," said Tom Malinowski of State, who boasted last week of his role in blocking a rapprochement with Russia. State employees sabotaged one of the principal policies for which Americans had voted, and they substituted their own.

So much for constitutional government and the rule of law . . .

But now it gets even worse. This week Congress moved legislation designed to codify in statute sanctions imposed on Russia by Barack Obama over Ukraine and evidence-free charges of Russian election interference. Provisions for a presidential waiver, which are standard in any sanctions legislation, are unusually narrow. Congressional proponents are clear that their aim is to take the matter out of the president's hands. Democrats, seemingly devoid of any other policy agenda or ideas, vow to keep banging the Russia drum through the 2018 Congressional elections.

When all is said and done, there are lots of reasons the political class hates Trump. His heresies on immigration and trade are near the top of the list. But make no mistake: for the Deep State and its mainstream media arm, demonizing Russia and Vladimir Putin personally is a dangerous obsession. (There is reason to suspect "Russian collusion" figured in the thinking of a fanatical Leftist's shooting attack on Republican Congressmen: "The shooter also signed a petition calling for an investigation into Trump-Russia ties, confirming he was radicalized by the mainstream media's obsession with conspiracy theories about Russia interfering with the election.")

It remains to be seen whether Oliver Stone's extended interview with Putin on the *Showtime* network will have any impact. So far the commentary seems to be divided between descriptions of the substance of the discussion and attacks on Stone for talking with such a bad, bad man: "Speaking after the interview, Stone refuted allegations that he became an unwitting messenger of pro-Putin propaganda or of dishonest information given by the president."

With regard to substance, relatively little attention has been accorded in American media to Putin's flat accusation that U.S. "special services" have supported terrorists, including in Chechnya. Of course anyone paying attention would know that arming jihadists is a standard part of U.S. policy, going back at least to Afghanistan in the 1980s and repeated in Bosnia, Kosovo, Libya, and today in Syria. Indeed, as early as the 1950s the U.S. had established a very close relationship with the Muslim Brotherhood and its terrorist elements as a weapon against Egypt's Gamal Abdel Nasser and Baathists in Syria and Iraq, who Washington thought were a little too cozy with the Soviet Union and far too socialist and secular for the taste of our pals in Saudi Arabia and the Gulf.

There is a real symbiosis between the anti-Russian imperative in American foreign policy and support for radical Islamic elements. It did not end when the Soviet Union and communism collapsed but rather was intensified. This is why Moscow's constant calls for a common front against terrorism are always rebuffed. Such cooperation doesn't make any sense for a *nomenklatura* whose number one goal is hostility to Moscow and for whom jihadists are at worst "frienemies"—people who may be troublesome but useful.

We can only imagine how completely different the world would be if the U.S. were to recognize that Russia is a country that in many respects is not that different from the United States or Europe and that we had common interests. But for the U.S. Deep State, that would amount to switching sides in a global conflict, where we see jihadists essentially as "freedom fighters" against a geopolitical adversary. These same clueless "elites" are then puzzled when their carefully nurtured, cuddly, "moderate" jihad terrorists attack us back here at home.

This irrational pattern is at the root of the hostility of American policymakers toward Russia and any prospect of normalizing bilateral ties. In large part, it's what underlies the "soft coup" being directed against Trump, of which the Sessions pillorying was an episode. (A late report based on unreliable, unverified sources suggests that Special Counsel on the Russia probe, Robert Mueller, is expanding his investigation to include potential obstruction of justice by President Donald Trump. Mueller, a close personal friend of ousted FBI Director James Comey, has already packed his team with partisan Democrats.)

Those behind this attempted coup think we can continue to treat Russia as though it were a minor power of the magnitude of Serbia, Iraq, Libya, or Syria, or even Iran. They think if we just keep pushing, pushing, pushing, either the Russians will collapse or back down. They will do everything possible to box Trump in and prevent him from pursuing any path other than the disastrous course laid out by Bill Clinton, George Bush, and Barack Obama. They can see no other outcome than removing Putin and returning Russia to the condition of a Yeltsin-era vassal state—a term Putin used in the Stone interview—or, better yet, its territorial breakup along the lines suggested by the late Zbigniew Brzezinski.

Will the Oliver Stone interview change any minds? It's too soon to tell. But if the soft coup against Trump succeeds, it might not matter, since then America could not be considered a self-governing constitutional republic even in a residual sense. We may have already passed our own Rubicon and just don't know it yet.

"Merkel Is Angry with America over Russia Sanctions but Will Do Nothing"

Jim Jatras | *Strategic Culture* | June 23, 2017

The tenure of Angela Merkel as Chancellor of the Federal Republic of Germany has been a disaster for her country and for Europe. That's why it's a refreshing change finally to have an issue where it is possible to agree with her.

Merkel, along with other voices in Germany and Austria, has denounced a bill (S. 722) passed by the U.S. Senate to impose new sanctions on Russia and Iran. In particular, Merkel has observed, correctly, that the legislation, if adopted, would negatively impact oil and gas pipeline deals with Russia. She evidently objects that this would be a unilateral U.S. action that would harm the interests of Germany and other countries without even consulting them.

As declared in a joint statement by German Foreign Minister Sigmar Gabriel and Austrian Chancellor Christian Kern: "Europe's energy supply is a matter for Europe, and not the United States of America!" (Wow! An exclamation point! From Teutonic officials! They must *really* be angry.)

Further:

> We cannot accept threatening European companies that contribute to the development of the European energy supply [system] with extraterritorial sanctions that violate international law! [Another exclamation point! They must be really, really angry!]
>
> Sanctions as a political instrument should not be linked to economic interests . . . Threatening German, Austrian and other European enterprises, which take part in the gas supply projects such as the Nord Stream II together with Russia or finance them, with penalties on the US market would add an absolutely new and highly negative aspect in relations between the US and Europe. [JGJ: Oddly, Berlin didn't seem quite so concerned about linking politics to economic interests when the interests were those of Italy, Greece, Hungary, Bulgaria, Serbia, and other countries that would have benefitted from South Stream.]
>
> This issue is all about the sales of the US condensed gas [to Europe] and pressing the Russian energy supply companies from the European market. The actual goal [of such sanctions] is to provide jobs for the US gas and oil industry. [JGJ: *You mean the U.S. may be exhibiting an element of export-oriented, pro-jobs mercantilism in its policy toward Europe? Surely, Germany never conducts trade relations on such a basis.*]

There's no doubt that S. 722—which passed the Senate by a vote of 98–2, with only Rand Paul and Bernie Sanders voting No—is a terrible piece of legislation. Its fundamental purpose is to tie President Trump's hands so that he cannot exercise his constitutional authority to conduct relations with foreign states. Specifically, Senators of both parties want to ensure that he doesn't have the ability to reach out and normalize ties with Moscow. To do that, a super-majority of Senators is willing to violate every principle of international law and comity, as well as damaging relationships with our top security and trade partners.

Even the broad authority for the president to waive sanctions when he deems it in the national interest, a standard feature in U.S. sanctions legislation, is denied Trump in this bill without Congressional permission. Whether this defect may be remedied in the House of Representatives is unclear. (Meanwhile, the power of Congress to decide upon war continues to be usurped by the Executive Branch without a murmur of protest. As the late Joseph Sobran once observed, the nice thing about the U.S. Constitution is that it poses no serious threat to our form of government.)

Perhaps the most entertaining aspect is Mrs. Merkel's threat to "retaliate" if the new sanctions bill becomes law. Who says Germans don't have a sense of humor! This, from someone who folded like a house of cards when she found out Barack Obama had the NSA tap into her mobile phone. The emptiness of Merkel's threat is an illustration of the point recently made by President Vladimir Putin that Russia is one of the few states in today's world that has the luxury of being truly sovereign. Germany does not have that luxury. The Germans' foreign policy, their intelligence policy, and other security institutions are essentially controlled by their American counterparts. Their financial sector is extremely vulnerable to any retaliation from Washington. So what can Merkel do to us? Not much.

The sanctions bill, if it becomes law, will be just another illustration that Germany and all other members of NATO and the EU are vassal states of Washington. If the likes of Merkel were replaced by decent national leaders of the caliber of Viktor Orbán or Václav Klaus, it might be another story. (While Europe will succumb to Washington's diktat on Russian sanctions, the European Commission—meaning Germany—is suing Poland, Hungary, and Czechia for refusing to import the migrant mobs invited by "Mutti Merkel." So much for her priorities.)

To add one more interesting twist, this week Trump met in Washington with Ukrainian President Petro Poroshenko. Natural gas seems to have been high on the agenda ("Ukraine Goes On Anti-Russia Pipeline Offensive As Europe Goes Nuts," by Kenneth Rapoza, *Forbes*, June 20):

> With Washington's blessing, Ukraine is going on the offensive against a Baltic Sea pipeline it deems a death knell to state controlled Naftogaz. Naftogaz is one of the most important companies in the country, and the gateway between Russian gas fields and the European market. This is the ultimate fight. Only this time, it pits Ukraine and the U.S. on one side with the Europeans and Russians—oddly enough—on the other. [. . .]
>
> Anti-Russia Senators, most of them Republican Never Trumpers, are turning the screws on Russian oil and gas firms. They have three hopes here: punish Russia for supporting anti-government forces in Ukraine; ban Trump from his constitutional duties of being able to call off the sanctions regime and help U.S. natural gas drillers and potential exporters. [. . .]

Naftogaz gave a hint to its lobbying efforts in the E.U. against Nord Stream. They said in a note that the European Commission 'should use its mandate as a guardian of the interests of the European consumers and insist on the application of the Third Energy Package to the Nord Stream II project.' [JGJ: *The Third Energy Package was Brussels' and Berlin's excuse to kill South Stream. Ironically, Ukraine and powerful elements in the U.S. now want to use it against the Germans themselves.*] [. . .]

Naftogaz is getting skillful at tugging at the heart strings of the E.U., which already has a political bias against Russia. The Congress's anti-Russia stance is counter to President Donald Trump's, but Trump has been beat up so severely on Russia that defending any sort of detente with the Kremlin seems futile. Russia is an energy rival to the U.S., but it is an energy partner to Europe. Adding Nord Stream to the bill creates more tensions. For all its talk about belonging in the European community, Ukraine has chosen Uncle Sam instead. [. . .]

"The Nord Stream II project undermines the solidarity in the E.U.," the company said in a statement yesterday as if that's Naftogaz's real concern.

What sense does any of this make in terms of U.S. national interests? The key is Rapoza's observation that "Trump has been beat up so severely on Russia that defending any sort of detente with the Kremlin seems futile." As with the worsening danger of U.S.-Russian confrontation in Syria, American policy on Europe, Ukraine, and Russia, along with related energy issues, is still in the hands of the Swamp Creatures. Nothing good can come of it unless and until Trump manages to gain effective control of the government of which he is the constitutionally elected head.

"'Collusion' Claims Backfire on Democrats Threefold, but Russia is More Evil Than Ever"

Jim Jatras | *Strategic Culture* | October 27, 2017

For months America and the rest of the world have been bombarded with hysterical claims from sore-loser Democrats, GOP Never-Trumpers, and their media shills that Donald Trump only won the 2016 election thanks to the hidden hand of that Mephistopheles of contemporary geopolitics, Vladimir Putin. Never mind that no evidence of any collusion between the Russians and anyone on the Trump team has been found, despite millions of dollars spent by Special Counsel Robert Mueller and several Congressional committees.

With the growing sense that there's no collusion to be found, the narrative lately had shifted towards a new story: maybe what the Russians were really doing was planting discord among Americans to exacerbate our social problems and destroy our faith in our democratic institutions. So, for a measly few hundred thousand dollars' worth of social media ads (many of them appearing after the election) on Facebook, Twitter, etc., Russian interests (we are never told who, exactly) aimed to "sow chaos and create divisions among Americans"—evidently in general, without any link to Trump or even particularly to help him. Among the favorite topics for socially divisive ads were left-leaning memes about Black Lives Matter and the environmental hazards of fracking, as well "a range of right-wing causes associated with Donald Trump's campaign," such as gun rights and illegal immigration. (Regarding the latter, let's not forget that, while remaining an unreconstructed KGB commie, Putin is also a tiki-torch wielding Grand Dragon of the global Alt-Right white nationalist movement. He's another Stalin and "literally Hitler" at the same time.) If not for dastardly Russian meddling, we would have no social problems at all, and everybody would be holding hands singing Kumabaya.

But now, with astonishing speed, just this week three stories have popped out that toss the whole Russian collusion tangle right back in face of Hillary Clinton and her party:

1. Hillary Clinton's presidential campaign and the Democratic National Committee paid for a defamatory "dossier" against Trump allegedly based on Russian sources:

> An explosive and salacious dossier alleging links between President Donald Trump and Russia was in part financed by Hillary Clinton's presidential campaign, according to a report Thursday.
> Marc E. Elias, a lawyer who represented Clinton's campaign and the Democratic National Committee, retained Fusion GPS, an intelligence firm that commissioned the former British intelligence officer Christopher Steele to produce the dossier, *The Washington Post* reported. . . . It has previously been reported that the dossier was financed by anti-Trump Republicans during the 2016 primary before Democrats picked up the tab. [. . .]
> The revelation comes amid increasing attempts by some Republicans on Capitol Hill to get Fusion GPS to reveal who financed the dossier. Last week, two Fusion GPS partners appeared before the House Intelligence Committee following a subpoena by the panel's Republican Chairman Devin Nunes. However, the firm's officials invoked their constitutional privilege not to answer any questions. [. . .]
> The dossier, first published by BuzzFeed News in January, garnered widespread attention in part to a particularly salacious allegation. It claimed that the Russian FSB spy agency possessed a compromising video of Trump getting Russian prostitutes to urinate on a Moscow hotel room bed once slept on by Obama and his wife, Michelle. [*Newsweek*, October 24: "TRUMP-RUSSIA 'PEE TAPE' DOSSIER WAS PAID FOR BY HILLARY CLINTON CAMPAIGN: REPORT"]

2. Russian investors are said to have paid millions of dollars to the Clinton Foundation and a half-million dollar speaking fee to Bill Clinton while Hillary, as Secretary of State, was considering approval of a controversial acquisition of a uranium-mining company:

> Multiple congressional committees are investigating an Obama-era deal that resulted in a Russian company purchasing American uranium mines.
> Lawmakers are also asking the Department of Justice to lift a reported gag order on a confidential informant who is expected to have more information about the agreement that allowed Russia to control about one-fifth of the uranium mining in the US—and former Secretary of State Hillary Clinton's involvement in it. [JGJ Note: The gag order was lifted shortly after this story was posted.]

President Trump called the Uranium One deal "the real Russia story" as federal investigators continue to probe Russia's alleged involvement in the 2016 election. And *The Hill* recently reported that Russian officials engaged in a "racketeering scheme" to further its energy goals in the US.

In 2013, Russian company Rosatom acquired a Canadian uranium mining company, now called Uranium One, which has assets in the US Uranium is key to making nuclear weapons. Through the deal, Russia is able to own about 20 percent of US uranium production capacity. [. . .]

The agreement was approved by nine government agencies with the Committee on Foreign Investment in the United States (CFIUS), an inter-agency group that reviews how certain foreign investments can impact national security. Clinton's State Department was one of those agencies, though the former secretary of state told WMUR-TV in 2015 that she was not "personally involved" in the agreement. [. . .]

Republicans have largely decried the deal, especially as some investors reportedly donated millions of dollars to the Clinton Foundation. Former President Bill Clinton also received a $500,000 speaking fee in Russia and reportedly met with Vladimir Putin around the time of the deal.

The FBI had looked into the agreement and uncovered that some Russian nuclear industry officials were engaged in nefarious dealings, which included extortion, bribery and kickbacks, *The Hill* reported. Evidence of wrongdoing by Vadim Mikerin, the Russian official overseeing Putin's nuclear expansion in the US who was eventually sentenced to prison, was discovered by the FBI before the deal was approved, according to *The Hill*. [Fox News, October 25: "Obama-era Russian Uranium One deal: What to know"]

3. A firm linked to Hillary Clinton's presidential campaign chairman, John Podesta, is reportedly under investigation by Mueller for influence-peddling on behalf of Russian interests:

Tony Podesta [John's brother] and the Podesta Group are now the subjects of a federal investigation being led by Special Counsel Robert Mueller, three sources with knowledge of the matter told NBC News.

The probe of Podesta and his Democratic-leaning lobbying firm grew out of Mueller's inquiry into the finances of former Trump campaign chairman Paul Manafort, according to the sources. As special counsel, Mueller has been tasked with investigating possible collusion between the Trump campaign and Russia.

Manafort had organized a public relations campaign for a nonprofit called the European Centre for a Modern Ukraine (ECMU). . . . The ECMU was reportedly backed by the Party of Regions, the pro-Russian and oligarch-funded Ukrainian political party for which Manafort worked as a consultant, and which paid his firm millions.' [NBC News, October 24: "Mueller Now Investigating Democratic Lobbyist Tony Podesta"]

At this point no one knows what impact these developments will have or how they relate to one another. But two things are certain. First, at least for a while, Trump supporters and much of the Republican party, plus media like Fox News, will be dancing with glee, whooping it up that the Democrats have now been caught in their own "RussiaGate" snare. How much real change there will be in the political landscape, either in getting rid of the collusion cloud over Trump's head or dragging down Hillary, the Podestas, and their cronies, remains to be seen.

Second, it's already clear that Trump's defenders are at least as thrilled to play the anti-Russian card as the Democrats have been:

- What does Democratic funding of the Christopher Steele dossier mean? The Democrats were implementing a Russian *"Chekist provokatsiya"* to smear Trump! (Never mind that there's no evidence the Russians had anything at all to do with what may well be a total fabrication by Steele and his pals in the shadowy world of British intelligence. (Let's not forget the possible role of GCHQ in monitoring then-candidate Trump.) Or maybe it's the fruit of the warped imagination of the yet-to-be identified Republican who funded Steele. Or maybe the FBI, which also paid Steele.)
- Why did the Russians bribe Bill and Hillary with speaking fees? To get their filthy paws on American uranium and "corner the market" on "the foundational material for nuclear weapons"! (Never mind that no less than the United States, Russia—which sits right next to friendly Kazakhstan, the world's top uranium producer—can make as many warheads as desired; access to sufficient uranium isn't an issue. As for the bribes, why should it be a surprise that some Russians would play the same game as the Saudis, Emiratis, Qataris, Ukrainians, and others who "contributed" the coffers of the likely next, and highly corrupt, president of the United States?)
- What were the Podesta Group and Manafort doing working for an NGO supported by Ukraine's Party of Regions? Peddling influence for Putin! (Just try to explain to anyone in Washington that working for Yanukovych and "Putin lobbying" weren't necessarily the same thing.)

In short, whatever the fallout in terms US internal politics, the root of all evil, for Republicans and Democrats alike, will remain the vast Russian conspiracy and its demon mastermind in the Kremlin.

"Attack on RT Is Another Step Towards Sovietization of American Media"

Jim Jatras | *Strategic Culture* | November 18, 2017

This week the US Department of Justice Criminal Division forced the Russian-funded television network RT (formerly Russia Today) to register as a "foreign agent" under the Foreign Agents Registration Act (FARA). Failure to comply would have risked arrest of RT's management and seizure of its assets. The move comes on the heels of Senators' recent demands that terrified tech giants Twitter, Facebook, and Google act as ideological filters.

With no discernable defenders among America's media establishment, RT rightly denounced the selective FARA mandate as an attack on media freedom—which it is. But more ominous is what the move against RT says about America's rulers' further intention to limit the sources of information available to its subjects.

As Daniel McAdams of the Ron Paul Institute writes:

> RT America is a news organization operating in the United States that is funded at least partly by a foreign government. So is the BBC. So is Deutsche Welle, France24, Al-Jazeera, and numerous other foreign media organizations. It is assumed that they all to a degree reflect the editorial interests of those who pay the bills.
>
> The same is true with other, non-state funded media outlets, of course. It's up to us to factor these things in when we consume media. That's what it means to be a free people.
>
> A core value in a free society is that our own government has zero power over what we read, what we watch, how we think, how we come to interpret current events, the conclusions we draw based on these inputs, and so on. These are private matters over which any government that is not tyrannical should have no sway.
>
> The real insidiousness of tyrannical systems is that the government most lasciviously seeks control over most private spaces—including the most private space called our brain, our intellect, our conscience. We must be free to follow our interests down whatever path they may lead us so that we may reach our own conclusions and then perhaps test them ourselves in the marketplace of ideas.

The attack on RT (and another Russian network, Sputnik, which evidently has not yet been given a deadline for registration) is a milestone in the degeneration of the American official (call them what you want—corporate, legacy, mainstream) media into PR agencies for the governing establishment and its ideological imperatives. We've been moving along this path for a while now, and it's going to get worse.

Long gone are those halcyon days of yore when Americans could just sit back and watch CBS's Walter Cronkite with total confidence they were getting the truth, the whole truth, and nothing but the truth. (For youngsters who have no idea who the hell Cronkite was, just Google "most trusted man in America.") Back in the naïve infancy of the TV age, from about the 1950s until the beginning of the 1990s, there was a common national media culture that reflected the established, generally liberal, mainly Democratic tilt of the American *inteligentsiya* that was almost uniform among the (then only) three networks and a handful of major newspapers and magazines. To be sure, that was also a ruling class media of a sort, but it reflected a broad and deep social consensus.

Those days are no more. Perhaps the unraveling of media trust and social consensus alike started in earnest with Vietnam. But still, for decades afterwards there still seemed to be plenty of empty cranial receptacles for government and corporate propaganda of the first Gulf War under Bush 41, Bill Clinton's phony humanitarian wars in the Balkans, Bush 43's Iraq War, and Obama's Libyan and Syrian imbroglios. Sadly, there are many such cranial receptacles even today.

By its attack on RT, the US government is officially telling us that only the mainstream media (MSM) can be regarded as are purveyors of Truth (with a capital T) and that anybody not on the approved list is fake. How do we know? Why, the MSM themselves tell us! *The Washington Post*'s "Democracy Dies in Darkness." CNN's "Facts First." *The New York Times*' "The Truth is Hard." (The fact that certifiably authoritative and truthful media are militantly hostile to Russia, not to mention to Donald Trump, is purely coincidental.)

A lot of Americans don't buy it anymore, though. Some of the skepticism falls along purely partisan lines reflecting increasing moral and political polarization: *our* media (which I exclusively consult) tells the truth, but *your* media (which I don't consult) are liars. About one-third of Americans get their talking points from, say, Michael Moore, and from Rachel Maddow on MSNBC, with their related internet echoes, while another third gets theirs from Rush Limbaugh, and from Sean Hannity on Fox News, and their internet echo chambers. Increasingly, there is nothing like a national dialogue on anything, but rather two entirely separate, diametrically opposed ideological cultures—and alternate realities—each demonizing "them." This is why when after Barack Obama's election the Tea Party appeared, the GOP fell over itself trying to co-opt them, while the Democrats denounced them as a mob of racists and subversives. When later the "Occupy" and Black Lives Matter movements broke out on the Left, the Democrats tried to figure out how to channel it while top Republicans denounced it as gang of commie anarchists and losers.

With the election of Donald Trump the divide intensified further to one of latent civil war.

At some point the false picture of pseudo-reality (as Alain Besançon called it in the late Soviet propaganda context) diverges so far from *real* reality that the official media narrative becomes useless and even counterproductive. While a majority of Americans probably are still glued to the partisan outlets of "their" side of the political divide, there is a growing sense across the spectrum that not only the MSM but even partisan media like Fox News and MSNBC are untrustworthy.

In the past, notably in the totalitarian societies of the 20th century, maintaining the credibility of official media required the physical repression of alternatives. Today, such a crude approach is unnecessary and almost technologically unfeasible, even for such undemocratic countries as Iran, Cuba, and Saudi Arabia (though North Korea may be successful through the sheer unavailability of modern communications technology to most of the population). Instead of suppressing dissent, is it sufficient to maintain major media's role as gatekeeper and certifier of reliability.

Which brings us back to the impact of foreign media like RT, Sputnik, Strategic Culture Foundation, Al-Jazeera, CGTN, Press TV, often in parallel with alternative media like Zero Hedge, Lew Rockwell, Antiwar.com, Ron Paul Institute, and others, to break through the information firewall but arguably then being influenced by the agenda of the sponsoring foreign governments. In any case, a growing segment of the American public is discovering a skill once well-honed by the citizens of the former communist countries: reading between the lines of the official media (which is assumed to be full of lies) and making informed comparisons to *samizdat* alternative media, foreign sources, and the rumor-mill to guess what the truth might be.

Make no mistake—what has started with RT won't end with RT. Our betters have decided they need to protect our minds from "propaganda" penetration that might cause us to doubt the truth of what CNN and the Washington Post tell us.

Citizens! Be grateful for such wise leaders and dedicated information workers! Smash the enemy voices that seek to undermine our democracy as we march boldly into the radiant future!

"Can the Impending Collapse of Russiagate Halt the Slide Toward a Nuclear 1914?"

Jim Jatras | *Strategic Culture* | February 2, 2018

In the period preceding World War I how many Europeans suspected that their lives would soon be forever changed—and, for millions of them, ended? Who in the years, say, 1910 to 1913, could have imagined that the decades of peace, progress, and civilization in which they had grown up, and which seemingly would continue indefinitely, instead would soon descend into a horror of industrial-scale slaughter, revolution, and brutal ideologies?

The answer is, probably very few, just as few people today care much about the details of international and security affairs. Normal folk have better things to do with their lives.

To be sure, in that bygone era of smug jingosim, there was always the entertainment aspect that "our" side had forced "theirs" to back down in some exotic locale, as in the Fashoda incident (1898) or the Moroccan crises (1906, 1911). Even the Balkan Wars of 1912–13 seemed less a harbinger of the cataclysm to come than local dustups on the edge of the continent where the general peace had not been disturbed even by the much more disruptive Crimean or Franco-Prussian wars.

Besides, no doubt level-headed statesmen were in charge in the various capitals, ensuring that things wouldn't get out of hand.

Until they did.

A notable exception to the prevailing mood of business-as-usual, nothing-to-see-here-folks was Pyotr Durnovo, whose remarkable February 1914 memorandum to Tsar Nicholas II laid out not only what the great powers would do in the approaching general war but the behavior of the minor countries as well. Moreover, he anticipated that in the event of defeat, Russia, destabilized by unchecked socialist "agitation" amid wartime hardships, would "be flung into hopeless anarchy, the issue of which cannot be foreseen." Germany, likewise, was "destined to suffer, in case of defeat, no lesser social upheavals" and "take a purely revolutionary path" of a nationalist hue.

When the great powers blundered into war in August 1914, each confident of its ability speedily to dispatch its rivals, the price (adding in the toll from the 1939–1945 rematch) was upwards of 70 million lives. But the cost of a comparable mistake today might be literally incalculable—if there's anyone left to do the tally.

During the first Cold War between the US and the USSR, there was a general sense that a World War III was, in a word, unthinkable. As summed up by Ronald Reagan: "A nuclear war cannot be won and must never be fought." Then, it was understood that all-out war, however it started, meant massed ICBMs over the North Pole and the "end of civilization as we know it."

Not anymore. What was unthinkable in the old Cold War has become all-too-thinkable in the new one between the US and Russia. As described by veteran arms control inspector Scott Ritter, in analyzing a draft of the 2018 US Nuclear Posture Review (NPR), the US threshold for the use of nuclear weapons has become dangerously low:

> The 2018 NPR has a vision of nuclear conflict that goes far beyond the traditional imagery of mass missile launches. While ICBMs and manned bombers will be maintained on a day-to-day alert, the tip of the nuclear spear is now what the NPR calls "supplemental" nuclear forces—dual-use aircraft such as the F–35 fighter armed with B–61 gravity bombs capable of delivering a low-yield nuclear payload, a new generation of nuclear-tipped submarine-launched cruise

missiles, and submarine-launched ballistic missiles tipped with a new generation of low-yield nuclear warheads. The danger inherent with the integration of these kinds of tactical nuclear weapons into an overall strategy of deterrence is that it fundamentally lowers the threshold for their use. [. . .]

Noting that the United States has never adopted a "no first use" policy, the 2018 NPR states that "it remains the policy of the United States to retain some ambiguity regarding the precise circumstances that might lead to a US nuclear response." In this regard, the NPR states that America could employ nuclear weapons under "extreme circumstances that could include significant non-nuclear strategic attacks." . . . The issue of "non-nuclear strategic attack technologies" as a potential precursor for nuclear war is a new factor that previously did not exist in American policy. The United States has long held that chemical and biological weapons represent a strategic threat for which America's nuclear deterrence capability serves as a viable counter. But the threat from cyber attacks is different. If for no other reason than the potential for miscalculation and error in terms of attribution and intent, the nexus of cyber and nuclear weapons should be disconcerting for everyone. [. . .]

Even more disturbing is the notion that a cyber intrusion such as the one perpetrated against the Democratic National Committee and attributed to Russia could serve as a trigger for nuclear war. This is not as far-fetched as it sounds. The DNC event has been characterized by influential American politicians, such as the Armed Services Committee Chairman John McCain, as "an act of war." Moreover, former vice president Joe Biden hinted that, in the aftermath of the DNC breach, the United States was launching a retaliatory cyberattack of its own, targeting Russia. The possibility of a tit-for-tat exchange of cyberattacks that escalates into a nuclear conflict would previously have been dismissed out of hand; today, thanks to the 2018 NPR, it has entered the realm of the possible.

The idea that a first-strike Schlieffen Plan could knock out the Russians (and no doubt similar contingencies are in place for China) at the outset of hostilities reflects a dangerous illusion of predictability. Truth may be the first casualty of war, but "the plan" is inevitably the second. That's because war planners generally don't consult the enemy, who—annoyingly for the planners—also gets a vote.

Recently US Secretary of Defense James Mattis declared that "great power competition—not terrorism—is now the primary focus of US national security," specifying Russia and China as nations seeking to "create a world consistent with their authoritarian models, pursuing veto authority over other nations' economic, diplomatic and security decisions." At least we can drop the pretense that US policy has been to fight jihad terrorism, not to use it as a policy tool in Afghanistan, Bosnia, Kosovo, Libya, Syria, and elsewhere. And of course Washington never, ever meddles in "other nations' economic, diplomatic and security decisions" . . .

There is much anticipation that release of a House Intelligence Committee memo "naming names" of those in the FBI and elsewhere inside and outside of government to thwart the election of Donald Trump and cripple his administration with a phony Russian "collusion" probe will be a silver bullet that upturns the Mueller probe and cleans the Augean stables of the Deep State. Even in that unlikely case, the damage is already done. The primary purpose of Russiagate was always to ensure Trump could not reach out to

Moscow, as seems to be his sincere desire. Even as the narrative began to boomerang against those who launched it, Trump's defenders (such as fanatical Russophobe Nikki Haley) are as adamant as his detractors that Russia is and will remain the main enemy: Russia was behind the Steele Dossier, Russia tried to "corner the market" on "the foundational material for nuclear weapons" with the Uranium One deal, etc. Hostility toward Russia is not a means to an end—it is the end.

At this point Trump is fastened to the neocons' and generals' axle, and all he can do is spin. Echoing Mattis, in his State of the Union speech Trump lumped "rivals like China and Russia" together with "rogue regimes" and "terrorist groups" as "horrible dangers" to the United States. (Note: The word "horrible" does not appear in the posted text. That evidently was Trump's adlib.) The recently issued "name and shame" list of prominent Russians is a veritable *Who's Who* of government and business, ensuring that there's no American engagement with anyone within screaming distance of the Kremlin.

To be fair, the Russians and Chinese are making their own war preparations. Russia's "Kanyon," a doomsday nuclear torpedo carrying a massive warhead, is designed to obliterate the U.S east and west coasts, rendering them uninhabitable for generations. (Wait a minute. Is it any coincidence, Comrade, that the coastal cities are just where the Democrats' electoral strength is? Talk about "collusion!" Somebody call Bob Mueller!) For its part, China is developing means to eliminate our white elephant carrier groups— handy for pummeling Third World backwaters but useless in a war with a major power—with drone swarms and hypersonic missiles.

Just as in 1914, when Durnovo referred to "presence of abundant combustible material in Europe," there is any number of global flashpoints that could turn Mattis's "great power competition" into a major conflagration that probably was not desired by anyone. However, if the worst happens, and the lamps go out again—maybe this time forever—Americans will not again be immune from the consequences as we were in the wars of the 20th century. The remainder of our lives, however brief, might turn out very differently from what we had anticipated.

"Is the Steele Dossier Full of 'Russian Dirt'—or British?"

Jim Jatras | *Strategic Culture* | February 9, 2018

With text messages between US Justice Department (DOJ) conspirators Peter Strzok and his adulterous main squeeze Lisa Page now revealing that then-President Barack Obama "wants to know everything we're doing," it now appears that the 2016 plot to subvert the rule of law and corrupt the US organs of state security for political purposes reached the very pinnacle of power. To call the United States today a "banana republic" increasingly may be seen as a gratuitous insult to the friendly spider-infested nations to our south.

Still, don't expect to see Barry Hussein Saetoro doing the perp walk anytime soon or even being deported back to Kenya. Don't expect to see orange prison suits on Strzok, Page, former FBI Director James Comey, former Associate Deputy Attorney General Bruce Ohr, former Deputy FBI Director Andrew McCabe, and others implicated in putting a political thumb on the scales to, first, get Hillary Clinton elected, and then, when that failed, to neuter Donald Trump's presidency with a phony Russiagate probe. Officials' getting "former-ed" is one thing, their getting prosecuted quite another. (Just imagine if a GOP administration had similarly skewed the supposedly non-political law enforcement and intelligence services for partisan reasons. We'd have Watergate on steroids. *The New York Times, Washington Post* and *CNN* would be calling for hanging, drawing, and quartering.)

Indeed, it's not even clear the Russiagate investigation itself will be impacted. After all, the narrative may have flipped on one *variable*—from Trump campaign collusion to Democratic and FBI collusion—but the constant remains the same: Russia. Trump's defenders are as insistent as his detractors that the *real* culprit is Russia! Russia! Russia!

Sean Hannity of Fox News has been particularly hyperventilative that the entire Steele Dossier lying at the black heart of the mess consists of "phony, fake-news Russian propaganda" and "Russian intelligence lies" from British MI6 (supposedly "former") spymaster Christopher Steele's "Russian sources." Even level-headed observers like Paul Sperry and Patrick Buchanan characterize the file as a "Kremlin-aided smear job" and "Russian dirt [that] Steele was spoon-fed by old comrades in the Kremlin's security apparatus."

Christopher Steele is not Russian

But what do we really know about Steele's claimed sources? Not much.

Sure, maybe Vladimir Putin personally whispered every word of the dossier into Steele's ear. Or maybe Steele invented his supposed sources from whole cloth: your clients are paying for sleaze, you give them sleaze. Or anything in between: maybe Steele consulted some imaginative Russian cranks with only a marginal, and most likely adversarial, relationship to the Russian authorities, whose "inside knowledge" Steele padded to justify his fee. (Steele claims he didn't pay his "sources"—assuming they exist at all—but that's no more worthy of credit than anything else he says.)

As analyzed by Russia expert Stephen F. Cohen:

Where, then, . . . did Steele get his information? According to Steele and his many stenographers—which include his American employers, Democratic Party Russiagaters, the mainstream media, and even progressive publications—it came from his "deep connections in Russia," specifically from retired and current Russian intelligence officials in or near the Kremlin. From the moment the dossier began to be leaked to the American media, this seemed highly implausible (as reporters who took his bait should have known) for several reasons:

- Steele has not returned to Russia after leaving his post there in the early 1990s. Since then, the main Russian intelligence agency, the FSB, has undergone many personnel and other changes, especially after 2000, and especially in or near Putin's Kremlin. Did Steele really have such "connections" so many years later? [JGJ: *Is it credible that the head of MI6's Russian branch is on a first-name basis with top Kremlin insiders? Turn the identities around and ask whether the chiefs of the US section of Russian or Chinese intelligence are on intimate speaking terms with the US president's top advisers or with the leadership of the CIA or FBI. Hardly.*]

- Even if he did, would these purported Russian insiders really have collaborated with this "former" British intelligence agent under what is so widely said to be the ever-vigilant eye of the ruthless "former KGB agent" Vladimir Putin, thereby risking their positions, income, perhaps freedom, as well as the well-being of their families?

- Originally it was said that his Russian sources were highly paid by Steele. Arguably, this might have warranted the risk. But subsequently Steele's employer and head of Fusion GPS, Glenn Simpson, wrote in *The New York Times* that "Steele's sources in Russia . . . were not paid." If the Putin Kremlin's purpose was to put Trump in the White House, why then would these "Kremlin-connected" sources have contributed to Steele's anti-Trump project without financial or political gain—only with considerable risk?

- There is the also the telling matter of factual mistakes in the dossier that Kremlin "insiders" were unlikely to have made, but this is the subject for a separate analysis.

And indeed we now know that Steele had at least three other "sources" for the dossier, ones not previously mentioned by him or his employer. There was the information from foreign intelligence agencies provided by Brennan to Steele or to the FBI, which we also now know was collaborating with Steele. There was . . . a "second Trump-Russia dossier" prepared by people personally close to Hillary Clinton and who shared their "findings" with Steele. And most intriguingly, there was the "research" provided by Nellie Ohr, wife of a top Department of Justice official, Bruce Ohr, who, according to the Republican memo, "was employed by Fusion GPS to assist in the cultivation of opposition research on Trump. Ohr later provided the FBI with all of his wife's opposition research." Most likely, it found its way into Steele's dossier. (Mrs. Ohr was a trained Russian Studies scholar with a PhD from Stanford and a onetime assistant professor at Vassar, and thus, it must have seemed, an ideal collaborator for Steele.)

The reference to "people personally close to Hillary Clinton and who shared their 'findings' with Steele" dovetails with another intriguing suggestion from former Clinton insider Dick Morris, who knows the modus operandi of the Clinton lie generator better than anyone else. On the Fox News "Ingraham Angle" show, Morris suggested to host Laura Ingraham that the bulk of the dossier was invented by veteran political dirty tricksters and Clinton-machine hatchet men Sid Blumenthal and Cody Shearer, who then engaged "former" spook Steele, because of the Brit's known relationship with the FBI, as their conduit to give their garbage credibility. (Never under-estimate the residual "colonial" mentality of Yanks to find any sort of gibberish convincing if delivered with a British accent, as confirmed by the ubiquity of posh Brit voices in American advertising.)

Andrew Wood is not Russian

But Steele isn't the only limey link to #Dossiergate. In late 2016, after Trump's election victory, Andrew Wood, a former British ambassador to Russia, told US Senator John McCain about the existence of compromising material on Donald Trump, according to Wood's account to BBC4. Wood then set up a meeting between Steele and David Kramer, an associate of McCain's. It's unclear whether McCain already knew about the dossier at that point or whether Wood alerted the Senator to its existence.

For what it is worth—not much—Wood states that McCain had obtained the documents from the Senator's own sources. "I told him I was aware of what was in the report but I had not read it myself, that it might be true, it might be untrue. I had no means of judging really," and that he served only to inform McCain about the dossier contents: "My mission was essentially to be a go-between and a messenger, to tell the Senator and assistants that such a dossier existed," Wood told Fox News. Wood elsewhere relates that McCain was "visibly shocked" at his description and expressed interest in reading the full report. That doesn't sound as though McCain had already obtained the dossier from his "own sources" but, rather, that Wood was the instigator.

So which is it? Did McCain already know about the dossier, and if so how did it "happen" to get raised with a British diplomat? Conversely, was the initiative from Woods to induce the Senator—known to be a strong Trump critic as well as for his hostility to Russia—to pass the dossier on in Washington? Keep in mind that the dossier had already been used to secure a Foreign Intelligence Surveillance Act (FISA) warrant to monitor Carter Page, a peripheral asteroid in the Trump orbit, and that Trump had already been elected. By this time the conspiracy's purpose had shifted from preventing Trump's victory to tying down his incoming administration, especially with respect to blocking any opening to Moscow as Trump said he intended to do. What better way to set the cat among the pigeons than for a supposedly totally non-political British diplomat (certainly no intelligence officer, he!) to quietly peddle the material from Steele (whom Wood called a "very competent professional operator... I do not think he would make things up.") to the right man in Washington?

GCHQ is not Russian

Finally, while it's clear the dossier served to get a FISA warrant for American services to spy on the Trump campaign and later the transition team, US agencies' might not have been the only eyes and ears monitoring them. Amid all the hubbub over Michael Wolff's slash-and-burn Fire and Fury, little mention (other than a heated denial on the floor of the House of Commons, from the notoriously truth-challenged former prime minister Tony Blair, and from the relevant British agency itself!) has been made of the suggestion that the UK's Government Communications Headquarters (GCHQ)—Britain's version of the NSA—was spying on Trump and providing their sister agencies in the US with additional data. Keep in mind the carefully worded deflection last year from James Clapper, former Director of National Intelligence (DNI), that "there was no wiretap against Trump Tower during the campaign conducted by any part of the national intelligence community... including the FBI," thus begging the question of whether Trump was spied on not by a US "national" agency but by one of the Anglosphere "Five Eyes" agencies—most likely GCHQ—which then passed the information back to their American colleagues. With Steele's and Wood's involvement, and given the virtual control of America's manifestly corrupted agencies of their counterparts in satellite countries like the United Kingdom, involvement by GCHQ and perhaps other "friendly" foreign agencies cannot be dismissed out of hand.

Madame Prime Minister is not Russian

To be sure, in 2016 the majority opinion in Russia was that Donald Trump's election would be preferable to Hillary Clinton's for the simple reason that the former openly advocated better relations with Moscow while the latter was a notorious warmonger. But there was also a strong minority view, especially among more pro-Western elements of the Russian establishment, that Hillary—"the devil you know"—was preferable to rolling the dice on an unpredictable and unknown quantity. Plus, Hillary was delightfully corrupt, with the Clinton Foundation an open invitation for many foreign powers to buy influence.

There was no ambiguity in the position of the British government, however. In 2016 Prime Minister Theresa May, like her German counterpart, made little effort to hide her disdain for the "just plain wrong" Trump and her preference for Hillary Clinton, whom she expected to win (as did most other observers). Why should anyone be surprised that her MI6 and GCHQ minions would share the same views and perhaps acted on them to provide some helping "hands across the water" to their US counterparts whose anti-constitutional conspiracy now stands exposed?

"The US–UK Deep State Empire Strikes Back: 'It's Russia! Russia! Russia!'"

Jim Jatras | *Strategic Culture* | February 18, 2018

There's no defense like a good offense.

For weeks the unfolding story in Washington has been how a cabal of conspirators in the heart of the American federal law enforcement and intelligence apparat colluded to ensure the election of Hillary Clinton and, when that failed, to undermine the nascent presidency of Donald Trump. Agencies tainted by this corruption include not only the FBI and the Department of Justice (DOJ) but the Obama White House, the State Department, the NSA, and the CIA, plus their British sister organizations MI6 and GCHQ, possibly along with the British Foreign Office (with the involvement of former British ambassador to Russia Andrew Wood) and even Number 10 Downing Street.

Those implicated form a regular rogue's gallery of the Deep State: Peter Strzok (formerly Chief of the FBI's Counterespionage Section, then Deputy Assistant Director of the Counterintelligence Division; busy bee Strzok is implicated not only in exonerating Hillary from her email server crimes but initiating the Russiagate investigation in the first place, securing a FISA warrant using the dodgy "Steele Dossier," and nailing erstwhile National Security Adviser General Mike Flynn on a bogus charge of "lying to the FBI"); Lisa Page (Strzok's paramour and a DOJ lawyer formerly assigned to the all-star Democrat lineup on the Robert Mueller Russigate inquisition); former FBI Director James Comey, former Associate Deputy Attorney General Bruce Ohr, former Deputy FBI Director Andrew McCabe, and—let's not forget—current Deputy Attorney General Rod Rosenstein, himself implicated by having signed at least one of the dubious FISA warrant requests. Finally, there's reason to believe that former CIA Director John O. Brennan may have been the mastermind behind the whole operation.

Not to be overlooked is the possible implication of a pack of former Democratic administration officials, including former Attorney General Loretta Lynch, former National Security Adviser Susan Rice, and President Barack Obama himself, who according to text communications between Strzok and Page "wants to know everything we're doing." Also involved is the DNC, the Clinton campaign, and Clinton operatives Sidney Blumenthal and Cody Shearer—rendering the ignorance of Hillary herself totally implausible.

On the British side we have "former" (suuure . . .) MI6 spook Christopher Steele, diplomat Wood, former GCHQ chief Robert Hannigan (who resigned a year ago under mysterious circumstances), and whoever they answered to in the Prime Minister's office.

The growing sense of panic was palpable. Oh my—this is a curtain that just cannot be allowed to be pulled back!

What to do, what to do . . .

Ah, here's the ticket—come out swinging against the main enemy. That's not even Donald Trump. It's Russia and Vladimir Putin. Russia! Russia! Russia!

Hence the unveiling of an indictment against 13 Russian citizens and three companies for alleged meddling in U.S. elections and various ancillary crimes.

For the sake of discussion, let's assume all the allegations in the indictment are true, however unlikely that is to be the case. (While that would be the American legal rule for a complaint in a civil case, this is a criminal indictment, where there is supposedly a presumption of innocence. Rosenstein even mentioned that in his press conference, pretending not to notice that that presumption doesn't apply to Russian *Untermenschen*—certainly not to Olympic athletes and really not to Russians at all, who are presumed guilty on "genetic" grounds.)

Based on the public announcement of the indictment by Rosenstein—who is effectively the Attorney General in place of the *pro forma* holder of that office, Jeff Sessions (R-Recused)—and on an initial examination of the indictment, and we can already draw a few conclusions:

- Finally, "collusion" is dead! If Mueller and the anti-constitutional cabal had any hint that anyone on the Trump team cooperated with those indicted, they would have included it. They didn't. That means that after months and months of "investigation"—or really, setting "perjury traps" and trying to nail people on unrelated accusations, like Paul Manafort's alleged circumvention of lobbying and financial reporting laws—and wasting however many millions of dollars, Mueller and his merry band got nothing. Zip. Zilch. Bupkes. Nada. The fake charge that Trump colluded with the Russians is exposed as the fraud it always was.
- And yet, "collusion" still lives! But while there is no actual allegation (much less evidence) that any American, much less anyone on the Trump team, "colluded" with the indicted Russians, the indictment makes it clear that Moscow sought to support Trump and disparage Hillary. Thus, Trump is guilty of being favored by Russia even if there was no actual cooperation. It's a kind of zombie walking dead collusion, collusion by intent (of someone else) absent actual collusion. Its purpose in the indictment is to discredit Trump as a Russian puppet, albeit an unwitting one. The indictment says the Russian desperados supported Bernie Sanders and Jill Stein too—so they're also Putin's dupes.
- Any and every Russian equals Putin. Incredibly, nothing in the indictment points to any connection of those indicted to the Russian government! This is on a par with the hysteria over social media placements by

"Russian interests" on account of which hysterical Senators demanded that tech giants impose content controls, or dimwit CIA agents getting bilked out of $100,000 by a Russian scam artist in Berlin in exchange for—well, pretty much nothing. (The CIA denies it, which leads one to suspect it is true.) Paragraph 95 of the indictment points to what amounted to a click-bait scam to fleece American merchants and social media sites from between $25 and $50 per post for promotional content. Paragraph 88 refers to "self-enrichment" as one motive of the alleged operation. That makes a lot more sense than the bone-headed claim in the indictment that the Russian goal was to "sow discord in the U.S. political system" by posting content on "divisive U.S. political and social issues." What! Americans disagree about stuff? The Russians are setting us against each other! In announcing the indictment, Rosenstein said the Russians wanted to "promote discord in the United States and undermine public confidence in democracy. We must not allow them to succeed." (He wagged his finger with resolve at that point.) It evidently doesn't occur to Rosenstein that he and his pals have undermined public confidence in our institutions by perverting them for political ends.

- Demonizing dissent. Those indicted allegedly sought to attract Americans' attention to their diabolical machinations through appeal to hot-button issues (immigration, Black Lives Matter, religion, etc.) and popular hashtags (#Trump2016, #TrumpTrain, #MAGA, #Hillary4Prison). Have you taken a stand on divisive issues, Dear Reader? Have you used any of these hashtags? *Are you reading this commentary?* You too might be an unwitting Russian stooge! Vladimir Putin is inside your head! Hopefully DOJ will set up a hotline where patriotic citizens influenced without their knowledge can now report themselves, now that they've been alerted. Are you a thought criminal, comrade?

- An amateurish, penny-ante scheme with no results—compared to what the U.S. does. At worst, even if all the allegations in the indictment are true—a big "if"—it would still amount to the kind of garden-variety kicking each other under the table that a lot of countries routinely engage in. As described in the indictment this gargantuan Russian scheme was (as reported by *Politico*) an "expensive [sic] effort that cost millions of dollars and employed as many as hundreds of people." *Millions* of dollars! *Hundreds* of people! How did the American republic manage to survive the onslaught? Rosenstein was keen to point out for the umpteenth time that nothing the Russians are alleged to have done (never mind what they actually might have done, which is far less) had any impact on the election. That stands in sharp contrast to the lavishly funded, multifaceted, global political influence and meddling operations the U.S. conducts in nations around the world under the guise of "democracy promotion." The National Endowment for Democracy (NED), along with its Democratic and Republican sub-organizations, can be considered the flagship of a community of ostensibly private but government-funded or subsidized organizations that provides the soft compliment to American hard military power. The various governmental, quasi-governmental, and non-governmental components of this network—sometimes called the "Demintern" in analogy to the Comintern, an organization comparable in global ambition if differing in ideology and methods—are also coordinated internationally at the official level through the less-well-known "Community of Democracies." It is often difficult to know where the "official" entities (CIA, NATO, the State Department, Pentagon, USAID) divide from ostensibly nongovernmental but tax dollar-supported groups (NED, Freedom House, Radio Free Europe/Radio Liberty) and privately funded organizations that cooperate with them towards common goals (especially the Open Society organizations funded by billionaire George Soros). Among the specialties of this network are often *successful* "color revolutions" targeting leaders and governments disfavored by Washington for regime change—a far cry from the pathetic Russian operation alleged in the indictment.

• "Mitt Romney was right." Already many of Trump's supporters are not only crowing with satisfaction that the indictment proves there was no collusion but refocusing their gaze from the domestic culprits within the FBI, DOJ, etc., to a bogus foreign threat. "This whole saga just brings back the 2012 election, and the fact that Mitt Romney was right" for "suggesting that Russia is our greatest geopolitical foe," is the new GOP meme. To the extent that Russiagate was less about Trump than ensuring that enmity with Russia will be permanent and will continue to deepen, this latest Mueller indictment is a smashing success already.

The Mueller indictment against the Russians is a well-timed effort to distract Americans' attention from the real collusion rotting the core of our public life by shifting attention to a foreign enemy. Many of the people behind it are the very officials who are themselves complicit in the rot. But the sad fact is that it will probably work.

"Russia Really Is America's No. 1 Enemy— Depending on Who 'America' Is"

Jim Jatras | *Strategic Culture* | April 29, 2018

US-Russia enmity is here to stay. Cold War II is a fact of life for the foreseeable future. The only questions are where, when, and how it might turn hot. That didn't happen in Syria this past Friday the Thirteenth, for reasons yet to be explained. But the danger is by no means gone.

Rather, the threat of a major war will continue to intensify as President Donald Trump continues to stack his team with GOP retreads who diametrically oppose his oft-repeated desire to improve ties with Moscow. Whether or not his desire is genuine is irrelevant. With each new appointment to the National Security Council and the State Department the Russophobic critical mass grows.

Personnel is policy. The door to rapprochement is being nailed ever more firmly shut. "FISAgate" and the Christopher Steele "dirty dossier," on top of bogus claims of Russian election meddling, have done their job. It would be remiss not to mention the major role played by British special services. The dossier itself, authored by a "retired" MI6 agent. The British diplomat (or another spook?) who passed it on to a top GOP Trump critic, and thence to then-FBI Director James Comey. The likelihood that GCHQ spied on Trump and his team. The Salisbury chemical provocation. The Douma chemical provocation.

Never forget that however culpable the likes of Comey, James Clapper, John Brennan, and others are, they had a lot of help from their "Five Eyes" pals abroad. There was foreign interference, alright, in what we still quaintly call "our democracy." But it was British, not Russian.

The fact that the House Intelligence Committee wrapped up its investigation having found no evidence of Russian collusion makes no difference.
Neither does the fact that Robert Mueller's probe won't turn up any evidence
either, since it doesn't exist. If Mueller nails Trump—and he well might—it
won't be because of anything to do with Russia, it will be a "process crime" like
perjury or obstruction trumped up during the investigation (cf., Flynn, Papadopoulos) or related to something in Trump's business and personal life (a
supposed election law violation for a payoff to Stormy Daniels, corners cut in
a sharp-elbowed New York real estate deal).

Again, the specifics hardly matter. If Trump's head rolls, the new
President Mike Pence—Vice President Nikki Haley Administration will be
even more anti-Russian. To quote America's schoolmarmish Metternich of
Turtle Bay: "Russia will never be our friend, we'll slap them when needed."
Surely Russia would never be crazy enough to slap back!

For Republicans, the factual vacuum at the heart of "Russiagate" only
means that the narrative of Trump's canoodling with the Kremlin just flips on
a partisan basis to a Democratic conspiracy. The DNC paid Steele for Russian
dirt! Hillary gave Putin our stocks of fissile material under the Uranium One
deal! The variable (Democrat vs. Republican) changes, the constant (Russia is
bad) doesn't. GOP NeverTrumpers and Trump supporters alike smugly
chortle that "Mitt Romney was right" when Barack Obama mocked him for
suggesting in 2012 that Russia was America's greatest geopolitical foe. (Note
that putting "Mitt Romney" and "was right" in the same sentence violates basic
grammar of the English language.)

To say that Russia is an adversary for "geopolitical" reasons is obvious to
many people whose views matter in Washington. Russia is the closest approximation of the "Heartland" of Halford Mackinder's "World Island": "Who
rules East Europe commands the Heartland; Who rules the Heartland commands the World Island; Who rules the World Island commands the World."
The United States is master of Mackinder's "Outlying Islands" (Western
Hemisphere and Australia) and "Offshore Islands" (British Isles and the
Pacific "First Island Chain").

So there you have it! According to the expert graduates of geopolitical
Mackinder-garten, Washington must confront Moscow over every square inch
of Eastern Europe and the Middle East! Otherwise the Russians will consolidate the "Heartland"—and then it's curtains for America! Never mind the
Mexican border, our frontline "self-defense" really lies in Ukraine, Moldova,
Georgia, and on Russia's Baltic and Black Sea littoral. (Ditto US naval
dominance in the South China Sea and East China Sea.) Anything less than
perpetual, full-spectrum, unipolar global domination by Washington would
be a dereliction of duty!

Of course we shouldn't overlook the fact that perpetual war (or at least
perpetual projection of power to the far corners of the earth at the risk of war)
is a breathtakingly profitable business—"doing well by doing good." If Russia
(and China) didn't exist our mandarin class would have to invent them.

At least, we are told, that unlike the first Cold War this second one is not
about ideology, like the struggle between "capitalism" (use of the term itself
was a bow to anarcho–socialist vocabulary) and communism. As summarized
by Susan B. Glasser of Politico:

> ... the new Cold War is not like the original Cold War because it lacks
> an ideological dimension.... the current tension between the United
> States and Russia is a Seinfeldian fight about nothing: Putin has no
> ideological goal beyond the elevation of the Russian state, ruled by
> him and his clan; he is not seeking adherents in the West, and there-

fore has brought about no great contest between two systems. . . .
After all, Putin does not preach worldwide revolution, which was a
key doctrinal element of Soviet communism.

Ah, but the new Cold War is ideological but with two critical differences from
the old one.

First, in the original Cold War the ruling cliques in Washington and
Moscow basically believed in the same ideology. While ordinary Americans
thought about communism as a murderous, godless machine of oppression
(think of the Knights of Columbus' campaign to insert "under God" into the
Pledge of Allegiance), many if not most of the irreligious intellectuals making
policy firmly believed that material progress, in a mildly socialist form, was
the duty of government—it was only the communists' *methods* they found
objectionable. As described by Professor Daniel J. Mahoney of Assumption
College:

> So many intellectuals were disarmed before the challenge of com-
> munism and could not see it for the radical evil that it was. For many,
> it was simply a more brutal means for achieving the desired ends of
> industrial modernity and social equality—"the New Deal in a hurry,"
> in Harry Hopkins's notorious formulation. That explains in part the
> divide between ordinary Americans, who . . . hated communism for
> its atheism as well as for its brutality, and elite opinion, which tended
> toward anti-anti-communism and refused to believe in the guilt of
> one of its own.

Second, while Glasser is right that "Putin does not preach worldwide
revolution," western governments do. Just as members of the old Soviet nomenklatura depended on Marxism-Leninism both as a working method-ology
and as a justification for their prerogatives and privileges, denizens of the
entrenched duopoly of Democrat liberal interventionists and Republican neoconservatives rely upon an ideological imperative of "democracy promotion"
for global empire and endless wars.

Perhaps the fullest expression of this was from a 1996 article by
neoconservative ideologists William Kristol and Robert Kagan, misleadingly
titled "Toward a Neo-Reaganite Foreign Policy," in which they called for the
US to establish and maintain indefinitely "benevolent global hegemony"—
American world domination. As scrutinized by this analyst the following year,
Kristol and Kagan laid down virtually all of the elements that have guided US
foreign policy and its media aspect during the ensuing years. It is no accident
that these same GOP neoconservatives were enthusiastic supporters of Bill
Clinton's Balkan interventions of 1990s, under the guidance of people like
then-Secretary of State Madeleine Albright, who once opined regarding the
sanctions-related deaths of a half million Iraqi children that "the price is worth
it." In the US establishment, there is little dissent on either side of the partisan
aisle with Albright's sincere conviction that a militant United States has a
special wisdom: "If we have to use force, it is because we are America; we are
the indispensable nation. We stand tall and we see further than other
countries into the future . . ."

So if some country doesn't agree with the "indispensable" opinion of
officials in Washington, they should prepare at least to get sanctioned, if not
bombed, occupied, targeted by terrorists, or set up for a "color revolution"
regime change, with the media cheering it on. Hence the succession of humanitarian, therapeutic wars of aggression in Serbia, Iraq, Libya, and Syria, plus
regime change operations in many, many other places.

After all, extremism is no vice in eliminating opposition to the inexorable forward march of "liberal democracy" against its benighted opponents: nationalists, neo-fascists, xenophobes, racists, anti-Semites, champions of neo-Marxism, protectionists, forces of illiberalism, conspiracy-mongers, fringe websites that spread "fake news," and other insects of their ilk. [From the "Renew Democracy Manifesto," paragraph 8. Somehow it's a bit reminiscent of *another* famous "Manifesto" . . .]

It's easy to see why a revived, national, non-communist Russia is the main enemy for the ideologists of this faux "America." The promise of putting America first, which is why the real America elected Donald Trump, terrified them.

Unfortunately, the ersatz America has taken firm hold of the key levers of power. Worse, Trump handed those levers to them.

"There Will Be No American–RussianAlliance Against China"

Jim Jatras | *Strategic Culture* | August 4, 2018

Since 1991 and the formal end of the first Cold War between the United States and the Soviet Union, the world has experienced an American "unipolar moment" as the bipartisan US policy establishment sought to consolidate and perpetuate its hegemonic control over the entire plant. Doomed to fail even before it received its fullest articulation in 1996 by neoconservative ideologists William Kristol and Robert Kagan (misleadingly billed as "Toward a Neo-Reaganite Foreign Policy"), that misbegotten moment thankfully is coming to an end.

The main question today is whether the grinding to a halt of a quest so foolish and destructive can peacefully devolve into a tripolar entente among the US, Russia, and China—or whether the entrenched Washington establishment will, Sampson-like, crash everything down in a desperate but futile attempt to hang on to its power and privileges. We appear to be approaching the cusp at which that question will be resolved one way or the other. What the Trump Administration does next with respect to Iran will be a key, perhaps decisive, indicator.

However, of late there has emerged an alternative concept that may be seen as a middle way between America's stubbornly hanging onto our diminishing hegemony versus working out a new Concert of Powers with the two countries the Trump Administration has dubbed rivals in a new "great power competition." This concept suggests that the United States should play odd-man-out, teaming up with one of the other two powers against the third. Such a triangulation conceivably could perpetuate and enhance America's global dominance (it is assumed the other nation would be the junior partner) while limiting the influence of the designated adversary.

Strangely, given the unhinged levels of Russia-hatred that define the American political class, no one seems to have proposed trying to flip Beijing away from its quasi-alliance with Moscow in a repeat of President Nixon's "playing the China card" against the USSR in the early 1970s. Rather, the hot talk is all the other way 'round, that the US should woo Russia as an ally against China. As presented by Harry J. Kazianis of the Center for the National Interest ("The Coming American-Russian Alliance Against China"):

> [T]here is a very real possibility that Washington and Moscow will collude for a very big reason—and soon.
>
> Both nations have a reason to fear a coming change in the international order that will impact them both. And as history shows us time and again, a rising power that seeks to overturn the international system can make the most dedicated enemies join forces—and fast.
>
> I can only be talking about one thing: a growing and more powerful China. [. . .]
>
> While it might not happen right away, and an armed clash over, say, Ukraine or Syria could delay or even destroy any chance of a geopolitical realignment, there is the very real possibility that the stars could align for Russia and America to take on China in the future. Stranger parings have occurred in the past. While we might rightly see Moscow as a rogue nation today, tomorrow it could be a partner in containing a common foe. History and circumstance still stand for no one.

Playing the Russia card against China is even presented by former Indian diplomat M. K. Bhadrakumar as part of a long-term strategy ("Trump Has a Grand Strategy, He Wants to Do a 'Reverse Nixon'—Partner Russia for an Alliance vs China") foreseen by the architect of Nixon's long-ago outreach to communist China, Henry Kissinger (who reportedly is advising Trump to this end):

> As far back as 1972 in a discussion with Richard Nixon on his upcoming trip to China, signifying the historic opening to Beijing, Kissinger could visualize such a rebalancing becoming necessary in future. He expressed the view that compared with the Soviets (Russians), the Chinese were "just as dangerous. In fact, they're more dangerous over a historical period." Kissinger added, "in 20 years your (Nixon's) successor, if he's as wise as you, will wind up leaning towards the Russians against the Chinese."
>
> Kissinger argued that the United States, which sought to profit from the enmity between Moscow and Beijing in the Cold War era, would therefore need "to play this balance-of-power game totally unemotionally. Right now, we need the Chinese to correct the Russians and to discipline the Russians." But in the future, it would be the other way around.

The possibility that Trump or some people in his Administration may be seriously considering the idea can't be dismissed. It should be noted that among the few sane voices about Russia in US public life, such as *Fox News'* Laura Ingraham (Trump "wants to triangulate China, Russia, does he not?") and Tucker Carlson, it is axiomatic that "China is the real threat, not Russia."

However, whether or not the US is open to teaming up with Russia against China doesn't address the question of whether such a ploy would be objectively viable. There are three strong reasons to suppose it wouldn't be:

1. *US hostility toward Russia is unalterable for the foreseeable future.* In a rational policymaking context, it should be obvious that there is no inherent reason for US-Russia animosity. The basic interests of the two states do not conflict and there is much, other than China, that should be a basis for coop-

eration, such as the common threat of Islamic terrorism (as opposed to the decades-long US penchant of employing jihadists against Russia and other countries, like Serbia, Libya, and Syria).

Unfortunately, there is little rationality about Russia in Washington. Diehard, uncompromising detestation of Russia, which decent people are not supposed to see as anything but an enemy, is inseparable from the transatlantic conspiracy to eject Trump from office. Indeed, Trump's pledge to improve relations with Moscow is among the top reasons Trump is being targeted for removal.

Hostility to Russia (and to any Trumpian hopes of détente) unites virtually all the Democrats, almost all prominent Republicans, the entire legacy media (of course), almost every prestigious think tank, and seemingly every high-level official on Trump's own team. In the wake of his Helsinki summit with Russian President Vladimir Putin and Trump's innocuous skepticism on supposed election "meddling," the hysteria of this phalanx of hate has reached new heights of derangement. Senators promise a new "sanctions bill from hell" even as Trump insists existing sanctions are here to stay, presumably forever. The new Senate measure even includes a preposterous requirement that the Secretary of State "submit a determination of whether the Russian Federation meets the criteria for designation as a state sponsor of terrorism"—evidently ignoring the fact that for over seven years the US has armed and funded bona fide al-Qaeda-linked terrorists in Syria while Russia has been killing them.

Trump's own top officials openly press him not only on bogus 2016 meddling but already accusing Moscow of interfering in advance in the 2018 Congressional vote with the intent, without any sense of irony, to "undermine our democracy." Social media like Facebook are on a search-and-destroy mission against anything even *suspected* of being "Russian-linked," whatever that means. A young Russian student advocating gun rights and networking in Washington is treated as a conflation of Anna Chapman and Natasha Fatale while being smeared and slut-shamed across the major media (and her lawyer is threatened with a gag order). Stepped-up military aid is being provided to Kiev. The NATO Pac-Man is set to gobble up next (the Former Yugoslav Republic of) Macedonia, while in the process alienating Russia from longtime Orthodox Christian friend Greece.

No wonder Russian Foreign Minister Sergey Lavrov can only look on with sardonic laughter.

In short, anything and everything Russian is toxic and becoming more so. Even if Trump really wanted to change this state of affairs—sure proof the evil Russians must "have something on him," according to former CIA Director Leon Panetta—he couldn't do it. Not only his opposition but his own team will see to that. US Ambassador to the United Nations Nikki Haley says Russia "is never going to be our friend." The Russians have every reason to take her at her word.

This makes any notion of enlisting Russia as an ally against China impractical, to say the least. To even contemplate it the US would have to be able to extend some sort of olive branch to Russia, but that can't happen anytime soon, if ever. You can't build a partnership on the basis of unremitting antagonism.

2. *Russia is once burned, twice shy.* Even in the event, currently inconceivable, that the US did offer to bury the hatchet with Russia, the Russians would have to be fools to accept.

They are not fools.

Apart from the most minimal, easily verified circumstances, why would anyone in Moscow believe any assurance from anyone in Washington? Did the US honor our commitment to Boris Yeltsin not to move NATO "one inch" further east following Germany reunification? Did the US respect the United Nations Charter, the Helsinki Final Act, and UN Security Council Resolution 1244 during the Bill Clinton Administration's 1999 military aggression against Serbia over Kosovo or the George W. Bush Administration's spearheading of Kosovo's purported secession in 2008? Does the US show good faith in baseless accusations of Russian guilt in false flag chemical attacks in Syria and the United Kingdom?

While Russian officials by nature remain open to "businesslike" and professional discussion with those they still insist on referring to as "partners," they also know blind ideological and zoological hatred when they see it.

Even if tomorrow the US would offer the Russians the sun, the moon, and the stars in exchange for cooperation against China, they wouldn't bite. Nor should they.

3. *Russia has more objective incentives to get along with China than with the US.* The main thing Russia needs from the US is basically—well, nothing. That is to say, there is very little of a practical, especially economic, nature Russia needs in a positive sense from the US, and vice versa. What Russia mainly wants from the US is negative: to stop regarding Russia as an enemy and get out of Moscow's face in regions vitally important to Russia but of little or no value to the US.

Without taking the analogy to George Orwell's *1984* too far (with America as the primary component of Oceania, Russia of Eurasia, and China of Eastasia), geographically America and Russia not only have no reason for conflict, they have little natural need for interdependence. Russia is the closest approximation of the "Heartland" of Halford Mackinder's "World Island. The United States is the principal in Mackinder's "Outlying Islands" (Western Hemisphere and Australia) and "Offshore Islands" (British Isles and the Pacific "First Island Chain"). But, *contra* the fantasies of some half-baked graduates of an elementary geopolitical "Mackindergarten," this configuration need not give rise to a predetermined and inevitable conflict but points as easily to the self-sufficiency of each dominant power within its own exclusive sphere.

With a common border of over 2,500 miles, Russia and China are locked into a relationship by the simple fact of geography in a way neither is with the United States, which inherently is in the most secure position of the three. The Russo-Chinese relationship can be hostile (as it notably was in the late 1960s, when the two then-communist giants fought a short border war that threatened to escalate into a nuclear conflict and set the stage for Nixon's China initiative) or it can be cooperative. Fueled in part by an entrenched American animus against Russia and a growing one towards China, Moscow and Beijing have chosen full-spectrum partnership via the Shanghai Cooperation Organization (SCO), the Belt and Road Initiative (BRI), Eurasia Economic Union (EAEU), the New (formerly BRICS) Development Bank (NDB), and other initiatives. Finally, Russia and China are working in concert to de-dollarize their financial systems in favor of local currency and of gold, which both countries have been buying in massive amounts.

Such ties between Russia and China are as natural, complimentary, and obvious as are America's with Canada and Mexico. It's hard to picture Moscow (or Beijing) abandoning them because someone in Washington flashes a come-hither look.

* * *

If Trump survives the efforts to remove him (either politically or physic-ally)—a tall order, given the forces arrayed against him—and doesn't plunge the US and the Middle East into an Iran misadventure that would destroy his presidency, it is still an open question whether he can deliver on an America First policy. Along with getting control of our borders and restoring America's industrial base eroded by bad trade policies, that must mean completing his demolition of the failed neoliberal order of which the US has been the guarantor and enforcer.

In its place the only stable and mutually advantageous arrangement for America is a Big Three accord with both Russia and China. The notion of turning one against the other should be dismissed as the distraction it is.

"Lenin Updated: 'Turn the Globalist War into a Race War'"

Jim Jatras | *Strategic Culture* | August 11, 2018

It's *déjà vu* all over again.

First US President Donald Trump meets with Russian President Vladimir Putin in Helsinki and appears to make some progress towards his stated goal of putting ties between Washington and Moscow on a positive course. Im-mediately, all hell breaks loose. Trump is a called a traitor. The "sanctions bill from hell" is introduced in the Senate. Trump is forced on the defensive.

Next Republican Senator Rand Paul of Kentucky visits Moscow, where he meets with Putin and gives him a letter from Trump proposing moderate steps towards rapprochement. Paul also talks with Russian Senators and invites them to come to Washington to continue the dialogue. Immediately, all hell breaks loose. Paul is called a traitor. The State Department "finds" the Rus-sians guilty of the using illegal chemical weapons (CW) in the United Kingdom and imposes sanctions. Trump is forced even more on the defensive.

In each instance the actions of the Washington establishment, both in Congress and in even in departments and agencies allegedly part of the Executive Branch of government headed by Trump, moved quickly to nip in the bud even the most tentative efforts by Trump to keep his campaign pledge. With regard to the new CW sanctions it is unclear whether Trump had anything to do with them at all; most likely they either were imposed without his participation or he acceded to them because he felt he had no other option.

It is debatable how much of the US government Trump actually controls. The baseless CW finding by the State Department (with heavy pressure from Congress) is the work of Trump's globalist enemies in the bureaucracy and in Congress (all of the Democrats, and almost all of the Republicans), with the complicity of his own appointees, to undermine his overtures to Moscow and further erode his Executive authority. Besides blocking every possible path to détente with Russia, this is another step to setting Trump up for removal from office.

Regarding the timing of a second set of sanctions set to kick in November, it's hard to see how that will be avoided. Russia will not submit to inspections, which the US is arrogantly demanding of Russia, as if she were some pipsqueak country like Libya. Given that the OPCW certified in 2017 that the Russians had completed destruction of 100% of their CW stockpile (cf., the US still has almost 10% of our stocks, which are not expected to be completely gone until 2023), the demand is the equivalent of proving that you have stopped beating your wife (to the satisfaction of someone who admittedly continues to beat his own wife).

In the absence of capitulating to the US demand, which Russia will not do, legally Trump can waive the sanctions. But that option is no doubt part of the political trap being laid for him, presenting him a Hobson's choice. On the one hand, he can waive the sanctions, further hyping the charges of treason against him (and, if the waiver is before the elections, giving the Democrats another red flag to wave), as well as inviting new legislation passed by a margin "Putin's puppet" cannot veto; or he can let them go into effect.

If, as seems likely, the harsher measures are applied it is hard to overstate the danger created. These are the kind of things that countries do just one step from totally breaking relations in advance of war: cutting off access to American banks, barring Aeroflot from the US (in context, the least of our concerns, though symbolic), effectively blocking all exports and imports, and downgrading or suspending diplomatic ties. With respect to the last—a direct assault on Trump's presidential authority to send and receive ambassadors under Article II of the Constitution (oddly, no one in Congress seems to care that presidents routinely usurp their authority to make war)—this likely would mean withdrawing the US ambassador from Moscow and expelling the Russian ambassador in Washington, while maintaining relations if at all at the *chargé d'affaires* level.

In word, this is insanity. What's perhaps worse is that this political warfare is being conducted with total disregard for the truth, much less an honest attempt to find it. It's worse than a presumption of guilt; it's a positive, unambiguous verdict of culpability under circumstances where the accusers in Washington and London (I would guess but cannot prove) know perfectly well that the CW finger pointing is false.

It has been clear from the beginning of Trump's meteoric rise on the American political scene that he and his American First agenda were perceived by the beneficiaries of the globalist, neoliberal order as a mortal danger to the system which has enriched them. Maintaining and intensifying hostility toward Russia, even at the risk of a catastrophic, uncontainable conflict, lies at the center of their efforts. This political war to save globalism at all hazards is intensifying.

It would be a mistake, however, to understand hostility to Russia as just a cold calculation of pecuniary and social advantage by a corrupt mandarin class. It is all that of course, but it is also deeply ideological, reflecting the agenda of the entrenched pseudo-elites to dismantle the traditional national identities and Christian moral values of the West—and impose their godless agenda on the East as well.

But there is something else too, something that touches the emotional heart of both Russophobia in a global context and anti-Trumpism domestically. That is the accusation of racism.

Unsurprisingly one of the first to give voice to this concept was Hillary Clinton, who in her August 2016 "tinfoil hat speech" sought to portray Trump as a creature of the "Alt-Right" because, among other things, he once complimented Infowars' Alex Jones: "Your reputation is amazing. I will not let you down." But in Hillary's estimation, who is "the grand godfather" of the worldwide Alt-Right? You guessed it: "Russian President Vladimir Putin." A month later she doubled down in her infamous "basket of deplorables" speech, branding Trump's tens of millions of supporters "racist, sexist, homophobic, xenophobic, Islamophobic—you name it." (In an evident oversight, she omitted mention of Putin.)

Give the warmongering old girl credit for her doggedness. Hillary has stuck to this theme even as she sinks into irrelevance (while still reportedly harboring ambitions of a 2020 presidential run!), in June 2018 calling Putin the leader of the worldwide "authoritarian, white-supremacist, and xenophobic movement" who is "emboldening right-wing nationalists, separatists, racists, and even neo-Nazis."

Hillary is not alone. As summed up by Jodi Jacobson of *Rewire.News* ("Putin, Trump, and Kavanaugh: A Triad of White Supremacy and Oligarchy"):

> Putin is a dictator. His interests are in amassing wealth and power at any cost, both in Russia and globally. . . . He is an ethnic nationalist, a white supremacist, and an Islamophobe. He aligns himself with radical right-wing religious and political groups to marginalize and attack the rights of women, LGBTQ communities, and religious and ethnic groups outside his power base.

But perhaps the most revealing description comes from putative comedian Bill Maher on a recent episode of his *HBO* program, explaining that "Race Explains Shift From Party Of Reagan To Party Of Putin" and excoriating not just Putin *but Russians as such* for their genetic characteristics:

> UPDATE, with video: The "dirty little secret" that explains how the Party of Reagan morphed into the Party of Putin is a four-letter word, Bill Maher said tonight: Race.
>
> "Russia," Maher said during his New Rules segment on HBO's Real Time With Bill Maher, "is one of the last places on earth to say, 'F**k diversity. We're here. We're white. Get used to it.'"
>
> Attempting to explain how 87% of Republicans (according to a recent poll) are fine with Russia's president Vladimir Putin visiting the White House, Maher chalked it up to racism, and even quoted a tweet from his old pal Ann Coulter.
>
> "Last year Ann Coulter tweeted that 'In 20 years, Russia will be the only country that is recognizably European.' As far back as 2013 Matt Drudge called Putin the leader of the free world. David Duke called Russia the key to white survival.
>
> "Today's Republicans, what's left of them, do not like the melting pot," he said. "And Russia? That pot don't melt."
>
> Making jokes about White Russians ("Let's see, I want to get drunk but I also want a glass of milk") and Russian basketball players ("the team that played against the Globetrotters"), Maher compared racial diversity (or lack thereof) in Russia to that of Western Europe.
>
> Ending the bit with a bite, Maher concluded, "A Barack Obama does not become the president of Russia. Wingnuts used to accuse Obama of being a foreign agent who took over America, but when a foreign power actually did take over America and it was the proudly white one, their response was 'come right on in.'
>
> "To the members of the Grand Old Party, Russia meddling in our elections isn't a breach of national security, it's just white people helping white people. Or what Republicans call governing."

Maher gives away more than he suspects. Very little in the foregoing says anything about racism, either Russian or American, but it does say a great deal about Maher's own disdain for Russia because it is "recognizably European," also known as (if you'll pardon the expression) white. One suspects he doesn't castigate, say, Koreans or Japanese for the fact that their countries are "recognizably Asian" and are going to stay that way.

Shifting to the US, it is increasingly obvious that what poses as antiracism and opposition to "hate" is little more than hostility to the identity and values of the core American *ethnos*: English-speaking Christians of European descent, including completely or partially assimilated descendants of immigrants. (In other countries this would be understood in specifically national terms—Russian, French, German, English, etc.—but for historical reasons too complex to summarize here, the core American demographic is generally seen in terms of race, not ethnicity. This stems in part from the absurd but widespread claim that the US not an ethnic state, only a civic one.) More and more this hostility is expressed as hatred of "whiteness" itself, in a manner that would be totally unacceptable applied to any other ethnic, racial, or religious group.

The current Exhibit A of such hatred is the controversy over a newly appointed member of the *New York Times* editorial board, Korean-born Sarah Jeong, whose expressions of anti-white bias were parodied by African-American conservative Candace Owens, only substituting "Jewish" and "black" for Jeong's "white." Unsurprisingly, Owens was suspended from Twitter while Jeong—who also trashes men and the police—is the beneficiary of fullthroated support from the assembled forces of diversity, tolerance, and overall wonderfulness.

Jeong is just one example of a phenomenon that has become fashionable among the haters. "White thoughts" are a disease, as is whiteness itself. Among the items various college professors have denounced as tainted by white racism are math, farmers' markets, interracial friendship, solar eclipses, the Bible (of course), environmental pollution, college football, the song "Jingle Bells," the nuclear family, punctuality, and (it goes without saying) supporting Trump. The existence of entire US states like New Hampshire and Vermont that are just "too white" is an affront to diversity, a problem demanding a solution. For the *über*-PC *HuffPost.com*, whiteness constitutes an entire issue category for the grievances of other racial, ethnic, religious, and sexual "communities," including helpful advice to liberal white feminists to just "shut the f**k up!" The inevitability of the United States' becoming a majority-minority country is stated as a fact as inevitable as sunrise and sunset, but it's "unabashed white nationalism" for even mainstream conservatives who are light-years away from the Alt-Right to point out that Americans never voted for or were asked their opinion about such a future. Conversely, "white-bashing" by self-loathers is a demonstration of the "nobility that flows from racial self-flagellation."

Connecting Putin and Russia with racism feeds into cockamamie phantasmagoria of Crimethink concepts that increasingly are considered outside the protection of what was once quaintly known as free speech: hate speech, fake news, conspiracy theories, white nationalism, white supremacy, patriarchy, "cisgenderism," and many more. (Astonishingly, this recent video from ADL's Orwellian-named "Center for Technology and Society," which claims to identify "online hate" with 78 to 85 percent accuracy through the use of artificial intelligence, is real, not a parody.) Just to be accused of subjectively and politically defined hate is now sufficient to trigger a coordinated muzzling of the offender's online presence by the lords of the Internet, getting them fired from their jobs, and even subjecting them to physical attack from violent enforcers like Antifa. Ostensibly these actions are undertaken by private entities, conveniently hiding the government hand encouraging tech companies to police content to counter "Russian meddling" and other thought crimes.

The current coupling of a globalist agenda with demonization of our country's majority demographic has a disquieting precedent. In August 1915 the committed internationalist Vladimir Lenin issued his infamous call to "turn the imperialist war into a civil war." In that, if in nothing else, his program was a smashing success, resulting in the deaths of up to ten million people through savage warfare, "Red Terror" repression, disease, and famine. As he summed it up, "I spit on Russia! That's only one stage we have to pass through on our way to world revolution!" No sacrifice of other peoples' lives was too high a price to be paid to implement Lenin's version of globalism.

As Anatoly Karlin notes ("The Real Lenin: Traitor, Parasite, Failure") the horrendous destruction inflicted by the Bolsheviks was motivated in part by Lenin's conscious hatred—perhaps not very different from Maher's today—of Russians as the majority ethno-religious group, who had to be crushed to liberate the certified oppressed minorities. That hatred gives "an inkling of the real reason why Western intellectuals like Lenin a lot more than Stalin," writes Karlin. Indeed, in light of the Russian experience there is a chillingly familiar ring to today's legitimatization of racial detestation of the American majority.

"Have You Committed Your Three Felonies Today?"

Jim Jatras | *Strategic Culture* | August 18, 2018

Several years ago the Commonwealth of Virginia enacted a law restricting firearms purchases to one per month. This was intended to discourage smuggling of weapons to urban areas outside Virginia with tight gun control laws and (unsurprisingly) high homicide rates. The law didn't seem to do much good and in a rare outbreak of common sense was later repealed, though there's recent misguided talk from Attorney General Mark Herring of reviving it.

During its short period in force, the prohibition spawned a popular saying in the Old Dominion: "Buy one gun a month—it's the *law*!"

A similar attitude may be appropriate in light of an estimate that due to vague statutes and the proliferation of federal regulations—which have the force of law—we wake up in the morning, go to work, come home, eat dinner, and go to sleep unaware we may have committed several federal crimes in the course of the day. The number varies but the average number of crimes per American seems to be about three.

The more important point is that every one of us is probably guilty of *something*. "There is no one in the United States over the age of 18 who cannot be indicted for some federal crime," retired Louisiana State University law professor John Baker told the *Wall Street Journal* in July 2011. "That is not an exaggeration."

- This means that if they want you, they can get you.
- That in turn means that who gets charged, prosecuted, and jailed is a matter of the relevant officials' discretion.
- And that in turn means that discretion can and will be politicized.

Like the *boychiks* used to say in the good ol' NKVD (People's Commissariat for Internal Affairs; *Народный комиссариат внутренних дел*): "Give Us the Man, and We Will Make the Case." (I guess nowadays, we should say "person.")

Let's stipulate that the true *Rechtsstaat,* where justice is administered in a politically neutral manner is few and far between in human history. The norm is politicized justice where holders of power—in an elective system, the winners—use the justice system to harass and terrorize the losers.

But America today must be the only country that's ever been so goofy that the losers are able to terrorize the winners. Whatever your feelings about the current administration, consider: the feds come in like gangbusters, breaking down doors, rousting targets from their beds, seizing their personal documents and devices, and subjecting them to piled-on charges and questioning designed to result in perjury, obstruction, and conspiracy charges—especially the phony crime of "lying to the FBI"—adding up to decades in jail. Those accused are forced to plead guilty to a lesser charge or bankrupt themselves hoping they will be vindicated by a jury of ~~sheep~~ their peers, where the feds have a 90 percent-plus conviction rate. That's treatment meted out to Paul Manafort, Mike Flynn, George Papadopoulos, Michael Cohen, and others.

Conversely, clear evidence of crime, such as mishandling classified material, is a freebie: "No reasonable prosecutor would bring such a case." Oh, some of the emails are "personal?" That's OK, you decide what's what—we trust you! There's a claim a foreign power hacked a computer server, which some compare to an act of war demanding retaliation—no, we don't need to see the server itself, your contractor's report is good enough for us! And while you're at it, go ahead and purge your electronic records (even material you're obligated to preserve) and smash up your smart phones and pull out SIM cards. Oh, hey, does anyone need immunity? No need to bargain, we're happy to provide! That's the treatment accorded to Hillary Clinton, Huma Abedin, Cheryl Mills, Tony Podesta, and their ilk.

It's no coincidence, Comrades, that this disparity is the work of denizens of a law enforcement and intelligence apparatus that is focused like a laser on two closely linked objectives: One, get Donald Trump. Two, at all costs, make sure that he cannot in any way move forward on his stated objective to improve ties with Russia. Those objectives are the two sides of the coin called Russiagate. All else, including the disparity of treatment given those close to Trump versus his opponents, is a function of Russiagate. Three other things also follow:

- Trump's powerlessness, even within his own administration. What kind of Chief Executive is reduced to tweeting what his subordinates *ought* to do—for example, providing Congress with documents demanded from the Department of Justice—versus *ordering* them to do it?
- Trump's personnel. People wonder, especially on foreign policy, why has Trump surrounded himself with a swarm of neoconservatives and Bush-retread Republicans? Maybe he is one of them. Or maybe anyone who dissented from the established warmongering line would be putting his head through a noose.
- Flipping the "Russians did it" narrative: Among the President's defenders, on say *Fox News*, no less than among his detractors, Russia is the enemy who (altogether now!) "interfered in our elections" in order to "undermine our democracy." Mitt Romney was right! The only argument is over who was the intended beneficiary of Muscovite mendacity, Trump or Hillary—that's the *variable.* The *constant* is that Putin is Hitler and only a traitor would want to get along with him. All sides agree that the

Christopher Steele dossier is full of "Russian dirt"—though there's literally zero actual evidence of Kremlin involvement but a lot pointing to
Britain's MI6 and GCHQ.

The Russia! Russia! Russia! hysteria is sometimes called a new McCarthyism,
but that's unfair—to Tailgunner Joe. In his day, whatever his excesses, there
really were Stalinist agents at the State Department. This new panic is nothing
we've seen before, except maybe during the Salem witch frenzy of the 1690s.
    Which brings us to Maria Butina, a Russian grad student and Second
Amendment advocate jailed (and refused bail) on thin allegations of unreg-
istered lobbying. As Phil Giraldi observes: "If you are a Russian and you are
caught talking to anyone in any way influential, there is potentially hell to pay
because the FBI will be watching you. You are automatically assumed to be
part of a conspiracy. Once 'evidence' is collected, you will be indicted and sent
to prison, mostly to send a message to Moscow. It is the ultimate irony that
how the old Soviet Union's judiciary used to function is now becoming
standing operating procedure in the United States." Butina has been portrayed as some kind of honey pot *femme fatale*, a cross between Anna
Chapman and Natasha from "The Adventures of Rocky and Bullwinkle," using
her Slavic charms to bewitch the naïve *MOΛΩN ΛABE* crowd at the National
Rifle Association. Among Butina's nefarious activities: networking at the National Prayer Breakfast. If they arrested everyone with foreign government
connections schmoozing at the Prayer Breakfast, they'd have to shut the thing
down. Honestly, I doubt even the investigators believe Butina is guilty of anything, and if she were any other nationality but Russian she wouldn't be facing
years in jail. [ATTENTION: A legal defense fund for Butina has now been
formed!]
    Which brings us to the biggest threat to what's left of our liberties as
Americans. (No, not the yanking of the security clearance of former CIA
Director John Brennan.) As is well known, we are facing an unprecedented,
coordinated campaign of deplatforming, shadowbanning, filtering, and other
foul means of putting dissenting voices into a digital GULag. While the glove
belongs to tech giants and their executives, *the hand inside is the government's*. Using Russian meddling as a pretext, companies that do billions of
dollars of business with the federal government are only too happy to police
the web of "suspected Russian-linked accounts." And since, as Hillary says,
Putin is the leader of the worldwide "authoritarian, white-supremacist, and
xenophobic movement" who is "emboldening right-wing nationalists, separatists, racists, and even neo-Nazis," anything and anybody that fails Virginia
Senator Mark Warner's or Mark Zuckerberg's sniff test is now fair game. We
are told that to sow discord and chaos Russian troll farms and social media
ads target "divisive" issues related to race, Black Lives Matter, and Ferguson,
absent which we'd all be holding hands singing Kumbaya. Connecting Putin
and Russia with racism feeds into a cockamamie phantasmagoria of Crimethink concepts that increasingly are considered outside the protection of what
was once quaintly known as free speech: hate speech, fake news, conspiracy
theories, white nationalism, white supremacy, white privilege, patriarchy,
"cisgenderism," and many more. The idea of "I disapprove of what you say,
but I will defend to the death your right to say it" is out the window. Instead
we have: anyone to the right of me gets what he deserves.
    While we hear a lot about the "input" end—violation of free speech rights,
a deadly, valid concern—even more worrisome is the "output": limiting what
Americans can see and hear that differs from the official media line, itself
largely a bulletin board for government sources. Unsurprisingly, that line is

unfailingly for war and intervention. As Patrick Armstrong puts it, maybe the censors could just buy some old Soviet jamming equipment.

It is hard to escape the notion that we are approaching the edge of some profound historical moment that will have far-reaching, literally life and death consequences, both domestically and internationally. In the period preceding World War I how many Europeans suspected that their lives would soon be forever changed—and, for millions of them, ended? Who in the years, say, 1910 to 1913, could have imagined that the decades of peace, progress, and civilization in which they had grown up, and which seemingly would continue indefinitely, instead would soon descend into a horror of industrial-scale slaughter, revolution, and brutal ideologies?

Whether opposition to the gathering darkness can be effective is uncertain. But what is not uncertain is our duty to oppose it, even at the risk of committing three felonies a day. "Fellow thought criminals—unite!"

"Will Someone in Washington Play the Ace of Spades before November?"

Jim Jatras | *Strategic Culture* | September 1, 2018

With regard to American foreign and security policy, President Donald Trump presents a paradox. Aside from some harsh bluster ("fire and fury" directed towards Pyongyang in the lead-up to an unprecedented US-North Korea summit), Trump generally seems to want more peaceful ties with the rest of the world and an end to wasteful and dangerous conflicts. On the other hand, if that is his intention, he's been unable to make much headway with an establishment that constitutionally is totally under his authority but in practice seems to be almost entirely independent of his supervision.

For example, Trump expresses his desire the get US forces out of Afghanistan but then announces that contrary to his own preferences he's putting more troops in. He meets in Helsinki with Russian President Vladimir Putin to achieve détente but then the State and Treasury Departments immediately poison the well with more sanctions and evidence-free accusations of Russian meddling in the upcoming Congressional elections. Trump announces his willingness to meet with Iranian President Hassan Rouhani without preconditions but then is immediately overruled by *über*-President (a/k/a Secretary of State) Mike Pompeo.

Much of this reflects the nature of his appointments. As Lawrence Wilkerson details ("The Neoconservative Comeback"), Trump's foreign and security policy apparatus is dominated by "the reentry into critical positions in the government of . . . the people who gave America the 2003 invasion of Iraq, [even] those many of them who declared 'Never Trump'" in 2016. Indeed, it's hard to think of a single member of his top team, or even anyone identifiable in the secondary rank, who agrees with the Trump campaign vision of an "America First" national interest-based strategy that means getting along with Russia and China, versus unending, reckless, global hegemonism.

Well fine, one might say, that's an explanation but not an excuse. In the end, it's his own fault. He picked these people.

That's true. But one still wonders *Why*. Does he not know better? Is he so supremely confident of his own ability to make the "final decision" that he doesn't care how his underlings might seek to stack the deck to implement their preferences, not his? Are there no alternative personnel available, given the danger of ending up like General Mike Flynn? Is he just paying off his donors?

In the end, the *Why* may not matter as much as the *What*—which is that Trump's policies, in substance, differ little in the end from what we would have gotten from a Mitt Romney or a Hillary Clinton administration:

- More NATO expansion, more deployments in the east, more sanctions and provocations against Russia. There is danger of an escalation in Ukraine, where Donetsk People's Republic leader Aleksandr Zakharchenko was just assassinated in a bomb blast and a major conflict—and perhaps a worldwide schism—may be about to break out over the status of the local Orthodox Church.
- Playing the "Muslim card" in the Balkans and against China in Xinjiang and in Myanmar (as a shot against Beijing's Belt and Road Initiative via the China-Myanmar Economic Corridor). When have western governments and media ever demanded that the so-called international community "do something" to save a non-Muslim population—anywhere?
- Further tightening the economic and financial screws on Tehran in the hopes of collapsing Iran's economy, forcing Iran's abrogation of the JCPOA with other powers (in the face of a predictable European wimp-out under threat of US secondary sanctions), and baiting Iran into some action such as a military move in the Strait of Hormuz that would "justify" an attack—all with the goal of regime change.
- Attempts to unravel the understandings reached at Singapore between Trump and North Korea's Kim Jong-un by accusing Pyongyang of dragging their feet on denuclearization while pressing for renewed US-South Korea military drills (which Trump appears to be resisting). As Justin Raimondo of *Antiwar.com* observes: "The North Koreans are no dummies: they know a regime change operation when they see one. As they watch our Deep State go after a democratically elected President whose hopes for peace complement their own, the North Koreans are waiting to see if Trump survives. I can't say that I blame them."

Raimondo's reference to regime change is important. Since before he took office Trump was besieged within his own administration by a hostile phalanx of Democrats, almost all of the GOP establishment, the federal law enforcement and intelligence *nomenklatura*, and the media. It doesn't help that his Attorney General, Jeff Sessions, seems to think he has nothing better to do than crank up the civil forfeiture machine and give states a hard time for playing fast and loose with federal marijuana laws, while a criminal anti-constitutional conspiracy operates under his nose at the Department of Justice and the FBI in cahoots with elements of the US and British intelligence agencies.

Certainly Trump's enemies and false friends, both inside and outside his administration, would love nothing better than to goad and cheer him into a splendid little war that, when it inevitably proves a disaster, would be blamed not on their globalist ideology but on someone they see as a shallow, superficial, unqualified, Twitter-addicted, unstable personality who never should have been allowed into the Oval Office. That would certainly alienate independents and maybe chip into his support even among his core Deplorables.

With the approach of an election that may produce a Democratic House of Representatives that almost surely will impeach him—a distinct possibility given voter fraud and government and corporate collusion to censor alternative and social media—Trump himself maybe be tempted to play the death card. Ordering military actions is one of the few commands to his subordinates he can be confident will be carried out, since that is their overwhelming preference too. Plus, as we must well remember, on previous occasions when he ordered military strikes on Syria he won a brief respite from the constant pounding from his political and media antagonists, who instead praised his "leadership," summed up in Fareed Zakaria's moronic observation after the April 2017 strike on Syria: "I think Donald Trump became President of the United States" last night.

Whether Trump decides to lay down the Ace of Spades or the self-guiding machinery of power seeking to undermine him does so on its own, we are in for a run of heightened danger between now and Election Day (November 6). While there are a number of possible flashpoints, one theater stands out: again Syria, where the impending government offensive against the last significant area still held by jihadists, al-Qaeda-occupied Idlib, sets the stage for yet another false flag chemical weapons attack.

In an unusual move, Russian officials briefed the State Department on plans for a chlorine gas strike by Hayat Tahrir al-Sham, formerly al-Nusra Front, formerly just plain old al-Qaeda, with British special services "actively involved" in the "provocation," which will "serve as another reason for the US, the UK, and France to hit Syrian government targets with air strikes." US, British, and French forces have concentrated in the eastern Mediterranean in preparation for an attack against Syrian government forces (effectively in support of the al-Qaeda-led jihadists), and Russia has also beefed up its naval presence. Without any sense of irony, the State Department summarily dismissed Moscow's warning as just "more false flag type reporting"—for the simple reason that it came from the Russians—and Deep State mouthpieces media like Bellingcat treat it as itself an indication that Damascus plans to use chemical weapons. As Caitlin Johnstone observes:

> This past April the US, UK and France launched airstrikes against Damascus in retaliation for an alleged chemical attack allegedly perpetrated by the Syrian government against civilians in the city of Douma. The strike was launched with no investigation having taken place whatsoever into the nature of the civilian deaths, and subsequent investigation found no evidence implicating the Syrian government in a chemical attack. This is unsurprising, because the Syrian government had no incentive to use chemical weapons in a battle it had already won at that point and every incentive not to provoke the wrath of powerful western military forces just to suffocate some kids to death. [. . .]

> Even if you dismiss the intelligence which Russia supplied to the US saying that a false flag chemical weapons attack is being prepared for in Idlib, it is self-evident that the jihadist militants would have every motive to stage one if given the opportunity.

> Keep an eye on this one, please. Syria is a key strategic region that the western power alliance has been plotting to take control of for decades, and it is entirely possible that they will pounce on any opportunity to prevent the Syrian government and its allies from shoring up control of the nation and bringing stability to the region. Stay skeptical.

It should also be noted that this scene is unfolding in the aftermath of an unusual peace overture to Damascus, under which the US offered to withdraw the illegal deployment of American troops on Syrian territory under three conditions. As described by Tom Luongo:

> According to a recent report by Joaquin Flores at Fort Russ News, the U.S. offered a withdrawal plan to Bashar al-Assad of Syria with three conditions. What should be immediately obvious is that the U.S. offered the meeting and opened up the talks.
>
> This is proof positive that the U.S. position in Syria is untenable and the U.S. [JGJ: or maybe just Trump?] is searching for a way out that will save a little face.
>
> From Fort Russ:
>
> First: Iran's full withdrawal from the Syrian south.
>
> Washington: withdrawal from the [al-Tanf] and eastern Euphrates against three conditions, including giving us a share of oil.
>
> Second: obtaining written assurances that US companies will receive a share of the oil sector in eastern Syria.
>
> Third, to provide the Syrian side with the Americans with full data on the terrorist groups and their members, including the numbers of foreign victims of these groups and those who survived, and those who have the possibility of returning to Western countries, considering that "the terrorist threat is intercontinental, we can get hurt in the service of international security."
>
> The Syrian response to this generous offer could easily be termed as dismissive. Assad has no reason to guarantee the U.S. anything after its shameful display over the past seven years. [. . .]
>
> Trump is surrounded by vipers and neocons (or do I repeat myself) who, despite his better instincts, fill him with nonsense which he then acts on without much reflection.
>
> I still feel that Putin laid on him some very eye-opening information behind closed doors in Helsinki which is why the intelligence agencies freaked out afterwards. But, this offer to withdraw from Syria is, yet again with Trump, two steps forward and one step back. [. . .]
>
> If Trump's goal is peace in the region, then this operation needs to go smoothly and it will if it's allowed to. But, that's the problem. Once Syria's settled it makes it easier for Trump to declare, "Mission Accomplished."
>
> If he doesn't he's going to have to go back to his base and tell them we need to stay to counter Iran? A country he keeps telling us is on the verge of collapse thanks to sanctions?
>
> That's not going to fly with his base who wants the empire dismantled. So, the argument for the false flag makes sense to trap Trump into having to stay, if not expand the conflict, to push Assad from office while damaging him at home on the eve of the mid-terms.
>
> This is the trap that's being laid right now because peace is not allowed to break out in the Middle East.

As Trump considers the next card he must play in the coming weeks and days, he needs to know that most of those advising him—the vipers and neocons he has surrounded himself with—have at heart neither his interests nor America's. If he plays the Ace of Spades and things go terribly wrong, he's the one who will end up the Joker—or switching game metaphors, draw the card that tells the millionaire "GO TO JAIL: Go directly to Jail. Do not pass Go. Do not collect $200."

Of course at that point, if things outside the US get really ugly, what happens to Trump's political fortunes could be the least of everybody's worries.

"Pelosi Prepares 'Second Pivot' of Regime Change in the United States"

Jim Jatras | *Strategic Culture* | November 10, 2018

The votes were barely counted before US President Donald Trump fired his Attorney General Jeff Sessions and began to prepare a showdown with the Deep State's effort to dethrone him. As Patrick Buchanan describes the stakes:

> For two years, Trump has been under a cloud of unproven allegations and suspicion that he and top campaign officials colluded with Vladimir Putin's Russia to thieve and publish the emails of the Clinton campaign and the Democratic National Committee.
>
> It is past time for Mueller to prove these charges or concede he has a busted flush, wrap up his investigation and go home.
>
> And now, in T.S. Eliot's words, Trump appears to have found "the strength to force the moment to its crisis."
>
> His attitude toward Mueller's probe is taking on the aspect of Andrew Jackson's attitude toward Nicholas Biddle's Second Bank of the United States: It's "trying to kill me, but I will kill it."

But oh wait—the votes aren't counted yet. In Arizona and, more dangerously, in Florida votes from Democratic precincts seemingly have appeared out of thin air to deny the Republicans additional seats in the Senate. (The governors' races in Florida and Georgia drag on as well, with Trump mockingly suggesting it's the Russians' fault.) In any US election now the side favoring the historic American nation must win big enough to overcome the growing, built-in advantage of an unknown number of illegal votes cast by non-citizens. But even that's not enough of a handicap, so the Evil Party of Certified Victims also gets to trot out for days and even weeks after election day however many provisional ballots, mail-in ballots, absentee ballots, and any other *verkackte* concoctions they can. It's the business end of multiplying measures supposedly designed to "increase voter participation," like automatic registration, same-day registration, online registration, and at-home voting, the cumulative impact (and no doubt intent) of which is not-quite knowing who's voting or how often—an old tradition of the Democratic Party. Above all, no ballot security measures can be implemented to require proof of citizenship to vote, as that clearly would be "voter suppression" and, it hardly needs to be added, racist (though demanding documentation of citizenship seems to work just fine in Mexico).

Trimming Trump's Senate advantage might be the least of his worries, though. Since he took office it's been clear that large parts of the Executive Branch—nominally under his total control—are instead part of the so-called "Resistance" dedicated to removing him. Most dangerously, this includes much of the Department of Justice and the intelligence agencies. (One can almost hear an audible sigh of relief from the rogues' gallery of criminal conspirators behind the phony Russiagate collusion story cooked up in the bowels of the US-UK Deep State with the aim of overturning the 2016 election. Now, after two years of the GOP's dithering in the area of investigations and hearings relevant to how the Trump campaign was put under politically motivated surveillance, those peccadilloes will be forever buried.) The Resistance also includes most of the judiciary, which can be counted on immediately to block any use of Trump's Executive authority individual judges don't like, even uses within his plenary Constitutional power, like command of the armed forces (for defending the US? No!) or immigration and border enforcement. Finally, a Senate Democratic block has existed in what is erroneously referred to as the filibuster, with which the GOP majority could dispense with but won't.

Now, however, with the House of Representatives flipped, we are about to see the consolidation in all three branches of what amounts to a rival government under incoming Speaker Nancy Pelosi. Gathering all resistance forces to herself Sauron-like as the focus of rival authority to Trump, she will hope first to render him powerless, then eliminate him. Accordingly, we can be sure that, both with the media's active complicity and via direct leaks, the House will receive a steady stream of confidential, politically valuable information from within the administration; collusion with the courts to further nullify Trump's actions will be standard operating procedure.

It's important to understand that the division of power confronting America in January 2019 will not be the usual circumstance of government divided on a partisan basis, "checks and balances," "gridlock," and all that sort of thing familiar from our history but the next phase of a second American civil war (or third, if we count Patriots vs. Loyalists during the War for Independence). Pelosi will lead the next revolutionary phase in which one part of the apparatus of government becomes what Alexander Shtromas called "the Second Pivot," an alternative, opposing source of official power.

(Contrary to the Marxist myth, revolutions happen not when "The People" rise up spontaneously in righteous anger but when some part of the ruling establishment defects to the revolt (or "Resistance") and becomes the new conferrer of legitimacy. There are obvious historical examples: Parliament in the English Civil War, the Third Estate's declaring itself the National Assembly of France, the Petrograd Soviet's coup against the Provisional Government, Boris Yeltsin's Russian government when Mikhail Gorbachev's Soviet government was under threat of the State Committee on the State of Emergency (itself an aspiring second pivot that failed), and the communist cabals in the various Warsaw Pact countries that ousted little Brezhnevs and installed little Gorbachevs.)

In seeking to overthrow the constitutionally elected president who was himself an insurgent against the cozy duopoly in Washington, it might seem the Democrats and their GOP "Never Trump" fellow travelers are actually the counterrevolutionaries against the populist "revolution" two years ago. However true that observation might be in a mechanical sense, it fails to encompass the anti-American, revolutionary—indeed, Leninist—substance of the party that has just captured the House.

Like the bush-league Bolshies they are, the Democrats have already dropped the sotto voce tone they adopted during the closing weeks of the campaign concerning impeaching Trump and now are "all-in" to get rid of him. In doing so, not only can they guarantee the perpetual dominance of their replacement voting bloc, the GOP establishment can purge the Republican party of Trump populism and—dare we say the word!—nationalism once and for all while happily settling in as a permanent, pampered minority with a share of the spoils.

An early test will be if Trump can resist calls for acting Attorney General Matthew Whitaker to recuse himself from the Mueller probe as Sessions had, leaving in charge Deputy AG Rod Rosenstein—the fox watching the henhouse. Mueller is widely expected to wrap up before the end of the year and he'll look for some additional scalps to hang to the wall to justify his existence. But the Democrats, now that they've taken the House, are more anxious to get on to other things that they can use to justify impeachment. This will of course not be found in any phony Russian collusion (the Democrats will play out the hand, just to keep their base on the edge of hysteria) but the real meat and potatoes will be elsewhere: Trump's tax returns and his business life back in New York. Contrary to most assurances that a Republican Senate guarantees Trump's survival, take note that it was Richard Nixon's own party that threw him to the wolves.

In two months the Second Pivot under Pelosi will rapidly become a state-within-a-state, a Petrograd Soviet at one end of Pennsylvania Avenue, with a Provisional Government—alas, that's all it is—headed by Trump at the other end. Hopefully the rivalry between them will not turn out as bloody as the one in Russia a century ago. But in terms of the gulf in values and identity that separates the two sides, it is no less of another phase of a civil war, a cold one—for the time being.

In any case, the country those of us of middle age grew up in is gone. The question now is what comes next: consolidation of a restored American order or some sort of collapse?

"'The People' Know What They Want and Just Might Get It—Good and Hard"

Jim Jatras | *Strategic Culture* | January 19, 2019

A survey of nations in what was once known quaintly as the Free World shows some of them engaged in what could best be described as a cold civil war.

Such a condition is inherently unstable. One possible future is one where the cold conflict becomes hot with unforeseeable consequences. Another is that one side successfully represses the other before violence reaches a certain threshold.

Now before we go any further, let's make one thing clear. Whatever the country and its specific ills, we can be sure that Vladimir Putin is the culprit. According to Stephen Collinson of *CNN* ("Another good day for Putin as turmoil grips US and UK"):

> In London, Theresa May on Tuesday suffered the worst defeat in the modern parliamentary era by a prime minister, as lawmakers shot down her Brexit deal with the European Union by a staggering 432 votes to 202.
>
> The United States, meanwhile, remains locked in its longest-ever government shutdown, which is now entering its 26th day, is no-where near ending and is the culmination of two years of whirling political chaos sparked by President Donald Trump.

It's hard to believe that two such robust democracies, long seen by the rest of the world as beacons of stability, have dissolved into such bitter civic dysfunction and seem unmoored from their previous governing realities. [. . .]

The result is that Britain and the United States are all but ungovernable on the most important questions that confront both nations.

That's music to Putin's ears.

The Russian leader has made disrupting liberal democracies a core principle of his near two-decade rule, as he seeks to avenge the fall of the Soviet empire, which he experienced as a heartbroken KGB agent in East Germany.

Russia has been accused of meddling in both the Brexit vote and the US election in 2016—the critical events that fomented the current crisis of the West.

It isn't exactly clear how the "meddling" of which the coryphaeus of the Kremlin is merely "accused" managed to entice Theresa May into botching (or sabotaging) Brexit talks or to embolden Donald Trump into finally standing his ground on his top campaign pledge. Even Collinson admits that folks in the US and UK may have had something to do with the ruckus: "Supporters of Trump in the US and Brexit in Britain see their revolts as uprisings against distant or unaccountable leaders who no longer represent them or share their values."

Harrumph! Why should anyone care what the great unwashed think about accountability or values? What matters, say "skeptics" like Collinson, is that the proles' getting uppity might be "deeply corrosive to the international political architecture that has prevailed for over 70 years." Let's get our priorities straight!

While Britain and the US are entertaining distractions, the current main feature is the *jacquerie* going on in France. To be sure, many wonder if *les gilets jaunes* are a genuine, grassroots rebellion of ordinary Frenchmen, or some kind of Astroturf comparable to "color revolutions" that western governments and their accomplices like George Soros have sponsored in many countries. While there is some evidence of *agents provocateurs* (the expression is French, after all) working for the Emmanuel Macron regime—can we start using that word now, like "Assad regime," "Putin regime," etc.?—and minor involvement of groups like Antifa committing vandalism with an aim to discredit the yellow vests, the definitive attestation of authenticity was pronounced by world-class poseur and shill for plutocracy and warmongering, Bernard-Henri Lévy: "It's a real social movement, but it's one driven by sad, mortifying, and destructive forces."

Any movement Lévy calls sad, mortifying, and destructive—that's French for "deplorable"—can't be all bad, especially with some monarchists involved. It's rather ironic, though, given that barely a year ago some were comparing vain little Macron to Napoleon.

What is perhaps most detestable to *bien pensants* like Collinson and Lévy is that the social basis of the yellow vests is readily identifiable. They're who we used to call simply French working people. As geographer Christopher Guilluy describes in Spiked:

> Paris creates enough wealth for the whole of France, and London does the same in Britain. But you cannot build a society around this. The *gilets jaunes* is a revolt of the working classes who live in these places.

They tend to be people in work, but who don't earn very much, between 1000€ and 2000€ per month. Some of them are very poor if they are unemployed. Others were once middle-class. What they all have in common is that they live in areas where there is hardly any work left. They know that even if they have a job today, they could lose it tomorrow and they won't find anything else.

Not only does peripheral France fare badly in the modern economy, it is also culturally misunderstood by the elite. . . . One illustration of this cultural divide is that most modern, progressive social movements and protests are quickly endorsed by celebrities, actors, the media and the intellectuals. But none of them approve of the *gilets jaunes*. Their emergence has caused a kind of psychological shock to the cultural establishment. It is exactly the same shock that the British elites experienced with the Brexit vote and that they are still experiencing now, three years later.

The Brexit vote had a lot to do with culture, too, I think. It was more than just the question of leaving the EU. Many voters wanted to remind the political class that they exist. That's what French people are using the *gilets jaunes* for—to say we exist. We are seeing the same phenomenon in populist revolts across the world. [. . .]

The Parisian economy needs executives and qualified professionals. It also needs workers, predominantly immigrants, for the construction industry and catering et cetera. Business relies on this very specific demographic mix. The problem is that 'the people' outside of this still exist. In fact, 'Peripheral France' actually encompasses the majority of French people. [. . .]

Think of the 'deplorables' evoked by Hillary Clinton. There is a similar view of the working class in France and Britain. They are looked upon as if they are some kind of Amazonian tribe. The problem for the elites is that it is a very big tribe.

The middle-class reaction to the yellow vests has been telling. Immediately, the protesters were denounced as xenophobes, anti-Semites and homophobes. The elites present themselves as anti-fascist and anti-racist but this is merely a way of defending their class interests. It is the only argument they can muster to defend their status, but it is not working anymore.

Now the elites are afraid. For the first time, there is a movement which cannot be controlled through the normal political mechanisms. The *gilets jaunes* didn't emerge from the trade unions or the political parties. It cannot be stopped. There is no 'off' button. Either the intelligentsia will be forced to properly acknowledge the existence of these people, or they will have to opt for a kind of soft totalitarianism.

Unfortunately, "soft totalitarianism" is not out of the question, whether in France or other countries in which populism threatens to upend the elites' neoliberal gravy train and all the social and moral baggage that comes with it. Guilluy sees the revolt in France as beyond control by the "normal political mechanisms." That may be true, at least in France, at least for now.

But the US may be another story. At the end of this week all Washington was atwitter with an alleged bombshell (relax, in the US legacy media every other story is a "bombshell," especially if it involves dirt on Trump) that former Trump attorney, "fixer," and alleged literal bagman Michael Cohen had actually been instructed by his erstwhile client to commit perjury. Unlike much else thrown at Trump, this story (reported in *Buzzfeed*, which by total coincidence played a key early role in publicizing the US-UK Deep's State's "dirty dossier") would constitute an impeachable crime. In an extraordinary move, Grand Inquisitor Robert Mueller released a statement through a spokesman indicating the report was "not accurate" but not specifying in what regard. As of this writing *Buzzfeed* stands by the story and asked for clarification by Mueller's office, which may or may not be forthcoming.

Whatever the fate of this report, make no mistake: there will be more of the same, an endless parade of them. The fact that such reports might turn out not to be true makes little difference. Their existence is sufficient to keep Trump constantly on the defensive pending his removal, one way or another.

Elizabethtown College Professor Emeritus Paul Gottfried describes how grandees of the GOP are already getting set to restore the *status quo ante* in collusion with their nominal Democrat adversaries once the interloper is gone:

> . . . in the next few years, a working alliance will develop between regular Democrats—particularly New Democrats from red states—and the milquetoast Republican establishment. . . . Such an alliance would reflect electoral reality, as the Right seems to be growing weaker, not stronger, since the election of Trump two years ago. The ever ambitious Mitt Romney fired on his party's leader prematurely, but his political instincts may be right after all. The GOP is likely to move leftward because that's where a majority of the voters are, and if this happens to Trump's detriment, Romney will hope to pick up the pieces. Neoconservatives and much of the authorized conservative movement would no doubt welcome the Utah senator or someone like him as the kind of "conservative" they could work with were he to run for the presidency.
>
> If the elections since 2018 have shown anything, it's this: blue electoral areas have remained quite solid, while traditionally red ones, even in the Deep South, are up for grabs. That's because the party perceived as being further to the left has benefited from its growing coalition. If there's another explanation, I can't seem to find it. It would not be unusual to have two national parties that are recognizably on the left contending for power. The parties now running the major Western European countries are all to the left of our present GOP.
>
> In a possible alliance, the GOP, as the ideologically and electorally weaker side, will readily cooperate with establishment Democrats. They will undoubtedly find such shared concerns as confronting Putin "the thug" and supporting the Likud Party in Israel. They should have no trouble reaching an agreement on giving amnesty to all non-criminal illegal immigrants once Trump is no longer on the scene.
>
> There is no reason to think that this political shift won't continue. We are looking at a process that's been brought about by college educators, the culture industry, the mass media, and mass immigration, and the momentum may be extremely hard to reverse or even to stop. America's future won't necessarily be British Columbia's, whose provincial legislature features only parties of the left and which hasn't elected a conservative to a provincial office since the early 1990s.

The celebrated Sage of Baltimore, H. L. Mencken observed that "Democracy is the theory that the common people know what they want, and deserve to get it good and hard." This begs the question, though, of who the "common people" are. In contrast to France, where Guilluy's "peripheral France" is still a majority of the French population, US elites in both parties are looking to the day when America's "deplorables" are a minority (which we already may be) that will continue to shrink. Anyone who might object to ethnic and moral replacement is clearly a racist and "white supremacist," comparable to France's "xenophobes, anti-Semites and homophobes." In the not-too-distant future, Guilluy's "normal political mechanisms" may be more than sufficient to handle what's left of a disappearing America.

If Trump is going to build that Wall, he'd better do it damn fast.

"In Ukraine's Presidential Vote the Joker's Wild"

Jim Jatras | *Strategic Culture* | March 23, 2019

The moment of truth is fast approaching in the high-stakes game of Three-Card Monte also known as Ukraine's presidential election. Following a March 31 first-round vote only two of the three leading candidates will make it to a runoff slated for April 21.

The Joker in the deck is, literally, a joker. Volodymyr Zelensky, a comic actor who played President of Ukraine in a popular TV series is now, according to all polls, the leading candidate for the position he once spoofed. Initially considered only a protest candidate funded by Dnipro-based oligarch Ihor Kolomoyskyi as a foil against his erstwhile ally turned bitter enemy, current president Petro Poroshenko, Zelensky seems to have hit a nerve with a public sick of the same old, corrupt faces. "People want to show the authorities the middle finger, and he is playing the role of this middle finger," says one Ukrainian analyst. Donald Trump would understand.

No one better embodies the old guard than the perennial Queen of Diamonds, former prime minister Yulia Tymoshenko. Long a fixture in Ukrainian politics, Tymoshenko, also known as the "Gas Princess" (for her prominent role in the shady natural gas industry), "goddess of the Revolution" (for her firebrand image in Ukraine's turbulent post-Soviet history), and the "Princess Leia of Ukrainian politics" (for her trademark folk-motif braids) maintains both her populist base and her high-style image: "a kind of Eva Peron figure," according to one US analyst, "on the side of the poor but in a fur coat."

After losing the presidency in 2010 to Viktor Yanukovych (who in 2014 was unconstitutionally ousted), Tymoshenko was jailed for allegedly having abused her power when she negotiated a sweetheart deal with the Kremlin for transit of Russian gas to Europe on pricing terms disastrous for Ukraine. Her imprisonment became a cause célèbre among western governments as "selective prosecution" (few insisted the charges were false), claiming, correctly, that she was singled out for political reasons while others guilty of as bad or worse walked. Paul Manafort would understand.

Rounding out the troika of frontrunners is the incumbent President Poroshenko, known as the oligarchic "Chocolate King" because of his confectionary company, *Roshen*. He's also sought to emulate another king, England's Henry VIII, through creation of his own Ukrainian church, which late last year Poroshenko declared independent of the Russian Orthodox Church with assistance from the Greek Orthodox Patriarch in Istanbul and the US State Department.

Coupled with his hard line on Russia demonstrated by the Kerch Strait naval confrontation in November 2018, Poroshenko's religio-nationalist campaign theme of "Army! Language! Faith!" seemed to give him a boost last month. It doesn't seem to have lasted, though, with his church project stalled by internal dissention and rejection from worldwide Orthodox prelates. Worse, prompted by Tymoshenko, Ukraine's parliament, the *Verkhovna Rada*, reluctantly has begun impeachment proceedings against Poroshenko for alleged involvement in a scheme to skim money from Ukraine's military industry in the form of kickbacks for smuggling spare military equipment parts from Russia at inflated prices. Jokester Zelensky accordingly provided his own interpretation of Poroshenko's slogan: "To steal from the army, to selectively split people by language, so that there will be no *faith* in you."

The accusations against Poroshenko highlight his (at best) mixed record when it comes to curbing Ukraine's notorious corruption, which has been called so bad a Nigerian prince would be embarrassed. Poroshenko supporters, which include most western governments and think tanks, say he's making progress. "Although the crooks remain at liberty, Poroshenko has done much to reduce the institutional and structural sources of corruption," writes Rutgers professor Alexander J. Motyl. "Poroshenko is right to believe that institutional change is much more effective in rooting out corruption than convicting a handful of criminals." Ukrainians, he says, should just "ask themselves just which candidate Putin hates most. That's who should be president."

While Washington applauds Poroshenko's firm anti-Russian line, his performance on corruption lags in the eyes of US Ambassador to Ukraine, Marie Yovanovitch, who says efforts have "not yet resulted in the anti-corruption or rule of law reforms that Ukrainians expect or deserve." As reported by Voice of America, Yovanovitch specifically wants Poroshenko to fire his special anti-corruption prosecutor Nazar Kholodnytsky. "Nobody who has been recorded coaching suspects on how to avoid corruption charges can be trusted to prosecute those very same cases," said Yovanovitch, referring to Kholodnytsky. "Those responsible for corruption should be investigated, prosecuted, and if guilty, go to jail."

Yovanovitch may face her own pot/kettle problem when it comes to turning a blind eye to corruption. Ukrainian Prosecutor General Yuriy Lutsenko told Hill.TV's John Solomon that in their very first meeting Yovanovitch gave him a "do not prosecute" list. "My response of that is it is inadmissible," says Lutsenko—who is also is also investigating a claim from a member of the Verkhovna Rada that the director of the National Anti-Corruption Bureau of Ukraine (NABU), Artem Sytnyk, attempted to assist the 2016 US presidential election of Hillary Clinton. "Nobody in this country, neither our president nor our parliament nor our ambassador, will stop me from prosecuting whether there is a crime," continued Lutsenko to Solomon. Yovanovitch has also reportedly badmouthed US President Donald Trump to Ukrainian officials, telling them to ignore him because he's going to be impeached. Predictably, Secretary Mike Pompeo's State Department has rushed to the defense—not of Trump, but of Yovanovitch, who has also ruffled conservative moral sensibilities in Ukraine with her showy support for LGBT issues.

Paradoxically—given the "selective prosecution" accusation against Yanukovych for locking up Tymoshenko—one of the few high-profile prosecutions under Poroshenko has been against a political adversary, former parliamentarian Aleksandr Onyshchenko. *The Washington Times* reported in 2017 that Onyshchenko "was forced to leave Ukraine after being exposed as an opposition supporter. Charges and arrest warrants were issued as a result of Onyshchenko revealing audiotapes that exposed high level corruption in President Poroshenko's inner circle."

It's virtually assured that Zelensky will pass the March 31 first round, leaving Tymoshenko and Poroshenko to fight it out for the other spot in the runoff. Tymoshenko is already laying the groundwork to cry foul if she comes in third. In Strasbourg, pro-Tymoshenko demonstrators recently urged "deputies of the European Parliament to join the electoral process in Ukraine as international observers with the view to preventing massive payoff of voters and to ensuring fair and transparent presidential elections."

Interior Minister Arsen Avakov, who heads the national police, also is looking into Poroshenko's alleged vote buying and has brought one of Poroshenko's campaign heads in for questioning. He also has accused Poroshenko-loyal agencies, such the prosecutor general's office and the SBU (the successor to the Ukrainian branch of the Soviet KGB), of harassing the opposition.

The bottom line is that in the first round, Poroshenko probably doesn't even need to outpoll Tymoshenko to get into the second round. It would be enough to get within five points of her and let what are called locally "administrative measures" take care of the deficit.

In the second round, whether against Poroshenko or Tymoshenko, it's increasingly plausible that Zelensky could become Ukraine's next president on what, for Americans, would be a familiar wave of populist dissatisfaction. Nina Khrushcheva, vocal Putin critic and great-granddaughter of Soviet premier Nikita Khrushchev, thinks that would be a mistake:

Ukraine cannot afford to take a Trump-size risk with someone like Zelensky. But nor should Ukrainians have to put up with another five years of Poroshenko, whose primary focus is on feathering his own nest. That leaves Tymoshenko. Despite her faults, she is the only realistic choice for Ukrainians. And, having survived an unjust prison sentence, she has already proved her willingness to make hard choices on behalf of her country, despite the personal consequences. Whereas a win for Tymoshenko would offer Ukraine its best chance in these tumultuous times, a victory for Zelensky would turn Marx's famous dictum on its head: America's farce would reappear as Ukraine's tragedy.

The bottom line is that at this point, anything can happen. The relevant question may be less who will win than who will lose and what he (or she) will do next. If Tymoshenko doesn't make the second round she will be sure she was cheated, and so will many of her supporters. If the past is any guide, in Ukraine that means taking to the streets. The recent clash in Kiev between police and anti-Poroshenko demonstrators may be a harbinger of things to come.

Whatever the outcome, even if peace is maintained, the eventual winner will face the same intractable problems that have stymied Poroshenko, above all the sputtering conflict in Donbass, high prices, a weak currency, and a struggling economy. There's no reason to think Poroshenko will do any better if reelected, nor that his opponents have a magic wand either.

It bears keeping in mind that in Three-Card Monte the "mark" always loses. In this case, the mark may well be Ukraine's voters.

"War with Russia is Not 'Inevitable.' Keep Repeating That"

Jim Jatras | *Strategic Culture* | April 6, 2019

Well, that didn't take long! No sooner had Robert Torquemada Mueller wrapped up his obscenely expensive inquisition without finding any so-called collusion with Russia than the obstacles to rapprochement between Washington and Moscow immediately dissipated. Calls for a new détente issued from sound thinkers such as Daniel R. DePetris of *The American Conservative* (Trump now has his "first opportunity to settle on a Russia policy without the risk of an extreme political backlash") and Srdja Trifkovic of *Chronicles*:

> Now that the Russian Collusion Myth has been revealed to be a mendacious conspiracy by the Deep State, the Democratic Party and the media, President Donald Trump needs to move on with his election promise to improve relations with Moscow. That is a geopolitical and civilizational necessity.

The undeniable wisdom of such recommendations was instantly recognized by the Washington establishment. Not only did Democrats and Never-Trump Republicans back off their Nazi-Putin paranoia, Trump's own team, starting with National Security Adviser John Bolton and Secretary of State Mike Pompeo rushed copies of DePetris' and Trifkovic's musings onto their boss's desk.

The most striking (though, oddly, little commented upon) evidence of the now-liberated Trump administration's beeline towards a new realist overture towards Moscow was explicit US recognition of Crimea as part of Russia. The newfound respect for Russia's security needs is evident:

The White House
Proclamation on Recognizing Crimea as Part of the Russian Federation
Issued on: March 25, 2019

> The Russian Federation took control of Crimea in 2014 to safeguard its security from external threats. Today, aggressive acts by NATO, including US forces, in the Black Sea and Ukraine continue to make Crimea a potential launching ground for attacks on Russia. Any possible future peace agreement in the region must account for Russia's need to protect itself from NATO and other regional threats. Based on these unique circumstances, it is therefore appropriate to recognize Russian sovereignty over Crimea.

> NOW, THEREFORE, I, DONALD J. TRUMP, President of the United States of America, by virtue of the authority vested in me by the Constitution and the laws of the United States, do hereby proclaim that, the United States recognizes that Crimea is part of the Russian Federation.

> IN WITNESS WHEREOF, I have hereunto set my hand this twenty-fifth day of March, in the year of our Lord two thousand nineteen,

and of the Independence of the United States of America the two
hundred and forty-third.

DONALD J. TRUMP

Oh wait, that actually didn't happen. The genuine March 25 proclamation
related to something entirely different.

Nevermind.

Let's get something straight. It is a fantasy to believe that Trump has been
freed by Mueller's goose egg. The Democrats will use his work as a starting
point (not as a finish) to keep digging into Trump's private and business affairs
to find something for which they can impeach him. As far as Russia goes, sure
there was no direct "collusion," but on the other hand the report, even before
its release, is being cited across the political spectrum as proof that Russia
"interfered" in our election to undermine our "democracy" and thus as reason
to keep the demonization campaign against Russia going. Pathetically, Trump
will continue to defend himself by boasting that "nobody's been tougher on
Russia" than he has while futilely calling for better relations (and even mutual
decreases in military spending, which will join his nonexistent Mexican wall,
his national infrastructure rehab, his Syria pullout, his . . .).

In that sense Mueller has changed nothing. We will continue to sputter
along like this for the remainder of Trump's presidency in a continued
downward slope. If anyone in Moscow thinks Trump now will be able to move
towards normalized relations they are sadly mistaken.

Aside from occasional pipe dreams that supposedly "declining power"
Russia can be pressed into service as a check against China (without offering
Moscow any positive incentive, of course) what we can count on is continuation of the coordinated campaign to render Russia's strategic situation
untenable: deployment of intermediate-range weapons in Europe to make
warning virtually nonexistent (and a strong possibility that START will follow
INF into oblivion); strategic bomber probes with prototype nuclear-armed
cruise missiles to prepare the aircraft for the possibility of launching the Long
Range Stand Off (LRSO) weapon; NATO maneuvers around Russia's land and
sea borders (but only to deter aggression, of course!); more sanctions; yet
more expansion of NATO (Ukraine and Georgia still on the agenda!);
vilification of Russia and, particularly, of President Vladimir Putin; militarization of Ukraine; attacking the Orthodox Church; the Skripal hoax; more
chemical false flags in Syria; trying to tank South Stream 2; blaming Russia
for "undermining democracy" in every western country in addition to the US—
all are components of a full-spectrum operation to destroy Russia's economy,
to destabilize its society, to replace its "regime" with one more to their
"partners'" liking, and ultimately to dismember Russia.

In the face of this, one is mystified why Putin, Foreign Minister Sergei
Lavrov, and other Russian statesmen continue to refer politely to their
Western "partners" even when it's painfully clear that they *have* no Western
partners. While these "partners"—who, it should be noted, *never* that use that
term about the Russians—claim they only want to change Moscow's "behavior," that isn't true. There is nothing Russia could do short of surrendering
its sovereignty and returning to the 1990s that would even begin TO mollify
Russia's "partners." As US Secretary of State Mike Pompeo put it in December
2018, America's "mission is to reassert our sovereignty [and] reform the
liberal international order," and "we want our friends to help us and to exert
their sovereignty as well." But Russia and other countries that haven't
"embraced Western values of freedom and international cooperation" to

Pompeo's satisfaction aren't our "friends" and thus have no such sovereign liberty.

In short, these Western "partners" hate Russia not for what it does, but for what it *is*: an obstacle to absolute global domination by a US-led "liberal international order." Russia's deployment of the most powerful weapons imaginable perhaps can limit the military aspect of that agenda, but it cannot reverse it. Quite to the contrary, such actions, like Moscow's defensive moves after the 2014 regime change in Ukraine or Russia's 2015 deployment in Syria or current presence in Venezuela, are held up as further "proof" of Russians' "typically, almost genetically driven" aggressiveness, in the words of former CIA Director James Clapper.

Does this mean that western war planners are preparing for a redux of the 1812 Grande Armée or 1941 Operation Barbarossa rolling across Belarus or Ukraine into Russia? No. Rather, western officials, mainly in the US, are confident (aren't they always?) that under constant moral, economic, financial, and military pressure a tipping point will be reached in Russia's internal instability and strategic vulnerability (the latter including the knowledge that leadership decapitation without warning is possible), forcing Moscow to fold, either through revolution, or coup, or inflicting a (we would hope, limited) military humiliation on them somewhere.

Notwithstanding their soft rhetoric, the Russian leadership understands this quite well. As Professor Stephen Cohen observes:

> Moscow closely follows what is said and written in the United States about US-Russian relations. Here too words have consequences. On March 14, Russia's National Security Council, headed by President Putin, officially raised its perception of American intentions toward Russia from "military dangers" (*opasnosti*) to direct "military threats" (*ugrozy*). In short, the Kremlin is preparing for war, however defensive its intention.

Just over a year ago, in March 2018, Putin unveiled a new set of deterrent capabilities against "all those who have fueled the arms race over the last 15 years, sought to win unilateral advantages over Russia, [and] introduced unlawful sanctions aimed to contain our country's development."(Hint: he was talking about the US and NATO.) "Nobody listened to us," Putin said then. "Well, listen to us now."

Of course, they didn't listen a year ago. And they're not listening today, either.

Gilbert Doctorow likens the current situation to that in depicted by Leo Tolstoy in *War and Peace*. Today as then, what happens next will be less due to this or that policymaker making this or that bad decision as much as the existence of a "near universal acceptance of the logic of the coming war" (Must read: "'War and Peace': The Relevance of 1812 as Explained by Tolstoy to Current Global Affairs," *Antiwar.com*):

> Transposed to our own day, this issue finds its parallel in the informational war the United States and the West more generally have been waging against Russia. The defamation of Putin, the denigration of Russia all have been swallowed whole by the vast majority of our political classes, who today would view with equanimity, perhaps even with enthusiasm any military conflict with Russia that may arise, whatever the immediate cause.

Hardheaded observers, notably military men, might reject this notion. Where is mobilization of NATO armies in offensive strength? The Russians know

NATO is a joke—they won't even cough up Trump's lousy two percent of GDP! General Shoigu isn't stupid!

Objectively that's true. But that doesn't change the fact that western, especially American, policymakers have defined our attitude towards Russia as an existential struggle that can have only one outcome—Russia's collapse, leading to regime change—either via war or means short of war. All elements of western policy are geared to that one inalterable objective.

That this policy won't and cannot succeed is never even considered by its authors. It continues because, literally, they cannot think of Russia in any other way. Nikolai Gogol likened the Russia of his day to a speeding troika, wordlessly hurtling towards its fate while "all things on earth fly by and other nations and states gaze askance as they step aside and give her the right of way."

Today, that reckless plunge describes not Russia but America and our craven satellites. As Israel Shamir concludes:

'Russians have few ambitions. They do not want to rule the world, or even to dominate their neighbors. They do not want to fight the Empire. They would be content to be left in peace. But if pushed, and now they are being pushed, they will respond. In [the] Russian view, even the most hostile American politicians will desist before the Doomsday collision. And if not, let it be.'

The question that no one in Washington seemingly is asking themselves is not whether war is inevitable but whether the Russian leadership, despite their polite talk, have come to believe (rightly) that positive change in their "partners'" behavior is very unlikely and that therefore war is much more likely than not, according to the "logic" of things described by Doctorow. "Fifty years ago, the streets of Leningrad taught me one rule: if a fight is inevitable you have to strike first," Putin told journalists at the 2015 Valdai conference. Even if, from the west's point of view war is not inevitable, what if the Russians have come to believe it is? (Suggested viewing: the films *1612* (2007) and the *Taras Bulba* (2009) as psychological war preparation of the population comparable to Sergei Eisenstein's World War II-era *Alexander Nevsky* (complete with a western bishop with a swastika on his miter) and the two-part *Ivan the Terrible*.)

Even more than a year ago, when the writing was already on the wall that Russiagate would turn out to be a whiff as far as nailing Trump goes, it was clear that in one important sense it had exceeded beyond all expectations: achieving permanent enmity between the US and Russia. Now, with the pointless investigation concluded, nothing has improved, nor can there be much expectation that it will. As Doctorow notes:

'Indeed, no one wants war, neither Washington nor Moscow. However, the step by step dismantling of the channels of communication, of the symbolic projects for cooperation across a wide array of domains, and now dismantling of all the arms limitation agreements that took decades to negotiate and ratify, plus the incoming new weapons systems that leave both sides with under 10 minutes to decide how to respond to alarms of incoming missiles—all of this prepares the way for the Accident to end all Accidents. Such false alarms occurred in the Cold War but some slight measure of mutual trust prompted restraint. That is all gone now and if something goes awry, we are all dead ducks.'

Barring a miracle, this does not end well.

Ukraine's Unheeded Warning

Immediate Course-ChangeNeeded to Put the Ukrainian Humpty-DumptyBack Together Again

James George Jatras | *American Institute in Ukraine* | March 26, 2014

Almost all current Western media commentary and analysis on Ukraine centers on the East-West spitting match over Moscow's incorporation of Crimea, and whether Russian forces may move into other areas. Little attention is being paid to the circumstance that gave rise to the crisis—the effective collapse of Ukraine's constitutional order and the dire political, economic, and fiscal consequences. Even less consideration is given to what interested countries, East and West, can and must do to put the Ukrainian humpty-dumpty back together again.

Any serious analysis of how we have arrived to where we are now must start with the fact that the current administration in Kiev has little claim of constitutional legitimacy. Even the new provisional "authorities" (for want of better term) effectively concede that the proper constitutional order was not followed with respect to the physical, if not legal, removal of President Viktor Yanukovych.

Articles 108 through 112 of the Ukrainian constitution allow the removal of a president only for medical incapacity, resignation, death (none of which occurred) or impeachment. Impeachment under Article 112 requires, first, that following a "special *ad hoc* investigating commission, composed of special prosecutor and special investigators to conduct an investigation"—which, needless to say, did not take place—"the Verkhovna Rada shall, by at least two-thirds of its constitutional membership, adopt a decision to bring charges against the President of Ukraine." Then, the "decision on the removal of the President of Ukraine from the office in compliance with the procedure of impeachment shall be adopted by the Verkhovna Rada of Ukraine by at least three-quarters of its constitutional membership." In the 450-seat body, that would require 338 votes (ten more than the actual number cast on February 22) followed by a review of the case by the Constitutional Court of Ukraine, which requirement also was not met. No Rada deputies voted against Yanukovych's removal, with dissenters either abstaining or absent from a chamber in which armed men stood watch to assure the expected outcome.

Still, the unelected Kiev administration and the Western countries that uncritically accept it as "the new Ukrainian government" claim that Yanukovych was properly ejected because he had "fled" first from Kiev, then from Ukraine, immediately following the February 21 power-sharing agreement signed by him and by three Opposition figures: Arseniy Yatseniuk, now regarded as "prime minister" by Western governments; Vitaly Klitschko, left out of the new administration"; and Oleh Tyahnybok, whose extreme nationalist "Svoboda" party effectively holds Kiev hostage, with five ministers in the new "administration" (including the Defense and Education Ministries and a Deputy Prime Minister) and "street cred" with armed groups like the even more extreme "Praviy Sektor," which remain camped out in Maidan. Left unmentioned is that Yanukovych had little option to remain in place (unless he wished to consider his removal under Article 108(4), death in office), given that immediately after the agreement was signed and co-signed by the foreign ministers of three European Union countries (Poland, Germany, France), and witnessed by a Russian representative, "the Maidan" rejected it, with armed men occupying government buildings as soon as they were vacated by the police in compliance with the agreement.

Besides lacking legal or constitutional authority, the Kiev administration has no serious claim to representing Ukraine as a whole. Overwhelmingly stacked with membership from the far west of Ukraine, one of the first acts of the new administration was to pass a law downgrading the status of the Russian language from the limited official use it had been accorded under Yanukovych. For cosmetic reasons, the law was quietly shelved—for the time being . . .

Quite aside from voters in the south and east of Ukraine whose votes in the 2010 presidential election and 2012 parliamentary vote effectively have been stolen from them, the Kiev administration cannot be said to be representative even of all forces *in opposition* to Yanukovych. The "interim" administration includes no members of Klitschko's UDAR or anyone representing the "Solidarity" party of former minister Petro Poroshenko, shown by polls to be one of the country's most popular politicians and a likely contender for the presidency. Indeed, how could Klitschko or Poroshenko be expected to join hands with a party dominated by ultranationalists and anti-Semites, a direct negation of the "European values" the Kiev administration claims to advocate? Or participate in an administration that takes its cues from radical groups whose "authority" (in Chairman Mao's famous phrase) comes from the barrel of a gun?

These flaws are not just academic. They relate directly to the collapsing state of law and order in Ukraine and the physical safety of Ukrainian citizens, and a deadly threat to anyone who doesn't toe the line of extreme pro-Bandera, UPA/OUN ideology. The growing anarchy has run the gamut from the forced "resignation" of the CEO of Ukraine's National Television Company, Aleksandr Panteleymonov, beaten over the head by Svoboda deputies, to a robbery of train passengers bound for neighboring Moldova. Recently police gunned down Oleksandr Muzychko, a/k/a Sashko Bily, a thuggish leader of Praviy Sektor, with retaliation expected. Is the new, "pro-Europe," "democratic" Ukraine about to descend into its own downward spiral of internecine brutality? Early presidential elections, now scheduled for May as a means to keep voters in the south and east marginalized and prevent their mobilizing any credible electoral force in the face of violent provocations, can only aggravate the current trend toward chaos.

The western governments who have granted the Kiev administration a moral *carte blanche* (in place of a monetary blank check that will not arrive), need to take a step back and consider can be done to prevent Ukraine's slide from bad to worse. Among the first items must be to neutralize the poisonous atmosphere between Ukraine's regions and language zones. These should include:

- Agreement on a return to the 2004 mixed presidential-parliamentary constitution.
- Decentralization, perhaps in a federal structure, to give real power to local and regional governments, and to assure the south and east they will not be dominated by radical groups from the west.
- Giving Russian status as a national language, with official use of Ukrainian and Russian according to which language predominates locally.

- To hold off on tying Ukraine exclusively to either the EU or the Russian-led Customs Union until a balance can be struck that ensures the country's cooperation with both blocs in a way that protects and restores all sectors of the rapidly sinking economy.
- Ukraine's foreign and security policy should be "Finlandized," as suggested by Henry Kissinger and others. (NOTE: The recent signing of the "political chapters" of the Association Agreement with the EU, in which Kiev would harmonize its policies with Brussels, which in turn is subordinated to NATO, was a serious step in the wrong direction.)
- Any questions of Ukraine's fundamental political, military, and economic orientation should be addressed by referendum.

Since achieving independence in 1991, the key vulnerabilities of Ukraine have been both its centrifugal regional tendencies (which might be more manageable in a federal structure) and the weakness of its state institutions in the face of oligarchic interests (likely to be an intractable as ever, noting that both the interim prime minister and president of the Kiev administration are lieutenants of Yulia Tymoshenko). To an extent greater than western governments care to admit, the violent overthrow of Yanukovych—whatever his faults—in effect "broke" the Ukrainian state, and all of Washington's horses, and all of Brussels' men have been unable to put it back together again. As things stand, the disorders promise to get worse not better, making the future unity of the country doubtful unless a rapid course change occurs soon.

"Why Do the 'Authorities' in Kiev Reject Federalism and Language Rights?"

Kiev "Administration" Prefers to Flirt with NATO

James George Jatras | *American Institute in Ukraine* | April 2, 2014

In the not-too-distant past, "federalism" was not a dirty word in Ukrainian politics, even from a western-oriented, nationalist perspective. For example, Professor Alexander J. Motyl of Rutgers University, a frequent commentator on Ukrainian affairs, last year made some thoughtful suggestions why decentralization made sense, especially in combating corruption (as AIU commented at the time, see "Decentralizing Ukraine: an Issue that Deserves Serious Discussion," August 2013).

Now, however, western governments view the prospect of federalism as just a ploy to break Ukraine up. Secretary of State John Kerry has deferred the question of federalism to the unelected Kiev "administration," which the U.S. and Europe uncritically accepted collectively as the legitimate government and the authoritative voice of all of Ukraine's people. Their rant is unsurprising:

> "Why does Russia not introduce federalism . . . Why does it not give more powers to national regions of the (Russian) Federation . . . Why does it not introduce state languages, other than Russian,

including Ukrainian, which is spoken by millions of Russians?" it
asked.

"There's no need to preach to others. It's better to put things in
order in your own house," it said. [*Reuters*, "Ukraine hits back at
proposals by Russia's Lavrov," March 31, 2014]

Of course, the Russian Federation does in fact have a functional federal structure. Under Article 68 of the Russian Constitution, subjects of the Federation
have the right to adopt state languages, which is more than Ukrainian oblasts
can do. There are dozens of republican official languages, in fact including
Ukrainian and Crimean Tatar, as well other languages with official status.
Conversely, since no language other than Russian has a nationwide presence
it is the only state language on the entire territory of the federation.

This contrasts sharply to Ukraine, where Ukrainian-Russian bilingualism
is a matter of daily life in much if not most of the country, but Article 10 of
Ukraine's constitution declares absurdly that Russian is the language only of
a "national minority." If and when Ukraine decides to take a hard look at
federalism, the *fact* of Ukraine's functional bilingualism needs to be given a
more realistic legal framework that promotes unity, not disunity, benefiting
from the experience of other bilingual or multilingual countries. One way to
do that would be in the form of a national accord that defines the roles of
Ukrainian and Russian as national languages in a federalized constitutional
structure. In addition, Kiev's performance under the European Charter for
Regional or Minority Languages remains inadequate with respect to truly
minority languages like Romanian, Bulgarian, or Gagauz—or Rusyn, which
Kiev refuses to recognize at all, even though it is protected as an official
minority language in Slovakia, Serbia, Romania, and elsewhere.

The harsh and misplaced response of the Kiev "administration" rejecting
even a discussion of federalism and language rights can only lead to further
weakening of Ukraine's cohesion, not its strengthening. Unfortunately, it's
clear where the Kiev "administration" is placing its priorities: on its geopolitical and military-strategic agenda. Yesterday, the NATO-Ukraine Commission issued a statement that included (presumably not as an April Fool's
joke):

We welcome Ukraine's signature of the political chapters of the
Association Agreement with the European Union on 21 March.

One would think the "political chapters" in an agreement with a completely
different organization—the European Union—would be none of NATO's
concern. But of course it is very much NATO's business, as the agreement
signed on March 21 obligates Kiev to harmonize its foreign and security
policies with Brussels, which in turn is subordinated to NATO under the 2002
"Berlin Plus" agreement.

Continued misplacement of priorities by western governments in their
determined support for the unrepresentative and unelected Kiev "administration" can only threaten Ukraine's already fragile already fragile unity.

Europe should be wary of the official "U.S. position" on Ukraine

James George Jatras | *American Institute in Ukraine* | April 7, 2014

With the declaration this week of a "Donetsk Republic" and pro-Russian activists' seizure of public buildings in Lugansk and Kharkov, the European Union is once again presented with the dilemma of how to respond to the enduring Ukraine crisis. So far, as was the case with Crimea, the EU position seems to be one of "American lite": mimicking Washington's rhetorical hard line while dragging their feet on sanctions in deference to Europe's greater exposure to possible Russian retaliation.

But qualified endorsement of tough U.S. talk while attempting to moderate actions isn't much of a strategy, starting with a mistaken reading of the mood in the United States. While it might seem reasonable to take hawkish statements by President Barack Obama and Secretary of State John Kerry as definitive of "the American position" on Ukraine, the reality of American opinion is far more complex. It is a complexity of which Europe should take note.

The "American position" as Europeans may hear it comes mostly from a relatively limited range of sources: a bipartisan, Washington-based foreign policy establishment; a group of think tanks, most of them financed directly or indirectly by the U.S. government; and publications with a mostly "inside the Beltway" audience that both reflect and reinforce government and think tank opinion.

It should be remembered that last year the same closed echo chamber was overwhelmingly supportive of President Obama's threat to launch airstrikes against Syria over claims the Assad regime had used chemical weapons. At seemingly the last minute, Mr. Obama referred the matter to Congress, which was buried by a tsunami of public opposition. After Afghanistan and Iraq, Americans—particularly younger voters—have had enough.

We have not yet arrived at either the prospect of military involvement or sanctions severe enough to endanger the European economy, but it's clear that most Americans' attitude toward Ukraine is that it is not our problem. While polls show some support for the kind of symbolic sanctions we've seen so far, Americans oppose either military intervention or military assistance to Ukraine. Even advocates of intervention, such as former Secretary of State Condoleezza Rice, admit and lament that their fellow Americans just are not with them. Nor is this a matter of knowledge and interest: a recent poll shows that the *less* Americans knew about Ukraine, including its location, the *more* they favored U.S. involvement.

European self-interest would be well served by listening to recommendations from the "other America" that differs from the official line and covers the spectrum from the Left (*The Nation*); Libertarianism (the CATO Institute, *Reason* magazine), to the Right (*The American Conservative*), the moderate center (*The National Interest*). Particularly significant are the voices of some respected "old gray heads," themselves products of the Washington establishment but advocate a different line: that Europe, Russia, and the U.S. need to cooperate and compromise in putting Ukraine back together again.

For example, former Secretary of State Henry Kissinger advocates internally a "policy of reconciliation between the various parts of their country" and internationally a "posture comparable to that of Finland." Former National Security Council adviser to President George W. Bush Thomas Graham has suggested an outline designed of restoring regionally balanced government, power-sharing, constitutional reform, and trade ties to both the EU and Russia. The common theme is that within Ukraine and internationally "compromise" must stop being a dirty word.

It is underestimated the extent to which the February unconstitutional seizure of power in Kiev fractured the Ukrainian state. All the talk of "taking Ukraine into Europe" doesn't change the fact that an elected president was chased out of office, with the participation of some violent, radical elements that make, say, Greece's Golden Dawn seem tame. (By contrast, protesters in Donetsk are rising up against an oligarch installed as governor, elected by nobody.) Restoring a functioning country will demand insistent negotiations across the range of issues: the balance between presidential and parliamentary powers, language rights, reigning in extremists, delaying presidential elections (now scheduled for next month) to allow Ukraine's south and east to have a fair voice, and the relative strength of the "center" and the regions in a decentralized or even federalized order that restores local confidence.

As cooler heads can agree, Ukraine's future viability—if it has one—depends on restoring its status as a "bridge" between Europe and Russia and a balance among its regions. Failure to achieve that can only lead to more "Crimeas" and "Donetsks," perhaps at some point spreading to western regions as central authority continues to break down. Even more dangerously, the unelected "administration" in Kiev may decide that the only way to rescue the situation is a declaration of martial law and total crackdown, something the legally elected Viktor Yanukovych only threatened in Kiev. That could open the door to a level of violence we have not yet seen, with unforeseeable consequences.

If Europeans don't want to get trapped into a downward spiral of incendiary threats and escalating reprisals—which however much they might pain Russia will hurt Europe significantly, America hardly at all, and Ukrainians most—they would do well to listen to the "other" American voices that are more accord with Europe's own interests.

Geneva Agreement on Ukraine Barely a Pause in Deepening Confrontation

James George Jatras | *American Institute in Ukraine* | April 22, 2014

Last week's announcement in Geneva of a consensus among four concerned parties—the United States, the European Union, the Russian Federation, and the interim administration in Kiev—on a common framework for defusing the Ukraine crisis was widely greeting with cautious hope. It turns out even that modest level of optimism was premature.

The short (just over 200 words) statement was extremely vague, amounting to little more than a general declaration of principles that armed groups should end their occupations of public places and that Ukraine should undertake a broad-based constitutional reform. It included no details on a timetable for implementation, no specific actions to be taken by any side, and no follow-up steps.

Even aspects of the agreement critical to any success were left undefined, perhaps because no real agreement existed. For example, a key requirement is that "all illegal armed groups must be disarmed; all illegally seized buildings must be returned to legitimate owners; all illegally occupied streets, squares and other public places in Ukrainian cities and towns must be vacated." But what constitutes an "illegal armed group"? Who is "illegally occupying" which "public places"? Who will decide? The agreement gives no indication.

Thus, within a day of the Geneva announcement western governments were denouncing pro-Russian activists in east Ukraine for refusing to leave regional and municipal government buildings—and threatening Moscow with new sanctions if they failed to do so immediately. The activists responded that they were not a party to the agreement and were not bound by it. (Perhaps by design, this echoes the response from protesters on the streets of Kiev when told of the February 21 power-sharing agreement between President Viktor Yanukovych and then-Opposition leaders.) They also insisted that since the unelected Kiev administration itself in an "illegal armed group" that took power by means of street violence, it should stand down first: "We absolutely agree that all buildings should be vacated—including the buildings taken by [Prime Minister] Yatsenyuk and [Acting President] Turchynov. If they leave their buildings, we shall do the same too," said Mr [Denis] Pushilin [of the self-proclaimed Donetsk Peoples Republic]. "Our position is absolutely neutral: if everybody will do it, we will do it as well."

Not only does the Kiev administration have no intention of relinquishing any authority, it has taken no steps to dislodge occupiers of the Maidan (falling literally under the rubric of "squares" in the Geneva agreement). Instead, it has moved to integrate personnel from radical groups like Praviy Sektor into a new "National Guard"—which, having been "legalized" can no longer be considered among "illegal armed groups" that must be "disarmed."

Perhaps each side simply hoped to use the Geneva forum as a means to achieve some more limited goal. For example, the unelected Kiev administration was effectively treated as representing the state of "Ukraine" for purposes of the negotiations, largely negating Moscow's pro forma position of not recognizing the post-Yanukovych leadership in the capital. Kiev also needed a breathing space in the face of the embarrassing collapse of its armed "anti-terrorist operation" last week. On the other hand, no mention was made of the status of Crimea, which even western observers noted was tantamount to Kiev's conceding its loss.

Meanwhile, U.S. Vice President Biden arrived in Kiev today to pledge full American support for the Kiev administration and to issue new threats to Russia that "time is short" to keep its Geneva commitments or face new sanctions. "Now it is time for Russia to stop talking and to start acting on the commitments that they made to get pro-Russia separatists to vacate buildings and checkpoints," Biden said. Kiev then announced it was resuming its armed action against eastern "separatists" under a newly formed commando group: "Ukraine's interior ministry has reportedly created a special 'Timur' battalion to fight separatism in the Luhansk region. Although the unit would appear to take its name from its commander, army veteran and champion power lifter Timur Yuldashev, he said on Ukrainian television it was so named because Timur in the Uzbek language means 'ironclad.'"

In short, it seems the Geneva agreement has set the stage for more violence, not less. Rather than a genuine meeting of the minds on joint steps to resolve the Ukraine crisis and to engage the U.S., EU, and Russia on a cooperative effort to maintain Ukraine as a viable state, it seems Geneva has turned into an excuse for each side to accuse the other of bad faith. In the end, Geneva may simply end up as a set of talking points for each side as the confrontation escalates further and Ukraine spirals deeper into a political and economic abyss.

German Report: European Union's Demand of 'Either–Or Choice' Pushed Ukraine Over the Brink

James George Jatras | *American Institute in Ukraine* | June 6, 2014

Since its inception in 2009, the American Institute in Ukraine (AIU) consistently has advocated the position that balance and compromise were essential to preserving Ukraine's stability and the country's essential role between East and West. This is a position also taken by many mainstream, respected commentators on both sides of the Atlantic, both before and during the current crisis. For example, just today, director of the Belfer Center for Science and International Affairs at Harvard University's John F. Kennedy School of Government, proposed the well-known key elements of an enduring settlement: neutrality, balanced trade ties, decentralization, minority and language rights, disarmament of armed groups both east and west, and international security guarantees. (See "How to Solve the Ukraine Crisis," *The National Interest*)

Unfortunately, this is not the course the west (preeminently the United States but also the European Union (EU)) has chosen to take. Instead of balance and compromise, the EU—spearheaded by the misguided "Eastern Partnership" (EaP), about which more below—insisted on forcing Ukraine into a single-vector, pro-western course of "Euro-Atlantic integration," with the disastrous results we have seen. As reported by *Deutsche Welle*:

> The European Union has been given a poor report card for its foreign policy by a group of prominent peace researchers who point to shortcomings in how the EU has dealt with its neighbors in the Ukraine crisis.
>
> The assessment was made by five leading research institutes in their "Friedensgutachten 2014" (Peace Report 2014), presented jointly in Berlin on Tuesday (03.06.2014).
>
> "The European Union policy of essentially presenting Ukraine with an either-or choice in the form of the association agreement was a momentous mistake," said Ines-Jacqueline Werkner of the Protestant Institute for Interdisciplinary Research in Heidelberg (FEST). According to her analysis, the EU has contributed to the development of the Ukraine crisis and has done little to resolve it.

EU's mistake

> "When the EU sided with the opposition on the Maidan—against the regime with which it previously wanted to sign an agreement—it increased internal political polarization and excluded itself as a mediator and conflict manager," said Werkner.
>
> The report recommends that the OSCE maintain an ongoing presence in Ukraine
>
> Bruno Schoch of the Peace Research Institute Frankfurt (PRIF) argued that the EU was overwhelmed when confronted with a player like Russia at a geopolitical level.
>
> Attempts by the foreign ministers of Germany, Poland and France to mediate in Kyiv in February came too late, according to the report.

By their own account, the five institutes hope their findings will enable them to influence foreign policy discourse in Germany. [. . .]

The researchers also made other suggestions for resolving the conflict. Among them: Ukraine should hold roundtable talks on regional and local levels, and supporters of the former President Viktor Yanukovych's Party of Regions should be included in the government.

Ukraine should also be clearly denied possible NATO membership. The long-term goal should be to make Ukraine a "connecting bridge" between the EU and Russia.

It bears shining a light on not only the fact that the EU made the mistake of pushing the "either-or choice" on Ukraine, but why that mistake was made at all. First, as is obvious, the U.S. bipartisan foreign policy establishment has consistently pushed the EU to pursue geopolitical, rather than purely economic, goals in its policies toward Ukraine and other former Soviet republics, notably Moldova and Georgia. Second, the major players in the EU, notably Germany, were largely "asleep at the switch" while they allowed an *ad hoc* "coalition of the willing" pursue their own agendas, in which the entire EU became trapped willy-nilly. As earlier noted by AIU:

> The Eastern Partnership was never a project to which all of the EU's members were fully committed but was always the pet project of Sweden and (especially) of Poland, for whom the eastern partners— and Ukraine in particular—were a "strategic" backyard. Even Romania has been supportive of the EaP only insofar as it advances its own goals regarding Moldova, while giving priority to other instruments for the same purpose, such as the Organization of the Black Sea Economic Cooperation. (Likewise, the EU's parallel initiative for North Africa and the Middle East, the "Union for the Mediterranean," reflects the priorities of Spain, France, and Italy.) To an extent, EaP can be seen as an analogue to the similarly incoherent GUAM (Georgia-Ukraine-Azerbaijan-Moldova), a U.S.-backed grouping with a vague security mission, valuable only to thwart Russia.

It remains to be seen whether the EU can take a step back and institute an eastern policy that reflects the interests of the EU as a whole, and not primarily the enthusiasms of the EaP's active supporters, backed by Washington.

A good measure of whether such a reassessment is likely is whether the EU can rein in the EaP's one-sided "integrationist" impulses when it comes to Moldova, a country that in its way exhibits fault lines and the need for balance and compromise reminiscent of Ukraine. For example, a recent study by the London School of Economics (LSE) suggests the EU-Moldova Association Agreement (AA), due to be signed later this month, has become more complicated in light of the continuing turmoil in neighboring Ukraine. As in Ukraine, forcing Moldovans to make an "either-or choice" between the EU and the Moscow-led Customs Union could exacerbate existing political and ethno/linguistic divisions, with unpredictable consequences we have seen all too well in Ukraine.

Nonetheless, as of this writing both the EU and the governing authorities in Chișinău seem prepared to press forward on the AA with single-minded determination.

Ceasefire and Talks in Ukraine: a Chance for Peace, Or Just an Opportunity for More Confrontation?

James George Jatras | *American Institute in Ukraine* | June 24, 2014

The unilateral ceasefire declared on June 20 by Petro Poroshenko, installed as president in Kiev earlier this month, initially was rejected as a mere ultimatum by leaders of the independent republics declared in Donetsk and Lugansk oblasts. Eastern fighters were particularly disparaging of Poroshenko's demand that they disarm. As reported by *The Guardian*: "Mikhail Verin, commander of the Russian Orthodox army, one of the most powerful militias in Donetsk, said Poroshenko was 'deceiving Russia and the European Union' and playing for time to reposition his forces for further attacks.'"

But upon Kiev's grudging acceptance of the need to negotiate with the easterners' representatives—albeit through the mediation of former President Leonid Kuchma as a face-saving buffer to allow Poroshenko to claim his administration was not talking directly to "terrorists" and those with "blood on their hands"—the ceasefire is now acknowledged, at least in principle, by both sides. The question is, does the will and ability exist to negotiate a political solution, or is this just a time-out before a new round of fighting in Ukraine and of stepped-up geopolitical confrontation?

Yesterday, June 23, an initial meeting conducted by Kuchma was held in Donetsk. Also participating was Viktor Medvedchuk, the head of the pro-Russian non-governmental organization (and close acquaintance of Russian President Vladimir Putin); Russian Ambassador to Ukraine Mikhail Zurabov; representative for the Organization for Security and Cooperation in Europe (OSCE) and chairman-in-office Heidi Tagliavini; Prime Minister of the contested Donetsk People's Republic Aleksandr Borodai; and southeast movement leader and former candidate for Ukraine's presidency Oleg Tsariov, representing the Lugansk People's Republic. Media reported no substantive progress, other than the fact of the meeting itself and the participants' commitment to meet again. "Both sides will respect this, God willing," Kuchma told reporters after the meeting, saying that he hoped to get a peace process on track during the break in hostilities.

Not that fighting has ceased entirely. In the initial days of the truce—which is only scheduled to last until June 27, not coincidentally the date when Poroshenko expects to sign an Association Agreement with the EU—each side has blamed the other for continuing hostilities. Today, pro-Kiev forces reportedly shelled the village of Semyonovka near the town of Sloviansk. Not far away, a MI–8 helicopter was shot down by a missile fired from a man-portable air defense system, killing nine Ukrainian fighters.

If the shaky ceasefire continues, at least for now, three factors will be crucial to whether it leads to a broader peace settlement or to further bloodshed:

> First, it is critical whether progress can be made on the substance of the negotiations themselves, specifically on the status of the eastern oblasts. As initially formulated in Poroshenko's plan, concessions fall far short of easterners' demands for local self-rule, much less of federalization. Offers of local autonomy would be limited to the creation of regional executive committees, with Kiev still retain-

ing the right to overrule governors. Use of the Russian language would be similarly revocable by Kiev. It is difficult to see how easterners could accept such terms as sufficient incentive to abolish their independent republics declared in Lugansk and Donetsk.

Second, it remains to be seen how much control Poroshenko actually has over "his side" of the negotiations. Even assuming he does control the official Ukrainian armed forces, the same cannot necessarily be said for groups like the "Azov battalion," which is manned largely by recruits of the extremist Praviy Sektor and funded by Dnepropetrovsk oligarch Igor Kolomoisky, who has refused to accept Poroshenko's ceasefire declaration. If Kiev were to agree to terms acceptable to the east, it's not clear Poroshenko would be able to implement it in the face of anticipated opposition from extreme nationalists. Perhaps Poroshenko's threatened "Plan B" of resumed attacks if the ceasefire fails indicates limited expectations.

Third, it is still unclear whether western governments will urge restraint on both sides and genuine negotiations for a peaceful solution, or whether a policy of sanctions threats and tough rhetoric will prevail to further agendas not directly relating to Ukraine. Continuing to exonerate Kiev of all responsibility for bloodshed in the east while placing all the blame on local militias—and on Moscow—is not likely to help produce a solution both sides can live with. As noted by Ted Carpenter, a longtime analyst with Washington's CATO Institute:

> There is a disturbing pattern over the decades in Washington's negotiations with countries deemed to be adversaries. It is a tendency to adopt a rigid stance marked by unrealistic demands that make achieving a settlement virtually impossible. Often, harsh economic sanctions against the target country reinforce the provocative diplomatic posture.

An illustration of what Carpenter means is the extent to which other voices in Washington see the Ukraine crisis an *opportunity* to give NATO a "new narrative": agreement on a "common threat," permanent deployment of NATO (i.e., American) forces to Poland and the Baltic States, potential membership of Finland and Sweden, and "reforming" the North Atlantic Council to put more authority into the hands of the (U.S.-compliant) Secretary General instead of member states' ambassadors. As they say: never let a good crisis go to waste.

Poroshenko's On–Again, Off–Again Offensive Shows His Narrowing Options

James George Jatras | *American Institute in Ukraine* | July 3, 2014

As was expected, on June 27 Petro Poroshenko joined representatives of Moldova and Georgia in Brussels to sign an Association Agreement (AA) with the European Union.

But once the smiles and congratulatory handshakes over Ukraine's "European choice" ended, Poroshenko had to return to Kiev to face the grim facts: fiscal insolvency heading for default, a plunging economy and national currency, a cutoff of gas supplies for non-payment, the continued presence of protesters occupying parts of the capital, and an unresolved security crisis in the Donetsk and Lugansk oblasts.

Regarding the last, on the day he signed the AA Poroshenko extended the ceasefire he had originally declared unilaterally (which was later accepted by armed militias in the east, upon the opening of negotiations) for an additional 72 hours, until Monday, June 30. Hopes of sustainable peace were raised in quadripartite discussions between Poroshenko and other Kiev officials with leaders of France, Germany, and Russia, all of whom supported continued suspension of hostilities to allow talks on humanitarian relief and border security. While during the truce each side accused the other of violations, the level of fighting nonetheless had subsided, to the relief of the locals.

But at 10 PM Kiev time on June 30, Poroshenko abruptly declared the truce at and end, with the immediate start of a new offensive to rid the region of people he called "dirt and parasites." The operation he earlier had ominously described only as "Plan B," to "destroy" all those who refused to disarm and submit to Kiev's authority, had begun.

In returning to the war option, and ignoring pleas from Paris, Berlin, and Moscow, Poroshenko seemed to be heeding two other constituencies.

First, his ceasefire had never been popular with more radical nationalist elements that formed the core of the movement that brought down the Yanukovych administration, and without which Poroshenko would not now be installed as president. During the extension, thousands gathered in the streets of Kiev to demand an "end to the ceasefire, introduction of martial law and provision of weapons to volunteer units" such as the "Donbas" battalion, whose commander, Semyon Semenchenko, addressed the pro-war crowd. Semenchenko—who reportedly is an ethnic Russian—later posted on *Facebook* what could be seen as an ultimatum to Poroshenko: "They say this was 'the last peaceful demonstration'. It seems they're right."

Second, despite French, German, and Russian calls for peace, the voice of the United States in support of peace was conspicuously absent. Perhaps pending another leaked phone call, it is not knowable what U.S. officials might have told Kiev privately. However, from public comment made *before* Poroshenko's announcement, Washington's favorable view of renewed military action may be inferred:

> The United States have made an early signal that they will support Poroshenko's decision. State Department spokesperson Jen Psaki said during her daily press briefing on June 30 that a ceasefire extension is up to Ukraine, and that the U.S. will support whatever decision the president makes.

Upon resumption of Kiev's hostile actions, Psaki called them "moderate and measured." This would come as news to civilians under Kiev forces' shelling in Slavyansk (according to *Reuters*):

> Mortars regularly hit apartment buildings, supermarkets, cars, hospitals and schools. Some people have been wounded inside their homes.
>
> A 63-year-old man who gave his name only as Valery pointed to what used to be the brick wall of his apartment.

"A shell came in this morning and there's no more apartment", he says. "My wife and my granddaughter had just come into the room. They were covered in brick and plaster."

His 14-year-old granddaughter was taken to hospital with minor injuries and concussion.

A callous attitude toward eastern civilians is hardly a surprise, given Kiev's inability to rely on Ukraine's regular army (according to *TIME* magazine):

Ukrainian conscripts serving in eastern Ukraine tend to be from the region, where the majority of the population is Russian-speaking. Many conscripts may have little loyalty to the Kiev government or openly support the separatists.

Accordingly, Kiev needs to rely on "National Guard" units, heavily manned by activists from western Ukraine, to spearhead the operation. Just as many members of the so-called "Azov" battalion are from Ivano-Frankivsk, many of the "Donbas" battalion fighters are from Lutsk, also in Ukraine's far west. For them, residents of eastern are not fellow countrymen but treacherous aliens to be suppressed by force:

Ten of the soldiers killed [in May] were from Lutsk or nearby, including Maj. Leonid Polinkevych, a 30-year-old battalion commander from the village of Kolky.

His family complains that the army leadership and the government didn't give the men the right equipment or orders to protect themselves.

"They were told they were on a peaceful mission. They said they should smile at the locals like clowns in the circus," said Maj. Polinkevych's father, Oleksandr, the head of the village council.

Local residents had hindered the unit's attempts to erect a checkpoint between two villages south of Donetsk. In a video from the day before the attack, men harangue the soldiers, who sit on a grass verge on the side of the road.

Finally, in yet another indication the on-again offensive has not gone well in any case, Poroshenko today replaced his defense minister, appointing Colonel General Valeriy Heletey, who promptly vowed to recover Crimea: "There will be a victory parade—there will be for sure—in Ukraine's Sevastopol." Also, yesterday in Berlin, a four-party foreign ministerial meeting (France, Germany, Russia, and Ukraine) again sought to reinstate talks and "to pave the way for a new ceasefire, despite continued fighting that Kyiv says has now killed 200 of its troops."

Today in Kiev, Poroshenko indicated, after talking on the phone with U.S. Vice President Joseph Biden, that a renewed ceasefire may be possible.

Meanwhile, the walls will keep closing in: "Ukrainian inflation in 2014 could speed up to 17–19 percent due to the hryvnia devaluation and the rise in regulated tariffs, said Valeriya Gontareva, the head of the National Bank of Ukraine (NBU)."

Poroshenko's 'Hail Mary' Pass: Kiev bets everything on military victory, may cut off gas and oil to Europe

James George Jatras | *American Institute in Ukraine* | August 8, 2014

For those not acquainted with American football, a "Hail Mary" pass is the desperation move of a losing team. The quarterback sends downfield all possible receivers, says a quick prayer, and hurls the ball high and far in the direction of the opposing end zone with the hope that one of his players will catch it. It rarely succeeds.

This roughly describes the position of Petro Poroshenko, installed in Kiev as president barely two months ago. Amid uncertainty over a pledge to cease hostilities around the MH17 crash site to allow investigation and recovery to proceed, Ukrainian military and "National Guard" forces continue to insist they can wrap up within weeks the anti-Kiev insurgency in the southeast and capture the insurgent strongholds of Donetsk and Lugansk. In choosing a completely military approach to what it calls "terrorism" by "dirt" and "parasites," Kiev is keeping the door closed on any negotiations toward a political resolution to the conflict, which is taking an increasing toll of civilian lives and has forced hundreds of thousands to flee their homes.

Whether this exclusively military "solution" can succeed remains to be seen. Meanwhile, on the international front, the Kiev administration now appears ready to add its own somewhat paradoxical contribution to the growing sanctions war between the West (primarily, the United States and the EU) and Russia. Today (August 8) Prime Minister Arseny Yatseniuk announced that new sanctions legislation against Russian interests would include "the possible halting of all types of transit, from air flights to transit of resources"—in other words, Russian natural gas and oil to European customers. The evident hope would be that European governments and consumers would not blame Ukraine—already shut off from gas imports due to nonpayment of its bills—but Russia, as was the case in earlier cutoffs in 2006 and 2009.

Like its military approach to the eastern Ukraine's political problems, Kiev interruption of energy deliveries to European countries would be a big political gamble, one that could easily backfire. But looking at the broader picture, it's not hard to see the confluence of circumstances that are forcing Kiev to risk a "long pass" towards the end zone:

Politics: Yesterday (August 7) violence returned to the Maidan when police and municipal workers trying to reopen normal traffic attempted to dismantle the tent city diehards have maintained since the violent demonstrations that led to the ouster of President Viktor Yanukovych earlier this year. Today, two people were injured in an explosion of unknown origin near the square. Recently, Poroshenko accused members of the Verkhovna Rada of being a traitorous "fifth column" for refusal to accept his demand that they recognize the Lugansk and Donetsk "peoples republics" as terrorist groups. Ukraine's legendary corruption is a continuing concern:

> , a journalist and Maidan activist who now leads the Lustration Committee—a body that wants to force all Ukrainian public officials to undergo checks for past links to corruption and misgovernance—

says Poroshenko has not done nearly enough during his time in charge.

"I see little evidence that he wants to change the corrupt system, just that he wants to lead it," says Sobelev. "I think there will be a new Maidan led by the people who come back from the front lines in the east, who have seen the effect that corruption and mismanagement has first hand. And I'd be surprised if all our current political leaders make it through that Maidan with their lives intact."

Economy and finances: Due to lack of fuel, hot water has had to be shut off even in Kiev. The free fall of the economy is accelerating: according to the *Wall Street Journal*, Ukraine's GDP will decline 6% to 7% this year, and the country's unemployment rate (even according to official statistics, which no doubt are low-balled) has already jumped from 7.7% last year to 9.3% Government bond offerings of up to 16.75% coupon yield reportedly have gone begging. According to *Bloomberg*, the hryvnia has depreciated 34 percent against the dollar this year (the second-worst performing currency tracked) and the corporate bond market is roiled by uncertainty about the country's future.

In short, even if the current offensive in Donetsk and Lugansk is successful—and there is no guarantee it will be with reports of high casualties and in locations across the country protests, led mostly by women, against the call-up of soldiers—Kiev will hardly be out of the woods. Indeed, any such victory may only presage the beginning of a protracted brushfire rebellion, comparable to those against "the PKK in Turkey, ETA in Spain or the IRA in the Northern Ireland." And if the offensive does falter, the other problems tearing the country apart can only become worse.

Once again, the available "off-ramp" is staring Poroshenko in the face: to halt hostilities and begin genuine negotiations with credible representative of the eastern and southern oblasts towards local self-rule, the rights of the Russian language, and restoration of the regional and international balance that is integral to Ukraine's survival as a unified state. Unfortunately, there is no indication that he is inclined to consider it, or that his supporters at home or abroad will let him.

Arrival of Humanitarian Convoy in Eastern Ukraine and Upcoming Poroshenko–Putin Meeting: Is a Real "Game-Changer" in the Offing?

James George Jatras | *American Institute in Ukraine* | August 22, 2014

Up to now, the Kiev administration under President Petro Poroshenko has placed all its eggs in the basket of achieving a short-term military victory over insurgents in Donetsk and Lugansk oblasts. That increasingly looks unlikely. Even western media has begun to notice a growing gulf between reality and the scattershot claims by "Anti-Terrorism Operation" spokesman Colonel

Andriy Lysenko of the National Security and Defense Council. Whether allegations of a Russian armored incursion (immediately destroyed by Kiev's forces), of an anti-Kiev militia attack on refugees, or of Kiev's capture of most of downtown Lugansk, the credibility of this new form of "Lysenkoism" is suffering, as are expectations of a "victory parade" through Kiev on August 24 Independence Day.

Arrival of the Russian "White Convoy" humanitarian aid trucks into the insurgent-controlled zone of fighting further complicates Kiev's efforts. Implausibly dubbed by Kiev a "direct invasion"—despite excruciating delays while the Red Cross, Ukrainian officials, and world media verified beyond doubt that the almost 300 trucks contained nothing but relief goods—the convoy as of today is rolling into areas where civilian hardship from relentless shelling and bombing by Kiev forces is reaching catastrophic proportions. Finally, in light of Kiev's obvious foot dragging, the trucks moved across the border without a final green light from the Ukrainian side and without Red Cross personnel accompanying them. Kiev has responded with the implausible claim that insurgent forces would themselves attack the trucks to "justify" a Russian invasion (and how would they know that?), which may or may not signal Kiev's own intentions. Perhaps most worrisome for the Ukrainian side is the possibility that the very presence of the relief convoy could impose a de facto localized ceasefire, as well as dramatizing the suffering inflicted by Poroshenko's offensive.

Meanwhile, the economic situation in Ukraine grows ever worse as the conflict in the east drags on. The hyrvnia has reached a new low (approaching 14 to the U.S. dollar), coal production (needed for electrical generation) centered in the conflict zone is collapsing (added to the increasing toll of the cutoff of Russian gas for nonpayment), and Economy Minister Pavlo Sheremeta has tendered his resignation in frustration of the slow pace of economic reforms (themselves problematic in terms of Kiev's urgent plea for the International Monetary Fund to combine the third and fourth pending tranches of stand-by lending). The impact of sanctions on Europe's agricultural sector, especially hard hitting in countries already in steep economic crisis like Spain and Greece, is deepening, adding to the pressure on Brussels and Berlin for a settlement.

Eyes increasingly are focused on a meeting scheduled for next week in Minsk, where Poroshenko will meet with Russian President Vladimir Putin. The European Commission (but not the United States) will be represented, with energy and economic ties between the EU and the Moscow-led Customs Union on the agenda:

> Asked by *EurActiv* what the Commission expected to achieve at the 26 August meeting in Minsk, Commission spokesperson Chantal Hughes said that Commission President José Manuel Barroso was unable to respond to the invitation of Russian President Putin to attend, but the EU executive would be represented by Vice President Catherine Ashton, Vice-President Günther Oettinger, responsible for energy, and Commissioner for Trade Karel de Gucht.
> "The purpose of the Commission is threefold [. . .]: to discuss the implementation of the EU-Ukraine Association agreement and the Deep and Comprehensive Free Trade Agreement, to explain once again why we believe these agreements are positive for the region, secondly to explore the possibility of re-launching energy talks possibly in a trilateral format [EU-Ukraine-Russia] in September [. . .] and finally to discuss the wider political security concerns and

to reiterate the EU's concern regarding the security and human-itarian situation in Eastern Ukraine."

Asked why the meeting was at the invitation of the Russian President, although it took place in Belarus, she said this was a meeting of the Customs Union, and that the issue had been discussed and agreed with Ukrainian President Poroshenko.

As always, the wild card is the position of the United States. Some in the Washington establishment, such as the ever-bellicose *Washington Post*, insist that only a zero-sum military solution is acceptable, never mind the human cost ("On Ukraine, any bargain is a bad bargain," August 21):

> With so many innocent civilians caught up in lethal combat, it is tempting to look for a cease-fire or some kind of time out that would lead to a period of diplomatic negotiation. But what would a pause and diplomacy accomplish? Any negotiations that leave this blight festering in Ukraine must be avoided.

But in what some are taking as a signal that the establishment consensus is beginning to crack, Professor John J. Mearsheimer called in the authoritative *Foreign Affairs* for a compromise settlement in Ukraine that will be familiar to AIU readers ("Why the Ukraine Crisis Is the West's Fault," September/October issue):

> There is a solution to the crisis in Ukraine, however—although it would require the West to think about the country in a fundamentally new way. The United States and its allies should abandon their plan to westernize Ukraine and instead aim to make it a neutral buffer between NATO and Russia, akin to Austria's position during the Cold War. Western leaders should acknowledge that Ukraine matters so much to Putin that they cannot support an anti-Russian regime there. This would not mean that a future Ukrainian government would have to be pro-Russian or anti-NATO. On the contrary, the goal should be a sovereign Ukraine that falls in neither the Russian nor the Western camp.

To achieve this end, the United States and its allies should publicly rule out NATO's expansion into both Georgia and Ukraine. The West should also help fashion an economic rescue plan for Ukraine funded jointly by the EU, the International Monetary Fund, Russia, and the United States—a proposal that Moscow should welcome, given its interest in having a prosperous and stable Ukraine on its western flank. And the West should considerably limit its social-engineering efforts inside Ukraine. It is time to put an end to Western support for another Orange Revolution. Nevertheless, U.S. and European leaders should encourage Ukraine to respect minority rights, especially the language rights of its Russian speakers.

Will the arrival of the "White Convoy" and next week's Minsk meeting set the stage for a shift in western policy in the direction suggested by Dr. Mearsheimer, or will the *Post*'s "damn the torpedoes" cruise to disaster continue to prevail? We soon shall see.

Worldwide Jihad

"Insurgent Islam and American Collaboration"

James George Jatras | *Chronicles* | February 1999

The cultural schism between the Western and Eastern halves of European Christian civilization—marked principally by their respective religious traditions, Roman Catholic and Protestant in the West and Orthodox in the East, may or may not prove fatal. One issue stands above all others in determining the outcome: the Islamic resurgence that has rapidly come to mark the post-Cold War era. For the East, which borders on the Muslim world, the problem continues to be, as it has been since Islam first appeared in the seventh century, primarily one of direct, violent confrontation, which today stretches from the Balkans to the Caucasus, and throughout Central Asia. For the West, on the other hand, the problem today is primarily internal, a result of ideological confusion (which in many instances leads to active collaboration), coupled with demographic infiltration.

Last year, the county board of Loudoun County, Virginia, just a few miles down the road from the federal capital, granted a zoning variance, over vigorous local opposition, to facilitate the construction of a new Islamic academy. The institution is one of a number being constructed nationwide, and it will cover some 100 acres, include elementary, middle, and high schools, feature an 800-bed dormitory, and grace the rolling hills of the Virginia horse country with a 65-foot mosque dome and an 85-foot minaret.

County residents opposed the academy on a variety of grounds, notably the loss of tax revenue on land that was otherwise zoned for business uses and the security threat posed by the school, either from Muslims who would be attracted to the county or from the possibility that anti-Saudi Islamic groups might see the academy as a tempting target. But the critics' central issue—and the one that highlights Western incomprehension of the phenomenon in question—was the character of the Saudi regime, which, according to the school's bylaws, exercises total control, to the extent that the school is part of the structure of the Saudi Ministry of Education: an establishment of a foreign sovereign on American soil. Indeed, the Saudi ambassador is *ex officio* chairman.

Predictably, as soon as Saudi Arabia and Islam became the issues, progressive opinion responded that rejection of the school would be intolerance of "diversity." One county resident displayed a crescent and star in the window of her home to show symbolically that "Islam is welcome here." The ever-vigilant *Washington Post* weighed in with an editorial blasting opposition to the school as "religious intolerance" and "the worst kind of bigotry" on the part of retrograde denizens of the Old Dominion. "Ugly statements that have been made in public meetings on the issue have run the range of mean-spiritedness," sniffed the Post, "with some residents asserting that the school should be rejected because 'the Saudis execute their own people who convert from Islam.'"

In point of correction to the *Post*'s sarcastic quotation marks, the 1997 U.S. Department of State Report on Human Rights Practices states the following about Saudi Arabia:

> Freedom of religion does not exist. Islam is the official religion and all [Saudi] citizens must be Muslims. . . . Conversion by a Muslim to

another religion is considered apostasy. Public apostasy is considered a crime under *Shari'a* law and punishable by death.

So which is more "ugly" and "mean-spirited"—the fact that the Saudis do indeed behead those who abandon Islam or that Loudoun citizens have been
tactless enough to take note of that fact? One witness before the county board
testified that her daughters, who are U.S. citizens, have been prevented from
leaving Saudi Arabia for over 13 years because, as women, they may not travel,
even though the elder one is now an adult, without their Saudi father's permission. The girls have been forcibly converted to Islam and can only look
forward to their eventual marriage, for which their consent is at best a
formality.

Fawning by Loudoun County authorities extended even to a blatant disregard of the county's own laws. A Loudoun ordinance defines a private
institution as one that is neither funded nor controlled by any government:
On both counts, the Loudoun Islamic academy fails. Yet the county board
rejected testimony by a former board member—the author of the relevant
ordinance —that the academy was not a private institution. No matter. Today,
neither Loudoun County, nor the Commonwealth of Virginia, nor the United
States would be able to create and run an educational institution based on any
religious doctrine. But a foreign government—a government that is every bit
as bigoted, intolerant, and ugly as the *Post* wrongly accused the school's critics
of being—may do so.

Especially illuminating in the Loudoun controversy was the position of
local Christian social conservatives, who stayed neutral or even supported the
academy. In the dimmer recesses of the American Christian mind, the only
concern was what precedent denying the variance might set for private
Christian schools, or the availability of public vouchers. The importation of
Shari'a into a once-Christian commonwealth seemingly registered not at all
in evangelical minds blissfully unaware of Islamic aims. But as Bat Ye'or wrote
in *The Decline of Eastern Christianity Under Islam,*

> The Islamist movement makes no secret of its intentions to convert
> the West. Its propaganda, published in booklets sold in all European
> Islamic centers for the last thirty years, sets out its aim and the
> methods to achieve them, they include proselytism, conversion, mar-
> riage with local women, and, *above all, immigration* [emphasis
> added]. Remembering that Muslims always began as a minority in
> the conquered countries ("liberated," in Islamic terminology) before
> becoming a majority, the ideologists of this movement regard Islamic
> settlement in Europe, the United States, and elsewhere as a chance
> for Islam.

The element of willful blindness in Western perspectives on Islam cannot be
overestimated. So deeply embedded is the notion that all religions are fundamentally the same that evidence to the contrary is simply wished out of
existence. When the Ayatollah Khomeini states that

> Muslims have no alternative . . . to armed holy war against profane
> governments, . . . the conquest of all non-Muslim territories. . . . It
> will be the duty of every able-bodied adult male to volunteer for this
> war of conquest, the final aim of which is to put Koranic law in power
> from one end of the earth to the other . . .

Such utterances are as little heeded as were similar statements by Lenin
during the Cold War. After all, Khomeini is a known "fundamentalist." Surely,

his statements cannot be held against the moderates, the "mainstream," who represent "*real* Islam," whose beliefs and values are not so different from ours—*can they?* The contention that Khomeini and his ilk *are* in fact Islam's historical "mainstream" not only is dismissed but is considered evidence of a dangerous "Christian fundamentalism," which is every bit as bad as the Muslim variety, probably worse. The growing number of Muslims in America (Islam, according to some claims, has already overtaken Judaism as the nation's largest non-Christian religion) and the irrefutable presumption of Muslim peaceableness have set the stage for Islam to become both a social and political force. Under the Clinton administration, Islam has made major strides to join denatured, humanized Protestantism, Catholicism, and Judaism in their semi-established status as kindred denominations of a single American civic creed, symbolized by Hillary Rodham Clinton's sponsorship last year of the *Eid al-Fitr* end-of-Ramadan celebration at the White House.

Likewise, the idea that Islam shares an Abrahamic pedigree with Christianity and Judaism, that we are all, in the Islamic phrase, "peoples of the book," is now almost universally accepted. But suppose that, during the early Christian era, a pagan philosopher from Athens had claimed to have received a vision from a divine messenger (*angelos*) to the effect that Zeus/Jupiter, the Greco-Roman "father god," was the one and only God —in fact, was the same God the Father worshipped by the Christians; that the Christians had corrupted their Scriptures to hide the fact that Jupiter had been worshipped by Adam, Noah, Abraham, Moses, and Jesus; that only the self-proclaimed prophet's recitation of his own vision was authoritative; that the rites and sacred places of the Olympian gods (the Eleusinian Mysteries, the Delphic Oracle) had always pertained to Jupiter alone and indeed had been established by earlier Abrahamic prophets; and that those who had surrendered their will to Jupiter were commanded to wage holy war under his thunder-bolt symbol on "infidels" who resisted the divine will. Is there any doubt that Christians then would have rejected the supposed kinship of the new teaching to their own faith as quickly as today's Christians rush to accommodate Islam?

There is little doubt that Islam's god is the former chief deity of the polytheistic Arab pantheon, stripped of his consorts and offspring—a variation on the moon god common throughout the ancient Middle East, among the Babylonians known as Sin (the Sinai peninsula is probably named after him) and among the Sumerians as Nanna. Among the pagan Arabs, he was usually called simply "the god," *al-ilah*: Allah. The moon god Allah, whose crescent symbol today caps mosques the world over, headed a pantheon of over 300 lesser divinities, including three daughters called Lat, Uzza, and Manat. In fact, the controversy over *The Satanic Verses* by Salman Rushdie centers upon an embarrassing (and historically documented) episode during Muhammad's evolving "revelation" (after his death collected as his Koran—*Qur'an*, "recitation") in which he admitted the possibility of retaining the three daughter-goddesses under his new dispensation. He later rescinded this idea as having been of false—"satanic"—inspiration. Muhammad (the son of Ab-dallah, "slave of Allah," a further attestation of the deity's pre-Islamic origin) was of the Quraysh tribe, the custodians of the Meccan shrine to the pantheon known as the *Ka'bah* ("cube"), which houses a black stone (probably a meteorite) that Muslim pilgrims continue to venerate. Pilgrims also perform other pre-Islamic pagan rites such as stoning the devil at Wadi Mina and partaking of the waters of the Zamzam well.

In short, Islam is a self-evident outgrowth not of the Old and New Covenants but of the darkness of heathen Araby. Despite ludicrous historical suggestions to the contrary (such as the idea that the *Ka'bah* was built by

Abraham), Muslim apologists have strained to find evidence in the Bible that a new prophet would arise *after* Jesus, seeing Muhammad in obvious prophecies of the Holy Spirit (that were fulfilled on Pentecost) or of the Second Coming of Christ. One could find no better refutation of Islam's efforts to appropriate Christian Scripture (here, Matthew 24:27) than that of the 14th-century Byzantine saint, Gregory Palamas, to his Turkish captors:

> It is true that Muhammad started from the east and came to the west, as the sun travels from east to west. Nevertheless he came with war, knives, pillaging, forced enslavement, murders, and acts that are not from the good God but instigated by the chief manslayer, the devil.

St. Gregory's answer is no less devastating to Islam's self-depiction as a pacific creed. Islam was born in violence, from Muhammad's sanction of raids of pillage and plunder (starting with attacks against his own Quraysh tribe, which initially rejected his revelation) to his savage execution of hundreds of men of the Qurayzah clan (which professed Judaism) and the enslavement and forced concubinage of their women and children. From its inception, first within Arabia and then against all unbelievers, Islam has been unthinkable without its mandate for violence, war, terror—in a word, *jihad*—itself codified in Muhammad's Koran (notably Sura 9:29). Today, Islamic apologists in America have been quick to latch on to the vocabulary of grievance, denouncing the association of Islam with its violent past (and present) as "stereotyping," "bigotry," and "ignorance." Even American elementary school texts have been rewritten to suggest that once-Christian Egypt, Syria, and Palestine became Muslim because their conquerors were "invited" in; Muslims are quick to remind Christians of the Crusaders' later "aggression," but they do not consider as aggression their own unprovoked seizure of the Christian Middle East.

In the application of *jihad*, as documented by Bat Ye'or and others, Islam divides the world into two domains, or "houses": the House of Islam (*Dar al-Islam*), where Islam rules and *Shari'a*, the law of Allah, has been realized; and the House of War (*Dar al-Harb*), where the rebellious unbelievers persist in their (or rather, our) lawlessness. In Islamic terms, we unsubdued Christians are *harbi*, and as such we have no legitimate right to our lands, our property, or even our lives, which by right belong not to us but to the Muslims; that which we now have we enjoy only until Islam becomes strong enough to impose *Shari'a*. As the highly respected and influential 14th-century authority Ibn Taymiyya explained:

> These possessions [i.e., the things taken away from the non-Muslims upon their conquest] received the name of *fay* [war booty] since Allah had taken them away from the infidels in order to restore them to the Muslims. In principle, Allah has created the things of this world only in order that they may contribute to serving Him, since He created man only in order to be ministered to. Consequently, the infidels forfeit their persons and their belongings which they do not use in Allah's service to the faithful believers who serve Allah and unto whom Allah restitutes what is theirs; thus is restored to a man the inheritance of which he was deprived, even if he had never before gained possession.

It is worthy of note that Ibn Taymiyya is particularly revered by the Wahabi sect, which is the ruling doctrine of Saudi Arabia; students at the Saudi-controlled Loudoun Islamic Academy will no doubt receive benefit of his wisdom. But Ibn Taymiyya's sentiments are not unique to him. On the contrary.

Bat Ye'or quotes comparable passages from Islamic sages of many eras and locales, from the time of Muhammad to the present day.

Surveying the long history of the Islamic assault on the Christian world, it is sobering to consider how close the latter has come to annihilation on more than one occasion. In the initial offensive during the first decade after Muhammad's demise, Christendom lost its birthplace in the Levant, with the front of the East Roman Empire only being stabilized at the approaches to Asia Minor. Meanwhile, the Arab armies swept west from conquered Egypt, subduing the whole north coast of Africa and crossing into Visigothic Spain in 711. They were finally stopped by the Franks under Karl the Hammer at Poitiers in 732, the centenary of Muhammad's death. The conversion of the Turkish tribes to Islam in the ninth century' lent *jihad* renewed impetus; the erosion and final collapse of East Roman power opened the eastern door to Europe in the 14th century, and the Ottomans were turned back only at the gates of Vienna in 1683. The site of the first high-water mark at Poitiers and the later one at Vienna are only some 700 miles apart—so narrow has been Christendom's brush with extinction!

The Turkish defeat at Vienna marked the beginning of two centuries of remission during which European technology, particularly military technology, seemed to have resolved the contest between the Cross and the Crescent decisively in favor of the former. During the 19th century, the Christian nations of the Balkans—the only conquered Christian lands since the Spanish *reconquista* in which the Muslims had not yet reduced the indigenous population to a minority, as they had in Egypt and Syria, or eliminated them utterly, as in the Maghreb—cast off their Muslim masters, and by the end of World War I, most of the Muslim world (with the exceptions of the Arabian heartland itself and of a truncated Turkey which had adopted the modernizing, secular ideology of Kemalism) was subject to European rule. But at the very time that Europe achieved its military and geopolitical advantage, the moral and religious decline that culminated in the autogenocides of 1914 and 1939 had become evident. Having found in their grasp places their Crusader predecessors had only dreamed of reclaiming—Jerusalem, Bethlehem, Antioch, Alexandria, Constantinople—effete and demoralized European governments made no effort to re-christianize them and, within a few decades, meekly abandoned them.

The moral disarmament of contemporary post-Christian Europe is now nearly universal. If, in the more remote past, Bourbon France had made common cause with the Sublime Porte (the scandalous "union of the Lily and the Crescent") against Habsburg Austria, the arrangement at least had the virtue of cynical self-interest: Catholic France was hardly expected to praise the sultan's benevolence as part of the bargain. But by the 1870's, Disraeli's obsession with thwarting Russian ambitions in the Balkans prompted the Tories' unprecedented depiction of Turkey as tolerant and humane even in the face of the Bulgarian atrocities. Even so, Britain's Christian conscience, prodded by Gladstone's passionate words, was sufficient to bring down Lord Beaconsfield's government in 1880.

After World War I, with the installation of nominally "pro-Western" governments in many Muslim countries fashioned from the wreckage of the Ottoman Empire, the West seems to have convinced itself of the existence of benign Islam. Indeed, the promotion of "moderate" Muslim regimes—especially those willing to make peace with Israel, and, even better, those that have a lot of petroleum—has become a linchpin of U.S. global policy. Egypt, Saudi Arabia, Jordan, Turkey, Pakistan, Morocco, the Gulf states, Bosnia-Herzegovina, Nigeria, Indonesia, and a few others have become the darlings of U.S. policy, valued as supposed bulwarks against "fundamentalism" of the Iranian variety (Iran itself having lately been a member of the favored assembly). Operationally, this means not only overlooking the radical activities of the supposedly "moderate" Muslim states—for example, Saudi Arabia's and Pakistan's support for the Taliban regime in Afghanistan (whom even the Iranians denounce as dangerous fanatics), and assistance by virtually all Islamic nations to the thinly disguised radical regime in Sarajevo—but also a consistent American bias in favor of the Muslim party in virtually every conflict with a Christian nation. The most prominent exception to date has been a pro-Armenian tilt in the Nagorno-Karabakh question, a function of Armenian-Americans' early cultivation of Congress, but this anomaly will undoubtedly soon shift to Azerbaijan's favor under the combined pressure of the Turkey/Israel lobby, of residual Cold War antipathy for Russia (seen as Armenia's main protector), and of American oil companies fixated on an energy El Dorado in the Caspian Basin.

It is hardly a surprise that business executives who would sell their grandmothers to Abdul Abulbul Amir for oil drilling rights would see the world as a reflection of their balance sheets, nor is it a surprise that secular, socially progressive opinion is viscerally anti-Christian. What is not expected is that so many Western Christians, Americans in particular, are willing to believe the worst about their Eastern Christian cousins, who, only lately freed from Islamic (and later, in most cases, communist) servitude, are desperately attempting to avoid a repeat of the experience. Today, when all of the Russian North Caucasus is subject to plunder and hostage-taking raids staged from *Shari'a*-ruled Chechnya, when not just Nagorno-Karabakh but Armenia proper is in danger of a repeat of 1915, when Cyprus and Greece receive unvarnished threats to their territorial integrity on a weekly basis for the offense of purchasing defensive weapons, and when the borders of Serbia are rapidly approaching those of the *pashaluk* of Belgrade in order to appease America's new friends in Bosnia and Kosovo, organized Roman Catholic and Protestant sentiment in America overwhelmingly sides with non- and anti-Christian elite opinion in its pro-Muslim, anti-Orthodox tendency.

For example, in 1993, statements were issued by a number of Roman Catholic, Protestant, and Anglican spokesmen in the United States urging military intervention on behalf of the Islamic regime in Sarajevo. "We are convinced that there is just cause to use force to defend largely helpless people in Bosnia against aggression and barbarism that are destroying the very foundations of society and threaten large numbers of people," wrote the chairman of the U.S. Catholic Conference, at a time when the Muslim beneficiaries of the intervention were not only impaling Serb POWs on spits but also were slaughtering Roman Catholic Croats by the hundreds in an offensive in central Bosnia. "What is going on in Bosnia is genocide by any other name," observed a prominent Baptist spokesman. "The ghosts of Auschwitz and Dachau have come back to haunt us. If we do nothing we are morally culpable." "Those of us who opposed the Gulf War believed that war was not the answer," opined the presiding bishop of the Episcopal Church, "but today we find ourselves confronted with an evil war, the sure elimination of which may be possible only by means of armed intervention." Thus did the high-minded guardians of the West's Christian integrity give their blessing for NATO to aid the resumption of *jihad* in Europe. Granted, they were to some extent victims of the melodramatic media coverage that has characterized the Balkan war, but that is not much of an excuse: Who told them to believe everything dished up by CNN?

In a previous article in *Chronicles*, I have noted that Western anti-Orthodox bias, which I have dubbed Pravoslavophobia, rarely means antipathy for Orthodoxy as such. Most serious Protestants and Roman Catholics often have a fairly positive attitude toward Orthodox Christianity as a morally conservative and liturgically traditional bulwark within the spectrum of Christian opinion. Perhaps it has been so long since Western Christians have had to defend themselves physically as Christians (as opposed to Americans, Englishmen, Germans, etc.) that they just do not understand those for whom it is a current concern.

On the other hand, there are Westerners for whom antipathy is based on the traditional Orthodox character of the front-line states bordering on Islam. Indeed, from this viewpoint, the desire of these countries to avoid not only islamicization but Westernization as well is a major count against them. Though differing in the specifics, the overall attitude toward Orthodox nations today is strongly reminiscent of that of the West toward the East as the dying Byzantine, Bulgarian, and Serbian states faced Ottoman conquest in the 15th century. The West then was explicit: We will help you only if you renounce Orthodoxy and adopt Roman Catholicism. The Orthodox East is being told today that unless they unquestioningly submit to the West's tutelage in political, social, moral, and economic matters—the collective "religion" of the Enlightenment heritage—they again will be thrown to the wolves. In fact, the West will even help the wolves to devour them.

The immorality, not to mention the stupidity, of this should be obvious. Maybe Christians will never come to agreement on doctrinal matters; maybe the East will insist on retaining its distinctive religious and cultural heritage. Whatever happens, the survival of Orthodox Christian civilization in the East should be hardly less important to the West than to the Orthodox themselves, and indeed over the long term, the West's own fate may depend on it. The fact that the West cannot recognize this reality is evident in the forest of minarets going up mainly in Western Europe but also now in North America.

Some Christians see the Muslim influx primarily as an opportunity for evangelization, and indeed we should never neglect to share the Gospel, the only real liberation, with Muslims, who should not, as individuals, be held responsible for the violent system into which they were born and of which they are—perhaps more than anyone else—victims. At the same time, in light of the growing volume of Muslim immigration. Western Christians will soon find out—maybe sooner than they think, given Western birthrates—that confronting the Islamic advance has become, as it has always been for Eastern Christians, a simple matter of physical survival. But by that time, it may be too late for the West as well.

This article was adapted from a May 1998 speech at "Overcoming the Schism: European Divisions and U.S. Policy," a conference sponsored by the Rockford Institute and The Lord Byron Foundation for Balkan Studies.

"Is There a Khilafah in Your Future? The Coming Islamic Revolution"

James George Jatras | *Chronicles* | February 2005

Discussions of *jihad* terrorism and the best defense against it rarely avoid entanglement in the contentious question of the relationship of terrorist actions to Islam as a religion. Is the terrorism an aberration of Islam, or is it, judged in light of history, the prevailing orthodoxy? Indeed, the question is an important one, and, in a society that avoids uncomfortable realities, answering it honestly is less a matter of analysis than of moral courage.

Perhaps less important in theory, but more central in terms of policy, is a question less commonly asked: *What is it, exactly, that the terrorists mean to achieve?* Nonstate violence as a political/military methodology is not new, nor does it exist in a vacuum. It proceeds from a worldview and, in almost all cases, has stated, ideologically defined, conscious goals. The question then becomes one of whether the terrorists' motivations are essentially *reactive* (*i.e.*, they are offended by the presence of infidels on the sacred soil of Arabia, they are opposed to U.S. policy in the Middle East, they are trying to preserve a traditional way of life from the depredations of modern moral corruption, *etc.*), in which case we would need to stop doing something (pull U.S. forces out of Saudi Arabia, stop supporting Israel, stop exporting trashy movies, *etc.*). Or is what they want something affirmative, something that has an independent, positive imperative?

In suggesting an answer to the question, I ask the reader to do a quick Google search for the word *khilafah*. When I first tried this about a year ago, the result was in the range of 26,000 to 29,000 links (some of them redundant). Now, the results are above 50,000, and, by the time you read this, maybe more. Almost all of these sites link to material available in English; I can only guess what is out there in Arabic, Urdu, Farsi, Turkish, Malay, and other languages. The location of the site operators is not always clear, but many of them seem to be based in the United Kingdom. (Since many of the quotations in this article were downloaded a few months ago, some of the sites have been removed, to some extent because of action of the British government. Since the sentiments expressed on the sites are unlikely to have disappeared as conveniently as the sites themselves, this appears to be, at best, treating the symptom.)

Khilafah—perhaps more familiar in the common form in English, *caliphate*—historically refers to the state ruled by a successor (called *khalifah* or, in English, *caliph*) of Muhammad, beginning in the seventh century. The *khilafah*, in one form or another, lasted until it was abolished in 1924 by Mustafa Kemal Ataturk at the founding of the Turkish Republic.

Even a cursory review of these websites shows that in only a very few of them does the *khilafah* reference pertain to this purely historical entity. On the contrary, as far as I can see, most of them are found on advocacy sites. These are people who date the current decrepitude of the Islamic world in comparison with the West to abolition of the *khilafah* and insist that all Muslims are obligated to work for its revival. For example, the following is from the website (*hizb-ut-tahrir.org*) of the Turkish branch of an international political party whose stated goal is reviving the *khilafah*:

> It was a day like this 79 years ago, and more specifically on the 3rd of March 1924 that . . . the criminal English agent, Mustafa Kemal (so-called Ataturk, the "Father of the Turks"!) announced that the Grand National Assembly had agreed to destroy the Khilafah; and . . . he establish . . . a secular, irreligious, Turkish republic. . . .
>
> Since that day the Islamic ummah [nation, community] has lived a life full of calamities; she was broken up into small mini states controlled by the enemies of Islam in every aspect. The Muslims were oppressed and became the object of the kuffar's [unbelievers'] derision in Kashmir, Philippines, Thailand, Chechnya, Iraq, Bosnia-Herzegovina, Afghanistan, Palestine and other lands belonging to the Muslims . . .

So the crime took place and the kuffar tightened their grip over the Islamic lands and tore it up into pieces. . . . In place of a single Khilafah state they established cartoon states and installed rulers as agents to carry out the orders of their kuffar masters. They abolished the Islamic Sharee'ah [sic; religious law] from the sphere of ruling, economy, international relations, domestic transactions and judiciary.

Without the Khilafah, the Islamic lands will remain torn up and the Islamic peoples will remain divided. Without the Khilafah the kafir, crusader and colonial states will continue to control us, plunder our resources and create divisions amongst us. Without the Khilafah, the Jews will continue to occupy our sacred places and kill and humiliate our brothers in Palestine. Without the Khilafah, the Islamic peoples in Bosnia, Chechnya, Afghanistan, Iraq, Kashmir, Uzbekistan and so on will continue to be killed. . . . Without the Khilafah, those Muslims who do not work seriously for its implementation will be sinful and incur the anger of Allah, even if they fast, pray, make Hajj [pilgrimage] and pay Zakah [alms]. This is because the work to establish the Khilafah Rashidah is a fard [duty] on every Muslim, and it should be conducted with the most extreme effort and utmost speed. . . .

The Khilafah Rashidah on the way of the Prophethood is coming soon by the help of Allâh. Its prerequisites in terms of system and statesmen are present. The voices of the Muslims in all parts of the world from Turkey to Nigeria, and from Uzbekistan to Indonesia are resoundingly demanding its return. It will come back despite the efforts and money spent by the kuffar and the agents to prevent its return. So strengthen your resolve and work seriously with the sincere da'wah ["invitation" to Islam; *i.e.*, proselytizing] carriers who are working to re-establish the Khilafah, so that you may attain the victory that Allâh has promised.

Two things in particular should be noted in this exposition: First, all existing governments—including those in power in the Islamic world, here called "cartoon states"—are illegitimate (or based on *kufr*, "unbelief") and must be overthrown; and, second. Islamic law, *sharia*, must be established as the ruling legal system.

Some of these sites detail what the *khilafah* will look like when it is reestablished, and what powers would be exercised by the man, the *khalifah*, who will rule it. In summary (from *al-isIami.com/islam/estaMish_khilafah .php?p=4*):

- The Khilafah [state] must include all Muslim nations in the world.
- There must be only one Khaleefah or Ameer [ruler], with all Muslims giving him their bay'ah or allegiance. . . .
- Shariah law must be implemented in the Islamic state regarding all issues.
- There must be only one military, with a single leadership appointed by the Khaleefah.

If the end sought by people of this persuasion is reestablishment of the *khilafah*, to what extent do they recognize the legitimacy of using violent struggle—*jihad* and, by extension, what we call terrorism—as a means to achieve it? There is actually sharp debate in this community about that issue. Some take the view that what leads to the reestablishment of legitimate authority is itself legitimate. This side generally takes a very expansive view as to what constitutes self-defense in such places as Chechnya, Kashmir, Bosnia, Palestine, Kosovo, the Philippines, Uzbekistan, Xinjiang, Sudan, Aceh, Afghanistan, and other places. Some drop hints, rather than state outright, about how they would answer this question. One British-Islamic website, *muslim-student.org.uk* (now removed), stated:

> Sharia'ah verdict obliges the Muslims to abolish the present puppet regimes in the Muslim World, and to establish the Islamic system and unite all the Muslim countries, bringing them back under the banner of one single state, and one single Khalif who would rule by the Holy Qur'an and the Sunnah of the Messenger (SAW). The duty of all Muslims is not only limited to working towards overthrowing the regimes ruling the Muslim countries nowadays, and in liberating occupied Muslim land from the unbelievers [*sic*] dominance, even if an Islamic rule is put in force, but it includes the work for unification of Muslim countries. This is a duty and it must not be stalled for any reason even the absence of an Islamic state, for the texts of the Sharia'ah concerning the unity of Muslim land are general and not limited to the presence of a Khalif. . . . Fighting and exterminating Israel is an obligation even if the Muslims fighting are Arab armies loyal to regimes of unbelief, like the Egyptian soldiers when they fought Israel during the Sinai war. . . . The uniting of Muslim [lands] includes the land that Muslims lost control of, including, Turkistan, Bulgaria, Cyprus, Greece and the land that Muslims had lost like Andalous (Spain) . . . Our duty as Muslims . . . [is] to kick the American, British, and Israeli forces from Hijaz (Saudi Arabia) and Palestine, and to overthrow all these non-Islamic regimes in order to establish the Islamic state on their ruins.

Others take the view that, strictly speaking, *jihad* can only be unconditionally legal once the *khilafah* is reestablished. If that were to occur, there is little disagreement that the foreign policy of the caliphate would be one of *jihad*. For example, *khilafah.com* says:

> Thus Islam has come for the whole of mankind and Allah has obliged the Muslims to convey it in a manner which draws attention. . . . [W]hoever stands as an obstacle and prevents Islam from reaching the people, it is an obligation to fight him in order to remove this obstacle, and thus to open the way for the people to Islam: so either they embrace Islam or they submit to the laws of Islam . . . The true and effective jihad which uproots kufr [unbelief] and liberates the land of the Muslims from the Yahud [the Jew] and Kuffar cannot take place without the existence of the Khilafah State which will unite the Muslims in a single state and under the leadership of one Khalifah who will rule them with the Book of Allah and the Sunna [traditions] of His Messenger, and lead them into the battlefields of jihad to spread Islam and protect the Muslims.

And, according to another site, *almuhajiroun.com* (currently offline, but this site has a remarkable tendency to reappear following periodic interruptions):

> Once the Islamic State is established anyone in Dar Al Harb [realm of war] will have no sanctity for his life or wealth hence a Muslim in such circumstances can then go into Dar Al Harb and take the wealth from the people unless there is a treaty [of temporary truce] with that

state. If there is no treaty individual Muslims can even go to Dar Al Harb and take women to keep as slaves.

Where will *khilafah* be instituted? The short answer is, *wherever it can be.* Commonly, two general areas have been discussed. One is in the zone stretching from the Ferghana Valley in Central Asia (overlapping the former Soviet republics of Uzbekistan, Kyrgyzstan, and Tajikistan) to Pakistan, which includes Afghanistan. Taliban-ruled Afghanistan would have been the embryo for the Khilafah's reestablishment in that region, with the eventual subversion of an already semi-Talibanized, nuclear-armed Pakistan, fostering the creation of a *sharia* superstate with over 200 million people and armed with nuclear weapons. The other candidate is in Southeast Asia, with the creation of a *sharia* state in the Aceh region of the northwestern part of the Indonesian island of Sumatra as the initial beachhead, to include eventually all of Indonesia, Malaysia, Singapore, and parts of the Philippines, Thailand, and Burma, and possibly Bangladesh.

What does all this have to do with anything? Just this: What we have here is an ideology, one with clearly defined goals, in search of a host—a land and a people in which to bring it to life. Some might dismiss this kind of talk as the ravings of just a few lunatics, albeit violent lunatics. Perhaps some might have taken the same view of an Austrian former corporal sitting in the Landsberg am Lech fortress prison in 1924, writing a book about his "struggle," or of a couple of obscure German scribblers issuing some kind of "manifesto" in 1848.

These disparate elements promoting *khilafah* share a common, clearly defined vision—one with a lot more moral, historical, and demographic depth than a Hitler or a Marx could have claimed—that should not be discounted. To call the violence associated with this movement merely "terrorism," without an awareness of what the violence is meant to achieve is to miss the whole point. The khilafists have their collective manifesto, and perhaps, with September 11 and its aftermath, they have had their Paris Commune. Maybe the next big attack will be their guns of the cruiser *Aurora*, leading, they hope, to their own October Revolution and the long-awaited rebirth of *khilafah*.

If this specter is haunting not just Europe but the whole world, why has hardly anyone noticed? To my knowledge, the only political leader of a major power who has publicly acknowledged the existence of this movement is President Vladimir Putin of the Russian Federation, who has observed that Chechen terrorism is an initial step in the reconstitution of a "global caliphate," which amounts, he said, to "world supremacy." Mr. Putin also took note of the radicals' willingness to kill Christians, atheists, and nonradical Muslims who oppose the effort. There seems to have been absolutely no resonance among other world leaders to this identification. In fact, in the media, there has been some criticism, as if Putin had made it up.

American policymakers seem unable or unwilling to take *khilafah* seriously, though they can hardly be unaware of it. U.S. policy is focused on "state-supported terrorism" and a list of "rogue states" instead of targeting the global *khilafah* movement and its subsets: *jihad* ideology and the demand to install sharia. Indeed, the major bases for that movement are not in the rogue states (with the partial exception of Iran) but in countries regarded by Washington as allies in the "coalition against terrorism": Saudi Arabia, Egypt, and Pakistan—all close, long-time friends of the United States. This does not even take into account khilafist strongholds in Europe, especially in Great Britain.

Dealing with this seeming incomprehension of the problem is a far more urgent task than the endless tinkering with the structure of law enforcement and intelligence agencies that disproportionately occupies the attention of

official Washington. Perhaps America—having seen her survival of the Cold
War primarily as a vindication of an end-of-history global order based on her
materialistic ideology of democratic capitalism—is incapable of recognizing an
opposing force based on completely different assumptions about God and
man and the purpose of human life. Even more troubling, we appear to be
guided by a worldview that proceeds from philosophical assumptions derived
from the Enlightenment that are almost designed to lead to incomprehension.
Our military prowess, though impressive, is only tangentially related to the
real threat.

"Grasping the Inexplicable"

James George Jatras | *Chronicles* | October 2005

The U.S. government has a new official program called "Orthodox Christian
World Outreach." Tens of millions of dollars will be spent to counter distrustful perceptions of the United States in Orthodox countries such as Serbia,
Greece, and Russia—perceptions resulting, in part, from our policies with
respect to Bosnia and Kosovo. Under this new program, American tax dollars
will support Orthodox Christian broadcasting, church schools. Orthodox think
tanks, and restoration of churches and monasteries in Kosovo and Cyprus and
of ancient icons and manuscripts in Orthodox monasteries. Perhaps the most
positive aspect is that, for the first time, the United States will ally herself
politically with national movements and parties that seek to bring an
Orthodox Christian moral and spiritual agenda to their societies. This is a
most welcome and unexpected development.

Alas, there is no such effort as "Orthodox Christian World Outreach."
Everything in the above paragraph is not true. Instead, Washington actually
has launched this same program with respect to the Islamic world. According
to *U.S. News & World Report,*

> In at least two dozen countries, Washington has quietly funded Is-
> lamic radio and TV shows, coursework in Muslim schools, Muslim
> think tanks, political workshops, or other programs that promote
> [so-called] moderate Islam. Federal aid is going to restore mosques,
> save ancient Korans, even build Islamic schools. ... Another strategy
> being pursued is to make peace with radical Muslim figures who
> [supposedly] eschew violence. At the top of the list: the Muslim
> Brotherhood, the preeminent Islamist society, founded in 1928 and
> now with tens of thousands of followers worldwide. . . . Indeed,
> sources say U.S. intelligence officers have been meeting not only with
> the Muslim Brotherhood but also with members of the Deobandi sect
> in Pakistan, whose fundamentalism schooled the Taliban and
> inspired an army of al Qaeda followers.

Particular attention is being focused on various groups based on Sufism (defined as "tolerant," notwithstanding plentiful evidence to the contrary),
exemplified by the tolerant, pluralistic Ottoman empire, about which no more
needs to be said.

If Washington's policy of subsidizing "*sharia* with a human face" seems vaguely familiar, it should. It was consciously modeled on America's Cold War policy of promoting social democracy as an antidote to communism. Even decades later, Washington's leading lights have been unable to see what was painfully obvious then: that sponsoring socialism only advanced the moral case for collectivism, materialism, and the growth of state power over society, accompanied by de-Christianization—a devolution that influences our thinking today.

We cannot presume that the result of "Muslim World Outreach" will be a stumbling into victory, a la the Cold War. Whereas then the noncommunist world did not support communist states and movements as a consistent policy—though they did so on occasion—American support for radical Islam is a longstanding pattern. Muslim World Outreach is the logical conclusion of policies dating, at least, back to the Afghan war of a quarter-century ago. This orientation can be summarized as follows: In local conflicts, promote Islamic interests; ally ourselves with *jihad* as long as itis directed against someone else. The underlying logic is this: If we—the United States, the West—support Islamic interests, the result will be a moderate Islam that will, perhaps, threaten others but not us; if we do not, those interests will be championed by "extremists" (or at least by extremists we have not co-opted and redefined as "moderates").

One would have thought this pattern would have been reconsidered after September 11. Instead, it has been reinforced and expanded. Even the official September 11 Commission said that

> The United States defended, and still defends, Muslims against tyrants and criminals in Somalia, Bosnia, Kosovo, Afghanistan, and Iraq. If the United States does not act aggressively to define itself in the Islamic world, the extremists will gladly do the job for us.

Evidently, the commission missed the obvious absurdity of the notion that, as of 2004, we are "still defending" Muslims in Bosnia or Kosovo. (Against whom? A Republika Srpska that is being systematically dismantled by Paddy Ashdown? Against terrified, isolated Serb enclaves in Kosovo?) Equally ignored is that our interventions have brought us no praise in the Islamic world but have simply augmented the list of Muslim grievances: Chechnya, Kashmir, Palestine, the Philippines, Iraq, etc.

While the explicit link between U.S. policy and appeasing Muslim sensibilities was first applied to the Balkans under President George H.W. Bush, the American dance with jihad vastly expanded under President Clinton. Regarding radical Islamic influence in Bosnia, Clinton's April 1994 "green light" for covert shipments of Iranian weapons through Croatia to the Muslim regime of the late Alija Izetbegovic is old news. Less well known is the contemporaneous presence in Bosnia of a second aid network—working parallel to the Iranians and, to some extent, in competition with them—that also brought in arms, funds, and mujahideen from around the world. Loosely patterned on—and, to some degree, an outgrowth of—the effort begun to assist Afghan resistance to the Soviet occupation in the 1980's, this parallel network in Bosnia was largely funded from Saudi Arabia through an intricate web of untraceable sources and was administered through a number of phony "charities." In short, this parallel network was what we now refer to as Al Qaeda.

While there are numerous references to Bosnia and even to Kosovo in the official September 11 Commission report, these have led neither to wide public comment nor to official inquiry into the extent to which the jihad terror that struck America in 2001 was empowered to do so because of mistakes made a decade ago in the Balkans.

While what became Al Qaeda was hatched in the 1980's in the Afghan-Pakistan border region, it was mostly in the context of the Balkan conflicts of the 1990's that (according to the commission report) the "groundwork for a true global terrorist network was being laid"—a network capable of striking the United States. Amazingly, this is the same report that recommends more pro-Islamic interventions along the lines of our policies in Bosnia and Kosovo.

What to many may seem simply a nonsensical orientation needs to be understood in a larger context. The overall tendency in American global policy, going back to the end of the Cold War, can be summed up in one word: hegemony. This means not only hegemony in Europe through NATO—which had specific application in the Balkan interventions—but in what is called the Broader Middle East, which includes the Caucasus and Central Asia and of which the Balkans is seen to be as much a part as it is of Europe. In its wider application, it means that the opinion of any other power, or any possible combination of powers, may not outweigh that of the United States on any point of the globe.

An important corollary of the foregoing is the effort to undermine the status of certain regional powers, notably Russia. This includes the current effort to dominate Russia's Near Abroad, an effort that has accelerated with the successful "Orange Revolution" in Ukraine and parallel advances elsewhere (Moldova, Kyrgyzia, and, perhaps next, Belarus and Kazakhstan, and likely Russia herself in 2008). Especially with the growing American rapprochement with our European allies—for which support for "democracy" in such places as the Ukraine has served as a catalyst—Russia's strategic isolation is deepening. With respect to diminution of Moscow's status as a power, it is significant that the *Washington Post* editorialized that "[neither Serbia nor Russia . . . should be allowed to stand in the way of resolving Kosovo's future"—that is, independence.

Consider Serbia's situation with respect to the elements of the policy I have outlined. First, she is part of the Broader Middle East, a particular focus for hegemonic control, where assuaging Muslim sentiments is a major imperative. Second, she is in Europe, where again, hegemonic control via NATO is imperative. Add another element, great-power chauvinism: Like the NKVD, we never make mistakes. No American policy mistakes of the past—by either party—can ever be reexamined, because this would compromise our infallibility.

This largely explains why the expected reappraisal of Bill Clinton's flawed Balkan policy never occurred in the George W. Bush administration. (Particularly puzzling to some was that an administration in which self-identified Christian conservatives figure so prominently would continue the decidedly anti-Christian policies of its predecessor.) Besides an imperious inability to admit error, two other factors should be noted: first, the continuing influence of the permanent foreign-policy bureaucracy, centered at the State Department, including many officials who held responsible jobs under Clinton and were retained under Bush; second, the dominance of the neoconservatives, for whom global hegemony was, and remains, an article of faith. Regarding the latter, even when Republicans in the House of Representatives voted against the Kosovo war by a margin of more than nine to one and, in fact, defeated the resolution of authorization, important figures now staffing the Bush administration faulted Clinton only in that his policy was not aggressive enough.

We will soon see a push for settling the "final status" of Kosovo. I will not review the details of the background noise—the Contact Group, Richard Holbrooke's recent essay in the *Washington Post*, the January 2005 International Crisis Group report, the hair-splitting over whether "standards" come before "status" (or vice versa) or whether the progression is from occupation to "independence without full sovereignty" or "guided sovereignty" or "shared sovereignty" with the European Union. There is no doubt that the United States, together with the European Union, will soon solemnly conclude that Kosovo's "progress" toward "standards" is sufficient to "move forward."

Predictably, Serbs will torture themselves over how to engage, as they have with other issues such as The Hague. "Do we participate in status talks? Do we boycott them? What should local Serbs do? How will cooperation benefit Serbia? How will resistance hurt us?"

The answers Serbs give to immediate questions concerning Kosovo, The Hague, etc., are less important for the short-term costs and benefits than they are for preserving any part of the Serbian national patrimony, encouraging national unity—spiritual and moral accord even more than political harmony. Serbs must decide what they would want for Serbia if the United States and the European Union did not exist, and only then decide how to engage them.

At the same time, Serbs should not think that the situation is hopeless or that nothing useful can be done. Even in the current climate, it is possible for incremental but significant gains to be made, as is occurring in the commercial sector.

More broadly speaking, whether Washington's agenda is sustainable over the long term—geopolitically, militarily, economically—is still unknown. Also, there are many in the United States, distributed across the political spectrum, who are skeptical that the prevailing program of global hegemony is in the American national interest; rather than bringing us "national greatness," it will lead us to ruin. While those who hold this view do not dominate U.S. foreign policy, neither are they entirely inconsequential. There is reason to think that even some who support hegemony as a global concept are receptive to the idea that our current orientation in the Balkans is counterproductive to their broader goals.

A version of this article was delivered as a speech at a conference on terrorism held in Belgrade in May 2005 and cosponsored by The Rockford Institute's Center for International Affairs.

"'With Us or with the Terrorists': It's clear which side Turkey is on."

Jim Jatras | *TheJIM!gram No. 5* | November 28, 2015

What Was the Level of U.S. Complicity?

What happened: Turkey claims the Russian plane crossed into Turkish airspace and failed to respond to repeated warnings. Russia claims it can prove its plane was over Syria the whole time. We will see if one version or the other will be generally accepted or whether a contentious muddle will continue indefinitely (cf. MH–17). However, even if the Turkish version prevails, the Russian plane at most would have been over Turkey for a well under a minute and presented no threat to anything or anyone inside Turkey. As stated by

Valeriy Burkov, a Russian military pilot and recipient of the Hero of Russia medal: "It's clear that this was a premeditated action, they were prepared and just waited for a Russian plane to show up. It wasn't downed because of pilot error, or because he was trigger-happy or whatever. This is preplanned, premeditated action." That assessment is likely true even if the aircraft passed momentarily into Turkey.

[UPDATE NOV. 27: Not only is it almost certain that Turkey was waiting in ambush to shoot down a Russian plane when the opportunity presented itself, it is increasingly clear it did so using information provided by Russia to the "US-led coalition"—that is, the United States—as to the Su-24's flight path. Put another way, Russia provided information about its operations to the US as part of a supposed cooperation against ISIS, which information the U.S. then shared with Turkey, which then used the information to shoot down the Su-24. Whether that is the extent of likely US complicity is unknown. For example, did Turkey proceed with its attack after consulting with the coalition—again, meaning the US—or did they proceed on their own without consulting or seeking clearance from anyone? One of the two Su-24 crew were killed by "moderate" terrorists supported by Turkey (and the U.S.?) as they parachuted to safety, a war crime in itself. Another Russian, a marine, was reported killed when his rescue helicopter searching for the Su-24 crew was shot down with a US-made TOW missile supplied to the jihadists.]

Motives: While the facts of the incident are murky, the motives on the part of Turkey—and specifically, of President Recep Tayyip Erdoğan—are not. They include:

- *Derailing any possibility of Russia-West accord on Syria and common action against ISIS*: This is Erdoğan's top goal. Since the Paris attacks, there has been a huge growth in Western opinion favoring cooperation with Russia on crushing a common enemy: ISIS. While the fate of Assad remains a sticking point, public opinion, media, and even officials of western governments, especially in Europe, increasingly see the need to worry about ISIS first, Assad later—if at all.

- *Saving ISIS and comparable jihad terror groups*: There can now be no doubt that in the confrontation between ISIS, al-Nusra (al-Qaeda), Ahrar ash-Sham, the "Army of Conquest" and the rest of the jihad menagerie against the civilized world, Erdoğan and Turkey are on the side of the former. The canard that Russia is not hurting ISIS, already punctured by the downing of the St. Petersburg airliner in the Sanai, can now be laid to rest. ISIS and Turkey's other proxies are in danger, and cooperation between Russia and the West could seal their fate. In particular, Turkey needs to keep control of part of its border with Syria to maintain ISIS's lifeline for oil exports and for the traffic of terrorists in and out of Syria.

- *Cash cow*: ISIS's oil exports depend on access to Turkey, reaping millions for Turkish middlemen. Whether or how Erdoğan's AK Party and cronies [or his family] may profit from this trade is not clear, but it would be naïve to rule it out. At the recent G-20 summit in Antalya, Turkey, Russian President Vladimir Putin embarrassed Western leaders—and in particular his host, Erdoğan—by presenting undeniable proof of how ISIS funds itself through oil exports via Turkey. It was only after this that the U.S.

joined in strikes against ISIS oil tanker trucks, something that presumably American intelligence had been aware of already. (Reportedly the U.S., unlike Russia, has given ISIS truck convoys 45 minutes' notice prior to striking them—certainly more consideration than the Su-24 was afforded.)

- *Turkish ground presence in Syria*: The Su-24's two-man crew parachuted down into an area controlled by Turkmen militia, which fired on them with small arms as they descended. Their fate is not reliably known. [Russian and Syrian commandos later recovered surviving Capt. Konstantin Murakhtin. He said there were no warnings from Turkey.] The Turkmen militia, who cooperate with al-Nusra and other jihad groups against the Syrian government and Kurdish militias—both enemies of ISIS—are an essential asset of Ankara's in keeping control of the portion of the border abutting Turkey's Hatay Province. They are controlled by embedded Turkish intelligence officers. The firing on the parachuting Russian crew, irrefutably recorded on video, is a war crime, for which the Turkish government bears command responsibility and criminal accountability. (One online comment on a video of a "militia" commander claiming "credit" for shooting at the Russians asserts that from his accent he is identifiable as a Turk, presumably an intelligence officer, not a local Syrian Turkman. I am unable to confirm this claim.) [In a further aggravating development, a Russian marine was reported killed when "moderate" Free Syrian Army terrorists shot down a Russian rescue helicopter with a U.S.-supplied TOW missile.]

Western reactions: Mixed. Some media have taken evident glee in the downing of the Russian plane, as stated in one headline: "The Russians had it coming." In his Washington meeting today with French President François Hollande, U.S. President Barack Obama seemingly accepted the Turkish version of events and justified the shootdown, stating that "Turkey, like every country, has a right to defend its territory and its airspace." (One wonders if "any country" includes Syria, whose airspace is violated daily by U.S., French, and other countries' aircraft striking targets without permission from Damascus in support of jihadists seeking to overthrow that country's government.) At an emergency NATO meeting, some skepticism was expressed about Turkey's action: "Diplomats present at the meeting told Reuters that while none of the 28 NATO envoys defended Russia's actions, many expressed concern that Turkey did not escort the Russian warplane out of its airspace." The NATO governments are no doubt aware of Turkey's past provocations against Syria, well before the advent of the Russian air campaign, staging border incidents seeking to trigger a Syrian response that could be depicted as an "attack on Turkey" justifying an Article 5 response. [UPDATE NOV. 26: One American military expert concludes the Turkish claim does not hold up and is a clear attempt to "NATO-ize" the conflict. Democrat-GOP establishment "Hillary Christie" may finally get the NATO-Russia clash they crave.]

Russian response: Putin made a harsh statement at Sochi prior to a meeting with King Abdullah of Jordan: "Today's loss is linked to a stab in the back delivered to us by accomplices of terrorists. Today's tragic event will have serious consequences for Russian-Turkish relations." Some form of retaliation is widely expected. Among the options are energy supply and tourism. Turkey is heavily dependent on Russian gas, but withholding it would hurt Russia financially as well and damage Russia's reputation as a reliable supplier. Already, there has been some indication that Russians will curtail vacations in

Turkey (a popular beach destination, both for price and because Russians don't need a visa) and of tour companies dropping Turkish vacations packages. Ironically, tourism retaliation primarily will hurt people in Turkish coastal areas, which are generally more secular and Europeanized than central Anatolia—in short, those disadvantaged would be disproportionately Erdoğan opponents, not supporters. Possible military responses include directing intensive airstrikes on Turkmen militia positions [which appears already to have begun], with the aim of killing Turkish intelligence personnel; and stepping up supply to and cooperation with Kurdish forces. The latter would be a deft move, given the popularity of the Kurds in the U.S.

> [UPDATE Nov. 27: Among Russia's responses, the big news may turn out to be Moscow's deployment in Syria of its state-of-the-art S-400 anti-aircraft missile system, which the Russians have long threatened to do but now have finally followed through on, prompted by what they see as Erdoğan's treachery. Based on the S-400 system's maximum range, its deployment could allow Russia to declare what in effect would be a no–fly zone that encompasses most of Syria, as well as all of Cyprus, all of Lebanon, and large parts of Israel, Jordan—and Turkey itself.]

MY PLEDGE: If I am selected for the Republican Vice Presidential nomination and am privileged to assume that august post in January 2017, I pledge to use my considerable influence with President Fill-in-the-blank to (1) break the pattern of bipartisan American cooperation with jihad terrorists supported by Turkey, Saudi Arabia, and other facilitators of Sunni extremism displayed since the Afghan jihad against the USSR, through the Balkan wars in the 1990s, until the present; and (2) review the U.S. relationship with Turkey with an eye to ending the U.S.-Turkish alliance (as suggested by Doug Bandow), either by expelling Turkey from NATO or—preferably—U.S. withdrawal from an alliance that has long outlived its successful defensive purpose and now has become a danger, not least to the United States.

An earlier version of this commentary appeared in Antiwar.com.

"If He Doesn't Like Trump's Exclusion of All Muslims, Obama Must Exclude Advocates of Sharia and Caliphate"

Jim Jatras | *Jihad Watch* | February 23, 2016

The smart and beautiful in both parties have been prostrate with the vapors ever since Donald Trump called for a temporary timeout on admitting all Muslims into the United States until "we can figure out what the hell is going on." Such a blanket exclusion, his critics claim, not only would be illegal (questionable), but would alienate "moderate" Muslims whose cooperation is essential to combating jihad terrorism (arguable).

After all, everyone agrees that not every Muslim is a jihadist.

Conversely, though, all jihadists are by definition Muslims.

So how do we sort them out? That is, if we don't exclude all members of the larger set (Muslims), how do we define and identify the subset (active or potential jihadists)? On that score, Trump is correct on one essential point: we *don't* know what the hell is going on.

Here's an illustration. Most Americans probably assume that when we screen people for admission into the United States, we not only look for terrorist connections but also weed out people promoting the radical ideology and goals that *motivate* the terrorists. This should at least include advocacy of creating a worldwide Caliphate state and imposition of Sharia law in place of the U.S. Constitution. One should also expect exclusion of members of the Muslim Brotherhood, the international pro-Caliphate political party Hizb ut-Tahrir, and similar organizations.

That assumption is dead wrong. Members of such groups and partisans of jihad ideology are not barred from entering our country unless there is a link to "terrorism" narrowly defined to include only detectable violent activity ("premeditated, politically motivated violence perpetrated against noncombatant targets by subnational groups or clandestine agents," 22 U.S.C. 2656f (d)). This is because a 1990 statutory revision virtually abolished so-called "ideological" grounds for exclusion as had previously been used against Nazis, communists, and anarchists.

Today, no one can be barred for adhering to the political and moral principles that justify jihadism or for advocating doctrines contrary to the Constitution, U.S. and American values, such as Sharia's blatant discrimination on the basis of religion and sex. Indeed, one can come into the U.S. even while pushing for the legal adoption of such barbarities as stoning adultresses, be-heading apostates from Islam, slavery and sex slavery, or pedophilic "child marriage"—or maintaining the legitimacy of such horrors as "honor" kill-ing or female genital mutilation, which are not strictly Islamic but endemic to some Muslim-majority countries—so long as there's no indication the appli-cant actually intends or has been linked to "premeditated, politically motiv-ated violence." (Interestingly, an 1891 inadmissibility of "any immigrant who is coming to the United States to practice polygamy" (8 U.S.C. 1182(a)(10) (A))—directed at the time against Mormons, not Muslims—remains on the books, though it's unclear how strictly it's enforced.)

Indeed, not only are Sharia and Caliphate advocates not barred from entry, under applicable standards such advocacy might actually *help* qualify them for admission as refugees, or for claiming asylum if already present in the United States. That's because in many countries the Muslim Brotherhood, Hizb-ut-Tahrir, and similar groups are illegal and subject to government re-presssion. In such countries, repression may under U.S. law constitute "perse-cution" for purposes of establishing asylum or refugee status. In effect, we're issuing an invitation: *Is your nasty government giving you a hard time because you're calling for Sharia and the Caliphate? You poor dear! Come take refuge in the U.S. so you can freely call for the same here—if you promise scout's honor to keep it non-violent.*

(Contrast that with the virtual exclusion of Syrian Christians under the same criteria. Christians make up about 10 percent of Syria's population, but they make up less than three percent of Syrians admitted so far as refugees or asylees. Why? Because under US law, only *government* persecution counts. Being raped, tortured, enslaved, and beheaded by non-governmental jihad groups such as ISIS doesn't. Since the Syrian government *protects* Christians, few of them qualify for admission, but a Muslim Brotherhood member calling for a Sharia-ruled Caliphate might be quite qualified).

Preferably, Congress should fix this egregious omission by legislating appropriate exclusions. However, President Obama—who reminded us he has a pen and phone—certainly could do it himself, at least temporarily until Congress acts, under statutory authority that allows him to bar any class of aliens he deems a danger to the U.S.: "Whenever the President finds that the entry of *any aliens or of any class of aliens* into the United States would be *detrimental to the interests of the United States*, he may by proclamation, and for such period as he shall deem necessary, *suspend the entry* of all aliens or any class of aliens as immigrants or nonimmigrants, *or impose on the entry of aliens any restrictions* he may deem to be appropriate." (18 USC 1182(f), emphasis added)

I'm not holding my breath. But the slim expectation that Mr. Obama might do the right thing isn't a reason not to try to force the issue. Conveniently, Mr. Obama has provided a mechanism to do so—on his own White House website. (A recent petition asking to list Turkey as a terrorist state reached almost 40,000 signatures, despite an almost total lack of media attention until the final two days.)

So on February 22, I posted a petition on the White House site, as follows:

We want the Obama Administration to:

1. Exclude from the US advocates of Sharia, Caliphate, sex slavery, killing apostates/adulteresses, "honor killing," or FGM
2. Exclude or deport from the US and bar from naturalization any person who, regardless of religious belief, advocates or condones the following principles that are contrary to the American Constitution and values: Sharia law, a Caliphate state, violent jihad, child marriage, slavery or sex slavery, "honor" killing, stoning adulteresses, killing apostates, female genital mutilation, or devaluation of inheritance or of legal testimony based on gender or religion; or who is or has been a member of any organization, or a participant in any of its activities, that advocates or condones any of the above. Such exclusion should not depend on any connection to terrorism or other violent actions, and should apply to visitors, immigrants, and refugees/asylees.

With the White House site only allowing 800 characters, this text is just an outline building upon programs for excluding Islamic radicals on ideological grounds proposed by Srdja Trifkovic, Daniel Pipes, and James Edwards, among others. If any such standard is adopted, it would have to be fleshed out and codified. Regulations would have to be issued to set out the methodology, including a well-crafted battery of questions to identify the targeted individuals and groups. It would not be perfect, any more than other law enforcement measures are perfect. But it would constitute a start towards figuring out "what the hell is going on."

Under White House rules, there are only 30 days from the time of posting to reach 100,000 signatures to trigger an official response, which anyway would amount to just some fibs drafted by the State, Justice, and Homeland Security departments. More important than any expected response, the petition allows an official government site to be used as a bulletin board for excoriating the Obama Administration's (and let's be honest, most Republicans') malfeasance in "Keeping America Safe"©.

Anyone wishing to sign the White House petition may do so **here**. (Only your initials are posted, and entry of zip code is optional).

"Groundhog Day on the Promenade Des Anglais"

Jim Jatras | *Chronicles* | July 15, 2016

We've watched this movie before. We will soon watch it again.

In mere minutes following the latest jihad attack in Nice—assuming another hasn't occurred before this appears in print—the script had already written itself.

Shockingly, it seems the perpetrator is—again!—a Muslim. What are the odds? Evidently, a Tunisian who moved to Nice is a "Frenchman." So there's no point in stemming the migrant flood; this is all "home-grown" now.

[The mass-murderer has reportedly been identified as Mohamed Lahou-aiej Bouhel, who (according to the *Telegraph*) "hailed from the Tunisian town of Msaken, which is close to the seaside city of Sousse, where 38 people, including 30 Britons, were gunned down by terrorists in June 2015."]

The responsible authorities will scramble around looking for "ties" to known jihadist terror groups as though ferreting out a ring of bank robbers.

The mainstream media will pronounce itself as puzzled, perplexed, flummoxed, and mystified as to the killer's real motivations as they were by those of the shooters in Orlando ("Allahu akbar!") and Dallas ("Kill white people"). No such uncertainty in Charleston, though.

Another "*Je suis . . .* " hashtag is born. The Eiffel Tower will be lit up in pretty colors. That'll show 'em!

The usual suspects—Hollande, Obama, the Clintons—will mouth the usual platitudes ("resolve," "thoughts and prayers" "the egalitarian and demo-cratic values that underpin our very way of life" "strong solidarity" "cowardly attack"). This, of course, has nothing to do with Islam, the "religion of peace©."

Most importantly, the "far right" dark forces of intolerance and Islamo-phobia (Marine Le Pen, Donald Trump) cannot be allowed to exploit Nice for their own nefarious schemes.

The surveillance state will tighten the screws across the board, without reference to ethnicity, religion, age, or sex. Not profiling Muslims, that would be racist. (What "race" is Islam again?)

Obama will renew his calls for gun control. He might now add federal truck control and a ban on multiple-axle "assault" vehicles.

Advocates of past interventionist fiascos in Bosnia, Kosovo, Iraq, Afgha-nistan, Libya, Syria—all noble quests to help oh-so-grateful Muslims—will strengthen their calls for boots on the ground against ISIS. Preferably Amer-ican boots, or maybe those of our Sunnis "allies," the ones arming and funding jihadists. Assad must go. We need "regime change" in Iran.

NATO and EU bureaucrats in Brussels, Washington, and capitals across Europe will spring into action: "Right! This calls for immediate discussion!" Then they will go back to addressing the "real threat to Europe"—posed by Russia.

After a few days, when the blood is washed off the promenade, after the customary solemnities and moments of silence, the sense of urgency will wear off. As it has for Paris (twice), Brussels, Sinai (Russians don't count, do they?), San Bernardino, Orlando, Istanbul, Baghdad, Dhaka, and lots of places we never noticed anyway.

The New Normal will reassert itself.

Until next time.

The sick institutions that prevail in the West at the national and international level assure that there indeed will be a next time.

Yes, there will be many, many next times unless and until people get really, really sick of this charade and do something about it.

And that starts with throwing the bums out.

"JASTA: Usual Suspects Get Ready to Gut Law Letting 9/11 Families Sue Saudis"

Jim Jatras | *Chronicles* | October 17, 2016

You'd think that after three and a half decades' working in Pergamum-on-the-Potomac, not to mention over 17 years' service with the U.S. Senate, one's capacity to be scandalized would have been exhausted. But even this jaded observer can't help being a bit shocked by the sheer sleaziness of the Obama Administration, Congressional leaders of both parties, lobbyists for Saudi Arabia, and the Wahhabist head-choppers who virtually own the three aforementioned categories as they prepare to make sure that American families of those killed or injured on 9/11 with the complicity of Riyadh are denied their day in court.

A clue should have been the ease with which a bill as controversial as the "Justice Against Sponsors of Terrorism Act" (JASTA; S. 2040) became law. There was no floor fight or roll call vote in either the House or the Senate, just a voice vote. There was no go-to-the-mat mobilization by the White House, Pentagon, State Department, or the Saudis' horde of Gucci-shod fixers to avert the overwhelming override of Barack Obama's veto.

We soon saw why. Even before the override vote took place the media began cranking out stories, seemingly written by the same person, that Congress was experiencing "buyer's remorse." (On the GOP side, the list of lawmakers suddenly pained by JASTA's supposed flaws overlaps strikingly with those rushing to throw Donald Trump under the bus for allegations of lewdness, but that's another story.) By the time JASTA was enrolled as Public Law No: 114-222 a bill to "correct" it reportedly was already in the works, with Congressional, Obama Administration, and Saudi participants up to their elbows tinkering with substitute language to be quietly passed during the Lame Duck session, *after* the November election.

This activity began belatedly, we are supposed to believe, when JASTA was just about to become law because it was only then that legislators experienced pangs of anxiety about the possible boomerang impact on the United States of the "precedent" created by an exception to the doctrine of sovereign immunity. Hogwash. Those concerns, overblown if not specious (as noted below), were well-known beforehand.

This was not a case of buyer's remorse. This was scripted jiu-jitsu to make a big show of standing up for Americans before an election and then quietly do the Saudis' dirty work once safely past those pesky voters.

To his credit, Donald Trump came out firmly for JASTA and against the Obama veto, despite advice to the contrary from some of the more establishment Republicans lately to board the Trump Train. Hillary Clinton says she would have signed JASTA into law, which given her reputation for honesty can be taken about as seriously as her stated opposition to the Trans-Pacific Partnership, which her longtime crony and felons' suffrage champion Virginia governor Terry McAuliffe says will be quickly reversed after November 8. (Conveniently absent from the floor of The World's Greatest Deliberative Body on the day of the JASTA veto override vote was McAuliffe's fellow Virginian and Hillary's running mate, Senator Tim Kaine.)

Exactly how JASTA would be ~~reformed~~ gutted to meet Riyadh's imperious favor is not yet clear and is less relevant than the intended result: the Saudis must not be subjected to legal accountability or even to further embarrassment or inconvenience. While there are a number of technical options available, the most likely one is simply to insert a presidential waiver clause. This would allow the White House to nullify the legal recourse of aggrieved American families (even retroactively shutting down those filing lawsuits immediately after JASTA became law) just by having the President formally attest to what anyone familiar with the Saudis' domestic and international behavior knows to be damnable lies.

Here is some suggested language from one highly skilled functionary of the Oligarchy under the Orwellian heading of "lawfare":

> Congress might require the President to determine that A) Saudi Arabia continues to be a reliable ally of the United States and partner in combating international terrorism; and B) Saudi Arabia is taking strong actions to prevent support inside and outside Saudi Arabia for religious extremism.

And they say Vaudeville is dead! What the USSR was to communism Saudi Arabia is to "international terrorism" and "religious extremism" (gee, which religion?). But does anyone doubt Barack Hussein Obama would rush to certify the truth of these rank fictions?

It should be noted that JASTA does not single out or even mention the Saudis by name. On its face, the law pierces the veil of sovereign immunity for *any* government that is implicated in an "act of international terrorism in the United States" on or after September 11, 2001. The fact that the Saudis and their hirelings and fellow-travelers both in and out of government are about the only ones trying to nullify JASTA approaches an admission of guilt.

The supposed need to fix JASTA reflects in part Saudi threats of financial retaliation, such as dumping U.S. Treasuries or switching their massive purchases of American-made weapons to competitors. But the big hammer is the claim that the JASTA "precedent" would open up the United States government to myriad foreign lawsuits, for example from the families of people killed by Obama's drone strikes. Leaving aside the question of whether the U.S. should be so blasé about our killing and maiming people in other countries with impunity, the argument of precedential danger is exaggerated:

- First, the United States *already* has statutorily waived sovereign immunity on a limited basis with respect to countries we don't like, notably Iran, Iraq (under Saddam Hussein), North Korea, and Cuba, even for actions that took place outside the U.S., which don't fall under JASTA In general, our rule has been that if a country is on our "bad guys" list—and specifically, if they are officially designated a "state sponsor of terrorism"—their sovereign immunity can be abridged however it suits us. Evidently, JASTA opponents don't think a little thing like official Saudi complicity in 9/11, which American plaintiffs would bear the burden of proving, should put Riyadh in that category.

- Second, some of the suggestions made that the U.S. could be subject to claims from Iraqis for the 2003 invasion and subsequent occupation, Palestinians for U.S. military assistance to Israel, Syrians for U.S. arming of terrorists in that country (which of course Obama is doing), and Yemenis for helping the Saudis commit war crimes on a massive scale in that country (which he is also doing), and others are not patterned directly on JASTA, which specifically applies only to international terrorism as defined in U.S. law but "does not include any act of war," also as defined in U.S. law.

The bald fact is, with or without the JASTA "precedent," other countries have *always* had the ability to pass domestic legislation allowing their citizens to sue the U.S. government in their courts for anything they want. They haven't done so, and are unlikely to do so even if JASTA stands in its current form, not because of some American precedent or absence thereof but because such laws wouldn't do them much good and could do them a lot of harm.

This is because of the huge disparity between American financial power, legal reach, and military might—and everyone else's. If any foreign country's government gets sued in American courts, it matters for the simple reason that *we can inflict pain on them.* Because international financial transactions typically are routed at some point through an American intermediary bank (and most such transactions are conducted in U.S. dollars, the world's "reserve currency"), a judgment in U.S. federal court can be enforced by intercepting funds belonging to that government. The same mechanism was key to forcing Iran to negotiate on its nuclear program by making it almost impossible for Tehran to conduct business internationally. Ditto the at-best questionable claims of U.S. "jurisdiction" over alleged corruption in the FIFA soccer federation, Russian sports doping (but nobody else's), non-U.S. companies doing business with regimes Washington has branded as "terrorist" (but the companies' own governments have not), subordinating all other countries' financial institutions to IRS regulation and potential intelligence penetration on the pretense of fighting tax evasion, and other occurrences taking place abroad but via the banking system supposedly "continuing" in the United States "constructively" (a fancy legal term meaning "not in actual fact, but let's pretend").

What admirers of the "lawfare" concept may applaud as the long arm of law enforcement others may decry as anti-sovereign, arrogant, imperial overreach. Either way, the fact remains that no country presently is capable of enforcing in its courts a judgment against the United States government unless Washington acquiesces. Suppose an award were made to citizens of Iraq, Yemen, or wherever under an analog to JASTA for some real or supposed misdeed by our government. How exactly would they collect on it? Seize a U.S. government-owned building? Impound a U.S. Navy ship in port? Shoot down an American drone? It's not hard to see why those would be bad ideas.

What it all boils down to is that fixing JASTA has little or nothing to do with fear of analogous legal retaliation or even Saudi threats to take their dirty money elsewhere. Rather, it is a reflection of the fact that when given a choice between justice for American citizens and nurturing a cushy, lucrative relationship with the most despicable human rights violator on the planet with the possible exception of North Korea and the by-far biggest wellspring of global jihad terrorism, mandarins of the Washington duopoly instinctively choose the latter. The long and the short of neutering JASTA is that the Saudis demand to be given what might be called the Clinton Privilege: what is law for thee is not law for me.

There's still time to stop this outrage. Americans can email and call their Senators and Congressman and tell them: "Hands off JASTA! It's only two years until the next election—and we will remember!" Pay particular attention to the Senate. As Kentucky Senator Rand Paul has heroically demonstrated in holding off some nasty, unconstitutional tax treaties, it only takes *one Senator* to put a hold on a bill. Often that hold can't be maintained for long, but a Lame Duck session lasts only a few weeks at most.

In overriding Obama's veto for the first time to enact JASTA, Congress, whatever the legislators' individual motivations, put Americans first—for a change. Now let's see if they stick to it by rejecting any changes to JASTA.

"How Far Will Trump's Enemies Push to Drag Him and America Down?"

Jim Jatras | *Chronicles* | February 10, 2017

As he completes his third week in office, Donald Trump has already stunned the world with his "shock and awe" campaign to keep promises made when he was a candidate. The mere fact of a politician doing what he said he would do seems to have unsettled the nerves of his opponents. What is called "Trump Derangement Syndrome" is already reaching critical proportions.

Withdrawing from the Trans-Pacific Partnership, ordering a start on his Mexican border wall, ordering an investigation into voter fraud (if conducted properly, almost certain to uncover widespread unlawful voting by non-citizens both legally and illegally present in the U.S., since no proof of citizenship is required to register), insisting he wants to get along with "killer" Vladimir Putin, and cutting short a call with Australia's prime minister over Barack Obama's idiotic promise to take in Muslim refugees that our mates Down Under don't want themselves—all of these have infuriated the usual suspects.

But the declaration of war was his order to impose restrictions on entry from seven majority-Muslim countries designated as trouble spots by Obama with nary a peep from the progressive watchdogs of "tolerance" and anti-"Islamophobia." As Srdja Trifkovic has noted, Trump's order is the first step in instating an ideological test to bar jihad ideologues from the United States. (See Trifkovic's "The Real 'Muslim Ban'" and my "If He Doesn't Like Trump's Exclusion of All Muslims, Obama Must Exclude Advocates of Sharia and Caliphate").

If Trump prevails on his exclusion order, he has the high ground to crush his opponents in both political parties—and they know it. That's why the reaction has been both hysterical and cynical. Mainstream media, inveterate enemies of Trump and the American people, rarely mention the list of countries was Obama's. (Frankly, it's a bad list. Iran is on it—how many terrorist attacks by an Iranian, or by any Shiite, have we seen in the U.S. or Europe? But look who's not on it: Saudis (9/11), Pakistanis (San Bernardino), Palestinians (Fort Hood), Afghans (Orlando). For that matter, where are the Federation of Bosnia and Herzegovina and the criminal pseudo-state of "Kosova"?) Still, you have to start someplace, and the order can be refined as it moves forward.

If it gets a chance. In a barefaced political move, a federal district judge in Washington State enjoined the order, and his injunction was upheld by three judges of the Ninth Circuit, the worst in the country. (As they say at the

Supreme Court: "This case comes on appeal from the Ninth Circuit. Other reasons for reversal include . . . ") Trump can ask for review by the full Circuit *en banc* (a futile undertaking) or more likely turn to the Supreme Court. If the Supreme Court agrees to hear the case, which is far from certain, a probable split of 4 to 4 (at best) would affirm the injunction. Or, as some consider likely, pseudo-conservative Justice Anthony Kennedy, of same-sex marriage infamy, could side with the terrorists-welcome crowd, handing Trump a 5 to 3 defeat.

Either result would kill Trump's order. He could always withdraw it and reissue it in modified form crafted to survive judicial scrutiny, but the lesson would be clear: questions of who can safely be let into the U.S. will no longer be governed by the duly elected president, whom the Constitution and federal statute empower to make such assessments, but by unelected judges' according to their personal preferences. This is the antithesis of the rule of law.

Clipping Trump's wings early to prevent his protecting our country from dangerous intruders is only one element of the threat he faces. Of even greater menace is the effort to create what amounts to a "color revolution" regime change on America's streets, in a replay of the tried-and-true method used in other countries: Philippines, Serbia, Georgia, Ukraine (twice), Egypt, Lebanon, just to name some that succeeded. Now the same Deep State and George Soros team are setting their sights on overturning the will of the American people to restore and preserve our country.

Violence against political speech of the wrong kind is being legitimated and mainstreamed by the media. Black-clad "anti-fascist action" reincarnations of Mao's Red Guards and Röhm's brownshirts beat up and mace peaceful citizens. So-called journalists openly mull whether the president should be assassinated. A celebrity fantasizes about blowing up the White House.

Americans are more divided than any time since 1861. The term "civil war" is heard more and more, both in the "cold" variety and the prospect it could turn hot. Half of America hates the other half. We have become virtual aliens to one another who don't agree on even the most basic principles of God, man, and the purpose of life. Secessionist movements are gathering unprecedented levels of support (notably in California—please, please, please let them go and take their 55 Democratic Electoral Votes with them!).

Taken together, there's reason to be cautiously pessimistic. Trump beat his GOP rivals, he beat Hillary, and maybe he can beat the confederacy of scoundrels mobilizing against him. But it's far from a sure thing. It's a fight in which he's virtually alone, with few trustworthy allies within his own party and even in his own nascent administration. (This is a particular concern in the national security area, which I will touch upon at another time.)

If Trump is to win, he needs to stick to his own instincts and vision. Compromising in the hopes of wooing those opposed to him would be fatal. Those who can be reconciled will be won only by delivering on his primary pledge to restore the economy and jobs for working people.

Actually, Trump is not totally alone. There are still the tens of millions of people who voted for him and who disdain his enemies as much as Trump's enemies hate him.

For the media, the "antifa" thugs, the fantasists of assassination, it may now seem all in good fun to trash every rule of civil and moral restraint in their quest to bring Trump down. But they should think twice, and then think again. The side that starts a civil war isn't necessarily the side that finishes it.

"Terror in Tehran, Qatar Spat, and Race for Syria–Iraq Border: the Washington 'Swamp' Gives Green Light for Saudi Arabia's Jihad Agenda"

Jim Jatras | *Strategic Culture* | June 9, 2017

This week's attacks in Tehran, for which the Islamic State (ISIS) promptly claimed responsibility, are at this writing the latest incidents to roil the troubled waters in an increasingly turbulent "Broader Middle East." They will not be the last.

The terror in Tehran comes as the threats from Saudi Arabia against Qatar on the surreal charge of supporting terrorism have reached a fever pitch. Observers openly discuss the possibility of a coup against the ruling Sheikh Tamim bin Hamad al-Thani, or even a Saudi invasion. Regarding a possible regime change, Saudi media note that Tamim's father, Hamad, came to power in a coup against his father; coups are not rare in Qatari history, and there's always another al-Thani brother, cousin, or nephew who could be installed as a suitable puppet for Riyadh. As for an invasion, keep in mind that Qatar was a part of the first and second Saudi states (defunct in 1818 and 1891, respectively) and could end up that way again. Given depressed oil prices and Qatar's massive natural gas reserves, the Saudis would welcome a quick and lucrative diversification of their portfolio. Qatar has placed its armed forces on the highest state of alert.

Meanwhile, in Syria, on June 6, U.S. planes for the second time put in an airstrike on pro-government forces near the al-Tanf border crossing with Iraq, near Jordan. The stated purpose was to protect U.S.-supported "moderate" jihadists in a "de-confliction zone" unilaterally declared by Washington. The U.S. also has reportedly established a presence at al-Zkuf, another border point to the north and east, with the obvious aim of blocking any link-up of Syrian and Iraqi forces fighting against ISIS. This coincided with announced launch of an offensive to capture ISIS's nominal capital at Raqqa, spearheaded by the U.S.-sponsored Syrian Democratic Forces—of which the main element by far is the Kurdish YPG, denounced as PKK terrorists by America's unreliable NATO ally Turkey.

All three of these destabilizing developments stem from a common root: the agenda of Saudi Arabia to further its Wahhabist agenda of violence and intolerance, which are notorious even by the inhumane standards prevailing in the Islamic world. Worse, that agenda has gotten a major boost from U.S. President Donald Trump's ill-advised visit to Riyadh last month, where he pledged what amounts to unlimited military and political support to 31-year-old Minister of Offense Defense and Deputy Crown Prince Muhammad bin Salman, who is effectively the country's ruler in the name of his doddering father, King Salman. Muhammad is the man behind the ongoing carnage Saudi Arabia and its Gulf allies (including Qatar!) are inflicting on Yemen, with U.S. and British help, and he no doubt would not shy from adding Qatar to his list of atrocities. Whether he would go as far as provoking open war with Iran, confident that the U.S. has his back, remains to be seen. Indeed, given Riyadh's support for jihadist groups, including ISIS, it can't be dismissed that the Saudis had a hand in the Tehran attacks in order to draw a response. No doubt the Iranians suspect as much.

The Saudi accusation that Qatar is abetting terrorism is true in the sense that Doha has been aiding jihadists in Syria, including ISIS, al-Qaeda, and their motley offshoots. Riyadh should be well aware of that, since the Saudis are arming the very same terrorists. That's not what the row is about, though. What the Saudis object to is, in part, Qatari support for the Muslim Brotherhood, a group Riyadh also helped for more than half a century before finally withdrawing their support with the Brothers' rise to power in Egypt in 2012. To be sure, the Muslim Brotherhood is a nasty piece of work, though the United States has not listed it as a terrorist organization. The Saudis' main objection to the Brothers isn't their radicalism—Riyadh gladly and lavishly supports far worse in many countries—but their populism and perceived threat to the royal pretentions of the House of al-Saud and those of other hereditary dictatorships in Muslim countries.

But Tamim al-Thani's real offense is his apparently willingness to talk with the Iranians, whom with American and Israeli backing the Saudis—the world's top state sponsor of terrorism, both in the "hard" form of money and arms and the "soft" form of Wahhabist ideology—fault for all the ills of the Middle East and the world. (In an inventive new wrinkle, a CNN report seeks to blame to the whole quarrel on—you guessed it—the Russians! According to one of America's leading fake news purveyor, "U.S. investigators believe Russian hackers breached Qatar's state news agency and planted a fake news report [that] . . . attributed false remarks to the nation's ruler that appeared friendly to Iran and Israel and questioned whether President Donald Trump would last in office." To the extent that report actually triggered the crisis, which is doubtful, it seems convenient for a number of parties to avoid the probability that the report was an accurate account of Tamim's views.) It remains to be seen if Riyadh can force Qatar to heel in short order. With mediation efforts by Oman, Kuwait, and other countries, Qatar may seek to appease it more powerful neighbor by reining in Al-Jazeera, expelling Muslim Brotherhood leaders, and cutting off dialogue with Tehran. Washington will also press for Doha's capitulation, having put all its eggs in the Saudi basket while not wanting to jeopardize the U.S. Central Command's forward headquarters in Qatar.

On the other hand, the Qataris may decide to stand their ground. Doha is not without supporters. German Foreign Minister Sigmar Gabriel blamed the U.S. (and by extension, the Saudis) for the crisis, denouncing the "Trumpization" of relations in the Gulf region. Iran has offered to send food shipments to Qatar to compensate for the closing of Saudi Arabia's land border. Turkey, which is favorable to the Muslim Brotherhood, has a base in Qatar, and the Turkish parliament is fast-tracking a bill to deploy forces there. It should be noted that Turkey, while a NATO ally, is increasingly estranged from the U.S., largely over U.S. support for the Syrian Kurds. Turkey and Iran, together with Russia, are participants in the legitimate de-escalation zones under the Astana process, which is acceptable to Damascus but at odds with Riyadh and Washington.

This is where it comes back to Syria. Despite all the talk of fighting ISIS and "terrorism" it is clear that the main demon in American policy remains Iran. Not only has the U.S. sought to block pro-Iranian Syrian and Iraqi control of their mutual border, it is clear that a redeployment of ISIS fighters from Raqqa to the south and east towards Mayadeen and Abu Kamal in Deir ez-Zor Governorate is not entirely accidental. This puts the U.S. presence at al-Tanf and al-Zkuf in a *de facto* partnership with ISIS against Damascus and Baghdad, creating what the Israeli outlet *Debkafile* security analysis site calls "the approach of a major showdown for control of southeastern Syria and its strategic multiple border assets." This is why, despite bluster from Defense

Secretary James Mattis that the U.S.-directed Kurdish offensive would subject ISIS to "annihilation" tactics, the reality is that ISIS fighters—or perhaps some Sunni ISIS-"light" to be assembled after Raqqa falls—are a strategic asset not to be discarded. (On June 1, Kurdish and allied groups allowed ISIS fighters safe passage out of Raqqa, but once out in the open the Russians—who were not party to the arrangement—slaughtered them with air power. Now that's annihilation!) As one neoconservative reflecting the view that Iran must be thwarted at any cost has suggested, the key is Deir ez-Zor, where an isolated Syrian army force has been valiantly holding out for years under sustained ISIS attack. (It should be recalled that in September 2016 U.S. planes "mistakenly" bombed Syrian positions in Deir ez-Zor, killing dozens of soldiers and aiding an ISIS attack.)

Thus, the Broader Middle East is beginning to resemble a room full of gasoline, with the Saudis gleefully striking matches. The underlying question is why the Trump Administration is backing them up and giving them the confidence they can get away with it. Foreign Minister Gabriel's reference to "Trumpization" is somewhat off the mark. The Qatar confrontation, U.S. actions to block link-up of Syrian and Iraqi forces (with ISIS and their Saudi sponsors the main beneficiaries), and at least indirectly the Tehran attacks, all proximately reflect the blank military and political check Trump has given Muhammad bin Salman.

This isn't "America First" but as described by Srdja Trifković it's "Wahhabism First." It's a manifestation not of "Trumpization" of American policy but of "de-Trumpization" and the Washington "Swampization" of his administration. Sad!

"Trump Tiptoes on Treacherous Tehran Tightrope as He Ends Support for Terrorists in Syria"

Jim Jatras | *Strategic Culture* | July 21, 2017

U.S. President Donald Trump has taken two seemingly incongruous actions with respect to Iran. On the one hand, he has slapped new economic sanctions on that country over its ballistic missile program and Tehran's alleged "malign activities", including targeting 18 entities and people for supporting "illicit Iranian actors or transnational criminal activity."

On the other hand, Trump certified to Congress that Iran is still complying with the terms of the 2015 nuclear deal negotiated by his predecessor, Barack Obama. Regarding that agreement, critics, such as the fake news *Los Angeles Times*, immediately attacked Trump for breaking his campaign promise "to 'rip up' the nuclear deal with Iran as soon as he took office."

Of course that's not what Trump had said when running for the presidency. While he criticized the deal in very harsh terms, he was the only GOP candidate other than Kentucky Senator Rand Paul who did not vow to trash the agreement on the first day of taking office:

"We have a horrible contract, but we do have a contract," Mr. Trump said on MSNBC's "Morning Joe." "I have all my life—I love to buy bad contracts where . . . people go bust, and I make those contracts good. This is a perfect example of taking over a bad contract. I will find something in that contract that will be very, very well-scrutinized by us, and I think they will not be able to do it, whatever it may be."

"I know it would be very popular for me to do what a couple of 'em said—'we're gonna rip it up,' 'we're gonna rip it up,'" he said. "Iran is going to be an absolute terror, and it's horrible that we have to live with it. Nevertheless, we have a contract. We've lost the power of sanctions because all of these other folks, all of these other countries that were with us, are gone now." [. . .]

"I would much rather . . . give you an answer that I would rip up the contract, I'm going to go in there . . . you can't do that," Mr. Trump said. "I have to do what's right. Politically and certainly for the nomination, I would love to tell you I'm going to rip up this contract, I'm going to be the toughest guy in the world, and I'm just rippin' it up, but you know what? Life doesn't work that way."

This position shows a businessman's common sense—a rare commodity in Washington. While career politician Barack Obama disingenuously commented that "no deal is better than a bad deal," real-world Donald Trump was smart enough to know that sometimes a bad deal is better than no deal if the latter leads to a worse outcome.

That was clearly the case with the Iran nuclear agreement. Whatever its flaws, no one really believed critics' claims that the "alternative to this bad deal is a much better deal." Iran conceded as much as it did only because the Obama Administration—in its single positive achievement in foreign policy, in my opinion—was able to secure the support of Russia and China in addition to our European satellites.

Without that common front, certainly no "better" deal would be possible if the U.S. were now to walk away. The only alternative to even a flawed deal would be war, and everyone knows it. Many of those who urged Trump against certification of Tehran's compliance have been agitating for war against Iran for years. (It goes without saying they also advocated regime change in Iraq and Libya.) According to press reports of unknown accuracy, the certification decision was a near thing, with Trump's advisers sharply split on their recommendations and the president initially leaning against certification. Some observers took the sanctions accompanying the decision as an indication Trump will kill the deal at a future point.

But there's another possible interpretation. Trump knows that war with Iran would destroy his presidency as the Iraq war destroyed that of George W. Bush. What if Trump applied the new sanctions as a tactical move to allow him to blunt criticism for keeping the nuclear deal in place?

Compare Trump's seemingly contradictory actions on Iran to the late bombshell news that he has ordered the cutting off of the CIA's program to arm "moderate rebels"—or rather, al-Qaeda-linked terrorists—in Syria. It comes after the minor miracle of a Trump's agreement with Russian President Vladimir Putin for a ceasefire in southwest Syria, which seems to be holding despite its repudiation by Israeli Prime Minister Binyamin Netanyahu. Given the state of siege Trump is under because of the Russian "collusion" accusations, could these positive steps have been taken in the absence of the largely symbolic April cruise missile strike on a Syrian base, which won him praise from his domestic enemies—despite having being told by intelligence that Damascus was not responsible for the April 4 chemical attack in Idlib?

Perhaps the seeming contradictions in Trump's approach to Iran and Syria are just the result of confusion and dissension. Or perhaps they are part of a deliberate strategy?

"Bombshell Revelation of US and Saudi Culpability in Creating ISIS Ignored by Mainstream Media"

Jim Jatras | *Strategic Culture* | November 3, 2017

Here it is, right from the horse's mouth! Qatar's former prime minister spills his guts about how his country worked with Saudi Arabia and Turkey under the direction of the United States—meaning then the Obama Administration—to funnel arms and money to jihad terrorists in Syria:

The explosive interview constitutes a high level "public admission to collusion and coordination between four countries to destabilize an independent state, [including] possible support for Nusra/al-Qaeda." . . . Former Prime Minister Hamad bin Jassim bin Jaber al-Thani, who oversaw Syria operations on behalf of Qatar until 2013, . . . said while acknowledging Gulf nations were arming jihadists in Syria with the approval and support of US and Turkey: "I don't want to go into details but we have full documents about us taking charge [in Syria]." He claimed that both Saudi Arabia's King Abdullah (who reigned until his death in 2015) and the United States placed Qatar in a lead role concerning covert operations to execute the proxy war.

The former prime minister's comments, while very revealing, were intended as a defense and excuse of Qatar's support for terrorism, and as a critique of the US and Saudi Arabia for essentially leaving Qatar "holding the bag" in terms of the war against Assad. Al-Thani explained that Qatar continued its financing of armed insurgents in Syria while other countries eventually wound down large-scale support, which is why he lashed out at the US and the Saudis, who initially "were with us in the same trench." ["In Shocking, Viral Interview, Qatar Confesses Secrets Behind Syrian War," *Zero Hedge*, October 29]

Busted! Consider the vulnerability of the former U.S. officials who were in charge at that time, President Barack Obama and Secretary of State Hillary Clinton. Just now, the latter had had her worst week since losing the election with the revelations about the Steele dossier, the Uranium One caper, and the Podesta Group's implication in "RussiaGate." The only thing now is to sit back and watch the fireworks show! From Tom Luongo (citing *Zero Hedge*):

Folks, I've been telling you for days now that the containment wall around Hillary Clinton has been breaking down. Now Qatar, which really has nothing to lose at this point outing the Obama Administration's complicity in this, especially since the Saudis turned on them and tried to make them the scapegoat for the failed insurgency in Syria.

But, to directly finger the U.S. CIA and State Departments, then under the control of Hillary Clinton, is absolutely the most damaging thing they could possibly do at this point in time.

Here it comes! You almost have to feel sorry for poor Hillary! The Trump team and their media supporters—starting with *Fox News*, which had been dancing on Hillary's political grave all last week—will be all over this story in no time!

Except they weren't. While Luongo pointed to what *should* have happened, there was not a peep from anyone in the Administration. Nor anything on *Fox*. Both were as mum as the mainstream media, which predictably were as silent as the graves of the hundreds of thousands of Syrians slaughtered by the jihadists.

No fireworks, just the chirping of crickets. As I predicted at the time, the Qatari story would be totally ignored by the American mainstream media. In fact, not a single major outlet in the United States ran the story, though there were a few English-language articles in the Middle East. The only appearances in the U.S. were alternative media like *Zero Hedge, the Ron Paul Institute, Antiwar.com*, and a few others, mostly bloggers picking up from *Zero Hedge*.

In short, far from a blockbuster, it was a non-event. Non-news. *It didn't happen*. The story wasn't even noticed by those who had a direct, partisan political interest in hyping it.

Just like last time.

Recall: in August 2016 Donald Trump accused Barack Obama and Hillary Clinton of being respectively the "founder" and "co-founder" of ISIS. Outrage across the media and political world! The supposedly neutral fact-checkers leaped into action to denounce Trump. "False," declared *FactCheck.org*. Flirting with "conspiracy theories," sniffed *Snopes*. "Pants on Fire," pronounced *PolitiFact*.

Well, sure, what do you expect from the MSM and their pet gatekeepers? How much sweeter the victory would be when Team Trump hits back with the proof! In eager anticipation I emailed a few contacts working on the campaign (August 11, 2016):

> Gents,
> We all know MSM are liars, but DJT's accusation that Obama and Hillary are founder and co-founder of ISIS is true. Putting money and weapons into support for jihadists was foreseen (when Hillary was SecState) in 2012 DIA memo to result in "salafist principality," what became ISIS in 2013. Flynn has said this was not a "blind eye," it was a "willful decision"!
> I haven't seen a peep about this memo and Flynn's comments in any outlet yet re the "founder/co-founder" accusation. Are you going to put out something from the campaign? Do you want me to draft something?
>
>   Jim

The response: "Write something from your angle first." Sure, no problem, I'm happy to serve it up. For the good of the cause! Make America Great Again! I wrote back:

> Feel free to use—let me know.

MEDIA IGNORE D.I.A. MEMO THAT PROVES TRUMP'S CLAIM THAT OBAMA AND CLINTON "FOUNDED" I.S.I.S.

The latest example of the major media's "in the tank for Hillary" behavior is the hysterical response to Donald J. Trump's accusation that President Barack Obama and former Secretary of State Hillary

Clinton are the "founder" and "co-founder," respectively of the Islamic State (ISIS, ISIL).

Not one major media outlet has bothered to mention the official document that proves the absolute truth of Mr. Trump's charges.

In 2015, subject to a FOIA request from Judicial Watch, an August 2012 Defense Intelligence Agency (DIA) report was made public. It specified that outside support for jihadist forces—in which al-Qaeda in Iraq (AQI) and the Muslim Brotherhood figured prominently—fighting against the Syrian government created the "possibility of establishing a declared or undeclared Salafist [radical Islamic terrorist] principality in Eastern Syria, and this is exactly what the supporting powers to the opposition want, in order to isolate the Syrian regime." Hillary Clinton was at that time Barack Obama's Secretary of State.

The following year, in April 2013, the predicted "Salafist principality" did indeed come into existence, with the AQI's declaring itself as the "Islamic State of Iraq and Syria"—ISIS.

As Mr. Trump has pointed out, a necessary precondition for the emergence of ISIS was Barack Obama's precipitous withdrawal of American forces from Iraq, which facilitated AQI's extending its operations into Syria. But also essential was the reckless decision of the Obama White House and Clinton State Department to pursue in Syria the same "regime change" policy that had led to disaster in Libya. This meant pumping money and weapons into the Syrian war in support of al-Qaeda-led jihadists.

Last year, commenting on the 2012 report, General Michael Flynn, formerly DIA director and now an adviser to Mr. Trump, commented that the rise of what became ISIS was not a result of turning a "blind eye" but of a "willful decision" to allow the anticipated "Salafist principality" to come into being. As General Flynn commented in an Al Jazeera interview:

> Hasan: You are basically saying that even in government at the time you knew these groups were around, you saw this analysis, and you were arguing against it, but who wasn't listening?
> Flynn: I think the administration.
> Hasan: So the administration turned a blind eye to your analysis?
> Flynn: I don't know that they turned a blind eye, I think it was a decision. I think it was a willful decision.
> Hasan: A willful decision to support an insurgency that had Salafists, Al Qaeda and the Muslim Brotherhood?
> Flynn: It was a willful decision to do what they're doing.

The record is clear. Barely a year into the Syrian war, the Obama Administration knew a jihadist quasi-state would form if support for terrorists continued. As a "willful decision," the Obama Administration, in cooperation with regional allies, continued that support that led to the formation of ISIS, exactly as expected. Obama's role as the "founder" and Hillary's as "cofounder" couldn't be clearer.

After that there was no response from Team Trump. Even Flynn, who was already on the record as of 2015, made no reference to the smoking gun from DIA—the very agency he had once headed!

In short, for whatever reason, even at that early date—August 2016—Trump's operation was already in the hands of people who were committed to the Deep State's perspectives. No, arming jihadists in Syria wasn't the problem. Nor was overthrowing Kaddafi and sloshing the region with Libyan weapons. Nor was ousting Saddam Hussein and opening up Iraq to both Iran and al-Qaeda. The only admissible mistake was *pulling out* from someplace we had deployed American forces.

For what it was worth, I decided to publish a version of my spurned talking points as a commentary in *Chronicles magazine*. A few others also took note of the DIA memo, such as Alex Newman of *The New American*. That was about it.

Ever the masochist, I decided to contact Louis Jacobson and Amy Sherman, the two relevant hacks at *PolitiFact* (August 12):

Dear Mr. Jacobson and Ms. Sherman,

This is Jim Jatras. I am a former US diplomat and former foreign policy adviser to the US Senate Republican leadership.

I don't know how it is possible give a "truth-o-meter" rating of "pants on fire" to Trump's claim that Obama and Hillary founded ISIS without even passing reference to the August 2012 DIA report that said if the western powers, Gulf States, and Turkey kept aiding radical Islamic forces in Syria—led by al-Qaeda in Iraq and the Muslim Brotherhood—it could result in the appearance of a "Salafist principality" in eastern Syria. That is just what happened, in the form of ISIS's declaration of statehood a few months later in April 2013. General Michael Flynn, formerly DIA director, has said on the record that that result was not a result of a "blind eye" but was a "willful decision." The memo itself also is specific that that outcome was desired by the "supporting powers" and that they knew the nature of the forces they were supporting.

Consider intent, causation, and effect. An intelligence service says, in sum, if you keep doing A you're likely to get B. So they keep doing A as a deliberate policy choice, B results right on cue. "Sarcasm" aside, what Trump said is accurate.

On the assumption that your omitting this aspect was a simple oversight and not evidence that *Politifact* is "in the tank" for #WarmongerHillary like the rest of the MSM, please consider amending your judgment to refer to and cite my commentary below. I am available to answer any questions or provide more information, either by email or at [*xxxxxxx*].

> Regards
> Jim

I should learn not to waste my time.

"The OIC Is the Muslim World's Voice. Christian Countries Should Have One Too!"

Jim Jatras | *Strategic Culture* | December 12, 2017

The Organisation of Islamic Cooperation (the OIC) bills itself as "the collective voice of the Muslim world." Founded in 1972 as the "Organisation of the Islamic Conference" and adopting its current name in 2011, the OIC joins 57 Member States in what is billed as the second-biggest intergovernmental organization after the United Nations. The OIC's declared mission is —

> . . . to safeguard and protect the interests of the Muslim world in the spirit of promoting international peace and harmony among various people of the world. . . . The Organization has the singular honor to galvanize the Ummah [i.e., all Muslims as a community] into a unified body and have actively represented the Muslims by espousing all causes close to the hearts of over 1.5 billion Muslims of the world. The Organization has consultative and cooperative relations with the UN and other inter-governmental organizations to protect the vital interests of the Muslims and to work for the settlement of conflicts and disputes involving Member States. In safeguarding the true values of Islam and the Muslims, the organization has taken various steps to remove misperceptions and has strongly advocated elimination of discrimination against Muslims in all forms and manifestations.

Despite intra-Islamic conflicts—notably the Sunni-Shiite divide led by Saudi Arabia and Iran respectively—the OIC is vocal in promoting a unified Muslim perspective on issues where there is a broad consensus. For example, the OIC recently issued a strong statement denouncing U.S. President Donald Trump's declaration that the United States considers Jerusalem to be Israel's capital. The OIC's information chief also took a position on the internal affairs of traditionally Christian European countries, to the effect that mass Muslim migration—what Srdja Trifkovic has called the Third Muslim Invasion—is really doing Europe a big favor. *No, it's no bother at all—we'll just help ourselves!*

Whatever one thinks of the OIC's activities and perspectives on various issues, one should nonetheless commend Muslim countries for their activism. Keep in mind, the OIC is an official organization of *governments* in the Islamic world, not of religious, academic, or NGO activists, though the latter contribute to the OIC's mission. Again, give credit where credit is due.

But where is the comparable activism by the governments of *Christian* countries? There is certainly an ample empirical basis for a Christian version of the OIC. Consider:

- There are almost two and half billion Christians in the world. The number of Muslims is about 1.8 billion. Granted, the reality behind such numbers largely reflects formal identification rather than active belief and worship, but the social importance of even *pro forma* self-description or communal tradition should not be dismissed.
- Approximately 120 sovereign states have a Christian majority. This compares to about 50 countries with a Muslim majority.
- There are four countries formally called Islamic republics (Afghanistan, Iran, Mauritania, and Pakistan), plus approximately 20 others where Islam's leading status is defined in law. For example, Article 2 of the Constitution of Oman states that "The religion of the State is Islam and Islamic Sharia is the basis for legislation"; Article 1 of the Basic Law of Saudi Arabia states that the kingdom "is a sovereign Arab Islamic state with Islam as its religion," with the Sunni Wahhabist sect in practice given preeminence over the minority Shia. By

contrast, because of Christianity's inherent distinction between the kingdom of God and the kingdom of Caesar, it would be hard to envision comparable "Christian states," though the Holy See (the Vatican) is a Christian theocracy. Nor is there a Christian counterpart to Sharia as a religious basis for civil law. Nonetheless there are approximately 30 states where Christianity, or a particular Christian church, is singled out for a unique legal status or described as the traditional or leading faith. These include the Church of England, the Lutheran churches in Scandinavia, the Orthodox churches of Greece and Georgia, and the Roman Catholic Church in Argentina (Constitution, Article 2: "The Federal Government supports the Roman Catholic Apostolic religion."), Costa Rica, Panama, Malta, Monaco, Liechtenstein, and others. For example, the Lateran Treaties regulating relations with the Vatican are affirmed in the Italian Constitution (Article 7). The Constitution of Georgia states (Article 9(1)) that "State shall recognise the outstanding role of the Apostolic Autocephalous Orthodox Church of Georgia in the history of Georgia and its independence from the State." Several other states grant *de facto* primacy to a church without formal legal sanction, with the primacy accorded the Russian Orthodox Church a notable example. Finally there are many secular countries where Christian morality and heritage are central to national identity and state policy. Even the United States once prided itself on calling itself a Christian nation, in substance if not in law, in the words of many prominent statesmen well into the 20th century.

• The flags of about 20 countries include specifically Islamic symbols, either the crescent moon or the *shahada* statement of faith (notably on the flag of Saudi Arabia). About 30 national flags carry a depiction of the Christian cross, with an additional dozen or so if naval ensigns are counted (for example the Saint Andrew's cross on the flags of the Russian and Belgian fleets, and the Saint George's cross on the ensigns of India, South Africa, Latvia, Lithuania, Ukraine, Trinidad and Tobago, and others whose civil flags do not display a cross).

What would be the purpose of a Christian version of the OIC? (For purposes of discussion, let's call it the *"Organisation of Christian Cooperation,"* or the *OCC*.) Let's take a leaf from the OIC and paraphrase: the mission of the OCC would be to –

> . . . protect the vital interests of Christians and to work for the settlement of conflicts and disputes involving Member States. In safeguarding the true values of Christianity and Christians, the OCC will take various steps to remove misperceptions and strongly advocate elimination of discrimination against Christians in all forms and manifestations.

That would be a pretty good start, wouldn't it? We could perhaps begin inside some of the nominally Christian countries, like the United Kingdom, where a spokesman for the government of Prime Minister Theresa May recently refused to confirm that publicly affirming the divinity of Jesus Christ could not land a person in jail for "hate speech." The notion that simple expression of Christian belief and adherence to Christian moral principles, notably in the area of sexuality, constitutes *hate* has become a global phenomenon. No other religion's believers are routinely defamed in this way.

Of course, as with the OIC a prospective OCC could and should be vocal on international issues. Starting in the 1990s, it began to be apparent even in polite, secular company that persecution of Christians was rampant in some countries, and that indeed more Christians died for their faith in the 20th century alone than in all the 19 centuries preceding it. To come to grips with anti-Christian persecution, the U.S. Congress enacted the 1998 International Religious Freedom Act, which in implementation unfortunately soon veered towards promoting generic "religious liberty" and away from countering actual persecution—chiefly of Christians at the hands of communist regimes (mainly in the past) and Muslim militants (now). Perhaps Christian persecution would be a good topic for an Organisation of Christian Cooperation to raise with the OIC, asking it as an intergovernmental organization to take forceful action to "remove misperceptions" that Islam is intolerant by insisting that all persecution of and discrimination against Christians by Muslims cease! After all, even the Administration of President Barack Obama, who proudly declared that the U.S. was no longer "just" a Christian nation, was eventually shamed into declaring that the Islamic State was committing genocide against Christians in Iraq and Syria (though Secretary of State John Kerry took care to put Yezidis first, and then added Shia Muslims and others to avoid any appearance of caring about Christians in particular). In "safeguarding the true values of Islam and the Muslims" the OIC rarely has taken note of maltreatment of Christians. If an OCC comes into being, it must vigorously champion persecuted Christians.

Another example where Member States of a future OCC could make a positive contribution is help with postwar reconstruction in Syria, including the rebuilding of churches. The Russian government has pledged its assistance with the participation of the Orthodox Church and religious organizations. Why shouldn't other Christian countries pitch in—not just in generic reconstruction aid but specifically to help maintain Christians in the region where Christianity was born? This kind of effort would be relevant not only in Syria but across the Middle East.

Which countries might be candidates to join a hypothetical Organisation of Christian Cooperation? Again, let's look at the OIC, the membership of which mainly consists of countries with a Muslim majority but also includes eight countries where Muslims are a minority: Ivory Coast, Gabon, Guyana, Mozambique, Nigeria, Suriname, Togo, and Uganda. Russia and Thailand, which are majority Christian and Buddhist respectively but have significant Muslim minorities, are OIC Observers. Thus a future OCC should not only welcome all majority Christian countries—including some that may also belong to the OIC—but others where Christians are numerically or socially significant. For example, while South Korea is only about one-third Christian, Christians form a solid majority of that country's citizens participating in organized religious activities. About thirty countries in sub-Saharan Africa would be obvious OCC Member State candidates, as would virtually all of Latin America. China and India, where Christian minorities outnumber the total populations of many majority-Christian countries, should certainly be welcomed as Members or Observers. Paradoxically, the main reluctance is likely to be found among such historically Christian countries as Britain, France, Germany, the Low Countries, Scandinavia, and—alas!—the U.S. and Canada, where the forces of militant secularism have become increasingly intolerant of any indication of Christian public identity among officialdom.

That leaves the question of which states might take the initiative in forming an Organisation of Christian Cooperation. The Vatican would be an obvious key player but might not want to take the lead to avoid perceptions that the OCC might become a mechanism for Roman Catholic influence. The same could be said for Russia, whose leadership could be taken to be a front for Russia's narrow state interests. But it should be noted that both the Holy See and the Kremlin have indicated their willingness to partner in defense of Europe's historic Christian identity and social mores. What is notable is that this is *state-to-state* discourse, not just religious dialogue between the Roman Catholic and Russian Orthodox churches.

Perhaps the most promising current trend is the revival of national traditions that incorporate Christian consciousness in Central Europe. For example, Poland's new Prime Minister Mateusz Morawiecki has declared: "My dream is to make [Europe] Christian again, since unfortunately, in many places, people no longer sing Christmas carols, the churches are empty and are turning into museums, and this is very sad." Likewise, Hungary's Prime Minister Viktor Orbán (a Protestant in a majority Roman Catholic country) has spoken out boldly and eloquently in defense of the Christian character of his own country but of Europe as a whole, as well as of Christians persecuted in the Middle East:

> A great many times over the course of our history we Hungarians have had to fight to remain Christian and Hungarian. For centuries we fought on our homeland's southern borders, defending the whole of Christian Europe, while in the twentieth century we were the victims of the communist dictatorship's persecution of Christians. . . . For us, therefore, it is today a cruel, absurd joke of fate for us to be once again living our lives as members of a community under siege. For wherever we may live around the world—whether we're Roman Catholics, Protestants, Orthodox Christians or Copts—we are members of a common body, and of a single, diverse and large community. Our mission is to preserve and protect this community. . . . Today it is a fact that Christianity is the world's most persecuted religion. It is a fact that 215 million Christians in 108 countries around the world are suffering some form of persecution. It is a fact that four out of every five people oppressed due to their religion are Christians. It is a fact that in Iraq in 2015 a Christian was killed every five minutes because of their religious belief. It is a fact that we see little coverage of these events in the international press, and it is also a fact that one needs a magnifying glass to find political statements condemning the persecution of Christians. But the world's attention needs to be drawn to the crimes that have been committed against Christians in recent years. The world should understand that in fact today's persecutions of Christians foreshadow global processes. The world should understand that the forced expulsion of Christian communities and the tragedies of families and children living in some parts of the Middle East and Africa have a wider significance: in fact they threaten our European values. The world should understand that what is at stake today is nothing less than the future of the European way of life, and of our identity.

As the neo-liberal international order (symbolized by twin EU and NATO bureaucratic centers in Brussels) continue their decline, a revival of the national—and dare we hope, Christian?—spirit may be possible even in Europe. Such a revival could be an important impetus to creating an Organisation of Christian Cooperation, and in turn an OCC could help encourage that revival. This is not to minimize historic animosities even among Christians. The Polish-Russian and Croatian-Serbian enmities come readily to mind. But if Iranians and Saudis can come together when the practical needs of Muslims *per se* require it, can Christians do any less? Does Christianity's *Founder*, Who commanded His followers to love one another, expect any less from us? Perhaps an OCC could itself become a catalyst for reconciliation among Christians as much as a voice within the global community.

We can maybe even dare to hope that the United States is not quite lost. After all, Barack Hussein Obama is out, Donald John Trump is in. He's even told Americans it's alright to say "Merry Christmas!" again. If an Organisation of Christian Cooperation were to be formed, Melania Trump would make a great honorary patroness!

"Is Langley Unleashing Jihad Against China in Xinjiang?"

Jim Jatras | *Strategic Culture* | September 15, 2018

One of the early indicators that the Trump administration's foreign and security policies would not be guided by the President's own preferences but by those of the supposed "experts"—globalists, neoconservatives, and assorted retreads from the George W. Bush administration—with whom he unwisely has surrounded himself was the announcement of a "new" strategy on Afghanistan in August 2017. It was neither new nor a strategy. President Donald Trump allowed his publicly stated preference to get the hell out to be overruled by the guys with the short haircuts who want to stay in Afghanistan, in effect, forever.

But why? What possible national interest could be advanced from a permanent American military presence in a godforsaken piece of real estate about as remote from the United States as it is possible to get while staying on this planet?

One answer was suggested by Colonel Lawrence Wilkerson (US Army-Ret.), former chief of staff to US Secretary of State Colin Powell, at the August 18, 2018, conference of the Ron Paul Institute. Wilkerson's description of the subjective thinking of the US military has the ring of truth (presented here in authentic Pentagonese BLOCK LETTERS, emphasis added in bold):

HERE IS WHAT THE MOST POWERFUL AND MOST STRATEGIC-ALLY-ORIENTED BUREAUCRACY IN OUR GOVERNMENT, THE MILITARY, HAS DECIDED FOR AFGHANISTAN.

THERE ARE THREE STRATEGIC REASONS WE WILL BE IN AFGHANISTAN, AS WE HAVE BEEN IN GERMANY SINCE WWII, FOR A VERY LONG TIME—WELL BEYOND THE ALMOST TWENTY YEARS WE HAVE BEEN THERE TO DATE.

THESE REASONS HAVE LITTLE TO DO WITH STATE-BUILDING, WITH THE TALIBAN, OR WITH ANY TERRORIST GROUP THAT MIGHT BE PRESENT. THESE THINGS ARE ANCILLARY TO OUR REAL OBJECTIVES.

THE FIRST REAL OBJECTIVE IS TO HAVE HARD POWER DIRECTLY NEAR THE CHINESE BASE ROAD INITIATIVE (BRI) IN CENTRAL ASIA.

ASK DONALD RUMSFELD HOW DIFFICULT IT WAS TO GET
MAJOR MILITARY FORCES INTO THIS EXTRAORDINARILY
DIFFICULT LAND-LOCKED TERRAIN IN THE FALL OF 2001.
FOR THAT REASON, WE ARE NOT ABOUT TO DEPART.

SECOND, IN AFGHANISTAN WE ARE RIGHT NEXT TO THE
POTENTIALLY MOST UNSTABLE NUCLEAR STOCKPILE ON
EARTH, PAKISTAN'S. WE ARE NOT ABOUT TO LEAVE THAT
EITHER. WE WANT TO BE ABLE TO POUNCE ON THAT STOCK-
PILE VERY SWIFTLY SHOULD IT BECOME A THREAT.

**THIRD, WE WANT TO BE ABLE TO MOUNT AND COVER
WITH HARDPOWER CIA OPERATIONS IN XINJIANG
PROVINCE, CHINA'S WESTERNMOST SECTION. THESE
WOULD BE OPERATIONS AIMED AT USING THE SOME
20 MILLION UIGHURS IN THAT PROVINCE TO DESTAB-
LIZE THE GOVERNMENT IN BEIJING SHOULD WE SUD-
DENLY FIND OURSELVES AT WAR WITH THAT COUN-
TRY.**

I WILL WAGER THERE ARE NOT A HANDFUL OF OUR CITIZENS
WHO REALIZE THAT WE—OUR MILITARY, THAT IS—PLAN TO
BE IN AFGHANISTAN FOR THE ENTIRE TIME WE ARE CON-
SIDERING FOR OUR GRAND STRATEGY—AND PERHAPS BE-
YOND.

We are not yet overtly at war with China, but given Beijing's quasi-alliance
with Moscow and the growing prospect of a clash between the US and Russia
in Syria or Ukraine it's not too soon to suppose the self-proclaimed "steady
state" already thinks of China as an enemy, or at least as a "great power
competitor" that needs to be taken down a peg. Of particular importance, as
noted by Wilkerson, is the Belt and Road Initiative (BRI), the centerpiece of a
greater Eurasian partnership, a key component of China's bid to become a
military superpower as well as an economic one.

Beijing's geographical weak link to Eurasian partnership is Xinjiang,
which is BRI's logistics hub and China's gateway to the west towards Central
Asia, Russia, and Europe. It also conveniently happens to be the home of
restive Muslim ethnic Uyghurs.

In short, Xinjiang is an ideal place for the CIA (per Wilkerson) to give
Beijing a hotfoot and try to throw an impediment in the way of BRI and thus
of Eurasian integration.

Whenever you see western governments and the legacy media wailing
about the plight of "persecuted Muslims" somewhere (in a way they never do
for Christians anywhere) it should be a tipoff the boys and girls over at Langley
are pushing the start button on a jihad against someone for geopolitical
reasons having nothing to do with human rights, religious freedom, or other
ostensible bleeding heart concerns. That appears to be what we're seeing today
in the strident chorus of alarm from Congress calling for sanctions against
Chinese officials.

We've seen this movie before. Today we see it against China and Beijing's
Belt and Road Initiative (the Uyghurs, and connectedly the Rohingya in Myanmar, directed against BRI's China-Myanmar Economic Corridor through Rakhine State on the Bay of Bengal). In the past we saw it in Afghanistan (against
the USSR), in the Balkans on behalf of Bosnian Muslims and Kosovo
Albanians (against the Serbs), in the Caucasus on behalf of the Chechens
(against Russia). Of course the successful overthrow and murder of the Libya's

Muammar Kaddafi and the not-yet-abandoned effort to effect regime change in Syria depend heavily on support for various al-Qaeda affiliates and offshoots.

It's significant that in all of our post-Cold War 1 military interventions every one (except for Bill Clinton's invasion of Haiti) was ostensibly to free or rescue some suffering Muslims—never mind that in Afghanistan, Iraq, Libya, Syria, Yemen, Somalia, etc. we somehow ended up killing large numbers of the supposed beneficiaries. Just imagine how many oppressed Muslims we would need to kill liberating Iran! Meanwhile, as we continue to support the Saudi slaughter in Yemen with a US quasi-alliance with al-Qaeda there, there's nothing to see, folks . . .

Recognizing these crocodile tears for what they are isn't to suggest that bad things aren't happening in Xinjiang. But based on past experience it's reasonable to think that behind the fog of state-sponsored media propaganda the reality is more complex and involves a substantial element of western intelligence ginning up the jihadis against the kaffir Han as we have against many other targets.

As is the case with Myanmar, where the government's claims of actual jihad terrorism—including massacring Hindu villagers—are dismissed out of hand, China's policy in Xinjiang is condemned without reference to the demonstrable reality of outside-supported attacks. As noted by Moon of Alabama:

> Since the early 1990s a number of terror incidents by the East Turkistan Islamic Movement (ETIM) [also known as the Turkestan Islamic Party] killed several hundred people in China. ETIM is sanctioned by the UN as an al-Qaeda aligned movement. Three years ago China decided to attack the problem at its roots. It prohibited Salafist-Wahhabi Islamic practice, which was only recently imported into the traditionally Sufi Uyghur-Muslim areas, and it tries to weed out any such ideology. It also fears the potential growth of an ethnic-nationalistic Turkic Uyghur movement, sponsored by Turkey, that could evolve into a separatist campaign.
>
> People who are susceptible to such ideologies will be put through a reeducation training which includes language lessons in Mandarin and general preparation for the job market. This may not be the way 'western' countries mishandle a radicalization problem, but it is likely more efficient. There surely are aspects of the program that can be criticized. But to claim that these trainings happen in "concentration camps" and for nonsensical reasons is sheer propaganda.

Further:

> Xinjiang province is larger than Great Britain, France, Spain, and Germany combined. It is a mostly uninhabitable landscape of mountainous and desert terrain with a tiny population of some 24 million of which only 45% are Muslim Uyghurs of Turkic ethnicity. It would be rather unimportant outer province for China were it not at the core of the new Silk road connections.
>
> It is a vulnerable point. An established insurgency in the area could seriously interrupt the new strategic communication lines.
>
> Chinese strategists believe that the U.S., with the help of its Turkish, Saudi and Pakistani friends, was and is behind the Islamic and ethnic radicalization of the Turkic population in the province. It is not by chance that Turkey transferred Uyghur Jihadis from Xinjiang

via Thailand to Syria to hone their fighting abilities. That the *New York Times* publishes about the Xinjiang re-education project, and also offers the report in Mandarin, will only confirm that suspicion. China is determined to end such interference.

The fact is that the CIA and MI6 spooks love jihadis—they're very "operational" as well as expendable. Case in point are several thousand Chinese Uyghurs fighting with the al-Qaeda-led terrorists in Syria's Idlib province, where China's President Xi Jinping no doubt will help Syria's Bashar al-Assad and Russia's Vladimir Putin ensure as many of them as possible never make it back home.

One inescapable irony is that the US and other intelligence services likely siccing their terrorist hounds on China represent governments that worship at the absurd altar of "diversity is strength," unlike the countries they are targeting. Unashamed of their identity and culture, the Han Chinese aren't buying it. As American nationalist Patrick Buchanan observes:

> Consider China, which seeks this century to surpass America as the first power on earth. Does Xi Jinping welcome a greater racial, ethnic and cultural diversity within his county as, say, Barack Obama does in ours?
>
> In his western province of Xinjiang, Xi has set up an archipelago of detention camps. Purpose: Re-educate his country's Uighurs and Kazakhs by purging them of their religious and tribal identities, and making them and their children more like Han Chinese in allegiance to the Communist Party and Chinese nation.
>
> Xi fears that the 10 million Uighurs of Xinjiang, as an ethnic and religious minority, predominantly Muslim, wish to break away and establish an East Turkestan, a nation of their own, out of China. And he is correct.
>
> What China is doing is brutalitarian. But what China is saying with its ruthless policy is that diversity—religious, racial, cultural—can break us apart as it did the USSR. And we are not going to let that happen.
>
> Do the Buddhists of Myanmar cherish the religious diversity that the Muslim Rohingya of Rakhine State bring to their country?

If Donald Trump really were master of his own house, maybe he could move forward on his pledge of an America First, national interest-based policy that finds "common ground" (as articulated at the same Ron Paul Institute conference by Colonel Doug Macgregor (US Army-Ret.)) with countries like Russia and China we continue to treat as adversaries.

But as things stand now, Trump's nominal subordinates continue to do as they please as though someone else occupied the Oval Office. Perhaps they anticipate that will soon be the case.

"Converting Khashoggi into Cash"

Jim Jatras | *Strategic Culture* | October 20, 2018

The hazard of writing about the Saudis' absurd gyrations as they seek to avoid blame for the murder of the late, not notably great journalist and Muslim Brotherhood activist Jamal Khashoggi is that by the time a sentence is finished, the landscape may have changed again.

As though right on cue, the narrative has just taken another sharp turn.

After two weeks of denying any connection to Khashoggi's disappearance, Riyadh has 'fessed up (sorta) and admitted that *he was killed by Saudi operatives but it wasn't really on purpose*:

> *Y'see, it was kinda'f an 'accident.'*

> *Oops. . .*

> *Y'see the guys were arguing, and . . . uh . . . a fistfight broke out.*

> *Yeah, that's it . . . a 'fistfight.'*

> *And before you know it poor Jamal had gone all to pieces.*

> *Y'see?*

Must've been a helluva fistfight.

The figurative digital ink wasn't even dry on that whopper before American politicos in both parties were calling it out:

- "To say that I am skeptical of the new Saudi narrative about Mr. Khashoggi is an understatement," tweeted Republican Sen. Lindsey Graham of South Carolina. "First we were told Mr. Khashoggi supposedly left the consulate and there was blanket denial of any Saudi involvement. Now, a fight breaks out and he's killed in the consulate, all without knowledge of Crown Prince. It's hard to find this latest 'explanation' as credible."

- California Rep. Adam Schiff, the ranking Democrat on the House Intelligence Committee, said in a statement that the new Saudi explanation is "not credible." "If Khashoggi was fighting inside the Saudi consulate in Istanbul, he was fighting for his life with people sent to capture or kill him," Schiff said. "The kingdom and all involved in this brutal murder must be held accountable, and if the Trump administration will not take the lead, Congress must."

Turkish President Recep Tayyip Erdogan must think he's already died and gone to his eternal recreation in the amorous embraces of the dark-eyed houris. The acid test for the viability of Riyadh's newest transparent lie is whether the Turks actually have, as they claim, live recordings of Khashoggi's interrogation, torture, murder, and dismemberment (not necessarily in that order)—and if they do, when Erdogan decides it's the right time to release them.

Erdogan has got the Saudis over a barrel and he'll squeeze everything he can out of them.

From the beginning, the Khashoggi story wasn't really about the fate of one man. The Saudis have been getting away with bloody murder, literally, for years. They're daily slaughtering the civilian population of Yemen with American and British help, with barely a ho-hum from the sensitive consciences always ready to invoke the so-called "responsibility to protect" Muslims in Bosnia, Kosovo, Libya, Syria, Xinjiang, Rakhine, and so forth.

Where's the responsibility not to help a crazed bunch of Wahhabist head-choppers kill people?

But now, just one guy meets a grisly end and suddenly it's the most important homicide since the Lindbergh baby.

What gives?

Is it because Khashoggi was part of the MSM aristocracy, on account of his relationship with the Washington Post?

Was it because of his other, darker, connections? As related by Moon of Alabama: "Khashoggi was a rather shady guy. A 'journalist' who was also an operator for Saudi and U.S. intelligence services. He was an early recruit of the Muslim Brotherhood." This relationship, writes MoA, touches on the interests of pretty much everyone in the region:

> The Ottoman empire ruled over much of the Arab world. The neo-Ottoman wannabe-Sultan Recep Tayyip Erdogan would like to regain that historic position for Turkey. His main competition in this are the al-Sauds. They have much more money and are strategically aligned with Israel and the United States, while Turkey under Erdogan is more or less isolated. The religious-political element of the competition is represented on one side by the Muslim Brotherhood, 'democratic' Islamists to which Erdogan belongs, and the Wahhabi absolutists on the other side.

With the noose tightening around Saudi Crown Prince Mohammad bin Salman (MbS), the risible fistfight cock-and-bull story is likely to be the best they can come up with. US President Donald Trump's having offered his "rogue killers" opening suggests he's willing to play along. Nobody will really be fooled, but MbS will hope he can persuade important people to *pretend* they are fooled.

That will mean spreading around a lot of *cash*. The new alchemy of converting Khashoggi dead into financial gain for the living is just one part of an obvious scheme to pull off what Libya's Muammar Kaddafi managed after the 1988 Lockerbie bombing: offer up some underlings as the fall guys and let the top man evade responsibility. (KARMA ALERT: That didn't do Kaddafi any good in the long run.)

In the Saudi case the Lockerbie dodge will be harder, as there are already pictures of men at the Istanbul Consulate General identified as close associates of MbS. But they'll give it the old madrasa try anyway since it's all they've got. Firings and arrests have started and one suspect has already died in a suspicious automobile "accident." Heads will roll!

Saving MbS's skin and his succession to the throne of his doddering father may depend on how many of the usual recipients of Saudi—let's be honest—bribery and influence peddling will find sufficient pecuniary reason to go along. Saudi Arabia's unofficial motto with respect to the US establishment might as well be: "The green poultice heals all wounds."

Anyway, that's been their experience up to now, but it also in part reflects the same arrogance that made MbS think he could continue to get away with anything. (It's not shooting someone in the middle of Fifth Avenue, but it's close.) Whether spreading cash around will continue to have the same salubrious effect it always has had in the past remains to be seen.

To be sure, Trump may succeed in shaking the Saudi date palm for additional billions for arms sales. That won't necessarily turn around an image problem that may not have a remedy. But still, count on more cash going to high-price lobbying and image-control shops eager to make obscene money working for their obscene client. Some big American names are dropping Riyadh in a sudden fit of fastidiousness, but you can bet others will be eager to step into their Guccis, both in the US and in the United Kingdom. (It should never be forgotten how closely linked the US and UK establishments are in the Middle East, and to the Saudis in particular.)

It still might not work though. No matter how much expensive PR lipstick the spinmeisters put on this pig, that won't make it kissable. It's still a pig.

Others benefitting from hanging Khashoggi's death around MbS's neck are:

- Iran (the drive for regime change rests on twin Israeli and Saudi pillars, and the latter is shaky right now);
- Yemen (support is building for Kentucky Senator Rand Paul's bill to cut of support for the Saudi war effort against that unfortunate country); and
- Qatar (after last year's invasion scare, there's no doubt a bit of *Schadenfreude* and (figurative) champagne corks popping in Doha over MbS's discomfiture. As one source close to the ruling al-Thani family relates, "The Qataris are stunned speechless at Saudi incompetence!" You just can't get good help these days).

Among the losers one must count Israel and especially Prime Minister Bibi Netanyahu. MbS, with his contrived image as the reformer, was the Sunni "beard" he needed to get the US to assemble an "Arab NATO" (as though one NATO weren't bad enough!) and eliminate Iran for him. It remains to be seen how far that agenda has been set back.

Whether or not MbS survives or is removed—perhaps with extreme prejudice—there's no doubt Saudi Arabia is the big loser. Question are being asked that should have been asked years ago. As Srdja Trifkovic comments in Chronicles magazine:

"The crown prince's recklessness in ordering the murder of Khashoggi has demonstrated that he is just a standard despot, a Mafia don with oil presiding over an extended kleptocracy of inbred parasites. The KSA will not be reformed because it is structurally not capable of reform. The regime in Riyadh which stops being a playground of great wealth, protected by a large investment in theocratic excess, would not be 'Saudi' any longer. Saudia delenda est."

The first Saudi state, the Emirate of Diriyah, went belly up in 1818, with the death of head of the house of al-Saud, Abdullah bin Saud—actually, literally with his head hung on a gate in Constantinople by Erdogan's Ottoman predecessor, Sultan Mahmud II.

The second Saudi state, Emirate of Nejd, likewise folded in 1891.

It's long past time this third and current abomination joined its antecedents on the ash heap of history.

"Christchurch, Birmingham, and the Power of Islamic Victimhood"

Jim Jatras | *Strategic Culture* | March 16, 2019

It's the massacre heard 'round the world! Leaders react across the globe! Religious bigotry and hate must be rooted out!

Oh wait, not *this* one. This is just another Muslim massacre of Christian villagers in Nigeria. Ho-hum, nothing to see here folks. Just move along now . . .

Ah, *here's* the right one! In the initial hours following the fatal shooting of several dozen Muslims at two mosques in Christchurch, New Zealand, the verdict was already in: this was a manifestation of white nationalism, which is a kind of "white ISIS."

The only secondary question left to settle remains: Who bears the most blame, Donald Trump individually, Serbs collectively, or Robert E. Lee posthumously?

One thing we will not see is any effort to avoid a *"backlash"* from Christchurch. Remember in 2015, "After Charlie Hebdo attack in France, backlash against Muslims feared"? Well, as one Twitter user notes, you won't see any headlines like "After Christchurch attack in New Zealand, backlash against white males feared."

Quite to the contrary, backlash against the perceived ideology behind the mosque attack and its presumed toxic racist purveyors will be front and center worldwide. (How soon before it's Putin's fault?) Nor will we see the killings breezily dismissed as just "part and parcel of living in a big city," as London's mayor Sadiq Khan waved away the threat of terror after a bombing in New York.

As pointed out by Srdja Trifkovic (himself a deplorable Serb by birth) in *Chronicles* magazine ("New Zealand Attacks: Repercussions and Perspective," March 15):

> The developing frenzy of compassion with the victims of Christchurch will result in a number of mathematically predictable consequences:
>
> - The ruling elites and their media cohorts all over the Western world will have a field day equating "violent extremism" (which has nothing to do with "true Islam," of course) with the neo-nazi, right-wing, white, Christian-inspired racism, xenophobia, Islamophobia, and all other traits of the deplorables; and yes, it will be Trump's fault to boot.
> - Various Islamic activist in the West, such as the sharia-promoting CAIR in the US and its fellow-conspirators elsewhere, will clamor for ever more stringent laws criminalizing "Islamophobia," effectively defined as any form of meaningful debate of Islam, its scriptural message, historical practice, and current ambitions.
> - Such demands will be promptly translated into legislative proposals by the jihadophile liberal class which will proclaim zero tolerance of "Islamophobia" as defined by CAIR et al. And, of course, they will demand additional Soviet/Nazi style gun laws.'
> [. . .]

There will be no attempt to place today's killings "in perspective," as is invariably the case after Muslim terrorists strike Western targets—in Nice, Paris, Berlin etc.—killing hundreds of people. That "perspective" should include the fact that some 30 million Muslims reside in the Western world today (many more on their own reckoning), which makes the probability of any one of them falling victim to a *deplorable* attack in any given year roughly *one in ten million* . . . The odds of a Christian in a majority-Muslim country being murdered by a

Muslim—simply for being what he is—approximately one in 70,000. This means a Christian living in a majority Muslim country is 143 times more likely to be killed by a Muslim for being a Christian than a Muslim is likely to be killed by a non-Muslim in a Western country for being what he is.

Despite what by any metric is a gross imbalance between Islamic violence committed against the innocent and violence committed against innocents *by* Muslims, the Christchurch attack will be a new milestone in Islam's empowerment as an aggrieved category, along with "other marginalized groups [that] have become victims of white supremacist ideologies in recent years." Victimhood is the ultimate form of empowerment, with CAIR already calling for social media to further muzzle criticism of Islamic intolerance and opposition to jihad terror.

Another testament to the power of victimhood was provided recently in Birmingham, England, where angry parental opposition successfully, for now, beat back efforts to institute a program aimed at primary school pupils "to promote LGBT equality and challenge homophobia." The parents, citing offense to their religious sensibilities, organized, protested strenuously, and threatened to yank their kids from the school in question. The school shelved the program.

Yay! Bravo for the parents! A win for the good guys!

Of course it's relevant that 98 percent of the families in the school are Muslim. As Rod Dreher comments in *The American Conservative*:

> Good for those Muslim parents! They have guts. They have a hell of a lot more courage than many US Christians do. What they are standing up to is not homosexuality, but the state's sexual indoctrination of little children. Andrew Moffat, the gay teacher who came up with the program, and who has been teaching it to Muslim students in that school, knows perfectly well what he's doing. The strategy liberals use in cases like this is that they have to make schools "safe" for kids, and to fight bullying. It's nonsense. What they are doing is trying to sexualize little children, and to destroy the substance of what their religiously and socially conservative parents teach them, and in so doing undermine the authority of the parents.

How would such a protest have worked out for any Christian parents with "guts"? It's no mystery. First, we can be sure they'd have lost. Second, they'd be vilified and likely subjected to reprisals.

Birmingham illustrates the rock-paper-scissors nature of intersectionality. On this occasion anti-Islamophobia and the educational establishment's dread of being called racist outweighed what in other contexts would be the invincible LGBT++ doubleplusgood ideology. The remnants of a disenfranchised Christian England are literally irrelevant spectators watching a fight between two empowered certified victim groups sparring with each other.

As pointed out by "Seoulite" in *TAC*, in the victim grievance department:

> Muslims will continue to come out on top, for several reasons.
>
> 1. They have the numbers and will steadily keep increasing in relation to the LGBT brigade, especially in particular locales.
> 2. They can always play the race card, which will always beat the LGBT card.

3. They can always make subtle references to "marginalization" and "radicalization." These are basically threats of blackmail: let us do what we want or we might start blowing ourselves up at pop concerts.

Unless the LGBT brigade start actually murdering Muslim children, bombs will always trump twitter criticism.

In the intersectional pecking order the trump card is anti-racism (of which "Islamophobia" is a subset, even though Islam isn't a race). Similarly, anti-racism and migrants' rights outweighed feminism and #MeToo, resulting in the dropping of charges against two illegal aliens who repeatedly raped and sodomized a 14-year-old middle school girl in Maryland. Ditto European authorities' inaction against migrant abuse of local women in Germany and Sweden and cover-up of Muslim "grooming gangs" raping girls throughout the United Kingdom. No price in native European women's flesh is too high to pay to signal virtuous rejection of racism and Islamophobia.

Thus, while LGBT++ and feminism might yet win an occasional skirmish, in the long run these are nothing more than noxious precipitates of the demoralized, decaying homegrown culture. Once that culture is gone, sexual pathologies will have no ability to sustain themselves against the militant, unapologetic newcomer that, ironically, embodies the very anti-homosexual and misogynistic attitudes they deplore.

That's no reason to celebrate, though. Pick your metaphor: rearranging deck chairs on the Titanic, choosing which sauce you wish to be eaten with, damned if you do, damned if you don't. It's all just sound and fury unless and until we see the (very unlikely) resolve of English (and French, German, Dutch, Swedish,—and American, Australian, and New Zealander) parents and the rest of the native population join Poles, Hungarians, Russians, Italians, and other nations still determined to exist on their own historical cultural and moral terms, not the ones allowed them by this or that faction among their gravediggers. As noted by Christine Douglass-Williams of *Jihad Watch*:

> At Parkfield Community School in Birmingham, we see a possible collision between two unlikely allies in the West: the socialist Left and Islamic supremacists. Such a collision is inevitable, as neither believes in freedom of belief and thought, or in the freedom of speech. For example, Christians who fully believe in the equality of rights of all people before the law but do not believe in promoting LGBT causes have been mercilessly attacked by LGBT socialist-Left activists for having a difference of faith and opinion, despite supporting the human rights of gays. Yet peculiarly, social justice warriors have given Islamic supremacists a free pass, despite their opposition to gay rights and the equality of rights of all people before the law, and also despite the gay hate-preaching from many mosques and the call for the murder of gays in many Islamic states.

Whether in Christchurch or Birmingham, or anywhere else in what until recently were indisputably societies that were ethnically European and spiritually, or at least culturally, Christian, the forces of the rising dictatorship of victims, despite their internecine squabbles, understand all too well who their common enemy is. Whichever faction might have the upper hand at any moment just boils down to scavengers scrapping over the rotting, barely living carcass of a legacy society begging to be put out of its misery.

"There'll always be an England"? Don't count on it. Or a New Zealand or an America, for that matter.

What Is an American?

"Rainbow Fascism at Home and Abroad"

by James George Jatras | *Chronicles* | June 1998

Some years ago, when I was a consular officer in the once-notorious border city of Tijuana, I spent a few days in Mexico City on my way back from a temporary assignment in Matamoros, another border town just across the Rio Grande from Brownsville, Texas. At a social function, I was cornered by a typically irate group of young Mexican intellectuals, who proceeded to lecture me on the evils of my country, in particular the manner in which (they claimed) we brutalize Mexican illegals caught crossing into the United States. After a few minutes of the standard exposition—genocide, racism, imperialism, and so forth—I posed a question: "In light of all your complaints about us, why do you Mexicans treat Guatemalans caught crossing your southern border the way you do?"—it being common knowledge that beatings, torture, rape, and even murder are prevalent.

My interrogators were astounded—then enraged. With a mixture of wounded pride and arrogance, they stormed back at me: "But, it's not the same thing—they have violated the laws of *la patria!*" The fatherland. Their fatherland. It was evidently clear to them, as Mexicans, that their fatherland was something as dear to them as the word implies. It was equally inconceivable to them that I, an American, might feel about my own country the way they felt about Mexico (maybe because, in their experience, Americans typically do not seem to have such feelings, at least the kind of Americans they would have occasion to know). After all, how can a *norteamericano* have a *patria*? For them, and for the rest of the world, the United States is not the unique home of a particular people—it is more like a natural resource. Everyone has a right to it.

La patria. La patrie. Das Vaterland. Otyechyestvo. For most nations, the fatherland is an obvious fact, like their own father and mother, like the air they breathe. In contrast, it seems that for Americans (and for that matter, all other English-speaking peoples) "fatherland" is a foreign-sounding word that applies to other countries, never to our own. We talk about our country in terms of ideals, principles, maybe traditions, even Founding Fathers, and we might be "patriots"—but we have no fatherland. We are explicitly told that American identity—the "American Creed" even—has nothing to do with "nationality" in the traditional understanding of the concept, much less with the related idea of "ethnicity." We talk as if there is no people, no nation (as opposed to ideological identity), no family (as the Greek *patria* is translated in the authorized version of Ephesians 3:15) for which America is home. Instead, we seem determined to turn our country into a boarding house, where each visitor—come one, come all—stays as long as he likes and takes what he will but owes no deeper loyalty.

This attitude affects our relationship with the rest of the world and our inability to base a policy on national interests. "Efforts to define national interest presuppose agreement on the nature of the country whose interests are to be defined," writes Samuel P. Huntington in the September/October 1997 issue of *Foreign Affairs*. "National interest derives from national identity. We have to know who we are before we can know what our interests are." Citing the "disintegrative" effects of non-European immigration in recent years and an increasingly intolerant cultural diversity, Huntington warns:

Without a sure sense of national identity, Americans have become unable to define their national interests, and as a result subnational commercial interests and transnational and non-national ethnic interests have come to dominate foreign policy.

In short, the negation of American national identity—which, in the domestic sphere, we see in Bill Clinton's gleeful projection of a non-European ethnic majority in the next century, America as a scene out of *Blade Runner*—dominates our relations abroad as well. Our anti-national, pseudo-intellectual elites are not content just with destroying the American nation; they want to eliminate everybody else's national identity too. The budding totalitarianism inherent in the domestic concept of group rights based on "diversity"—race, ethnicity, language, religion, sex, age, economic class, handicap, sexual preference, and so on (the breeding of the new and improved American "rainbow" analogue to *Homo Sovieticus*)—needs little elaboration. Of course, the means employed—open trade and immigration, federalized education and health care, gun control and the inversion of traditional morality, feminization of the military and more federal, state, and local criminalization of "hate crimes"—may, in the long run, prove as destructive to some of the currently favored groups as it is to the traditional American identity that is being broken down: *E pluribus nullum*.

The same impulse operates in the international sphere, in which the denationalized "new" United States is rapidly becoming both enforcer and prototype for a new global order. Last November the *Washington Post*, a publication that is anything but hostile to globalization, ran an article entitled "Even Allies Resent U.S. Dominance: America Accused of Bullying World." The *Post* quotes the German newsmagazine *Der Spiegel*:

Never before in modern history has a country dominated the earth so totally as the United States does today. American idols and icons are shaping the world from Katmandu to Kinshasa, from Cairo to Caracas. Globalization wears a "Made in USA" label. The Americans are acting, in the absence of limits put to them by anybody or anything, as if they own a blank check in their "McWorld."

Of course, not all foreigners object to "McWorld." As one commentator in Germany put it: "American values and arrangements are most closely in tune with the new *Zeitgeist*. . . . And that makes for a universal culture with universal appeal."

Several years ago. Strobe Talbott, Bill Clinton's Oxford housemate and now Deputy Secretary of State, wrote an essay for *Time* entitled "America Abroad: The Birth of the Global Nation." In it, he expresses his prediction—and his hope, which he is now in a position to help realize—that in the next century "nationhood as we know it will be obsolete; all states will recognize a single, global authority. A phrase briefly fashionable in the mid-20th century—'citizen of the world'—will have assumed real meaning by the end of the 21st" (and if Talbott gets his way, a lot sooner than that). The established consensus, differing only in details between the Talbott/Madeleine Albright internationalist left and the "national greatness" pseudo-conservatism of the *Weekly Standard*, ensures that for the foreseeable future American "benevolent global hegemony" (the *Standard's* expression), in symbiosis with the United Nations, will be the order of the day. As I have outlined previously in *Chronicles*, this impulse is a continuation of those of the pretenders to global domination that were born in the First World War and figured so prominently in the Second. The 20th century has been the century primarily of red fascism and briefly of brown fascism. The 21st century begins as the era of rainbow fascism, stamped "Made in USA," an America none of the Founding Fathers—with the possible exception of Tom Paine—would recognize, much less countenance.

What is a nation? The following can serve as a useful working proposition from the pen of a man who had some experience with nations (mainly with destroying them), Iosif Vissarionovich Dzhugashvili, better known as Stalin, wrote:

> A nation is an historically formed community of people (but one neither racial nor tribal), possessing a common territory, a common language, and a commonly shared economic life, a community of psychological outlook which is manifested in a community of culture.

Not too bad for a guy who dropped out of the seminary to become a bank robber, although one might quarrel with the part about "neither racial nor tribal," since indeed most nations come into being precisely as organic extensions of the family, the clan, and the tribe.

In the American context, this was obvious to John Jay, who noted in *Federalist* 2 that America was—

> one connected country, . . . one united people, a people descended from the same ancestors, speaking the same language, professing the same religion, attached to the same principles of government, very similar in their manners and customs.

Indeed, to Jay it was self-evident that, contrary to the prevailing delusion that national culture is irrelevant to national creed, "the creed," as Huntington puts it, is "a product of the culture."

Huntington suggests that "the values and institutions of the original [American] settlers, who were Northern Europeans, primarily British, and Christian, primarily Protestant," were "modified but not fundamentally altered" by later waves of Western, Southern, and Eastern European immigration. Still, we all instinctively recognize that there is something more characteristically "American" about that original stock: it has long been possible to be an "ethnic" or "hyphenated American" who was also Italian, Greek, Polish, Jewish, or Irish. But an American cannot be "English" or an "English-American" unless he himself actually is from England. (The seldom-encountered "French-American" would sound almost as silly.) According to the "American Creed," it is heresy to admit what we all know to be true: that on a certain level, those of us who are hyphenated are not as unambiguously "American" as those who have no other ethnic identity.

In general, nations are built in part through the suppression or absorption of competing national, regional, tribal, or religious identities. The relatively late unifications of Germany and Italy illustrate the extent to which the result is sometimes little more than a set of conventions. For example, we all acknowledge that a Bavarian is a German, along with, say, a Prussian, with whom (according to John Jay's criteria of ancestry, language, religion, customs, etc.) the Bavarian has far less in common than he does with an Austrian. But an Austrian, as we all know, is not a German, never has been a German, and is not allowed even to think about possibly being a German. By the same token, a Sardinian or a (German-speaking) South Tyrolian is an Italian, but a Corsican or a (German-speaking) Alsatian is a Frenchman. A Rhinelander who speaks Plattdeutsch or Niederdeutsch at home is a German, but someone a few miles away, where the almost identical speech is the state language, is a Dutchman or maybe a Fleming (which is to say, a Belgian).

Interestingly, suppressed nationality seems to translate at times into nationalist attachment to the suppressing power. The most obvious example is the American South, which, after its forcible reincorporation into the Union became, and by most accounts remains today, the most nationalist region of the country. The same might be said of the Scottish Highlanders, who, within decades of Culloden and the genocidal Highland Clearances, became an indispensable element in the growth of a minor island kingdom into a worldwide empire. (Oddly enough, the Lowlanders, who mostly are ethnic Teutons rather than Celts and who have always been English-speaking, today are devotees of the sacred moor and seem to have forgotten entirely on whose side the bulk of their ancestors fought in the Forty-Five.)

To sum up, the concept of nationhood, though deeply rooted in immutable ancestral origins as well as historical experience, is at the same time subject to *ex post facto* interpretation, which lends not only a certain flexibility but even, in the wrong hands, a dangerous malleability.

How does this observation apply to the behavior of the dominant globalist elite? A quick glance at any historical atlas reveals that, prior to 1945, hardly a decade passed without significant shifts in European borders. (We do not even need to talk about the ridiculous lines on the map of Africa.) The post-World War II ossification of territorial arrangements should be seen as an anomaly occasioned by an unusual circumstance, the Cold War division of Europe. The first meaningful postwar shift in borders occurred in 1990 with the reunification of Germany, ending a division that mirrored that of the continent as a whole. In short order followed the dissolution of Yugoslavia, the Soviet Union, and Czechoslovakia.

Two seemingly contradictory trends are taking place simultaneously: on the one hand, the resurgence of nationalisms that a century ago would have been thought long dead—Scottish, Welsh, Breton, Cornish, Basque, Catalan, Flemish, Walloon, Corsican, Moldovan, Abkhazi, Gagauz—and, on the other hand, European integration. Indeed, it is striking that in most cases the resurgent sub-nationalisms, in asserting their independence from the states of which they had been a part, often for centuries, do not seem to have much interest in attacking the larger trend of transnational integration. Nor do the globalist elites in Washington or at Turtle Bay seem unduly dismayed by these resurgences. One is struck, for example, by how easily Bill Clinton's Europhile clone, Tony Blair, accepts what only a few years ago would have been unthinkable: a Scottish parliament, even the devolution of Wales. The fact is, today it matters little whether the nominal capital of Scotland is Edinburgh or London, or if Northern Italy claims to be governed from Milan or Rome, because in any case the real power will be in Brussels, if not in New York or Washington. The breakup of Czechoslovakia—the "velvet divorce" hailed as a model of peaceful democratic political change, though neither the Czechs nor the Slovaks nor the federation as a whole ever had an opportunity to vote on the question—boiled down to whether Germany would eat it up in one bite or two, with Prague becoming the proud new capital of *Das Bundesprotektorat von Böhmen und Mähren*, a hewer of wood and drawer of water for the economic hegemon of United Europe. (Not, by the way, the worst of fates.)

The rainbow fascist nexus is this: Both secession and integration strike at the same enemy, the only entity with even a chance of defying the new globalism—the historic nation-state. That is why Strobe Talbott finds very exciting the "devolution of power not only upward toward supranational bodies and outward toward commonwealths and common markets but also downward toward freer, more autonomous units of administration that permit distinct societies to preserve their cultural identities and govern themselves as much as possible." The fact that virtually all nation-states today are clamoring to cede their sovereignty to global institutions is a commentary on the quality of their leadership. But if those states are broken up, losing in the process their military strength and their political institutions, their weak successors cannot possibly avoid integration into the new imperium. This is especially likely when we consider that most contemporary secessionist movements, such as the Scots National Party (not to mention La Raza in this country), are at least as far to the left as the national governments they hope to supplant, ensuring that the prospects for improved leadership are hardly promising.

The question of nationality (and its accompaniment, self-determination), has become putty in the hands of the global elite. Srdja Trifkovic has noted the international role in the breakup of Yugoslavia and the Soviet Union, which may be taken as cautionary examples. (Huntington observes: "If multi-cultur-alism prevails and if the consensus on liberal democracy disintegrates"—if?— "the United States could join the Soviet Union on the ash heap of history.") Many people may still remember the 1946 book *I Chose Freedom*, the classic Cold War defector story by Victor Kravchenko. The author was an ethnic Ukrainian, which he obviously regarded as a certain type of Russian—his recollection of his early years is entitled "A Russian Childhood," and his grandfather's account of the 1878 Russo-Turkish war celebrates feats of Russian arms. Kravchenko recounts his dismay, during the official "Ukrain-ianization" program in the 1920's, at being forced to learn from textbooks written in the same Ukrainian speech he spoke at home, in lieu of the standard Russian texts to which he was accustomed, texts which he and his classmates had to consult on the sly. One might imagine someone in southern France being forced, for political reasons, to conduct formal business in Provençal instead of standard French, or of a Swiss German having to struggle through technical manuals in his native Allemannic dialect. The fact is, the distinction between a dialect and a language has long since become more a question of politics than of linguistics. In the Soviet Union, the idea of "Ukrainian" (and, even more absurdly, "Byelorussian") language and nationality was first en-couraged because it was useful to Lenin and company to break up the Russian nation; and then, at the appropriate time, the parts were beaten into conform-ity with the artificial formula "national in form, socialist in content." In the post-communist era, rainbow fascism finds the dissolution of historic nation-hood in the formerly communist world one accomplishment of Lenin, Stalin, and Tito that should not only be maintained but will, in Talbott's mind, set the stage for the final rejection of "tribalism" and the creation of a multi-national global state. His claim that the United States is already a precursor of such a state points to a similar manipulation of ethno-linguistic identity; if yesterday Byelorussian turned out to be a national language, who is to say Ebonics will not be tomorrow?

Rainbow fascism is very fond of what someone has called the "Stone in the Garden of Eden" thesis. This is the notion that there was a flat rock lying around somewhere on Day Six of creation, with the 1998 borders of all the countries scratched on it, borders which are sacrosanct and enforceable by the United States. One odd thing about this idea—really, a rank superstition—is that it is subject to mindless, even arbitrary revision. If a recognized state— say, Yugoslavia or the Soviet Union—ceases to exist, then its former internal administrative lines become imbued with eternal Edenic inviolability. Federal states, in particular, seem to be susceptible to this now-you-see-it, now-you-don't standard. I expect that, in the not-too-distant future, certain states in the American Southwest, having been for decades little more than administrative appendages of Washington, will miraculously rediscover their sovereignty once they become officially Spanish-speaking.

There is one area in which Huntington is somewhat deficient: he correctly focuses on the minority ethnic and commercial skew to non-national American policy but does not really examine the deeper philosophical mandate inherent in globalization. We should bear in mind that rainbow fascism, like its red and brown kin, is above all an ideology, a malignant derivative of the moral corruption and demographic collapse of Christian civilization. Indeed, it might be more accurate to say that, in its messianic aspect, it is a sort of Christian heresy. With its predecessors, rainbow fascism shares a basically materialistic core combined with a flexibility and spiritual sensitivity that is far more subtle and seductive. If, in theological terms, communism was the temptation to change stones into bread, if national socialism was a genetic and materialistic perversion of the idea of the "peculiar people" elect of God, then rainbow fascism has an aspect of a materialized Pentecost run riot, from its seemingly endless ability to incorporate subordinate ideologies (New Age, environmentalism, feminism) to its claim to bestow complete freedom within "diversity." This "white noise" babble of a multitude of voices, each in its own distinctive way expressing the same vacuity, may indeed turn out to be the "end of history" prophesied by Francis Fukuyama. That the United States—responding to an ill-conceived summons to "national greatness"—would find itself the indispensable midwife for the birth of such a monster should be repugnant to any real patriot, to any true son of our fatherland.

"It's Time for a Protestant on the Supreme Court"

Jim Jatras | *TheJIM!gram No. 2* | October 15, 2015

From the founding of the Republic until 1836, every Justice on the U.S. Supreme Court was not only male but a WASP (White Anglo-Saxon Protestant).

That changed with the first Roman Catholic elevated to the Court, Roger B. Taney of Dred Scott infamy. Two other Catholics were appointed in the 1890s. The idea took hold of an informal representative "Catholic seat" on the Court.

The first Jewish Justice, Louis Brandeis, was confirmed in 1916. Thurgood Marshall, the first African-American, in 1967. The first woman, Sandra Day O'Connor, in 1981. The first Hispanic, Sonia Sotomayor, in 2009. Given our admirable passion for representative fairness, I suppose we should be scouting out talented jurists who are (fill in the blank) Asian, Native American, Mormon, Muslim, Scientologist, avowedly atheist, openly gay, bisexual, transgender, differently abled, and so forth.

But hold on a minute! In our zeal for diversity on the Court, we somewhere seem to have lost track of somebody. There is not a single WASP on today's Supreme Court—indeed not a single Protestant of any racial, linguistic, or gender description.

Especially as the Court has become less and less a judicial referee—as the Obergefell decision on same-sex marriage recently reminded us—than effectively a super-legislature that feels entitled to impose the robed Solons' personal preferences on the nation, fair representation is more important than ever. It is intolerable that not one member of America's founding ethnos and core demographic sits on our highest panel as it just makes up stuff nowhere to be found in the Constitution.

I am not a WASP or even a Protestant, but I believe it's time for a Protestant to be named to fill the next Supreme Court vacancy. Ideally, the nominee should be from one of the confessions that dominated the United States at our founding (an Episcopalian, a Congregationalist, or a Quaker), but I could be persuaded of the merits of a Methodist, a Lutheran, a Baptist or other Evangelical, or even (going out on limb here) a Presbyterian. Note that nothing in the Constitution requires Justices to be lawyers—another testament to the Founding Fathers' timeless perspicacity.

MY PLEDGE: If I am selected for the Republican Vice Presidential nomination and am privileged to assume that august post in January 2017, I pledge to use my considerable influence with President Whoever-ends-up-the-GOP-nominee to ensure that at least one qualified Protestant is named to the Supreme Court.

"'Hispandering' in Miami: Flouting the Presidential Oath"

Jim Jatras | *Chronicles* | March 10, 2016

Tuning in last night, one could be forgiven for thinking the United States (or at least Miami) was no longer functionally an English-speaking land. Taking place under a backdrop proclaiming *El Debate Demócrata*, the exchange pretty much dispelled any lingering doubt that the Democrats are in any sense a party serving the interests of a united American nation, regardless of our various ethnic, racial, or cultural roots. Engaging in a two-hour-long exercise in what even one of the moderators called "hispandering," Hillary and Bernie made it clear their policies would be directed specifically toward the needs, wants, and demands of Latinos *qua* Latinos, not to Americans as a whole. What's next, specialized debates for African-Americans, Asian-Americans, the LGBTLSMFT "community," the "differently-abled," Muslims, Rastafarians, vegans, whoever?

To note this does not excuse the Republicans (Trump conditionally excepted), but it does show that the Democrats don't even seem to care that non-Latino Americans watching last night would start to feel they are aliens in their (formerly, our) own country. At least in the Democrats' projections to TV-land, we are well on our way to the replacement America called for by Illinois Congressman Luis Gutiérrez: a "new American political coalition," a self-selected ruling class that posits its interests and values against those of the historic Christian (mainly Protestant), English-speaking American nation, which will be consigned to the status of a permanent disenfranchised, vilified minority:

> . . . a million Latinos turn 18 every year in the United States of America. And . . . they're all American citizens of the United States. And here's what happens: they become the basis of the new American political coalition. That is young people, that is Latinos, that is immigrants, it's African Americans, it's Asians, it's gay people, it's peo-

ple that care about the economy [translation: "Gimme free stuff"], and it's people that care about the environment [translation: carbon cultists]. . . . look: you're never going to take the White House with this kind of politics ever again because there's a new American politics.

In a word, it's Balkanization, a coalition of vested group entitlements, spearheaded by recent immigrants and their "anchor baby" descendants who reject assimilation to a common American identity and in fact define themselves in opposition to it.

Even more importantly, as far as I have heard so far no pundit noted what should have been the blaring headline from the debate: "Democratic Candidates Vow to Break Presidential Oath of Office." On taking office, the President swears that he (or she) *"shall take Care that the Laws be faithfully executed. . . . "* (Art. II, Sec. 3) Exceeding even Barack Obama's malfeasance on "Dreamers," Hillary and Bernie both insisted they would *not* honor their Constitutional duties with regard to deporting aliens, whether children or adults, who don't have criminal records. That in itself should bar them from the office they seek. (You take for what it's worth whether these two supporters of "Sanctuary Cities" would deport criminal aliens, either.) Neither left any doubt that their "constituency" is not the historic American nation but the Guatemalan woman in the audience asking for help in getting her deported husband back into the country, Constitution or no Constitution.

"Death of a Nation"

Jim Jatras | *Chronicles* | August 17, 2017

Every living nation needs symbols. They tell us who we are as one people, in what we believe, and on what basis we organize our common life.

This fact seems to be very clear to the current leadership in Russia, particularly to President Vladimir Putin, in restoring and reunifying a country rent by three generations of Red and White enmity to achieve a national synthesis. With regard to things spiritual, this meant first of all the world-historic reunification of the Russian Orthodox Church, between the Moscow Patriarchate and the New York-based Russian Orthodox Church Outside of Russia. It also meant the rebuilding of the Cathedral of Christ the Savior dynamited by the communists in 1931, not coincidentally the recent target for desecration by degenerates hailed by western "democracy" advocates.

Civic and military symbols matter as well. After 1991 there were those who wanted landmarks of the communist era to be ruthlessly expunged the way the Bolsheviks had themselves sought (in Solzhenitsyn's description) to rub off the age-old face of Russia and to replace it with a new, ersatz Soviet image. Instead, wisdom prevailed. The national anthem adopted in 2001 retains the Soviet melody but with new lyrics (written by Sergey Mikhalkov, who with Gabriel El-Registan had penned the original lyrics in 1944!)—Lenin and Stalin are out, God is in. The old capital is again Saint Petersburg, but the surrounding district still bears the name Leningrad. The red star marks Russia's military aircraft and vehicles, while the blue Saint Andrew's cross flies over the fleet. The red stars likewise are still atop the Kremlin towers while the Smolensk icon of Christ once again graces the Savior Gate. The red banner that was hoisted triumphantly on the Reichstag in 1945 is carried on Victory Day. The remains of exiled White commanders like Anton Denikin and Vladimir Kappel were repatriated and reburied at home with honor.

I may be wrong, but I would like to think that perhaps Russia took a lesson from what until recently had been the American example. In his Second Inaugural Address in March 1865, as the "brothers' war" was drawing to a close, Abraham Lincoln spoke of the need to "bind up the nation's wounds." In striving to do so, nothing was more important than our honoring the heroes of both the Blue and the Gray, perhaps most poignantly demonstrated decades later in the veterans' reunions at Gettysburg. "Unconditional Surrender" Grant and "Marse Bobby" Lee, "Uncle Billy" Sherman and "Stonewall" Jackson, naval legends David "Damn the torpedoes" Farragut and Raphael "Nelson of the Confederacy" Semmes, cavalrymen "Fightin' Phil" Sheridan and J.E.B. Stuart, and many, many others—these names belong to all of us. As Americans.

To say this is not to avoid the centrality of slavery in the southerners' attempted secession or to address the constitutional question of whether they were legally entitled to do so. (Maybe California will have better luck heading for the exit. *¡Adios, amigos!*) Nor does it sugarcoat white southerners' perception of Reconstruction as a hostile, armed occupation or of the institution of Jim Crow racial segregation after federal troops were withdrawn and the Democratic Party assumed power. But the fact is that the *mythos* of North-South reconciliation in a reunited American nation was a foundation of our becoming an economic giant by the late 19th century, a world power at the beginning of the 20th (at the expense of the decrepit Spanish empire, with the celebrated military participation of former Confederates), and a dominant power after two victorious world wars.

That America may soon be gone with the wind. The violence at Charlottesville, the pulling down of a Confederate memorial by a mob in Durham, the removal of four monuments from Baltimore (which has one of America's highest homicide rates) under the cowardly cloak of night, and calls for getting rid of many more are simultaneously the death throes of the old America built on one national concept and the birth pangs of a new, borderless, multiethnic, multilingual, multireligious, multisexual, ahistorical, fake "America" now aborning in violence and lawlessness.

He who says A must say B. When one accepts demonization of part of our history and placing those who defend it beyond the pale of legitimate discourse, one should hardly be surprised when the arrogant fury of the victors is unleashed. That takes two forms: the nihilist street thugs of "Antifa" and "Black Lives Matter," and the authorities (both governmental and media, a/k/a the Swamp) who confer on them immunity for violent, criminal behavior. The former are the shock troops of the latter.

They've been at it for months, well before Charlottesville, across the country, with nary a peep from the party that supposedly has uniform control over the federal government. Our First Amendment rights as Americans end where a black-clad masked thug chooses to put his (or her or indeterminate "gender") fist or club. To paraphrase U.S. Chief Justice Roger Taney in *Dred Scott*, loyalists of the old America have no rights which the partisans of the new one are bound to respect. Where's the Justice Department probe of civil rights violations by this organized, directed brutality? (Or maybe there will be one, including looking into George Soros's connection. If not, what's the point of having RICO?)

To be sure, the spectacle of genuine racists on display in Charlottesville provided the perfect pretext for these people, but they're not the cause. Far from forestalling the violent, revolutionary abolition of the historic America (definitively described by Pat Buchanan) by inciting some kind of white backlash—perhaps in the form of a race war as some of them despicably hope—the "Unite the Right" organizers at Charlottesville have accelerated the revolution. It's a revolution that dovetails with the anti-constitutional "RussiaGate" coup in progress against President Trump, who is the last hope for preserving the historic American nation. If he is removed (is he the *only* one, even in his own Administration, fighting back?) and the nice *respectable* anti-Trump Republican party is restored, they'll gladly join hands with their Democratic and media Swamp buddies in dragging what remains of America down.

If anyone is tempted to think that the new America will be more peaceful in world affairs, think again. It's no coincidence that the same forces that want to bring Trump down and also redefine our country's identity coincide almost entirely with those who want America aggressively to impose "our values"— meaning *their* values—on the globe. As I put it almost 20 years ago in *Chronicles* magazine, in a somewhat different context, this fake "America" is the vanguard of Rainbow Fascism, at home and abroad.

No doubt the same terrible sense of foreboding, even worse, must have occurred to Russians in 1920, when they saw their country bloodily sacrificed on the altar of a crazed, internationalist ideology. Somehow, after paying an unimaginable price in war and repression, they emerged three quarters of a century later still remembering how (as the late General Aleksandr Lebed put it) "to feel like Russians again."

If we fail to avoid the impending long night, will we Americans be so lucky?

"Death of a Nation" was simultaneously published on the online magazine Strategic Culture, *August 17, 2017.*

"Don't Defund 'Sanctuary' Jurisdictions, Prosecute their Officials"

Jim Jatras | *Chronicles* | September 25, 2017

Letter from Pergamum-on-the-Potomac

One of President Donald Trump's first actions after taking office was his Executive Order of January 25, 2017, instructing the Departments of Justice (DOJ) and Homeland Security (DHS) to deny federal grant money for local law enforcement activities to cities and counties refusing to cooperate with the federal government in dealing with illegal aliens. As night surely follows day this defunding strategy has gotten gummed up in the federal courts, similar to the limbo in which Trump's order restricting visas from specified Muslim-majority countries languishes.

Leaving aside the legal merits one way or the other, trying to use federal funds as a club for beating sanctuary jurisdictions into submission is the wrong approach for at least two reasons. First, it allows city, county, and state officials to grandstand as champions of their citizens facing collective punishment from the evil, racist, overbearing feds. *Sanctuarista* officials can claim with some degree of justification that withholding funds endangers their communities by denying local governments tools to do their job—effectively distracting from the greater danger presented by the presence of the criminal aliens themselves.

The second problem stems from the feds' use of "detainer" requests to local jurisdictions asking them to take the positive action of holding a named alien whom DHS (specifically, Immigration and Customs Enforcement) believes is subject to removal from the country. As the name implies, that's just what these detainer notices are: *requests*, not orders, to hold the alien for up to 48 hours beyond the time he would ordinarily have been released from custody. As judge Andrew Napolitano has correctly pointed out, there is no legal obligation on the part of local authorities to help the feds with manpower or resources to enforce federal law. Plus, there's a strong argument based on federalism and division of powers that the federal government can't force—"commandeer"—state and local officials to carry out a federal function.

This puts the Administration in the position of punishing states, counties, and municipalities—and more precisely, their citizens, even those who may support Trump's deportation policy—for their officials' declining to do something they are not legally obligated to do. Politically, and probably legally, it's a loser.

Luckily, there's a more direct and almost certainly more effective approach available. Instead of asking for help from local and state officials, the feds (either DHS or DOJ) can notify the relevant custodial official (police chief, commissioner of corrections, etc., whoever has effective control of access to a prisoner and can sign him over) that an arrest warrant has been issued for a named individual and that federal officers will show up at such-and-such date and time to take him into federal custody. The recipient official will also be notified that he will *personally face criminal prosecution* if he seeks to interfere, either by shielding the alien or helping him to evade arrest (i.e., releasing him before the time when he would otherwise have been released).

At least two federal statutes give the Administration powerful leverage. Consider 18 U.S. Code § 1071, "Concealing person from arrest":

> "**Whoever** harbors or conceals any person for whose arrest a warrant or process has been issued under the provisions of any law of the United States, so as to prevent his discovery and arrest, **after notice or knowledge** of the fact that a warrant or process has been issued for the apprehension of such person, shall be fined under this title or imprisoned not more than one year, or both; except that if the warrant or process issued on a charge of felony, or after conviction of such person of any offense, the punishment shall be a fine under this title, or imprisonment for not more than five years, or both." [Emphasis added]

A similar provision exists for anyone who—

> " . . . knowing or in reckless disregard of the fact that an alien has come to, entered, or remains in the United States in violation of law, conceals, harbors, or shields from detection, or attempts to conceal, harbor, or shield from detection, such alien in any place, including any building or any means of transportation;" 8 U.S. Code § 1324(a)(1)(A)(iii), "Bringing in and harboring certain aliens."]

In Section 1071, "whoever" unquestionably would include a local custodial official. The words "any" provide very broad purview, certainly sufficient to cover taking custody of an illegal alien. The words "after notice or knowledge" are also important, as they place the official receiving the notification in the position of risking prosecution under the cited provisions if he intentionally hurries the prisoner's release prior to the feds' arrival, somewhat analogous to destruction of evidence following issuance of a subpoena. Issuing a federal warrant for a named alien's arrest and informing the relevant local police or detention official that federal officers will arrive at a specified date and time to seize him would, if the official harbored or sprang the alien, satisfy all the elements of a federal crime, namely that—

> "(1) a federal warrant has been issued for the fugitive's arrest; (2) the defendant had knowledge that a warrant had been issued for the fugitive's arrest; (3) the defendant actually harbored or concealed the fugitive; and (4) the defendant intended to prevent the fugitive's discovery or arrest."

This proposed use of arrest warrants would reverse the dynamic of the current detainer requests. Instead of asking the locals affirmatively to *do* something which they have discretion to refuse, the feds would be demanding, under pain of felony prosecution, that they *not* do something, namely not to harbor, conceal, or block discovery and arrest. Thus there is no attempt to commandeer local/state to perform a federal task, just warning them not to violate the law by interfering with federal officers in the course of doing their job. Keep in mind that there is nothing inherent in a prisoner's being held by state or local authorities that immunizes him from federal arrest.

If this proposal is adopted, there would still be issues relevant to execution. Upon being informed that a sought alien had been booked into local or state custody (via the FBI, which automatically is informed of arrests and passes the information on to DHS) the feds would have to move fast, in most cases not giving notification until the federal arrest is imminent. No doubt increased manpower and federal detention space would be needed, and in turn increased funding. Evidentiary questions would arise as to whether in a given case an alien's release may have been hastened to keep him out of federal custody. There would also still be the dilemma, as exists now, of whether it would be better to leave an illegal alien accused of a serious crime, like murder or rape, to face state prosecution, as deportation amounts to putting him at liberty in his own country without punishment but with the attendant danger of his illegal return.

Finally, there is the possibility that state and local custodial officials might defy the federal arrest warrant by shielding or releasing the alien anyway, citing sanctuary policies or (as California's Governor Jerry Brown is now considering) state law. Well, bring it on! That could mean not only prosecution of the relevant custodial officials but of the culpable politicians—governor, mayor, cabinet officials, city councilmen, state legislators—on a charge of conspiracy and possibly solicitation.

Just picture 'em—all cuffed and taking the perp walk: Governor Brown, California Attorney General Xavier Becerra, San Francisco Mayor Ed Lee and City Attorney Dennis Herrera, Los Angeles Mayor Eric Garcetti, Washington, DC, Mayor Muriel Bowser, New Orleans Mayor Mitch Landrieu, Chicago Mayor Rahm Emanuel, New York Mayor Bill de Blasio, and many others.

That would be quite a show!

"Who 'Fought to Preserve Slavery'?"

Jim Jatras | *Chronicles* | November 29, 2017

The campaign against memorials to long-dead Confederates seems to have taken a bit of a sabbatical. Perhaps the media have only paused the hype in favor the celebrity groping mania, or maybe pulling down or defacing outdoor art is not a cold-weather activity. In any case, the relative calm was a blessing worth counting.

Nonetheless, in the supposition that Dixiephobic iconoclasm will return in full force in the not too distant future, it's perhaps appropriate to address a canard favored by *moderate* historical revisionists. This is the claim that Lee, Jackson, Stuart, and other Confederate notables are duly consigned to eternal opprobrium because they "fought to preserve slavery" while Washington, Jefferson, Madison, Monroe, and other Founding Fathers, although slave owners themselves, did not.

Neither point of that distinction is as clear as its proponents would have us believe.

With respect to the Confederates, the centrality of African slavery to the South's determination to secede is unavoidable. While apologists sometimes raise such issues as the Morrill Tariff, the state declarations of secession are quite unambiguous that the Northern states' hostility to slavery, and in particular their refusal to comply with their constitutional obligation to return escapees, was the primary, if not the sole, cause for (in the words of Mississippi) "dissolving its connection with the government of which we so long formed a part."

The states declaring their departure precisely and repeatedly cited Northern states' violation of Article IV, Section 2, Clause 3, of the Constitutional "compact":

> "No person held to service or labour in one state, under the laws there-of, escaping into another, shall, in consequence of any law or regulation therein, be discharged from such service or labour, but shall be delivered up on claim of the party to whom such service or labour may be due."

At the time of its adoption, the scope of what came to be known as the Fugitive Slave Clause was applicable across the Republic, with the arguable except of Massachusetts, where slavery had been declared illegal by that state's Supreme Court under the 1780 state constitution. Elsewhere, despite the adoption of gradual emancipation laws, slaves were held in Northern states for years, even decades, after the Constitution's entry into force. Also note that the Clause applied originally not only to slaves (persons "held to labour") but to apprentices and indentured servants (persons "held to service").

Still, by 1861 the Clause was relevant only to black slaves escaping from Southern states. The latter argued that since the Northern states were not honoring the "compact," they likewise were no longer bound by it. As argued by South Carolina: "We maintain that in every compact between two or more parties, the obligation is mutual; that the failure of one of the contracting parties to perform a material part of the agreement, entirely releases the obligation of the other; and that where no arbiter is provided, each party is remitted to his own judgment to determine the fact of failure, with all its consequences." In the layman's terms: we had a deal but you welched on it, so the deal's off.

But while slavery was certainly the cause of secession, it wasn't the cause of the *war*. Nobody would have fought to preserve or abolish anything if the North had been willing to let the South go in peace. An independent South had no desire to overturn the federal government of a rump Union, nor to invade

Northern states and impose dominion over them. When the Southerners fought, they fought because the North was willing to resort to arms for the sole purpose of keeping them in the Union. Thus, if the North was not fighting to abolish slavery, how could Southerners be fighting to preserve slavery?

The fact that secession itself, not slavery, was the cause for which the Union was willing to resort to war—in time racking up a death toll (as revised upwards in 2012) of 750,000 souls, the proportional equivalent of over 7.5 million Americans today—is evidenced by the amendment proposed by Ohio Republican Congressman Thomas Corwin, and approved by both the House of Representatives and the Senate just days before Abraham Lincoln's inauguration, to guarantee slavery forever in the places where it existed:

> "No amendment shall be made to the Constitution which will auth-orize or give to Congress the power to abolish or interfere, within any State, with the domestic institutions thereof, including that of persons held to labor or service by the laws of said State."

The Corwin Amendment proves that *for the North* slavery wasn't the bone of contention and that indeed the United States would be willing to accept it in perpetuity (or at least would promise to do so) if the southern states would remain in the Union. Outgoing President James Buchanan signed the Amend-ment, though that was legally superfluous. Lincoln pronounced the substance of the Amendment already to be "implied constitutional law" but added that he had "no objection to its being made express and irrevocable." He even sent copies to southern governors as an inducement not to secede. The latter were unimpressed. If the Yankees would not honor words already in the Constit-ution, what good were new ones?

To be sure, few Southerners could have entertained much of an expect-ation that the North would allow their peaceful separation. Some "fire-eaters" no doubt welcomed the prospect of war, sure of their victory and of the despised Yankees' humiliation. Achieving a moral advantage sought by many initiators of war both before and since, Lincoln was successful in getting the Confederates to fire the first shot, abetted by hotheads like Edmund Ruffin. Sam Houston warned that Southerners' "fiery, impulsive" nature would prove their undoing. He was right.

Of course, by 1863 the Civil War did become a fight against slavery. Lincoln's Emancipation Proclamation foreclosed the possibility of the Confed-eracy's recognition by Great Britain, which Southerners had hoped might be as critical as French intervention had been during the Revolution. Lincoln was clear that the Proclamation was a wartime expedient; his own opinions on racial matters are today as inadmissible as any secessionist's. Once the Lee and Jackson memorials are down, we can look forward to those of Honest Abe following suit, a phenomenon perhaps already underway.

But at least Washington and Jefferson are safe. Nobody can accuse them of "fighting to preserve slavery," right?

Not so fast . . .

Lincoln wasn't the first to see emancipation of an enemy's slaves as a tool of military policy. During the American Revolutionary War, the British issued two "emancipation proclamations" of their own. (The British did not abolish slavery in their own empire until 1833. Unlike us, they somehow managed to do it without killing each other in the hundreds of thousands.)

In November 1775, John Murray, 4th Earl of Dunmore, royal governor of Virginia, issued a proclamation of martial law, which included a promise of freedom to "all indentured Servants, Negroes, or others, (appertaining to Rebels,)" if they would defect to His Majesty's forces to bear arms. (At the time, British and Americans alike daintily avoided the distasteful term "slave," preferring "Negro," "servant," or "person." The 1861 secession proclamations were not so fastidious.) While only a few hundred black slaves (there is no estimate of response from white indentured servants) reached safety with the British to be enrolled in "Lord Dunmore's Ethiopian Regiment," up to 100,000 may have fled servitude—from Patriot and Loyalist owners alike.

A second proclamation from General Sir Henry Clinton, the Commander-in-Chief of British forces fighting the Americans, was not contingent on fugitives' enlisting in the royal service. Issued in June 1779, when the war was going poorly for England, it may have been something of a desperation measure that nonetheless had some impact:

> "First published in loyalist printer James Rivington's *New York Gazette* of July 21, 1779, news of the proclamation—subsequently named for Philipsburg Manor in what's now Sleepy Hollow, New York, where Clinton had his headquarters—quickly spread through the colonies. When British troops captured Charleston, South Carolina, in 1780, thousands of slaves joined them. The same pattern was replicated in Virginia in 1781, where thousands more joined the British armies and naval warships that were freely operating on its land and rivers. Both George Washington and Thomas Jefferson lost slaves to Clinton's strategy as British commanders such as Charles Cornwallis upheld its provisions."

Whatever the numbers that had availed themselves of Dunmore's and Clinton's appeals, the American side was sufficiently exercised about the matter to seek reversal of the results in the final resolution of the war. The Treaty of Paris of September 1783, which is the official "deed" to American independence from our former sovereign—"In the name of the most holy and undivided Trinity," as solemnly invoked in the preamble—specified (Article 7):

> ... his Brittanic Majesty shall with all convenient speed, and without causing any destruction, or carrying away any Negroes or other property of the American inhabitants, withdraw all his armies, garrisons, and fleets from the said United States, ...

So, it seems that, at least in part, Washington and Jefferson were fighting to preserve slavery after all. Or at least fighting to recover slaves that had slipped their grasp.

Upon Washington's triumphant entry into New York to accept the handover of authority from Clinton's successor, General Sir Guy Carleton, and provide for the evacuation of British forces on November 25 (long known thereafter as Evacuation Day, but now largely forgotten), the American commander raised the issue of Article 7. Carleton, with the poise befitting his station, replied that the Article applied to no such persons under his authority, since having already been set at liberty by His Majesty, they no longer constituted "property" within the meaning of the treaty language. This left only the question of compensation of their *former* masters, for which purpose Carleton prepared a registry called the *Book of Negroes* to record the 3,000 or so erstwhile slaves embarking to Nova Scotia, some of whom later resettled in the British manumission colony of Sierra Leone.

As recorded in his published correspondence, the Father of Our Country told Carleton that his position was "totally different from the letter and spirit of the Treaty" but, presumably having more important priorities, chose not to press the point. There is no indication any compensation was ever paid.

"Mutti Merkel's Muddle"

Jim Jatras | *Strategic Culture* | December 1, 2017

Is there any sight more delicious than that of German Chancellor Angela "Mutti" Merkel squirming around like a worm on a hot sidewalk?

When the most recent German election yielded an inclusive result, Merkel was presented with several options—all of them bad (for her):

Plan A: Go back to the well for a Grand Coalition between her Christian Democratic Union/Christian Social Union (CDU/CSU) grouping with the Social Democrats (SPD). The SPD immediately rejected that idea in light of a plunge in their party's popularity that has tracked with Merkel's. They no doubt had in mind the fate of the last party that spent too long shackled to Merkel, the Free Democrats (FDP), who in 2013 elections as part of a coalition government failed even to meet the five percent threshold for representation in the Bundestag and only were able to claw themselves back in this year under the dynamic leadership of Christian Lindner. Besides, a renewal of a CDU/CSU-SPD Grand Coalition would mean elevating the upstart populist-conservative, bring-back-the-Deutschmark, Eurosceptic, anti-migrant, anti-Islamic Alternative für Deutschland (AfD) as the official Opposition.

Plan B: After the SPD's telling her to "include us out," Merkel's next obvious choice was a Black-Yellow-Green "Jamaica Coalition" to form a majority with the FDP and the goofy Greens. It's a combination as absurd it sounds. Conceivably, Merkel could form a coalition with either the FDP or the Greens alone—probably better with the Greens, given how far Left the CDU has drifted under Merkel, much to the chagrin of many in the conservative Bavarian CSU—but that wouldn't be enough for a majority. But getting the Yellows and Greens to agree with each other proved impossible. Mercifully, FDP leader Lindner finally pulled the plug on what would have been an unviable, monstrous chimera.

Plan C: One option that has been mentioned as a hypothetical but evidently not given serious consideration is a minority government, possibly with the FDP (which would be unlikely to accept an invitation) but more likely with the Greens, with the SPD acting as the coalition's guarantor without actually being in the government. This would be a novelty in postwar Germany and would run across the Germans' legendary terror of instability. But actually, it has a lot of political advantages. For Merkel, it would give her what she wants most: to remain Chancellor. For the SPD, it would allow them the advantages of a governing party (no legislation could pass without their approval) without any of the responsibility. It would also allow the Socialists to pull down the government whenever they chose, which is maybe why Merkel is avoiding it. Happily for all the "respectable" parties a Merkel-led minority government would anoint SPD as the official "Opposition"—playing dog in the manger to keep the AfD from that starring role—while in reality being Merkel's collaborator. If I were Merkel, this is the route I'd take. (I hope she doesn't read this!)

Plan D: There has been some talk of new elections but it doesn't seem to have gained much traction. The obvious drawback is the possibility another ballot would just be the longest, ugliest route back to the same stalemate that exists now, unless there is some dramatic shift in the results. For Merkel, the big plus might be that if she can budge a little to the Right, some disaffected Christian Democrats who had in the last round voted for the AfD (virtually all of AfD's support has come right out of the CDU's hide) might "come home" to Mutti on account of "buyer's remorse" of causing "instability." While a roll of the dice, new elections might be Merkel's second best option. (Again, Angie, please don't read this!)

Plan E: Surprise! It turns out that the last available scheme is right back to Plan A, a Grand Coalition with the Socialists. But for that, it appears Merkel will have to move even farther to the Left on migration policy, the key issue that has led to the CDU's decline—and the AfD's rise—in the first place:

> German Chancellor Angela Merkel is determined to avoid a snap election by seeking another "grand coalition" with the Social Democrats (SPD), but she might have to scrap a proposed cap on immigration to secure her fourth term in office.
>
> Merkel's decision to open the doors to migrants has shaken up German politics during the fall. Her party, the Christian Democratic Union (CDU), suffered its worst election result since the 1940s in September after some voters turned to anti-immigration party the Alternative for Germany (AfD) in protest of Merkel's migrant policies. The chancellor is now struggling to form a new government because potential coalition partners disagree with her plans to put a cap on the annual immigration level. [. . .]
>
> Immigration is set to take a central role in coalition talks. Merkel wants to cap the annual migrant influx at 200,000, which SPD considers to be a breach of the German constitution.

Really, the show can't get any better than this. What else could AfD ask for? If a new Grand Coalition is assembled, AfD will have a field day throwing bombs in what American military planners call a "target-rich environment." They don't need to accuse Merkel and the Christian Democrats of being the tired, stale clones of the SPD presiding over the demise of Germany, and with it the moribund "European Project"—that reality will be on display for all to see. I'm sorry if it sounds a little Bolshie, but the phrase "the worse, the better" comes to mind.

If Merkel had any dignity left, much left a shred of patriotism, she'd quit now and let history be her judge. If she vacated the leadership of the CDU, the possibility exists that a new leader would pull the party in a more responsible direction. The model, right next door, is Sebastian Kurz's revitalization of the Austrian Peoples Party (ÖVP), which hopefully will soon finalize a coalition with the Freedom Party of Austria (FPÖ), Austria's rough equivalent of the AfD.

For Germany, maybe it's too soon to contemplate a post-Merkel CDU/CSU-AfD coalition, maybe also including the FDP. But we can dream, can't we?

"Trump Sinks a 'Sweet Hole' on DACA"

Jim Jatras | *Chronicles* | January 18, 2018

It's just incredible what a hullabaloo can erupt from the garbled account of just one spoken word.

All week long the national media and political class have been in a tizzy over what Donald Trump was reported to have said in a closed-door White House meeting with Senators over DACA and immigration policy.

Does nobody recall that Trump is an avid golfer and resort developer? *Obviously*, he was characterizing certain garden spot countries in analogy to a "sweet hole" on a golf course. But he was misheard and misreported, or perhaps deliberately misrepresented.

Clearly, his actual words *must* have been: "Why are we having all these people from *sweet hole* countries come here? These places are so nice, why would anyone want to leave?"

That puts everything in a very different light.

Take Haiti, for example. Those in the know can tell you that the horrific scenes of squalor plastered on the internet showing slapdash shacks sur-rounded by mud and raw sewage are in fact a carefully contrived ruse to bilk unsuspecting foreigners of their money via corrupt NGOs like the Clinton Foundation—a kind of reverse Potemkin village. The real Haiti, cunningly hidden from prying eyes, is a Caribbean version of Wakanda.

Or why would Trump unfavorably compare El Salvador to Norway? It makes no sense. Sure, El Salvador has MS13, but Norway has its violent gangs too. They're called "Vikings." (Admittedly, they've not been much heard from lately.)

Alright, so maybe Trump didn't really say "sweet hole." (There evidently is some question of whether the second syllable was "hole" or "house.") Is this the worst word ever uttered in a non-public meeting in the Oval Office? At least nobody claims Trump said whatever he said like Lyndon Johnson, perched on the presidential throne.

Perhaps the real offense is less the word itself than its implication that certain Countries ABCD are horrible, while other Countries WXYZ are quite the opposite. And since Countries ABCD are pretty much full of black and brown people, and Countries WXYZ are by and large the abodes of white and yellow people, he's a *racist* for noticing the difference. Hence, the media and Trump's critics' manic repetition of the R-word, as though it were a sort of magical charm that at some point will cause him to crumble into dust.

There are over seven and a half billion people inhabiting this orb of woe. Probably somewhere in the range of 90 percent of them would dramatically improve their lives if they left where they are and moved to the United States. Aside from the clear benefit to the Democratic Party in welcoming spanking new voters, how does it profit the American nation to import hordes of poor and uneducated people to drag down wages, especially in low-paying job categories, and consume a disproportionate share of public benefits?

Keep in mind too that because a very high proportion of migrants in this category would be considered "minorities" under U.S. law, they and their off-spring would immediately qualify upon arrival for affirmative action status in hiring and education. What kind of idiot country imports foreigners and then discriminates in their favor against the natives? For what purpose—to offset historical wrongs to which the newcomers were never victim?

Conversely, the President's defenders suggest that what's really needed is to switch from a country-of-origin basis for our immigration system to a merit-based system. Let's take only the best and the brightest, from whatever place they hail.

That's a bad idea too. First off—let's show a little altruism here—it would make the plight of the "sweet hole" countries worse. I am not generally a fan of Pope Francis with respect to his views on migration, but he has a point when he says, like Pope John Paul II before him, that a "brain drain" from Third World countries robs them of much of their best talent and hope for improving their own homelands.

However, to note that is not to suggest that importing them into the U.S. is such a blessing for us. Just as we don't need a migrant underclass, neither do we need an imported overlord class taking the best jobs from American kids who have busted their humps getting through school and in many cases gone heavily into debt.

This is a particular problem in high-tech and IT, where massive companies with near-monopoly market control—and consequently almost total obsequy from the bipartisan political class—demand the importation of ever more foreign talent, particular in STEM fields. This is despite serious uncertainty as to whether there are enough jobs even for Americans trained in those fields.

A special area of concern is pushback against the Trump Administration's modest effort to trim the much-abused H–1B program for supposedly "temporary" workers. Not only would reform transgress the left's multi-culturalism and plutocratic corporations' demand for cheap, docile indentured labor, it's being opposed by foreign governments, notably of India (which Trump is cultivating under a misguided "Indo-Pacific" strategic concept, as analyzed by Srdja Trifkovic).

Immigration has become the object of a kind of reverse-nativism, according to which America needs a vital "transfusion of fresh blood" from lots and lots of bright, energetic foreigners. You see, American-born people are just too lazy and stupid to succeed on their own and deserve to be replaced. If you or your brat loses out to an "insourced" immigrant or H–1B visa-holder, maybe one who can trump you on an affirmative action preference, too bad for you.

Here's a suggestion. Let's nix both immigrant underclass and overclass and have a long (if not permanent) immigration timeout like we had from the end of the first Great Wave of immigration in the mid-1920s until the current wave was set off by the 1965 immigration act. For four decades, those who entered in that previous wave (such as all of this writer's grandparents) and their progeny had time to assimilate and become Americans. Unless and until those who arrived in the past few decades have likewise assimilated to the extent possible—and the millions now here illegally have been repatriated— entry should be cut down to the absolute minimum. That should be not much more than spousal visas, and those should be strictly scrutinized for fraud.

It remains to be seen whether Trump's language, whatever it was, will translate into good policy. In the wake of Sweethole-Gate, he's in a strong position. Republicans can move a clean federal government funding bill and dare the Democrats to block it because it doesn't save the "Dreamers." But never underestimate the potential for panic among Congressional Republicans and their ability to throw away a winning hand.

Meanwhile, there's a news report from Florida about the discovery of the carcasses of about 20 stolen horses that appear to have been killed in Santeria or other "black magic" rituals, stripped of their meat, and then dumped.

Police suspect it may be the work of Norwegians.

"American Politics Is Now Just Civil War by Other Means"

Jim Jatras | *Strategic Culture* | November 3, 2018

In the wake of the sending of bomb-like devices of uncertain capability to prominent critics of US President Donald Trump and of a mass shooting at a Pittsburgh synagogue (both Trump's fault, of course)—plus a migrant invasion approaching the US through Mexico—there have been widespread calls for toning down harsh and "divisive" political rhetoric. Of course, given the nature of the American media and other establishment voices, these demands predictably have been aimed almost entirely against Trump and his Deplorable supporters, almost never against the same establishment that unceasingly vilifies Trump and Middle American radicals as literally Hitler, all backed up by the evil White-Nationalist-in-Chief, Russian President Vladimir Putin.

Those appealing for more civility and a return to polite discourse can save their breath. It's much, much too late for that.

When Trump calls the establishment media the enemies of the people, that's because they—together with their passive NPC drones and active Antifa enforcers—are enemies, if by "the people" we mean the historic American nation. Trump's sin is that he calls them out for what they are.

Trump didn't cause today's polarization, he only exacerbates it because he punches back. Good, may he continue to do so. Pining for a more well-mannered time in a country that belongs to another, long-gone era is futile.

American politics is no longer about a narrow range of governing styles or competing economic interests. It is tribal. Today's "tribes" are defined in terms of affinity for or hostility to the founding American *ethnos* characterized by European, overwhelming British origin (a/k/a, "white"); Christian, mainly Protestant; and English-speaking, as augmented by members of other groups who have totally or partially assimilated to that *ethnos* or who at least identify with it (think of Mr. Hamadura in *The Camp of the Saints*).

(Unfortunately we don't have a specific word for this core American ethnic identity to distinguish it from general references to the United States in a civic or geographic sense. (Russian, by contrast, makes a distinction between ethnic русский (*russkiy*) and civic/geographical российский (*rossiiskiy*).) Maybe we could adapt Frank Lloyd Wright's "Usonian"? Or "Americaner," comparable to Afrikaner? Or "Anglo-American"?)

Since the Left gave up on its original focus on industrial workers as the revolutionary class, the old bourgeois/proletarian dichotomy is out. Tribes now line up according to categories in a plural Cultural Marxist schematic of oppressor and victim pairings, with the latter claiming unlimited redress from the former. As the late Joe Sobran said, it takes a lot of clout to be a victim in America these days. The following is a helpful guide to who's who under the new dispensation:

Category	Oppressor	Victim
Sex	Male	Female
Race	White	"Person of Color" (POC)
Language	English	Non-English
Religion	Christian	Non-Christian

Sexual Orientation	"Cis"/"Straight"	LGBTQQIAPP+
Sovereign allegiance	US citizen	Non-US citizen
Legal status	Citizen/legal resident	Illegal/"Undocumented"
Criminality	Law-abiding	Offender
Origin	Native	(Im)migrant
Physical condition	Able	Disabled
Economic	Self-supporting	Dependent

In most of the above categories there are variations that can increase the intensity of oppressor or victim status. For example, certified victimhood in a recognized category confers extra points, like Black Lives Matter for race (it is racist to suggest that "all lives matter") or a defined religious group marginalized by "hate" (mainly anti-Jewish or anti-Muslim, but not something like anti-Buddhist, anti-Rastafarian, or even anti-atheist or anti-Satanist because no one bothers about them; anti-Christian victimhood is an oxymoron because "Christian" is inherently an oppressive category). In addition, meeting the criteria for more than one category confers enhanced victimhood under a principle called "intersectionality."

In the same way, there are aggravating factors in oppressor categories, such as being a policeman (an enforcer of the structure of oppression regardless of the officer's personal victim attributes, but worse if straight, white, Christian, etc.) or a member of a "hate" subculture (a Southerner who's not vocally self-loathing is a presumed Klan sympathizer; thus, a diabetic, unemployed, opioid-addicted Georgia cracker is an oppressor as the beneficiary of his "white privilege" and "toxic masculinity," notwithstanding his socio-economic and health status). Like being Southern, living while genetically Russian is also an aggravating factor.

Creatively shuffling these descriptors suggests an entertaining game like Mad Libs, or perhaps an endless series of jokes for which you could be fired if you told them at work:

> Two people walk into a bar.

> One is a Baptist, straight, male Virginia state trooper whose ancestors arrived at Jamestown.

> The other is a one-legged, genderqueer, Somali Dervish WIC-recipient illegally in the US on an expired student visa.

> So the bartender says . . . [insert your own punch line here]

While Patrick Buchanan is right that the level of domestic violence today is not up to what the US experienced in 1968, the depth of the existential divide is much greater. This is why it's perfectly acceptable for a homosexual, black MSM news anchor to describe "white men" collectively as a "terror threat," but when a straight white, female counterpart makes a clumsy but mild observation about ethnic role-playing it's a firing offense. (Note that while "female" is an assigned victim category, white females can be "gender traitors" if they are seen as putting their "racial privilege ahead of their second-class gender status"; to remain victims in good standing and as "allies" of higher-caste victim groups they need to learn to just "shut the f**k up" when POC sisters with superior oppressed status are holding forth.)

The victim side accuses its opponents of a litany of sins such as racism, sexism, homophobia, Islamophobia, etc., for which the solution is demographic and ideological replacement—even while denying that the replacement is going on or intended. This is no longer ordinary political competition but (in an inversion of von Clausewitz attributed to Michel Foucault) politics "as the continuation of war by other means." In its immediate application this war is a second American civil war, but it can have immense consequences for war on the international stage as well.

To attain victory the forces of victimhood championed by the Democratic Party need to reclaim part of the apparatus of power they lost in Trump's unexpected 2016 win. (Actually, much of the apparatus in the Executive Branch remains in Democratic hands but is only of limited utility as a "resistance" under the superficial Trumpian occupation.) As this commentary appears it is expected that on November 6 the GOP will retain control of the US Senate but the House of Representatives will flip to the Democrats.

That's what's "supposed" to happen, just as Hillary Clinton was "supposed" to win the White House two years ago. How things will actually play out though is anybody's guess.

But for the sake of discussion, if the expected scenario comes to pass the last chance Trump's election afforded to save what is left of the American nation is likely to come to an end. We can anticipate three results:

- First, on the domestic political front, while Democrats and their MSM echo chamber have cooled down talk of impeaching Trump, it will return with a vengeance on November 7 (coincidentally, Great October Socialist Revolution Day) if the House changes hands. In contrast to the GOP's dithering in the area of investigations and hearings relevant to the US-UK Deep State conspiracy to overturn the 2016 election (which will be buried forever), the Democrats will be utterly ruthless in using their power with the single-minded purpose of getting Trump out of office before 2020. They won't waste much time on the phony Russian "collusion" story (Robert Mueller's report will be an obscenely expensive dud), they'll focus like a laser on getting Trump's tax returns and dredging up anything they can from his long involvement in the sharp-elbowed, dog-eat-dog world of New York property development and construction, confident they can find something that qualifies as a high crime or misdemeanor. (Some racist language couldn't hurt, either.) The model will be Richard Nixon's Vice President Spiro Agnew, who was forced out of office on charges relating to his time in Maryland politics years earlier. Even the GOP's retention of the Senate would be far from a guarantee that Trump won't be removed. It's easily foreseeable that a dozen-plus Republican Senators would be thrilled to get rid of Trump and restore the party's *status quo ante* with Mike Pence in the Oval Office. As with Nixon, Republicans will panic at whatever dirt the Democrats dig up and demand Trump resign for the "good of the country and the party," as opposed to the way Democrats formed a protective phalanx around Bill Clinton. Unlike Nixon, Trump might choose to fight it out in the Senate and might even prevail. In any case, a change in control of just one chamber means an extended political crisis that will keep Trump boxed in and perpetually on the defensive.

- Second, for Trump's supporters and other dissenters from the Regime of Certified Victims, the walls will continue to close in. The digital ghetto-ization of alternative views to "protect our democracy" from supposed outside meddling conflated with "hate online" will accelerate, with social media a particular target for censorship. The Deep State's intelligence and law enforcement organs will step up actions to penalize any resistance to Leftwing violence, while perpetrators of such violence will rampage with impunity. Trump has done nothing to protect free speech online or in public places while his enemies continue to contract the space for both—but things can and likely will get much, much worse if the Democrats feel the wind at their back after next week. Such vestigial protections of religion, free speech, right to bears arms, and others that we still possess —for now—aren't likely to survive much longer as the edifice of the old America continues to crumble under the malfeasance of the very Executive, Legislative, and Judicial officials who pretend to be its custodians.

- Third and most ominously, chances of a major war could increase exponentially. If Trump is fighting for his life, chances of purging his terrible, horrible, no good, very bad national security team will go from slim to none. Any hope of a national interest-based policy along the lines Trump promised in 2016—and which still seems to be his personal preference—will be gone. Thankfully, South Korea's President Moon Jae-in has run with the ball through last year's opening and hopefully the momentum for peace in Northeast Asia will be self-sustaining. With any luck, the Khashoggi imbroglio between Washington and Riyadh will lead to America's "downplaying and eventually abandoning the anti-Iranian obsession that has so far overshadowed our regional policy" and to an end the carnage in Yemen, even as the Syria war lurches toward resolution. Still, the US remains addicted to ever-increasing sanctions, and despite warnings from both Russia and China that they are prepared for war—warnings virtually ignored by the US media and political class—the US keeps pressing on all fronts: outer space, the Arctic, Europe (withdrawal from the INF treaty), Ukraine, the South China Sea, the Taiwan Strait, Xinjiang, and elsewhere. Trump is expected to meet with Putin and Chinese President Xi Jinping following the US election, but they may have to conclude that he is not capable of restraining the war machine nominally under his command and will plan accordingly.

"The Dictatorship of Victims Strikes Back"

Jim Jatras | *Chronicles* | November 08, 2018

One can almost hear an audible sigh of relief from the rogues' gallery of criminal conspirators behind the phony Russiagate collusion story cooked up in the bowels of the US-UK Deep State with the aim of overturning the 2016 election. Now, after two years of the GOP's dithering in the area of investigations and hearings relevant to how the Trump campaign was put under politically motivated surveillance, those peccadilloes will be forever buried. Instead, with a unity of purpose alien to the Stupid Party, the Evil Party taking over the House of Representatives in January 2019 will be utterly ruthless in using their power with the single-minded purpose of getting Trump out of office before 2020.

They'll still wail about "The Russians! The Russians! The Russians!" of course, but that will be just for show. (Robert Mueller's report will be an obscenely expensive dud.) Instead, Speaker Nancy Pelosi and her minions will focus like a laser on getting their mitts on Trump's tax returns and dredging up anything they can from his long involvement in the sharp-elbowed, dog-eat-dog world of New York property development and construction, confident they can find something that qualifies as a high crime or misdemeanor. (Some racist language couldn't hurt, either. He's literally Hitler, y'know.)

The model for impeaching Trump will be Richard Nixon's Vice President Spiro Agnew, who was forced out of office on charges relating to his time in Maryland politics years earlier. The GOP's retention of the Senate and even picking up a few seats will be far from a guarantee that Trump won't be removed. It's easily foreseeable that a dozen-plus Republican Senators (think Mitt Romney) will be thrilled to get rid of Trump and restore the party's *status quo ante* with Mike Pence in the Oval Office. As with Nixon, Republicans will panic at whatever dirt the Democrats dig up and demand Trump resign for the "good of the country and the party," as opposed to the way Democrats formed a protective phalanx around Bill Clinton. Unlike Nixon, Trump might choose to fight it out in the Senate and might even prevail. In any case, a change in control of just one chamber means an extended political crisis that will keep Trump boxed in and perpetually on the defensive.

Independently of the impeachment sound and fury in Washington, the walls will continue to close in on domestic dissenters. The digital ghettoization of alternative views to "protect our democracy" from supposed outside meddling conflated with "hate online" will accelerate, with social media a particular target for censorship. The Deep State's intelligence and law enforcement organs will step up actions to penalize any resistance to Antifa violence, while perpetrators of such violence will rampage with impunity. Trump has done nothing to protect free speech online or in public places while his enemies continue to contract the space for both—but things can and will get much, much worse. Such vestigial protections of religion, free speech, right to bears arms, and others that we still possess—for now—aren't likely to survive much longer as the edifice of the old America continues to crumble under the malfeasance of the very Executive, Legislative, and Judicial officials who pretend to be its custodians.

It's important to understand that the division of power confronting America in two months will not be the usual circumstance of government divided on a partisan basis, "checks and balances," and all that sort of thing familiar from our history but the next phase of a second American civil war (or third, if we count Patriots vs. Tories). In this phase we are confronted with a revolutionary situation in which one part of the apparatus of government potentially forms what Alexander Shtromas called "the second pivot," an alternative source of official power. (Contrary to the Marxist myth, revolutions happen not when "The People" rise up but when some part of the ruling establishment defects to the revolt and becomes the new conferrer of legitimacy. There are obvious historical examples: Parliament in the English Civil War, the Third Estate's declaring itself the National Assembly of France, the Petrograd Soviet's coup against the Provisional Government, Boris Yeltsin's Russian government when Mikhail Gorbachev's Soviet government was under threat of the State Committee on the State of Emergency (itself an aspiring second pivot that failed), and the communist cabals in the various Warsaw Pact countries that ousted little Brezhnevs and installed little Gorbachevs.)

In seeking to overthrow the constitutionally elected president who was himself an insurgent against the cozy duopoly in Washington, it might seem the Democrats and their GOP "Never Trump" fellow travelers are actually counterrevolutionaries against the populist "revolution" two years ago. However true that might be in a mechanical sense, it fails to encompass the anti-American, revolutionary—indeed, Marxist—substance of the party that has just captured the House.

Increasingly and irreversibly American politics is no longer about a narrow range of governing styles or competing economic interests. It is tribal. Today's "tribes" are defined in terms of affinity for or hostility to the founding American *ethnos* characterized by European, overwhelming British origin (a/k/a, "white"); Christian, mainly Protestant; and English-speaking, as augmented by members of other groups who have totally or partially assimilated to that ethnos or who at least identify with it (think of Mr. Hamadura in *The Camp of the Saints*).

(Unfortunately we don't have a specific word for this core American ethnic identity to distinguish it from general references to the United States in a civic or geographic sense. (Russian, by contrast, makes a distinction between ethnic *russkiy* and civic/geographical *rossiiskiy*.) Maybe we could adapt Frank Lloyd Wright's "Usonian"? Or "Americaner," comparable to Afrikaner? Or "Anglo-American"? Or "Murican"?)

Since the Left, of which the Democratic Party is a wholly-owned subsidiary, gave up on its original focus on industrial workers as the revolutionary class, the old bourgeois/proletarian dichotomy is out. Tribes now line up according to categories in a plural Cultural Marxist schematic of oppressor and victim pairings, with the latter claiming unlimited redress from the former.

As the late Joe Sobran said, it takes a lot of clout to be a victim in America these days. The following is a helpful guide to who's who under the new dispensation:

Category	Oppressor	Victim
Sex	Male	Female
Race	White	"Person of Color" (POC)
Language	English	Non-English
Religion	Christian	Non-Christian
Sexual Orientation	"Cis"/"Straight"	LGBTQQIAPP+
Sovereign allegiance	US citizen	Non-US citizen
Legal status	Citizen/legal resident	Illegal/"Undocumented"
Criminality	Law-abiding	Offender
Origin	Native	(Im)migrant
Physical condition	Able	Disabled
Economic	Self-supporting	Dependent

In most of the above categories there are variations that can increase the intensity of oppressor or victim status. For example, certified victimhood in a recognized category confers extra points, like Black Lives Matter for race (it is racist to suggest that "all lives matter") or a defined religious group marginalized by "hate" (mainly anti-Jewish or anti-Muslim, but not something like anti-Buddhist, anti-Rastafarian, or even anti-atheist or anti-Satanist because no one bothers about them; anti-Christian victimhood is an oxymoron because "Christian" is inherently an oppressive category). In addition, meeting the criteria for more than one category confers enhanced victimhood under a principle called "intersectionality."

In the same way, there are aggravating factors in oppressor categories, such as being a policeman (an enforcer of the structure of oppression regardless of the officer's personal victim attributes, but worse if straight, white, Christian, etc.) or a member of a "hate" subculture (a Southerner who's not vocally self-loathing is a presumed Klan sympathizer; thus, a diabetic, unemployed, opioid-addicted Georgia cracker is an oppressor as the beneficiary of his "white privilege" and "toxic masculinity," notwithstanding his socio-economic and health status). Like being Southern, living while genetically Russian is also an aggravating factor.

Creatively shuffling these descriptors suggests an entertaining game like Mad Libs, or perhaps an endless series of jokes for which you could be fired if you told them at work:

Two people walk into a bar.

One is a Baptist, straight, male Virginia state trooper whose ancestors arrived at Jamestown.

The other is a one-legged, genderqueer, Somali Dervish WIC-recipient illegally in the US on an expired student visa.

So the bartender says . . . [insert your own punch line here].

While Patrick Buchanan is right that the level of domestic violence today is not up to what the US experienced in 1968, the depth of the existential divide is much greater. This is why it's perfectly acceptable for a homosexual, black MSM news anchor to describe "white men" collectively as a "terror threat," but when a straight white, female counterpart makes a clumsy but mild observation about ethnic role-playing it's a firing offense. (Note that while "female" is an assigned victim category, white females can be "gender traitors" if they are seen as putting their "racial privilege ahead of their second-class gender status"; to remain victims in good standing and an "allies" of higher-caste victim groups they need to learn to just "shut the f**k up" when POC sisters with superior oppressed status are holding forth.)

The victim side accuses its opponents of a litany of sins such as racism, sexism, homophobia, Islamophobia, etc., for which the solution is demographic and ideological replacement—even while denying that the replacement is going on or intended. This is no longer ordinary political competition but (in an inversion of von Clausewitz attributed to Michel Foucault) politics "as the continuation of war by other means." Things will continue to get ugly.

"O Canada! The True North Strong and Free— Not"

Jim Jatras | *Strategic Culture* | April 20, 2019

Canadian visitors to Washington sometimes wonder why their embassy stands at the foot of Capitol Hill.

The answer? To be close to where Canada's laws are made.

A main showcase of Ottawa's craven servility to Washington is Prime Minister Justin Trudeau's complicity in the US-led regime change operation being conducted against Venezuela. Not content with ruining his own country with multiculturalism, polysexualism, and the like, Li'l Justin has acted in lockstep with Big Brother to the south in slapping sanctions on Venezuelan officials and serving as a US agent of influence, especially with other countries in the western hemisphere:

> A Canadian Press report published at the end of January revealed that Canadian diplomats worked systematically over several months with their Latin American counterparts in Caracas to prepare the current regime-change operation, pressing [Venezuelan President Nicolás] Maduro's right-wing opponents to set aside their differences and mount a joint challenge to the government. "The turning point," said the Canadian Press [Global News], "came Jan. 4, when the Lima Group . . . rejected the legitimacy of Maduro's May 2018 election victory and his looming January 10 inauguration, while recognizing the 'legitimately elected' National Assembly." The report cited an unnamed Canadian official as saying the opposition "were really looking for international support of some kind, to be able to hold onto a reason as to why they should unite, and push somebody like Juan Guaidó."
>
> One day prior to Maduro's inauguration, [Canadian Foreign Minister Chrystia] Freeland spoke to Guaidó, the newly-elected National Assembly speaker, by telephone to urge him to challenge the elected Venezuelan president.

But that's not all. Canada is out front and center in the "Five Eyes" intelligence agencies' war on China's Huawei—with direct prompting from US legislators and intelligence. As explained by Col. Larry Wilkerson, former chief of staff to Gen. Colin Powell, it's not that Huawei violated any law when circumventing US sanctions but it is the US that is acting illegally by unilaterally imposing sanctions that were never agreed to internationally. But that's OK—when it comes to Washington's claims of jurisdiction over every human being on the planet, Justin and Chrystia are happy to oblige!

Also, let's not forget Chrystia's role in keeping the pot boiling in Ukraine. It would of course be cynical (and probably racist) to attribute anything relating to Ukraine to her own interesting family background. . . .

To be fair, the lickspittle attitude of Canadian officials towards their masters south of the 49th parallel is hardly unique in the world. Also to be fair, it's natural and would be generally beneficial for Canada to have a positive relationship with a powerful, kindred neighbor rather than a negative one. Think of Austria's ties to Germany, or the Trans-Tasman relationship of Australia and New Zealand, or the links that still exist between Russia and Ukraine despite efforts by the west to set them against each other (as, for example, Spain and Portugal were at loggerheads for several centuries, when the latter was a loyal ally of Spain's foe, Great Britain, to such an extent that Portugal was sometimes shown on maps and globes in the same pink as British possessions; a similar situation existed between Argentina and British ally Chile).

A close and mutually advantageous relationship is one thing, but Canada's de facto loss of independence is another. Not only does the US control Canada's diplomacy, military, and intelligence but also her financial system (with, among other levers, the notorious FATCA law, which places Canadian institutions under the supervision of the IRS, with Canada's revenue service acting, care of the Canadian taxpayer, as a cat's paw for not only the IRS but the NSA and other snooping agencies). As explained by one Canadian nationalist (yes, they do exist!), the redoubtable David Orchard, trade is also a critical issue:

> Canada . . . , after almost three decades of "free trade" with the U.S., has more than $1.2 trillion in federal and provincial debt, large deficits at every level, no national child or dental care, high university tuition, miserly old age pensions, years of massive budget cuts, and giveaway prices for its exports of oil, gas, timber and minerals.
>
> For 150 years, great Canadian leaders have warned that without an economic border with the United States, we would soon no longer have a political border.
>
> We once owned the world's largest farm machinery maker, Massey Harris, headquartered in Toronto; built the world's largest and most respected marketer of wheat and barley, the Canadian Wheat Board, based in Winnipeg; created a great transcontinental railway system, beginning in Montreal, which tied our country together; and saw Vancouver's shipyards produce the beautiful Fast Cat ferry.
>
> Instead of spending hundreds of billions on foreign-made machinery, electronics, automobiles, ships, fighter jets and passenger aircraft (even payroll systems for federal employees!), we can build our own, both for the domestic and export market.
>
> We once designed and built the world's most advanced jet interceptor, the Avro Arrow, so we know it can be done. With Canada's resources and ingenuity, it could create a prosperous, domestically controlled economy that would give Canadians multiple benefits, security and pride of ownership. All that is required is some of the will that drove our ancestors to create an alternate power in North America. As George-Étienne Cartier, the great Québécois Father of Confederation, put it, "Now everything depends on our patriotism." [Note: Orchard is the author of the must-read book *The Fight for Canada: Four Centuries of Resistance to American Expansionism*. To begin at the beginning, in the late 1680s, as part of English-French rivalry in North America, Massachusetts Puritans sought to root out the nest of popish deviltry known as Quebec. Following their disastrous 1690 defeat, they decided to fight Satan closer to home by hanging witches. The rest, as they say, is history . . .]

Scratch a Canadian patriot and you'll hear about the Avro Canada CF–105 Arrow. As a watershed moment in Canada's downward slide into subservience, the cancellation of what by all accounts was a magnificent aircraft—and a snapshot of what Canada's international competitiveness (including in advanced aerospace) could have looked like had it been able to develop inde-pendently—might have been the point of being sucked into the American vortex. As noted by one response to my suggestion that Ottawa's stance on Venezuela amounted to Canada's annexation by the US:

> Canadian here. . .unfortunately, the above is true (not literally of course, but in practice). It goes back even before the time of Diefen-baker, who canceled our Avro Arrow program on demand from the US—thus destroying our aerospace industry and causing brain drain to the US/Europe.

To this day, the decision of then-Prime Minister John Diefenbaker to kill the Arrow project (and "put 14,528 Avro employees, as well as nearly 15,000 other employees in the Avro supply chain of outside suppliers, out of work") on what came to be known as "Black Friday," February 20, 1959, remains controversial and shrouded in mystery. A mix of budgetary, political, technological, and personality factors has been cited, none of them conclusive. Pressure from the US side, including unwillingness of Washington to purchase a Canadian aircraft when the US could pressure them to buy American planes and mis-siles, no doubt played a key role: "Instead of the CF–105, the RCAF invested in a variety of Century Series fighters from the United States. These included the F-104 Starfighter (46 percent of which were lost in Canadian service), and (more controversial, given the cancellation of the Arrow) the CF–101 Voodoo. The Voodoo served as an interceptor, but at a level of performance generally below that expected of the Arrow."

While we may never know reliably why Diefenbaker cancelled the Arrow or how Canada or Canadian industry might have followed a different path, there's no question of the superior capabilities of the Arrow. As it happens, one of the few pilots who had a chance to test the Arrow in an impromptu friendly dogfight is now-retired USAF fighter pilot Col. George Jatras, later US Air Attaché in Moscow (also, this analyst's father). As he related in 2017:

> I've received a number of messages in the last couple days about this bird, including some that say it may be revived. I don't know how The Arrow would compare to today's aircraft, but I had a first-hand lesson on how it faired against the F–102.
>
> In 1959, I was stationed at Suffolk County AFB on Long Island with the 2nd Fighter Interceptor Squadron. We had an informal exchange program with a Canadian fighter squadron stationed near Montreal. From time to time, two or four aircraft from one of the squadrons would fly to the other's base on a weekend cross country.
>
> On one such exchange, I was #3 in a four-ship formation led by [former Tuskegee airman] Ernie Craigwell (I don't recall who the other pilots were). As we entered Canadian airspace, cruising at about 40,000 ft., we spotted a contrail well above our altitude (probably at 50,000ft.) and closing very fast. As the other aircraft appeared to be passing by, we could clearly see the delta shaped wing and knew it was the Avro Arrow that the Canadian pilots had told us about. Then, instead of just passing by, he rolled in on us! Ernie called for a break and we split into elements. When we talked about the encounter afterwards we all agreed that our first thought was, "This guy is in for a surprise; he doesn't know that he's taking on the F–102." Well, we were the ones in for a surprise. Even with two ele-ments covering each other, not one of us could get on his tail. His power and maneuverability were awesome. After he had played with

us for a few minutes, like a cat with four mice, he zoomed back up to
about 50K and went on his way. What an aircraft! What a shame that
it never went into production.

What is perhaps most curious about the Arrow's demise is that "everything
was ordered brutally destroyed; plans, tools, parts, and the completed planes
themselves were to be cut up, destroyed, scrapped and everything made to
disappear." Why? Well, security of course! Don't engage in conspiracy theories
. . .

The Canadian national anthem finishes with a pledge: "O Canada, we
stand on guard for thee." It should be noted that understandably resentful
Loyalists fleeing the US following the American Revolution were a major
contribution to the growth of Canada's English-speaking population. American troops—back when we were the plucky underdog fighting the mighty
British Empire—invaded Canada in 1775 and during the War of 1812 but were
defeated. Relations got testy during the American Civil War as well, and even
afterwards the US was wary of a proposed united "Kingdom of Canada," hence
the choice of the name "Dominion" in 1867. If today's Canadians think we-all
down here don't know whom they've mostly had in mind to "stand on guard"
against all this time, they'd better think again.

Maybe it's past time for Canadians to get serious again about their independence—eh?

Evil Party, Stupid Party

"It's the Cloture, Stupid! Bring Back the Filibuster to Restore 'Power of the Purse'"

Jim Jatras | *TheJIM!gram No. 1* | October 12, 2015

TheJIM!gram© *is a publication of **Jim Jatras**, the only announced prospect for the 2016 GOP Vice Presidential nod, addressing the daunting challenges facing our great country. Reposting and re-distribution with attribution is permitted and encouraged.*

The chaos surrounding selection of a replacement for House Speaker John Boehner is a symptom of the ongoing civil war tearing the GOP apart.

On the one side, we have Tea Partiers and other conservatives who want Republicans to play hardball with the Obama administration and use Congress's "power of the purse" to defund Obamacare, Planned Parenthood, amnesty via Executive Order, and other outrages. On the other, there is the establishment (of which Boehner is a symbol), who advise caution—in effect, capitulation—in the face of "reality": the MSM will blame any government shutdown on the GOP-ruled Congress, so let's avoid damage that could lessen chances of putting a Republican in the White House in January 2017.

Republicans would have a far better chance of winning the budget blame game if they would send funding bill after funding bill, minus the targeted items, to Barack Obama's desk and force him to veto them. Sure, the media would still blame the GOP, but at some point it would start to dawn on the American people that Congress is sending Obama money for 99.99 percent of the government's operations and *he* is the one forcing a shutdown over the 00.01 percent he imperiously demands.

That hasn't happened, though. In fact, during his tenure Obama has cast only *four* vetoes, far fewer than any recent president. (Counting pocket vetoes, George W. Bush cast 12, Clinton 37, George Bush the Elder 44 (in just one term), Ronald Reagan 78. FDR still holds the record with a whopping 635!) Failure of the Republican Congress to dump spending bills in Obama's lap continues to give him a free ride while degrading the GOP brand and spurring Republicans' intra-party bloodletting.

Observers of this failure often blame the "Democratic filibuster" in the Senate for blocking House-passed legislation. (A *Google News* search of "Democratic filibuster" yields over a thousand hits.) Some deride Majority Leader Mitch McConnell for failing to apply the "nuclear option" used in 2013 on Executive nominations by his Democratic predecessor, Harry Reid. It's a step Republicans are loath to take in anticipation of the day they are back in the minority.

But the fact is, *there is no Democratic filibuster in the Senate*. The filibuster in its classic form—a tag-team of minority-party Senators inveighing at length on the floor to delay a vote they are sure to lose—hasn't existed for decades. (The commendable filibuster-like speeches by GOP Senators Rand Paul and Ted Cruz in 2013 were essentially dramatizations.) Today, the proximate obstacle to getting legislation through the Senate with a simple majority of 51 votes is *cloture*, specifically Senate Rule XXII, which provides for limiting debate following a vote of three-fifths of Senators present.

Ironically intended as a means to streamline Senate business, in practice Rule XXII means not much can get done without a 60-vote super-majority.

The cloture rule enables a lazy man's filibuster. It allows a minority (today, the Democrats) of 41 Senators to "filibuster" a bill—including spending bills that ax funds for Obamacare, Planned Parenthood, etc.—from the comfort of their offices or fundraising receptions. They don't have to haul their carcasses down to the Senate floor and speechify as long as their feet and bladders can hold out before they eventually have to fold and a simple majority vote proceeds.

Let's stop making it easy for them. The Senate should revoke Rule XXII and go back to the archetypal filibuster that generally existed in the 19th and early 20th centuries. Set up the cots in rooms abutting the Senate chamber, empty the spittoons, send out the Sergeant-at-Arms to round up stragglers! It's *Mr. Smith Goes to Washington* on live TV! Especially with C-SPAN coverage, let's see how much time Democrats want to burn defending Obama's enormities in front of the nation—and then make 'em vote, up-or-down.

A return to the old-timey real-life filibuster would be magnificent political theater and valuable public education on the issues. It would also respect the World's Greatest Deliberative Body's tradition of affording the minority their right of unlimited debate while allowing for an eventual majoritarian vote to proceed. Best of all, it would provide a much better chance of throwing the dead cat of the spending issue on Barack Obama's desk, where it belongs.

MY PLEDGE: Presiding over the Senate is the Vice President's only specified Constitutional duty [Art. I, Sec. 3, Cl. 4], yet no incumbent in that office has assiduously applied himself to that task. If I am selected for the Republican Vice Presidential nomination and am privileged to assume that august post in January 2017, I pledge to be the most active President of the Senate in American history, in which my almost 18 years of experience working at the U.S. Senate will serve me in good stead. I further pledge to use my influence as presiding officer to ensure, without favor or bias, full and fair debate of public business followed by a simple majority vote.

"Let Them Be Red While We Take Back Reagan's Blue"

Jim Jatras | *TheJIM!gram No. 3* | October 23, 2015

There has been understandable chortling among Republicans that at the Democrats' first debate they finally came clean on the "S-word." Long considered almost taboo in American politics, the term socialism can now be considered mainstream in the party of (for now, anyway) Jefferson, Jackson, and FDR.

Snarkiness aside, it's about time. Whether some of us conservatives like it or not, approximately half of our fellow citizens are attracted to ideas tilting to portside. In that sense, the Democrats' "outing" themselves as socialists is simple truth-in-labeling and not an excuse-for-libeling.

After all, some of America's best foreign friends are avowed socialists, for example the British Labour Party's Tony Blair, a/k/a "Bush's Poodle." One could add the Socialist, Social Democratic, and Labour parties of our NATO allies in Germany, France, Spain, Italy, Netherlands, Denmark, Portugal, and so forth. Let's not forget Canada's answer to Bernie Sanders, Liberal Prime Minister-designate Justin Trudeau.

One thing common to all these parties is their signature color: some shade of red. Red is also the color of the European Parliament's Progressive Alliance of Socialists and Democrats and of the worldwide Socialist International (SI), of which almost all these parties are members. (Red was also the color of the SI's rival, the now-defunct Communist International.)

Historically, America's Republicans and Democrats had no official color. Campaign colors varied from year-to-year and candidate-to-candidate (remember Jimmy Carter's green?), though some combination of red-white-and-blue was standard. In 1980 and 1984, Ronald Reagan's deep blue became close to a Republican trademark.

Color-coding of states on TV networks' Election Night maps also varied by year, though generally Republicans were blue and Democrats red. "'It's beginning to look like a suburban swimming pool,' the television anchor David Brinkley noted on election night 1980, as hundreds of Republican-blue light bulbs illuminated NBC's studio map, signaling a landslide victory for Ronald Reagan over the Democratic incumbent Jimmy Carter. Other staffers, *Time* magazine wrote, called it 'Lake Reagan.'"

The GOP-blue vs. Democrat-red scheme not only accorded with the profiles of conservative and socialist parties internationally, it reflected the subliminal and emotional impact colors have on the human psyche:

> That is, the cooler color blue more closely represented the rational thinker and cold-hearted and the hotter red more closely represented the passionate and hot-blooded. This would translate into blue for Republicans and red for Democrats. Put another way, red was also the color most associated with socialism and the party of the Democrats was clearly the more socialistic of the two major parties. [Clark Bensen, "RED STATE BLUES: Did I Miss That Memo?", *POLIDATA*, 5/27/04]

The current counterintuitive scheme arose only during the prolonged Bush-Gore standoff in 2000 as (argued implausibly by numerous sources, most of them liberal-leaning) the supposed "need for consistency across media outlets became paramount." And since the Democrats just happened to be blue in some outlets that year (so the story goes), the current pattern was established—and stuck with the monikers "red states" and "blue states" attributed first to *NBC*'s Tim Russert.

Many conservatives, including this writer, suspect but can't prove that the real reason was the MSM's desire to scrub socialistic red from the Democrats and strip the GOP of Reagan's color. [NOTE: If you have any proof of how the red/blue switcheroo actually happened, tweet me!] Republicans have reinforced our reputation as the Stupid Party by meekly allowing the Evil Party to get away with it.

Enough is enough! In 2014 the Republican National Committee declared blue to be the party's color. The same year activists in the California Republican Party called for the party to return to its chromatic roots: "'Should the Republican Party choose its own principles and symbols, or should we let the national media do that for us?' asked Rep. Doug LaMalfa, R-Richvale, in an email to delegates. 'Well, the answer should be obvious.'"

Yes, it should be obvious but evidently it isn't—even to Republicans. Amazingly, contrary to its own 2014 declaration the RNC itself *displays red logos* on its official website, on its Twitter account, and on its Facebook page!

Now that the Democrats are openly a red socialist party, it's time Republicans got serious about reclaiming *our* color. RNC, please change the logo to blue and display it consistently on party sites. GOP candidates, please ensure that blue predominates on your campaign materials. Republican voters—refuse to accept paraphernalia in red. Ask for blue instead: a deep, rich Reagan blue, not the insipid shade favored by the Democrats.

And *everybody*, please stop enabling of the Democrats' appropriation of the GOP's cool, trustworthy, responsible, if slightly boring true blue by parroting the "red state" "blue state" dichotomy—and insist on the same when speaking with media. (One admirable example: *WorldNetDaily*'s Joseph Farah rejection of the "media-manipulated color narrative.")

As Congressman LaMalfa (*see his principled **blue** campaign site!*) observed, we can't let someone else choose the GOP's symbols. Symbols matter. They tell the world who we are—and who our opponents are.

It's time to set the visual record straight.

MY PLEDGE: Starting now, and especially if I am selected for the Republican Vice Presidential nomination and am privileged to assume that august post in January 2017, I pledge to maintain consistently the GOP's historic blue identification in all relevant contexts and insist on referring to the Democrats as the red socialist party they now acknowledge themselves to be.

"The Benghazi Hearing: What Neither Hillary nor the Republicans Want to Talk About"

Jim Jatras | *TheJIM!gram No. 4* | October 29, 2015

As I write this, Hillary Clinton's appearance before the House panel investigating the 2012 terrorist attacks that killed four Americans is still going on. I wasn't able to listen to all of it live, and will plow through the transcript in due course.

Two things already are notable: one concerning the impact of the hearing itself—plus another aspect marked only by the sound of crickets chirping.

First, as one would have expected, the hearing has generated more heat than light. As has been the case to date, Republican lawmakers seem mainly interested in granular details of the State Department's bureaucratic handling of the Benghazi post's requests for more security, what did then-Secretary Clinton know and when did she know it, whether help could have and should have been sent and who stopped any such attempt, whether prompt action might have changed the outcome, questionable claims regarding a movie riling up the Muslim rabble, Hillary's reliance on the expertise (or lack thereof) of Sidney Blumenthal, and all the other back-and-forth that's dominated the issue since the events in question.

Democrats predictably shilled for her, the poor innocent victim of a GOP Star Chamber.

In short, nothing new.

Hillary boosters will be reinforced in their conviction that the inquiry is a witch hunt to hurt political prospects of the still-presumptive (especially with "Uncle Joe" Biden's declining to run) Democratic presidential nominee. In supporting that conviction, the ill-phrased comments of abortive House Speaker candidate Kevin McCarthy were a godsend.

Conversely, Hillary-haters (who outnumber her fans, according to polling) will be buttressed in their conviction that she's a lying incompetent with the blood of four Americans on her hands. (There's nothing wrong with a witch hunt if you catch a real witch.)

Aside from digging Americans more firmly into the partisan points of view they already hold, little of importance is likely to result.

Which is unfortunate, because the hearing could have been a watershed in American foreign policy if someone on either side of the aisle had wished to pillory Hillary on an issue that screams out for *public* answers. But certainly no Democrat would do so for partisan reasons, and no Republican seemed to care. (One can only wish that Ron Paul or Dennis Kucinich, or both, had been on that panel!)

That issue is *what was really going on in Benghazi*. Unremarked upon from the lawmakers' bench was Clinton's admission that the post in Benghazi was *not* a consulate, as it is uniformly reported in the media. She did refer several times to the CIA compound.

No Sherlock Holmes is needed here. The facts have been in plain sight *for over three years*. As just one example, the following is a good summary from October *2012*, barely a month after the murders of Ambassador Chris Stevens and three other Americans:

> [T]here's growing evidence that U.S. agents—particularly murdered ambassador Chris Stevens—were at least aware of heavy weapons moving from Libya to jihadist Syrian rebels.
>
> In March 2011 Stevens became the official U.S. liaison to the al-Qaeda-linked Libyan opposition, working directly with Abdelhakim Belhadj of the Libyan Islamic Fighting Group—a group that has now disbanded, with some fighters reportedly participating in the attack that took Stevens' life.
>
> In November 2011 *The Telegraph* reported that Belhadj, acting as head of the Tripoli Military Council, "met with Free Syrian Army [FSA] leaders in Istanbul and on the border with Turkey" in an effort by the new Libyan government to provide money and weapons to the growing insurgency in Syria.
>
> Last month *The Times* of London reported that a Libyan ship "carrying the largest consignment of weapons for Syria . . . has docked in Turkey." The shipment reportedly weighed 400 tons and included SA–7 surface-to-air anti-aircraft missiles and rocket-propelled grenades.
>
> Those heavy weapons are most likely from Muammar Gaddafi's stock of about 20,000 portable heat-seeking missiles—the bulk of them SA–7s—that the Libyan leader obtained from the former Eastern bloc. Reuters reports that Syrian rebels have been using those heavy weapons to shoot down Syrian helicopters and fighter jets.
>
> The ship's captain was "a Libyan from Benghazi and the head of an organization called the Libyan National Council for Relief and Support," which was presumably established by the new government.
>
> That means that Ambassador Stevens had only one person—Belhadj—between him and the Benghazi man who brought heavy weapons to Syria.
>
> Furthermore, we know that jihadists are the best fighters in the Syrian opposition, but where did they come from?

Last week *The Telegraph* reported that an FSA commander called them "Libyans" when he explained that the FSA doesn't "want these extremist people here."

And if the new Libyan government was sending seasoned Islamic fighters and 400 tons of heavy weapons to Syria through a port in southern Turkey—a deal brokered by Stevens' primary Libyan contact during the Libyan revolution—then the governments of Turkey and the U.S. surely knew about it.

Furthermore there was a CIA post in Benghazi, located 1.2 miles from the U.S. consulate, used as "a base for, among other things, **collecting information on the proliferation of weaponry looted from Libyan government arsenals, including surface-to-air missiles**" . . . and that its security features "were more advanced than those at [the] rented villa where Stevens died."

And we know that the CIA has been funneling weapons to the rebels in southern Turkey. The question is whether the CIA has been involved in handing out the heavy weapons from Libya. ["How US Ambassador Chris Stevens May Have Been Linked To Jihadist Rebels In Syria," *Business Insider*, by Michael B Kelley, October 19, 2012]

In short, to an extent still undisclosed to the American people, U.S. agencies (and specifically the CIA) were at least aware of—and almost certainly complicit in—a pipeline to ship weapons from Gaddafi's captured stocks to jihad terrorists in Syria seeking to overthrow the government of President Bashar al-Assad. The key actors were jihadists, including elements of al-Qaeda, that NATO had assisted in overthrowing Gaddafi.

Shockingly, such savages don't always remain on the leash and sometimes bite the hand that fed them. In a word, the Benghazi debacle was *blowback* from a "regime change" operation in which our allies and clients were the very terrorists we've been told for 14 years by both parties are the greatest threat to Americans' lives and freedoms.

It's then clear why Republican Congressmen declined to grill Hill' on the details of our canoodling with terrorists: to do so would be to call into question the bipartisan penchant for supporting jihadists in multiple conflicts. Perpetuating a pattern established no later than the 1980s in Afghanistan (under Ronald Reagan, when at least Cold War vicissitudes could be considered a partial excuse), terrorists inspired by Saudi Wahhabist ideology were "our guys" in Bosnia and Kosovo (under Bill Clinton) and in Libya (under Barack Obama).

While the presidents in the post-Cold War cases were Democrats, most Republican criticism was not that supporting people of that ilk was a bad idea but that, respectively, Clinton or Obama wasn't moving decisively *enough* to empower the terrorists. Hence, the familiar refrain that Obama was "leading from behind" in Libya. If only we had moved faster, critics claimed, pro-American, democratic "moderates" might have gained power . . . Sure.

The same pattern continues today, in Syria. Just this week, in light of Russia's airstrikes against the Islamic State (ISIS, ISIL, Daesh), the al-Nusra Front (the *official* al-Qaeda affiliate), Ahrar al-Sham, and other jihadists, the Obama administration boldly responded—with arms drops to "trusted" terrorists. Having been up to their elbows in supporting jihad in Libya, Saudi Arabia, Turkey, and the Gulf States are now doubling down on their aid to terror groups in Syria, while publicly members of the U.S.-led "anti-ISIL coalition." Some allies.

And where is the GOP? Aside from a few noble exceptions, Republicans are faulting Obama for not providing *more* help to the jihadists, even joining with none other than *Hillary Clinton* in calling for a no-fly zone. How little we've learned.

Other angles could also have been explored at the hearing, such as Hillary's *faux* Caesaresque cackle regarding Gaddafi's murder: "We came, we saw, he died!" One yearns to ask her if extrajudicial murder of foreign heads of state is now official U.S. policy, or is that just her private peccadillo? Can she suggest a list of other countries' leaders who, without benefit of trial, should have a knife shoved up their rectum, then get shot in the head?

Inquiring minds want to know.

MY PLEDGE: If I am selected for the Republican Vice Presidential nomination and am privileged to assume that august post in January 2017, I pledge to use my considerable influence with GOP President Yet-To-Be-Named to ensure that America's unholy alliance with jihad terrorists is put to an immediate halt.

"Will the GOP Establishment Opt for President Hillary?"

Jim Jatras | *Chronicles* | January 7, 2016

The Iowa caucuses are under a month away, and the GOP Establishment is in white-knuckle panic that Donald Trump's candidacy has not imploded. His rather moderate proposal for a temporary time-out on Muslims' entry into the U.S. has gone the way of its predecessors in actually boosting his numbers. Allegations of sexist misuse of a Yiddish expression have fallen as flat as Trump's other supposedly fatal gaffes.

The Republican donor class claims pragmatic concerns. If Trump is the nominee, they moan, we're sure to hand victory to Hillary Clinton. We need to nominate someone who can win, and Trump can't.

But the Establishment's real worry is not that Trump might lose to Hillary. What terrifies them is that he might *win*. Make no mistake: most of those warning of Trump's adverse impact on Republican prospects would prefer a President Hillary Rodham Clinton and are prepared to help achieve that outcome.

That's because this is not just a replay of the tiff we've seen in the past couple of cycles between Tea Partiers and RINOs. Nor does it mostly concern the hot-button issues of abortion, LGBTQLSMFT "rights," or even guns.

Rather, this showdown relates to a basket of issues reflecting an irreconcilable divide over whether an "American nation" (a quaint expression most people under the age of 50 have never heard of) even exists—not just as a propositional "creed" but as a real, natural nation with its own history, traditions, and narrowly defined interests. In symbiosis with the entrenched Deep State the money boys will brook no heterodoxy on three interconnected imperatives:

> *Foreign interventionism*: Whether America leads from the front or behind (the parties can sham-fight over that), not a sparrow falleth to earth anywhere but that the Inside-the-DC-Beltway crowd must have the

prevailing opinion about it—generously lubricated with rhetoric about democracy, human rights, rule of law, and other invocations of "universal principles." We don't concede even the possibility that other powers might have genuine, national interest-based concerns in their own neighborhoods that we'd do well to weigh against our own. Policymakers of both parties are more preoccupied with Ukraine's border with Russia and with Syria's border with Turkey (or for that matter, with the South China Sea) than they are with our own country's border with Mexico. Continued cooperation with jihadists in the name of "fighting terrorism" is a must, as is kowtowing to a grab-bag of foreign regimes that leaven Washington with billions in lobbying dollars.

Immigration: The Democrats' multiculturalism and lust for an endless inflow of people who will vote for them against the GOP doesn't match that of Republican big shots' suicidal hankering for what amounts to open borders. Even Bernie Sanders understands that uncontrolled immigration depresses wages—and for much of the GOP's corporate sponsors and their stock values, that's a big plus. In some circles it's an article of faith that U.S. enterprise and innovation would barely exist if not for bright and eager H–1B indentured workers from the Far East and the Indian Subcontinent. Whether on amnesty for illegal aliens or the prospect of profiling against advocacy of Sharia and the Caliphate, GOP elites are hardly distinguishable from Barack "That's not who we are" Obama.

Trade: Our trade policy seems deliberately designed to penalize American producers and to favor foreign competitors penetrating our domestic market. Actually, maybe it was. Starting with postwar Germany and Japan, the deal has been: *we* give you privileged market access, *you* submit to Washington on all security matters. (Beijing has agreed to the one from Column A but not from Column B.) With the predictability of Charlie Brown kicking the football, each new trade deal is touted as "opening new markets for American goods" and "creating millions of good-paying jobs," and each with clockwork regularity leads to bigger deficits and lost jobs. Taking time out from their ritual denunciations of Obama's abuse of his Executive Authority, the "Stupid Party's" leadership steamrolled blank-check presidential trade authority through Congress.

Trump has stepped over the no-go line in each of these three areas. He has said Crimea is none of our concern (let the Europeans deal with it) and that Russia's bombing the Islamic State is just fine. His heresies on immigration need no comment. He denounces trade agreements with Mexico and China as the fruit of American negotiators' ineptitude; the author of *The Art of the Deal* insists that he could do a better job.

Whether Trump's policy proposals can garner a win in November 2016 if he is the Republican nominee, whether they can be implemented if he is elected, or whether they would prove successful is not at issue here. What is relevant now is that the GOP Establishment needs hear no more. Taken together, Trump's deviationism on these three points constitutes an existential threat to their control over the party and (in condominium with the Democrats) the country. In response, at least four options are available to them:

Go scorched earth to block Trump's nomination. Who knows how many highly paid political operatives have been wracking their brains to no avail trying to figure out what else they can throw at Teflon Don. The lack of an obvious alternative to Trump doesn't help. At this point, Ted Cruz seems the best-positioned, but the fifth candidates' debate only accentuated his unacceptable (to the Establishment) move toward the foreign policy realism of Trump and Rand Paul. Marco Rubio, who is "safe" on all three of the issues noted above, has been nailed on amnesty, an attraction for the donors but poison with the base. Establishment faves Jeb Bush, John Kasich, and Chris Christie are moribund. The clock is ticking, and Trump still stands.

Force Trump to go independent. If the Establishment can find a way to rig the nomination mechanics against Trump in either the primaries (difficult) or at the Convention (probably too late), he might still go independent—pledge or no pledge. The party at that point would happily welcome Hillary's victory in gleeful anticipation of blaming the Republican sacrificial lamb's defeat on Trump and his boorish followers. This would be the bigwigs' optimal path, one that hopefully would chastise the rabble for several cycles to come. Unfortunately, it depends on Trump's decision to pull the ripcord, which his detractors can't guarantee.

Let Trump be the Republican nominee, help Hillary win. If Trump does walk out of Cleveland the king of all he surveys, many GOP moneybags will refuse to support him. But it might not matter. First, Trump doesn't need their damn money. Second, more cash won't improve Hillary's attractiveness as an uninspiring candidate who long ago lost that "new car" smell. On the other hand, even a lousy Democratic nominee arguably starts with 242 electoral votes of the 270 needed, largely a function of immigration-fed demographic changes in swing states. A little help from ineligible Democratic voters (the courts effectively bar requiring actual proof of citizenship, not just the registrant's certification) might do the trick.

Let Trump be the nominee, see if he wins. Talk about heresy. Anti-Trumpians could swallow their bile and back him with varying degrees of enthusiasm, much like conservatives grudgingly endorsed "presidents" Dole, McCain, and Romney. The obvious risk is that Trump might win. If that happens, it could be hoped that his presidency would prove such a disaster as to vindicate the wisdom of profligate global meddling, dispel the mirage that we can control foreigners' access to our country and deport those here illegally, and demonstrate the impracticality of American producers' recapturing our own domestic market. Then maybe those tricked by Trump's flim-flammery would throw themselves abjectly at the feet of those who *tol' ya so*. Yeah, that'll happen.

"Swan Song from Our Second Worst President"

Jim Jatras | *Chronicles* | January 14, 2016

President Obama's final State of the Union address was long on themes and short on specifics. It clearly was an attempt to secure a legacy of accomplishment. That attempt is at best questionable.

It is important to divide Obama's record between what he failed to do and what he has succeeded in doing—most of it bad. Either way, it is not a record to be proud of.

Start with his failures. In foreign affairs, he has barely changed course from the disastrous policies of George W. Bush. "Regime change" remains the order of the day: Bush had his in Iraq; Obama had Libya and has tried, but so far failed, in Syria. The "Arab Spring" has become the "Jihadist Winter."

Obama pretends the Islamic State is just a rag-tag band with some pickup trucks—at least he refrained from again calling them the "J.V." About the only specific difference is that Bush "renditioned" suspected terrorists and water-boarded them, Obama just kills them with drones. The Ukraine crisis, in which Obama's administration has played a destabilizing role, festers.

This continuity reflects the fact that Obama doesn't much care about foreign policy. He reads what Samantha Power and Susan Rice (and before that, Hillary Clinton) put on his teleprompter. His real mission is to fundamentally transform America domestically. On that, he has largely succeeded—to the detriment of our country.

His signature "accomplishment" is Obamacare. While perhaps providing some expansion of healthcare availability, it has made health services more expensive for most Americans. It also has expanded the federal purview over previously private activity.

Obama wants to decrease the prevalence of guns in American life. On that score, his leaving office can only help, because every time he opens his mouth, millions of Americans run out to buy weapons. An armed citizenry is fundamental to Americans' traditional notion of ourselves as a free people. Some people disagree, they would prefer to be more like England or other countries where private citizens don't have guns, only the police and army do. That's a legitimate opinion to hold, but it's not the American tradition. Tens of millions of us distrust Obama when he proposes "moderate, common-sense reforms"—none of which will reduce violence anyway—because we suspect what he really wants is move the ball from where we are now to a disarmed public.

He promised the Trans-Pacific Partnership (TPP) will support "more good jobs." Translation: get ready for massive job losses after the GOP helps pass TPP.

Obama's contempt for the traditional American identity is palpable. His guests at the speech featured an illegal alien "Dreamer" from Mexico and a plaintiff in the case that forced same-sex "marriage" on all 50 states. He slandered as people who vandalize mosques and bully kids Americans who worry that Syrian "refugees" (most of whom are neither Syrians nor refugees but Muslim migrants from many countries) might include terrorists like the Tsarnaev brothers. He won't be happy until we duplicate in America what we saw on New Year's Eve in Cologne care of "Mutti Merkel." Characteristically, he calls for mutual respect and accord among Americans while caricaturing and demonizing those who disagree with him.

Obama has made great strides in transforming a center-right, basically conservative country with a recognizable national culture and historic traditions into a mini-United Nations: a multicultural, multiethnic, multi-religious microcosm of the world with no defining core and devoid of a moral center-of-gravity except a gender-bending attitude of "if it feels good, do it."

All in all, even with a year left to go Obama should go down in history as our second worse president ever. I make that caveat only because first prize should go to his predecessor. On top of his own considerable errors, George W. Bush made the GOP brand so toxic, we ended up with Obama. So Bush needs to take the blame not only for his own poor performance but for Obama's too. Of course it might get even worse, if Hillary Clinton is our next president. Or for that matter, most of the Republican contenders.

"I Stand with America. I Stand with Trump. An Endorsement from 'the Man You've Never Heard Of'"

Jim Jatras | *TheJIM!gram No. 7* | March 6, 2016

In part because no one else in American history had ever done so, in September of last year I announced my interest in and availability for my party's vice presidential nomination. I so informed each GOP presidential candidate by letter and Twitter. ABC News promptly dubbed me "the Man You've Never Heard Of Who Desperately Wants to Be Vice President." (I'd have preferred "diligently" to "desperately," but why quibble.)

I was content to let my offer lie on the table pending the Republican Convention and the eventual presidential nominee's selection of a running mate, who I assumed almost certainly would be someone other than my humble but eminently qualified self. Despite repeated media inquiries, I saw no need to state a preference for any of the contenders for the top office.

Things have changed. As of this moment, I formally announce my endorsement of Donald John Trump for President of the United States.

What has prompted this less than earth-shattering decision? Essentially, two factors:

- First, with increasing urgency good friends have been insisting to me that Donald Trump is a disaster for the country and for the Republican Party. He's a liberal Democrat only pretending to be a conservative. He's an avatar of nativism, racism, and hatred. He's a "plant" by the Clintons to throw the election to Hillary. He's "unpresidential," he's crude, and he's a misogynist. He's an egomaniacal con man and a lousy businessman who hates old ladies.

- Second, and more importantly, my decision to endorse Mr. Trump is prompted by the unleashing of what appears to be the most formidable defamation campaign in American history. Fueled to the tune of tens of millions of dollars and keynoted by failed presidential candidate Mitt Romney (who reportedly was scared away from the 2016 race by the fearsome ¡Jeb! Bush), the #NeverTrump jihad recites the full litany of charges. But central is the claim that if Trump is the nominee, he'll not only lose in a landslide to Hillary Clinton but drag the GOP "brand" down to catastrophic defeat, costing the Grand Old Party the Senate, the House, governorships, state legislatures, and local offices down to sheriff and dogcatcher.

I don't imagine the voice of one near-unknown can counter such a massive effort. At the same time, maintaining neutrality could be construed as concurrence or even complicity.

It's time to choose a side. I stand with America. I stand with Trump.

I will not here pick through the hail of darts furiously being flung Trumpwards, which on their merits I find mostly though not entirely unconvincing. Suffice it to say that with regard to the most potent accusation—that Trump's nomination means electoral disaster for Republicans—the Trumpophobes do not really talk or behave as though they believe their own propaganda. As I wrote two months ago, in an analysis even more relevant now than it was then:

> . . . the Establishment's real worry is not that Trump might lose to
> Hillary. What terrifies them is that he might *win*. Make no mistake:
> most of those warning of Trump's adverse impact on Republican
> prospects would prefer a President Hillary Rodham Clinton and are
> prepared to help achieve that outcome.

Why? Primarily, it's not Trump's personal qualities, it's his positions on three
related issues where both the GOP and the Democratic establishments have
stood foursquare against the interests of the American people, as I identified
in January: **immigration, trade, and war**:

> Trump has stepped over the no-go line in each of these three areas.
> He has said Crimea is none of our concern (let the Europeans deal
> with it) and that Russia's bombing the Islamic State is just fine. His
> heresies on immigration need no comment. He denounces trade
> agreements with Mexico and China as the fruit of American nego-
> tiators' ineptitude; the author of *The Art of the Deal* insists that he
> could do a better job.

But because a broad swath of the American people clearly is enthusiastically
for Trump, his opponents sense they can't beat him on issues. They have to
rely on personal smears and electoral trickery.

Let's remember that early in the nominating process, when GOP insiders
considered Trump a kind of joke, the party insisted he sign the no-independ-
ent-run pledge for fear he'd run as spoiler after he inevitably fizzled. Now that
he's not fizzling and looks increasingly likely to take the nomination (notwithstanding the usual blather about a brokered Convention), it's the paladins of
Beltway Conservatism threatening to go "Dixicrat" with some rump-GOP,
faux conservative alternative like Romney (or even more absurdly, #Draft
Condi Rice) if Trump takes the official nomination in Cleveland. They themselves, Trump's *critics,* are the ones contemplating splitting the Republican
party on purpose, and serving the election up on a platter to Hillary. And
despite the increasing likelihood that Trump will garner the Republican
nomination, they continue to savage him, doing Hillary's work for her.

Does that sound like the strategy of people afraid that Trump will *lose*?

No, they are rightly afraid that Trump's possible victory as a populist-
nationalist Tribune of the Plebs, with his deviationism on immigration, trade,
and war, would constitute an existential threat to their control over the party
and (in condominium with the Democrats) the country, as well as debunking
their phony "conservatism" that conserves nothing. For many of the Brahmins
of the Stupid Party, President Hillary Clinton would be a hundred times more
palatable.

The decline of America's moral and constitutional integrity is less a
matter of narrowly-defined "conservatism" than a function of the fact that we
are losing even our semblance of representative self-government by a free
people who, whatever our diverse ethnic, racial, or religious origins, share the
core values and loyalties of the historic American nation. As Laura Ingraham
recently observed:

> Yes, there will be times when the populists disappoint pure conser-
> vatives. But populists and pure conservatives each have the same
> basic goal—a great country where the average person has a chance at
> a better life. By contrast, the Establishment already has what it wants
> and will do everything it can to maintain the status quo. Ted Cruz
> and his supporters have to make their own decision, but in the long
> run they need a major shakeup in the GOP Establishment to have a

chance of seeing their ideas become law. Rubio (and his donors) have no intention of making such a change. In fact, they will support policies—open borders, new trade deals, more government debt—that will make any such change much harder to achieve.

For social conservatives in particular, it's time to recognize the decades-long come-on by the GOP and "Conservatism, Inc." for the scam it is: *"Vote for us, we'll get a majority in Congress, we'll take the White House, we'll appoint good 'strict constructionist' Justices* [like Anthony Kennedy, David Souter, Sandra Day O'Connor . . . well, you get the picture] *and return decency to America."* Uh-huh. That's been our Plan A, and we see how well it's worked out. It won't get better as our country is abolished out from under us. As one Roman Catholic writer observes ("Yes, Catholics Can Vote For Trump"):

> No other candidate is serious about the Mexican-Muslim invasion. Trump is the only candidate promising to do something about it. Either Trump gets elected, or the bishops will destroy the pro-life movement with all their new pro-abortion voters.

The alternative to a populist revolution—and with it at least the hope of a conservative social restoration—is continuing down the path set by the duopoly of the Democrats (no comment needed) and the GOP open borders donor class (ditto). For a look into a non-Trump future, consider what Illinois Congressman Luis Gutiérrez calls a "new American political coalition," a self-selected ruling class that posits its interests and values against those of the historic Christian (mainly Protestant), English-speaking American nation, which will be consigned to the status of a permanent disenfranchised, vilified minority:

> . . . a million Latinos turn 18 every year in the United States of America. And . . . they're all American citizens of the United States. And here's what happens: they become the basis of the new American political coalition. That is young people, that is Latinos, that is immigrants, it's African Americans, it's Asians, it's gay people, it's people that care about the economy [translation: "Gimme free stuff"], and it's people that care about the environment [translation: carbon cultists] . . . . look: you're never going to take the White House with this kind of politics ever again because there's a new American politics.

In a word, it's Balkanization, a coalition of vested group entitlements, spearheaded by recent immigrants and their "anchor baby" descendants who reject assimilation to a common American identity and in fact define themselves in opposition to it. It's the political equivalent of American workers' training their foreign replacements for their own jobs. Gutiérrez is telling us: a new, substitute America is here—*another people*—ready to take power. As Jacob Heilbrunn cited Bertolt Brecht's poetic mockery (in the context of the 1953 East Berlin uprising):

> The Secretary of the Writers Union
> Had leaflets distributed in the Stalinallee
> Stating that the people
> Had forfeited the confidence of the government
> And could win it back only
> By redoubled efforts. Would it not be easier
> In that case for the government
> To dissolve the people
> And elect another?

Thus, what is really at stake is whether our country will irrevocably cease to be a *res publica*—the property of a self-aware, sovereign citizenry. If the historic America is not to be "dissolved" and transformed into Gutiérrez-land, the power of the bipartisan "oligarchy" (as Senator Jeff Sessions, a Trump supporter, calls it) or of the "Deep State" (as author Mike Lofgren, not a Trump supporter, calls it) must be broken. On the Democratic side, Sanders is trying to do that (in his own flawed way, but weighed down by the required idols of the Left, from #BlackLivesMatter to "sanctuary cities" to a blank check for abortion) but is unlikely to succeed. Hillary, the corrupt *Picture of Dorian Gray* face of the Democratic faction of the oligarchy, maintains a commanding lead. Trump's prospects in the GOP are better, perhaps much better.

Can we trust Trump? Will he build his wall and secure our borders? Renovate our deteriorating infrastructure? Restore our manufacturing base? Audit the Federal Reserve and defenestrate the banksters? Restore the GOP's long-lost reputation (now hardly remembered by anyone) as the "Peace Party" that got us out of wars the Democrats started? Sign a bill to defund Planned Parenthood, as long as they continue to perform abortions (which they will)? Exclude actual or potential Islamic terrorists? Dump our freeloading so-called "allies"? Cease the PC trashing of every tradition in which Americans once took pride? Reunite a nation sundered by Barack Obama and the GOP mandarins, with their *divide et impera* Punch and Judy show of class and racial discord?

Can Trump really "Make America Great Again"? Or at least slow our decline and give our country another chance?

I don't know. But I do know that none of the more mannerly politicians served up by the oligarchy will.

"Trust not in princes . . ." (Ps. 146:3) Neither Trump nor any other politician should be accepted on blind faith. Who really can say if Trump can win or if he does how he would govern. Who can say what's really in his mind and heart or if, in God's eyes, he's a good man or a bad one. But given the dire warning from the likes of Romney, I like the odds with Trump better than with any of the available alternatives. When the character of his enemies is considered—particularly Warfare State neoconservatives (some of whom at least have the honesty to defect openly to Hillary)—my willingness to gamble on him only increases.

Finally, a warning. As Stalin observed: "Death solves all problems. No man, no problem." Trump, who for many powerful people is quite a problem indeed, has been recklessly compared to Jean-Marie Le Pen, Silvio Berlusconi, Vladimir Putin—even to Hitler and Mussolini. In an American context, to Andrew Jackson, Huey Long, and George Wallace. Let's note that each of those three Americans was the target of assassination. Jackson survived by a failure of his attacker's pistols, hailed by some as miraculous. "The Kingfish" was killed. Wallace was crippled for life.

If you think there is any length to which Trump's enemies will not go, think again.

MY PLEDGE: Whether or not I am selected for the Republican Vice Presidential nomination and am privileged to assume that august post in January 2017, I will remain committed to the core principles I announced in September 2015, which I hope will be furthered under a Trump presidency: "I am pro-life, pro-gun, pro-traditional marriage, pro-immigration control, anti-war, pro-privacy, pro-tax reform, anti-phony 'free trade' deals. We need to feel like Americans again!"

"The Two Faces of #NeverTrump: Those Who Know and Those Who Don't"

Jim Jatras | *Chronicles* | May 4, 2016

With his resounding victory in Indiana, the forces denoted by the Twitter hashtag #NeverTrump should fold up shop and accept the inevitable.

Some of them will. Senator Ted Cruz had the sense to realize that his play to deny Donald J. Trump a first-ballot victory in Cleveland would find even less favorable ground in New Jersey and California. We'll see how many of the foot soldiers follow suit.

But the money side of #NeverTrump vows to fight on, even in the wake of Indiana: "The biggest anti-Trump super-PAC, Our Principles PAC, said it will continue pushing to force a contested convention as long as Trump remains short of the 1,237 delegates needed to win the nomination outright." Our Principles PAC reportedly has a $2 billion war chest provided by Wall Street heavyweights with one mission: stop Trump.

The question is, why?

For a tiny but influential (and very wealthy) subgroup lurking under the #NeverTrump rubric, the answer is simple: they want to ensure that Hillary Rodham Clinton and her sex predator husband move back into the White House in January. Beltway Brahmin George Will and neoconservative ideologue Max Boot (settling for Hillary because Stalin is unavailable) have said as much.

There's no mystery here. The Brahmins, neocons, and plutocrats are the #NeverTrump Who Know Why They Do What They Do.

For this faction, Trump is perceived as a threat to the bipartisan oligarchy whose wealth, power, and privileges depend on uncontrolled borders, globalized trade, and endless wars. The *nomenklatura* of the U.S. Deep State still hopes to throw Cleveland into chaos by denying Trump a first-ballot win, splitting the GOP, and offering up some luckless victim (until Indiana maybe Ted Cruz) as the Designated Loser. Or, failing that, if Trump does prevail, to have poisoned enough minds against him to cripple him in November.

With regard to this faction, there is little to be said. They are irredeemable enemies of the historic American nation. They cannot be appealed to, they can only be defeated and their snouts yanked out of the trough they've been slopping at for decades.

The mystery has been the motivations (in the plural, since they seem to have myriad reasons) of the other, more numerous faction of #NeverTrump, who now face a hard choice. These are overwhelmingly dedicated Republicans, often religious, Middle Class social conservatives, who don't like Trump because (choose one or more of the following): he's a liberal Democrat in sheep's clothing, not a real, Constitutionalist, small-government, "Movement" conservative; he's going to lose big time to Hillary (look at the polls!); he's said lots of things to offend lots of people, and we can't have someone that rude in the Oval Office. These are the ones who have been using every procedural tactic in the book to secure as many delegates as possible for Ted Cruz on a second ballot at a contested Convention, for example in the adroit heist of 10 of 13 at-large delegates for Cruz in Virginia, a state Trump won in the primary.

What has this other, much larger group been hoping to accomplish? This is where they have proved to be the #NeverTrump Who Don't Know Why They Do What They Do.

What these people have *intended* to achieve is fulfillment of a desperate wish. They have wished that someone else more to their liking could secure the GOP nod and then whup Hillary in the fall.

If wishes were horses, beggars would ride. The fact is, there was no way their wish was going to come true. If, in the unlikely event Trump is denied 1,237 delegates by July, there is no way any alternative can be installed without incurring the just accusation by pro-Trumpers that they wuz robbed. Even if Trump were copasetic with that outcome (not likely . . .), his followers would erupt. The scenario of the moneyed #NeverTrump Who Know folks would become inevitable: Hello President Hillary.

The irony is, the design of Those Who Know can only succeed with the unwitting assistance of Those Who Don't. Can the latter be reasoned with? The more decent if not necessarily more clever members of #NeverTrump Who Don't Know need to wake up to the fact that they are following an agenda set by those like Our Principles PAC who consciously intend exactly the harm conservatives most seek to avoid and are using them to that end.

They now need to start using their brains, not just their hearts.

"If Trump Loses, a 'Transformed' GOP Might Not Get a Second Chance"

Jim Jatras | *Chronicles* | July 25, 2016

Donald Trump has made it clear from the beginning that he's in it to win it. He has said that if he ends up losing the presidential race it will all have been for nothing: "If I don't go all the way, and if I don't win, I will consider it to be a total and complete waste of time, energy, and money."

For what it is worth, I think he's right.

Men wiser than I have suggested that even if Trump loses, the Republican Party and the nation will have been transformed:

> Patrick J. Buchanan: "Trump's nomination represents . . . a repudiation of much of post-Cold War party dogma. . . . Even should Trump lose, there is likely no going back. Does anyone think that if Trump loses, we are going back to Davos-Dubai ideology, and Barack Obama's Trans-Pacific Partnership is our future? Even Hillary Clinton has gotten the message and dumped TPP. Economic nationalism is the future."

> Scott McConnell: "Trump's weaknesses as a candidate, well known to everyone, may keep him from winning. But his run will change the nature of the GOP, and it is very hard to see how the old GOP elites and neoconservative establishment will put the lid on the aspirations Trump has unleashed, in this election cycle or those to come."

> Leon Hadar: "If Trump loses, a Republican political entrepreneur searching for ways to revive the GOP should try to refashion Trumpism—not as a white ethno-nationalist ideology, but as a new and inclusive political movement along the lines of a New Nationalism,

an American Gaullism, or a modified version of globalism that places the national interest at its center."

If the worst happens on November 8, I really do hope they are right. But I fear they are not.

This election is for all the marbles. This moment for America, not to mention the GOP, may not come again anytime soon, if ever.

Sure, if Trump loses—I don't think he will, but "if"—the grandees of the Republican Party will fault him personally. Even more will they blame Trump's defeat on his deviations from neoconservative-globalist orthodoxies about immigration, trade, and war. A vengeful donor class will seek to banish to perpetual outer darkness Trump's heresies from the respectable Republican catechism by instituting structural "reforms" to make sure this never, ever happens again. The oligarchy that got sucker-punched by Trump will not twice make the mistake they made this cycle of letting a blaspheming infidel slip into the sacred precincts. As *National Review* #NeverTrump-er Kevin Williamson has suggested, "the Democratic party and its undemocratic 'superdelegate' system sure is looking smart right about now."

In a similar vein, witness a recent "small gathering of influential conservative and libertarian leaders who came together for three days to imagine a 'more evolved' version of right-wing politics," after the hoped-for Trump loss to Hillary Clinton (as described by participant Steve McIntosh of the Institute for Cultural Evolution):

> The group included distinguished author Charles Murray, Republican gay rights activist Margaret Hoover, and anti-tax icon Grover Norquist. Also present were prominent libertarians, right-leaning political scientists, and numerous Republican media personalities. And while we did not reach a clear consensus on the 'future of the right,' we did find remarkable agreement around the potential for a revitalized center-right coalition that could offer a viable alternative to unprincipled right-wing populism.

> By the end of the three-day meeting, many were optimistic that a fresh kind of conservative and libertarian politics will rise from the ashes of Trump's impending loss. The group was excited by the possibility of a new American right that could be 'radically innovative and radically inclusive.' We agreed that a key strength of the right is found in its championing of entrepreneurial innovation and the values of personal and economic liberty. And this same spirit of creative innovation can be used to craft positive proposals for market-based healthcare reform and a meritocratic immigration policy.

> By freeing itself from the backward-looking concerns of nativists, Tea Partiers, and some religious conservatives, this emerging center-right coalition could embrace political issues currently owned by the left—issues such as income inequality, environmentally friendly energy policy, immigration reform, and even a conservative plan for affordable health care. By advancing solutions to these issues that are primarily market-based, and thus more acceptable to conservative and libertarian sensibilities, this center-right political alliance could make progress in areas that are currently stymied by hyper-partisan polarization.

> Moreover, by working to restate the platform of the American right to make it more socially liberal, even while it remains fiscally conservative, this emerging center-right coalition could also attract a poli-

tically significant number of millennial voters who would help make
up for the loss of social conservatives in the Republican base.

In short, the "New Republican Party" advocated by these lofty intellects would
not only jettison the GOP's most reliable, socially conservative base, it would
double down on rejecting precisely the populist economic agenda for which
Trump is the standard-bearer.

To be sure, if Trump loses, there will be an enraged backlash against
#NeverTrump backstabbers who saddled America with President Hillary.
While some of this would be from "party regulars" who just hate losing
(though you'd think they would be used to it by now), the bulk would be
ordinary citizens, many of them not self-defined Republicans.

Still, populists/nationalists would probably lose a contest for control of
the party. Arrayed against them, the "New Republicans" would likely prevail
for three reasons:

1. They would have lots and lots of money at their disposal. Duh.
2. They would not be blindsided as they were in this election. Trump only
    got this far because an establishment thoroughly alienated from its
    voter base never saw it coming. (Their error was comparable to David
    Cameron's miscalculation that he could defang the Euroskeptics once
    and for all by allowing them a referendum and then beating them.) But
    their eyes sure are open now.
3. They would not be facing Trump, who was able to prevail because of his
    celebrity status and independent wealth, without either of which he
    would not now be the nominee. Plausible populist champions with both
    of those qualities do not grow on trees.

This is not to discount the rising tide of populism and nationalism that Trump
has set loose, which in similar form is sweeping Europe. It is only to suggest
that a post-Trump Republican Party is unlikely to be the vehicle for that
movement. And because of the lock the two established parties have on the
U.S. electoral system, a third party based on Trump-style populism can't
successfully compete in the manner the Eurocrat establishment is being
challenged from both the right and the left by groups like UKIP (Britain), the
National Front (France), PEGIDA, Alternative für Deutschland (Germany),
Movimento Cinque Stelle (Italy), Partij voor de Vrijheid (Netherlands),
SYRIZA (Greece), Podemos (Spain), and others.

Thus, if the donors successfully reestablish their hold on the GOP and
move it in the direction of a "revitalized center-right coalition" purged of hated
"unprincipled right-wing populism," the latter will essentially become a
sullen, politically disenfranchised, demographically shrinking rump, at least
at the national level.

Which of course would be just fine with the aspirant "New Republican
Party" freed from those loathsome nativists, Tea Partiers, and religious conservatives. A restored GOP establishment, reveling in Trump's defeat, would
be more than happy to play second fiddle to a permanently dominant Democratic Party, with which they share both a consensus on policy fundamentals
and donor interests.

Take one example: the threat of Islamic terrorism is central to Trump's
immigration views and his "Make American Safe Again" plank. As we await
the next, inevitable attack inside our borders, we increasingly are supposed to
accept that even here in our own home the "new normal" is that we are rabbits
hunted by human wolves (gratuitously imported ones at that), and that we can
only be relatively safe by cowering behind elaborate security measures. Under

the GOP-Democrat duopoly the U.S. government—indeed all western governments and international organizations, like the useless and dangerous NATO —have failed in their most basic duty, that of protecting the lives and safety of their citizens.

No less than Obama (and of course anyone named "Clinton") a restored Republican establishment would be unable and unwilling to fix the deficiencies we see. They are the wrong human material. They are incapable of instituting the measures needed to detect and uproot the wolves from the larger societies in which they are lurking, or even to exclude them from the U.S. in the first place. Besides launching new misadventures abroad, they would rather screw down surveillance-state security measures—militarization of police, wholesale data collection, gutting the Second Amendment (approved by Hillary-appointed justices)—on everyone regardless of national origin, religion, age, or sex than profile actual or potential jihadists, bar or deport sharia and caliphate activists, stop the migrant influx, and of course cease supporting jihadists in Syria and elsewhere who share the same Wahhabist ideology as those committing attacks at home. Such "leaders" are more concerned about possibly being called "racists" than about endangering their own citizens. In the end they have more in common morally with the terrorists than with the interests and values of ordinary Americans, whom they despise as rubes and bigots.

If Trump loses, I am not saying definitively that the "Middle American Radicals" unleashed by Trump will be disempowered, just that that is the likelier outcome.

Conversely, if Trump wins, we won't have to find out. That would be a far more attractive prospect.

"A Reader Has a Historical Note on Sam Francis's 'Evil Party' and Stupid Party'"

James Jatras | VDARE.com | July 27, 2016

From: James Jatras

If in due course Donald J. Trump ends up saving (only in the temporal sense) what remains of the historic American nation from the devil named Hillary Rodham Clinton, with all her works and all her pomp, the chroniclers will record that his John the Baptist was Patrick J. Buchanan, who on the critical issues of immigration, trade, and war was Trump before there was Trumpism.

In turn, the role of Prophet Elijah would justly belong to the late, lamented Samuel T. Francis. Sam's was a voice crying in the wilderness, prophesying what then seemed the improbable, if not impossible, revolt of the "Middle American Radicals"—an event that, lo, in the fullness of years may now be upon us, smiting the Republican and Democratic establishments hip and thigh and putting them to ignominious flight.

Among Sam's lesser though still noteworthy achievements was his popularization of the characterizations of the Republicans as the "Stupid Party" and the Democrats as the "Evil Party":

> "IN AMERICA, WE have a two-party system," a Republican congressional staffer is supposed to have told a visiting group of

Russian legislators some years ago. "There is the stupid party. And
there is the evil party. I am proud to be a member of the stupid party."
He added: "Periodically, the two parties get together and do
something that is both stupid and evil. This is called—"bipartisanship." [*Immigration policy stupid, evil and hurting Americans* by Peter Brimelow, *Contra Costa Times,* December 4, 1999]

For the record, I am the staffer to whom Sam referred, having been for many
years a foreign policy adviser to the Senate GOP leadership. Unfortunately, I
don't remember which group of Russians I was talking with at the time, but it
was during the chaotic Yeltsin years. I may have also said something to the
effect (as quoted) of being "proud to be a member of the stupid party," but I
am not sure—it was a while back.

As I also recollect, I gave the Russians (and afterward related to Sam) this
explanation of the labels:

> "The evil party wants to bankrupt the country and destroy its morals.
> The stupid party is, in principle, opposed to those things but doesn't
> have a clue what to do about it. And when something is really
> evil *and* stupid, we call that 'bipartisan.'"

I must admit that at the time (early 1990s) I underestimated the potential of
either party all by itself to be evil and stupid simultaneously, without the
participation of its nominal rival. Live and learn, I guess. In many subsequent
conversations with foreigners confused about our weird party system, I have
found that this explanation clarifies things for them and often elicits a gleam
of sad recognition: "Ah, yes. Unfortunately, we have something similar . . ."

"Running the Big Khan in Philly"

Jim Jatras | *Chronicles* | August 2, 2016

If patriotism is the last refuge of scoundrels, Scoundrel Time to the nth degree
was on full display in Philadelphia last week. The closing days of the Democratic Convention featured an orgy of frenzied flag-waving (never mind the
minimal presence of Old Glory at the opening) and orchestrated chants of
"USA! USA! USA!" (doing double duty to drown out dissent from Sanderistas).

On NPR, Audie Cornish's guests David Brooks of the *New York Times* and
E.J. Dionne of *Pravda on the Potomac* (a/k/a the *Washington Post*) chortled
with glee that Hillary had successfully stolen the jingoism card from Trump.
In Brooks' absurdly sweeping claim:

> The Trump campaign, the one thing they've really, completely lost is
> their core argument. They were trying to portray themselves as the
> nationalists and the Democrats as the globalists. The Democrats
> have completely established themselves as the patriotic nationalists.

Seriously, he said that. But nary an opposing voice was heard to disturb a
consensus worthy of the Bandar-log: "We are great. We are free. We are
wonderful. We are the most wonderful people in all the jungle! We all say so,
and so it must be true."

Scoundrels feigning patriotism is one thing, but the starring act in Philly was the appearance of Mr. and Mrs. Khizr Khan, parents of Captain Humayun Khan, killed in Iraq in 2004 in a pointless war Hillary supported but Trump didn't. Ever since, Mr. Khan's accusations have been accorded saturation coverage, amplified by a full-spectrum media echo chamber featuring a parade of expert commentators scrupulously balanced between liberal Democratic Trump-haters and "conservative" GOP Trump-haters. (If nothing else, everyone's now forgotten all about the DNC's thumb on the scale to fix the Democratic race for Hillary, except to note that the Russians must be behind hacking the patriotic Democrats' emails because Moscow wants to elect Treasonous Trump, the ultimate Putin Troll.)

Let's stipulate that by all accounts Captain Khan died "a hero to our country," and his dad seems a "nice guy," as Trump has said. But how does that validate the substantive points that Mr. Khan made? Let's address just two:

1. Mr. Khan: *"If it was up to Donald Trump, he [Captain Humayun Khan] never would have been in America."* Mr. Khan refers to Trump's earlier advocacy of a temporary ban on Muslims' entering the United States, not his later shift to restricting anyone—not just Muslims—seeking entry from a "terrorist nation." (For what it is worth, Trump was right the first time. Who's more of a potential threat entering the U.S.: a Christian from Syria, Iraq, or Iran, or a Muslim from Paris, Brussels, or London?)

But let's take Mr. Khan's point at face value and suppose that he and his wife, and hence their son, would not have been in America under the original Trump concept. That would also mean we would not have had admitted the Afghan parents of the Orlando killer, the Pakistani parents of the San Bernardino killer (and his co-jihadist Pakistani bride), the Palestinian parents of the Fort Hood killer, the Chechen parents of the Boston bombing killers, and others less well known. So what is the fair tradeoff between the harm inflicted on America and the mourning families of dozens of victims by the jihadist progeny of these aliens, versus the good Captain Khan did that presumably would have been lost? (Let's leave aside the unknowable *It's a Wonderful Life* hypothetical about what would have happened in an alternate universe: "Every man on that transport died. Harry wasn't there to save them, because you weren't there to save Harry.")

2. Mr. Khan: *"Donald Trump, you are asking Americans to trust you with our future. Let me ask you: Have you even read the U.S. Constitution? I will gladly lend you my copy. In this document, look for the words 'liberty' and 'equal protection of law.'"* Has Mr. Khan, or any of those trashing Trump, even read the Constitution? Can they show one place where it requires the U.S. to apply domestic "equal protection" standards to admission of aliens? Our laws on issuance of visa to immigrants and visitors contain all sorts of criteria that would be impermissible at home. We favor admission of the wealthy (so-called "millionaire" investor visas) and disfavor the poor (barring those "likely to become a public charge"). We effectively discriminate on the basis of national origin via several visa categories that impose country quotas. We have even discriminated on the basis of religion, for example during the 1970s and 1980s favoring Soviet Jews, Pentecostals, and Evangelical Baptists over other groups. At this very

moment, the Obama administration effectively gives Syrian Muslims preference for refugee and asylum status over Syrian Christians, despite the fact that the latter are targeted by the Islamic State, al-Qaeda, and U.S.-supported "moderate" jihad terrorist groups opposed to the Damascus government. So why should it be out of bounds to give disparate treatment to members of the one religion (guess which!) that is linked to a basket of undesirable features such as sharia law, the caliphate, stoning adulteresses, killing apostates, and (in some areas) female genital mutilation? Nothing in the Constitution Mr. Khan has kindly offered to Donald Trump prevents such scrutiny.

As of this writing, the anti-Trump Two Minute Hate has lasted several days and shows no sign of abating. One senses the Philly scoundrel-patriot Democrats, Establishment Republicans, and their media lapdogs believe they have finally found the right harpoon to kill the Great White Whale and will keep hurling it with gusto. Whether it works or not remains to be seen.

Trump Claims Obama and Hillary Are 'Founder' and 'Co-Founder' of ISIS, Media Feign Amnesia

Jim Jatras | *Chronicles* | August 12, 2016

No one paying attention with even one eye and half an ear can be ignorant of the fact that when it comes to this year's election the MSM are lying shills for Hillary. But now it seems they're all suffering from amnesia too.

The latest "OMG, Trump said *that*!" moment is The Donald's claim that Barack Obama and Hillary Clinton are, correspondingly, the "founder" and "cofounder" of ISIS. True to form, the media reaction has been to shriek in outrage that he would cast aspersions on such august personages.

As of this writing, not one American media source of which this writer is aware has brought up in relation to Trump's claims the August 2012 report (declassified and released in 2015 under a FOIA request from Judicial Watch) from the Defense Intelligence Agency (DIA) stating that "there is the possibility of establishing a declared or undeclared Salafist principality in Eastern Syria, and this is exactly what the supporting powers to the opposition want, in order to isolate the Syrian regime." The "supporting powers" are identified as "western countries" (no doubt including and led by the United States), "the Gulf States" (presumably including and led by Saudi Arabia), and "Turkey" (just Turkey).

In August 2012 the Secretary of State at the time was one Hillary Rodham Clinton. The President was and still is one Barack Hussein Obama.

The DIA report said, in essence, that if we (the U.S. and our local cronies) keep aiding al-Qaeda, the Muslim Brotherhood, and other such sterling democrats, something really nasty would arise in eastern Syria. Several months later, it did, when ISIS declared itself a state straddling the Syria-Iraq border.

At some point, even a three-year-old picks up on the concept of causation. "Johnny, if you keep doing that, you'll [break it, hurt yourself, whatever]." The MSM would have us think that Obama and Hillary are less intelligent than a three-year-old. By dumping funds and arms into the hands of terrorists—only the supposedly "moderate" head-choppers, of course—they had no idea, poor dears, what might happen.

Except they did. Aside from the cautionary example of the chaos Libya was thrown into by "regime change" in 2011, not to mention the appearance of al-Qaeda in the first place as a precipitate from the Afghan war against the Soviets, they had every reason to heed what amounted to a forewarning from DIA. Instead, they decided to press on, aware of the likely result. This was intended: " . . . this is exactly what the supporting powers to the opposition want."

General Michael Flynn, currently a Trump adviser, took over as head of DIA a month before the issuance of the report in question. Whether it was his personal effort to caution the administration or simply the professional analysts in the DIA apparatus laying out the facts as they saw them, the 2012 report made no difference. As Flynn confirmed last year [to Al Jazeera's Mehdi Hasan], this was not a matter of the administration's turning a "blind eye" but of their "willful decision" that led to ISIS:

> **Hasan**: You are basically saying that even in government at the time you knew these groups were around, you saw this analysis, and you were arguing against it, but who wasn't listening?
> **Flynn**: I think the administration.
> **Hasan**: So the administration turned a blind eye to your analysis?
> **Flynn**: I don't know that they turned a blind eye, I think it was a decision. I think it was a willful decision.
> **Hasan**: A willful decision to support an insurgency that had Salafists, Al Qaeda and the Muslim Brotherhood?
> **Flynn**: It was a willful decision to do what they're doing.

Let's put into broader context the Fourth Estate's malfeasance in not connecting the 2012 DIA report to Trump's accusation. In the last couple of weeks we've seen a steady parade of Republican poobahs and mandarins coming out against Trump (some overtly for Hillary though most pretending there's some other alternative), plus a veritable *Who's Who* of the Deep State responsible for every God-awful mess abroad, in both a GOP lineup and a bipartisan one. (If Trump does win, he'll at least save time not having to draw up his own Enemies' List.) And let's not forget the former Acting CIA Director who's calling for assassinations of Russian personnel (and Iranians) in Syria. Sure! It's all in good fun! What could possibly go wrong?

In a decent society, most of these people would be in jail, not telling us who's "unqualified" to keep implementing the same disastrous policies they've given us all these years. Instead, their sage pronouncements are given saturation media exposure while the smoking gun that proves Trump's case on ISIS gets the Memory Hole.

To say the playing field is tilted doesn't even begin to describe it. The real question is whether the American public can see it for what it is.

"The Oligarchy is Losing Its Grip, But Its Death Throes May Prove Fatal—to Us"

Jim Jatras | *Chronicles* | September 21, 2016

How American Media Serves as a Transmission Belt for Wars of Choice

Several weeks ago the mainstream media (MSM) gave saturation coverage to a picture of a little boy pulled from the rubble of Aleppo after his home and family were crushed in what was dubiously reported as a Russian airstrike. Promptly dubbed "Aleppo Boy," his dusty image immediately went viral in every prestige outlet in the United States and Europe. The underlying message: we—the "international community," "the Free World," the United States, you and I—must "do something" to stop Syrian President Bashar al-Assad and his main backer and fellow Hitler clone Vladimir Putin.

Not long before, another little boy, also in the area of Aleppo, was beheaded on video by the "moderate" U.S.-supported jihad terror group Harakat Nour al-Din al-Zenki. The images of his grisly demise received far less media attention than those of official Aleppo Boy. This other kid received no catchy moniker. No one called for anyone in power to "do something." In fact, western support for the al-Zenki jihadists—which the Obama administration refused to disavow even after the beheading and allegations of chlorine gas use by al-Zenki—can itself be seen as part of "doing something" about the evil, evil Assad.

Another small detail readily available in "alternative media" but almost invisible in the MSM: Mahmoud Raslan, the photographer who took the picture of Aleppo Boy and disseminated it to world acclaim, also took a smiling selfie with the beaming al-Zenki beheaders of the other kid. But, hey, says Raslan, I barely know those guys. Now let's move on . . .

For those who have been paying attention for the past couple of decades, Aleppo Boy is a familiar example of what is known as "atrocity porn," titillating the audience through horror and incitement to hatred of the presumed perpetrators. Atrocity porn has been essential for selling military action in "wars of choice" unconnected to the actual defense of the U.S.: incubator babies (Kuwait/Iraq); the Racak massacre (Kosovo); the Markale marketplace bombings, Omarska "living skeletons," and the Srebrenica massacre (Bosnia); rape as calculated instrument of war (Bosnia, Libya); and poison gas in Ghouta (Syria). Never mind that the facts, to the extent they eventually become known, may later turn out to be very different from the categorical black-and-white accusations on the lips of western officials and given banner exposure within hours if not minutes of the event in question.

As I have detailed in a recently posted study, *How American Media Serves as a Transmission Belt for Wars of Choice*, atrocity porn doesn't exist in isolation. Rather it is part of a well-established pattern. Whenever a U.S. president, whether Democrat or Republican, plots a military intervention in another country, media (particularly the MSM) dutifully parrot government-provided content. Among the key features analyzed:

- Deficiency of knowledge as the American norm: The less we know, the more likely we are to believe what we're being told. Those least informed are most persuaded of the need to "do something."
- Reliance on government sources, "ventriloquism," and information incest: Unknown to the public, much MSM "information" comes from government sources. Ask White House aide Ben Rhodes.
- Centralized corporate ownership: You can't serve both God and Mammon, but Caesar and Mammon get along just fine. Propaganda interfaces with ratings dollars for six giant corporate conglomerates.

- "Para-journalism," "infotainment," and "atrocity porn" as a war trigger: Once government decides on war, they need to sell it. The MSM duly serves up made-to-order atrocities.
- Demonization "Hitler" memes and "weaponization" of media: It's all black and white, no shades of gray. Compromise and negotiation have no role in confronting absolute evil. War is the default option.
- America and the "international community," the "Free World," and "American exceptionalism" and "leadership": What normal Americans understand by our country's "exceptional" character is very different from the malign use to which political and media elites put it.
- Disregarding "alternative" media, American samizdat: Accurate information is available in "alternative" media, but the MSM still decide if it exists or not.
- "We never make mistakes," "stay the course," and "MoveOn-ism": U.S. policy has no rearview mirror. Authors of past disasters are not discredited. Those who said "tolya so" are ignored.

The media's acting as a transmission belt for war is best understood by seeing the MSM as themselves an integral part of a multifaceted, hybrid public-private entity encompassing an astonishing range and depth. Centered in Washington with secondary concentrations in New York and Silicon Valley, it is variously known as the Establishment, the Oligarchy (as called by Alabama Senator Jeff Sessions), or the Deep State (as analyzed in depth by my longtime Congressional colleague Mike Lofgren). This entity includes elements within all three branches of the U.S. government (especially in the military, intelligence, and financial sectors), private business (the financial industry, government contractors, information technology), think tanks, NGOs, the "Demintern," both political parties and campaign operatives, and an army of lobbyists and PR flacks. Students of history will note a startling resemblance to the old Soviet *nomenklatura*.

The Deep State is not just Dwight Eisenhower's "Military-Industrial Complex." Compared to these guys, Curtis LeMay was a peacenik. The Oligarchy's propensity for war is inseparable from its media falsehood-generator. As Solzhenitsyn observed: "Anyone who has proclaimed violence his method inexorably must choose lying as his principle." Both have become deeply engrained in our public life and especially in our foreign and military policies.

There is hope, though. Under assault from this year's anti-Establishment challenges from Donald Trump and Bernie Sanders, the failure of Barack Obama's policies in Syria and Ukraine, and boiling anger from a shrinking American Middle Class, both the Oligarchy and its media component show signs of losing their grip. Of particular note is growing public skepticism of the MSM in favor of digital "alternative media" across the political spectrum: Antiwar.com, OpEdNews, RonPaulInstitute.org, zerohedge.com, LewRockwell.com, Infowars.com, Counterpunch.com, Unz, Takimag, Consortiumnews, and many others, including upstart independent conservative TV network One America News. Some other publications are open to alternative views and serve as conduits to more mainstream opinion, such as *Chronicles* Magazine on the (genuine, not Neocon) Right, *The Nation* on the Left, the libertarian *Reason*, and the foreign policy realist publication *The National Interest*. At the same time, the MSM increasingly must take note of "alternative" information in an attempt to preserve some of its diminishing credibility. The most obvious success in this regard is DrudgeReport.com, especially in its Trump-friendly coverage of the presidential race, with Breitbart also worth mentioning. A growing segment of the American public is discovering a

skill once well-honed by the citizens of the former communist countries: reading between the lines of the official media (which is assumed to be full of lies)
and making informed comparisons to *samizdat* alternative media, foreign
sources, and the rumor-mill to guess what the truth might be. An encouraging
sign is Obama's failure to herd the country into the Syrian war in 2013 in the
face of an outpouring of public opposition across the political spectrum. The
possibility exists for a peaceful evolution over the next few years to a less
warlike posture that would refocus on America's domestic needs.

There is also grave, perhaps growing, danger. The Deep State's servitors
and beneficiaries could risk a major war in a desperate bid to save their wealth,
power, and privileges—with dire consequences for America and the world.
Most people may be inclined to dismiss the idea of "kickstarting World War
III" as alarmism, if not conspiracy-mongering. Maybe that is the case. On the
other hand, such speculation isn't entirely baseless in light of the willingness
of some American politicians, including some who aspire to the Oval Office
(and one who might actually get there) to impose a no-fly zone or "safe area"
in Syria, and threaten to shoot down Russian aircraft to do it; give lethal aid
to Ukrainian forces, along with putting American and other NATO advisers'
and trainers' "boots on the ground"; or directly challenge Beijing's claim of
sovereignty over rocks in the South China Sea through U.S. and allied air and
naval transit despite Chinese warnings of a military response. If such a confrontation were to get out of control, either by design or accident, the resulting
conflict could assume unexpectedly catastrophic proportions. Instead of saving the Deep State, a world war (one that is presumed to go nuclear) could
hasten its extinction, along with much else besides.

How American Media Serves as a Transmission Belt for Wars of Choice:
Please read it.

"If #NeverTrumpersHelp Elect the Clinton Crime Family, We Can't Expect a 'Do–Over'— Ever"

Jim Jatras | *Chronicles* | November 3, 2016

Every election cycle, we are told that "this" might be the most important ballot
we ever cast. What if this time it turns out to be true?

Maybe this election isn't like the Super Bowl or the World Series, where
fans of the defeated team can console themselves with "Wait 'til next year!"
What if there is no "next year"?

As what's left of the American nation contemplates whether to send a
known criminal and her rapist husband back to the White House, some are
already contemplating how to contain the damage. As one faux-conservative
commentator put it, even if Hillary Clinton wins she'll be "boxed in by a
Republican Congress for the first two years; much more probably so in 2019
and 2020. By then, it'll be time to try again, this time with a Republican
nominee not suffering from a major personality disorder."

Apart from the snide reference to Donald Trump's personality (the notion
that a "sane Donald Trump" would win in a romp has been soundly debunk-
ed), the mirage of a "do-over" after what former assistant FBI director James

Kallstrom has called the Clinton "crime family" is re-ensconced at 1600 Pennsylvania Avenue is, depending on the intention of anyone so claiming, a mirage or a fraud. As I have noted before, this one is for all the marbles, in all likelihood permanently.

If Hillary manages to claw out a win (perhaps with the help of enough dead and non-citizen voters and ballot-flipping machines), we can count on a Republican-controlled Congress to be, at best, even more pathetically ineffective at "boxing" her in than they were against Barack Obama. More likely, we can expect active complicity on critical issues. There won't be much to "try again" in 2020 under three all-too-foreseeable scenarios:

A. BEST CASE scenario: Trump/Buchananite populism is purged from the GOP, the old, Bushist regime is restored (amnesty, "free" trade, endless "wars of choice"), and by some fluke an off-the-shelf conventional Republican stiff manages to win in 2020. In other words, the bipartisan Oligarchy (to which Trump is the only alternative in sight) plays the red card one more time before turning back to blue for good in 2024. Nothing of substance changes, at least not for the better. PROBABILITY: less than 5%.

B. MUCH MORE LIKELY scenario: Trump/Buchananite populism is purged from the GOP, the old, Bushist regime is restored (amnesty, "free" trade, endless "wars of choice"), and an off-the-shelf conventional Republican stiff gets shellacked by the permanent Democratic majority Hillary has enhanced pursuant to her little-noted pledge *not* to enforce the immigration laws. (Which constitutes breaking her oath of office in advance, but no one seems to care.) A collaborationist GOP settles in for permanent minority status: cushy for the *apparatchiki*, disaster for a dwindling number of dispirited conservative voters. PROBABILITY: much more than 5% but how much depends on Scenario C.

C. ALL TOO POSSIBLE scenario: The most pathological warmonger in American history gets into the White House, bringing in her entire merry band of neoconservatives and liberal interventionists regardless of party affiliation. She starts a splendid little war someplace—Syria, Iran, South China Sea, it doesn't much matter where. Bushist Republicans and a bellicose media transmission belt cheer her on. To "unite a divided country" in wartime she quashes domestic opposition with punitive measures that make Abe Lincoln and Woodrow Wilson look like Ron Paul, effectively ruling by Executive decree. (A few terrorist attacks by jihadists she lets in to the U.S. will nicely justify anti-gun measures while being sure no one "blames Islam.") In due course, World War III ensues. Scenarios A and B are overtaken by events. Forever. PROBABILITY: It would be nice not to find out.

In the wake of FBI Director James Comey's reopening Hillary's Emailgate investigation, there's been loose talk about what happens if Hillary is indicted while President-elect or about impeaching her after she takes office—"Hello President Tim Kaine!" Nonsense. If Barack Obama and Loretta Lynch wouldn't allow Hillary and her henchpersons to be indicted in July, they sure won't after she is invested with the power to dispense a "Get Out Of Jail Free" card for any possible inconveniences after they leave office. As for impeachment, keep in mind that Richard Nixon was forced from office only when it became clear enough Senate Republicans would vote to remove him. To take Trump's hypothetical, Hillary could stand in the middle of 5th Avenue and shoot somebody and a solid phalanx of Democratic Senators would deny the necessary two-thirds majority to convict her, as they did for her husband. Knowing that to be the case, House Republicans would not even bother to vote articles against her.

Let's be honest. If Hillary wins, we're stuck with her for the duration, or until her concealed health problems catch up with her.

Or until Scenario C kicks in.

Which brings us again to the deplorable (not in the good sense) stance of diehard #NeverTrumpers. In the law, there's a concept called the "but for" test. It's the venerable, commonsense, balance-of-probabilities notion that you can be liable for damages if someone suffers a harm that would not have occurred "but for" your action. If Hillary becomes President and foreseeable, irreparable harm accrues to America and the world, particular blame and opprobrium should fall upon the brow of Christian commentators who, not content with personally declining to support the only declared pro-life candidate among the top four contenders, have used their soapboxes to discourage others from voting for Trump—whose victory is the only proximate chance to avert Scenarios A, B, or C above.

Indeed, notables in this category state in so many words that Hillary's election would be preferable to Trump's, which if not exactly constituting an endorsement is awfully close to it. This includes one writer (already roundly rebuked by *Chronicles*' Tom Piatak) who morally condemns Christians who stand with Trump as "indelibly stained" and posits that for "religious and social conservatives, a Clinton presidency would be terrible [but] it would not the worst thing imaginable"—that Trump would be worse because he's a "dirtbag." Another such writer compares Trump to the degenerate emperor Elagabalus (though Hillary is a far better match) and opines that it is "a hard thing to accept that some elections should be lost, especially in a country as divided over basic moral premises as our own, [but]. . . . today's conservatism has far more to gain from the defeat of Donald Trump, and the chance to oppose Clintonian progressivism unencumbered" by Trump's alleged personal flaws. (Make no mistake. Although these barbs are directed in name against Trump, the real target is the mass of spiritually benighted Americans like me who are depraved enough to support him. At root, it's just another elitist version of Hillary's *irredeemables* and *deplorables* cross-dressing as piety.)

If Donald Trump loses, it may be for lack of conservative and Christian voters these worthies have actively dissuaded. Empirically, it would be hard to prove that "but for" their active discouragement of votes for Trump, he might have won, and that the agony our country would then face might not have occurred. But that is certainly the *intent* of their repeated jeremiads against the Republican nominee. If, God forbid, Hillary Clinton wins, and we wake up on November 9 lamenting the country we have lost, probably forever—and even facing a qualitatively heightened peril of nuclear holocaust—every decent American should remember those indelibly stained personages who knowingly sought that outcome out of what they touted as their righteous concern for Christian and conservative principles. I hope then they would at least have the decency to shut up and spare us their moralizing and complaints under the regime they preferred and energetically sought to install. It would in part be *their* regime. They must own up to it.

But thankfully that horrifying prospect is not yet upon us. There's only one way to keep it from becoming a reality, and it's in our hands, at least for those of us who live in "swing states." For what it's worth, I've already voted.

"Could Stay-at-HomeMoms Help Put Trump Over the Top?"

Jim Jatras | *Chronicles* | November 16, 2016

Donald Trump caught a lot of people off guard with his proposal, spearheaded by daughter Ivanka, on child-care benefits. This is not familiar Republican territory. Of course, Hillary Clinton's plan is more "generous," promising 12 weeks of paid leave to Trump's six.

But there's one, big fat difference that has been underreported: Hillary's plan only applies to work outside the home. Trump's applies equally to stay-at-home parents, the vast majority of whom are moms. As Ivanka spelled out in the *Wall Street Journal*:

> And what if one parent staying home to raise the children is the best option for a family? This is the praiseworthy choice of many, yet there's zero value or recognition by our government for this hard and meaningful work. Under my father's proposal, stay-at-home parents will receive the same tax deduction as their working peers.

Ivanka later joined her father on television with Dr. Oz, speaking movingly on behalf of mothers who care for their own children. Where, when, and from whom in this age of Sheryl Sandberg's Lean In have we heard someone from the "One Percent" suggest that human beings, especially those of the female persuasion, might have something more valuable to do with their lives than claw their way to the top of the corporate ladder? (Of course in Sheryl's case, it helped to start near the top with a bit of a boost from "Larry Summers at Treasury; Sergey Brin, Larry Page and Eric Schmidt at Google; and Mark Zuckerberg at Facebook." Just lean in, girls, anyone can do it—as long as you have the right patrons. Sheryl is reportedly in line to be Hillary's Treasury Secretary.)

Obviously, as with any plan the devil is in the details: how much would Trump's proposal cost (not only the tax deduction for those in fact paying taxes but EITC for those at lower income levels), impact on hiring, quantifying stay-at-home work in monetary terms, and so forth. You also have predictable complaints from the Left and the "free market *über alles*" pseudo-Right, respectively, that the plan assumes most of the parents impacted would be women (The horror! The horror!) and that it constitutes more federal government interference with business. And don't forget the pinheaded attack on Ivanka from that bastion of natalism and maternalism, *Cosmopolitan* magazine, as to how or if her plan would cover same-sex "couples."

Giving the gender-warriors the dismissive brush-off they deserve, let's ask regarding the free-marketeer critics: how many of them are the same "conservatives" cheering on the open borders and "free trade" that have helped drive down wages, forcing each parent to work for what amounts to half of the salary paid to our fathers and grandfathers only a few decades ago? (That is, if they can find jobs at all, or even contract work with no employee benefits.) Maybe we should be less worried about "conserving" market principles that long since have been skewed against the Middle Class and more worried about conserving American families. Was man (or woman, or child) made for the market, or the market for the family?

Leaving aside the details, the key to the Donald-Ivanka plan is the recognition that we need to stop pretending that, as a common good, parents', especially mothers', caring for their own children is worth exactly zero, and child care is only of value if you pay a stranger (almost always another woman, preferably a foreigner) to do it. It's time to stop denigrating stay-at-home parents, especially moms, as "not working" and in effect subsidizing, even coercing, their exit from the home by squeezing them economically with worker-hostile trade, tax, and immigration policies imposed by a donor class that won't be happy until American wages are on a par with those of Bangladesh. It is precisely this calculated war on home moms that Obama has waged, and which Hillary would prosecute further.

Approximately ten-and-half million American women are stay-at-home moms, and in the phony Obama Recovery that number appears to be growing. Trump's family-friendly plan could have an impact on the election, especially in light of the Republican candidate's polling shortfall with women. Married women are a key GOP voting bloc with which the polls show Trump lagging, but that might change—if they take note of his plans to help them.

"Battle over Healthcare: Just Another Theater in the War to Remove Trump"

Jim Jatras | *Strategic Culture* | March 17, 2017

Ever since the November 2016 election and the defeat of the horrible war-monger Hillary Clinton, I have been flooded with inquiries from Serbia, Russia, and other countries asking how and when American foreign policy will change for the better. Will NATO back off from provocations in the Baltic and Black seas? Will Trump accept a compromise over Crimea? Will Washington cease its 100 percent bias in favor of Zagreb, Sarajevo, and Priština against the Serbs? Why has nothing changed yet? Will America go to war with Iran? North Korea? China?

Keep in mind that Donald Trump's appointments within his own administration are proceeding with glacial sluggishness, in part though not entirely due to Senate Democrats' slowing down the confirmation process. It also doesn't help that Trump seems to have a penchant for appointing people to foreign policy and national security posts who in no way reflect what appear to be his sincerely held views. Sometimes it seems that the only ideological Trump-ist in his administration is Trump himself.

But most importantly, keep in mind that Trump mainly ran on what he would do for the American people *at home*: police our borders ("Build the Wall!"), deport criminal aliens, end the glut of cheap illegal labor that drives down wages (and drives up medical costs with illegals' uninsured visits to the emergency room); reverse one-sided trade deals and restore manufacturing; and rebuild our infrastructure, which was once the envy of the world and is now its laughingstock.

These promises, which impact the everyday life of Americans at home, will determine if his presidency is a success or if he gets tossed out on his ear in 2020, with the warmongering Deep State majestically reassuming its right-ful patrimony. That's if the ongoing "soft coup" being waged against him by the Deep State and MSM hasn't succeeded in removing him before then. With that in mind, Trump's only *essential* foreign task is not to stumble into another catastrophic war somewhere.

Among his domestic promises that are make-or-break for him, and for the Republican Party in which he is locked in an uncomfortable symbiosis, Trump's promise to repeal and replace "Obamacare" (formally, the "Affordable Care Act") is front and center. Keep in mind that for historical reasons too complicated to describe here, the United States doesn't have a healthcare system like most other countries. While the federal government has a large role in regulating the system, the major players are private companies providing insurance to pay for medical services, much as we have life insurance or car insurance.

But medical insurance is much more heavily regulated, and as one might expect the companies themselves have a lot of influence about how they are regulated. The result is something like a system of state capitalism which satisfies nobody, neither those who advocate the kind of universal "single payer" socialist model practiced by other developed countries (but which often results in waiting lists, shortages, and lower quality of care) versus those who claim that a purer free market model of the sort we have for other essential services, like food, would work better. American prices for prescription drugs, many of them developed in the U.S., are among the world's highest, because other countries' governments insist on buying them in bloc at set prices, leading the companies to make up the difference in America where they can charge whatever they like. Among Trump's heresies with many Republicans is that he'd like the U.S. federal government also to purchase in bulk and drive prices down.

American health services are prohibitively expensive for anyone who doesn't have insurance, and not everyone does. Most Americans who have insurance get it through their employers (where the worker also must pay into the system), itself a problem as more and more companies hire people as "contract workers," not as employees who must be offered such benefits. Millions of working people are uninsured, either because their employers don't offer insurance or they can't afford the premiums. Some young and healthy people—they call them "young immortals"—have access and can afford insurance but would rather spend their money on something else. The Medicaid program provides basic services for the poor. As it stands, American healthcare generally is considered as having a high quality of care and quick availability—if you have insurance, you won't die waiting for your heart bypass, you'll get it right away.

Obamacare adjusted this system, largely by trying to force young immortals to buy insurance by fining them if they don't. In the end, American healthcare became even more complex and expensive, though several million people who were uninsured now have it on a subsidized basis.

For a number of reasons, the Republican Congress has decided that keeping their promise to repeal and replace Obamacare is first on their legislative agenda. This in effect means that almost nothing else can get done until Congress takes care of that. (As the American expression has it, they aren't coordinated enough to walk and chew gum at the same time.) Similarly, the forces eager to bring down Trump—for other reasons, especially to prevent him from changing American foreign and security policy—are doing their very best to ensure that the first item on the Republicans' domestic agenda turns into a disastrous failure.

Certainly, there is disagreement in the Republican ranks on how to proceed. There are procedural problems on how to get legislation through the Senate, where the Democrat minority can block it. A powerful Democratic ally is the supposedly non-partisan Congressional Budget Office, which just released a skewed estimate on costs of the Republican replacement plan and how many people might not be forced to buy insurance and will therefore be presumed uninsured. In the media, that becomes a depiction of cruel Republicans kicking sick grandmothers out to the curb to die for the sheer evil fun of it.

In short, the healthcare debate will proceed with the same scorched-earth ferocity we've seen on "Russian hacking" and the political assassination of Mike Flynn, except the theater of civil war has shifted to a domestic issue. But the real issue isn't health care at all, it's how to cripple Trump and then remove him before he can do real damage to the Deep State.

And now, just as I write this, someone at the Internal Revenue Service has criminally leaked part of Trump's 2005 tax return. The hunt is on!

"Dump Senate Cloture, Bring Back 'Mr. Smith's' Filibuster"

Jim Jatras | *Chronicles* | March 29, 2017

As the Stupid Party licks its wounds after the not-too-surprising disintegration of its bid to repeal and replace Obamacare, talk is again turning to abolishing the Senate filibuster with a "nuclear options" that would allow legislation to clear the World's Greatest Deliberative Body (WGDB) with a simple majority of 51 votes (or 50 plus the Veep in case of a tie). While this latest fiasco took place solely among House Republicans, it happened in large part because of the need to craft a bill that would qualify for filibuster-proof Budget Reconciliation procedural consideration by the Senate. The result was a flawed, unviable piece of legislation that in the end satisfied nobody.

Threats from Senate Democrats to filibuster the nomination of Judge Neil Gorsuch to the Supreme Court have fed more talk of "going nuclear." Senate Republicans are loath to take that step, anticipating the day they are back in the minority, even though it's increasingly clear that they can pass almost nothing while the minority party still has blocking power in the upper chamber.

"Filibuster" has become almost a household word. A *Google News* search for "Democratic filibuster" yields about eight thousand hits, "Senate filibuster" some five thousand.

There's just one little problem. There *is* no filibuster in the Senate.

The filibuster in its classic form—a tag-team of minority-party Senators inveighing at length on the floor to delay a vote they are sure to lose—hasn't existed for decades. (The commendable filibuster-like speeches by GOP Senators Rand Paul and Ted Cruz in 2013 were essentially dramatizations.) Today, the proximate obstacle to getting legislation through the Senate with a simple majority is *cloture*, specifically Senate Rule XXII, which provides for limiting debate following a vote of three-fifths of Senators present. Ironically intended as a means to streamline Senate business, in practice Rule XXII means not much can get done without a 60-vote super-majority. Once Senators inform their respective leaderships they have 41 votes against a bill, it's *sayonara*, time move on to something else.

The cloture rule empowers a lazy man's filibuster. It allows a minority (today, the Democrats) of 41 Senators to "filibuster" a bill—including bills to repeal Obamacare, defund Planned Parenthood, confirm judges, building the Mexican Wall, etc.—from the comfort of their offices or fundraising receptions. They don't have to haul their carcasses down to the Senate floor and speechify as long as their feet and bladders can hold out before they eventually have to fold and a simple majority vote proceeds.

Let's stop making it easy for them. The Senate should revoke Rule XXII and go back to the archetypal filibuster that generally existed in the 19th and early 20th centuries. Set up the cots in rooms abutting the Senate chamber, empty the spittoons, send out the Sergeant-at-Arms to round up stragglers! Let's watch the assembled solons reenact *Mr. Smith Goes to Washington* on live TV! Especially with C-SPAN coverage, we'll see how much time and political capital Democrats want to burn defending their enormities in front of the nation—and then make 'em vote, up-or-down.

A return to the old-timey real-life filibuster would be magnificent political theater and valuable public education on the issues. It would also respect the WGDB's tradition of affording the minority their right of unlimited debate while allowing for an eventual majoritarian vote to proceed. Best of all, it would provide a much better chance of getting Donald Trump's legislative agenda to his desk.

"Waiting for John Brown"

Jim Jatras | *Chronicles* | June 16, 2017

Just imagine if a deranged Tea Party activist known to rant on social media against Barack Obama and Hillary Clinton had gunned down a bunch of Democrats. Would Republican officials get away with saccharine expressions of "this is an attack on all of us," "we stand united," and similar vacuities?

Hardly. They'd be dunned mercilessly by media and their Democratic colleagues demanding they own up to "the climate of hate" they'd created, condemn any and every group the Southern Policy Law Center had ever looked at cross-eyed, and disavow anyone to the right of Mitt Romney or more of an American nationalist than George Soros.

Actually, we don't need to imagine. Just remember how the media rushed to blame Sarah Palin and the Tea Party (and of course guns) for the 2011 shooting of then-Congresswoman Gabby Giffords by an unstable man of hard-to-define political leanings. In fact, in the wake of this week's attack on Republicans in Alexandria, Virginia, the *New York Times* saw fit to print the same baseless charge.

Hillary Clinton crony and Virginia Governor Terry McAuliffe rushed to raise the gun issue, noting that firearms kill 93 million Americans every day. Virginia State Senator Richard Black notes that at that rate in three and half days there won't be any Americans left.

But rather than blaming the Alexandria attack on the ongoing hate campaign stoked by media and Democrats against Donald Trump and his deplorable supporters, namby-pamby Republicans (do I repeat myself?) rushed to depoliticize its manifestly political nature. At worst, we hear, the shooting punctuates the need to tone down partisan bickering from both sides, "to find America's middle again and return to civility." On the practical side, maybe we need to think about whether Congressmen need more protection. Evidently the mutual bonds of membership in a mandarin ruling class take precedence over acknowledging the one-way ideological animus behind the violence.

While professional Republicans studiously avoid the legitimization of violence against opinions deemed unacceptable by the Left, some populist conservative media, and even the semi-mainstream *Fox News*, have not. A New York theatrical assassination of Trump as Caesar, a mock Trump beheading by someone claiming to be a comedienne, and a rapper's firing a prop pistol at the head of a Trump-themed clown have been mentioned as incitements.

Less well-publicized is the day-in and day-out violent abrogation of the rights of ordinary citizens who don't have the protection of the Secret Service or Capitol Police at the hands of black-clad, masked "Antifa" (i.e., "anti-fascist") thugs, against which no known Democrat and precious few Republicans have raised their voices. As Tea Party activist Judson Phillips recently commented (evidently written before Alexandria):

> The first skirmishes of a second American civil war have begun.
> No, this is not a metaphorical analogy to that bloody conflict that killed approximately 620,000 Americans. It is an objective statement of the reality in America.
> Since the election of 2016, the left has gone crazy. Their version of the tea party is called Resistance, and the spearhead of that is a loosely formed terrorist group called Antifa. Antifa is short for Anti-Fascist. The irony of their name is not lost on those who actually know history, as their tactics are straight from the fascist playbook.
> In the past few months, these groups have repeatedly disrupted peaceful pro-Trump rallies. They have called for and used violence against people who support the president or disagree with them and even against members of the media who will report things Antifa doesn't want reported.
> Just a few days ago, a woman associated with Antifa attacked a police horse, using a flagpole with nails extending from it. At the same incident in Pennsylvania, other Antifa terrorists had sharpened bamboo poles and baseball bats.
> Conservatives and those perceived to be conservatives have been attacked. The weapons have included glitter-filled gel, urine bombs, chains, bicycle locks and baseball bats. As their violence becomes more intense, it is now only a question of when, not if, someone will be killed.

This is not, as the media would have us think, just a matter of tit-for-tat confrontations between pro-Trump and anti-Trump groups. These are planned calculated armed assaults on ordinary, decent Americans who have been demonized as "white nationalists, neo-Nazis, and Klansmen along with other provocateurs from the so-called 'alt-right.'" Add to that the certainty that Trump and his team stand condemned as conscious traitors who have "betrayed our democracy" to the evil Vladimir Putin. So really, how is violence not justified?

Little in the aftermath of the Alexandria attack indicates that this epidemic of what is already being called Hodgkinson's Disease will be recognized for what it is and dealt with accordingly. (Both the ideological motivation and the authorities' determination to avoid it are reminiscent of those in American and Europe who hasten to declare "this has nothing to do with Islam" after every instance of "sudden jihad syndrome.")

The unanswerable question is how far this will go. We can hope the duly constituted authorities will rein in this violence but that's unlikely. At the national level, the Trump administration is too busy defending itself against a soft coup to crack down on organized Antifa groups and those that fund them. Even if they tried, most GOP officeholders would remain at best silent and useless, as they have on voter fraud and sanctuary cities, but many would join Democrats in denunciation. The courts would play the same malign role as they have on the Administration's travel order, gutting any initiative on the basis of political "discrimination" (never mind that the violence is itself politically discriminatory). Meanwhile, local authorities in "progressive" jurisdictions will continue to treat the expression of "provocative" views they don't agree with as the problem, not the violent suppression of such views, which they view with apathy if not approval.

So perhaps what remains of America will just meekly allow itself to be deprived of its rights of speech, assembly, and the constitutional effectiveness of their votes by third-rate reenactors of Mao's Red Guards and Röhm's *Sturmabteilung*. Or maybe things will calm down on their own.

Or maybe not. Maybe Americans who up until now have been confident their rights as citizens would be protected by the authorities will finally be disabused of that notion and begin to respond in kind. We have historical examples of how civil wars start, as in Spain in 1936. It's not pretty.

At this writing we don't know if the Alexandria shooter simply sought to kill as many people as possible, or whether he hoped to spark something bigger. We have an example of how that happens too, at Harper's Ferry in 1859.

It's not clear whether James Hodgkinson intended to be a new John Brown. But the way things are going, one will show up sooner than later.

"Bipartisanship! The Evil Party and the Stupid Party Team Up to Cripple Trump, Subvert the Rule of Law, and Put the US on a Road to War"

Jim Jatras | *Strategic Culture* | July 28, 2017

The overwhelming approval by both chambers of the US Congress of a bill imposing new, permanent sanctions on Russia, Iran, and North Korea puts President Donald Trump in an impossible position. He can either sign the bill or allow it to become law without his signature, in which case he has acquiesced in the Legislative Branch's usurpation of what is supposed to be among the Executive's primary constitutional responsibilities, the conduct of relations with foreign states.

Or he can veto it, but with a total of only five votes against it in both the Senate and the House together, an override is almost certain. Trump would still find his authority curtailed, on top of crippling his clout during the infancy of his term.

Keep in mind that this is being inflicted on Trump mainly by members of his own party. The Republican Congressional leadership can't manage to repeal Obamacare, reform taxes, stop voter fraud, keep dangerous people out of our country, build the Mexican Wall, or renew our national infrastructure. But they find plenty of time to hold hands with the Democrats, who are trying to unseat the constitutionally elected president in a "soft coup" over phony "Russiagate", to enact a misguided piece of legislation that is expressly intended to guarantee that Trump can't, under any foreseeable circumstances, improve ties with the one country in the world with which we absolutely must get along, at least on some minimal level: "It's the Russia, Stupid!"

This is bipartisanship at its worst. In case we need to be reminded, America does not have a multiplicity of parties like most other countries. Instead, we have just two: an "Evil Party" and a "Stupid Party"—and when something is really evil *and* stupid, we call that "bipartisan."

To appreciate how corrosive of the rule of law this bill is, consider the status of an authority the Constitution does put firmly into the hands of Congress: the power to make war. Congress has uttered hardly a peep of protest over the decades as their most solemn trust has effectively become a dead letter. Successive presidents have conducted operations in or against dozens of countries without authorization from Congress in clear violation of international law. (In fact, during President Bill Clinton's aggression against Serbia in 1999, Congress affirmatively *voted down* his request for war authority. He and lapdog NATO proceeded anyway.)

Recently the Pentagon was enraged at Turkey's revealing the existence of at least 10 secret American bases in northern Syria. The anger was over the exposure of the bases' existence, not the fact that they had no legal justification to be there at all, under either US domestic law or binding international law. With respect to both the military presence in Syria is lacking, but no one in Congress cares. They're too busy clipping Trump's wings.

Let's keep in mind that in addition to the illegal bases, the US is busy conducting military activities in Syria under the bizarre fiction of acting pursuant to the Authorization for the Use of Military Force (AUMF) passed in September 2001 after the 9/11 attacks. Under that resolution, the President is authorized to wage war against entities that "authorized, committed, or aided the terrorist attacks that occurred on September 11, 2001." That might conceivably be applicable to the operations of al-Qaeda in Syria, although until President Trump's recent decision to cut off CIA arms supplies to jihadists in Syria, al-Qaeda linked groups seemed to be mostly *beneficiaries* of Washington's involvement, not military targets. It can't possibly apply to ISIS, which didn't even exist in 2001. Even more blatantly illegal is the repeated targeting of Syrian governments forces operating on their own territory and fighting *against* al-Qaeda, among other terrorist groups.

With respect to international law there is no murkiness at all: US actions in Syria are flatly illegal. First, let us keep in mind that treaties and conventions, like the UN Charter, are not optional; they are *binding* on state parties, and in the US legal system have the same weight as federal statute. Under the Charter, which is the fundamental law of the international system, there are two—and only two—legitimate uses of military force.

- First, authorization by the UN Security Council under Chapter VII "ACTION WITH RESPECT TO THREATS TO THE PEACE, BREACHES OF THE PEACE, AND ACTS OF AGGRESSION." Clearly, that justification is inapplicable, since the UNSC has authorized no US action in Syria.
- Second, there is Article 51, which upholds the "inherent right of individual or collective self-defense if an armed attack occurs against a Member of the United Nations." Nobody in Syria has attacked us or any US treaty ally, though Turkey has occasionally flirted with invoking NATO (a collective self-defense organization subject to Article 51, which is cited in Article 5 of the North Atlantic Treaty) while itself aggressing against Syria.

On point of comparison, let's remember the *ex post facto* rationales trotted out after the 1999 Kosovo war. As stated by Dr. Richard Falk, in arguing the illegality of military actions against Syria:

> In the aftermath of the Kosovo NATO War of 1999 there was developed by the Independent International Commission the argument that the military attack was "illegal but legitimate." The argument made at the time was that the obstacles to a lawful use of force could not be overcome because the use of force was non-defensive and not authorized by the Security Council. The use of force was evaluated as legitimate because of compelling moral reasons (imminent threat of humanitarian catastrophe; regional European consensus; overwhelming Kosovar political consensus—except small Serbian minority) relating to self-determination; Serb record of criminality in Bosnia and Kosovo) coupled with considerations of political feasibility (NATO capabilities and political will; a clear and attainable objective—withdrawal of Serb administrative and political control—that was achieved). Such claims were also subject to harsh criticism as exhibiting double standards (why not Palestine?) and a display of what Noam Chomsky dubbed as "military humanism."

None of these Kosovo elements are present in relation to Syria.

But of course none of those "compelling moral reasons" were really "present" in Kosovo, either. They were lies then and remain lies today.

In any case, Trump is about to suffer a debilitating wound to his authority, care of the Republican-controlled Congress. Meanwhile the lynch mob led by Special Counsel Robert Mueller, with his unlimited budget and all-star lineup of partisan Democrat lawyers, will broaden and dig till they can find someone they can nail for something, dragging it out into the 2018 Congressional election year.

If the Republicans lose the House next year, Trump without any doubt will be impeached. And unlike Democrats, who rallied around "their" president Bill Clinton, enough GOP Senators will rush to convict Trump. He'll have to resign or be removed. The Deep State's soft coup will have succeeded.

As the noose tightens around Trump's neck, there's only one apparent way out: a splendid little war. Whether it's against Iran or North Korea may be decided by the flip of a coin.

"Isolated Trump Flails Helplessly as He Bows to Irrational Policies on Russia and Europe Imposed by Congress"

Jim Jatras | *Strategic Culture* | August 4, 2017

President Donald Trump has signed the sanctions bill against Russia, North Korea, and Iran. With the near-unanimous, veto-proof margin by which the so-called "Countering America's Adversaries Through Sanctions Act" was passed by both the House and the Senate, Trump was in a lose-lose position.

In the signing statement issued by the White House, Trump and his advisers tried to put a brave face on what can only be seen as a humiliating defeat. Despite some cosmetic changes–

> . . . the bill remains seriously flawed—particularly because it encroaches on the executive branch's authority to negotiate. Congress could not even negotiate a healthcare bill after seven years of talking. By limiting the Executive's flexibility, this bill makes it harder for the United States to strike good deals for the American people, and will drive China, Russia, and North Korea much closer together. The Framers of our Constitution put foreign affairs in the hands of the President. This bill will prove the wisdom of that choice.
>
> Yet despite its problems, I am signing this bill for the sake of national unity. It represents the will of the American people *to see Russia take steps to improve relations with the United States*. We hope there will be cooperation between our two countries on major global issues so that these sanctions will no longer be necessary. [Emphasis added]

To suggest this absurd, dangerous, and unconstitutional law can be characterized as representing a desire "to see Russia take steps to improve relations" with the US is the opposite of the truth.

The conscious purpose of this law is to make sure that no steps to improve ties can be taken for decades to come. In that, it will be a success. The US Deep State has boxed Trump in, there's nothing he or anyone else can do about it. Cold War 2 will almost certainly be a fact of life—for many, many years.

Unless we stumble into a Hot War between the US and Russia, which could be of considerably shorter duration . . .

Trump's ubiquitous critics slammed his disparagement of the bill even as he signed it. "I built a truly great company worth many billions of dollars," Trump jabbed. "That is a big part of the reason I was elected. As President, I can make far better deals with foreign countries than Congress." True of course. But this is less defiance than helpless flailing at the air. Trump is alone. He knows it, and so does everyone else.

Not only is Congress almost totally united against his foreign policy campaign positions, almost everyone in his own administration is too. Personnel selections in foreign and national security policy are overwhelmingly from the neoconservative and Republican "Never Trump" camp informally led by former losing GOP presidential candidate Mitt Romney. Trump loyalists and people who might actually agree with his campaign positions are systematically blackballed. Those getting jobs in the administration are sometimes, to the extent humanly possible, even worse than the Obama appointees they are slowly supplanting. On Russia, anyway, it seems about the only Trumper in his administration is the president himself. Even his cutoff of CIA weapons to al-Qaeda-linked jihadists cannot be secure as the *"al-Assad has no role in the future governing of Syria"* meme returns.

In the end, Moscow has accepted the reality that "US politics have been captured by the Russophobic forces that have been pushing Washington toward the path of confrontation." While *pro forma* Russia continues to hold out the principle that it still "stands ready to normalize bilateral relations with the United States and cooperate on major international issues. . . . on the basis of equality, mutual respect and a balance of interests", they know the real score. The new law signed by Trump is tantamount to a "full-scale trade war," conceded Russian Prime Minister Dmitry Medvedev. "The hope that our

relations with the new American administration would improve is finished."
Finished.

No one can take seriously the spin from Vice President Mike Pence that the US continues "to believe that if Russia will change its behavior, our relationship can change for the good and improve for the interests in both of our countries and the interest of peace and stability in this region and around the world." Putting aside the air of lecturing an unruly child, "behavior" has nothing to do with it. Moscow could hand Crimea back to Ukraine, escort Kiev's troops into the Donbass on a red carpet, and hang Bashar al-Assad from a Damascus lamp post, but the sanctions would remain and be progressively tightened. Look how long it took to get rid of Jackson-Vanik far after its ostensible purpose was long since moot.

Note that the Vice President's comments took place on a tour of Estonia, Montenegro, and Georgia, three countries (one really can't call Montenegro a "nation") that are totally useless for defending America against Russia or anyone else but constitute part of a "C"-shaped loop around Russia's western perimeter. Also note that Macedonia may soon also get pulled in, stepping up the pressure for Serbia's and Bosnia-and-Herzegovina's absorption. Even the mafia-ruled, terror-rife pseudo-state of Kosovo is getting come-hither looks.

The more the merrier! Tighten that noose! When all's said and done, the Russophobic impulse controlling US policy is not about what the Russians have done but who they are: *Russia delenda est.* Hostility toward Russia is not a means to an end—it *is* the end.

Meanwhile, American prestige media post literally irrational headlines like "Russia's Military Drills Near NATO Border Raise Fears of Aggression." This refers to circumstances where (1) we pull in "allies" that are useless in defending us but are ideal forward offensive platforms, (2) we string our military bases around Russia, and (3) make a big show of provocative troop, air, and naval movements right on the Russians' borders and on the edge of their territorial waters, but (4) *they're* the provocative and "aggressive" ones for moving troops around *on their own territory.*

With this bill now signed into law, we presumably will see some Russian response, without the delay of the ill-founded delusion that restraint will be rewarded. But the fact is, when it comes to sanctions ping-pong, Russia is in an inherently weaker position. While western observers often overestimate the damage sanctions do to the Russian economy, there's very little Russia can do to the US economy. The volume of bilateral trade is too low, the disparity in economic and financial power is just too great, the US role in the world financial system is too pervasive, as is our hold over our subservient satellites, who will likely suffer more damage than Russia.

Perhaps the Europeans will begin to see that the people making policy in Washington are not really their friends, though that would require both courage and wisdom from the likes of Merkel, Macron, and May—not a good bet. So far, it's just noise:

> European Commission President Jean-Claude Juncker warned of potential collateral damage to Europe's energy market, as the sanctions could inadvertently hit European companies involved with Russia's energy-export pipelines. One such pipeline, the Nord Stream 2 [JGJ: The EU Commission didn't worry about their policies' "collateral damage" to South Stream, when the beneficiaries would have been southern Europe and the Balkans], which aims to carry natural gas from Russia to Germany through the Baltic Sea, involves several European companies. "'America First' cannot mean that Europe's interests come last," Juncker said, adding that the

Commission would be ready to act "within a matter of days" if their concerns were not addressed.

The irony of course is that it's not Trump's "America First" that is responsible but exactly the opposite: the efforts of the US establishment—which the EU loves, and vice versa—to torpedo Trump! But if Trump's unpopularity in Europe can be used as a means to rally opposition to the US sanctions, it may have some value. Hypocrisy has its uses.

As we move forward into an increasingly dangerous world perhaps Moscow will focus less on striking back against the US than on self-protection: breaking off reliance on the US dollar, refocusing their energy and other vital sectors toward Asia and Eurasian economic integration. If the Europeans are smart (big "if") they will think in that direction themselves.

If so, that would lead to another, supreme irony. An article of faith of western Russophobes is that Moscow's top goal is to "decouple" the US from Europe. If that ends up happening, to whatever extent, Trump's enemies may end up accomplishing it for them. Perhaps Trump isn't the Russian plant—perhaps his domestic opponents are.

"It's Time for Deplorables to March on Washington"

Jim Jatras | *Chronicles* | August 10, 2017

Letter from Pergamum-on-the-Potomac

The Trump presidency eerily inhabits two diametrically opposed realities.

On the one hand, we have the *Beltway Reality*.

This is a world where Donald Trump is friendless and on the ropes, the Kevin McCallister of American politics. His legislative agenda, starting with repeal of Obamacare, is stalled if not moribund at the hands of a Congress ostensibly controlled by his own allies. He got a Supreme Court justice confirmed but other priorities—from building the Mexican Wall to rebuilding our infrastructure to tax reform to defunding Planned Parenthood to putting a stop to "sanctuary" cities and states—are going nowhere fast. A solid phalanx of hostile Democrats, with their media and Deep State allies, join hands with Republicans who are either incompetent or complicit, or both, to thwart him at every turn. Even his own administration is rife with untrustworthy neoconservatives, treacherous #NeverTrump Republicans, and even alleged cronies of George Soros, whom Trump has drawn to his bosom like so many asps.

Within this Beltway Reality, the one area of bipartisan "progress" is the Kumbaya moment of hand-in-hand Evil Party and Stupid Party collusion to strip Trump of his constitutional authority to make foreign policy, especially toward Russia. Unchecked criminal leaking of classified material to a hostile media keeps him perpetually on the defensive. Meanwhile, with full Congressional (of course including GOP) backing of Robert Mueller and his all-star team of partisan Democrats, Trump may well have entered into what Pat Buchanan calls a kill box that can only culminate in a silent coup that removes him from office.

Inside this Beltway Reality, the Swamp is winning.

On the other hand, we have the *Heartland Reality*.

Among Americans who lead normal lives—that is, lives unclouded by breathless outrage over his latest tweet—Trump's tenure so far has been a smashing success. Legislative shortfalls barely register in a happy-news list of improved job creation, stock market record highs (though how much of that represents real economic growth and how much a ballooning investment bubble is open to debate), low oil prices, higher consumer confidence, and an apparent drop-off in illegal alien entries (and even indications of self-deportations). In the Heartland Reality, Trump is moving decisively to dredge the Swamp via a flurry of Executive actions to step up border enforcement, cancel the Paris Climate Agreement, pull out of the Trans-Pacific Partnership, unblock the Keystone Pipeline, eject from the military people with delusions they are not of the sex they really are, and rescind job-killing regulations.

At Trump's campaign-like rallies out in what one sleazy Trump-hater calls "knuckle-drag America," mainly in states that voted for him, the Deplorables are as fired up as ever. They love him and he loves them. Like the giant Antaeus renewing his strength against his foe Heracles by making contact with his mother, the Earth, Trump is visibly energized and reinvigorated when he renews the bond with "his" people.

In this Heartland Reality, Trump is winning and making America great again.

It is in the nature of things that two such radically different but manifestly linked realities cannot indefinitely endure. One or the other must triumph over its rival.

How the Beltway can vanquish the Heartland is painfully obvious. Mueller and his merry band will broaden their probe and dig until they can find someone they can nail for something, dragging things out into the 2018 Congressional election year. Meanwhile, if the Republicans lose the House, Trump without any doubt will be impeached. Unlike Democrats, who rallied around "their" president Bill Clinton, enough GOP Senators will rush to convict Trump. He'll have to resign or be removed. The Deep State's soft coup will have succeeded, in large part thanks to the hostility of the hefty percentage of Republican officeholders who were even more appalled at Trump's victory than their Democratic pals, and who purposefully are torpedoing his agenda in the hopes of eventually eroding the support of his base. (The woefully misunderstood *cloture* rule—not some nonexistent "filibuster"—has been useful in this regard.)

There are also scenarios that would have Trump out before the next election, but the foregoing is enough for now. Whatever the timing, the prospect of removing Trump before the end of his term is all too real. It already has evinced dire warnings of a reaction from his supporters after the coup succeeds, even calls to civil war or massacre. Even assuming such warnings should be taken seriously (personally, I don't) what good would an insurrection do *after* Trump is toppled? Barn door, horse . . .

The more difficult question is how the transparent effort to reverse the results of last year's election can be scotched *before* it attains its goal—how the Heartland can vanquish the Beltway. In some form, this must mean that Trump's support cannot be confined to rallies back home but must make an impact in Washington, to put the fear of God and the American people into the black hearts of the Swamp critters.

A few thoughts come to mind:

—Trump can start playing hardball with recalcitrant Republicans, calling for primary challenges against incumbents who have thwarted his agenda. (Given the timing, however, this alone will not be enough.)

—He can give a detailed televised speech to the American people laying out what he has sought to do, where he has succeeded and where he has failed—and who's to blame. Name names, especially Republican names. Demand the end of the 60-vote threshold in the Senate and passage of the stalled initiatives. Demand confirmation of his nominees. Ask his supporters to light up the House and Senate switchboard, crash the Congressional email servers. (But would the networks even agree to give, or even sell, him time? Would internet and social media distribution be enough?)

—But most powerfully, he can ask his Deplorables to come to Washington It should be on a weekday when Congress is in session. Following a half-hour Trump rally at the east end of the National Mall, they will fan out to mob Senators' and Representatives' offices to tell them and their staffs first hand, in person, what they must do.

But whatever Trump does, he needs to do it soon. The Swamp has a plan to up-end the constitutional order. Trump needs one to preserve it. Tweets and rallies out in the real America won't get the job done. The America of the Deplorables must make its presence powerfully felt in Washington.
Mr. President, call us! We will come!

"If War Comes, Don't Blame the 'Military-Industrial Complex'—Things Are Even Worse Than You Think"

Jim Jatras | *Strategic Culture* | August 12, 2017

As the drumbeat intensifies for what might turn out to be anything but a "splendid little war" against North Korea, it is appropriate to take stock of the ongoing, seemingly successful effort to strip President Donald Trump of his authority to make any foreign and national security policies that fly against the wishes of the so-called Military-Industrial Complex, or MIC. A Google search for "Military-Industrial Complex" (in quotation marks) with "Trump" yields almost 450,000 hits from all sources and almost 26,000 from just news sources.

During the 2016 campaign and into the initial weeks of his administration, Trump was sometimes described as a threat to the MIC. But over time, with the appointment to his administration of more generals and establishment figures (including some allegedly tied to George Soros) while purging Trump loyalists, it's no surprise that his policies increasingly seem less a departure from those of previous administrations than a continuation of them (for example, welcoming Montenegro into NATO). Some now say that Trump is the MIC's best friend and maybe always was.

There are those who deny that the MIC exists at all. One self-described conservative blogger writing in the pro-war, pro-intervention, and mostly neoconservative *National Review* refers to the very existence of the MIC as a "myth" peddled by the "conspiracy-minded." Sure, it is conceded, it was appropriate to refer to such a concept back when President Dwight Eisenhower warned against it in 1961 upon his impending departure from the White House, because back then the military consumed some 10 percent of the American GDP. But now, when the percentage is nominally just 3.2 percent, less than $600 billion per year, the term supposedly is inapplicable. (There are those who argue that the real cost annually is over $1 trillion, but why quibble.)

There is a germ of truth contained in the reference to money. Compared to the "wars of choice" that have characterized US global behavior since the end of the Cold War with the Soviet Union, the MIC of the 1950s and 1960s was relatively less likely to embark upon foreign military escapades. The existence of a world-class nuclear-armed foe in the form of the USSR moderated tendencies toward adventurism. The most serious "combat" the classic MIC preferred to engage in was inter-service battles for budgetary bounty. Reportedly, once General Curtis LeMay, head of the Air Force's Strategic Air Command, was briefed by a junior officer who repeatedly referred to the USSR as "the enemy." LeMay supposedly interrupted to correct him: "Young man, the Soviet Union is our *adversary*. Our *enemy* is the Navy."

But today the "Military-Industrial Complex" is an archaic term that doesn't begin to describe the complexity and influence of current structures. Indeed, even in Eisenhower's day the MIC was more than a simple duplex consisting of the Pentagon and military contractors but also included an essential third leg: the Congressional committees that provide the money constituting the MIC's lifeblood. (Reportedly, an earlier draft of the speech used the term "military-industrial-Congressional" complex, a fuller description of what has come to be called the "Iron Triangle." Asked about the omission from the final text, Eisenhower is said to have answered: "It was more than enough to take on the military and private industry. I couldn't take on the Congress as well.")

Not only did the Iron Triangle continue to expand during the Cold War, when production of military hardware established itself as the money-making nucleus of the MIC, it swelled to even greater proportions after the designated enemy, the USSR, went out of business in 1991. While for one brief shining moment there was naïve discussion of a "Peace Dividend" that would provide relief for American taxpayers from whose shoulders the burden of a "long twilight struggle" against communism (in John Kennedy's phrase) had been lifted, that notion faded quickly. Instead, not only did the "hard" side of the MIC maintain itself—first in Iraq to fight "naked aggression" by Saddam Hussein in Kuwait, then in the Balkans in the 1990s as part of NATO's determination to go "out of area or out of business"—it then branched out into "soft" areas of control.

In the past quarter century what began as Eisenhower's MIC has become a multifaceted, hybrid entity encompassing an astonishing range and depth in both the public and private sectors. To a large extent, the contours of what former Congressional staffer Mike Lofgren has called the "Deep State" (which largely through Lofgren's efforts has since become a household word) are those of the incestuous "expert" community that dominates mainstream media thinking but extend beyond it to include elements of all three branches of the US government, private business (especially the financial industry, government contractors, information technology), think tanks, NGOs (many of which are anything but "nongovernmental" but are funded by US official agencies and those of our "allies", satellites, and clients), higher education (especially the recipients of massive research grants from the Department of Defense), and the two political parties and their campaign operatives, plus the multitude of lobbyists, campaign consultants, pollsters, spin doctors, media wizards, lawyers, and other functionaries.

Comparing the MIC of 1961 to its descendant, the Deep State of today, is like comparing a horse and buggy to a Formula One racecar. The Deep State's principals enjoy power and privileges that would have brought a blush to the cheeks of members of the old Soviet *nomenklatura,* of which it is reminiscent.

Indeed, the Deep State's creepy resemblance to its late Soviet counterpart is manifest in its budding venture into the realm of seeking to brand domestic American dissent as treason, to the hearty approval of the loony Left. As described by Daniel McAdams of the Ron Paul Institute for Peace and Prosperity:

> The government would never compile, analyze, and target private news outlets just because they deviate from the official neocon Washington line.
>
> Perhaps not yet. But some US government funded "non-governmental" organizations are already doing just that.
>
> The German Marshall Fund has less to do with Germany these days than it did when founded after WWII as a show of appreciation for the US Marshall Fund. These days it's mostly funded by the US government, allied governments (especially in the Russia-hating Baltics), neocon grant-making foundations, and the military-industrial complex. Through its strangely Soviet-sounding "Alliance for Securing Democracy" project it has launched something called "Hamilton 68: A New Tool to Track Russian Disinformation on Twitter."
>
> This project monitors 600 Twitter accounts that the German Marshall Fund claims are "accounts that are involved in promoting Russian influence and disinformation goals." Which accounts does this monitor? It won't tell us. How does it choose which ones to monitor? It won't tell us. To what end? Frighteningly, it won't tell us. How ironic that something called the German Marshall Fund is bringing Stasi-like tactics to silence alternative media and opinions in the United States!

The Soviet *nomenklatura* gave up without a fight. It's unlikely its American counterpart will. Whether Trump in the end decides to fight or to seek accommodation is still under debate. Some suggest that by signing the recent bill imposing sanctions on Russia, Iran, and North Korea, he has already surrendered. But either way, war or not, things are going to get very rocky.

"Democratic Win in Alabama Senate Race Signals Big Trouble for Trump"

Jim Jatras | *Strategic Culture* | December 15, 2017

On December 12 Democrat Doug Jones narrowly defeated Judge Roy Moore in a special election to fill the U.S. Senate seat vacated by Jeff Sessions (R-Alabama) to serve as President Donald Trump's attorney general. While on the surface Jones's victory signals a turnover of just one seat in the narrowly divided upper chamber, it points to potentially huge—possibly fatal—consequences for Trump's presidency.

First, there's the numbers in the Senate to consider. Today, Republicans hold a nominal 52–48 edge, "nominal" because there is a handful of "squeaky wheel" Republicans who on most issues would prefer to vote with the Democrats anyway and whose votes can only be purchased at extortive price. This means that the Republican leadership—which itself has an uneasy and at times contentious relationship with Trump—doesn't really have a working majority in the Senate. The flip of just the Alabama seat (meaning a net shift of two votes, one loss for the GOP and one gain for the Democrats) to 51–49 means that on any vote the Republicans can afford the defection of just one senator to the Democrats' monolithic bloc, with Vice President Mike Pence casting a tiebreaking vote.

This means that the Republican Senate is crippled. Any one GOP senator has near-veto power over anything he (or very likely, she) pleases. While the Republicans still hope they can get their tax bill conferenced, voted on, and on Trump's desk before January when Jones takes over the Alabama seat, that legislation may signal not only the first but also the last and only major legislative achievement the Republicans can point to before next year's election. (Senate Democratic Leader Chuck Schumer (D-New York) has already called for the final tax vote to be put off until after Jones is seated.) As we move into the 2018 campaign year, we can expect what amounts to a complete shutdown of already meager legislative activity and a total roadblock of Executive nominations. Of particular concern will be if a Supreme Court justice dies or retires.

> *Result*: The Democrats are in a strong position to frustrate anything resembling a Trump legislative agenda or even (they are not the same thing) a Republican agenda, allowing them to claim in 2018 that Trump and the GOP have failed to deliver on their promises.

Second, the fact that the GOP could lose in Alabama, one of the most conservative, Republican, and pro-Trump states in the country, is ominous. A month ago Republicans were badly defeated in an off-year state election in Virginia. The Old Dominion calamity, however, could be blamed on both the Republican candidates' attempt to straddle the intraparty conflict between the GOP's populist-nationalist and establishment wings (about which more below) and on Virginia's increasingly inhospitable demographics (between the influx of federal government employees and contractors and of both legal and illegal immigrants, the heavily populous suburbs near Washington, DC, are less part of Virginia than they are a mélange of Massachusetts and El Salvador, and vote accordingly). There are no such excuses available in Alabama. Simply put, if Republicans can't reliably win there, they can't win anywhere.

Granted, Moore himself was the target of unproven, decades-old of sexual allegations fueled by the national hysteria over groping and other misconduct and hyped by the major media. Not coincidentally, the media also gave prime coverage to a rehash of accusations against Trump just a day before the Alabama vote to set up Trump and Moore as the molester twins. The Democrats, who recently defenestrated Senator Al Franken (D-Minnesota) and Representative John Conyers (D-Michigan), despite the latter being a civil rights "icon" in the description of House Democratic Leader Nancy Pelosi, have positioned themselves to play "identity" politics with women as they have with "people of color," notably in the Black Lives Matter movement.

This showed in the Alabama voting. One verdict: "#BlackWomen Are The Reason Why Roy Moore Lost The Alabama Senate Race." While Jones lost white women overall, he did much better among them than Barack Obama did, no doubt largely due to the sex allegations against Moore. Plus, Jones outspent Moore 10-to-1, as the national Democrats poured in money largely aimed at mobilizing African-Americans—a whopping 96 percent of whom supported Jones, similar to Obama's 95 percent support among blacks in 2012. A last-minute push by George Soros-funded operatives to register felons to vote can't have hurt either; of course reference to such activity is open-and-shut proof of anti-Semitism as well as racism.

By contrast, Republicans were divided and many stayed home. Compared with the 2016 presidential turnout, the Republican vote in Alabama fell by 51 percent, while the Democratic turnout declined by only eight percent. The Republican National Committee, which had earlier shut off support to Moore when the sexual allegations surfaced, turned it back on only after Trump came out in support of Moore. The Republican Senatorial Committee stiff-armed him to the end.

For the GOP the more disruptive subtext is the feud between the populist-nationalist wing of the party personified by former Trump adviser Steve Bannon and an establishment faction symbolized by Senate Majority Leader Mitch McConnell (R-Kentucky). Moore's candidacy was the first litmus test of Bannon's ability to deliver on his threat to recruit populist candidates to defeat establishment GOP incumbents. Moore's loss seriously damages the credibility of Bannon's ability to deliver.

Keep in mind that even if there had not been a single sexual allegation against Moore much of the GOP establishment would still have been desperate to keep him out of the Senate. A longtime favorite with populists and, especially, with Christian social conservatives, Moore was twice removed as Chief Justice of the Alabama Supreme Court for refusing an order from the federal courts to remove a depiction of the Ten Commandments he had installed on the Court's official premises. He is outspoken in his hostility to Islam and anything related to the LGBT agenda, and has voiced a positive attitude toward Vladimir Putin. (Moore allegedly was a Putin puppet, just like Trump.)

> *Result*: The Democrats are united and can deliver to the polls their anti-Trump base, bolstered by media hype of sexual misconduct allegations and racial identity politics. Republicans are divided, demoralized, and unfocused.

Given the disunity within his own party, it is strange to note the lack of serious engagement by Trump himself. To be sure, as President and leader of the party, Trump has to try to balance factions to try to get his agenda through Congress—a balancing act that so far has produced few results. Also, he knows that in their preferences, many if not most GOP officeholders are not on his side; they're happy to work with him on tax cuts (a perennial Republican favorite) but most are indifferent or hostile to his views on immigration and trade. That said, as with his habit of staffing his administration with people who disagree with his campaign promises (which soon will likely yield a cabinet even more out of touch with his populist and America First agendas, particularly as relates to neoconservative dominance in foreign and security policy) he seems only partially aware of the need to support Republicans who are more aligned with him and his agenda over those who don't.

Thus, Moore's loss will likely only reinforce Trump's ongoing metamorphosis into a standard, off-the-shelf Republican, in substance if not in rhetoric. Sadly, that will not be his salvation if he cannot find a way to ensure that the Virginia and Alabama debacles are not replicated next year. Given Republican internecine bloodletting and his opponents' success so far in blocking Trump's initiatives, the Democrats are anticipating big wins in next year's Congressional races. Even given the fact that they have many more

Senate seats to defend than the GOP does, they hope a sweep similar to what happened in Virginia could put them in control of that body. The path is harder for getting control of the House, where the Democrats would have to flip 24 seats, but their chances are growing better by the day.

The outcome of the 2018 elections is critical to Trump's political future. If the Democrats take the House, Trump certainly will be impeached—whether on some collateral, concocted "RussiaGate" charge (like "obstruction") or on sexual misconduct antedating his election is irrelevant. He then would be removed, even if the Republicans retain control of the Senate. Unlike Democrats, who uniformly rallied around Bill Clinton when he was impeached—not a single Democrat senator voted to remove him—there are undoubtedly many Republicans who would jump at the chance to get him out of office and replace him with Pence.

"'Treasonous' Trump in the Conspirators' Crosshairs"

Jim Jatras | *Strategic Culture* | July 21, 2018

At least the White House can be happy that the resident Hitler-in-Chief's inhuman separation of innocent migrant children from adults caught illegally crossing the US border with Mexico matters to nobody anymore.

Everyone's moved on. "Children in cages" is yesterday's news.

The issue now is treason, a crime carrying the death penalty.

On that score America and the entire world owe former CIA Director and onetime communist voter John Brennan a debt of gratitude for pointing out that President Donald Trump's expressing the slightest hint of doubt about conclusions reached by the US Intelligence Community is both impeachable and treasonous.

Brennan didn't just make that up, you know. It's in the Constitution of the United States, right there in black and white:

Article II, Section 1
The executive Power shall be vested in an Intelligence Community of the United States of America.

Article III, Section 3
Treason against the United States, shall consist in doubting the Intelligence Community in any way, shape, or form.

There you have it, it's an open and shut case of treason, committed in full view of the global public within feet of Russian President Vladimir Putin—who, as the crack journalists of our intrepid Fourth Estate have now revealed through their diligent investigative work, *was once an officer in the Soviet KGB!* Trump's unmasking, through his very own perfidious words, now adds "traitor" to all the other terms of opprobrium already justly appertaining to him.

We all know what happens to traitors, don't we?

A day later Trump hastily sought to cover up his treachery with the lame suggestion that he had inadvertently dropped the semi-syllable "-n't" during his Helsinki press conference with his Russian "handler." (Actually, that "wouldn't/would" dodge is pretty cute. Who thought it up—Steve Miller? Sarah Huckabee Sanders? Trump himself? Genius! One can almost hear them brainstorming over what explanation would most insult the limited intelligence of their critics.)

But try as he might, Trump can't escape. His media pursuers have caught on to his Houdini routine:

> President Donald Trump's attempt on Tuesday to backpedal on his disastrous remarks siding with Russian President Vladimir Putin, in which the stone-faced president read from a monotone prepared statement but deviated several times from it, was eerily reminiscent of the way he handled his infamous false equivalence in response to the deadly white supremacist rally in Charlottesville, Virginia, last summer.
>
> After accepting Putin's denial instead of affirming U.S. intelligence agencies' conclusion that Russia interfered in the 2016 election, Trump on Tuesday tried to reverse course. Reading from prepared remarks, he said that he accepts the intelligence agencies' conclusion and claimed that he misspoke during Monday's press conference. (He added 'that perhaps "other people" were responsible, and reverted to his usual talking point that "there was no collusion" between his campaign and Russia, which appeared to be unscripted.) [. .]
>
> Many reporters, commentators and other political observers made similar observations, noting that Trump could quickly reverse himself again, just as he did in his response to the events in Charlottesville.

Indeed, just the day after his "stone-faced," "monotone" semi-contrition, Trump was right back at it, colluding with fellow Putin-puppet Tucker Carlson on *Fox News*. (Even worse, the Trump-Carlson duo even blasphemed against the holiest of holies of US national security, Americans' willingness to risk nuclear annihilation in World War III over tiny, corrupt Montenegro.)

Not only did this two-man, latter-day analogue to the Gunpowder Plot belittle the supposedly *proven* fact of Russian hacking of the 2016 election (which nonetheless is still disbelieved by almost 40% of Americans!), they took the opportunity to inject a note of—you guessed it!—racism:

> Carlson used literal white supremacy to defend Trump's news conference.
>
> "I mean I'm not a shrink, so I don't fully understand it. I mean I don't think Russia is our close friend or anything like that. I mean, of course, they tried to interfere in our affairs; they have for a long time. Many countries do. Some more successfully than Russia, like Mexico which is routinely interfering in our elections by packing our electorate," Carlson said, suggesting Mexican immigrants who become naturalized citizens and vote are somehow illegitimate voters.
>
> Former FBI Director James Comey criticized Trump for sitting down with Hannity and Carlson.
>
> Having sold out our nation on an international stage, Mr. Trump will now explain it all to Sean Hannity and Tucker Carlson? I'm guessing *RT* and [*Sputnik*] were unavailable.

But aside from Carlson, virtually all of Trump's supposed defenders (mostly on *Fox News*) agreed entirely with the President's accusers that questioning the intelligence community was totally impermissible. Indeed, both his defenders and even Trump himself have tried to deflect criticism by citing the myriad ways in which his Administration has been "tough" on the Russians: sanctions, expelling diplomats, striking Syria twice, and most of all reveling in the slaughter of Russian contractors in Syria.

This reflects a troubling fact that undermines optimism that the Helsinki summit will herald a change for the better in the US-Russia relationship. The fact is, Putin is master in his own house but Trump is not. There is no order or instruction Trump can give that he can be sure will be carried out, either by the Pentagon or the intelligence community—and certainly not the Justice Department, which blatantly tried to sabotage the summit with Deputy Attorney General Rod Rosenstein's issuance of a vacuous indictment of 12 GRU officers. As described by former CIA intelligence officer Michael Scheuer:

> Why should any American worry about the unending, manic claims that Russia interfered in the 2016 election? This story, after all, has been made up and perpetuated by aspiring traitors like Clapper, Hayden, Tapper, Acosta, Hillary Clinton, Comey, John Podesta, Maddow, McCabe, Brennan, Page, Strzok, Wray, the reporting staffs of the Washington Post and the New York Times, the Council on Foreign Relations, and most of all, by the foreign-born Obama. To believe this crew's statements about anything at all is to believe that John McCain and Lindsey Graham can open their mouths without lying us into yet another interventionist war. [. . .]
>
> In the face of what Jefferson surely would call a "long train" of perfidy, treason, obsessive avarice, and murder by the national government, one must ask why would any commonsensical American fail to see that the Russian-meddling narrative is transparently an attempt by Obama leftovers and the seething, quite mad Neocons to push the United States into a new Cold War with Russia, one that would lead to a hot war, as well as a means of keeping themselves out of the slammer and off the gallows.
>
> Indeed, there is not a loyal American citizen who has a single credible reason to believe any intelligence-based claims made by the Obama administration, or the Obama leftovers in Trump's administration, about Russian interference in the 2016 election. The citizenry's only fair-minded conclusion is that Obama ordered his intelligence and military lieutenants to stand down on responding to "Russian hacking" in summer, 2016, because no such hacking occurred. Certainly, the two indictments of Russians—written by Obama acolytes led by Rosenstein, Strzok, and old-man, disgrace-to-the-Marines Mueller and his merry band of Trump-hating attorneys—are clearly dreamed-up travesties that would disgrace a first-year law-school student and get him the boot therefrom.

The bottom line is that, even after Helsinki, Trump remains besieged inside his own Administration. It cannot be said with any assurance that there is a single high official, including Trump's own appointees, who agrees with the President's desire for rapprochement with Russia. Congress is almost entirely against him, as evidenced by a virtually unanimous Senate vote on a non-binding resolution against treaty-based law enforcement cooperation with Russia (as discussed by the two presidents) and talk of fast-tracking more sanctions legislation.

Even in areas theoretically under Trump's full control, most importantly his constitutional command of the military, there is pushback. One early deliverable of the summit should be US-Russia cooperation in Syria to help wind down that war. But General Joseph Votel, who leads U.S. Central Command, was quick to point out that he's received no instructions and that under prohibitory legislation enacted in 2014 no such cooperation would be legal without Congressional action to create an exception—which will not be forthcoming.

In a rule of law state, law enforcement should be politically neutral. In most countries it's not, with those in power using police, prosecutors, and courts as weapons against the opposition. Only in America, and only since Trump's election, has anyone seen the bizarre phenomenon of election losers abusing law enforcement against the winner. Even as Trump talks optimistically of a second summit with Putin in Washington in a few months, the criminal Deep State conspiracy against him rolls on with the complicity of top appointees like Rosenstein.

Every effort will continue to be made to ensure no concrete progress can be made on whatever was discussed in Helsinki while maintaining the 24/7 drumbeat of demonization. (There's even an attempt to force Trump's interpreter in Helsinki, Marina Gross, to divulge what transpired in private between the presidents. Gross herself may draw suspicion on account of an unconfirmed report that *she may actually speak Russian.* . . .)

For his part, Trump must seek support from the only direction he can: the tens of millions of "Deplorables" who voted for him. The more the media, the Democrats, and the GOP establishment trash him, the more they are convinced he is on the right track. By doubting the truth of Russian hacking and our sacred NATO obligation to every insignificant country few ordinary Americans could find on a map, he has increasingly mainstreamed those notions with his base.

Trump's only way forward is continuing to be the wrecking ball he was elected to be. Twitter and his ability to change the subject with outrageous and "impermissible" utterances and actions are his main weapons. In that vein, as long as he's being accused of treason, he might as well make the most of it:

Mr. Trump, fire Rosenstein and let the chips fall where they may.

"A Bang or a Whimper: If TrumpIs Overthrown What ComesNext?"

Jim Jatras | *Strategic Culture* | January 12, 2019

It's a new year and the American cold civil war has shifted to its next phase with the Petrograd Soviet (formerly the Smolny Institute for Noble Maidens), a/k/a Speaker Nancy Pelosi's Democrat-controlled House of Representatives ensconced at one end of Pennsylvania Avenue. Pelosi leads the revolutionary "second pivot" and rival center of authority to the embattled Provisional Government headed by President Donald Trump, headquartered 16 blocks to the northwest.

As of this writing Trump is fighting for his political life. If he loses the Mexican standoff over the government shutdown and his border wall, he's essentially finished. At this juncture, it looks as though he is prepared to declare a state of emergency and use Pentagon or FEMA funds to order the emplacement of a barrier as a military construction project. This is something for which he has the clearest black-and-white statutory authority under 10 US Code § 2802.

Nonetheless, if he goes that route, any such effort will be gummed up in the courts, just like his use of his plenary authority under 18 US Code 1182(f) to exclude "any aliens or . . . any class of aliens" whose entry into the US would in his judgment "be detrimental to the interests of the United States"—the germ of his campaign's promised "Muslim ban"—was wimped down into supposedly "extreme vetting" of aliens from a handful of countries without much indication of what the "vetting" is supposed to filter. It's likely such litigation would delay the wall or prevent its being built at all.

As of now, Trump states his preference to let the Democrats stew. After all, those immediately inconvenienced, such as federal workers and beneficiaries of some federal programs, are primarily Democrat constituencies. Let's see how many more hysterical bleeding hearts like Cher pressure Pelosi to throw in the towel: "NANCY YOU ARE A HERO LET HIM HAVE HIS FKNG MONEY!!."

In any case, as even Senator Lindsey Graham recognizes, if Trump loses this battle—one he should have fought a year and a half ago—"it's probably the end of his presidency." If Trump wins, or more properly he avoids losing, he only lives to fight another day.

And, fight he must, despite his defenders' truthful and entirely irrelevant bleating that there was no Russian "collusion." Notwithstanding Democrats' tap-dancing during the 2018 campaign on whether or not they would seek to impeach Trump, right out of the box articles of impeachment were filed within days of the House's changing hands. Trump's disgraced lawyer and "fixer" Michael Cohen will testify before the House Government Oversight Committee in February. While the weight of opinion suggests that Grand Inquisitor Robert Mueller will wrap up his *auto-da-fé* in a few months if not weeks, that would seem to be throwing away a powerful synergy with a House that is just beginning to gear up for multiple investigations into every aspect of Trump's private and professional life, as well as his kids'. Add to that New York State Attorney General Letitia James on the warpath against Trump and "anyone" associated with him. Given Trump's years in the sharp-elbowed world of high-end New York real estate and numerous business enterprises, as well as the Trump Foundation, there's no limit to the number of regulatory, tax, and other violations the putsch plotters will construe as federal and state crimes, the latter of which can't be pardoned by the President.

In short, it's now a question not if Trump will be impeached but when and on what accusations. Adding fuel to the Democrats' determination to bring him down before he's up for reelection is the fear that if Trump survives until then he might well win, something no other Republican is likely to be able to do given the GOP's tin ear to working class concerns, especially in the Rust Belt states that were Trump's margin of victory. If Trump is successfully removed before 2020, whomever the Democrats nominate will beat Mike Pence or any other Republican nominee in a romp. After that, especially if Trump's wall hasn't gotten built, a sufficient number of imported new voters, many of them illegal, will ensure a permanent Democratic lock hold on power.

When Trump is impeached there may not be enough GOP votes in the Senate to remove him—as things stand now. But never underestimate Republicans' propensity to cut and run when the going gets tough. It is suggested that any Republican who votes against Trump would seal his own political fate. Don't be so sure. Those not up for reelection until 2022 and 2024 (like Utah's newly elected Senator Mitt Romney, who didn't even wait to be sworn in to volunteer for the role of Brutus) will feel insulated. Besides, when the crunch comes establishment Republicans fear a harsh word from the *Wash-*

ington Post and *New York Times* editorial pages more than they do their own voters.

This is not to say that after impeachment Trump *will* be removed, just that it is well within the realm of possibility. But if it does happen, then what?

One anti-Trumper (who prides himself on "poking Trump's meth-addled, under-educated fans with a pointy stick." No elite contempt for the Deplorables there!) ponders whether there would be—

> . . . a civil war if Trump is driven from office—e.g., conviction after impeachment, resignation, 25th Amendment—that depends on what happens after, and there is no denying there is a chance of it, but it is highly unlikely. Many—possibly a great many—would believe they were wronged by this outcome, but how many would take up arms, and start shooting? Very few, if any at all. Trump would leave, Pence would become President, and Pence would be given credit for calming and healing the nation.
>
> There would be no civil war.
>
> But what happens after? Suppose Trump is put on trial for criminal charges, and then convicted? Or suppose he is pardoned or let off the hook, and then begins a sore-loser populist campaign all over the country, complaining that the Presidency was "stolen" by the "deep state" and that Hillary and "fake news" are responsible? That is when we should reopen the question of civil war.

Of course if Trump is forced out, it would be *precisely* a stolen election—in effect, a regime change operation of the sort the same US-UK Deep State has staged in so many other countries—abetted by the lying, fake news (no need for sarcasm quotes) worthy of the former USSR and the Democratic establishment, with the collusion of a substantial element of the GOP. But in the improbable suggestion of Trump's leading a post-White House rebellion, one raises a valid point: if Trump were removed, either politically or physically, what—or who—would be the Deplorables' rallying point? What or who would constitute the second pivot in what would then aspire to leadership in a new revolutionary situation?

The answer is not obvious. Those threatening various degrees of violent or even "gruesome" responses if the ongoing, anti-constitutional soft coup were to succeed never seem to address the question of what, exactly, the revolt would intend to achieve. Reinstate Trump, assuming that's even possible? If not him, who—Ivanka? Where and how would pathologically law-abiding middle-class Americans, many of them older and in questionable health, vent their rage? March on Washington—and do what when they got there? Torch the local post office?

Sure, devotees of the Second Amendment own more private weapons, so Trump supporters are better armed. But that may change as the violent Left gears up its own paramilitary capabilities secure in the knowledge that authorities turn a blind eye to their violence while regarding even non-violent civic nationalism as subversive.

Unlike the circumstance when the Constitution was adopted and private firearms were as good or better than military ones, there is no comparison today in delivery of devastating, deadly force. Trump himself seems to anticipate that the military would come out on his side:

> "These people, like the Antifa—they better hope that the opposition to Antifa decides not to mobilize," Trump said recently. "Because if you look, the other side, it's the military. It's the police.

It's a lot of very strong, a lot of very tough people. Tougher than them. And smarter than them . . . Potentially much more violent. And Antifa's going to be in big trouble." [. . .]

Some on far-right social media sites are all excited about what they're calling "Civil War 2.0." As documented by Dave Neiwert, there are various "Proud Boys" and "Patriots" living a fantasy version of Hank Williams Jr.'s "Country Boys Can Survive" almost entirely online.

"If they succeed in impeaching President Trump, then we will back President Trump," one Georgia militiaman told reporters. "With a use of force if need be."

Well, maybe. In a conflict that would look nothing like America's organized and relatively polite War Between the States (1861–1865) and more like the brutal communal conflicts in Yugoslavia (1991–1995), Spain (1936–1939), or Russia (1917–1922) estimates vary widely on how the military would divide. The same can be said for police forces, some of them heavily militarized.

Or perhaps the historic American nation, whose last-chance champion Trump was elected to be, would give up without a fight and submit to a tyranny that would, eventually, result in some even more fundamental societal collapse. Americans like to imagine ourselves as rough-hewn, freedom-loving, don't-tread-on-me rebels. But after decades of corruption and conditioning by politicians, judges, bureaucrats, educators, entertainers, media, advertising, pharmaceuticals, processed foods, etc., today's Americans may well be among the most docile people on earth.

Maybe that's how America ends: not with a bang but a whimper. Let's hope we don't have occasion to find out.

"I'm Jumping Off the Trump Train: Assange Was the Last Straw"

Jim Jatras | *Strategic Culture* | April 13, 2019

The saddest thing is that even if he survives in office until the 2020 vote (and he might not) Trump still will almost certainly be the lesser of two evils, in the manner to which we have become accustomed.

On March 6, 2016, this Deplorable issued a statement formally endorsing Donald J. Trump for the presidency of the United State.

I now hereby withdraw that endorsement.

No doubt this declaration from your Working Boy will be greeted with the same deafening indifference as my earlier less than earth-shattering announcement of support.

Keep calm. The planet will continue to spin on its axis at a 23.44 degree tilt.

As I tweeted on April 4, when it appeared that Ecuadorian President Lenín [sic] Moreno was going to cough up Julian Assange:

If this comes to pass & #JulianAssange is brought to #US in chains like a Gaulish chieftain in a Roman triumph can we definitively declare that any possible #Trump revolution is over & the #Deep-State won?

A quick perusal of social media since Assange's arrest shows that many others have reached a similar conclusion.

But why? To be sure, there have been other betrayals. The two strikes on Syria on phony chemical warfare accusations come immediately to mind. Or Trump's failure to build the Mexican wall, coupled with repeated humiliating defeats in Congress with the predictability of Charlie Brown's getting suckered by Lucy into trying to kick the football.

At the same time there were excuses. On Syria, maybe the President was fed false intelligence. Or maybe Ivanka was upset: *Daaaddyyy, you have to dooo something!* Or maybe Trump knew the CW accusations against Damascus were fake but felt he had to act (an ominous sign in itself) to deflect charges of being Putin's puppet, hence what could be deemed deliberately pinprick *pro forma* strikes. On the wall, well you can't trust lawyers' advice, he just doesn't understand his legal authority well enough, or maybe he . . .

But the Assange arrest and his upcoming renditi—oops!—extradition to the United States are different. There's no nuance. No excuse. No false intel report. No poor legal advice.

It's plain and simple. The same entities (Deep State, permanent government, the oligarchy, the Borg, whatever term you like) that targeted Trump with the phony Russia collusion narrative want Assange's scalp nailed to the wall. It's one thing for favored outlets like the *Washington Post* and CNN to disseminate classified information that favors the Deep State, quite another to reveal information contrary to its interests. As the premier dispenser of embarrassing secrets that facilitates online dissidence from the established narrative (also under attack by governments and their tech giant accomplices) an example must be made of Assange *pour encourager les autres*. He can count on being sentenced to rotting for decades in a nasty *Office Space* federal prison (the US will gladly waive the death penalty to spare the Brits' prissy Euroconsciences) but may very well die soon enough of natural causes, perhaps like Slobodan Milošević.

An essential role in Assange's betrayal by Moreno was played by Trump's Veep Mike Pence and Secretary of State Mike Pompeo. Former President Rafael Correa says a direct condition of Moreno's getting a $4.2 billion IMF loan was Assange's head on a platter. That's a lot more plausible than establishment media reports that Assange was ejected for transgressing the Ecuadorians' fastidious hygiene standards, which (whether based in fact or not) are just cynical defamations to justify his upcoming lynching.

It's irrelevant whether Trump—who theoretically is the boss of all US agency operatives working with their Brit colleagues to get their mitts on Assange—let the nab go forward because he was unwilling to order his minions to stand down or was powerless to do so. In that regard, it's similar to pointlessly asking *why* he has the terrible, horrible, no good, very bad national security team he does. Is it because of "Javanka"? Is it because he's beholden to a gaggle of oligarchs? (Supposedly his being a self-financed billionaire made him immune from such influences.) Is it a reflection of a personality disorder?

In the end it doesn't matter *why*, all that matters is what *is*. With Assange's arrest Trump is now exposed as the wholly owned subsidiary of the Swamp he ran against. He's now just a wheel fixed to an axle. All he can do now is it spin.

In my 2016 endorsement I asked the questions—only questions, not predictions—of what Trump might hopefully accomplish:

Can we trust Trump? Will he build his wall and secure our borders? Renovate our deteriorating infrastructure? Restore our manufacturing base? Audit the Federal Reserve and defenestrate the banksters? Restore the GOP's long-lost reputation (now hardly remembered by anyone) as the "Peace Party" that got us out of wars the Democrats started? Sign a bill to defund Planned Parenthood, as long as they continue to perform abortions (which they will)? Exclude actual or potential Islamic terrorists? Dump our freeloading so-called "allies"? Cease the PC trashing of every tradition in which Americans once took pride? Reunite a nation sundered by Barack Obama and the GOP mandarins, with their *divide et impera* Punch and Judy show of class and racial discord?

Can Trump really "Make America Great Again"? Or at least slow our decline and give our country another chance?

I don't know. But I do know that none of the more mannerly politicians served up by the oligarchy will.

"Trust not in princes . . ." (Ps. 146:3) Neither Trump nor any other politician should be accepted on blind faith. Who really can say if Trump can win or if he does how he would govern. Who can say what's really in his mind and heart or if, in God's eyes, he's a good man or a bad one. But given the dire warning from the likes of Mitt Romney, I like the odds with Trump better than with any of the available alternatives. When the character of his enemies is considered—particularly Warfare State neoconservatives (some of whom at least have the honesty to defect openly to Hillary)—my willingness to gamble on him only increases.

Even in retrospect it was then a gamble worth taking, indeed the only responsible choice given the horrifying alternative. More, given what Trump promised that departed from the usual nonsense served up by the GOP, the fact that Trump got the nomination instead of the NPCs on the shelf was itself perhaps a sign of that the historic American nation still had a fighting chance.

As for what we hoped he might deliver to "Make America Great Again," we can see now that the answers to all of the above questions are and will remain an emphatic No. Sure, we got a marginally better tax bill passed, something that any Republican White House and Congress would have done. He may have made minor progress on trade. If we are really lucky, he'll get another Supreme Court pick and *Roe v. Wade* will be overturned—marvelous to be sure, but it won't save this country.

Trump has utterly failed to control the border, much less deal with related issues like remittances, birthright citizenship, and aliens illegally voting. As retired Army Colonel Douglas Macgregor observes: "Surely, Trump should have concluded by now that without an Executive Order that commits the U.S. Army to the defense of the southern border and limits cross-border traffic to legitimate commercial activity, mass illegal immigration will not stop. . . . In a word, Trump refuses to take command and match rhetoric with action, then he will join the pantheon of failed presidents that promised the world only, this time, the American Republic's existence hangs in the balance."

Unfortunately, Trump's appointees—uniformly neoconservatives, Bush-era warmongers, and GOP *apparatchiki*—have better things for our military to do than defending our own country, to which they are at best indifferent. We can be thankful that Trump hasn't started any new wars, *yet*, but his underlings' dogged commitment to regime change in Venezuela and Iran may change that. His outreach to North Korea hangs by a thread in the face of blatant attempts to sabotage it.

One hopes that at least some animal-level gut instinct will preclude Trump's crossing that dark river and ruining what's left of his presidency as George W. Bush did in Iraq. If his lunatics are reckless enough to stumble us into a war with Russia, Trump's reelection will be the least of anyone's concerns.

Even without a war his remaining time in office will not be the revival of America that he promised. Let's keep in mind that for many decades now transformative Democratic presidents have not left this country the same way they found it: FDR, LBJ, Clinton, Obama. By contrast, Republican presidents' tenures have been at best plateaus along our decline (Eisenhower, Reagan) or positively contributed (Nixon, the two Bushes) to the march of what the Left regards as "Progress" toward their abolition of the historic America and birth of a dystopian Cultural Marxist dictatorship of victims: a borderless, multi-ethnic, multilingual, multireligious, multisexual, ahistorical, fake country.

Perhaps the saddest thing is that even if he survives in office until the 2020 vote (and he might not) Trump still will almost certainly be the lesser of two evils, in the manner to which we have become accustomed. Despite his no longer representing a threat to the Swamp, the critters will continue to hate him anyway as an avatar of the America they seek to destroy: European ethnicity, Christian (culturally if not spiritually or morally), English-speaking, toxically masculine. He might even win, given the Wall Street and Democratic Socialist Democrats' ripping each other's guts out and the solid 35 to 40 percent of the folks who think from Trump's tweets and stump speeches he's actually delivering on his promises.

Either way, though, the outcome will be the same. The man who had what is almost certainly to have been the last peaceful, political chance save what's left of the American republic will thrash around for a few more years, having become little more than a catalyst for our nation's demise and perhaps its dissolution.

This is not to say that there is no hope. Maybe tomorrow Trump will pardon Assange. Maybe he'll decide to militarize the Mexican border. Maybe he'll fire his whole national security team and, for good measure, pull us out of Afghanistan, Syria, Iraq—and NATO. Maybe Barr really will hold the FISA miscreants to account. Maybe . . .

. . . maybe there will be an outpouring of miracles that match the one that occurred when Trump improbably was elected in the first place. But as is the case with miracles, the odds are not good.

"Trump Will Be Impeached. The Stupid Party Says, 'Bring It On!'"

Jim Jatras | *Strategic Culture* | June 1, 2019

In the wake of Robert Mueller's calculated handoff of the "Get Trump" portfolio to the Democrat-controlled House of Representatives, two things are evident.

First, President Donald J. Trump is virtually certain to be impeached. That's manifest despite doddering House Speaker Nancy Pelosi's playing cute for now, seeking to ensure first that "we do want to make such a compelling case, such an ironclad case that even the Republican Senate, which at the time seems to be not an objective jury, will be convinced." Translation: We don't have the goods yet, but we expect to.

Second, like generals proverbially fighting the last war—namely, Republicans' failed 1998 effort to oust Bill Clinton—many in the GOP have convinced themselves that a Trump impeachment will be unsuccessful and will only hurt the Democrats. Put another way, the Stupid Party once again rises to the occasion. Cue Karl Rove:

> Knowing what they know today, if House Democrats move forward on the impeachment of President Trump, five things will happen.
>
> First, swing voters will conclude the Democrats are conducting a highly partisan exercise.
>
> Second, impeachment talk will largely or completely obscure anything else House Democrats will do legislatively. Voters could decide the Democrats are a do-nothing bunch.
>
> Third, impeachment will play a much larger role in the Democratic presidential primary. The issue of impeachment will obscure the other messages of the Democratic presidential hopefuls and raise the prospect of a backlash against candidates like former Vice President Joe Biden and Sen. Bernie Sanders of Vermont, who have yet to embrace impeachment.
>
> Fourth, the Republican Senate will quickly dismiss any impeachment resolution passed by the House, killing the issue.
>
> And finally, any of the dozens of vulnerable House Democrats in Republican-leaning districts who back impeachment will have given their GOP opponents a big issue.

Make no mistake, while the Democrats hope to wound Trump even if the attempt to remove him fails, they are deadly serious that they have a realistic shot at finishing him off. Moreover, they know that removing him by impeachment is a better prospect than beating him at the polls.

The Democrats are not at all sure about winning in 2020, not least because of the pathetic gaggle of so-called candidates they've got to offer. Thus their main goal in pursuing impeachment will not be to weaken Trump for 2020, it is—still—to get him out of the White House.

That's because, as was the case in 2016, Trump's the only GOP candidate who has a shot at winning. The Democrats want a sure thing. Having underestimated him in 2016 they don't want to roll the dice again. Even though Trump has not turned out to be the transformative president that many of his supporters might have hoped for, he certainly will be the lesser of evils compared to whoever ends up the Democratic nominee. (Spoiler alert: it won't be Tulsi Gabbard.) Worse from their point of view, he remains a toxic avatar of the old America they thought well and truly laid to rest once and for all. They can't breathe easy while he remains in office lest he, however unlikely in view of his failures of performance, serve as a catalyst for revival of the historic American nation facing extinction at the hands of certified victim classes.

Rove refers to the Democrats' "knowing what they know today," but Pelosi has made it clear that they intend to know a lot more before they pull the trigger. All the fluff over "obstruction" is just to keep the pot boiling while they get to the real meat and potatoes. Let House Judiciary Committee Chairman Jerry Nadler and House Intelligence [sic] Committee Adam Schiff yammer about obstruction while multiple committees and New York state and city prosecutors keep digging: taxes, business skullduggery in New York real estate, babes, racism. Remember, they don't need to find a *crime*, only something that will give enough Republicans in the Senate an excuse to give Trump the heave-ho.

Rove says the "Republican Senate will quickly dismiss any impeachment resolution passed by the House." That's nonsense, and Rove knows it. The relevant analogue to the upcoming Trump impeachment isn't Clinton 1998, it's Richard Nixon 1974. Bill Clinton literally could have raped Juanita Broaddrick in the middle of Fifth Avenue in broad daylight and the Democrats still would have circled the wagons to defend him, as they in fact did, without a single Democratic vote to convict. As it hardly needs be added, the media unanimously supported them.

Nixon, however, was done in by his own party when Senate GOP leaders told Tricky Dick (loathed by most of his party, as Trump is) that he had to resign or they would vote to remove him. That's because Republicans are not only the Stupid Party, they're the Cowardly Party. Depending on what the Democrats dig up on Trump, Republicans can be counted on to see scary editorials in the *Washington Post* and *New York Times* and run away in panic: "I've always been supportive of the president, but I can't defend *that*. So I have no choice but to . . . ."

Add in the fact that between a quarter and a third of GOP Senators would jump at the chance to put a knife in Trump's back if they got the opportunity, with prospective Brutus and sanctimonious warmonger Mitt Romney at the front of the line. At the appropriate time, establishment Republican poobahs like Rove will join them, basking in media praise for "putting country above party."

Note that this is *not* a prediction that Trump *will* be removed, only that his impeachment will not be necessarily the futile exercise some claim because of the GOP majority in the Senate. It's possible Trump will survive. The Democrats might come up empty on the required dirt. They may fall short of the number of Republicans they need to give him the "Nixon talk." Even if Trump is given an ultimatum, he may decide, unlike Nixon, to fight—and he might actually win. But don't take it as a given that impeachment won't be a serious attempt to remove Trump that will only backfire on the Democrats. It might succeed.

If it doesn't, with the advantages of incumbency Trump's chances of winning reelection are better than even, though the landscape has become less favorable than it was in 2016. His base remains strong (most of his Deplorables think he's actually delivering on his promises, because he says so in tweets and at his rallies. Look at that big, beautiful invisible nonexistent Wall! Winning!). On the other hand, failure to control our border means the demographic shift against Republicans has continued unabated, coupled with zero efforts to police voting by non-citizens and (notably in Florida) letting felons vote. If Trump loses either Florida or Pennsylvania, it's probably all over even with a lousy Democratic opponent. That's aside from whatever economic hiccup might occur between now and next fall. Or if Trump gets us into a war somewhere.

Finally, let's note what was the most important substantive message from Mueller's swan song: Russia! Russia! Russia! Mueller both began and ended his ramble with a denunciation of Russia's supposed attack on the United States in 2016. Citing Mueller, Ranking Democrat on the Senate Intelligence [sic] Committee Mark Warner has called for redoubled efforts to pass "legislation that enhances election security, increases social media transparency": a dog-whistle for the real threat to honest elections: using "Russian bots" and "hate speech" as justification for tech companies' clampdown on dissent. Whatever happens to Trump, our dangerous enmity with Russia is permanent—and possibly passing the point of no return—while erosion of Americans' freedoms will continue apace.

"We Live in Hysteric Times: What Trump's Impeachment Really Means"

Jim Jatras | *Strategic Culture* | December 21, 2019

> *"America is a corpse being consumed by maggots. Liberals are rooting for the maggots. Conservatives are rooting for the corpse."*
> *@Vendee_Rising*

For a century and a half American political life has been the exclusive preserve of the duopoly of Democrats and Republicans, also known as the Evil Party and the Stupid Party. (If something is both Evil and Stupid, we call that "Bipartisan.") But the familiar Evil-Stupid dichotomy doesn't even begin to describe the descent into national dysfunction and galloping irrationality that characterizes the Trump impeachment hysteria.

Media chatter now centers on the nuts-and-bolts questions of "what's next?" Will House Speaker Nancy Pelosi send the articles of impeachment over to the Senate? (Yes. Even one of the legal "scholars" enrolled in the impeachment lynch mob avers that Trump isn't actually impeached until the Senate receives the articles.) Who will be the trial managers? (Who cares.) Will there be a "real trial," with witnesses? (It hardly matters.) Will Trump be removed? (Unlikely unless some bolt from the blue flips 20 GOP Senators.) Will impeachment be the Democrats' albatross going into November 2020? (Most polls show independents are turned off, but there's still almost a year to go.)

None of these questions, which are meaningful only in a mental universe of the Evils and the Stupids shadowboxing over a partisan allocation of political spoils, touch upon the grim—and occasionally sardonic—symptoms of America's seemingly unstoppable terminal slide.

With Trump's impeachment it's time to say goodbye to yesteryear's Team Evil and Team Stupid. Say hello in 2020 to Team Maggot and Team Corpse!

Even though Trump has not turned out to be the transformative and restorative president that many of his supporters might have hoped for, he certainly will be (assuming he survives impeachment, which he probably will) the lesser of evils in November 2020 compared to whoever ends up as the Maggot Party nominee. Worse from his opponents' point of view, he remains a toxic avatar of the old America they thought would be well and truly laid to rest for ever and ever, amen, when Hillary Clinton came into her kingdom. That having misfired in 2016, partisans of that legacy America's marginalization, displacement, and eventual extinction can't breathe easy while Trump remains in office lest he, however unlikely in view of his failures of performance, serve as a catalyst for revival of the historic American nation facing loss of its birthright: an organic, uncontrived, living *ethnos* characterized by European, mainly British origin (a/k/a, "white"); Christian, mainly Protestant; and English-speaking, as augmented by members of other groups who have totally or partially assimilated to it. The certified victim classes standing on the threshold of the permanent, total power that eluded them

three years ago are haunted by the knowledge that *there's still lots of them Muricans in red MAGA hats rallying to Trump out there in Flyover Country.*
. . .

In short, Democrats hate Trump not so much for what he's done (which, contrary to what his passionate supporters think based on his Tweets, isn't much) but as an expression of an amorphous dread that by some mysterious populist alchemy he might still breathe life back into the Corpse Party's deplorable base. With that in mind, here are a few things to note as we cruise on into Bizarro World:

- *"What do you mean 'we,' white man?"* As the impeachment spectacle unfolded in the House, one could not fail to be touched by the hushed, heartfelt reverence with which Democrat after Democrat cited the sage words of the Founding Fathers: Madison especially, but also Jefferson and Washington. No doubt they can hardly wait for this spectacle to be over so they can go back to denouncing the Founders as dead, racist, Christian, patriarchal, "Anglo," and (presumably) heterosexual slave-holders in wigs and knee-breeches whose memory should be expunged from the historical record. It's instructive to glance at the members of the House Judiciary Committee who—solemnly, reluctantly, and prayerfully, they assure us!—voted out articles of impeachment in the name of "the American people." But which "people" might that be? Of the 23 Demo-crats who voted, *only four* even arguably fit the heritage American, male profile of the Founding Fathers. The "gender balance" (as it's ungram-matically called nowadays) on the voting majority side of the Committee is 12–11. That's not quite up to Barack Obama's exhortation that "every nation on earth" should be "run by women," but it's progress in that direction! (Just imagine how much more serene the world would be if all countries were ruled by peaceniks like Hillary Clinton, Madeleine Albright, Condi Rice, Susan Rice, Samantha Power, Anne-Marie Slaugh-ter, Michèle Flournoy, Evelyn Farkas, etc., plus a bevy of Deep State Democrats now installed in Congress.) By contrast, the 17 Republicans on the Committee have approximately the same demographic composition they'd have had in 1950—and aside from the inclusion of two women, that of the First Congress seated in 1789.

In short, in the Congressional Maggot Caucus the approaching Dictatorship of Victims defined by race, sex, ethnicity, sexual orientation, language, religion, migratory status, etc., is already becoming a reality, and they voted to get rid of Trump. Members of the Corpse Caucus defending him still belong demo-graphically and morally to the declining legacy America, though they'd never, ever admit it. Impeachment is thus more than just the latest iteration of the years-long anti-constitutional coup to overturn a presidential election, though it is that too. Even more fundamentally, it's a coup against the people whose identity, traditions, and values the Constitution was intended to ensure for themselves and their posterity.

- *Foreign interference in our deMOCKracy.* Even more absurd than Dem-ocrats' presumption in lip-synching the venerable principles of an Ameri-can constitutional tradition they despise almost as much as they loathe the *ethnos* that ordained and established it is their feigned horror—horror!—that Trump's phone chat with Ukraine's Volodymyr Zelensky realized the Founders' worst fears of *foreign* influence over American domestic politics. Leaving aside the fact that Ukraine under Zelensky's predecessor, Petro Poroshenko, *did* try to queer the 2016 election in favor of Hillary, and that Hunter and Joe Biden *are* crooks, the Maggoteers' ability to maintain a straight face of shocked indignation smack in the middle of a souk, a flea market, a bazaar where both domestic and foreign interests buy, sell, and trade favors like vintage baseball cards is nothing less than heroic.

While the bipartisan leadership has not yet taken up the helpful suggestion that barcodes be affixed to legislators' foreheads so that interested persons and organizations can conveniently scan prices and self-checkout, they have provided a helpful guide to what are called "Congressional Member Organizations (CMOs)," also called coalitions, study groups, task forces, or working groups. Memberships in many but not all CMOs serve as virtual barcodes for potential (mostly legal) campaign donors, including, in the case of "friends of" this or that foreign country, contributions from ethnic compatriots who are US citizens, or at least are supposed to be. Here's a partial selection:

- Argentina Caucus, Armenian Issues Caucus, Azerbaijan Caucus, Bangladesh Caucus, Bosnia Caucus, Brazil Caucus, Cambodia Caucus, Central America Caucus, Colombia Caucus, Congressional Caucus on Bulgaria, Croatian Caucus, Czech Caucus, Ethiopian-American Caucus, Ethnic and Religious Freedom in Sri Lanka, EU Caucus, Friends of Australia Caucus, Friends of Denmark Caucus, Friends of Egypt Caucus, Friends of Finland Caucus, Friends of Ireland Caucus, Friends of Liechtenstein Caucus, Friends of New Zealand Caucus, Friends of Norway Caucus, Friends of Scotland Caucus, Friends of Spain Caucus, Friends of Sweden Caucus, Friends of the Dominican Republic Caucus, Friends of Wales Caucus, Georgia Caucus, Hellenic Caucus, Hellenic Israel Alliance Caucus, House Baltic Caucus, Hungarian Caucus, India and Indian Americans Caucus, Iraq Caucus, Israel Allies Caucus, Israel Victory Caucus, Kingdom of Netherlands Caucus, Korea Caucus, Kyrgyzstan Caucus, Macedonia and Macedonian-American Caucus, Moldova Caucus, Mongolia Caucus, Montenegro Caucus, Morocco Caucus, Nigeria Caucus, Pakistan Caucus, Peru Caucus, Poland Caucus, Portuguese Caucus, Qatari-American Strategic Relationships Caucus, Republican Israel Caucus, Romania Caucus, Serbian Caucus, Slovak Caucus, Sri Lanka Caucus, Taiwan Caucus, UK Caucus, Ukraine Caucus, U.S.-Bermuda Friendship Caucus, U.S.-China Working Group, U.S.-Japan Caucus, U.S.-Kazakhstan Caucus, U.S.-Lebanon Friendship Caucus, U.S.-Philippines Friendship Caucus, U.S.-Turkey Relations and Turkish American, Uzbekistan Caucus, Venezuela Democracy Caucus

Recalling Your Working Boy's years at the State Department—where there still exists no "American Interests Section"—the reader can search the above in vain for anything that looks remotely like "Friends of the United States of America."

- *Russia! Russia! Russia!* In fact, the Democrats' core impeachment narrative—Russia bad, Ukraine good—is itself an example to which American policy is in the grip of foreign antipathies and attachments against which the Father of Our Country warned us in his 1796 farewell address:

    "[N]othing is more essential than that permanent, inveterate antipathies against particular nations, and passionate attachments for others, should be excluded; and that, in place of them, just and amicable feelings towards all should be cultivated. The nation which indulges towards another a habitual hatred or a habitual fondness is in some degree a slave. It is a slave to its animosity or to its affection, either of which is sufficient to lead it astray from its duty and its interest."

In his closing statement before the impeachment vote House Judiciary Chairmaggot Adam "Captain Ahab" Schiff, in his frenzied hunt for the Great Orange Whale, provided a textbook example of what Washington feared:

"[W]e should care about our allies. We should care about Ukraine. We should care about a country struggling to be free and a Democracy. We used to care about Democracy. We used to care about our allies. We used to stand up to Putin and Russia. We used to. I know the party of Ronald Reagan used to. 'Why should we care about Ukraine?' But of course it's about more than Ukraine. It's about us. It's about our national security. Their fight is our fight. Their defense is our defense. When Russia remakes the map of Europe for the first time since World War II by dint of military force [JGJ: Well, there was Kosovo, but never mind . . .] and Ukraine fights back, it is our fight too."

Indeed, one wonders how hysterical Democrats missed accusing Trump outright of *treason*, which actually is specified as grounds for impeachment in Article II, Section 4. After all, as described by Schiff, didn't Trump's actions constitute (under Article III, Section 3) "adhering" to our evil enemies the Russians, and "giving them aid and comfort"? It's an open and shut case of a capital crime—and the House Majority Whip is ready to get the rope! (Really, how did the Democrats miss this? Maybe GOP stupidity has migrated to the other side of the aisle. . . .)

It is noteworthy that not a single House Republican dared or even cared to question Schiff's framing of the issue, which was bolstered by witnesses from the permanent military, intelligence, and diplomatic establishment, including Trump's appointees. Nor is any Republican Senator likely to point out the inconvenient truth that we have no defense treaty with Ukraine, which thus is not really our "ally." Partisanship is the variable; Russophobia is the constant. The sole retort from Trump's establishment defenders: *He released the aid to Ukraine, including the Javelin missiles Obama denied them! He's every bit the warmonger you want him to be! So there!*

Thus, even with Trump's almost (at this point) certain survival of a Senate impeachment trial, the relevant foreign inveterate antipathies and passionate attachments will remain entrenched. (Not just in the case of Ukraine/Russia but with respect to the rest of the world our habitual hatreds and fondnesses remain firmly in place and are unlikely to change for the balance of Trump's presidency, if ever. Trump's Korea initiative is on life support. Israel/Iran is a flashpoint that could explode at any time: "Israel, even less than the US, cannot take casualties. A couple of bull's eyes, a lot of Israelis go back to Brooklyn. The 82 million people in Iran have no place else to go.")

Senate Demaggotic Leader Chuck Schumer gave the game away when he demanded that the World Greatest Deliberative Body receive testimony from cashiered National Security Adviser John Bolton and acting White House Chief of Staff Mick Mulvaney but *not* from the man at the center of the whole Ukraine "drug deal" (as Bolton described it): Rudy Giuliani. Why wouldn't the assembled Maggotrats jump at the chance to grill him under oath? Because he'd dole out the real dirt on Ukraine and its legendary corruption that would make a Nigerian prince blush. For the same reason, Corpsublicans won't want to hear from him either, any more than they're interested in whether the "sub-sources" of the Steele Dossier—whose identity the US Justice Department knows and who were available to the IG's investigators—really had anything to do with the Russian government. We wouldn't want to debunk all that yammering about "fake Kremlin dirt," would we.

Meanwhile, back in what remains of America, regardless of how impeachment turns out, the lines of irreconcilable division deepen. Whether or not Trump is reelected (the politics look good for him, the demographics don't) he will eventually be gone, whether in 2020, 2021, or 2025. He will almost certainly be the last Republican president, depending on when Texas goes the way of Virginia. One way or the other, we'll soon see whether the corpse has any fight left in it.

"Before the Bidens 'Did' Ukraine, There Was Iraq—and Serbia"

Jim Jatras | *Strategic Culture* |October 16, 2020

The United States approaches the November 2020 election with growing apprehension, even dread. Among the possibilities:

- Protracted uncertainty about the presidential contest. Think Florida 2000 but with several states' results unresolved for weeks or even months ("Experts held 'war games' on the Trump vs. Biden election. Their finding? Brace for a mess");
- A disputed outcome, perhaps with Donald Trump and Joe Biden both claiming victory, compounded by a "blue shift," where states are claimed by Trump on election night but flip over to Biden as additional absentee and mail-in ballots conveniently turn up days or weeks later;
- Violent civil conflict, spurred on in the streets by goon squads mobilized and funded by a *Who's Who* of the corporate and foundation establishment; and
- A color revolution style regime change operation staged by groups like the Soros-linked "Transition Integrity Project" and managed by people like "legal hatchet man" Norm Eisen, perhaps culminating in a military coup to remove Trump and install Biden in the Oval Office (as detailed by former Virginia State Senator and Judge Advocate General officer Richard Black).

For those who have followed events outside the United States during the past few decades, much of this sounds familiar. We've seen it before—inflicted on other countries.

Now It's Coming Home to the U.S.

As explained by *Revolver News*, what happens in America next to a great extent may be a form of *blowback* from a specific event: the U.S.-supported 2014 regime change operation in Ukraine:

A "Color Revolution" in this context refers to a specific type of coordinated attack that the United States government has been known to deploy against foreign regimes, particularly in Eastern Europe deemed to be "authoritarian" and hostile to American interests. Rather than using a direct military intervention to effect regime change as in Iraq, Color Revolutions attack a foreign regime by contesting its electoral legitimacy, organizing mass protests and acts of civil disobedience, and leveraging media contacts to ensure favorable coverage to their agenda in the Western press.

It would be disturbing enough to note a coordinated effort to use these exact same strategies and tactics domestically to undermine or overthrow President Trump. The ominous nature of what we see unfolding before us only truly hits home when one realizes that the people who specialize in these Color Revolution regime change operations overseas are, literally, the *very same people* attempting to overthrow Trump by using the *very same playbook*. Given that the most famous Color Revolution was the [2004] "Orange Revolution" in the Ukraine, and that Black Lives Matter is being used as a key component of the domestic Color Revolution against Trump, we can encapsulate our thesis at Revolver with the simple remark that "Black is the New Orange."

This hardly should come as a surprise. The same government agencies and their corporate, NGO, and think tank cronies that are now weaponizing Black Lives Matter, Antifa, other Wokesters, and military putsch plotters here at home to remove Trump have turned regime change abroad into an art form. Ukraine was one of their signal successes, featuring a cast of characters later key to the failed "Ukrainegate" impeachment.

Another consequence of regime change: corruption. As the old saying goes, any idiot can turn an aquarium into fish soup, but no one has yet figured out how to reverse the process. Once a country gets broken it tends to stay broken, whether the "breaking" is accomplished by military means (Serbia 1999, Iraq 2003, Libya 2011) or by a color revolution from the streets (Serbia 2000, Georgia 2003, Ukraine 2004–2005 and again in 2014, Kyrgyzstan 2005, Lebanon 2005, Armenia 2018, plus many others of varying degrees of success, and failures in Iran, Russia, Venezuela, China (Hong Kong), and Belarus). With the target nation's institutions in shambles, the dregs take over—in Libya, for example, even to the point of reintroducing trade in sub-Saharan African slaves, whose black lives evidently don't *matter* to anyone at all.

Iraq: Crush, Corrupt, Cash In

Finally, once regime change occurs and corruption is rampant, another shoe drops: foreign vultures descend on the carcass, profiteers who in many cases are *the very same people that helped to create the chaos on which they are cashing in*. Invariably, these carpetbaggers are well-connected individuals in the aggressor states and organizations positioned on the inside track both for the carve-up of the target country's resources and (the word "hypocrisy" doesn't begin to describe it) for funds to implement "reform" and "recon-struction" of the devastated target.

The showcase of this scam, pursuant to Colin Powell's reported "Pottery Barn Rule" (*You break it, you own it*) was the money ostensibly spent on rebuilding Iraq, despite assurances from the war's advocates that it would pay for itself. With the formal costs conservatively set at over $60 billion to $138 billion out of a tab for the war of over two trillion dollars, the lion's share of it went to U.S. and other vendors, including the notorious $1.4 billion no-bid contract to Halliburton subsidiary KBR, of which then-Vice President Dick Cheney, a major proponent of the war, had been a top executive. ("Rand Paul Says Dick Cheney Pushed for the Iraq War So Halliburton Would Profit.")

In Ukraine, Biden's Son Also Rises

The predatory cronyism vignette most pertinent to the Black/Orange regime change op now unfolding before us with the intent of installing Joe Biden in the Oval Office is that of his son, Hunter, and a Ukrainian energy company with a sketchy reputation, Burisma Holdings. (Right at the outset, even some of Hunter's associates thought the gig with Burisma was too "toxic" and broke off ties with him.) Though ignored or dismissed as fake news and a conspiracy theory by Democrats and legacy media (or do I repeat myself?), the facts are well enough known and fit the Iraq pattern to a T: then-Vice President Joe Biden pushed for regime change in Ukraine, which succeeded in February 2014 with the ouster of the constitutionally elected president, Viktor Yanu-kovych. In April 2014, Joe Biden's son, Hunter, was brought onto Burisma's board (along with a fellow named Devon Archer, later convicted of unrelated fraud) at an exorbitant level of compensation that made little sense in light of Hunter's nonexistent expertise in the energy business—but which made plenty of sense given that his dad was not only Veep but the Obama administration's point man on policy toward Ukraine, including foreign assistance money. [NOTE: It now has come out that in 2015 Hunter put his dad, the U.S. Vice President, in direct contact with Burisma, news the giant tech firms sought to suppress on social media.]

When a troublesome Ukrainian prosecutor named Viktor Shokin seemed to be taking too much interest in Burisma, Papa Joe came to the rescue, openly threatening the western-dependent politicians installed after Ukraine's 2014 color revolution with withholding of a billion dollars in U.S. aid until Shokin, whom Joe unironically alleged to be "corrupt," got the heave-ho. As Tucker Carlson nails it, Shokin's ouster followed a direct request from Burisma's Clinton-connected PR firm, Blue Star Strategies, to Hunter to lobby his dad to get Shokin off their back. Joe did just what was asked. He later bragged: "I said, 'You're not getting the billion. I'm going to be leaving here [i.e., Kiev] in, I think it was about six hours.' I looked at them and said, 'I'm leaving in six hours. If the prosecutor is not fired, you're not getting the money.' Well, son of a bitch. He got fired."

But First There Was Serbia

Today many people remember Iraq, some have a clue about Ukraine. But Serbia, which preceded them, is off the radar screen of most Americans. To recap:

As a Senator in the 1990s, Joe Biden was one of the most militant advocates of U.S. military action against Serbs during the breakup of the Yugoslav federation, first in Croatia (1991–95), then in Bosnia (1992–95), and then in Serbia's province of Kosovo (1998–1999). (As has been said about others like Hillary Clinton and the late John McCain, Biden evidently has never met a war he didn't like. Along with Hillary, in 2003 Biden helped to whip Senate Democrat votes for the Bush-Cheney Iraq war.) Channeling his inner John McCain, Biden continually called for the U.S. to bomb, bomb, bomb, bomb the Serbs while (in a foreshadowing of the Obama-Biden administration's support for jihad terrorists in Libya and Syria, which ultimately resulted in the appearance of ISIS) pushed successfully for sending weapons to the Islamist regime in Bosnia and then for the U.S. to arm the Islamo-narco-terrorist group known as the "Kosovo Liberation Army" (KLA).

Joe Biden was the primary sponsor of the March 1999 Kosovo war authorization for military action against Serbia and Montenegro, S. Con. Res. 21. (As a little remembered historical note, Biden's resolution might be seen as the last nail in the coffin of Congress's constitutional war power. While S. Con. Res 21 passed the Senate, it failed in the House on a 213–213 tie vote, with Republicans overwhelmingly voting Nay. It didn't matter. Bill Clinton, reeling from the Lewinsky scandal, went ahead with the bombing campaign anyway.) The ensuing 78-day NATO air operation had little impact on Serbia's military but devastated the country's infrastructure and took hundreds of civilian lives. (Even now, more than 20 years later, Serbia suffers from elevated cancer levels attributed to depleted uranium munitions.) But for Jihad Joe even that wasn't punishment enough for people he collectively demonized as "illiterate degenerates, baby killers, butchers, and rapists." In May 1999, at the height of the NATO air assault, he called for the introduction of U.S. ground troops ("we should announce there's going to be American casualties") followed by "a Japanese-German style occupation."

Eventually the bombing stopped in June 1999 when then-Serbian strongman Slobodan Milošević acceded to temporary international occupation of Kosovo on the condition that the province would remain part of Serbia, as codified in United Nations Security Council Resolution 1244. It was a promise the U.S. and NATO, not to mention their European Union (EU) concubine, had no intention of keeping. Under the nose of the NATO occupation, ostensibly demobilized KLA thugs were given virtually free rein to terrorize the Serbian population, two-thirds of whom were driven out along with Jews and Roma, the rest sheltering in enclaves where they remain to this day. Orthodox Christian churches and monasteries, many of them centuries old, were particular targets for destruction and desecration. KLA commanders—who were also kingpins in the Kosovo Albanian mafia dealing in sex slaves, drugs, weapons, and even human organs—were handed local administration.

In 2007 Senator Biden praised the new order as a "victory for Muslim democracy" and "a much-needed example of a successful U.S.-Muslim partnership." A year later, the Bush administration sought to complete the job by ramming through Kosovo's independence in barefaced violation of UNSCR 1244 and despite strong Russian objections. But instead of resolving anything the result was a frozen conflict that persists today, with about half of the United Nations' member states recognizing Kosovo and half not. Touting itself as the most pro-American "country" [sic] in the world, the Kosovo pseudo-state became a prime recruiting ground for ISIS.

But hey, business was good! Just as in Iraq, the politically well-connected, including former officials instrumental in the attack on Serbia and occupying Kosovo, flocked to the province fueled by lavish aid subsidies from the U.S. and the EU, which for a while made Kosovo one of the biggest per capita foreign assistance recipient "countries" in the world. One such vulture—sorry, entrepreneur—was former Secretary of State Madeleine we-think-a-half-million-dead-Iraqi-children-is-worth-it Albright, a prominent driver of the Clinton administration's hostile policy on top of her personal Serb-hatred. Albright sought to cash in to the tune of hundreds of millions of dollars on the sale of the mobile telephone company PTK, originally a Yugoslav state-owned firm that was "privatized" (i.e., stolen) in 2005 as a joint stock company, but she later dropped her bid when it attracted unwanted publicity. Also in the hunt for Kosovo riches was former NATO Supreme Commander and operational chief of the Kosovo war General Wesley Clark, who reportedly cornered a major share of the occupied province's coal resources under a sweetheart deal that seems to have vanished from public scrutiny since first reported in 2016.

At the moment there seems to be no smoking gun of a direct Biden family payout, à la Ukraine, but there is a possible trail via Hunter's Burisma-buddy Devon Archer and Archer's fellow-defendant John "Yanni" Galanis, who in turn is connected to top Kosovo Albanian politicians. In any case, the Biden clan seems to have paid a lot of attention to Kosovo for not having skin in the game. Joe's late son and Delaware Attorney General, Beau, worked in Kosovo following the war to train local prosecutors as part of an OSCE (Organisation for Security and Cooperation in Europe) "rule of law" mission (admittedly a big task in a mafia-run pseudo-state), for which a road was named after him near the massive U.S. base Camp Bondsteel. With Hunter on hand for the naming ceremony, Joe Biden took the opportunity to express his "condolences" to Serbian families who lost loved ones in the NATO air assault—of which he was a primary advocate.

A "Shokin" Demand

Perhaps the best parallel between Biden's handiwork in Ukraine and his interest in Kosovo also relates to getting rid of an inconvenient individual. But in this case, the person in question wasn't a state official like Burisma prosecutor Viktor Shokin but a hierarch of the Serbian Orthodox Church.

In May 2009 Vice President Biden insisted on visiting one of Kosovo's most venerable Serbian Orthodox Christian sites, the Visoki Dečani monastery. Ruling Bishop Artemije of the Eparchy of Raška and Prizren, which includes Kosovo and Metohija, refused to give his blessing for the visit, in effect telling Biden he was not welcome. Bishop Artemije long had been a bane of Biden and others advocating detachment of Kosovo from Serbia, starting with his first mission to Washington in 1997 as war clouds gathered. In 2004 Bishop Artemije sued the NATO powers in the European Court of Human Rights in Strasbourg following their inaction to protect his flock during an anti-Serbian rampage by Muslim Albanian militants in March of that year. Then, in March 2006, as preparations were underway for a "final solution" to the Kosovo issue, Bishop Artemije launched an intensive multinational lobbying and public relations effort (in which Yours Truly was the lead professional) to try to derail the U.S. policy to which Biden had devoted so much attention. While the Bishop's campaign was unsuccessful in reversing U.S. policy it was instrumental in delaying it for over a year—to howls of outrage from Biden's associates in Washington. Thus, for Biden, the monastery visit snub by Bishop Artemije was adding insult to injury.

The end for Bishop Artemije came a few months later, at the beginning of 2010, at the time of two visits to Kosovo by U.S. Admiral Mark P. Fitzgerald, then Commander, U.S. Naval Forces Europe and Africa, and Commander, Allied Joint Force Command (JFC) Naples (who retired later that year, becoming, unsurprisingly, a consultant "with numerous defense and comercial maritime and aviation contractors"). At that time, an unconfirmed report indicated that a high NATO officer (whether Admiral Fitzgerald or someone else is not specified) stated in the course of one of his local meetings (this is verbatim or a close paraphrase): "What we need here is a more cooperative bishop." (More details are available here. Since that posting last year the NATO command in Naples seems to have scrubbed the items about Fitzgerald's 2010 visits from their site.)

Shortly afterwards, Biden's troublesome priest was forcibly removed by police and exiled from his see, without ecclesiastical trial, by Church authorities in Belgrade under pressure from compliant Serbian politicians installed after the October 2000 color revolution, in turn pressured by NATO. The pretext? Transparently baseless charges of financial wrongdoing. In other words, bogus accusations of "corruption"—like against Ukraine's Shokin.

One could almost hear Joe Biden chortle: "Well, son of a bitch. He got fired."

But Look at the Bright Side. . .

Back to the incipient coup facing the United States, there should be no illusion that what's at stake in the unfolding scenario for the removal of Donald Trump is not just his presidency but the survival of the historic American *ethnos* of which he is seen as an avatar by both his supporters and detractors. Remember, we're dealing with predators and scavengers who are happy to burn the old, evil America down as long as they can achieve total power and continue to feather their cushy nests. Short of a blowout Trump victory by a margin too big to hijack, we're headed for a dystopian state of affairs.

If they do manage to remove Trump, "by any means necessary," and Joe Biden takes the helm, we can anticipate a bevy of globalist warmonger appointees that make Trump's team look like disciples of Mahatma Gandhi. Among the names floated like Nicholas Burns, Antony Blinken, Michele Flournoy, Evelyn Farkas, and Anne-Marie Slaughter, all were on board with Bosnia, Kosovo, Iraq, Libya, Ukraine, Syria . . . [NOTE: The Atlantic Council, known as NATO's semi-official think tank in Washington and which will be instrumental in staffing a future Joe Biden administration, also has been the beneficiary of generous donations from Hunter Biden's paymaster, Burisma.]

It's a recipe for wars, regime changes, and color revolutions galore.

But to finish on a positive note, the potential future business opportunities will be endless!

America First!

"Benevolent Global Hegemony"

James George Jatras | *Chronicles* | June 1997

Every once in a great while, an article appears in a mainstream publication that lets the cat out of the bag, by spelling out ideas that have long been dominant in public life but are usually seen only in vague or implicit form. One such appeared in the July/August 1996 edition of *Foreign Affairs*. Entitled "Toward a Neo-Reaganite Foreign Policy," it was intended as a blueprint for a Dole administration, and no doubt also a claim for high appointment for its authors, William Kristol and Robert Kagan, both editors of the neoconservative *Weekly Standard*. It could best be summed up as an appeal for America to become the embryo of a world empire.

The American role in the post-Cold War international order, according to Kristol and Kagan, should be "benevolent global hegemony." After defeating the "Evil Empire," the United States—

> enjoys strategic and ideological predominance. The first objective of our foreign policy should be to enhance that predominance by strengthening America's security, supporting its friends, advancing its interests, and standing up for its principles around the world. The aspiration to benevolent hegemony might strike some as morally suspect. But a hegemon is nothing more or less than a leader with preponderant influence and authority over all others in its domain. That is America's position in the world today.

Other powers, they argue, notably Russia and China, will bristle at American hegemony, but we should take their displeasure "as a compliment."

Predictably, the authors call for a military buildup unconnected to any identifiable military threat. They call for "citizen involvement," in effect, a militarization of the populace (in a complete perversion of the traditional citizen-soldier concept) and their seduction into the imperial enterprise: to "close the growing separation of civilian and military cultures in our society," to "involve more citizens in military service," to "lower the barriers between civilian and military life." Perhaps most disturbing about the Kristol/Kagan call to greatness is how they define our interests. "Americans," they write, "have never lived in a world more conducive to their fundamental interests in a liberal international order, the spread of freedom and democratic governance, [and] an international economic system of free-market capitalism and free trade." Of course, this has nothing to do with how we will preserve the traditional moral and economic interests of our own people or with keeping other powers out of our traditional empire in this hemisphere—what we usually mean by national interests—and everything to do with the blessings we will supposedly bestow upon the rest of benighted humanity, assumed to be, as Kipling put it, half devil and half child.

They continue: "American hegemony is the only reliable defense against a breakdown of peace and the international order. The appropriate goal of American foreign policy, therefore, is to preserve that hegemony as far into the future as possible." In sum, hegemony for hegemony's sake: we are obligated to take up the white man's burden, to take on the Sisyphean task of preserving the existing international order, seemingly forever. In fairness to the Republicans, it should be noted that there is greater uneasiness on the GOP right about this trend than there is on the Democratic left, whose noninterventionism seems to have evaporated with the demise of communism. Note the *New York Times'* piece (December 19, 1996) on Madeleine Albright's "Munich Mindset" by Owen Harries, editor of the *National Interest.* Harries takes Albright to task for her "enthusiasm for action [of an] apparently indiscriminate nature," her seeming to "favor intervention generally and on principle," and her viewing the world as "an endless series of Munich-like challenges." Whatever one might think of Colin Powell, one can only agree with Harries that the question she once put to the general—"What's the point of having this superb military that you're always talking about if we can't use it?"—is nothing less than simpleminded. Harries' warning fell on deaf ears as Albright was unanimously confirmed as Secretary of State by the Senate, 99 to nothing. For those who lament the demise of bipartisanship: Madame Albright meet Messrs. Kristol and Kagan, or for that matter, Jeane Kirkpatrick.

This is now the norm—Tweedledee Anthony Lewis, Tweedledum William Safire. Make no mistake, whatever ordinary Americans might think, the political, media, and intellectual elites, regardless of their party affiliation, are firmly behind America's global enterprise.

It is hard to believe that just a few decades ago, before 1914, the Western World—Europe, Christendom—little doubting its obvious superiority, cultural as well as technological, over all other peoples, exercised direct authority over virtually the entire world, over all other civilizations. The only serious exception was Islam, as represented by the Ottoman Empire, which was widely seen to be on its last legs; the Christian peoples of the Balkans had lately thrown off the Turkish yoke, and prospects loomed for the reconquest of Anatolia and the Levant.

All of this came crashing down in 1914. Due largely to the same arrogance that had fed the rush for empire, and which, with little modification, impels our contemporary neo-imperialists, the European powers embarked upon an orgy of autogenocide that probably has never been equaled at any time on any continent. And not content with that, they gave it another go 20 years later, and, at the conclusion of their second world war, they embarked upon the Cold War. The result is a civilization that is a shadow of its former self, crippled, wounded—perhaps fatally—that is culturally, morally, religiously moribund. Perhaps most telling, it is demographically moribund: when people refuse to produce offspring at even replacement level, this is sure evidence that the disease is terminal.

We are still living in the wreckage left from World War I. It is generally acknowledged that among its results was the spawning of two very similar, crassly materialistic, antitraditional ideologies, each of which had found a home in one of the defeated empires: Bolshevism in Russia and, largely a reaction to communism, National Socialism in Germany. The activities of these two states—twins, in many ways—and the other powers' concerns about them, were primarily the occasion of World War II; the activities of the twin that survived and expanded its power in that conflict, the Soviet Union, were the occasion of the ensuing Cold War. This much is obvious. But what is not generally acknowledged, and what perhaps is only now becoming obvious, is that the war did not produce (and by produce I mean serve as a catalyst, not cause: the roots are much deeper) just two such ideologies but three: the twins were actually triplets. While the third child of the war superficially resembled the old empires that had gone to war in 1914—there was still a king in London, the Third Republic continued to sputter along in France—what was missing was even the pretense that civilization rested upon the old certainties, primarily religious in origin, without which, it had been assumed, ordered and moral life was impossible. Men were no longer ashamed to admit they were atheists; after all, if God really existed, how could He have permitted that slaughter? The antitraditional impulse that had been growing for decades, perhaps centuries, before 1914, vastly accelerated after the war and, bit by bit, subtly but inexorably, established itself in academia, the media, and in government. Today it holds untrammeled sway over virtually all formerly Christian countries. What had once been apostasy had become the ruling religion.

As evidence, consider the celebrated article by Samuel Huntington, "The Clash of Civilizations?" in the June 1993 issue of *Foreign Affairs*. Huntington's thesis is that in the post-Cold War world the clash of ideologies (which had superseded, in turn, clashes among nation-states, dynasties, and religions) would itself be superseded by a clash of civilizations, which he designates as Western, Islamic, Confucian, Japanese, etc. Despite some serious flaws in his presentation, I think the overall thrust is correct. Consider, however, what Huntington sees as the distinguishing core concepts of the West: individualism, liberalism, constitutionalism, human rights, equality, liberty, the rule of law, democracy, free markets, the separation of church and state. These are criteria (identical to those assumed by Kristol and Kagan, and all of them amenable to manipulation) that could not by any means have described European civilization during most of its long history but are only applicable to its current decrepitude. One would never know that European civilization has been characterized, primarily, by the Christian religion (though divided into a number of communions) and shared ethnic and linguistic origins, specifically the various branches of the Indo-European family: a discernible local ethno-religious culture occupying a defined homeland in the Northern part of the planet.

Finally, with regard to the post-Cold War world, the power relationship between the European and non-European worlds has almost been completely reversed. The shattered self-confidence of even the victors in World War I made the liberation of their colonies a foregone conclusion, the only real question being one of timing. When the liberation came, during the Cold War, the non-European world generally sided with either the United States or the Soviet Union while the outcome was in doubt, but this only temporarily masked a deeper reality, which is now coming to light: that the non-Western cultures are no longer cowed by Western technical and military superiority. Perceiving our moral weakness and their demographic strength, they increasingly see European wealth and land as a prize to be expropriated: in short, *The Camp of the Saints*, or what my friend has called the candy store with the busted lock. Our hegemonist elites seem to believe that man does live by Big Mac alone, and they delude themselves with the specious idea that our culture (by which they mean our movies, our rock music, our fast food) is all the rage from Beijing to Bujumbura. And finally, there is only a dim recognition that in the centuries-old struggle between Cross and Crescent the latter has decisively returned to the offensive after a hiatus of some three centuries.

When future generations look back on today, they will see that the United States' emergence as the world's only superpower is one of the biggest and crudest practical jokes in history. For if there is one country that is utterly incapable of perceiving its interests and constructively acting upon them, it is the United States. This is due partly to our national temperament and institutions. Some of these may have their roots in the founding of the country, but the focus here is on contemporary characteristics that are relevant to the political elite's ability to manipulate a people into supporting a globalist agenda. For example, of any European or derivative people, Americans are most ignorant of their own history and know even less about other peoples. Historical knowledge is mainly limited to ethnic or hyphenated Americans, who are familiar with their own distinctive tribal renditions: black Americans, who know that we had slavery and Jim Crow; and some white Southerners, who can recite in minute detail the particulars of the great Lost Cause. Other than that, the American store of history consists of the latest O.J. story, some sports statistics, and the complete lyrics to the theme songs to *The Beverly Hillbillies* and *Gilligan's Island*. We have forgotten who we are, and when our hegemonist elites decide to bomb or starve some other people, we do not know who, let alone where, these people are.

Until the Civil War, American national consciousness was primarily regional and local; shared ethnic origins in the British Isles was assumed. In retrospect, we can now say the heyday of a unified American identity was the interval between the end of Reconstruction and the end of World War II; that identity was defined by ethnicity (Northwest European) and religion (Protestant), as well as by shared historical experience. Immigration during this period was almost exclusively European, and to the extent that it increasingly consisted of Eastern and Southern Europeans and non-Protestants, the immigrants were expected to Americanize, that is, dress, talk, and act like WASPs. Today, we give lip-service the WASP principles upon which this Republic was built while vilifying as racist the notion that WASP ethnicity has any relationship to American nationality. The result is progressive Balkanization: the multiculturalism of the left and the pluralism of the neoconservatives, which, as Joe Sobran has noted, are pretty much the same thing. In short, we have accepted the notion that the United States is not the home of a distinct people but a community of shared ideals, as interpreted by the elites—ideals that are available for export.

Unlike European countries, we have never had a monarch, a nobility, an established church. We really do believe in every man a king. Among the consequences is the fact that such elites as we do have tend to exercise their power not by open appeal to their legitimate authority (because they cannot) but by manipulation of images: Joseph Goebbels, meet Madison Avenue. We are suckers for the claim that any social institution based on privilege, tradition, or, worst of all, discrimination must be destroyed. When the internationalist elites call for making the world safe for democracy, they are singing our song. We are ever ready to "level the playing field" on behalf of the little guy, the underdog, or the victim, a propensity artfully mobilized first by the Croats and then even more effectively by the Muslims in the Yugoslav war. In its extreme, this phenomenon takes the form, as Joe Sobran has described it, of an inversion of sympathies, an altruistic identification with the "other" against one's own: the alien against the native, the non-European against the European, the non-Christian against the Christian.

Americans like to bask in their self-image of rough-and-ready, free-living individualism: Don't tread on me. However accurate that might have been at one time, it is not so now. Despite the fact that Americans are increasingly suspicious of their public institutions and are increasingly aware that their laws are made not by elected representatives but by nonelected judges and bureaucrats, it would seldom occur to most Americans to disobey their illegitimate edicts. Indeed, the more fundamentally decent and traditionally-minded Americans are precisely those who are most obedient to commands from on high that undermine their core values. Their respect for the law, ordinarily a virtue, is used against them by the lawless. This phenomenon is particularly evident among Southern families with strong traditions of military service, whose sons (and now daughters) are sent abroad to risk their lives not for the defense of their homeland but for a globalist agenda.

Even as Americans have abandoned Puritanism for hedonism as their guiding principle for good living, they have not given up their assumption that the essential question in any conflict is figuring out who are the white hats and who are the black hats. This tendency, coupled with a naive faith in our own national righteousness—truth, justice, and the American way—plus ignorance of the outside world, plays into the hands of the hegemonist elite.

In general. Congress—members and staff of both established parties—might be seen as occupying a middle ground between the people and the political elite. Some of the inhabitants of Capitol Hill fully share in the dominant internationalist mindset, others are fellow-travelers, and still others attempt to oppose it, usually unsuccessfully. Three influences on Congress, as well as the Executive Branch, deserve mention.

Among the two most potent foreign lobbies on Capitol Hill are those pleading the causes of Israel and the pro-Western Muslim states, notably Saudi Arabia and the Persian Gulf oil monarchies. It is often wrongly assumed that these lobbies are mutually antagonistic, when in fact their interests, while certainly not identical, are often congruent. This congruence was most evident during the Persian Gulf War and has affected America's pro-Muslim policy in the Balkans. The latter reflects the obvious sympathies of our Muslim client states, the cynical but skillful manipulation (as the Israeli analyst Yohanan Ramati has pointed out) by Croatian and Muslim propaganda of holocaust themes to mobilize American Jewish opinion, and the desire of some Israeli policymakers to be in accord with American support for friendly, pro-Western Islamic states. Summing up this orientation in the *New York Times* (January 2, 1996), in an op-ed with the revealing title of "The Third American Empire," Jacob Heilbrunn and Michael Lind, both editors at the *New Republic*, wrote:

> The fact that the United States is more enthusiastic than its European allies about a Bosnian Muslim state reflects, among other things, the new American role as the leader of an informal collection of Muslim nations from the Persian Gulf to the Balkans. The regions once ruled by the Ottoman Turks show signs of becoming the heart of a third American empire.

Perhaps partly a function of historical and geographic illiteracy, most American policymakers seem to have trouble with the notion of a world characterized by several competing powers, similar in many respects to that of pre-1914, though today the powers are mostly non-European. Additionally, there is a heavy element of inertia, particularly among those associated with the defense establishment: post-communist Russia may not be the Soviet Union, but it is the best we can come up with. Awareness that the Cold War was itself the latest unfortunate installment of the fratricidal intra-Christian, intra-European self-immolation (which, with the toll of both world wars and internal repression by totalitarianism, has cost us tens of millions of the best people our civilization has produced) is almost nonexistent; on the contrary, the thrust of American policy is not to unify Europe but to set it at daggers against itself yet again.

As a rule, each country in Europe feels entitled to look down its nose on its immediate neighbor to the east. Several countries, notably Russia, Poland, Germany, and Croatia, like to flatter themselves with the notion that they are Europe's eastern bulwark against the Asiatic hordes. The Poles consider the Russians barbarians, the Germans believe they are superior to all Slavs, the French see Germans as the uncouth Hun, and, in British eyes, the wogs begin at Calais. In America, this phenomenon manifests itself in the vague notion that the "West" is synonymous with a host of Goodthink concepts (enlightenment, progress, democracy, etc.) and the "East" with their antitheses. An important reinforcement of this notion was the supposition, during the Cold War, that communism was somehow more natural to Eastern Europeans (i.e., "Bohunks") than it is to people that are more like us. There is also an identifiable bias among American elites, particularly in the media, against national cultures based on Eastern Orthodox Christianity and perhaps against Orthodoxy itself. The upshot is that in the conflicts that define the line between the European and non-European world—notably in the Balkans, in the Caucasus, and in Central Asia, where Orthodox nations are in conflict with Islam—the hegemonist elite is almost uniformly hostile to the Christian, European side. NATO expansion up to Europe's East/West fault line, with Orthodox countries excluded, should be seen in the same light.

As both Alain Besançon (*The Rise of the Gulag: Intellectual Origins of Leninism*) and Igor Shafarevich (*The Socialist Phenomenon*) have shown, among the characteristic features of modern ideologies, of socialism in particular, is a completely closed, circular system of thought. Indeed, it might be more correct to refer to a nullification of thought, an antidote to rational discourse and description of social and political phenomena. What appeared instead was epitomized by Marxism-Leninism, a dualistic pseudo-reality where words and concepts are given a special ideological significance distinct from their normal real-world meanings and which insists that the real world conform to the ideological vision. Ideology does not appear fully mature, like Athena springing from the forehead of Zeus, but rather, as Besançon observed, becomes apparent when—

> it has attained its pure, developed form, [having] gone through a historical cycle. The history of ideology could be compared to the different successive stages in the lives of certain parasites, which go through a cycle which is apparently capricious, but which is in fact necessary to their complete development. They must, for instance, go through a river mollusc, then pass into a sheep, and finally lodge, not without deleterious effects, in the body of a human. [In the case of ideology, the host organism is a nation], whence it will return to the river. At every change of location, there is an equivalent change of form.

At this point, I think it is possible to state that the third child of the 20th century, the sibling of communism and national socialism, is finally reaching its ideological synthesis. That ideology, which I will call by the name it has proudly chosen for itself, democratic capitalism, having completed its incubation period and outlasted its rivals—and indeed having absorbed a number of their impulses and even, in many cases, their former personnel, much as in the post-World War II period, in many European countries, former fascists flocked to the Communist Party—is finally taking center stage as the ruling ethos of the world's only surviving superpower. While it would take another Besançon writing another *The Rise of the Gulag* to detail what may be an incipient totalitarianism, three key features deserve comment.

Marxism-Leninism styled itself the champion of peace, progress, and socialism, terms that had meaning only within the closed world of ideology. Likewise democratic capitalism touts as its principles a trinity of democracy, human rights, and free markets, the latter being very broad and encompassing exchange of people—i.e., unrestricted immigration—as well as goods and services. These concepts do not necessarily have any relationship to the normal, nonideological meaning of the words and are in fact endlessly manipulated by the political elite. Democracy does not mean simply broad participation of citizens in the business of governance, but is an ideological concept that encompasses the progressive social content of the popular decision. Accordingly, if the citizens of California vote to withdraw benefits to illegal aliens or to repeal affirmative action, or if voters in Colorado prohibit localities from passing gay rights ordinances, this is not an exercise of democracy but a violation of democracy, and the courts are obligated to overturn the vote. Likewise, if the Danes vote against the Maastricht agreement, they have to vote again until they get it right; the same thing happened in Ireland on the question of divorce. Free markets generally do not mean just the private exchange of goods and services for mutual benefit but encompass, for instance, the right of financial elites closely tied to the government to have their risks underwritten by their less-well-off fellow-citizens, as in the Mexican bailout; profits are privatized, losses socialized. As was the case with communism, the core concepts are understood to be manifest in an inevitable global march of progress toward (in Francis Fukuyama's famous phrase) the "end of history." We are building Utopia.

Morality is a function not of objective behavior but of the place of the actor within the ideological system. Marxism-Leninism expressed the concept in terms of *kto-kogo*, "who-whom," and Maoism employed it to the extent of recognizing entire nations as either progressive or reactionary. We see the same dualistic concept applied by the democratic capitalists today: if Iraq kills Kurds, it is bad; if Turkey kills Kurds, it is good. If Muslims and Croats want to secede from Yugoslavia, it is democracy; if Serbs (and now, Croats) want to leave Bosnia, it is aggression. If NATO warplanes overfly Bosnian Serb territory, the Serb air defenses are a threat to the planes, but the planes are not themselves threatening. The Soviet Union, as leader of the "socialist camp," authoritatively judged states and their actions within this dualist scheme during the Cold War, and the United States, having assumed leadership of the "international community," makes similar judgments today. The *kto-kogo* parallel with communism even extends to the domestic sphere, with, for example, the Bolshevik concept of the "socially friendly," i.e., common criminals that the regime considered class allies against the bourgeoisie. We see a similar phenomenon in what Samuel Francis has called "anarchotyranny," meaning the seemingly helpless posture assumed by the reigning authorities in the face of real crime (murder, rape, drug dealing) as juxtaposed with the brutality to which ordinary citizens are often subjected.

In general, while the use of force is available to the elites, more useful is the employment of secondary concepts and movements such as feminism, environmentalism, homosexualism, consumerism, evolutionism, hedonism, educationism, antidiscriminationism, etc. They are used to further destroy traditional moral restraints, the family, and national identity, leaving an atomized population without resistance to ideological direction. Force is less necessary than it was in the case of communism or national socialism: there is no need (yet) to jail or commit to punitive psychiatry Joseph Sobran or Samuel Francis—only to brand them as being outside the mainstream. As one policy analyst has put it, the main levers of control are not Pavlovian but Freudian, the message more subliminal than conscious. A symptom of the tension between rulers and ruled is the prevalence of conspiracy theories (usually involving the Council on Foreign Relations, the Trilateral Commission, etc.), which, as Francis has observed, fall into the error of mistaking for ruling organizations the organizations to which the ruling elites often belong.

Finally, while the United States is without doubt the main host for the globalist ideology (analogous, in the case of communism, with the Soviet Union), it is not the only one. One of the sharp divisions among the hegemonist elites is whether, as the Clinton administration believes, the United States should be the principal enforcer for an international order legitimated by the United Nations, or whether, as the neoconservatives believe, the United Nations should be brought into line with the dictates of a hegemonist United States.

It is hard to say whether the above consolidation of power is already an accomplished fact, or whether it is still short of its completed form. Has the United States already been irrevocably transformed into a second evil empire or not? I can say that even today in Washington it is almost impossible to have a serious discussion with most policymakers about our country's interests without entering the world of pseudo-reality, without being treated to an endless ode to the shared values of democracy, human rights, and free markets, along with a defense of the righteousness of forcibly sharing them with lesser breeds. I concede that one of the disabilities of living and working in the capital of the New World Order is a lack of appreciation for the common sense that I trust still remains in the country at large, which some believe will eventually beat back the ideological tide. Conversely, I submit that those living in the real America—which I assume is out there somewhere—little suspect how bad things really are. I would be glad to be proved wrong.

"Trump Is Right about NATO, Brussels Attacks"

Jim Jatras | *Chronicles* | March 24, 2016

This week Donald Trump ignited another furor, this time for asking the simple question of whether America's commitment to NATO is worth it. The following day, Brussels was hit by jihad terror attacks.

Johnny on the spot, Senator Ted Cruz accused Trump of surrendering to ISIS and to Putin in the face of the Brussels attacks. How Putin is responsible for Brussels, or how the attacks relate to NATO—an alliance mobilized against a USSR that went defunct a quarter century ago—is anyone's guess.

The following day, the *Washington Post*—house organ of the liberal interventionist establishment—hit the same theme: Trump's "radical isolationism" is to blame.

Contra Cruz and the *Post*, the fact is, Donald Trump, and only Donald Trump, is calling for shutting the door on what made Brussels possible: barring Muslim migrants until "we can figure out what the hell is going on." If Europe is unwilling to do that, these attacks will continue and escalate. And America can look forward to the same if we don't start taking Trump's advice.

NATO made sense when the alliance was formed in 1949 to defend a devastated and impoverished Europe against Stalin, who had communized all of Eastern Europe. During Senate ratification, one of the clinching arguments was that it would last only a few years, until Europe got back on its feet. When future president Dwight D. Eisenhower took command of NATO in 1951, he said: "If in ten years, all American troops stationed in Europe for national defense purposes have not been returned to the United States, then this whole project will have failed."

Now, almost seven decades later, with a Europe more populous and richer than the U.S., European freeloaders still depend on the US. According to the *WSJ* in 2014, "The U.S. accounts for about 73% of the roughly $1 trillion in total military spending by NATO countries each year." It's not getting better. Of NATO's 28 member countries, only four others besides the U.S. (the UK,

Estonia, Greece, and Poland) spend more than the targeted two percent of GDP on defense. (And Greece does so only out of fear of its fellow NATO "ally" Turkey.)

Even worse, NATO has become a vehicle for mischief that doesn't advance American security but undermines it. When French President Nicolas Sarkozy wanted to strut his stuff in 2011 in support of his reelection bid (he lost anyway), he called on NATO (meaning the U.S.) to do the heavy lifting for "regime change" in Libya. Barack Obama and Hillary Clinton gladly obliged him. The result: Hillary's Benghazi debacle and a failed state that's become a terrorist playground.

Even more dangerously, President Recep Tayyip Erdogan of Turkey has been playing "chicken" with the Russians in Syria. Why? So that if in his zeal to support jihad terrorist forces in Syria he gets into a tussle with the Russians, he can call on NATO (meaning us) to bail him out. Even Obama has been smart enough not to fall for that.

Still more perilous is the fact that with its 1998 and 2004 expansions, NATO has taken in former Warsaw Pact countries and the former Baltic republics of the USSR—places we have no hope of defending except with the use of nuclear weapons. Under NATO's Article 5 guarantee, an attack on one is an attack on all. How many Americans are willing to risk a nuclear strike on, say, New York or Chicago to defend Tallinn or Riga? And now some, including Hillary, want to extend those guarantees further afield, to Ukraine and Georgia.

And Trump should not even *ask* whether or how any of this makes Americans more secure or prosperous?

When NATO was first expanded in 1998, only a few brave Americans stood against it. One was conservative icon Phyllis Schlafly. She wrote then that "Western Europe, which has grown wealthy on U.S. handouts over the past 50 years, is today's 'welfare queen.' The Senate should terminate welfare for foreigners now." Well, the Senate didn't take her advice, and the European welfare queen has totted up 20 more years of sandbagging the U.S. taxpayer. (Note that Trump has also questioned security welfare to Japan and South Korea.)

Schlafly also warned that the treaty to expand NATO would commit "us to permanent involvement in foreign conflicts. It should be called Clinton's Go-To-War Treaty." We should have listened to her. As night follows day, expanding NATO was followed by Kosovo (1999), Iraq (2003), Libya (2011), Syria (ongoing). What do Americans have to show for the trillions of dollars wasted?

Donald Trump has not even said (yet) that we should pull out of NATO but just consider ways we might make our participation more cost-effective. The hysteria with which his modest suggestion simply to "rethink" a commitment that was never meant to be eternal should be a clue. What is it that the NATOphile crowd fear will not survive scrutiny? If NATO is such a great deal for the United States, they should be happy for the attention. The fact that they demand *no thinking allowed* when it comes to NATO speaks volumes.

"Hillary's Warped Notion of American Exceptionalism and Indispensability"

Ed Lozansky and Jim Jatras | *Chronicles* | October 27, 2016

Perhaps one of the most used and abused political expressions in recent years
has been that of "American exceptionalism." Politicians and commentators
routinely invoke it as high principle and accuse their opponents of insufficient
devotion to it, or contrariwise blame it for all the ills of the world.

For example, in 2013, Russian President Vladimir Putin ruffled many
Americans' feathers:

> It is extremely dangerous to encourage people to see themselves as
> exceptional, whatever the motivation. . . . We are all different, but
> when we ask for the Lord's blessings, we must not forget that God
> created us equal.

Hillary Clinton weighed in on exceptionalism in an August speech before the
American Legion, in which she also took a swipe at Donald Trump:

> The United States is an exceptional nation. . . . But, in fact, my
> opponent in this race has said very clearly that he thinks American
> exceptionalism is insulting to the rest of the world. In fact, when
> Vladimir Putin, of all people, criticized American exceptionalism, my
> opponent agreed with him, saying, and I quote, 'if you're in Russia,
> you don't want to hear that America is exceptional.' Well maybe you
> don't want to hear it, but that doesn't mean it's not true.

It needs to be asked, though: when people praise or criticize "American exceptionalism," are they always talking about the same thing?

America, like any country, has its own distinctive history, culture, and
traditions. America's unique founding principles—consent of the governed,
due process, constitutionally limited division of powers, representative
government—justly have been an inspiration to the world for over two centuries. Thomas Jefferson wrote of the "palpable truth, that the mass of mankind has not been born with saddles on their backs, nor a favored few booted
and spurred, ready to ride them legitimately, by the grace of God."

This "exceptional" idea was new in human history. Any American worthy
of the name justly takes pride in it. This is the genuine American exceptionalism of Washington, Jefferson, and Madison, lately championed by Reagan. The fact that we have strayed so far from it, both domestically and internationally, is shameful.

The unique moral revolution to which the Founding Fathers pledged their
lives, their fortunes, and their sacred honor has little connection to the bastard
term (usually capitalized as "American Exceptionalism") that describes post-
Cold War U.S. global behavior, by which policymakers in Washington assert
both an exclusive "leadership" privilege and unsupportable obligation to
undertake open-ended international missions in the name of the "Free World"
and the "international community." This is the counterfeit "Exceptionalism"
of a tiny clique of bipartisan *apparatchiki*—GOP "neoconservatives" and
Democrat "liberal interventionists" and their mainstream media mouthpieces—who have little regard for our country's oldest traditions or the security and welfare of the American people.

This second kind of Exceptionalism means that the rules we demand of
other countries don't apply to us (so much for Jefferson's appeal in the Declaration of Independence to "a decent respect to the opinions of mankind"). Its
proponents justify "regime change" in Iraq, Libya, Syria, and Ukraine, maybe
in Russia too. They have wasted trillions of Americans' tax dollars in the

process of making us less safe, not more. Now the Obama Administration is willing to risk confronting Moscow and sparking a new world war in a bid to save al-Qaeda in Aleppo. As Trump has noted: "You're going to end up in World War Three over Syria if we listen to Hillary Clinton."

It is this debased and dangerous kind of Exceptionalism that Hillary represents. Closely related is her concept of America's "indispensability":

> We are the indispensable nation. People all over the world look to us and follow our lead. . . . When America fails to lead, we leave a vacuum that either causes chaos or other countries or networks rush in to fill the void.

It's no coincidence she is preferred by self-regarded *indispensable* hacks of both parties who have been up to their elbows in every foreign mess since Reagan. Starting next year, they are eager to give us more of the same.

For genuine patriots, the true, uniquely American exceptionalism of the Declaration of Independence and the U.S. Constitution is our precious inheritance. America's true exceptionalism is the antithesis of what Hillary and her acolytes intend, as attested by John Quincy Adams: "Wherever the standard of freedom and independence has been or shall be unfurled, there will [America's] heart, her benedictions and her prayers be. But she goes not abroad in search of monsters to destroy. She is the well-wisher to the freedom and independence of all. She is the champion and vindicator only of her own."

In scouring the world for monsters to destroy Hillary's perversion of authentic American principles has more in common with Soviet universalism than the vision of the Founders. In pursuing "benevolent global hegemony" the supposed indispensables suggest that other countries and peoples are dispensable—or disposable. In the process, Americans' freedoms have become disposable too. This is, in a word, *un-American*—a good old expression that needs to make a comeback.

Genuine American exceptionalism and the "America First" policies of Donald Trump don't mean our withdrawal from the world. U.S. primacy in a multipolar system is something most countries, including Russia and China, would be prepared to accept, however grudgingly. But continuing down the road Hillary Clinton, Barack Obama, and George W. Bush have blazed for a quarter century promises us just more war, more enemies, and eventual catastrophe. It's a mistake America cannot afford to make.

Edward Lozansky is president of the American University in Moscow.

Jim Jatras is a former U.S. diplomat and foreign policy adviser to the Senate GOP leadership. He recently published a major study, "How American Media Serves as a Transmission Belt for Wars of Choice."

"Mr. Trump: America Doesn't Need Tiny, Corrupt Montenegro in NATO"

Jim Jatras | *Chronicles* | December 1, 2016

During the presidential campaign Donald Trump horrified the bipartisan foreign policy mandarinate by suggesting that NATO was "obsolete" and useless against the only real threat faced by Europe: the massive influx of violent Muslims applauded by German Chancellor Angela Merkel, the "EuSSR" bureaucracy in Brussels, and the Obama Administration. Trump also indicated that America's treaty pledge to defend alliance members was not absolute, especially for moochers unwilling to pony up for their own security.

Even before he takes office, Trump has a golden opportunity to show he means business with the pending NATO accession of Montenegro, a former constituent republic of Yugoslavia. With one word, he can put the kibosh on it.

If there was ever an ideal candidate to demonstrate a "Trump Doctrine" on ending NATO's profligate freeloading, Montenegro is it. A tiny state—it really can't be called a "nation"—of barely 600,000 people (fewer than half of whom identify as ethnic Montenegrins) and a nominal GDP of about $4 billion (roughly a tenth that of New Haven, Connecticut), Montenegro makes even neighboring Albania (another unqualified recent NATO acquisition) look formidable. With fewer than two thousand personnel in its armed forces, Montenegro obviously would contribute zilch to America's security, despite the rumored prowess of its crack three-man mess kit repair team.

Accepting Montenegro into NATO wouldn't make Americans any safer, but it would lay on our plate that country's problems. To be sure, Montenegro is a lovely and picturesque vacation spot. Its people are proud and freedom-loving, as they have repeatedly shown over the centuries in tenacious and brutal wars against occupiers—mainly Turks and Teutons—with whom they would now be allied in NATO. Resentment against NATO itself, which bombed Montenegro for 78 days in 1999 as part of the Bill Clinton Administration's illegal war against then-Yugoslavia over Kosovo, is reflected in the fact that despite massive propaganda there is still no majority support for joining the bloc. (The pro-NATO government claims a plurality in favor of accession but won't risk a referendum.) In fact, the only real security threat to Montenegro is internal: a persistent slow-burn separatist insurgency by Albanian Muslims to snip off the border region they call "Malesia," as part of their aspiration for a "Greater Albania" that includes Kosovo, other parts of southern Serbia, a third of (the Former Yugoslav Republic of) Macedonia, and part of northern Greece.

Why is the U.S. even considering admitting Montenegro to NATO? Mainly because, as lame duck President Barack Obama stated in his transmittal message to the Senate asking for its advice and consent to ratification of the relevant protocol, "Montenegro's accession to NATO will demonstrate to other countries in the Balkans and beyond that NATO's door remains open to nations that undertake the reforms necessary to meet NATO's requirements and contribute to the security of the alliance, and is yet another milestone in advancing the Euro-Atlantic integration of the Balkans." Evidently the kind of "reforms" Obama means is the cosmetic stepping aside of the notoriously corrupt ex-Prime Minister Milo Đukanovic, who effectively still controls Montenegro's shaky "pro-western" government despite serious corruption allegations that include gun-running, cigarette smuggling, banking fraud, and scams involving the privatization of state-owned utility firms.

But more important is showing that "NATO's door remains open" to other countries, many of them even more unstable and mired in dangerous disputes than Montenegro: Bosnia-and-Herzegovina (a synthetic state that remains under outside supervision to manage its jerry-built balance among mutually suspicious Muslims, Serbs, and Croats); FYRO-Macedonia (as noted, under threat from Albanian secessionists, barred anyway because of its name trademark dispute with Greece); Serbia (where despite a government under western control a solid majority of citizens are confirmed NATO-phobes); and Kosovo (Serbia's NATO-occupied province administered by a gaggle of Albanian mafia kingpins, terrorists, and human organ-harvesters, not to mention being a top hotbed of ISIS activity in Europe along with the Muslim part of Bosnia).

Then, after wrapping up Obama's "Euro-Atlantic integration of the Balkans," we can get on to his "and beyond." This means the real third-rail, world-war risks that beset the former Soviet republics on NATO's wish list: Georgia, Azerbaijan, Ukraine, and Moldova. The United States doesn't need this parade of horribles. If Trump follows through with putting "America First!" an early item must be making sure that further NATO expansion is one door that is firmly and finally shut. That should be followed by a thorough zero-baseline reassessment of why we are in NATO at all a quarter century after the Warsaw Pact and the USSR dissolved. What's in it for us?

Nonetheless, the same Washington establishment that just got its head handed to them on November 8 is still determined to press ahead. Globalists of both parties are urging the Senate's rubber stamp of Montenegro's entry prior to Obama's departure from office, before the incoming Trump Administration can reassess it—and hopefully the rest of our long-outdated relationship with NATO too. The Committee on Foreign Relations has yet to report out Montenegro's resolution of ratification so it can be slipped through the Senate and flopped onto Obama's desk before he leaves office, presenting his successor with a fait accompli.

Luckily, there is more than one bite at the apple to stop Montenegro's accession. First, the Foreign Relations Committee can decline to take action on significant matters before Trump takes office in January. (That would be a good rule for the GOP-controlled Congress to follow generally. Why help Obama lob parting stink-bombs at Trump? Another item that should not get action in the lame duck Congressional session is the Saudi lobbyists' plotted revision to gut JASTA, "Justice Against Sponsors of Terrorism Act" (S. 2040). Also beware any ploy to move the abominable TPP "Trans-Pacific Partnership," which some are still hoping can be spirited through by complicit Republicans notwithstanding the election results.)

Second, even a lone Senator can place a "hold" on a treaty resolution, just as with any other bill. To his credit, Kentucky Senator Rand Paul has held up a series of defective tax treaties for months. The same can be done with the Montenegro protocol if it gets out of committee.

Finally, Trump himself can weigh in. He can make it clear that America's fetish for collecting useless satellites like so many "meaningless Facebook friends" is over and done with. Making a commitment to go to war, including the risk of nuclear war, to defend some country nowhere near the United States is a deadly serious business, not a grand gesture of some absurd "Euro-Atlantic trajectory." On any hard-headed cost/benefit analysis, Montenegro is all cost, no benefit.

Mr. Trump, please pull the plug.

"The Big Three: America, Russia, and China Must Join Hands for Security, Prosperity, and Peace"

Ed Lozansky and Jim Jatras | *Washington Times* | December 16, 2016

With the defeat of Hillary Clinton by Donald Trump, we may never know how close America and all mankind came to nuclear war. Driven by the globalist agenda of the "indispensable" neoconservatives and liberal-interventionists calling the shots in a Clinton administration, it would have been only a matter of time before the United States found itself at war with Russia, or China, or both.

When Trump takes office, for the first time since Ronald Reagan we will have a president with the stature and vision to put the interests of the American people first. Trump's firm hand on the tiller of the American ship of state combined with his business sense will enable him to deal confidently but fairly with the formidable, no-nonsense leaders of the world's next two major powers: Russia's Vladimir Putin and China's Xi Jinping. This is a unique historic opportunity that must not be wasted.

Trump can move decisively to restore stability to a global order that has been spinning out of control. It is a good sign that he held cordial phone conversations with both Putin and Xi soon after his victory. It's time to cement mutual goodwill with both Russia and China, which have established a *de facto* alliance in response to the mishandling of American policy under Trump's immediate predecessors.

No one should pretend Trump's task will be easy in light of the world's many contentious issues. Trump's "America First!" policy to make the United States secure, prosperous, and great again is a welcome change from decades of globalism. Similarly, Putin and Xi also put their countries' interests first— that's their job. But Trump has dealt with "tough customers" before, and that hasn't stopped him from making great, mutually beneficial deals.

Among our suggestions:

Dispense with the "indispensables": Trump is right when he says he doesn't need smug, self-anointed "experts" who have "perfect résumés but very little to brag about except responsibility for a long history of failed policies and continued losses at war." *None* of those who denounced Trump during the campaign should be allowed to serve in his administration, no matter how contritely they beg. This is not vindictiveness, is it good sense. As they say, "personnel are policy": Trump must keep out of his Administration people whose only "contribution" would be to try to steer him back to the failures of the past.

Make the common struggle against "radical Islamic terrorism" a priority: Trump has rightly faulted his erstwhile opponent and the lame duck sitting in the White House for their failure to name the principal security threat to America and the whole civilized world. To say the least, that threat is neither Russia nor China, who themselves are battling jihadism at home. It is urgent to settle the dangerous flashpoint in Syria. Aid to so-called "moderate" terrorists from western and regional patrons like Saudi Arabia must end, immediately. Coordination among the U.S., Russia, and China, and with Syrian and Iraqi forces, must aim to destroy all jihadist groups, not just the Islamic State. NATO should reach out to the Shanghai Security Organization to coordinate a worldwide anti-terrorism strategy.

Defuse regional tensions where America's vital interests are not at stake: Despite suggestions from the foreign policy establishment, neither China nor anyone else is threatening the sea lanes in the South China

Sea. As Philippine President Rodrigo Duterte's opening to Beijing shows, even America's closest regional partners do not want to be pushed into a military confrontation to suit the agenda of "indispensables" in Washington. American concerns about North Korea can only be solved with Beijing's security respected. In Europe, NATO forces should stand back from Russia's borders and territorial waters. NATO expansion should be ended—starting with the U.S. Senate's declining to act on the accession of tiny and corrupt Montenegro—while a new security architecture in Europe takes shape. The Alliance's 2008 pledge to bring in Georgia and Ukraine should be withdrawn. We and our European allies should find a way to cooperate with Russia on pulling Ukraine out of its political and economic crisis as a united, neutral state.

Russia boasts the world's greatest landmass and natural resources unrivalled by any other country. She also has the only nuclear arsenal comparable to America's. China is the most populous country in the world, with an economy achieving a par with ours and a burgeoning military sector. If American policy had been designed to alienate both of these giants and drive them to cooperate against us, it could not have been more successful.

President Donald Trump can correct the mistakes of past U.S. presidents. Rather than adversaries, Russia and China can become America's essential partners and are, we are convinced, ready to respond positively. It's time for Trump and America to take the initiative for U.S-Russia-China cooperation towards a secure, prosperous, and peaceful future. A Trump-Putin-Xi "Big Three Summit" should be a priority for the new U.S. President's first 100 days.

Edward Lozansky is president of the American University in Moscow. He is the author of the book Operation Elbe, which describes joint US-Russia anti-terrorist efforts.

Jim Jatras is a former U.S. diplomat and foreign policy adviser to the Senate GOP leadership. He is the author of a major study, "How American Media Serves as a Transmission Belt for Wars of Choice."

"In Astana, a Demonstration of Leadership is Needed—But Whose?"

Jim Jatras | *Strategic Culture* | January 19, 2017

One of the most commonly heard buzzwords heard around Washington is "American leadership." America must lead, we are told, or nothing good can happen. No matter what the issue or relevant locale, no matter how far from American shores or insignificant the impact on Americans' safety or prosperity, the whole world waits with bated breath for the wizards of Washington to "lead."

Only rarely does anyone ever address the questions of "leading" to where, to what end, to accomplish what? And how does the end benefit the United States? One would think those questions would be decided first with only then considering the matter of who leads, who follows, and who gets out of the way.

The issue of American leadership, or absence thereof, is relevant to next week's kickoff of Syria peace talks in Astana, Kazakhstan, brokered by Russia, Turkey, and Iran. The United States—or more properly, the Obama administration—was not invited at all, much less leading anything. That's all to the good.

Without the Obama-ites mucking up the table, perhaps there's finally a chance for peace after six years of carnage. The key is that after repeated rounds of the fruitless "Geneva Process" between Russia's Foreign Minister Sergei Lavrov and U.S. Secretary of State John Kerry, the Russians finally decided that the Obama administration could not be a productive interlocutor. (I've lost track of how many times Lavrov and Kerry cheerfully announced an understanding on how to move forward, with the U.S. immediately declaring afterwards, ." . .BUT, Assad must go!")

After having had quite enough of Washington, or at least enough of the outgoing Obama crew, Moscow decided to deal with Ankara instead. Despite the notoriously erratic tendencies of Turkish President Recep Tayyip Erdogan during the almost six years of war, he's turned out to be more reliable than U.S. President Barack Obama and Kerry. The first evidence of that was the relatively quiet wrap-up of east Aleppo, which was far less than the humanitarian catastrophe many in the west predicted, and perhaps were hoping for.

As to the role and impact of each side on the process of the Astana negotiations, Moscow, closely working with Damascus and Tehran has the upper hand. Most importantly, the government of Syrian President Bashar al-Assad stays—period. There will be no "regime change."

Among the three sponsors, Turkey remains the odd man out. On the other hand, in these talks Ankara, and only Ankara, speaks for the "opposition"—that is, the terrorists (most of them non-Syrians) fighting against the Syrian government. If Erdogan has abandoned his unreal, maximalist goals, as appears to be the case, he can secure terms that wind the war down in a way that lessens the terrorist blowback Turkey has already experienced.

It's been reported that Kazakhstan may itself join the talks, though that's unlikely to impact the substance. The main foundation in Astana is unity of purpose among Syria, Russia, and Iran, which has been essential to their success on imposing their agenda on their adversaries. Turkey has been forced to come to terms, the Obama Administration has been dealt out, and other powers—notably Saudi Arabia and Qatar—now need to consider how disruptive they intend to be even though they cannot prevail in their initial goals. Qatar is probably smart enough to figure that out. Saudi Arabia probably isn't, as its behavior in Yemen shows.

So where does this leave American leadership, with President Donald Trump now taking the helm in Washington? Some media have reported that Russia has invited the incoming Trump administration to the Syrian peace talks, putting it the context of an expected cooperation between Trump and Russian President Vladimir Putin. Reportedly, Iran has objected to having the U.S. there at all. It's too soon to tell yet what the American presence (if there is one) in Astana might have, but the invitation—as, I assume, only an observer for now—is a positive sign. If Trump keeps faith with his campaign promises to work with Russia and destroy, not just contain, Daesh, their participation could be a big positive as opposed to the Obama approach, which could only be a "spoiler."

Keep in mind that during the 2016 campaign, Trump had strongly criticized Obama's policy in Syria, saying President Assad's ouster should not be a primary US interest. So far so good. However, it's not clear to what extent other "baggage" might complicate things. There are many "Iran hawks" coming into the Trump administration. The ridiculous and false phrase "Iran is the world's leading sponsor of global terrorism" is commonly heard. Recently, a group of former officials, including many close to the incoming Trump team, issued a letter calling for what amounts to "regime change" in Iran and support for the notorious terrorist Marxist-Islamic cult, the "Mojahedin-e Khalq (MEK)." In effect, it's a call for Trump to destroy his administration over Iran the way George W. Bush destroyed his in Iraq.

On the other hand, Trump himself has noted that Iran, along with Syria and Russia, are fighting Daesh. He has said that the days of "regime change" and "nation-building" are over. As a businessman, he's smart enough to know that dumping a few trillion dollars down the drain will ruin his primary goal to restore the American economy and create jobs. He has to choose. Unfortunately, even in his own administration he may find himself lonely. We shall see.

If the partial success in Aleppo of the tripartite Moscow-Tehran-Ankara entente can be replicated countrywide, and if Trump makes good on his pledge to work with Moscow to destroy Daesh (and hopefully al-Qaeda and its many offshoots), we could see this war wind down quickly. To be sure, some resistance will continue in the eastern part of the country. Pacifying Syria also depends to some extent on events in Iraq, notably in Mosul (where lack of reports in western media suggest things are not going as well as hoped). But the prospect exists to liberate and restore peace to the major population centers, which would be a great start.

It's too soon to be wildly optimistic. But if Astana sees Washington (under new management) taking the uncharacteristic step of exercising leadership by not messing things up and instead letting the countries more directly concerned work things out, we may have reason to be encouraged. More importantly, we may have reason to hope that there are at last people in Washington who have learned to distinguish between when to act in defense of vital interests and when to decline to act when such interests are not at stake.

"Do Obama's Sanctions on Dodik Signal the Last Desperate Gasp of a Failed Policy?"

Jim Jatras | *Strategic Culture* | January 26, 2017

With only days to go before leaving the White House, Barack Obama's ambassador in Sarajevo slapped sanctions on Milorad Dodik, President of Republika Srpska (RS). The supposed cause, according to the official statement, was that Dodik had "actively obstructed" or posed "a significant risk of actively obstructing" the 1995 Dayton Accords, and in so doing posed "a significant threat to the sovereignty and territorial integrity of Bosnia and Herzegovina" (BiH).

That's quite a mouthful for the "offense" of standing up for Bosnian Serbs' choice, via public referendum, of a day to mark their national and spiritual identity. Despicably, Valentin Inzko, the unelected "High Representative" of Nobody in Particular, compared RS's Day of the Republic to the founding of the World War II-era Ustaša-ruled "Independent State of Croatia" (NDH), infamous for its genocidal slaughters of Serbs, Jews, and Roma.

The Dodik sanctions episode is noteworthy for what it tells us about three related factors: the future of BiH as a state (or something pretending to be a state); the desperate effort by the late, unlamented Obama administration and their Republican and European collaborators to perpetuate their failed policies of the past quarter century; and the hope for (but not certainty of) a more enlightened U.S. policy in the Balkans, in Europe, and globally, particularly to the need to combat Islamic radicalism, not support it.

First, regarding the future of BiH, it's not looking good. Dodik called BiH "a project with no future", saying the only viable path is a "peaceful divorce along entity lines." In response, American and EU diplomats called for more "reforms", which in practice means pushing for greater centralization of power in the hands of the Muslims at the expense of Serbs and Croats. In response to Inzko's tirade, the RS has cut contacts with his office and endorsed a call by war veterans "to apologize to the Serb people for the insults he uttered."

Thus, this latest episode can be taken as another turn in BiH's spiral into dysfunction. In principle, it might still be possible for the Muslims to enter into genuine negotiations with Serbs and Croats for a authentic federation that respects the rights, security needs, and identities of all three communities—the only way BiH has a chance of staying together. But that's unlikely with the Muslims' conviction that outside powers, notably the U.S., will maintain a thumb on the scale to assure their dominance.

Second, the Dodik sanctions need to be seen in context with other efforts of the Obama administration to "poison the well" for the Trump team as the transfer of power approached. This mostly concerned Russia: expulsion of diplomats, military deployments on Russia's borders, and contrived hysteria over "Russian hacking" of the U.S. election. Put in its simplest form, the two interlocking defining principles of the bipartisan U.S. foreign policy establishment (or the Deep State) since the breakup of the Soviet Union and the Warsaw Pact has been continued determination to maintain Russia as the vassal state it was under Boris Yeltsin (and failing that, to break it up, for example according to the three-way partition floated by Zbigniew Brzezinski); and, as a tool in achieving the subjugation of Russia (as well as appeasing our "friends" like Saudi Arabia), championing Islamic causes, particularly against Orthodox Christian opponents. This means support for jihadist elements that began in Afghanistan in the 1980s (which gave birth to al-Qaeda) and then in Bosnia (the Iranian arms "green light" and covert U.S. air delivery of weapons and, reportedly, jihad fighters), in Kosovo (Fatos Klosi, the former head of that Albanian secret police, said he had twice seen Osama bin Laden in Tirana consulting with "prime minister" and Kosovo mafia leader Hashim Thaci planning their terrorist campaign against Serbia), and then in Libya and Syria.

In a Balkan context, the fact is that U.S. support was given to Bosnian Muslims *as Muslims* for the specific purpose of currying favor with the Islamic world. For example, the late Rep. Tom Lantos (Democrat, California)—then-Chairman of the Foreign Affairs Committee—said the following at a Congressional hearing on Kosovo in 2007 in the lead-up to the 2008 illegal declaration of independence:

> Just a reminder to the predominantly Muslim-led government[s] in this world that here is yet another example [i.e., "another" example after BiH] that the United States leads the way for the creation of a predominantly Muslim country in the very heart of Europe. This should be noted by both responsible leaders of Islamic governments, such as Indonesia, and also for jihadists of all color and hue. The United States' principles are universal, and in this instance, the United States stands foursquare for the creation of an overwhelmingly Muslim country in the very heart of Europe.

Not to be outdone, Mr. Lantos' Senate counterpart at the time, recently departed Vice President Joseph Biden, expressed similar views (Financial Times, January 3, 2007): "[A]droit diplomacy to secure Kosovo's independence could yield a victory for Muslim democracy. . . . a much-needed example of a successful US-Muslim partnership . . ."

In other words, American support for Islamic communities in the Balkans is not primarily driven by Balkan realities. Rather, it is guided by a larger, global concept regarding how the United States wants to be perceived in the Islamic world. It is of course a concept that has yielded only disaster. The biggest European recruiting grounds for ISIS and hotbed for its activities are in America's "Muslim democratic" pets Kosovo and Bosnia (the Federation of BiH of course, not RS).

Third and finally, there is a chance this could change because of a transfer of power at the source of the problem: in Washington. President Donald Trump boldly declares his desire to improve ties with Russia and join with Moscow to combat radical Islamic terrorism, starting in Syria. This would be a direct repudiation of the policies of Obama, George W. Bush, and the pathological Bill Clinton. He has indicated a willingness to work with forces all over the world that will join with us in that perspective. Seen through such a lens Milorad Dodik is a natural ally, as is Russia's Vladimir Putin.

This brings us back to why the specific last-minute decision to slap sanctions on Dodik. As he observed:

These are not sanctions of the United States, these are sanctions of those who were defeated in elections in the U.S. and I'm not surprised by this move, because I have heard so many threats from this outgoing administration over the last ten years. . . . The reprisal followed, but it probably wouldn't have happened had I not been invited to the inauguration of U.S. President-elect Donald Trump. They could not bear to see me. The sanctions are a personal move of those who understand politics as a policy of force. . . . The decision was announced by an administration that will two days from now go into political history, and it yet remains to be seen whether they had any suggestions from here for such a decision.

Put another way, Obama's and Hillary's rear guard—who unfortunately have many supporters in the neoconservative wing of the Republican Party—lashed out any way they could. As a principled and strong (one might say, "Trumpesque") figure Dodik was a tempting target.

The Trump administration is still very much in formation, and one assumes that there's no possible way it could be worse than its predecessors. But caution is in order. When Bush was elected in 2000, and even more after the al-Qaeda attacks of 2001, there were those who flatly predicted that the U.S. would rapidly switch sides in the Balkans to confront the jihad threat. Instead, the clueless Bush, guided by neoconservatives who had supported the Clinton aggression, intensified their pro-Islamic bias across the globe, and in the Balkans most of all. Convinced that "moderate" Islam was the only antidote to "radical" Islam, they wanted to prove all the more desperately how much they favored Muslim causes in the Balkans and any terrorists opposed to Russia or friends of Russia.

It's clear where Trump wants to go. The problem is, he needs to populate his administration with credentialed professionals. These will mainly be veterans of the administration of Bush the Younger, whose tendency will be to try to drag Trump back to the failures of that era. Whether they will succeed or whether Trump can break them to his will is not yet known.

"Milo Djukanovic's Claims of Russian Assassination Plot Are a Desperate Ploy to Further NATO Bid"

Jim Jatras | *Strategic Culture* | February 26, 2017

Reports surfacing in the British media of a Russian plot to kill Montenegro's former prime minister Milo Djukanovic should be seen for the cynical ploy they are. To give just the smallest bit of defense to these British publications—yes, it is true Djukanovic is making these allegations. Is there any substance or proof to these allegations? No. The UK media has shown it is as politicized as its American mainstream counterparts like *CNN* by publishing such fake news.

Good reason to doubt these baseless charges starts from the fact that they come from Djukanovic, who has a stupendous reputation for corruption and is trying to move forward desperately with NATO accession for Montenegro which has stalled in the U.S. Senate for about two months. At this point if he were to say the sky is blue, it would be reason to disbelieve him and look for an ulterior motive.

Djukanovic transparently is throwing this red meat on the table in the context of hysteria that is going on in Washington concerning allegations of Moscow's hacking the American election ("the Russians did it!") and the open attack by the "deep state," by elements of the intelligence community with their leaks, and by the mainstream media that just claimed the scalp of general Mike Flynn, President Donald Trump's former National Security Adviser. Besides criminally seeking to overthrow the constitutionally elected government—as they have imposed "regime change" on other countries—they want to do anything they can to block any rapprochement from the Trump administration with Moscow.

Djukanovic has very artfully inserted himself into this narrative. His message is simple: you can't let the Russians win. Nothing else matters. He is trying to use "the Russians are coming" meme as a way to jumpstart Montenegro's stalled NATO bid. Let's remember the debate in Washington isn't about letting Montenegro into NATO because having it as an ally makes American more secure. Montenegro obviously does nothing for our defense. The question is whether the NATO door will remain open, particularly for Georgia and Ukraine.

It seems no one cares to ask why America should be allied with a nation that doesn't particularly what to be allied with us. According to opinion polls, it is far from clear that most Montenegrins want to be in NATO and aligned to us in the first place. Most recent polls indicate a slight plurality in the "against" camp despite relentless government propaganda and the braying of Soros-controlled media. A recent survey indicated that some 84% of Montenegrins want a vote on the matter. Even a solid majority of NATO supporters favor a referendum. Djukanovic won't hold a referendum because he knows he would lose it.

Djukanovic's ploy is well timed. It both feeds and feeds off of the anti-Russian frenzy, which is the basis of what former Congressman Dennis Kucinich has called an attempted coup to bring down the Trump administration. Calls are openly heard for "patriots" in the intelligence services to overthrow Trump for the "good of the country."

It is uncertain whether Djukanovic will successfully ride the wave of Russophobia to get Montenegro into NATO. What is certain is that America is on the edge of turning into a banana republic. Trump has very little time to strike back, hard. One way for him to show who's boss is to turn thumbs down on Djukanovic and his trickery.

"Trump Leaves Direction of US Foreign Policy Hanging"

Jim Jatras | *Strategic Culture* | March 6, 2017

During his first five weeks in office, Donald Trump has faced an unprecedented (inside the United States, anyway) effort at regime change operation engineered by elements of the Deep State and the mainstream media. Time will tell whether he can beat back the threat of forces that seek above all to prevent any American rapprochement with Russia and are staging a "soft coup" to stop it.

On February 28, Trump gave his first formal speech as president to the Congress and American people, and informally to the rest of the world. He returned to many of the themes of his campaign, in particular to put America and the American people first, not the interests of the global elite. He also signaled his desire for peace and avoiding foreign conflicts:

> Free nations are the best vehicle for expressing the will of the people—and America respects the right of all nations to chart their own path. My job is not to represent the world. My job is to represent the United States of America. But we know that America is better off, when there is less conflict—not more.
>
> We must learn from the mistakes of the past—we have seen the war and destruction that have raged across our world.
>
> The only long-term solution for these humanitarian disasters is to create the conditions where displaced persons can safely return home and begin the long process of rebuilding.
>
> America is willing to find new friends, and to forge new partnerships, where shared interests align. We want harmony and stability, not war and conflict.
>
> We want peace, wherever peace can be found. America is friends today with former enemies. Some of our closest allies, decades ago, fought on the opposite side of these World Wars. This history should give us all faith in the possibilities for a better world.

What Trump did not make explicit is what he intends to do about the most fundamental principle of U.S. foreign policy, which the coup-plotters against him are desperate to maintain at any cost. For decades U.S. policy has been predicated on the notion that Russia (and before that, the USSR) is the main enemy and a mortal threat the United States; and that radical Islam (mainly Sunni and linked with Saudi Arabia) are a "frienemy": a secondary danger but one that can be usefully sicced onto the main enemy, Russia. Exhibits of this abound: Turkish, Saudi, and Georgian complicity aiding Chechen "freedom fighters"; harboring Ilyas Akhmadov, supposed "foreign minister" of the defunct terrorist "Chechen Republic of Ichkeria"; neoconservative *Schadenfreude* over the Beslan school and Nord-Ost theater massacres, as though the Russians brought it on themselves and deserved to be slaughtered. The same pattern is visible elsewhere: in the past Serbia mainly, but later Libya and Syria, where the United States supported jihadist forces against governments friendly to Russia.

Trump was again clear that for him the main enemy is not Russia (widely seen as a one of the potential "new friends" he referred to) but, with great emphasis, "radical Islamic terrorism." If he is sincere about that, it doesn't mean Russia is necessarily a friend but it does mean the U.S. needs to prioritize. If Trump means to destroy the Islamic State (and also al-Qaeda and, if we are honest, the rest of the gaggle of Salafist jihad terrorists in Syria and Iraq), we need to at least understand that there's no such thing as a moderate terrorist. It also means that the Saudis—with whom we've been partnered at least since Afghanistan in the 1980s—are not our friends. It means we must have at least a working relationship against radical Islamic terrorism with Russia, which means also the Iraqi and Syrian armies, and at least to some extent (admittedly, with some concern) Iran.

From his words, Trump seems to understand this. One suspects that top policy advisers sharing his populist and nationalist views, Steve Bannon and Stephen Miller, do too. Probably also Chief of Staff Reince Priebus and media adviser Kellyanne Conway. But his national security team (with the possible exceptions of Secretary of State Rex Tillerson and National Security Council chairman Lt. Gen. Keith Kellogg) still seem stuck in the pre-Trump model that equates Russia with everything bad and sees jihadists as a strategic asset. The latter would include Vice President Mike Pence, plus Defense Secretary James Mattis (reportedly he wanted to bring a bunch of Democrats into top jobs at the Pentagon, including Hillary Clinton's shadow Defense Secretary Michele Flournoy), National Security Adviser Lt. Gen. H.R. McMaster, United Nations Ambassador Nikki Haley (who so far seems just to read talking points prepared for her by Samantha Power's staff) and several others. The latter crowd even routinely twists the radical Islamic terrorism meme into "get Iran", even though Iran didn't create the Islamic State and in fact is fighting against it. Rather, ISIS was created by U.S. "allies" Saudi Arabia, Qatar, and Turkey, with the Obama Administration's acquiescence. Even when calling for action against the Islamic State, the latter group want to turn to these same "Sunni allies" and somehow transform the fight against Sunni jihadists to a regional confrontation with Iran, which, among other things, would complicate if not scuttle cooperation with Russia.

Whatever the details, the stark policy choice before Trump boils down to one question: do we still see jihadists as an asset against Main Enemy Russia (in which case, start stocking up on iodine pills), or do we see Russia as asset against radical Islamic terrorism? Most of Trump's team unfortunately leans to the former, while he rhetorically leans to the latter.

He needs to choose.

"Wikileaks CIA Document Dump Heats Up Fight Between Trump and Deep State/MSM"

Jim Jatras | *Strategic Culture* | March 9, 2017

The latest release of a massive trove of apparently genuine documents originating with the Central Intelligence Agency comes as Donald Trump's grudge match with the Deep State and its Mainstream Media (MSM) allies was already reaching the boiling point. It will now get even hotter, if that's possible.

On the details, so-called "Vault 7" consists of some 8,761 documents evidently originating in the CIA's Center for Cyber Intelligence. According to Wikileaks, it shows that U.S. intelligence agencies have developed effective methods to break into devices from iPhones and Android phones to Samsung "smart" televisions, allowing them to monitor communications even when devices are turned off. The documents also disclose malware, viruses, and security vulnerabilities known as "zero days" and several hundred million lines of code used by the CIA, as well as the agency's ability to break into devices and intercept messages before they can be encrypted by applications such as WhatsApp, Signal, Telegram, Confide, and others many people wrongly considered to be secure.

In short, in case anyone had any doubts, privacy is a fiction, for any person or any organization. Not that that's much of a surprise, but it's still disquieting to see the details. Only the naïve would believe that several other countries with advanced cyber-technology don't have similar capabilities as the U.S., if not exactly with the depth and breadth of those now on display.

Trump and his supporters now can point to the pervasiveness and sophistication of these techniques in support of the President's claim that his predecessor, Barack Obama, bugged his communications at Trump Tower in New York. Deep State and MSM enemies of the President will cite the same evidence as support for the kind of capabilities that Russia likely also has, feeding their unsupported claims that Russian hackers tried to, and perhaps succeeded in, skewing the election in favor or Trump and against Hillary Clinton. The release of these new documents at a time when anti-Trumpers already had claimed Lt. Gen. Mike Flynn's scalp and are aiming for that of Attorney General Jeff Sessions will be taken as further confirmation of their claim that Wikileaks is a tool of Moscow.

The new document cache will be picked over for some time and new conclusions drawn, but even now there are some lessons to be learned.

First, Vault 7 completely demolishes the already meager claim in December 2016 from the outgoing Obama administration that evidence of "Russian code" in alleged hacking of the Democratic National Committee proved Moscow's involvement. That argument was absurd on its face even when it was made, roughly equivalent to suggesting that because a gang of bank robbers used a Volkswagen for a getaway car they must have been Germans. Clearly Russian hackers would use anything but Russian software to avoid pointing back to themselves. Wikileaks now confirms the CIA's use of Russian software for false-flag effect:

> The CIA's Remote Devices Branch's UMBRAGE group collects and maintains a substantial library of attack techniques 'stolen' from malware produced in other states including the Russian Federation.
>
> With UMBRAGE and related projects the CIA cannot only increase its total number of attack types but also misdirect attribution by leaving behind the 'fingerprints' of the groups that the attack techniques were stolen from.

Second, Vault 7 should be scrubbed for evidence of coordination between American agencies and those of the other "Five Eyes" Anglosphere countries with which the U.S. closely shares intelligence: the United Kingdom, Canada, Australia, and New Zealand. Why? There's a saying in Washington: never believe anything until it's been officially denied. Obama has been lawyerly definitive in his denials of ordering taps on Trump and his team or on any American citizen, ever. More precise in his language has been James Clapper, former Director of National Intelligence (DNI), who states that "there was no wiretap against Trump Tower during the campaign conducted by any part of the national intelligence community." This begs the question of whether Trump was tapped not by a U.S. "national" agency but by one of the Five Eyes sister agencies, which then passed the information back to their American colleagues, a ploy to avoid legal prohibitions on domestic spying or even a *pro forma* warrant requirement. A U.S. former intelligence official familiar with the practice tells me that such a maneuver was not only a possible means for the espionage against Trump but probable. The most likely agency to have carried out the task is the UK's Government Communications Headquarters (GCHQ), formal counterpart of the U.S. National Security Agency and its virtual satellite.

"GCHQ: You Read It Here First"

Jim Jatras | *Strategic Culture* | March 23, 2017

This is a fast-moving story, so there's a chance that more may have happened by the time you read it.

On March 9, *Strategic Culture Foundation* published in English and Serbian my commentary about Wikileaks' release of its "Vault 7" of CIA documents. It concluded with the following speculation as to who might have spied on the incoming team of Donald Trump on behalf of his predecessor Barack Obama and elements of the Deep State still effectively working for him:

> Vault 7 should be scrubbed for evidence of coordination between American agencies and those of the other "Five Eyes" Anglosphere countries with which the U.S. closely shares intelligence: the United Kingdom, Canada, Australia, and New Zealand. Why? There's a saying in Washington: never believe anything until it's been officially denied. Obama has been lawyerly definitive in his denials of ordering taps on Trump and his team or on any American citizen, ever. More precise in his language has been James Clapper, former Director of National Intelligence (DNI), who states that "there was no wiretap against Trump Tower during the campaign conducted by *any part of the national intelligence community.*" This begs the question of whether Trump was tapped not by a U.S. "national" agency but by one of the Five Eyes sister agencies, which then passed the information back to their American colleagues, a ploy to avoid legal prohibitions on domestic spying or even a pro forma warrant requirement. A U.S. former intelligence official familiar with the practice tells me that such a maneuver was not only a possible means for the espionage against Trump but probable. The most likely agency to have carried out the task is the UK's Government Communi-

cations Headquarters (GCHQ), formal counterpart of the U.S. National Security Agency and its virtual satellite.

As far as I know, no one else had conjectured in print specifically about GCHQ's possible role. Keep in mind, it was only a theory. I didn't have then, and I don't have now, any hard evidence to back it up. I simply said: here's a place the specialists might want to look for evidence. As might be expected, my comments attracted no further attention of which I'm aware.

Several days later, on March 13, Judge Andrew Napolitano, a longtime, widely respected legal commentator on *Fox News*—closely followed by the White House—stated that he had three intelligence sources independently confirm to him that in fact GCHQ had spied on Trump:

> "Three intelligence sources have informed *Fox News* that President Obama went outside the chain of command—he didn't use the NSA, he didn't use the CIA, he didn't use the FBI and he didn't use the Department of Justice," Napolitano said, adding that the former president "used GCHQ."

As later published by Napolitano in print by *Fox*:

> Enter James Bond.
>
> Sources have told me that the British foreign surveillance service, the Government Communications Headquarters, known as GCHQ, most likely provided Obama with transcripts of Trump's calls. The NSA has given GCHQ full 24/7 access to its computers, so GCHQ—a foreign intelligence agency that, like the NSA, operates outside our constitutional norms—has the digital versions of all electronic communications made in America in 2016, including Trump's. So by bypassing all American intelligence services, Obama would have had access to what he wanted with no Obama administration fingerprints.
>
> Thus, when senior American intelligence officials denied that their agencies knew about this, they were probably being truthful. Adding to this ominous scenario is the fact that three days after Trump's inauguration, the head of GCHQ, Robert Hannigan, abruptly resigned, stating that he wished to spend more time with his family.

There's no reason to think that Napolitano was in any way basing his claim on what I had written. It's also perhaps of note that while he claimed three sources on the air on March 13, he declined to do so later in print, referring only to "sources."

As one might expect, GCHQ instantly denied the accuracy of the judge's claim, on March 14 calling it (through an unnamed "security official"—though some stories identified the source as being with MI6, a different British agency) "totally untrue and quite frankly absurd." That itself is unusual. Intelligence agencies usually prefer the formula of "neither confirm nor deny" and avoid getting pulled into definitive statements of fact that could prove problematic later.

As we say in Washington, never believe anything until it's been officially denied. I would apply the same rule in London.

The row kicked up again on March 16, when White House spokesman Sean Spicer quoted at length from Napolitano's comments. He was clear to point out that he was not making the assertion himself, simply noting what Judge Napolitano had claimed. Spicer's comments prompted further outraged howls from the UK, including calls to the White House from the British

Embassy in Washington on March 17. That same day, National Security Adviser Lt. Gen. H.R. McMaster was reported as having given the British assurances that the claims about GCHQ would not be repeated, prompting debates as to whether or not the U.S. had apologized. As reported by the militantly anti-Trump *Washington Post*:

> At a news briefing Friday, a spokesman for British Prime Minister Theresa May said: "We have received assurances from the White House that these allegations would not be repeated." The spokesman would not confirm reports in the British media that the White House had apologized to Britain. . . . "Recent allegations made by media commentator Judge Andrew Napolitano about GCHQ being asked to conduct 'wire tapping' against the then President Elect are nonsense. They are utterly ridiculous and should be ignored," GCHQ said in a statement.

But later that same day, March 17, Trump himself went right back to the same allegations, during a frosty joint press conference with German Chancellor Angela Merkel:

> "We said nothing," Trump said when asked about the former judge's claims regarding the Government Communications Headquarters (GCHQ). "I didn't make an opinion on it. All we did was quote a certain very talented legal mind who was the one responsible for saying that on television," Trump said. "That was a statement made by a very talented lawyer on Fox [News]. And so you shouldn't be talking to me, you should be talking to Fox."

Trump's comments prompted *Fox News* host Shepard Smith to deny it had information validating Napolitano's claims: "*Fox News* cannot confirm Judge Napolitano's commentary. Fox News knows of no evidence of any kind that the now-President of the United States was surveilled at any time in any way. Full stop." On March 20 media reported that *Fox News* had indefinitely dropped Napolitano's appearances on the network as a legal analyst.

End of story, right? Napolitano was wrong and got the sack.

Not so fast. On March 21:

> A longtime friend of Trump's, Stone told *DailyMail.com* that "despite the quick denials", he thinks "Judge Napolitano is correct."
>
> My own sources high up in the Tory government, who are quite powerful, assured me that there was surveillance by the Brits", he stated. "Of course they deny it. That's their job to deny it."
>
> Stone believes that Trump was under surveillance during both George W. Bush's and Barack Obama's presidencies.
>
> "We know from the government's database, that was leaked by CIA, veteran CIA operatives, who had realized the extra-constitutional nature of this program and spilled the beans, who became whistleblowers' that Trump's New York apartment and Palm Beach residence were monitored, Stone said, as well as "several of his resorts, his cell phone and so on."
>
> The information cited by Stone appeared Monday on *Infowars.com*.
>
> Infowars says the information it received from law enforcement suggests that Trump and site founder Alex Jones "were under illegal, unauthorized government monitoring" from 2004 to 2010.

So was he monitored this fall? I believe he was," Stone said Monday evening of Trump.

One late-breaking piece to the puzzle: Paul Mulshine of the *Star-Ledger of New Jersey* (Napolitano's home state) suggests the *Fox News* threw the judge under the bus knowing full well that no less than the *New York Times*—the unofficial U.S. "newspaper of record"—had on March 1 reported British and Dutch agencies spying on Trump, based on what may be the same three sources Napolitano referred to ("Fox News or Weasel News? Why did the network scapegoat Andrew Napolitano?"):

> American allies, including the British and the Dutch, had provided information describing meetings in European cities between Russian officials—and others close to Russia's president, Vladimir Putin— and associates of President-elect Trump, according to three former American officials who requested anonymity in discussing classified intelligence.

At this point, it's hard to know what the truth is. But I'm willing to guess there's more to come on this story—which, remember, you saw here first.

"What Can Be Expected from the Trump—Xi Mar-a-LagoSummit?"

Jim Jatras | *Strategic Culture* | March 30, 2017

The upcoming summit between US President Donald Trump and Chinese President Xi Jinping offers an early test of the Trump Administration's willingness to depart from the policies of global "unipolar" domination and pointless confrontation that have characterized the past three American presidencies. The very fact that the summit is taking place this early in the Trump presidency is an encouraging sign.

The first thing to keep in mind is the American side's lack of unity of purpose. Trump himself, and probably Secretary of State Rex Tillerson, can be expected to approach the summit in a businesslike "let's make a deal" fashion. Their primary goal, far more important than anything else, can be expected to be redressing what they see as a massive imbalance in US-China trade.

But we also have to consider the influence of Trump's national security team, which is dominated by military men who think all problems derive from insufficient American "leadership" and inadequate use or threat of force. While they are more circumspect in relation to China than they would be about, for example, how to approach ISIS or Iran, their default position is defined by military responses: air and naval challenges to China's claims in the South China Sea, deploying the THAAD system in South Korea (ROK), threatening a military response to North Korean (DPRK) missile tests.

Finally, we still have the baneful influence of the US permanent ("Deep State") bureaucracy and Barack Obama holdovers, for whom American global dominance and attempts to dictate other countries' internal affairs and external policies are an article of faith. (We can probably thank this group for ramming through Montenegro's NATO accession this week, after months of heroic resistance by Senator Rand Paul.)

Knowing these divisions, the Chinese will certainly approach the Americans with wariness. Beijing's task will be how to assess the relative weight of Trump's economic and trade imperatives—which China will be loath to rebalance in the Americans' favor but may have little choice—versus the PRC's vital national security interests. Regarding the latter, the two most important are the Korean Peninsula and the South China Sea, where the American military men and the Deep Staters will want to dictate to Beijing. The challenge for the Chinese will be how to leverage Trump's relative lack of interest in security matters and give primacy to his economic goals.

In my view, the optimal outcome for both sides would be for Beijing to make compromises on trade in exchange for American concessions in the security sphere that in effect recognize a Chinese security sphere in the western Pacific. This can and should result in significant US walk-back of policies that pointlessly threaten China's security but don't enhance American security:

Korea

US policymakers routinely demand more "pressure" on Beijing to restrain the DPRK. Reasonable Chinese initiatives, such as the recent proposal for mutual moratoria on DPRK missile tests and on US-ROK military exercises were summarily dismissed by the US. Chinese (and Russian) concerns about THAAD system coverage of their sovereign territory were similarly ignored. Seemingly the US side does not comprehend that American military threats and countermeasures encourage even more warlike and erratic responses from Pyongyang. Failure to appreciate the counterproductive impact of America policy is largely due to the conviction that no bad result can ever be Washington's fault—which would constitute "blaming America." It will be a formidable task for the Chinese to convey why they have a vital, nonnegotiable security interest in the survival of the DPRK: if the DPRK were, for any reason, to cease to exist, a unified Korea under the Seoul government allied with the US would mean the prospect of American forces on the Chinese border. (The Americans might deny that, but consider the expansion of NATO with the dissolution of the Warsaw Pact and collapse of the USSR.) Such a presence would be an intolerable threat to China's vital national security interests, hence Beijing's need for the DPRK to continue to exist as long as the Americans are in the ROK. Given Trump's expressed concerns about how our allies take advantage of us and don't pay for their own defense (and in the case of the South Koreans, also are killing US jobs in a lopsided trade relationship), an open-ended discussion should be proposed as to under what circumstances US forces might eventually be withdrawn from the peninsula. Washington must understand that stepping back from current provocative actions could, with Chinese help, achieve future conditions where US security guarantee to the ROK become irrelevant.

The South China Sea

American critics of Beijing's claims in the South China Sea cite two principles: a supposed US interest in freedom of navigation and open sea lanes, and the claimed illegality of China's building militarized artificial islands and claiming the waters around them. Regarding navigation of the South China Sea, it seemingly escapes American notice that China in no way is threatening sea lanes and that, given the relative volume of container shipping, the sea lanes are of benefit to the PRC much more than to the US. Regarding the islands, the American position is largely an expression of our desire always to be the referee of the legitimacy of other nations' actions, whether we have an interest or not. (Would China care if the US built artificial islands in the Caribbean and claimed them as sovereign American territory? Of course not.) Xi no doubt will make it clear that her islands in the South China Sea are sovereign Chinese territory and that military probing by the US will eventually lead to unfortunate consequences that neither side wants. Proposals guaranteeing other countries' rights to legitimate transit could have some positive impact, especially if they would be acceptable to US regional partners, notably the Philippines.

It will not be an easy task for Xi to extract meaningful retreat by Washington on either of these strategic issues. Nor will Trump find the Chinese a pushover on trade. But if deal-making impulses can replace the policies of diktat that have characterized American policymaking for a quarter of a century, as successful "win-win" summit could set a standard for future progress in other forums.

"Tillerson in Moscow: Is World War III Back on Track?"

Jim Jatras | *Strategic Culture* | April 14, 2017

If anyone is worried whether the prospect of a major war, which many of us considered almost inevitable if Hillary Clinton had attained the White House, is back on track, Secretary of State Rex Tillerson's visit to Moscow was cold comfort. From his remarks together with his counterpart Sergey Lavrov, there is now little reason to expect any improvement in US-Russia ties anytime soon, if ever, and much reason to expect them to get worse—a lot worse.

There has been a great deal of speculation as to why President Donald Trump, who promised a break with the warmongering policies Hillary would have implemented, and which characterized the administrations of Barack Obama, George W. Bush, and Bill Clinton, would have bombed Syria's Shayrat airbase in retaliation for a supposed chemical weapons (CW) strike without evidence or authorization from either Congress or the UN Security Council.

(I won't bore anyone familiar with Balkan affairs with the almost certain origin of the gas attack in Idlib. The odds that it was a false flag by the jihadists far, far outweigh any chance of a CW attack by Syrian government forces. To cite the "Markale market massacres" is enough. Ghouta September 2013 wasn't the first such deception in Syria, and Idlib April 2017 won't be the last. American media condemning Assad for the CW attack and demanding justice for the victims never mention that the site is held by al-Qaeda and that they themselves have a CW capability. Nor that the jihadists likely knew when and where Syrian planes would be operating, since the Russians would have notified the US under the deconfliction agreement. This is not to rule out the Russian explanation that the release was due to Syrian bombing of the jihadists' CW cache but I consider the planned provocation more likely based on the timing. Predictably, an amateurish four-page paper issued by the US intelligence community to justify accusations against Assad contained zero evidence.)

Among the reasons speculated for President Trump's abrupt reversal of his campaign positions:

–   Trump actually believes Assad was responsible, based on false intelligence fed to him by National Security Adviser H.R. McMaster and others, or on an emotional appeal from his daughter, Ivanka, based on sensational media coverage.
–   Trump doesn't believe it but someone gave him The Talk: "Do what you're told, Mr. President, or you and Barron will end up like Jack Kennedy."
–   Whether or not he believes Assad is to blame for the CW attack, Trump wants to improve ties with the Russians and work together with them to defeat the jihadists in Syria and end the war, and perhaps cut a "grand bargain" that includes Ukraine, but he can't because of the domestic pressure from the media, the Deep State, almost all of the Democrats, and a lot of Republicans on the evidence-free charge that Moscow tried to skew the 2016 election. (That seems to be partly working, with many formerly harsh critics now praising him. On the other hand, his own base is now split between those who cheer any jingoistic use of force and those who see that another optional war will doom his domestic priority to "Make America Great Again!") The one piece of evidence that supports this conjecture is the extremely limited pinprick nature of the US strike on Shayrat.
–   Related to the previous point, given the power of the domestic forces conspiring against him, Trump needed to project strength. (My guess is that Moscow, Beijing, and others will conclude just the opposite: he is weak and not even master in his own house.)
–   Trump is impulsive and lacking in substance, so he goes for the quickest and easiest path to what he perceives to be current advantage. The praise of his former detractors—mainly those who have denigrated and derided him—will prove short-lived. At the earliest opportunity those hailing him now as "presidential" will be the first to call for his head.
–   Trump's real priority was to impress the Chinese on Korea, with a show of force during President Xi Jinping's summit in the US. Sending an aircraft carrier group to the waters near Korea with a barrage of bellicose rhetoric that the US will resolve the North Korea issue if China doesn't reinforces this theory, at least in part. Whether Xi was impressed the way Trump might have intended it is another conjecture.

Whatever the motives, the real question is what comes next. Aside from when another false flag may occur—which Washington in effect invited with threats of a further, more devastating military action against Syria—it matters whether behind closed doors Tillerson's proposals differed from his public comments. Broadly speaking, there are two possibilities:

1.   Tillerson may have said, in effect, that Trump has laid down a marker, neutralized domestic critics, and shown he's a big dog—now let's get down to business. All the accusatory language is just for show, so Trump will have greater flexibility of action. In the weeks prior to the Idlib CW attack, Washington and Moscow had seemed to be coordinating on plans for an offensive against Daesh in Raqqa and airstrikes against al-Qaeda in Idlib. The US and Russia together need to find a way to wrap up this war that defeats the enemy Trump campaigned against: radical Islamic terrorism. It's up to the Syrian people to work

out who their leaders should be. If there are security concerns America's Israeli, Turkish, and Sunni friends have, let's find a way to address them within that larger context—

or

2. Tillerson's private comments were consistent with his public statements, amounting to imposing the US Deep State's agenda on Moscow. That diktat gives priority to blocking some mythical "Shia Crescent" to keep our Sunni "allies" and Israel happy. Assad must go on some specified timetable, though we may grandly allow him so preside over a rump Alawite state in western Syria on a temporary basis; if Assad goes along, we'll let him retire to Moscow, but if he waits until the next chemical provocation it's off to The Hague or we'll kill him ourselves. Syria must be partitioned: we will allow Moscow to participate in a marginal role on the "defeat" of Daesh with a blitzkrieg on Raqqa but then create a "Sunnistan" (or maybe more than one) in eastern Syria, run by some hand-picked jihadi group friendly to the Saudis—basically Daesh with new hats and flag: Islamic State "lite." To limit Kurdish aspirations Turkey might be awarded a "Turkmen" zone in the new Syria, as well as primacy over a neighboring al-Qaeda-administered area. Also, we can anticipate a demand that Russia be prepared to step aside and not oppose an operation for regime change in Tehran.

Even the first message might have been a hard sell given how poisoned the well is and the depth of the abyss of Russian mistrust of the United States. No matter how positive anything Tillerson might have said privately, can anyone in Moscow now believe anything from Washington?

But if the message was the second one, as I believe it was, the Russians would have little choice but to conclude that a major war may be unavoidable and they will plan accordingly. (China would reach the same conclusion.) Plans being made when it was assumed Hillary Clinton was going to win but tentatively mothballed with Trump's election will be pulled out and updated. Paradoxically, Moscow might still acquiesce to Tillerson's demands on Syria but only in the spirit of August 1939—a temporary expedient to buy time and space for what must come.

I of course hope the message was the first but fear it was the second. The white-hot rhetoric coming out of Washington is far in excess of that needed to position US opinion for a reasonable deal with Moscow. Quite to the contrary, it seems calculated to burn any bridges back from anything but regime change and more war. Once again, as has been the case since the Cold War ended in 1991—but only on the Russian side—US goals look to be geopolitical and ideological, not based on American national interest. The agendas of the Deep State and our regional "allies" will continue to set US policy. Russia must be destroyed as an independent power, right after Syria, Iran, and North Korea but before China. (In a Balkan sideshow, Trump this week signed the NATO accession of Montenegro, effectively completing encirclement of Serbia. At a White House meeting with Jens Stoltenberg, Trump praised NATO.) As was the case in Bosnia, Kosovo, and Libya, and today in Syria, the US is happy to use jihadists as proxies while coldly watching them eliminate centuries-old Christian communities.

In short, the usual. If such a path has been chosen by Trump, as appears likely, it may well doom his presidency to failure. But in context, that would be the least of our worries.

I would be very, very glad to be proved wrong.

"Has the Globalist Establishment Defeated the Populist–NationalistRevolt?"

Jim Jatras | *Strategic Culture* | April 27, 2017

Last year, when the people of the United Kingdom voted in favor of leaving the European Union, the Establishment in Europe and the United States was stunned. All the polls had predicted a win for the Remain camp. Everyone who counted, including Hillary Clinton and Barack Obama, made it clear that staying within the increasingly dysfunctional EU was the only acceptable option.

The friendly advice of global elites, from all the smart, beautiful, and rich people on both sides of the Pond, was rejected by the people of Britain—or by the people of England and Wales, anyway. What was considered unlikely or even impossible nonetheless happened. Britain, it seemed, was not dead yet.

Next came the United States. All the experts said Hillary Clinton's victory was a foregone conclusion. The only serious questions were how large her win would be, whether other Republicans running for Congress and state offices could escape the vortex of Donald Trump's debacle of historical proportions, whom would she select for her Cabinet, and when would World War III start. (Indeed, some seriously suggested that Trump had run solely to help ensure Hillary's path to the White House, as the only Republican who could manage to lose to such a flawed Democratic standard-bearer.) But working-class voters in America's Rust Belt—Pennsylvania, Ohio, Wisconsin, Michigan—flipped the Establishment a rude gesture and elected Trump. America, it seemed, was not dead yet.

On both sides of the Atlantic the revolt had been unleashed! Ordinary citizens demanding to claw back power from the Davos class were on the march! What began in 2016 would surely continue in 2017.

Except it didn't.

Actually, the counterattack of the Establishment began already in 2016. In Austria, Norbert Hofer of the Freedom Party of Austria (FPÖ), who earlier in the year had initially squeaked out a narrow win, which was then reversed by questionable absentee ballots, only then to be nullified by a court challenge, lost to an establishment candidate in a December re-run. The loss came after a predictable campaign of vilification of the FPÖ and Hofer as (choose your favorite) racist, anti-Semitic, Islamophobic, fascist, Nazi, and so forth.

The first test of what some have called the "Trump effect" had failed.

Next came the Netherlands. The March 15 vote saw the defeat of the Party for Freedom of Geert Wilders, who promised to hold a Brexit-style referendum to take the Netherlands out of the EU—"Nexit." Focused heavily on to the harmful impact of Islamic immigration and Muslims' refusal to integrate into Dutch society and accept Dutch social standards, Wilders made an even more attractive target than Hofer for those whose concept of Europe includes abolishing its traditional identity. Even though polls showed most Dutch voters favoring a referendum, the result was another defeat for the "far-Right." (Why is there never a "far-Left"?)

Now we come to France. Three-quarters of French citizens cast their ballots in the first round for candidates who to one extent or another wanted to renegotiate or end France's relationship with the EU ("Frexit"), and maybe

NATO too, and to restore ties with Russia. The only top contender who did not make such an offer, Emmanuel Macron—an Establishment candidate fraudulently branded an "outsider" by the servile media—is heavily favored to win over (you guessed it) "racist" "far-Right" "fascist" "Islamophobic" "xenophobic" Marine Le Pen of the National Front. Some media are already warning in grim terms about Russian intrigues to secure her victory, preemptively discrediting her if she does somehow manage to win, or at least to sow "doubt/discord/confusion."

Which brings us back the United States again. Trump won, but he is far from fully in control of the apparatus of the US government. Congressional inquiries into Russian influence in the election and on his team now suggest that General Michael Flynn, Trump's first National Security Adviser, could face criminal charges. Federal judges brazenly disregard the laws and the Constitution to strike down Trump's efforts to police America's borders and deport illegal aliens.

Taking what may seem now to him the path of least resistance, Trump and his appointees have instituted a national security policy that hardly differs from Obama's or what Hillary's would have been if she had won:

- Vilify Russia, maintain sanctions, and keep expanding NATO (welcome Montenegro!), which turns out not to be "obsolete" after all;
- Bomb Syria and demand "regime change" in Damascus;
- Expand military operations in Afghanistan, including dropping the "Mother of All Bombs";
- Threaten North Korea and Iran with military action; and
- Press China on Korea and the South China Sea, while offering concessions on trade—a complete reversal of what should have been Trump's deal.

Part of this reflects bad personnel selections. Part of it may be a calculation born of necessity—one step forward, two steps back. (After all, Steve Bannon has called himself a Leninist.) The pinprick strike on Syria indicates it may have been mainly for show.

But most of all we see how weak Trump's position is, election or no election. The Establishment may not have been able to stop him at the ballot box, partly because of how horrible the competing candidate and her campaign were. But they still may get the last laugh.

If indeed Le Pen is defeated, it may show that the corrupt, plutocratic, anti-Christian, anti-national pseudo-elites have found the formula to ensure their perpetuation in power, for a while anyway. That, however, will do nothing to address the political, economic, demographic, and above all spiritual crises that characterize their misrule. It means only that they have beat back orderly and peaceful attempts by decent citizens to change course before it's too late. If that turns out to be the case, it will only mean that the collapse, when it comes, will be all the more terrible.

"A Splendid Little War Could End Trump's Presidency"

Jim Jatras | *Chronicles* | May 02, 2017

Letter from Pergamum-on-the-Potomac

Here's an interesting hypothetical.

Suppose the Trump Administration's game of chicken with Pyongyang goes wrong. Suppose it results in the vaporization of a goodly portion of Seoul's 10 million-plus population, not to mention almost all of the 28 thousand or so American troops in South Korea.

It's not an unrealistic scenario. Sure, there are those who say it can't happen, that common sense will prevail—as though common sense were a plentiful commodity. But pretty much every gaming out of "kinetic military action" (to use the buzzword *du jour*) in Korea leads to a grim outcome.

Never mind the human cost for a moment, or the devastating reprisal that would be visited on millions of North Koreans, almost all of them hapless victims. Ask: What would be the impact on Donald Trump's political fortunes? Would he be impeached for what would be a self-inflicted catastrophe of world historical proportions?

Even if he remained in office, would he be rendered nothing more than a pathetic, disgraced placeholder? Say goodbye to the Mexican wall, to restructured trade ties, to the whole MAGA agenda.

Why is it hard to shake the sense that some of those egging on Trump's newfound bellicosity in Korea and elsewhere would be thrilled with such a development?

Ever since he unleashed cruise missiles on a Syrian airbase in reprisal for an extremely dubious claim that the Damascus government had used chemical weapons against civilians, Trump seemingly has gotten in touch with his inner neoconservative. Repudiating in deed if not in word the America First policy on which he pledged his sacred trust during the campaign, Trump and his appointees have instituted a national security policy that hardly differs from Obama's or what Hillary's would have been if she had won:

- Vilify Russia, maintain sanctions, and keep expanding NATO (welcome Montenegro!), which turns out not to be "obsolete" after all;
- Bomb Syria and demand "regime change" in Damascus;
- Expand military operations in Afghanistan, including dropping the "Mother Of All Bombs";
- Threaten North Korea and Iran with military action; and
- Press China on Korea and the South China Sea, while offering concessions on trade—a complete reversal of what should have been Trump's deal.

Part of this reflects bad personnel selections. Boxed in by Russia-gate, part of it may be a short-term calculation born of perceived necessity—one step forward, two steps back. (After all, Steve Bannon has called himself a Leninist.) The pinprick strike on Syria indicates it may have been mainly for show.

Most of all, though, we see how weak Trump's position is, election or no election. The Establishment may not have been able to stop him at the ballot box, largely because of how horrible the competing candidate and her campaign were. But they still may get the last laugh.

Perhaps more is at work than just flipping Trump to the neocon team, the way George W. Bush, who had promised a more "humble" foreign policy, was converted after 9/11. Can the Deep State and the MSM really rest easy with Trump in the White House? Goading and cheering him into a senseless war maybe provide a definitive solution to the Trump problem.

However bad it goes, the President's newfound admirers certainly would not blame the disaster on their globalist ideology. Rather, the scapegoat would be readily at hand: a shallow, superficial, unqualified Twitter-addicted unstable personality who never should have been allowed into the Oval Office. "We supported him all the way but he just messed it up."

If and when catastrophe strikes, in Korea, or Syria, or Iran or any one of the other places where Trump is being encouraged to press the envelope, former Trump critics now hailing the return of "leading from the front" will not take the fall. No, the albatross will be hung around Trump's neck and those of the benighted deplorables who elected him.

Who then would be left to defend him?

"Attack on Media May Presage Return of Donald Trump of 2016"

Jim Jatras | *Strategic Culture* | May 6, 2017

In what may be the shortest revolution on record, Donald Trump's performance on national security affairs has been a tremendous disappointment to those of his supporters who took seriously his pledge of an America First foreign policy. Seemingly controlled or intimidated by the very Deep State and mainstream media (MSM) he denounced during the campaign, he has looked to be going out of his way to adopt globalist and belligerent policies toward Russia in Europe and especially in Syria, toward China over North Korea, and of course towards Iran.

In recent days, in classic Trump style, he appeared to soften his tone on Korea by suggesting he'd be "honored" to meet with Kim Jong-un. He talked with Russian President Vladimir Putin about possibly getting cooperation in Syria back on track. But most significantly of all, he re-launched his assault on the same media that had at least briefly praised him for his foreign bellicosity, especially for the needless, unjustified, and militarily insignificant strike on Syria's Shayrat airbase after what almost certainly was a false flag attack by jihad terrorists supported by the U.S. Deep State and our regional allies.

The annual White House Correspondents' Dinner in Washington is a posh affair that embodies the cozy, incestuous relationship between the Deep State and the MSM. Even Republican presidents despised by the media, like George W. Bush and Ronald Reagan, were expected to be "good sports" playing along with the vanity of narcissists who imagine themselves walking, talking embodiments of freedom of the press enshrined in the First Amendment to the U.S. Constitution. (That vanity is itself part of the problem. Freedom of the press is a right of all citizens, not just self-anointed media professionals. Saying it only pertains to certified journalists would be comparable to limiting the First Amendment's freedom of religion to clergymen.)

In place of going to the Dinner, Trump instead went to Harrisburg, Pennsylvania, the capital of a working-class Rust Belt state that no Republican had won in decades and without whose votes he would not today be president. Speaking at a campaign-style rally roughly at the same time the Dinner was proceeding without him, Trump and his supporters reveled in their contempt for the MSM:

As you may know, there's another big gathering taking place tonight in Washington D.C. Did you hear about it? A large group of Hollywood actors [*the crowd boos*] and Washington media [*more boos*] are consoling each other in a hotel ballroom in our nation's capital right now. . . . I could not possibly be more thrilled than to be more than 100 miles away from Washington's swamp . . . with a much, much larger crowd and much better people. . . . They are gathered together for the White House Correspondent's Dinner—without the president! Media outlets like CNN and MSNBC are fake news, fake news.

So, just as an example of media, take the totally failing New York Times. Pretty soon they'll only be on the Internet—the paper's getting small and smaller. You ever notice? It's starting to look like a comic book, it's getting small.

Back in Washington at the Dinner, as though on cue, the president of the White House Correspondents' Association stated: "We are not fake news. We are not failing news organizations. We are not the enemy of the American people."

Like Richard Nixon's infamous "I am not a crook", there are some denials that cannot sound like anything but a confirmation of the accusation. Who would stand on a dais to give a nationally televised speech to deny being a fake, a failure, and an enemy of the people except someone who knows that he and his associates are in fact all of those things? And more, that Americans also know they are those things and despise them for it.

The battle lines of America's cold civil war are becoming clearer all the time. Free speech and freedom of the media are at the heart of the struggle, as witnessed by "Antifa" mobs violently shutting down speakers with which they disagree, with barely a murmur of protest from "journalists" of the sort gathered at the Dinner.

As the old saying goes, one robin does not a spring make. Harrisburg may be a start if it's followed by action. It's too soon to say that Trump's flirtation with the warmongering ways of his predecessors was just a feint to position himself for a counterattack that may now be starting. But perhaps it's reason to hope.

"Trump Tries to Get His Footing in the Washington Swamp: Firing James Comey While Moving Forward with Russia in Syria"

Jim Jatras | *Strategic Culture* | May 12, 2017

The sudden firing of FBI Director James Comey has become the newest bright, shiny object distracting everybody in Washington. Predictably, reaction falls sharply down the usual lines of division.

For Trump supporters, Comey's dismissal is a needed step in "draining the Washington Swamp", as he promised during the campaign. Given that Comey is someone so detested by Democrats, who blame him (and Vladimir Putin) for Hillary Clinton's defeat, perhaps choosing that particular scalp to nail to the wall was calculated to confuse and split the opposition.

If so, it didn't work very well. Barely had the news of Comey's dismissal been reported than Democrats shrieked it was for the purpose of crippling investigation into baseless allegations of collusion between the Trump campaign and the Kremlin. On the mainstream American media, that's all you hear: Russia, Russia, Russia, cover-up, cover-up, cover-up. Unsurprisingly, Congressional Republicans, many of them Trump-haters anyway, are intimidated. Those calling for a Special Counsel to conduct the investigation may finally get their way.

In short, what may be the first decisive counterattack from President Trump against the permanent government in Washington may have the effect of turning up the heat on him from the same forces that are determined to destroy him. Most of all, they hope they can forestall any opening to Moscow by beating the drum on Russian interference with the US election and accusing Trump of removing Comey to hide his misdeeds.

The Comey firing comes just as we are beginning to see some small signs that Washington and Moscow are finally making a start in a common effort against the threat of radical Islamic terrorism. Throughout the 2016 campaign then-candidate Donald Trump repeatedly voiced the need to get along with Russia.

For Trump's opponents, such thoughts confirmed their accusations that he was Vladimir Putin's puppet, the "Siberian Candidate." Many of his supporters saw it as part of his America First policy, the end of foreign nation-building and unnecessary wars.

Unfortunately, the direction Trump had signaled in 2016 didn't materialize in 2017. Perhaps daunted by critics determined to block any possible US-Russia rapprochement, the first three months of the current administration were framed by the same anti-Russian rhetoric that characterized that of Barack Obama and the campaign of Hillary Clinton. Things got even worse with the April chemical weapons attack in Syria, which the US immediately and without evidence blamed on Syrian government forces supported by Russia. Prospects increased for American and Russian direct military confrontation.

During his trip to Moscow last month, Secretary of State Rex Tillerson told Putin that the "relationship between our two nations was the lowest it's been since the Cold War and it's spiraling down, it's getting worse. . . . the two greatest nuclear powers in the world cannot have this kind of relationship. We have to change it." According to Tillerson, the Russian president nodded in agreement.

Change seems to be happening, however slowly. The dismissal of Comey came on the eve of a meeting between Tillerson and Foreign Minister Lavrov in Washington to discuss Syria. Responding the Senate Democratic Leader Charles Schumer's accusation that removing Comey was related to Russia, Trump tweeted: "Cryin' Chuck Schumer stated recently, 'I do not have confidence in him (James Comey) any longer.' Then acts so indignant. #draintheswamp." In a last-minute announcement calculated to enrage his enemies, Trump also met with Lavrov. Seemingly joining in the taunts, when asked by media whether the Comey firing would cast a shadow over his talks, Lavrov quipped, "Was he fired? You are kidding. You are kidding."

More importantly, Lavrov commented following the meeting:

"Our dialogue as of now is free from ideology that was very typical for Obama's administration. . . . Both Trump and Secretary of State and his administration as I realized today once again are business-like people and they want to reach agreements not for the sake of

demonstrating their achievements to anyone in terms of their ideological preferences."

On substance, the United States now seems to be prepared to cooperate, on
some level, with an arrangement for safe zones jointly guaranteed by Russia,
Turkey, and Iran. While fraught with difficulties and potential for renewed
conflict, the arrangement may finally set the stage for progress towards a
political settlement to the Syrian war and common action against the Islamic
State, al-Qaeda, and their allies. In a decision sure to aggravate relations with
NATO ally Turkey, Trump also has announced providing advanced weapons
to Kurdish forces in preparation for an offensive against Raqqa.

Such moves are bound to provoke furious attempts at disruptions.
Topping the list of immediate concerns is the danger of a replay of the April
false flag chemical attack in Idlib. There are reports that General H.R.
McMaster, Trump's National Security Adviser and the rumored force behind
the strike against a Syrian air base, is in the president's disfavor and may also
get the sack.

More dangerous in the long run are the many domestic US special interest
groups who place their narrow goals and ambitions above the interests of
American people. These groups, aided by the mainstream/fake news media,
do not care about the misery and destruction around the world or the cost to
America in blood and treasure caused by our misguided foreign policy since
collapse of USSR. For them Russia is more useful as an enemy than as a friend.

It remains to be seen if Trump can beat back his domestic foes sufficiently
to escape the straitjacket on his policy options. That is the real battle, and it's
beginning to get serious.

"Trump's UN Speech: the Swamp's Wine in an 'America First!' Bottle"

Jim Jatras | *Strategic Culture* | September 22, 2017

In his maiden speech to the United Nations General Assembly, President
Donald Trump invoked the terms "sovereign" and "sovereignty" 21 times. In a
manner unimaginable coming from any other recent occupant of the White
House, the President committed the United States to the principle of national
sovereignty and to the truth that "the nation-state remains the best vehicle for
elevating the human condition." More, Trump rightly pointed out that these
pertain not just to the US and the safeguarding of American sovereignty but
to all countries:

> In foreign affairs, we are renewing this founding principle of sove-
> reignty. Our government's first duty is to its people, to our citizens—
> to serve their needs, to ensure their safety, to preserve their rights,
> and to defend their values.
>
> As President of the United States, I will always put America first,
> just like you, as the leaders of your countries will always, and should
> always, put your countries first.

Then he took it all back.

Listening to the president, one would almost think Trump was giving two different speeches, one rhetorical and one substantive. The rhetorical speech (reportedly authored by Stephen Miller) was the most stirring advocacy one could hope for of the rule of law and of the Westphalian principle of the sovereign state as the bedrock of the international order. The substantive speech, no doubt written by someone on the National Security Council staff, abrogates the very same Westphalian principle with the unlimited prerogatives of the planet's one government that reserves the right to violate or abolish the sovereignty of any other country—or to destroy that country altogether—for any reason political elites in Washington decide.

Numerous commentators immediately rushed to declare that Trump had dialed back to George W. Bush's 2002 "Axis of Evil" speech. (The phrase is attributed to then-speechwriter David Frum, now a moving figure behind the "Committee to Investigate Russia," which in the sage opinion of Rob Reiner and Morgan Freeman claims "we are at war" with Russia already.) Trump has now laid down what amounts to declarations of war against both North Korea and Iran. On both he has left himself very little room for maneuver, or for any compromise that would not be regarded as weakness or Obama-style "leading from behind." While hostilities against both countries may not be imminent (though in the case of North Korea, they might be) we are, barring unforeseen circumstances, now approaching the point of no return.

With respect to North Korea, some people assume that because the consequences would be patently catastrophic the "military option" *must* be off the table and that all this war talk is just bluster. That assumption is dead wrong. The once unthinkable is not only thinkable, it is increasingly probable. As Trump said: "The United States has great strength and patience, but if it is forced to defend itself or its allies, we will have no choice but to totally destroy North Korea." This is exactly backwards. Threatening North Korea with total destruction doesn't equate to the defense of the US (forget about our *faux* allies South Korea and Japan, which contribute nothing to our security), it positively increases the danger to our country and people. The Deep State would rather risk the lives of almost 30,000 American military personnel in Korea, of hundreds of thousands and perhaps millions of South Koreans, and of even more millions in North Korea—not to mention prodding Pyongyang to accelerate acquisition of a capability for a nuclear strike on the United States itself—than pry its grip off of a single square meter of our forward base against China on the northeast Asian mainland.

With respect to Iran, the relevant passages of Trump's speech could as well have been drafted in the Israeli and Saudi foreign ministries—and perhaps they were. Paradoxically, such favoritism toward some countries and hatred for others is the exact opposite of the *America First!* principle on which Trump won the presidency. As stated in his Farewell Address by our first and greatest president (wait—are we still allowed to say that? George Washington was a slave-owner!), a country that allows itself to be steered not by its own interests but the interests of others negates its own freedom and becomes a slave to its foreign affections and antipathies:

> "The nation which indulges toward another an habitual hatred or an habitual fondness is in some degree a slave. It is a slave to its animosity or to its affection, either of which is sufficient to lead it astray from its duty and its interest. Antipathy in one nation against another disposes each more readily to offer insult and injury, to lay hold of slight causes of umbrage, and to be haughty and intractable when accidental or trifling occasions of dispute occur."

Not to belabor the obvious, at least as far as foreign policy goes, the would-be Swamp-drainer has lost and the Swamp has won. We can speculate as to why. Some say Trump was always a liar and conman and had no intention of keeping his promises. (Let's see what he does on the "Dreamers" and throwing away his wall on the Mexican border. As Ann Coulter says, "If Trump doesn't get that wall built, and fast, his base will be done with him and feed him to Robert Mueller.") Others say Trump meant what he said during the campaign but now surrounded by generals and globalists that dominate his administration, and with populists in the White House now about as common as passenger pigeons, he's a virtual captive. If so, it's a captivity of his own making.

To be fair, Trump's populism was never based on consistent non-interventionism. In 2016 he promised more money for the Pentagon and vowed to be the most "militaristic" president ever. Still, he seemed to understand that wars of choice unrelated to vital national interests, like Bush's in Iraq and Obama's in Libya, were a waste of untold billions of dollars and produced only disasters.

His acceptance of the Swamp's continuation of the war in Afghanistan was his first major stumble towards the dismal path of his predecessors. War against North Korea or Iran, or God forbid both, would wreck his presidency and his pledge to "Make America Great Again!" even more surely than Iraq ruined Bush's.

Still unanswered: does Trump know that, does he care, and does he have the wherewithal to do anything about it? At the moment, it doesn't look good.

"Fake News Media Suppress Two Blockbuster Stories on Syria"

Jim Jatras | *Strategic Culture* | June 29, 2017

It has become the conventional wisdom that the information world has been forever changed by the advent of the Internet Age. Whereas in the past the established media were the only source of news and opinion, we are led to believe that now, with a virtually unlimited availability of independent voices, facts cannot be concealed and "the truth will out."

Unfortunately, that notion is far from reality, at least when issues of war and peace are concerned. While proliferation of first cable channels and then online publications means the establishment American networks (*ABC, CBS, NBC,* plus *CNN*) and newspapers (*New York Times* (a/k/a, the "newspaper of record"), *Washington Post*) have a smaller market share than in the past, they still have a near monopoly on the legitimacy and public significance of information. This means that while "alternative media"—itself a dismissive term relating to the presumed unreliability of contents—might report and document information contrary to the official line emanating from prestige media operating in symbiosis with their government sources, they can be ignored.

Despite the ubiquitous accessibility of online independent media, news and commentary about national security issues in the U.S. and Western Europe displays an almost Soviet-style façade of uniformity. Unlike the practice of the totalitarian states of the 20th century, maintaining the credibility of official media does not require the physical repression of alternatives. Instead of suppressing dissent, is it sufficient to maintain major media's role as gatekeeper and certifier of reliability. Information originating in "alternative" circles becomes reliable and publicly actionable only when picked up and disseminated by the "mainstream media" (MSM), thus validating the information and its ostensibly "alternative" source. Unless and until that happens, alternative information and opinion, especially that which runs counter to the MSM/government/corporate narrative, is ignored and relegated to "conspiracy theory," "internet chatter," or even subjected to the dread label of "denier" of some established, obligatory truth, for example the "Bosnian genocide" and Serbian guilt.

Non-validated information and views thus become a kind of American *samizdat,* which is tolerated but has no impact on public affairs. For example, with respect to the 1990s Balkan conflicts (Markale, Srebrenica, Racak, organ-trafficking by leaders of the "Kosovo Liberation Army," etc.), information discrediting the official versions of the same events has long been available but has no ability to dislodge the established accounts, even in retrospect.

This week we have been given two startling examples of how this marginalization of factual reporting and analysis can take place in plain sight. Both relate to Syria, the hottest current danger of touching off a major global conflagration. One example is an exposé of the role the United States and its allies have played in turning Syria into a playground for jihadists groups aligned with al-Qaeda. The other debunks claims that the Syrian government of President Bashar al-Assad has "used chemical weapons against his own people."

"How America Armed Terrorists in Syria" (*The American Conservative*) by Gellhorn Prize award winning investigative journalist Gareth Porter is the definitive analysis of how U.S. agencies—in particular the CIA—have been pumping money and weapons into the Syrian conflict for the past six years. They have been doing so in the full knowledge that the recipients of the assistance were not only Islamic terrorists but affiliates, allies, or offshoots of al-Qaeda. Writes Porter:

> The supporters of this arms-supply policy believe it is necessary as pushback against Iranian influence in Syria. But that argument skirts the real issue raised by the policy's history.
> The Obama administration's Syria policy effectively sold out the U.S. interest that was supposed to be the touchstone of the "Global War on Terrorism"—the eradication of al Qaeda and its terrorist affiliates. The United States has instead subordinated that U.S. interest in counter-terrorism to the interests of its Sunni allies. In doing so it has helped create a new terrorist threat in the heart of the Middle East.

Porter further details how the CIA served as a conduit for weapons from the stocks of the deposed and murdered Muammar Kaddafi to ship them from Libya to their terrorist colleagues in Syria. Even more disturbing for those following the rise of Islamic radicalism in Europe is the participation of countries in Central Europe in the Balkans—including Serbia, which one would think has had enough experience with U.S.-supported jihadists not to get involved:

> The CIA's covert arms shipments from Libya came to an abrupt halt in September 2012 when Libyan militants attacked and burned the embassy annex in Benghazi that had been used to support the operation. By then, however, a much larger channel for arming anti-

government forces was opening up. The CIA put the Saudis in touch with a senior Croatian official who had offered to sell large quantities of arms left over from the Balkan Wars of the 1990s. And the CIA helped them shop for weapons from arms dealers and governments in several other former Soviet bloc countries.

Flush with weapons acquired from both the CIA Libya program and from the Croatians, the Saudis and Qataris dramatically increased the number of flights by military cargo planes to Turkey in December 2012 and continued that intensive pace for the next two and a half months. The *New York Times* reported a total 160 such flights through mid-March 2013. The most common cargo plane in use in the Gulf, the Ilyushin IL-76, can carry roughly 50 tons of cargo on a flight, which would indicate that as much as 8,000 tons of weapons poured across the Turkish border into Syria just in late 2012 and in 2013.

One U.S. official called the new level of arms deliveries to Syrian rebels a "cataract of weaponry."

And a year-long investigation by the Balkan Investigative Reporting Network and the Organized Crime and Corruption Reporting Project revealed that the Saudis were intent on building up a powerful conventional army in Syria. The "end-use certificate" for weapons purchased from an arms company in Belgrade, Serbia, in May 2013 includes 500 Soviet-designed PG–7VR rocket launchers that can penetrate even heavily-armored tanks, along with two million rounds; 50 Konkurs anti-tank missile launchers and 500 missiles, 50 anti-aircraft guns mounted on armored vehicles, 10,000 fragmentation rounds for OG–7 rocket launchers capable of piercing heavy body armor; four truck-mounted BM–21 GRAD multiple rocket launchers, each of which fires 40 rockets at a time with a range of 12 to 19 miles, along with 20,000 GRAD rockets.

The end user document for another Saudi order from the same Serbian company listed 300 tanks, 2,000 RPG launchers, and 16,500 other rocket launchers, one million rounds for ZU–23–2 anti-aircraft guns, and 315 million cartridges for various other guns.

The other "must-read" article ignored in official circles in Washington is "Trump's Red Line" in the German publication *Die Welt,* by prominent investigative reporter Seymour Hersh. Without going into the details, Hersh confirms what independent observers said at the time: that the incident on April 4 in an al Qaeda-controlled town in Syria's Idlib governorate was not a chemical weapons attack by Syrian government forces. Worse, according to Hersh, U.S. military and intelligence officials immediately informed President Donald Trump that that was the case. Nonetheless, before any examination of the facts could take place, on April 7 he ordered a retaliatory attack against the Syrian airbase supposedly responsible—to the applause of his detractors. For example, CNN's Fareed Zakaria, previously a harsh critic who had derided Mr. Trump's "rocking horse presidency" as a "circus," intoned the next day: "I think Donald Trump became president of the United States last night."

The blockbuster *Die Welt* article by Hersh has been ignored to the point of invisibility by the MSM. It should be noted that Hersh, a longtime contributor to prestigious MSM outlets like the *New Yorker* and the *New York Times,* had published an earlier exposure of a 2013 sarin gas attack in Ghouta, Syria, that was falsely blamed on the Syrian government, in the *London Review of Books* (*LRB*), since no U.S. publication would take it. But this latest piece was refused by the *LRB,* according to *Die Welt:* "The [*LRB*] editors accepted it, paid for it, and prepared a fact checked article for publication, but decided against doing so, as they told Hersh, because of concerns that the magazine would vulnerable to criticism for seeming to take the view of the Syrian and Russian governments when it came to the April 4th bombing in [Idlib]." The fact that the Syrian and Russian governments might be right evidently carried little weight with the editors.

Perhaps coincidently, perhaps not, less than two days after the appearance of the Hersh article, White House spokesman Sean Spicer put Damascus on notice that U.S. intelligence had detected activity indicating preparation by Syrian forces of "another" (i.e, a repeat of the April non-attack in Idlib). If "Mr. Assad conducts another [sic] mass murder attack using chemical weapons, he and his military will pay a heavy price," said Spicer. Piling on, U.S. ambassador to the United Nations Nikki Haley said that the U.S. would respond harshly to "any" use of chemical weapons, not even qualifying whether the Syrian government were the responsible party—a dangerous invitation for the jihadists to stage a false flag chemical attack. Haley also threatened to hold Russia and Iran accountable.

Within two days of Spicer's warning, Secretary of Defense James Mattis claimed the threat had been successful, and that Syria was not going to launch a chemical attack: "They didn't do it." Or to put it in more accurate terms, Mattis was taking credit for the non-occurrence of something that wasn't going to happen anyway, which would supposedly have been a repeat of a prior event that hadn't happened either.

If this all sounds convoluted and bizarre, that's because it is. Perhaps the whole Spicer threat and Mattis claim that it worked were contrived as what they call at the Pentagon a "Kabuki dance", an empty show and noise, possibly to look tough in advance of an anticipated Trump meeting with Russian President Vladimir Putin at the July G20 meeting. Or maybe this episode is part of an effort by Mattis and Secretary of State Rex Tillerson to clean up Middle East messes created by Trump's son-in-law Jared Kushner.

The fact is, no one knows for sure except those directly involved. But it's certain that U.S. fake news media, ever a reliable transmission belt for unnecessary wars, are small help in ascertaining the truth.

"Trump's New Strategy for Afghanistan Is Neither New, nor a Strategy, nor Trump's"

Jim Jatras | *Strategic Culture* | August 24, 2017

For some time it has been clear that the White House of President Donald Trump was convulsed with a struggle among various court factions vying for the Emperor's ear. Crudely oversimplified, these are variously described as:

1. The military "Junta" (Generals McMaster, National Security Council; Mattis, Pentagon; and Kelly, White House Chief of Staff;
2. The Goldman-Sachs "Globalists" (preeminently First Daughter Ivanka and First Son-in-Law Jared Kushner);
3. The "Populist-Nationalists" ("the two Steves" Bannon and Miller); and
4. The Regular Republicans who, to their credit, in 2016 chose to join the Trump populist movement over more conventionally "conservative"

GOP candidates (Former Chief of Staff Reince Priebus, Counselor to the President Kellyanne Conway).

It is understood that the first two factions were generally allied against the second two. Following Priebus's ouster, the bellwether would be who got tossed out next: Bannon or McMaster. It was Bannon.

On August 18, with Bannon's defenestration, it became clear that the Junta and the Globalists were firmly in charge. The only outliers left—besides somebody named Trump—are Conway and Miller. We'll see how long they last. Any of them.

The immediate impact of the Junta/Globalist victory in the internal struggle was renewed sharp rhetoric against North Korea (Bannon's suggestion the there was no acceptable military option may have been one proximate cause of his ejection) and, even more so, Trump's speech on Afghanistan on August 21 in front of a military audience.

Before addressing the specifics, it's important to note that his remarks not only signaled a humiliating defeat of Trumpism within Trump's own administration but reflected the damage done by the vicious attacks he has suffered for speaking the truth about events in Charlottesville. His offense: to affirm that responsibility for violence lay not only with the "white nationalists" but also with the armed Antifa "protesters" bent on attacking them. In fact, to anyone with a fair mind watching the TV coverage, it was clear that the violence overwhelmingly came from the latter, abetted by the evidently deliberate decision of Virginia Governor and likely 2020 Democratic presidential hopeful Terry McAuliffe to withdraw police separation of the two sides and herd the nationalists up against Antifa.

While not mentioning Charlottesville by name, the entire beginning section of Trump's Afghanistan speech—his first prime time televised address to the nation as president—stuck to a politically correct script, ritually intoning that "there is no room for prejudice, no place for bigotry, and no tolerance for hate." (In yet another zigzag, the very next night, at a rally with cheering supporters in Phoenix, Trump read back aloud his previous comments on Charlottesville and denounced Antifa. The media, notably *CNN*, dissolved in a deranged fit of rage.)

As to what he now plans for Afghanistan:

It's not new, it's same-old same-old: Aside from a few Trumpish rhetorical flourishes, it was a speech that could have been given by President Hillary Clinton or President Jeb Bush. In substance, it was a rehash of the failures of Barack Obama and George W. Bush. Only a few details changed. He will loosen rules of engagement for U.S. forces, which among other things will mean more dead Afghans and more Taliban recruits. He will boost troop numbers but won't tell the enemy—or the American people—by how many; the number 4,000 has been kicked around, but who knows. Finally, no timetables will "guide our strategy," just "conditions on the ground," but what those conditions need to be for us to finally get out are not described either. Nor is there any clue as to how boosting American numbers to about 13,000 will accomplish what 100,000 couldn't.

"We will ask our NATO allies and global partners to support our new strategy with additional troop and funding increases in line with our own," said the President. "We are confident they will." Pure fantasy. On the other hand, Trump completely ignored Afghanistan's record opium production. Evidently promising to stamp that out would be just too fantastical.

It's not a strategy, it's just a policy: One of the problems with being entirely guided by military men is their tendency to focus on their tactical tradecraft. Hopefully that's something they're good at. But their knowledge and skill, though vitally important, doesn't of itself constitute a strategy. Or put another way, professional military men can tell a policymaker *how* to accomplish what he wants, but they can't tell him *what* he wants. The result is a policy composed of various tactics that don't add up to much of anything except more of what we've seen since 2001.

We will not engage in nation-building, said Trump, or tell Afghans how to live. This could mean no more nagging them over laws mandating the killing of apostates or about women's rights. ("Don't throw acid in the face of little girls because they attend school. That's not nice.") We weren't doing much of that anyway, but now it's official: Americans are fighting to make Afghanistan safe for *Sharia*. (Paradoxically, Trump was reportedly convinced that Afghanistan is not doomed to be a Hobbesian abode of savages by McMaster's showing him a picture of mini-skirted Afghan female students from the 1970s. As Justin Raimondo points out, the good general surely neglected to mention the reason there are no more mini-skirts to be seen is because of our support, with Pakistan and Saudi Arabia, for Osama bin Laden and his ilk. Mission accomplished!)

On the other hand, is it telling Afghans how to live when Trump promised to root out corruption? (What Americans are calling corruption is what in Afghanistan is usually just called "life.") Indeed, very little was said about what the Afghan government thinks about the "new" plan. But then again, we barely care what Seoul thinks about deploying the THAAD system in South Korea, so why should we ask the opinions of an Afghan government that wouldn't last a week without American support? One is reminded of the Soviet-era quip that Afghanistan was the most peace-loving country in the world. Why? Because it doesn't even interfere in its own internal affairs.

Regionally, Trump vowed to force Pakistan to stop providing safe haven for the Taliban (sure, that will work) and to get India more involved. U.S. Ambassador to the United Nations Nikki Haley said that in addition to "putting the pressure on Pakistan" Washington would "put the pressure on India that they have to be part of the political solution." Just like we "pressure" North Korea, or "pressure" China on Korea and the South China Sea, and "pressure" Russia on Syria, Ukraine, what have you. Pressure, pressure, pressure! Doesn't anyone in Washington know how to talk with anyone to seek common interests? Why no mention of the three regional powers—Russia, China, and Iran—that like India (but unlike Pakistan) don't want an Afghanistan ruled by Salafists? Now that could be a *strategy*.

It's not Trump's policy, it's the Swamp's: Trump pretty much let the cat out of the bag when he conceded that his first impulse was to get out of Afghanistan. (Interestingly the reflexively pro-war *Washington Post* and *National Review* published calls for the U.S. to withdraw our forces, saying Trump's earlier instinct was right! Be prepared for them to rip out his liver when things turn out badly.) But then Trump talked with the big boys with the short haircuts who explained the facts of life to him. He seems to have bought the Swamp's line that because Obama "hastily and mistakenly withdrew from Iraq" the result was ISIS. Nonsense. ISIS came into being because (a) we invaded Iraq in the first place and (b) for years Obama armed terrorists seeking to overthrow the government of Syria, continuing a policy in place since the 1980s Afghanistan war against the USSR. Given such assumptions, the most optimistic hope is for a "surge" like that in Iraq in 2007, which at least superficially stabilized Anbar province and Baghdad. Again, very optimistically, that could provide cover for us to withdraw our forces. More likely, given the fear of "hastily and mistakenly" withdrawing Obama-style, we will stay for an indefinite period amounting to a permanent occupation. After all, look how long we've been successfully stabilizing Germany, Japan, and South Korea!

The sad fact is that Trump almost certainly knows all this, at least on a gut level. What exactly the exact political alchemy is that has led him to this juncture is open for speculation. But what is not speculative is the grim fact that whether or not this is Trump's policy, Afghanistan is now Trump's war.

"Three Dangerous Delusions about Korea"

Jim Jatras | *Strategic Culture* | September 2, 2017

They say that most of the world's real dangers arise not because of what people don't know but because of what they do "know" that just ain't so.

As a case in point, consider three things about Korea that the bipartisan Washington establishment seems quite sure of but are far removed from reality:

Delusion 1: All options, including U.S. military force, are "on the table."

- Everyone knows there are no military "options" the U.S. could use against North Korea that don't result in disaster. The prospect that a "surgical strike" could "take out" (a muscular-sounding term much loved by laptop bombardiers) Pyongyang's nuclear and missile capabilities is a fiction. Already impractical when considered against a country like Iran, no one believes a limited attack could eliminate North Korea's ability to strike back, hard. At risk would be not only almost 30,000 U.S. troops in Korea but 25 million people in the Seoul metropolitan area, not to mention many more lives at risk in the rest of South Korea and perhaps Japan.
- Hence, any contemplated U.S. preemptive strike would have to be massive from the start, imposing a ghastly cost on North Koreans (do their lives count?) but still running the risk that anything less than total success would mean a devastating retaliation. That's not even taking into account possible actions of other countries, notably China's response to an American attack on their detestable buffer state.

Delusion 2: North Korea must be denuclearized.

- Whether anyone likes it or not, North Korea is a nuclear weapons state outside the Nuclear Non-Proliferation Treaty and will remain so. Kim Jong-un learned the lessons of Saddam Hussein and Muammar Gaddafi. Because Kim has weapons of mass destruction, especially nukes, he gets to stay alive and in power. If he gives them up, he can look forward to dancing the Tyburn jig or getting sodomized with a bayonet, then shot. That's not a difficult choice.

Delusion 3: If the U.S. presses China hard enough, Beijing will solve the problem for us.

- There is no combination of U.S. sanctions, threats, or pressures that will make Beijing take steps that are fundamentally contrary to China's vital national security interests. (Here, the "vital national security" of China means just that, not the way U.S. policymakers routinely abuse the term to mean anything they don't like even if it has nothing to do with American security, much less with America's survival.) Aside from speculation (which is all it is) that China could seek to engineer an internal coup to overthrow Kim in favor of a puppet administration, maintaining the current odious regime is Beijing's only option if they don't want to face the prospect of having on their border a reunited Korean peninsula under a government allied with Washington.

- After Moscow's experience with the expansion of NATO following the 1990 reunification of Germany, why would Beijing take credibly any assurances from Washington (of which there is no indication anyway) not to expand into a vacuum created by a collapse of North Korea? Quite to the contrary, it has been suggested that if China refuses to deal with the North Korea problem on Washington's behalf, then the U.S. would do it on its terms, presenting Beijing (in the description of former U.S. ambassador to the United Nations John Bolton) with "regime collapse, huge refugee flows and U.S. flags flying along the Yalu River." Adds Bolton, "China can do it the easier way or the harder way: It's their choice. Time is growing short." If under such a scenario U.S. forces end up on China's border, suggests Bolton, they wouldn't be leaving anytime soon. Don't be so sure. In 1950, the last time American forces were on the Yalu River, they weren't there very long when hundreds of thousands of Chinese soldiers crossed into Korea. Keep in mind that happened when China didn't have nuclear weapons but the U.S. did.

The seemingly weekly rise and fall of the decibel level of bellicose rhetoric coming out of Washington and Pyongyang obscures the realities behind these three delusions. Little change can be expected from Pyongyang, whose policy at least has the virtue of simplicity: "if you do anything bad to us, we'll do something really, really bad to you."

So then, what are the prospects Washington could jump off the hamster wheel and come up with something besides threats and sanctions? The omens are not auspicious. Just before he left the White House, Steve Bannon violated the taboo surrounding Delusion 1: "Until somebody solves the part of the equation that shows me that ten million people in Seoul don't die in the first 30 minutes from conventional weapons, I don't know what you're talking about, there's no military solution here, they got us." Then he was gone.

But let's be optimistic. There have been reports of direct "back channel" contacts between North Korea and the U.S. at the United Nations in New York. Even Bolton suggests that some kind of accommodation could be made to China in the form of a pullback of U.S. forces down to the south, near Pusan, so as to be still "available for rapid deployment across Asia." (Certainly, that's one idea. Here's a better one: how about getting us out of Korea entirely and not having Americans available for deployment across Asia?)

The definitive clarification should have been the Beijing-based *Global Times* editorial of August 10, 2017 ("Reckless game over the Korean Peninsula runs risk of real war"), universally seen as reflecting the position of the Chinese government:

> China should also make clear that if North Korea launches missiles that threaten U.S. soil first and the U.S. retaliates, China will stay neutral. If the U.S. and South Korea carry out strikes and try to overthrow the North Korean regime and change the political pattern of the Korean Peninsula, China will prevent them from doing so.

That means that if Kim attacks the U.S., he's on his own. If we attack Kim, we're at war with China. In the latter case, while Russia would not likely directly join the fray we can be sure Moscow would provide China total support short of belligerency. Put mildly, this would not be in the American interest.

There is one, and only one overriding priority that should now guide U.S. policy on Korea. It's not regime change in North Korea—despite that regime's loathsomeness—or even the wellbeing of South Korea or Japan. It's avoiding Kim's developing a missile system capable of delivering a nuclear weapon to the United States. How close North Korea might be to such a capability is the subject of wildly conflicting estimations. (Regarding the American lives hung out on the DMZ, there's a simple solution to ensuring their safety—get them the hell out of there.)

But what about South Korea and Japan? Our "alliances" with them are a fiction. The U.S. guarantees their security but other than cooperating on the defense of their own territory they do nothing to safeguard ours, nor can they. The U.S. derives no benefit in continuing to make ourselves a target on account of a place that's more than five thousand miles from the American mainland.

It's time that "America First!" meant something. As a start, Washington could take seriously Beijing's proposal for a double-freeze. On the one hand, Pyongyang would suspend its nuclear and missile programs, in particular halting tests of weapons with potential intercontinental range. Washington and Seoul would suspend joint military exercises, including practicing so-called "decapitation strikes" aimed at North Korea's leadership.

If protecting our own territory and people is American officials' top priority, and not, as they implausibly claim, "regime change" in North Korea, it's hard to see why a double-freeze would not be a sensible first step. It would be largely up to China to see that the North Koreans complied with their part of the deal. If they did, perhaps it could lead towards a long-overdue settlement of this Cold War-era standoff and, in time, a reunited, *neutral* Korea. If not, all bets are off—but we'd be hardly worse off than we are now.

"Is a New 'Kosovo' Brewing in Myanmar?"

Jim Jatras | *Strategic Culture* | September 8, 2017

Whenever western governments and mainstream media start shedding crocodile tears over a minority community of "peaceful Muslims"© being persecuted by some nasty non-Muslim government somewhere, with demands that the "international community" do something about it, it should be treated with a big, fat dollop of skepticism.

At issue at the moment are the Rohingya, approximately one million of whom constitute a large minority in Rakhine (formerly Arakan) state in Myanmar (formerly Burma). According to reports in the prestige media and from (government-funded) human rights groups, Myanmar's government is oppresssing the Rohingya, many of whom have fled next door into predominantly Muslim Bangladesh.

We are told that the Rohingya, "often described as 'the world's most persecuted minority'" at the hands of Rakhine Buddhists incited by fanatical monks backed up by the national government, are facing genocide and ethnic cleansing. The international community must do something! Where's Samantha "the Genocide Chick" Power when we need her?

If all this sounds familiar, it is. Almost word-for-word the foregoing could describe the western official and media narrative of the Serbian province of Kosovo and Metohija in the late 1990s. Just replace "Rohingya Muslims" with "Albanian Muslims," "Rakhine" with "Serb," "Theravada Buddhist" with "Orthodox Christian."

Of course the Kosovo official narrative was, and remains, almost a total perversion of the truth. In the late 1990s, western intelligence services and their friends in the Islamic world, notably Saudi Arabia, the Gulf States, and Turkey, as well as al-Qaeda-linked Islamic "charities", pumped weapons into Kosovo to support armed terrorist groups known as the "Kosovo Liberation Army" (KLA). Headed by kingpins in the Albanian mafia, the KLA attacked Serbian officials and civilians, as well as murdered insufficiently militant Albanians, in a bid to invite a government crackdown which would serve as a pretext for intervention by the international community, meaning the U.S. and NATO, to stop a fictional Serbian genocide of Albanians. As I noted in an August 1998 U.S. Senate report months before the supposed massacre that "justified" the NATO attack on Serbia, military action had already been decided upon and awaited only a suitable "trigger":

> As of this writing, planning for a U.S.-led NATO intervention in Kosovo is now largely in place, while the Clinton Administration's apparent willingness to intervene has ebbed and flowed on an almost weekly basis. The only missing element appears to be an event—with suitably vivid media coverage—that would make intervention politically salable, even imperative, in the same way that a dithering Administration finally decided on intervention in Bosnia in 1995 after a series of "Serb mortar attacks" took the lives of dozens of civilians—attacks, which, upon closer examination, may in fact have been the work of the Muslim regime in Sarajevo, the main beneficiary of the intervention. [For details, primarily reports from European media, see RPC's "Clinton-Approved Iranian Arms Transfers Help Turn Bosnia into Militant Islamic Base," 1/16/97] That the Administration is waiting for a similar "trigger" in Kosovo is increasingly obvious: "A senior U.S. Defense Department official who briefed reporters on July 15 noted that 'we're not anywhere near making a decision for any kind of armed intervention in Kosovo right now.' He listed only one thing that might trigger a policy change: 'I think if some levels of atrocities were reached that would be intolerable, that would probably be a trigger'" [*Washington Post*, 8/4/98]. The recent conflicting reports regarding a purported mass grave containing (depending on the report) hundreds of murdered Albanian civilians or dozens of KLA fighters killed in battle should be seen in this light. [from "Bosnia II: The Clinton Administration Sets Course for NATO Intervention in Kosovo," August 1998]

To note the similarities between official and media about the Rohingya in 2017 and "Kosovars" in 1998–99 is not to say that armed outside intervention against Myanmar is imminent or even in the cards. Nor does it disprove the claim that the Rohingya, or some of them, may indeed be suffering persecution. It is only to suggest that when the usual manipulators in the media and the self-appointed international community get on their genocide high horse, caution is in order. It needs to be asked, what is the other side of the story?

For example, as analyzed by Moon of Alabama:

Media attention is directed to some minor ethnic violence in Myanmar, the former Burma. The story in the 'western' press is of Muslim Rohingya unfairly vilified, chased out and killed by Buddhist mobs and the army in the state of Rakhine near the border to Bangladesh. The 'liberal' human interventionists like Human Rights Watch are united with Islamists like Turkey's President Erdogan in loudly lamenting the plight of the Rohingya.

That curious alliance also occurred during the wars on Libya and Syria. [JGJ: And in Kosovo.] It is by now a warning sign. Could there be more behind this than some local conflict in Myanmar? Is someone stoking a fire?

Indeed.

While the ethnic conflict in Rakhine state is very old, it has over the last years morphed into a Jihadist guerilla war financed and led from Saudi Arabia. The area is of geo-strategic interest:

> Rakhine plays an important part in [the Chinese One Belt One Road Initiative] OBOR, as it is an exit to the Indian Ocean and the location of planned billion-dollar Chinese projects—a planned economic zone on Ramree Island, and the Kyaukphyu deep-sea port, which has oil and natural gas pipelines linked with Yun-nan Province's Kunming.

Pipelines from the western coast of Myanmar eastwards to China allow hydrocarbon imports from the Persian Gulf to China while avoiding the bottleneck of the Strait of Malacca and disputed parts of the South China Sea.

It is in 'Western interest' to hinder China's projects in Myanmar. Inciting Jihad in Rakhine could help to achieve that. . . . A clearly Islamist insurgency was build up in the area. It acts under the name Arakan Rohingya Salvation Army (ARSA) and is led by Ataullah abu Ammar Junjuni, a Jihadist from Pakistan. (ARSA earlier operated under the name Harakah al-Yakin, or Faith Movement.) Ataullah was born into the large Rohingya community of Karachi, Pakistan. . . . Reuters noted in late 2016 that the Jihadist group is trained, led and financed through Pakistan and Saudi Arabia:

> A group of Rohingya Muslims that attacked Myanmar border guards in October is headed by people with links to Saudi Arabia and Pakistan, the International Crisis Group (ICG) said on Thursday, citing members of the group. . . . "Though not confirmed, there are indications [Ataullah] went to Pakistan and possibly elsewhere, and that he received practical training in modern guerrilla warfare," the group said. It noted that Ataullah was one of 20 Rohingya from Saudi Arabia leading the group's operations in Rakhine State. Separately, a committee of 20 senior Rohingya emigres oversees the group, which has headquarters in Mecca, the ICG said.
>
> The ARSA Jihadists claim to only attack government forces but civilian Arakaness Buddhists have also been ambushed and massacred. Buddhist hamlets were also burned down.

Finally, it needs to be noted that showing sympathy for Muslim victims, real or fake, has several attractions for western governments and media:

- It pleases western elites' friends in Riyadh, Ankara, Islamabad, etc., to see effete post-Christians take the Muslim side in a way none of them would ever stick up for Christians. How nice to see how weak, corrupt, and cowardly the unbelievers are! (How many protests did we hear from our Saudi, Turkish, Pakistani, and other supposed friends about the suffering of Christians in Syria and Iraq at the hands of al-Qaeda and Daesh? For that matter, how much did we hear about it from western governments? When have western governments and media ever demanded that the so-called international community "do something" to save a non-Muslim population—anywhere?)
- It allows western elites to scrub away the suspicion that somewhere, somehow any hint of concern about Islamic terrorism or Muslim mass migration into Europe is evidence of "racism" and "Islamophobia." Championing persecuted Muslims like the Rohingya and Kosovo Albanians shows the west harbors no such biases.
- Perhaps most importantly, standing up for allegedly persecuted Muslim minorities allows western governments and media to deflect any blame for the hundreds of thousands—in all likelihood millions—of Muslims killed in the process of "democracy promotion" in majority Muslim countries like Afghanistan, Iraq, Syria, Yemen, Somalia, and other places, or the many more who would be killed in the process of "bringing freedom" to Iran. Sure, many non-Muslims have also been killed in these noble humanitarian efforts, but their deaths are not politically actionable—no government or terrorist movement will threaten retribution.

"Political Earthquakes in Diverse Places"

Jim Jatras | *Strategic Culture* | September 29, 2017

> *"For nation shall rise against nation, and kingdom against kingdom: and there shall be famines, and pestilences, and earthquakes, in diverse places."*—Matthew 24:7

Certainly there's never been a time when nation hasn't risen against nation. Likewise, earthquakes, such as the one that this month killed some 300 people in Mexico, are hardly a rarity.

But it's not often you see political earthquakes that shake the structure of world politics occurring in such a short span of days: the German national election of September 24, the independence referendum in Iraqi Kurdistan on September 25, and the upcoming independence vote in Catalonia on October 1. Each in its way shows that the "End of History" post-Cold War world order is a mirage, now in the process of dissipating.

Germany

Thankfully the era of Angela Merkel is over. Not formally of course. For a while she will linger on as Chancellor, inflicting ever more damage on her Christian Democratic Union (CDU) and Christian Social Union (CSU) faction, on her country, and on European civilization. But she's a lame duck, and everyone knows it. At least the British Conservatives, after suffering earlier this year a pyrrhic victory similar to the CDU/CSU's, acknowledge that Theresa May will step down as party leader after a decent interval. If Merkel had any dignity left, she would announce her retirement.

Instead she has made it her mission to stop the ascent of the true victor in the election: the populist-patriotic *Alternative für Deutschland* (AfD), whose rise in political fortunes almost entirely tracks with loss of support for the CDU/CSU, whose political and moral bankruptcy is matched only by their erstwhile Grand Coalition partner, the Social Democratic Party (SPD). A renewed less-grand CDU/CSU-SPD government is ruled out, both because the SPD and its lackluster leader Martin Schulz (an even lamer duck than Merkel) could not risk even further erosion in their brand and because of the establishment's hysterical need to block the AfD's becoming the official Opposition. This leads Merkel to try to negotiate a bizarre "Jamaica" black-yellow-green coalition with the Free Democrats (FDP) and the Greens. Even if the Christian Democrats did not exist, getting the FDP and Greens into a coherent governing program would be a formidable task. Any new coalition, even if one can be formed, will be shaky and new elections are likely within two years. Hopefully they will take place with Merkel having fled to Chile.

But the real news is the AfD, now the third largest party in the Bundestag. Germany, it seems, is not dead yet. As Srdja Trifkovic has observed:

> For over seven decades since the *Untergang* it has been first desirable, then necessary, and ultimately mandatory for a mainstream German to be ashamed of his past. De-nazification of the early occupation years had morphed into de-Germanization. An integral part of the final package is to subscribe to the postmodern liberal orthodoxy in all its aspects. It must include the willingness to welcome a million "migrants" in a year (with millions more to come if the Duopoly so decides—and Merkel and Schulz both agree that there must be no upper limit.) The AfD begs to differ, but when its leaders make a reality-based statement like "Islam does not belong to Germany," or a common sense one like "We don't need illiterate immigrants," they are duly Hitlerized. [. . .]

It is not by chance that the survivors of red totalitarianism in the former German Democratic Republic and their descendants are voting for the AfD *en masse*. They know ideologically driven cretins when they see them, and they can tell who is able and willing to stand up to them. It is ironic that *hoi polloi* of old Prussia and Saxony may yet prove to be the liberating pathfinders for the ever-so-sophisticated multiculturalists on the Rhine insistent on self-annihilation. There is still hope for Germany.

Iraqi Kurdistan

The overwhelming vote in favor of independence by residents of Iraq's Kurdish Regional Government (KRG) may prove the fuse that ignites what already was shaping up as follow-on regional war to the impending defeat of Daesh and Damascus's victory. While Syria has given lukewarm indication that some sort of Kurdish autonomy may be possible, the vote in Iraq to force the issue of independence has pulled Turkey even closer to the existing Iran-Iraq-Syria regional axis backed by Moscow. The vote in the KRG prompted immediate threats of military action by Baghdad.

The Kurdish move comes at a time when U.S.-backed, mainly Kurdish "Syrian Democratic Forces" (SDF) are moving into Daesh-vacated areas in eastern Syria in a clear effort to block the Russian-backed Syrian Arab Army

(SAA). It is alleged that the US—or more particularly, the Pentagon, primary sponsor of the SDF—has two goals: first, to block Iran's so-called "land bridge to the Mediterranean stretching from an Iraq run by their Shiite allies to Lebanon, where their Hezbollah auxiliaries dominate"; and to seize oil fields in eastern Syria for the economic support for a north Syrian Kurdish statelet, where a dozen or so undisclosed (and illegal) US bases have already been established. To achieve these goals, powerful influences in Washington are willing to risk a military clash with Moscow.

With one war winding down, another war—or perhaps two or three wars—may be about to start.

Catalonia

As some of us warned at the time, when in February 2008 the West insisted that pushing for the illegal detachment of the province of Kosovo and Metohija from Serbia was a "unique case," it has instead proved to be a prototype. One of the first aftershocks came in August of the same year, soon after the west almost unanimously recognized the independence of a supposed "Republic of Kosovo," when South Ossetia and Abkhazia declared their independence from Georgia with Russian support.

The fact is, every separatist movement is "unique" and valid in the eyes of the minority that wants the separation. That's why despite the large majority of European Union states' moving quickly to follow the US lead in recognizing Kosovo, five did not: Cyprus (because of the breakaway "Turkish Republic of Northern Cyprus," really Ankara's occupation zone), Greece (to support Cyprus); Slovakia (concerned about Magyar irredentism in its southern region); Romania (also Magyars, in Transylvania), and Spain (not only Catalonia but the Basque country and possibly Galicia). One aspect of Catalonia is that it is another Kosovo chicken coming home to roost.

Recently President Donald Trump expressed mild opposition to Catalan independence, but the EU is strongly opposed. The latter is a bit ironic, since both sub-national separatists and supra-national entities like the EU have the same enemy, the historic nation-state. Most of the Catalan "independists" are on the moral and political level very much Brussels' type of people. As one Spanish blogger has remarked:

> The Independists are mostly hipsters, SJWs [social justice warriors], feminists and all kinds of degenerates who welcome with open arms the Islamists (as they breed fast, hate the Spanish for their expulsion in 1492 and the Church and do not speak Spanish), the same Islamists who will be a majority in a hypothetical Catalan Republic in two generations and will impose the Sharia. In a way, it will be fun to watch, in another way we cannot leave over half the population of that region, the silent majority, in the hands of those lunatics ... This is a distraction for their larger plans for the EU superstate. Thus, they are divided, on the one hand the MSM [mainstream media] is, albeit with little enthusiasm, pro-Independence. On the other hand, the EU has expressed a very mild support for their vassal Spain whose populace is the most enthusiastically pro-EU (little they know). You can be sure that should Catalonia become independent, they will de facto stay in the EU. Nobody is allowed to leave the EU plantation. At the end the EU does not care if its member states are nation states or regions, it could be argued that weaker mini states will be easier to rule.

"All of Spain Should Vote on Catalan Independence"

Jim Jatras | *Strategic Culture* | October 6, 2017

There is a certain frame of mind that believes that secession by ethnic min-orities is an absolute good in itself. Asked the question, "*Should Region X have the right to secede from Country Y?*" a lot of people will answer with a resounding "*Yes!*" without knowing or even caring where X and Y are or who lives there.

Others are more selective, relying instead on the Bolshevik principle of *kto-kovo* ("who-whom"), which relegates the righteousness of secession to whether or not the observer likes or dislikes the state in question. This is typical of western governments. Good secessions are from countries we don't like—Serbia above all, of course. Independent Kosovo: good. Montenegro's separation from its union with Serbia: good. But Republika Srpska's possible separation from Bosnia and Herzegovina: bad. Independence of Serbian Kraijinas from secessionist Croatia: emphatically bad. Northern Kosovo and Metohija's separation from "sovereign, independent Kosovo": very, very bad.

The only constant: Serbs are always wrong.

The same subjective *kto-kovo* frames conflicts in the former Soviet Union. The *deus ex machina* independence of all the former Union Republics was an automatic and positive development. But the desire of any portion of them—Abkhazia, South Ossetia, Adzharia (Georgia), Pridnestrovie, Gagauzia (Mol-dova), Crimea, Donbass (Ukraine)—to leave its former Union Republic is per se illegitimate, notwithstanding the 1990 Soviet law on secession requiring separate referenda in such entities.

The desire of Catalans—or more precisely, of some undetermined portion of people living in Catalonia—to secede from Spain is different because it doesn't fit into the usual *kto-kovo* international lineup. One finds among Catalan sympathizers many of the usual partisans of biased western selectivity as well as some of their fiercest critics (such as the usually sound Pepe Escobar). Likewise, members of both of the usual camps have expressed opposition to Catalan secession, either out of mechanical support for "western institutions" (the European Union, the US) or consistent support for the principle of state sovereignty (the government of Serbia and most of the countries that oppose an independent Kosovo).

In the court of public opinion, the pro-independence camp has gained the upper hand. While the Catalan referendum was clearly illegal under Spanish law and the Spanish authorities had every right to shut it down, the TV images of police using physical force to prevent people from casting a ballot played badly against Madrid—which is no doubt what was intended. If, as expected, Catalan independence is declared in the coming days, Madrid will have little choice but to suspend Catalonia's autonomy, further radicalizing the situation. (Remember how the west falsely cited Slobodan Milosevic's supposedly "abolishing" of Kosovo's "constitutionally guaranteed autonomy" in 1989 as proof of an impending "final solution" against the province's Albanians.)

The morality play of Madrid's "authoritarian" violation of "democracy" brings us to another canard: the notion that the "will of the Catalan people" is paramount. This is misguided for at least two reasons. First, who decided that

Catalonia as a subdivision of Spain, or of Catalans as a distinct nation, is in a position to asset a sovereign, united "will" apart from the rest of Spain? As was the case with Kosovo (and just a week ago, in Iraqi Kurdistan), Catalonia demonstrates the futility of granting autonomy to a region based on a minority ethnic, linguistic, or religious identity. Doing so only whets that minority's demand for more cession of power, culminating in the demand for independence. (Hence, in Serbia the League of Social Democrats of Vojvodina endorsed the Catalan referendum.)

Second, granting presumptive sovereignty to an aspiring secessionist entity always ends up shortchanging those who don't want to secede. This can take more than one form. One example is the "West Virginia" model, whereby one region within the entity doesn't want to leave; comparable to Pridnestrovie, South Ossetia, Republika Srpska, etc. Another is intimidation of citizens who are loyal to the common state—who according to polls represent a majority in Catalonia. As stated by film director Isabel Coixet i Castillo in *El País*:

> I see now, with horrifying clarity, that no matter what happens next, there is no room here for me or for anybody who dares to think independently, even though this is my birthplace. Today it is insults against me, yesterday it was insults against members of my family; the day before it was insults against friends of mine whose other friends openly criticize the fact that the former are still friends with me. And tomorrow, it will be something worse. [. . .]
>
> Because if, when you condemn the (Spanish) government's actions, you don't also condone the Catalan government's actions, you immediately become an enemy, a fascist, a fascistoid, a Franco follower, the scum of the earth. And you think about the fear that has already covered, like spores, the skin of all those people who keep quiet but who secretly come tell you that they're on your side—that they are grateful for what you are doing, and then they tell you that they don't even talk about the situation inside their own homes, for fear that their children will hear them and get into trouble at school.
>
> These are not mere anecdotes. This is the reality on the ground for those of us who live here. This is the new, shocking fracture of a society that used to live in peace and without fear, with logical differences of opinion and different values and different criteria, but always on a foundation of respect.

Madrid has stumbled badly. Whether the situation is already unsalvageable is unclear at this point. What is clear is that increasing confrontation and represssion, however legal and even necessary, will bolster the intolerant, revolutionary repression of Spanish patriots and embolden secessionists.

When Catalan authorities scheduled their referendum, Madrid could have coopted it by saying, "Great idea! The whole of Spain will vote on whether Catalonia should be independent." Not only would that have given the rest of the country a voice, it would have allowed the cowed and silent majority within Catalonia to express its will. Perhaps even at this late date it's an idea the Spanish government should consider.

"An Attack on Iran or North Korea Wouldn't Be Putting 'America First'"

Jim Jatras | *Strategic Culture* | October 20, 2017

Almost every day I am asked by someone what the likelihood is that we may soon be at war with Iran or North Korea, or conceivably both. As it's unlikely either of those countries will attack the United States since it would be suicidal, the question of war really means: are we going to attack them?

There are those who say all the tub-thumping emanating from Washington is just bluster. For example, Justin Raimondo of *Antiwar.com* writes that President Donald Trump is just engaging in "rhetorical pyro-technics and scor[ing] political points with certain [domestic] constituencies while maintaining the status quo: in short, he gets to engage in what is essentially a theatrical performance entirely unrelated to what is actually occurring on the ground. His enemies, mistaking rhetoric for reality, have risen to the bait."

I hope Raimondo is right but I fear otherwise. Underlying his analysis is the all-too-factual reality that attacking either country would result in catastrophe. "Millions would die, on both sides of the demilitarized zone," if we were to move first, he writes. "For this reason, the US—despite Trump's tweets—is not going to launch an attack on North Korea." Similar logic applies to Iran.

Unfortunately, if a prudent assessment of costs and benefits had guided American policy in recent years, none of our other wars of choice would have taken place either—yet they did. The fact that foreseeable consequences may appear "unthinkable" to rational minds does not mean they are not regarded as quite thinkable to those making the decisions.

The potential for war is not, as Trump's enemies and even some of his lesser-informed supporters would have us think, the product of his populism or nationalism. Quite the contrary, in 2016, Trump excoriated the globalist establishment's interventions under Presidents George W. Bush and Barack Obama in Iraq, Afghanistan, Libya, and Syria. Now he's adopted those very same policies clothed in Trumpish "America First!" bombast. Why he has done that is unclear and in the end not particularly relevant to what happens next.

To be sure, I do not think that the generals and globalists who now guide Trump's policies want war with either country, but they are willing to risk war to get what they want. On Korea, they insist on North Korea's de-nuclearization, which would likely set the stage for regime change in Pyongyang—which Kim Jong-un well knows, and why he will never agree to it. "The 'America First' solution is clear: Kim's threat to the U.S. is present only for as long as America remains engaged in Korean affairs," writes Srdja Trifkovic. "Disengage, and it disappears." But Washington will not countenance ever giving up the U.S. military foothold on the Korean peninsula. To keep it, they would rather put in jeopardy the almost 30,000 American personnel in South Korea and the lives of countless Koreans on both side of the 38th parallel.

Given that any U.S. attack on North Korea, or even Pyongyang's coming to believe that such an attack may be imminent, would almost certainly trigger a devastating counterstrike against South Korea and perhaps Japan, any American military action would have to be overwhelming from the start. Recent speculative talk of Kim's ability to wipe out up to 90% of the American population with an electromagnetic pulse (EMP) attack can have only one aim—to lay out a justification for a preemptive U.S. strike, perhaps a nuclear one. Perhaps Trump will wave that scenario under Chinese President Xi Jinping's nose at their summit next month based on delusions in Washington that if the U.S. can appear sufficiently bellicose, the Chinese will be panicked into solving the problem for us, either by a coup to remove Kim and his entourage or even via an invasion of North Korea.

Trump's belligerence towards Iran is similarly divorced from American national interests. To start with, the Administration's claim that Iran is violating the "spirit" of the JCPOA (Joint Comprehensive Plan of Action) is a tacit admission that Tehran is in fact meeting its obligations. Decertification of the agreement has less to do with actual concern about an Iranian nuclear device than seeking to neuter Iran as a regional power. This is clear from Trump's recently announced new strategy towards Iran, directed against the IRGC (Islamic Revolutionary Guard Corps), Iran's missile program, and Iran's state integrity and regional interests generally. Many of those pushing Trump in this direction make no secret of wanting military action achieve "regime change" in Tehran to install in place of the current theocratic government the so-called Mojahedin-e Khalq-e Iran (MEK) terrorists—subsidized by Saudi Arabia—much as we parachuted the ersatz Iraqi National Congress into Baghdad after overthrowing Saddam Hussein in Iraq.

Full-spectrum hostility to Iran has nothing to do with putting America first. Critics of U.S. foreign policy have long pointed out that we tend to act less in accord with the interests of our people than those of trans-national corporations (notably those connected to what is known anachronistically as the Military-Industrial Complex, more properly called the Deep State) and those of supposed "allies" that do nothing to safeguard our security but are all too happy to drag us into their quarrels to further their interests, not ours. Two of the most powerful foreign lobbies in Washington are those of Israel and Saudi Arabia, which are increasingly linked based on their shared hostility to Iran. It is significant that Trump's first two destinations abroad as president were to Saudi Arabia and Israel.

Trump seems to have entirely bought the false line that Iran is the world's foremost supporter of terrorism. Really? How many Shiite, Iranian-supported terrorist attacks have taken place in Europe or North America? No, the dubious honor of top sponsor of jihad terror belongs far and away to Saudi Arabia and its Wahhabist ideology that inspires Daesh, al-Qaeda, Boko Haram, al-Shabaab, and many other groups. In an inversion of reality, the U.S. administration blames global terrorism explicitly on Iran (including the IRGC), Syria, and by extension Russia, all of which are fighting against al-Qaeda and Daesh, as Trump himself acknowledged during the 2016 campaign, to the chagrin of GOP "experts."

Now Trump has decertified the Iran nuclear deal as expected but has not withdrawn the U.S. from it. The next move is up to Congress, whether to re-impose sanctions lifted under the agreement. If they do so, that would effectively mean the U.S. is withdrawing from the JCPOA, whether or not there is a formal repudiation by the U.S.—a step Trump could have taken but didn't. Based on my conversations on Capitol Hill this week, immediately restoring sanctions is improbable. Keep in mind that Democrats, even those deeply hostile to Iran, will wish to preserve what may be Obama's only significant foreign policy achievement from his time in office and will be loath to endorse the action of a president they despise. Many Republicans, much as they railed against Obamacare for seven years but then fumbled when they had an opportunity to repeal it, will find it easier to sound belligerent than to take a real action that might have consequences.

If Congress does not re-impose sanctions within the 60-day window, that effectively means that for now the U.S. will formally remain within the JCPOA despite the decertification, which even bellicose Ambassador to the United Nations Nikki Haley has conceded. (Giving some hope for Raimondo's thesis, this could be what Trump intended—a way to look strong and hairy-chested, and to appease the partisans of Israel and Saudi Arabia, while leaving responsibility for staying in the agreement with Congress.) It's likely, though, that eventually we will see some sort of measure from Congress condemning Iran for the usual laundry list of "bad behavior"—mostly untrue, and mostly not related to nuclear weapons development—with a sanctions trigger at some point in the future, perhaps in one year. Meanwhile, the U.S. will demand that Tehran agree to "improving" the deal with respect to ceasing development of missile technology, stopping aid to Hezbollah, Hamas and the Houthis, desisting from bad-mouthing Israel, pulling the IGRC out of Syria and Iraq, and swallowing pretty much anything else anyone can think of that would be fundamentally unacceptable to Iran.

If U.S. does at some point pull out of the JCPOA, or re-impose sanctions (which amounts to the same thing), it would be to the horror of the other signatories, who are anxious to preserve it. It would then be up to Iran to decide if pulling out of the agreement to which all the other parties except the U.S. remained committed were in her national interest. In my opinion that would be a foolish move and Iran would gain nothing from it. First, Iran has repeatedly said she does not wish to develop nuclear weapons and that doing so would contrary to her principles. Second, even if the U.S. were to re-impose sanctions, their effectiveness would be limited by the non-participation of even America's closest allies and trading partners, not to mention rejection by Russia and China. Third, Iran's remaining in the agreement with the other parties would create an advantageous circumstance for Tehran on one side with London, Paris, Berlin, Brussels, Moscow, and Beijing, while Washington is isolated on the other. (Or maybe this is part of Trump's clever plan to disengage us from the Middle East! We go so far out on the limb that no one's with us.) Finally and most dangerously, if Iran did denounce the JCPOA because the U.S. had, the hawks would claim it signaled a premeditated "breakout" toward acquisition of nuclear weapons, leaving Trump with "no choice" but to preempt it militarily.

While Patrick Buchanan writes that we are already on the road to war with Iran, there are many more relevant variables than is the case with North Korea. Moreover, while the fate of the JCPOA remains in limbo, it would take several months, perhaps a year, for the U.S. to assemble the forces necessary in the region to launch an attack on Iran. At this point I'd assess the odds of war with Iran holding at about 15%, but they could increase substantially and quickly depending on what happens next.

By contrast, assets for an attack on North Korea are already mostly in place on a hair trigger, awaiting only the order to engage. About a month ago, former NATO commander Admiral James Stavridis estimated a 10% chance of a nuclear war between the U.S. and North Korea, and a 20% to 30% chance of a conventional one. I think that assessment was optimistic then and things are getting worse. With regard to any attempt at "limited" conventional strike targeting specific missile and nuclear facilities, plus a decapitation of the North Korea leadership, it's not a realistic option—at that point Kim would have nothing to lose. I suggest that the odds of war have passed 30% and are increasing almost weekly but with strong possibility that any conflict could turn nuclear.

"Whatever happened to 'America First'?" asks Paul Mulshine. One can't help but suspect that Trump doesn't fully appreciate the box in which he now finds himself. If he does decide on war against North Korea or Iran, or God forbid both, with the anticipated horrible consequences, he will be blamed, not his newfound neoconservative fans. In that case, the Never-Trumpers won't have to wait for impeachment, they can activate the 25th Amendment to remove him for what they will claim is proof of his mental illness.

"'America First!' AWOL from Beijing, War with North Korea Looms"

Jim Jatras | *Strategic Culture* | November 11, 2017

There's no indication that President Donald Trump's summit with China's Xi Jinping achieved any breakthrough on North Korea. But why didn't it? After all, Trump said that China could "fix" the North Korea problem "easily and quickly" and it was just a matter of Xi's making up his mind to do so.

No less divorced from reality was Trump's half-hearted pitch on the US trade imbalance with China. The problem, he said, was not the Chinese—whom he complimented on their cleverness in exploiting our stupidity—but on the flaccid policies of prior American administrations. Quite true! But what will he do differently? Not much it seems, except maybe give a big tax cut with no strings attached to fat corporations that are thrilled to keep moving their operations overseas. Global market *über alles*! And here we all thought Hillary Clinton lost the election . . .

All in all, Trump's China visit was characterized by putting his "America First!" campaign principles on ice in favor of the globalist agenda of his economic advisers and subordination of trade to the geopolitical concerns of the military Junta that runs his administration for him. Sure, there might some tinkering here and there, like the recent hit against Chinese aluminum foil dumping. But plutocrats worried about a "trade war" with China can sleep easy.

On North Korea—the overwhelming US preoccupation at the Trump-Xi summit—Trump came up empty. For months observers have fretted over Trump's oscillating rhetoric from fire and destruction one day to let's-make-a-deal the next. He's his own good cop, bad cop act.

In principle there's nothing wrong with bluster and unpredictability. The art of the deal, you know. Despite the claims of Trump's detractors, the President's supposed irresponsibility and impulsiveness aren't the problem. Trump's personal style hasn't yet resulted in war, and if war comes, that wouldn't be the reason for it. Rather the real danger comes from the ostensible experts who set the parameters within which Trump operates, to whom he's unwisely outsourced his foreign and security policies. The following articles of faith are baked into the cake:

- First, it's nice that there has evidently been a back channel for direct US talks with North Korea, but from Washington's perspective there is nowhere for negotiations to go past demands for denuclearization. Any kind of concession to Pyongyang is out of the question, as it would mean "rewarding aggression" and "showing weakness." There are no evident contours for a deal when only one side is expected to make concessions.

- Second, because Washington has defined North Korea's nukes as *ipso facto* a vital threat to the US, the minimum acceptable US goal is Pyongyang's dumping its weapons. (Regime change would better, since it would also mean denuclearization.) The fact that Pyongyang is unlikely to give up its nukes under any circumstances means there can no deal.

- Third, in Washington's collective mind the crisis is 100 percent the fault of North Korea, zero percent the result of our presence in Korea, of our threats against Pyongyang, or of our actions elsewhere. How can you blame us—we tried diplomacy for 20 years and all it did was lead to a bomb! Any suggestion that Kim Jong-un is responding to threats from George W. Bush's 2002 Axis of Evil speech or to the disposal of Muammar Qaddafi and Saddam Hussein (who, unlike Kim, were foolish enough not to have WMDs) would be "blaming America!" Taking responsibility for past mistakes is not our forte. The prospect that the US mainland might in a few months be targetable by a nuclear-tipped North Korean ICBM has nothing at all to do with anything the US has said or done.

- Fourth, we know China can solve this at will—easily and quickly, as the President said. As former US ambassador to the UN John Bolton says: "That's why you say to China: 'we're gonna see reunification here. Do you want to do it the hard way or the easy way?'" This means China can do the job for us, or we'll do it. The notion that Beijing will not take an action fundamentally inconsistent to China's national security because of American flattery or threats is almost inconceivable. But if they fail to do as we demand, what comes next will be their fault, not ours.

- Fifth, the military option is still very much on the table. The Junta are not strategic thinkers but they are very, very certain of their technique. If worst comes to worse, and they are "forced to act" (from their point of view) they are supremely (and dangerously) confident that good execution can minimize the damage. Preparations for a preemptive strike continue apace. In Seoul Trump touted the prowess of the three US carrier groups off the peninsula. Maybe it's all just a bluff to get the Chinese to act (as we know they can; see the preceding paragraph). But if worse comes to worst, and it turns out horribly for a lot of people: We had no choice in light of China's inaction. Does this mean the planners are sitting around scheming to sacrifice Seoul so as not to look weak? No, but they are prepared to risk that outcome because they are boxed in by all the other elements of their approach. Worse, they are sure they call pull it off. After all, look at how well our other recent wars have gone!

- Sixth, Trump has made it clear that his instincts are on hold and he'll be guided by "the professionals." (Compare Afghanistan, where his "new" same-old non-strategy was dictated by the Junta against what he admits were his own inclinations.) On Korea, the "experts" mainly refers to the Junta but also Nikki Haley (!!!!) and probably John Bolton. (There's also a possibility that David Petraeus, the genius advocate of arming al-Qaeda in Syria, has a thumb in the pie as well.) Plus, keep in mind that Trump isn't a neoconservative but he is an Andrew Jackson, or perhaps Teddy Roosevelt, nationalist. "Do not underestimate us," Trump warned Kim. "And do not try us." When the "experts" tell him that North Korea is "trying" us, what else can he do but act? After all, in April the "experts" told him that al-Assad gassed children in Syria—and boom!—he launched cruise missiles to the applause of both the Swamp critters and much of his populist base that has no idea where Syria is.

- Seventh—and here's the fun part—if it does all turn into a huge disaster involving hundreds of thousands of deaths, who will take the fall? Not [H.R.] McMaster or Haley. No, it will all be blamed on Trump and the "America First!" path he failed to follow. The establishment on both sides of the aisle, including many who prodded him toward a more aggressive policy, will rush to denounce him: See, we told you he's nuts! The professionals gave him good advice but he messed everything up! In that case, they wouldn't have to wait for impeachment, the 25th Amendment would be invoked. Talk about a "win-win" for the Deep State warmongers: getting rid of Kim and Trump!

"Jerusalem and American Problem–Solving"

Jim Jatras | *Strategic Culture* | December 9, 2017

Once upon a time, before France abolished the death penalty, three condemned terrorists were led to the guillotine. They were a Japanese, a German, and an American.

The Japanese went first. To show his bravery, he demanded to be laid on his back glaring up at the suspended blade. The switch was triggered, the blade was released, the condemned man shouted "Banzai!" in defiance . . .

But there was a malfunction in the mechanism! Just short of the man's neck the blade *stopped.*

Well, the French were so impressed by the Japanese terrorist's bravery, they pardoned him on the spot. He was lifted to his feet, kissed on both cheeks in the Gallic fashion, and sent on his merry way.

Next came the German. Not to be outdone by his comrade, he too demanded to look death boldly in the face. A flick of the switch, a cry of "Sieg Heil!", a flash of the blade—which again stopped short. Following the Japanese precedent, the German was pardoned as well. With a kiss on both cheeks, off he went.

Last was the American. Like his predecessors, he too faced up toward the blade, scrutinizing it.

But just an instant before the switch was to be triggered, the American called out:

"Hey wait! I see the problem. Let me up—I can fix it!"

For better or worse, that is how we Americans tend to see the world. Nothing can ever just *be*, everything is a *problem*. And as night follows day, we are sure all problems have *solutions*. Whatever it is, we can *fix* it!

Which brings us to Jerusalem. It is the core problem within a bigger problem, the Israel-Palestinian conflict.

Americans are certain there is a solution. That certainty fails to take into account two factors:

1. The Israelis
2. The Palestinians

From the Israelis' point of view, there actually isn't a Jerusalem problem at all. They have it—all of it—and they're going to keep it.

For the Palestinians, there definitely is a Jerusalem problem. They don't have it but want it—or part of it anyway—as the capital of a Palestinian state. Which in turn leads to their next problem: that there isn't a Palestinian state, and it's unlikely there will be one.

Not a real state, anyway. The Israelis will never risk it. As Srdja Trifkovic explains:

The structural problem in the Arab-Israeli conflict which remains overlooked by the media—the mother of all problems—is not Trump's recognition of Jerusalem as Israel's capital. It is whether the Palestinian Arabs can ever recognize Israel as a legitimate entity.

From the orthodox Muslim point of view, the struggle against Israel is more than a "war of national liberation": it is *an act of worship* for which God rewards a struggler in the form of victory in this life and eternity the hereafter. In line with this teaching, Hamas' military wing, the Brigades of Martyr 'Izziddin Al-Qassam, call their attacks *'amaliyyat Istish-hadiyah*, or "martyrdom operations." The religious contextualization of the Arab-Israeli dispute makes its resolution structurally impossible. The conflict is no longer stated in the secular, "rational" terms of power, territory, resources, and guarantees. Hamas, Hizballah, and other Islamic groups have brought a qualitative change to the Middle Eastern discourse: from their point of view no permanent peace is possible because it would be against Allah's will to grant any piece of land once controlled by the faithful to non-Muslim infidels.

In short, President Donald Trump's recognition of Jerusalem as Israel's capital is the end of a long pretense. In keeping a campaign pledge to domestic constituencies, he has visibly changed the American role in the Israel-Palestinian dynamic. In the opinion of Marc Ginsberg, former U.S. ambassador to Morocco and White House Middle East adviser, Trump's declaration is—

> . . . the culmination of a concerted effort by American uber Jewish and Christian evangelicals to put an end to the façade of America as an "honest broker" of Middle East peace. A façade that successive American diplomats have tried to sell to the Palestinians and Arab nations like a used car. [. . .]
>
> For decades, successive American presidents have inserted themselves into the peacemaking business giving rise to a diplomatic industrial complex dedicated to forging a peace between Israel and the Palestinians. Anyone who has made the effort has failed, and the failures have piled up like layers of Jerusalem stone. . . . For whatever may come of Trump's actions it may at least finally, finally, send a message to the Palestinians that the long, painful era of America acting as their "impartial" intermediary with Israel, is over.

Let's take a moment to catch our breath after we've stopped laughing at the notion—worthy of a used car salesman indeed!—that the U.S. could ever have been considered an "honest broker" or "impartial" in pretty much any international context these days, much less this one. Still, Ginsberg has a point. Whatever the delusions anyone might have entertained that the U.S. would hold both sides' feet to the fire to get a viable two-state deal, forget it. The Palestinians will get what, and only what, the Israelis are prepared to give them.

The suggestion has been made that Trump has undercut some super-secret, super-genius peace plan concocted by his son-in-law, Jared Kushner. Likewise, that the Administration's and (Israeli Prime Minister Netanyahu's) favorite Arab, Saudi Crown Prince Mohammad bin Salman was not fully on board. The patent absurdity of such claims isn't worth refuting. Mohammad, no less than Netanyahu, couldn't care less about the Palestinians. He's preoccupied with figuring out how to drag the U.S. into a war with Iran.

Trump "recognized" Jerusalem as Israel's capital—which in substance already was the position of the United States as codified in 1995 legislation—but did not immediately move the U.S. Embassy to Jerusalem. (Despite the nonsense about a process taking months or even years, the formalities could be accomplished instantly by just switching the signs on the Embassy in Tel Aviv and on the U.S. Consulate General in Jerusalem.) This "split the baby" approach bears a striking similarity to Trump's action on the Iranian nuclear deal, where he symbolically kept another campaign pledge by "decertifying" the agreement but didn't pull the U.S. out of it.

On both Jerusalem and the Iran deal, the outrage around the world was deafening, but in the end nothing much happened. The world kept spinning on its axis.

Meanwhile, the problems fester, with no solutions in sight.

"Iran and Myths of Revolution"

Jim Jatras | *Strategic Culture* | January 5, 2018

In just the past few days during which Iran has seen anti-government protests, much has been written and said about Iranians' desire for freedom, mixed with speculation about whether or not the ayatollahs' Islamic republic is in danger of collapse.

The following is not another such analysis. Rather, this is an attempt to address the underlying assumptions of most of the sage pronouncements to which we are treated—assumptions that are as lacking in substance as they are ubiquitous. Three of these myths are noted below.

Spontaneous popular uprising—not

"Arise ye pris'ners of starvation, Arise ye wretched of the earth!" The stirring words of the socialist and communist anthem, *The Internationale*, encapsulate the sense most people have of revolution as the result of unbearably oppressive conditions. At some point "The People" can stand no more, and in noble wrath they rise up as one against their tormenters!

There's just one little problem. That has never happened, it isn't happening now, and it never will happen.

Revolts and revolutions (see below) almost always occur when things are getting better but expectations have outpaced performance. Or when things had been getting better but there's been a setback, either economically (like in Iran today, where President Rouhani's neoliberal economic reforms have cut consumer subsidies paid under his predecessor, Ahmadinejad) or in 1917 Russia (problems with the conduct of the war and the economy).

Even then, revolts and revolutions don't take place unless other conditions are present. One of them is relative freedom to protest and even, in some cases, to engage in subversive activities. For example, why did revolt "spontaneously" break out in Russia in 1917 but not in the Soviet Union in 1941, when, in the latter case, the losses on the war front were far greater in terms of men and territory and the privations of the home population far more severe? Because, Tsar Nicholas did not impose all-pervasive wartime discipline on the home front or even in the army, allowing anti-war agitators to operate within the ranks. Where would that have got you with Stalin in 1941? Or in North Korea or Saudi Arabia today?

"The People" don't all of one accord suddenly decide to shift direction like a flock of birds or a school of fish. Movements by human beings need to be planned, led, and incited. Consider the role of the Masonic lodges in revolutionary France, the Bolsheviks in Russia, the religious establishment in Iran that in 1979 brought the mullahs to power in the first place, and the Muslim Brotherhood and other Salafist groups in the so-called "Arab Spring" starting in 2011.

The Iranian government says the disorders are instigated from the outside. They would say that even if it weren't true, but public support from President Donald Trump, Ambassador Nikki Haley, and Prime Minister Binyamin Netanyahu adds credence to the charge. So does news of a Trump-Netanyahu "strategic work plan" to counter Iran following a December 12 White House meeting. So does the appointment earlier this year of the "Dark Prince," "Ayatollah Mike," the "Undertaker" and convert to Islam Michael D'Andrea to run the CIA's Iran operation. (One Langley insider's simple comment on the D'Andrea appointment: "All I can say is that war with Iran is in the cards.")

"Freedom!"—but for whom?

Well-wishers of the Iranian demonstrators laud their quest for: *Freedom!* For most of the world, that word usually implies a set of related values: political freedom, democracy, the rule of law (versus the rule of the ayatollahs and their security services); economic freedom (Stefan Molyneux has spoken eloquently about the venerable Persian civilization whose creative potential had been stultified under the Islamic republic); and social and personal freedom (the image of the woman holding her hijab aloft, "Tiananmen-Square-style.")

One is reminded of the idealistic, cosmopolitan, pro-"democracy" young ladies who in 1979 voluntarily donned hijab or chador in "solidarity" with Islamic protests against the "repressive, corrupt, and pro-American regime" of Reza Shah Pahlavi—and who then found themselves confined in such garb for the rest of their lives. An inconvenient truth for many advocates of "freedom" in Iran is that while in non-Islamic countries there is generally a congruency between democracy and social liberties, in Muslim societies there is an inherent and underlying conflict.

Here's the tradeoff. You can push for more "democracy"—and end up with an illiberal, Sharia-ruled state that oppresses women and non-Muslims. Or you can have an enlightened autocrat or military caste that imposes a secular order in which women can run about with uncovered hair and minorities are equal citizens. The mid-20th century saw various movements and regimes that enforced the latter: Kemalism in Turkey, Baathism in Iraq and Syria, Nasserite pan-Arabism in Egypt, military rule in a number of countries (Algeria, Pakistan (until Zia-ul-Haq's imposition of Sharia), and Egypt today after a brief run of Islamist "democracy").

Certainly there are many, many people in Iran who would like to see the restoration of the socially liberal state that existed under the Shah—and maybe restoration of the monarchy itself. But no one should imagine such a restoration would be particularly *democratic*. (Maybe some of those no-longer-young girls stuck in their hijabs for almost four decades may have reconsidered their priorities.) To survive, such a restoration, even if it commands the support of a majority of the population would have to contend with a very substantial portion of the population for whom secularism and liberalism are not just wrong but *shirk* (idolatry) and *ridda* (apostasy)—and are prepared to act accordingly.

Revolt or Revolution?

"Treason doth never prosper: what's the reason? Why, if it prosper, none dare call it treason." The self-evident observation of John Harington (also famed as the inventor of the flush toilet) is that if a revolt succeeds, it is no longer just a revolt. Those who launched it are no longer traitors, those who opposed the revolution are.

The conversion from revolt to revolution almost never happens unless there is a split in *l'ancien régime* to create what Alexander Shtromas called "the second pivot," a second source of official power. This happens not when "The People" rise up but when some part of the ruling establishment defects to the revolt and becomes the new conferrer of legitimacy. There are obvious historical examples: Parliament in the English Civil War, the Third Estate's declaring itself the National Assembly of France, the Petrograd Soviet's coup against the Provisional Government, Boris Yeltsin's Russian government when Mikhail Gorbachev's Soviet government was under threat of the State Committee on the State of Emergency (itself an aspiring second pivot that failed), and the communist cabals in the various Warsaw Pact countries that ousted little Brezhnevs and installed little Gorbachevs.

In Iran today, the question isn't whether "The People" will topple "the regime." It's whether, when, and where a split might occur in the ruling establishment to create a rival point of authority. If that doesn't happen, a revolt it will remain, either being suppressed or dying out on its own.

Ironically, in Iran's 1979 revolution, the Islamic establishment itself may be regarded as having been a kind of second pivot. Keep in mind that in 1953, the Islamic clergy—most prominently Ayatollah Abol-Ghasem Kashani, friend and mentor to Ruhollah Khomeini, the future Supreme Leader of the Islamic Republic—was allied with the Shah in the CIA-sponsored overthrow of the left-leaning Mohammad Mosaddegh. Without such support it's unlikely the Shah would have succeeded.

Most of the mullahs were content to stay in their well-paid government sinecures under royal authority, even after 1963, when the Shah launched his "White Revolution" modernization program of land reform, privatization, and most controversially women's rights and legal equality of non-Muslims. But Khomeini, forced into exile, led the denunciation that the reforms were an "an attack on Islam." From his place of exile in Paris, Khomeini inveighed against the threat to Islam and eventually became the second pivot that brought down the Shah.

"Trump at One Year: His Fate May Hang on What He Does Next About Immigration"

Jim Jatras | *Strategic Culture* | January 19, 2018

When in 2016 Donald Trump mugged the bipartisan political establishment in the United States, there were three issues that put him beyond the pale:

- Rejection of the globalist meddling, mindless confrontation with Russia, and interventionist wars of Bush Sr., Bill Clinton, Bush Jr., and Barack Obama in favor of America First nationalism—which critics equated with phony memes of "isolationism" and even flirtation with Nazism;
- Restructuring America's trade relations to favor American workers and producers, not international corporations keen to dump their costly domestic employees and relocate abroad, sending in their products tariff-free; and
- Stopping the migration invasion of the US, symbolized above all by building The Wall on the Mexican border—and making Mexico pay for it.

As Trump's first year in office comes to a close, where do we stand?

War and Foreign Policy

The neoconservatives who have made a disaster of American policy for almost three decades are exultant that Trump is dancing to their tune. In the Middle East, "America First" has turned into "Israel and Saudi Arabia First" and a vendetta against Iran. While Trump has taken credit for the possible outbreak of peace between the two Koreas, that is a byproduct of the intransigence and bluster coming from Washington—which may resume as soon as the Olympics are over.

With respect to Russia, the picture is dreary and the trend worrisome. The absurdly named "Countering America's Adversaries Through Sanctions Act," passed last year with a bipartisan, veto-proof supermajority, stripped Trump of his constitutional authority to make policy toward Russia. A new round of legislatively mandated sanctions designed to block any possible outreach to Moscow by criminalizing contact with any Russian within screaming distance of the Kremlin is imminent. Early hopes of US-Russia cooperation in Syria against jihad terrorist have given way to a continued (illegal) US military presence east of the Euphrates, talk of a "New Syrian Army" (recycled Daesh and al-Qaeda terrorists, with a push to turn the CIA aid spigot back on), plausible Russian suggestions of a US hand in a drone attack on Russian personnel, and back to square one with "Assad must go!" Providing lethal weapons to Ukraine—which could entail American advisers on the ground near the conflict line in the Donbas—moves us closer to military confrontation.

All that said, there is a school of thought that says Trump is in so precarious a position vis-à-vis a Deep State working overtime to remove him (and if pushed too hard, might just "JFK" him), that he has no choice but to adopt a "rope-a-dope" strategy. Patrick Armstrong thinks that Trump is purposely undermining the imperial order bit by bit by degrading the narcissistic notion of US global "leadership." This means Trump's seeming to go along with his ubiquitous adversaries' bellicose agenda to the Nth degree but in the process making the US less and less relevant.

Korea may be an example: bluster and threaten, so the panicked South reached out to the North. Recognize Jerusalem as Israel's capital: the US is no longer the mediator between Israel and the Palestinians, and we defund the Palestinian Authority and the UN to boot. Threaten to pull out of the Iran nuclear deal: nervous Europeans distance themselves from Washington and cozy up to Moscow, Beijing, and Tehran, which may in turn lead to a diminished US enthusiasm for defending "disloyal" NATO allies. Double down on the failed Afghanistan non-strategy: blame Pakistan and cut off their money. Impose economic and financial sanctions with reckless abandon: an alternative international finance system is in the works.

In any case, among Trump's three populist heresies from the bipartisan Swamp's agenda, this is the least well articulated and least important to his base in Flyover Country, many of whom reflexively if ignorantly respond positively to anything that sounds "tough" and militaristic ("Support our troops!"—so how about we stop getting them killed and crippled in unnecessary missions?). Whatever Trump thinks he's doing, as long as he doesn't stumble us into a war somewhere like Korea, Iran, Ukraine, or Syria, things are still better than if Hillary had won.

- *Verdict after one year*: Let's call it a wash. But there's still reason to worry.

Trade

Not much can be said about trade at this time. Maybe that's good. There are solid America First people in the administration, such as U.S Trade Representative Robert Lighthizer and Peter Navarro, who heads the White House Office of Trade and Manufacturing Policy, backed up by speechwriter Stephen Miller, the main nationalist-populist left in the Trump inner circle. Commerce Secretary Wilbur Ross is generally counted in this camp. Perhaps a low decibel level means quiet progress.

Or not. The trade nationalists are at daggers drawn with the globalists and generals: National Economic Council chief Gary Cohn, Treasury Secretary Steven Mnuchin, White House Chief of Staff John Kelly, and National Security Adviser H.R. McMaster. The former two are ideological free traders and advocates for global corporations and banks. The latter favor the tried-and-failed decades-long policy of buying geopolitical and strategic advantage by taking it out of the hide of American workers and producers: we give our satellites like Germany, Japan, South Korea, etc., etc., free, non-reciprocal access to our domestic market, they hand over their sovereignty. What a deal!

Who will come out on top is unclear. Pulling out of TPP was a positive sign. What Trump does about NAFTA will be a critical, which is why the usual suspects are in full-throated hysteria over his threat to insist Canada and Mexico renegotiate it or to pull the US out. With respect to the 800-pound gorilla of America's trade woes, an America First pitch to China ought to be getting us out of Korea and the South China Sea while rebalancing our enormously one-sided trade relationship. Unfortunately, the globalists and generals would rather do the opposite: keep sacrificing Americans' economic wellbeing in an effort to "contain" China strategically.

Trade won't matter much in the November elections amid happy-news perceptions of improved job creation, stock market record highs (though how much of that represents real economic growth and how much a ballooning investment bubble is open to debate), and higher consumer confidence. But over the long term, if this opportunity is lost to put Americans' interests ahead of those of transnational corporations it might not come again.

- *Verdict after one year*: It could go either way.

Immigration

Of the three Trumpish heresies from bipartisan orthodoxy, this is the most important. While for the establishment it ranks with foreign policy and is closely tied to it ("Invade the world, invite the world"), for Trump's base is it head and shoulders above the other two. If not for his pledge to build The Wall and make Mexico pay for it, Trump never would have been the Republican nominee and won the presidency.

For the past week the American media and political class have been in a tizzy over precisely what scatological term Trump may have used in a closed-door White House meeting over DACA ("Deferred Action on Childhood Arrivals," Obama's so-called "Dreamers") and immigration policy generally, including funds to build The Wall. (There evidently is some question of whether the second syllable was "hole" or "house.") Is this the worst word ever uttered in a non-public meeting in the Oval Office? At least nobody claims Trump said whatever it was he said like Lyndon Johnson, perched on the presidential throne.

Trump's real offense was less the word itself than its implication that certain Countries ABCD are horrible places to live, while other Countries WXYZ are quite the opposite. And since Countries ABCD are pretty much full of black and brown people, and Countries WXYZ are almost exclusively the abodes of white and yellow people, he's a racist for noticing the difference. Hence, the media and Trump's critics' frenzied repetition of the R-word word, as though it were a sort of magical incantation that at some point will cause him to crumble into dust.

There are over seven and a half billion people inhabiting this orb of woe. Probably somewhere in the range of 90 percent of them would dramatically improve their lives if they left where they are and moved to the United States. Aside from the clear benefit to the Democratic Party in welcoming spanking new voters, how does it profit the American nation to import mobs of impoverished and uneducated people to drag down wages, especially in low-paying job categories, and to consume a disproportionate share of public benefits?

Keep in mind too that because a very high proportion of migrants in this category would be considered "minorities" under US law, they and their progeny would immediately qualify upon arrival for affirmative action status in hiring and education. What kind of idiot country imports foreigners and then discriminates in their favor against the natives? For what purpose—to offset historical wrongs to which the newcomers were never victim?

Conversely, the President's defenders suggest that what's really needed is to switch from a country-of-origin and family-reunification basis for our immigration system to a merit-based system. Let's take only the best and the brightest, from whatever place they hail.

A supposed merit-based system is a bad idea too. First off—let's show a little altruism here—it would make the plight of the horrible countries worse. I am not generally a fan of Pope Francis with respect to his views on migration, but he has a point when he says, like Pope John Paul II before him, that a "brain drain" from Third World countries robs them of much of their best talent and hope for improving their own homelands.

However, to note that is not to suggest that importing cherry-picked high-achievers into the US is such a blessing for us. Just as we don't need a migrant underclass, neither do we need an imported overlord class taking the best jobs from American kids who have busted their hump getting through school and in many cases gone heavily into debt.

This is a particular problem in high-tech and IT, where massive companies with near-monopoly market control—and consequently almost total obsequy from the bipartisan political class—demand the importation of ever more foreign talent, particular in STEM fields. This is despite serious uncertainty as to whether there are enough jobs even for Americans trained in those disciplines.

A special area of concern is pushback against the Trump Administration's modest effort to trim the much-abused H−1B program for supposedly "temporary" workers, a transgression against both the left's multiculturalism and corporate plutocrats' demand for cheap, docile indentured labor. There exists a kind of reverse-nativism, according to which America needs a vital "transfusion of fresh blood" from lots and lots of bright, energetic foreigners. You see, American-born people are just too lazy and stupid to succeed on their own and deserve to be replaced. If you or your offspring lose out to an "insourced" immigrant or H-1B via-holder, maybe one who can trump you on an affirmative action preference, too bad for you.

Here's a suggestion. Let's nix both imported underclass and overclass and have a long (if not permanent) immigration timeout like we had from the end of the first Great Wave of immigration in the mid-1920s until the current wave was set off by the 1965 immigration act. For almost half a century, those who entered in that previous wave (such as all four of this writer's Spartan grandparents) and their progeny had time to assimilate and become Americans. Unless and until those who arrived in the past few decades have likewise Americanized (are we allowed to say that?) to the extent possible—and the millions now here illegally have been repatriated—entry should be cut down to the absolute minimum. That should be not much more than spousal visas, and those should be strictly scrutinized for fraud.

It remains to be seen whether Trump's language, whatever it was, will translate into good policy. In the wake of "S-Gate," he's in a strong position. Republicans can move a clean federal government funding bill and dare the Democrats to block it and shut down the government of the whole country because it doesn't save the "Dreamers." But never underestimate the potential for panic among Congressional Republicans and their ability to throw away a winning hand.

That's where the risk for Trump is. If he falls for a chump's deal on immigration, where he yields on DACA in exchange for promises and gestures the way Ronald Reagan got suckered on the last big amnesty in 1986, his base—which indeed wouldn't care if he gunned down someone in the middle of 5th Avenue—might not be so forgiving. They can overlook a lot, but not that. And if his base stays home this November, we're looking at a Democratic Congress, impeachment, and President Mike Pence.

- *Verdict after one year*: Trump's rough talk and the hateful reaction to it increase the chances he will stand his ground. But it still could go either way. This is the one to watch.

"Playing 'Kurdish Card' in Syria Backfires on US As Turks Move In"

Jim Jatras | *Strategic Culture* | January 25, 2018

What the result will be of Turkey's offensive against the Kurdish-held enclave of Afrin in northwest Syria may not be clear for a while, but two things are already certain. Bad decisions in Washington provided the trigger, and

Washington's regional position will suffer as a result of Ankara's Orwellian-named "Operation Olive Branch."

The offensive is the latest twist from Turkey's erratic and unpredictable leader, President Recep Tayyip Erdogan. Let's recall that "Sultan" Erdogan was an early and active participant in what was supposed to have been a relatively easy regime change operation in Syria starting in 2011, on the pattern of NATO's overthrow of Libya's Muammar Qaddafi that same year. Turkey, with its lengthy border with Syria, was (and to some extent still is) a major supporter of al-Qaeda-linked jihadist groups in Syria, working with Saudi Arabia and Qatar under American guidance, with Israel as a silent partner. The appearance of ISIS (Daesh, ISIL) as an outgrowth of al-Qaeda in Iraq was a direct and foreseen consequence of that effort, as the Obama Administration was warned in 2012 by the U.S. Defense Intelligence Agency (DIA), then under the command of General Michael Flynn.

To the surprise of many, the Syrian government under President Bashar al-Assad didn't just roll up and die but displayed an unexpected tenacity in defending that country's secular, multi-religious society against outside efforts to impose a Wahhabist sectarian state. The clincher came with Russia's September 2015 intervention, a distinctly unwelcome development for the "Assad must go!" crowd.

Two months later a crisis erupted between NATO-member Turkey and Russia when Turkish planes shot down a Russian Su–24 fighter (ostensibly for crossing into Turkish airspace) and ethnic Turkish (also called Turkmen) fighters murdered one of the two Russian airmen who parachuted from the plane. Perhaps Erdogan thought he could give Moscow a bloody nose and, with NATO's backing him up, the Russians would turn tail and run. That didn't happen, giving Erdogan reason to feel hung out to dry.

Then came the July 2016 coup attempt against Erdogan, orchestrated, he claims, by his former ally businessman, educator, and cleric Fethullah Gülen, resident in the U.S. Despite the deep freeze in Russia-Turkey ties since the Su–24 shootdown, Russian covert assistance reportedly was critical to saving Erdogan's regime and perhaps his life. At the same time, his U.S. ally—which denies involvement in the coup attempt—still refuses to hand over Gülen, whose supporters in Turkey have been repressed in a massive purge of real or imagined opposition to Erdogan's consolidation of power.

Internationally, the upshot of the coup's failure was a turnaround in ties between Ankara and Moscow. In December 2016, Erdogan joined Russia and Iran, the principal supporters of the Syrian government against terrorists armed by Turkey among others, in the Astana peace process.

Erdogan, if not completely breaking with the anti-Assad coalition, at least started to hedge his bets, for example not reacting to the Syrian liberation of Aleppo from Ankara's al-Qaeda clients. When Syrian forces relieved the ISIS siege of Deir ez-Zor in eastern Syria in late 2017, and the Syrian army linked up with the Iraqi army (supported by the U.S. and Iran) at their common border, ISIS was almost finished as a territorial "caliphate." This in turn has allowed Damascus to shift its focus elsewhere, notably to al-Qaeda-held Idlib. This wasn't yet the end of the Syrian war but the end was coming into view.

Or so it seemed—which brings us back to U.S. policy.

In July 2017, Ankara had leaked the existence of U.S. bases in Kurdish-held northwestern Syria. Not that it matters to anyone in Washington, this presence is totally illegal under both U.S. law (there's no Congressional authorization) and international law, which in U.S. politics counts for nothing (no UN Security Council authorization, no self-defense justification, and of course no invitation from the Syrian government). The U.S. presence with the Kurds is positioned on the eastern bank of the Euphrates River, while the

Russians and Syrians stay mainly on the western bank. Aside from some scary air incidents, it seems both sides seem to have been careful not to come into conflict.

If Washington had been content to leave it that, President Donald Trump—who had campaigned on a promise to "crush and destroy ISIS"—was in a great position to declare victory and get out. Keep in mind that despite ordering a demonstrative cruise missile strike on a Syrian air base in April 2017 (in reprisal for a chemical attack that almost certainly was not the work of the Syrian government), he had not indicated an appetite for digging deeper into an involvement in a conflict where he had once praised Assad, Russia, and Iran for fighting ISIS. He even reportedly cut off CIA aid to "rebels," i.e., al-Qaeda, in July.

That was then, this is now. The U.S. is not leaving Syria. The globalists, generals, and other Swamp-monsters, plus their Israeli and Saudi pals, have won and "America First!" has lost. Recently Secretary of State Rex Tillerson announced a new "way forward" in Syria, which in effect is an old way back towards the Obama policy. There are five pillars:

- Defeat of ISIS and al-Qaeda. [The first is almost finished in Syria and Iraq, and regarding the second there seems to be some confusion about whose side we've been on for almost seven years];
- Assad must go [Seriously; the fact that regime change in Syria would mean curtains for the Christians evidently is of no concern in Washington];
- Block the Iranians [The "Shiite crescent" bogeyman is now a "northern arch"];
- Return of refugees to their homes [Is that why the U.S. and the EU maintain sanctions on government-held areas?]; and
- No weapons of mass destruction [Someone seems to have picked up by mistake the old talking points regarding Iraq, circa 2002].

The linchpin of this concept, if it can be called that, is using the Kurds as America's boots on the ground. (It should be noted that when CIA assistance to its al-Qaeda clients was stopped last year, the Pentagon's support for the Kurdish YPG (*Yekîneyên Parastina Gel*, "People's Protection Units") was maintained or stepped up; at the time the move seemed largely a bureaucratic tiff between Langley and DoD. Now however there are rumblings that the CIA aid spigot may be turned back on.) But for Erdogan, the icing on the cake was U.S. announcement of plans to create a 30,000 "Border Security Force." For Turkey, this amounts to U.S. sponsorship, perhaps with partition of Syria in mind, of a Kurdish quasi-state comparable to Iraqi Kurdistan, in league with the Kurdish PKK (*Partiya Karkerên Kurdistanê*, "Kurdistan Workers Party") —designated a terrorist group by the U.S., Turkey, and NATO. Hence Erdogan's claim he is acting against a U.S.-armed "terror army," which he vows to "strangle . . . before it's even born."

Perhaps U.S. officials thought they could manage Ankara's response, or that the bombastic Erdogan was just bluffing. If so, they were mistaken. It now remains to be seen how far the Turks plan, or are able, to advance in Afrin. There is also speculation whether an assault may also be directed toward Manbij in the main, eastern Kurdish-held area known as Rojava, where some 2,000 or more American troops are present. In addition, Erdogan, who has progressively dismantled the Kemalist secular order in Turkey seems bent on whipping the offensive up as an Islamic ideological jihad in 90,000 mosques across the country.

Afrin, with its rough terrain, is a tough nut to crack. Manbij might be even harder and risk confrontation with the U.S. In either case the Kurds are fighting on their home turf against the Turkish army with their local Turkmen militia and al-Qaeda allies. Damascus reportedly has allowed Kurds from the main Rojava area they hold further east to cross government-held territory to reinforce Afrin. Meanwhile, the expectation of some Kurds that the United States would create a "no-fly zone" to defend them from America's own NATO ally was comically unrealistic.

While it's hard to say in the short term if the Turks or Kurds will come out ahead, there's no doubt that strategically the big loser is the U.S.—and it's a totally self-inflicted wound. If Trump had stuck to his original goal of just defeating ISIS, he could take credit for the efforts of the Syrian army and Russian air force and soon truthfully proclaim "Mission Accomplished" (in contrast to George W. Bush's notorious Iraq declaration in 2003). But now, with the foolish adventure into which his generals (National Security Adviser H.R. McMaster, Defense Secretary James "Mad Dog" Mattis, and White House Chief of Staff John Kelly) have led him, with Tillerson's agreement or acquiescence, he now has on his hands a conflict between our *de jure* NATO ally Turkey and our *de facto* ally, the Kurds.

If the Kurds win, Turkey is in effect lost to NATO—we're close to that already. If Turkey wins, the misguided U.S. plan to stay in Syria is finished—a likely outcome anyway.

As far as the impact within Syria, the Kurds are about to find out, as did the Iraqi Kurds following their abortive independence declaration last year, that they likewise have pressed their luck too far and were foolish to count on "friends" in Washington, for whom they are disposable. In the end, the Turkish attack is likely to accelerate the Kurds' outreach to Damascus, with whom they have never entirely burned their bridges.

"What Would an 'America First!' Security Policy Look Like?"

Jim Jatras | *Strategic Culture* | February 23, 2018

Republicans love to caricature Democrats as big spenders whose only approach to any problem is to throw money at it. As with most caricatures, it is made easy by the fact that it is mostly true. At least when it comes to domestic entitlement programs, nobody can top the party of FDR and LBJ when it comes to doling out goodies to favored constituencies paid for by picking someone else's pocket.

However, Republicans are hardly the zealous guardians of the public purse they would have us believe. While quick to trash their partisan opponents for making free with taxpayers' money, they are no less happy to do the same—at least when it's called "national defense."

Over the next five years, the Trump administration will spend $3.6 *trillion* on the military. The GOP-controlled Congress's approved, with Republicans voting overwhelmingly in the affirmative, the "Bipartisan Budget Act of 2018" (HR 1892) and the "National Defense Authorization Act for Fiscal Year 2018" (HR 2810). With respect to the former, the watchdog National Taxpayers Union urged a No vote:

An initial estimate of approximately $300 billion in new spending above the law's caps barely scratches the surface in terms of total spending. The two-year deal also includes $155 billion in defense and non-defense Overseas Contingency Operations (OCO) spending, $5 billion in emergency spending for defense, and more than $80 billion in disaster funding. $100 billion in proposed offsets are comprised of the same budget gimmicks taxpayers have seen used as pay-fors over and over and are unlikely to generate much of a down-payment on this new spending.'

Senator Rand Paul (R-Kentucky) poses the question that few in Washington—and certainly few Republicans—are willing to ask: *"Is our military budget too small, or is our mission too large?"* He notes:

Since 2001, the U.S. military budget has more than doubled in nominal terms and grown over 37% accounting for inflation. The U.S. spends more than the next eight countries combined.

It's really hard to argue that our military is underfunded, so perhaps our mission has grown too large. That mission includes being currently involved in combat operations in Iraq, Syria, Afghanistan, Somalia, Niger, Libya, and Yemen. We have troops in over 50 of 54 African countries. The wars in Iraq and Afghanistan have cost over a trillion dollars and lasted for over 15 years.

Defense spending is about survival, right? If you need to spend it, you spend it. But realistically, how does one assess whether spending is too much or too little without looking at the strategy the military is tasked with carrying out, and whether it makes any sense?

Proponents of increased—always increased—spending, like Defense Secretary James Mattis, point to real problems with increased accident rates due to poor training or equipment maintenance or the fact that most army brigades and navy planes are not ready for combat. But is that a symptom of too little money or of a force stretched beyond its limits by conducting operations anywhere and everywhere with little regard for actual U.S. interests?

That doesn't matter politically, though. The message is, if you don't support giving more money, you are guilty of neglecting the nation's security and of killing service personnel. No wonder only a brave handful of Republican legislators consistently are willing to say No, like Senator Paul and a few House members: Justin Amash (Michigan), John Duncan (Tennessee), Walter Jones (North Carolina), Raul Labrador (Idaho), and Thomas Massie (Kentucky).

Here's a crazy idea. What if instead of taking for granted a national security policy that seeks to maintain U.S. supremacy over every square inch of the globe we figure out what our real defense needs are—protecting our own country, not mucking about in the rest of the world—and *then* structure and fund the forces we need? What would that look like?

To start with, we know what it *doesn't* look like: the policies followed by Presidents and Congresses of both parties for the past three decades since the Berlin Wall came down. While the Trump administration's new National Security Strategy (NSS) takes a commendable but befuddled nod toward genuine American interests—Pillar I (defense of American borders and tightening immigration controls to keep dangerous people out) and Pillar II (ending unfair trade practices and restoring America's industrial base)—the real meat and potatoes is in Pillar III ("Preserve Peace Through Strength"), which could have

been drafted by any gaggle of George W. Bush retreads—and no doubt was—
or for that matter by Obama holdovers.

The NSS's Pillar III is little more than a rehash of the usual litany of
"threats" from China, Russia, North Korea, Iran, etc. It's symptomatic that
these are clustered under "Strategy in a Regional Context" as Indo-Pacific (a
perfectly ridiculous concept that could best be summed up as "China—bad!"),
Europe ("Russia—bad!"), Middle East ("Iran—bad!"), and South and Central
Asia. Next comes the region that should be our first concern, but isn't: the
Western Hemisphere ("Cuba and Venezuela—bad!"). Last comes Africa (well,
at least we can agree on something), but we still need a dedicated Africa
Command (which for some reason is located not in Africa but in Stuttgart,
Germany).

Still, just suppose that by some wild unpredictable accident we ended up
with a strategy that in some way resembled the "America First!" prioritization
Donald Trump promised us? Here's a possible broad sketch:

- *Western Hemisphere comes first, not last.* As they say in New England,
  "Good fences make good neighbors." Presumably good walls make even
  better neighbors. Whatever happened to controlling our own border with
  Mexico, which was the cornerstone of President Donald Trump's campaign? That remains hostage to political horse-trading and a budgetary
  game of chicken in the Washington Swamp. As far as the political class is
  concerned, the Wall can wait until *mañana.* At the same time, the U.S. is
  all too happy to meddle in our neighbors' internal affairs under the justification of "democracy promotion." Recently Secretary of State Rex Tillerson claimed such meddling was an expression of the Monroe Doctrine,
  which he said "clearly has been a success, because . . . what binds us
  together in this hemisphere are shared democratic values." Really? That
  would have been big news to President James Monroe, who promulgated
  the Doctrine back in 1823 when no other country in the Americas could
  be described as a democracy and when even most of the U.S. Founding
  Fathers would have disputed that label for the Republic they sought to
  create. Monroe's declaration had nothing to do with democracy. Rather,
  its core was a warning to other powers not to establish colonies in our
  hemisphere, an exclusion which we have considered essential to our
  security for almost two centuries. Even as a relative infant on the international scene, long before our young nation had emerged as a power on
  a par with those of Europe, the United States considered it reasonable to
  ask other powers not to step on our toes in our own neighborhood.

- *Respecting the "Monroe Doctrines" of other powers:* The regional deference the United States has demanded in our own area for nearly 200 years
  is precisely the one we today refuse to accord to other respectable powers,
  namely China and Russia, by conceding the primacy of their security
  interests in, respectively, the former Soviet space and in the western
  Pacific. Instead—as under Bill Clinton, Barack Obama, George W. Bush—
  the Trump administration still rejects the principle of "spheres of influence," which in practice means not only asserting mastery in the Western
  Hemisphere but over every square inch of the globe. Today not a single
  sparrow falls to the ground anywhere but that a divinely omniscient and
  omnipotent Washington must have the last word about it—generously
  lubricated with rhetoric about democracy, human rights, rule of law, and
  other invocations of "universal principles." Despite suggestions from the
  foreign policy establishment, neither China nor anyone else is threatening
  the sea lanes in the South China Sea. Even America's closest regional

partners do not want to be pushed into a military confrontation with China to suit the agenda of "indispensables" in Washington. American concerns about North Korea can only be solved with Beijing's security respected—and without the presence on the peninsula of almost 30,000 American "tripwire" troops and tens of thousands more in Japan.

In Europe, NATO forces should stand back from Russia's borders and territorial waters. NATO expansion should be ended—even after the Trump administrations ill-advised decision to induct tiny and corrupt Montenegro—while a new security architecture in Europe takes shape. The Alliance's 2008 pledge to bring in Georgia and Ukraine should be withdrawn. Better yet, get us out of NATO entirely! We and our European friends should be finding a way to cooperate with Russia on pulling Ukraine out of its political and economic crisis as a united, neutral state, not pumping in lethal weapons so touch off renewed large-scale fighting.

An American accord with Russia and China is the stable tripod of any rational global peace, and no one else really matters at the moment. Russia boasts the world's greatest landmass and natural resources unrivalled by any other country. She also has the only nuclear arsenal comparable to America's. China is the most populous country in the world, with an economy achieving a par with ours and a burgeoning military sector. If American policy had been designed to alienate both of these giants and drive them to cooperate against us—and maybe it was designed to do that—it could not have been more successful.

- *Get the hell out of the Middle East and Central Asia.* The NSS risibly refers to the undesirability of America's earlier "disengagement" from the region, evidently a reference to the Obama administration's not being quite as bellicose as its authors might prefer (for example, only support-ing terrorists in Syria, not invading the place outright), Of dubious value even in its time, President Jimmy Carter's 1980 declaration that the Persian Gulf region lies within the vital interests of the United States is only a dangerous absurdity now. The entire region designated under the goofy moniker "Greater Middle East" is a welter of ethnic and religious antagonisms and unstable states that for America have only two things in common: (1) they ain't us, and (2) they ain't nowhere near us. It's not America's job to sort the place out, via such fool's errands as nation-wrecking in Libya and Syria, nation-building in Afghanistan and Iraq (after wrecking them), and "mediating" to "solve the problem" of the Israelis and the Palestinians.

  The sole interest the U.S. and the American people have in the region is to ensure that jihad terrorism doesn't achieve a sufficient foothold as to present a threat to us here. However, our regional efforts have instead served to increase and import that threat, not diminish it. American policy toward the region should rest on two pillars: (1) limiting our contact with it, above all drastically cutting down immigration from the area and, hence, the prospect of importing more terrorists; and (2) instead of favoring terrorism-supporting regimes like Saudi Arabia and Pakistan, defer to countries with more direct interests in the region but who also have a fundamentally anti-jihad outlook, principally Russia, China, and India. Let them babysit Afghanistan.

  Other than that—include us out.

Granted, this is only an outline, but it's a start. Back to the matter of Repub-licans' penchant for overspending on the military, the force needed for this concept of "America First!"—one that focuses first of all on defending our territory and people—could only be a fraction of what we spend now. Wouldn't it be great to finally get that "Peace Dividend" we were promised until George H.W. Bush decided he'd rather build a New World Order starting in Kuwait?

"Mikhail Octavian Trump"

Jim Jatras | *Strategic Culture* | April 6, 2018

It is said that during the 1990s' time of troubles in Russia a popular view held that the prevailing chaos and ruin could only be redressed by a leader meeting the description of "Adolf Vissarionovich Pinochet." *(Адольф Виссарионович Пиночет).* The composite name of this hypothetical rescuer featured (1) the surname "Pinochet" of the anti-communist Chilean military strongman, (2) the patronymic "Vissarionovich" of Joseph "the Great Helmsman" Stalin, and (3) the first name "Adolf" of—well, you know. . . .

Let's leave aside for now whether Vladimir Vladimirovich Putin bears any remote resemblance to this imaginary (but 20 years ago, much hoped-for) personage except to note that Russia under his tenure has made an astonishing comeback. As described by historian Vladimir Brovkin:

> What Putin has accomplished or what Russia has accomplished since 2000 is astonishing. It amounts to a political, economic, and moral revolution. Any aspect of Russia's existence you take, you see measurable progress. The standard of living has grown, pensions are paid, factories are working, and unemployment is lower than in most European countries. Life expectancy has steadily increased, birth rates have increased, and incomes have increased. Education is back, Russian research and development is back again, one of the best in the world and not staffed by foreigners who flock to Silicon Valley, but staffed by Russians educated in Russia.
>
> Military technology made a breakthrough of historical significance. For the first time ever Russia has weapons superior to those of the US, not to mention Britain, France and Germany combined.
>
> For the first time in a hundred years Russian agriculture is producing for export and for the first time ever, Russia exported more grain than the US.

One should add that this has been accomplished along with a dramatic revival of Russia's prerevolutionary Orthodox Christian identity and commitment to traditional moral authority in the family and the nation, including in public institutions like the armed forces. This adds to post-modern western elites' hatred for Putin personally and Russia generally.

So if Russia under Putin has been given at least a shot at becoming great again, what about America's chances under Donald John Trump?

This is not the time to rehash America's self-evident decades-long decline under the predatory ministrations of Republicans and Democrats alike. Suffice it to say that Donald Trump was elected by a fluke of history about as improbable as Putin's emergence from the Yeltsinite "Swamp." The question is: is it conceivable that Trump could accomplish for our country anything remotely approaching what Putin has done for his?

For some, merely to pose the question in such terms is not only to exonerate (altogether now!) the evil, murderous, KGB thug Putin but to consign the American experiment in democracy to extinction under Trump's alleged autocracy envy. In an Aesopian warning against Trump, generally level-headed Bruce Fein warns that the growth of Executive power, no matter how well-guided by a latter-day Cicero (not anywhere in sight anyway), presents a mortal danger to constitutionalism:

> Cicero foolishly believed that he could salvage the Roman Republic from Julius Caesar's dictatorship by inculcating Republican virtue in Octavian, his would-be successor. Following his defeat of Mark Anthony in the last Roman civil war, Octavian exercised, de facto, all of the dictatorial powers of Julius Caesar. Cicero's tutorials proved trifles light as air. The Roman Senate became ornamental only, and the Republic became an Empire. Octavian changed his name to Caesar Augustus, and the Senate deified him.
>
> The Republic was never restored. The Empire, earmarked by limitless executive power, began spiraling downward featuring the likes of Nero, Caligula, Tiberius, and Elagabalus. It collapsed in 410 A.D. with the sacking of Rome by the Visigoth King Alaric. More enlightened Emperors like Trajan, Hadrian, and Marcus Aurelius were at best speed bumps in the Empire's road to self-ruination. [. . .]
>
> The Constitution embodies more collective wisdom about human nature, the corruption of power, and the majesty of liberty and justice than any other government charter that has been conceived or tried. We must elude the Cicero Trap. Our plight is not the absence of a Sir Launcelot to rescue Guinevere. It is the withering of our constitutional institutions calculated to protect against limitless executive power and tyranny.

The warning against a Lancelot or some other man on a white horse as our would-be deliverer presumes that there is a modicum of constitutional integrity left to salvage. That is not self-evident. In 2005 the late Joseph Sobran called our country "Post–Constitutional America," adding that nowadays "the U.S. Constitution poses no serious threat to our form of government." Things have gotten a lot worse since.

Again, one hardly need supply the details. We have presidents who make war at will, with Congress at best compliant enablers; a supposed "legal tender" printed by fiat of the Federal Reserve and underwritten by Wahhabist despots; legislative authority wielded by unelected bureaucrats in cahoots with the corporate interests they supposedly police; centralization of national power that renders the several "sovereign" states little more than federal administrative districts; an imperial Judiciary that usurps Executive and Legislative authority alike with nary a murmur of protest, while making up constitutional "rights" that appear nowhere in the text; human wreckage in what had been our manufacturing heartland; a "democracy" consisting of a corrupt market-sharing deal between two entrenched parties whose main activity is spending obscene amounts of money; collusion of multiculturists and plutocrats to debase the value of citizenship by mass importation of aliens, both legal and illegal, coupled with court-mandated lack of ballot security; a massive military structure designed for global power projection but which has been useless for defending our own borders.

In short, whatever the Founding Fathers meeting at Philadelphia in 1787 had sought to ordain and establish for themselves and their posterity, their work has long since become window-dressing for lawless, arbitrary power. As Robert E. Lee warned in his day, "The consolidation of the states into one vast empire, sure to be aggressive abroad and despotic at home, will be the certain precursor of ruin which has overwhelmed all that preceded it." He hardly could have imagined how "aggressive abroad and despotic at home" the post-constitutional order would turn out to be. (But who cares about the opinion of a "traitor" who "fought to preserve slavery"?)

Fein writes that under Octavian, having morphed into the divine Augustus, "the Republic was never restored." But perhaps "restore" is the wrong word. More to the point, was the Roman polity preserved? Citing Ohio State University Professor of Classics at Anthony Kaldellis, Brian Patrick Mitchell argues in the affirmative:

> The standard story that the Roman republic ended with Caesar Augustus becoming emperor is therefore simply wrong, says Kaldellis. The republic lived on, albeit in a new phase, the Principate, in place of the earlier Consulate. Historians call the republic's later, third phase the Dominate—during which military emperors, ruling from wherever military necessity demanded, came to be addressed for the first time in Roman history as *Domine*, or "Lord." The fourth, final, and longest phase, by far, was Byzantium, lasting from the fifth to the 15th century, during which emperors ruled as civilians from the city officially named New Rome but commonly called Constantinople ("Constantine's city") and founded originally as Byzantion (Byzantium in Latin).

Given the terminal breakdown confronting the Roman state and society in the days of the first century BC Triumvirs—comparable to that of the USSR in the late 1980s and the Russian Federation of the 1990s, and of America on the eve of Trump's election—it's hard to see how Rome could have been preserved as a unified, functioning society other than the way Octavian did it: save what can be saved, trash what can't, and move on. Contra Fein, the result was not a downward spiral but the consolidation and perpetuation of the Roman order, notably in its Christian form that was to last for more than a millennium. It is no accident that it is the glory of this Rome, not of the pre-Principate republic, that European states for centuries have sought to emulate, from the Carolingians, to the Holy Roman Empire, to the Russian Third Rome, to Napoleon, and even somewhat to the United States.

Supposed "constitutional conservatives" of the #NeverTrump hue doggedly appeal to an ahistorical originalism reminiscent of dissatisfied Soviet liberals during the 1960s–70s Brezhnevite "stagnation" who sought a return to "pure" Leninism purged of Stalin's supposed deviations. (A.I. Solzhenitsyn wrote of himself in an earlier period: "The author of these lines, who in his day landed in jail precisely because of his hatred of Stalin, whom he reproached with his departure from Lenin, must now admit that he cannot find, point to, or prove any substantial deviations.") Certainly America's founding was far more humane and decent than that of the bloody-handed Bolsheviks. But a time machine back to the habits, expectations, and morals that undergird our second and theoretically current Constitution, today honored mainly in the breach, is a fantasy.

This is not to argue against such vestigial protections of religion, free speech, right to bear arms, and others that we still possess—for now—but to suggest that they aren't likely to survive much longer as the edifice of the old

America continues to crumble under the malfeasance of the very Executive, Legislative, and Judicial officials who pretend to be its custodians. Trump's critics on the establishment Right know this, reserving their heavy fire for his 2016 campaign pledges to control America's borders (and build The Wall), rectify one-sided trade relations with our supposed "partners" (and restore our manufacturing base), and withdraw us from the global empire business (get along with the Russians, stop mucking about in Syria and Ukraine, no more regime change or nation-building).

Such detractors have been only too happy to team up with the Left, the Deep State (FBI, CIA, and their pals in the United Kingdom, notably MI6 and GCHQ), and the media to beat back Trump's threat to business as usual and allow the rot to continue apace. Sad to say, even many of Trump's backers concede that they have largely succeeded. While there has been some stepped up immigration enforcement, The Wall has not been built, extreme vetting (forget the Muslim ban) remains tied up by the courts, and Sanctuary jurisdictions flout federal law with impunity; some partial progress has been made on trade, but the jury is still out; on foreign and security policy, Trump administration personnel and policy alike amount to a third Bush presidency.

Nonetheless, one can't help thinking that inside President Trump there's a tiny little Candidate Trump from 2016 fighting to get out. Against the recommendations of his advisers, he decided to meet with North Korea's Kim Jong-un—whether the meeting comes off remains to be seen. Seemingly on a whim, he has declared we'll be withdrawing our (illegal) presence in Syria "very soon," to the horror of the supposed experts. Even a possible meeting—at the White House!—with Putin has been floated.

Thus, there's still a ray of hope—if Trump manages to avoid getting sucked into a war against Iran or North Korea (or God forbid, Russia) and somehow manages to avoid impeachment if, as many expect, the House flips to the Democrats. As an aspiring Octavian goes it's not much, but it's better than anything else we could have expected.

On the other hand, if Trump is removed or falters further from his populist campaign promises (that is, even worse than his underwhelming delivery so far), America's decline will accelerate and soon become irreversible. In that case, history will rank him with another leader who sought to save the failing system he inherited but instead ended up a catalyst for its further destabilization, ushering in its final collapse.

His name is Mikhail Gorbachev.

"Did the West Just Lose World War III by Forfeit?"

Jim Jatras | *Strategic Culture* | April 20, 2018

In the fall of the year 1480, at a point not far from Moscow, two armies faced each other on the opposite banks of the Ugra River.

On the one side were the forces of the Grand Duchy of Moscow, whose ruler, Grand Prince Ivan III (known as "the Great" and the "gatherer of the Russian lands"), had recently rejected further payment of tribute to the Great Horde.

On the other were the forces of Grand Khan Ahmed bin Küchük, who had come to lay waste to Moscow and instruct the impudent Prince Ivan to mend his ways.

For weeks the two assembled hosts glared at one another, each wary of crossing the water and becoming vulnerable to attack by the other. In the end, as though heeding the same inaudible signal, both withdrew and hastily returned home.

Thus ended more than two centuries of the Tatar-Mongol yoke upon the land of the Rus'.

Was this event, which came to be known as "the great standing on the Ugra River," a model of what happened in Syria last week?

Almost immediately upon reports of the staged chemical attack in Douma on April 7, speculation began as to the likely response from the west—which in reality meant from the United States, in turn meaning from President Donald J. Trump. Would Trump, who had repeatedly spoken harshly of his predecessors' destructive and pointless misadventures in the Middle East, and who just days earlier had signaled his determination to withdraw the several thousand Americans (illegally) stationed in Syria, see through the obvious deception?

Or, whether or not he really believed the patently untrue accusations of Syrian (and Russian) culpability, would Trump take punitive action against Syria? And if so, would it be a demonstrative pinprick of the sort inflicted almost exactly a year earlier in punishment for an obvious false flag chemical attack in Idlib? Or would we see something more "robust" (a word much beloved of laptop bombardiers in Washington) aimed at teaching a lesson to both Syrian President Bashar al-Assad and his ally, Prince Ivan III's obstreperous heir Russian President Vladimir Putin?

The answer soon came on Twitter. Assad was an "animal." Putin, Russia, and Iran were "responsible" for "many dead, including women and children, in mindless CHEMICAL attack"—"Big price to pay."

Around the world, people mentally braced for the worst. Would a global conflagration start in Syria with an American attack on Russian forces? A grim trepidation reminiscent of the October 1962 Cuban Missile Crisis gripped the hearts of those old enough to remember those thirteen days when the fate of all life on our planet was in doubt.

Certainly there were enough voices in the US establishment egging Trump on. Besides, at home he still had the relentless pressure of the Mueller investigation, intensified by the FBI's April 9 raid on his lawyer Michael Cohen. Trump's only respite from the incessant hammering was his strike on Syria last year.

During the first Cold War both American and Soviet forces took great care to avoid direct conflict, rightly afraid it could lead to uncontrolled escalation. But now, in this second Cold War, western commentators were positively giddy at the thought of killing Russians in Syria. . . .

. . . or rather killing *more* Russians, citing the slaughter of a disputed number of contractors (or "mercenaries" as western media and officials consistently called them, implying they deserved to have been exterminated). *That'll teach 'em not to tangle with us!* It was unclear whether the warning from Russian Chief of Staff General Valery Gerasimov that Russia would respond against an attack by striking both incoming weapons as well as the platforms that launched them would be taken seriously.

After a slight softening of tone by both Trump and Defense Secretary General James "Mad Dog" Mattis on April 12, during which a team from the Organisation for the Prohibition of Chemical Weapons (OPCW) was approaching Douma to conduct an on-site examination, there emerged a slim ray of hope that Trump would step back from acting on the transparently false provocation. (The slimness of any such hope was illustrated by the fact that seemingly the most restrained of Trump's advisers was somebody nicknamed "Mad Dog.")

When on the evening of Friday the Thirteenth (Washington time) news came that the US had initiated military action, together with France and (the country Russia had accused of staging the Douma fraud) the United Kingdom, many feared the worst. The hasty timing was clearly aimed at preempting the arrival of the OPCW inspectors.

Of greater concern was the extent of the assault? If Russians were killed, Gerasimov was serious.

As it turned out, the worst didn't come. World War III didn't happen. Or hasn't—yet.

In fact nothing much happened at all. According to the official US reports, something over a hundred missiles were launched at three targets. All missiles reached their targets—"Mission Accomplished!" The other side, however, claimed to have shot down roughly 75 percent of the incoming Tomahawks.

In the end, the damage was even less than from the follow-up to Idlib last year. No one was reported killed, neither Syrian nor Russian nor Iranian. Western governments claimed to have struck a serious blow at Syria's chemical weapons capability. Syrians and Russians scoffed that the missiles had hit empty buildings and that Syria had no CW to hit since 2014, as certified by the OPCW.

In the aftermath of the missile show, media carried unverified reports that Trump had wanted a stronger campaign but deferred to Mattis's caution, no doubt reflecting the views of professional military men who didn't want to find out whether Gerasimov was bluffing. Mattis also reportedly wanted Congress to vote on any action before it was taken but was overruled by Trump.

There was even some speculation that the whole thing was a charade worked out in cooperation with the Russians. Even if true (and it's unlikely) the mere fact that Trump would have to engage in such a ruse speaks volumes about the weakness of his position. "Whatever Trump says, America is not coming out of Syria," writes Patrick Buchanan. "We are going deeper in. Trump's commitment to extricate us from these bankrupting and blood-soaked Middle East wars and to seek a new rapprochement with Russia is 'inoperative.'"

That's clear from the comments of US Ambassador to the United Nations Nikki Haley. She states that America won't disengage until three objectives have been met: that ISIS has been defeated (a pretext, since ISIS is on the ropes and remains alive only because of hostile actions taken by the US and others against Syria); Damascus is finally deterred from using chemical weapons (a falsehood, since they don't have any); and Iran's regional influence is blocked (which means we're staying in effect permanently in preparation for a larger war against Iran and perhaps eventually Russia).

The last point is unfortunately true, as plans are underway to beef up a Sunni anti-Iran bulwark in eastern Syria to cut off Tehran's so-called "land bridge" to the Mediterranean. Most Americans in Syria are to be replaced with a so-called Arab force—the "Arab NATO" touted last year in connection with Trump's maiden foreign trip as president. (As though the one NATO we already have weren't bad enough!)

Saudi Foreign Minister Adel al-Jubeir has suggested troops from his country would participate. Aside from whether Riyadh can spare them from their ongoing task of wrecking Yemen, Saudi personnel are likely to become a prime target for Syrians itching to get a crack at their chief tormenters over the past seven years.

So was anything really settled on April 13? On this occasion the West chose not to "cross the river," much as Khan Ahmed's force declined to do in 1480. For their part, the Russians in Syria, like their ancestors on the Ugra, were on defense and had no need to risk offensive action.

Unfortunately, unlike the "the great standing on the Ugra River," which resolved the question of Russian independence and sovereignty in that era, nothing has been resolved now. The question remains: will the US peacefully relinquish its position as the sole arbiter of authority, legality, and morality in a unipolar world in favor of a multipolar order where Russia's and China's legitimate interests and spheres of influence are respected? Or will we continue to risk plunging mankind into a global conflict?

Syria remains a key arena where one path or the other will be taken to finally wrap up what US Army Major Danny Sjursen calls "Operation Flailing Empire." The irony is that peacefully "losing" our pointless and dangerous attempt to rule the world would only be to Americans' benefit. That's what Trump promised in 2016. He hasn't delivered and it's increasingly doubtful he can.

In the end, the threat of World War III hasn't vanished. It has just been postponed.

"Is 'Wrecking Ball' Trump Undermining America's Global Clout? Let's Hope So!"

Jim Jatras | *Strategic Culture* | May 18, 2018

However much Donald Trump's loyal base in the United States continues to love him (while the other half of the American population loathes him), it's safe to say that the overwhelming consensus among foreign leaders is one of contempt mixed with fear. While not identifying Trump by name, European Union (EU) foreign policy chief Federica Mogherini left no doubt about what she thinks of the current hand on the tiller of the American ship of state in the aftermath of US withdrawal from the Iran nuclear deal:

> It seems that screaming, shouting, insulting and bullying, system-atically destroying and dismantling everything that is already in place, is the mood of our times. . . . This impulse to destroy is not leading us anywhere good . . . It is not solving any of our problems.

Let's take a look at some of the primary breakage in the wake of what some see as Trump's bull-in-a-china-shop path of destruction:

- Pulling out of the Paris Climate Agreement and the Trans-Pacific Partnership: This, we are told, amounts to America's "withdrawing from our role as unelected (but de facto) global leader." The new international rules on the environment and trade will not be made in Washington.
- Moving the US embassy in Israel to Jerusalem: The US is no longer (and really, never was) the "honest broker" or "impartial" mediator for a dead-end Middle East peace process.
- Thwarted in Syria: Despite two pinprick strikes against Syrian forces, President Bashar al-Assad (a "monster," according to Trump) will remain

in office, with the Astana process of Russia, Iran, and Turkey sidelining the moribund Geneva talks under the US and Russian auspices. That outcome is unlikely to be changed by plans to block Iranian influence by introducing a Sunni foreign legion into the Kurdish-held areas under US sponsorship, but their deployment could provide cover for US forces to slouch out.

- Loss of influence in Iraq and Lebanon: Despite Washington's support (in awkward, unacknowledged partnership with Tehran) for Baghdad's recovery of areas earlier held by ISIS, Iraqi voters placed Shiite cleric and longtime US antagonist Muqtada al-Sadr in the catbird seat for forming the next government. Likewise, gains for Hezbollah in Lebanon's election can't be spun as a win for Washington.

- Korean accord, less excuse for America's presence: Trump's domestic fans like to credit his tough talk for bringing North Korea's Kim Jong-un to the table and agreeing to give up his nuclear weapons. It remains to be seen what actually will happen when Trump and Kim meet in Singapore next month, assuming the summit takes place as planned. But there's no doubting the real breakthrough—perhaps impelled by Trump's threatening language—was South Korea's Moon Jae-in's first making an overture to the north, evidently with American blessing. Just the prospect of a settlement has prompted speculation on whether or not it would lead to a drawdown of the US military presence.

- US withdrawal from the Iran nuclear deal: To date the big kahuna of Trumpian applecart-upsetting is his decision to terminate American participation in the Joint Comprehensive Plan of Action (JCPOA) placing caps on Iran's nuclear program in exchange for international sanctions relief. Not only has Trump trashed the deal, his administration has reimposed unilateral US sanctions on Iran and is threatening America's closest allies and trading partners with secondary sanctions. More worrisome is what the US action indicates about a possible drive for regime change in Tehran and of the prospect of war to achieve it. Adding insult to injury, Trump played for chumps French President Emmanuel Macron, German Chancellor Angela Merkel, and British Prime Minister Theresa May (with her Foreign Secretary, Boris Johnson), treating with contempt their pathetic personal pleas to stay in the deal. The jury is out on whether tough talk from May, Macron, Merkel, and Mogherini (4M) pledging to stay in the JCPOA and foil US sanctions on their companies doing business with Iran will translate into action; EU blocking measures could be key. Those predicting a 4M wimp-out have strong arguments. On the other hand, if the Euro-poodles do manage to hang tough, break with the US, and stand with Russia and China, it would be declaration of independence of historic proportions. Anything that could cause the likes of migrant-loving "Mutti" Merkel to behave like a patriot would be a minor miracle in itself.

Taken together, critics say these and similarly irresponsible actions by Trump and his team have thrown into doubt the reliability of the US as an international partner and have degraded the value of US "global leadership." According to a recent Gallup poll (gleefully cited by MSNBC's dreadful Rachel Maddow):

One year into Donald Trump's presidency, the image of US leadership is weaker worldwide than it was under his two predecessors. . . . With its stable approval rating of 41%, Germany has replaced the US as the top-rated global power in the world. The US is now on nearly even footing with China (31%) and barely more popular than Russia (27%)—two countries that Trump sees as rivals seeking to "challenge American influence, values and wealth."

Nicholas Burns, a former senior American diplomat under Republican and Democratic administrations, harrumphed, "Trump is weak on NATO, Russia, trade, climate, diplomacy. The US is declining as a global leader." Former National Security Adviser Susan Rice sneeringly calls Trump "our wrecking ball in chief."

But hold on. That sounds familiar. As *Dilbert* creator Scott Adams wrote in March 2016: "If you think the government is broken, and you want to send a wrecking ball to Washington D.C., Trump offers that possibility."

Well, that's what we Deplorables voted for. Maybe that's what we got. Anything that makes Maddow, Burns, and Rice unhappy can't be all bad!

To be sure, Trump has not delivered on one of his signature campaign promises, to improve ties with Russia. With some help from across The Pond, the essence of the entire Russiagate witch hunt has been to block any hope of US-Russia rapprochement, a necessary element for significant progress on almost any important international issue. By all external indications the campaign to turn Trump's foreign policy into a repeat of that of George W. Bush but with a harsher edge has been a smashing success.

Or has it? As one commentator suggests:

> Appearances can be deceiving. The Russo-Sino-Persian axis is secretly aligned with Trump, who they know is an enemy of the Deep State/Bilderberger empire. I expect Iran to make a few concessions and Trump will come out looking stronger, just as he did in Korea. Trump believes in the 'Great Man' theory of history and he and Putin and Xi are secretly working together. Russia will let Trump bomb Syria (no great consequence), Xi will compromise on trade a bit (no great consequence), and Iran will probably make a few inconsequential concessions. Trump's concessions will occur later (pulling some troops out of South Korea, letting Putin handle Syria, no serious military action against Iran). As Pepe [Escobar] has pointed out in the past, Xi will get Pakistan to lean on the Taliban and Trump will be even able to pull US troops out of Afghanistan. In the end, the Deep State will lose control of Eurasia while Trump with his false bluster will paradoxically seem strong. Hold onto your hats!

This is all speculation of course. Evidence for such a secret alignment is scant to none, except perhaps the suspiciously meager strikes on Syria and the clearly deliberate care not to hit Russia's forces. One also wonders why, if this were really Trump's intention, would he not proceed in a more direct way? For that matter, why would he not appoint to a top policymaking position even a single person who conceivably could share this agenda?

One answer is that Trump is aware of the fate of the last president who tried to buck the Deep State and rein back our global meddling. On this theory he literally cannot tell a soul of his intentions, which he must keep strictly *in pectore* while outwardly pursuing a blustering "policy of strength" that perversely results in cutting the legs from under the very American "leadership" he pretends to champion. If such jiu-jitsu lies at the heart of Trump's policy, he really is some kind of genius!

Another, and perhaps more likely, answer is that he is achieving the same goal not through a thought-out program but more as the product of (to him) unconnected, instinctual actions, the consequences of which he only dimly foresees. That is, Trump doesn't necessarily have the path or the desired outcomes clearly plotted in his mind, just a gut-level sense of what he wants to do at each decision point. The result still might have some underlying internal logic which he only partly appreciates on a cognitive level.

Or maybe all the foregoing is just grasping at straws. Perhaps Trump really has no idea what he's doing. It's possible that through the quirks of his impulsive personality he's just taking the decades-old thrust of America's hegemonic bullying to its logical absurdity—with counterproductive results. The chickens of the Pox Americana are finally coming home to roost. It's then tempting for America's customary foreign enablers—notably those in Europe, who invariably submit supinely to every *diktat* from Washington, especially with respect to hostility to Russia—to recoil from the uncouth Trump and his arrogant "America First!" attitudes in effusive horror (Mogherini: "screaming, shouting, insulting and bullying, systematically destroying and dismantling").

In any case, if we ignore the bleating and whining from those lamenting the decline in US "leadership" we can perhaps be thankful for anything that undercuts the global hegemonic project and, perhaps in spite of the worst intentions of Trump's appointees, moves us incrementally towards a national interest-based policy. Putting the individual issues in context, the only real question before us whether the US persists in the insane quest for unipolar world domination that shifted into high gear in 1991 and must inevitably lead to a cataclysm of unimaginable proportions; or whether there can be a soft landing into a multipolar order, where the US accepts the status of *primus inter pares* in concert with Russia and China, with side-understandings with Europe, India, Japan, and so forth.

Let us hope it is the latter. If so, whether that is the result of deliberate policy calculations or of policy failures is less important than the outcome itself.

"Forget Kim. It's Time for a Trump–Putin Summit—Now!"

Jim Jatras | *Strategic Culture* | May 25, 2018

In the aftermath of US President Donald Trump's cancellation of his scheduled June 12 summit with North Korea's Kim Jong-un, the gathering clouds of global conflict are getting thicker and darker:

Korea: The cancellation is a triumph for Trump's national security team, most if not all of whom were horrified at the prospect of his meeting personally with Kim. (There was no telling what the Big Man might agree to if he met Little Rocket Man face to face. What if Korea actually were denuclearized? There would be no more excuse for keeping American troops on the peninsula! Disaster!) From the team's perspective, scuttling the meeting altogether would be the best outcome, but derailing the date and cranking the nasty rhetoric back up will do for now. Talk of a Libyan model, even more than inclusion of B-52s in exercises with South Korea (which Trump reversed), got the job done. Now it's imperative for the national security establishment to load Trump up with nonnegotiable demands (maybe patterned on Pompeo's

Iran provocation; see below) that Kim would have no choice but to refuse on the chance the summit gets rescheduled through the frantic efforts of South Korea's Moon Jae-in—and maybe of Trump himself, if he still wants a shot at that Nobel Peace Prize. Pyongyang's continued willingness to talk will register in Washington as desperation and an invitation for renewed pressure.

Iran: Secretary of State Mike Pompeo has delivered to Tehran what only can be deemed an ultimatum. It makes Austria's 1914 demands on Serbia look mild in comparison. Ultimata are designed to be rejected, "justifying" whatever action the threatening power has already decided upon. Tehran is being told to dismantle its entire regional security presence—or else. The "or else" means initially a campaign of destabilization (assassinations, fomenting domestic unrest, and insurrections by disgruntled ethnic and religious communities; see Syria 2011) or, if that fails, direct military action (see Libya 2011 and Iraq 2003). To trigger the latter look for a false flag or contrived "Iranian attack," such as a naval incident in the Persian Gulf (see Gulf of Tonkin 1964). Also targeted by the ultimatum are the European countries aghast at US withdrawal from the Iran nuclear deal. In addition to smacking secondary sanctions on our satellites (officially, "allies" and "partners"), the harshness of Pompeo's terms is designed to spook the Europeans into the vain hope they can restrain a reckless US bent on war by meeting Washington halfway (or three-quarters of the way, or nine-tenths of the way . . .) in helping to corner Tehran. Watch to see who will crack first: London, Paris, or Berlin?

Syria: Despite Trump's repeated assertion that he wants to get Americans out of Syria, there is reason to think we are digging in further. This has nothing to do with defeating ISIS. Rather, along with a planned buildup of Saudi and other foreign Sunni troops in the US- and Kurd-controlled zone, the principal target is Iran (see above). US policy in Syria is driven by Israeli and Saudi hostility to Iran, and Pompeo's list of nonnegotiable demands includes withdrawal of Iranian (and Hezbollah) forces from that country. It is a mystery how the US, whose troop presence in Syria violates international law and probably American domestic law as well, has the right to demand the departure of forces present legally by invitation of the internationally recognized government. Punctuating US determination to confront Iran were new strikes this week against Syrian government forces, while Israel flaunted its first-ever combat use of the US F–35.

Ukraine: The level of fighting on the Donbas line of control has intensified. Meanwhile Kiev forces show off tests of the Javelin antitank missiles they received from the Trump administration, which the Obama administration had earlier declined to provide. Ostensibly intended to deter a Russian attack—in which case they would make little difference—the Javelins could be used in an offensive against Donbas forces (perhaps in concert with an attack on the Kerch bridge connecting mainland Russia to Crimea) followed by a call for insertion of international peacekeepers. Russia considers the FIFA World Cup from June 14 to July 15 a prime-time window for such an assault. A Dutch report assigning blame to—surprise!—Russia for downing MH17 comes at an opportune moment.

Balkans: Prestigious think tanks call for "action" to intensify the same policies that have made a wreck of the Balkans for a quarter of a century. Why? To counter Russian influence, of course! The only shortcoming in US and European policy is that we haven't been aggressive enough.

Sitting at the geographic and political junction of these seemingly disparate theaters of active or potential conflict is the US establishment's entrenched hostility to Russia. Despite the accelerating unraveling of the anticonstitutional plot to dump Trump by elements of the US Deep State (in the CIA, FBI, Department of Justice, and elsewhere) together with their British counterparts (MI6 and GCHQ), the effort's primary policy objective was achieved: President Trump has been blocked from his oft-stated desire to improve ties with Moscow. Addressing the regional issues above—any one of which could reach dangerous crisis proportion at any moment—would be far more feasible with Washington and Moscow working in cooperation instead of at cross-purposes or daggers drawn. But instead, we have a new cold war care of James Clapper, John Brennan, Christopher Steele, Peter Strzok, Stefan Halper, and their ilk—possibly even including Barack Obama.

In some ways this second Cold War is even more dangerous than the first one. The instincts of restraint and prudence that had been built up over decades of confrontation have atrophied. While both the US and Russia still maintain massive nuclear arsenals, new military technology has continued to make rapid progress in such areas as hypersonic weapons and cyber-warfare. Also, while during the first Cold War American and Soviet planners consciously sought to avoid direct contact between their forces in Third World proxy wars, today American and Russian forces come into perilous proximity to one another. Given Washington's relentless determination to press Moscow to the brink in every theater, the consequences of even an unintended clash are not given the gravity they demand.

It is impossible to know from outside of Trump's own mind to what extent he has abandoned his pledge to improve relations with Russia (or never meant it in the first place), or whether he might simply be biding his time to make his move. But it is clear what that move must be if there is any possibility of cutting the Gordian knot that binds shut the gate to rapprochement: Trump and Russian President Vladimir Putin should meet in a formal and substantive summit at the earliest possible date. A productive understanding between the United States and Russia must start at the top, on the personal level or it will not happen at all.

To that end, recently this analyst joined other activists in posting the following petition on the official White House website:

President Donald Trump should hold early summit
with Russian President Vladimir Putin
Created by J.J. on May 21, 2018

Ronald Reagan famously said: "A nuclear war cannot be won and must never be fought. The only value in our two nations possessing nuclear weapons is to make sure they will never be used." Unfortunately, today a new Cold War between the US and Russia again poses an existential threat to the people of both nations and to the whole world. Therefore, we urge President Trump to follow in the steps of Ronald Reagan and to start a direct dialogue with President Putin in search of solid and verified security arrangements. As President Trump said repeatedly "only haters and fools" do not understand that good US-Russia relations are also good for America. By all indications President Putin feels the same way for his country. A summit should be arranged as soon as possible.

The petition is open for signature until June 20. When signing, use of Gmail is recommended to facilitate registration of your vote.

No one should imagine a White House petition can by itself change the direction of American policy. However, if there are elements on Trump's team who are not entirely against the idea of a summit, a show of public support may serve to strengthen their case against those opposed.

Most important is a constituency of one: Mr. Trump himself. If Trump was at all willing to hold a summit with Kim because of his handful of nukes, he can certainly do so with the leader of the one country on the planet with enough nuclear weapons to destroy the US.

Obama got his Peace Prize presented to him on a platter simply for getting elected while being black. By contrast, if Trump wants his Peace Prize he's going to have to work for it. With Kim off his dance card, he's got plenty of time to take a spin with Putin.

"When, Where, and How Will the Empire Strike Back?"

Jim Jatras | *Strategic Culture* | June 9, 2018

In any analysis of contemporary international politics it pays to be cautiously pessimistic. As the default mode one can generally expect that any way in which things *can* go wrong to threaten the peace and security of the planet, they *will*. Anticipation of improvement is a chump's bet.

That's why this analyst's gut instinct rebels at any indication that things overall may be moving in a positive direction, however haltingly or indirectly. But consider:

- Trump-Putin summit: President Donald Trump has again indicated his interest in finally holding a formal summit with President Vladimir Putin. Austria has offered Vienna as a venue.
- Trump-Kim summit: Despite what was almost surely a deliberate effort in Washington to torpedo the June 12 Singapore meeting, it's back on. To the chagrin of many in the US *nomenklatura* dedicated to a permanent American presence on the East Asian mainland, there's perhaps even a danger of peace breaking out on the Korean peninsula. Oh no! How do we then justify keeping American troops there? What happens to the happy prospect of US forces confronting China on the Yalu River in the event of regime change in North Korea? Might a Trans-Korean Railway connecting the South to Russia and China get built? The possibilities are too horrible to contemplate.
- Goodbye Russiagate, hello Spygate: Allegations of Trump's and his team's collusion with the Kremlin are increasingly exposed as what they are: a cover for an anti-constitutional conspiracy within the structures of the US Deep State (CIA, NSA, FBI, Department of Justice, etc.) in complicity with—the Russians?—no with their British sister agencies (MI6, GCHQ), first to deny Trump the presidency, then to neuter him and remove him from office, and above all to block any chance of a patch-up with Russia. While Robert Mueller and his merry band of Democratic donors certainly have not given up, their prospects are fading and the Russia obsession is beginning to turn into a political liability for the DNC in the November Congressional elections.
- European populism marches on: *Viva l'Italia!* The European Union's (EU) favorite Sicilian, Italian President Sergio Mattarella, tied to whack the M5S/Lega coalition. The hit failed. Now Italy, the third-largest economy in the eurozone—too big to be smacked around like Greece—joins

the populist bloc centered in the Visegrád Group, plus Austria. This has particular importance with respect to the EU's (and Germany's) disast-rous open door migration policy.

- Trade: In his boldest "America First!" move to date, Trump has slapped higher steel and aluminum tariffs on—well, pretty much everybody. While the move itself may be a bit ham-fisted, it has signaled that the days of the US attachment to one-way free trade while our trade partners practice mercantilism are over.

- Europe's anti-Russia sanctions: American pressure on Europe with re-spect to trade with Iran, added to Trump's new tariffs, feeds resentment across Europe, especially in powerful Germany, which especially objects to Washington's threatening sanctions on companies participating in Nord Stream 2. It may be too soon to guess how soon the EU will pull the plug on anti-Russian sanctions, but there's something in the air when even the likes of European Commission President Jean-Claude Juncker can say that "Russia-bashing has to be brought to an end." Italy's voice will be key.

- G7—or G6+1, or again G8?: Trump's trade move has set a cat among the pigeons at this month's Group of Seven (G7) summit in Canada, hosted by alleged groper Prime Minister Justin Trudeau. (To be fair, perhaps image-conscious Justin was just trying to stay in close, intimate touch with the media.) Trade differences add to disagreements over climate issues, leading to a Twitter spat between Trudeau and his francophone pal French President Emmanuel Macron against Trump, who plans to skip the climate portion of the summit which is likely to produce a statement from the other six countries but not the US, effectively creating a G6+1. Meanwhile Trump has exploded the heads of Russian collusion conspiracy-mongers with his suggestion that Russia should be readmit-ted to the club, bringing it back to a G8. Italy has seconded the suggestion. Russia has indicated its lack of interest.

At the epicenter of each one of these earthshaking developments is one man: Donald Trump.

It would be inaccurate to say that these are even moves of the US government, of which Trump is only in partial control. With the permanent government—not to mention some of his own appointees—seeking to under-mine him at every step, Trump seems to be resorting to the one tool he has at his personal disposal: disruption.

Let's remember that, especially in the Rust Belt states of Pennsylvania, Ohio, Michigan, and Wisconsin, those who voted for Trump wanted some-thing radically different from business as usual. They voted for him because they wanted a bull in a china shop, a wrecking ball, a human hand grenade, a big "FU" to the system.

Maybe that's what we got.

To be sure, none of the foregoing itemized developments is dispositive. But taken together they point to a remarkable confluence of good omens, at least from the point of view of those who wanted to shake up, even shatter, the cozy arrangements that have guided the so-called "liberal global order."

But those whose careers and privileges, and in some cases their freedom and even lives, depend on perpetuating that order will not go gentle into that good night. They are getting nervous. This means in particular the elements of the US-UK special services, their Democratic and GOP Never-Trump fellow travelers, the Trump-hating fake news media, and the bureaucratic non-entities in Brussels (not only at the European Commission but at NATO headquarters).

If past is prologue, the Empire will strike back—hard and dirty.

One is reminded of the past seven years of war in Syria, where every time the US indicated a willingness to disengage, or when Syrian forces had made major military gains, then—BAM!—a chemical weapons attack immediately and without evidence is attributed to government forces, followed by renewed cries of "Assad is killing his own people! Assad must go!" (This is a ploy that goes back at least the Bosnian war of the 1990s. Every time a negotiated ceasefire seemed to be taking shape, another "Serb mortar attack" on civilians took place, leading to calls for NATO military action.)

The question is not "if" there will be a provocation, rather it's one of when, where and how. While it's difficult to make predictions, especially about the future, it's nonetheless possible to anticipate some possibilities:

- FIFA World Cup 2018 in Russia (June 14 to July 15): Given the huge expense and effort Russia has put into the World Cup as a favorable showcase to the world, it will be a tempting target. Let's remember that the unconstitutional ouster of Ukraine's elected government took place as Putin's attention was presumably distracted by his pride and joy, the 2014 Sochi Winter Olympics. The 2008 attack by Georgia's then-president, Mikheil Saakashvili, on South Ossetia, was launched while the world's eyes were focused on the Summer Olympics in Beijing. Both initiatives led to a strong counteraction by Moscow, leading in turn to worsened relations between Russia and the West—including Russia's suspension from the G8 in 2014. (Though in the fevered imagination of western Russophobes, Putin was the one using the games as a cover, not the other way around.) A provocation could be directed against the FIFA events themselves—perhaps a terrorist attack by ISIS operatives reportedly being ferried out of the Middle East to Russia—or something elsewhere timed to coincide with matches being played all over Russia.
- Ukraine: Regarding President Petro Poroshenko's actions, everything must be put into the context of upcoming presidential elections in 2019. Poroshenko has to find a way to get into a runoff, presumably against Yulia Tymoshenko. The most beneficial thing he could do would be somehow to pull a rabbit out of his hat and achieve a peace deal in the Donbas. But chances of that are slim to none, as it would require flexibility from Kiev that Poroshenko can't afford to show lest he be accused of being a Russian puppet. Conversely, he can up the ante with the Russians and hope the West will line up behind him. Perhaps the recent fake news murder fiasco regarding the still very much alive Arkady Babchenko was to have been one such ploy but it misfired. But there are other options, such as a provocation along the line of control in the Donbas (the newly delivered US Javelin missiles are handy, as is the Dutch MH17 report), maybe a covert attack on the Kerch bridge, as well as other less obvious possibilities.
- Syria: It's high time for another malevolent, militarily pointless, and counterproductive chemical attack "against his own people" by "monster"© Assad, who must be eliminated by any means necessary. Who's responsible? Russia of course!
- Incident between NATO and Russian forces: NATO forces are stepping up provocative maneuvers on Russia's doorstep in the Baltic and Black seas—purely to deter Moscow's aggression, mind you. An incident could occur as any time, either by accident or on purpose. Either way, it would be the hostile Russians' fault for putting their country so close to our bases and the venues of our military exercises.

- The Balkans: Never forget that those Serbs just can't be trusted. *Srbe na vrbe!*
- Assassination: One of Putin's well-known predilections is for killing, or at least attempting to kill, anyone who might displease him. Or like Assad with his chemical weapons, maybe Putin kills just for the sheer, malicious fun of it. The list of victims is long: Babchenko (except, not), the two Skripals (except, not them either), political opponents like Boris Nemtsov and Sergei Yushenkov, muckraking journalists like Anna Politkovskaya and Natalia Estemirova, former *chekist* Aleksandr Litvinenko, *RT* network founder Mikhail Lesin, crusading lawyers like Stanislav Markelov and Sergei Magnitsky, oligarch Boris Berezovsky, and so on. A well-timed rubout of a suitably visible figure would have a salubrious impact on any annoying moves towards East-West rapprochement. No evidence is needed—the mere identity of the victim would be irrefutable proof of Putin's guilt.

Regarding the last item, assassination, it should always be kept in mind that in the end the man threatening to upset the applecart of the liberal global order isn't Putin—it's Trump. That suggests an ultimate solution that might become tempting if The Donald's continued functioning at higher than room temperature becomes just too much to endure.

As Joseph Stalin is reputed to have remarked, "Death solves all problems. No man, no problem." Trump, who for many powerful people is quite a problem indeed, has been recklessly compared to Jean-Marie Le Pen, Silvio Berlusconi, Vladimir Putin—even to Hitler and Mussolini. In an American context, to Andrew Jackson, Huey Long, and George Wallace. Let's note that each of those three Americans was the target of assassination. Jackson (someone Trump is known to admire) survived by a failure of his attacker's pistols, hailed by some at the time as miraculous. "The Kingfish" was killed. Wallace was crippled for life.

There is reason to think that Trump is well aware of the fate of the last American president who so threatened the habitual order of things and the entrenched, ruthless establishment that profits so mightily from it. He has repeatedly indicated his interest in releasing the full file on Jack Kennedy's assassination, then backed off from it for undisclosed reasons. The shooting death of the president's brother Robert Kennedy, who had he been elected president in 1968 would have had the opportunity to reopen the investigation into his brother's murder, is back in the news with Robert Kennedy, Jr., expressing doubt about the official conclusion that his father was killed by Sirhan Sirhan.

If anyone thinks there is any length to which Trump's enemies will not go, think again.

"Atrocity Porn and Hitler Memes Target Trump for Regime Change"

Jim Jatras | *Strategic Culture* | June 23, 2018

American and global audiences have been bombarded with media images of wailing children in holding facilities, having been separated from adults (maybe their parents, maybe not) detained for illegal entry into the United States. The images have been accompanied by "gut-wrenching" audio of distraught toddlers screaming the Spanish equivalents of "Mommy!" and "Daddy!"—since, as any parent knows, small children never cry or call for their parents except in the most horrifying, life-threatening circumstances.

American and world media have provided helpful color commentary, condemning the caging of children as openly racist atrocities and state terrorism comparable to Nazi concentration camps and worse than FDR's internment of Japanese and Japanese-Americans. Indeed, just having *voted* for Trump is now reason enough for Americans to be labeled as Nazis.

Finally, the presumptive Hitler himself, also known as President Donald Trump, citing the pleas of First Lady Melania and First Daughter Ivanka, signed an Executive Order to provide for adults and (their?) children to be detained together. However, the order is unlikely to hold up in court, with sanctuary-minded states aiming to obstruct border enforcement the way Trump's earlier order on vetting arrivals from terrorism-prone countries has been crippled by the federal judiciary. His media and bipartisan political opposition will be happy only when all border violation detentions cease and America has gone full Merkel, starting with ending Trump's declared zero tolerance for illegal crossings and restoration of Barack Obama's catch-and-release policy.

Even then, Trump will be vilified for taking so long to do it. Whether or how Trump may yield further is not clear, but rather than slaking the hate campaign against him, his attempted effort at appeasement has put the smell of political blood in the water with the November 2018 Congressional midterm elections looming.

Some images of small children have become veritable icons of Trumpian brutality. One photo, reportedly of a two-year-old Honduran girl (who in fact had not been separated from her mother), graced the cover of *Time* magazine, confronting the black-hearted tyrant himself. Another, of a little boy in a cage, went viral before it was revealed that this kid had nothing to do with the border but rather was briefly inside a staged pen as part of a protest in Dallas.

The reality behind the pictures doesn't matter, though. More important are the images themselves and their power, along with dishonest media spin, to produce an emotional response that short-circuits critical thinking. Never mind what the facts are! Children are suffering! Trump is guilty! We need to "do something"!

On point of comparison, let's remember the saturation media distribution given in 2016 to a picture of a little boy, Omran Daqneesh, said to have been pulled from the rubble of Aleppo after what was dubiously reported as a Russian airstrike. Promptly dubbed "Aleppo Boy," his pathetic dusty image immediately went viral in every prestige outlet in the United States and Europe. The underlying message: we—the "international community," "the Free World," the United States, you and I—must "do something" to stop Syrian President Bashar al-Assad and his main backer and fellow Hitler clone Vladimir Putin.

(Not long before, another little boy, also in the area of Aleppo, was beheaded on video by the "moderate" US-supported jihad terror group Harakat Nour al-Din al-Zenki. The images of his grisly demise received far less media attention than those of official Aleppo Boy. This other youngster received no catchy moniker. No one called for anyone in power to "do something." In fact, western support for the al-Zenki murderers—which the Obama administration refused to disavow even after the beheading and allegations of chlorine gas use by al-Zenki—can itself be seen as part of "doing something" about the evil, evil Assad. (Reportedly Trump's viewing the beheading video led to a cutoff of CIA aid to some jihad groups.) Another small detail readily available in alternative media but almost invisible in the major outlets: Mahmoud Raslan, the photographer who took the picture of Aleppo Boy and disseminated it to world acclaim, also took a smiling selfie with the beaming al-Zenki beheaders of the other kid. But, hey, says Raslan, I barely know those guys. Now let's move on . . .)

For those who have been paying attention for the past couple of decades, the Trump border crisis kids, like Aleppo Boy before them, are human props in what is known as "atrocity porn" designed to titillate the viewers through horror and incite them to hatred of the presumed perpetrators. Atrocity propaganda has long been a part of warfare—think World War I claims of Belgian babies impaled on German bayonets—but with modern digital technology and social media the impact is immediate and universal.

It's irrelevant whether what is identified in images corresponds to reality. What matters is their ability to evoke mindless, maudlin emotionalism, like *MSNBC*'s Rachel Maddow choking up in tears over the border children or the similar weepy display in 2016 by *CNN*'s Kate Bolduan over Aleppo Boy.

Now being deployed in an American domestic context over whether or not the US should be allowed to control its borders, for decades atrocity porn has been essential for selling military action in wars of choice unconnected to the actual defense of the US: incubator babies (Kuwait/Iraq); the Racak massacre (Kosovo); the Markale marketplace bombings, Omarska "living skeletons," and the Srebrenica massacre (Bosnia); rape as calculated instrument of war (Bosnia, Libya); and false flag poison gas attacks in Ghouta and Douma (Syria). Never mind that the facts, to the extent they eventually become known, may later turn out to be very different from the categorical black-and-white accusations on the lips of western officials and given banner exposure within hours if not minutes of the event in question.

Atrocity porn dovetails closely with another key meme, that of Hitler-of-the-month. In painting Trump as *der Führer* on the border, we see coming home to America a ploy that has been an essential element to justify foreign regime change operation, each of which has been spelled out in terms of black-and-white, good-versus-evil Manichaean imperatives, with the side targeted for destruction or replacement having absolutely no redeeming qualities. This entails first of all absolute demonization of the evil leader in what is called *reductio ad Hitlerum*, a concept attributed to philosopher Leo Strauss in 1951. Russia's Vladimir Putin has been characterized by name as another Hitler by Hillary Clinton and others. Among the prominent "Hitlers" since 1991 have been Saddam Hussein (Iraq), Slobodan Milosevic (Yugoslavia/Serbia), Radovan Karadzic (Republika Srpska), Moammar Qaddafi (Libya), and Bashar al-Assad (Syria), with less imposing *Führer* figures to be found in Mohamed Farrah Aidid (Somalia), Manuel Noriega (Panama), Mahmoud Ahmadinejad (Iran), and Omar al-Bashir (Sudan).

With apologies to Voltaire, if Hitler had not existed it would be necessary for the US-UK Deep State to invent him . . .

Today the atrocity porn and Hitler memes that have been so useful in justifying regime change in other countries are being directed with increasing intensity against America's own duly elected president. This is at a time when the original conspiracy to discredit and unseat him, the phony "Russian collusion" story, is in the process of unraveling and being turned back on its originators. Horror of horrors, Trump is now feeling free enough to move forward on a meeting with Putin.

Keep in mind that Putin is, according to Hillary Clinton, leader of the worldwide "authoritarian, white-supremacist, and xenophobic movement" who is "emboldening right-wing nationalists, separatists, racists, and even neo-Nazis." So he and Hitler-Trump should get on famously! The prospect of any warming of ties between Washington and Moscow has elements of the US intelligence agencies, together with their British coconspirators in MI6 and GCHQ, in an absolute panic.

That's why desperate measures are in order. As noted earlier, when confronted with a reincarnation of the most evil personage in history, even the most extreme actions cannot be ruled out. Demonizing the intended target neutralizes objections to his removal—by any means necessary.

After all, how can any decent person oppose getting rid of Hitler?

"Will Next Steps on Iran Point towards a New 'Big Three' or World War III?"

Jim Jatras | *Strategic Culture* | July 28, 2018

On July 22 US Secretary of State Mike Pompeo delivered a bizarre speech on Iran. Delivered from the Ronald Reagan Presidential Library in Simi Valley, California, and ostensibly addressed to the Iranian-American community, the speech's staging clearly sought to evoke the fall of communism, casting the Ayatollahs in the role of Leonid Brezhnev and company.

Iranian "regime change" is not the publicly stated goal of the Trump Administration's policy. But it is hard to see how US demands on Tehran don't amount to exactly that, with Pompeo comparing the Iranian "regime" (a term used dozens of times to imply illegitimacy) to a "mafia." He asserted that Iran's behavior is "at root in the revolutionary nature of the regime itself." What can change its "root" or "nature" without ceasing to be itself?

Pompeo demanded not just a total change in policy from Tehran but a different mode of governance amounting to Iran's ceasing to be an independent regional power. The Reagan venue's analogy to the collapse of communism in the USSR and Eastern Europe echoed in the Secretary's heavy emphasis on "a new 24/7 Farsi-language TV channel" spanning "not only television, but radio, digital, and social media format, so that the ordinary Iranians inside of Iran and around the globe can know that America stands with them."

The US position on Iran is that it is solely a question of removing a layer of malign governance, after which democracy, tolerance, peace, and general niceness will spontaneously break forth, and justice will roll down like water and righteousness like a mighty stream. Just like happened in Iraq after 2003. Just like in Libya.

Never mind that Iran isn't North America or Europe. Never mind that American and European ideas of social and personal liberty would be anathema to an unknown but significant percentage of Iran's population. Never mind that the replacement for the Ayatollahs envisioned by many Administration big shots, the cultish People's Mojahedin Organization of Iran (Mojahedin-e Khalq, MEK), may not be particularly democratic or popular with Iranians. Don't bother us with details—the neo-Bolshevik myth of a spontaneous uprising by the oppressed masses (with a little help from outside, like the Kaiser's generals were kind enough to provide Lenin) is alive and well in Washington.

One is reminded of "true believer" Condoleezza Rice in 2006 denouncing as—you guessed it!—*racist* any objections to militant democracy promotion in the Middle East, specifically in Iraq:

> "Well, growing up in the South and having people underestimate you because one of the reasons for segregation, one of the reasons for the separation of the races was supposedly, the inferiority of one race to the other," she explains. "And so when I look around the world and I hear people say, 'Well, you know, they're just not ready for democracy,' it really does resonate. I hear echoes of, well, you know, blacks are kind of childlike. They really can't handle the vote. Or they really can't take care of themselves. It really does roil me. It makes me so angry because I think there are those echoes of what people once thought about black Americans."

Pompeo heavily emphasized Iran's internal problems, such as political represssion, corruption, economic distress, many of which are no doubt are quite real. Still, it was hard to listen to the Secretary without mentally comparing how the identical litany of abuses would apply to Washington's perennial darling of the Islamic world, Saudi Arabia, which in every particular is far, far worse than Iran. But nobody is talking about what amounts to regime change in Riyadh or even any sanctions against them. Accusations of Iranian state support for terrorism would be risible if arming myriad Sunni jihadist groups by the US and our various partners, the Saudis chief among them, were a laughing matter.

Pompeo's speech triggered a rebuke by Iranian President Hassan Rouhani that "peace with Iran is the mother of all peace, and war with Iran is the mother of all wars"—an unfortunate choice of words given how Saddam Hussein's "mother of all battles" turned out. Trump immediately shot back with a tweet threatening that Iran could "SUFFER CONSEQUENCES THE LIKES OF WHICH FEW THROUGHOUT HISTORY HAVE EVER SUFFERED BEFORE." Predictably, Trump's ubiquitous critics focused as much on the all-capital letters as on the substance of the exchange.

No one knows where any of this is leading. The memory immediately triggered was that of harsh verbal exchanges between North Korea's "Little Rocket man" Kim Jong-un and the "mentally deranged US dotard" Trump prior to their love fest in Singapore. Justin Raimondo of *Antiwar.com* was succinct in his optimism: "This means he'll be scheduling a Rouhani summit in a few months."

On the other hand, instead of Singapore 2018 we could be seeing a repeat of the lead-up to Iraq 2003. So many of the same people who were beating the drums for the war with Iraq under President George W. Bush are playing the same tune now with respect to Iran. It is significant that whereas with respect to North Korea our foremost regional partner, South Korea, is pushing hardest for a peaceful outcome, Israel and Saudi Arabia, the two foreign states that exercise almost total control over the political class in Washington, are itching for the US to take care of their Iran problem for them. The hare-brained "Arab NATO" idea has been revived.

Defense Secretary James "Mad Dog" Mattis has denied a report that the US was identifying targets in Iran to be struck as early as next month and disowned regime change. For what it is worth (probably not much) a recent poll shows that Americans are against war with Iran by a better than two-to-one margin. But, as Raimondo observes, "there are plenty of warmongers in Washington who just can't wait for the shooting to start in the Middle East again, and they have targeted Iran as their next victim. . . . [S]uch a war would destroy Trump's presidency precisely because his base would oppose it. And yet, . . . despite the fact that the President's advisors are pushing war with Iran, Trump routinely ignores them and does exactly as he pleases: that's why we had the Singapore summit and the Helsinki meeting with Putin."

We can hope that Trump will decide on his next steps with regard to Iran based on much broader international considerations that impact his domestic goals. Taken most optimistically, that could mean a concept that some of us have been suggesting for almost two years: a new "Big Three" understanding among Trump, Putin, and Chinese President Xi Jinping. Indeed, Professor Michael T. Klare, writing in *TomDispatch.com*, claims this is Trump's conscious intention:

> An examination of his campaign speeches and his actions since entering the Oval Office—including his appearance with Putin—reflect his adherence to a core strategic concept: the urge to establish a tripolar world order, one that was, curiously enough, first envisioned by Russian and Chinese leaders in 1997 and one that they have relentlessly pursued ever since.
>
> Such a tripolar order—in which Russia, China, and the U.S. would each assume responsibility for maintaining stability within their own respective spheres of influence while cooperating to resolve disputes wherever those spheres overlap—breaks radically with the end-of-the-Cold-War paradigm. During those heady years, the United States was the dominant world power and lorded it over most of the rest of the planet with the aid of its loyal NATO allies.
>
> For Russian and Chinese leaders, such a "unipolar" system was considered anathema. After all, it granted the United States a hegemonic role in world affairs while denying them what they considered their rightful place as America's equals. Not surprisingly, destroying such a system and replacing it with a tripolar one has been their strategic objective since the late 1990s—and now an American president has zealously embraced that disruptive project as his own. [. . .]
>
> The big question in all this, of course, is: Why? Why would an American president seek to demolish a global order in which the United States was the dominant player and enjoyed the support of so many loyal and wealthy allies? Why would he want to replace it with one in which it would be but one of three regional heavyweights? [. . .]
>
> In the Trumpian mindset, this country had become weak and overextended because of its uncritical adherence to the governing precepts of the liberal international order, which called for the U.S. to assume the task of policing the world while granting its allies economic and trade advantages in return for their loyalty. Such an assessment, whether accurate or not, certainly jibes well with the narrative of victimization that so transfixed his core constituency in rustbelt areas of Middle America. It also suggests that an inherited burden could now be discarded, allowing for the emergence of a less-encumbered, stronger America—much as a stronger Russia has emerged in this century from the wreckage of the Soviet Union and a stronger China from the wreckage of Maoism. This reinvigorated country would still, of course, have to compete with those other two powers, but from a far stronger position, being able to devote all its resources to economic growth and self-protection without the obligation of defending half of the rest of the world.

Listen to Trump's speeches, read through his interviews, and you'll find just this proposition lurking behind virtually everything he has to say on foreign policy and national security. "You know . . . there is going to be a point at which we just can't do this anymore," he told Haberman and Sanger in 2016, speaking of America's commitments to allies. "You know, when we did those deals, we were a rich country . . . We were a rich country with a very strong military and tremendous capability in so many ways. We're not anymore."

The only acceptable response, he made clear, was to jettison such overseas commitments and focus instead on "restoring" the country's self-defense capabilities through a massive buildup of its combat forces. (The fact that the United States already possesses far more capable weaponry than any of its rivals and outspends them by a significant margin when it comes to the acquisition of additional munitions doesn't seem to have any impact on Trump's calculations.)

If such is indeed Trump's calculation, his likelihood of attacking Iran is very low.

Conversely, the forces benefitting from the status quo Trump would dismantle cannot be expected to accept such a future with equanimity: the Pentagon and NATO military establishments, the intelligence community, the hordes of contractors and think tank denizens, and others. Perhaps even worse, Trump's domestic critics face the terrifying prospect that he could emerge as the greatest peacemaker in modern history, as well as restorer of America's economic might.

We can thus expect an added zeal born of desperation from former "CIA director John Brennan, FBI director James Comey, Robert Mueller, James Clapper, Andrew McCabe, Peter Strzok, Deputy Attorney General Rod Rosenstein, and the Democratic National Committee," who, Paul Craig Roberts aptly says, are "engaged in high treason against the American people and the President of the United States and are actively engaged in a plot to overthrow the President of the United States." Just in recent weeks the intensity of this campaign prevented Trump from agreeing to anything of substance with Putin in Helsinki, forced him to tap-dance around what he did or didn't say at the post-summit press conference, and postpone according to Grand Inquisitor Mueller's convenience a follow-up US-Russia summit (no doubt to the delight of his own appointees no less than to his enemies').

We can expect that between now the November 2018 Congressional elections Mueller will come out with several indictments against Trump associates with the hope of tipping the House of Representatives to the Democrats. If that happens, despite an anticipated GOP retention of the Senate, Trump will be removed or forced to resign in 2019, with a substantial percentage of Republicans ready to jump at the prospect of putting Mike Pence into the Oval Office, with current UN Ambassador Nikki Haley a virtual shoo-in as Vice President.

Such a development would prompt an anguished but futile outburst from Trump's base. But with *l'ancien régime* back in power, the guardians of the neoliberal, unipolar order the interloper had imperiled will move quickly to repudiate any understandings he might have had with Moscow and Beijing. The slide toward a catastrophe of literally unimaginable proportions, which Trump had sought to arrest, will become for all intents and purposes irreversible.

At that point Iran will be the least of our worries.

"Trump's Terrible, Horrible, No Good, Very Bad National Security Team"

Jim Jatras | *Strategic Culture* | October 6, 2018

Gareth Porter paints a dismal picture. Time and again, President Donald Trump indicates he wants to do the right thing: get out Afghanistan, get out of Syria, get out of South Korea.

Every time, his national security team—the people he appointed—sends him to "the tank" and hotboxes him with all the reasons he's wrong and why the US needs to "stay the course" in multiple wars and absurd deployments.

If the account of Bob Woodward is to be believed, Trump's flailing against his own appointees is nothing less than pathetic, that of a pitiable Gulliver roped down by Lilliputians of his own installation. As described by Tom Engelhardt:

> After all, from National Security Advisor John Bolton (the invasion of Iraq) and Secretary of State Mike Pompeo (a longtime regime-change advocate) to CIA Director Gina Haspel (black sites and torture), Secretary of Defense James "Mad Dog" Mattis (former Marine general and CENTCOM commander), and White House Chief of Staff John Kelly (former Marine general and a commander in Iraq), those adults [sic] and so many like them remain deeply implicated in the path the country took in those years of geopolitical dreaming. They were especially responsible for the decision to invest in the U.S. military (and little else), as well as in endless wars, in the years before Donald Trump came to power. And worse yet, they seem to have learned absolutely nothing from the process. [. . .]
>
> In his book, Woodward describes a National Security Council meeting in August 2017, in which the adults [sic] in the room saved the president from his worst impulses. He describes how an impatient Donald Trump "exploded, most particularly at his generals. 'You guys have created this situation. It's been a disaster. You're the architects of this mess in Afghanistan. . . . You're smart guys, but I have to tell you, you're part of the problem. And you haven't been able to fix it, and you're making it worse. . . . I was against this from the beginning.' He folded his arms. 'I want to get out . . . and you're telling me the answer is to get deeper in.'"
>
> And indeed almost 16 years later that is exactly what Pompeo, Mattis, former National Security Advisor H.R. McMaster, and the rest of them were telling him. According to Woodward, Mattis, for instance, argued forcefully "that if they pulled out, they would create another ISIS-style upheaval. . . . What happened in Iraq under Obama with the emergence of ISIS will happen under you, Mattis told Trump, in one of his sharpest declarations."

There's every indication that Trump's heart is in the right place but he hasn't got either the awareness of his own vast Executive authority (for example his ability to withdraw us from entangling treaties, *including NATO*, with the stroke of a pen!) or the detailed factual knowledge to refute the lies fed to him by his own team. Symptomatic is Trump's seeming acceptance of the canard that ISIS arose because of "what happened in Iraq under Obama"—supposedly that a "premature" American withdrawal created a "vacuum"—rather than as a *foreseen and intended result* of the Obama administration's aim to create a "salafist principality" in the Syria-Iraq border region, as attested to by his own first National Security Adviser, General Mike Flynn, whom Trump shamefully threw to the wolves when things got hot.

Porter nonetheless concludes on an optimistic note: "Trump's unorthodox approach has already emboldened him to challenge the essential logic of the US military empire more than any previous president. And the final years of his administration will certainly bring further struggles over the issues on which he has jousted repeatedly with those in charge of the empire."

So maybe we can still hold out hope for the human wrecking ball.

Still, whatever Trump's sound personal impulses, what have we got to show for it? Let's look at the score so far:

- The bad news: Under Trump we've stayed bogged down in all the messes he inherited. And worse, in Syria he even took direct military action (which his predecessor declined to do) and has set us up for multiple rounds of nuclear chicken with Russia. In Afghanistan, we've added troops, not withdrawn them. Our no-questions-asked support for Saudi Arabia's sickening war against Yemen continues. We've given Ukraine lethal weapons, another aggravating action Barack Obama hesitated to take, and given Kiev a green light to open a new front against the Russian Orthodox Church. Despite Trump's summit with Russia's Vladimir Putin ties with Moscow worsen by the day. Things with China don't look so rosy either, with a major US Navy "show of force" set for the South China Sea.
- The good news: Though the outcome is still in doubt harsh rhetoric against North Korea's Kim Jong-un led to the billing and cooing in Singapore.
- The best news: Trump hasn't started any new wars of his own.

Not yet, anyway.

If Trump plans to launch a spanking new useless conflict of his own (launching at least one war has become something of a presidential prerogative, the Constitution notwithstanding), Iran seems to be the place. The portents are all bad. Despite his long-term optimism Porter notes that by adopting a policy of regime change against Iran urged on him by National Security Adviser John Bolton and financier Sheldon Adelson, Trump "may finally give up his resistance to the multiple permanent US wars."

Sharp attacks on Iran by Trump and other top US officials, as well as by Israeli Prime Minister Binyamin Netanyahu, defined last month's United Nations General Assembly (UNGA) meeting. Superficially, this resembled Trump's verbal assaults last year on "Little Rocket Man" Kim Jong-un and North Korea, which eventually set the stage for the Singapore summit, a lowering of tensions on the Korean peninsula, an opening between the two Koreas which could become self-sustaining, and an uncertain path to denuclearization.

However, it is unlikely the current vilification of Tehran will lead to a comparable outcome. All signs indicate that Washington is serious about regime change in Tehran, either via sponsorship of internal unrest that would topple the current government, or by military action a la Iraq 2003. While the former is certainly Washington's preferred option, the latter cannot be ruled out. This orientation may be considered fundamental to the administration's current course both because of the composition of Trump's team and because of the insistence of America's regional partners, above all Israel and Saudi Arabia.

In pursuing this course, we will continue to see on-and-off confrontation with Russia, stepped up pressures on China, and a divergence of views with America's European allies, especially on sanctions policy. Iran may be the focus, but this is a full-spectrum global policy long in preparation. In July 2018 it was reported that a few months earlier the US and Israel formed a joint working group focused on internal efforts to encourage protests within Iran and to undermine the country's government. The point men are Bolton and his Israeli counterpart Meir Ben-Shabbat.

Of a piece is Pompeo's July speech from the Ronald Reagan Presidential Library in Simi Valley, California, in which he clearly sought to evoke the fall of communism, casting the Ayatollahs in the role of Leonid Brezhnev and company. While Iranian "regime change" is not the publicly stated goal of the Trump Administration's policy, it is hard to see how US demands on Tehran don't amount to exactly that, with Pompeo comparing the Iranian "regime" (a term used dozens of times in his speech to imply illegitimacy) to a "mafia." He asserted that Iran's behavior is "at root in the revolutionary nature of the regime itself"—suggesting that no real change can be expected and that removal is the only remedy. Pompeo demanded not just a total change in policy from Tehran but a different mode of governance amounting to Iran's ceasing to be an independent regional power.

Also of note were reports in late 2017 of a Trump-Netanyahu "strategic work plan" to counter Iran following a December 12 White House meeting and, before that in June 2017, the appointment of the "Dark Prince," "Ayatollah Mike," the "Undertaker" and convert to (Sunni) Islam Michael D'Andrea to run the CIA's Iran operation. (One Langley insider's simple comment on the D'Andrea appointment: "All I can say is that war with Iran is in the cards.")

In short, this is a coordinated, strategic effort using every lever of national power to achieve its objective. It would be naïve to expect that this does not include the use of covert action, including support for terrorism inside Iran (such as the recent attack on a parade in heavily ethnic Arab Khuzistan), if not directly then via proxies armed and funded by Saudi Arabia and the Gulf States on the pattern of Libya and Syria.

For anyone desperately seeking a parallel between Trump's harsh rhetoric towards North Korea at last year's UNGA, which led in time to the Singapore summit with Kim Jong-un, there is little to indicate that this is simply Trump's "art of the deal" to achieve a similar outcome with Iran. There are three key distinctions between the two theaters. First, US demands regarding North Korea were focused on its nuclear program, while demands on Iran are comprehensive and are tantamount to demanding that the current government abolish itself. Second, while America's top partners in northeast Asia, Japan and especially South Korea, welcome a warming to Pyongyang, US partners in the region of Iran, notably Israel and Saudi Arabia, are themselves the engines pushing for a more bellicose policy.

Third, Trump's national security team is totally committed to the Israel-Saudi line. This was illustrated at the conference held in sync with the UNGA of the group United Against Nuclear Iran (UANI) at which Bolton and Pompeo both appeared. According to one attendee, the atmosphere was one of cultic surrealism: Iran is responsible for every problem in the broader Middle East if not the whole world, including the Taliban, al-Qaeda, and ISIS; all Sunni terror groups ultimately trace their origin and funding back to Tehran; Tehran was responsible for 9/11; the terrorist MEK is the true representative of the Iranian people and is being groomed to be inserted as a replacement as soon as the "regime" crumbles. The UANI event was eerily reminiscent of the atmosphere in Washington in 2002, only replacing one letter to change Iraq to Iran.

Iran is also central to the confrontation in Syria, from which Trump evidently would like to disengage but has been overruled by his underlings. The US, backed by Britain and France, threatened action against Syria and even Russia if chemical weapons were used "again" in a now-postponed offensive on Idlib province. The standoff dramatically escalated with the Russian introduction of S–300 anti-aircraft systems, now reportedly being delivered, in the aftermath of the downing of a Russian surveillance aircraft and the killing of 15 crewmen as a consequence of an Israeli strike near Russia's Khmeimim airbase ostensibly against Iranian targets. The S–300 deployment creates a flexible, de facto no-fly zone against Israel in western Syria and even can neutralize onboard electronic systems within a 250-km radius—effectively including all of Israel. How and when the next confrontation will take place is unclear.

By early November we can expect further tightening of sanctions on number of countries continuing to do business with Iran, especially energy purchases. Among these are China and Turkey, and possibly India. (India is a special case because of Washington policymakers' efforts to woo New Delhi as the linchpin of the anti-China "Indo-Pacific Quad" along with Japan and Australia.) But the most important targets will be countries of the European Union. Much is being made of a so-called "clearing house," or Special Purpose Vehicle (SPV) for conducting business with Iran to avoid the SWIFT system and US sanctions.

The SPV concept is supported by the European Union, the United Kingdom, France, and Germany, as well as China and Russia. But the SPV or any other mechanism for the Europeans to defy the US is only as good as the weakest link. Simply the suggestion of the mechanism has infuriated Washington, which will seek to peel off one or another of the European participants in the hopes of collapsing their common action. It should also be kept in mind that the US Treasury Department *can simply sanction the SPV clearing house itself*, applying secondary sanctions to any European companies that interact with it.

Predictions that the Europeans are steeling their jelly-like nerves to defy Washington are laughable. The US treats our supposed allies with contempt because that's what they deserve. (This is broader than just Iran. For example, Washington is also threatening Europe with secondary sanctions on companies participating in Nord Stream 2 (NS2).) The Europeans, even if they had the will, can't just pull a SWIFT alternative out of a hat. It would take time, resources, and determination, which they are unlikely to expend once the US seriously starts to threaten them. Finally, it is well known that US intelligence has strong influence over many European politicians (including compromising material on them), as well as control of media, special services, military commands, and think tanks. In short, their ability to behave independently is small.

Russia is supposedly prepared to use its Financial Communications Transfer System (SPFS) based on blockchain technology to protect itself, especially when new, extremely harsh financial sanctions are set to kick in in November, close to the time full anti-Iran sanctions go into effect. It will be interesting to see if they can pull it off. With the knowledge that they are the number one target for US financial sanctions, the Russians have had time to work on protective alternatives, including local currency arrangements that bypass the dollar—and Moscow still doesn't know how well it will work when the time comes. The most recent round of indictments against the GRU over a bizarre witch's brew of supposed offenses including election meddling,

chemical weapons, doping, and MH17 (with London's malign hand much in
evidence) is just a taste of what is to come, even now including direct threats
of war.

To sum up, Iran is the *proximate* target of a policy that has only one
direction (forward) and one speed (fast). But the *ultimate* target is Russia,
with no possible improvement in sight and a state of relations that worsens by
the week; this is designed to crush its economy and financial system, render
its security posture untenable, and lead to a reinstallation of a puppet government of the sort that existed in the 1990s, pending breaking up Russian into
more manageable pieces. Finally, after Iran and Russia are disposed of next in
line is China, against which covert action to sabotage the Belt and Road
Initiative may already have begun.

There isn't anything remotely America First about any of this. It's certainly not what this Deplorable voted for. But with the terrible, horrible, no
good, very bad national security team Trump has saddled himself with, what
else can we expect? They are in charge. Things are going to get a lot worse
before they get better—if ever.

"Britain on the Leash with the United States— but at Which End?"

Jim Jatras | *Strategic Culture* | October 13, 2018

The "special relationship" between the United States and the United Kingdom
is often assumed to be one where the once-great, sophisticated Brits are
subordinate to the upstart, uncouth Yanks.

Iconic of this assumption is the mocking of former prime minister Tony
Blair as George W. Bush's "poodle" for his riding shotgun on the ill-advised
American stagecoach blundering into Iraq in 2003. Blair was in good practice,
having served as Bill Clinton's dogsbody in the no less criminal NATO
aggression against Serbia over Kosovo in 1999.

On the surface, the UK may seem just one more vassal state on par with
Germany, Japan, South Korea, and so many other useless so-called allies. We
control their intelligence services, their military commands, their think tanks,
and much of their media. We can sink their financial systems and economies
at will. Emblematic is German Chancellor Angela Merkel's impotent ire at
discovering the Obama administration had listened in on her cell phone, about
which she—did precisely nothing. Global hegemony means never having to say
you're sorry.

These countries know on which end of the leash they are: the one attached
to the collar around their necks. The hand unmistakably is in Washington.
These semi-sovereign countries answer to the US with the same servility as
member states of the Warsaw Pact once heeded the USSR's Politburo. (Sometimes more. Communist Romania, though then a member of the Warsaw Pact
refused to participate in the 1968 invasion of Czechoslovakia or even allow
Soviet or other Pact forces to cross its territory. By contrast, during NATO's
1999 assault on Serbia, Bucharest allowed NATO military aircraft access to its
airspace, even though not yet a member of that alliance and despite most
Romanians' opposition to the campaign.)

But the widespread perception of Britain as just another satellite may be misleading.

To start with, there are some relationships where it seems the US is the vassal dancing to the tune of the foreign capital, not the other way around. Israel is the unchallenged champion in this weight class, with Saudi Arabia a runner up. The alliance between Prime Minister Bibi Netanyahu and Saudi Crown Prince Mohammad bin Salman (MbS)—the ultimate Washington "power couple"—to get the Trump administration to destroy Iran for them has American politicos listening for instructions with all the rapt attention of the terrier Nipper on the RCA Victor logo. (Or did, until the recent disappearance of Saudi journalist Jamal Khashoggi. Whether this portends a real shift in American attitudes toward Riyadh remains questionable. Saudi cash still speaks loudly and will continue to do so whether or not MbS stays in charge.)

Specifics of the peculiar US-UK relationship stem from the period of flux at the end of World War II. The United States emerged from the war in a commanding position economically and financially, eclipsing Britannia's declining empire that simply no longer had the resources to play the leading role. That didn't mean, however, that London trusted the Americans' ability to manage things without their astute guidance. As Tony Judt describes in *Postwar*, the British attitude of "superiority towards the country that had displaced them at the imperial apex" was "nicely captured" in a scribble during negotiations regarding the UK's postwar loan:

> In Washington Lord Halifax
> Once whispered to Lord Keynes:
> "It's true they have the moneybags
> But we have all the brains."

Even in its diminished condition London found it could punch well above its weight by exerting its influence on its stronger but (it was confident) dumber cousins across the Pond. It helped that as the Cold War unfolded following former Prime Minister Winston Churchill's 1946 Iron Curtain speech there were very close ties between sister agencies like MI6 (founded 1909) and the newer wartime OSS (1942), then the CIA (1947); likewise the Government Communications Headquarters (GCHQ, 1919) and the National Security Administration (NSA, 1952). Comparable sister agencies—perhaps more properly termed daughters of their UK mothers—were set up in Canada, Australia, and New Zealand. This became the so-called "Five Eyes" of the tight Anglosphere spook community, infamous for spying on each others' citizens to avoid pesky legal prohibitions on domestic surveillance.

Despite not having two farthings to rub together, impoverished Britain— where wartime rationing wasn't fully ended until 1954—had a prime seat at the table fashioning the world's postwar financial structure. The 1944 Bretton Woods conference was largely an Anglo-American affair, of which the aforementioned Lord John Maynard Keynes was a prominent architect along with Harry Dexter White, Special Assistant to the US Secretary of the Treasury and Soviet agent.

American and British agendas also dovetailed in the Middle East. While the US didn't have much of a presence in the region before the 1945 meeting between US President Franklin Delano Roosevelt and Saudi King ibn Saud, founder of the third and current (and hopefully last) Saudi state—and didn't assume a dominant role until the humiliation inflicted on Britain, France, and Israel by President Dwight Eisenhower during the 1956 Suez Crisis—London has long considered much of the region within its sphere of influence. After World War I under the Sykes-Picot agreement with France, the UK had expanded her holdings on the ruins of the Ottoman Empire, including taking a decisive role in consolidating Saudi Arabia under ibn Saud. While in the 1950s the US largely stepped into Britain's role managing the "East of Suez," the former suzerain was by no means dealt out. The UK was a founding member with the US of the now-defunct Central Treaty Organization (CENTO) in 1955.

CENTO—like NATO and their one-time eastern counterpart, the Southeast Asia Treaty Organization (SEATO)—was designed as a counter to the USSR. But in the case of Britain, the history of hostility to Russia under tsar or commissar alike has much deeper and longer roots, going back at least to the Crimean War in the 1850s. The reasons for the longstanding British vendetta against Russia are not entirely clear and seem to have disparate roots: the desire to ensure that no one power is dominant on the European mainland (directed first against France, then Russia, then Germany, then the USSR and again Russia); maintaining supremacy on the seas by denying Russia warm-waters ports, above all the Dardanelles; and making sure territories of a dissolving Ottoman empire would be taken under the wing of London, not Saint Petersburg. As described by Andrew Lambert, professor of naval history at King's College London, the Crimean War still echoes today:

> In the 1840s, 1850s, Britain and America are not the chief rivals; it's Britain and Russia. Britain and Russia are rivals for world power, and Turkey, the Ottoman Empire, which is much larger than modern Turkey—it includes modern Romania, Bulgaria, parts of Serbia, and also Egypt and Arabia—is a declining empire. But it's the bulwark between Russia, which is advancing south and west, and Britain, which is advancing east and is looking to open its connections up through the Mediterranean into its empire in India and the Pacific. And it's really about who is running Turkey. Is it going to be a Russian satellite, a bit like the Eastern Bloc was in the Cold War, or is it going to be a British satellite, really run by British capital, a market for British goods? And the Crimean War is going to be the fulcrum for this cold war to actually go hot for a couple of years, and Sevastopol is going to be the fulcrum for that fighting.

Control of the Middle East—and opposing the Russians—became a British obsession, first to sustain the lifeline to India, the Jewel in the Crown of the empire, then for control of petroleum, the life's blood of modern economies. In the context of the 19th and early 20th century Great Game of empire, that was understandable. Much later, similar considerations might even support Jimmy Carter's taking up much the same position, declaring in 1980 that "outside force to gain control of the Persian Gulf region will be regarded as an assault on the vital interests of the United States of America, and such an assault will be repelled by any means necessary, including military force." The USSR was then a superpower and we were dependent on energy from the Gulf region.

But what's our reason for maintaining that posture almost four decades later when the Soviet Union is gone and the US doesn't need Middle Eastern oil? There are no reasonable national interests, only corporate interests and those of the Arab monarchies we laughably claim as allies. Add to that the bureaucracies and habits of mind that link the US and UK establishments, including their intelligence and financial components.

In view of all the foregoing, what then would policymakers in the United Kingdom think about an aspirant to the American presidency who not only disparages the value of existing alliances—without which Britain is a bit player—but openly pledges to improve relations with Moscow? To what lengths would they go to stop him?

Say 'hello' to Russiagate!

One can argue whether or not the phony claim of the Trump campaign's "collusion" with Moscow was hatched in London or whether the British just lent some "hands across the water" to an effort concocted by the Democratic National Committee, the Hillary Clinton presidential campaign, the Clinton Foundation, and their collaborators at Fusion GPS and inside the Obama administration. Either way, it's clear that while evidence of Russian connection is nonexistent that of British agencies is unmistakable, as is the UK's hand in a sustained campaign of demonization and isolation to sink any possible rapprochement between the US and Russia.

As for Russiagate itself, just try to find anyone involved who's actually Russian. The only basis for the widespread assumption that any material in the Dirty Dossier that underlies the whole operation originated with Russia is the claim of Christopher Steele, the British "ex" spy who wrote it, evidently in collaboration with people at the US State Department and Fusion GPS. (The notion that Steele, who hadn't been in Russia for years, would have Kremlin personal contacts is absurd. How chummy are the heads of the American section of Chinese or Russian intelligence with White House staff?)

While there are no obvious Russians in Russiagate there's no shortage of Brits. These include (details at the link):

- Andrew Wood, a former British ambassador to Russia
- Stefan Halper, a dual US-UK citizen.
- Ex-MI6 Director Richard Dearlove.
- Robert Hannigan, former director of GCHQ; there is reason to think surveillance of Trump was conducted by GCHQ as well as by US agencies under FISA warrants. Hannigan abruptly resigned from GCHQ soon after the British government denied the agency had engaged in such spying.
- Alexander Downer, Australian diplomat (well, not British but remember the Five Eyes!).
- Joseph Mifsud, Maltese academic and suspected British agent.

At present, the full role played by those listed above is not known. Release of unredacted FISA warrant requests by the Justice Department, which President Trump ordered weeks ago, would shed light on a number of details. Implementation of that order was derailed after a request by—no surprise— British Prime Minister Theresa May. Was she seeking to conceal Russian perfidy, or her own underlings?

It would be bad enough if Russiagate were the sum of British meddling in American affairs with the aim of torpedoing relations with Moscow. (And to be fair, it wasn't just the UK and Australia. Also implicated are Estonia, Israel, and Ukraine.) But there is also reason to suspect the same motive in false accusations against Russia with respect to the supposed Novichok poisonings in England has a connection to Russiagate via a business associate of Steele's, one Pablo Miller, Sergei Skripal's MI6 recruiter. (So if it turns out there is any Russian connection to the dossier, it could be from Skripal or another dubious expat source, not from the Russian government.) Skripal and his daughter Yulia have disappeared in British custody. Moscow flatly accuses MI6 of poisoning them as a false flag to blame it on Russia.

A similar pattern can be seen with claims of chemical weapons use in Syria: "We have irrefutable evidence that the special services of a state which is in the forefront of the Russophobic campaign had a hand in the staging" of a faked chemical weapons attack in Douma in April 2018. Ambassador Aleksandr Yakovenko pointed to the so-called White Helmets, which is closely associated with al-Qaeda elements and considered by some their PR arm: "I am naming them because they have done things like this before. They are famous for staging attacks in Syria and they receive UK money." Moscow warned for weeks before the now-postponed Syrian government offensive in Idlib that the same ruse was being prepared again with direct British intelligence involvement, even having prepared in advance a video showing victims of an attack that had not yet occurred.

The campaign to demonize Russia shifted into high gear recently with the UK, together with the US and the Netherlands, accusing Russian military intelligence of a smorgasbord of cyberattacks against the World Anti Doping Agency (WADA) and other sports organizations, the Organization for the Prohibition of Chemical Weapons (OPCW), the Dutch investigation into the downing of MH–17 over Ukraine, and a Swiss lab involved with the Skripal case, plus assorted election interference. In case anyone didn't get the point, British Defense Secretary Gavin Williamson declared: "This is not the actions of a great power. This is the actions of a pariah state, and we will continue working with allies to isolate them."

To the extent that the goal of Williamson and his ilk is to ensure isolation and further threats against Russia, it's been a smashing success. More sanctions are on the way. The UK is sending additional troops to the Arctic to counter Russian "aggression." The US threatens to use naval power to block Russian energy exports and to strike Russian weapons disputed under a treaty governing intermediate range nuclear forces. What could possibly go wrong?

In sum, we are seeing a massive, coordinated hybrid campaign of psyops and political warfare conducted not by Russia but against Russia, concocted by the UK and its Deep State collaborators in the United States. But it's not only aimed at Russia, it's an attack on the United States by the government of a foreign country that's supposed to be one of our closest allies, a country with which we share many venerable traditions of language, law, and culture.

But for far too long, largely for reasons of historical inertia and elite corruption, we've allowed that government to exercise undue influence on our global policies in a manner not conducive to our own national interests. Now that government, employing every foul deception that earned it the moniker Perfidious Albion, seeks to embroil us in a quarrel with the only country on the planet that can destroy us if things get out of control.

This must stop. A thorough reappraisal of our "special relationship" with the United Kingdom and exposure of its activities to the detriment of the US is imperative.

"Sayonara, 'America First'! We Hardly Knew Ye!"

Jim Jatras | *Strategic Culture* | December 1, 2018

President Donald Trump's cancellation of his planned meeting with Russian President Vladimir Putin at the Buenos Aires G20 is another sign of the now almost certain demise of his declared "America First" agenda—and perhaps of his presidency. Supposedly decided in response to a Ukraine-Russia naval incident in the Kerch Strait, dumping the meeting is universally and correctly seen as a response to the guilty plea of his former lawyer and "fixer," Michael Cohen, to lying to Congress (notice that James Clapper isn't forced to plead to his perjury before the Senate) and Cohen's disclosure of Trump's fruitless business dealings in Russia.

Keep in mind that this comes at a time when grand inquisitor Robert Mueller is on thin ice—or would be, if Trump and his team had a clue. Consider: in just the past few days Jerome Corsi, Roger Stone, and belatedly perhaps even Paul Manafort have delivered what amounts to a case against Mueller's underlings, including subornation of testimony they knew to be false—a felony punishable by five years in the slammer (18 US Code § 1622—Subornation of perjury). Is Trump or any of his lawyers thinking of having the victims swear out a complaint and instructing the Justice Department actually to *prosecute* these miscreants? No, of course not, even though at least Corsi appears to be willing.

Likewise Trump threatens to declassify "a wide swath of 'devastating' documents related to the Mueller probe, which he had initially planned to do in September before changing his mind" on the beseeching of British Prime Minister Theresa May. Britain's worst prime minister ever is desperate to hide the fact that at its root there's nothing Russian about "Russiagate" but there's lots and lots of British MI6, GCHQ, and other Five Eyes skullduggery aimed at subverting the 2016 US election and preventing any possible rapprochement between Washington and Moscow. With respect to both goals this massive PSYOP and political warfare campaign by the US-UK Deep State has been a smashing success.

Trump has the goods on them but just sits on his hands and threatens. (He should heed that great philosopher Tuco from *The Good, the Bad, and the Ugly*: "When you have to shoot, shoot—don't talk.") For those patiently waiting for Trump's "4D chess" game to unleash QAon's "Storm," here's a news flash: the cavalry is not coming to the rescue. The following are just a few names that will never be brought to justice: Rod Rosenstein, Peter Strzok, Bruce Ohr, Andrew McCabe, James Comey, Lisa Page, Andrew Weissmann, Stefan Halper, Christopher Steele, Joseph Mifsud, Richard Dearlove, Andrew Wood, Susan Rice, Loretta Lynch, Cheryl Mills, Huma Abedin, Samantha Power, Sally Yates, Jeannie Rhee, Eric Holder, James Clapper, John Brennan, and Barack Hussein Obama. Oh, and Hillary Clinton of course (while the whistleblower on her corrupt activities gets raided by the FBI).

These august personages are not subject to the laws binding on ordinary mortals like thee and me. These scoundrels will skate. All of them. That's why a smug, world-class criminal like Brennan can mock Trump's complaints as similar to how "corrupt authoritarian leaders abroad behaved before they were deposed." He already anticipates dancing on Trump's (probably figurative) grave.

Back to the Cohen plea, it's entirely likely it was timed to have precisely the result of scuttling the Trump-Putin meeting. There can be no better illustration of the weakness of Trump's position than his inability to engage in even a semblance of statesmanship with respect to the leader of the one power on the planet with which the US absolutely must have some minimal working relationship.

With the Democrats set to take over in the House of Representatives in just over a month, we'll soon see intensified investigations coordinated with Mueller to find any possible pretext for impeachment in Trump's business or private life. It's conventional wisdom that even if the Democrat-controlled House can find something to support articles of impeachment the GOP-held Senate will be Trump's firewall. Bunk. Democrats rallied around their president Bill Clinton but it was Republicans who threw Richard Nixon to the wolves. Are there a dozen or so Republican Senators who would be ready to dump Trump and install Mike Pence in the Oval Office? You betcha. Start with Mitt Romney.

As the noose around Trump's neck continues to tighten, his response will be to keep on carping about how unfair it all is, that there was no collusion with Russia, that it's a "total witch hunt" that should be ended. All true, all meaningless. He has the weapons to fight back but lacks the knowledge or personnel to use them. So he complains. He tweets. Meanwhile, on substance he's jumping up and down like a monkey on a string.

Which leaves us asking: *Why?*

One of the burdens carried by those of us Deplorables who early in 2016 declared our support for the then-improbable candidacy of Donald Trump has been the taunts of those who "knew better." Trump was a fraud, they said, "just a BS-ing con man who would say anything to get elected." He was a stalking horse to help usher in President Hillary (what other Republican could she possibly beat?). He was crude, impulsive, irritable, egotistical, dyslexic, and incapable of and uninterested in learning anything he doesn't already know. He was a flimflam artist who had cheated everyone he'd ever done business with or been married to and would abuse his *lumpen* Murican political supporters in Flyover Country accordingly. He was just another globalist neocon flunky of the Israelis, the Saudis, and the Deep State who was only mouthing populist rhetoric to get elected. He was a shyster on the make whose only goal was to enhance his "brand" to get even richer. He was a huckster with big assets in Russia, Saudi Arabia, China, and other nasty, nasty places, who just wanted to make a killing on his investments. And so on . . .

Those of us who supported Trump (and who still struggle to support him) point to his repeated use of America First and national interest language even when it was politically counterproductive and only served to subject him to vilification by Democrats and establishment Republicans alike. Ditto his repeated appeals for better relations with Russia, even at the cost of being accused of treason by the same antagonists and their media shills. Ditto the claim from a hostile source like Bob Woodward that behind doors Trump repeatedly tries to do the right thing, like get the US out of Afghanistan and Syria, but then is overruled by "experts" who are his nominal subordinates. Ditto his seeming "art of the deal" transformation of his bluster and threat competition with "Little Rocket Man" into the best chance for peace on the Korean peninsula in seven decades. From his unscripted comments and tweets, there always seems to be a little 2016 Candidate Trump fighting to get out of President Trump but never quite succeeding. . . .

But how then to explain his terrible, horrible, no good, very bad national security team? His beeline to Saudi Arabia, Israel, and NATO headquarters in his maiden foreign policy trip to reaffirm mindless hostility to Iran and America's suicide pact with useless so-called "allies" in Europe? His authorization of lethal weapons to Ukraine? His two cruise-missile strikes on Syria on transparently bogus claims of chemical weapons use? His ever-tightening of sanctions on Russia and nonstop expansion of NATO? His continued naval provocations against China?

To characterize as "low" expectations of any Trump-Putin sidebar meeting that might have happened at the G20 is putting it extremely mildly. (Who knows, maybe they'll still manage to steal a few sweet moments for a quick *tête-à-tête*, like a secret tryst of illicit lovers. Maybe Strzok and Page can provide some pointers.) Even laying aside the endless navel-gazing about what President Trump *really* wants, and why his administration's foreign policy bears almost no resemblance to his 2016 America First platform, it's pretty clear that in practice the US course will remain essentially a continuation of the failed policies of the past three decades: a futile attempt to maintain US global hegemony indefinitely at any cost. That can have only one hideous outcome.

With regard to Russia, the Kerch Strait incident will serve as another pretext for sanctions that will soon be added with the predictability that night follows day. The ongoing trade war with China (on purely economic grounds not wrong in itself) serves as a backdrop for continued dragon-baiting in the South China Sea, the Taiwan Strait, and Xinjiang, all places where the US has no actual interests. Even Trump's minimal potential as a wrecking ball to disrupt the dysfunctional commitments he inherited doesn't seem to be working out. The Swamp-critters to whom he's entrusted his administration dance along their merry way as though Mitt Romney or ¡Jeb! Bush were president, with little or no interference from their nominal boss.

On top of hastening the bankruptcy of the US, the danger of war with Russia, or China, or both will continue to increase. Neither Russian President Putin nor Chinese President Xi Jinping can still have any illusions about that and are planning accordingly. No one knows exactly when or where we will reach the point of no return.

Russian and Chinese officials have warned the US about their preparedness for war in so many words. No one in Washington is listening, except to the extent that the new report of a Congressionally mandated commission has concluded that despite spending on our military *ten times* what Russia does and *three times* China's outlays, we still might lose a war to either of those powers.

So what do the Swamp-critters draw from that? We need to spend even *more!* And Trump will accommodate them.

The one bright spot so far has been on the Korean peninsula—for which Trump deserves great credit, though his minions are working overtime to avert the horrid prospect that peace might break out and we'd no longer have an excuse to keep troops in South Korea. On everything else, even where developments favor disengagement from involvements not conducive to American interests, Trump's administration insists on digging back in.

For example, France's "Little Macro" wants a European army. It's a ridiculous pipe dream, especially since Europe faces no external threat except migration, against which a conventional force is mostly useless. But Trump should be thrilled to take him up on the offer and turn European security over to Europeans. Instead, he's trying to sink the idea.

Likewise, in the Syrian conflict it's clear that with Russian and Iranian help President Bashar al-Assad's government has beaten the jihadists sicced on that unfortunate land by the US and our so-called allies, but Washington won't admit it and still hopes to leverage Assad's departure. Why, because of ISIS, which Trump said was the sole reason we have thousands of US troops (illegally) in that country? No, but because of the need to oppose Iran and impose regime change in Tehran, as well as denying Moscow a "win."

Iran (an Israeli obsession having no bearing on US security) is also the reason Trump declined to take the exit ramp the Khashoggi murder offered from our unnecessary commitment to the despicable Wahhabist regime in Riyadh. Instead, he has doubled down on US support for Mohammed bin Salman while absurd plans for an "Arab NATO" proceed, as though one NATO weren't already bad enough.

None of this is America First. In a sane policymaking world, Trump should be looking to cut a spheres of influence deal with Putin (and with Xi and maybe with India's Narendra Modi). Maybe that's what Trump really wants, maybe it isn't. Or maybe someone just gave him The Talk: "Do what you're told, Mr. President, or you and maybe your kid will end up like Jack Kennedy."

In the final analysis, it doesn't seem to matter much what Trump wants. It would be only a small exaggeration to say that with respect to foreign and security policy Trump is now a mere figurehead of the permanent state. Even if Trump and Putin do happen to meet again, what can the latter expect the former to say that would make any difference?

As a signal of the approaching end of the short-lived hope of America First, cancellation of Trump-Putin is the penultimate act but not yet the final one. The fat lady's aria will be when Julian Assange is dragged to Washington in chains, like some barbarian chieftain paraded in a Roman triumph.

Ultimately, as Ann Coulter writes (with respect to the Mexican border crisis, where Trump is at least doing slightly better than in foreign affairs but not by much), Trump might "only be remembered as a small cartoon figure who briefly inflamed and amused the rabble." If so, his failure will have frittered away the only peaceful chance to avert the looming death of our nation at the hands of the Cultural Marxist duopoly, as well as to turn aside from the real prospect of a world war—one from which America cannot emerge undamaged as we did from the first two.

P.S. I would be genuinely thrilled to be wrong about all of the foregoing.

"The 'America Last' Express Hurtles On: Saudi Arabia, INF, Ukraine"

Jim Jatras | *Strategic Culture* | December 8, 2018

As the façade of 2016 Candidate Donald Trump's promised "America First" continues to crumble away, the baked-into-the-cake pathologies of the foreign and security policy "experts" who monopolize President Trump's administration plunge forward along their predetermined paths. Any realistic notion of American national interests comes last after the priorities of—well, pretty much everyone else with leverage in Washington.

Case in point, let's start with Saudi Arabia and all the breast-beating over whether Saudi Arabia's Mohammed bin Salman (MbS) really is guilty of ordering the killing of Jamal Khashoggi. (Spoiler Alert: You betcha!)

American and western media were all a-twitter last week with Russian President Vladimir Putin's high five to Crown Pariah MbS at the G20. Amid the *faux* outrage—come on, does anyone really think MbS was the *only* killer in that room?—the gesture received America's highest media tribute: a parody on "Saturday Night Live."

What a circus. Apart from Putin's greeting, the assembled hypocrites went out of their way to shun the leprous MbS, even shunting him to the margins of the group picture—as though the killing of one dodgy journalist outweighed their abetting MbS's business-as-usual slaughter in Yemen. *Really! I barely know the guy. We were never actually friends . . .*

Khashoggi's gruesome death is the gift that keeps on giving, exacerbating as it does both international and domestic American fault lines. Let's keep in mind that his affiliation was with the Muslim Brotherhood (and Turkish President Recep Tayyip Erdoğan), the CIA, and (almost the same thing) the *Washington Post*. Internationally these line up with Turkey, Qatar, and Saudi elements currently on the outs with MbS and who would like to send him to join Khashoggi. Domestically in the US these add up to the Deep State and "the Resistance" to President Donald Trump, who are thrilled to be able to hang Khashoggi around his neck like an albatross, which he's foolishly allowing to happen.

On the other hand, MbS is supported by Israel, which has a lot of clout on Capitol Hill (duh) and virtually owns the Trump administration (also duh). Prime Minister Bibi Netanyahu has Trump dancing to his tune via Jared Kushner (Trump and Kushner may now in fact be the same person), Ivanka Trump, and Sheldon Adelson, plus his entire foreign policy team, starting with National Security Adviser John Bolton and Secretary of State Mike Pompeo. Rather than wisely using the Khashoggi imbroglio as an opportunity to take the exit ramp away from US support for the crazed Wahhabist head-choppers in Riyadh of *any* faction, Team Trump is doggedly defending their line in the sand in support of MbS personally as the spearhead of their anti-Iran, "Arab NATO" program.

The Resistance side is no less anti-Iran, but beating the Khashoggi drum and even tying it to support for Yemen slaughter (not that they really give a damn about Yemen, except for a few bleeding hearts like Senator Rand Paul and Representative Tulsi Gabbard, who even have the temerity to oppose the CIA's arming of al-Qaeda in Syria!) is a twofer: to weaken and humiliate Trump, plus hoping at some point to install a replacement to MbS who would be a more reliable tool for their anti-Iran vendetta. The big break, if it comes, will be if Bibi's foot soldiers around Trump decide they need to dump MbS as counterproductive to their agenda on Iran. Then they'll stop resisting the Resistance, MbS will be removed (with extreme prejudice), and Trump will have egg on his face for having supported him for so long. For the Resistance, it's win-win . . .

. . . *if* it happens that way. On the other hand, even exposed as the bloody-minded killer he is, it's not impossible MbS, with Israel backstopping him, can just tough it out. After all, those waiting in the wings in Riyadh are no angels either. At least in the short term MbS may still have the upper hand via squatter's rights; he's in power and the guy everybody still has to deal with. He can also still spread a lot of cash around as Khashoggi recedes into the rearview mirror.

If things really look as though they are going south on him, MbS might think to take leaf from the playbook of Georgia's Mikheil Saakashvili in 2008 and Ukraine's Petro Poroshenko a couple of weeks ago (more below) and provoke an incident with Iran on his own to force Washington back him up. That would be risky, to say the least. It's unlikely that even Bolton and Pompeo are ready for war—yet. They seem to believe their own propaganda about regime change via sanctions and economic collapse and the supposedly yuge popularity of the "People's Mojahedin" (MEK), our designated replacement waiting to be parachuted into Tehran. They'll at least want to run the sanctions game a while longer to weaken Iran (and humiliate the Europeans some more) before they go for Plan B if necessary. Also, they'd need a phony pretext along the lines of Iraqi WMDs, Benghazi, Racak, and it's uncertain MbS is competent give them one all by himself.

If MbS does hazard to strike out on his own before they (Donald Kushner and Boltpeo) are ready, he may end up chewing on his tie like Saakashvili (or whatever the equivalent of that is with a thobe and gutra). At that point he would be universally seen as a liability and removed. Nothing can be ruled out of course, and if MbS thinks things are getting really shaky he just might do it, figuring he's got nothing to lose . . . but his head.

Shifting gears to the big league between the US and Russia, it's virtually certain the Trump administration will follow through on its threat to pull out of the Intermediate-Range Nuclear Forces (INF) Treaty, originally concluded between the US and the USSR in 1987. Pompeo's ultimatum to Russia to confess they were cheating and dispose of the offending 9M729 missiles was couched in a laundry list of "admit when you stopped beating your wife" charges: "These violations of the INF treaty cannot be viewed in isolation from the larger pattern of Russian lawlessness on the world stage. The list of Russia's infamous acts is long: Georgia, Ukraine, Syria, election meddling, Skripal and now the Kerch Strait, to name just a few."

Pompeo's ultimatum came literally one day after Trump signaled in a Tweet that he does not want a new arms race:

> I am certain that, at some time in the future, President Xi and I, together with President Putin of Russia, will start talking about a meaningful halt to what has become a major and uncontrollable Arms Race. The U.S. spent 716 Billion Dollars this year. Crazy!

Ha! Who does this Trump fellow think he is—the President? He doesn't want a "crazy" arms race? Too bad. He'd better check with the guys he's picked to run his administration for him. They're completely copasetic with crazy—and then some!

Perhaps we can hold out a desperate hope that Trump's intention is to replicate his tentative win on Korea, that threatening to pull out of the INF Treaty and accusing Moscow of every sin under the sun is just part of the "art of the deal," "little rocket man" versus "mentally deranged dotard," etc., with the real goal a new and better deal with Russia, maybe including China as well. But if that were so (there's no evidence for it) there's no need to trash the current agreement or even to threaten to do so. There is a lot that has changed technologically since 1987, and updates and revisions, perhaps in a protocol to the existing treaty might make sense.

That's unlikely to happen though. Instead, not only will there be a new arms race in the intermediate range—which Moscow declares its willingness to undertake, however reluctantly—the flaccidity of America's European so-called allies is again relevant. US threats to deploy intermediate-range missiles in Europe would be meaningless if European countries refused to host them because doing so would make them a target for Russian weapons. But while the European Union whines it would be better to keep the Treaty (just like it whined impotently about the JCPOA), NATO—mainly the same countries as belong to the EU—dutifully backed up the US position. There's no evidence Europeans are prepared to confront Washington with a firm *"Ohne uns!"* if the INF agreement is terminated. Servility to their Transatlantic hegemon outweighs even their instinct for self-preservation. Whereas in the 1980s the first intermediate-range deployment of US Pershing missiles sparked a huge, mainly Leftist, European peace movement—which in turn helped lead to the INF Treaty in the first place—nothing of the sort exists now. This perhaps reflects the fact that today's Left, which has little affinity with ordinary working people and is obsessed with Cultural Marxist identity politics, has become quite anti-Russian with the demise of communism.

Finally, moving to Ukraine, one would think the Trump Administration would not be particularly friendly towards a government that was complicit in the attempt to use the Christopher Steele dossier to put Hillary Clinton in the White House and then, when that failed, to cripple the Trump administration through the witch hunt known as Russiagate. While the major players were intelligence and law enforcement agencies of the United States and the United

Kingdom (not necessarily in that order), other countries were involved too. One of the prominent ones was Ukraine, whose President Petro Poroshenko feared he could be left out in the cold if Trump improved ties with Russia per his oft-stated intent– since after all, nobody in Washington could care less about Ukraine except as a club to beat Russia with. Steps were taken to avert that:

> Andrii Telizhenko, a former high-ranking Ukrainian diplomat known well in Washington circles, had vital information about collusion between elements of Ukraine's Petro Poroshenko administration and the US' Democratic National Committee (DNC) to dig up—or create—dirt on Donald Trump, but he has been chronically ignored by US investigators.
>
> Telizhenko appeared as a key source in a January 2017 Politico article by Ken Vogel titled, "Ukrainian efforts to sabotage Trump backfire: Kiev officials are scrambling to make amends with the president-elect after quietly working to boost Clinton."

Whatever concerns Poroshenko might have had that his complicity in the anti-Trump US-UK Deep State plot would hurt his standing with the administration of his target have long since been put to rest. Trump's turning his administration into a haven for Bush-era recidivists and others of the sort who have turned American policy into a shambles for the past three decades has seen to that. Hostility to Russia is and will remain a lodestar of US policy, which *ipso facto* makes Poroshenko our "friend."

That means that Poroshenko need only poke the bear to get a growl and kneejerk pledges of support will click into place. While Ukraine may not be a full member of the golden circle of countries like Israel, Saudi Arabia, and the United Kingdom that have the US on a leash, it's not too far from it either.

With his reelection prospects in March 2019 appearing dismal, Poroshenko decided to "wag the dog" with a stunt in the Kerch Strait connecting Crimea to the Russian mainland that he knew would provoke a Russian response. As *Moon of Alabama* reports:

> The Ukrainian president Petro Poroshenko sent the boats with the order not to coordinate their passage with Russian authorities. The captured sailors confirm that. He obviously wanted to provoke a violent Russian reaction.
>
> The government of Ukraine practically admitted that the mission had nefarious intent:

>> Ukraine's state security service [SBU] says that its intelligence officers were among the crew on Ukrainian naval ships seized by Russia in a standoff near Crimea.
>>
>> The SBU agency said in a statement Tuesday that the officers were fulfilling counterintelligence operations for the Ukrainian navy, in response to "psychological and physical pressure" by Russian spy services. It didn't elaborate, but demanded that Russia stop such activity.
>>
>> Russia's FSB intelligence agency said late Monday that that there were SBU officers on board the Ukrainian ships, calling that proof of a 'provocation' staged by Ukraine.

Moscow is acutely aware of the danger of an attack to disable the Kerch Strait Bridge, built quickly and at great expense (a fact that undermines the oft-repeated anti-Russian claim that Moscow is plotting to seize Mariupol,

Zaporozhye Oblast, and part of Kherson Oblast to establish a mainland route from Donbas to Crimea from the north). There have been rumors (perhaps no more than that) that Ukraine seeks to deploy a Special Atomic Demolition Munition (SADM), a small, man-portable, low-yield (circa one kiloton) device developed by NATO in the 1950s for destroying European infrastructure in advance of a Soviet invasion. Such a device would be deployable by divers if they had access to the bridge. Whether or not there's any factual basis for such concerns, Moscow takes threats to the bridge seriously. In May 2018 the Russian Investigative Committee opened a criminal case against establishment commentator Tom Rogan and his *Washington Examiner* editor for advocating blowing up of the bridge, which Russian officials called incitement to terrorism.

Right on cue, Washington is preparing new sanctions, planning to send US warships into the Black Sea in a show of support for a country to which we are not allied (amid a lunatic call from the Atlantic Council to force an entry into the Sea of Azov as well!), and conducting "extraordinary" observation flight over Ukraine. What could possibly go wrong?

The bottom line is that Poroshenko now can jerk our chain and we will respond. While this time he failed to get a nationwide, 60-day martial law declaration approved by a Rada concerned he'd use it to cancel next year's election, he did get 30 days in oblasts bordering Russia and Pridnestrovie. This will be useful not only for hampering electoral activities of his opponents in areas where he is even more unpopular than in the rest of Ukraine, it will facilitate seizures of churches and monasteries from the canonical Ukrainian Orthodox Church—a process that has already begun. He is secure in the knowledge that another provocation is always an option, in Kerch again, or the Donbas, or a grab against a major Church site like Pochaev or Pechersk.

Perhaps the saddest thing is that it has now become all so predictable. We were told that Donald Trump's administration would put America and American interests first. But instead, those acting in his name tell us through their actions: "Get in line, peasants."

"'New World Order' Wine Pompoured into a Pro–'Sovereignty' Rhetorical Bottle"

Jim Jatras | *Strategic Culture* | December 15, 2018

Secretary of State Mike Pompeo began his December 4 speech in Brussels at the German Marshall Fund with "a well-deserved tribute to America's 41st president, George Herbert Walker Bush," whom he praised as "an unyielding champion of freedom around the world." It was fitting that he did so. The heart and soul of Pompeo's remarks extolling the return of "the United States to its traditional, central leadership role in the world" were little more than a rehash of Bush the Elder's aggressive internationalism.

Pompeo (or his speechwriter) should be given credit for a masterpiece of misdirection. While the substance of his speech was a blast of stale air from the 1990s, the rhetoric was all Trumpism and national sovereignty—but only for countries obedient to Washington: "Our mission is to reassert our sovereignty, reform the liberal international order, and we want our friends to help us and to exert their sovereignty as well."

What about the sovereignty of countries the US doesn't count as "friends"? Well, that's a different story: "Every nation—every nation—must honestly acknowledge its responsibilities to its citizens and ask if the current international order serves the good of its people as well as it could. And if not, we must ask how we can right it."

So according to Pompeo, the United States and our vassals ("we") have an obligation ("must") to fix international actors that in our infinite wisdom are not serving "the good of their people." For example, "Russia hasn't embraced Western values of freedom and international cooperation." (Why should Russia care what "we" think of its values—and why should its values be "western," anyway? Never mind! We "must" do something about it!)

This assertion constitutes not only a right but a duty of the US to dictate not only the external policies of every country on the planet but even their internal order as well if judged by all-knowing Washington to be insufficiently serving the good of their people. This means that some countries (the US and our "friends") are sovereign, but countries we deem to be failing their people are not. Even Leon Trotsky would shrink from making such a declaration.

This alone gives the lie to the claims of the Swamp-critters Trump has put in charge of his administration that the US is "only" trying to impact behavior. (As in Pompeo's "We welcomed China into the liberal order, but never policed its behavior." So now we're the police too.)

Would the Russians meet Pompeo's standard if, say, they returned Crimea to Ukraine (presumably over the strong objections of the large majority of its residents who voted to join Russia)? Of course not. Russia would still be our No. 1 enemy.

What if the Russians "admitted" to Pompeo's self-certifying accusations of violations of the INF Treaty and Chemical Weapons Convention, and then took the actions the US demands? Not good enough.

Maybe a gay parade through Red Square to show love of "Western values"? Getting warmer, but still no . . .

Admittedly, this arrogant attitude of being both the big player on the geopolitical field as well as the globocop referee (and enforcer) didn't originate with Pompeo. Let's recall how George H. W. Bush described America's mission in his 1991 State of the Union:

> What is at stake is more than one small country [i.e., Kuwait], it is a big idea—a new world order, where diverse nations are drawn together in common cause to achieve the universal aspirations of mankind: peace and security, freedom, and the rule of law. Such is a world worthy of our struggle, and worthy of our children's future. . . . The world can therefore seize this opportunity to fulfill the long-held promise of a new world order—where brutality will go unrewarded, and aggression will meet collective resistance. Yes, the United States bears a major share of leadership in this effort. Among the nations of the world, only the United States of America has had both the moral standing, and the means to back it up. We are the only nation on this earth that could assemble the forces of peace.

Notably missing is any concern about the United States itself, the security of our own borders and territory, and the welfare and prosperity of the American people. Instead, American "leadership" is needed to usher in a globalist utopia defined by Goodthink "universal aspirations of mankind: peace and security, freedom, and the rule of law."

One would think that at this point in the 21st century people would be wary of regurgitated Leninist claptrap, especially since it has dominated US policy for almost three decades. It's all here:

- Democratic centralism (which is NATO's operating principle: there's democratic debate until the US decides, after which there's centralism; US "allies" in NATO have less independence than members of the Warsaw Pact did).
- Control of mass communication and information that are closely in sync with the ruling apparatus and have about as much diversity of viewpoint as Soviet media circa 1980 (though more and more American Thought Criminals are seeing the shutdown of dissent on the internet and social media through deplatforming, shadowbanning, skewing search results, and cutting off domains and payment systems as an attack on our samizdat alternative to the official media).
- The bipartisan establishment would never admit that killing millions of people is a valid way to bring about utopia, but they have been willing to do just that in wars of choice in the Greater Middle East (including the Balkans and Afghanistan) and willing to risk far, far more deaths by pushing Russia (and China) to the brink. This is facilitated by sophisticated information control with features such as "atrocity porn" that acts as a transmission belt.

Not only is all of this Bolshevik to the core, much of it is specifically Trotskyite. That's literally true at least for the influence of the neoconservative movement as it developed originally out of the exodus of Max Schachtman and his followers, who were expelled from the official US communist party in 1928, and then went through several party name changes, finally ending up as Social Democrats USA. As Justin Raimondo of *Antiwar.com* summarizes it:

> . . . [T]here is plenty to see, first and foremost the Trotskyist DNA embedded in the neocon foreign policy prescription. . . . The Trotskyists argued that the Communist Revolution of 1917 could not and should not be contained within the borders of the Soviet Union. Today's neocons make the same argument about the need to spread the American system until the U.S. becomes a "global hegemon," as *Weekly Standard* editor Bill Kristol puts it. Trotsky argued that socialism in one country was impossible, and doomed to failure: encircled by capitalism, surrounded by enemies constantly plotting its downfall, the "workers state" would not survive if it didn't expand. The neocons are making a similar argument when it comes to liberal democracy. Confronted by an Islamic world wholly opposed to modernity, Western liberal democracy must implant itself in the Middle East by force—or else face defeat in the "war on terrorism." Expand or die is the operative principle, and the neocons brought this Trotskyist mindset with them from the left.

Very few Americans who don't themselves come from far-left and émigré fever swamps have much of an idea of any this to this very day. Starting in earnest in the 1980s under Reagan, large numbers of neocons, who had previously styled themselves Henry "Scoop" Jackson Democrats, began to enter the governing apparatus on the strength of their intellectual and academic credentials and their strong anti-Sovietism. Regarding the neocons's hostility to the USSR, originally an expression of their anti-Stalinism, "regular" Americans conservatives, whose own moral views were closer to ordinary Americans', mistook it for simple anti-communism. Little did most of them suspect that the neocons were even more devoted to world revolution than was Brezhnev's Politburo, and that to them the US was little more than a base of operations, just as the Bolsheviks had earlier viewed Russia.

The neocons' influence leveled out but did not disappear under the presidency of George H.W. Bush (1989–1993), to whose credit also had some balance from relative "realists" like Henry Kissinger, Brent Scowcroft, and James Baker. However, neocons were able to make major gains under Bill Clinton (1993–2001) in alliance with so-called "liberal internationalists" like Madeleine Albright, Strobe Talbott, Richard Holbrooke—and of course Hillary Clinton. While reflecting somewhat different priorities (notably on the mix between America as the engine of world revolution vs. the role of the United Nations), the neocons and liberal internationalists found common ground in so-called "humanitarian interventionism," notably in the Balkans. The neocons' only criticism of Clinton's actions in Bosnia and Kosovo (and later of Obama's in Libya and Syria) was not being militant enough; accordingly, the neocons (mostly outside of the Executive Branch in those years but well-represented on Capitol Hill and in think tanks) helped the liberal internationalists beat back partisan Republican and residual realist skepticism for Clinton's wars.

When the GOP again controlled the White House under George W. Bush (2001–2009), the liberal internationalists returned the favor by whipping up Democratic support for the invasion of Iraq. By that time the neocons were in virtually total control of the Republicans' foreign policy in powerful alliance with representatives of the Deep State complex centered on the Pentagon and military industries. This latter group, known as the "Vulcans," included people like Dick Cheney, Donald Rumsfeld, Colin Powell, Paul Wolfowitz, Richard Armitage, and Condoleezza Rice. Then, when the Democrats took over again under Barack Hussein Obama (2009–2017), the liberal internationalists' militancy was championed by a "triumfeminate" of Hillary Clinton, Susan Rice, and Samantha Power (known as the "genocide chick"), under whom "responsibility to protect" (R2P) became a dominant principle of US policy, again with vocal neocon support.

With Donald Trump's election, it was hoped by many of his supporters that his "America First" views and stated desire to get along with Russia and to get the US out of places like Afghanistan and Syria, as well as his criticism of NATO, signaled a sharp departure from the influence of the neocons and their liberal interventionist and Vulcan allies. Alas, that was not to be. As Pompeo's Max-Schachtman-masquerading-as-Pat-Buchanan speech shows, the neocon/Deep State lock remains on a policy that hurtles heedlessly forward towards disaster.

"Did Someone Slip Donald Trump Some Kind of Political Viagra?"

Jim Jatras | *Strategic Culture* | December 22, 2018

This has been an extraordinary week. After two years of getting rolled by the Washington establishment, it seems that President Donald Trump woke up and suddenly realized, "Hey—*I'm* the president! I have the legal authority to *do* stuff!"

- He has announced his order to withdraw US troops from Syria.
- His Defense Secretary James Mattis has resigned. There are rumors National Security Adviser John Bolton may go too. (Please take Secretary of State Mike Pompeo with you!)
- He announced a start to withdrawing from Afghanistan.
- He now says he will veto a government funding bill unless he gets $5 billion for his Wall, and as of 12:01 AM Washington time December 22 the federal government is officially under partial shutdown.

All of this should be taken with a big grain of salt. While this week's assertiveness perhaps provides further proof that Trump's impulses are right, it doesn't mean he can implement them.

The Syria withdrawal will be difficult. The entire establishment, including the otherwise pro-Trump talking heads on *Fox News*, are dead set against him—except for Tucker Carlson and Laura Ingraham.

Senator Lindsey Graham is demanding hearings on how to block the Syria pullout. Congress hardly ever quibbles with a president's putting troops into a country, where the Legislative Branch has legitimate Constitutional power. But if a president under his absolute command authority wants to pull them out—even someplace where they're deployed illegally, as in Syria—*well hold on just a minute!*

We are being told our getting out of Syria and Afghanistan will be a huge "gift" to Russia and Iran. Worse, it is being compared to Barack Obama's "premature" withdrawal from Iraq (falsely pointed to as the cause of the rise of ISIS) and will set the stage for "chaos." By that standard, we can never leave anywhere.

This will be a critical time for the Trump presidency. (And if God is *really* on his side, he soon might get another Supreme Court pick.) If he can get the machinery of the Executive Branch to implement his decision to withdraw from Syria, and if he can pick a replacement to General Mattis who actually agrees with Trump's views, we might start getting the America First policy Trump ran on in 2016.

Mattis himself said in his resignation letter, "Because you have the right to have a Secretary of Defense whose views are better aligned with yours on these [i.e., support for so-called "allies"] and other subjects, I believe it is right for me to step down from my position."

Right on, Mad Dog! In fact Trump should have had someone "better aligned" with him in that capacity from the get-go. It is now imperative that he picks someone who agrees with his core positions, starting with withdrawal from Syria and Afghanistan, and reducing confrontation with Russia.

Former Defense Secretary Chuck Hagel complains that "our government is not a one-man show." Well, the "government" isn't, but the Executive Branch is. Article II, Section 1: "The executive Power shall be vested in a President of the United States of America." Him. The President. Nobody else. Period.

Already the drumbeat to saddle Trump with another Swamp critter at the Pentagon is starting: "Several possible replacements for Mattis this week trashed the president's decision to pull out of Syria. Retired Gen. Jack Keane called the move a "strategic mistake" on Twitter. Republican Sens. Lindsey O. Graham (R-S.C.) and Tom Cotton (R-Ark.) signed a letter demanding Trump reconsider the decision and warning that the withdrawal "bolsters Iran and

Russia." If Trump even considers any of the above as Mattis's replacement, he'll be in worse shape than he has been for the past two years.

On the other hand, if Trump does pick someone who agrees with him about Syria and Afghanistan, never mind getting along with Russia, can he get that person confirmed by the Senate? One possibility would be to nominate someone like Acting White House Chief of Staff Mick Mulvaney specifically to run the Pentagon bureaucracy and get control of costs, while explicitly deferring operational decisions to the Commander in Chief in consultation with the Service Chiefs.

Right now on Syria Trump is facing pushback from virtually the whole Deep State establishment, Republicans and Democrats alike, as well as the media from *Fox News*, to *NPR*, to *MSNBC*. Terror has again gripped the establishment that the Trump who was elected president in 2016 might actually start implementing what he promised. It is imperative that he pick someone for the Pentagon (and frankly, clear out the rest of his national security team) and appoint people he can trust and whose views comport with his own. Just lopping off a few heads won't suffice—he needs a full house-cleaning.

In the meantime in Syria, watch for another "Assad poison gas attack against his own people." The last time Trump said we'd be leaving Syria "very soon" was on March 29 of this year. Barely a week later, on April 7, came a supposed chemical incident in Douma, immediately hyped as a government attack on civilians but soon apparent as likely staged. Trump, though, dutifully took the bait, tweeting that Assad was an "animal." Putin, Russia, and Iran were "responsible" for "many dead, including women and children, in mindless CHEMICAL attack"—"Big price to pay." He then for the second time launched cruise missiles against Syrian targets. A confrontation loomed in the eastern Med that could to have led to war with Russia. Now, in light of Trump's restated determination to get out, is MI6 already ginning up their White Helmet assets for a repeat?

Trump's claim that the US has completed its only mission, to defeat ISIS, is being compared to George W. Bush's "Mission Accomplished" banner following defeat of Iraq's army and the beginning of the occupation (and, as it turned out, the beginning of the real war). But if it helps get us out, who cares if Trump wants to take credit? Whatever his terrible, horrible, no good, very bad national security team told him, the US presence in Syria was never about ISIS. We are there as Uncle Sam's Rent-an-Army for the Israelis and Saudis to block Iranian influence and especially an overland route between Syria and Iran (the so-called "Shiite land bridge" to the Mediterranean).

For US forces the war against ISIS was always a sideshow, mainly carried on by the Syrians and Russians and proportioned about like the war against the Wehrmacht: about 20% "us," about 80% "them." The remaining pocket ISIS has on the Syria-Iraq border has been deliberately left alone, to keep handy as a lever to force Assad out in a settlement (which is not going to happen). Thus the claim an American pullout will lead to an ISIS "resurgence" is absurd. With US forces ceasing to play dog in the manger, the Syrians, Russians, Iranians, and Iraqis will kill them. All of them.

If Trump is able to follow through with the pullout, will the Syrian war wind down? It needs to be kept in mind that the whole conflict has been because we (the US, plus Israel, Saudi Arabia, Qatar, Turkey, UAE, the United Kingdom, etc.) are the aggressors. We sought to use al-Qaeda and other jihadis to effect regime change via the tried and true method. It failed.

Regarding Trump's critics' claim that he is turning over Syria to the Russians and Iranians, Assad is nobody's puppet. He can be allied with a Shiite theocracy but not controlled by it; Iran, likewise, can also have mutually beneficial ties with an ideologically dissimilar country, like it does with Christian Armenia. The Russians will stay and expand their presence but unlike our presence in many countries—which seemingly never ends, for example in Germany, Japan, and Korea, not to mention Kosovo—they'll be there only as long and to the extent the Syrians want them. (Compare our eternal occupations with the Soviets' politely leaving Egypt when Anwar Sadat asked them, or leaving Somalia when Siad Barre wanted them out. Instead of leaving, why didn't Moscow just do a "Diem" on them?) It seems that American policymakers have gotten so far down the wormhole of their paranoid fantasies about the rest of the world—and it can't be over-emphasized, concerning areas where the US has *no actual national interests*—that we no longer recognize classic statecraft when practiced by other powers defending genuine national interests (which of course are legitimate only to the extent we say so).

What happens over the next few days on funding for the Border Wall—which is fully within the power of Majority Leader Mitch McConnell to deliver—and over the next few weeks over Syria and Afghanistan may be decisive for the balance of the Trump presidency. If he can prevail, and if he finally starts assembling an America First national security team beginning with a good Pentagon chief, he still has a chance to deliver on his 2016 promises.

Anyway, if this week's developments are the result of someone putting something into Donald's morning Egg McMuffin, America and the world owe him (or her) a vote of thanks. Let's see more of the wrecking ball we Deplorables voted for!

Woking the World

"Lewd for Thought"

Jim Jatras | *Chronicles* | October 11, 2016

In view of the ongoing partisan MSM feeding frenzy over Donald Trump's hot microphone comments about women, the question is raised over what constitutes impermissibly lewd thoughts, words, and actions. The following is a helpful guide:

   1. LEWD. This means the way virtually all men sometimes think about women, with varying degrees of frequency; the verbal expression of such thoughts by some but far from all men, usually in circumstances of privacy; or acting on such thoughts by a distinct minority of men who assume, often correctly, that they can get away with it because of their wealth, fame, social standing, or good looks. Lewdness, so defined, is inherently threatening and demeaning to women, frail flowers that they are, whom society must rigorously defend against men's lewd thoughts, words, and actions pending final eradication of testosterone.

   2. NOT LEWD: ACCEPTABLE. This means that because women are rough and tough and can do anything a man can do except way better, they may, to varying degrees, think about, talk about, or act towards men in a manner analogous to men's lewdness towards women. This is entirely acceptable. However, if men respond positively to women's non-lewdness, so defined, that may constitute lewdness on their part depending how women feel about such response.

   3. NOT LEWD: VIRTUOUS AND PRAISEWORTHY. This means any thoughts, words, or actions formerly considered immoral and falling under any category of the designation LGBTQILSMFT [*watch this space for future additions*] or certain artistic genres (e.g., hip hop). Such virtuous, praiseworthy non-lewdness, so defined, must be celebrated in parades, awards, and government-sponsored expression. Criticism of or disrespect for—or even insufficient enthusiasm for—this category of non-lewdness constitutes hate speech and is grounds for social ostracism, economic ruination, and, increasingly, legal sanction.

"The West's Quest to 'Save the World Through Degeneracy'"

Jim Jatras | *Strategic Culture* | September 15, 2017

Analysts of world affairs tend to fall into certain traps concerning the motivations and behavior of political actors. We consistently look at politicians' electoral support, states' access to resources, lines of offense or defense, traditional alliances and enmities, the profits of empowered interests, geography, demography, and many other objective factors.

But the subjective ideological, spiritual, and moral motivations that loom high in the self-conscious actions of movers and shakers are seldom given the attention they deserve. That is, what do the presidents, government ministers, military officers, bureaucrats, oligarchs, and NGO gurus themselves *think* they are doing when they advocate for or against a certain set of policies?

Sometimes the answers seem to make no sense at all in terms of the usual analyses of objective "interests." The easiest resolution to such puzzles is usually found in Occam's razor: just follow the money. Somebody, somewhere, is making a buck. Usually lots of bucks.

But even the money trail fails to answer some questions. For example, as part of their foreign policies why are western (North American and western European) governments, NGOs, etc., so insistent on demanding action on a "progressive" program to advance "gender" issues such as same-sex "marriage," "transgenderism," and so forth? After all, if Americans want to pump little kids full of "gender-reassignment" hormones, or if the citizens of (big surprise) California wish to subject kindergarten children to an abomination like "drag queen story hour," that would be bad enough. Certainly in the fullness of time there will be enough millstones and depths of the sea, figuratively speaking, to give the culpable their just deserts. (By the way, can we please dispense with the notion that LGBTQI-etc. "recruitment" of children is just a paranoid fantasy of "haters"? If "drag queen story hour" isn't recruitment into, first, a mindset, and then in at least some cases, participation—then what is it? America can be proud we don't have evil laws like they have in Russia aimed at protecting children from "propaganda of non-traditional sexual relationships." The brutes!)

The West's demand for new, post-Christian social and moral values is a particular danger to some of the countries that emerged from communism in the 1990s. Paradoxically, given Marxism-Leninism's claim to be the godless science of social progress, post-communist Central and Eastern Europe is generally far more traditional and—dare we say it?—Christian, if not particularly churchgoing, in its social conscience compared to the West. Perhaps that is because communist materialism was such a failure compared to consumerist materialism that the West provided much more fertile ground for transforming an ideology of class struggle into a struggle against the spiritual and moral values upon which society is rooted. The paradox is that today the roots of what was once quaintly known as Christendom are still relatively stronger in the East—and thus must be destroyed.

Hence the threats from western governments to some countries—Poland, Hungary, Russia, Belarus, Serbia, Ukraine, Georgia, etc.—to improve their "human rights" performance on "gender issues." Hold a gay parade! Recognize same-sex unions! Pretend that boys can turn into girls and vice versa! Or else—sanctions! (Similar pressures are put on majority-Christian countries in sub-Saharan Africa. Islamic countries are oddly immune from criticism.)

As it happens, there is a decades-old blueprint for imperialism based on sexual degeneracy. It is found in an unlikely place, the novel *A Confederacy of Dunces* by John Kennedy Toole. Written in 1963 but not published until 1980, the book takes its title from the epigram of Jonathan Swift's essay, *Thoughts on Various Subjects, Moral and Diverting*: "When a true genius appears in the world, you may know him by this sign, that the dunces are all in confederacy against him."

In this case, the genius in question is Toole's fictional protagonist, the brilliant but lazy Ignatius J. Reilly (a disciple of the late-Roman philosopher Boethius), who encounters on the streets of his native New Orleans a member of what today would be called a sexual minority. The chance meeting sparks in Reilly a bold, revolutionary burst of insight that fits so well into our contemporary world that it's hard to believe it's a depiction from over half a century ago. There's no proof that this passage was in fact the inspiration for our present-day fanatics of imperialist gender revolution, but the stunning parallels, including a call for regime change in "reactionary countries," speak for themselves:

> As I was wearing the soles of my desert boots down to a mere sliver of crepe rubber on the old flagstone banquettes of the French Quarter in my fevered attempt to wrest a living from an unthinking and uncaring society, I was hailed by a cherished old acquaintance (deviate). After a few minutes of conversation in which I established most easily my moral superiority over this degenerate, I found myself pondering once more the crises of our times. My mentality, uncontrollable and wanton as always, whispered to me a scheme so magnificent and daring that I shrank from the very thought of what I was hearing. "Stop!" I cried imploringly to my godlike mind. "This is madness." But still I listened to the counsel of my brain. It was offering me the opportunity to Save the World Through Degeneracy. There on the worn stones of the Quarter I enlisted the aid of this wilted flower of a human in gathering his associates in foppery together behind a banner of brotherhood.
>
> Our first step will be to elect one of their number to some very high office—the presidency, if Fortuna spins us kindly. Then they will infiltrate the military. As soldiers, they will all be so continually busy in fraternizing with one another, tailoring their uniforms to fit like sausage skins, inventing new and varied battle dress, giving cocktail parties, etc., that they will never have time for battle. The one whom we finally make Chief of Staff will want only to attend to his fashionable wardrobe, a wardrobe which, alternately, will permit him to be either Chief of Staff or debutante, as the desire strikes him. In seeing the success of their unified fellows here, perverts around the world will also band together to capture the military in their respective countries. In those reactionary countries in which the deviates seem to be having some trouble in gaining control, we will send aid to them as rebels to help them in toppling their governments. When we have at last overthrown all existing governments, the world will enjoy not war but global orgies conducted with the utmost protocol and the most truly international spirit, for these people do transcend simple national differences. Their minds are on one goal; they are truly united; they think as one.
>
> None of the pederasts in power, of course, will be practical enough to know about such devices as bombs; these nuclear weapons would lie rotting in their vaults somewhere. From time to time the Chief of Staff, the President, and so on, dressed in sequins and feathers, will entertain the leaders, i.e., the perverts, of all the other countries at balls and parties. Quarrels of any sort could easily be straightened out in the men's room of the redecorated United Nations. Ballets and Broadway musicals and entertainments of that sort will flourish everywhere and will probably make the common folk happier than did the grim, hostile, fascistic pronouncements of their former leaders.
>
> Almost everyone else has had an opportunity to run the world. I cannot see why these people should not be given their chance. They

have certainly been the underdog long enough. Their movement into power will be, in a sense, only a part of the global movement toward opportunity, justice, and equality for all; (For example, can you name one good, practicing transvestite in the Senate? No! These people have been without representation long enough. Their plight is a national, a global disgrace.)

Degeneracy, rather than signaling the downfall of a society, as it once did, will now signal peace for a troubled world. We must have new solutions to new problems.

"The Less We Believe Them about Las Vegas, the More They Want Our Guns"

Jim Jatras | *Strategic Culture* | October 13, 2017

Once again, there has been a mass shooting in the United States and the usual script is in play. America's 'gun culture' is to blame! Before the blood was dry gun control advocates had trotted out their standard list of remedial measures, none of which would have prevented what had just taken place.

Since the Las Vegas massacre we have been regaled about evil guns by factually ignorant buffoons like Bill Maher, Colin Jost, Michael Che, Jimmy Kimmel, Stephen Colbert, Trevor Noah, and John Oliver—the last two not even Americans. Anyone who disagrees is just wrong and callous about the loss of innocent life. We now import foreigners to insult us and our institutions and pay them outrageous salaries to do it.

Las Vegas was a bit different from previous mass shooting in at least two glaring respects. First, the inability of law enforcement to discover a motive remains the biggest mystery. Admittedly, these same authorities in the US— and even worse in Europe—typically find themselves scratching their collective head in puzzlement after a murderer shouting "Allahu Akbar" kills a bunch of people. (*What did he mean by that? Maybe that's Arabic for "Merry Christmas"! We're still trying to figure out why he did it, but we're sure it had nothing to do with Islam. And anyone who says it did is a racist.*) At this point, the actions of the person identified as the Las Vegas killer (whose name will not be mentioned here to deny whatever immortality he may have sought) are attributed to mental instability. That's not good enough. Subjectively, even maniacs *think* they are doing something. Even a total lunatic who believes he is, say, fighting Martians or chopping potatoes, *intends* that outcome. But here, supposedly, someone stockpiles weapons for months, meticulously plans a murderous onslaught—and maybe had contingencies for attacks else- where—and there's not a hint of what he thought he was up to. That's simply not plausible. (Repeated claims by Daesh that the Las Vegas killer was one of their "soldiers" have not yet been substantiated but authorities were lightning- quick to dismiss the possibility. Meanwhile, despite a total lack of evidence, multiple "RussiaGate" investigations of the Trump Administration roll on and on. *Let's not be hasty, some connection to the Kremlin might eventually turn up . . .*)

Second, there's the money. The individual in question, as confirmed by his girlfriend as well as by his brother and other family members, was quite rich. Supposedly his initial wealth was made via savvy real estate deals (possible) but later was sustained by being really, really good at video poker at Las Vegas casinos, where he was a welcome regular "comped" by the House with food, drinks, hotel rooms, and other goodies. That's not just implausible, it's virtually impossible. As Ann Coulter points out, the fact that he was "was treated like royalty by the casinos . . . means he was losing. . . Anyone who plays video poker over an extended period of time will absolutely, 100 percent, by basic logic, end up a net loser." If anyone would know this, it's police in Los Vegas, where casino operators are pillars of the community and gambling is the major industry. It's clear to anyone with half a brain that the killer was laundering money—from somewhere yet to be disclosed. In our age of digital financial surveillance, casinos are among the last places someone can anonymously churn large amounts of unsourced cash, no questions asked. Maybe the police and FBI haven't figured out where the money was coming from, or maybe they have and are protecting someone.

In any case, the inability to get a straight answer to the questions, or even to ascertain simple facts like whether a hotel security guard was shot before or after the mass killing began, or when the first call was made to police, feeds public distrust and speculation as to what the hell is really is going on. That is turn prompts establishment gatekeepers like Snopes to denounce as "conspiracy theorists" (mainly of the "far right" variety, because the existence of a far left is itself a conspiracy theory) folks trying to make sense of the nonsense we're being force-fed.

At least Las Vegas has shined a light on one deception that has long been standard in the American media: the notion—no doubt believed by many outside the US—that Americans routinely run around with machine-guns shooting each other. This impression is fed by false claims of gun-control advocates that "assault rifles"—semiautomatic guns (where one trigger-pull equals one round fired)—are "weapons of war." What makes them not like contemporary weapons of war is that they are not fully automatic (hold the trigger down for multiple, rapid rounds), which is why gun control advocates abuse the trick designation "military *style*"—they look scarier than semi-automatic hunting rifles because of cosmetic features like pistol grips and folding stocks. Fully automatic weapons (i.e., machine guns) have been virtually impossible acquire legally in the US for decades. The evident use in Las Vegas of a so-called "bump stock" to allow a semiautomatic to fire in a manner similar to a machine gun has forced even our fake news outlets to note the distinction. It's a rare breakout of actual facts.

Ironically, when the Second Amendment to the US Constitution, which protects Americans' fundamental right to keep and bear arms, was adopted, ordinary civilian guns really *were* equal to weapons of war. In fact, they were sometimes better. Think of how the standard British "Brown Bess" smoothbore was outclassed by the far more accurate Pennsylvania Rifle—perfect for picking off Redcoat officers at long range.

Advocates in gun control in America are always saying they just want "common-sense gun control" laws, like "closing the gun show loophole," having stricter background checks, limiting the size of magazines, restricting the number of weapons or amount of ammunition someone can buy, and other seemingly innocuous measures. Each is a fraud. For example, closing the so-called gun show loophole would be basically a ban on private transfers from one citizen to another—such as a man selling, or giving, a pistol or rifle to his cousin—without all the reporting and red tape federally licensed arms dealers must deal with. This is despite the fact that none the notable killings that supposedly justify more controls was carried out with a weapon from such a sale or would have been prevented if the demanded reform had been in place.

Meanwhile, the real American slaughter continues in cities where gun laws are as strict as those in any country in Europe, and it is virtually impossible for an honest citizen to acquire and carry a legal weapon. For example, last month Chicago reached its 500th homicide so far this year, and by New Year's Day 2018 is on track to rack up a total exceeding *ten times* that of the Las Vegas massacre. What's the solution? Evidently to infringe on the constitutional rights of honest, peaceful, law-abiding citizens who are armed and increasingly distrustful of what they are being told by their supposed betters.

"Lewd for Thought: America Is Groping Towards Peak Stupidity"

Jim Jatras | *Strategic Culture* | November 25, 2017

We've long known that *Whom the gods would destroy they first make mad.* Now it appears that the gods make those marked for destruction really stupid, too.

I don't know how many people outside the United States have noticed the roaring frenzy of sexual abuse allegations that has now become a centerpiece of American public life. Each news roundup leads with the latest accusations. Every day a new alleged miscreant pops into view. It's a wonder that London bookmakers haven't yet started taking bets on who's going to be next.

The allegations range from forcible rape to lewd comments to kissing "without consent," and everything in between. (How many first kisses take place *with* consent? "You may kiss me now." You want that in writing? Witnessed and notarized?) The most common alleged offense seems to be groping.

Rarely are distinctions made between actions that constitute serious crimes that ought to be punished accordingly as opposed to what until recently was considered ordinary male initiative. For example, the charge that decades ago Alabama Senate candidate Roy Moore sexually fondled a 14-year-old girl (criminal and disqualifying, *if true*) is conflated with having taken a 17-year-old on a date (with her mother's permission and without any allegation of sexual contact) or maybe having signed a high school yearbook.

The undifferentiated mixing of felonious and—dare I say it?—normal behaviors amid a welter of allegations shouldn't be surprising when we consider that the real target isn't so much sexual assault or misconduct as commonly understood but masculinity itself. *Lean in! Smash the Patriarchy!* (Does anyone have any idea what a functioning society would look like once any remnant of patriarchy is rooted out? Has there ever been an example of one, aside from some marginal little group starving in a jungle or desert somewhere?)

Never mind that for centuries our society held up a concept of the gentleman who was obligated to respect, protect, and defer to women, reinforced by customary sex roles and Christian moral restraints. *But women don't need that kind of oppression! A woman needs a man like a fish needs a bicycle!* We are then shocked that the social breakdown of moral traditions leaves women face to face with the savages among us.

Stupidity reigns. Reflecting the demented certainty that "there's no difference" between predatory older men preying on younger females and the much rarer cases where the sexes are reversed, judges have made a point of handing down draconian sentences to women involved with teenage boys. (Mysteriously, the youngsters themselves usually don't appear to be particularly upset.) In Nevada, a 34-year-old woman was convicted of lewdness with a minor for kissing a 13-year-old boy and putting his hand on her breast—and was given a *life sentence*. She'd have gotten off lighter if she had killed the kid. (Meanwhile, on the homosexual side of the ledger, the "twink" culture is alive and well.)

Last year, in view of the media feeding frenzy over Donald Trump's hot microphone comments about women's allowing rich and famous men to take sexual liberties, it became clear that there was little clarity about what does or doesn't constitute impermissibly lewd thoughts, words, and actions. The following helpful guide is even more applicable today:

1. LEWD. This means the way virtually all men sometimes think about women, with varying degrees of frequency; the verbal expression of such thoughts by some but far from all men, usually in circumstances of privacy; or acting on such thoughts by a distinct minority of men who assume, often correctly, that they can get away with it because of their wealth, fame, social standing, or good looks. Lewdness, so defined, is inherently threatening and demeaning to women, frail flowers that they are, whom society must rigorously defend against men's lewd thoughts, words, and actions pending final eradication of testosterone.

2. NOT LEWD: ACCEPTABLE. This means that because women are rough and tough and can do anything a man can do except way better, they may, to varying degrees, think about, talk about, or act towards men in a manner analogous to men's lewdness towards women. This is entirely acceptable. However, if men respond positively to women's non-lewdness, so defined, that may constitute lewdness on their part depending how women feel about such response.

3. NOT LEWD: VIRTUOUS AND PRAISEWORTHY. This means any thoughts, words, or actions formerly considered immoral and falling under any category of the designation LGBTQILSMFT [*watch this space for future additions*] or certain artistic genres (e.g., hip hop). Such virtuous, praiseworthy non-lewdness, so defined, must be celebrated in parades, awards, and government-sponsored expression. Criticism of or disrespect for—or even insufficient enthusiasm for—this category of non-lewdness constitutes hate speech and is grounds for social ostracism, economic ruination, and, increasingly, legal sanction. [And in the international arena is it justification for aggression against retrograde countries.]

"'He Beareth Not the Sword in Vain'"

Jim Jatras | *Strategic Culture* | August 24, 2018

"Nothing wrong with shooting as long as the right people get shot."
—San Francisco Police Inspector *"Dirty Harry"* Callahan, played by Clint Eastwood (Magnum Force, *1973*)

The modern world is remarkably blasé and hypocritical when is comes to who gets killed, whether by shooting, by sword, or by other means. This is especially true of the *bien pensants* of the globalist order, who from their perch high atop their moral Mount Olympus are more than happy to set the *lumpen* straight on when and how killing is good or bad.

For example, government, media, and think tank mouthpieces of the western establishment are quick to scream that the designated Hitler-of-the-month–Milosevic, Hussein, Kaddafi, Assad–is "killing his own people" and that it's a humanitarian duty for the so-called "international community" to engaging in killing to put a stop to it. On the other hand, cuddly Saudi "reformer" Mohammad bin Salman kills lots and lots of innocent civilians in Yemen–though admittedly, not his "own" people–with lavish help from the same governments that in other contexts favor humanitarian killing. (With friends like Mohammad, who needs Yemenis?)

Or consider abortion. Every right-thinking sophisticate knows that innocent unborn children are expendable and that it is a mark of a country's respect for women's rights to dismiss their lives as worthless (predictably, this video was pulled down). (Also worthless are some children with medical issues like little Alfie Evans, condemned to death by the enlightened conscience of British medicine and jurisprudence; or elderly and others now considered candidates for euthanasia.) That's why once-Catholic Ireland felt the need in a recent referendum to modify protective language in its constitution so they could be like the rest of the chic free-thinking countries in the European Union, which at the moment still excludes Poland and Malta. (Most of Latin America, including perpetual American *bêtes noires* Venezuela and Nicaragua, has strongly protective laws. An exception is Cuba, which approximates the US policy of abortion at any time in pregnancy for any or no reason.)

But when it comes to killing, the hot topic these days is capital punishment in view of Pope Francis' recent pronouncement that seemed to change his confession's teaching on the subject. The previous Catechism of the Catholic Church (Paragraph 2267) promulgated by Pope John Paul II held that "traditional teaching of the church does not does not exclude recourse to the death penalty, if this is the only possible way of effectively defending human lives against the unjust aggressor." That section now has been modified to read:

> Recourse to the death penalty on the part of legitimate authority, following a fair trial, was long considered an appropriate response to the gravity of certain crimes and an acceptable, albeit extreme, means of safeguarding the common good.
>
> Today, however, there is an increasing awareness that the dignity of the person is not lost even after the commission of very serious crimes. In addition, a new understanding has emerged of the significance of penal sanctions imposed by the state.
>
> Lastly, more effective systems of detention have been developed, which ensure the due protection of citizens but, at the same time, do not definitively deprive the guilty of the possibility of redemption.
>
> Consequently, the Church teaches, in the light of the Gospel, that 'the death penalty is inadmissible because it is an attack on the inviolability and dignity of the person', and she works with determination for its abolition worldwide.

One could argue with the rationale for the change. Few who affirm the moral acceptability of capital punishment would suggest that that the "dignity of the person is lost" because of "the commission of very serious crimes." Quite the contrary, some would argue, on very high authority indeed, that it is precisely *because* of human dignity with its divine origin that death is the proper consequence of murder: "Whoso sheddeth man's blood, by man shall his blood be shed: for in the image of God made he man." (Genesis 9:6) As Aaron Wolf of *Chronicles* magazine observes: "Capital punishment is necessary to preserve the dignity of man, the honor (marred by sin yet still present) bestowed upon man which distinguishes him from the gibbon and the orangutan and the shrimp and the house cat. Certain crimes against God's image-bearers have mortal consequences."

Lest one suppose this is a standard laid down only for ancient Israel (though, given to Noah, it preceded the Old Covenant and applied to all postdeluvian humanity), note that the Apostle Paul laid out the godly duty of secular rulers to enact justice by violent means: "For rulers are not a terror to good works, but to the evil. . . . if thou do that which is evil, be afraid; for he beareth not the sword in vain: for he is the minister of God, a revenger to execute wrath upon him that doeth evil." (Romans 13:3–4)

There's also a sharp debate on the consequences of the Pope's making the change itself and whether it means other seemingly long-settled teachings are up for redefinition, including on matters like homosexuality. As Rod Dreher of *The American Conservative* comments:

> So, today, there is no "if" about it: Pope Francis has said flat-out that the death penalty is immoral, and has ordered the Catechism to be written to reflect this new teaching. . . . It seems to me that the Pope has crossed a bright line. He is denying, for the first time in nearly two millennia of Catholic teaching, and in direct contradiction to the Fathers of the Church, that the state has the right to impose capital punishment. That's a meaningful difference from saying that the state has that right, but shouldn't use it.
>
> Even if you disfavor the death penalty, understand what this means: this Pope has claimed forthrightly that the Catholic Church taught error, but now, at long last, he has set the Church straight. [. . .]
>
> Catholic friends keep saying to me how much they hope that the Catholic Church and the Orthodox Churches can end our thousand-year schism, and reunite. I would love for that to happen myself, but I keep telling them that even if the Orthodox set aside the historical prejudices that stand in the way, there is no way that Orthodoxy is going to take the chance of reunion with the Latin church that is so unstable, liturgically and doctrinally.

However, there are those in the Orthodox Church (as well as in mainstream Protestant denominations, most of which have long supported abolition of capital punishment, along with various non-Christian groups) who are thrilled with Francis' change and who call for following his lead. Notable is Jim Forest, a principled and passionate advocate for the unborn, the disabled, and the imprisoned, as well as a committed opponent of war as international secretary of the Orthodox Peace Fellowship, writing recently in support of the new Roman Catholic position and advocating its adoption by Orthodoxy ("POPE FRANCIS'S CHALLENGE TO ALL CHRISTIANS: END THE DEATH PEN-ALTY").

There are at least three things wrong with Forest's article:

First, its placement in Public Orthodoxy, the publication of the "Ortho-dox Christian Studies Center" of Fordham University is problematic. Along with The Wheel and Orthodoxy in Dialogue, Public Orthodoxy seems little more than a vehicle for revisionist academics to stir ecclesial discord and advocate the importation into Orthodoxy of moral pathologies that have wrought havoc among the western confessions and in society at large. (See "A Two-Pronged Attack on Orthodoxy and Russia.") It's a questionable venue for someone of Forest's quality.

Second, Forest cites the views of a number of early Christian authorities in a manner that implies they said what they did not say. St. Hippolytus of Rome, St. Basil the Great, St. John of Kronstadt, and Athenagoras of Athens– these, like many others throughout the ages, have spoken in favor of mercy, of inducing repentance by the wrongdoer, and of the terrible gravity of taking human life under any circumstances, even accidentally or in self-defense. That attitude is reflected in historic Orthodoxy's hesitance to inflict death on criminals (as compared to Western Europe, where in some countries mere thieves were hanged until the 19th century, notably in England). In Byzantium this meant mitigating the many capital offenses in Roman law and even sparing the lives of those guilty of crimes of state, substituting corporal mutilation as a more humane and Christian alternative ("And if thy right eye offend thee, pluck it out, and . . . if thy right hand offend thee, cut it off, . . . for it is profitable for thee that one of thy members should perish, and not that thy whole body should be cast into hell." Matthew 5:29–30). Similarly, until the Bolshevik orgy of slaughter (of course, that wasn't capital punishment but the "supreme measure" of "social prophylaxis"!) Imperial Russia made sparing use of the death penalty even for murder, as illustrated in Dostoyevsky's *Crime and Punishment* by Rodion Raskolnikov's eight-year sentence for a double murder–something that would be unheard of in Europe or America. But mercy and forbearance are quite different from claiming that the death penalty is wrong in and of itself and impermissible in all circumstances, which, as Forest must be aware, no Ecumenical or Regional Synod has ever decreed, nor (to this writer's knowledge) has any Church Father ever taught. Certainly one may personally adhere to an abolitionist view just as one can be an absolute pacifist, but it cannot be claimed that is the Church's position.

Third, *misleading references to two important historical episodes refute Forest's own argument.* Forest cites the action of St. Nicholas of Myra in rushing to the defense of three men condemned to be beheaded by an official, Eustathios, where the holy hierarch "took the sword from the executioner's hands and threw it to the ground, then ordered that the condemned men be freed," forcing Eustathios's repentance. He also describes how the fierce convert from paganism, Saint Prince Vladimir, Enlightener of Rus', became so meek a Christian that he ceased putting anyone to death.

With respect to St. Nicholas, Forest omits (no doubt inadvertently, since he mentions it elsewhere) one key fact: that the three men were *innocent*. Hence, not only were they spared death by the saint's intervention but *all punishment*. This account is hardly a basis for arguing that those guilty of terrible crimes should never be executed.

The reference to Saint Prince Vladimir is even more inapt, and Forest has neglected to give us the rest of the story. As related in *The Primary Chronicle (or Tale of Bygone Years, Повесть временных лет):*

> While Vladimir was thus dwelling in the fear of God, the number of bandits increased, and the bishops, calling to his attention the multi-plication of robbers, inquired why he did not punish them. The Prince answered that he feared the sin entailed. They replied that he was appointed of God for the chastisement of malefaction and for the practice of mercy toward the righteous, so that it was entirely fitting for him to punish a robber condignly, but only after due process of

law. Vladimir accordingly abolished *wergild* and set out to punish the brigands.

Plainly, the very priests sent from Constantinople to nurture the sprouts of the Christian faith in Vladimir's newly planted land told him in no uncertain terms that the sword on his hip wasn't just a fashion statement. It was Vladimir's job as prince, they admonished him, to go out and use deadly force as justly as he could within the limits of human fallibility, whatever the hazards to his own soul. (The reference to wergild is significant. Even Vladimir-baptized-Basil seemed to prefer the Germanic custom of paying restitution for harm, including even taking a life; he was counseled otherwise by Christian catechists who knew their Saint Paul.)

Contra Forest, and with due respect to Pope Francis, the historic, scriptural, patristic teaching that balances clemency with justice was summarized by the Moscow Patriarchate in its *Bases of the Social Concept of the Russian Orthodox Church*: "IX. Crime, punishment, reformation"—as posted on Forest's website, where it is inaccurately claimed that "the death penalty is condemned":

> The death penalty as a special punishment was recognised in the Old Testament. There are no indications to the need to abolish it in the New Testament or in the Tradition or in the historical legacy of the Orthodox Church either. At the same time, the Church has often assumed the duty of interceding before the secular authority for those condemned to death, asking it show mercy for them and commute their punishment. Moreover, under Christian moral influence, the negative attitude to the death penalty has been cultivated in people's consciousness. Thus, in the period from the mid-18th century to the 1905 Revolution in Russia, it was applied on very rare occasions. For the Orthodox church consciousness, the life of a person does not end with his bodily death, therefore the Church continues her care for those condemned to capital punishment.
>
> The abolition of death penalty would give more opportunities for pastoral work with those who have stumbled and for the latter to repent. It is also evident that punishment by death cannot be reformatory; it also makes misjudgement irreparable and provokes ambiguous feelings among people. Today many states have either abolished the death penalty by law or stopped practicing it. Keeping in mind that mercy toward a fallen man is always more preferable than revenge, the Church welcomes these steps by state authorities. At the same time, she believes that the decision to abolish or not to apply death penalty should be made by society freely, considering the rate of crime and the state of law-enforcement and judiciary, and even more so, the need to protect the life of its well-intentioned members.

It should be noted that while the Russian Federation has observed a moratorium on capital punishment since 1996, the law still remains on the books. If that changes in the future, either by abolishing the death penalty entirely or by reinstating its use, it should be, as the *Social Concept* states, a matter to be determined by society freely in light of all the issues involved put into proper context. The same is true for other countries, whether or not they are Orthodox or even Christian.

"The Sexual Subversion of Ukraine"

Jim Jatras | *Strategic Culture* | December 29, 2018

In the aftershock of US President Donald Trump's bombshell decision to pull American troops out of Syria and to draw down US forces in Afghanistan, plus the resignation of Defense Secretary James Mattis and Brett McGurk, the Special Envoy to the anti-ISIS Coalition [*sic*: never mind who created ISIS in the first place . . .], we are already seeing progress. The Syrian flag has been raised over Manbij as the Kurds scramble for protection from Damascus against threatening Turkish forces.

We're not out of the woods yet though. Given the "orgy of shrieking and caterwauling," "the horrifying collective scream" emanating from Washington, a pushback from the Deep State and the bipartisan Washington establishment is inevitable and possibly imminent. A false flag chemical attack blamed on the Syrian government but perpetrated by the jihadists (and likely cooked up with assistance from the British MI6) remains a looming danger. Also unpredictable is the next move by Israel, whose jets operating in Lebanese airspace struck targets near Damascus following Trump's withdrawal order. In turn, Syria and Russia responded by considering extension of air protection to Lebanon and declaring that future Israeli strikes on Syria will prompt counterattacks on targets inside Israel. The danger of escalation should not be underestimated.

But the big worry remains Ukraine. Given the more than two-year long Russiagate witch hunt, the most toxic smear against Trump's Syria withdrawal is that it's a big "gift" to Russian President Vladimir Putin. As shown by the unanimous western response to the November Kerch Strait incident, Ukrainian President Petro Poroshenko knows he can do pretty much anything and any Russian response will be blamed on Russia.

Poroshenko has a menu of options. He can go back the well at the Sea of Azov and the Kerch Strait, a tempting possibility if the British (who are at the root of Russiagate and are at least as desperate to prevent a Washington-Moscow détente than Poroshenko is) are dumb enough, or cynical enough (they don't call them Perfidious Albion for nothing), to risk the lives of sailors of Her Majesty's Navy on a confrontational stunt where Moscow has an overwhelming preponderance of power. Likewise, Poroshenko could launch an attack on the Donbas. Kiev's forces recently occupied most of the "gray zone" separating forces at the Minsk agreement ceasefire line. There are also concerns over reports of chemicals stockpiled at Mariupol (hey, if a chemical provocation works in Syria, why not Ukraine?).

But the most likely proximate avenue for Poroshenko may be an attack on the canonical Ukrainian Orthodox Church, which is an autonomous (self-governing) part of the Russian Orthodox Church. Following what some are already calling the Robber Council of Kiev on December 15, which purported to create an "autocephalous" (independent) church headed by "Metropolitan" Epiphany (Dumenko) from a merger of schismatic groups, Poroshenko and the Ukrainian parliament are moving with alacrity to strip the canonical Church of its legal status and turn its property over to Dumenko's bogus church (which actually isn't independent at all but is subject to the Patriarchate of Constantinople). Lists of monasteries for seizure are being prepared. Canonical clergy are investigated and harassed by the SBU, Ukraine's successor to the old Soviet KGB. Any resistance or disorders these actions will provoke are already being blamed in advance on—you guessed it—Putin and the canonical Church.

Where is the US government, that great proponent of human rights and religious freedom? Cheering it on of course. On the day of the Robber Council, the US Embassy in Kiev tweeted out its congratulations in English and in Ukrainian (not in Russian of course, the language of *Untermenschen*). Secretary of State Mike Pompeo placed a personal call to Dumenko as the "newly elected head of the Orthodox Church of Ukraine Metropolitan Epifaniy." US Ambassador Marie Yovanovitch extended her congratulations to Dumenko in person. When the trouble starts, there's no mystery as to on whose side the US government, or at least the State Department, will come down.

One might well ask *why*? Aside from the obvious impropriety of the United States' taking sides in a question of the Orthodox Church's internal governance, *why* is the State Department so committed to promoting a transparently political power grab by Poroshenko, the schismatics, and the Ecumenical Patriarch Bartholomew I of Constantinople?

The short answer is that it is strictly geopolitics. From the point of view of the State Department, the Russian Orthodox Church—and hence the canonical autonomous Ukrainian Orthodox Church—is nothing more than an instrument of the Kremlin's soft power. According to one person rather new to the relevant issues but nonetheless considered authoritative by the State Department:

> The Church, for its part, acts as the Russian state's soft power arm, exerting its authority in ways that assist the Kremlin in spreading Russian influence both in Russia's immediate neighborhood as well as around the globe. The Kremlin assists the Church, as well, working to increase its reach. Vladimir Yakunin, one of Putin's inner circle and a devout member of the ROC, facilitated in 2007 the reconciliation of the ROC with the Russian Orthodox Church in Exile (which had separated itself from the Moscow Patriarchate early in the Soviet era so as not to be co-opted by the new Bolshevik state), which reconciliation greatly increased [Patriarch of Moscow] Kirill's influence and authority outside of Russia.
>
> Putin, praising this event, noted the interrelation of the growth of ROC authority abroad with his own international goals: "The revival of the church unity is a crucial condition for revival of lost unity of the whole 'Russian world,' which has always had the Orthodox faith as one of its foundations."

Hence, weaken "Russian state's soft power arm," weaken the Russian state.

But unfortunately there is even more to it than that.

The authors of the current US anti-Russia, anti-Orthodox Church policy know, or at least instinctively sense, that the revival of Russia's Church-State *symphonia* after a hiatus of eight decades is not just a political alliance of convenience but is the source of deep spiritual, moral, and social strength. This is reflected, for example, in Putin's warm remarks on the dedication of a Moscow monument to Aleksandr Solzhenitsyn, the acknowledged godfather of Russia's restoration as a Christian country, on the centenary of the writer's birth.

In Russia's reborn *symphonia*, President and Patriarch speak as one:

> At the height of the Cold War, it was common for American conservatives to label the officially atheist Soviet Union a "godless nation."

More than two decades on, history has come full circle, as the Kremlin and its allies in the Russian Orthodox Church hurl the same allegation at the West.

"Many Euro-Atlantic countries have moved away from their roots, including Christian values," Russian President Vladimir Putin said in a recent keynote speech. "Policies are being pursued that place on the same level a multi-child family and a same-sex partnership, a faith in God and a belief in Satan. This is the path to degradation." [. . .]

Mr. Putin's views of the West were echoed this month by Patriarch Kirill I of Moscow, the leader of the Orthodox Church, who accused Western countries of engaging in the "spiritual disarmament" of their people.

In particular, Patriarch Kirill criticized laws in several European countries that prevent believers from displaying religious symbols, including crosses on necklaces, at work.

"The general political direction of the [Western political] elite bears, without doubt, an anti-Christian and anti-religious character," the patriarch said in comments aired on state-controlled television.

"We have been through an epoch of atheism, and we know what it is to live without God," Patriarch Kirill said. "We want to shout to the whole world, 'Stop!'" ["Who's 'godless' now? Russia says it's U.S.: Putin seizes on issue of traditional values," by Marc Bennetts, *Washington Times*, January 28, 2014]

Such sentiments can hardly sit well with Western elites for whom the same-sex partnerships decried by Putin (and placed by him on a moral level with belief in Satan) are esteemed as a mark of social enlightenment. That's why an inseparable part of the "European choice" the people of Ukraine supposedly made during the 2014 "Revolution of Dignity" is wholesale acceptance of "European values," including the kind of "Pride" symbolized by LGBT marches organized over Christian objections in Orthodox cities like Athens, Belgrade, Bucharest, Kiev, Odessa, Podgorica, Sofia, and Tbilisi. (Note that after the march in Odessa in August of this year a priest of the canonical Church targeted by Poroshenko cleansed the street with Holy Water.)

It is hard to assess exactly how significant the moral/sexual component of undermining Orthodoxy in Ukraine is, but there is no denying it is a factor. There is a curious consistency between advocacy for non-traditional, post-Christian sexual morality and support for the schismatic pseudo-Church sponsored by Poroshenko and Patriarch Bartholomew.

To start with, the relevant US government officials cheering the church schismatics are also upfront and visible in Ukraine in their advocacy of the LGBT agenda. The US Embassy Kiev website displays Pompeo's declaration on behalf of all Americans that "The United States joins people around the world in celebrating Lesbian, Gay, Bisexual, Transgender, and Intersex (LGBTI) Pride Month, and reaffirms its commitment to protecting and defending the human rights of all, including LGBTI persons." As of this writing, the press release describing the Secretary's call to "Metropolitan" Dumenko appears just below the "Pride Month" message.

Ambassador Yovanovitch has really gone the extra mile—literally. Not only did she tweet out her Pride message, she also participated in the parade (and took 60 Embassy personnel and family members with her!) proudly marching behind the American flag. Your tax dollars at work! (Must watch video posted by *HromadskeUA*, an "independent" Ukrainian media outlet reportedly funded by, among others, the US Embassy, the Canadian Embassy, and George Soros's International Renaissance Foundation, though the cited

HromadskeUA financial reports no longer seem to be available.) Both
Yovanovitch's remarks in the video and the posted text draw an explicit
connection between the "freedom" of the 2014 regime change and the new
sexual morality (Google autotranslation from Ukrainian):

> The atmosphere is wonderful. It is important for us because we main-
> tain equal rights. In 2014, people in Ukraine were in favor of
> freedom, and this is an organic continuation—US Ambassador Marie
> Yovanovich goes to the March of Equality Column. With her together
> with about 60 representatives of the American embassy.

The locals were quick to make the same connection. "KyivPride," a local LGBT
advocacy group supported by (surprise, surprise) the US Embassy, the Canadian government, the German embassy, the US Agency for International
Development (USAID), and Freedom House were quick to hail creation of the
new pseudo-church, no doubt reflecting the deep piety of the group's
members. As posted by *OrthoChristian.com*, The organization posted a
message on several platforms, including Facebook and Instagram, reading:

> KyivPride congratulates all LGBTI Orthodox believers on the forma-
> tion of a united and independent Ukrainian Orthodox Church and
> reminds everyone that love does no harm to others! Also remember
> that article 35 of the constitution of Ukraine states: "Everyone has
> the right to freedom of personal philosophy and religion. This right
> includes the freedom to profess or not to profess any religion."
> Human rights above all!

Last but certainly not least is the involvement of certain fringe elements in the
Orthodox Church itself, plus at least one not-so-fringe element. As this analyst
warned months ago the Ukrainian church crisis seemingly facilitates the anti-
Christian moral agenda of certain marginal "Orthodox" voices like "Orthodoxy
in Dialogue," Fordham University's "Orthodox Christian Studies Center," and
The Wheel. As Anatoly Karlin points out, "many of the biggest supporters of
Ukrainian autocephaly in the West are for all intents and purposes SJWs. The
website Orthodoxy in Dialogue, for instance, wants Orthodoxy to get with the
times and start sanctifying gay marriage":

> We pray for the day when we can meet our future partner in
> church, or bring our partner to church.
> We pray for the day when our lifelong, monogamous commitment
> to our partner can be blessed and sanctified in and by the Church.
> We pray for the day when we can explore as Church, without
> condemnation, how we Orthodox Christians can best live our life in
> Christ in the pursuit of holiness, chastity, and perfect love of God and
> neighbour.
> We pray for the day when our priests no longer travel around the
> world to condemn us and mock us and use us as a punching bag.
> We pray for the day when the one, holy, catholic, and apostolic
> Church of Christ ceases to be our loneliest closet.

Sadly, Metropolitan John (Zizioulas) of Pergamon is anything but marginal.
Considered one of the world's most prominent Orthodox intellectuals, his
titular see in Asia Minor has been devoid of Christians for many decades, a sad
example of the "rotten boroughs" that make up the Patriarchate of Constantinople apart from its extravagant assertions of universal authority based on
an imperial reality that died centuries ago. Metropolitan John is one of the

foremost polemicists in asserting Constantinople's fictional claims over Ukraine in the lead-up to the Robber Council.

Not surprisingly, there is reason to suppose Metropolitan John also shares the revisionists' views on sexual morality. As this analyst was recently informed by a knowledgeable Church source:

> I have a friend who just came back from an academic conference in Greece. He told me about an incident at the council in Crete [i.e., presumably a reference to the abortive 2016 "Eighth Ecumenical Council"] where [Metropolitan John] Zizioulas had the doors closed and regaled the bishops about how they needed to support the LGBT agenda and gay marriage. How much is the [Ecumenical Patriarchate] pushing this agenda, albeit quietly?

This report is not inconsistent with the Metropolitan's public views. As one Orthodox blogger commented in 2015:

> Another example of gravely twisting the teachings of the Holy Fathers is [Metropolitan John] Zizioulas's view on homosexuality, quoted by an Anglican publication (the Tablet): *"When I raise the question of homosexuality he claims that the Greek Church is traditionally flexible and non-Judgement on such issues (!!!), but is now becoming more puritanical—due to Western Influence."* So, after Zizioulas, the Orthodox tradition does not condemn homosexuality, but the condemnation of this sin would be a Protestant influence! What would the Ap. Paul, St. John Chrysostom and all the saints of the Orthodox Church would say about these serious and blasphemous statements?

To sum up, we can expect the crisis in Ukraine to get worse, with malign geopolitical and moral agendas both making their mark. It is not easy to sort out which in the end may have the most deadly impact.

"Violence Erupts as West Turns Its Sexual Subversion Weapon on Georgia"

Jim Jatras | *Strategic Culture* | June 22, 2019

With apologies to Alfred, Lord Tennyson, it's June, when a young man's (or woman's, or sexually indeterminate person's) fancy lightly turns to thoughts of nontraditional "love" of any variety expressed by the ever-growing LGBTT QQIAAP alphabet soup. In downtown Washington it's impossible to swing a cat without hitting a rainbow flag or a "Pride" enthusiast.

If anyone was under the impression that established religion was a thing of the past in secular, postmodern societies, he, she, it, they, ze, sie, hir, co, or ey are mistaken. There is in fact an official religion of the "democratic" West, and LGBT++ etcetera is it.

A symptom of that is corporations' display of rainbow versions of their logos, a demonstration that their plutocratic money-grubbing is duly balanced by piety. This includes the *Cartoon Network*, a sign that the effort to initiate kids into the satanic LGBT++ "church" is becoming increasingly overt. Really, with abominations like "Drag Queen Story Hour" they hardly even bother to hide it anymore.

Ending the traditional family founded on marriage and the birth of children is the intended but hidden goal, as confirmed in 2012 by Soviet-born LGBT activist Masha Gessen, prior to the US Supreme Court's establishing same-sex marriage nationwide:

> [I]t is a no-brainer that the institution of marriage should not exist. . . . Fighting for gay marriage generally involves lying about what we're going to do with marriage when we get there, because we lie that the institution of marriage is not going to change, and that is a lie. The institution of marriage is going to change, and it should change, and again, I don't think it should exist.

For the past several years governments of formerly Christian countries in North America and Europe have made LGBT ideology an integral element of their promotion of "human rights" and "democracy" in formerly communist countries. This includes pressuring compliant governments of European countries recently emerged from communism to hold "Pride parades" that offend local sensibilities. (Mystifyingly, there is no effort to force such demonstrations on Riyadh, Islamabad, etc.) Recent targets of such sexual subversion have been Ukraine (where it has been a key element of the US State Department's and the Ecumenical Patriarchate's attack on the canonical Orthodox Church) and Moldova (where the US embassy took the lead in a joint statement hailing the "the International Day Against Homophobia, Transphobia and Biphobia [and] . . . support for lesbian, gay, bisexual, transgender and intersex (LGBTI)"). Our tax dollars at work!

The message to traditional societies still grounded in Christian morality but with elites committed to "a European course," meaning membership in NATO and (perhaps *someday*. . .) the European Union is that it's a package deal. You don't get to pick which part of western "democracy, human rights and free markets" you want and which you don't. You can't have transatlanticism without transgenderism. So shut up, grit your teeth, and *take it* . . .

At this very moment Ground Zero for the West's campaign to undermine the traditional Christian concept of the family is Georgia, where the usual suspects—foreign embassies and their controlled NGOs, working in concert with George Soros's Open Society groups—were determined to hold Tbilisi's first Pride parade this week. As reported by *Orthodox Christianity* on June 17:

> Georgia is a deeply traditional country, with more than 80% of the population belonging to the Orthodox Church, and the battle between traditional, Orthodox values and more liberal, secularized values is being prompted and aggravated not only by the nation's LGBT community, but by the great Western powers, Archpriest David Isakadze, and others, believes.
>
> "It is clearly evident who is controlling the processes in Georgia," Fr. David said. "We truly want to be an independent country, not in word, but in deed. The U.S. authorities, in the person of the ambassador [Elizabeth Rood—O.C. (JGJ: Rood is actually *Chargé d'Affaires*, a.i., not ambassador)] directly interfere in our internal affairs. She wants to control the processes here and exacerbate the situation, knocking people against one another," Fr. 'David explained, noting that he and those of like mind are prepared to

demand that the U.S. withdraw its acting ambassador if she does not immediately appeal to the participants in the LGBT event to disband.

The Georgian Patriarchate issued a statement on Friday, calling on the authorities to prevent the event, citing the divisions it causes in the traditional society that largely stands against the sinful nature of the LGBT lifestyle. At the same time, the Church declared that there must be no violence surrounding the events.

Faced with massive public opposition—over 97 percent of respondents in a TV poll opposed the march!—Georgian authorities cancelled the parade. Opposition to the Pride event is being spearheaded by businessman and father of eight children Levan Vasadze, who predictably (along with conservative Christian American supporters, like Brian Brown of the International Organization for the Family) has been smeared by Soros-funded hate outfits like the Southern Poverty Law Center and *RightWingWatch*, together with solidly pro-LGBT Western media reporting (with the commendable exception of *CBN*'s George Thomas's must watch interview with Vasadze) for stating what any unbiased observer knows is the truth in Georgia, as well as other post-communist countries:

> Vasadze portrayed the LGBTQ movement as part of the "ugly heritage" of the "liberal domination" that "befell upon the world" after the collapse of the Soviet Union. Georgians had hoped to embrace western freedoms, he said, but instead the country is being destroyed by poverty and liberal abortion laws and he portrayed the push for LGBTQ equality as "the last nail in our coffin." He said "our fragile puppet state is under tremendous pressure from the likes of George Soros" and the U.S. embassy.

(If anything, Vasadze is being optimistic about his country's demographic health: 'In 2015, the National Statistics Office of Georgia released the results of the first census in more than a decade reflecting that the country's population as of 2014 reduced to 3.7 million from 5.4 million in 1989. . . . "The United Nations has put Georgia on the list of 'Dying Nations' and 'Dying Languages'," [National Statistics Office of Georgia head] Zviad Tomaradze warned adding that according to the UN experts, in 2050 the Georgian population would decrease by 28 percent, while among the ethnic Georgians the depopulation will amount to 50 percent.")

On June 19 the organizers of "Tbilisi Pride" and their foreign mentors and funders had declared that despite lack of a permit they would go through with their demonstration at an undisclosed time by Sunday, June 23. Then, late on Friday, June 21, local time, organizers declared the event postponed but "the rally would be held at a later date that was yet to be confirmed." *Translation*: "We'll be back when our opponents have been battered sufficiently into line. You can't stop 'democracy'!"

But don't think the forces of Western progress and enlightenment are just sitting on their hands. The most effective defense is an offense. And, as the anti-Trump conspirators in the US-UK Deep State know, the best offense always is "Russia! Russia! Russia!"

A pretext came on Thursday, June 20, when an international group of legislators visited the Georgian parliament under the auspices of the Athens-based Interparliamentary Assembly on Orthodoxy (IAO). Uniting lawmakers from over a dozen countries, the IAO includes "parliamentarians throughout the world, Christian Orthodox in faith, with the aim of joining our common cultural aspect, that of religion, as the meeting point in the participation of structuring a contemporary complex reality." During the visit, the president of IAO's General Assembly, Russian State Duma Deputy Sergei Gavrilov, sat in the Speaker's chair in the Georgian parliamentary chamber. While no doubt impolitic given strained relations between Georgia and Russia (which had recently been incrementally improving ties following their short war in 2008) the move was "standard practice," according to a statement from the IAO.

Nevertheless, opposition forces, stung by growing opposition to their Pride provocation, used the Gavrilov incident as an excuse to launch a violent attack on the parliament on a scale that could only have been preplanned and awaiting activation. (It should be noted that, in keeping with the anti-Russian theme, Tbilisi Pride organizers tweeted their support for the parliament attack, doubtlessly expecting reciprocation for their cause.) Spearheaded by the United National Movement, the party of disgraced former president and Western favorite Mikheil Saakashvili (who is in self-imposed exile, fleeing from his conviction on corruption charges), the attack mimicked violent actions of "peaceful protesters" in Kiev five years ago with the end of pro-voking forceful police resistance and numerous injuries, which duly occurred. As of this writing the Georgian parliamentary Speaker was forced to resign and questions are being raised as to whether the ruling Georgian Dream reformist party can retain power—which surely was the point in the first place.

In short, in the context of two seemingly unrelated but in spirit closely linked events—the postponed Pride parade and the assault on the parliament—we may be seeing the beginning of a regime change operation like that in Ukraine in 2014 and in Georgia in 2003. Indeed, it was the latter that brought Saakashvili to power in the first place.

As things stand as of this writing, Georgia is simmering in a national crisis with deep political, social, moral, and spiritual consequences for the country's future. Any small progress in improved relations with Russia has been scuttled. As Gavrilov notes on the Duma website:

"Our common opinion is that now in Georgia there is an obvious attempt of a coup d'état and the seizure of power by radical extremist forces, which are guided in many respects from abroad and, as we think, are associated with Mr. [Mikhail] Saakashvili," said Sergei Gavrilov at a press conference.

"The meeting of the Interparliamentary Assembly on Orthodoxy was the ground for inciting anti-Russian hysteria and discrediting Georgia, as an Orthodox country, to strike at Georgian Orthodoxy and the Georgian Orthodox Church," he added.

He also admitted that Western secret services could be involved in these events.

As if to confirm Gavrilov's suspicions of Western involvement, in a June 21 statement the US Embassy in Georgia placed full blame on the police (regarding the parliament) and "anti-American rhetoric from anti-LGBT groups" (regarding the Pride march):

'Following the violent escalation of last night's demonstrations in downtown Tbilisi, including use of tear gas and rubber bullets by police, additional protest activity is expected to occur tonight and possibly throughout the weekend. Public Pride Week events may also occur over the weekend at undisclosed locations in Tbilisi. Based on violent, anti-American rhetoric from anti-LGBT groups, the embassy has determined that there is increased risk that Americans could be targeted. U.S. government personnel have been directed not to part-

icipate in any demonstrations and to avoid any areas where a large
crowd is gathering.'

The bureaucrats and Sorostitutes at the US Embassy in Tbilisi are in serious
need of adult supervision from the Trump Administration. Earlier this week
pro-family leader Vasadze directly appealed personally to US President
Donald Trump to clean out the nest of "Swamp" globalists running the US
embassy in Tbilisi. What are the odds that he will heed it—or even be informed
of it by his advisers? After all, they wouldn't want him to be accused of
"colluding" with Moscow by standing up for Georgia's Christian, pro-family
people targeted by American officials who constitutionally are under the
President's authority.

Fatuous FATCA

"Rand Paul's Stand against Tax Treaties Is More Important than You Think"

Jim Jatras | *Accounting Today* | May 13, 2016

President Barack Obama has now joined personally in renewed efforts to pressure Kentucky Senator Rand Paul to stop blocking the ratification of eight tax treaties pending before the U.S. Senate. Paul is sticking to his guns, and it's important for Americans to understand why these treaties present a grave threat to our constitutional liberties.

Of the eight treaties, seven of them are bilateral agreements with various countries to facilitate cooperation to avoid double taxation and to lower compliance costs. Regrettably, these agreements also unnecessarily change the standard for providing personal financial information to law enforcement agencies from probable cause of criminal behavior, such as fraud—which Paul correctly regards as the only constitutionally permissible standard under the Fourth Amendment—to what amounts to wholesale bulk collection on the pattern of the NSA's violations of email and phone privacy.

This is Paul's only concern with these seven bilateral treaties. A simple amendment could conform them to constitutional standards and they could move forward expeditiously.

However, that reasonable solution is not acceptable to Secretary Jack Lew's Treasury Department. That's because the Department also insists on using the treaties as a Trojan Horse for one of the most dangerous and dysfunctional laws enacted under the presidency of Barack Obama: the Foreign Account Tax Compliance Act, or FATCA.

FATCA, which few Americans have ever heard of, was passed by a Democrat-controlled Congress in 2010, supposedly as a weapon against "fatcat" offshore tax evasion. Disdaining the constitutional path of investigating individuals who are suspected of wrongdoing and securing a warrant for accessing their private records, FATCA takes the NSA approach: to require all non-U.S. banks to hand over information on U.S. private persons (not corporations, by the way) absent any requirement of reasonable suspicion, due process, or a court order. If banks fail to do so, they face crippling sanctions that essentially shut them out of the American market. FATCA has led many foreign banks to deny services to Americans rather than deal with the burdens and crushing compliance costs, thus impeding U.S. business and export opportunities and risking economic harm.

To enforce FATCA, Treasury has concocted a series of so-called "Intergovernmental Agreements" (IGAs) with foreign governments to provide for "exchange" of private financial information. These IGAs are not authorized under FATCA or any other law, nor are they treaties submitted to the Senate for advice and consent under the U.S. Constitution. They are at best legally dubious. Nonetheless, in the IGAs with many countries Treasury has promised that the U.S. will report "reciprocal" information from American banks for foreign governments, something the Obama administration currently has no legal authority to do but repeatedly has requested from Congress.

Because the IGAs designate tax treaty mechanisms for FATCA information "exchange," Paul's holding up the bilateral treaties also impedes indiscriminate FATCA reporting. Conversely, if the treaties were amended to allow information transfer only under the probable cause standard, the higher constitutional standard would govern. That, not double tax relief, is why Treasury is so desperate to approve these treaties without amendment.

That this is Treasury's real agenda is further confirmed by the eighth treaty the Senator is foiling, a so-called "Protocol amending the Multilateral Convention on Mutual Administrative Assistance in Tax Matters." The Protocol, along with a follow-up "Competent Authority" agreement, is an initiative of the G20 and the Organization for Economic Co-operation and Development (OECD), with the support, unsurprisingly, of the Obama Administration.

Unlike the seven bilateral tax treaties, the Protocol cannot be repaired. It is utterly inconsistent with any concept of American sovereignty or Americans' constitutional protections. Ratification of the Protocol would mean acceptance by the United States as a treaty obligation of an international "common reporting standard," which is essentially FATCA gone global—sometimes called GATCA. Ratifying the Protocol arguably would also provide Treasury with backdoor legal authority to issue regulations requiring FATCA-like reporting to foreign governments by U.S. domestic banks, credit unions, insurance companies, mutual funds, etc. This would mean billions of dollars in costs passed on to American taxpayers and consumers, as well as mandating the delivery of private data to authoritarian and corrupt governments, including China, Saudi Arabia, Mexico, and Nigeria.

Citing "tax evasion" is no more an excuse for trashing constitutional protections than invoking terrorism. Senator Paul insists that, no less than email and phone metadata, details of our financial affairs—among the most private of any individual's possessions—must remain confidential. As Paul stated in his hold letter to Majority Leader Mitch McConnell, "An individual's bank account is the epitome of who they are as a private citizen; a bank account reveals where someone is shopping, what foods they like, the medicines they're taking, the doctors they're visiting, and the places they're traveling."

Make no mistake: if today governments can disregard privacy because accounts happen to be held in another country, tomorrow they will do the same domestically under the misguided "third party doctrine" (which Paul has challenged in court with respect to cell phones).

For that reason, the Senator is right to insist that the OECD Protocol is dead on arrival. The other seven tax treaties should proceed with one simple but essential fix.

It is noteworthy that in both this Congress and the previous one Paul has introduced legislation to repeal FATCA and also is a plaintiff in a lawsuit to challenge its constitutionality (recently dismissed on a rubber-stamp standing ruling, with an appeal expected). In 2014 and 2015 respectively, the Republican National Committee unanimously passed resolutions to repeal FATCA and stop GATCA. Early in 2017, Congress needs to send a FATCA repeal bill to President Donald Trump for his signature, finally getting rid of "the worst law most Americans have never heard of."

"Why Is the Senate GOP Leadership Helping Obama Pass Job-Killing Treaties?"

Jim Jatras | *Conservative Review* | June 16, 2016

As Barack Obama becomes the lamest of Lame Ducks, you can count on him to take every opportunity to aim a parting shot at what's left of the American economy and the U.S. Constitution. In recent weeks he has abused his Executive authority on guns, overtime pay, imposing gender-bending bathroom rules on states and parents, and slipping U.S. "boots on the ground" into Libya, Yemen, and Syria.

Unsurprisingly, the GOP leadership in Congress is utterly ineffective in blocking him.

Even worse, on some matters top Congressional Republicans have shown their readiness to carry Obama's water for him. The best-known examples are the 2014 $1.1 trillion "Cromnibus" abomination (which funded Obama's illegal actions on immigration) and approval of "Obamatrade" authority last year to expedite horrible deals like TTIP (the "Transatlantic Trade and Investment Partnership" with the European Union) and TPP (the "Trans-Pacific Partnership"), which Donald Trump rightly has called "insanity."

Now there's yet another monstrosity waiting in the wings. Obama and Treasury Secretary Jack Lew are trying to shoehorn the United States into a global financial reporting scheme that would trash American sovereignty, suck money out of the U.S. economy, and violate constitutional principles, such as respecting the Senate's advice and consent to treaties and requiring warrants for searches of personal data.

Unfortunately, the Republican leadership in the Senate is lining up to help Obama and Lew do it.

At issue are seven obscure tax treaties being held up by Senators Rand Paul (R-KY) and Mike Lee (R-UT). Foreign Relations Committee Chairman Bob Corker (R-TN) is trying to pry loose Paul's and Lee's "hold" on the treaties and to rubber stamp them without fixing data reporting standards that violate the 4th Amendment to the U.S. Constitution. The two Senators are happy to quit blocking the pacts, which are otherwise acceptable, if they are amended to remedy that defect.

A Dear Colleague letter signed by Corker—but clearly drafted by Lew's Treasury Department—claims to debunk Paul's and Lee's objections in what amounts to a rehash of Obama Administration talking points. For example, the letter (evidently prompted by my recent commentary opposing the treaties) claims blocking them won't prevent operation of a little-known 2010 law called the "Foreign Account Tax Compliance Act" (FATCA), which the Obama administration has sought to implement using a series of unauthorized and unratified "intergovernmental agreements." With all due respect to Chairman Corker, this claim is inaccurate. For example, Article 5(1) of the relevant agreement with Switzerland says in so many words that FATCA requests 'shall not be made prior to the entry into force' of a treaty the two Senators have a hold on. If that's not blocking, what is?

From the standpoint of American jobs and foreign investment in the U.S., there is even more at stake. Since the "Panama Papers" story broke, foreign officials have accused the United States of acting as a tax haven as well as permitting states like Delaware, Nevada, and Wyoming not to disclose "beneficial ownership" of corporations. There have been calls to blacklist the United States, and even to apply sanctions against us.

Barack Obama has invited these attacks on America by his administration's practice over the past five years of subjecting our trading partners to one-sided, costly, and humiliating FATCA demands under threat of financial sanctions. They have capitulated, in part because Obama—as noted above, with no legal authority—has promised foreign governments the U.S. would provide reciprocal data under the FATCA agreements he refuses to submit to the Senate as treaties. Now he expects Congress to make good on his imprudent and legally deficient pledges.

It's important to keep in mind the seven tax treaties are themselves innocuous and even desirable from the standpoint of avoiding double taxation for Americans doing business overseas. But contrary to Chairman Corker's letter, ratifying them without fixing their constitutional defects facilitates their use as vehicles for data reporting under the legally dubious FATCA "intergovernmental agreements," many of which also require "reciprocal reporting" from domestic U.S. institutions to foreign governments. This would hit U.S. banks, credit unions, insurance companies, mutual funds, etc. with costs comparable to those FATCA imposes on foreign institutions, which run into the millions *per* financial institution (for example, Canada's Bank of Nova Scotia alone already had spent $100 million as of 2013). Imposing the same burdens here in the U.S. would mean billions of dollars extracted from American consumers and taxpayers, spurring massive capital flight from the United States and lost jobs. That's why U.S. credit unions have written to the Congressional leadership to oppose domestic expansion of FATCA, which would "increase regulatory burdens on American credit unions and banks without resulting in a single dollar of new tax revenue to the Treasury."

Finally, the seven treaties are a stalking horse for another item on Obama's and Lew's political bucket list: a so-called "Protocol amending the Multilateral Convention on Mutual Administrative Assistance in Tax Matters" that would lock in a FATCA-like international "common reporting standard" as treaty obligation. The result would be essentially FATCA gone global—sometimes called GATCA—which in would be set for a global tax under United Nations auspices, pressure on the U.S. to raise our domestic tax rates, and subjecting our country to the oversight of bureaucrats at the Organization for Economic Cooperation and Development and other international organizations.

Republican leaders should not provide *ex post facto* authority for Obama's and Lew's reciprocal FATCA and GATCA schemes, which would also hand embattled IRS Commissioner John Koskinen sweeping new regulatory powers. It comes as no surprise that President Obama seeks to impose these burdens on America as his parting gift. What is deplorable is that any Republican leader would help him do it. Instead of promoting Obama's global regime, it's time for Senate Republicans to put America first. They should join Senators Paul and Lee in ensuring these treaties are not ratified until Obama leaves office, and get ready to send President Donald Trump a FATCA repeal bill early next year.

"Now That It's Clear the U.S. Will Not 'Reciprocate' on FATCA, Will 'Partner' Countries Wise Up?"

Jim Jatras | *JIMGram No. 10* | June 25, 2016

As I have warned for several years now (for example, see with respect to **Europe**, **Canada**, and **Cayman**), "partner" governments signing legally defective "Foreign Account Tax Compliance Act" (FATCA) "intergovernmental agreements" (IGAs) under "promises" from the U.S. Treasury Department that the U.S. would provide reciprocal information from domestic American institutions was at best a long shot, more likely just a deception. *Almost three years ago*, in July 2013, Florida Congressman Bill Posey made it clear requests for legislative authority to provide "reciprocity" were *dead on arrival.*

Yet foreign governments have continued to deceive themselves—or their publics, or both—that American participation in a global GATCA, or intergovernmental "automatic exchange of information" (AEOI), "disclosure of corporate beneficial ownership," and a "common reporting standards" (CRS) regime, probably under OECD auspices, were just around the corner . . .

Well, it isn't. Period. Full stop.

With Senators Rand Paul's and Mike Lee's stalwart block of tax treaty provisions as backdoor mechanisms for securing the Obama Administration's sought-for authority, the matter is deader than ever here in Washington. (See "Rand Paul's Stand against Tax Treaties Is More Important than You Think," *Accounting Today*, May 13, 2016; and "Why Is the Senate GOP Leadership Helping Obama Pass Job-Killing Treaties?" *Conservative Review*, June 16, 2016.)

Belatedly, some elements abroad are waking up to the fact they've been had. They have only themselves to blame, really. Not only were they warned by this writer time and again, they at least should have had the common sense (and an elementary understanding of our non-parliamentary Constitutional system) to know that Treasury's promises had no legal authority and were worthless. But so intimidated were they by America's mighty threat of FATCA sanctions (which now seem ready to be unleashed, with the expiration of a two-year "grace period"), or deceived by the siren-song of the compliance industry that "there is no alternative" to an inevitable (and for the industry, highly lucrative) acquiescence to Washington's demands, or perhaps slavering with the sheer greedy lust of an expected tax revenue bonanza (a mirage, of course) *if only* they would throw their citizens' privacy concerns under the bus, our so-called "partners"—more properly called satellites—meekly handed over the keys of their financial institutions to the IRS (not to mention, to the NSA, CIA, etc.).

But still, our "partners" now pronounce themselves shocked—shocked!—that "the Yanks" aren't keeping their promises. Since the "Panama Papers" story broke, foreign officials have accused the United States of acting as a tax haven as well as permitting states like Delaware, Nevada, and Wyoming not to disclose "beneficial ownership" of corporations. There have been calls to blacklist the United States, and even (from the Greens/EFA group in the European Parliament) to apply sanctions against us. Cayman **Premier Alden McLaughlin** has called for a level playing field in terms of financial transparency and stated that a standard without U.S. participation "is not a global standard."

Good luck with that.

At this point, as our foreign partners finally notice the raw deal they've gotten, they have three choices:

1. Keep beating their collective heads against the wall, futilely demanding that IGA reciprocity promises be honored, that American states disclose "beneficial ownership," that the U.S. sign on to the so-called "Protocol amending the Multilateral Convention on Mutual Administrative Assist-

ance in Tax Matters," along with a follow-up "Competent Authority" agreement, etc. To which Congress in effect answers: "Yeah, you and what army?"

2. Accept that Washington will treat international information ex-change like we treated the League of Nations or the International Criminal Court: those lesser, not-fully-sovereign countries will comply with whatever we dictate to them, and we will ignore their requests to us. Have a nice day!

3. Finally admit to themselves that FATCA, GATCA, AEOI, CRS, and the rest of the whole rotten OECD-Obama scheme was a bad idea to start with. They must then tell Treasury they will not comply with FATCA and will pull out of arrangements that violate state sovereignty and personal privacy—and if Treasury does attempt to impose illegal sanctions for FATCA non-compliance, determined resistance and asymmetrical responses will follow. (Granted, small countries like, say, Cayman, are in a weak position to defend themselves directly, though they could support anti-FATCA efforts inside the United States, which they haven't. Other countries do have significant options. For example, Canada and the United Kingdom are in a strong enough financial relationship vis-à-vis the U.S. to tell Treasury that any FATCA "withholding" to their institutions will be met dollar-for-dollar with withholding from transfers to the U.S. Or Canada could inform the U.S. that an equal sum of FATCA withholding would be imposed in added fees on American air carriers transiting Canadian airspace on Atlantic flights. Let's get creative, people!)

The bottom line is this: if there's a will to resist, the means will be found. But if "partners" continue to cower as they have thus far, they deserve whatever they get. Based on past performance I remain skeptical that our satellites will summon the wherewithal actually to stand up for themselves. But the successful Brexit vote gives even this most hardened cynic pause and renewed hope in the spirit of liberty.

Meanwhile, at least the sense unfairness and the need to do something about it appear to be growing. The following is a survey by country of reactions to the accurate perception that FATCA is an unfair, one-way street, especially for "Accidental Americans," who are local citizens who for a variety of reasons are considered "U.S. Persons" for tax purposes by the U.S. (Edited below, the source is Jude Ryan on the Accidental Americans group on Facebook, where the original text and further details are available.)

France: The Assemblée Nationale has set up a fact-finding mission to investigate the extraterritorial reach of U.S. laws and in particular the invidious position French "Accidental Americans" find themselves in. Several recent events have highlighted the propensity of the U.S. courts and the US administration to purport to impose sanctions against foreign corporations and foreign individuals in respect of events occurring outside of US territory. Based on the feedback of a wide array of experts, the factfinding mission will attempt to define the contours of US extraterritoriality, exhaustively identify all cases of extraterritorial application of US laws, assess their impact and in particular their impact on fair competition and the economic losses suffered by French companies as a result, and to study ways in which to counter such practices both at a national and European level. The mission hopes that its findings will lead to concrete implementation measures. A hearing of French "Accidental Americans" was held on 8 June 2016 and at which issues raised by FATCA and the US practices of Citizenship Based Taxation, particularly as regards "Accidental Americans" were discussed. The mission questioned and heard testimony from five accidental Americans. Also, French Parliamentarian Seybah Dagoma wrote to the President Hollande's office drawing his attention to the issues faced by French citizens who are also Accidental Americans. In her letter, Ms. Dagoma denounced the unintended consequences of FATCA, the absurdity of Citizenship Based Taxation, the extra-territorial reach of U.S. laws and the living nightmare French Accidental Americans and their families are enduring.

Italy: Massimiliano Fedriga, leader of the parliamentary Lega Nord group recently posed a question to the Italian government regarding the situation of Accidental Americans and in particular how the Italian government proposes to safeguard Italian citizens caught up in this mess (in addition to questions regarding infringement of Italian sovereignty, compliance costs and related matters). Senator Comarloi for the Lega Nord is apprised of the situation and is also looking into this and Matteo Salvini (member of the Lega Nord and fellow MEP) has also been informed of the issues.

Canada: In Canada, the Alliance for the Defence of Canadian Sovereignty has initiated a lawsuit against the Government of Canada legislation that enables the FATCA IGA "agreement" between Canada and the United States. The Defendants in the lawsuit are Canada's Attorney General and Revenue Minister. The Plaintiffs are two women from Ontario, Canada, both born in the United States, but who left the United States at an early age and have no meaningful ties with United States—yet they are deemed by the United States to be "tax citizens." The Plaintiffs Claim that the legislation violates Canada's Charter of Rights and Freedoms, Constitution, and it sovereignty as a nation. The trial is likely to take place in Canada Federal Court later in 2016. Plans are also afoot to mount a legal challenge in the US courts to the US practice of Citizenship Based Taxation.

Israel: Two actions are ongoing in Israel. The first is an appeal to Israel's Supreme Court, contesting the right of banks to transfer information pertaining to local accounts of dual citizens to the IRS. If this appeal is successful, the problems of accidentals will also be solved. The second revolves around banking problems faced by the many small charities popular in Israel's ultra-Orthodox communities. These charities rely on foreign donations. Requiring them to report on all donators will effectively ruin them. This issue is being discussed by the finance committee in the Israeli parliament. This committee also promised to discuss the Accidental Americans issue.

It still remains to be seen where these efforts will amount to anything serious. Likewise, even if they are, it is essential they are directed not towards pulling the U.S. into the financial fishbowl—which I repeat again for the record, just will not happen—but for scuttling it entirely. In that regard, it's belatedly time to create what never has existed from the time FATCA was launched in 2010: a dedicated, funded Washington-based lobby and media effort to repeal this misbegotten, wasteful, invasive, and dysfunctional law.

EurAlfabet

"EurAlfabet™"

Omniplot.com

EurAlfabet™ was devised by Jim Jatras as a way to facilitate phonetic conversion among the principle alphabets used to write European languages: Latin, Cyrillic and Greek. The name stands for "European Universal Recognition Alphabet."

EurAlfabet is based on "visual phonetic conversion" (VPC), an original concept that corresponding letters in different alphabets can be designed to convey the same phonetic value. For example, the Latin letter "S" is written in Cyrillic as "C" and in Greek as "Σ." EurAlfabet provides a single letter design that is mentally "heard" by the reader as /s/, so that where an American sees an "S", a Russian looking at the same letter would see a "C." The same VPC principle is applied to all other letters in all three alphabets.

Because readers of the Cyrillic and Greek alphabets generally are more familiar with the Latin alphabet than vice versa, EurAlfabet is particularly useful in parts of Central and Eastern Europe where western speakers of English, French, German, etc., may have difficulty in recognizing the local letters.

Notable features

Type of writing system: alphabet
Direction of writing: left to right in horizontal lines
Used to write: European languages
There are Latin, Cyrillic and Greek versions of the alphabet

EurAlfabet™ (Cyrillic)

Аа	Бб	Вв	Çç	Дд	Ее	Ёё	Жж	Зз
Аа	Бб	Вв	Гг	Дд	Ее	Ёё	Жж	Зз
a	b	v	g	d	e	ё	zh	z

Ии	Йй	Кк	Лл	Мм	Нн	Оо	Пп	Рр
Ии	Йй	Кк	Лл	Мм	Нн	Оо	Пп	Рр
i	j	k	l	m	n	o	p	r

Çç	Тт	Уу	Фф	Нн	Цц	Чч	Шш	Щщ
Cc	Тт	Уу	Фф	Хх	Цц	Чч	Шш	Щщ
s	t	u	f	x	ts	ch	sh	shch

Ъъ	Ыы	ь	Ээ	Юю	Яя
Ъъ	Ыы	ь	Ээ	Юю	Яя
"	i	'	e	ju	ja

EurAlfabet™ (Latin)

Ɑɑ Бб Cc Ðð Eє Ƒƒ Çç Hн Іі
Aa   Bb   Cc   Dd   Ee   Ff   Gg   Hh   Ii

Ɉɉ Кк Λλ Мм Ɲɲ Oo Ππ Qq Ɽɽ
Jj   Kk   Ll   Mm   Nn   Oo   Pp   Qq   Rr

Çç Tt Ʊʊ Ѵѵ Ѡѡ Ӿӿ Үү Ʒʒ
Ss   Tt   Uu   Vv   Ww   Xx   Yy   Zz

EurAlfabet™ (Greek)

Ɑɑ Ѵѵ Çç Ðð Eє Ʒʒ Hн Θθ Іі
Aα   Bβ   Γγ   Δδ   Eε   Zζ   Hη   Θθ   Iι
a   b   g, y d   ē   z   ē   th   i

Кк Λλ Мм Ɲɲ Ξξ Oo Ππ Ɽɽ Çç
Kκ   Λλ   Mμ   Nν   Ξξ   Oο   Ππ   Pρ   Σσς
k   l   m   n   ks, x o   p   r, rh s

Tt Үү Ƒƒ Hн Ѱѱ Ωω
Tτ   Yυ   Φφ   Xχ   Ψψ   Ωω
t   u, y ph   kh, ch ps ō

Sample words in EurAlfabet™

Тєλєƒон | ƦЄÇTOƦΑNT | TOЇΛЄT | TЄƦМЇNΑΛ

ÐєπαƦTМЄNT | ЇNTЄƦNЄT | HOTЄΛ | ÇTΑÐHON

Παƙ | ΠΑÇÇΠОƦT | Çʊѵєнв♯ | Bαnƙ | МЄTƦO

Ʒооπαƙ | ÇTОП | ÇʊπєƦМΑƦƙЄT

Sample texts in EurAlfabet™

Russian version

Vҫɛ ʌюьн ɾoжьɑютҫiɑ ҫvoбoьннмн н ɾɑvннмн v ҫvoɛм
ьoҫтoннҫтvɛ н ɾɾɑvɑн. Oнн нɑьɛʌɛнн ɾɑzумoм н ҫovɛҫтью н
ьoʌжнн ɾoҫтуɾɑть v oтнoшɛннн ьɾuҫ ьɾuҫɑ v ьuнɛ бɾɑтҫтvɑ.

Все люди рождаются свободными и равными в своем
достоинстве и правах. Они наделены разумом и совестью и
должны поступать в отношении друг друга в духе братства.

Greek version

'Όλοι οι άνθρoπoι ҫɛннιoύнтɑι ɛʌɛύθɛɾoι κɑι íҫoι ҫтнн
ɑξιoɾɾέɾɛιɑ κɑι тɑ ьικɑιóмɑтɑ. Εíнɑι ɾɾoικιҫмένoι мɛ ʌoҫική
κɑι ҫyнɛíьнҫн, κɑι oϝɛíʌoyн нɑ ҫyмɾɛɾιϝέɾoнтɑι мɛтɑξý тoyҫ
мɛ ɾнɛýмɑ ɑьɛʌϝoҫýннҫ.

'Όλοι οι άνθρωποι γεννιούνται ελεύθεροι και ίσοι στην
αξιοπρέπεια και τα δικαιώματα. Είναι προικισμένοι με λογική και
συνείδηση, και οφείλουν να συμπεριφέρονται μεταξύ τους με
πνεύμα αδελφοσύνης.

English version

Αʌʌ нuмɑн бɛiнҫҫ ɑɾɛ бoɾн ϝɾɛɛ ɑнь ɛquɑʌ iн ьiҫнiтγ ɑнь
ɾiҫнтҫ. Тнɛγ ɑɾɛ ɛньoшɛь шiтн ɾɛɑҫoн ɑнь coнҫҫiɛнcɛ ɑнь
ҫнouʌь ɑcт тoшɑɾьҫ oнɛ ɑнoтнɛɾ iн ɑ ҫɾiɾiт oϝ бɾoтнɛɾнooь.
(Αɾтicʌɛ 1 oϝ тнɛ Uнivɛɾҫɑʌ Ьɛcʌɑɾɑтioн oϝ Нuмɑн ɾiҫнтҫ)

All human beings are born free and equal in dignity and rights.
They are endowed with reason and conscience and should act
towards one another in a spirit of brotherhood. *(Article 1 of the
Universal Declaration of Human Rights)*

"Attention foundries! New Phonetic Latin/Cyrillic/Greek Conversion Font Launched: 'EurAlfabet™' Key to Business in Multi-Language Europe"

NEWS PROVIDED BY
EurAlfabet
12 Sep, 2013, 01:57 ET

WASHINGTON, Sept. 12, 2013/PRNewswire-USNewswire/—The following is being released by EurAlfabet™:

A unique font designed to aid universal comprehension of all alphabets used in Europe is now available. Intended to give readers of different alphabets phonetic access to previously indecipherable script, "EurAlfabet" is suited especially for business applications in regions where diverse alphabets are in use.

EurAlfabet (for "European Universal Recognition Alphabet") facilitates universal phonetic recognition in all European languages, including English, French, German, Spanish, Italian, Dutch, Russian, Ukrainian, Serbian, Bulgarian, Greek—regardless of which alphabet is used. This is because EurAlfabet phonetically converts letters between the LATIN (e.g., English, French, etc.), CYRILLIC (e.g., Russian, etc.), and GREEK alphabets. All three alphabets are in official use by the European Union.

EurAlfabet is based on "visual phonetic conversion" (VPC), an original concept that corresponding letters in different alphabets can be designed to convey the same phonetic value. For example, the Latin letter "S" is written in Cyrillic as "C" and in Greek as "Σ" (the familiar "Sigma"). EurAlfabet provides a single letter design that is mentally "heard" by the reader as "ess," so that where an American sees an "S," a Russian looking at the same letter would see a "C." The same VPC principle is applied to all other letters in all three alphabets.

Because readers of the Cyrillic and Greek alphabets generally are more familiar with the Latin alphabet than vice versa, EurAlfabet is particularly useful in parts of Central and Eastern Europe where western speakers of English, French, German, etc., may have difficulty in recognizing the local letters. This has great functionality for electronic applications and for understanding of displays relating to—

- Everyday needs (telephone, hotel, restaurant, park, internet);
- Place names (city names, districts, sites of interest);
- Company names; and
- People's names.

According to its purchase license, buyers of EurAlfabet have unlimited rights to use the font in company names, logos, emblems, stationary, signs, and advertising. In addition to standard characters, EurAlfabet provides supplemental symbols, such as accented vowels, the German "Eszett" (ß), and the new sign for the Russian ruble. EurAlfabet is under trademark and design patent protection.

ATTENTION FOUNDRIES: Contact EurAlfabet to arrange distribution rights.

Contacts: office@euralfabet.com and EurAlfabet1@gmail.com or 202–375–1007

Open Letter to Michael Dukakis

Open Letter to Michael Dukakis

Dimitrios Georgiou Iatreidis, March 25, 1988

ORIGINAL COVER LETTER

The enclosed document (AN OPEN LETTER TO GOVERNOR MICHAEL DUKAKIS FROM A GREEK ORTHODOX LAYMAN) addresses matters that must be of grave concern to you. It is an appeal to Governor Dukakis to abandon positions publicly held by him—*particularly his zealous advocacy of abortion and public funding of abortion*—that contradict the teachings of the Orthodox Church. Copies have been sent to all Orthodox bishops in the U.S. as well as to many priests and laymen.

In the event that the Governor will not return to the Church's teachings, this letter asks him to explicitly acknowledge his apostasy from the Orthodox Christian faith and, thereby, from the moral basis of the Greek nation. It also asks Orthodox Christian, both clergy and laity, to cease their silence concerning Governor Dukakis's impious views, speak the truth about them, and cease their support for him and, by extension, his assault on decent people.

Some of us, both clergy and laity, may be of a mind to "pass the buck" with regard to Governor Dukakis. We may think: this is all "just politics," or "let his priest or his bishop discipline him." I cannot accept that. The Governor's anti-Christian positions are a public assault on the reputation of the Orthodox Church and on the name of the Greek nation. If we remain silent, we become the Governor's accomplices. In particular, I ask the Orthodox clergy, both Greek and non-Greek, the bishops especially: do not assume that your flock knows better, or that it is clear to them the Governor has placed himself outside the Church. Many people, your flock, do *not* know better. Many are helping him because they think he is a fellow Greek or a fellow Orthodox.

The Governor's pro-abortion responsibility is not abstract or theoretical but concrete. In 1977 and 1978 Governor Dukakis vetoed efforts by the Massachusetts legislature to cut off or restrict Medicaid funding of abortions. ABORTIONS WERE FUNDED AND PERFORMED THAT WOULD NOT HAVE OCCURRED EXCEPT FO THE GOVERNOR'S ACTION. Thus, Governor Dukakis, wielding his veto pen, is as directly culpable in those killings as the abortionist wielding his suction tube. Governor Dukakis is an impenitent mass murderer; he is proud of himself.

The year 1988 is a watershed for Orthodoxy in America. One way or the other, we will be sending a loud message to our fellow citizens about who we are and what our Church stands for. We can stand up and say: No, Governor Dukakis is NOT an Orthodox Christian, and his message is in direct opposition to the true Apostolic faith to which we hold fast. Or we can remain silent in the face of the Governor's cynical use of our name and reputation for his obscene purposes, perhaps irreparably damaging Orthodox witness in this country. "Look" people will say, "there is Michael Dukakis, the first Greek Orthodox presidential candidate—pro-abortion, pro-communist, pro-sodomy."

We cannot sit quietly by while unknowing Orthodox Christians help the Governor. All of us clergy and laity, must speak out, talk to our priests and bishops, and demand action.

The faithful must be warned, and it is YOUR responsibility to do so.

/signed/

Dimitrios Georgiou Iatreidis
(in English: James George Jatras)
[address redacted]

(PUBLICATION OR REPRODUCTION IS NOT ONLY PERMITTED
BUT ENCOURAGED)

AN OPEN LETTER TO GOVERNOR MICHAEL DUKAKIS FROM A GREEK ORTHODOX LAYMAN

March 25, 1988 (n.s.)
Feast of the Annunciation
Greek Independence Day

The Honorable Michael Dukakis
Governor, Commonwealth of Massachusetts
State House, Boston

Dear Governor Dukakis:

For several years, with great pride, many Americans of Greek origin have intently followed your political career—first as a Massachusetts legislator, then as governor, now as a leading contender for the presidency of the greatest republic in the Free World. Conscious of this attention, you have openly proclaimed your ethnic roots, in seemingly your every public utterance pointing to the unprecedented achievements of "this son of Greek immigrants." In turn, the breadth of the Greek community in America has responded, providing you (according to press accounts) with some 20 percent of the funds available to your campaign.

But as you well know, your self-identification as a Greek has not only ethnic but religious implications. Your religious affiliation is noted matter-of-factly in the press as Greek Orthodox, and that is how you identified yourself in an interview earlier this year with the *National Catholic Register*. Your campaign office in Washington responds to inquiries about your religious views likewise: Governor Dukakis is Greek Orthodox. Archbishop Iakovos, primate of the Greek Orthodox Church in the Americas, writing in the *Orthodox Observer* in January about the advances made by Greek Orthodox people in the New World, enthused: "We have a presidential candidate! And if we are united we can advance still further." The public conclusion is obvious: you are Greek, you are Greek Orthodox, you are one of us . . .

But are you really one of us?

For almost two thousand years, since Saint Paul preached on Mars' hill to the Athenians, since Saints Peter and Paul laid the foundations of the Church at Corinth, the Greeks have professed the Christian faith and supplied numberless witnesses and martyrs for Christ Who preserved them through centuries of hardship, war, and poverty, and enslavement under an alien yoke. It was in recognition of this that the superiors and representatives of the sacred and pious monasteries of the Holy Mountain of Athos, in an extra-ordinary council in 1980, referred to the Orthodox Church as the "Mother and Nourisher of our [i.e., the Greek] nation." Without Her protection, you and I, Governor Dukakis, would not have had any opportunity to be Americans or to enjoy the benefits of this blessed land—we would never have been born, our race long since extinguished many centuries ago, lost in the mists of time with the Galatians, the Phrygians, and the Thracians. Thus, the Greek nation, and every Greek-American, lives only by the grace of our eternal Lord and Savior, the God-man Jesus Christ, and of His Church. Certainly, it is possible to be an Orthodox Christians without being an ethnic Greek (and indeed the great majority of Orthodox Christians are not Greeks). But the converse is not true: To be a Greek, one must be an Orthodox Christian; a Greek who apostatizes from the Orthodox Christian faith is also a traitor to his ethnic origins. Such an apostate turns his back not only on Christ and salvation but assaults the memory of his holy Christ-ransomed forebears and the blood of those countless among them who laid down their lives for His sake.

Thus, Governor Dukakis, I ask you: are you one of us, are you an Orthodox Christian? I understand perfectly that being a politician is no easy matter, that there are difficult ethical and practical questions to be faced that may not always be held to account in a strictly religious context. So perhaps we can dismiss as "just politics" allegations that your liberal furlough policy for violent criminals is a public danger, or that your Massachusetts "economic miracle" is not how you depict it; these areas of political disagreement are not the crucial matters that concern me or those that should concern your Greek Orthodox supporters. Rather, there are other questions, relating to your religious values and your position with respect to our Holy Orthodox Church, that must be addressed. These are, primarily, three: your attitude toward communism; your family status with respect to the Church; and, worst of all, your zealous advocacy of abortion and public funding of abortion.

First, it must be understood that communism is not just another political viewpoint. Through its violent attack on human society and religion it leaves scarcely any of the Ten Commandments unbroken: by murder, stealing, coveting, blasphemy, and the usurpation of God's place by a new materialistic god, History. Communism's record of holocaust against the Church, begun in Russia in 1917 with the massacre of clergy and wholesale destruction of churches, can leave little doubt of its fundamental motivation in militant atheism. No, it is more than atheism; it is hatred of God, it is war against Him (literally, from the Greek: *Theomachy*). One would think that anyone of Greek origin would recall that just 40 years ago Greece narrowly escaped a cruel fate at the hand of red Theomachists aided by then-dictator Joseph Stalin and all the resources of the world communist movement. Only after a bitter and brutal struggle, with the communists at one point holding virtually the entire country and subjecting it to their savagery (as depicted in the motion picture and book *Eleni* by Nicholas Gage), did Greece emerge victorious. And if the Greek nationalists had not received crucial aid from the United States, the communists certainly would have won.

Perhaps this is old history to you, Governor Dukakis, but it should not be. At this very moment in which you aspire to the most responsible secular office in the world, we find ourselves and our neighbors threatened here, right on our own North American continent, with the very same Theomachy defeated four decades ago in Greece. Motivated by one and the same God-hating communist worldview, Marxism-Leninism, the nine-man Sandinista leadership in

Nicaragua, with the support of the Soviet Union, Castro's Cuba, East Germany, North Korea, Vietnam, Libya, and a host of other communist and terrorist entities, has declared a "revolution without borders." By the Sandinistas' own admission, this revolution is aimed initially at the other countries of Central America, and then to Mexico; but the ultimate target is the United States. As *Comandante* Tomas Borge, Minister of the Interior and a member of the nine-man Sandinista junta, stated to North Korean audience in 1980 (when Nicaragua's largest aid donor was the United States under the Carter Administration): "The Nicaraguan revolutionaries will not be content until the imperialists have been overthrown in all part so the world. . . . We stand with the forces of peace and progress, which are socialist countries." In 1981, another of the nine *comandantes*, Defense Minister Umberto Ortega, told army officers: "We are anti-Yankee, . . . we are guided by the scientific doctrine of the revolution, by Marxism-Leninism."

Even as Greek patriots in the 1940s took up arms in defense of their country and their faith, Nicaraguan patriots—the Nicaraguan Resistance, the "Contras"—have done likewise in the 1980s. In the 1940s, America stood by the Greeks. But what is your answer, you "son of Greek immigrants," to the Nicaraguans today? A kick in the teeth. Let's face it, Governor: if in 1947 we had had a "Dukakis Doctrine" in place of the Truman Doctrine, Greece today would be a member of the Warsaw Pact. We cannot now, four decades later, afford to be so stupid as to permit a little Warsaw Pact to form right here in our own front yard.

I have watched you debate with the other Democratic candidates, who also opposed aid to the Nicaraguan democratic resistance, and I have noted the passion, the commitment you bring to this issue. You even interject the "not another dollar for Contra aid" theme into discussion of unrelated matters. Visibly, your heart is in this. You really want to see the Contras lose and the communist Sandinistas win. For you it is, perversely, a moral issue. Just as I look at both the Greek civil war in the 1940s and the Nicaraguan civil war today as a clash of moral visions, good guys against bad buys, Christian against antichrists, you see it the same way—the only difference being that you see the communist God-hating Sandinistas, about whom I have never heard a bad word from you, as the good guys.

I reiterate, the communists are Theomachists, strugglers against God; those who call themselves Greeks, children of the only Orthodox Christian nation that has not fallen to communist terror and slavery, have a special moral obligation to be truthful about this. Neither you nor I are absolved from this obligation because others do not perceive it or shoulder it.

I am sorry if I appear to assume too much about what you believe in your heart of hearts, as if any man (certainly not I) were capable of reading what lies within. But in this imperfect world we have to rely on outward indices and form opinions on the information available to us, as *evidence* of what probably lies within. We are not to judge or condemn one another, leaving that to the Judge of all men. I would hesitate to analyze the motives of another Christian, a private citizen, preferring to leave the welfare of his soul to himself. But when a man embarks upon the path of seeking public power, we are forced to form a judgement, whether we want to or not, based on the best guess we can make of who this man is and for what purposes he seeks power. I suppose this is what they call nowadays (post Gary Hart) the "character issue"; if we want to know what a president would do, we must know who he is; we do not judge the man, lest we be judges, but we must, as believers and as citizens, assess his actions and the motivations underlying them. And with regard to you, Governor Dukakis, every outward indication is that you have turned your back on your religious and ethnic origins, regarding the latter as just a convenient prop for your stump speech. As for genuine religious values, whatever you may feel inside (about which we can only guess), we must draw the conclusion from outward appearances that you have renounced the Christian faith and severed your ties to the Orthodox Church, in which you were born, baptized, and chrismated.

Which brings us to my second point: clearly, from a formal standpoint, your membership in the Church has been severed by your marriage outside the Church. To be specific, your marriage to a non-Christian, which cannot be sanctified by the Church, suspends you from the sacraments. So that your defenders will not try to raise the false spectre of anti-Semitism, because your wife is Jewish, it needs to be spelled out: the situation would be the same if she were a Buddhist, a Muslim, a Hindu, or, for that matter, a Unitarian. The important thing is that the Church can accept only a marital union with a Christian who professes the Holy Life-Giving Trinity; even a Christian who is not Orthodox is tolerable. So, even in this minimum sense, your Orthodoxy is negated.

I do not mean to emphasize this too strongly. Love, as they say, is blind. We do not deliberately choose with whom to fall in love, and it is not hard to understand that a man could fall in love with a non-Cristian woman and could not find life bearable without her. Perhaps such a situation should be regarded more as tragic than as a willful rebellion against the Church, and I cannot speak to the motivations of this matter either of you or your wife, neither of whom do I know personally. Perhaps we should accept that one could enter into a marriage outlawed by the Church, to all appearances choosing one's own spouse over the Bride of Christ, but still harboring in one's soul a love of Christ. This cannot be judged but by Him who reads the secrets of all men's hearts . . .

But children are another matter. Here, the natural stirrings of a parent's love must, if that parent has the slightest residue of Orthodox Christian belief, dictate the child's baptism. Any loving parent, Christian or non-Christian, gives his children, his own flesh and flood, whatever good things he can—food, clothing, shelter, education, warmth, guidance—not out of obligation but because he loves his children more than he loves himself. But for a Christian, to give his children all the good things life has to offer, but to deny them Christ, is to give them nothing. What good is it, for a Christian, to give children material life, which lasts but a day, and to hide from them the knowledge of the life in Christ, which is forever? What good is it, for a Christian, to see his children gain the whole world but lose their souls? We know that even the most sincere Christian parent cannot ensure his child's salvation any more than he can ensure he will turn out well in other respects as he grows up. But at least he can, he must, point these young souls entrusted to his care in the right direction—and for an Orthodox Christian, this means presenting the new infant to the Church for baptism, even as our Lord was presented in the Temple in Jerusalem on the eighth day after his birth, with Saint Simeon as His witness.

Whether or not an infant is baptized is key evidence not of a parent's love but of his faith: non-Christians do not baptize their children (and some Christians who do not believe in infant baptism delay in baptizing them) not because they hate their children but because they do not consider it necessary for the infant's welfare. It is not lack of parental love but a difference of faith. Thus, a purported Orthodox Christian who does not baptize his children is thereby denying the Orthodox faith through his inaction. A believing Orthodox Christian (even one of weak faith) knows that baptism is a beginning of life in the spiritual sense; it is Christ taking the child by the hand before he is even capable of thought. The child's mind might not yet comprehend but his soul does.

It is my understanding, Governor Dukakis, that none of your three children is baptized. Reportedly, when asked about this, you have responded that you and your wife have tried to "raise them in both cultures." But it is not culture you have denied your children but Christ. It is the light of Christ that enters the child's soul at baptism, the gift of the Holy Spirit conferred upon that soul at chrismation, that you have denied. This is the antithesis of faith.

Not long ago, in Russia, a woman brought her infant daughter to a priest for baptism. After baptizing the child, the priest was amazed to find out that the woman was not a Christian and that she could not even bring herself to believe in the existence of God. He asked her, naturally enough, why she had had her daughter baptized. She replied: "So that her life will not be empty like mine." We see that this woman, calling herself an unbeliever, nonetheless had *faith*. Despite her doubts and her unbelief, like those of Saint Thomas, God had reached out His hand and touched her.

Or consider another example, from my own life. Early last year, my second daughter, Christina, was born two months premature. Initially very healthy at birth, she was afflicted with a serious respiratory virus when she was a few weeks old. She was helicoptered to an intensive care unit, where (as the little boy in the next room died of the same illness) superbly skilled doctors and nurses tried, on an hour-by-hour basis, to keep her alive. She finally pulled through, though afterward the medical people told us that they had not expected her to live. That her doctors' skill, the prayers of man, and the donation of friends of, literally, their lifeblood are responsible for her recovery is undoubted; so too is the intervention of the Most-pure Mother of God, from whose miraculous myrrh-streaming icon Christina was anointed while she lay on what was, for all we knew, her deathbed. But the point here is this: the priest (her godfather) baptized Christina as soon as she arrived at the hospital, when the gravity her illness became apparent. At that point a great load was lifted from our shoulders, as we (my wife and I) continued to pray that her earthly life would not yet end; but we were secure in the knowledge that her eternal life was not at risk. Even if we had not been able to baptize her and if she had died, I cannot say that I would have been too unsure of her fate in God's merciful hands. But as Orthodox Christians, for us to know that she had become Christ's maidservant was the most important thing: even if she had lived no longer on this earth, the purpose of her short life would have been fulfilled. Anyone who retains a smidgen of Orthodox feeling could not deny this fulfillment of his child.

Which brings me to the third and final, the most important, point of this letter: the issue of abortion. When Christina was born, she weighed in at not much more than two pounds. Her crying sounded more like a kitten than a baby. It occurred to me as the nurse put her in my arms (actually, my *hands*—she was that small) that somewhere, at that very moment, for all I knew right there in that same hospital, another infant just like her was being placed not in the hands of her father but in a trash receptacle. *This one*, Christina, by accident of birth, was to be loved and cared for; *those other ones*, nameless, thousands of them each day, are consigned to drainpipe, dumpster, or incinerator.

Since that black day, January 22, 1973, when the Supreme Court handed down the infamous *Roe v. Wade* decision, striking down the abortion laws of all fifty states, from the most restrictive to the most liberal, some *twenty million* infants have been legally murdered. This means that on average, over 3,000 are killed *per day*, through all nine months of pregnancy, many of them with the use of tax dollars. The fact that abortion is so widespread and so accepted by many elements of our society stands as the foremost moral indictment of America today and a measure of how far we have fallen from the principles of the Christian faith. The legal "reasoning" behind *Roe v. Wade* has in turn spawned new horrors, justifying infanticide, euthanasia, and even the cutting off of food and water to comatose patients. Beholding this descent into barbarism, an Orthodox Christian—indeed, any decent American of any faith —must stand aghast and shudder for the fate of his country.

For its part, the Orthodox Church has never deviated from its condemnation of abortion, based not only on numerous Scriptural references but on the teaching of the Holy Fathers of the Church, who with one voice condemned the taking of human life in the womb. From the very beginning of the Church, abortion was considered the equal of murder, and aborters were sentenced to lifelong penance. In the area of Canon law, the reginal Council of Ancyra (A.D. 314) prescribed a period of ten years' penance, the reduction from the life sentence previously in force evidencing not a change of view as to the gravity of the offense but of mercy for the penitent. In A.D. 691, the representatives of the entire Church assembled in council in the city of Constantinople (called variously the Quinisext Council, or the Council in Trullo; see *The Rudder*) and decreed, Canon XCI, that the punishment for anyone who procures an abortion is the same as that for a murderer. I emphasize that Canon XCI, which is still in force, is effective over the entire Church and is binding on all Orthodox Christians without exception.

Some other churches, with a more legalistic frame of mind, might quibble about "attenuated causality" or "indirect responsibility" or engage in similar pettifoggery, saying that a pro-abortion legislator, judge, or executive official cannot be held responsible by the Church for the consequences of his actions. Orthodox Christians should not put up with any of that nonsense: we know when a person is guilty of abortion—when he advocates it, justifies it, forces people to pay for it, and opposes and frustrates efforts to stop it. If a man is guilty of the murderous crime of "procuring" abortion when he uses his own money to kill his own unborn child, how much worse is a government official who uses his office to force unwilling citizens to pay for the killing of thousands, perhaps millions, of children!

Your record on abortion is as clear as it is evil and impious. Even before *Roe v. Wade*, as a Massachusetts legislator, you introduced a bill [H. 3756] to repeal all restrictions on abortion then part of Massachusetts statute. As governor, after *Roe v. Wade*, you have fought all efforts arising in the legislature to restrict the use of public monies to pay for abortions, liberally employing your veto power. In November 1986, you actively opposed a ballot referendum that would have restricted abortion, and you consistently have championed Medicaid funding for abortions. You do not even have the decency to be hypocritical about your support for abortion (like such nominal Roman Catholics as Mario Cuomo and Geraldine Ferraro, with their famous, "I'm personally opposed to abortion, *but* . . ." stance). No, you are an advocate, a zealot, a veritable Apostle of Abortion, an Evangelist of Infanticide, a keynote speaker at a 1986 Planned Parenthood "celebration" in Boston of the *Roe v. Wade* death decision.

At that ghoulish "celebration" you said: "I don't know when life begins. I'm not sure I ever will." Governor, the Church *tells* you when life begins. If you don't know, it is because you refuse to listen.

In a predominantly non-Orthodox society you may try to hide under the threadbare rug of "pluralism," saying you have no right to "impose morality" on people. But *all law* is an imposition of morality, often if not always based on religious views: murder is illegal because it is *wrong*; stealing is illegal because it is *wrong*. After a great civil war, we outlawed slavery in this country because it is *wrong* to hold human beings, created in the image and likeness of God, as chattels. Would you trot out "pluralism" in defense of slavery? Would you advocate a "pro-choice" stand on human bondage, allowing each slave-owner to consider the question of whether or not to own slaves is not a human rights issue but a property issue, that every man has the right to "control his own property"? Would you swear fealty to the *Dred Scott* decision with the same inflexibility with which you support *Roe v. Wade*? Your answer is clearly no; in defense of your support of public funding of abortion you answered in 1977: "No, I would not have supported the idea of providing poor whites with slaves in the last century, simply because the Supreme Court sanctioned the rights of whites to own slaves, *because I am against slavery.*" Exactly so: you are *against* slavery but *for* abortion, and that is all the difference; it is wrong, in your mind, to imprison people for their race but alright to kill them for their tender age.

One could go on and on to chronicle your sustained assault on everything good and decent, both as legislator and governor, revealing your efforts to leave not one stone upon another in the edifice of Christian morality—your fervent support for so-called "gay rights" (actually, special status for Sodomites), your veto of a 1988 Massachusetts budget provision prohibiting the placement of foster children with homosexuals and bisexuals, your legislative efforts to repeal laws against blasphemy [H. 3483], and so much more that the heart sickens at the retelling of it. In what frenzy have you done these things, by what demon are you driven?!

You may ask: who is this loudmouth, this scribbler, this troublemaker, to sit in judgement over me? And I answer: just another sinner, who—like you and the Publican and all other miserable souls—is in desperate need of Christ's saving grace, crying out: "Lord, have mercy on me (*Kyrie eleison*)." As I stated near the outset of this letter, I would not consider it my place to question, like the Pharisee, your motivations, your thoughts, your faith, the state of your soul. For you, as a private person, it is your responsibility to look into your own soul, with the help of your priest (if you have one) and your bishop. I am well aware of my failings, maybe more than yours, and it is not my place to judge you or anyone else.

But at the same time, I cannot sit by silently while a public figure, to all appearances using our name but not sharing our faith, stands up and attacks our Church and attacks Christ. This is not "just politics"! You may say: but other Greeks, bishops even, give me friendship and support. And I answer: let it be on their heads. When the Last Day comes, when all the world, both the living and the dead, stand before Christ the Ruler of All to be judged, let them admit to Him: "Yes, I was a friend of Michael, the killer of babes; yes, I helped him and promoted him to power; yes, I did not oppose the evil he did to God and man but assisted him." Trembling before Him and the assembled multitude, my heart black with my own transgressions, I even now give thanks that *that*, by the Lord's infinite mercy, will not be among them.

Michael: Addressing you not by your gubernatorial title but by your Christian name, I implore you: *turn away* from the Godlessness and the lawlessness you have adopted as your principle! Listen to the teachings of the Holy Fathers, heed the prayers of the glorious and victorious Saints and Martyrs, respect the blood of the innocent. Cease trampling upon the divine seed that was planted in you in your infancy more than a half century ago and let it grow. Return, Michael, to faith in the God-man Jesus Christ, our one True God, and to the communion of His One, Holy, Catholic and Apostolic Orthodox Church—for the sake of your own soul and our country.

Does my appeal fall on deaf ears? I pledge, Governor Dukakis, that if you answer my appeal in the affirmative, that if you return to the Church and renounce your blasphemies—indeed, if only you will cease complicity in the murder of unborn infants—I will be the first to welcome you back and call you brother. And if I have cited anything incorrectly, in any of the foregoing with respect to communism, your family status, or abortion, I will issue a full and abject retraction, even as I have sent forth this letter.

But if, Governor Dukakis, the facts are as I have set them out, and if you retain your hardness of heart and persist in your chosen path, you must take the following steps:

Firstly, that you announce, publicly and categorically, that you are an apostate from the Orthodox Christian faith and a pagan, having by your own word and deed demanded that your name be stricken from the Book of Life.

Secondly, that you also announce that, on account of your apostasy from the Church, you no longer regard yourself as Greek, having turned your back on the essence of the Greek nation, which is its faith in Christ.

Thirdly, that you cease milking the Greek community, or any other community of pious Orthodox Christians, for donations to support your campaign, based on false perceptions of ethnic or religious solidarity, and confine your efforts in this regard to such organizations that share your Godless views: Planned Parenthood, National Abortion Rights Action League, National Organization for Women, the American Civil Liberties Union, People for the American Way, and other such groups with which I assume you to be far more familiar than I.

Rest assured, Governor, that I am not the only Greek Orthodox Christian who feels this way. Laity as well as clergy, we have an obligation to defend our Church. As the *Circular Epistle of the Eastern Patriarchs* of 1848, a declaration of the four ancient sees of Constantinople, Alexandria, Antioch, and Jerusalem, co-signed by twenty-nine metropolitans, stated: "No patriarch or council has ever been able to introduce any novelty among us, since the Body of the Church, that is, the people themselves, is the guardian of religion." And this letter is an appeal precisely to the entire Body of the Church, in all of the its members, the strength of Orthodoxy. Accordingly, I have sent copies of this letter to the bishops and the priests (both of the Archdiocese and of other jurisdictions), to Greek publications and organizations, to other Orthodox publications, and to concerned laymen, as well as to many American public figures and press commentators who wish us well. From these readers, I ask:

From the bishops, both Greek and non-Greek: do not stand silently by while this imposter defames our Church. With all due filial respect, I beg you: pronounce this man Michael to be *anathema*, in keeping with the Canons and your consciences.

From the priests, both Greek and non-Greek: be not silent in the face of the insults hurled by this man Michael, for without your guidance members of your flock may unwittingly aid him in his evil. Speak the truth.

To the Greek laity, in America and abroad, and to all Orthodox Christians of whatever nationality: do not be fooled by Governor Dukakis into thinking that he is one of us. He is a traitor and a renegade, an outcast, a member of the foul tribe of Cain and Judas. Lend him no support, oppose him at every turn.

To all decent people of all races, creeds, and national origins: do not believe that Governor Dukakis is what he represents himself to be. Expose his evil deeds, and help him to ruin. Do not think badly of us because of him.

Governor Dukakis, this is a free country. Here anyone is free to hold any view on any topic, to advocate any position or policy, for good or for ill. You may do as you please. But as a simple matter of "truth in labeling" you should not pretend to be what you are not. You cannot have your cake and eat it too. You cannot be a Greek Orthodox Christian—and also be pro-abortion, pro-communist, pro-blasphemy, pro-sodomy, and so on. You must choose. I do not want my daughters growing up in a country where Michael Dukakis is a national figure, a governor, or (God forbid!) president, so that people will say to them or think: oh, you're Greek Orthodox—you must be pro-abortion, pro-communist, and all the rest of it. We are decent Christian folk. Your continued identification with us is a standing slap in the face of our Holy Church and an indelible stain blackening the ancient name of the Hellenic race. This is not "just politics"; this is a spiritual assault against us. And it is spiritual suicide against yourself.

For ultimately, whatever I or other men say or write about you, remember always that there is One above us who watches and judges all things. Remember the fate of your predecessor in the slaughter of innocents, an earlier governor who exalted himself: Herod the Great, King of Judea, who massacred the infants of Bethlehem in his vain attempt on the life of our Savior. Remember how God smote him with an agonizing death, exuding worms and a terrible stench. For your welfare, above all else, open your eyes and see the blood on your hands, take fear, and repent.

May God have mercy on you, on me and on all of us.

/signed/

Dimitrios
an unworthy servant of our redeemer,
Jesus Christ, Who rose from the dead
and lives forever

Dimitrios Iatreidis
   in English: James George Jatras
Alexandria, Virginia

Reply to a Roman Catholic

Reply to a Roman Catholic

James George Jatras | August 22, 1995

This letter was my last in an exchange with a well-known Roman Catholic apologist who was born into an Orthodox family and specializes in opposing Orthodoxy. In order to keep the focus on substance, not personalities, the gentleman's name and identifying information has been redacted, though discerning readers can probably figure out who he is.

James George Jatras
[address redacted]

August 22, 1995 (n.s.)
Martyrs Agathonikos and Charisimos
[name redacted]
[address redacted]

Dear Mr. [name redacted],

Please accept my abject and genuine apologies for not having replied sooner to your letters to me of October 1, 1993, and August 23, 1994. To answer the question posed in your second epistle (of which I have enclosed a copy for your easier reference, along with copies of its predecessor and my reply to it of November 10, 1993): No, your not receiving a return letter from me was not due to misdirection caused by [*organization redacted*]'s offices having moved. Rather, this unconscionable failure was entirely mine, due to (1) my initial (and perhaps excusable) desire to research the matters to which you referred in your first letter and to seek guidance from other, more knowledgeable Orthodox sources; (2) my unfortunate (and not so excusable tendency to be distracted other, not necessarily more urgent, matters; and (3) my *extremely* disorganized (and absolutely inexcusable) manner of handling correspondence—to the effect that I had misplaced your last writing to me for quite some months and have only recently relocated it. I can very much understand if you have lost interest in this matter and do not wish to continue the exchange; also, I am not sure if I should write to you at this address or at [*organization redacted*]'s office in [*location redacted*]. Nonetheless, I believe you deserve a response, however belated. Here it is. I have endeavored to elucidate what I regard as the essential problems that separate Rome from Orthodoxy, and have included illustrative enclosures; I have also relied heavily on quotations from relevant authorities (and consequently increased the length of the letter) so as to ensure, to the best of my ability, that I am giving not just my personal opinion (which has no intrinsic value) but a response that accords with Church teaching. In order to be as direct as possible, I thought it best to first address the issues you raised in your letter and their enclosures.

However, at the outset—even at the risk of beginning this letter on some-thing of a harsh note—I wish to be clear on one point: in answering you in detail I do not mean to suggest that the difference between Orthodoxy and Roman Catholicism should be understood to be merely the sum of the dif-ferences on the various "points of disagreement" (the *filioque*, the papacy, Purgatory, *azymes*, etc.). Rather, in a real sense, these are symptoms of a more profound divergence between two entirely differently religions. As one of my consultants on this matter, Fr. Steven Allen, a former Roman Catholic, has put it (this is a close paraphrase): "Orthodoxy is the divinely revealed and divinely instituted Christianity of the Gospels and the early Church, and Roman Catholicism is not. . . . No one who has embraced the Holy Fathers as true Fathers in the Faith, and has taken even one feeble but sincere step on their sorrowful, narrow, and stony path, the path indicated by Our Savior as the only way to salvation, would mistake the path of Roman Catholicism for anything but what it is, one of the countless varieties of the broad path which leads to perdition."

To take last matters first, with your August 1994 letter you enclosed your article "Testimony to the Primacy of the Pope by a 17th Century Orthodox Prelate" from the January/February 1992 issue of *Social Justice Review*. In it you discuss, with substantial excerpts, the favorable attitude toward papal primacy of Peter of Moghila (or Mohila), Metropolitan bishop of Polish-occupied Kiev from 1633 until his death in 1647. A few observations appear to be in order:

• Not in any way to detract from his merits, Peter's tendency as a Latinizer is well-known, as is the reason for that tendency, to wit, the necessity to refute the perhaps even worse Protestantizing found in the writings of his contemporary, Patriarch Cyril (Lukaris) of Constantinople (1572–1638). As Bishop Kallistos (Ware) points out:

> Cyril's Calvinism was sharply and speedily repudiated by his fellow Orthodox, his *Confession* [of 1629] being condemned by no less than six local councils between 1638 and 1691. In direct reaction to Cyril two other Orthodox hierarchs, Peter of Moghila and Dositheus of Jerusalem, produced Confessions of their own. Peter's *Orthodox Confession*, written in 1640, was based directly on Roman Catholic manuals. . . . On the whole, however, the *Confession* of Dositheus is less Latin than that of Moghila, and must certainly be regarded as a document of primary import-ance in the history of modern Orthodox theology. Faced with the Calvinism of Lukaris, Dositheus used the weapons which lay nearest to hand—Latin weapons (under the circumstances it was perhaps the only thing that he could do); but the faith he defend-ed with these Latin weapons was not Roman, but Orthodox. [*The Orthodox Church*, Timothy (Kallistos) Ware, 1964 Penguin edi-tion, pp. 107–108]

• In charity, what is said for Dositheus might be said for Peter; after all, when it came to doctrinal polemics, the "less Latin" Dositheus enjoyed the relative "luxury" of living under Ottoman, not Polish, rule. In a period when, with the sole, and often precarious, exception of Muscovy, the entire Orthodox world was under the political domination and religious oppression of Muslims or Roman Catholics, and when Orthodox scholar-ship had fallen to an all-time low, it is not surprising that our doctrinal defenses against the Scylla of Protestantism would be influenced by the Charybdis of Roman Catholicism, and vice versa.

In any case, Peter's prescription is no solution to the Orthodox/Roman Catholic disagreement about authority in the Church. (By the way, I am relying on your translated text and have no independent confirmation that this was indeed his position; but I do not dispute it.) As you summarize Peter, his views "anticipate by 3 centuries the . . . counsels set forth in Vatican II's Decree on Ecumenism . . ."; "the need to respect the liturgical heritage of the Eastern churches; lessening Roman centralization over the Eastern rites; and restoring the historical canonical prerogatives of the patriarchs." As I will address later in this letter, this seeming compromise, as with parallel "solutions" to the *filioque* controversy, does nothing to clarify the issue.

Suffice it for the moment to say, whatever Peter may have intended, these recommendations can only amount in practice to our total submission the papacy. They constitute no more than revocable dispensations granted by an absolute sovereign, not evidences of the fraternal love that properly exists between one successor to the holy Apostles and another.

In assessing Peter's possible contribution to a resolution of the Orthodox/Roman Catholic separation, it is illustrative of the difficulties involved that you make passing mention of another major figure of the time: "In 1623 the Ruthenian Catholics saw their holy Archbishop of Polostk, St. Josaphat Kuntsevich, receive the crown of martyrdom at the hands of opponents of union." Our recollection of this worthy, which is somewhat at odds with your characterization, perhaps sheds some light on the circumstances of the Orthodox under 17th century Polish rule (from "The Vatican and Russia," by Deacon Herman Ivanov-Treenadzaty in *Orthodox Life*, date unknown, published by Holy Trinity Monastery, Jordanville, NY; notes omitted):

> The very memory of this most evil of personalities is inconceivably scandalous. To recall his last name is in itself a "casus belli." Just before his "martyr's end," which occurred on November 12, 1623, in Vitebsk, Kuntsevich ordered the disposal of dead Orthodox by having their corpses exhumed and thrown to dogs. In all of his Polotsky diocese, both in Mogilyov and in Orsha, he pillaged and terrorized the Orthodox, closing and burning churches. Eloquent complaints were sent to judges and to the Polish Sejm. The most convincing condemnation of Kuntsevich's character is found in a letter dated March 12, 1622, one and a half years before his death, from the Lithuanian chancellor Leo Sapiega, clearly a Roman Catholic, the representative of the Polish king himself: "By thoughtless violence you oppress the Russian [incidentally, "Rut(h)enian" is merely a Medieval Latin rendering of the word Russian and does not convey a separate ethnic identification] people and urge them on to revolt. You are aware of the censure of the simple people, that it would be better to be in Turkish captivity than to endure such persecutions for faith and piety. You write that you freely drown the Orthodox, chop off their heads, and profane their churches. You seal their churches so the people, without piety and Christian rites, are buried like non-Christians. In place of joy, your cunning Uniatism has brought us only woe, unrest, and conflict. We would prefer to be without it. These are the fruits of your Uniatism." Let us remember that these words are not fantasies or the slanders of a fanatically-tempered Orthodox, but the contents of a historical letter from the head of a Roman Catholic state, the Chancellor of the Grand Duchy of

Lithuania, written on behalf of the Polish King to a turbulent Uniate bishop. In the very same letter and with much foresight Leo Sapiega writes, "It would have been better not to have given us nationwide strife and hatred, and instead to have preserved us from nationwide condemnation."

Arriving in Vitebsk on the 12th of November, 1623, with a band of his cohorts, Kuntsevich proceeded to knock down the tents where the Orthodox secretly held divine services. One of Kuntsevich's deacons attacked an Orthodox priest. The crowd, which had run out of patience, then turned on Kuntsevich, who was personally heading the pogrom, and with sticks and stones beat him to death. His maimed body was placed in a sack and tossed into the Diva River. Such was the inglorious end of the earthly life of this alleged 'apostle of unity' as none other than Pope John Paul II shamelessly dares to call him. Before John Paul II, Pius IX on June 19, 1867, already glorified Josaphat Kuntsevich as a saint. In 1923, on the occasion of the 300th anniversary of Kuntsevich's death, Pius XI published an encyclical *Ecclesiam Dei (The Church of God)* in which Kuntsevich is named "hieromartyr," a "righteous person," and where it is said that such an example of "holy life" should aid in unifying all Christians.

On November 25, 1963, during the rule of Paul VI, Kuntsevich's remains were brought to Rome to the papal basilica of St. Peter, where they now "rest" under the altar of St. Basil the Great, near the relics of Sts. Gregory the Theologian and John Chrysostom. Without any remorse and at the same time scorning historical truth in order to satisfy his petty interests in a struggle with Orthodoxy, John Paul II is not afraid to speak about the "noble personality" of Josaphat, "whose spilled blood has forever fortified the great work of the Unia." In his message to his Ukrainian flock, *Magnum Baptismi Donum (The Great Gift of Baptism)*, published on April 19, 1988, not a single word rectifies the now established (false) representation of Uniatism and the actions of Kuntsevich. [John Paul's praise for Josaphat Kuntsevich calls to mind his similar accolades during his 1994 visit to Zagreb for the late archbishop of that city, Aloyius Cardinal Stepinac, an enthusiastic supporter of the World War II pro-Nazi regime of Croatian dictator Ante Pavelic, which slaughtered hundreds of thousands of Orthodox Serbs.]

I now turn to the points you raised in your letter of October 11, 1993:

- The citation from St. Gregory the Dialogist purporting to show that he taught the *filioque* is not one that is usually raised in connection with that debate. As you recall, St. Gregory, in this passage (*Dialogues*, Book 2:38), is relating the miracle of a woman cured of madness by spending the night in the cave where St. Benedict had once lived. In his characteristic format, St. Gregory answers the question put to him by his deacon, Peter: Why do the martyrs often grant greater miracles in locations where they are not buried than in places where they are? St. Gregory answers with an analogy to the fact that the Holy Spirit, who is sent into the world by the Father (John 14:26) and by the Son (John 15:26, 16:7), is made more greatly manifest after the Son is taken up into heaven than when He was still present in the flesh: "The point is that as long as the disciples could see our Lord in His human flesh they would want to keep on seeing Him with their bodily eyes. With good reason, therefore, did He tell them, 'If I do not go, the Advocate with not come.' What He really meant was, 'I cannot teach you spiritual love unless I remove my body from your sight; as long as you continue to see me with your bodily eyes you will never learn to love me spiritually.'" [*The Fathers of the Church: A New Translation, Saint Gregory the Great: Dialogues*, translated by Odo John Zimmerman, O.S.B., published by Fathers of the Church, Inc., New York, 1959, pp. 109–110] In this context, it is clear that St. Gregory is referring to the temporal mission of the Holy Spirit, Who is indeed "from the Son" in the limited sense that He is sent by the Son (John 15:26). The fact that, in the Latin, St. Gregory uses the preposition *a*, rather than *ex*, is also indicative (though not dispositive) that he means a "sending forth from" not "originating out of." Likewise indicative, though not dispositive, is his use of *semper* ("always"), which would tend to indicate repeated or continuing action—that is, temporal action—rather than eternal origin.

- With regard to your other citation of St. Gregory's work (*Dialogues* Book 4:39; actually, the edition cited above has it as 4:41), I believe you are interpreting his expressions in light of a system of thought that arose long after his death, thus drawing from it a meaning he could never have intended or even imagined. St. Gregory's reference to fire here is based on 1 Cor. 3:11–15, which he himself goes on to quote. The Dialogist's writings, as of course the Corinthian passage that undergirds it, were noted by St. Mark of Ephesus in his refutation of the Latin teaching on purgatory at the "Union Council" of Ferrara-Florence (1439–39), in which he reiterated the authentic apostolic and patristic teaching:

> But if souls have departed this life in faith and love, while nevertheless carrying away with themselves certain faults, whether small ones over which they have not repented at all, or great ones for which—even though they have repented of them—they did not undertake to show fruits of repentance: such souls, we believe, must be cleansed from this kind of sins, but not by means of some purgatorial fire or a definite punishment in some place (for this, as we have said, has not at all been handed down to us). But some must be cleansed in the very departure of the body, thanks only to fear, as St. Gregory the Dialogist literally shows [Author's note: in Book IV of the Dialogues]; while other must be cleansed after the departure from the body, either while remaining in the same earthly place, before they come to worship God and are honored with the lot of the blessed, or—if their sins were more serious and bind them for a longer duration—they are kept in hell, but not in order to remain forever in fire and torment, but as it were in prison and confinement under guard." ["First Homily: Refutation of the Latin Chapters Concerning Purgatorial Fire," from *The Soul After Death*, by Hieromonk Seraphim Rose, Saint Herman of Alaska Brotherhood, Platina, CA, 1980, Appendix I, p. 207, 209; the texts of St. Mark's First and Second Homilies are enclosed.]

Three points illustrated in this passage deserve particular mention. First, the Orthodox do not deny, as do the Protestants, that some sins are forgiven only after death (Matt. 12:32). Second, it is clear that St. Mark was familiar with St. Gregory's *Dialogues* (albeit in Greek translation) and did not see in them a refutation of the Orthodox doctrine but rather its confirmation. Third, the *Dialogues* themselves supply, in the same sequence, the examples cited by St. Mark:

→ *"Some must be cleansed in the very departure from the body, thanks only to fear."* See *Dialogues* 4:48, a man who is purified of his minor faults "by the very dread that grips a departing soul" at the hour of death.

→ *"Other must be cleansed after the departure from the body . . . while remaining in the same earthly place."* See *Dialogues* 4:57, a man whose soul was sentenced after his death to serve as a bath attendant at a hot spring of which he had formerly been the owner until, through the intercessions made for him in the Divine Liturgy by the living, he was forgiven. Note the absence of any mention of fire in this account.

→ *"Or . . . they are kept in hell, but not in order to remain forever in fire and torment, but as it were in prison."* See, also in *Dialogues* 4:57, the account of the disobedient and gold-loving monk Justus, who, through the efforts of St. Gregory himself, is released over a period of 30 days from "suffering the torments of fire." However, Justus' experience of hellfire—which, in his case, was not intended for eternity but only for a short period—should be compared to the many instances in Orthodox literature where persons at the edge of death were shown hell's fiery torments (and in a few cases, briefly made to feel them) before being returned to their bodies to repent properly. (cf. *Dialogues* 4:37, the experience of the Spanish monk, Peter.) In short, there is only one punishing fire after death: that of hell.

So, if the Orthodox accept the need for some souls to be cleansed of sins after death, and if that cleansing can in some cases involve the experience of fire, does that not mean that we (much less St. Gregory!) accept Purgatory? The answer, clearly, is No. The crucial difference between our teaching, which is in complete harmony with St. Gregory and the other Fathers, Latin and Greek, and yours, which only became distinct since the time of Anselm of Canterbury, is again pointed out by St. Mark (from his "Second Homily," p. 220):

> You [i.e., the Latins] have made a certain astonishing division, saying that every sin must be understood under two aspects: (1) the offense itself, which is made to God, and (2) the punishment which follows it. Of these two aspects (you teach), the offense to God, indeed, can be remitted after repentance and turning away from evil, but the liability to punishment must exist in every case; so that, on the basis of this idea, it is essential that those released from sins should all the same be subject to punishment for them.
>
> But we allow ourselves to say that such a stating of the question contradicts clear and commonly-known truths: if we do not see a king, after he has granted an amnesty and pardon, subject the guilty to yet more punishment, then all the more God, among Whose many characteristics love of mankind is an especially outstanding one, even though He does punish a man after a sin which he has committed, still after He has forgiven him He immediately delivers him from punishment also. And this is natural. For if the offense to God leads to punishment, then when the guilt is forgiven and reconciliation has occurred, the very consequence of the guilty—the punishment—of necessity comes to an end.

Thus, we say that forgiveness of sins applies to punishment along with guilt, although these should be seen as two aspects of the same thing, not, as the Latins teach, as two different things. In opposing the idea that forgiveness of guilt is one thing and remittance of punishment another, St. Mark cannot be accused of setting forth a caricature or a misrepresentation of the Roman Catholic teaching. For example:

> By an indulgence (*indulgentia*) is under-stood the extra-sacramental remission of the temporal punishments of sins remaining after the forgiveness of the guilt of sin. . . . Remission is not a forgiveness of sin, but it presupposes as a necessary condition that the sin has been forgiven. [Dr. Ludwig Ott, *Fundamentals of Catholic Dogma*, Tan Books and Publishers, Inc., Rockford, IL, 1960, p. 441]

Likewise:

> God **could** remit the sins of mankind without any satisfaction and without violating justice (S. Th. III 46 2 ad 3). **But, in fact**, in the order of grace established by God through Christ, all forgiveness of sins is granted in virtue of a corresponding satisfaction. In the extra-sacramental remission of temporal punishments for sins in Indulgences, the Church offers to the Divine Justice a substitute satisfaction—that is, the infinite satisfaction of Christ and the superabundant satisfaction of the Saints. [Ott, p. 442, emphasis added]

Interestingly, Ott does not explain how it is known that God does not "in fact, in the order of grace" do what He admittedly "could" do, and what we Orthodox claim he does in fact do: forgive the punishment of sins when He forgives the sin itself. (Also interestingly, as support for the concept of Purgatory, Ott cites [p. 483] what appears to be your same quotation from St. Gregory, based on Matt. 12:32, wherein Christ says that some **sins** will be **forgiven** in the world (or age) to come, as if He had in fact said that the **temporal punishment for some sins already forgiven** in this world will be **remitted** in the next.) The Latin idea—that redeemed Christians must be tortured after death for sins that have been forgiven—is entirely alien to the world in which the Fathers lived and taught. A product of the intellectual climate of the High Middle Ages, it is completely anachronistic when super-imposed on St. Gregory's work, and I have not the least doubt that he would have found it as repellant as did St. Mark. In short, neither Christ nor St. Gregory teach what you claim they teach.

In closing this topic, it remains to explain the much-cited 1 Cor. 3:11–15:

> For other foundation can no man lay than is laid, which is Jesus Christ. Now if any man build upon this foundation gold, silver, precious stones, wood, hay stubble; Every man's work shall be made manifest: for the day shall declare it, because it shall be revealed by fire; and the fire shall try every man's work of what sort it is. If any man's work abide which he hath built thereupon, he shall receive a reward. If any man's work shall be burned, he shall suffer loss; but he himself shall be saved; yet so as by fire.

As St. Mark comments, "This citation, it would seem, more than any other introduces the idea of purgatorial fire; but in actual fact it more than any other refutes it." Even St. Gregory, as well as Blessed Augustine of Hippo, seems to have misunderstood it, as judged by his use of it in *Dialogues* 4:41; all the more reason why, as the Orthodox pointed out at Ferrara-Florence, "Greeks should understand Greek words better than foreigners." (I do not know whether an erroneous sense of this passage is fostered by the wording in the

Vulgate.) As St. John Chrysostom pointed out in a treatise against the Origenists (who did not believe that hell was eternal), the "day" written of by St. Paul is the Day of Judgement; the "wood, hay, and stubble" mean bad deeds, as food for the eternal fire; "saved" here means not "salvation," "deliverance from punishment," "going through purgatorial fire," or (as Blessed Augustine understood it) "bliss," but "continued existence," or "preservation" in eternal punishments; "suffer loss" means eternal tortures, loss of the divine light, perdition; and the "fire" spoken of refers to the fiery presence of God on that day (Ex. 24:17, Heb. 12:29, Dan. 7:10, Ps. 28[29]:7, 103[104]:4, 96[97]:3, Heb. 1:7, II Pet. 3:12), which shall illumine the righteous and burn (while not consuming, along with their evil works) the unrighteous, as explained by St. Mark, drawing upon the words of St. Basil the Great:

> "Basil the Great also speaks of this in the 'Morals,' in interpreting the passage of Scripture, *the voice of the Lord Who divideth the flame of fire* (Ps. 28:7): 'The fire, prepared for the torment of the devil and his angels, is divided by the voice of the Lord, so that after this there might be two powers in it: one that burns, and another that illumines; the tormenting and punishing power of that fire is reserved for those worthy of torments; while the illuminating and enlightening power is intended for the shining of those who rejoice. Therefore the voice of the Lord Who divides and separates the flame of fire is for this: that the dark part might be a fire of torment and the unburning part a light of enjoyment.' (St. Basil, Homily on Psalm 28)

> "And so, as may be seen, this division and separation of that fire will be when absolutely everyone will pass through it: the bright and shining works will be manifest yet brighter, and those who bring them will become inheritors of the light and will receive that eternal reward; while those who bring bad works suitable for burning, being punished by the loss of them, will eternally remain in fire and will inherit a salvation which is worse than perdition, for this is what, strictly speaking, the word 'saved' means—that the destroying power of fire will not be applied to them and they themselves be utterly destroyed." ["First Homily," *The Soul After Death,* pp. 215–216; also see *The History of the Council of Florence* by Ivan N. Ostroumoff, Holy Transfiguration Monastery, Boston, 1971, pp. 49–55 (first published in Moscow, 1847).]

• You ask, "What Ecumenical Council has ever explicitly condemned the doctrine of the *filioque*," further asserting that (1) it "was held as correct doctrine throughout the Church in the West from the 4th to the 9th centuries," and that (2) if it is heretical, then we "were equally heretical in maintaining for centuries [our] communion with 'heretical' Rome." Leaving aside for the moment the question regarding the Ecumenical Council, I note that these two assertions are in disagreement with the historical facts:

→ Acceptance of the *filioque* (and the comparable expression, *ex filio*) in the West was both gradual and spotty. As Bishop Kallistos explains:

> It is not certain when and where this addition was first made, but it seems to have originated in Spain, as a safe-

guard against Arianism. At any rate the Spanish Church interpolated the *filioque* at the third Council of Toledo (589), if not before. From Spain the addition spread to France and thence to Germany, where it was welcomed by Charlemagne and adopted at the semi-Iconoclast Council of Frankfort (794). It was writers at Charlemagne's court who first made the *filioque* into an issue of controversy, accusing the Greeks of heresy because they recited the Creed in its original [!] form. But Rome, with typical conservatism, continued to use the Creed without the filioque until the start of the eleventh century. In 808 Pope Leo III wrote in a letter to Charlemagne that, although he himself believed the *filioque* to be doctrinally sound, yet he considered it a mistake to tamper with the wording of the Creed. [In 809] Leo deliberately had the Creed, without the *filioque,* inscribed on silver plaques and set up in Saint Peter's. [*The Orthodox Church,* pp. 58–59. The silver plates, which I believe are still there, are in Latin and Greek, which latter tongue, according to St. Photios, was to assure that "the unspotted pattern of true piety might not in any way be falsified by a barbarous language." Leo explained his action by also engraving on the plates: "These words I, Leo, have set down for love and as a safeguard of the orthodox faith." (*Haec Leo posui amore* et *cautela fidei orthodoxae.*)]

→ Thus, the East, which had little contact with the West except via Rome, became aware of the magnitude of the problem only at a comparatively late date. Moreover, it is inaccurate to suggest that the increasing prevalence of a misguided expression (which may reflect nothing more than confusion) is identical to acceptance of a false **doctrine** (which constitutes heresy). As an illustration, consider a formulation. sometimes put forth as a possible solution to the *filioque* controversy: that the Holy Spirit proceeds from the Father and *through* the Son. This phrase is found in the Church Fathers, and it is even, beginning with St. Maximus the Confessor in the 7th century, used in reference to the *filioque.* But it is anything but a compromise. Consider the following explanation (from *Orthodox Dogmatic Theology: A Concise Exposition,* by Protopresbyter Michael Pomazansky, p. 90):

> To this one should add that the expression, 'through the Son,' which is found in certain Holy Fathers, in the majority of cases refers definitely to the manifestations of the Holy Spirit *in the world,* that is, to the providential actions of the Holy Trinity, and not to the life of God in Himself. When the Eastern Church first noticed a distortion of the dogma of the Holy Spirit in the West and began to reproach the Western theologians for their innovations, St. Maximus the Confessor (in the 7th century), desiring to defend the Westerners, justified them precisely by saying that by the words 'from the Son' they intended to indicate that the Holy Spirit is *given* to creatures through the Son, that He is *manifested,* that He is *sent*—but not that the Holy Spirit has His existence from Him. St. Maximus the Confessor himself held strictly to the teaching of the Eastern Church con-

cerning the profession of the Holy Spirit from the Father
and wrote a special treatise about this dogma. [original
emphasis]

Similarly, we might accurately say that "the Son is born of the Father
and the Holy Spirit," or that He is "born of the Father and *through*
the Holy Spirit"—*if and only if* we understand that in the former
instance, "born" means begotten of the Father before all ages, while
in the latter instance "born" means as a man, in a stable, in the town
of Bethlehem, in the province of Judaea, sometime around 4 B.C., of
Mary the Virgin, through the agency of the Holy Spirit. But if we were
to mean for "born" to indicate, in the latter instance with respect to
the Holy Spirit as well as the Father, the *eternal cause* of the Son's
existence, this would be a new and Trinity-attacking heresy. The
issue isn't so much the words used as the thought the words convey.
Thus, St. Maximus did not condemn the Westerners, nor should he
have. He was convinced, probably correctly, that there was, as yet, no
heretical content to the novel Western formulation: that the Western
expression still connoted that the Spirit's eternal origin is from the
Father only and that the interpolation was an unfortunate and
imprecise allusion to His temporal activity. No doubt too, the fact
that the Roman see generally opposed the *filioque* would have been
an important consideration. But two centuries later, during the
patriarchate of St. Photios, it was clear that the Latins had come to
mean by the *filioque* precisely that the Spirit has His eternal origin
from both the Father and the Son: it was from *that* point that further
communion with the West was unwarranted. Note also that at the
close of the "Photian Schism," with the all-too-brief restoration of
Orthodoxy at Old Rome, one of the last Orthodox popes, John VIII,
asked St. Photios to be patient with his efforts to correct the
misguided among his flock:

> We know the unfavorable accounts that you have heard
> concerning us and our Church; I therefore wish to explain
> myself to you even before you write to me on the subject.
> You are not ignorant that your envoy, in discussing the
> Creed with us, found that we preserved it as we originally
> received it, without adding to or taking anything from it; for
> we know what severe punishment he would deserve who
> should dare to tamper with it. To set you at ease, therefore,
> upon this subject, which has been the cause of scandal to
> the Church, we again declare to you that not only do we thus
> recite it, but even condemn those who, in their folly, have
> had the audacity to act otherwise from the beginning, as
> violators of the divine word, and falsifiers of the doctrine of
> Christ, of the Apostles, and of the Fathers, who have
> transmitted the Creed to us through the councils; we
> declare that their portion is that of Judas, because they have
> acted like him, since, if it be not the body of Christ itself
> which they put to death, it is, at all events, the faithful of
> God who are his members, whom they tear by schism,
> giving them up, as well as themselves, to eternal death, as
> also did that base Apostle. Nevertheless, I think that your
> Holiness, so full of wisdom, is aware of the difficulty of
> making our bishops share this opinion, and of changing at

once so important a practice which has taken root for so many years. We therefore believe it is best not to force any one to abandon that addition to the Creed, but we must act with moderation and prudence, little by little, exhorting them to renounce that blasphemy [i.e., the *filioque*]. Thus, then, those who accuse us of sharing this opinion do not speak the truth. But those who say that there are persons left among us who dare to recite the Creed in this manner, are not very far from the truth. Your Holiness should not be too much scandalized on our account, nor withdraw from the healthy part of the body of our Church, but zealously contribute by your gentleness and prudence to the conversion of such as have departed from the truth, so that with us, you may deserve the promised reward. [*The Papacy*, by the Abbe Guettee, Minos Publishing Co., NY, 1866, pp. 337–338, emphasis omitted]

In any case, the futility of "through the Son" was finally demonstrated during Ferrara-Florence, when it was suggested as a solution that the desperate Byzantines could live with. But the victorious Latins insisted: does "through" [Greek: *dia*] mean the same thing as "from" [Greek: *ek*]? No, the Byzantines answered, the former refers to the actions in the world and in time, the latter to eternal causation. So, the Greeks, in a pathetic and unprincipled attempt to save their doomed country, placed unity above truth and capitulated, accepting the Latin dogma. The only condescension Pope Eugene IV was willing to make was, having *accepted* the validity of the *filioque*, we were not actually obliged to *recite* the Creed in the interpolated form but could continue to say it in our traditional manner. (As you know, Rome's policy toward the Uniates today is generally the same.)

→ Seen in this light, the uncompromising response of St. Photios, to the effect that the Holy Spirit proceeds from the Father "alone" (which expression, in keeping with the same canonical principles we urged in vain upon the Latins, we have refrained from inserting into the Creed), was neither "radical" nor an "innovation." Again, consider the following analogy: The Creed states that the Son "is begotten of the Father before all ages." It is not stated that He is begotten of the Father "alone" (though he is the "only-begotten Son," John 3:16, *uios monogenis*), but that is clearly understood. But if someone were to come along and suggest that the Son is born eternally of the Spirit (and not just born of Him with respect to the Incarnation, i.e., temporally), and we were to respond by insisting that the Son's eternal generation is of the Father *alone* would that be a "radical innovation," of which you accuse St. Photios?

At this juncture, I wish to skip to your 6th point, regarding "Petrine supremacy," not because your 2nd through 5th are unimportant but because this matter has, along with the *filioque*, figured so prominently in the discord between Orthodoxy and Roman Catholicism. To begin with, I am glad you used the correct word, "supremacy" since in the Roman Catholic system, if the pope is not supreme, he is nothing—in place of the less-exalted attribution of "primacy," once accorded to the pope of Old Rome and now to the archbishop of New Rome. It has unfortunately become customary, on both sides of the ongoing (and I believe, misguided) "ecumenical dialogue" to evade, with all the verbal gymnastics that human rhetorical ingenuity can devise, the central question with respect to authority: Is the Bishop of Rome simply one *among* his brother bishops, having a "primacy of honor" due to the former Imperial City over which he has pastoral care? Or is he the "Vicar of Christ," the "Supreme Pontiff," with universal jurisdiction *over* all bishops, holding in his hands alone the Keys of Peter? Again, if we are being honest, not "ecumenical," the Roman Catholic view can only agree with the second expression. Consider the following iterations: "It is necessary to salvation that every human creature be subject to the Roman Pontiff." [*Unam Sanctam*, Pope Boniface VIII, 1302; this is, I believe, *de fide*.] "The Pope is Christ in office, Christ in jurisdiction and power . . . We bow down before thy voice, O Holy Father, as we would before Christ Himself." [First Vatican Council Proclamation of Infallibility, Pope Pius IX, 1870] "We hold upon this earth the place of God Almighty." [Pope Leo XIII, Encyclical Letter, June 20, 1894] Admittedly, I have taken these not from the original sources but from their secondary citation in Orthodox anti-Latin polemical works. But I do not think their authenticity is at issue. Neither is the fact that the last few Popes have chosen to style themselves with a somewhat different image than that projected by these passages, without, however, repudiating the authority claimed in them. Even the relatively restrained Dr. Ott states (under an explanation of "primacy" that is far better suited to the term you chose, "supremacy"):

> Christ appointed the Apostle Peter to be the first of all the Apostles and to be the visible Head of the whole Church, by appointing him immediately and personally to the primacy of jurisdiction. *(De fide.)* [p. 279]

> According to Christ's ordinance, Peter is to have successors in his Primacy **over** [Note: "over," not "within"] the whole Church and for all time. *(De fide.)* [p. 282]

> The successors of Peter in the Primacy are the bishops of Rome. *(De fide.)* [p. 282]

> The Pope possesses full and supreme power of jurisdiction **over** the whole Church, not merely in matters of faith and morals, but also in Church discipline and in the government of the Church. *(De fide.)* [p. 285]

> The Pope is infallible when he speaks ex cathedra. *(De fide.)* [p. 286]

> [T]he Primatial power is: . . . A true power of jurisdiction, that is, a true governing power, not merely a warrant of supervision or direction . . . ; A **universal** power, that is, it extends personally to the pastors (bishops) and to the faithful, totally and individually, of the whole Church . . . ; Supreme power in the Church, that is, there is no jurisdiction possessing a greater or equally great power. . . ; A full power, that is, the Pope possesses of himself alone the whole fullness of the Church power of jurisdiction and not merely a greater share than the other bishops taken individually or conjointly . . . ; An ordinary power, that is, it is connected with the office, by virtue of divine ordinance, and is not delegated from a higher possessor of jurisdiction . . . ; A truly episcopal power, that is, the Pope is just as much a **"universal bishop"** of the whole Church as he is bishop of his diocese of Rome ("Episcopus Urbis et Orbis": Jacob of Viterbo). Thus, the Papal power, like any other episcopal power, embraces the legislative, the juridical, and the punitive power. . . ; An immediate power, that is, the Pope can exercise his power, without the inter-

vention of an intermediary, **over** the bishops and the faithful of the whole Church. [pp. 285–286; I think it is hardly necessary here to reiterate what St. Gregory wrote about anyone calling himself the "universal bishop" being the "precursor of Antichrist."]

Our answer to these assertions is twofold: (1) the kind of absolute supremacy claimed here can only belong to Christ Himself, and (2) nowhere can it be documented that authority of this description was wielded, even if it was claimed now and then, by pre-schism Roman popes and acknowledged by the rest of the Church. (Indeed, even the occasional extravagant and self-aggrandizing demands made by occupants of the see of Rome during that period hardly rise to these heights, and were, in most cases, greeted by other bishops, East and West, with charitable silence.)

→ Your first letter to me included a one-page enclosure, "Pope St. Gregory the Great, Defender of the Papacy," from *Serviam*, January-February 1992. In it you attack an article called "The Universal Patriarch" published in *The Orthodox Christian Witness* of August 16, 1981, which, from your response, evidently featured lengthy quotations from St. Gregory's correspondence with and about Patriarch St. John the Faster of Constantinople regarding the honorific title "Ecumenical" bestowed upon the latter by the Emperor. In disputing the clear meaning of the Gregorian quotations you close with the following, which you claim "destroy[s] the fundamental rationale for the Byzantine Schism":

> Who does not know that the holy church is founded on the solidity of the Chief Apostle, whose name expressed his firmness, being called Peter from Petra (Rock)? . . . Though there were many Apostles, only the See of the Prince of the Apostles . . . received supreme authority in virtue of its very principiate. [Letter to Patriarch Eulogius of Alexandria, Ep. 7]

I must remark that upon first seeing your use of this passage I was reminded of the abuse by papal apologists of the famous words of Tertullian (." . . thou hast Rome, whose authority is near us. How happy is that church to whom the Apostles [Note: evidently not just St. Peter but St. Paul, and in the context, St. John as well] have given all its doctrine with their blood. . .") without noting the sentences immediately before it, which refer to the similar apostolic authority of Corinth (St. Peter and St. Paul) and Ephesus (St. John).

The following is a fuller rendering of your quotation from St. Gregory; the translation is slightly different, so I have boldfaced the words you quoted:

> Your Holiness [i.e., Eulogius of Alexandria] has spoken to me at large, in your letters, of the see of St. Peter, prince of the Apostles, saying that he still resides here by his successors. Now, I acknowledge myself unworthy not only of the honor of the chiefs, but even to be counted in the number of the faithful. Yet I have willingly accepted all that you have said, *because your words regarding the see of Peter came from him* [i.e., Eulogius himself] *who occupies that see of Peter. A special honor* has no charms for me; but I greatly rejoice that you, who are very holy, only ascribe to me what you also give to yourself. Indeed, **who is ignorant that the holy Church has been made fast upon the solidity of the prince of the Apostles, whose name is the**

type of the firmness of his soul, and who borrowed from the rock his name of Peter? . . . Therefore, **though there were many Apostles, the single see of the prince of the Apostles prevailed by his princedom;** which *now exists in three places;* for it is he that *made glorious* that see where he condescended to rest *(quiescere)* and close his present life [i.e., Rome]. It is he who *adorned* the see [i.e., Alexandria], whither he sent the Evangelist, his disciple [i.e., St. Mark]. It is he who *strengthened* the see, which he occupied for seven years, although finally compelled to leave it [i.e., Antioch]. Since then there is but one see of the same Apostle, and three bishops now hold it by divine authority. All the good I hear of you I also impute to myself. [*The Papacy*, pp. 228–229, emphasis added. The portions of *The Papacy* dealing with the St. John the Faster controversy, pp. 206–237, are enclosed.]

A few things are evident here. First, if we wish to impute to St. Gregory any concept of successive Petrine authority from these words, it must be in the form of a kind of Petrine "triarchy," a triumvirate consisting of Rome, Alexandria, and Antioch; but since no one has ever put forth any such bizarre idea which would, in any case, itself destroy the notion of a unique Roman supremacy based on Petrine authority—he must mean something else. Second, the "something else," which is plain from his own words, is to pay Eulogius back in he same coin for the lavish Petrine honorifics he had previously heaped upon St. Gregory. Third, supporting the idea that, in St. Gregory's words, a *special honor*, rather than a claim of power, is meant to be conveyed, are the expressions "made glorious," "adorned," and "strengthened," as applied to the *three* occupants of the *one* Petrine see; of these, only "strengthened," which pertains to Antioch, remotely hints at the usual assertions of Petrine authority (cf. Luke 22:32). Fourth, in other correspondence with Eulogius and with Anastasius of Antioch, St. Gregory uses comparable expressions: "remember what was said of him whose seat you fill," followed by a quote of John 21:18, a well-known reference to St. Peter [See *The Papacy*, pp. 229–230]; "Praise and glory be in the heavens to my saintly brother, thanks to whom the voice of Mark is heard from the chair of Peter . . . [p. 230]; and so forth. Fifth, one should not read too much into the terms "prince" or "principiate/princedom/principality," which, deriving from the Latin *princeps* (literally, "he who takes first place"; see *The American Heritage Dictionary of the English Language,* "Appendix: Indo-European Roots," Houghton Mifflin Company, Boston 1976, p. 1534), are the functional equivalent of such words as "primacy," "primate," "prime," etc., from *primus,* also meaning "first," "foremost." These terms, along with similar designations such as "leader," "preeminent," "chief," and "coryphaeus" (i.e., "head" or leader of a chorus), are often found in Orthodox literature with the understanding of *primus inter pares* ("first among equals"). The Fathers wrote in the same manner, for example Blessed Augustine: "He [i.e., St. Peter] had not the primacy over the disciples *(in discipulos)* but among the disciples *(in discipulis)*. His primacy among the disciples was the same as that of Stephen among the deacons." [*The Papacy*, p. 176, emphasis and citations deleted.]

→ I have devoted such attention to the foregoing excerpts from St. Gregory because your citation of them is representative of the way in which patristic extracts have been employed to accomplish a complete inversion of the Fathers' actual teaching. At this point, it might be appropriate to supply those quotations, most of which are to be found in *The Papacy*, from the most prominent Western Fathers and writers, not only St. Gregory but St. Ambrose of Milan, St. Hilary of Poitiers, St. Cyprian of Carthage, Blessed Augustine of Hippo, Tertullian—not to mention those of the East, which utterly demolish the papal pretensions. But I think this is not necessary, both because I assume you to be familiar with them and because I have no desire, in this letter, to recreate the Abbe Guettee's admirable work. In closing this topic, I only wish to emphasize the following: A Church claiming to be *The* Church (as do both Orthodoxy and Roman Catholicism) cannot—with regard to government no less than doctrine and worship—be built upon foundations that are demonstrably a- or even anti-historical. Accordingly, I have enclosed the speech by the Roman Catholic bishop Georg Strossmayer of Diakovar in Croatia, delivered in 1870 at the First Vatican Council against the new doctrine of papal infallibility. The facts he adduces are self-explanatory in their impact: not only are there several documented examples of popes who taught heresy, but, as put by the Fr. Steven mentioned at the beginning of this letter, a "deeper and more important issue is the connection between discernment and holiness of life." He continues:

> The church of the first millennium knew of *no* great theologians and Fathers who rightly divided the word of truth and at the same time were hardened fornicators or murderers or occultists. . . . This is an insult to God and the dignity of human nature; it makes a degraded man who is deeply in communion with the demons into a mechanical oracle of divinely revealed truth. . . . Of course, we [Orthodox] believe that 'valid' sacraments can be 'performed' by a priest who has fallen into serious sin, but we would not trust such a person's theological judgment, much less claim for him some kind of guaranteed infallibility.

Which raises another question: Does the pope still lay claim to ultimate temporal, as well as spiritual, sovereignty? That is, if (as formerly held by papal apologists) the "two swords" of Luke 22:38 represent the two powers—one, the spiritual, wielded by the pope himself, and the other, the temporal, which he *delegates* to lay rulers as his subordinates—can he any more renounce, in principle, the divinely-bestowed primacy over temporal rulers than he could supremacy over the Church, which (the Roman Catholic view has it) was similarly vested in Matt. 16:18?

- To return to your points 2 through 5, you ask: "What Ecumenical Council ever condemned . . ." Baptism by sprinkling or pouring, Eucharistic *azymes*, Purgatory (which I have already touched upon), and the Immaculate Conception. I will not answer these at length, as I did in the previous sections, but will simply note the following:

  → When examined in detail, these Roman Catholic doctrines and practices rely on syllogisms and Scholastic convolutions (and the same contempt for Holy Tradition) comparable to those underlying the *filioque* and papal supremacy. (cf. Col. 2:8)
  → As to substance, not only do the Latin practices with regard to Baptism and *azymes* depart from the universal tradition of the Church, they destroy the relationship between type and antitype. In

the case of Baptism, the typology is based on both the Old Testament "Baptism" in the Red Sea (I Cor. 10:2) and the fact that in passing into the water of Baptism we are buried with Christ, and rising from the water we are reborn in His Resurrection (Col. 2:12). As for the *azymes*, they are symbolic of the Old Testament priesthood of Aaron, not the New Testament priesthood of Melchizedek (Gen. 14:18, Ps. 109 [110]:4, and Heb. 5:6); a similar typology exists between the wafer-like manna of Exodus and the Body of Christ, the "true bread from heaven" (John 6:32–33); in the Eucharistic bread, the leaven represents the presence of the Holy Spirit, which, since Pentecost, resides in the Church; and the Greek words for unleavened wafer (*azymos*) and bread (*artos*) are distinct. If Melchizedek had presented wafers in place of bread to Abraham, or if Christ had celebrated His New Passover in His Body and Blood with wafers of the old Passover, we would know from the text. With regard to the Immaculate Conception, besides being an innovation opposed by many Latin thinkers, notably Bernard of Clairvaux, it is entirely dependent on a distorted understanding of original sin; indeed, as the newly glorified St. John of Shanghai and San Francisco has pointed out, the Roman Catholic view, far from praising the Most Holy Theotokos, denies her all virtues in holding that she was in a condition of being unable to sin! [See *The Orthodox Veneration of the Mother of God,* by Blessed Archbishop John Maximovich, pp. 35–47.]

→   Your question as to "Which Ecumenical Council . . ." misinterprets the concept of authority as it exists in our Church, as if wherever you write "pope" we write "Ecumenical Council." It suggests that because such a council has not met since 787, and since most of the Roman Catholic errors only manifested themselves well after that date, *ergo*, they are not errors! (Of course, there are the standard statements by which the Orthodox have repeatedly and consistently condemned the Latin divergences from Holy Tradition; these include, but are not limited to: *The Mystagogy of the Holy Spirit,* by St. Photios the Great, c. 880, which, as the title suggests, is an exhaustive demolition of the *filioque; The Synodicon of the Holy Spirit,* issued under Patriarch Germanos the New, 1222–1261 —that is, during the period of exile from Constantinople forced upon the Byzantines by the sanguinary ministrations of the Fourth Crusade, which had founded the so-called Latin Empire, 1204–1261, again mostly concerning the *filioque;* the Encyclical Letter of St. Mark of Ephesus, 1440–1441, against the "Union Council" of Ferrara-Florence; the *Sigillion* of 1583, issued by the Patriarchs Jeremiah of Constantinople, Silvester of Alexandria, and Sophronius of Antioch in response to Rome's promulgation of the Julian calendar, which also condemned the *filioque, azymes,* Purgatory, and papal supremacy; The Reply of the Orthodox Patriarchs to Pope Pius IX, 1848, covering a number of topics; the Encyclical Letter of 1895, issued by the Synod of Constantinople headed by Patriarch Anthimos VII in reply to an appeal for reunion issued that year by Pope Leo XIII, condemning the *filioque,* Baptism by sprinkling, *azymes,* Purgatory, the Immaculate Conception, papal supremacy and the newly proclaimed dogma of infallibility, and many other errors.) In short, the Latin doctrines and practices are well understood, as are the Orthodox objections to them in light of the consensus of the authentic Holy Tradition: to translate into a colloquialism (at the risk of seeming flippant), when it comes to heresy, "we know it when we see it." In my original interim reply to you of November 10, 1993, I noted an assertion (found in your book *Ending the Byzantine Greek Schism,* pp. 74–75) by Thomas Aquinas: "To say that the Vicar of Christ, the Roman Pontiff, does not hold the primacy in the universal Church is an error analogous to that which denies that the Holy Ghost proceeds from the Son." *(Contra Errores Graecorum,* 1264) Indeed, there is no doubt a close link between false teaching on authority in the Church and false teaching on the Holy Spirit. As you quoted, in the same place, Fr. Yves Congar:

> It has often been observed that a theology which denies the eternal procession of the Holy Spirit from the Word tends to minimize the part played by definite forms of authority in actual life, and this leaves the way open to a kind of independent inspiration. The ecclesiology of the Orthodox Churches has a distinctly 'pneumatic' tendency and declines to accept Catholic ideas of authority which seem to savor of legalism. [This is a remarkable passage, and I thank you for including it in your book. I have no doubt that a Church in which the Holy Spirit dwells seems oddly "pneumatic" from the perspective of one where He does not. That is, Fr. Congar and, making a similar point on the same page in your book, Fr. Dismas Purcell find it peculiar that, having no pope, we are forced to "make do" with the Holy Spirit!]

In general, it seems that Roman Catholicism reasons from authority: if the pope says it, it is true. (Similarly, Roman Catholicism's descendent, Protestantism, accords similar "infallible" authority to their "paper pope," the Bible, which is nonetheless filtered through the minds of fallible men.) From this standpoint, I suppose it is natural for Roman Catholics to look at the Orthodox and conclude, "Ah, what the pope is for us (and the Bible is for the Protestants), the council is for them: truth is what a council proclaims, heresy is what a council condemns." This is exactly backwards. For us, the Truth is Christ himself, who is also our eternal Bishop (Heb. 3:1, 4:14, I Pet. 2:25, 5:4) and the Head of the Church (Eph. 1:22–23, 4:16); the Holy Spirit abides in the Church, which is why the gates of hell cannot prevail against it. (Matt. 16:18) Accordingly, Truth in the Church is an objective, vital quantity *that does not change* (Heb. 13:8), contrary to the Roman Catholic idea of "development of doctrine"; it is precisely that Truth that will never leave the Church (Matt. 28:20). Because of that Truth (Who is begotten of the Father) and the Spirit (Who proceeds from the Father), neither of Whom is ever absent from the Church, the Father is also made known (John 4:23–24, chs. 15–17 passim, esp. 16:13–15). *The Church, beginning with the Apostles and continuing with the Fathers, is well aware of the objective Truth that is in it and, with the power of the Spirit, rejects any error attacking that Truth* (Acts 2:42, II Thes. 2:15, I Pet. 1:5, Jude 3). Lawful authority in the Church is inseparable from this criterion of truth: Whoever speaks truly, to that extent has true authority; whoever teaches wrongly, to that extent his authority is forfeit. Any Orthodox Christian, speaking the truth of Orthodoxy, outweighs any number of exalted names and titles—be they theologians, emperors, kings, popes, patriarchs, metropolitans, bishops, or monks if such teach falsely. This is precisely the criterion that separates the seven authoritative Ecumenical Councils from the "Robber Council" of Ephesus of 449 and the "Council of Constantinople" of 869, which purported to depose St. Photios, and which is considered the

"Eighth Ecumenical Council" by the Roman Catholic Church. This is precisely the criterion, not some mythical Petrine infallibility, that separates the acclaim given to Pope Celestinus ("Celestinus the new Paul! Celestinus, defender of the faith!") by the Council of Ephesus (431) and that given to Pope St. Leo the Great ("Peter has spoken by Leo! Leo teaches according to piety and truth!") at the Council of Chalcedon (451) from the condemnation meted out to the Monothelite Pope Honorius I by the third Council of Constantinople (680), and confirmed by later popes: "Anathema to Honorius the heretic!"

- Finally, in closing your letter of October 1993, you quoted St. Cyril of Jerusalem to the effect that, in "sojourning in any city," one should not just ask "where the Church is, but where is the Catholic Church," with the further recommendation that I "ask any passerby or policeman where the nearest Catholic church is," and that I will invariably "be directed to a church in communion with the See of Peter." In this observation, you are correct. This only proves that St. Cyril could not foresee that the very title of "Catholic" would, in popular usage, have acquired a meaning as distorted, in its application to the religious organization headed by the pope of Rome, as is the doctrine taught by that organization. One might as well say that the terms "Church of Christ," or "Christian Church," or "Church of the Disciples" refer uniquely to the Protestant denominations that use those and other similar labels.

  → More pertinent than the exact words St. Cyril chose is the meaning he gave them. That is, in advising sojourners to ask for the "Catholic church," did he intend for this query to yield the result it admittedly does today to distinguish a church "in communion with the See of Peter," i.e., Rome? You are of course aware that St. Cyril was a participant in the Second Ecumenical Council, held at Constantinople in 381. Not only was the reigning pope of Old Rome, Damasus I (famous for being the first to claim his office was uniquely *the* Apostolic see, as well as for the dozens of corpses that littered the basilica during his election, the result of a fight between his supporters and those of an Arian rival, Ursinus), not present, he did not even send a legate; in fact, not a single Western bishop attended the Council. Nonetheless, it was and is accepted by the whole Church, Rome included, as having been ecumenical. Moreover, the bishop presiding at the Second Council was St. Meletius of Antioch, *who was not even in communion with Pope Damasus,* who supported a rival for the Antiochian see, Paulinus. That is to say, St. Cyril was a leading figure in a Council at which the pope was neither present nor represented, and which was presided over by a bishop regarded by the pope as a schismatic. Is it reasonable, then, to assume that St. Cyril would not have regarded the Second Ecumenical Council as "catholic"—and presumably not "orthodox," either—because Pope Damasus had nothing to do with it? How, then, can we take "in communion with Rome" to be the standard that St. Cyril really had in mind when he wrote "Catholic"?

  → I cannot overlook the fact that, besides "Catholic," there is another adjective that is inseparable from the ecclesiastical identity to which you seek to lay claim, and which also has a bearing on the continued accuracy of St. Cyril's method for ascertaining a church's orthodoxy: *Roman.* As you know, it was this same Second Council which added a 9th paragraph to the Creed authored by the First Council, regarding belief in "One, Holy, Catholic, and Apostolic Church." In so doing, the collected Fathers apparently forgot to add what would appear to be, for your doctrine, this other essential modifier, (although, if they had thought to include it, the word almost certainly would have been taken not as a reference to the then-embryonic papacy but to the Empire). That is, the Council adopted, as part of the Church's fundamental creedal statement, a definition of the Church that does not mention the pope, or his city, or even the state of which that city was still a capital. Its omission increases the likelihood that Roman communion held little or no weight in St. Cyril's and the Fathers' notion of catholicity.

→ The whole issue of why the Roman Catholic church is known, in popular speech, as "Catholic" and why the Church to which that adjective more properly refers is known primarily under the denotation "Orthodox" is an interesting historical inquiry. Indeed, it seems that the "Catholicism" of the Roman church is to some extent a reaction to the "Orthodoxy" of the Orthodox Church. As Fr. John A. Hardon, S.J., explains it *(The Catholic Catechism,* Doubleday & Company, Inc., Garden City, NY, 1966, p. 218):

> . . . Christian missionaries since the time of St. Paul labored to make this intentional catholicity also actual. They succeeded to such a degree that, since apostolic times, the faithful have professed in the liturgy their belief "in the holy catholic Church," where the original Greek is never capitalized. The custom of using the separate title "Catholic Church" (initial capital letters) can be certainly traced to the time of the Eastern Schism, finalized in 1054, when oriental Christians isolated the term "Orthodox Church" to identify themselves as distinct both from the Nestorians and Monophysites. Consistent with this approach, the Council of Florence (1445 [this is an error: the date was 1438–1439]) speaks of the "holy Roman Church," to emphasize acceptance of Rome as a condition for complete unity.

To turn around your suggestion that I ask any passerby or policeman today where the "Catholic" church is, I ask to you to imagine yourself back in the fourth century walking up to a passerby or whatever was the equivalent of a policeman and asking him, "Where is the nearest *Roman* Catholic church?" Is there any doubt that he would either be completely baffled at your question or that he would, at best, ignore the word "Roman" (perhaps assuming that you were a barbarian who was unsure of what polity he was travelling through) and direct you to an Orthodox church that is, one that gives "true glory" *(orthodoxia)* to God, beginning with adherence to the Niceno-Constantinopolitan Creed co-authored by St. Cyril? (By the way, it was this same Second Ecumenical Council that wrote the 8th paragraph of the Creed concerning the Holy Spirit, Who "proceeds from the Father.") And if you were to then insist on knowing if that local church were in communion with the pope of Rome, our same passerby—who almost certainly would not know the answer, unless you happened to be *in* Rome—would no doubt lose his patience and leave you to your irrelevant investigations.

Having finally completed my comments on the issues raised in your letters, I now wish to turn to what, as a I stated at the beginning, is the more fundamental difference between Orthodoxy and Roman Catholicism: the palpably different spirit that animates and permeates each, and the inevitable intel-lectual and other consequences. As Fr. Alexey Young, a convert from Roman Catholicism, pointed out in a work with which you are familiar:

> . . . [S]piritual life in the Orthodox Church differs so dramatically from spiritual life in the Catholic Church; there is, in fact, hardly any similarity at all. External similarities (belief in sacraments, liturgical worship, government by bishops, etc.) are of almost no significance whatever compared to the abyss that separates spiritual life and living between the two Churches, as any convert from Catholicism to Orthodoxy will readily testify. [*Winds of Change in Roman Cathol-icism: An Appeal to Roman Catholics*, Nikodemos Orthodox Public-ation Society, Etna, CA, 1979, p. iv]

Now, it is one thing to make this assertion, but it is another thing to show why the assertion is true. I have been pondering how to approach this task in my reply to you, since we are talking about a distinction that, for us anyway, is more *felt* than *thought*. It occurs to me that instead of trying to *explain* a phenomenon that defies rational analysis and description it would be better to set out a practical aspect of Christian life that *exemplifies* the phenomenon. Taking that approach, I have selected the matter of **fasting**. As Bishop Kal-listos writes:

> [The] effort to purify the passions needs to be carried out on the level of both soul and body. On the level of the soul they are purified through prayer, through the regular use of the sacraments of Con-fession and Communion, through daily readings of Scripture, through feeding our mind with the thought of what is good, through practical acts of loving service to others. On the level of the body they are purified above all through fasting and abstinence, and through frequent prostrations during the time of prayer. Knowing man is not an angel but a unity of body and soul, the Orthodox Church insists upon the spiritual value of bodily fasting. We do not fast because there is anything in itself unclean about the act of eating and drinking. Food and drink are on the contrary God's gift, from which we are to partake with enjoyment and gratitude. We fast, not because we despise the divine gift, but so as to make ourselves aware that it is indeed a gift—so as to purify our eating and drinking, and to make them, no longer a concession to greed, but a sacrament and a means of communion with the Giver. Understood in this way, ascetic fasting is directed, not against the body, but against the flesh. . . . Its aim is not destructively to weaken the body, but creatively to render the body more spiritual.
> Purification of the passions leads eventually, by God's grace to what Evagrius [of Pontus, a monk and mystical writer, 346–399] terms *apatheia* or 'dispassion.' By this he means, not a negative condition of indifference or insensitivity in which we no longer *feel* temptation, but a positive state of reintegration and spiritual free-dom in which we no longer *yield* to temptation. Perhaps *apatheia* can best be translated "purity of heart." [*The Orthodox Way*, St. Vladimir's Seminary Press, Crestwood, NY, 1990, pp. 155–156, original emphasis.]

Elsewhere Bishop Kallistos explains:

The primary aim of fasting is to make us *conscious of our dependence upon God*. If practiced seriously, the Lenten abstinence from food—particularly the opening days—involves a considerable measure of real hunger, and also a feeling of tiredness and physical exhaustion. The purpose of this is to lead us in turn to a sense of inward brokenness and contrition; to bring us, that is, to the point where we appreciate the full force of Christ's statement: "Without Me you can do nothing." (John 15:5) If we always take our fill of food and drink, we easily grow over-confident in our own abilities, acquiring a false sense of autonomy and self-sufficiency. The observance of a physical fast undermines this sinful complacency. Stripping from us the specious assurance of the Pharisee—who fasted, it is true, but not in the right spirit—Lenten abstinence gives us the saving self-dissatisfaction of the Publican. (Luke 18:10–13) Such is the function of the hunger and the tiredness: to make us "poor in spirit," aware of our helplessness and of our dependence on God's aid.

Yet it would be misleading to speak only of this element of weariness and hunger. Abstinence leads, not merely to this, but also to a sense of lightness, wakefulness, freedom, and joy. Even if the fast proves debilitating at first, afterwards we find that it enables us to sleep less, to think more clearly, and to work more decisively. [. . .]

If it is important not to overlook the physical requirements of fasting, it is even more important not to overlook its inward significance. Fasting is not merely a matter of diet. It is moral as well as physical. True fasting is to be converted in heart and will; it is to return to God, to come home like the Prodigal to our Father's house. In the words of St. John Chrysostom, it means "abstinence not only from food but from sins." "The fast," he insists, "should be kept not by the mouth alone but also by the eye, the ear, the feet, the hands and all the members of the body": the eye must abstain from impure sights, the ear from malicious gossip, the hands from acts of injustice. It is useless to fast from food, protests St. Basil, and yet to indulge in cruel criticism and slander: 'You do not eat meat, but you devour your brother.' [. . .]

. . . [T]he Lenten fast is not intended only for monks and nuns, but is *enjoined on the whole Christian people*. Nowhere do the Canons of the Ecumenical or Local Councils suggest that fasting is only for monks and not for the laity. By virtue of their Baptism, all Christians—whether married or under monastic vows—are Cross-bearers, following the same spiritual path. The exterior conditions in which they live out their Christianity display a wide variety, but in its inward essence the life is one. Just as the monk by his voluntary self-denial is seeking to affirm the intrinsic goodness and beauty of God's creation, so also is each married Christian required to be in some measure an ascetic. The way of negation and the way of affirmation are interdependent, and every Christian is called to follow both ways at once. [*The Lenten Triodion,* Faber and Faber, London, 1978, pp. 16–17, 21, original emphasis, notes omitted.]

I have cited these passages to show that this one aspect of Orthodox spiritual life, central though it is, cannot be appreciated except within a broader context which includes not only correct doctrine but prayer, almsgiving, the liturgical life of the Church, and a proper sense of the interdependence between body and soul. Only in this way can we say we have, as the Apostle instructs us, "crucified the flesh with its passions and desires," so that we can "live in the

Spirit" and "walk in the Spirit" (Gal. 5:24–25). As Fr. Michael Pomazansky writes:

> The Orthodox path of the Christian is *the path of the cross and of struggle*. In other words, it is the path of patience, of the bearing of sorrows, persecutions for the name of Christ, of despising the goods of the world for the sake of Christ, of battling against one's passions and lusts. . . . All believers are called to struggle according to their strength: *They that are Christ's have crucified the flesh with the passions and lusts.* (Gal. 5:24) The moral life cannot exist without inward battle, without self-restraint. The Apostle writes: *For many walk, of whom I have told you often, and now tell you even weeping, that they are the enemies of the cross of Christ; whose end is destruction, whose god is their belly, and whose glory is in their shame, who mind earthly things.* (Phil. 3:18–19) [*Orthodox Dogmatic Theology*, pp. 327–328, original emphasis]

Only by engaging in this struggle, we believe, can we cooperate with God (I Cor. 3:9) in restoring the divine image placed in us by our Creator, and, in so doing, restore our spiritual fellowship with Him (Ps. 50[51]:10–11). Again, as Bishop Kallistos illustrates with the example of St. Seraphim of Sarov (the most famous of modern Russian monastic saints, 1759–1833):

> Saint Seraphim of Sarov briefly described the whole purpose of the Christian life as nothing else than the acquisition of the Holy Spirit, saying at the beginning of his conversation with Motovilov:
>
> > Prayer, fasting, vigils, and all other Christian practices, however good they may be in themselves, certainly do not constitute the aim of our Christian life: they are but the indispensable means of attaining that aim. For *the* true *aim of the Christian life is the acquisition of the Holy Spirit of God.* As for the fasts, vigils, prayer, and almsgiving, and other good works done in the name of Christ, they are only the means of acquiring the Holy Spirit of God. Note well that it is only good works done in the name of Christ that bring us the fruits of the Spirit.
>
> "This definition," Vladimir Lossky has commented, "while it may at first sight appear oversimplified, sums up the whole spiritual tradition of the Orthodox Church." As Saint Pachomius' disciple Theodore said: "What is greater than to possess the Holy Spirit?" [*The Orthodox Church*, p. 235]

But it cannot be overlooked that the foregoing *assumes doctrinal orthodoxy— that is, that the struggler is a member of the Orthodox Church.* As St. Seraphim stated in the same conversation with Motovilov:

> The grace of the Holy Spirit which was given to us all, the faithful of Christ, in the sacrament of Holy Baptism, is sealed by the sacrament of Chrismation on the chief parts of the body, as appointed by the Holy Church, the eternal keeper of this grace. . . . The Lord listens equally to the monk and the simple Christian layman, provided that both are Orthodox. [Found in *Orthodoxy and the Religion of the Future*, by Hieromonk Seraphim Rose, Saint Herman of Alaska Brotherhood, Platina, CA, 1975, p. 219, emphasis deleted.]

In light of these examples, some might be tempted to say that it all sounds nice, but obviously very few Orthodox people completely succeed in following the regime of fasting established in Holy Tradition much less practicing charity as we are enjoined (Luke 18:23) and praying as we should (I Thes. 5:17), i.e., to give away all we have and to pray without ceasing. But that is partly the point: while even those who earnestly engage in these spiritual labors often fail to attain, to the letter, the standard set out for us, even that standard is measured against perfection itself: "Be ye therefore perfect, even as your Father which is in heaven is perfect" (Matt. 5:48). So, in falling short of that perfect standard, much less of the attainable but still difficult traditional regime, we become even more aware of our own sinfulness and shortcomings and the need to labor even more diligently. As one monk responded, when asked what they do in the monastery: "We fall and get up, fall and get up, fall and get up again." Indeed, *even when we do achieve* the strict fasting standards established by the Church (and we are advised *not* to try to exceed them, to succumb to the demonic temptation to overreach our spiritual powers by being "self-willed" in our approach), we come to the same realization, feeling even more acutely (again, referring to fasting) the sinful, gluttonous pleasure of even the meager fare permitted under the rules. Thus, as I have tried to show, fasting is merely a means but an indispensable one, if applied with an understanding that true practice (*orthopraxia*) is inseparable from true doctrine (*orthodoxia*): "As we worship (or fast, etc.), so we believe (*lex orandi, lex credendi*)."

How different all this is from Roman Catholicism, "which," writes Fr. Alexander Schmemann in his monumental *Great Lent,* "long ago replaced the spiritual understanding of fasting with a juridical and disciplinary one (cf. for example, the power to 'dispense' from fasting as if it is God and not man who needed fasting!)." [St. Vladimir's Seminary Press, Crestwood, NY, 1969, p. 50] Fr. Alexey Young further comments:

> The Catholic Church has now almost completely lost the ascetic, other-worldly spirit. Whereas Orthodoxy still proclaims that the *essence* of Christianity is asceticism, and to this end gives Orthodox Christians strict fasting rules as the *standard* for true Christian life, Catholicism has almost completely abandoned any such idea. To take fasting before communion as an example, it was not so many years ago that the faithful were required to fast from all food and drink from midnight on. Later this was changed to three hours, and finally in the wake of Vatican II, to one hour. In some places fasting has been completely forgotten.
>
> One Orthodox theologian says this about the Roman Catholic spirit of reform: 'The papal idea, based upon the corrupt modern principle of spiritual self-satisfaction, is either to give a special "dispensation" from the standard . . . or else to change the standard itself so that the believer can fulfill it easily and thereby obtain a sense of satisfaction from "obeying the law." This is precisely the difference between the Publican and the Pharisee: the Orthodox man feels himself constantly a sinner because he falls short of the Church's exalted standard (in spirit if not in letter), whereas "modern" man wishes to feel himself justified, without any twinge of conscience over falling short of the Church's standard." [*Winds of Change*, p. 11, original emphasis.]

As a final illustration, it goes without saying that for Orthodox married people fasting, both with regard to ascetical fasts and to the total fast preceding Holy

Communion, includes abstention from sexual relations (cf. I Cor. 7:5, Ex. 19:15). Even observant Roman Catholics, for whom abstaining from relations to avoid conceiving a child has becoming a shibboleth of "orthodoxy"—a proof of their devotion to "natural family planning" in place of "artificial birth control"—would hardly imagine that indulging in relations is inconsistent with even the minimal fasts now observed by their church.

Again, lest it be suspected that these passages are a caricature of or a slander against Roman Catholicism, I tried to find a description of fasting from the Roman Catholic perspective in the works of Dr. Ott and Fr. Hardon already cited. As far as I could find, Dr. Ott did not mention it at all; granted, his is a book on dogma, but surely the practice of prayer, fasting, and almsgiving as the means by which dogma is realized in the human heart deserves some attention. Fr. Hardon discusses "Fast and Abstinence" under the heading "Sacramentals," but his treatment tells little about the purpose of fasting, consisting mainly of a review of the changing (i.e., relaxed) fasting standards in the context of "doing penance . . . [as] a necessary condition for salvation." [p. 555] In general, one gets the distinct impression that, in the entire Roman Catholic scheme of things, this matter is vestigial, an afterthought, a dim memory of an outmoded but not-entirely-abandoned duty. However, this should not be surprising if we accept, as the Orthodox viewpoint has it, that the essence of fasting cannot be summed up in the term "penitential" (per Fr. Hardon) but is primarily "pneumatic" (to borrow the terminology of Fr. Congar). That is, if, as St. Seraphim states, the precise aim of the Christian life is to acquire the Holy Spirit, and if fasting is one of the primary disciplines for doing so, it is to be expected that that discipline would atrophy in a church whose departure from the truth began with an attack on that same Holy Spirit (i.e., the *filioque*).

As I stated earlier, the radical difference between Orthodox and Roman Catholic spirituality, of which the various Latin deviations from Orthodoxy are both cause and symptom, have produced very significant consequences in the intellectual, social, political, and other spheres of Christian life. Indeed, we should say in terms of outlook basic assumptions about God and man, the relationship between Church and society, between *cultus* and *cultura* Roman Catholicism has far more in common with its Protestant offspring, with which it shares its function as the spiritual progenitor of a Western Civilization now entering what I believe to be its terminal stages of decrepitude, than it does with Orthodoxy.

This aspect of our discussion is important, perhaps not so much from the Orthodox standpoint than from the Roman Catholic, since "admir[ation of] the Catholic Church for its intellectualism and its contributions to Western Civilization" is, as you wrote in your "To Be Truly Orthodox Is to Be in Communion with Peter's See," one of the main attractions of that church to many. By contrast, we Orthodox are often accused of being anti-intellectual or even obscurantist. (I observe from having read your *Ending the Byzantine Greek Schism* shortly after receiving your first letter to me that a major, and perhaps the only, factor in Demetrios Kydones' conversion to Roman Catholicism was his utter conviction of his own intellectual superiority—and that of his Latin mentors, Aquinas in particular, over his countrymen.) My approach to this issue, like that of spirituality, is more exemplary than explanatory; for this purpose, I have enclosed an introduction by Fr. Michael Azkoul for an English translation of *On the Mystagogy of the Holy Spirit*, written by St. Photios the Great in the mid-ninth century. (As you know, the *Mystagogy*, referred to previously in this letter, is the first systematic Byzantine attempt to come to grips with the doctrinal ramifications of the *filioque*.) Fr. Michael's article conveys a good sense of the history and substantive problems connected with the *filioque,* as well as its damaging spiritual effects. But there is also something else—a sense of not just *what* Orthodoxy thinks that differs from Roman Catholicism but *how* it thinks. Indeed, the *how* is probably more important, in that this is the difference that first permitted the specific doctrinal deviations, such as the *filioque,* to creep into the Western Church. Fr. Alexey Young summed it up this way, in his *Winds of Change* in *Roman Catholicism* (p.4):

> In Latin Christianity there is a great emphasis on defining and analyzing, by philosophical processes, the great mysteries of the Faith, whereas in Eastern Orthodox Christianity these mysteries are gazed upon with wonder and reverence and humility. In other words, in Latin Christianity one comes to a knowledge of the truth primarily just by *thinking,* by bringing all the rational powers of one's mind to a point of concentration on a given question or concept. There is no other prerequisite than that a person be reasonably intelligent and informed and prepared to do the job of thinking. Thomas Aquinas or John Calvin might add to this thinking process a prayerful request for inspiration, but the process remains essentially the same: it is human logic that guides the thinker. This has now been for so many centuries the *norm* in Western Christianity (for this same approach has been inherited by the Protestant offspring of Roman Catholicism) that no one today thinks there is anything wrong with it, in spite of the fact that individuals starting with the same basic set of facts come to quite different conclusions. Thus, it seems quite 'logical' to some that there should be an infallible papacy, while to others this is offensive and repugnant; both of them appeal to Scripture for support.

And, one might add, both of them find in Scripture what they are looking for. This description, by the way, refers to what is called cataphatic, or "positive," theology, which attempts to make positive assertions, by a deductive process, from what is already revealed. Thus, for the Latin mind, if we know A and B from the Scriptures and the Church Fathers, and if C and D can be shown to follow logically from A and B then C and D *must also be true.* If Saint Peter was the leader of the Apostles, the Pope *must* be infallible; if the Mother of God was sinless and ever-virgin, she *must* have been conceived without original sin; if Heaven and Hell are the respective abodes of saints and sinners pending the Last Judgment, Purgatory *must* exist now. At root, this is an attempt to shrink the wisdom of God down to a size circumscribable by man's finite and sin-enfeebled intellect, to treat God as if He were something we can dissect, slap onto a slide, and put under our microscope.

Orthodoxy, however, does not think in this manner. That is, the Church is a divine organism—the Body of Christ, filled with the Holy Spirit. The Church does not think as man thinks, if "thinking" is even the right word at all. The faith once delivered to the Apostles cannot be improved upon through human vanity. On the contrary, one must apply every aspect of the human personality, not least the intellect, to be in accord with the Spirit that guides and preserves the Church, for which reason the gates of Hell cannot prevail against it. This is the manner of apophatic, or "negative," theology, which Fr. Michael very accurately describes beginning on p. 18 of the enclosed article. This is not any sort of obscurantism or gnosticism. On the contrary, it is a recognition that one must think about divine things in the divine manner— "mystagogically." The human mind must be used in a manner that strives, first of all, to be in one accord with the "mind of the Church." How else can one apprehend a faith so fundamentally based on antinomies (God is One but He is Three; Christ is God and He is man; man is predestined but he has free will, salvation by faith versus good works; etc.), unless one transcends the human temptation to try to "reconcile" or "solve" or "explain" them?

A few closing points. First, it is hard to overstate how much a departure from pre-schism theology the *filioque* is and how profound have been the consequences of the West's acceptance of it. Fr. Michael summarizes St. Photios' arguments (which, by the way, cannot begin to substitute for reading the *Mystagogy* itself) as follows: The *filioque* "abrogates the monarchy of the Father, emasculates His hypostasis, unbalances the Trinity with a filial causation which also subordinates the Spirit, and depersonalizes and denatures the 'peculiar characteristics' *(idiomata)* of the divine Persons." [p. 26] This is the basis of the charges of semi-Sabellianism and semi-Macedonianism. However, it would be a mistake to think this only an abstract theological question: the *filioque's* conquest of the West has had devastating consequences in the political, cultural, and social spheres as well. For example, Fr. Michael notes [p. 11, n. 36] the political and iconographic ramifications; one thinks of the materiality, sentimentality, and even eroticism that has in the West long characterized religious art no less than secular art. (With regard to this last feature in Western religious art, one immediately thinks of the Baroque sculptor Gianlorenzo Bernini's scandalous modeling of Teresa of Avila, whose overwhelmed expression of ecstasy is anything but spiritual.) Or contrast the spirit seen in a Roman Catholic cathedral—grandly reaching up to the heavens towards God from an earth from which He is seemingly absent (and presumably needs a "vicar" to represent Him)—from that of an Orthodox church: a tiny cosmos, a foretaste of eternity where God reigns in the hearts of His people.

In pondering this, I was reminded of the passage in Eric Voegelin's *The New Science of Politics* (p. 105 in the 1987 University of Chicago edition), where he attributes Christianity's failure to "re-divinize" man and society in the Roman world to the defeat of Arianism, because Athanasian Christianity does not believe in a personal monarchy within the godhead (which latter view Voegelin mistakenly attributes to St. Gregory Nazianzus). But that is the whole point: the Orthodox teaching preserves the monarchy of the Father within the Trinity, while the *filioque* destroys it. (The Orthodox find the unity of the Trinity in the Father's hypostasis, the Roman Catholics in the divine nature, which is common to all three Persons.) Elsewhere, Voegelin notes that the Orthodox east, Byzantium and Russia, did not suffer from the "de-divinization" that occurred in (and has come to typify) the West, resulting in a reemergence of gnosticism in increasingly virulent outbreaks. The parade of horribles that followed the Reformation, the Enlightenment, the Age of Progress, and modernism in all its myriad forms (socialism, enviromentalism, feminism, homosexualism, etc.)—should hardly come as much of a surprise.

There are other social observations I could touch upon along the same line of analysis: the myth of "caesaropapism" in the east versus the very real and continual conflicts between established "papocaesarism" in Rome and aspiring western "caesaropapists" from Charlemagne to Henry VIII to Bonaparte (see Fr. Michael, p. 16); or Voegelin's description of what one might call a progressive "inoculation" of western societies as the intensifying gnostic outbreaks occur, a factor that may account for the way Marxism tore through Russia as smallpox did through the New World—but I think the point is clear.

Clear, but largely irrelevant. If religion is true, it must be true apart from the social consequences. Indeed, if a person is looking for cultural or intellectual validation, I might even suggest he become a Roman Catholic. After all, the Western Civilization has produced a secular (or neo-pagan) high culture of unequalled brilliance and beauty, not to mention technical achievement. Perhaps the contemporary phenomenon that Tom Wolfe refers to as "the worship of Art" has a more legitimate pedigree than he might have realized. Perhaps the very fact of the West's "de-divinization," and the constant gnostic threat inherent in it, is inseparable from its cultural success, much like we assume almost as a matter of course that a great artist is a very troubled man. In any case, the Orthodox east has not produced such a culture and I think it is incapable of doing so. It is my sense that very often converts to Rome are really "converts" to Western Civilization in a broader sense, with their entry into the Roman communion being simply the logical spiritual consequence. So, in the end, I suppose it depends on what one is looking for in a church: truth and salvation, or culture.

Finally, I would be remiss if I failed to note the most important recent developments, such as the visit to Rome of Ecumenical Patriarch Bartholomew, Pope John Paul II's issuance of *Ut Unum Sint*, and the 1993 Balamand declaration. To put it succinctly, the latter-day heirs of John Beccos, Demetrios Kydones, and Cardinals Isidore and Bessarion are much mistaken (I am of course referring to those representing *our* side of the "ecumenical dialogue") if they believe that all the issues which have divided Orthodoxy and Roman Catholicism can be waved away with a cleverly-worded concordat, an unworthy and even more dishonest successor to Lyons and Ferrara-Florence. Still more are those representing *your* side fooling themselves if they believe likewise. When the new *Unia* now in the works is finalized and made public, the result for us will no doubt be a painful schism. But there is likewise no doubt that the Orthodox Church, however small at that point, will continue to trust in the promise made to Her by the heavenly Bridegroom (Matt. 16:18), to Whom She will be presented at the appointed hour in holiness, without spot or blemish (Apoc. 21:2, Eph. 5:27). Contemplating the current direction of events, I could not help feeling a sense of bitter irony when I read your article in *Serviam,* where you refer (in St. Gregory's time) to "the battered Church in the East torn by various schisms and heresies and increasingly subject to Imperial interference." Compare that description—which in fact is fairly accurate as to the state of affairs at that time—to the following description of Roman Catholicism today, by Malachi Martin (quoted in *Winds of Change in Roman Catholicism*, pp. 13–14):

> [Pope] Paul [VI] realized in his last two years that something unimaginably ominous had been moving inexorably toward them, was already in their midst, and that it had nothing to do with the Holy Spirit. "The smoke of Satan has entered the Church, is around the altar," he remarked somberly and helplessly. ... Nothing he did could stem the onslaught on him—for had he not espoused a "people's church" where all had equal voice? . . . women who wanted to be priests, priests who wanted to be married, bishops who wanted to be regional popes, theologians who claimed absolute teaching authority, Protestants who claimed equality and identity, homosexuals and divorced people who called for acceptance of their status on their terms, Marxist priests and bishops and nuns and layfolk who claimed his approval to destroy the social order. ... It was the new "people" let loose on the old kingdom, and Paul had no defense against them. Increasingly he reacted with tears.

Leaving aside the motives of our unionists, it is clear why Rome—despite all protestations of its Rock-like solidity—is desperate for the new *Unia:* (1) on the one hand an instinctive sense that the annexation of the liturgically and theologically "conservative" Orthodox would buoy the foundering Western vessel and, (2) on the other hand, the desire to finish off, once and for all, the millennium-old reproach our Church represents—a standing reminder of what you once were and now no longer are, of what you once had and are now lacking. The second point I admit I cannot prove. As to the first, consider the words, which need no commentary, of a devoted Roman Catholic, a sincere and fair-minded supporter of union:

> "[W]hat the East has to offer the West is infinitely more important [than what Papal leadership offers the East]. The Western Church, including the Roman Catholic Church, is in real danger of ceasing to be a Christian body. Neither St. Augustine nor St. John Chrysostom would recognize as Christian much of what goes on in Roman Catholic parishes. A quiet advocacy of homosexuality goes on unimpeded by rebukes from the Vatican. Belief in the sacraments is rapidly evaporating. Confirmation and confession are almost totally neglected. Feminism is the reigning ideology, and bishops promote it as much as they can without provoking direct action from Rome. Reports of concelebrations by laywomen are increasing, and the archdiocese of Chicago plans to put women in charge of dozens of parishes." ["All That Separates Must Converge," by Leon Podles, *Touchstone: A Journal of Ecumenical Orthodoxy*, Chicago, Summer 1995, pp. 9, 12]

In closing, let me emphasize that nothing here suggests that Orthodox *people*, considered as individuals distinct from the Orthodox Church *per se*, have any monopoly on virtue: when it comes to mustering an array of fools, scoundrels, and sluggards, we can compete with any religion on earth. Indeed, if it were not so, we wouldn't have to worry about Rome and our "dialogue" with it at all. As some of us like to say, we are the Right Church with all the Wrong People in it. But this too, is part of the essential mystery of the Church, how each of us, a chief among sinners (cf. I Tim. 1:15)—that same compound fool, scoundrel, and sluggard we each see when we look in the mirror every morning, if we are honest with ourselves—is made perfect, despite his baser inclinations. "I am the Vine, ye are the branches: He that abideth in Me, and I in him, the same bringeth forth much fruit: for without Me ye can do nothing" (John 5:5; see the enclosed icon). When all is said and done, the life-giving sap of the true Vine is what Orthodoxy offers and what cannot be taken away. Conversely, in a promotional for your book that appeared in the November 1992 *Serviam*, you write: "Because of the crisis of faith afflicting the Church in the West, *Ending the Byzantine Greek Schism* is a timely book . . . to place in the hands of those tempted to lapse into a centuries-old schism [i.e., Orthodoxy]." That is, because you, not we, are suffering a "crisis of faith," you are losing people to us, and you hope to stop their ears to the Voice that calls them to Orthodoxy. But you will not succeed in this, neither with your book nor by any other means, any more than Rome can successfully "unite" with some part of the Orthodox Church without destroying in it precisely those qualities that you hope will repair your own church's deficiencies; as is plain from the results of Lyons and Ferrara-Florence, and will soon become plain once again, such a part manifests itself as but a broken-off branch (cf. Rom 11:17–20), as dry and lifeless as that onto which it has chosen to be grafted. "If a man abide not in Me, he is cast forth as a branch, and is withered; and men gather them, and cast them into the fire, and they are burned" (John 5:6).

If you are interested in writing back, please note my new address.

With regards,

James George Jatras

How American Media Serves as a Transmission Belt for Wars of Choice

"How American Media Serves as a TransmissionBelt for Wars of Choice"

James George Jatras | Social Science Research Network (SSRN) | June 2016

> *"In war-time, truth is so precious that she should always be attended by a bodyguard of lies." (Winston Churchill)*

> *"You furnish the pictures and I'll furnish the war." (attributed to William Randolph Hearst)*

Introduction

The propaganda of war is almost as old as war itself. Both for mobilizing the home front and demoralizing the enemy, packaging war as "our" noble cause against a depraved and deadly "them" has long been a standard, if distasteful, part of the human condition.

But with the advent of modern communications, and especially in the digital age, war propaganda has reached an unprecedented level of sophistication and influence, primarily with regard to the international behavior of the United States. The formal end of the U.S-Soviet Cold War in 1991 left the U.S. with no serious military or geopolitical opponent just at a time when the role of global media was undergoing a significant shift. Earlier that same year, the First Gulf War had featured the debut of *CNN* as a provider of ubiquitous, real-time, 24-hour conflict coverage, setting a standard for later hostilities. Also that same year, the Internet went public.

The decades following 1991 saw a qualitative evolution in the role of media as not just a reporter of events but as an active participant. No longer simply an accessory to conflict, the art and science of media manipulation has perhaps become the core of modern warfare. Indeed, it may even be possible to assert that the psychological aspect of war has become its most important deliverable, eclipsing traditional objectives such as territory, natural resources, or money. (The analogy can be made to the religious wars of 17th century Europe or the ideological conflicts of the mid-20th century, but the technological aspects of information production and dissemination in those eras were insufficient to produce what we see today.)

Below we will examine the unique—and uniquely dangerous—role belligerent media, especially American media, play in contemporary warfare; survey the extent, origins, and evolution of the state apparatus lying behind this phenomenon; and suggest the possibility of remedial action.

Belligerence of the Post-Cold War America Media

The First Gulf War of 1991 marked a watershed both for America's propensity for military action and for the media's role in it. Claims of legality and righteousness from the administration of President George H. W. Bush regarding its decision to expel the Iraqi forces of erstwhile American client Saddam Hussein from Kuwait met with little dissent, least of all from major American news organizations. A similar media chorus of approval if not outright encouragement characterized Bill Clinton's interventions in Somalia (1993), Haiti (1994), Bosnia (1995), and Kosovo (1999), as well as those of George W. Bush in Afghanistan (2001) and Iraq (2003) after the 9/11 attacks. Even President Barack Obama's regime change operation in Libya (2011) benefitted from the same pattern. Only with Obama's intended attack on Syria in September 2013 over a supposed use of chemical weapons by the Syrian government did the established symbiosis between media advocating "humanitarian" or "preemptive" action and the application of American military force misfire.

In each of these episodes the media's uncritical repetition of government-issued "information" and opinions was a key factor in setting the stage for war. Given that in *none* of these enterprises was the territorial integrity or independence of the United States at stake, each can be regarded as a "war of choice" requiring the creation and selling of a rationale not directly based on American national defense. In that context it is important to note the presence in each of some common features that are seldom commented upon—certainly not by American media themselves—that characterized the media's role as the government's transmission belt for implanting pro-war justifications into the public consciousness.

Deficiency of knowledge as the American norm

- Americans are poorly informed about events in the outside world, and younger Americans appear to be even more ignorant than their elders. This means that when policymakers cite the need for action in a given country and news feeds shift to "crisis" coverage, few people have a contextual reservoir of knowledge that may run counter to the official narrative. This largely nullifies the target audience's capacity for critical evaluation.

As the imperative for intervention in a given country arises, both government and media can be sure that they are depicting their rationale on a nearly blank canvas and that the consumers will have little or no context within which they are being told that America "must do something." Americans know, and in general care, little about the outside world. (In fairness to Americans, while we rank particularly low on geographic literacy, knowledge in the rest of the world in many cases is only marginally better. Ignorance in the U.S. matters more because we are more likely to be the initiator of military action than other countries are.) Perhaps the most stunning recent example of how lack of knowledge dovetails with bellicosity was an April 2014 survey at the height of the Ukrainian crisis, where only one-sixth of Americans polled could find Ukraine on a map, but the less they knew about where the conflict was the more they favored forceful American action.

This knowledge deficit is reflected in and reinforced by a paucity of international coverage by American media. Despite the growth of Internet-based alternatives, the majority of the American public still gets most of its news from television, specifically from the networks (*ABC, CBS, NBC,* plus *FoxNews, CNN, MSNBC*) and their local affiliates. Moreover, these are their most trusted news sources, as opposed to web- and social media-based information. (It is true that dependence on TV news falls off dramatically for Millennials, who prefer social and interactive media sources such as *Facebook* and *YouTube*. However, this largely means that Millennials are simply uninterested and uninformed regarding anything they consider as not having immediate personal relevance, consume news only accidentally on a pick-and-choose basis, and in fact are even "dumber" than their elders.)

One feature of American TV news programming that is strikingly different from that found outside the United States (for example, on *BBC1, TF1, ARD, ZDF, RaiUno, NHK,* etc., and their international counterparts like *BBC, Deutsche Welle, France 24, NHK World,* etc.) is a notable scarcity of substantive international news stories. It is not uncommon that an entire half-hour evening network news program will not feature a single event outside the United States. A typical program will begin with inclement weather somewhere in the country, a transportation accident, or a lurid crime story (preferably a murder with sensational features, such as a youthful victim or with a racial aspect, or a mass shooting prompting renewal of the perennial American debate about gun control). A significant portion will be devoted to celebrity gossip, consumer features (such as tips on how to save on your utilities or credit card bill, or turn clutter into cash), and health (new findings on weight loss, recovering from cancer, etc.) In an election season, which because of the length of U.S. campaigns consumes about half the calendar, there may be political news, but much of that will center on the colorful aspects of personality clashes and "gaffes," with little attention paid to the substance of war and peace or foreign affairs.

Reliance on government sources, "ventriloquism," and information incest

- The official media are less a watchdog over government than themselves part of the governing structure, a bulletin board for government propaganda.

Any small attention to "news" from, say, Ukraine or Syria-Iraq, largely consists of "journalists" reporting what they were told by their government contacts. It is understood on both sides that uncritical reporting of the contact's message is the price of continued access. Unsurprisingly, the prevailing bias in such reports is for sanctions, military action, the surveillance state, and the rest of the all-too-familiar script. Hard questions about goals, costs, or legality are seldom asked. This means that when a "crisis" atmosphere is generated about the "need" for U.S. military engagement, virtually the only views presented to the public are those generated by government officials or those friendly to the government's position in the think tank and nongovernmental organization community.

A vivid illustration of how government influence takes the form of a kind of "ventriloquism," with poorly informed, mostly young Washington-based journalists playing the role of puppet was given in a candid interview of Ben Rhodes, Obama's White House "Assistant to the President and Deputy National Security Advisor for Strategic Communications and Speechwriting." At once cynical and evidently proud of his success, Rhodes described to David Samuels of the *New York Times Magazine* how even the journalists being used only dimly perceive their function as conveyors of official "content" with self-generating "force multipliers." As this analyst has commented, Rhodes has "actually cut a window into the belly of the beast and allowed us to see what is going on." Writes Samuels:

It is hard for many to absorb the true magnitude of the change in the news business—40 percent of newspaper-industry professionals have lost their jobs over the past decade—in part because readers can absorb all the news they want from social-media platforms like Facebook, which are valued in the tens and hundreds of billions of dollars and pay nothing for the "content" they provide to their readers. . . . Rhodes singled out a key example to me one day, laced with the brutal contempt that is a hallmark of his private utterances. "All these newspapers used to have foreign bureaus," he said. "Now they don't. They call us to explain to them what's happening in Moscow and Cairo. Most of the outlets are reporting on world events from Washington. The average reporter we talk to is 27 years old, and their only reporting experience consists of being around political campaigns. That's a sea change. They literally know nothing." . . .

In this environment, Rhodes has become adept at ventriloquizing many people at once. Ned Price, Rhodes's assistant, gave me a primer on how it's done. The easiest way for the White House to shape the news, he explained, is from the briefing podiums, each of which has its own dedicated press corps. "But then there are sort of these force multipliers," he said, adding, "We have our compadres, I will reach out to a couple people, and you know I wouldn't want to name them . . . And I'll give them some color," Price continued, "and the next thing I know, lots of these guys are in the dot-com publishing space, and have huge Twitter followings, and they'll be putting this message out on their own." . . .

Now the most effectively weaponized 140-character idea or quote will almost always carry the day, and it is very difficult for even good reporters to necessarily know where the spin is coming from or why. . . . Price turns to his computer and begins tapping away at the administration's well-cultivated network of officials, talking heads, columnists and newspaper reporters, web jockeys and outside advocates who can tweet at critics and tweak their stories backed up by quotations from "senior White House officials" and "spokes-people." . . .

The narratives [Rhodes] frames, the voices of senior officials, the columnists and reporters whose work he skillfully shapes and ventriloquizes, and even the president's own speeches and talking points, are the only dots of color in a much larger vision about who Americans are and where we are going that Rhodes and the president have been formulating together over the past seven years. [from "The Aspiring Novelist Who Became Obama's Foreign-Policy Guru," May 2016]

Buttressing government/media ventriloquism, content of information used in the formulation of American global policy is dominated by a few hundred certified "experts" sharing a remarkable uniformity of opinion regardless of party affiliation. These experts, who inhabit a closed loop of Executive Branch departments and agencies, Congress, media, think tanks, and nongovernmental organizations (NGOs), are responsible for the generation of policy initiatives and their implementation. It should also be noted that many of the most prominent NGOs themselves receive significant funding from government agencies or contractors and could more properly be termed "quasi-nongovernmental," or QuaNGOs. In addition, as with private industry, particularly in the military and financial sectors, there is a brisk rotation of personnel between government and think tanks and other nonprofits in what is called the "revolving door." The presence of past, future, and returning personnel of Goldman Sachs (also, known as the "great vampire squid wrapped around the face of humanity, relentlessly jamming its blood funnel into anything that smells like money") in government agencies tasked with regulating the financial industry is especially notorious.

In short, the people who play key roles in the government and nongovernmental sectors not only think alike, in many cases they are in fact the very same people who have simply switched positions within what could best be understood as a single, hybrid public-private entity (which we will examine in greater detail below at "Behind Media Belligerence: The American Deep State"). These sources of expert views also overwhelmingly dominate the content of news and information (for example, serving as media "talking heads" or publishing commentaries), ensuring that what the public sees, hears, and reads is in accord with the analytical papers issued by think tanks, Congressional reports, and official press releases. The result is a closed loop that is almost completely impervious to views regarded as "outside the mainstream" because they do not originate in or accord with the incestuous "consensus" that exists inside the loop.

Centralized corporate ownership

- Corporate consolidation feeds the tendency toward ratings-based sensationalism, not critical public-interest programming.

The servility of privately owned U.S. media in conveying government views superficially may seem a paradox. It is seldom commented upon that compared to the large majority of other countries, the most prominent and accessible media outlets in the United States are not publicly owned or operated. Whereas outside the U.S. the principal media giants are wholly or majority government-owned entities (*BBC* in the United Kingdom, *CBC* in Canada, *RAI* in Italy, *ABC* in Australia, *ARD* and *ZDF* in Germany, *Channel One* in Russia, *NHK* in Japan, *CCTV* in China, *RTS* in Serbia, etc.), the American public broadcasters *PBS* and *NPR* are dwarves alongside their privately owned competitors. News and information becomes less a question of professional journalistic integrity than maximizing advertising dollars for corporate ownership, a fact that can impact coverage.

While in the past U.S. regulators were keen to ensure diversity of private ownership as a condition of using "public airwaves" (a condition that has never applied to print media, though some limits remain on corporate "cross-ownership" of broadcast and print by the same company), recent decades have seen increasing consolidation. As of 2015, the large majority of American media were owned by six conglomerates: Comcast, News Corporation, Disney, Viacom, Time Warner, and CBS. That's down from 50 companies that controlled that same share as recently as 1983. This also applies to online media: "In raw numbers, 80 percent of the top 20 online news sites are owned by the 100 largest media companies. Time Warner owns two of the most visited sites: *CNN.com* and *AOL News*, while Gannett, which is the twelfth largest media company, owns *USAToday.com* along with many local online newspapers." The average viewer ingests some 10 hours of programming daily from a seeming variety of outlets that the consumer may not realize have the same corporate owners.

"Para-journalism," "infotainment," and "atrocity porn" as a war trigger

- The major media's function as a conduit for government-generated content dovetails with chasing advertising dollars. Consumers are less informed than entertained with prurient images and messages that serve both Caesar and Mammon.

News has always been a money loser for privately owned American broadcast networks. Until the 1970s, networks allocated resources to their unprofitable news operations as a public obligation, in effect subsidizing news—which networks were required to provide as a percentage of their airtime—from entertainment programming that attracted advertising dollars. But with the push for deregulation in recent decades, news has been under intense pressure to generate its own ratings that justify its existence by in effect becoming entertainment programming itself –

> . . . in the form of "low end" in a proliferation of shows that practice what might be called "para-journalism." The most important new form is the "tabloid" news magazine, . . . They are not news shows that borrow conventions from entertainment television, but the other way around: entertainment programs that borrow the aura of news. The forms and the "look" are news—the opening sequences frequently feature typewriter keys and newsroom-like sets with monitors in the background. The content, however, has little of the substance of journalism; above all, little about public affairs.

The tabloid format in turn impacts what little coverage of foreign matters that does appear in hard news programming, as viewers brought up on "Sesame Street" have come to expect to be entertained more than informed. The result is "infotainment," a market-driven product that "critics say . . . is based increasingly on what will interest an audience rather than on what the audience needs to know. Former FCC chairman Newton Minow says that much of today's news is 'pretty close to tabloid.' Former *PBS* anchor Robert MacNeil says that the trends 'are toward the sensational, the hype, the hyperactive, the tabloid values to drive out the serious.'" The ultimate expression of sensationalized, entertainment content in the context of global conflict is known as "atrocity porn," which titillates the audience through horror and incitement to hatred of the presumed perpetrators (as described by William Norman Grigg):

> Atrocity porn plays a critical role in the process of mobilizing mass hatred on the part of the state's designs. Like its sexual equivalent, atrocity porn (especially, and obviously, in the case of stories describing rape and other sexual abuse) appeals to prurient interests to manipulate base impulses. . . . Authors of atrocity porn also cynically exploit the predictable reactions it will provoke from decent people.

Atrocity porn has been an essential element for selling military action: incubator babies (Kuwait/Iraq); the Racak massacre (Kosovo); the Markale marketplace bombings, Omarska "living skeletons," and the Srebrenica massacre (Bosnia); rape as calculated instrument of war (Bosnia, Libya); and poison gas in Ghouta (Syria). Moreover, as blogger Julia Gorin has noted, the recycling of victim memes has begun, including prodding from governments:

> Columnist David P. Goldman (a.k.a. Spengler) had an article in *Asia Times* this month ("To be kind is to be cruel, to be cruel is to be kind," Apr. 14), citing a recent migrant incident in Europe, first reported by UK *Daily Mail*:

The 240ft Monica had been spotted in international waters during the night. When Italian coastguard boats drew along-side, the crews were shocked to see men and women on board begin dangling the infants over the side. The refug-ees—mostly Kurds and many said to be heading for Britain—calmed down only when they were assured they would not be turned away from Italy. . . . When in world history has one side in negotiations threaten[ed] to kill its own people in order to gain leverage?

Here I started getting antsy, yelling at the computer screen, "When in world history? *When*? Try the '90s!" That is, when Bosnian pres-ident Alija Izetbegovic followed through on Bill Clinton's suggestion that he needed to cough up at least 5,000 dead bodies if he wanted a NATO intervention on his side of a turf war against Serbs.

Gorin's insightful observation that prompting from politicians for media coverage to "justify" an attack already decided upon was further borne out in Kosovo. As noted by this analyst in a U.S. Senate report during the buildup to the March 1999 NATO assault on Serbia, lying in plain sight since mid-1998 was what amounted to an invitation from the Clinton Administration: give us a suitable atrocity, and we'll give you a war:

As of this writing, planning for a U.S.-led NATO intervention in Kosovo is now largely in place, while the Clinton Administration's apparent willingness to intervene has ebbed and flowed on an almost weekly basis. The only missing element appears to be an event—with suitably vivid media coverage—that would make intervention pol-itically salable, even imperative, in the same way that a dithering Administration finally decided on intervention in Bosnia in 1995 after a series of 'Serb mortar attacks' took the lives of dozens of civilians—attacks, which, upon closer examination, may in fact have been the work of the Muslim regime in Sarajevo, the main beneficiary of the intervention. [For details, primarily reports from European media, see RPC's "Clinton-Approved Iranian Arms Transfers Help Turn Bosnia into Militant Islamic Base," 1/16/97] That the Admin-istration is waiting for a similar "trigger" in Kosovo is increasingly obvious: "A senior U.S. Defense Department official who briefed reporters on July 15 noted that 'we're not anywhere near making a decision for any kind of armed intervention in Kosovo right now.' He listed only one thing that might trigger a policy change: 'I think if some levels of atrocities were reached that would be intolerable, that would probably be a trigger.'" [Washington Post, 8/4/98]. The recent conflicting reports regarding a purported mass grave containing (depending on the report) hundreds of murdered Albanian civilians or dozens of KLA fighters killed in battle should be seen in this light. [from 'Bosnia II: The Clinton Administration Sets Course for NATO Intervention in Kosovo,' August 1998]

In due course, the January 1999 "Racak Massacre"—the details of which still have not been adequately explained, 17 years later—provided the required "trigger." It's hard to escape the notion that politics and media had melded into a kind of reality show (from the same Senate report):

The foregoing review of the Clinton Administration's prevarications on Kosovo would not be complete without a brief look at one other possible factor in the deepening morass.

Consider the following fictional situation: A president embroiled in a sex scandal that threatens to bring down his administration. He sees the only way out in distracting the nation and the world with a foreign military adventure. So, he orders his spin-doctors and media wizards to get to work. They survey the options, push a few buttons, and decide upon a suitable locale: Albania.

The foregoing, the premise of the recent film *Wag the Dog*, might once have seemed farfetched. Yet it can hardly escape comment that on the very day, August 17 [1998], that President Bill Clinton is scheduled to testify before a federal grand jury to explain his possibly criminal behavior, Commander-in-Chief Bill Clinton has ordered U.S. Marines and air crews to commence several days of ground and air exercises in, yes, Albania as a warning of possible NATO intervention in next-door Kosovo. Perhaps life does imitate art, and here the coincidence tends toward the surreal. Certainly there is one clear difference between the movie and the Kosovo crisis, in that the former was a media fraud with simulated violence while there is indeed a real shooting war in Kosovo (though not without some degree of media slant that would do justice to Stanley Motss, the fictional Hollywood producer played by Dustin Hoffman).

Not too many years ago, it would not have entered the mind of even the worst of cynics to speculate whether any American president, whatever his political difficulties, would even consider sending U.S. military personnel into harm's way to serve his own, personal needs. But in an era when pundits openly weigh the question of whether President Clinton will (or should) tell the truth under oath not because he has a simple obligation to do so but because of the possible impact on his political "viability"—is it self-evident that military decisions are not affected by similar considerations? Under the circumstances, it is fair to ask to what extent the Clinton Administration has forfeited the benefit of the doubt as to the motives behind its actions.

Demonization "Hitler" memes

- Demonizing the intended target neutralizes objections to his removal. How can any decent person oppose getting rid of Hitler?

Post-Cold War conflict can never be a clash of legitimate subjective interests. Rather, each of America's adventures must be spelled out in terms of black-and-white, good-versus-evil Manichaean contests. The side targeted for destruction or replacement has absolutely no redeeming qualities and represents an existential threat not only to the United States but to the entire world, most of all to the people of the country in question. This entails first of all absolute demonization of the evil leader in what is called *reductio ad Hitlerum*, a concept attributed to philosopher Leo Strauss in 1951. Russia's Vladimir Putin has been characterized by name as another Hitler by Hillary Clinton and others. Among the prominent "Hitlers" since 1991 have been Saddam Hussein (Iraq), Slobodan Milosevic (Yugoslavia/Serbia), Radovan Karadzic (Republika Srpska), Moammar Qaddafi (Libya), and Bashar al-Assad (Syria), with less imposing *Führer* figures to be found among Mohamed Farrah Aidid (Somalia), Manuel Noriega (Panama), Mahmoud Ahmadinejad (Iran), and

Omar al-Bashir (Sudan). (Paradoxically, successive rulers of the despotic Kim clan ruling North Korea have not been singled out for the same treatment. This perhaps reflects that country's almost total blockage of outside news access required to supply enough raw material for the Hitler meme, or the reluctance of policymakers to stoke a need to "do something" about a target that actually *does* have weapons of mass destruction and might consider using them if attacked.)

In due course, the targeted "Hitler" will be accused of "killing his own people" to invoke the doctrine of "responsibility to protect" (R2P) as a trump to state sovereignty and territorial integrity. Inflated death tolls of selected conflicts are all attributed to the demonized leader, none to the "moderate, democratic, pro-western, pro-American" opposition, who in many cases are terrorists, jihadists, or criminals of various stripes. Indictment of the targeted leader by international tribunals authorized, funded, and controlled by the U.S. and western countries (for example, Milosevic and Karadzic by the International Tribunal for the former Yugoslavia, al-Bashir by the International Criminal Court (ICC), and repeated calls by R2P advocates for the ICC to indict al-Assad) effectively removes the figure in question from the realm of politics—and the potential for negotiation and compromise—to an imperative that the "accused" be "brought to justice" as determined by the powers controlling the tribunal.

"Weaponization" of media

- In weaponized media, information does not exist to provide insight into objective reality. Rather it is a tool that has meaning only with reference to its subjective purpose.

Demonization of targeted countries and leaders fits into a broader narrative of conflict that builds upon the American penchant for understanding all conflicts as pitting the "good guys" in white hats vs. "bad guys" in black hats. While this attitude may have its roots in Americans' frontier heritage and our somewhat naïve sense of idealism, it lends itself to cynical manipulation by political operations whose ideological principles are most strongly shaped by 20th century ideologies, notably Trotskyism. Having determined that the current "Hitler of the month" has no redeeming qualities, events in a current or planned conflict zone are useful only insofar as they can be used pedagogically for their predetermined purpose.

In addition, similar events can have a totally different moral character depending whether they are caused by the good side or bad side. Thus, U.S. airstrikes are "humanitarian," our "collateral damage" is excusable (bombing of a Doctors Without Borders hospital in Kunduz, Afghanistan, by the U.S. is a regrettable error by low-level personnel—oops!), while others' strikes are criminal (Syrian "barrel bombs," Russians hitting hospitals and a school in Syria). Weaponization of news especially applies to selective finger pointing of war crimes, especially genocide, which as an accusation that completely delegitimizes the enemy can be considered the nuclear bomb of propaganda memes.

America and the "international community," the "Free World," and "American exceptionalism" and "leadership"

- America, like any country, has its own distinctive history, culture, and traditions. Additionally, America's unique founding principles—

consent of the governed, due process, division of powers, limited
government—justly have been an inspiration to much of the world
for over two centuries and are a valid point of American pride.
However, neither of these venerable "exceptional" qualities has
much connection to the much-used and abused bastard term (usually
capitalized as "American Exceptionalism") that describes contemporary U.S. global behavior, by which policymakers in Washington
assert both an exclusive "leadership" privilege and unsupportable
obligation to under-take open-ended, international missions in the
name of the "Free World" and the "international community."

A further notable feature of global discourse is the ritual application of a family
of terms characterizing America's role in the world. All are routinely used by
U.S. officials and repeated by media. The term "international community" is a
favorite of American presidents when invoking their claimed authority for the
use of military force: Bush the Elder in Kuwait, Clinton in Bosnia and Kosovo,
Bush the Younger in Afghanistan and Iraq, and Obama in Libya and Syria.
(Indeed the term is cited far more than either the imperative of American
national security or legality based on constitutional authority.) As noted by
British journalist and academic Martin Jacques "We all know what is meant
by the term 'international community,' don't we? It's the west, of course,
nothing more, nothing less. Using the term 'international com-munity' is a
way of dignifying the west, of globalising it, of making it sound more respectable, more neutral and high-faluting." Indeed, more precisely than the simply
"the west," the "international community" means the geo-political bloc of
countries led (or less charitably, controlled) by Washington.

Closely linked is the concept of the "Free World," a rhetorical relic of the
Cold War that originally was juxtaposed to the communist camp headed by
the USSR but which now has become almost synonymous with "international
community." In any given instance, despite talismanic usage by western
officials (especially the U.S. president, routinely tagged as the "Leader of the
Free World" as though Stalin and Mao were still extant), either expression
might represent at any given time a distinct minority of the world's population
consisting of the U.S. and our satellites. (Even the word "ally" no longer has
the meaning of a mutual, treaty-based defense obligation. As Christopher
Preble of the CATO Institute has suggested: "Essentially any country that buys
into Washington's hegemonic program, any country willing to go along with
the proposition that the United States is and should be the world's policeman,
is an ally.")

Finally, the expression "American Exceptionalism" has become a litmus
test both domestically in the United States (for example, in the accusation that
Obama is a bad president because he "doesn't believe in American Exceptionalism," at least not sufficiently) and abroad as an accusation against the
U.S. for claiming an extraordinary privilege and unique exemption from the
rules of international behavior binding on other states. It is the latter understanding of the expression that has been become most current, despite a
minority view that American Exceptionalism construed as a special license for
empire is ahistorical, un-American, and un-Christian, as well as inconsistent
with older and better American traditions.

Taken together with some degree of interchangeability, these three expressions depict an America (and the incumbent White House resident)
invested with practically unlimited legal and moral authority to act as a
progressive global force, including the use of military power. You are either
with us or against us: our actions are absolutely good by definition, not
relatively good in comparison to the actions of other powers, which on some

level are at best only conditionally legitimate to the extent the U.S. President regards them as such. The result is an approximation of the old Soviet concepts of the "vanguard of all progressive humanity" and the dichotomy of *kto/kogo* ("who/whom") in a predetermined, inevitable historical progression. When we act, "history" is on our side. In such a moral universe, compromise is equated to unacceptable weakness (the charge against Obama of "leading from behind") and contrary to objective social forces and global processes, which depend on "American leadership." The questions of "leading" to what ends, or how those ends benefit the American people are seldom asked.

Disregarding "alternative" media, American samizdat

- As we will see at the end of this analysis, "alternative" media may be part of the eventual breakdown of the system we are describing. But currently the major media operating in concert with their government and corporate sponsors still are in a position to validate what appears in alternative sources by repeating it or to relegate it to a politically powerless realm by ignoring it.

While proliferation of first cable channels and then online publications means the major American networks (*ABC, CBS, NBC*) and newspapers (*New York Times* (a/k/a, the "newspaper of record"), *Wall Street Journal, Washington Post*) have far smaller market share than in the past, they still have a near-monopoly on the legitimacy and public significance of information. This means that while "alternative media"—itself a dismissive term relating to the presumed unreliability of contents—might report and document information contrary to the official line emanating from prestige media operating in symbiosis with their government sources, they can be ignored.

In the past, notably in the totalitarian societies of the 20th century, maintaining the credibility of official media required the physical repression of alternatives. Today, such an approach is unnecessary and almost technologically unfeasible, even for such undemocratic countries as China, Iran, Cuba, and Saudi Arabia (though North Korea may be successful through the sheer unavailability of modern communications technology to most of the population). Instead of suppressing dissent, is it sufficient to maintain major media's role as gatekeeper and certifier of reliability. Information originating in alternative circles becomes reliable and publicly actionable only when picked up and disseminated by the "mainstream media" (MSM), thus validating the information and its ostensibly "alternative" source. Unless and until that happens, alternative information and opinion, especially that which runs counter to the MSM/government/corporate narrative, is ignored and relegated to "conspiracy theory," "internet chatter," or even subjected to the dread label of "denier" of some established, obligatory truth. Non-validated information and views thus become a kind of American *samizdat* (the Russian term for Soviet-era illegal "self-publishing"), which is tolerated but has no impact on public affairs. For example, with respect to the Balkan conflicts (Markale, Srebrenica, Racak, organ-trafficking by leaders of the "Kosovo Liberation Army"), information debunking the official versions of the same events has long been available but has no ability to dislodge the established accounts, even in retrospect.

"We never make mistakes," "stay the course," and "MoveOn-ism"

- American policy evidently has no rear-view mirror, no lessons are ever learned. Being right bestows no credit, giving birth to catastrophes incurs no costs.

Like the Stalin-era NKVD political police, the United States never makes mistakes. To be fair, the U.S. government and media are hardly unique in their rare willingness to admit errors. This is especially true in the case of U.S. use of military force, where the decision for war remains the "responsible" path as opposed to the unknowable "what if we hadn't gone in?" Thus, President Obama, in answer to the question of what was his biggest mistake as president, replied "not having done enough" in Libya after overthrowing Qaddafi. That "regime change" might have been a bad idea in the first place was not even a point of consideration. At most, mistakes concerning details of execution can be admitted (and then immediately discounted in terms of importance), for example the decision to disband the Iraqi army and Baath party after the 2003 invasion and occupation of Iraq. But the invasion itself and the reasons for it are off limits, at least for those who had built their reputations and lined their nests on the basis of the decision for war.

Even in the midst of an action abroad, it is difficult for American policymakers to readjust to mistaken assumptions. Instead, the preferred course is simply to redouble our efforts (William Astore, citing Professor Andrew Bacevich):

> Whether [under] a Clinton or a Bush or an Obama matters little. The U.S. can't help but meddle, using its powerful military as a more or less blunt instrument, at incredible expense to our country, and at a staggering cost in foreign lives lost or damaged by incessant warfare. And no matter how catastrophic the results, that national security state can't help but find reasons, no matter how discredited by events, to 'stay the course.'

Similarly, the consequences of policy decisions are never relevant as future lessons. Instead, they are treated with what Dmitry Babich of *RT* has called "MoveOn-ism":

> Take the example of the torture carried out by Americans during the War on Terror. Nobody apart from whistleblowers has been jailed. Why? According to President Obama, because "we need to look forward, not back." Likewise, consider the invasion of Iraq. "I know a large part of the public wants to move on', said former British Prime Minister Tony Blair, "I share that point of view." And so on. Nobody is ever held to account—and, it should be added, no lessons are learned for "next time."

MoveOn-ism also means not only that authors of past disasters are not held to account, they are not even discredited. Supposed experts who made the crucial bad decisions on Iraq had no compunction about sharing their wisdom on Libya. Those who wrecked Libya then called for the same in Syria. In ancient Israel false prophets were put to death, but in contemporary America they are awarded cushy sinecures at prestigious think tanks and lucrative lobby shops. Conversely, those who correctly predicted the consequences of earlier follies and said "toldja so" are given no credit, their warnings still unheeded.

Behind Media Belligerence: the American Deep State

The American media's role in war cannot be understood without a brief examination of the governing apparatus in whose service the media operates. But first it is important to dismiss a myth persistently peddled with regard to the media's role in unleashing wars of choice. This is the so-called "CNN Effect," the idea that because of the emotive power of media coverage, and especially graphic TV images of human suffering (as we have seen, "atrocity porn"), reluctant governments are compelled to intervene in conflicts of which they would otherwise choose to stay out:

> It is over 20 years since debate over the relationship between TV news coverage of war, and resulting decisions to intervene for what appeared to be humanitarian purposes, occupied a good deal of scholarly and political attention. Back then, it was the *newly emerging global media players such as CNN* that were seen by many to be *the driving force* between purportedly humanitarian interventions during crises in countries such as Somalia (1992–1993) and Bosnia (1995). The term the CNN effect came to be understood as shorthand for the notion that mainstream news media in general, not just CNN, were having an increased effect upon foreign policy formulation. [emphasis added]

There are at least three things wrong with the notion that media are the active "driving force" forcing passive governments to act. First, as shown in the section above ("'Para-journalism,' 'infotainment,' and 'atrocity porn' as a war trigger"), government sometimes invites the coverage that then "forces" them to act on a course upon which they'd already decided and were only awaiting a "justification" that is duly served up by compliant media. Second, as we have seen in the preceding section, media are themselves largely submissive and uncritical conduits for government information. That is, when media dutifully convey to the public shocking stories, with appropriately graphic footage, of real or concocted atrocities attributable to the designated Hitler figure, government sources (and their satellites in the think tanks, NGOs, etc.) conveniently have already made that identification for them. Third, just as media know which topics and themes for coverage fit into the approved narrative, they also know what is not acceptable for reporting. (For example, from this analyst's personal experience, early in the Bosnian war of 1992–95 American media refused first-hand accounts of atrocities committed against Serbs by neo-Ustaša Croatian militias. Why? Because they already "knew" from their government-connected network that "the story" was atrocities committed by Serbs against Croats (and Muslims), not the other way around. Likewise today the almost total blackout on civilian casualties caused by the U.S.-supported Saudi bombing campaign in Yemen.)

This should not be a seen as a simple question of government officials giving specific instructions to journalists as to what they should or should not cover. Self-interested journalists instinctively know that stories that promote the official narrative lead to fame, fortune, and professional awards, and stories that run counter to it lead to career suicide. As described by Robert Parry:

> The reason for this conformity among journalists is simple: If you repeat the conventional wisdom, you might find yourself with a lucrative gig as a big-shot foreign correspondent, a regular TV talking head, or a "visiting scholar" at a major think tank. However, if you don't say what's expected, your career prospects aren't very bright.

If you somehow were to find yourself in a mainstream setting and even mildly challenged the "group think," you should expect to be denounced as a fill-in-the-blank "apologist" or "stooge." A well-paid avatar of the conventional wisdom might even accuse you of being on the payroll of the despised leader. And, you wouldn't likely get invited back.

In sum, both journalists and government officials belong to what can be seen as a single, interlocking network in which war, largely for "humanitarian purposes" unrelated to direct or even indirect American national interests, is a necessary "deliverable." At all levels and in all functions, this network operates as an efficient distributor of vast amounts of money.

Media as an expression of the American Deep State

When we think of the relationship between the government and media, it would be a mistake to think of the former simply as the official apparatus of the state carrying out its constitutionally mandated duties. Rather, it is necessary to understand it as multifaceted, hybrid entity encompassing an astonishing range and depth in both the public and private sectors. To a large extent, the contours of what former Congressional staffer Mike Lofgren has called the Deep State are those of the "expert" community that dominates media thinking, but extends beyond it to include elements of all three branches of the U.S. government, private business (especially the financial industry, government contractors, information technology), think tanks, NGOs and QuaNGOs, higher education (especially the recipients of massive research grants from the Department of Defense), the political parties and their campaign operatives, and lobbyists and PR flacks for any of the foregoing.

As Lofgren explains, the core of the Deep State resides in Washington, with secondary concentrations on Wall Street and in Silicon Valley:

> There is the visible government situated around the Mall in Washington, and then there is another, more shadowy, more indefinable government that is not explained in Civics 101 or observable to tourists at the White House or the Capitol. The former is traditional Washington partisan politics: the tip of the iceberg that a public watching C-SPAN sees daily and which is theoretically controllable via elections. The subsurface part of the iceberg I shall call the Deep State, which operates according to its own compass heading regardless of who is formally in power. [. . .]
>
> The Deep State does not consist of the entire government. It is a hybrid of national security and law enforcement agencies: the Department of Defense, the Department of State, the Department of Homeland Security, the Central Intelligence Agency and the Justice Department. I also include the Department of the Treasury because of its jurisdiction over financial flows, its enforcement of international sanctions and its organic symbiosis with Wall Street. All these agencies are coordinated by the Executive Office of the President via the National Security Council. Certain key areas of the judiciary belong to the Deep State, such as the Foreign Intelligence Surveillance Court, whose actions are mysterious even to most members of Congress. Also included are a handful of vital federal trial courts, such as the Eastern District of Virginia and the Southern District of Manhattan, where sensitive proceedings in national

security cases are conducted. The final government component (and possibly last in precedence among the formal branches of government established by the Constitution) is a kind of rump Congress consisting of the congressional leadership and some (but not all) of the members of the defense and intelligence committees. The rest of Congress, normally so fractious and partisan, is mostly only intermittently aware of the Deep State and when required usually submits to a few well-chosen words from the State's emissaries. [. . .]

[T]he Deep State does not consist only of government agencies. What is euphemistically called "private enterprise" is an integral part of its operations. In a special series in *The Washington Post* called "Top Secret America," Dana Priest and William K. Arkin described the scope of the privatized Deep State and the degree to which it has metastasized after the September 11 attacks. There are now 854,000 contract personnel with top-secret clearances—a number greater than that of top-secret-cleared civilian employees of the government. While they work throughout the country and the world, their heavy concentration in and around the Washington suburbs is unmistakable: Since 9/11, 33 facilities for top-secret intelligence have been built or are under construction. Combined, they occupy the floor space of almost three Pentagons—about 17 million square feet. Seventy percent of the intelligence community's budget goes to paying contracts. And the membrane between government and industry is highly permeable: The Director of National Intelligence, James R. Clapper, is a former executive of Booz Allen Hamilton, one of the government's largest intelligence contractors. His predecessor as director, Admiral Mike McConnell, is the current vice chairman of the same company; Booz Allen is 99 percent dependent on government business. These contractors now set the political and social tone of Washington, just as they are increasingly setting the direction of the country, but they are doing it quietly, their doings unrecorded in the *Congressional Record* or the *Federal Register*, and are rarely subject to congressional hearings. [. . .]

Washington is the most important node of the Deep State that has taken over America, but it is not the only one. Invisible threads of money and ambition connect the town to other nodes. One is Wall Street, which supplies the cash that keeps the political machine quiescent and operating as a diversionary marionette theater. Should the politicians forget their lines and threaten the status quo, Wall Street floods the town with cash and lawyers to help the hired hands remember their own best interests. . . . It is not too much to say that Wall Street may be the ultimate owner of the Deep State and its strategies, if for no other reason than that it has the money to reward government operatives with a second career that is lucrative beyond the dreams of avarice—certainly beyond the dreams of a salaried government employee. [. . .]

After Edward Snowden's revelations about the extent and depth of surveillance by the National Security Agency, it has become publicly evident that Silicon Valley is a vital node of the Deep State as well. Unlike military and intelligence contractors, Silicon Valley overwhelmingly sells to the private market, but its business is so important to the government that a strange relationship has emerged. While the government could simply dragoon the high technology companies to do the NSA's bidding, it would prefer cooperation with so important an engine of the nation's economy, perhaps with an implied *quid pro quo*. Perhaps this explains the extraordinary indulgence the government shows the Valley in intellectual property matters. If an American 'jailbreaks' his smart-phone (i.e., modifies it so that it can use a service provider other than the one dictated by the manufacturer), he could receive a fine of up to $500,000 and several years in prison; so much for a citizen's vaunted property rights to what he purchases. The libertarian pose of the Silicon Valley moguls, so carefully cultivated in their public relations, has always been a sham. Silicon Valley has long been tracking for commercial purposes the activities of every person who uses an electronic device, so it is hardly surprising that the Deep State should emulate the Valley and do the same for its own purposes. Nor is it surprising that it should conscript the Valley's assistance.

Still, despite the essential roles of lower Manhattan and Silicon Valley, the center of gravity of the Deep State is firmly situated in and around the Beltway. The Deep State's physical expansion and consolidation around the Beltway would seem to make a mockery of the frequent pronouncement that governance in Washington is dysfunctional and broken. That the secret and unaccountable Deep State floats freely above the gridlock between both ends of Pennsylvania Avenue is the paradox of American government in the 21st century: drone strikes, data mining, secret prisons and Panopticon-like control on the one hand; and on the other, the ordinary, visible parliamentary institutions of self-government declining to the status of a banana republic amid the gradual collapse of public infrastructure. [. . .]

The Deep State is the big story of our time. It is the red thread that runs through the war on terrorism, the financialization and deindustrialization of the American economy, the rise of a plutocratic social structure and political dysfunction. Washington is the headquarters of the Deep State, and its time in the sun as a rival to Rome, Constantinople or London may be term-limited by its overweening sense of self-importance and its habit, as Winwood Reade said of Rome, to "live upon its principal till ruin stared it in the face." "Living upon its principal," in this case, means that the Deep State has been extracting value from the American people in vampire-like fashion. [from "Anatomy of the Deep State," February 2014; now expanded into a book, *The Deep State: The Fall of the Constitution and the Rise of a Shadow Government*]

The Deep State is not synonymous with the "Military-Industrial Complex" (MIC) against which President Dwight Eisenhower warned in 1960 upon his impending departure from the White House, though Ike's MIC is entirely included within the Deep State and historically provided its core. Ironically, compared to today's structure, the MIC of the 1950s and 1960s was relatively less likely to embark upon foreign military escapades. The existence of a world-class nuclear-armed foe in the form of the USSR moderated tendencies toward adventurism. The most serious "combat" the classic MIC preferred to engage in was inter-service battles for budgetary boodle. Reportedly, once General Curtis LeMay, head of the Air Force's Strategic Air Command, was briefed by a junior officer who repeatedly referred to the USSR as "the enemy." LeMay supposedly interrupted to correct him: "Young man, the Soviet Union is our adversary. Our enemy is the Navy."

Even in Eisenhower's day, the MIC was more than a simple duplex consisting of the Pentagon and military contractors but also included an essential third leg: the Congressional committees that provide the money constituting the MIC's lifeblood. (Reportedly, an earlier draft of the speech used the term "military-industrial-Congressional" complex, a fuller description of what has come to be called the "Iron Triangle." Asked about the omission from the final text, Eisenhower is said to have answered: "It was more than enough to take on the military and private industry. I couldn't take on the Congress as well.")

Not only did the Iron Triangle continue to expand during the Cold War, when production of military hardware established itself as the money-making nucleus of the MIC, it swelled to even greater proportions after the designated enemy, the USSR, went out of business in 1991. While for one brief shining moment there was naïve discussion of a "Peace Dividend" that would provide relief for American taxpayers from whose shoulders the burden of a "long twilight struggle" against communism (in John Kennedy's phrase) had been lifted, that notion faded quickly. Instead, not only did the "hard" side of the MIC maintain itself—first in Iraq to fight "naked aggression" by Saddam Hussein in Kuwait, then in the Balkans in the 1990s as part of NATO's determination to go "out of area or out of business"—it then branched out into "soft" areas of control including the financial and IT aspects Lofgren describes. As with the older hardware-based deliverables, the new "soft power" feeds a New Class of privilege mainly centered in the Washington, DC, suburbs, symbolized by extravagant and tasteless "McMansions" that "resemble the architecture of the Loire Valley, Elizabethan England, or Renaissance Tuscany as imagined by Walt Disney, or perhaps Liberace." The media themselves are no less a part of this new pseudo-aristocracy than are government agencies and "Beltway Bandits."

In describing the soft structure of the Deep State, it is important to note also the following, all of which interface closely with the media.

Lobbyists and PR shops

One could argue that the old, Eisenhower-era MIC at least claimed defense of the American homeland as its justification—after all, the heavily armed Soviet bloc really did exist—and that arms manufacturers were essentially the World War II-era "arsenal of democracy" that defeated Nazism, fascism, and Japanese militarism updated to face communism. As part of the justification for a substantial chunk of the federal budget, Pentagon contractors developed and still maintain an army of lobbyists and media spin doctors to secure their positions on Capitol Hill and in the bureaucracy.

But increasingly the same influence community is dominated by interests whose claim to "defend America" is slim to none, and whose client interests often are those of transnational corporations or foreign states. As Justin Raimondo of *Antiwar.com* recently observed, it's possible to see the lobbying and PR industries as a veritable "Fifth Estate" within the governing structure, an estate whose very purpose is to skew the loyalty of a huge portion of the Washington establishment toward corporate or foreign interests that are not necessarily compatible with those of the American people (here, with particular reference to Saudi Arabia, a conspicuous consumer of PR and lobbying services):

> The Constitution provides for three branches of government: the executive, Congress, and the judiciary—but there have been a few additions lately. With the rise of mass communications, common

parlance has designated the media as the "Fourth Estate," because—
in theory—it is supposed to act as a 'watchdog" on the activities of the
other three. (Although in practice, as we have seen, it often doesn't
work out that way.) And as America entered the age of empire, stepping out on the world stage and exerting its power, a development
the Founders foresaw—and greatly feared—became a reality: the rise
of foreign lobbyists, i.e. the Fifth Estate, as a power in our domestic
politics.

This was inevitable as we took the road to empire. Our foreign
clients, protectorates, and sock puppets have a material interest in
maintaining the status quo: their life blood depends on the smooth
workings of the political machinery that keeps the gravy train flowing
from Washington to every point on the globe. 'Foreign aid,' arms
deals, overseas bases that boost their economies, the deployment of
'soft power,' and the architecture of entangling alliances that have
enmeshed us all over the world—all of this is defended and relentlessly extended by foreign lobbyists who work day and night to
protect and expand their very profitable turf.

The latest newsworthy example is the Saudi lobby, which is
working overtime these days to burnish the Kingdom's badly
tarnished image. The recent agitation for the release of the censored
28 pages of the joint congressional report on the 9/11 terrorist
attacks—and news reports of their horrific war crimes in Yemen—
has them on the defensive. [. . .]

Drinkers at the American trough 'are worried about what it means
for them: for their arms deals, for their trade deals, for international
funding and alliances that they depend on.' They are, in short,
worried about the possible loss of all that free stuff they're getting . .
. . This is the price we pay for empire: interventionism is a two-way
street. We send the Marines to foreign lands—and they send their
lobbyists to Washington. Our overseas client-states have every
interest in maintaining the level of financial and military support
that flows out to them, and it's no surprise that they're fighting to
retain it. The question is: are the American people finally beginning
to realize that their overseas empire is a burden rather than a boon?
[from "The Fifth Estate: Foreign Lobbyists," April 2016]

In the same category can be placed non-profit foundations that ostensibly
serve altruistic functions but which often serve as conduits for peddling
influence and, not incidentally, sometimes for enriching prominent political
figures. Such figures can even include a possible future President of the United
States, with a prime example of corruption provided by the Clinton Foundation, which is as well documented (here by investigative journalist Ken
Silverstein) as it is ignored by major media and even by the token "opposition"
on the Republican side of the aisle:

One money-laundering expert and former intelligence officer based
in the Middle East who had access to the foundation's confidential
banking information told me that members of royal families in Middle Eastern countries, including Kuwait and the United Arab Emirates, have donated money to the CGEP [Clinton Giustra Enterprise
Partnership, a Canadian organization run by one of Bill Clinton's
close friends, Frank Giustra] that has then been sluiced through to
the Clinton Foundation. He added that the CGEP has also received
money from corrupt officials in South Africa during the regime of

Jacob Zuma and from senior officials in Equatorial Guinea, one of the most brutal and crooked dictatorships in the world. "Equatorial Guinea doesn't give to the Clinton Foundation in New York because it's too embarrassing," he said. "They give the money anonymously in Canada and that buys them political protection in the United States. The Clinton Foundation is a professionally structured money-laundering operation." [. . .]

Its biggest donors include some truly wonderful people and countries. There are, to name a few, the torture-happy, terror-exporting government of Saudi Arabia; a foundation controlled by Victor Pinchuk, a Ukrainian oligarch accused of bribery and corruption; and Frank Giustra, a penny-stock artist who became filthy rich with the generous assistance of Bill Clinton. In 2008, a former Kazakh official told reporters that Giustra, who established the CGEP with Clinton, donated millions to the foundation after Clinton helped him purchase uranium deposits in Kazakhstan. (At the time, Giustra denied this claim, pointing out that he had been engaged in mining deals in Kazakhstan since the 1990s.) [from "Shaky Foundations," November 2015]

"Democracy promotion"

In the preceding section, we touched upon the role of think tanks, NGOs, and QuaNGOs as an integral part of the information and analysis that fills media with views supportive of wars of choice. The same entities can be considered less as servants of the Deep State than themselves part of it. As the Cold War was winding down in the 1980s, the U.S. ramped up what was billed as "democracy promotion" activities through a variety of entities, most notably through the establishment of the National Endowment for Democracy (NED) in 1983. But as with the hard military side of the Deep State's activities, notably NATO, far from fading away along with the Soviet threat it ostensibly was tasked with opposing, the new apparatus of "democracy promotion" vastly expanded its mandate. NED, along with its Democratic and Republican sub-organizations, can be considered the flagship of a community of ostensibly private but government-funded or subsidized organizations that provides the soft compliment to American hard military power.

The various governmental, quasi-governmental, and nongovernmental components of this network—sometimes called the "Demintern" in analogy to the Comintern, an organization comparable in global ambition if differing in ideology and methods—are also coordinated internationally at the official level through the less-well-known "Community of Democracies." It is often difficult to know where the "official" entities (CIA, NATO, the State Department, Pentagon, USAID) separate from ostensibly nongovernmental but tax dollar-supported groups (NED, Freedom House, Radio Free Europe/Radio Liberty) and privately funded organizations that cooperate towards common goals (especially the Open Society organizations funded by billionaire George Soros). As described by commentator and author Srdja Trifkovic, among the specialties of this network are "color revolutions" targeting leaders and governments disfavored by Washington for regime change, a soft power analogue to wars of choice:

Even a seasoned cynic sometimes gasps in disbelief. "President Putin misinterprets much of what the U.S. is doing or trying to do," U.S. Secretary of State John Kerry told a press conference in Geneva on

March 2. "We are not involved in 'numerous color revolutions' as he asserts. In the case of Ukraine, such assumptions are also wrong. The United States support international law with respect to the sovereignty and integrity of other people."

This is akin to Count Dracula asserting his strict adherence to a vegan diet and his principled respect for the integrity of blood banks worldwide. Various quasi-NGOs funded by American taxpayers and funneled through organizations such as the National Endowment for Democracy, Freedom House and the National Democratic Institute, not to mention George Soros's Open Society Foundations (partly funded by U.S. and other Western governments), have been actively engaged in dozens of "regime-change" operations for a decade and a half. Their work is conducted in disregard of international law and in violation of the sovereignty and integrity of the people whose governments are thus targeted.

The overthrow of Slobodan Milosevic in Belgrade (October 2000) provided the blueprint, in strict accordance with Gene Sharp's manual. Widespread popular discontent was manipulated by the U.S./Soros funded and trained Otpor! network to bring to power a government subservient to Western political and economic interests. ... Georgia's 2003 "Rose Revolution" was carried out by the *Kmara* ("Enough") network, a carbon copy of Serbia's "Otpor," including the clenched fist logo. Its activists were trained and advised by the U.S.-affiliated Liberty Institute and funded by the Open Society Institute. ... The march of history continued with the 2004 "Orange Revolution" in Ukraine—that grand rehearsal for the Maidan coup a decade later—and the 2005 "Cedar Revolution" in Lebanon, which was given its name by then-U.S. Under Secretary of State for Global Affairs Paula J. Dobriansky. Also in 2005 the "Tulip Revolution" in Kyrgyzstan had as its chief foreign advisor Givi Targamadze, an official of Georgia's aforementioned Liberty Institute, who at the time chaired Saakashvili's parliamentary committee on defense and security. [from "Lies, Kerry's Lies, and Color Revolution Statistics," March 2015]

U.S. financial power and "lawfare"

Washington holds tremendous leverage over the financial stability of almost every other government because of the status of the dollar as the world's reserve currency and the fact that virtually all international financial transactions—most of which are conducted in dollars, especially in the energy sector (in which the "petrodollar" is the standard unit)—at some point pass through an American intermediary institution, thus triggering U.S. claims of "jurisdiction." Even the SWIFT system, formally based in Europe, is under heavy U.S. influence if not control. This allows American officials to threaten other countries, even our closest allies, with crippling financial sanctions of dubious legality if they don't accede to Washington's demands.

A prime example of this is the so-called Foreign Account Tax Compliance Act (FATCA), which requires foreign financial institutions to hand over to the IRS a treasure trove of private information (which under U.S. law can, and undoubtedly will, be passed to intelligence agencies such as the CIA and NSA) and subject other countries' financial sectors to regulatory administration by the U.S. Treasury Department. (Paradoxically, the same Department doesn't control America's own central bank, the Federal Reserve, which is essentially a private entity.) FATCA was built upon earlier "successes" such as the U.S.

Justice Department's imposing penalties on an extraterritorial basis against Swiss banks for violating American tax laws and a $9 billion-dollar shakedown of France's BNP Paribas for violating U.S. sanctions laws with respect to Sudan, Cuba, and Iran. Media coverage of the practice of using a combination of financial power and U.S. law against entities not under American juris-diction—sometimes referred to as "lawfare"—is almost entirely generated from U.S government sources, with journalists uniformly cheering yet another victory over the forces of corruption, tax evasion, money-laundering (in which Dodd-Frank provides another lever), and terrorism.

Rarely are concerns raised about what gives the United States such sweeping and exceptional authority in violation of other countries' sover-eignty. In addition to finance-related issues (in which the latest episode is the "Panama Papers," which some believe to have originated in U.S. agencies, with Russia's President Putin the primary intended target), the lawfare concept has also branched into sports: FIFA corruption charges (which is mainly driven by the U.S. Department of Justice (DOJ), despite only incidental U.S. connect-ions) and the allegations of doping by Russian athletes (also now involving DOJ), including Maria Sharapova.

Simply put, the United States government considers the entire globe under the jurisdiction of American law, in effect whenever, wherever, and on whatever issues officials in Washington may choose. However, the line between legal and political objectives often is far from clear.

Political Parties and superficial partisan clashes

One of the hypocritical quirks of America's "democracy promotion" activities is criticism of other countries for electoral practices that are even more prevalent in the United States. For example, in 2010 NED's Republican and Democratic QuaNGOs, respectively the International Republican Institute (IRI) and the National Democratic Institute (NDI), faulted Ukraine's (then) new electoral law as a "retreat" from democracy, asserting that it favored incumbents over challengers, allowed plurality winners without a runoff, and gave an edge to established national parties over startups.

Of course all three of the IRI-DNI points of criticism of Ukraine virtually define the American party system. Congressional districts are drawn to eliminate serious challenge to incumbents of either party (nobody has yet figured out how to gerrymander a Senate race, though), and runoffs, with the exception of Louisiana's "jungle primary," are unknown. But the critical abuse—and the factor that makes the two established parties an integral part of the ruling structure no less than the Communist Party of the Soviet Union (CPSU) was in its day—is the Republican-Democrat "duopoly" that has effectively divided the U.S. political "marketplace" ever since 1860 when the Republican Party first won the presidency under Abraham Lincoln.

For over a century various "third parties"—Libertarian, Green, Socialist, Constitution, American Independent, Reform, etc.—have sought to replicate the Republicans' displacement of the Whigs. But our legal and electoral systems place severe roadblocks in the path of potential third parties; in most American states, the "two major parties" automatically qualify for a place on the ballot, while other parties and independents often must undergo an expensive and cumbersome petition process. If two commercial firms were to carve up the marketplace between them the way the Republicans and Democrats do access to the ballot, they would be prosecuted for violation of antitrust laws and their executives put in jail.

Especially in hard economic times, the perception of hand-in-glove collusion of the two established American parties feeds the cynical public belief that there is no real difference between them. Huey Long, a populist Democratic senator and governor of Louisiana, once compared American politics to a restaurant: "They've got a set of Republican waiters on one side and a set of Democratic waiters on the other side, but no matter which set of waiters brings you the dish, the legislative grub is all prepared in the same Wall Street kitchen." (Long was gunned down in 1935 while running for president.)

This doesn't mean, however, that public feelings are not highly polarized on a partisan basis. Traditionally, for most of the 20th century, the Democrats could count on about 40–45% of the electorate, the Republicans about 35–40%, with a slim group in the middle up for grabs. (In spite of the Democrats' greater percentage, the GOP benefits from its more reliable turnout.) Because of increasing skepticism about the established parties, those numbers are now about one-third solid Republican, about one-third solid Democratic, and about one-third "independents" who constitute the majority of the flip-flop in sequential "referendum" elections, where the only alternative to the Republicans is the Democrats, and vice versa.

At the same time, we have an increasingly polarized political media culture, reflecting not only the multiplicity of cable and satellite channels but the internet and "new media" like Facebook and Twitter. Back in the infancy of the TV age, from about the 1950s until the 1990s, there was a common national media culture that reflected the established, generally liberal, Democratic tilt of the American *inteligentsiya* that was almost uniform among the (then only) three networks and a handful of major newspapers and magazines. That has now changed superficially into a sharp partisan divide, where about one-third of Americans get their talking points from, say, Michael Moore, and Rachel Maddow and Chris Matthews on *MSNBC*, with their related internet echoes, while another third gets theirs from Rush Limbaugh, and Sean Hannity and Bill O'Reilly on *Fox News*, and their internet echo chamber. Increasingly, there is nothing like a national dialogue on anything, but rather two entirely separate, diametrically opposed ideological cultures, each demonizing "them." This is why when after Barack Obama's election the Tea Party appeared, the GOP fell over itself trying to co-opt them, while the Democrats denounced them as a mob of racists and subversives. When later parallel grassroots Occupy movements broke out on the Left, the Democrats tried to figure out how to channel it while top Republicans denounced them as commie anarchists and loons.

The same partisan division of labor is found with regard to international policy, where there are also two dominant camps—both of them pro-war. As already noted, American foreign policy is dominated by a narrow clique of supposed "experts." While almost of them agree on the basics regarding the American role in the world and the advisability of wars of choice and replacing uncooperative governments via "color revolutions," they also maintain a pro forma division that reflects the partisan duopoly. These fall generally into the camps of the "liberal interventionists" (Democrats like Hillary Clinton, U.N. Ambassador Samantha Power, and former Secretary of State Madeleine Albright) or, on the Republican side, "neoconservatives" (like the late U.N Ambassador Jeane Kirkpatrick, former Secretary of State Condoleezza Rice, and architects of the Iraq war such as Paul Wolfowitz). Between these camps there is virtually no difference when it comes to getting rid of the next "Hitler of the Month" but perhaps mainly for appearance's sake they engage in noisy but meaningless shadow-boxing with their partisan opposite numbers over details. Thus, under Obama Democrat-leaning media accuse the Republicans of "undermining our President," just as GOP-friendly media did when George W. Bush held the office. Republicans howl that Obama has weakened America through "leading from behind," not from the front—whatever that means. But underlying the acrimony is a deep consensus on ends and means: For example, in the summer of 2013 the pro-Republican and pro-Democrat media vied with one another in screaming for U.S. bombing of Syria over what even then seemed false charges of chemical weapons use, while accusing their political opponents of being simultaneously weak and dangerous. A similar bipartisan accord demands so-called "lethal aid" to Ukraine.

Finally, it should be noted that the multitude of campaign consultants, pollsters, spin doctors, media wizards, lawyers, and other functionaries in the party mechanisms (and non-party fellow-travelers, like operators of "independent expenditure committees" whose titles run the alphabet with the exception of "Q" and "Z") are themselves members in good standing of the political establishment, with the cash flow to prove it. Unsurprisingly, a good percentage of the McMansions in the Washington suburbs belong to people in this category, a numerous class on the payroll of an astonishingly small set of ultra-wealthy funders. As *One America News* producer April LaFever sums up the parties as money machines: "Turns out a small core group of uber rich people control all the money in politics, about 50 people to be exact. Donors on both sides of the aisle are expected to shell out even more money this [i.e., 2016] cycle and surpass the $828 million groups paid for the 2012 election."

In sum, the U.S. political system is dominated by a formal bifurcation that more resembles a one-party state with two factions than an open competition among a multiplicity of truly diverging principles. The well-remunerated participants, both inside and outside of the formal organs of government—and including media—are effectively part of the governing structure and almost uniformly hew to a consensus line.

A note on the role of ideology

While a full examination of the ideological issues related to the American media's pro-war tilt is beyond the scope of this analysis, the reader should not have the impression that the U.S. Deep State is solely a moneymaking enterprise, though money generates the power that makes all the wheels turn. But just as members of the old Soviet *nomenklatura* depended on Marxism-Leninism both as a working methodology and as a justification for their prerogatives and privileges, denizens of the entrenched duopoly of Democrat liberal interventionists and Republican neoconservatives rely upon an ideological imperative for global empire and endless wars. Perhaps the fullest expression of this was from a 1996 article by neoconservative ideologists William Kristol and Robert Kagan, misleadingly titled "Toward a Neo-Reaganite Foreign Policy," in which they called for the U.S. to establish and maintain indefinitely "benevolent global hegemony"—American world domination. As scrutinized by this analyst the following year, Kristol and Kagan laid down virtually all of the elements that have guided U.S. foreign policy and its media aspect during the ensuing years. It is no accident that these same GOP neoconservatives were enthusiastic supporters of Bill Clinton's Balkan interventions of 1990s, under the guidance of people like then-Secretary of State Madeleine Albright, who once opined regarding the sanctions-related deaths of a half million Iraqi children that "the price is worth it." In the U.S. Deep State, there is little dissent on either side of the partisan aisle with Albright's sincere conviction that a militant United States has a special wisdom: "If we have to use force, it is because we are America; we are the indispensable nation. We stand tall and we see further than other countries into the future . . ."

And if some country doesn't agree with the "indispensable" opinion of officials in Washington, they should prepare at least to get sanctioned, if not bombed, occupied, targeted by terrorists, or set up for a "people power" regime change, with the MSM cheering it on.

Is a Remedy Possible?

When this analyst served at the U.S. Department of State in the (then) Office of Soviet Union Affairs, starting in early 1981, it was possible to count on one hand the number of other people at the entire Department who admitted to even the possibility that the status of Marxism-Leninism as the ruling ideology in Russia was not permanent. The overwhelming, self-evident assumption was that the Soviet system as it then existed and had perpetuated itself for three generations was here to stay. The destabilization of that system—and part- icularly the adverse impact on the USSR's agreed-on "narrative" of Gor- bachev's *glasnost'*—was unforeseen by American policy-makers. What had been a powerful mutual reinforcement of the Soviet political structure and its propaganda operations instead turned into a downward spiral as the regime and the carefully articulated narrative that had justified its existence for so many years broke down.

Like the still-formidable and dominant MSM, the U.S. Deep State and its machinery for advocating wars of choice, regime change operations, color revolutions, and sanctions may seem a dauntingly solid enterprise. That appearance has been fed by a combination of American geopolitical hegemony internationally and submissive media hegemony domestically. The very per- ception of overwhelming power and the pointlessness of opposition has itself been a factor in perpetuating this structure. Channeling The Borg, the message is (here with reference to Montenegro, which has just acceded to NATO membership): WE ARE THE UNITED STATES. RESISTANCE IS FUTILE. YOU WILL BE ASSIMILATED.

Nonetheless, there are indications that all is not well for the hegemonic enterprise. At the interlocking political/geopolitical, economic/financial, and information levels, there are warning signs. As was the case with the late USSR, it is likely that the decline and ultimate dissolution of the structure we have been describing will involve all three sectors:

Political/geopolitical and economic/financial

For the first time in decades, a significant challenge is being mounted dom- estically against the policy consensus of the Republican-Democrat duopoly. Because of the lock the two established parties have on the U.S. electoral system, that can't happen via a third party in the manner the European Union establishment (itself essentially a satellite of the U.S.) is being challenged from both the Right and the Left by groups like UKIP (Britain), the National Front (France), PEGIDA, Alternative für Deutschland (Germany), Movimento Cinque Stelle (Italy), Partij voor de Vrijheid (Netherlands), SYRIZA (Greece), Podemos (Spain), and others. While myriad "third parties" exist in the United States, they have no chance of taking power, even at the local level, and serve primarily as vehicles for "protest" votes, the equivalent of voting "none of the above" or "a pox on both your houses!" The combination of corporate interests with fixing of the political marketplace been the GOP and the Democrats leaves little opportunity for positive development.

Thus, the only path for even marginal change is an insurgency within one of the two established parties. As it happens, in 2016 there is rebellion in both parties. This is not coincidental. The failures of the two-party consensus are evident in voter fury directed against Republicans and Democrats alike in light of a shrinking Middle Class, flat or falling income levels (reflecting in large part loss of high-paying manufacturing jobs), crippling debt levels ("nearly half of Americans would have trouble finding $400 to pay for an emergency"), a rising mortality rate (notably among the white working class, dubbed "the White Death" from suicide, substance abuse (with about five percent of the world's population, the U.S. consumes 80 percent of the world's opioid prescriptions), and a diet of processed foods and GMOs, in a pattern reminiscent of collapsing life expectancy of Russian males as the USSR imploded), and a record low labor participation rate. There is a widespread sense of foreboding that the future will be even worse, with prospects of a new financial crisis that would dwarf the mortgage-based securities collapse of 2008. Despite an ostensible "recovery"—mostly in the form of record profits on Wall Street generated by the Fed's throwing free money at the investor class, while the real economy remains flat-line—public unease is palpable, along with most Americans' expectation of a lower standard of living for their children and grandchildren. Somebody is making a lot of money out of "benevolent global hegemony," but it sure isn't the ordinary folk in what the elite of both parties concentrated on the coasts disdain as "Flyover Country."

While very different in their proposed remedies, the candidacies of Bernie Sanders in the Democratic Party and of Donald Trump in the GOP tap into this rising tide of resentment. At this writing, it appears that Sanders has been beaten back by Hillary Clinton (the corrupt Picture of Dorian Gray face of the Democrat side of the establishment) while Trump has seized the high ground in the Republican race. In his challenge to what Trump-supporter Senator Jeff Sessions (R-Alabama) calls the "oligarchy" (comparable to Lofgren's Deep State), it is significant that Trump has defied Republican (i.e., neoconservative) orthodoxy on the Iraq war and the Ukraine crisis, as well as on Libya and Syria, and questioned the cost of ties with many supposed "allies," for which reason some panicked neoconservatives have openly defected to Clinton. Trump's critics desperately wish to hide the fact that his supposedly isolationist "America\ First" views are closer to those of our Founding Fathers than are the interventionists'. Unsurprisingly, the relationship between the pro-war media and Trump is one of open mutual loathing—but he still gets saturation news coverage because of his impact on ratings.

The domestic political challenge occurs at a time when U.S. hegemony is not going well internationally. As noted above, for the first time the media-interventionist bandwagon failed in its attempt to unleash American air attacks on Syria in 2013. That failure was followed in September 2015 by launch of the successful Russian intervention in that country and the general recognition that the Assad government will not be overthrown. The Ukraine crisis has settled into a sullen standoff, with Ukraine sliding down toward failed state status and thus completely lacking in usefulness as a NATO/EU salient against Russia. Return of Crimea to Ukraine is off the table, and sanctions by Europe—which even Obama admits are maintained under U.S. pressure—are more of a problem for the governments imposing them than for Moscow. The European Union's woes are compounded by a looming "Brexit" vote, Dutch voters' rejection of an Association Agreement with Ukraine, the failure of the European Central Bank's negative interest rate policies, and the migrant crisis, throwing the very existence of the EU into doubt. In the South China Sea and Korean Peninsula, Washington's imperial overreach risks war with Beijing over what a growing number of observers see as issues of limited importance to the United States. As governments (notably Russia and China) stockpile gold, there is increasing, though perhaps premature, talk of a BRICS-based alternative to the U.S. and dollar-dominated global financial system and breaking away from the dollar in energy pricing.

To sum up, on the substantive side, the media narrative that the establishment—the oligarchy, the Deep State, the Republican-Democratic duopoly—depends on is looking almost as threadbare as the "radiant future of communism" did in 1985, the year Gorbachev became General Secretary of the CPSU Central Committee. As characterized by Ralph Nader: "Our political system is decaying. It's on the way to gangrene." The rot no longer can be hidden.

Skepticism of the official media narrative and alternatives

At some point the false picture of pseudo-reality (as Alain Besançon called it in the late Soviet propaganda context) diverges so far from real reality that the official media narrative becomes useless and even counterproductive. While a majority of Americans probably are still glued to the partisan outlets of "their" side of the political divide, there is a growing sense across the spectrum that not only the MSM but even partisan media like *Fox News* and *MSNBC* are untrustworthy. The decline of the credibility of established media is of major proportions (*Associated Press*, via alternative site *Activist Post.com*):

> Trust in the news media is being eroded by perceptions of inaccuracy and bias, fueled in part by Americans' skepticism about what they read on social media.
>
> Just 6 percent of people say they have a lot of confidence in the media, putting the news industry about equal to Congress and well below the public's view of other institutions. In this presidential campaign year, Democrats were more likely to trust the news media than Republicans or independents. [. . .]
>
> Nearly 90 percent of Americans say it's extremely or very important that the media get their facts correct, according to the study. About 4 in 10 say they can remember a specific incident that eroded their confidence in the media, most often one that dealt with accuracy or a perception that it was one-sided.
>
> The news media have been hit by a series of blunders on high-profile stories ranging from the Supreme Court's 2012 ruling on President Barack Obama's health care law to the Boston Marathon bombing that have helped feed negative perceptions of the media.
>
> In 2014, *Rolling Stone* had to retract a vivid report about an alleged gang rape at a fraternity party at the University of Virginia. The Columbia Graduate School of Journalism, asked by *Rolling Stone* to investigate after questions were raised about the veracity of the story, called it an avoidable journalistic failure and 'another shock to journalism's credibility amid head-swiveling change in the media industry. [from "New Poll Shows Only 6% Of People Trust The Mainstream Media," April 2016]

American conservative hatred of the MSM has a long history, in large part due to the conviction that the prestige media tilted toward the liberal side. But the failure of the major parties also negatively impacts the credibility of their media mouthpieces, helping the proliferation of alternatives like *OpEdNews*, *zerohedge.com*, *Antiwar.com*, *TheSaker*, *LewRockwell.com*, *Russia-Insider*,

Chronicles magazine, *Infowars.com, Counterpunch.com, RonPaulInstitute-*
.org, Consortiumnews, and many others, including upstart conservative
network *One America News.* Some other publications are open to alternative
views and serve as conduits to more mainstream opinion, such as *The*
American Conservative on the Right, *The Nation* on the Left, the libertarian
Reason, and the foreign policy realist publication *The National Interest.*

As would be expected, the emergence of alternative media is messy and
chaotic, with controversies over what and what does not qualify as "alternative," and even that alternatives are themselves sucked into the MSM ambit.
At the same time, "mainstream" media increasingly must take note of "alternative" information in an attempt to preserve some of its diminishing credibility. The most obvious success in this regard is *DrudgeReport.com,*
especially in its coverage of the presidential race. As summarized by Mike
Adams of *NaturalNews* (as picked up by *Infowars.com,* a major alternative
source):

> The bottom line is that the mainstream media thinks you are
> incredibly stupid and will buy anything they say, no matter how
> illogical or irrational it might be. What the alternative media has now
> proven is that the mainstream media is largely irrelevant. It matters
> nothing what they print or broadcast. The people who are informed
> know it's all lies, and the mind-numbed propaganda victims who still
> watch shows like CNN and MSNBC are irrelevant to the march of
> history anyway.
> Real history is being shaped, investigated and reported by the
> alternative media. We are the ones who have no big corporate spon-
> sors and no million-dollar budgets, but we have the hearts and minds
> and passion for truth and justice that drives our work to levels of
> authenticity that the mainstream media can never hope to attain. . .
> regardless of production budgets. [. . .]
> For once-grand institutions of news reporting like the New York
> Times and the Washington Post, the era of honest journalism con-
> ducted in the public interest is a long-faded shadow. Today, main-
> stream media exists solely to catapult corporate propaganda and fill
> the minds of the American people with useless drivel as a distraction
> from the real history bring shaped around them.
> In fact, internet-savvy viewers and readers of today automatically
> distrust any news reporter who is obviously reading a teleprompter.
> If there's a teleprompter involved, it's obviously scripted news. And
> if it's scripted news, it's probably pure bunk.
> Real journalism isn't scripted. Today's viewers would rather see an
> honest person with a rag-tag wardrobe reporting the news on the side
> of the road than from a person with a million-dollar smile and a
> thousand-dollar suit reporting from a flash-and-dazzle studio by
> reading a teleprompter. Everybody knows the teleprompter news is
> fake. Everybody knows the 'news barbie' who was hired for her good
> looks has no real clue what she's even reading or saying. Everybody
> knows the mainstream media is far more interested in BLOCKING
> important stories than reporting them. [from "Alternative Media
> Upstages Lamestream Media In World-Class Coverage Of Historic
> Bundy Ranch Showdown," April 2014]

It should also be noted that domestic alternative media sometimes interact
with foreign media (such as *RT, Al-Jazeera, CCTV, PressTV*) to break through

the information firewall but arguably then being influenced by the agenda of the sponsoring foreign governments. In any case, a growing segment of the American public is discovering a skill once well-honed by the citizens of the former communist countries: reading between the lines of the official media (which is assumed to be full of lies) and making informed comparisons to *samizdat* alternative media, foreign sources, and the rumor-mill to guess what the truth might be.

The U.S. government's denunciation of *RT* in particular as a "propaganda bullhorn," in Secretary of State John Kerry's description, is well known. There is now evidence of enough official U.S. concern about the influence of Russian (and Chinese) media that measures may be soon taken to try to blunt their impact, particularly in Europe. In a step that was not even taken during the Cold War, some in Congress are seeking to create a dedicated service at the State Department, a "Center for Information Analysis and Response"—characterized by some as a budding "Ministry of Truth"—to "expose and counter foreign information operations directed against United States national security interests and proactively advance fact-based narratives that support United States allies and interests." The bill authorizing the Center, called the "Countering Information Warfare Act of 2016," would apply "a whole-of-government approach leveraging all elements of national power," including participation of the Director of National Intelligence, to "provide grants or contracts of financial support to civil society groups, journalists, nongovernmental organizations, federally funded research and development centers, private companies, or academic institutions." This effort, if approved, would coordinate with organizations such as the NATO Center of Excellence on Strategic Communications, the European Endowment for Democracy, and the European External Action Service Task Force on Strategic Communications.

Conclusion

Developments in the coming few years could rival the consolidation of political, economic, military, and information power that occurred in the early 1990s and in which we are still living today. As both the American political establishment and Washington's global hegemony enter a period of growing uncertainty, the media establishment that supports them is suffering a related loss of influence and credibility. Possibilities include a transition internationally to a more multi-polar order, with foci of authority not ultimately answerable to the U.S., which itself would have major repercussions within the United States, including further erosion of media's efficacy as a bellicose transmission belt. Far from hurting the U.S., in this analyst's opinion, we might finally be able to realize the Peace Dividend that eluded us a quarter of a century ago, rechanneling our energies and resources towards our domestic economy, our infrastructure, and our festering social problems.

But such a development would take some time, probably about five years. Conversely, as is often the case when an entrenched oligarchy is facing a loss of power and privilege, it doesn't give up without a fight. At any time, with little notice, the duopoly could resort to adventurism, a roll of the dice to preserve the existing order. The notion that some policymakers in United States might decide upon, or at least risk, a major conflict in order to prevent the emergence of new arrangements has been suggested by alternative writers, such as Paul Craig Roberts, Philip Giraldi, Joe Lauria and Robert Parry of *ConsortiumNews.com*, Gilbert Doctorow, Alex Jones's *Infowars.com*, Justin Raimondo of *Antiwar.com*, Patrick Martin and Timothy Gatto of Rob Kall's *OpEdNews.com*, Joachim Hagopian, Michael Snyder, and others.

Most people may be inclined to dismiss the idea of "kickstarting World War III" as alarmism, if not conspiracy-mongering. Maybe that is the case. On the other hand, such speculation isn't entirely baseless in light of the willingness of some American politicians, including some who aspire to the Oval Office—and one who might actually get there—to impose a no-fly zone or "safe area" in Syria, and threaten to shoot down Russian aircraft to do it; give lethal aid to Ukrainian forces, along with putting American and other NATO advisers' and trainers' "boots on the ground"; or directly challenge Beijing's claim of sovereignty over rocks in the South China Sea through U.S. and allied air and naval transit despite Chinese warnings of a military response. If such a confrontation were to get out of control, either by design or accident, the resulting conflict could assume unexpectedly catastrophic proportions. Instead of saving the Deep State, a world war (one that is presumed to go nuclear) could hasten its extinction, along with that of much else besides.

But if the worst were to occur in the near future, there's one thing we could be sure of, however briefly: the official U.S. and western media would tell Americans that is wasn't "our" fault, it was "theirs." And most people would believe them, even if they have only the vaguest idea who "they" are.

James George Jatras is a media and government relations specialist with extensive experience in international relations, government affairs, and legislative politics. Before entering the private sector he served for many years (1985–2002) as a policy adviser and analyst for the Republican leadership in the U.S. Senate; before that (1979–1985), he was a U.S. Foreign Service Officer with the US Department of State, with service in Mexico and in Soviet affairs and public diplomacy. Since entering the private sector in 2002, Jatras's work has spanned a range of legislative and political issues and international affairs, including matters related to foreign policy, international security, human rights, public diplomacy, immigration, international trade and finance, and the global terror risk environment, as well as domestic issues. His international experience includes work relevant to Belgium, Canada, China, Cuba, France, Georgia, Germany, Hungary, India, Iran, Iraq, Japan, Mexico, Philippines, Russia, Saudi Arabia, Serbia, Syria, Ukraine, United Arab Emirates, the UK, and Yemen. He has also advocated in the legislative process in diverse areas such as appropriations, healthcare, tax, energy (including renewable), pharmaceuticals and cosmetics, immigration, security services, transportation, bioterrorism, and criminal defense. Jatras is a frequent speaker, panelist, and seminar participant on numerous topics. He has made numerous media appearances and is a frequent contributor to print and online publications, both in the United States and abroad. He holds a J.D. from Georgetown (1978) and a BA from Penn State (1974). He is a member of the U.S. Supreme Court Bar and the Pennsylvania and District of Columbia bars. Jatras is married, with two grown daughters and three grandchildren. He can be reached on Twitter @JimJatras.

An Orthodox View of Abortion

The Amicus Curiae Submitted

to the Supreme Court of the United States

The following brief to the U.S. Supreme Court was submitted at the initiative of Deacon John (of blessed memory) and Valerie Protopapas of the pro-life group Orthodox Christians for Life. The brief is notable both as a formal statement of Orthodox teaching in an American legal context and as an unprecedented cooperative effort among jurisdictions in the United States. The substantive legal and constitutional argument is primarily the work of Subdeacon Paul Farley (currently of St. Andrew Orthodox Church in Lockhart, TX), a distinguished attorney with extensive state and federal experience. My contribution, as Counsel of Record, is mainly in the historical and doctrinal argumentation.

An Orthodox View of Abortion

The Amicus Curiae Submitted to the Supreme Court
No. 88–605

In the Supreme Court of the United States

October Term, 1988

WILLIAM L. WEBSTER; STATE OF MISSOURI, *Appellants,*
v. REPRODUCTIVE HEALTH SERVICES;
PLANNED PARENTHOOD OF GREATER KANSAS CITY;
HOWARD I. SCHWARTZ, M.D.; ROBERT L. BLAKE, M.D.; CARL C.
PEARMAN, M.D.; CARROLL METZGER, R.N.C.;
MARY L. PEMBERTON, B.S.W., *Appellees.*

On Appeal from The US Court of Appeals for the 8th Circuit

BRIEF *AMICUS CURIAE* OF THE HOLY ORTHODOX CHURCH

+ + +

The Holy Orthodox Church respectfully submits this brief amicus curiae on behalf of itself & its members.[1]

INTEREST OF *AMICUS CURIAE*

The Holy Orthodox Church was founded by Jesus Christ & the Apostles & bears witness to that continuous & unbroken faith.[2] The precepts of the Orthodox Christian faith mandate the protection of innocent human life, especially that of unborn children. The Church regards abortion as murder, & as such, takes a very active role in opposing legalized abortion. That the issue of abortion has both a moral & a legal dimension to it, is indisputable. However, this cannot in any way be equated to an assertion that the 2 aspects are disparate, or unrelated. Rather, the 2 have historically been intertwined; it must be recognized that laws have traditionally been positive expressions of moral norms.

The Framers of the Constitution discerned a divine presence not only in daily living, but as reflected in the Constitution itself. "It is impossible for any man of pious reflection not to perceive in it a finger of that Almighty hand which has been so frequently & signally extended to our relief in the critical stages of the revolutionary."[3] That is, a law must of its very nature have a moral component to it, which cannot be divorced from the law itself.

Legal precepts, particularly those of constitutional proportions, simply cannot be judged in a vacuum. This notion not only predates the Constitution;[4] it is at the very heart of our civilization. The foundations of our morality can be found in the dawn & early morning light of the Judeo-Christian tradition, of which the Orthodox Church is a unique custodian. From its inception nearly 2,000 years ago, it has never deviated from its condemnation of abortion, based on numerous scriptural references & the teaching of the Holy Fathers of the Church. The Church regards the *Roe v. Wade* decision as a gruesome turn on the road of judicial activism, having resulted in a holocaust which has claimed at least 20,000,000 innocent lives.[5]

STATEMENT OF THE CASE & STATEMENT OF FACTS

Amicus curiae adopts the statement of the case & the statement of the facts as set out in the Appellants' Brief.

SUMMARY OF ARGUMENT

In this case, the Holy Orthodox Church seeks to restore to our nation's law the highest principle which a civilized society can espouse—the recognition that all human life is sacred. In *Roe v. Wade*, 410 U.S. 113 (1973), the Supreme Court relied heavily upon its presentation of historic Christianity's teaching & practices. The assertions made in *Roe* were erroneous & have no foundation in the church's traditions. Rather than being ambivalent, or even condoning abortion, as suggested by the *Roe* Court's opinion, historic Christianity has always condemned abortion as murder, without regard for any distinctions as to fetal development or viability.

The *Roe* Court also blurred the factual question of when life begins with the distinct legal question of what constitutional value attends to that life. The resulting confusion has tied the hands of legislators & elevated abortion to the status of a near-absolute right. Unless this Court takes judicial notice, the factual question of when life begins is properly a subject for legislative findings. The strictly legal question of a life's constitutional value is the clear issue before this Court, as the State of Missouri has made an appropriate factual determination.

Science & history both mandate a conclusion that human life & constitutional personhood are co-extensive, & any other result is without foundation in American jurisprudence. Consequently, the Holy Orthodox Church urges this Court to overrule *Roe v. Wade* & accord full constitutional protection to all human life beginning at conception.

ARGUMENT

I. THIS IS AN APPROPRIATE CASE IN WHICH TO RECONSIDER ROE v. WADE

In *Roe v. Wade*, 410 U.S. 113 (1973), & in subsequent cases, this Court has never reached the critical legal & public policy issue, that of when life begins. *Id.* at 159. However, for constitutional purposes, it is entirely appropriate for this Court to undertake to construe the term "life" as it appears in both the 5th & 14th Amendments.[6] In the absence of a judicial determination, such matters have traditionally been committed to the political processes. Unfortunately, the Court has nonetheless proceeded to preclude any legislative determination of the question. *Akron v. Akron Center for Reproductive Health,* 462 U.S. 416, 444 (1983).

This has created the confusing & circular assertion that life & personhood are unrelated, but nonetheless it is impermissible for legislatures to make findings as to when life begins. Unlike any other factual question, the political processes are now forbidden from employing the fruits of scientific research. If elected officials are to be prohibited, as a matter of law, from making necessary & proper factual findings, then this Court must determine for purposes of the Constitution, whether or not life is present in an unborn fetus. The State of Missouri has undertaken to make such a determination & to address the merits of this case, this Court must make a ruling upon the validity of that assertion. Even though the question of when life begins may be difficult,[7] that does not remove the necessity of a just & proper judicial disposition of this case.

The Court has elevated abortion above all other constitutional rights; in practice, it may not be restricted, even if a life is indeed present. Unlike other constitutional rights, abortion need not be balanced against competing governmental interests. The implication is that the right to an abortion is more central to the tradition of individual liberty in America than the cherished rights of free speech & religion.

The Missouri statute at issue here presents an important opportunity for this Court to resolve the ambiguities created by previous decisions & clarify the precise relationship between human life & constitutional personhood. The Court need not make a ruling on the factual question of when life begins; indeed, this is properly left to legislatures & trial courts. However, it is imperative that there be a clear statement of the constitutional value of human life, *whatever* point science indicates it begins. If personhood does not attach until birth, then it is crucial to have guidance as to the legal status of prenatal human life. The instant case frames the issue as clearly as is possible.

II. ROE v. WADE WAS WRONGLY DECIDED & OUGHT TO BE OVERRULED

Amicus does not suggest to this Court that the theology or canons of the Orthodox Church, or of any other religious body, should form the basis of American constitutional law. However, in its lengthy historical exegesis, the *Roe* Court sought to show that abortion was philosophically & morally grounded in the Judeo-Christian tradition. To the extent such a perception is the foundation of *Roe,* the Orthodox Church bears an undivided witness to the fact that it is a perception which is utterly inconsistent with the experience of historic Christianity.

In the early centuries of the Church, its moral traditions & teachings were universally embraced, holding sway over almost the whole of Europe, the Middle East & northern Africa, from Hadrian's Wall to the frontiers of the Persian Empire. Though this unanimity was later lost, the divergent moral strands of western thought, including Anglo-American jurisprudence, ultimately trace their lineage to this rich heritage.

A. The Court's Finding in *Roe v. Wade,* That Abortion is Consistent with Historic Moral Practices, Is Erroneous

The *Roe* Court relied heavily upon the contention that "Christian theology & canon law came to fix the point of animation at 40 days for a male & 80 days for a female, a view that persisted until the 19th century," & that "there was otherwise little agreement about the precise time of formation or animation." 410 U.S. at 134. The Court apparently found that Aristotle's 3 stage theory of life formed the basis of Christianity's beliefs & "came to be accepted by early Christian thinkers." *Id.* at 133, n.22. The implicit conclusion is that the ancient Christian Church did not consider abortion in early pregnancy to be the taking of a human life. With all due respect to this Honorable Court, such was simply not the case.

Early Christian thought was not in any sense comparable or equivalent to prior Jewish or Greco-Roman traditions. The Church's teaching represented a significant departure from Aristotelian thought & from the beginning regarded abortion as abhorrent & an abomination before God. The biologically erroneous Aristotelian view was rarely alluded to, & even in such cases where mention was made of the attempted distinction between "formed" & "unformed" fetuses, it was for the purposes of reiterating its moral irrelevance. To the extent that some western Christian writers espoused certain elements of Aristotelian philosophy, they must be regarded as rather exceptional scholastic forays, whose basic premises & ultimate results have now been conclusively demonstrated to be false. The Christian Church, from its inception, expressed a distinct & fundamental horror of abortion, at whatever stage of pregnancy, & considered it to be the killing of a human being.

1. Early Christian Writings & the Fathers of the Church All Condemned Abortion as Murder

Among the most highly regarded of ancient Christian writings is the *Didache*, which dates from the late 1st century.[8] Its teaching is unambiguous:

> Do not murder a child by abortion or kill a newborn infant. *Id.* at II, 2.

This is echoed in another didactic writing universally esteemed in the ancient Church, the *Epistle of Barnabas,* from the early 2nd century:

> Never do away with an unborn child or destroy it after its birth. *Id.* at XIX, 5.

The writings of the Fathers of the Church & other authorities further attest to the unanimity with which abortion was condemned. Among the earliest was the philosopher & apologist Athenagoras of Athens, who wrote to the Emperor Marcus Aurelius (c.177) to defend Christians against false charges of murder:

> What reason would we have to commit murder when we say that women who induce abortions are murderers & will have to give account of it to God?[9]

St. Basil the Great (c.330–379) was unequivocal:

> A woman who deliberately destroys a fetus is answerable for murder."[10]

St. John Chrysostom (c.345–407) who in his famous homilies railed against men who secured the abortions of their illegitimate offspring, called their actions "even worse than murder." Of such men who impelled women to have abortions, he said,

> You do not let a prostitute remain a prostitute, but make her a murderer as well.[11]

Finally, Canon 91 of the Quinisext Ecumenical Council (691), decreed that people

> who furnish drugs for the purpose of procuring abortion, & those who take fetus-killing poisons, they are made subject to the penalty prescribed for murderers.

The same canonical position along with the opinions of individual Church Fathers, were compiled in the *Photian Collection,* which was adopted as the official ecclesiastical law book of the Orthodox Church in 883.

2. The Early Church Recognized That Life Begins at Conception & Rejected Distinctions Based upon Fetal Development or Viability

The *Roe* Court observed that there was "little agreement about the precise time of formation or animation.

There was agreement, however, that prior to this point the fetus was to be regarded as part of the mother, & its destruction, therefore, was not homicide." 410 U.S. at 134. This assertion has no basis in the practices or theology of historic Christianity.

Among the earliest testimonies that fetal development was irrelevant is that of St. Basil the Great, who wrote that "any hairsplitting distinction as to its being formed or unformed is inadmissible with us."[12]

He also condemned suppliers of abortifacients, regardless of the stage of pregnancy:

> Those who give potions for the destruction of a child *conceived* in the womb are murderers, as are those who take potions which kill the child.[13]

St. Basil's brother, St. Gregory of Nyssa (c.335–394), saw the fetus as a complete human being from the time of conception & specifically rejected theories based upon formation or quickening:

> There is no question about that which is bred in the uterus, both growing & moving from place to place. It remains, therefore, that we must think that the point of commencement of existence is one & the same for body & soul.[14]

Even Tertullian of Carthage (c.160–c.230), a prominent Latin ecclesiastical writer who seemed to accept the formed/unformed distinction as a biological matter, dismissed its moral importance:

> Abortion is a precipitation of murder, nor does it matter whether or not one takes a life when formed or drives it away when forming, for he is also a man who is about to be one.[15]

Though less specific, Holy Scripture also recognizes that an unborn child's life is sacred & begins no later than conception:

> Before I formed you in the womb, I knew you, & before you were born
> I consecrated you; I appointed you a prophet to the nations. *Jeremiah* 1:5, 6.[16]

Also noteworthy is St. Luke's use of the same Greek word, *brephos* (baby), for both the unborn St. John the Baptist (*Luke* 1:44) & the newly born Christ child (*Luke* 2:12). Even more indicative are those examples, in both Old & New Testaments, where God enters into a direct personal relationship with a specific individual before birth, by "consecrating," "appointing," "calling & setting apart" the unborn child through His grace.[17] This testifies to the Bible's view that the fetus is not only a human being but a person. That this understanding of an unborn person's receptivity to divine grace extends back to conception is further evidenced by the ancient practice, as formalized in the Church calendar, of celebrating not only the conception of Christ (Annunciation, March 25), but that of His mother (Dec. 9) & St. John the Baptist (Sept. 23).

The canon law of the ancient Church, still in effect in the Orthodox Church today, is entirely consistent with the foregoing exposition of theological, patristic & scriptural evidence. The 1st canonical pronouncement specifically on abortion was that of the regional Council of Elvira, Spain (c.303), imposing life-long excommunication. In 314–315, the regional Council of Ancyra adopted Canon 21:

> Regarding women who become prostitutes & kill their babies & who make it their business to concoct abortives, the former rule barred them for life from communion, & they are left without recourse. But, having found a more philanthropic alternative, we have fixed the penalty at 10 years, in accordance with the fixed degrees.

The reference to prostitutes attests to the Fathers' recognition that abortion was only resorted to by women in the most desperate social circumstances. 3 centuries into the Christian era, abortion was unthinkable to the broad mass of Christian people; canon law was adopted which lightened the penalty imposed upon those most in need of mercy. More importantly, the "former rule," imposing life-long excommunication, is Apostolic Canon 66, which pertains to homicide.[18] The fact that for centuries the Church treated abortion at any stage of pregnancy as homicide, without regard to fetal development, is indicative of the illusory nature of the formed/unformed distinction.

In addition, the *Roe* Court's reliance upon the writings of Augustine of Hippo (354–430) & Thomas Aquinas (1225–1274), as indicative of early Christian thought was misplaced.[19] While concepts such as "ensoulment" or "quickening" gained some currency in certain ecclesiastical circles beginning in the 5th century, this serves only to underscore the danger inherent in drawing broad-based conclusions based upon excerpts of writings from selected theologians. Augustine never laid claim to being infallible, nor did he presume to speak for the entire Church.[20] In fact, in the conclusion of his final treatise, he offered his opinions humbly to the judgment of the Church:

> Let those who think that I am in error consider again & again carefully what is here said, lest perchance they themselves may be mistaken. And when, by means of those who read my writings, I become not only wiser, but even more perfect, I acknowledge God's favor to me.[21]

However, there is no doubt that despite their misunderstanding of fetal development, they sought to protect the fetus & considered its destruction homicide. We can, with the benefit of historical & scientific hindsight, attribute the misapplication of a correct impulse to a biological error stemming ultimately from Aristotle. The *Roe* Court adopted this error as the basis of its analysis of the moral acceptability of abortion over the past 2,000 years; but as would be the case with a hypothetical body of jurisprudence based on the Ptolemaic geocentric system or the phlogiston theory of combustion, this Court should not hesitate to look beyond what we now understand to be a factual error, albeit a persistent one.

Historic Christianity recognized conception as the time at which life & soul were united, & regarded abortion at any stage of pregnancy as homicide. Though the Orthodox Church, for historical reasons relating to its organizational & doctrinal continuity with historic Christianity, is more acutely aware of this fact, this should not be taken as sectarian pleading. Rather, it is a unique witness to an older & sounder tradition that is our common heritage. The fact that the theological writings of Christian antiquity were formulated by men with little understanding of biology, but whose views are entirely compatible with our modern understanding, is further testament to their moral perspicacity.

B. Human Life Begins at Conception

The incorrectness of the *Roe* Court's assertion that there has been a historic lack of consensus on abortion has been demonstrated in section II A, supra. Even so, it is not the judiciary's proper role to evaluate consensus. *The Federalist No. 78* (A. Hamilton.) The legal & social morass resulting from the *Roe* decision is in large part a product of the confusion over what was actually decided. The *Roe* Court blurred the strictly *factual* question of when life begins with the quite distinct *legal* determination of what constitutional value attends to that life.

Modern science has borne out the prescient wisdom of the Holy Fathers of the Church, that life begins at conception, & at no other arbitrary or scholastically derived juncture.[22] However, this Court need not make a scientific determination of when life begins, any more than it was necessary in *Roe* to determine when a fetus is "viable;" this is a matter which is properly committed to the political processes. The Missouri legislature has undertaken to make findings of fact, as is appropriate in matters of social & economic regulation. It is improper for the judiciary to enjoin the political processes from determining the factual basis for proposed legislation. Traditionally, the federal courts give the greatest possible deference to legislative determinations with respect to such questions.[23]

This Court need only interpret the term "person," & thereby determine the constitutional value of unborn human life. Unless this Court should foreclose the option by taking judicial notice, or adopting a constitutional definition of "life" embracing a manifest legal fiction, the State of Missouri is entitled to make a judgment as to when life begins. The judiciary's role is to determine the constitutional value of that life.

C. A Human Life is a "Person" for Purposes of the Constitution

To the extent that a construction of the term "person," as used in the Constitution, was made in *Roe,* it was done on the basis of the facts as presented & understood by the Court as that time. *Amicus* respectfully submits that the factual underpinnings of *Roe v. Wade* were erroneous or, at best, incomplete. Reliance upon Aristotle & other selected writers from antiquity do not validate the *Roe* Court's conclusion that the morality of abortion has traditionally been ambivalent. As shown *supra,* some theorists have had erroneous views of the factual question of when life begins, but there has been no divergence as to the legal & moral value of that life once it has been established.

In *Roe* the Court went to some lengths to demonstrate that most references to "persons" in the Constitution had solely a postnatal connotation. However, this begs the question as to what "person" means in the 14th Amendment. It must also be observed that most constitutional references to persons only dealt with adults, & in the original intent of the document, only white males. However, again, this still does not speak to the 14th Amendment, which obviously was intended to vindicate the rights of black children as well as adults, & has subsequently been applied to protect the rights of women as well as men. There is no basis in history, jurisprudence, or simple logic to justify specially exempting the unborn from the scope of the Amendment.

Furthermore, the appropriate constitutional definition of "person" has already been made by this Court. Justice Douglas, writing for the Court, found that illegitimate children are "persons," on the grounds that:

> They are humans, live & have their being. They are clearly "persons" within the meaning of the 14th Amendment. *Levy v. Louisiana,* 361 U.S. 68, 70 (1968).

Unborn children clearly are human, do live & have their being, in accordance with Justice Douglas' perceptive holding. An unborn child has as little control over its status as an illegitimate child & is far more vulnerable. They are "persons" under the Constitution, & there is no rational basis whatsoever for creating an arbitrary or scholastic distinction so as to exclude them.

Another critical distinction which the *Roe* Court ignored was the 14th Amendment's differentiation of citizenship & personhood:

> No State shall make or enforce any law which shall abridge the privileges or immunities of *citizens* of the United States; nor shall any State deprive any *person* of life, liberty or property, without due process of law; nor deny to any *person* within its jurisdiction the equal protection of the laws.[24]

As understood by the Framers of the 14th Amendment, citizenship relates to political rights, while personhood deals with the more basic rights inherent in all human beings. *See, e.g.,* Bishop, *The Privileges or Immunities Clause of the 14th Amendment,* 79 Nw. U. L. Rev. 142, 151–153 (1984). The latter is a much broader classification than the former, encompassing both citizens & noncitizens; all citizens are persons, but the reverse is not true. Even a decision as monstrous as *Dred Scott v. Sanford,* 60 U.S. (19 How.) 393 (1857), conceded that slaves were persons under the Constitution, but denied them the privileges of citizenship.

Therefore, the many references to "persons" cited by the *Roe* Court in support of its finding of purely postnatal application were, contextually, referring to persons who were also citizens.[25] The references to "persons" relied upon by the *Roe* Court were made in political contexts, such as eligibility to vote or to hold political office, which of course would preclude *all* persons under a certain age, whether born or not. Such strict textual interpretation, done without regard for historical meaning & context, is devoid of constitutional justification.

In addition, this Court had already, some 87 years prior to *Roe,* recognized corporations as "persons" under the 14th Amendment. *Santa Clara County v. Southern Pacific Railroad Co.,* 118 U.S. 394, 396 (1886). That corporations are not male, female, black, white, prenatal, nor postnatal, is transparently obvious. There is also no conflict between the recognition of personhood, but simultaneous denial of citizenship, as corporations cannot vote nor hold political office. Thus, while Santa Clara is entirely consistent with the 14th Amendment, *Roe* is not. The distinctions made in *Roe* & its progeny are artificial & have no basis in the adjudication of constitutional claims. This is made readily apparent through attempting to reconcile Santa Clara & *Roe*. Reading them together creates a result which is "hauntingly Orwellian—something can be a person without being human, & can be human without being a person.²⁶ No civilized society can possibly endorse such a conclusion.

The instant case clearly frames the contradictions & ambiguities precipitated by the *Roe* decision, & *Amicus* urges this Court to resolve them by reaffirming the moral, social & legal recognition of the value of unborn human life.

CONCLUSION

The historic morality which forms the foundation of American constitutional thought is firmly grounded in the Judeo-Christian tradition. That tradition has unambiguously recognized that life begins at conception & that abortion is murder. The notion that abortion on demand is an inherent right which cannot be denied, is of recent origin. Samuel Adams recognized that such innovations should be resisted:

If the liberties of America are ever completely ruined, . . . it will in all probability be the consequence of a mistaken notion of *prudence,* which leads men to acquiesce in measures of the most destructive tendency for the sake of present ease.²⁷

The "present ease" of abortion on demand does not, & cannot, alter the historical & moral truth that "universal life would proceed according to nature if we would practice continence from the beginning instead of destroying, through immoral & pernicious acts, human beings who are given birth by Divine Providence."²⁸ The assembled jurisdictions of the Holy Orthodox Church in the United States speak with 1 voice in urging this Court to recognize the sanctity of human life & reverse the decision of the Court of Appeals.

Dated this 21st day of February, 1989.
Respectfully submitted,
JAMES GEORGE JATRAS
PAUL FARLEY

JAMES GEORGE JATRAS
PAUL FARLEY

¹ Counsel for *Amicus* has obtained the oral consent of both parties to this case. Written consent shall be filed with the Clerk of the Court immediately upon its receipt.

² The Holy Orthodox Church includes all major Orthodox Christian groups in the USA: Albanian, American, Antiochian, Bulgarian, Carpatho-Russian, Greek, Romanian, Russian, Serbian & Ukrainian. Regardless of the jurisdiction, all Orthodox Christians share a unity of faith & tradition extending back almost 2,000 years to the time of Jesus Christ & the Apostles.

³ *The Federalist, No. 37* (J. Madison). George Washington echoed this sentiment it would be peculiarly improper to omit, in this 1st official act, my fervent supplications to that Almighty Being, Who rules over the universe, Who presides in the council of nations & Whose providential aids can supply every human defect. . . . In tendering this homage to the great Author of every public & private good, I assure myself that it expresses your sentiments not less than

my own. . . . No people can be bound to acknowledge & adore the invisible Hand, Which conducts the affairs of men, more than the people of the United States." Washington, *1st Inaugural Address, quoted in,* Eliot, *American Historical Documents, 1000–1904,* at 226 (New York: P.F. Collier & Son Corp., 1938).

[4] *See, e.g.,* John Locke, *2nd Treatise on Civil Government,* ch. IV, secs. 22 & 23 (New York: Liberal Arts Press, 1952).

[5] This brief is filed with the blessings of: *The American Carpatho-Russian Orthodox Greek Catholic Diocese*: His Grace, Bishop Nicholas; V. Rev. Frank P. Miloro, Dean of Christ the Saviour Orthodox Theological Seminary; *The Anthiochian Orthodox Christian Archdiocese of North America:* His Eminence, Most Rev. Metropolitan Philip; Rt. Rev. Antoun, Auxiliary Bishop; V. Rev. Peter E. Gillquist, Chairman of the Council of Coordinators, Antiochian Evangelical Orthodox Mission & member, Worship & Evangelization Committee, National Council of Churches; V. Rev. Jack N. Sparks, Dean of St. Athanasius College; *The Greek Orthodox Archdiocese of North & South America:* Rt. Rev. Maximos, Bishop of Pittsburgh; Rev. Dr. Stanley S. Harakas, Archbishop Iakovos Professor of Orthodox Theology & Christian Ethics, Holy Cross Greek Orthodox School of Theology; Rev. Dr. Theodore Stylianopoulos, Professor of New Testament & Orthodox Spirituality, Holy Cross Greek Orthodox School of Theology & member of the Central Committee of the World Council of Churches; Rev. Fr. George A. Alexson, Secretary-Treasurer of the Greater Washington Orthodox Clergy Council & Pastor, St. Katherine's Greek Orthodox Church of Northern VA; *The Orthodox Church in America:* His Beatitude Theodosius, Archbishop of Washington, Metropolitan of All America & Canada; Rt. Rev. Peter, Bishop of New York & New Jersey; Rt. Rev. Dimitri, Bishop of Dallas & the South; Rt. Rev. Herman, Bishop of Philadelphia & Eastern PA; Rt. Rev. Gregory, Bishop of Sitka & Alaska; Rt. Rev. Nathaniel, Bishop of Detroit & the Romanian Episcopate; Rt. Rev. Job, Bishop of Hartford & New England; Rt. Rev. Tikhon, Bishop of San Francisco; Rt. Rev. Mark, Acting Bishop of Chicago & the Midwest; V. Rev. Leonid Kishkovsky, Secretary of External & Ecumenical Affairs & President-Elect of the National Council of Churches; V. Rev. John Meyendorff, Dean of St. Vladimir's Orthodox Theological Seminary & Professor of Church History & Patristics; V. Rev. Daniel K. Donlick, Dean of St. Tikhon's Orthodox Theological Seminary; V. Rev. Joseph P. Kreta, Dean of St. Herman's Orthodox Theological Seminary; V. Rev. Thomas Hopko, Associate Professor of Dogmatic Theology, St. Vladimir's Orthodox Theological Seminary & member, Faith & Order Commission of the World Council of Churches; V. Rev. John Kowalczyk, Adjunct Professor of Religious Education & the Christian Family, St. Tikhon's Orthodox Theological Seminary & Pro-Life Coordinator of the Diocese of Eastern Pennsylvania; V. Rev. Vladimir Borichevsky, Professor of Moral & Pastoral Theology, St. Tikhon's Orthodox Theological Seminary; Rev. Fr. Alexander F.C. Webster, Senior Research Associate, Ethics & Public Policy Center, Washington, D.C. (for identification only); Holy Transfiguration Orthodox Monastery, Elwood City, PA; Holy Dormition Orthodox Monastery, Rives Eaton, MI; *The Russian Orthodox Church in Exile:* His Eminence, Most Rev. Vitaly, Metropolitan of New York & Eastern America, 1st Hierarch of the Russian Orthodox Church in Exile; Most Rev. Anthony, Archbishop of Los Angeles & Southern California; Most Rev. Antony, Archbishop of San Francisco & Western America; Most Rev. Laurus, Archbishop of Syracuse & Holy Trinity Monastery, Rector of Holy Trinity Orthodox Seminary & Abbot of Holy Trinity Orthodox Monastery, Jordanville, NY; Rt. Rev. Alypy, Bishop of Chicago, Detroit & Midwest America; Rt. Rev. Hilarion, Bishop of Manhattan; Rt. Rev. Daniel, Bishop of Erie & Protector of the Old Rite; Rev. Fr.

Alexey Young, Editor of *Orthodox America*; Rev. Fr. Gregory Williams, Editor of *Living Orthodoxy*; *The Serbian Orthodox Church in the US & Canada:* His Grace, Bishop Christopher; *The Ukrainian Orthodox Church of America & Canada:* His Grace, Bishop Vsevolod.

In addition, this brief is endorsed by: Orthodox Christians for Life—John Protopapas, Co-Founder & Chairman; Rev. Fr. Edward Pehanich, Co-Founder & Spiritual Advisor, & Diocesan Representative for the Carpatho-Russian Orthodox Greek Catholic Diocese; Valerie Protopapas, Educational Director & Sanctity of Life Director for the Diocese of New York & New Jersey (OCA); & V. Rev. Gordon T. Walker, liaison to the Antiochian Evangelical Orthodox Mission. This brief is also endorsed by: Dr. Lewis J. Patsavos, Professor of Canon Law, & Dr. John Chirban, Professor of Psychology & Counseling, Holy Cross Greek Orthodox School of Theology; Dr. John Erickson, Professor of Canon law & Church History, St. Vladimir's Orthodox Theological Seminary; the Orthodox Christian Association of Medicine, Psychology & Religion; the Orthodox Brotherhood of the US; the National Association of Romanian Orthodox Women in America; & American Romanian Orthodox Youth.

[6] "No person shall be . . . deprived of life, liberty, or property, without due process of law . . . ." U.S. Const. amend. V. "No State shall . . . deprive any person of life, liberty, or property, without due process of law. . . ." U.S. Const. amend. XIV, sec. 1.

[7] *Roe v. Wade*, 410 U.S. 113, 159 (1973).

[8] Also known as *The Teaching of the 12 Apostles*, it is a codification of the oral tradition handed down by the Apostles to their successors. Cf. *II Thessalonians* 2:15. It was called "scripture" by Clement of Alexandria (+c.215) & was recommended for catechists by St. Athanasius (c.297–373).

[9] Athenagoras, *Legation for Christians*, 6 *Patrologia Graeca* 969 (Paris: J.P. Migne ed., 1844–1865).

[10] St. Basil the Great, *Letters* CLXXXVIII, Canon 2.

[11] St. John Chrysostom, *Homilies in Romans, XXIV*. *See also* the authoritative treatise by Fr. John Kowalczyk, *An Orthodox View of Abortion*, (Minneapolis: Light & Life Publishing Co., 2nd ed. 1979).

[12] St. Basil the Great, *supra* note 10.

[13] *Id.*, Canon 8 (emphasis supplied.)

[14] St. Gregory of Nyssa, On the Soul & the Resurrection.

[15] Tertullian of Carthage, *Apology IX*.

[16] *See also, Job* 10:8, 9, 11; *Psalms* 139:13–16; *Ecclesiastes* 11:5; *Luke* 1:41–44.

[17] See, e.g., Psalms 139:13–16; Isaiah 44:2; Isaiah 49:1, 5; Jeremiah 1:5; & Galatians 1:15–16.

[18] Apostolic Canon 66 permitted penitents to return to communion only on their deathbeds. As the name suggests, an Apostolic Canon is a teaching received directly from the 12 Apostles.

[19] 410 U.S. at 133 n.22.

[20] "If some have spoken imprecisely, or for some reason unknown to us, even deviated from the right path, but no question was put to them nor did anyone challenge them to learn the truth—we admit them to the list of Fathers, just as if they had not said it, because of their righteousness of life & distinguished virtue & their faith, faultless in other respects. We do not, however, follow their teaching in which they stray from the path of truth." St. Photius, *Letter to the Patriarch of Aquileia*, quoted in, Haugh, *Photius & the Carolingians*, 136–137 (Belmont, Mass: Nordland, 1975); & Archbishop Philaret of Chernigov, 3 *Historical Teaching of the Fathers of the Church*, 254–255 (St. Petersburg, 1882).

[21] Augustine of Hippo, *On the Gift of Perseverance*, ch. 68. *See also*, Fr. Seraphim Rose, *The Place of Blessed Augustine in the Orthodox Church* (Platina, California: St. Herman of Alaska Brotherhood, 1983).

[22] *See*, Subcommittee on the Separation of Powers, Senate Committee on the Judiciary, *The Human Life Bill*, S. 158, 97th Cong., 1st Sess. 7–13 (1981).

[23] United States v. Carolene Products Co., 304 U.S. 144, 152–153 n.4 (1938).

[24] U.S. Const. amend. XIV, sec. 1 (emphasis supplied).

[25] 410 U.S. at 157.

[26] East & Valentine, *Reconciling Roe v. Wade* in Horan, Grant & Cunningham, *Abortion & the Constitution*, at 90 (Washington: Georgetown University Press, *1987*).

[27] 2 *The Writings of Samuel Adams*, 287–288 (New York: G.P. Putnam's Sons, H.A. Cushing ed., 1904) (emphasis in original).

[28] Clement of Alexandria, II *Paedagogus*, ch. X, 96, I.

The Parable of the Bakers, the Dough, and the Special Bread

The Parable of the Bakers,
the Dough, and the Special Bread

Once upon a time, in a certain town, there lived a Baker. The Baker started a bread dough with his own special Leaven, which no other baker ever had. He used this leavened dough to bake a special bread unlike any other, and when people joined together to eat it, they were nourished in a special way. The leavened dough was intended to be continuous—that is, when the Baker baked, he never used up the whole lump, no matter how many loaves were baked and eaten. Instead, he always reserved some of the original leavened dough and added more ingredients to keep the dough going and to propagate new lumps in which the special Leaven lived and grew.

The Baker (who was much loved on account of his bread) needed to go away for a while, but would be coming back. Accordingly, he appointed other bakers to take care of the continuous leavened dough and to keep it going (he assured them it would last until he got back!), and to keep producing the special bread for the people who ate it and loved the original Baker. In time, these bakers appointed other bakers, who in turn appointed yet others. According to the original Baker's instructions, the appointed bakers had different jobs: some added the ingredients and mixed the dough, some kneaded the lumps, some shaped the loaves, some put the loaves in the oven and took them out, some delivered the bread to the people who ate it, and some were chief bakers who mostly oversaw the other bakers in doing all these things. Along with the leavened dough, the original Baker gave the appointed bakers detailed special baking knowledge as to how all this was to be done, so the leavened dough would keep growing and the special bread would be made just like he had first made it.

Some of these first-appointed bakers wrote down the dough ingredients and even some (but far from all!) of the special baking knowledge in a Recipe. This was very helpful, especially to later bakers who had not met the original Baker or seen for themselves how he made his special bread. But like all good cooking, this Recipe was only part of what a baker needed to know to produce the special bread. The bakers also needed the rest of the special baking knowledge—like how to knead the dough, how much dough to bake at a time and how much to keep, how to form the loaves *just so*, at what temperature to bake the loaves and for how long, how to preserve and propagate the leaven, and much, much more—a lot of things that were *not* written in the Recipe. Later on, some of this other special baking knowledge was sometimes written down here or there, in one form or another (as bakers and other cooks sometimes do, on little kitchen notes)—but some never was. According to the original Baker's instructions, only the bakers who had been appointed by the original Baker (or who had been appointed by appointed bakers) were taught this special baking knowledge, mostly by example. Even when other people who were not appointed bakers learned some of this knowledge (and after a while, a lot of people had some idea what was in the Recipe, too), no one could be a real baker and make the special bread unless he had the leavened dough kept going from the original Baker, with the original, special Leaven. And only real, appointed bakers had that leavened dough.

II.

This is the way things stayed for a long time. Years went by, generations of bakers lived and died, lots of new bakeries were started with lumps of the original leavened dough to produce the special bread, which came into ever-greater demand.

Not everybody was happy about this, though. Some other bakers who did not know the original Baker, or who didn't like him, or who just didn't like the special bread, or who maybe were just jealous, said *their* bread was better. Sometimes they tried to do bad things to the bakers appointed by the original Baker, or wreck their bakeries. Sometimes they beat up or even killed the appointed bakers, or stole their dough or bread and destroyed it when they could. Some people got the idea that the special bread itself was bad and convinced the police commissioner and the cops to punish people who ate it and to shut down bakeries! Other people even falsely claimed that *they* were actually the bakers appointed by the original Baker—and even had *secret* special baking knowledge they said came from the original Baker (but it didn't, really). Most people, though, weren't fooled—they could tell from the real, original, special bread.

The appointed bakers were not particularly surprised by all this kind of thing—in fact, the original Baker had told them to expect it. But because of these difficulties, the bakers who really were appointed by the original Baker started calling themselves the Original Bakery (and all their bakeries had signs saying "Original Bakery"), so that people would know who was who. They just carried on, in good times and bad (there were occasional fires and floods and crime that closed many bakeries, which was very sad), but the bakers' job was to keep on baking the special bread until the original Baker came back (he sure was taking his time!), and that's what they did. More and more people kept eating the special bread, and new bakeries sprang up all over town.

One day a new police commissioner started eating the special bread himself, and he liked it so much he made a point of protecting the bakers and their bakeries from crooks, and that helped a lot. He even asked the chief bakers of the Original Bakery to hold big conventions from time to time to help let people know which was the *real* special bread, so imitations wouldn't fool anyone. At the very first of these big conventions, the chief bakers wrote an official Certificate of Authenticity, attesting that the Original Bakery was the only bakery founded by the original Baker, using his original dough with his special Leaven, and producing the special bread—and they even mentioned some of the most important special baking knowledge that only the *real* Original Bakery used. They did this so that every Original Bakery bakery would hang a copy of the Certificate of Authenticity in a place where anyone could see it, near the "Original Bakery" sign. That way, people would know they were in a real Original Bakery bakery, not an imitation. It was kind of like a license for each bakery, and the chief bakers also said that if a bakery changed the Certificate of Authenticity by *even one word*, it could no longer be an Original Bakery bakery. (In a world full of frauds, you can't be too careful about these things, you know!)

III.

But one day, something bad happened, something that was even worse than the fires, floods, and crooks. One of the Original Bakery bakers in a certain part of town far from the original Baker's home neighborhood—he was a very important and highly respected chief baker, who oversaw many other bakers working under him—decided he was not important or highly respected enough. So he claimed (he even "found" some kitchen notes to "prove" it!) that the original Baker had put the first chief baker at his particular bakery in charge of the *whole* Original Bakery and over *all* the Original Bakery bakers— even the other chief bakers!—and that therefore (so this very important and highly respected chief baker said), he too must be in charge of everything. To make his point, this very important and highly respected chief baker even started calling himself the "Really Chief" baker. Most of the bakers working under him in his part of town went along with him (though a few, mostly those who had been in other parts of town at one time or another, objected in vain), and his Really Chief Bakery took over that whole part of town. The Really Chief baker also had a pretty good arrangement with the cops at the local precincts in that part of town, who didn't pay much attention to the police commissioner, who lived on the other side of town, where the Original Bakeries still operated near where the original Baker had once lived, before he went away. These local cops helped the Really Chief baker keep everybody in line—the bakers and the people who ate the bread alike. After a while, in that part of town there were no Original Bakery bakeries left—just Really Chief bakeries.

As the years passed, each Really Chief baker was succeeded by another Really Chief baker, each one after the other making the same claims.

The Really Chief baker sometimes even got the cops from his part of town to raid the Original Bakery bakers in other parts of town he did *not* control, to pressure them into joining the Really Chief Bakery, but that mostly wasn't successful. Every once in a while, the Original Bakery bakers would try to talk with the Really Chief baker and his bakers to see if they could work things out (the police commissioner tried to help too), but every time, the Really Chief Baker just demanded that they join *his* Really Chief Bakery. (He even claimed that the Original Bakery bakers had all worked for earlier Really Chief bakers in the Really Chief Bakery a long time ago, which totally puzzled them, since nothing of the sort had ever happened!) After trying a few times to work things out, the Original Bakery bakers pretty much left the Really Chief baker alone, though they did need to have the police commissioner chase his rogue cops back over to their own part of town from time to time.

But even this was not the worst of it. You see, the Really Chief baker wasn't content just to order around the other bakers in his part of town and try to force more Original Bakery bakers to join his Really Chief Bakery. Unthinkably, he began to fiddle around with how the special bread was made! He began to say that only *he* was authorized by the original Baker to explain how to use the Recipe, and he said that only *he* knew the *really* special baking knowledge—like how to knead the dough, how much dough to bake and how much to keep, how to form the loaves *just so*, at what temperature to bake the loaves and for how long, how to preserve and propagate the leaven, and all the rest which (conveniently for the Really Chief baker!) was mostly not written in the Recipe. He even claimed that he, of all the bakers, *never made a mistake* (at least when it came to baking)! Some of the Really Chief Bakery bakers knew better, but most didn't—and besides, there were those cops (some of whom were getting hard to tell from crooks). So everybody in that part of town went along with the Really Chief baker, willy-nilly. Some people noticed that the special bread wasn't tasting quite the same as it was supposed to, but most people didn't (you see, some hadn't eaten the *real* special bread, made the right way, for a very long time, and many had never eaten it or even heard of it).

In fact, what was happening (though nobody realized it at the time) was: the original, special Leaven in the dough used by the Really Chief Bakery was . . . dying. The Really Chief baker's explanations of the Recipe and his version of the special baking knowledge just didn't work with the special dough, and what leaven the dough still had wasn't the original Leaven it used to be, especially since in that part of town they weren't getting any more original dough with the live Leaven from the Original Bakeries. (And not only that, the Really Chief baker even added some new words to the Certificate of Authenticity—something about the Leaven—and made all his bakers change the copies hanging in their bakeries the same way. Some of them even took a pen and just squeezed the new words into the copies they already had—as if nobody would notice! So you see, right there, the Original Bakery bakers did not consider the Really Chief bakeries licensed bakeries at all anymore, so they sure wouldn't give them any more original dough even if they asked, which they didn't.) So in the part of town where the Really Chief Bakery was, the bread kept getting less and less special—and also, incidentally, more and more *flat*. And after a while, the people in that part of town forgot it had ever been any different.

Meanwhile, elsewhere, the Original Bakery bakers kept on making the special bread with the original, special Leaven, which only they had.

And would you believe it, the Really Chief baker said *they* were baking it wrong because their bread wasn't flat like his! He also said the Original Bakery bakeries were not real, licensed bakeries because *their* copies of the Certificate of Authenticity hanging in their bakeries didn't have the new words *he* had added! When the Original Bakery bakers heard these things they weren't sure if they should be angry or just very sad.

IV.

This went on for a while. Each Really Chief baker in turn kept charging more and more for his flat bread, which in his part of town was the only "special" bread there was (even though it wasn't all that special and was *really* flat). Finally, some of the people eating it (and even quite a few of the Really Chief Bakery bakers) began to wonder what was wrong. The bread costs too much, it isn't very special, it isn't particularly nourishing, and it isn't even filling! They *knew* something was wrong—and they were pretty sure the Really Chief baker was responsible—but they really didn't know *what* was wrong. You see, for most of them, the Really Chief Bakery was the only one they had ever known. They assumed there had been an original Bakery back at the time before the original Baker had gone away, back when the Recipe had been written down, but they weren't quite sure what had happened after that. They were pretty sure the Really Chief baker's explanation of the Recipe was mostly wrong and that his version of the special baking knowledge was worse, but they could only guess how things were supposed to be. You see, they all had been trained by the Really Chief baker and his bakers. They didn't know any other way to bake "special" bread. They didn't know much about the Original Bakery. Some had never heard of it, some weren't sure it still existed, and some assumed it was pretty much like the Really Chief Bakery—after all, the Really Chief baker claimed to *be* the Original Bakery! And almost none of them had any idea about the dough with the original, special Leaven or what the special bread made with it was really like.

So these dissatisfied Really Chief Bakery bakers and some the people who felt the same way did what seemed to be a pretty good idea at the time. They tried to correct, or fix, or restore the Really Chief Bakery to its proper form based on the only thing they were pretty sure was original: the Recipe. They said: "The Recipe alone! No Really Chief baker explanations, no special baking knowledge, no Certificate of Authenticity—just the Recipe. Let's get back to the Recipe!" When they said this, they hadn't mostly intended to *leave* the Really Chief Bakery—but that's what happened. The Really Chief baker told them: "It's my way, or the highway," and he sicced the cops on them. So the bakers and people who tried to restore the Really Chief Bakery did about the only thing they could: they started their own bakeries. Some of them had been bakers for the Really Chief baker (and for some reason thought this was important), and some had not and only just decided "I'm a baker because I've studied the Recipe. I can bake as well as anybody else." They gave their bakeries different names, mostly after the baker who started it (like: the Bob Bakery, or the Bill Bakery); as a group, they tended to call themselves the "Proper" bakers, since they thought they were restoring the Bakery to its proper and original form by following the Recipe alone.

But the Proper bakers soon found out they had a new problem: saying "The Recipe alone!" was easier than figuring out what that meant. To start with, each Proper baker had a different idea about how the Recipe was to be read. And some of them were not sure that the special baking knowledge they had learned in the Really Chief Bakery was *entirely* wrong—while some of it was the Really Chief baker's invention, some of it might be original (in fact, it was all mixed up together, but they had little way to know what was what.) Also, all kinds of questions about what was *not* in the Recipe kept coming up: "What about the leaven—should we use any and if so, what kind?" (You see, the Recipe *assumed* the original Leaven put there by the original Baker was *already* in the dough!) "The Recipe says 'flour,' but what kind? On what days should we bake? What different jobs should bakers do? Should there be chief bakers, or are all bakers in charge of each other?" And many other such things. So each Proper baker took his own best guess about what *ought* to be the answers to these questions. (Most of them claimed the answers were "clear from reading the Recipe," which was odd, since for a lot of other Proper bakers reading the same Recipe, the answers were "clearly" very different—in some cases the exact opposite!) So the Proper bakers kept arguing with each other, and as they argued more and more of them started their own bakeries: soon the Bob Bakery and the Bill Bakery were joined by bakeries named after Mike, and Elmer, and Floyd, and Tom, and Becky, and Sid, and Henrietta, and Tiffany, and who knows who else; some people even said that every person who ate the bread should be his (or her) *own* baker! (There was even one man who called himself a baker and claimed the original Baker *himself* had come to see him—he even showed people something called "Another Recipe of the Original Baker" he said the original Baker had given him to prove it!—and then had gone away again.)

Each Proper bakery had its own explanation of the Recipe, and each had to start its own dough from scratch or use some "flat" dough they had taken from the Really Chief Bakery. But with all their might, bake they did! They turned out all sorts of more-or-less bread (some of it not *bad*, exactly): rolls, and cakes, and bagels, and crackers, and muffins, and bread-sticks, and scones, and donuts, and even some stuff that was more like pudding, and who knows what else. The only thing the Proper bakers really agreed on was that the Recipe was the most important thing and the way *our* bakery (or *my* bakery) explains it is right—but all those *other* bakeries, and especially the Really Chief baker, were no good. (Actually, given how divided the Proper bakers were, the Really Chief baker might have been able to put them out of business, but luckily for them some of the local cops—who also were getting pretty tired of the Really Chief baker's bossiness!—in the precincts where they set up shop took them in hand and even helped shut down the remaining Really Chief Bakery bakeries. The Really Chief baker did, however, borrow some of the Proper bakers' ideas, just to be on the safe side.)

But for all this, none of the Proper bakers (nor, of course, the Really Chief baker) could make the real, original special bread, because they no longer had the dough with the original, special Leaven. This was sad, because in most cases these bakers were honest people trying their best with what they had.

V.

So, anyway, the Really Chief Bakery and the various Proper bakeries kept on *a-baking away* in their various parts of town, and people ate what they baked and assumed that's all there was. Meanwhile, in the *other* parts of town, opposite from where the Really Chief and Proper bakers plied their trade, things were not going well for the Original Bakery—yes, it was still there and still baking the real, original special bread from the dough with the original, special Leaven started by the original Baker—but it was having a tough time for completely different reasons. For one thing, a lot of new, out-of-town people had moved (actually, broken) into their parts of town and had pretty much taken over. These were rough people, and they didn't much care for any kind of bakery or for "bread-eaters" in general, whom they despised. These new people often burned down bakeries or killed the bakers. At times, they took over some of the bakeries and used them as places to prepare their own kind of food. The police commissioner and his cops had done their best to keep order, but eventually they were driven out or killed and the new people set up their *own* police force.

Soon, in some parts of town where the Original Bakery bakeries were, there were a lot more of the new people than those who ate the special bread. (It wasn't clear why the new people hated the special bread so much, but they did. When one of the new people decided he liked the special bread more than their own kind of food, which made them strong but also very mean-tempered, they it made a particular point to kill him! That was so mean!) Some people who ate the special bread couldn't stand all this meanness, so they gave up and stopped eating the special bread, and joined the new people. In many parts of town, all of the bakeries were closed or wrecked and all of the bakers and even the people who ate the special bread were gone: only the new people from out-of-town were left. In other parts, the Original Bakery barely managed to keep going and just had to make the best of things. The remaining bakers (the ones the new people hadn't killed) kept making the special bread, and the people who kept eating it needed its special nourishment more than ever, what with the difficulty of life under the new people.

The long and the short of it was: the real Original Bakery didn't pay much attention to what happened with the Really Chief Bakery and the Proper bakeries—they had too many problems of their own to worry about already, just keeping their own bakeries going. Once in a great while the Original Bakery bakers would talk with the Really Chief baker and his bakers, and even with the Proper bakers ("Maybe some of *your* cops could come over here and do something about the new people? You probably should—they don't like you either, you know!"), but nothing of much importance came of it. The Really Chief baker only wanted to get the Original Bakery bakers to join his operation. (He even offered to let them keep *calling* themselves the "Original Bakery" if they did join him, but they knew it wouldn't be true anymore. A few agreed, but most said No.) The Proper bakers tried to get the Original Bakery bakers to use their explanations of the Recipe, but this only confused the Original Bakery bakers—how could the Proper bakers even talk about explaining the Recipe (which they didn't even agree on among themselves!) without the special baking knowledge, much less without the original leavened dough! (Once, some Proper bakers asked the Original Bakery bakers how *they* explained the Recipe, so the Original Bakery bakers told them all about the original dough and advised them to get some—but the Proper bakers rejected that advice because it didn't fit the Proper bakers' own understanding of the Recipe.) And most of all, the Original Bakery bakers and the people who ate their special bread just wanted help. They had a hard time figuring out what was the difference between the Really Chief Bakery and the Proper bakeries, anyway. Neither of them had the dough with the original, special Leaven, neither could make the special bread, so what was their problem?

VI.

For the Original Bakery, there were better times, and there were worse times. In better times, the people who ate the special bread managed to chase the new people back out of town, and they even were able to set up their own police force again to protect the Original Bakery bakeries. (But only from some parts of town, where the new people from out-of-town had not become too numerous. In other parts, the new people have shut all the bakeries and there are no more "bread-eaters" at all.)

At other times, things got even *worse*. Some people who used to eat the special bread but who had gotten some half-baked (ha! ha!) ideas from the parts of town where people ate Really Chief or Proper bread decided that *all* bread was bad and that, in fact, there never had been any "original Baker" at all! (What were these half-baked ideas? Truth be told, for a long time many dissatisfied Really Chief and Proper bread-eaters had given up bread entirely and had serious doubts about the original Baker. They figured *their* bakers were wrong, so they *all* must be wrong. They figured the original Baker was probably just a myth invented by the bakers so they could sell bread. In the Really Chief and Proper bakeries' parts of town, people who thought like this considered themselves smarter than ordinary people who just ate the bread without asking too many questions. Eventually, some people in the Original Bakery part of town wanted to be smart too, so they started to think the same thing.) For a long time, these "half-baked" people tried to kill all the bakers and shut all the bakeries. They did a great deal of damage, and for a while it began to look like they might succeed in wiping out the Original Bakery and the original dough entirely (even though the original Baker had said that wouldn't ever happen). But one way or another, despite the difficulties, the Original Bakery bakers kept on baking and the people kept eating the special bread, and eventually that very bad time passed and things got a little better. Still, the people with "half-baked" ideas never quite went away and were to be found in all parts of town.

VII.

Then, finally, a funny thing happened. First, a lot more people who ate bread from all of the various bakeries—Original, Really Chief, and Proper—did a lot more visiting in each others' parts of town. In particular, a number of people from the Original Bakery parts of town had moved to the Really Chief and Proper bakeries' parts of town. When that happened, some of the Original Bakery bakers began to bake their special bread in those parts of town, where the people there had not seen it for a very long time (though some had heard of it), and of course none had ever eaten it. Most people figured: "OK, so what? It's all bread, there's lots of different kinds, every bakery or baker is just as good (or bad) as the next. They say *their* bread is different—but they'll turn out to be like all the other bakers. And even if their so-called 'special bread' seems pretty good now, we'll see what happens in a while." And in fact, some of the people who had arrived with the Original Bakery bakers believed that all bread and all bakeries were pretty much the same. Some of them stopped eating the special bread and began eating the local not-so-special bread. Others even gave up bread and joined the "smart" people with the "half-baked" ideas. Still others figured that if the various breads and bakeries weren't much different, they might as well combine all the bakeries into one big bakery (some of the bakers even tried to arrange a merger!). But a lot of other people (especially some bakers in the Original Bakery bakeries) didn't think this was a good idea at all. And besides, even the bakers trying to arrange the merger couldn't agree on how to do it (things like: which bakers would be in charge of which other bakers, which version of the special baking knowledge they would use, or even what kind of bread they would bake). But they kept on talking, anyway.

However, some of the people who had always lived in the Really Chief and Proper bakeries' parts of town (and even many of the good and honest Really Chief and Proper bakers, who had been trying so hard for so long to make the original Baker's special bread!) began to wonder: "Maybe this Original Bakery bread (which seems so strange to us, so different from the Really Chief and Proper bread!) is better than what we have? Maybe it really *is* the original special bread the original Baker made from the dough with the original, special Leaven, for which the Recipe was written so long ago? The original Baker assured the first-appointed bakers the original dough would last until he got back—it must exist *somewhere*! Maybe this is it. Maybe this is what we have been looking for." So some began to ask the Original Bakery bakers for the special bread, they ate it, and they found that it was so. They found out not because they had studied the Recipe a lot (though that helped some) or even because they had learned some of the special baking knowledge (though that helped some, too), but because they *ate* the special bread.

For you see, neither the Recipe, nor the explanations, nor special baking knowledge, nor the Certificate of Authenticity, nor anything else is much good without *eating* the special bread made from the original dough, with the original, special Leaven, just the way the original Baker started it and told the Original Bakery bakers to keep it going. (And they did!) And maybe more people at last began to understand this because of something that those who ate the Original Bakery's special bread always knew but couldn't exactly explain: that when the original Baker went away, he somehow wasn't *really* gone. They knew that in some mysterious way he had always still been with them, even though they couldn't see him. In some way, he was *in the special bread* (it must be something about the original, special Leaven!), and even more mysterious, *in the people who ate the special bread* (since, after all, whatever you eat becomes part of you), and in the bakers too. By eating it, they became more and more like the original Baker himself—that's why the special bread was so specially nourishing. And that's one reason the original Baker (who was no ordinary baker!) assured them the leavened dough would last until he would come back.

But someday, maybe very soon, everyone will see the original Baker again, just like he said. And maybe that's another reason why more people all the time are learning about the special bread and the Original Bakery, while there is still time.

THE END

KEY
To the Parable of the Bakers, the Dough, and the Special Bread

NOTE: To be consulted only AFTER reading the Parable in full!

I.

The original Baker: Christ
A certain town: first the Roman Empire, later the whole Christian world
The bread dough: the body of the Church, indwelt by the Holy Spirit
The Leaven: the Holy Spirit
Special bread: the Eucharist
The original Baker went away: the Ascension of Christ
The original Baker would be coming back: the Second Coming of Christ
First-appointed bakers: the Apostles
Appointed other bakers: Apostolic Succession
Bakers had different jobs: the degrees of priesthood (Bishop, Priest, Deacon), minor orders, laity
Chief bakers: Bishops
Original Baker's instructions: Holy Tradition
The Recipe: Tradition codified in the Holy Scriptures, particularly the New Testament
Special baking knowledge: Holy Tradition not in the Scriptures

II.

Production of more lumps, more bakeries: the growth of the Church in the Roman Empire
Bakers who did not know the original Baker: pagans and others who do not accept Christ
Wrecking bakeries, killing bakers, etc.: persecution of the Church by pagan Rome
Police commissioner and cops: the Roman Emperor and imperial authorities
Those claiming special baking knowledge: heretics, particularly Gnostics
Original Bakery: the One, Holy, Catholic and Apostolic Church, i.e., the Orthodox Church
New police commissioner: the Emperor St. Constantine
Big conventions of bakers: Ecumenical Councils
Certificate of Authenticity: the Niceno-Constantinopolitan Creed
Can't change the Certificate of Authenticity: Anathema against changing the Creed

III.

Part of town far from Original Baker's neighborhood: the West, far from Middle East
"Really Chief" baker: the Pope of Rome

Bakers in his part of town: other bishops and clergy in the West

He "found" some kitchen notes to "prove" it: forgeries like the "Donation of Constantine"

Local cops: secular rulers in West, notably barbarian kings

Each Really Chief baker in succession: papal claim of Petrine authority

Raids by cops on the Original Bakery: attacks by Roman Catholic rulers on Orthodoxy

Original bakers talk with Really Chief baker: failed reunion councils: Lyons, Florence

Really Chief bakery claims to be Original Bakery: Roman Catholic claims to be original Church

Police commissioner chases rogue cops back: defense of Orthodoxy by the Emperor

Really Chief baker changes special baking knowledge: Papal doctrinal innovations

Really Chief baker claims never to make mistakes: Papal Infallibility

Leaven dying in Really Chief bakery's dough: departure of the Holy Spirit from the West

New words in Certificate of Authenticity: addition of *Filioque* to the Creed

Bread getting flat: Roman Catholic use of unleavened wafers in place of bread for Eucharist

III.

Charging more for bread: indulgences, tribute to papacy in the West

Bakers blame Really Chief baker for problems: dissent in the Roman Catholic church

Reject special baking knowledge, Certificate of Authenticity: rejection of Tradition

"The Recipe alone": "The Bible alone"; *Sola Scriptura*

Try to correct Really Chief bakery: attempts to reform Roman Catholic church from within

"My way or the highway": Pope rejects internal reform

Sicced the cops on them: Pope asks secular rulers to suppress Luther, other Reformers

Started their own bakeries: Reformers start new churches

Bob, Bill bakeries: Lutheran church, Calvinist church, etc.

"Proper" bakeries: Protestant churches

Different ideas how to read the Recipe: Protestant disagreements on Biblical interpretation

Whether to put in Leaven: Protestant misunderstandings of role the Holy Spirit in the Church

More bakeries after Mike, Elmer, Floyd, etc.: proliferation of Protestant denominations

Man who claimed to see Original Baker, "Another Recipe": Joseph Smith, Book of Mormon

Rolls, cakes, bagels, etc.: widely differing Protestant understandings of the Eucharist

Really Chief baker borrows ideas from Proper bakers: the Counter-Reformation

V.

New people: Islam, Muslims

Burned down or destroyed bakeries, killed bakers: Muslim persecution of Orthodox Christians

Take over bakeries, use to prepare own food: turning churches into mosques

Police commissioner and cops killed, driven out: destruction of Empire by Islam

More new people than "bread eaters": Muslims becoming majority in formerly Christian areas

New people killed for eating special bread: Islamic law mandates killing of apostates

Some bread-eaters join new people: Christians who became Muslims

Original Bakery asks for help against new people: Empire asks West for help against Islam

Original bakeries who join Really Chief baker's operation: Uniates, i.e., Eastern-rite Catholics

Original Bakery talks with Proper bakers: letters between Orthodox and Lutherans in 1500s

VI.

Chased new people out of town: liberation of Orthodox nations in the Balkans in 19th century

All bakeries shut and no "bread-eaters": places where no Christians left, e.g., Anatolia

"Half-baked" people: communists and other atheists, modernists

Damage done by "half-baked" people: communist persecution of the Church

Bad time passed: end of communism in Orthodox countries

VII.

Original bakery people to other parts of town: Orthodox immigration to West, especially U.S.

Some stop eating special bread: Orthodox who join Western churches or become un-churched

Effort to arrange merger of bakeries: ecumenism

Really Chief/Proper people notice Original Bakery: Catholics/Protestants discover Orthodoxy

Original Bakery must exist somewhere: Christ said gates of hell not prevail against Church

Nothing good without original dough: Eucharist most important thing to life of the Church

Original Baker still present in bread: the Eucharist is Christ's Body and Blood

Something about the Leaven: Christ made present by action of the Holy Spirit

Original Baker present in people who eat bread: Eucharist makes Christians more Christ-like

Leavened dough lasts until Original Baker returns: the Church continues to end of the world

Everyone will see Original Baker soon: Christ will return soon to judge all the world

It's Later Than You Think

"It's Later Than You Think"

James George Jatras | Ron Paul Institute | September 16, 2021

I accepted the invitation to speak with you today only with great trepidation. This was for at least three reasons.

The first is that, both for self-protection in an increasingly unfree country and my growing sense that nothing I or anyone else can say will make much difference in averting the horrors I believe are coming our way, I had ceased my public writing and speaking life, such as it was. I reluctantly have made an exception to that less than momentous recusal but plan to resume it at the end of today.

Secondly, I was loath to contaminate the naturally ebullient optimism of youth with my crotchety Boomer pessimism. At your age you should feel that the world is, if not quite your oyster, at least pregnant with possibilities. How do I tell you that, in the layman's terms, your lives will probably suck? At least in the near future. But there is hope. I will return to that.

Thirdly, I thought it would be derelict of me not to provide you with some sage, old graybeard advice of a practical nature. If I were in your shoes today, what would I do, specifically, to try to make a positive contribution to the world around me? How best to serve God and my neighbor? To make my country and the world a better place? And to do it in relative safety, in a modest degree of economic sustainability, perhaps even comfort? To marry, start a family, and see your offspring rise in peace and prosperity?

This last is most daunting, because the world has changed so much, in such a short time, and the pace of change is accelerating. Back in the olden days of yore, in my case the late 1970s, when I entered government service, that was an honorable thing to do. (Allow me to note that there are some who still spotlessly preserve that honor, such as The—literally—Honorable Thomas Massie, who will address us today. But such examples are rare sightings nowadays. In the institution in which he serves, you could probably count them on one hand, and you might not need your thumb.)

But I digress. When I started out, I did so consciously following in the footsteps of my father, a career Air Force officer and fighter pilot, and my father-in-law, a career agent in the old Immigration and Naturalization Service. After law school and a bit of flirting with the FBI and CIA, I ended up at the State Department, as a commissioned Foreign Service Officer.

My first assignment was as a Consular Officer in the border city of Tijuana, Baja California, just across from San Diego. The usual duties: jails, hospitals, stolen planes and cars, but mostly visas. With respect to immigrant visas, virtually all the applicants were already living illegally in the US and in most cases receiving various forms of public assistance. In principle, they should have been denied resident alien status under Section 212(a)(15), "likely to become a public charge," but in practice they couldn't be denied for receipt of any plethora of benefits—Food Stamps, WIC, Aid to Families with Democratic Children, Medicaid, SSI, etc. etc.—unless it was actually called W-E-L-F-A-R-E, and sometimes not even then. Earlier this year the Catholic Legal Immigration Network, Inc. issued a statement lauding the final dropping of the pretense ("Public Charge Rule Is Dead: Hurrah!!"—two exclamation points, seriously. . . .) Lesson: permeable borders and a welfare state are not a good match.

My next assignment was in Washington in the Office of Soviet Union Affairs, a/k/a "the Soviet Desk." This was at the beginning of the Reagan Administration, but, naïve young fellow that I was, I was shocked—shocked!—to find out that there were hardly any actual anti-communists in the whole Department, not just at the Desk. Not so much communist sympathizers, mind you, just *blasé* about ideas and ideology, generally accepting of a kind of a mushy FDR/LBJ liberalism tending toward social democracy—in short, like most of the rest of the bureaucracy. Sure, the Soviet version of those values was annoying, but what do you expect from Russians? (It was no surprise that a bureaucracy that was mildly sympathetic to Moscow when it was run by communists—just New Dealers in a hurry—became implacably hostile once the red flag was lowered from the Kremlin.) I remember once when some initiative or other was being floated past the White House, a colleague asked the Desk director, "Do you think the president will go for this?" The Director replied, only partly in jest: "He's a political appointee. He'll do what he's told." Lesson: at least in foreign policy and national security, forget elections: the permanent bureaucracy rules.

Eventually I left the State Department to work for many years in the Republican leadership of the US Senate. My job was to prepare papers on upcoming legislation (with a partisan spin) and on topics of interest to GOP Senators and staff: the conflicts in Central America, Mozambique, Angola, Grenada; sanctions on South Africa; POWs left behind in Southeast Asia (despite the sanctimonious flying of all those black flags, "You Are Not Forgotten," they were indeed abandoned, care largely of two Senators with experience in Vietnam); the First Gulf War; the Somalia fiasco; the breakups of the USSR and Yugoslavia; Clinton's Haiti invasion ("Operation Uphold Democracy"—really!); 9/11 and the invasion of Afghanistan; and—worst of all—the US military intervention in the Balkans, first in Bosnia, then in Kosovo. The lesson you know already: a lie will travel halfway around the world while the truth is still putting on its running shoes, the first casualty of war is truth—you know the drill.

Likewise, it's hard to work on Capitol Hill without coming to see what a bazaar it is. (Well, bizarre too, but also a bazaar, a souk, a flea market.) While the bipartisan leadership has not yet taken up the helpful suggestion from the Babylon Bee that barcodes be affixed to legislators' foreheads so that interested persons and organizations can conveniently scan prices and self-checkout, they have provided a helpful guide to what are called "Congressional Member Organizations (CMOs)," also called coalitions, study groups, task forces, or working groups. Memberships in many but not all CMOs serve as virtual barcodes for potential (mostly legal) campaign donors, including contributions from ethnic compatriots who are US citizens, or at least are supposed to be, funneled to "friends of" this or that foreign country: like the "Argentina Caucus, Armenian Issues Caucus, Azerbaijan Caucus, Bangladesh Caucus, Bosnia Caucus, Brazil Caucus, Cambodia Caucus,. . ."—you get the idea, all the way to Uzbekistan and Venezuela (what, no Zimbabwe?), with at least four caucuses just for Israel. (Some might say the whole Congress is pretty much an "Israel Caucus," but that's a whole 'nother topic. . .) Perhaps it's the legislative counterpart to the infamous "clientitis" at the State Department, where—as we used to say, "there is no 'US Interests Section'"—and where diplomats come to see themselves as much or more as advocates for the countries they deal with than for the US. (We also liked to say there could never be a coup in the US overthrowing the Constitutional order because there's no American Embassy in Washington. I guess we got that one wrong . . .)

Like many people, I greeted the end of communism in the USSR and the Soviet bloc with a sense of hope. No more need for an ever-growing, ever-more invasive national security surveillance state! A peace dividend! Finally, back to a sane pre-1914 international order! But of course all of the malign trends we had seen during the Cold War, far from decreasing, increased as the—what do you want to call it, the Deep State, the Borg, the Blob, the Swamp, the MICIMATT (Ray McGovern's Military-Industrial-Congressional-Intelligence-Media-Academia-Think-Tank complex)—saw its chance to achieve total global domination—to rule the world—"benevolent global hegemony," in perpetuity, as neocon gurus William Kristol and Robert Kagan christened it in 1996. Lesson: folks who think night and day about nothing but achieving power, money, and influence tend to get them.

A little slow on the draw, I remember when my seven-and-a-half watt cranial light bulb finally sputtered into illumination. In 1992, I was attending a briefing of the International Republican Institute (IRI), one of the quasi-governmental entities set up to promote—get this!—"democracy" in the 1980s, regarding the recent election in Albania. An IRI staffer who had been working on the ground in that country proudly related how they had helped secure a victory for the Democratic Party over its rival, the former communists rebranded the Socialist Party, for a paltry eight million bucks. Even better, they managed to do it even though—it was clear to everyone, and the staffer was explicit on this point—the Socialists had more public support than the Democrats did! During Q&A, simple fellow that I was, I asked: "But if the Socialists were more popular than the Democrats, wouldn't the democratic outcome have been a win for the Socialists?" Oh, no no no, you silly boy, you! You see, the Democratic Party has democratic principles, so their win, even though fewer people support them, is the democratic result. It then struck me that we had gone through the looking glass, that words didn't mean anymore what normal people meant by them.

Well, that was then, this is now. Let's get something very clear. Back in my day, yes there was corruption, yes there was influence-peddling, yes there was contempt for truth and common decency. But these were debasements within what could still be argued was a structure built on a constitution and the rule of law. That is, something existed, though as with all human affairs, it was only as good as the people operating within that something. One could still, with a straight face, contend that if the good guys win, if wise policies prevail—audit the Fed, cut taxes, stop our interventionist foreign policy, ban abortion, legalize dope, whatever you want—there was enough integrity to the something to allow for such improvements. We were still living in a normal moral universe, where virtue and vice contended for dominance. We were still living in America.

We really can't say that anymore. It's not just that laws and the Constitution are violated—when were they not?—but that they now have almost no relevance to the nation, or perhaps former nation, we have become. When I say nation, I mean the core, founding American ethnos characterized by European ancestry, by the English language, and by the Christian religion, mostly Protestant. The constitutional order established by the Founding Fathers—you know, those racist, gun-toting transphobes in knee britches and powdered wigs—for themselves and their posterity is a secondary epiphenomenon, the ethos of the founding ethnos, their folkways and values. You know, all that quaint Anglo-Saxon due process, *habeas corpus*, presumption of innocence, limited powers stuff. The primary phenomenon, without which the erstwhile constitutional order would not have existed in the first place, from which it derived its values, principles, and structure, is the ethnos. That is what is under attack, even more than the order itself, which in my opinion is effectively gone.

And it's come with astonishing speed.

It is difficult to look back on the events of the *annus horribilis* of 2020—and to anticipate worse to come—without a foreboding that the world is nearing some sort of crescendo. The Gnostic tendency described by Eric Voegelin, in his landmark 1952 book *The New Science of Politics*—hey, don't immanentize the eschaton, bro'!—and fitfully growing year by year, decade by decade, century by century, seems to have achieved an unprecedented and decisive degree of domination in a few short months, and not just in America. It is increasingly difficult to see any signpost of restraint, much less of restoration.

Perhaps this crescendo will be similar to earlier ones: collapse of the Western Roman Empire, the Islamic conquest of the Eastern Empire, the East-West Great Schism and the Crusades, the neopagan humanism of the Renaissance, the religious strife of the Reformation, the misnamed Enlightenment with its malign offspring Revolution and "Progress," the world wars and totalitarianisms of the modern era. Yet with each seeming turn of the wheel, with each ebb and flow between disorder and partial re-stabilization, the net linear advance of Gnosticism is undeniable.

Even a cursory search of the internet yields multiple references to the congealing omnipresence of powerful actors in every sphere of life to implement a program called the "Great Reset." Released in May 2020 by Prince Charles of the United Kingdom and Klaus Schwab, founder and executive chairman of the World Economic Forum (commonly known as Davos, after its meeting place in Switzerland), the Great Reset takes its cue from the "Covid-19 crisis, and the political, economic and social disruptions it has caused" as—no, not as a misfortune, not a calamity—but as "*a unique window of opportunity* [emphasis added] to shape the recovery," informed by the insights of "global stakeholders" in "determining the future state of global relations, the direction of national economies, the priorities of societies [really, what doesn't come under the heading of "the priorities of societies"?], the nature of business models and the management of a global commons" in order to "build a new social contract that honors the dignity of every human being," summed up in the ubiquitous slogan "Build Back Better." The initiative's list of Partners ("global stakeholders") reads like a Who's Who of the most powerful international corporations.

While the provenance, natural or artificial, of the viral disease that served as the justification—or pretext—for this "unique opportunity" may remain forever in the shadows (except perhaps to the small group of *cognoscenti* who feel they are guiding the process) the primary manifestation of the crisis is all too public: a relentless incitement of paralyzing and irrational fear—of a malady that has an almost universal survival rate for anyone not in a handful of comorbidity categories. The very success of this terror campaign is a testament to the extent to which post-modern and (mostly) post-Christian society has reached the point of deeming physical death, though inevitable, as the worst possible fate, to be avoided at all costs. Imposed via *diktat* by the very government and corporate entities force-feeding the scare propaganda, the costs—in the form of lockdowns (heretofore a term relevant exclusively to prisons), travel bans, compulsory masking, denial of opportunity to earn a living, "distance learning" in place of education, "virtual" social interactions, mass transfer of assets from the middle class and small enterprises to a *rentier* elite, and the prospect of an unavoidable, and perhaps a mandatory, biometric "passport" as proof of vaccination—continue to rise.

No less dismaying is the propensity of many people, perhaps most, to go along with all this, running the gamut from sullen submission to loving embrace of their shackles and enthusiastic willingness to force others' compliance. What explains this? Fear of reprisal, fear of being thought of as a crank or "conspiracy theorist," terminal law-abidingness, a misplaced virtue of charity regarding others' intentions, naïve trust in "authority," "experts," "science" and claims of necessity to keep us and others "safe"? Or even worse, a sense of joining the worthy elites in their domination of lesser, insufficiently obedient and "caring" mortals? A totalitarian mindset is not solely an elite phenomenon.

In any case, these measures and their justifications, though constantly changing and often contradictory, are all the more obligatory. Taken together they have all the appearance of a controlled demolition of all established human interactions in anticipation of their replacement by something we are assured by our betters will be an improvement. The contours of the "new normal" in the post-American America hurtling in our direction have already become so familiar as to need little elaboration:

- A proletarianized middle class eager to exchange freedom for security and minimal support in the form of "relief"—no, not relief from governments' destruction of their livelihoods, but from the fearsome virus, leading to "universal basic income" (i.e., the dole in place of self-support), profligate production of fiat money (which unavoidably means inflation and destruction of whatever assets a shrinking middle class might have left), and moves toward a cashless society: in a word, serfdom. "You will own nothing, and you will be happy." You will eat bugs, and you will enjoy them;

- Elevated levels of substance abuse, mental and emotional illness, social alienation and isolation, domestic abuse, suicide, immune deficiency, and other morbidities caused not by the illness but by measures imposed supposedly to save lives but probably taking a higher toll than the disease itself, to which we can now add whatever the real toll of the vaccines might be;

- Immunization (with repetition ad infinitum via "boosters" required in light of "mutations" like the "Delta variant" and the expected future appearances of new plagues), if not legally required at least will be so universally demanded by ostensibly private business (notwithstanding real concerns about the vaccines' safety, efficacy, and long-term effects, including infertility and problems associated with genetic modification) that it amounts to a license for basic living—we offer a pinch of incense before the genius of "science," a false savior, a fake Caesar, required in order to be allowed to buy or sell, work, go to school, travel, etc. As a seamless, global regime of "vaccine apartheid" becomes inescapable, with every human being, whether small or great, rich or poor, bond or free, threatened with pariah status for refusing the injection of a substance of unknown safety (numbers of those suffering serious adverse consequences are suppressed), effectiveness (as new "variants" arise even many who have gotten jabbed get sick), and morality (how attenuated exactly are the aborted fetal cell lines used in development?), the enforcement mechanisms are becoming clearer as well: mandatory carrying of a scannable "health status" record on smart phones, QR app facilitating the precise location and activities of every human being on the planet every second of their lives. (So much for your HIPAA "privacy.") It's hard to avoid the suspicion that that was perhaps a goal of the entire pandemic response in the first place;

- Further blurring of the lines between Big Government, Big Finance, Big Pharma, Big Data, etc., amounting to corporate state capture ("Faucism");
- Travel limits on law-abiding people (but not for illegal migrants), not for the purpose of restoring sovereign state boundaries (which would be deplorably nationalist—just ask Viktor Orbán!) but for what amounts to herd control and monitoring;
- Not directly based on supposed anti-virus measures but closely tracking with them, joint government and corporate promulgation of socially destructive, historically counterfeit ideologies ("intersectionality," LGBTQI+, feminism, multiculturalism, "critical race theory" (a/k/a, hate whitey), suppression of "populism" in the name of "democracy") with principal targeting of children subject to sexualization and predation by those expressing what were once quaintly known as abnormal appetites and identities. (This of course has become a key component of the US and European global "human rights" and "democracy" promotion; evidently cultural imperialism and neo-colonialism are just fine and dandy when sufficiently Woke. Maybe you've seen that meme, with the fierce skull-masked fighter with an American flag: "Until I am out of ammo or out of blood, I will fight for homosexuality in Botswana!") These "values" in turn accelerate longstanding trends towards infertility and demographic collapse (decline in marriage, family formation, and childbearing) pointing to population reduction and replacement via post-human society, transhumanism, and bio-engineering; and not least—
- Replacement of "real" reality based on physical proximity with other people with virtual or augmented (i.e., fake) reality, combined with universal surveillance via artificial intelligence, 5G and blockchain technology, facial recognition, and biological tagging, backed up by omnipresent social credit, cancel culture, and digital censorship penalties. Replacement of the real universe with a virtual "metaverse."

In sum, what could not be implemented over decades solely by fear of climate change and "rising oceans" is now being swiftly achieved via fear of a submicroscopic infectious agent. No one should doubt that the old, pre-2020 world is forever gone.

This brave new world, my young friends, is your world. This is not something that is going to get fixed by the next election, or any election, by a new political party or movement, or by a convention of the states to write new Constitutional language for our Executive, Legislative, and Judicial authorities to ignore or pervert like they do the current language.

(Let me also mention in passing one of my pet peeves: while government at all levels bears a YUGE responsibility for all this, most of it is being carried out by private corporations. This leads some free-market advocates to shrug their shoulders: "Weeeell, they're private businesses, they're within their rights." I say: bunk. To start with, corporations are inherently creatures of the state. They wouldn't even exist were it not for legislation making them under the law "persons"—though they have neither body to be kicked nor soul to be damned. Given the incestuous "partnership" between government and the corporatocracy, the distinction is increasingly academic.)

Much of what I have described centers on the United States. To note that is not to be unduly parochial any more than would have been noting Russia's centrality to an earlier Gnostic outbreak a century ago. Given our country's global dominance in virtually every field of human endeavor—politics, military, finance, economy, science, medicine, media, popular culture, etc.—in the wake of the collapse of the earlier communist eruption (and before that, of national socialism), it is to be expected that this global crisis would begin, and perhaps will end, in the United States.

There is a remarkable congruence, though not an exact identity, between the divisions in American society pitting those who accept the therapeutic narrative on the virus and supposed countermeasures against those who reject them, and between those who accept and reject the violent "social justice" campaign championed by groups like Black Lives Matter and Antifa (themselves sponsored by the government and corporate establishment), culminating in a contested presidential election that half the electorate believes was the result of fraud. The conclusion that the US Constitution and the rule of law, which have been declining for many years, may have in fact reached a terminal point is reluctantly dawning on tens of millions of ordinary, generally apolitical Americans. Not only are we more divided than at any time since 1861–1865, we are even more aliens, indeed enemies, to one another than were Northerners and Southerners back then in terms of fundamental questions of who we are, what man is, Who God is, and how we should order our lives and our country. In 1861 they worshipped the same God, read the same Bible, honored the same Founding Fathers, claimed fidelity to the same Constitution. In today's America, like in the rest of the Woke Woke West, we can't even agree on our pronouns.

The term "cold" civil war, a war that might possibly turn "hot," has become a commonplace in American discourse. That should not come as a surprise when we remember how the Red Gnostic seizure of power in Russia, to which many draw parallels to America today, didn't triumph without bloodily overcoming ferocious popular resistance. The rising tide of Rainbow Gnosticism in America now, whether it succeeds or fails, may turn out to be just as destructive. Let's remember too that, if you credit the William Strauss and Neil Howe "Fourth Turning" cycle, we are only about halfway through a crisis that will totally transform this country, assuming there's a country left at all by the end of it.

Finally, "wars and rumors of war" may not be confined to the United States. As the dysgenic impacts of the virus scare affect other countries to a greater or lesser degree, so America's growing instability must have its international reverberations. Afghanistan is a bellwether. Suggestions have been made that overextension abroad and internal crises may force the United States, willy-nilly, to withdraw from the program of global hegemony launched after the demise of the USSR, with a multipolar world finally emerging. That could happen, but it's not likely, at least not smoothly. Despite the Kabul kick in the teeth, realism is still a scarce commodity among Washington's *nomenklatura*, where the penalties for strategic failure are few but rewards for aggression are great. As we will see, the Afghan humiliation will have little consequence for those culpable. While American "humanitarian intervention," "democracy promotion," and "regime change" have been to little advantage but much harm to the supposed beneficiaries (Haiti, Serbia, Iraq, Libya, Ukraine, Syria, Yemen, Afghanistan, etc.) the tangible benefits are clearly visible in the form of the "McMansions" around the Washington Beltway, which still sprout like mushrooms after heavy rains. As America continues down the road of confrontation with Russia, and increasingly with China, the prospect of the first major global conflict, now well overdue, since the Long War of 1914–1945 grows. A self-interested, arrogant, ignorant, and spiritually and intellectually stunted leadership class caught in a Thucydides Trap (a declining power confronted by a rising opponent or opponents) may well be tempted to launch a war to eliminate the "threat" if it feels victory may be in reach today but might not be tomorrow. To call such a prospect apocalyptic is not hyperbole.

In the end, my young friends, the impact any one of us can expect to have in the face of world-historic trends before which the fates of nations and empires fly like leaves in the autumn winds is vanishingly small. Already baked into the cake will be, I believe, hardships for you that we've become accustomed to think only happen to "other people" in "other countries" far away, not seen here since the Revolution and the Civil War, or maybe in isolated instances during the Great Depression: financial and economic disruption and, in some places, especially in urban areas, collapse; supply chains, utilities, and other aspects of basic infrastructure ceasing to function (what happens in major cities when food deliveries stop for a week?), even widespread hunger; rising levels of violence, both criminality and civil strife. These will be combined, paradoxically, with the remaining organs of authority, however discredited, desperately cracking down on the enemy within—no, not on murderers, robbers, and rapists, but on "science deniers," "religious fanatics," "haters," "conspiracy theorists," "insurrectionists," "gun nuts," "American Taliban," "purveyors of "medical misinformation," and, of course, "racists," "sexists," "homophobes," and so forth. It's the late Samuel Francis' "anarcho-tyranny" nightmare come to life with a vengeance.

As I say, I think your ability to impact the "big picture" regarding any of this is slim to none. Even our ability to discern the signs of the times in an era of pervasive Gnostic deceit abetted by technologies unimaginable just a few years ago is limited.

Nevertheless, for what it is worth, I put before you three practical tasks for your consideration.

Firstly, be vigilant against deception, in a day when assuredly evil men and impostors will grow worse and worse, deceiving, and being deceived. Admittedly, this is a tough one, given the ever-present lying that surrounds us and the suppression of dissent. Try to sift truth from falsehood but don't become obsessed because, in many cases, you won't be able to be sure anyway. Focus most on what's proximate to you and on the people most important to you. It sounds terrible, I know, because everyone who's denoted as an "expert" or an "authority" isn't necessarily unreliable, but that's a good starting assumption. Be skeptical—about everyone. In communist countries, this was the norm: listen to what the establishment media say, to foreign sources if you can access them, and to anti-establishment dissidents (then it was samizdat, now it's internet "conspiracy theorists"—but don't get sucked in by Trojan Horses like the infamous Q.): then triangulate and take your best guess. There may be a cost. As Solzhenitsyn said, "He who chooses the lie as his principle inevitably chooses violence as his method."

Secondly, as stewards of every worldly charge placed on us by God and by other people—as fathers and mothers, as husbands and wives, as sons and daughters, as neighbors, as students, as workers, as citizens, as patriots—we must prudently care for those to whom we have a duty within the limited power and wisdom allotted to us. Start with yourselves. Be as self-sufficient as possible. Get involved in your community; that leftist slogan is actually a good one: think globally, act locally. Befriend your neighbors. Learn a real skill—electricity, plumbing, carpentry. Farm! DON'T go to law school, for goodness' sake. Get in shape. Eat and sleep right. Have plenty of the essentials: food, fuel, gold, ammunition. Learn to shoot. Limit computer and phone time. Cultivate healthy personal relationships—real ones, not virtual ones. Marry young, have kids—especially women, don't get seduced by all that "career" nonsense. Read old books. Cultivate virtue. Go to church.

Simply being what used to be considered normal and leading a productive life is becoming the most revolutionary act one can perform. With that in mind, find the strength to be revolutionaries indeed!

You've seen the meme: Hard times create strong men; Strong men create good times; Good times create weak men; Weak men create hard times. Well, take it from the weakling generation that brought them to you: the hard times, they is a-coming. But they won't last forever. If you live through them—and some of you will not—we'll see what possibilities, as of now literally unimaginable, might then exist. But you will need to be personally fit to take advantage of them. You will also need to be part of some kind of sustainable community of likeminded people.

Third, for those of you who are believers, particularly Christians, we must pray without ceasing, firm in faith that, through whatever hardships may lie ahead, even the very hairs of our head are all numbered, and the final triumph of Truth is never in doubt.

Thank you, and good luck. You're going to need it.

These remarks were delivered to the Ron Paul Institute Student Seminar in Washington, DC, September 3, 2021.

It's Even Later Than You Thought

"It's Even Later Than You Thought"

James George Jatras | Ron Paul Institute | September 8, 2022

Allow me to say at the outset how pleased and not a little surprised I was to be invited to address this seminar for the second year in a row. Pleased, because I can't think of a better place than the Ron Paul Scholars Seminar to encounter bright young people who can afford even the most cranky old Boomer like myself grounds for hope. Surprised, because as I recall following last year's presentation the organizers were constrained to confiscate your predecessors' belts and shoelaces and place them under 24-hour protective watch. As I asked them last year: "How do I tell you that, in the layman's terms, your lives will probably suck? At least in the near future. But there is hope. I will return to that."

My talk last year was called "It's Later than you Think," and of course now it's even later still. On the off-chance that none of you has memorized that text, I will give a brief summary of what I said then—which as I noted even then ended with a dim glimmer of sunlight—and then review how the past year has, I believe, confirmed my assessment then and, somewhat paradoxically, made that glimmer shine just a bit brighter. All in all, I think we have grounds to be cautiously pessimistic.

In brief, my thesis last year was that the gathering clouds were not just those of a political crisis (presumably one that would be amenable to change through political means—"Vote harder next time! Vote harder, boy!") or just an economic and financial crisis (is two quarters of negative GDP growth by definition *really* a recession, or not—ah, the rollercoaster of the business cycle!). No, it was something more fundamental. Rather, the America we oldsters had grown up with, and which had been declining for decades, had fundamentally ceased to exist.

Indeed, what we're seeing here is something of world historic proportions that in some essential way breaks with anything seen in the lifetime of anyone now living. Sure, back in my day—

> there was corruption, yes there was influence-peddling, yes there was contempt for truth and common decency. But these were debasements within what could still be argued was a structure built on a constitution and the rule of law. That is, something existed, though as with all human affairs, it was only as good as the people operating within that something. One could still, with a straight face, contend that if the good guys win, if wise policies prevail—audit the Fed, cut taxes, stop our interventionist foreign policy, ban abortion, legalize dope, whatever you want—there was enough integrity to the something to allow for such improvements. We were still living in a normal moral universe, where virtue and vice contended for dominance. We were still living in America.
>
> We really can't say that anymore. It's not just that laws and the Constitution are violated—when were they not?—but that they now have almost no relevance to the nation, or perhaps former nation, we have become. When I say nation, I mean the core, founding [state-

building] American ethnos characterized by European ancestry, by the English language, and by the Christian religion, mostly Protestant. The constitutional order established by the Founding Fathers—you know, those racist, gun-toting transphobes in knee britches and powdered wigs—for themselves and their posterity is a secondary epiphenomenon, the ethos of the founding ethnos, their folkways and values. You know, all that quaint Anglo-Saxon due process, *habeas corpus*, presumption of innocence, limited powers stuff. The primary phenomenon, without which the erstwhile constitutional order would not have existed in the first place, from which it derived its values, principles, and structure, is the ethnos. That is what is under attack, even more than the order itself, which in my opinion is effectively gone.

It is difficult to look back on the events of the annus horribilis of 2020—and to anticipate worse to come—without a foreboding that the world is nearing some sort of crescendo. The Gnostic tendency described by Eric Voegelin, in his landmark 1952 book *The New Science of Politics*—"Hey, don't immanentize the eschaton, bro'!"—and fitfully growing year by year, decade by decade, century by century, seems to have achieved an unprecedented and decisive degree of domination in a few short months, and not just in America. It is increasingly difficult to see any signpost of restraint, much less of restoration. [A year later, there's no looking back.]

Perhaps this crescendo will be similar to earlier ones: collapse of the Western Roman Empire, the Islamic conquest of the Eastern Empire, the East-West Great Schism and the Crusades, the neopagan humanism of the Renaissance, the religious strife of the Reformation, the misnamed Enlightenment with its malign offspring Revolution and "Progress," the world wars and [socialist] totalitarianisms of the modern era. Yet with each seeming turn of the wheel, with each ebb and flow between disorder and partial re-stabilization, the net linear advance of Gnosticism is undeniable.

A watershed was passed with Covid and the measures—the lockdowns, the masks, social distancing and monitoring, the clot shot, censorship of dissent—supposedly intended to deal with a virus, accomplishing within a few short months what decades of climate hysteria could not, summed up under the moniker "the Great Reset" and its ubiquitous slogan "Build Back Better."

Taken together [what we have been seeing has] all the appearance of a controlled demolition of all established human interactions in anticipation of their replacement by something we are assured by our betters will be an improvement. The contours of the "new normal" in the post-American America hurtling in our direction have already become so familiar as to need little elaboration: infringement on traditional liberties based on "keeping us safe"; "cancel culture"; blurring of the lines between Big Government, Big Finance, Big Pharma, Big Data, etc., amounting to corporate state capture; and, not directly based on supposed anti-virus measures but closely tracking with them, joint government and corporate promulgation of socially destructive, historically counterfeit ideologies ("intersectionality," LGBTQI+, feminism, multiculturalism, "critical race theory,") . . . with principal targeting of children subject to sexualization and predation by those expressing what were once quaintly known as abnormal appetites and identities.

. . . these [so-called] "values" in turn accelerate longstanding trends towards infertility and demographic collapse (decline in marriage, family formation, and childbearing) pointing to population reduction and replacement via post-human society, transhumanism, and bio-engineering.

This brave new world, my young friends, is your world. This is not something that is going to get fixed by the next election, or any election, by a new political party or movement.

In the end, . . . the impact any one of us can expect to have in the face of world-historic trends before which the fates of nations and empires fly like leaves in the autumn winds is vanishingly small. Already baked into the cake will be, I believe, hardships for you that we've become accustomed to think only happen to "other people" in "other countries" far away, not seen here since the Revolution and the Civil War, or maybe in isolated instances during the Great Depression: financial and economic disruption and, in some places, especially in urban areas, collapse; supply chains, utilities, and other aspects of basic infrastructure ceasing to function (what happens in major cities when food deliveries stop for a week?), even widespread hunger; rising levels of violence, both criminality and civil strife. These will be combined, paradoxically, with the remaining organs of authority, however discredited, desperately cracking down on the enemy within—no, not on murderers, robbers, and rapists, but on "science deniers," "religious fanatics," "haters," "conspiracy theorists," "insurrectionists," "gun nuts," purveyors of "medical misinformation," and, of course, "racists," "sexists," "homophobes," ["Christian nationalists," "semi-fascist MAGA Republicans"], and so forth. [To paraphrase Barry Goldwater, extremism in defense of "democracy" and Joe Biden's "soul of the nation" is no vice. Moderation in pursuit of "social justice" and "equity" is no virtue.] It's the late Samuel Francis's "anarcho-tyranny" nightmare come to life with a vengeance.

Now. there's where I would have left it last year. We are a year further into a very dark tunnel, and there's nothing (in my very fallible opinion) anyone can do to stop an accelerating rush into the abyss.

But we can talk about probabilities. A year ago, if I had to guess, I'd have said chances of any kind of happy ending for this country or the world would be very slim indeed. Limitless tyranny at home, endless war abroad. George Orwell's boot stomping on a human face forever, but dragged out in rainbow glitter and a feather boa while carving up your kids' sexual parts. America: sliding quietly under the Woke waves never to be seen again while imposing the same poison on the rest of the world. There is no Transatlanticism without transgenderism! As Craig Murray memorably observed regarding the United Kingdom and the collapse of Boris "BoJo the Clown" Johnson's Prime Ministership, we could anticipate that America would draw to a close not with a bang . . . but with a fart (albeit one generating hurricane force winds).

My assessment radically changed on February 24, 2022, when Russia began what it called its Special Military Operation in Ukraine. Without going into all the details of the war itself and the reasons for it, I believe that the reverberations of that war are having and will continue to have serious consequences for the smooth fade into oblivion that had been our most likely doom. In a nutshell, the entire globalist program—Build Back Better, plans for Biden's renewable Gangrene New Deal energy economy, "you vill eat ze bugz," more "genders" than Heinz varieties—may come crashing down along with its premier instrumentalities, the evil twins NATO and the European Union. Can it be that there's a "soft landing" to this second cold war, that the US-led so-called "rules-based international order" might dissolve as (relatively) peacefully as did the Warsaw Pact and the USSR? Do miracles on that scale happen twice in one lifetime?

Put another way: what we're seeing now is in fact World War III between the Global American Empire (the G.A.E., or "the GAE") and a loose set of countries led by Russia and China: Eurasia. Only a small portion of that war is military, confined for the moment to Ukraine but with the danger of spreading. There is also the potential for an outbreak in the western Pacific over Taiwan., not to mention other flashpoints like Iran and North Korea. Most of this global war, though, is financial and economic, and of course in the informational and propaganda sphere. Bottom line: I see no way for the GAE to win, nor any way for its leaders to accept defeat. The risk of an accidental escalation to a nuclear conflagration exists, as does the possibility (albeit a slim one, I hope) of a so-called "Samson Option," deliberately bringing down the temple crushing all inside.

Well, if the worst happens, we won't have to worry because we'll all be dead. If it doesn't, what comes next won't be pretty though: a combination inflation/deflation in the form of inflation of daily living needs (food, fuel), deflation of stored wealth (stocks, bonds, crypto, real estate, maybe metals, durable goods and discretional purchases that people can't afford because all their money goes for food, gas, and keeping lights on). For the short term, cash will be king but eventually—maybe in a year, two years?—the US dollar will go down the tube as well. At this juncture it's hard to see what could replace it, but it sure won't be the Euro or the Pound.

In our post-industrial debt-based virtual economy we will be painfully educated as to how much our ability to buy underpriced imported stuff at Walmart and on Amazon rests on dollar "seigniorage," which in turn rests on global perceptions of American military superiority. As the *New York Times'* Thomas Friedman put it, "McDonald's cannot flourish without McDonnell Douglas, the designer of the F–15." Just as the USSR's international standing was inextricably linked to its internal stability, the visible failure of the empire will feed a crisis of legitimacy at home in the US and in our vassal states. The chickens of the US establishment's post-Cold War misguided and needless ideological quest for world domination, waged with all the Manichaean messianic zeal of 1920s Bolsheviks, are coming home to roost. It is a house built on sand: "And the rain descended, and the floods came, and the winds blew, and beat upon that house; and it fell: and great was the fall of it."

The real question I don't know the answer to is when we cease from a downward sloping glidepath to a sudden plunge. It will certainly hit Europe first. Indeed, that's already happening, with smelly Germans being told not to shower but wash with a wet rag and to gather firewood for the coming winter. There will be civil disorders and toppling of governments by nonconstitutional means, as we already saw some time ago in Sri Lanka. But unlike the AstroTurf color revolutions the US and our satellites have specialized in for decades these will be true grassroots outpourings of desperation. Some countries like France and Italy have a real proclivity for that sort of thing, others like Germany not so much.

What about the US? Maybe there's too much Anglo-Saxon law-abidingness—and for the time being, too much danger of harsh repression à la the January 6 "insurrection," crushing of alt-lite groups like the Proud Boys and Patriot Front, politization of law enforcement, and so forth. Things would only get "kinetic" here when cities dissolve into chaos and people outside rural areas starting pondering who gets to eat today and who doesn't, but I don't know how soon that might happen.

How bad will it get? Two of my former Senate colleagues, now at a major Washington think tank, on a recent podcast urged us to remember (specifically, in the aftermath of the *Dobbs* ruling overturning *Roe v. Wade*) that—

> ... we're fellow Americans, we're fellow citizens. We are not enemies.
> ... [to] quote Lincoln ..., he says in the first inaugural address, "We are not enemies, but friends. We must never be enemies." It's a nice thought, a pious wish. But is it true? Was it true in Lincoln's time? Bear in mind that both Northerners and Southerners –

> In 1861 . . . worshipped the same God, read the same Bible, honored the same Founding Fathers, claimed fidelity to the same Constitution. In today's America, like in the rest of the Woke Woke West, we can't even agree on our pronouns [or on what a "woman" is. We *are* moral aliens to one another. We are *not* "fellow" anythings except in the most superficial, formal sense.]. . . . The term "cold" civil war, a war that might possibly turn "hot," has become a commonplace in American discourse. That should not come as a surprise when we remember how the Red Gnostic seizure of power in Russia [a century ago], to which many draw parallels to America today, didn't triumph without bloodily overcoming ferocious popular resistance. The rising tide of Rainbow Gnosticism in America now, whether it succeeds or fails, may turn out to be just as destructive. Let's remember too that, if you credit the William Strauss and Neil Howe "Fourth Turning" cycle, we are only about halfway through a crisis that will totally transform this country, assuming there's a country left at all by the end of it.

There's also the ethnic factor, to which I alluded earlier. In addition to their terminal (and it may *be* terminal) law-abidingness, Americans have a poor understanding of their identity as an *ethnos*. If you ask the average American who doesn't belong to a "hyphenated" identity like African, Asian, Latinx, etc., or specifically Polish, Italian, Jewish, Greek, Cuban, Haitian, Japanese, whatever "What *makes* you an American, what *is* an American? *Who and what are you?*"—he or she would have no idea what you were talking about. "Uhhh. . .. muh 'Constitution' . . . muh 'democracy'?" "Uhhh. . . [looking at his arm] . . . I guess, uh, I'm 'white'?" "Uhhh. . . my grandfather was Dutch I think. . . or was that Danish?" "Uhhh . . . I think my mom's Presbyterian. . .?"

When I was a kid more than half a century ago, from a family of relatively recent immigrant origin, if you told the average non-hyphenated American that Americans weren't a nation, he'd have punched you in the nose, and deservedly so. Now, after decades of multi-culti propaganda based two great lies—one: that we're a "civic" nation, not an "ethnic" one, and two: that America is a "nation of immigrants"—we don't know who or what the hell we are. This is one reason, as the late Samuel Huntington put it, our relationship with the world is so messed up, dominated by foreign and corporate lobbies: if you don't know who you are, how can you tell what your interests are?

Mind you, I'm not saying the Constitution is unimportant, but as I mentioned, it's an epiphenomenon, not the foundation but an expression of something more fundamental: the people who created it who were, well, *Englishmen* who'd fought for their rights as Englishmen and separated from the Crown as a consequence. Hint: that's why we're speaking English. That's *why* we have the Constitution we do. That's the identity to which those of us not of Anglo-Saxon stock assimilated *to*, before assimilation became a hate concept. Observed John Jay, the first Chief Justice of the US Supreme Court: "Providence has been pleased to give us this one connected country to one united people—a people descended from the same ancestors, speaking the same language, professing the same religion, attached to the same principles of government, very similar in their manners and customs." Writes Huntington: "Subsequent generations of immigrants were assimilated into the culture of the founding settlers and modified it, but did not change it fundamentally. . . . Would America be the America it is [or was?] today if in the 17th and 18th centuries it had been settled not by British Protestants but by French, Spanish, or Portuguese Catholics? The answer is no. It would not be America; it would be Quebec, Mexico, or Brazil." The *ethnos* makes the constitution, not the other way around.

Point of illustration: We've only had two constitutions, the first one, the Articles of Confederation, was only in effect for a few years. How many constitutions has France had? Hint: the current setup since 1958 is called the Fifth Republic. Plus lots of monarchy, a couple of Napoleons. Yet France remained France because there are these people, an *ethnos*, called "Frenchmen," a unique historical mélange of Germanic Franks (hence the name) and Romanized Celtic Gauls. Sure, since even before the recent influx of migrants from Africa and the Middle East, there are other *ethnoi* indigenous to France: Basques, Bretons, German-speaking Alsatians (as Bonaparte—himself a Corsican, really a kind of Italian—once said, "Let the Alsatians speak German so long as their swords swing French"). But none of these are the "state-building nation" as it's known in political theory. We don't call that country "Alsatia," "Corsicania," or "Bretonia." France exists because of French people specifically, not these others.

My point here isn't really about France, which has its own elite pathologies. (The ridiculous current president, "Li'l Macro" as I like to call him, once said there is no such think as "French culture," notwithstanding the millions of people around the world who both know it and appreciate it.) The point is that states and their constitutional orders depend on the self-awareness of the people who created that state and their desire for a sovereign, independent political expression—even one along the lines of a limited, minimalist state most of us would prefer. To a greater or lesser extent, that self-awareness, which is usually though not always ethnic, is still to be found in some European countries (especially, and paradoxically, in the former communist countries) and even more so outside of Europe. In America that self-awareness is more questionable. Put another way, many Frenchmen still know they are French, Russians Russian, Poles Polish, Japanese Japanese, Yorubas Yoruba, and so forth. Americans—eh, it's at best an open question. In my opinion, that doesn't bode well for our long-term future as we enter a period of existential turmoil.

We also, in the short term, need to take into account a looming regime crisis: Uncle Joe Biden is incompetent and *everybody* sees he needs to go but there's nobody capable who will replace him—certainly not that cackling moron set to take his desk in the Oval Office. Meanwhile, the GOP, with very few exceptions, isn't much better. Also—spoiler alert!—watch for election fraud in November, for which we're already seeing the media spin, and which could itself be a trigger. In any case, we ain't gonna vote our way out of this. As someone on Twitter put it, "America today is like a corpse being consumed by maggots. Liberals are rooting for the maggots. Conservatives are rooting for the corpse."

All in all, it's a real Shinola Storm in which we'll be faced with a lot of what are called "known unknowns"—information deficits of which we are aware—plus no doubt a bunch of "unknown unknowns": you don't know what you don't know; too many variables, not enough constants. I do take some comfort in the hope that whatever happens, it very well may take down the globalist Davos Great Reset crowd. What comes next, I don't know. Once the GAE Sauron tanks, will it be replaced by a Eurasian Saruman—or will there be a genuine opportunity for global pluralism and, domestically, revival of some kind of healthy order reflecting our country's best traditions and values? Maybe I'm a giddy optimist after all. . . .

I do hope that once the ordeal is over, some sort of decent America can arise, perhaps only in part of what used to be the United States. Anticipating something comparable to what the Soviet Union went through in the 1990s, I reckon the whole thing should be over by about 2027, hopefully sooner but by 2030 at the latest.

But first we have to get through it. Which brings us back to my parting admonitions to your predecessors last year, which I see no need to change:

'I think your ability to impact the "big picture" regarding any of this is slim to none. Even our ability to discern the signs of the times in an era of pervasive Gnostic deceit abetted by technologies unimaginable just a few years ago is limited.

'Nevertheless, for what it is worth, I put before you three practical tasks for your consideration.

'Firstly, be vigilant against deception, in a day when assuredly evil men and impostors will grow worse and worse, deceiving, and being deceived. Admittedly, this is a tough one, given the ever-present lying that surrounds us and the suppression of dissent. Try to sift truth from falsehood but don't become obsessed because, in many cases, you won't be able to be sure anyway. Focus most on what's proximate to you and on the people most important to you. . . . Be skeptical—about everyone. . . . There may be a cost. As Solzhenitsyn said, "He who chooses the lie as his principle inevitably chooses violence as his method."

'Secondly, as stewards of every worldly charge placed on us by God and by other people—as fathers and mothers, as husbands and wives, as sons and daughters, as neighbors, as students, as workers, as citizens, as patriots—we must prudently care for those to whom we have a duty within the limited power and wisdom allotted to us. Start with yourselves. Be as self-sufficient as possible. Get involved in your community; that leftist slogan is actually a good one: think globally, act locally. Befriend your neighbors. Learn a real skill—electricity, plumbing, carpentry. Farm! *Don't* go to law school, for goodness' sake. Get in shape. Eat and sleep right. Have plenty of the essentials: food, fuel, gold, ammunition. Learn to shoot. Limit computer and phone time. Cultivate healthy personal relationships—real ones, not virtual ones. Marry young, have kids—especially women, don't get seduced by all that "career" nonsense. [Nobody on his or her deathbed ever said, "Gosh, I wish I'd spent more time at the office.] Read old books. Cultivate virtue. Go to church.

'Simply being what used to be considered normal and leading a pro-ductive life is becoming the most revolutionary act one can perform. With that in mind, find the strength to be revolutionaries indeed!

'You've seen the meme: Hard times create strong men; Strong men create good times; Good times create weak men; Weak men create hard times. Well, take it from the weakling generation that brought them to you: the hard times, they is a-coming. But they won't last forever. If you live through them—and some of you will not—we'll see what possibilities, as of now literally un-imaginable, might then exist. But you will need to be personally fit to take advantage of them. You will also need to be part of some kind of sustainable community of likeminded people.

'Third, for those of you who are believers, particularly Christians, we must pray without ceasing, firm in faith that, through whatever hardships may lie ahead, even the very hairs of our head are all numbered, and the final triumph of Truth is never in doubt.

'Thank you, and good luck. You're going to need it.'

These remarks were delivered to the 2022 Ron Paul Scholars Seminar in Washington, DC, Sept. 2, 2022.

The Only Thing We Have to Fear
Is Extinction Itself

"The Only ThingWe Have to Fear Is Extinction Itself"

James George Jatras | Ron Paul Institute | September 6, 2023

Today it's hard for anyone under the age of 50 to appreciate how genuine and pervasive was fear of a nuclear holocaust during the Cold War between the US- and Soviet-led blocs.

Books, movies, and TV both reflected and stoked popular anxiety about the possible "end of civilization as we know it." The heyday for this was in the 1950s and 1960s, with books like *The Long Tomorrow* (1955) and *On the Beach* (1957, with a 1959 film adaptation), and films like *Fail Safe, Seven Days in May, Dr. Strangelove* (all in 1964, while the real-life scare of the 1962 Cuban Missile Crisis was fresh in people's minds).

There appeared to be a bit of a lull during the 1970s era of US-Soviet *détente* under Nixon, Ford, and Carter, perhaps also reflecting elite sympathy for socialism and an expected future convergence between the ideological groupings, which on a basic level shared the same globalist, materialist values. But nuclear terror returned with a vengeance in the 1980s—for example, *The Day After* (1983) and the animated *When the Wind Blows* (1986). And who can forget (certainly no male person!) the delightful Nena's 1983 music video *Neunundneunzig Luftballons*.

The Left, both in the United States and worldwide, was unanimous that Ronald Reagan, a self-confessed anti-communist, was a reckless cowboy who wanted to blow up the planet. As that great philosopher, Sting, put it in his 1985 song "The Russians":

> *There is no historical precedent*
> *To put the words in the mouth of the president?*
> *There's no such thing as a winnable war*
> *It's a lie we don't believe anymore*
> *Mister Reagan says, "We will protect you"*
> *I don't subscribe to this point of view*
> *Believe me when I say to you*
> *I hope the Russians love their children too*

The irony is that Reagan's own views were hardly different from the ones the song sought to promote. As he stated jointly with Soviet premier Mikhail Gorbachev that very same year, 1985: "A nuclear war cannot be won and must never be fought," a view that prevailed until the USSR imploded just a few years later.

We live in a very different world now, where the prospect of nuclear annihilation barely registers with anyone.

Just as big earthquakes are often preceded by foreshocks, major wars are frequently heralded by smaller conflicts. Before World War I: the Franco-German Morocco crises (1906 and 1911), the Italo-Turkish War (1911–12), the two Balkan Wars (1912, 1913). Before World War II: the Second Italo-Ethiopian War (1935–37) and—the most famous pre-conflagration rumble of them all—the Spanish Civil War (1936–39).

Today, we are looking at a possible regional war in West Africa, centering on American and French demands that "democracy" be restored in Niger. (As one Indian publication put it, "Death follows Victoria Nuland.") Then, of course, there's China/Taiwan.

But the obvious Spanish Civil War-rank conflict of the moment is Ukraine.

I don't think we need to go into all the details of how we got here, but just in brief:

- Relentless NATO expansion after 1991;
- The 2014 US- and EU-backed coup that overthrew Victor Yanukovich, followed by the Russian annexation of Crimea and the new Kiev regime's launch of a war to repress rebellions in the Russian-speaking east and south of the country;
- The 2015 Minsk agreements, which provided for Ukraine's neutrality and decentralization, and for reintegration of the rebellious areas with protections of their language and culture—agreements that both Ukrainian and European former officials have admitted they never intended to implement, seeing them only as a delaying ruse for building up a force capable of conquering the Donbas;
- A relentless program of Ukraine's NATO-ization in all but name under Obama, Trump, and Biden; and
- Washington's peremptory rejection of Moscow's 2021 *ultimata* to the United States and NATO to resolve the conflict diplomatically, with the hope that Russia, baited into an incursion into Ukraine, would be bled white in an Afghanistan-style insurgency and by crushing sanctions that would "turn the ruble into rubble," pancake Russia's economy, and lead to regime change in Moscow.

Oops. Russia's expected ruin didn't happen. Even the mainstream media cheerleaders of only a fortnight ago now admit that Ukraine is losing, assigning the blame not to the geniuses that thought up this strategy (if it can be called that) but to Ukraine's being too "casualty averse"—even as that country is turning into one vast graveyard. There's speculation that some in Washington and other western capitals are seeking an "off-ramp"—if for no other reason than the need to focus on the really big show, a looming war with China. Some suggest that in the end, we'll just walk away, consigning Ukraine to the Memory Hole along with Afghanistan. All that's left then is for GOP neocons to whine that the Biden Administration was too stingy with their aid and "lost Ukraine" while they gear up for the main event in the western Pacific.

Personally, I don't think that will happen. Nobody cares about Afghanistan but the Afghans, but if Washington walks away from Ukraine it's effectively conceding that the US, through NATO, no longer is the security hegemon of Europe. That means the effective end of NATO, in fact if not in name; and where NATO goes, its concubine, the European Union, won't be far behind.

More to the point, though, the notion that this will soon end with a whimper misses the whole point. None of this is really about Ukraine, which is just an expendable tool to hurt Russia. (Maybe the Poles or Lithuanians or Romanians are eager to volunteer for the job once we're fresh out of Ukrainians.) Ukraine is just a variable; the constant is *Ruthenia delenda est.* Russia must be destroyed.

Gilbert Doctorow, a noted observer of Russian affairs, likens the current situation to that of Napoleon's 1812 Russian campaign depicted by Leo Tolstoy in *War and Peace*. Today as then, what happens next will be less due to this or that policymaker making this or that bad decision. Rather, "the precondition for war is the near universal acceptance of the logic of the coming war."

What is that logic today? It's simple: the ruling circles in the United States (needless to add, with their sock puppets in western capitals) are utterly, unself-consciously convinced that they are the living embodiment of all virtue, truth, and progress in what Russian Foreign Minister Sergei Lavrov described as the "replication of the experience of Bolshevism and Trotskyism"—to cite Reagan, morphing ourselves into a new Evil Empire in place of the old one. As neocon kingpins William Kristol and Robert Kagan put it in their 1996 manifesto, the policy of the United States in the coming era must be one of "benevolent global hegemony" intended to last—well, forever. Its moral content is exemplified, on the one hand, by US support for subjugation of the canonical Ukrainian Orthodox Church and, on the other, the spectacle of a transgender US serviceperson acting as a PR official for the Ukrainian military declaring that "we're human," and the Russians "most definitely aren't."

As I like to say: There's no Transatlanticism without transgenderism.

Unsurprisingly, regarding their alleged lack of human-ness, the Russians disagree. But who cares what they think? Our leaders see not only Putin but Russians in general as an obstacle to the radiant future, where every knee will bow before the sacred rainbow flag.

Sun Tzu says, "If you know the enemy and know yourself, you need not fear the result of a hundred battles. If you know neither the enemy nor yourself, you will succumb in every battle." The Russians more or less know themselves. They kind of know us, but not as well as they think they do, with rather a tendency to project normalcy onto fundamentally abnormal people. On the other hand, our rulers—dangerous people whose levels of arrogance and ignorance defy description: monkeys with nuclear hand grenades—know neither themselves nor the Russians.

On top of that, as Doctorow further observes, the mechanisms that lent some stability and restraint to the US-Soviet standoff are now all but gone, rendering the once-"unthinkable" of the 1950s' nuke horror films all-too-thinkable today:

> . . . no one wants war, neither Washington nor Moscow. However, the step-by-step dismantling of the channels of communication, of the symbolic projects for cooperation across a wide array of domains, and now dismantling of all the arms limitation agreements that took decades to negotiate and ratify, plus the incoming new weapons systems that leave both sides with under 10 minutes to decide how to respond to alarms of incoming missiles—all of this prepares the way for the Accident to end all Accidents. Such false alarms occurred in the Cold War but some slight measure of mutual trust prompted restraint. That is all gone now and if something goes awry, we are all dead ducks.

"No one wants war." A similar thought was expressed by Hermann Göring, when he was on trial at Nuremberg:

> Of course the people don't want war; neither in Russia nor in England nor in America, nor for that matter in Germany. That is understood. . . . But after all, it's the leaders of the country who determine the policy, and it's always a simple matter to drag the people along whether it's a democracy, a fascist dictatorship, or a parliament, or a communist dictatorship. Voice or no voice, the people can always be brought to the bidding of the leaders. That is

easy. All you have to do is tell them they are being attacked, and denounce the pacifists for lack of patriotism, and exposing the country to greater danger.

So I guess Doctorow is a bit off the mark in suggesting that "no one wants war." Clearly, *somebody* wants war. A lot of very important "somebodies" wanted this war in Ukraine. They wanted war in the Balkans in the 1990s. They wanted war in Afghanistan, Iraq (twice!), Libya, Yemen, Syria, and a dozen places in Africa where we have almost no idea what's going on.

"All you have to do is tell them they are being attacked . . ." I can't help but think of the meme with two blank-face NPCs, one wearing a pink knit hat mindlessly repeating "Russia! Russia! Russia!," the other with a red MAGA hat chanting "China! China! China!" Between them is the seal of the CIA with the eagle saying, "Yes, yes, my pretties. That's it. That's it."

Here we are, 60 years after the fact, with the growing recognition by even the most spoon-fed normies that the CIA had something to do with the assassination of Jack Kennedy. In fact, we have here today perhaps the foremost authority on the topic, Mr. Jacob Hornberger. Yet doubting our rulers' truthiness still is treated as a thought crime. A little while ago, Vivek Ramaswamy was the target of a media hate fest for (in the words of *The New Republic*) "spout[ing] conspiracy theories about January 6 and 9/11." Oh no! "Conspiracy theories"! (Or, as they are known when they turn out to be true, "spoiler alerts.") The heretic Ramaswamy evidently believes—shocking as this sounds—that our government has not been entirely honest about these matters. He must be a dupe for the Russians! Or for the Chinese!—which *The New Republic* also implies.

You may have heard some people compare the "lawfare" being directed against Donald Trump with the evident aim of eliminating the likely opponent next year of the desiccated-husk-of-Hunter-Biden's-dad (assuming ol' Joe will be the Democratic nominee, which I don't) to the behavior of a banana republic. This is a gratuitous insult to the friendly spider-infested nations to our south!

I recently suggested to a sober observer of public affairs that the strategic goal is keeping Trump off the ballot in one or more must-win states for him, like Pennsylvania, Michigan, Georgia, Arizona, to which he responded: "That's a recipe for civil war." (I tried to imagine what Republicans taking to the streets would look like. A mob of decrepit Boomers rolling their motorized wheelchairs down to the corner and burning down the post office?) Anyway, taking him out via lawfare seems to be Plan A. If that fails—well, Plan B would get us into Mr. Hornberger's area of expertise.

The term "cold civil war"—a war that might possibly turn "hot"—has become a commonplace in American discourse. So has the expression "national divorce." In 1861 Americans both North and South worshipped the same God, read the same Bible, honored the same Founding Fathers, claimed fidelity to the same Constitution. In today's America, we can't even agree on our pronouns or on what a "woman" is, much less on what it means to be an American. We are moral aliens to one another, indeed enemies. What actually holds the former American republic together? "Muh Constitution"? "Muh democracy"?

Keep in mind, we're not talking about a mere political crisis that will get solved in an election or two. Not even about political and constitutional collapse, or even a financial and economic calamity—that's coming too, in part because of the impact of the Ukraine war on the dollar-denominated global system—but a fundamental challenge to the social fabric itself, and not just in the United States.

A watershed was passed with covid and the measures—the lockdowns, the masks, social distancing and monitoring, the clot shot, censorship of dissent, all combined with a pervasive, inescapable external and internal panopticon: as the troubadour of transhumanism Yuval Harari writes, "we are seeing a change in the nature of surveillance from over the skin surveillance to under the skin surveillance"—supposedly intended to deal with a virus, accomplishing within a few short months what decades of climate hysteria could not, summed up under the moniker "the Great Reset" and its ubiquitous slogan "Build Back Better."

Taken together what we're experiencing has all the appearance of a controlled demolition of all established human interactions in anticipation of their replacement by something we are assured by our betters will be an improvement. The contours of the "new normal" in the post-American America hurtling in our direction have already become so familiar as to need little elaboration:

- Infringement of traditional liberties based on "keeping us safe";
- "Cancel culture";
- Blurring of the lines between Big Government, Big Finance, Big Pharma, Big Data, etc., amounting to corporate state capture; and, not directly based on supposed anti-virus measures but closely tracking with them,
- Joint government and corporate promulgation of socially destructive, historically counterfeit ideologies ("intersectionality," LGBTQI+++, feminism, multiculturalism, "critical race theory"), with principal targeting of children subject to sexualization and predation by those expressing what were once quaintly known as abnormal appetites and identities.

These so-called "values"—which, remember, are effectively the official ideology of the West, which we seek "benevolently" to impose on the rest of the world, by force if necessary—in turn accelerate longstanding trends towards infertility and demographic collapse pointing to thinning the human herd and replacement via post-human society, transhumanism, and bio-engineering. This is not just "political" but a strike at the heart of human existence: the spiritual, moral, and even biological basis for marriage, family formation, and production of the next generation. In a word: depopulation.

A few years ago, His Royal Highness, the late Prince Philip of the United Kingdom, perhaps half in jest delivered this thigh-slapper: "In the event that I am reincarnated, I would like to return as a deadly virus, to contribute something to solving overpopulation." Some of you may have heard of groups like Extinction Rebellion and BirthStrike: "Are you terrified about the future that lies ahead for contemporary and future youth? Do you want to maximize your positive impact on the Climate Change Crisis? You can protect children while fighting climate change and systematic corruption by refusing to procreate!" Makes perfect sense: preserve a better planet for future generations by eliminating future generations. It reminds me of Otto von Bismarck's comparing the idea of preventive war to committing suicide out of fear of death. (That's not as abstract as it might sound. Recently a young woman in Canada seeking help for depression and suicidal ideation was advised by hospital staff that she might be interested in their tried and Trudeau-ed "Medical Assistance in Dying (MAID)" euthanasia program. Tempted to kill yourself? Let us help you!)

But why stop at half measures? The Voluntary Human Extinction Movement, VHEMT (pronounced "vehement," according to their website): "We're the only species evolved enough to consciously go extinct for the good of all life, or which needs to. Success would be humanity's crowning achievement. May we live long and die out."

Maybe they're on to something! In his landmark work *The Socialist Phenomenon*, the late Russian mathematician and student of history Igor Shafarevich took note of what he believed is a collective human death impulse:

> The idea of the death of mankind—not the death of specific people but literally the end of the human race—evokes a response in the human psyche. It arouses and attracts people, albeit with differing intensity in different epochs and in different individuals. The scope of influence of this idea causes us to suppose that every individual is affected by it to a greater or lesser degree and that it is a universal trait of the human psyche.
>
>   This idea is not only manifested in the individual experience of a great number of specific persons, but is also capable of uniting people (in contrast to delirium, for example) i.e., it is a social force. The impulse toward self-destruction may be regarded as an element in the psyche of mankind as a whole. [...]
>
>   In the Freudian view (first expressed in the article "Beyond the Pleasure Principle"), the human psyche can be reduced to a manifestation of two main instincts: the life instinct or Eros and the death instinct or Thanatos (or the Nirvana principle). Both are general biological categories, fundamental properties of living things in general. The death instinct is a manifestation of general "inertia" or a tendency of organic life to return to a more elementary state from which it had been aroused by an external disturbing force. ["Dust thou art, unto dust shalt thou return."] The role of the life instinct is essentially to prevent a living organism from returning to the inorganic state by any path other than that which is immanent in it.
>
>   Marcuse [Shafarevich refers here to Herbert Marcuse, theorist of the Frankfurt School, known for his adaptation of the theory of class conflict in classical Marxism to other social divides, notably in the area of sex, setting the stage for "intersectionality"] introduces a greater social factor into this scheme, asserting that the death instinct expresses itself in the desire to be liberated from tension, as an attempt to rid oneself of the suffering and discontent which are specifically engendered by social factors.

With the failure of the Ukrainian offensive, Moscow now faces a dilemma. Do they move decisively to impose a military solution that ends the war, or do they continue to show restraint in the hopes that somebody, somewhere— Kiev, Washington, London, Brussels—decides it's time to sue for peace? Keen not to take a precipitous step that might bring about a direct clash of NATO and Russian forces, so far they've opted for the latter—I repeat: so far.

The West faces its own dilemma. Do our rulers concede defeat, which effectively means the end of the Global American Empire (the GAE)? Or do they drag things out as long as possible, hoping Moscow will fall for another Minsk-type ceasefire, with the Kremlin playing the part of Charlie Brown taking another run at kicking the football, having been promised that *this* time we'll keep our word? Or, mistaking Russian restraint for weakness, do they push the envelope by inserting a "coalition of the willing" into western Ukraine, challenging Russian naval forces in the Black Sea, encouraging and equipping the Ukrainians to step up attacks on Moscow and other Russian cities, staging some sort of false flag of the type that has proved so effective in other conflicts? In other words, do we double down? That's in addition to opening up other asymmetrical theaters in the Balkans, Syria, Iran, the Taiwan Strait, and elsewhere.

In mistakenly projecting a rational actor mentality onto their opponents, the Russians seem to be acutely aware of the legitimate concern that decisive military action on the ground could panic NATO and trigger an uncontrolled escalation. They seem oblivious to the contrary concern, that, by holding back and waiting for a reasonable dialogue that will never take place, they are in effect encouraging their adversary to stage one reckless provocation after another—in the sustained belief that some *deus ex machina* can snatch victory from the jaws of defeat—resulting in the very uncontrolled escalation that Moscow seeks to avoid.

Even these speculations assume that the miserable specimens of humanity calling the shots in Western capitals would only *risk* a direct conflict but would not *deliberately* choose it. But is that assumption correct? As Doctorow notes, the old Cold War restraints have broken down. Maybe demonstration of a teeny-tiny, low-yield nuke is just the thing to show that non-human Vladof Putler that the GAE is serious!

What could possibly go wrong?

Recently on his podcast Judge Andrew Napolitano showed part of a computer simulation of a US-Russia nuclear exchange in which the initial toll on the US population was only ("only"!) about nine percent, while on Russia it was around 62 percent. (Given that Russia has more warheads than we do, I don't know how they came up with that, but I didn't conduct the simulation.) Is it so impossible that somewhere, somebody might look at those data and decide it's a tolerable tradeoff? (Later on, the simulation has pretty much everyone on earth starving to death from nuclear winter, with agriculture in the northern hemisphere unviable for several years. Now *there's* a way to resolve both global warming and supposed overpopulation with one stroke! Hey, VHEMT, have we got a concept for you!)

Whether or not these dolts manage to kill us all, either by deliberate action or through sheer incompetence, it's hard to escape the notion that we are approaching the edge of some profound historical moment that will have far-reaching, literally life and death consequences, both domestically and internationally. In the period preceding World War I how many Europeans suspected that their lives would soon be forever changed—and, for millions of them, ended? Who in the years, say, 1910 to 1913, could have imagined that the decades of peace, progress, and civilization in which they had grown up, and which seemingly would continue indefinitely, instead would soon descend into a horror of industrial-scale slaughter, revolution, and brutal ideologies?

Which brings us to my parting admonitions to your predecessors in this seminar, which I see no need to change:

My young friends, the impact any one of us can expect to have in the face of world-historic trends before which the fates of nations and empires fly like leaves in the autumn winds is vanishingly small. Already baked into the cake will be, I believe, hardships for you that we've become accustomed to think only happen to "other people" in "other countries" far away, not seen here since the Revolution and the Civil War, or maybe in isolated instances during the Great Depression: financial and economic disruption and, in some places, especially in urban areas, collapse; supply chains, utilities, and other aspects of basic infrastructure ceasing to function (what happens in major cities when food deliveries stop for a week?), even widespread hunger; rising levels of violence, both criminality and civil strife. These will be combined, paradoxically, with the remaining organs of authority, however discredited, desperately cracking down on the enemy within—no, not on murderers, robbers, and rapists, but on "science deniers," "religious fanatics," "haters," "conspiracy theorists," "insurrectionists," "gun nuts," "purveyors of "medical misinform-ation," Russian or Chinese "stooges," and, of course, "racists," "sexists," "homophobes," and so forth. It's the late Samuel Francis' "anarcho-tyranny" nightmare come to life with a vengeance.

Nevertheless, for what it is worth, I put before you three practical tasks for your consideration.

Firstly, be vigilant against deception, in a day when assuredly evil men and impostors will grow worse and worse, deceiving, and being deceived. Admittedly, this is a tough one, given the ever-present lying that surrounds us and the suppression of dissent. Try to sift truth from falsehood but don't become obsessed because, in many cases, you won't be able to be sure anyway. Focus most on what's proximate to you and on the people most important to you. . . . Be skeptical—about everyone. . . . There may be a cost. As Solzhenitsyn said, "He who chooses the lie as his principle inevitably chooses violence as his method."

Secondly, as stewards of every worldly charge placed on us by God and by other people—as fathers and mothers, as husbands and wives, as sons and daughters, as neighbors, as students, as workers, as citizens, as patriots—we must prudently care for those to whom we have a duty within the limited power and wisdom allotted to us. Start with yourselves. Be as self-sufficient as possible. Get involved in your community; that leftist slogan is actually a good one: think globally, act locally. Befriend your neighbors. Learn a real skill—electricity, plumbing, carpentry. Farm! Don't go to law school, for goodness' sake. Get in shape. Eat and sleep right. Have plenty of the essentials: food, fuel, gold, ammunition. Learn to shoot. Limit computer and phone time. Experience nature. Cultivate healthy personal relationships—real ones, not virtual ones. Marry young, have kids, lots of them—especially women, don't get seduced by all that "career" nonsense. Nobody on his or her deathbed ever said, "Gosh, I wish I'd spent more time at the office." Read old books. Cultivate virtue. Go to church.

Simply being what used to be considered normal and leading a productive life is becoming the most revolutionary act one can perform. With that in mind, find the strength to be revolutionaries indeed! In the face of the culture of death and extinction, choose to affirm life.

You've seen the meme: Hard times create strong men; strong men create good times; good times create weak men; weak men create hard times. Well, take it from the weakling Boomer generation that brought them to you: the hard times, they is a-coming. But they won't last forever. If you live through them—and some of you will not—we'll see what possibilities, as of now literally unimaginable, might then exist. But you will need to be personally fit to take advantage of them. You will also need to be part of some kind of sustainable community of likeminded people.

Thirdly, for those of you who are believers, particularly Christians, we must pray without ceasing, firm in faith that, through whatever hardships may lie ahead, even the very hairs of our head are all numbered, and the final triumph of Truth is never in doubt.

Thank you, and good luck. You're going to need it.

A version of this presentation was given to the Ron Paul Institute's Scholars Seminar on September 1, 2023, in Washington, DC.

Only Systemic Change Can Save the U.S.

Only Systemic Change Can Save the U.S.

Executive Intelligence Review | January 28, 2022

This is an edited transcription of an interview with Jim Jatras, conducted by Mike Billington on Jan. 14, 2022. Mr. Jatras served in the State Department in Mexico and on Russian affairs. He also served for many years as an adviser to the Republican leadership in the Senate. He then worked in the private sector, while establishing himself as a leading analyst on political issues internationally. Subheads have been added.

EIR: *This is Mike Billington with the* Executive Intelligence Review, *the Schiller Institute, and The LaRouche Organization. I'm here speaking with Jim Jatras. Would you like to say anything else about your career, Jim?*

Jim Jatras: No, I don't think so, except to say that the extent to which somebody can be in the belly of the Beast for 30 years and come out relatively sane, I hope so. I guess we'll let the viewers decide that.

'It's Later Than You Think'

EIR: *You presented a speech to a student seminar at the Ron Paul Institute last September titled "It's Later Than You Think." What did you mean by that?*

Jatras: Well, we tend to think of political and economic developments in a kind of isolation—what are good policies, what are bad policies, what are constructive, what are destructive—rather than looking at the underlying health of society itself and macro historical trends that make such policy choices viable or not.

My concern was, and is, that we are approaching some kind of a crunch, some kind of a major crisis, not only in America but globally, that not only could totally remake what it means to be an American, but maybe means the end of the American nation and the republic itself. I would even go as far as to say, I don't think the American Republic, as we've known it, really exists anymore. I'd like to ask the question of people: how many republics have there been in France? Well, this is the Fifth Republic. Yet the French nation still exists.

Many Americans are so wedded to the notion of our constitution, our political structures, that they lose sight of the fact that that's all they are—they're just structures. Those structures are going through the biggest crisis, certainly since the Great Depression and possibly since the Civil War. And we don't really know what's going to come out on the other side of it. I think the problems America faces today are not going to get solved by an election or a political party or a political movement—we're going to have to go through a great destructive ordeal of some sort. And we cannot really envision what comes out on the other side.

On the Recent Russia-U.S. Diplomacy

EIR: *The talks this week between Russia and the United States, while not an absolute failure, were described by Russians as the West having failed to budge an inch on the fundamental issues of guarantees for Russian security. Nonetheless, several leading Russian experts, including Gilbert Doctorow and Dmitri Trenin, have described the talks as a victory for Russia by forcing the U.S. to admit that they would not conduct a war with a nuclear armed Russia over Ukraine. You have headed an organization called the American Institute in Ukraine and have insight into this. What's your view of this week's diplomatic efforts?*

Jatras: I'm basically in agreement with the analysts you cited, I think sometimes there's too much of a focus on, you might say, the CNN headline—which is: "Will Russia invade Ukraine?"—when that is not really what this is about. In fact, it's not even primarily about Ukraine, in the sense that it's really about NATO expansion and the United States and our satellites. Let's not even call them allies, they are satellites, basically on Russia's doorstep, its front porch, its back porch and everywhere else, threatening its vital security interests. And the Russians have basically signaled that they've had enough. As President Putin said, "We have no place left to retreat to." So, I think they're coming back to say, "All right, we're giving you one last chance to address our security concerns seriously, to provide us with guarantees."

I don't know what those guarantees would look like, by the way, since the West can never be trusted to keep its word. But, nonetheless, I think they're making one last chance to say, "Will you take our serious concerns seriously? Here are two draft treaties. Do we have a deal or not?" And I think the West is coming back and saying, "No, we don't have a deal."

We can delay Ukraine's accession to NATO for about 10 years. Maybe we can have some more confidence-building measures in Europe, things of that sort. I don't think that's going to wash with the Russians. As you mentioned, Gil Doctorow, as he's pointed out, thinks that the Russians are ready to act in some decisive and dramatic way, stationing advanced hypersonic weapons close to the United States that would give them the same flight time to our major cities as we are posing a threat to Russian cities. Maybe some kind of surgical strikes within Ukraine against hostile forces that would force NATO to wake up and smell the coffee and say, "We have to accommodate these concerns or else the pain level is going to keep getting ratcheted up."

NATO is no longer the master of all it sees in Europe, as we were, say, in the 1990s, and the Russians are in a position to act. They're acting unilaterally, and there's really not much we can do about it unless we want to start a major war.

Unfortunately, what I'm seeing from most of the establishment—there was an absurd discussion at the Atlantic Council, (which, just saying Atlantic Council almost tells you how absurd it was going to be), where the most reasonable person on the call, if you can believe it, was Evelyn Farkas—who had this horrible piece in *Defense One* basically talking about how we need to fight a war with the Russians in Ukraine. But she was the only one who took that seriously. The rest of them were all saying, "No, no, the Russians are just bluffing. We just need to crank up the weaponry going into Ukraine and crank up the sanctions threats, and the Russians will back down." That's what I think is the dominant view within the establishment.

On Those Who Propose Nuclear War

EIR: *This brings up the issue of some of the mad men who openly propose a nuclear war. The head of the U.S. Strategic Command, Admiral Richard, said earlier last year that because of the rise of Russia and China, nuclear war, which we used to consider unlikely, is now likely, which is literally madness. And Senator Roger Wicker directly calling for a first strike nuclear attack on Russia. Do you think these people have the power to influence decision-making on the questions of war?*

Jatras: I think they can influence it. Even I don't believe there are people who are crazy enough to actually deliberately push the button and say, let's have a nuclear war. Maybe there are. They've got to be out there somewhere. But the bigger concern I have is that we are in a very dangerous period, especially since I think the Russians will do something fairly dramatic before the end of the month, my guess is.

Then you always have the risk of unintended escalation. Increasingly for the last few years, you have American and Russian planes playing chicken over the Black Sea or the Baltic Sea, or with boats—something unintended could happen, leads to an escalation, and then we don't really know what happens after that. So, the risk is there. The question is, can we find some way to come to an understanding of security in Eastern Europe, which basically means getting out of Russia's face, or can we not? I find it very hard to believe this establishment can accommodate them. So that risk will be there.

On the 2014 Coup in Ukraine

EIR: *The Obama administration and the Trump administration and the Biden administration have all referred to the violent overthrow of the elected government in Ukraine in 2014 as a "democratic revolution." You know the situation well. What can you say about that coup and its aftermath today?*

Jatras: Let's remember what triggered it. You hear, again, misreported in the Western media, that it's because [President Viktor] Yanukovych was Moscow's stooge and he refused to proceed with a deal with the European Union. All Yanukovych did—first off, he wanted his country to be non-aligned, not either part of a Western bloc nor part of a Russian led bloc. He very much wanted to be a neutral country, which many people, by the way, are even proposing now as a solution to the problem. Well, that solution has never been acceptable to the West. We want Ukraine in our camp, by hook or by crook, despite the fact that Ukraine is a very, very divided country.

If you look at the electoral map, you look at the linguistic maps, the only way to hold Ukraine together is by having it straddle both sides of the East-West divide. Anybody with any sense knows that, but that's not good enough with Victoria Nuland and people like that. You have this almost Bolshevik mentality which says, "The people of Ukraine have chosen their historical path." No, they haven't. The people of Ukraine are certainly as divided as the people in the United States are. They haven't made a choice of any historical direction at all. It was, as you say, a coup, and it was clearly planned for many years in advance. A lot of money being poured in there by the National Endowment for Democracy (NED) and other Soros organizations and other outside groups, to prepare for a color revolution, the overthrow of the Yanukovych government, similar to what we saw recently in Belarus and very recently in Kazakhstan, an attempt to do that as well. These things don't just come out of thin air, whatever the local roots of those might happen to be. Yanukovych, unlike President Tokayev in Kazakhstan recently, dithered. He couldn't make up his mind whether to accommodate the demands or to try to defend himself and to crush what was an insurrection—a real one, not a fake one like we talk about a year ago here in this country. He ended up paying for it by being driven out of office. At that point, we had this triumphalism coming from the West. "Ukraine is ours! Ukraine is coming to the West! Ukraine is coming to Europe! NATO," blah blah blah.

Well, the Russians felt they had some cards they could play in the Donbas and supporting the local people there who, remember, were the people who voted for Yanukovych in the first place. They saw their vote taken away by a violent mob in the streets of Kiev, and they were not willing to accept it. Certainly, the people in Crimea were not willing to accept it, and the Russians took steps to secure their interests and the interests of those people in Ukraine.

We saw, as you know, the Minsk agreement by which Kiev was given an opportunity to repair some of this damage by saying, "OK, fine, let's have a federalization of Ukraine. Let's give self-rule to these areas and eastern Ukraine. Let's not repress the Russian language. Let's try to put Humpty Dumpty back together by accommodating the diversity of Ukraine." And of course, they and their Western sponsors had no intention of ever doing that, despite Kiev's legal commitment to the Minsk agreement. So that's where we are now.

In the meantime, the West has proceeded with NATO expansion. Right after Trump was elected, they swept Montenegro into NATO, even though the polls showed that, at best, there was an even split within the population about whether they should join NATO. I actually think the majority was opposed to that. They just swept in North Macedonia—a ridiculous name for a ridiculous excuse for a country.

Why are we doing all of this stuff? It has nothing to do with American security, certainly, but it does have to do with tightening a stranglehold around Russia, which has been the purpose of NATO ever since, supposedly, the Cold War ended in 1991.

On the Neo-Nazi Organizations in Ukraine

EIR: *What do you think of the relations between forces within the U.S. and Europe with the overtly neo-Nazi groupings within Ukraine? Even Israel has complained bitterly that Ukraine is allowing these neo-Nazi organizations to parade with swastikas and with pictures of Stepan Bandera and so forth. What's behind these institutions and how much influence do they have over actual policy?*

Jatras: It's hard to say, Mike, because we know that especially in the Republican Party—not exclusively—some of this kind of World War Two Losers Association stuff, goes all the way back to the 1950s, really, even in the late 1940s, where the CIA and MI6 and other—you may be familiar with something called the Anti-Bolshevik Bloc of Nations. This is something that was around largely led by West Ukrainian pro-Nazi elements that went all the way back to the late 1940s and was originally created by British intelligence and then was adopted by the Americans as well. But there were many groups like that. Now, some of them may have been simply people who were nationalists of various sorts and thought that their countries had gotten a raw deal on the territorial arrangements in Europe in both World Wars; others, I think, were very ideologically committed to something along the lines of fascism or Nazism. And we do see some elements like that in Ukraine.

I would draw a parallel to the way the United States, especially the intelligence agencies, have used jihadists of various sorts as proxies in various wars, going all the way back to Afghanistan in the 1980s. We used them in Bosnia, we used them in Kosovo, we used them in Libya. We are still using them today in Syria. There is, I think, a very cynical attitude of the intelligence agencies toward extremist groups, whether they're neo-Nazis or whether they're jihadists. They say, "Yeah, these people are operational, we can use them with a degree of plausible deniability. If they get into trouble, too bad for them. 'The secretary will disavow any knowledge of your actions.' But they can get the job done because they're ruthless." So, I think the degree of cynicism about groups like this is really hard for most Americans to believe, that their government would engage in this.

On the Orthodox Church in Ukraine and Russia

EIR: *The coup in Ukraine also included an effort to separate the Ukraine Orthodox Church from the Russian Orthodox Church as part of this anti-Russian hysteria. You are a member of the Greek Orthodox Church and you're active in issues regarding Orthodox Christianity. What can you tell us about what was going on in Ukraine and where that stands today?*

Jatras: Well, a lot of this is "inside baseball" in the Orthodox Church. I'm of Greek origin, personally. The parish I attend most of the time is a Russian parish although it's mostly full of just regular Americans. Some are Greeks, some Russians, some Serbs, Romanians and so forth, but it's mostly just Americans. We're still one Church at this point. We like to say the devil can never subvert our Church because he can't figure out the organization chart. We have this feud going on between Constantinople and Moscow over Ukraine and what really was the status of Ukraine in the 17th century and all this sort of thing. But I think we shouldn't lose sight of the fact that, again, just as I was mentioning with regard to jihadist and neo-Nazi groups, for outside meddlers, religion is simply another lever that they can use to try to manipulate society and to try to even break down society.

For example, we're talking about specifically the Orthodox Church. Back in 1948, there was essentially a coup in Constantinople (Istanbul) that removed the patriarch then, Maximos, who was considered to be too friendly toward the Russian Church—which, let's be honest, at the time was under the control of the Soviet authorities—and replaced him with the archbishop here in America, Athenagoras, who was actually flown over there on Truman's plane and installed by the U.S. government, the Greek government and the Turkish government acting in concert, and [the Ecumenical Patriarchate] has been an asset of the United States, the State Department and the CIA, ever since 1948. Of course, this is also consistent with Constantinople's kind of "neo-papal" aspirations within the Orthodox Church, which is itself a-historical.

At the same time, you've got Russia, which—again in a very peculiar structure among the local Orthodox churches—is itself a majority of the entire Orthodox Church, a good chunk of that being in Ukraine.

Now in Ukraine, the Orthodox Church is called the Ukrainian Orthodox Church. It is an autonomous part of the Russian Orthodox Church; it is self-ruling in virtually all aspects. That church is the canonical Church in Ukraine. Its status has not changed.

What has happened is, with U.S. support, Constantinople has tried to create a rival Orthodox church in Ukraine from a group of—actually several groups of—schismatics that they tried to cobble together into a new church. That's where we stand right now. We have two competing Orthodox churches in Ukraine. The canonical one aligned with Moscow, which is very much the majority, and a much smaller one supported by the United States and Constantinople, which is not acceptable to most of the rest of the world—in Romania and Jerusalem and Serbia and Bulgaria and the other places of the Orthodox Church.

Again, I know this is very complex "inside baseball," but what it shows is frankly a degree of sophistication, and again, cynicism of the Western powers that they're willing to manipulate this in order to make some kind of a political game. Because I think the way they see it is, just as the Maidan in 2014 was a political coup to try to separate Russia from Ukraine, this is, if you will, a spiritual coup to try to accomplish the same thing: to take two very closely kindred people in language, culture and especially religion, and set them at odds against each other. It's not working, it's not successful, but it is creating a lot of discord, a lot of unhappiness and hurt, and even to some extent, violence.

On the Various 'Color Revolutions'

EIR: *Georgia is yet another country where the NED/Soros apparatus ran a color revolution in 2003, the so-called "Rose Revolution," which saw the mobs connected to Mikhail Saakashvili overthrow the government of Eduard Shevardnadze, who himself had been the Soviet Union's Foreign Minister before becoming President of Georgia, a position that he kept after the falling apart of the Soviet Union and Georgia became independent. Then in 2019, you've pointed out, that there was a second color revolution—you could call it a "rainbow revolution"—which was unleashed by the Soros organization, and some people in the U.S. Embassy in Tbilisi, demanding support for an LGBTQ parade, a Pride parade, against the strong opposition of the 80% of Georgia's population who are Orthodox Christians. Where did this lead and what is the status of that at this point?*

Jatras: I think to a large part it is simply the application on the local level of what is a huge, huge part of Western policy, which is the promoting of—[pause] I'm trying to think of a socially and morally destructive force the equal of LGBTQ. As I like to say, there's no trans-Atlanticism without trans-genderism. This is a huge part of American and Western democracy promotion and human rights promotion.

There's a great meme out there of an American soldier with an automatic weapon and a flag and a skull mask saying, "Until I'm out of ammo or out of blood, I will fight for homosexuality in Botswana." This is one of the great causes for which Americans are willing to shed blood and treasure? Evidently so.

I think part of it has to do with the fact that if you look at maps of social attitudes like, for example, towards same-sex marriage or toward the role of religion and public life and things like that, you will notice a rather odd thing—that is, that Eastern Europe, the areas that were under communism, are much more conservative than the countries of Western Europe. Maybe it was because as a progressive Promethean force, communism was such a failure that the underlying social attitudes are actually much more pre-modern conservative when it comes to social and family values and religious values than Western Europe, and presumably the United States, which have been corrupted by decades of consumerism and all these other materialist forces.

I think that the Western policymakers instinctively understand that if we want to conquer these societies, we need to break down their social attitudes. And one way to do that is to tell them, "Hey, if you want to be part of the West, you want to be part of the EU and NATO, you want to be part of the democratic club? It's a full package. You have to take this as well." I think that's what they were doing there in Georgia, but they also do that in Ukraine.

I even remember there was one of the priests from the church in Odessa, after they had a big Pride parade there, he went out afterwards with holy water to re-sanctify the streets after the parade had passed through. People there don't like this sort of thing, but nonetheless, the Americans and the U.S. embassies with their rainbow flags and all that, they're all over it. They're being forced to do this because, well, "this is democracy. This is the West. You have to get used to it."

On the Changes in 'Western Values'

EIR: *I'm reminded that Russian Foreign Minister Lavrov once said, regarding the so-called "Western values" that you hear spoken of so often, that the West insists on defending, are not the values of their grandfathers.*

Jatras: No, they're not. And by the way, I can remember back in the 1990s, when I was at the Senate, there was a big issue about giving observer status to some big coalition of LGBT organizations, which included groups like NAMBLA, the North American Man/Boy Love Association, which is a pro-pedophile group. This was a very controversial thing at the U.N. This was under the Clinton administration.

North America, the U.S., Canada and all of Western Europe were really promoting this, and the countries in Eastern Europe—this was the 1990s—newly liberated from communism, were saying, "What is going on here? We have to accept *this?*" I mean, the communists there never would have accepted anything like that. So, you really had this kind of weird thing, where these Western countries, the paragons of democracy, are promoting this kind of depravity.

Latin America was opposed to it. The Islamic world was opposed to it. The Far East, I think, was mostly puzzled by it, by "what kind of people are these?" And then you had Eastern Europe, which was sort of on the fence, because they knew they should be integrating in with the democratic West, but at the same time they couldn't figure out why in the world we would be pushing something like this.

On the Balkan Wars

EIR: *You've noted often that the leaders in both parties—you've named in particular John McCain, Joe Biden and Hillary Clinton—have never seen a war they didn't like. Biden's push for the war started by George W. Bush and Tony Blair in Iraq is well known, that he strongly promoted it. But less well known is that Biden led the effort to launch a war on Serbia in 1999, which led to 78 days of bombing, without U.N. authorization, laying waste to much of that country. Biden also backed the al-Qaida-linked Kosovo Liberation Army in that conflict and the independence of Kosovo. You were involved in some of this; if you could explain that?*

Jatras: At the time I was the analyst at the Republican Policy Committee in the Senate, and the Clinton administration had decided on—"intervention" is a nice word—I would say on "aggression" in the Balkans, not only in Bosnia, but also in Kosovo. I tried, to whatever extent I could, to inform Republican Senators and their staff, which it was my job to do, as to what was the reality behind some of the claims of the Clinton administration. That was a little difficult to do when the leader of the Republican Party in the Senate at that time was Bob Dole, who was on the same program as Biden and the Clinton administration.

But I did my best to try, to say, "Look, here are the open sources. Here's what they're saying. Here's the various al-Qaida and other groups that are involved here in terms of the human rights and other claims. Here's what's really going on. Yeah, we've unleashed a brutal inter-communal war between Serbs and Muslims and Croats and Albanians. Rather than trying to find some way for a peaceful resolution, we're trying to aggravate it, in a conflict that was kind of a rock-paper-scissors thing." Well, the Serbs were always the bad guys, they said—let's just start with that and work from there.

And by the way, some of this goes back to what we were talking about earlier, as I mentioned, the World War Two Losers Association. If you look at a map of occupied Europe in the Balkans in 1943 and compare it to the way we carved up Yugoslavia, the two maps look awfully similar. We essentially adopted all of the Axis clients from during the war and said, "Oh, these are now democratic NATO clients." So, you know, again, the roots of these things tend to go back a long way.

In any case, obviously I was unsuccessful in trying to enlighten people about what was going on, although I will say that when the vote on the Kosovo War occurred in Congress, the Republicans voted primarily against it. Maybe a lot of it was just partisan because it was the Clinton administration, a Democratic administration. But even with Bob Dole in the Senate and Henry Hyde, at the time the Republican leader in the House, whipping votes in favor of the war, the Republicans in the Senate voted, I think very heavily in the majority, against the war, and in the House, not only a very heavy majority of Republicans voted no, they even voted down the war resolution. It failed on a tie vote in the House of Representatives.

Nonetheless, Clinton proceeded with the war, which tells you something about the integrity of our constitutional process, when a war can take place not only against international law, in violation of the U.N. Charter, aggression against another country, but even against American domestic law: When the Congress says "No, you do not have the authority to go to war," and they said, "Yeah, well, I'm going to do it anyway." And so, there are many things that are all wrapped up in these things.

The long and the short of it is that it is amazing to me how many people, even who are essentially anti-war and against these wars—You remember there was a great series by Oliver Stone about the history of American wars and aggression around the world. I notice he skipped over the Balkans. He sort of forgot that war. These are the wars everybody wants to not really pay attention to because they sort of went down in the history as the place where NATO, the West came as the cavalry with the rescue. We were there for mom and apple pie and human rights and democracy. Well, it really wasn't that way. Nonetheless, that then set the stage and the precedent for places like Iraq and Libya.

On Kosovo and the 'Rule of Law'

EIR: *On Kosovo: Secretary Tony Blinken and other U.S. officials have insisted that under the so-called "rule of law"—which means their own made-up rules—nations cannot change the borders of other nations by force. Maria Zakharova, the Russian Foreign Ministry spokeswoman, responded to that statement by saying, "Do we get it right? That Washington no longer supports Kosovo's sovereignty?" You were directly involved in much of this. What is Zakharova referring to?*

Jatras: Let's remember, under U.N. resolution 1244, which ended the war in Kosovo, Kosovo was supposed to remain part of Serbia, and there were supposed to be negotiations about its status with the fullest possible autonomy, which is what Belgrade was offering. They were willing to jump through any hoop requested of them in terms of whatever autonomy could ever exist anywhere on Earth, for any part of any country, they were willing to offer that to Kosovo. But the Western powers, especially Washington, had decided *ab initio*: "No, no. The only possible solution is independence." Well, the U.N. resolution doesn't say that.

At that time—I was in the private sector—I was involved in lobbying on behalf of the Bishop of Kosovo, Bishop Artemije, against the American policy of pushing for independence for Kosovo. I would say we met with some success. That was supposed to be resolved by the end of 2006. It wasn't. It was dragged out until the beginning of 2008, when I think the Western powers thought they were losing support, so they needed to push the button they needed to move quickly on unilaterally recognizing Kosovo as an independent state, even though there was no legal mandate for that at all. And certainly, there was no negotiated solution to that effect.

I think that's one reason why we have a stalemate now where you have about one hundred and ten countries at last count that recognized Kosovo, but a lot of those are micro-states. The vast majority of the world's population— India, China and so forth, not to mention Russia—even still today, five members of the European Union—Greece, Cyprus, Romania, Spain and Slovakia— have not recognized Kosovo's independence. So it's not an acceptable solution for anybody, but that's where we are right now.

I think the point that Zakharova is referring to is that you say you can't change borders by force. Well, what do you think the West did in 1999 in the war and then 2008 in recognizing Kosovo's independence? We did precisely that without any legal authority at all. We detached part of a state, or at least claimed to, and say this is now a new country. Well, OK, you know, some things, once you break them, stay broken. Once you have a principle like the inviolability of borders, and say, "Oh, well, *we* can break them when we want, but *you* can't." Well, the other side says, "Oh no? Watch." And then, if you want: might makes right. If you want the law of the jungle, if you want to say that the U.N. guarantees of the inviolability of borders and state sovereignty no longer matter, OK, they don't matter anymore, I guess. Well, who asked for that?

On Construction and Destruction

EIR: *On China's role in all of this: the Belt and Road Initiative, which is taking the economic miracle within China over these past decades through massive infrastructure, lifting the productive platform of the nation as a whole. They are taking that to the rest of the world. They are also very active in Eastern Europe in huge amounts of trade through the thousands of trains that now traverse the new China-Europe Silk Road routes; and also through investments in infrastructure across the region, especially in Eastern Europe. How do you see the difference between China's approach to international relations to that of the United States?*

Jatras: This is something we've discussed before, especially with regard to some of the ideas that Mr. LaRouche was championing for many decades. It really comes down to construction versus destruction: Are you going to build? Are you're going to integrate—a rising tide raises all boats? Or are you going to try to look at the other people trying to do that and say, "Let's beggar thy neighbor, let's try to throw roadblocks into that. Let's try to break it down." We've talked about this in the past.

For example, why don't we have a land bridge across the Bering Strait, with trade between Eurasia and North America? Why are we not building our

own Belt and Road Initiative here in the Western Hemisphere? Why are we
not trying to come up with a way that countries can act in a cooperative way
to build up their economies and to maximize their mutual advantages in the
way that I think the Chinese and the Russians and the other countries behind
Eurasian integration are doing that.

Our response is what? To try to give the Chinese the hotfoot in Xinjiang,
to try to give the Russians a hot foot in Kazakhstan with a coup there, rather
than trying to find a way to build up the world economy, build up standards of
living. We're trying to find a way to play "dog in the manger" by trying to retard
those efforts if it's being done by somebody else, while we neglect to do it
ourselves. We're not doing any of these things.

To put it in a nutshell: that is the distinction between construction and
destruction, and it's a really sad thing. But that gets back to what we're saying
about the nature of our ruling class and the duopoly in this country. They seem
to see eye to eye on these things, about preserving American hegemony,
primarily based on military power *ad infinitum* and using whatever dirty
tricks in the book they can, to try to preserve that and to keep the other guys
down.

On the Trump Administration as a 'Missed Opportunity'

EIR: *President Trump insisted—one of the reasons he got elected—that he
was going to rebuild the American industrial economy, and Wall Street
basically said, "Forget it. We have to bail out the bankrupt financial institutions," and as a result, really nothing, nothing has changed. We continue to
see no infrastructure and no development within the U.S. Do you have
thoughts on that whole financial situation?*

Jatras: I'm not an economist. I'm not an expert on financial matters. As I say,
I do understand the difference between construction and destruction. I think
Trump did want to do that. I think he did have a concept of a national
economy.

When it comes to China, yeah, I do think our trade relationship with
China is terribly lopsided. It seems to me that is because, frankly, it's beneficial
to a lot of corporate America to hollow out our industries, our production, and
ship those operations to foreign countries. China, certainly, but many other
countries as well. And then, of course, bring their goods back in the United
States, duty free, basically undermining our national economy.

At the same time—I was saying this back at the time of the Trump
administration—there's a natural deal here between the United States and
China, to where we rebalance our trade relationship to favor American
production and the American industrial base, but at the same time, we get out
of China's face in the South China Sea, the Taiwan Strait and so forth, the same
way that we should be getting out of Russia's face in Eastern Europe; that it
seems to me there's the making of a deal there.

I don't know that Trump really saw that. It seemed to me a lot of people
in his administration had a strong animus against China across the board, that
not only did they want to address the trade issues, which I think is legitimate,
but also wanted to threaten them on some of the security issues, which I
thought made no sense whatsoever.

But that's where we are. I do think Trump, on some level, at least in his
gut, had a sense that we need to build up our own national economy, get
control of our borders, get control of our trade. Unfortunately, like many other
things, I don't think he really had any idea how to do that. He certainly
populated his administration with all the wrong people when it came to
getting any of his agenda from 2016 done. When you turn to the Heritage

Foundation and the Republican National Committee to hire a bunch of Bush retreads for your administration, hey, you're going to get your tax cut, which any Republican president would want to push through the Congress, but you're not going to get an infrastructure bill, you're not going to get any of the other things you want.

I think looking back on it, Trump was a great missed opportunity and perhaps in some sense, the last missed opportunity for an America that, maybe, could have been revived.

On American Political Theory

EIR: *As to the two-party system, you were an adviser to the Republican Party in the Senate, as you mentioned, for many years. You have insight into the two-party system that we have today—what Lyndon LaRouche referred to as the "two potty" system. What is your view on democracy in America today, which the war party claims to be defending in their wars around the world?*

Jatras: To be precise, I was an adviser to the Senate Republican leadership, which is a Senate office, not a party office. The structure of the Senate, as in the House, is partisan, but it's the Senate, part of the U.S. government. It's not the Republican Party *per se.*

I don't know, Mike, we might not be fully in agreement on these things. I'm a pretty retrograde guy when it comes to political theory. I do notice that the founding fathers did not intend to create a democracy. They knew their history, they knew their Aristotle, they knew how democracies tend to end. For the first 80 or 90 years of our republic until the Civil War, we had a confederal republic. And then after the Civil War, until at least in the post-World War Two period, we had a federal democracy.

But then, increasingly in recent decades, we've had a consolidated administrative state, a managerial state. I don't think you would even call it democracy anymore. This is the way democracies tend to end. Once you have: everybody has the vote, everybody can say, "Well, I want, I want, I want." You tend to vote yourself benefits out of the other guy's pocket. And that goes for the plutocracy, too. They say, "Well, we can manipulate the levers of this thing too, and we have our propaganda machine in the media" and so forth. So none of this should be particularly surprising where you get to a moribund state where a constitution on paper is simply honored in the breach.

It's honored with fingers crossed behind your back, and it really doesn't exist anymore. The fact that we have this entrenched duopoly, which is as entrenched in America today as the CPSU was entrenched as a one-party system in the Soviet Union, is something that is—I don't know that there's any coming back from that, except in the same sense that, well, when the Soviet Union collapsed, so did the Communist Party of the Soviet Union, and something new arose from the ashes.

Unfortunately, I think that's sort of where we are now in America today, what that looks like, how bad it's going to be, with things like supply chain breakdown, collapse of the dollar. Who knows what else is going to come, whether it results in the breakup of the country or what level of violence? I don't think we really know. I explored some of this in the piece you mentioned earlier, the "It's Later Than You Think."

I think unfortunately—and again, we might disagree on this, Mike—a lot of this is baked into the cake. I don't know that there's much any of us can do by shouting from the rooftops that "bad things is a'comin." The bad things will come, and then we'll see how we get through it, who survives, who doesn't, and what comes from the ashes.

On the Human Factor in History

EIR: *At the end of that talk, you gave to the students at the Ron Paul Institute, you said: "I think your ability to impact the big picture regarding any of this is slim to none." That's somewhat like what you are saying right now. That's clearly rather pessimistic. As you know, LaRouche always told the youth, and others, that in a systemic crisis like we're in today—and you acknowledge it's a systemic crisis—the ability to make big changes is even greater than normal, rather than less, precisely because the old system is falling apart and people are forced to give up their delusions and look for new solutions, including outside of the United States, internationally. So how do you respond to that?*

Jatras: Well, I would say that it largely depends on the human factor and the mechanisms. I remember during the 2020 election, so many people were saying—people who believe that the vote was stolen, and I'm one of those people—"Well look, the Supreme Court's going to do this, or the state legislators are going to do that, or Congress is going to do this." And I kept saying, "No, no, no. None of those things are going to happen, because those people who are in charge of the system, in charge of being the guardians of the system, will not do their duty even when the facts are plain."

I think a lot of us have a kind of a naïve—and I'm not calling Mr. LaRouche naïve—but a lot of us have a naïve faith, in facts. If you throw the facts on the table—whether it's about COVID or whether it's about CRT [Critical Race Theory] and Black Lives Matter and Antifa, or whether it's about foreign policy—that people will wake up and say, "Oh my God, you're right, let's do the right thing." The trouble is that you have people holding all the levers of power who will not do the right thing. That means what you have is stasis. You have stasis until the collapse comes. Now what happens after that?

Yeah, I think there are things that people can do. I'm not advising complacency by any means. I just don't see the levers. I don't see the pathways to changing national policy even in the middle of a crisis until the collapse comes. That doesn't mean that the local, and to some extent at the state level, things can't be done. I live in a rural county in Virginia. We did pretty good in this last election here. We're very optimistic here at the county level, maybe even a little optimistic at the state level.

That may be a little naïve. But you look at states like Florida and Texas to some extent, maybe we have a kind of a soft secession going on in some of the states and localities in America where, yeah, a healthy America could still be sustained and provide the groundwork for a kind of a revival of the American spirit and something like an American republic in the future. But I think those pathways are not yet clear to us. I think being active at the local level, being active with your community, acting with likeminded people, and why conversations like this, I think are valuable, are something we should focus on. But not to expect that, "Oh great. The Republicans are going to take the House this year," and that goodness and niceness will break out, because it won't.

On Lyndon LaRouche

EIR: *Lyndon LaRouche always, always represented himself as an American, supporting the American System of Hamilton and Lincoln and Roosevelt, but he always insisted he represented the human race as a whole, and fought for the human race as a whole, rather than for one nation. You have followed LaRouche for many, many years, and you've been involved in many* *of our discussions and forums and conferences. How do you see LaRouche, his role in history and his impact on the international situation today?*

Jatras: I think he will be remembered as a visionary and maybe a reminder of what could have been; that if there had been people who were willing to listen to common sense at the right time, when opportunities had not been frittered away one after another, the outcome could have been different; that we would not have to go through this crisis or crunch or whatever you want to call it, which I think we will have to go through now.

I think one of the things that occurred to me, looking back on my comments at the time when we were asking about his exoneration to try to get a pardon and an exoneration for him from the unjust prosecution—persecution that he suffered, and that you and many others suffered, by the way, at the hands of Robert Mueller and the establishment. You think about that. What if those policies had been heeded at the time when they could have made a big difference, rather than them saying, "Let's squash this guy," which was the response of the powers at the time?

I think it could have made a big difference in the life of this country, but unfortunately that didn't happen. Remember, he was out talking about these things, how many decades ago? There were how many missed opportunities through all of those decades? And now here we are.

I'm not saying those ideas are not applicable now. As you point out, we do have to look at the rest of the world, that to a great extent some of the things he proposed, about a new Silk Road and so forth, are being followed by the Eurasian powers. I don't want to sound naïve in that regard. I'm sure the Chinese and the Russians and other countries are looking out for number one, the way, frankly, a national government should do.

I think, as we discussed a little earlier, we have so many people on the Right in this country today who are calling for the "China, China, China" alarm, the same way the Left fell for "Russia, Russia, Russia" during the Trump years: "Oh, the Chinese Communists, you know, they're behind everything."

Well, first off, despite the formality of the CCP [Chinese Communist Party] being the ruling party in China, I think it's pretty clear that it's not—I like to call it Han National Bolshevism. The bottle may be red and has a picture of Mao on it, but the wine inside the bottle is Han Nationalist and Confucian, and there's simply nothing really communist about it other than the name of the party. Now, it's authoritarian. In some ways, it behaves in ways that we would consider quite inhumane. But I think it reflects the long history of China as a civilization, and it is focused on China's national interest, but not in a kind of a "let's destroy everybody else" kind of mentality, but rather that China will have its greatest flowering and opportunity when other people do as well.

Why can we not see that in our leadership? I think it gets back to the level of corruption that has become almost ubiquitous at the upper ends of our system, whereas, hopefully, at the lower end, the local level, maybe to a lesser extent on the state level, there are still healthy things there that can be preserved.

On Optimism in the Future

EIR: *Thank you. Any further thoughts or last words for our readers and supporters?*

Jatras: No, not really, I would just ask people, if they want to see what I have written—I have lost my muse for writing; I do try to do interviews from time to time, but I am an incessant tweeter—until they kick me off. So go to @JimJatras on Twitter if you want to see my latest thoughts or dumb ideas.

I do want to say that, blackpilled as I do tend to sound—I am a Boomer after all—I am fundamentally an optimist in many respects. As I pointed out with respect to France, the fact that one republic is ending doesn't mean the nation goes away. I do believe there is an American nation. I realize that concept is not well understood or accepted in America today because we tend to think in "civic terms" rather than national terms. But I do think that there is a future for the American people as we come through this crisis, which still, I think, has another five to seven years to go. We'll see how bad it gets. But something, some phoenix, will arise from the ashes.

At the same time, even in a greater sense, on a moral, spiritual level, the hairs on our head are all numbered. God is in His heaven. Nothing happens without His allowance or His will. If we pray without ceasing and have confidence in the final triumph of good, it will sustain us through even very difficult times.

EIR: *Ok, thank you very much, Jim.*

Jatras: Thank you, Mike, for the opportunity.

ABOUT THE AUTHOR

James George Jatras was born in Harrisburg, Pennsylvania, and raised in a military family, growing up in several locations in the United States as well as in Germany and Greece. All four of his grandparents immigrated to the U.S. from Laconia (Sparta), Greece. His parents, George and Stella (Stavroula) were born in the U.S. His father, George, was a career U.S. Air Force fighter pilot who retired with the rank of Colonel after service including combat in Vietnam, as a U.S. Air Force adviser to the then-Royal Hellenic Air Force, and as U.S. Air Force Attaché in Moscow (USSR). His mother, Stella, was an active advocate for Serbia and Serbs, formally recognized by His Grace Bishop Artemije of Raška and Prizren (Kosovo) with a certificate of gratitude in 2004 and, posthumously, with a recognition by the Serbian government in 2014.

Jatras received his B.A. in Political Science, with Honors, in 1974 from the Pennsylvania State University, University Park, Pennsylvania, and his J.D. degree in 1978 from the Georgetown University Law Center, Washington, D.C. From 1979 to 1985, he was a commissioned Foreign Service Officer with the U.S. Department of State serving in the Office of the Under Secretary of State for Political Affairs on issues relating to public diplomacy and international broadcasting; in the then-Office of Soviet Union Affairs; and as a Consular Officer in Tijuana, Baja California Norte, Mexico. From 1985 to 2002, he was a senior advisor to the U.S. Senate Republican Policy Committee under Chairmen Bill Armstrong (Colorado), Don Nickles (Oklahoma) and Larry Craig (Idaho). While with the committee, he drafted and edited extensive portions of the Republican Party National Platforms of 1988, 1992, and 1996. In 1988, Jatras co-authored (with Paul Farley) an *amicus curiae* brief to the U.S. Supreme Court in the case *Webster v. Reproductive Health Services* on behalf of the Orthodox Church, advocating the reversal of *Roe v. Wade*. He remains a member of the U.S. Supreme Court bar and is retired from the Pennsylvania and District of Columbia bars.

It should be noted that Jatras's work in the Senate spanned the years of the collapse of the Warsaw Pact, the dissolution of the USSR and Yugoslavia, and the outbreak of the Yugoslav wars of the 1990s and demonization of the Serbs by western governments and media, during which time he sought to write and issue official reports that presented a balanced picture of events. As such, Jatras's office at the Senate was one of the few places in official Washington open for Serbs to receive a fair and sympathetic hearing for their point of view. During this time, he received and became acquainted with opposition political figures who later assumed an important role in Serbia. In 2004, he appeared as the second defense witness called by former Yugoslav and Serbia President Slobodan Milošević at his trial before the International Criminal Tribunal for the former Yugoslavia at The Hague.

Following his government service, Jatras worked for several years as a government relations and media specialist ("lobbyist") with two major Washington-based law firms, then with some smaller media companies. His international experience includes work relevant to Belgium, Bosnia and Herzegovina, Canada, China (Taiwan), Cuba, France, Georgia, Germany, Hungary, India, Iran, Iraq, Japan, Mexico, Philippines, Russia, Saudi Arabia, Serbia, Syria, Ukraine, United Arab Emirates, the United Kingdom, and Yemen.

From 2006 to 2009, in the course of his post-Senate lobbying work, Jatras conducted a campaign on behalf of Bishop Artemije to offset western policy with respect to the "final status" of Kosovo and Metohija at a time when the Serbian government and Church were passively inactive. Under the rubric of an NGO, the American Council for Kosovo, for which Jatras served as Director, this campaign on behalf of the Orthodox Serbian people cultivated not only government and media in the U.S. but in Russia, India, Israel, and locations in Europe, including the UK, Germany, Italy, and the European Commission in Brussels, holding conferences, publishing books, and placing advocacy ads and commentaries in diverse media. For these efforts he received a formal recognition from Bishop Artemije in 2022.

Jatras is now retired and lives in rural Virginia. Both during and following his working years, he has been a frequent speaker, panelist, and conference participant in U.S. and international venues, has made numerous media appearances, and is a frequent contributor to print and online publications, both in the U.S. and abroad. In 2024 he was awarded the Order of Njegoš (Second Class), from President Milorad Dodik of Republika Srpska.

Baptized into the Orthodox Church in infancy with the name Dimitrios, Jatras has been a life-long Orthodox Christian and is now a parishioner and warden at St. Herman of Alaska Orthodox Church under its rector, Metropolitan Jonah (Paffhausen). He was married for 45 years to his late wife, Kathy Helen (Pappas) Jatras, whom he met during their senior year in high school in Athens, Greece. She, like him, was an Orthodox Christian of Greek ancestry. They have two grown daughters and (at last count) six grandchildren. He can be reached on X @JimJatras.

TITLE INDEX

American Institute in Ukraine

"Arrival of Humanitarian Convoy in Eastern Ukraine and Upcoming Poroshenko-Putin Meeting: Is a Real "Game-Changer" in the Offing?" August 22, 2014 — 179

"Ceasefire and Talks in Ukraine: a Chance for Peace, Or Just an Opportunity for More Confrontation?" June 24, 2014 — 174

"Europe should be wary of the official 'U.S. position' on Ukraine," April 7, 2014 — 168

"Geneva Agreement on Ukraine Barely a Pause in Deepening Confrontation," April 22, 2014 — 170

"German Report: European Union's Demand of 'Either-Or Choice' Pushed Ukraine Over the Brink," June 6, 2014 — 172

"Immediate Course-Change Needed to Put the Ukrainian Humpty-Dumpty Back Together Again," March 26, 2014 — 165

"Poroshenko's 'Hail Mary' Pass: Kiev bets everything on military victory, may cut off gas and oil to Europe," August 8, 2014 — 178

"Poroshenko's On-Again, Off-Again Offensive Shows His Narrowing Options," July 3, 2014 — 175

"The Patriarch of Russia's Restoration," 2009 — 30

"Why Do the 'Authorities' in Kiev Reject Federalism and Language Rights?" April 2, 2014 — 167

Chronicles of Culture

"Appointment of Special Counsel for 'Russiagate' Could Derail Trump's MAGA Agenda, Lead to War," May 19, 2017 — 107

"Benevolent Global Hegemony," June 1997 — 337

Ron Paul Institute

Strategic Culture

Miscellaneous Articles, Letters, and Statements

GENERAL INDEX

Will, George, 281
Williams, Fr. Gregory, 585
Williamson, Gavin, 442
Williamson, Kevin, 283
Wolfe, Tom, 86, 537
Wolff, Michael, 127
Wolfowitz, Paul, 453, 564
Wood, Andrew, 126–129, 441, 443
Wood, Nathaniel, 62–64
Woodward, Bob, 434, 444
World War I, 21, 72, 122, 145, 189,
    236, 338–339, 429, 439, 625, 631
World War II, 17, 20, 32, 77, 84, 110,
    161, 238, 328, 338, 340, 342, 353,
    439, 514, 559, 625, 638, 642, 645
World War III, 87, 122, 292, 293, 314,
    365, 368, 415, 417–418, 430, 571,
    618, 654–656
Wrangel, Pyotr, 5
Wray, William, 315
Wright, Frank Lloyd, 254, 259
Xi Jinping, 226, 257, 350–351, 363,
    365–366, 392, 395, 420, 431, 445,
    448, 656
Xinjiang, China, 89, 146, 194, 223–
    227, 257, 445, 644, 654
Yakovenko, Aleksandr, 441
Yakunin, Fr. Gleb, 18
Yakunin, Vladimir, 79, 90, 471

Yanukovych, Viktor, 58, 119, 155–156,
    165–167, 170–173, 176, 178, 331,
    626, 637–638
Yates, Sally, 443
Yatseniuk, Arseny, 165, 171, 178
Yeltsin, Boris, 30–31, 103–104, 114,
    137, 150, 258, 286, 354, 401
Young, Fr. Alexey, 530, 533, 535, 585
Yovanovitch, Marie, 76, 81, 89, 92,
    156, 471–473
Yugoslavia, 19, 51, 54–55, 77, 94, 96,
    238–239, 319, 343, 348, 429, 550,
    604, 642, 649
Yuldashev, Timur, 171
Yushenkov, Sergei, 426
Zakaria, Fareed, 147, 378
Zakharchenko, Aleksandr, 146
Zakharova, Maria, 642–643
Zelensky, Volodymyr, 74–75, 82–83,
    155–157, 326
Zhirinovsky, Vladimir, 104
Zia-ul-Haq, 400
Zimbabwe, 604
Zimmerman, Odo John, 515
Zizioulas, John. *See* John (Zizioulas),
    Metropolitan
Zuckerberg, Mark, 144, 295
Zuma, Jacob, 561
Zurabov, Mikhail, 174
Zyuganov, Gennadi, 104